CONSTITUTIONALISM IN ASIA

This book is a collection of judiciously selected constitutio
Asia, designed for scholars and students of constitutional lav
stitutional law. The book is divided into 10 chapters, arranged thematically around key ideas and controversies, enabling the reader to work through the major facets of constitutionalism in the region. The book begins with a Introduction that critically examines the study of constitutional orders in 'Asia', highlighting the histories, colonial influences and cultural particularities extant in the region. This serves both as a provisional orientation towards the major constitutional developments seen in Asia – both unique and shared with other regions – and as a guide to the controversies encountered in the study of constitutional law in Asia. Each of the following chapters is framed by an introductory essay setting out the issues and succinctly highlighting critical perspectives and themes. The approach is one of 'challenge and response', whereby questions of constitutional importance are posed and the reader is then led, by engaging with primary and secondary materials, through the way the various Asian states respond to these questions and challenges. Chapter segments are accompanied by notes, comments and questions to facilitate critical and comparative analysis, as well as recommendations for further reading.

The book presents a representative range of Asian materials from countries including: China, Japan, Mongolia, Taiwan, South Korea, Hong Kong, the 10 ASEAN states, Timor-Leste, India, Pakistan, Bangladesh, Sri Lanka and Nepal.

Constitutionalism in Asia

Cases and Materials

Wen-Chen Chang, Li-ann Thio,
Kevin YL Tan and Jiunn-rong Yeh

·HART·
PUBLISHING

OXFORD AND PORTLAND, OREGON
2014

Published in the United Kingdom by Hart Publishing Ltd
16C Worcester Place, Oxford, OX1 2JW
Telephone: +44 (0)1865 517530
Fax: +44 (0)1865 510710
E-mail: mail@hartpub.co.uk
Website: http://www.hartpub.co.uk

Published in North America (US and Canada) by
Hart Publishing
c/o International Specialized Book Services
920 NE 58th Avenue, Suite 300
Portland, OR 97213-3786
USA
Tel: +1 503 287 3093 or toll-free: (1) 800 944 6190
Fax: +1 503 280 8832
E-mail: orders@isbs.com
Website: http://www.isbs.com

Hart Publishing is an imprint of Bloomsbury Publishing plc

British Library Cataloguing in Publication Data
Data Available

ISBN: 978-1-84946-234-1

Typeset by Hope Services, Abingdon
Printed and bound in Great Britain by
TJ International Ltd, Padstow, Cornwall

Acknowledgements

In the three years it took us to put this book together, we have accumulated many intellectual and other debts. We would like to first acknowledge the National University of Singapore, whose Academic Research Fund (ARF) enabled us to employ our various research assistants; acquire rare academic materials; and fund study trips to Sri Lanka and Bangladesh. We further acknowledge the research grants provided by the National Science Council in Taiwan and by the National Taiwan University Top University Projects in collaboration with the Institute for Advanced Studies in Humanities and Social Sciences.

At our respective institutions, our colleagues have been most supportive of our work and have given unstintingly of their time, energies and connections to facilitate our research and understanding of the various jurisdictions covered in this volume. At the Faculty of Law, National University of Singapore, we would especially like to thank Arun Kumar Thiruvengadam, Gary F Bell and Michael Dowdle. At the National Taiwan University, we especially thank Professor Chun-Chieh Huang, Dean of the Institute for Advanced Studies in Humanities and Social Sciences.

Many friends from overseas also helped us greatly in obtaining difficult-to-find materials on constitutional law. In this connection, we are grateful to: Ridwanul Hoque of the University of Dhaka, and Tom Temprosa and Mayla Germina Alonzo Ibanez of the Philippines. Thank you too to Ridwanul Hoque and former Dean N Selvakummaran of the Faculty of Law, University of Colombo, for so kindly arranging and facilitating our study visits to Bangladesh and Sri Lanka respectively, and taking every care to make our visits pleasant and productive.

In the course of writing this book, we have also benefitted greatly from our conversations, interviews and exchanges with: Md Ershadul Karim of Chancery Law Chronicles, Bangladesh; Justice Syed Refaat Ahmad; Dr Kamal Hossein; Ms Sara Hossein; Professor Md Maimul Ahsan Khan; Professor Sumaiya Khair; Professor Shahnaz Huda; Associate Professor Ridwanul Hoque; Professor Md Maimul Ahsan Khan; Professor Asif Nazrul; Dr Shaddeen Malik; and Mr Mahmudul Islam (from Bangladesh); and Dean Naganathan Selvakummaran, Dr Jayampathy Wickremaratne; Mr VT Thamilmaran; Ms Wasantha Seneviratne; Ms Rose Wijeyesekera; Dr Mario Gomez; and Dr Sivaji Felix (from Sri Lanka).

Last but not least, we thank our students and research assistants whose hard work in locating, collecting and systematising these materials made it much easier for us to think through and analyse them. In Singapore, we thank our team of student researchers at the Faculty of Law, National University of Singapore, especially Darius Lee, Michelle Virgiany and Audrey Wong. Thanks too to Cheryl Kam for helping prepare the manuscript and her editorial assistance. In Taiwan, we are grateful to Yi-Li Lee, Shao-Man Lee, Chun-Yuan Lin, Yen-Lun Tseng, Shang-Yun Lu, Sze-Chen Kuo, Yu-Teng Lin, Chun-Yin Hsiao, Chia-ching Chen, Pei-Jung Li, Po-Cheng Lin, Zo-Tzu Ma, Hsing-Jung Hsieh, Ju-Ching Huang, Pei-En Hsu, Adeline Suk Ching Ha, Ka Kit Hoi, Yaruo Lin, Huan Minh Duong, Somrudee

Kosanan, Batbold Enkhbold and Nyamgerel Sukhchuluun; and in Bangladesh, Emraan Azad.

We are grateful to the different generations of our students who were willing 'guinea pigs' in our various comparative constitutional law and human rights classes. Thank you for helping us.

It has been almost two and a half years since we met Richard Hart at the International Association of Constitutional Law Congress in Mexico City in December 2010, when this idea was first mooted. We are delighted to see the germ of the idea finally come to fruition. In this endeavour, we are deeply grateful to Richard Hart and his wonderful team at Hart Publishing for bravely agreeing to publish this volume, and doing all things possible to guide us all through getting the manuscript to press and for producing such a handsome book.

Wen-Chen Chang
Li-ann Thio
Kevin YL Tan
Jiunn-rong Yeh

The authors and publisher gratefully acknowledge the authors and publishers of extracted material which appears in this book, and in particular the following for permission to reprint from the sources indicated:

Adam Schwarz and Talisman Publishing Pte Ltd, Singapore, *A Nation in Waiting: Indonesia's Search for Stability* (2004)

Foreign Languages Press, Peking, *Selected Works of Mao Tse-tung*, vol 4 (1969)

Giuffre Editore, Rome, Andrew Harding 'Asian Law, Public Law, Comparative Law Stir-Fry: Theory and Methods Considered' in Tania Groppi, Valeria Piergigli & Angelo Rinella (eds), *Asian Constitutionalism in Transition: A Comparative Perspective* (2009)

Historia Constitucional, Eric Ip, *Building Constitutional Democracy on Oriental Foundations: An Anatomy of Sun Yat-Sen's Constitutionalism* (2008)

Islamic Publications Ltd, Lahore, Pakistan, Sayyid Abul Ala Maududi, 'Fundamentals of Islamic Constitution' in Khurshid Ahmad (ed), *The Islamic Law and Constitution*, (1955)

Princeton University Press, Princeton, NJ, Daniel A Bell, 'Introduction' in Jian Qing, *A Confucian Constitutional Order: How China's Ancient Past Can Shape Its Political Future* (2013)

St Martin's Press, New York, Brian Lapping, *End of Empire* (1985)

St Martin's Press, New York, WG Beaseley, *The Rise of Modern Japan: Political, Economic and Social Change Since 1850* (Rev edn 2000)

University of Hawai'i Press, Honolulu Suisheng Zhao, *Power by Design: Constitution-Making in Nationalist China* (1996)

University of South Carolina Press, Columbia, SC, Hungdah Chiu, 'Constitutional Development and Reform in the Republic of China on Taiwan' in Bih-Jaw Lin (ed), *Contemporary China and the Changing International Community* (1994)

Wiley Publishing, Lawrence M Friedman, 'Is There a Modern Legal Culture?' in *Ratio Juris* (1994)

Wiley Publishing, Maimon Schwarzchild, 'Constitutional Law and Equality' in Dennis Patterson (ed), *A Companion to Philosophy of Law and Legal Theory* (1999)

Summary Contents

Acknowledgements   v

Contents   xi

List of Displayed Extracts   xix

Table of Cases   xxxvii

Table of Legislation   lxiii

Introduction   1

1   Constitution Making and State Building   9

2   Constitutional Cultures in Asia   65

3   Government System and Structures   127

4   Constitutional Change and Amendments   219

5   Judicial Review   307

6   Democracy and the Right to Political Participation   463

7   The Right to Equality and Equal Protection   545

8   Free Speech and *Res Publica*   641

9   Religion and State   771

10   Socio-Economic Rights   943

Index   1023

Contents

Acknowledgements   v
Summary Contents   ix
List of Displayed Extracts   xix
Table of Cases   xxxvii
Table of Legislation   lxiii

Introduction: Asia, Constitutions and Constitutionalism   1

I.   Constitutionalism in Asia: The Legacy   1
II.   Aims and Ambit of This Book   5
III.   Our Approach   7

1. Constitution Making and State Building   9

I.   Introduction   9
II.   Early Inspirations   10

     A. Introduction   10
     B. Japan   10
     C. China   12
     D. The Philippines   14
     E. Siam (Thailand)   16

III.   Colonialism and Decolonisation   17

     A. The Colonisation of Asia   17
     B. Japan, Taiwan and Korea   18

        i.   Japan   18
        ii.   Taiwan   20
        iii   The Korean Peninsula   23

     C. British Devolution   26

        i.   Burma   29
        ii.   Ceylon   30
        iii. India   31
        iv. Pakistan   33
        v.   Malaysia, Singapore and Brunei   34

IV.   Revolutionary Moments   37

     A. Communist Revolutions   37

        i.   China   38
        ii.   Vietnam   45
        iii. Laos   48
        iv. Cambodia   50

B. Democratic Revolutions   51
  i.   Mongolia   52
  ii. Indonesia   52
  iii. The Philippines   54
  iv. Cambodia   56

V.   Constitution-making in Asia: Some General Observations   57

A. Epochs of Constitution-making and Asia   57
B. Constitutionalism and Legitimacy   58
  i.   Majoritarian Legitimacy   59
  ii. Economic and Legal Legitimacy   62

VI. Conclusion   63

2. Constitutional Cultures in Asia   **65**

I.   Introduction   65
II.   Law, Culture and the Constitution   66
III. Culture and Constitutions: A Functional Approach   76

A. Introduction   76
B. Culture as Normative Matrix   77
  i.   Visions of the Common Good   77
  ii. Novel or Unique Rights   83
C. Constitutional Culture and Instrumentalism   85
  i.   Constitution and National Identity: History, Constitutional
       Patriotism and Cosmopolitanism   85
  ii. Culture as a Platform for Political Ideology   100
  iii. Constitutional Cultism: North Korea   102
D. Culture and Paths of Institutional Interaction   103
  i.   Governing Institutional Interactions Through Culture   103

IV. Constitutional Culture and the Character of the Polity (Defining the 'We') 104

A. Cultures and Frameworks for Co-existence   104
B. Religion and Constitutional Identity   105
  i.   The Non-recognition of Buddhism as Official Religion in the
       2007 Thai Constitution   108
  ii. Nepal: From Hindu Kingdom to Secular State   109
  iii. Bangladesh: From Secular to Islamic Republic and Back:
       The Fifth Amendment Case of 2010   110
  iv. Malaysia: 'Islam' – The No Longer Innocuous Clause?   116

V.   The Influence of Constitutional Culture on the Style of Constitutionalism:
     Before and Beyond the Courts   118

A. Introduction   118
B. Intra-Party Democracy in Socialist States   121
C. Culture, Propriety and Persuasion: Virtuous Rulers and Internal
   Restraint of Leaders   122
D. Popular Petition and Populist Constitutionalism   123

E. Relational Constitutionalism: Beyond Sanctions and Rights to
Solidarity and Reconciliation   124

3. Government System and Structures   **127**

I. Introduction   127
II. Organisations of State   128

A. The Head of State and Symbolic Powers   128
B. The Head of Government and Administrative Unity   140

III. Separation of Powers and Government Systems   145

A. Parliamentary System   145

    i. The Legislative Power in the Parliamentary System   145
    ii. Executive Power in a Parliamentary System   146
    iii. Vote of No Confidence and Dissolution of the Parliament   148

B. Presidential System   157

    i. Domestic Affairs   157
    ii. Foreign Affairs   163
    iii. Presidential Immunity   167
    iv. The Impeachment of the President   170

C. Other Unique Systems   173

    i. The Chinese Communist Party and Government   174
    ii. Hong Kong: One Country Two Systems   178
    iii. Bangladesh: The Caretaker Government   180

IV. Political Branches: Conflict and Conciliation   181

A. Appointment   181
B. Policy and Budget   190
C. Foreign Policy and War   196
D. Emergency Power   203

    i. Taiwan   206
    ii. Malaysia   207
    iii. The Philippines   208
    iv. India   210
    v. Pakistan   212

E. The Court's Role in Mediating Political Conflicts   216

4. Constitutional Change and Amendments   **219**

I. Introduction   219
II. Constitutional Durability and Adaptability   220

A. Some Observations on the Durability of Constitutions in Asia   220
B. Constitutional Change, Sovereignty and Legitimacy   223
C. Imposed and Autonomous Constitutional Change   230
D. Constitutional Change in a Transitional Context   239
E. Constitutional Change during Revolutions and Emergencies   247

III. Constitutional Moments and Methods of Constitutional Change   255
      A. Constitutional Amendment and Procedure   256
      B. Political Actions and Referenda   265
      C. Judicial Decisions, Soft Constitutional Law and Custom   270
IV.   Limits to Constitutional Change   278
      A. Eternity Clauses   279
      B. Implied Limits ('Basic Structure' or 'Basic Features')   280
      C. International Law and Transnational Constitutionalism   299

5. Judicial Review   **307**
I.   Introduction   307
II.   Nature of Judicial Review   307
      A. Decentralised Systems of Review   308
      B. Centralised Systems of Review   309
      C. Judicial Power and the Assertion of Judicial Review Powers   311
III. Institutional Design of Judicial Review   324
      A. The Centralised Model: Constitutional Court   328
          i.   Primary Jurisdictions   328
          ii. Ancillary Jurisdictions   337
      B. The Decentralised Model   342
IV.   Subject of Judicial Review   349
      A. Constitutional Amendment   349
      B. Law or Parliamentary Resolution   352
      C. Administrative Rule   356
      D. Emergency Decrees   361
      E. Judicial Decision   365
V.   Judicial Appointment, Organisation and Independence   369
      A. Judicial Appointment   369
          i.   Judicial Appointment to Constitutional Court   369
          ii. Judicial Appointment to Ordinary Courts and Supreme Courts 373
          iii. Qualification of Judge and Procedure of Judicial Appointment 375
      B. Judicial Transfer   382
      C. Security of Remuneration and Judicial Budget   385
      D. Court Structure and Judicial Administration   389
VI.   Justiciability and *Locus Standi*   396
      A. Cases or Controversies   397
      B. Political Question   400
      C. *Locus Standi*   404
          i.   Individuals   404
          ii. Public Interest Litigation and Taxpayer Suits   411
VII. Approaches to Constitutional Interpretation   417
      A. Text-based Approach   417

B. The Historically-Based Approach 424
C. Purposive Approach 426
D. Use of Foreign and International Law 431

    i. Use of Foreign or International Law 432
    ii. Reticence Towards Foreign or International Law 436
    iii. Balancing: Referencing for Restricting Rights 438

VIII. Forms of Judicial Decisions and Remedies 443

A. Limited Constitutionality or Limited Unconstitutionality 444
B. Prospective Ruling, Temporal Validity and Judicial Deadlines 447
C. Unconstitutional Declaration without Invalidation and Judicial
    Warnings 456
D. Judicial Law-Making 459

6. Democracy and the Right to Political Participation **463**

I. Introduction 463
II. Democracy and Democratisation in Asia 464

A. Concepts and Types of Democracy 464
B. Waves of Democratisation 465
C. Forms of Political Representation 467

    i. Electoral Representation: Apportionment and Voting Disparity 467

D. Functional or Sectoral Representation 478
E. Proportional Representation and Anti-hopping Laws 481

    i. Proportional Representation 481
    ii. Anti-hopping Laws 490

F. Quotas 493

III. Institutions for Political Representation 497

A. Political Parties and Militant Democracy 497

    i. Formation of Political Parties 498
    ii. Dissolution of Political Parties 501

B. Elections 507
C. Election Commissions 511

    i. Independence of the Election Commission 511
    ii. Functions of an Election Commission 514

IV. Right to Political Participation 520

A. Qualification of Voters 521
B. Qualifications of Candidates 529

V. Referendum, Initiative and Petition 535

A. Referendum 536
B. Initiative 540
C. Petition 543

7. The Right to Equality and Equal Protection   545

I.   Equality and the Law   545
II. Equality Before the Law   550

   A. Introduction   550
   B. Meaning of 'Equality Before the Law'   553

III. Equal Protection of the Law   556

   A. Introduction   556
   B. Prohibited Categories of Discrimination   557
   C. Positive Discrimination   558

     i. Constitutional Protection of Indigenous Peoples   558

   D. Privilege and Equality   579
   E. Rational Classification and the Reasonable Nexus Test   589

     i.   The Indian Test and Its Progeny   589
     ii. The American Test   607
     iii. Beyond Classification: Proportionality   619

IV. Discrimination and the Protection of Minorities   622
   A. Introduction   622
   B. Gender Discrimination   624

     i.   Women   624
     ii. Gender Selection and Abortion   626
     iii. Homosexuals and the Third Sex   629

   C. Discrimination Against Indigenous Peoples   634

     i. Indigenous Peoples and the Right to Self-Determination   634

   D. Discrimination Against Aliens or Foreigners   637

8. Free Speech and *Res Publica*   641

I.   Introduction   641
II. Free Speech   643

   A. Prior Restraints on Speech   643
   B. Press, Media and Right to Reply   652

     i. Entry Regulation of Media   653
     ii. Access to Media and Right to Reply   659

   C. Sedition and Hate Speech   669
   D. Lèse Majesté, Contempt of Court and Symbolic Speech   682

     i.   Lèse Majesté   683
     ii. Contempt of Court   687
     iii. Symbolic Speech   700

   E. Political Defamation   704

     i. Defence of Truth   705
     ii. Fair Comment and Qualified Privilege   712

   F. Obscenity and Pornography   722
   G. Judicially Enforced Apologies   733

III. Right to Assembly and the Political Process   739

    A. Prior Notification or Approval   740
    B. Restrictions on Right to Assembly   742

IV. Freedom of Association and Civil Society   755

    A. The Right of Individuals to Associate/Disassociate   756
    B. Rights and Freedoms of Associations   763

9. Religion and State   **771**

I. What is Religion?   771

    A. Defining Religion: A Broad or Restrictive Approach?   771
    B. Religion or Custom?   776
    C. The Test of Essential Practice   779

II. Content of Religious Freedom   782

    A. Right to Profess   783
    B. Religious Conversion as a Public Order Issue   785
    C. Propagation and Conversion   798

        i. Constitutionalising the Right to Propagate Religion   799
        ii. The Right to Propagate Religion   802
        iii. Anti-Propagation Legislation   805
        iv. Legislative Schemes   807

III. Right to Practice   826

    A. Religious Dress Codes in Public Schools/Institutions   827

        i. State Enforcement   828
        ii. State Restraint (Singapore and Malaysia)   830

    B. Limits to Right to Religious Organisation – Public Order
       Considerations   833

IV. Religious Exemptions: Conscientious Objection   836

    A. Combative Sport in Schools   836
    B. Military Service   839
    C. Refusal to Participate in Flag and Anthem Ceremonies on
       Grounds of Religious Objections   851

V. The Diversity of Religion–State Constitutional Arrangements   859

    A. Introduction   859
    B. Secular Constitutional Models and Constitutional Theocracies   861

        i. Secular Liberal Constitutional Models   861
        ii. Secular Socialist Constitutions and Religion   862
        iii. Constitutional Theocracies   866

VI. Models of Secularism in Asia: What Separation of Religion and
    State Entails   870

    A. India and Ameliorative Secularism   870

        i. History of the Constitutional Principle of Secularity in India   870
        ii. Hindu Bias in the Indian Constitution and Threat of Hindutva   874

B. Philippines Secularism: Accommodation through Exemptions and
    Exceptions   878
    i. Church and State in the Philippines   878
C. Secular Government and Halal Certification   890
D. Japan: From State Shinto to a Secular State and Ceremonial Shinto   892

VII. State and Religion – The Protectionist State   904

A. The Protection of Religious Orthodoxy and State Regulation of
    Religious 'Words'   904
    i. Use of Religious Words   905
B. Blasphemy Laws and Protectionist Regimes   909
    i.   Cults and Deviant Sects   910
    ii.   Instrumentalism: Keeping Law and Order   911
    iii. Intrinsic Reasons for Preserving Orthodoxy   914
    iv.   On Blasphemy in General   915
    v.   Pakistan, Blasphemy and the Ahmadis   916
    vi.   Indonesia, Blasphemy and the Ahmadis   932

10. Socio-Economic Rights   **943**

I.   Introduction   943
II.   Express Socio-economic Rights: Judicial Review   945

A. Non-Discrimination Involving Fundamental Rights and
    Socio-Economic Considerations   946
B. Judicial Review of the Quantum of Social Benefits   949
C. Prioritising Competing Rights: Right to Smoke versus the Right to
    Avoid Smoke as a Facet of the Right to Life and Health   952
D. Social Insurance Schemes: Competing Rights   954
E. Regulation of Worker's Economic Rights and Collective Bargaining   957

III. Judicial Review and the Enforcement of Directive Principles: Implied
      Rights and Legislative–Executive Accountability   961
IV.   Economic Policy, Privatisation and Judicial Review in Indonesia   968
V.   Judicial Construction: Reading Directive Principles to Expand the
      'Right to Life' to Include Socio-Economic Rights   983

A. Right to Life and Livelihood: Housing and Unlawful Eviction   985
B. Right to Life and the Right to Food   994
C. Right to Life and Right to Health   1001
D. Right to Education   1006
E. Right to Life and Right to a Healthy Environment   1009
F. Right to Life Defined by Reference to ICESCR   1017
G. Right to a Healthy Environment and Sustainable Development   1019

Index   1023

List of Displayed Extracts

Chapter 1

Section II.B. WG Beaseley, *The Rise of Modern Japan: Political, Economic and Social Change Since 1850*, rev edn (New York: St Martin's Press, 2000) 76–77

Section II.C. Hungdah Chiu, 'Constitutional Development and Reform in the Republic of China on Taiwan' in Bih-Jaw Lin (ed), *Contemporary China and the Changing International Community* (Columbia SC: University of South Carolina Press, 1994) 3–34, 4–6

Section II.E. A Harding and P Leyland, *The Constitutional System of Thailand: A Contextual Analysis* (Oxford: Hart Publishing, 2011) 10–14

Section III.C. B Lapping, *End of Empire* (New York: St Martin's Press, 1985) 1

Section IV.A.i. Suisheng Zhao, *Power by Design: Constitution-Making in Nationalist China* (Honolulu: University of Hawaii Press, 1996) 25–26

Chapter 2

Section II. LM Friedman, 'Is There a Modern Legal Culture?' (1994) 7(2) *Ratio Juris* 117, 120–26

A Harding 'Asian Law, Public Law, Comparative Law Stir-Fry: Theory and Methods Considered' in T Groppi, V Piergigli and A Rinella (eds), *Asian Constitutionalism in Transition: A Comparative Perspective* (Rome: Giuffre Editore, 2009) 19, 28–32

Section II.B.ii. *Extracurricular Lesson Ban Case* 12-1 KCCR 427, 98Hun-Ka16, etc (consolidated) 27 Apr 2000 (Constitutional Court, South Korea)

Section III.C.i. A Schwarz, *A Nation in Waiting: Indonesia's Search for Stability* (Singapore: Talisman, 2004) 8–10

Li-ann Thio, 'Soft Constitutional Law in Non-liberal Asian Constitutional Democracies' (2010) 8(4) *I•CON* 766–99, 776–80

E Ip, 'Building Constitutional Democracy on Oriental Foundations: An Anatomy of Sun Yat-Sen's Constitutionalism' (2008) 9 *Historia Constitucional (revista electronica)*, available at <http://hc.rediris.es/09/index.html>

DA Bell, 'Introduction' in Jian Qing, *A Confucian Constitutional Order: How China's Ancient Past Can Shape Its Political Future* (Princeton, NJ: Princeton University Press, 2013) 1, 5–10

Section IV.B.iii.   *Khondker Delwar Hossain, Secretary, BNP Party v Bangladesh Italian Marble Works Ltd, Dhaka* Civil Petition for Leave to Appeal 1044 and 1045/2009 (the 'Fifth Amendment Case')

Chapter 3

Section II.A.   *Yong Vui Kong v Attorney-General* [2011] SGCA 9 (Court of Appeal, Singapore)

Action for Recognition of the Status as a Member of the House of Representatives and a Claim for Remuneration 14 Minshū 1206 (Supreme Court, Japan) *Tun Datu Haji Mustapha bin Datu Harun v Tun Datuk Haji Mohamed Adnan Robert, Yang di-Pertua Negeri Sabah & Datuk Joseph Pairin Kitigan (No 2)* [1986] 2 MLJ 420 (High Court, Malaysia)

Section II.B.   *JY Interpretation No 613* 21 Jul 2006 (Constitutional Court, Taiwan)

Section III.A.iii.   *Action for Recognition of the Status as a Member of the House of Representatives and a Claim for Remuneration* 14 Minshū 1206, (Supreme Court, Japan)

Rameshwar Prasad & Ors v Union of India & Anor [2006] AIR SC 980 (Supreme Court, India)

Section III.B.i.   *Ferdinand Marcos et al v Honorable Raul Manglapus et al* 177 SCRA 668 (1989) (Supreme Court, Philippines)

President's Proposition for National Confidence Referendum Case 2003Hun-Ma694, 27 Nov 2003 (Constitutional Court, South Korea)

In Re The Nineteenth Amendment to the Constitution (2002) 3 *Sri Lanka Law Reports* 85 (Supreme Court, Sri Lanka)

Section III.B.ii.   *Senator Aquilino Pimental et al v Ermita, Office of the Executive Secretary* GR No 158088, 6 Jul 2005 (Supreme Court, Philippines)

Concerning the Presidential Decision to Dispatch Korean National Armed Forces to Iraq 2006Hun-Ma1098, 1116, 1117 (Consolidated) 30 Oct 2006 (Constitutional Court, South Korea)

Francis Fukuyama, Bjorn Dressel & Boo Seung Chang, 'Facing the Perils of Presidentialism?' (2005) 16(2) *Journal of Democracy* 102

Section III.B.iii.   *Mallikarachchi v Attorney-General of Sri Lanka* (1985) 1 *Sri Lanka Law Reports* 74 (Supreme Court, Sri Lanka)

JY Interpretation No 627 15 Jun 2007 (Constitutional Court, Taiwan)

Section III.B.iv.   *Presidential Impeachment Case* 2004Hun-Na1, 14 May 2004 (Constitutional Court, South Korea)

Section III.C.ii.   *The Association of Expatriate Civil Servants of Hong Kong v The Chief Executive of HKSAR* 1 HKLRD 615 (CFI) (Court of First Instance, Hong Kong)

Section IV.A.   *Appointment of Acting Prime Minister Case* 98Hun-Ra1, 14 Jul 1998 (Constitutional Court, South Korea)

JY Interpretation No 632 15 Aug 2007 (Constitutional Court, Taiwan)

Arturo De Castro et al v Judicial and Bar Council et al Case GR No 191002, 17 Mar 2010 (Supreme Court, Philippines)

JY Interpretation No 613 21 Jul 2006 (Constitutional Court, Taiwan)

Section IV.B.   *JY Interpretation No 520* 15 Jan 2001 (Constitutional Court, Taiwan)

The President of the House of Representatives Requests for a Constitutional Court Ruling that the Enactment of Emergency Decrees were Inconsistent with Section 218 of the Constitution of the Kingdom of Thailand, BE 2540 (1997) Ruling No 1/2541, 23 May 1998 (Constitutional Court, Thailand)

Section IV.C.   *Judgment upon Case of the so-called 'Sunakawa Case' [Violation of the Special Criminal Law Enacted in Consequence of the Administrative Agreement under Article III of the Security Treaty between Japan and the United States of America]* 1959(A)No 710, 16 Dec 1959 (Supreme Court, Japan)

Judgment upon Case of Constitutionality of the Forced Leasing of Land for US Bases in Okinawa Prefecture 1996 (Gyo-Tsu) No 90, 28 Aug 1996 (Supreme Court, Japan)

Case Concerning the Presidential Decision to Dispatch Korean National Armed Forces to Iraq 2003Hun-Ma814, 29 Apr 2004 (Constitutional Court, South Korea)

Section IV.D.i.   *JY Interpretation No 543* 3 May 2002 (Constitutional Court, Taiwan)

Section IV.D.ii.   *Teh Cheng Poh v Public Prosecutor* [1979] 1 MLJ 50 (Privy Council, Malaysia)

Section IV.D.iii.   *Prof Randolf S David et al v Gloria Macapagal-Arroyo* GR No 171396, 3 May 2006 (Supreme Court, Philippines)

Section IV.D.iv.   *SR Bommai v Union of India* (1994) 2 SCR 644 (Supreme Court, India)

Section IV.D.v.   *Sindh High Court Bar Association v Federation of Pakistan* 31 Jul 2009 (Supreme Court, Pakistan)

Chapter 4

Section II.B.   *JY Interpretation No 31* 29 Jan 1954 (Constitutional Court, Taiwan)

JY Interpretation No 261 21 Jun 1990 (Constitutional Court, Taiwan)

Ng Ka Ling v Director of Immigration [1999] 1 HKLRD 315 (Court of Final Appeal, Hong Kong)

Section II.C.   *Judgment upon Case of Validity of Cabinet Order* 1952(A)No 2868, 27 Jul 1953 (Supreme Court, Japan)

Judgment upon the so-called Sunakawa Case [Violation of the Special Criminal Law Enacted in Consequence of the Administrative Agreement under Article III of the Security Treaty between Japan and the United States of America] 1959 (A) No 710, 16 Dec 1959 (Supreme Court, Japan)

Section II.D.   *May 18 Incident Non-institution of Prosecution Decision Case* 7-2 KCCR 697, 95Hun-Ma221, 15 Dec 1995 (Constitutional Court, Korea)

Siddique Ahmed v Bangladesh (7th Amendment Case) Writ Petition 696/2010, 26 Aug 2010 (Supreme Court, Bangladesh)

Section II.E.   *Habeas Corpus Petition of Benigno S Aquino, Jr et al v Sec Juan Ponce Enrile, Gen Romeo Espino & Gen Fidel Ramos* 59 SCRA 183; GR No L-35538, 17 Sep 1974 (Supreme Court, Philippines)

Watan Party v The Chief Executive/President of Pakistan & Anor Constitutional Petition No 36 of 2002, 7 Oct 2002 (Supreme Court, Pakistan)

Section III.A.   *JY Interpretation No 314* 25 Feb 1993 (Constitutional Court, Taiwan)

In Re The Eighteenth Amendment to The Constitution and The Provincial Councils Bill (2002) 3 *Sri Lanka Law Reports* 71, 3 Oct 2002 (Supreme Court, Sri Lanka)

Section III.B.   *Josue Javellana v The Executive Secretary & Ors* GR No L-36142 [1973] PHSC 43, 31 Mar 1973 (Supreme Court, Philippines)

Section III.C.   *Relocation of the Capital City Case* 2004Hun-Ma554, 21 Oct 2004 (Constitutional Court, Korea)

Cheng v Li [2009] HKEC 1587 (High Court, Hong Kong)

Section IV.B.   *Golak Nath v Punjab* [1967] AIR SC 1643 (Supreme Court, India)

Kesavananda v State of Kerala [1973] AIR SC 1461 (Supreme Court, India)

Minerva Mills Ltd v Union of India [1980] AIR SC 1789 (Supreme Court, India)

In Re the Thirteenth Amendment to the Constitution and the Provincial Councils Bill (1987) 2 *Sri Lanka Law Reports* 312 (Supreme Court, Sri Lanka)

In Re the Nineteenth Amendment to the Constitution (2002) 3 *Sri Lanka Law Reports* 85 (Supreme Court, Sri Lanka)

JY Interpretation No 499 24 Mar 2000 (Constitutional Court, Taiwan)

Section IV.C.   *Masykur Abdul Kadir Case* Constitutional Court Decision No 013/PUU-I/2003 (Constitutional Court, Indonesia)

Chapter 5

Section II.C.   *Ng Ka Ling & Others v Director of Immigration* [1999] 1 HKLRD
315 (Court of Final Appeal, Hong Kong)

Ng Ka Ling & Others v Director of Immigration (No 2) [1999]
1 HKC 425 (Court of Final Appeal, Hong Kong)

The Interpretation by the Standing Committee of the National
People's Congress of Articles 22(4) and 24(2)(3) of the Basic Law of
the Hong Kong Special Administrative Region of the People's
Republic of China 26 June 1999 (The Standing Committee of the
Ninth National People's Congress, China)

Director of Immigration v Chong Fung Yuen [2001] 2 HKLRD 533
(Court of Final Appeal, Hong Kong)

Qi Yuling v Chen Xiaoqi et al [1999] Lu Min Zhong No 258, 13 Aug
2001 (Higher People's Court of Shandong Province, China)

Section III.A.i.d. *JY Interpretation No 371* 20 Jan 1995 (Constitutional Court,
Taiwan)

*Re: The application to the Constitutional Court for the interpretation
of section 241 paragraph four and section 264 in conjunction with
section 6 of the Constitution of the Kingdom of Thailand, BE 2540
(1997)* Ruling No 5/2541, 4 Aug 1998 (Constitutional Court,
Thailand)

Section III.B.   *Case Concerning the National Police Reserve* 6 Minshū 9 (Supreme
Court, Japan)

Constitutional Reference No 1 of 1995 [1995] SGCT 1 (Constitution
of the Republic of Singapore Tribunal, Singapore)

Section IV.B.   *Adjudication on the Matters Whether the Interpretation of the
Constitution by the State Great Hural Breached or Not the Constitution*
23 Mar 2001 (Constitutional Court, Mongolia)

JY Interpretation No 419 31 Dec 1996 (Constitutional Court,
Taiwan)

Section IV.C.   *Re: The Phra Nakhon Si Ayutthaya Provincial Court referred the
objections of the defendants to the Constitutional Court for a ruling
under section 264 of the Constitution of the Kingdom of Thailand,
BE 2540 (1997)* Ruling No 14-15/2543, 4 Apr 2000 (Constitutional
Court, Thailand)

JY Interpretation No 216 19 Jun 1987 (Constitutional Court, Taiwan)

Rules implementing the Certified Judicial Scriveners Act Case
89Hun-Ma178, 15 Oct 1990 (Constitutional Court, South Korea)

May 18 Incident Non-institution of Prosecution Decision Case
95Hun-Ma221, etc, 15 Dec 1995 (Constitutional Court, South
Korea)

Section IV.D.   *Stephen Kalong Ningkan v Government of Malaysia* [1968] 2 MLJ 238 (Privy Council, on appeal from Malaysia)

JY Interpretation No 543 3 May 2002 (Constitutional Court, Taiwan)

Section IV.E.   *JY Interpretation No 154* 29 Sep 1978 (Constitutional Court, Taiwan)

Constitutional Review of Judgments Case 96Hun-Ma172, 24 Dec 1997 (Constitutional Court, South Korea)

Decision Number 001/PUU-IV/2006 25 Jan 2006 (Constitutional Court, Indonesia)

Section V.A.i.   *JY Interpretation No 601* 22 Jul 2005 (Constitutional Court, Taiwan)

Decision Number 005/PUU-IV/2006 23 Aug 2006 (Constitutional Court, Indonesia)

Section V.A.iii.   *Kilosbayab v Ermita* GR No 177721, 3 Jul 2007 (Supreme Court, Philippines)

De Castro et al v Judicial and Bar Council et al Case GR No 191002, 17 Mar 2010 (Supreme Court, Philippines)

SP Gupta v President of India and Ors [1982] AIR SC 149 (Supreme Court, India)

Section V.B.   *Union Of India vs Sankal Chand Himatlal Sheth and Anr* [1977] AIR 2328 (Supreme Court, India)

SP Gupta v President of India and Ors [1982] AIR SC 149 (Supreme Court, India)

Section V.C.   *JY Interpretation No 601* 22 Jul 2005 (Constitutional Court, Taiwan)

Bengzon v Drilon GR No 103524, 15 Apr 1992 (Supreme Court, Philippines)

Section V.D.   *Anwar Hossain Chowdhury v Bangladesh* 1989 18 CLC (AD) (Supreme Court, Bangladesh)

JY Interpretation No 530 5 Oct 2001 (Constitutional Court, Taiwan)

Secretary, Ministry of Finance v Md Masdar Hossain 29 CLC (AD) (Appellate Division, Supreme Court, Bangladesh)

Decision Number 005/PUU-IV/2006 23 Aug 2006 (Constitutional Court, Indonesia)

Section VI.A.   *Karpal Singh v Sultan of Selangor* [1988] 1 MLJ 64 (High Court, Malaysia)

Lim Mey Lee Susan v Singapore Medical Council [2011] 4 SLR 156 (High Court, Singapore)

Joya v PCGG GR No 96541, 24 Aug 1993 (Supreme Court, Philippines)

Section VI.B.   *Javellana v Executive Secretary* GR No L-36142, 31 Mar 1973 (Supreme Court, Philippines)

Marcos v Manglapus [1989] 177 SCRA 668 (Supreme Court, Philippines)

Action for Recognition of the Status as a Member of the House of Representatives and a Claim for Remuneration 14 Minshū 1206 (Supreme Court, Japan)

JY Interpretation No 328 26 Nov 1993 (Constitutional Court, Taiwan)

Section VI.C.i.   *Government of Malaysia v Lim Kit Siang* [1988] 2 MLJ 12 (Supreme Court, Malaysia)

Chan Hiang Leng Colin v Minister for Information and Arts [1996] 1 SLR 609 (Court of Appeal, Singapore)

Tan Eng Hong v Attorney-General [2012] SGCA 45 (Court of Appeal, Singapore)

Case to Seek Declaration of Illegality of Deprivation of the Right to Vote of Japanese Citizens Residing Abroad 59 Minshū 7 (Supreme Court, Japan)

Decision Number 010/PUU-IV/2006 25 Jul 2006 (Constitutional Court, Indonesia)

Section VI.C.ii.   *SP Gupta v President of India and Ors* [1982] AIR SC 149 (Supreme Court, India)

Chavez v Presidential Commission on Good Government GR No 130716, 9 Dec 1998 (Supreme Court, Philippines)

Section VII.A.   *JY Interpretation No 392* 22 Dec 1995 (Constitutional Court, Taiwan)

SP Gupta v Union of India and Ors [1982] AIR SC 149 (Supreme Court, India)

Director of Immigration v Chong Fung Yuen [2001] 2 HKLRD 533 (Court of Final Appeal, Hong Kong)

Section VII.B.   *JY Interpretation No 3* 21 May 1952 (Constitutional Court, Taiwan)

Section VII.C.   *Constitutional Reference No 1 of 1995* [1995] SGCT 1 (Constitutional Tribunal, Singapore)

Ng Ka Ling & Others v Director of Immigration [1999] 1 HKLRD 315 (Court of Final Appeal, Hong Kong)

Synthetics & Chemicals Ltd Etc v State of Uttar Pradesh [1990] AIR 1927 (Supreme Court, India)

Section VII.D.i.   *JY Interpretation No 582* 23 Jul 2004 (Constitutional Court, Taiwan)

Bangladesh Legal Aid and Services Trust (BLAST) v Bangladesh [2010] 39 CLC (HCD) (Supreme Court, Bangladesh)

Visakha v State of Rajasthan [1997] AIR SC 3011 (Supreme Court, India)

Section VII.D.ii. *Attorney-General v Chee Soon Juan* [2006] SGHC 54, 2 SLR 650 (High Court, Singapore)

Attorney-General v Hertzberg Daniel [2008] SGHC 218 (High Court, Singapore)

Section VII.D.iii. *Disclosure of the Identity of Sex Offenders Convicted of Acquiring Sexual Favors from Minors in Exchange for Monetary Compensation* 2002Hun-Ka14, 6 Jun 2003 (Constitutional Court, South Korea)

Section VIII.A. *Constitutional Review of Judgments Case* 96Hun-Ma172 et al, 24 Dec 1997 (Constitutional Court, South Korea)

Joint and Several Liability of Executive Officers and Oligopolistic Stockholders Case 2000Hun-Ka5, 29 Aug 2002 (Constitutional Court, South Korea)

Section VIII.B. *IC Golaknath v State of Punjab* [1967] AIR SC 1643 (Supreme Court, India)

Public Prosecutor v Dato' Tap Peng [1987] 2 MLJ 311 (Supreme Court, Malaysia)

Abdul Nasir bin Amer Hamsah v Public Prosecutor [1997] SGCA 38 (Court of Appeal, Singapore)

Koo Sze Yiu v Chief Executive of the HKSAR [2006] 3HKLRD 455 (Court of Final Appeal, Hong Kong)

The Right to Vote of Nationals Residing Abroad Case 2004Hun-Ma644 et al, 28 Jun 2007 (Constitutional Court, South Korea)

Section VIII.C. *JY Interpretation No 86* 15 Aug 1960 (Constitutional Court, Taiwan)

JY Interpretation No 211 5 Dec 1986 (Constitutional Court, Taiwan)

Section VIII.D. *Vishaka and others v State of Rajasthan and others* [1997] AIR SC 3011 (Supreme Court, India)

Chapter 6

Section II.C.i. *Case to Seek Invalidation of Election* 65 Minshū 2, 23 Mar 2011 (Supreme Court, Japan)

National Assembly Election Redistricting Plan Case 2000Hun-Ma92, 25 Oct 2001 (Constitutional Court, South Korea)

Robert v Tobias Jr v Hon City Mayor Benjamin S Abalos GR No L-114783, 8 Dec 1994 (Supreme Court, Philippines)

Bagabuyo v COMELEC GR No 176970, 8 Dec 2008 (Supreme Court, Philippines)

J & K National Panthers Party v the Union of India & Ors [2010] INSC 937 (Supreme Court, India)

Section II.D.   *Chan Yu Nam & Anor v the Secretary for Justice* [2010] 1 HKC 4937
                   (Court of First Instance, Hong Kong)

Section II.E.i.   *Case Seeking Nullification of an Election* 58 Minshū 1 (Supreme
                   Court, Japan)

                   One-Person One-Vote Case 2000Hun-Ma91, 19 Jul 2001
                   (Constitutional Court, South Korea)

                   Ang Bagong Bayani-OFW Labor Party v Commission on Elections
                   GR No 147589, 26 Jun 2001 (Supreme Court, Philippines)

                   Ang Ladlad LGBT Party v Commission on Elections GR No 190582,
                   8 April 2010 (Supreme Court, Philippines)

Section II.E.ii.   *JY Interpretation No 331* 30 Dec 1993 (Constitutional Court,
                   Taiwan)

                   National Seat Succession Case 92Hun-Ma153, 28 Apr 1994
                   (Constitutional Court, South Korea)

Section II.F.   *Dr Ahmed Hossain v Bangladesh* 21 CLC (AD) 109, 2 Mar 1992
                   (Supreme Court, Bangladesh)

                   Union of India v Rakesh Kumar and Ors [2010] AIR SC 3244
                   (Supreme Court, India)

Section III.A.i.   *Registration Requirement of Political Parties* 2004Hun-Ma246, 30
                   Mar 2006 (Constitutional Court, South Korea)

                   Dr Mohd Nasir bin Hashim v Menteri Dalam Negeri [2006] 6 MLJ
                   213 (Court of Appeal, Malaysia)

                   *Political Party Registrar's application for an order to dissolve Patiroop
                   Party* Ruling 2/2542, 4 Mar 1999 (Constitutional Court, Thailand)

Section III.A.ii. *Re: Request of the Attorney-General for dissolution orders against
                   Pattana Chart Thai Party, Paen Din Thai Party and Thai Rak Thai
                   Party* Ruling No 3-5/2550, 30 May 2007 (Constitutional Court,
                   Thailand)

                   *Re: The Attorney-General requested for a Constitutional Court order
                   to dissolve Neutral Democratic (Matchima Thippathai) Party* Ruling
                   No 18/2551, 2 Dec 2008 (Constitutional Court, Thailand)

                   Janata Dal (Samajwadi) v The Election Commission of India [1996]
                   AIR 577 (Supreme Court, India)

Section III.B.   *Day and Time of, and Method of Determining the Elect at the
                   Re-election and the Vacancy Election for Members of the National
                   Assembly* 2003Hun-Ma259, 27 Nov 2003 (Constitutional Court,
                   South Korea)

                   NP Ponnuswami v Returning Officer [1952] AIR 64 (Supreme Court,
                   India)

Section III.C.i.   *Macalintal v COMELEC* GR No 157013, 10 Jul 2003 (Supreme
                   Court, Philippines)

Sixto S Brillantes Jr v Yorac GR No 93867, 18 Dec 1990 (Supreme Court, Philippines)

Section III.C.ii.   *Mohinder Singh Gill & Anr v Chief Election Commissioner* [1978] AIR SC 851 (Supreme Court, India)

ABS-CBN Broadcasting Corporation v Commission on Elections GR No 133486, 28 Jan 2000 (Supreme Court, Philippines)

Jatiya Party v Election Commission and Ors 2001 BLD (AD) 10, 30 Nov 2000 (Supreme Court, Bangladesh)

Section IV.A.   *Kim v Osaka Electoral Commission* 49 Minshū 639 (Supreme Court, Japan)

Case to Seek Declaration of Illegality of Deprivation of the Right to Vote of Japanese Citizens Residing Abroad 59 Minshū 7 (Supreme Court, Japan)

Secretary for Justice v Chan Wah [2000] 3 HKCFAR 459 (Court of Final Appeal, Hong Kong)

Restriction on Prisoner's Right to Vote Case 2007Hun-Ma1462, 29 Oct 2009 (Constitutional Court, South Korea)

Section IV.B.   *Mercado v Manzano* 307 SCRA 630 (1999) (Supreme Court, Philippines)

JY Interpretation No 290 24 Jan 1992 (Constitutional Court, Taiwan)

Tse Hung Hing v Medical Council of Hong Kong [2010] 1 HKLRD 111 (Court of First Instance, Hong Kong)

Judicial Review on Regulation No 23 Year 2003 Regarding General Election of President and Vice President 007/PUU-II/2004, 23 Jul 2004 (Constitutional Court, Indonesia)

Section V.A.   *Impeachment of the President Case* 2004Hun-Na1, 14 May 2004 (Constitutional Court, South Korea)

Dharmadasa Gomes v Commissioner of Elections [2000] 3 SLR 207 (Court of Appeal, Sri Lanka)

Section V.B.   *Enrique T Garcia v Commission on Elections* 237 SCRA 279 (1994) (Supreme Court, Philippines)

Chapter 7

Section I.   RJ Pennock, 'Equality and Inequality' in Joel Krieger (ed), *The Oxford Companion to Politics of the World* (New York: Oxford University Press, 1993) at 271

M Schwarzchild, 'Constitutional Law and Equality' in D Patterson (ed), *A Companion to Philosophy of Law and Legal Theory* (Oxford: Blackwell Publishers, 1999) at 156–58

Section III.C.i.   *Adong bin Kuwau & Ors v Kerajaan Negeri Johor & Anor* [1997] 1 MLJ 418 (Court of Appeal, Malaysia)

Kayano et al v Hokkaido Expropriation Committee (The Nibutani Dam Decision) (Sapporo District Court, Civil Division No 3), 27 Mar 1997 (1999) 38 *International Legal Materials* 394 (trans MA Levin)

Section III.D.   *Judicial Yuan Interpretation No 649* 31 Oct 2008 (Constitutional Court, Taiwan)

Visually Impaired Massagers Case 20-2(A) KCCR 1089, 2006Hun-Ma1098•1116•1117 (consolidated), 30 Oct 2008 (Constitutional Court, South Korea)

Section III.E.i.   *The State of West Bengal vs Anwar Ali Sarkar* [1952] AIR 75, [1952] SCR 284 (Supreme Court of India)

Section III.E.ii.   *Quinto v Commission on Elections* GR No 189698, 22 Feb 2010 (Supreme Court, Philippines)

Act on the Immigration and Legal Status of Overseas Koreans Case 13-2 KCCR 714, 99Hun-Ma494, 29 Nov 2001 (Constitutional Court, South Korea)

Section III.E.iii.   *Pledge to Abide by the Law Case* 14-1 KCCR 351, 98Hun-Ma425, etc, (consolidated), 25 Apr 2002 (Constitutional Court, South Korea)

Section IV.B.ii.   *Centre for Enquiry into Health & Allied Themes (CEHAT) & Ors v Union of India & Ors* (2003) 8 SCC 398, [2003] AIR SC 3309 (Supreme Court, India)

Section IV.B.iii.   *Naz Foundation v Government of Delhi & Ors* WP(C) No 7455/2001, 2 Jul 2009 (High Court, Delhi)

Sunil Babu Pant & Ors v Government of Nepal Writ No 917 of 2007 (Supreme Court, Nepal) English translation in (2008) 2(1) *NJA Law Journal* 262

Section IV.D.   *Arudou v Earth Cure* Judgment of 11 Nov 2002 (Sapporo District Court, Japan) (2008) 9(2) *Asian-Pacific Law & Policy Journal* 297 (trans Timothy Webster)

Chapter 8

Section II.A.   *Brij Bhushan v Delhi* [1950] SCR 605 (Supreme Court, India)

Persatuan Aliran Kesadran Negara v Minister of Home Affairs [1987] 1 MLJ 442 (High Court, Malaysia)

Judgment upon Case of Injunctions against Publication In Relation To the Freedom of Expression 40 Minshū 872 (Supreme Court, Japan)

J Y Interpretation No 105 7 Oct 1964 (Constitutional Court, Taiwan)

South Korea Periodicals Registration Case 90Hun-Ka23, 26 Jun 1992 (Constitutional Court, South Korea)

Section II.B.i.   *J Y Interpretation No 678* 29 Jul 2010 (Constitutional Court, Taiwan)

Secretary, Ministry of I & B v Cricket Association of Bengal [1995] AIR 1995 SC 1236 (Supreme Court, India)

Section II.B.ii.   *J Y Interpretation No 364* 23 Sep 1994 (Constitutional Court, Taiwan)

Request for a Corrective Report Case 89Hun-Ma165, 16 Sep 1991 (Constitutional Court, South Korea)

Japan Communist Party v Sankei Newspaper Inc 875 Hanrei Jiho 30, 1977 (Supreme Court, Japan)

Life Insurance Corporation v Manubhai [1993] AIR 171, [1992] SCR (3) 595 (Supreme Court, India)

Section II.C.   *Praising and Encouraging under National Security Act Case* 89Hun-Ka113, 2 Apr 1990 (Constitutional Court, South Korea)

Public Prosecutor v Oh Keng Seng [1977] 2 MLJ 206 (Federal Court, Malaysia)

Public Prosecutor v Koh Song Huat Benjamin [2005] SGDC 272 (District Court, Singapore)

Virendra v The State of Punjab [1957] AIR 896 (Supreme Court, India)

Section II.D.i.   *Dr Eggi Sudjana, SH, MSi, Pandapotan Lubis* 013-022/PUU-IV/2006 [2006] IDCC 26, 6 Dec 2006 (Constitutional Court, Indonesia)

Section II.D.ii.   *Shadrake Alan v Attorney-General* [2011] SGCA 26 (Court of Appeal, Singapore)

Attorney-General v Tan Liang Joo John & Ors [2009] SGHC 41 (High Court, Singapore)

Wong Yeung Ng v Secretary for Justice [1999] 2 HKC 24, [1999] 2 HKLRD 293 (Court of Final Appeal, Hong Kong)

Attorney-General, Malaysia v Manjeet Singh Dhillion [1991] 1 MLJ 167 (Supreme Court, Malaysia)

Hewamanne v Manik de Silva & Another [1983] 1 Sri LR (Supreme Court, Sri Lanka)

Section II.D.iii.   *HKSAR v Ng Kung Siu* [1999] 8 BHRC 244 (Court of Final Appeal, Hong Kong)

Section II.E.i.   *Case to Seek Damages and Compensation for Non-Pecuniary Damages Caused by Libel and Damage to Credit* 20 Minshū 5 (Tokyo High Court, Japan)

Judgment Concerning the Case where a Newspaper Company, when Printing an Article Distributed from a News Agency in the Newspaper that it Publishes, is Deemed to have Reasonable Grounds for Believing the Fact Alleged in Said Article to be True 2009 (Ju) No 2057, 28 Apr 2011 (Supreme Court, Japan)

Case of Defamation 1966(A) No 2472, 25 Jun 1969 (Supreme Court, Japan)

J Y Interpretation 509 7 Jul 2000 (Constitutional Court, Taiwan)

Letter of Condolence for Kim Il-sung Case 97Hun-Ma265, 24 Jun 1999 (Constitutional Court, South Korea)

Section II.E.ii. *Albert Cheng & Anor v Tse Wai Chun Paul* 4HKC1, 13 Nov 2000 (Court of Final Appeal, Hong Kong)

Review Publishing Co Ltd & Anor v Lee Hsien Loong & Anor [2009] SGCA 46 (Court of Appeal, Singapore)

Section II.F. *Judgment Upon Case of Translation and Publication of Lady Chatterley's Lover and Article 175 of the Penal Code* 1953(A) No 1713, 13 Mar 1957 (Supreme Court, Japan)

Ranjit D Udeshi v Maharashtra [1965] 1 SCR 65 (Supreme Court, India)

J Y Interpretation No 407 5 Jul 1996 (Constitutional Court, Taiwan)

J Y Interpretation No 617 26 Oct 2006 (Constitutional Court, Taiwan)

Case to Seek Revocation of the Disposition of Notification to the Effect that the Goods to be Imported Fall Within the Category of Prohibited Goods 2003 (Gyo-Tsu) No 157, 19 Feb 2008 (Supreme Court, Japan)

Section II.G. *Notice of Apology Case* 89Hun-Ma160, 1 Apr 1991 (Constitutional Court, South Korea)

Ma Bik Yung v Ko Chuen [2001] 4 HKC 119 (Court of Final Appeal, Hong Kong)

J Y Interpretation No 656 3 Apr 2009 (Constitutional Court, Taiwan)

Section III.B. *Leung Kwok Hung v HKSAR* [2005] 8 HKCFAR 229 (Court of Final Appeal, Hong Kong)

Japan v Teramae (1975) 29 Keishu 489 (Supreme Court, Japan)

Chee Siok Chin & Ors v Minister for Home Affairs & Anor [2006] 1 SLR(R) 582 (High Court, Singapore)

J Y Interpretation No 445 23 Jan 1998 (Constitutional Court, Taiwan)

Himat Lal K Shah v Commissioner of Police [1973] SCR (2) 266 (Supreme Court, India)

Section IV.A.   *Ariyapala Gunaratne v The People's Bank* [1985] 1 Sri LR 338 (Supreme Court, Sri Lanka)

Judgment Concerning Whether the Agreement Concluded Between an Employee and Employer, which Obliges the Employee Not to Exercise the Right to Withdraw from a Particular Labour Union, is Contrary to Public Policy 2004 (Ju) No 1787, 2 Feb 2007 (Supreme Court, Japan)

Prohibition of Political Party Membership of Primary and Middle School Teachers 2001Hun-Ma710, 25 Mar 2004 (Constitutional Court, South Korea)

JY Interpretation No 373 24 Feb 1995 (Constitutional Court, Taiwan)

Sivarasa Rasiah v Badan Peguam Malaysia & Anor [2010] 2 MLJ 333 (Federal Court, Malaysia)

Section IV.B.   *JY Interpretation No 644* 20 Jun 2008 (Constitutional Court, Taiwan)

JY Interpretation No 479 1 Apr 1999 (Constitutional Court, Taiwan)

Damyanti Naranga v The Union of India & Ors [1971] AIR 966, [1971] SCR (3) 840 (Supreme Court, India)

Dr Mohd Nasir Hashim v Menteri Dalam Negeri [2006] 6 MLJ 213 (Court of Appeal, Malaysia)

Secretary of Aircraft Engineers of BD & Anor v Registrar of Trade Union & Ors 1993, 22 CLC (AD) (Supreme Court, Bangladesh)

Chapter 9

Section II.A.   *Daud bin Mamat v Majlis Agama Islam* [2001] 2 MLJ 390 (High Court, Malaysia)

Section II.B.   *Lina Joy v Majlis Agama Islam Wilayah & Anor* [2004] 2 MLJ 119 (High Court, Malaysia)

Lina Joy v Majlis Agama Islam Wilayah [2007] 4 MLJ 585 (Federal Court, Malaysia)

Section II.C.i.   Constituent Assembly of India Debates 6 December 1948, Vol VII (Article 25, Constitution of India) available at <http://www.indiankanoon.org/doc/1933556/>

Section II.C.iii.   Johor Legislative Assembly, Control and Restriction of the Propagation of Non-Islamic Religions Enactment 1991 (State of Johor) No 13 of 1991

Section II.C.iv.a.   *Rev Stainislaus v State of Madhya Pradesh* [1977] AIR 908, [1977] SCR (2) 611

Evangelical Fellowship of India v State of Himachal Pradesh CWP No 438 of 2011A (High Court, Himachal Pradesh)

Section II.C.iv.b.   *Teaching Sisters of the Holy Cross in Menzingen v Sri Lanka* SC
                     Special Determination No 19/2003 (Supreme Court, Sri Lanka)

Section III.A.i.   *Salahuddin Dolon v Government of Bangladesh* Writ Petition No
                     4495 of 2009 (High Court, Bangladesh)

Section III.A.ii.   *Meor Atiqulrahman bin Ishak v Fatimah bte Sihi* [2006] 4 MLJ 605
                     (Federal Court, Malaysia)

Section III.B.   *Decision Upon the Case Where the Dissolution Order on the Grounds
                     Provided by Article 81(1)(1) and (2) of the Law on Religious
                     Organizations is Not Against Art 20(1) of the Constitution* 1996 (ku)
                     8, Minshū Vol 50, No 1, at 199 (Tokyo High Court) (trans Sir Ernest
                     Satow)

Section IV.A.   *Matsumoto v Kobayashi* 50 Minshū 469, 8 March 1996 (Supreme
                     Court, Japan)

Section IV.B.   *Conscientious Objection to Military Service Case* 16-2(A) KCCR
                     141 2002 Hun-Ka1 (Constitutional Court, South Korea)

                     Judicial Yuan Interpretation No 490 1 Oct 1999 (Constitutional
                     Court, Taiwan) (trans Jiunn-rong Yeh)

                     Chan Hiang Leng Colin v Public Prosecutor [1994] 3 SLR(R) 209
                     (Court of Appeal, Singapore)

Section IV.C.   *Nappalli Peter Williams v Institute of Technical Education* [1992]
                     2 SLR 569 (Court of Appeal, Singapore)

                     Ebralinag v Division Superintendent of Schools of Cebu GR No
                     95770, 1 March 1993, 219 SCRA 256 (1993) (Supreme Court,
                     Philippines)

                     Resolution on Motion for Reconsideration GR No 95770 December
                     29, 1995

                     Bijoe Emmanuel v State of Kerala [1987] AIR 748, [1986] SCR (3)
                     518 (Supreme Court, India)

Section V.B.iii.   Sayyid Abul Ala Maududi, 'Fundamentals of Islamic Constitution'
                     in *The Islamic Law and Constitution*, Khurshid Ahmad (ed & trans)
                     (Lahore: Islamic Publications Ltd, 1955) ch 7, 271–91 (summary)

Section VI.A.i.a.   *Hinsa Virodhak Sangh v Mirzapur Moti Kuresh Jamat & Ors* Appeal
                     (Civil) 5469 of 2005 (Supreme Court, India)

Section VI.A.ii.   *Dr Ramesh Yeshwant Prabhoo v Shri Prabhakar Kashinath Kunte*
                     (1996) SCC (1) 130 (Supreme Court, India)

Section VI.B.i.   *Alejandro Estrada v Soledad Escritor* AM No P-02-1651 22 June
                     2006 (En Banc) (Supreme Court, Philippines)

Section VI.C.   *Islamic Da'Wah Council of the Philippines Inc v Office of the Executive
                     Secretary* GR No 153888, 9 July 2003 (Supreme Court, Philippines)

Section VI.D.   *Kakunaga v Sekiguchil (The Tsu City Shinto Ground-breaking Ceremony
                     Case)* 31 Minshū⁻ 533, 13 July 1977 (Supreme Court, Japan)

Judgment Upon Constitutionality of the Prefecture's Expenditure from Public Funds to Religious Corporations Which Held Ritual Ceremonies (*Yasakuni Shrine Case*) 1992 (Gyo-Tsu) No 156, 2 April 1997 (Supreme Court, Japan, Grand Bench)

Judgment on the Enshrinement of a Dead SDF Officer to Gokoku Shrine (*Self Defence Force Officer Enshrinement Case*) 1 June 1988, 1982(0) No 902 (Supreme Court, Japan)

Section VII.A.i.   *Titular Roman Catholic Archbishop of Kuala Lumpur v Menteri Dalam Negeri* [2010] 2 MLJ 78 (High Court, Malaysia)

Section VII.B.   *Junaid K Doja, International Book Agency Limited, Dhaka v The State* (2001) 21 BLD 573 (Supreme Court, Bangladesh)

Section VII.B.v.   *Majibur Rehman v Federal Government of Pakistan* PLD 1985 Federal Shariat Court 8 Vol XXXVII, at 71–72, 76–82, 87, 99–101, 114–15, 118–19

Zaheeruddin v The State (1993) 26 SCMR 1718 (Supreme Court, Pakistan)

Section VII.B.vi.   Presidential Decree No 1/PNPS/1965 on the Prevention of the Misuse/Insulting of a Religion Made into a Law by Law 5/1969

Decision of the Constitutional Court on the Blasphemy Law No 140/PUU-VII/2009, 19 April 2010 (Constitutional Court, Indonesia) [unofficial trans M Virgiany]

Chapter 10

Section II.A.   *Fok Chun Wa v The Hospital Authority* [2012] HKCFA 34, [2012] 2 HKC 413 (Court of Final Appeal, HKSAR)

Section II.B.   *Shigeru Asahi v Minister of Health and Welfare* Case Number Gyo Tsu No 14 of 1964 (Judgment of May 24, 1967) [edited for ease of reading]

Section II.C.   *No-smoking Zone and Right to Smoke Cigarette* 16-2(A) KCCR 355, 2003Hun-Ma457, 26 Aug 2004 (Constitutional Court, Korea)

Section II.D.   *Compulsory Subscription to the National Pension Plan* 13-1 KCCR 301, 99Hun-Ma365, 22 Feb 2001 (Constitutional Court, Korea)

Section II.E.   *Constitutional Complaint against the Proviso of Trade Union and Labor Relations Adjustment Act Article 81 Item 2* 17-2 KCCR 392, 2002Hun-Ba95•96, 2003Hun-Ba9 (consolidated) 24 Nov 2005 (Constitutional Court, Korea)

Section III.   *JY Interpretation No 578* 21 May 2004 (Constitutional Court, Taiwan)

Oposa et al v Fulgencio S Factoran Jr et al GR No 101083 (Supreme Court, Philippines)

Section IV.   *Judicial Review of the Electricity Law (No 20/2002)* Case No 001-021-022/PUU-I/2003 (Constitutional Court, Indonesia)

Judicial Review of the Law of the Republic of Indonesia Number 7 Year 2004 regarding Water Resources Case Number 058-059-060-063/PUU-II/2004; Case Number 008/PUU-III/2005 (Constitutional Court, Indonesia)

Section V.A. *Olga Tellis & Ors v Bombay Municipal Council* [1985] 2 Supp SCR 51, [1986] AIR SC 180 (Supreme Court, India)

Bangladesh Legal Aid and Services Trust and others v Government of Bangladesh Writ Petition No 5915 of 2005 (Supreme Court, Bangladesh)

Section V.B. *People's Union for Civil Liberties v Union of India & Ors* Writ Petition (Civil) No 196 of 2001 (Supreme Court, India)

Section V.C. *Laxmi Mandal v Deen Dayal Harinagar Hospital* WP(C) 8853/2008 (Supreme Court, India)

Paschim Banga Khet Mazdoor Samity & Ors v State of West Bengal & Anor [1996] AIR SC 2426, (1996) 4 SCC 37 (Supreme Court, India)

Section V.D. *Unni Krishnan, JP v State of Andhra Pradesh* [1993] AIR 217, [1993] SCR (1) 594 (Supreme Court, India)

Section V.E. *Shehla Zia v WAPDA (Water and Power Development Authority)* PLD (1994) SC 693, 712 (Supreme Court, Pakistan)

Section V.F. *Clean Air Foundation Ltd v The Government of the HKSAR* [2007] HKCFI 757 (Court of First Instance, HKSAR, No 35 of 2007)

Table of Cases

Australia

Adelaide Company of Jehovah's Witnesses Incorporated v Commonwealth
[1943] ALR 193.. 780, 848–9, 857, 925
Church of the New Faith v Commissioner of Pay-Roll (1982) 154 CLR 120......... 773
Gallagher v Durack (1983) 45 ALR 53 696
Kruger & Ors v Commonwealth of Australia 190 CLR 1; (1997) 146 ALR 126.... 851
Lange v ABC (1997) 145 LR 96... 712
Mabo & Ors v State of Queensland & Anor (1986) 64 ALR 1.............................. 562
Morgan Proprietary Ltd v Deputy Commissioner of Taxation for New South
Wales [1940] AC 838... 593
Pareroultja & Or v Tickner & Ors (1993) 117 ALR 206...................................... 562
Pell v The Council of Trustees of the National Gallery of Victoria [1998]
2 VR 391 915

Bangladesh

Ain o Salish Kendra (ASK) v Government of Bangladesh 19 BLD (1999) 488.. 990–1
Akramuzzaman v Bangladesh 52 DLR 209 605
Anwar Hossain Chowdhury v Bangladesh 1989 18 CLC (AD) (Supreme Court,
Bangladesh.. 114, 313, 351, 389–91
Bangladesh Jatiya Mahila Ainjibi Samity v Government of Bangladesh, (2009)
29 BLD (HCD) 415.. 829–30
Bangladesh Legal Aid and Services Trust (BLAST) and others v Government of
Bangladesh Writ Petition No 5915 of 2005 (Supreme Court, Bangladesh)... 988–91
Bangladesh Legal Aid and Services Trust (BLAST) v Bangladesh [2010] 39 CLC
(HCD) (Supreme Court, Bangladesh)...433–5, 441
Bangladesh National Women Lawyers Association (BNWLA) v Govt of
Bangladesh, Writ Petition No 5916 of 2008 (Supreme Court, Bangladesh).. 79, 829
Dr Ahmed Hossain v Bangladesh 21 CLC (AD) 109 (Supreme Court,
Bangladesh) 494, 496
Farooque v Bangladesh (1997) 49 DLR (AD) 1.. 416, 968,
1020 ....
Jatiya Party v Election Commission for Bangladesh and Ors 2001 BLD (AD)
10, 30 Nov 2000 (Supreme Court, Bangladesh)... 518–19
Jibendra Kishore v East Pakistan 9 DLR (SC) 21... 605
Junaid K Doja, International Book Agency Limited, Dhaka v The State (2001)
21 BLD 573 (Supreme Court, Bangladesh) 909–10
Kalam v Bangladesh 21 BLD-446.. 990
Khushi Kabir v Government of Bangladesh (WP No 3091 of 2000) 1000

Retired Government Employees Association v Bangladesh 46 DLR 426 605
SA Sabur v Returning Officer 41 DLR (AD) 30 605
Salahuddin Dolon v Government of Bangladesh Writ Petition No 4495 of 2009
    (High Court, Bangladesh) 828–30
Secretary, Ministry of Finance v Md Masdar Hossain 2000 29 CLC (AD)
    (Appellate Division, Supreme Court, Bangladesh) 389, 393–4
Secretary of Aircraft Engineers of BD & Anor v Registrar of Trade Union &
    Ors 1993, 22 CLC (AD) (Supreme Court, Bangladesh) 768–9
Siddique Ahmed v Bangladesh (7th Amendment Case) Writ Petition 696/2010,
    26 Aug 2010 (Supreme Court, Bangladesh) 244–6, 351
Society for the Enforcement of Human Rights (BSEHR) v Government of
    Bangladesh 53 DLR (2001) 1 991

Canada

Calder v Attorney-General of British Columbia (1973) 34 DLR (3d) 145,
    British Columbia 562
Donald v Board of Education for the City of Hamilton [1945] OR 518 852
Edwards v Canada (Attorney General) [1930] AC 124 (Privy Council on appeal
    from Supreme Court of Canada) 426
Eldridge v British Columbia (Attorney-General) [1997] 3 SCR 624 949
Multani v Commission Scolaire Marguerite-Bourgeoys (2006) SCC 6 (Supreme
    Court, Canada) 827
Newfoundland (Treasury Board) v NAPE [2004] 3 SCR 381 949
Ontario Human Rights Commission v Daiming Juang 2006 Human Rights
    Tribunal of Ontario 1 773
R v Butler [1992] 1 SCR 452 732
R v Keegstra [1990] 3 SCR 697 680–1
R v Kopyto (1988) 47 DLR (4th) 213 79
RJR-McDonald Inc v Attorney General of Canada [1995] 3 SCR 199 948
Robert Libman Equality Party v AG of Quebec 1997 3 RCS 569 948
Vriend v Alberta (1998) 1 SCR 493 631–2

China

Qi Yuling v Chen Xiaoqi et al [1999] Lu Min Zhong No 258, 13 Aug 2001
    (Higher People's Court of Shandong Province, China) 122, 314, 322–4

Columbia

Constitutional Court, T760/08 (Judgment of 31 July 2008) 945

European Court of Human Rights

Bayatyan v Armenia, App no 23459/03 (ECtHR, 7 July 2011)............................ 846
Dahlab v Switzerland App no 42393/98 (ECtHR, 15 February 2001).................... 827
Efstratious v Greece App No 24095/94 (ECtHR, 18 December 1996)................... 838
Kokkinakis v Greece App No 14307/88, 25 May 1993, (ECtHR) 805, 818
Larissis v Greece App nos 140/1996/759/958–960, (ECtHR, 24 February
    1998).. 818–19
Lautsi v Italy App no 30814/06 (ECtHR, 18 March 2011)..................................... 860
Leyla Sahin v Turkey, App no 44774/98 (ECtHR, 10 November 2005)................. 782
Lopez Ostra v Spain (1994) Series A no 303-C.. 1019
Melnychuk v Ukraine App No 28743/03 (ECtHR, 5 July 2005)........................... 667
Metropolitan Church of Bessarabia v Moldova App no 45701/99 (ECtHR,
    13 December 2001)... 861
Podkolzina v Latvia ECHR 2002-II 443 533
Refah Partisi v Turkey App no 41340/98 (ECtHR, 13 February 2003)................. 108
Sahin v Turkey App no 44774/98 (ECtHR, 10 November 2005) 827
Scoppola v Italy (No 3), App No 126/05 (ECtHR, 22 May 2012)...................... 528
Sentges v The Netherlands, App no 27677/8 July 2003... 947
Sporrong v Sweden (1982) 5 EHRR 35.. 947

Germany

1 BvR 1783/99 (15 Jan 2002) (Federal Constitutional Court)............................... 782
Flag Desecration Case (1990) 81 BVerfGE 278.. 683
Holocaust Denial Case [1994] 90BVerfGE 241 (Federal Constitutional Court)..... 682
Judgment of 9 February 2010, Bundesverfassungsgericht [BVerfG] [Federal
    Constitutional Court] 1 BVL 1/09, 1 BVL 3/09, 1 BVL 4/09 of 9 Feb 2010 (Hartz
    IV)... 952
Teacher Headscarf decision, Judgment of 24 September 2003-BVerfGE 108, 282;
    Case No 2 BvR 1436/02 (Bundesverfgassungsgericht [BVerfG] Constitutional
    Court, 24 Sept 2003) 827

Hong Kong

Albert Cheng & Anor v Tse Wai Chun Paul [2000] 4 HKC 1 (Court of Final
    Appeal, Hong Kong).. 712–16, 720
Association of Expatriate Civil Servants of Hong Kong v The Chief Executive
    of HKSAR 1 HKLRD 615 (CFI) (Court of First Instance, Hong Kong).... 179–80
Chan Yu Nam & Anor v the Secretary for Justice [2010] 1 HKC 4937 (Court of
    First Instance, Hong Kong)... 479–80
Cheng v Li [2009] HKEC 1587 (High Court, Hong Kong) 274–6
Chong Fong Yuen v Director of Immigration, FACV No 26 of 2000.................... 277
Chu Woan Chyi v Director of Immigration [2007] HKCFI 267 772

Clean Air Foundation Ltd v The Government of the HKSAR [2007] HKCFI
    757 (Court of First Instance, HKSAR, No 35 of 2007) 1017–19
Democratic Republic of Congo v FG Hemisphere Associates LLC [2011]
    4 HKC 151 326
Director of Immigration v Chong Fung Yuen [2001] 2 HKLRD 533 (Court
    of Final Appeal, Hong Kong).....................................320–2, 418, 421–3
Eastern Express Publisher Ltd v Mo Man Ching [1999] 2 HKCFAR 264 712
Fok Chun Wa v The Hospital Authority [2012] HKCFA 34, [2012] 2 HKC 413
    (Court of Final Appeal, HKSAR) 946–9
HKSAR v Ng Kung Siu [1999] 2 HKCFAR 442... 441
HKSAR v Ng Kung Siu [1999] 8 BHRC 244 (Court of Final Appeal, Hong
    Kong)...441, 700–3
Kong Yunming v Director of Social Welfare [2009] HKLRD 382 945
Koo Sze Yiu v Chief Executive of the HKSAR [2006] 3 HKLRD 455 (Court
    of Final Appeal, Hong Kong)..................................... 448, 452–3, 459
Lam Yuk Ming v AG [1980] HKLR 815... 179–80
Lau Cheong v HKSAR (2002) HKCFAR 415 946
Lee v Attorney-General [1996] 1 HKC 124 441
Leung Kwok Hung v HKSAR [2005] 8 HKCFAR 229 (Court of Final Appeal,
    Hong Kong)...739–40, 742–4, 752
Ma Bik Yung v Ko Chuen [2001] 4 HKC 119 (Court of Final Appeal, Hong
    Kong).. 735–6
Ng Ka Ling & Others v Director of Immigration [1999] 1 HKLRD 315; (No 2)
    [1999] 1 HKC 425 (Court of Final Appeal, Hong Kong).............. 227–30, 314, 318,
                                                                    320, 322, 324–6, 422, 428–30
Ng Ngau Chai v The Town Planning Board (unreported) HCAL 64/2007 dated
    4 July 2007 1017
R v Chan [1994] 3 HKC 145... 441
Secretary for Justice v Chan Wah [2000] 3 HKCFAR 459 (Court of Final Appeal,
    Hong Kong)..524–5, 527
Tse Hung Hing v Medical Council of Hong Kong [2010] 1 HKLRD 111 (Court
    of First Instance, Hong Kong)... 531–2
Vallejos v Commissioner of Registration & Anor [2012] 2 HKC 185 (Court
    of Appeal, Hong Kong SAR)... 639–40
Wong Yeung Ng v Secretary for Justice [1999] 2 HKC 24; [1999] 2 HKLRD
    293 (Court of Final Appeal, Hong Kong)..................................692–3, 698
Yau Yuk Lung (2007) 10 HKCFAR 335.. 948

India

Acharya Jagdishwaranand Avadhutta v Commissioner of Police, Calcutta
    AIR 1984 SC 51 924–5
Ahmedabad Municipal Corporation v Nawab Khan Gulah Khan [1997]
    AIR SC 123.. 988
Akhil Bhartiya Soshit Karmachari Sangh v Union of India [1981] AIR
    SC 298.. 984

AP State Pollution Control Board v MV Nayudu & Ors 2000(3) SCALE 354,
2000 Supp 5 SCR 249... 1019
Arun Ghosh v State of West Bengal, AIR 1970 SC 1228 810
Aruna Roy v Union of India (2002) 7 SCC 368 872
Arya Samaj [1971] AIR SC 1731... 877
Ashok Kumar Pandey v State of West Bengal [2004] 3 SCC 349..................... 414–15
Ashok Kumar Thakur v Union of India (2008) 6 SCC 1 1009
Bandhua Mukti Morcha v Union of India [1984] AIR 802, [1984] SCR (2)
67.. 984, 992, 1006–7
Basheshar Nath v The Commissioner of Income Tax, Delhi & Rajasthan & Anor
1959 SCR Supp (1) 528 553
Bennett Coleman v Union of India [1973] AIR 1973 SC 107.............................. 653
Bhagwan Koer v JC Bose 1904 ILR 31 Cal 11 876
Bhagwati Charan Shukla's case ILR 1946 Nag 865.. 604
Bijoe Emmanuel vs State Of Kerala [1987] AIR 748, [1986] SCR (3) 518
(Supreme Court, India)... 857–8
Bombay Dyeing & Mfg Co Ltd v Bombay Environmental Action Group (2006)
3 SCC 434, [2006] AIR SC 1489.. 1021
Brij Bhushan v Delhi [1950] SCR 605 (Supreme Court, India)........................... 644–5
Centre for Enquiry into Health & Allied Themes (CEHAT) & Ors v Union of
India & Ors (2003) 8 SCC 398, [2003] AIR SC 3309 (Supreme Court, India). 627–8
Chameli Singh v State of Uttar [1996] AIR SC 1051 984
Chiranjit Lal Chowdhury v The Union of India and Others [1950] SCR
869 .... 590, 594–5, 598–9, 605
Chng Suan Tze v Minister for Home Affairs [1988] AIR 2 SLR(R) 525................. 313
Commissioner, Hindu Religious Endowments, Madras v Sri Lakshmindra
Thirtha Swamiar of Sri Shirur Mutt AIR 1954 SC 282........ 771, 779, 834, 849, 924
Commissioner of Police v Acharya Jagdishwarananda Advadhuta [2004] INSC
155 (11 March 2004) 781
Consumer Education & Research v Union of India [1995] AIR 922, [1995]
SCC (3) 42.. 1001
Damyanti Naranga v The Union of India & Ors [1971] AIR 966, [1971] SCR
(3) 840 (Supreme Court, India) 765–6, 770
Delhi Development Horticulture Employee's Union v Delhi Administration
[1992] AIR SC 789 984
Dr KC Malhotra v State of Madhya Pradesh [1994] AIR MP 43........................ 1001
Dr Ramesh Yeshwant Prabhoo v Shri Prabhakar Kashinath Kunte (1996) SCC
(1) 130 (Supreme Court, India) 875–7
Durgah Committee Ajmer v Syed Hussain Ali AIR 1961 SC 1402; [1962] SCR
(1) 383... 780, 924
Evangelical Fellowship of India v State of Himachal Pradesh CWP No 438 of
2011A (High Court, Himachal Pradesh).. 810–16
Frances Mullin v Administrator, Union Territory of Delhi [1981]
AIR 746 .... 984, 1007, 1013
Frances Mullin v WC Khambra [1980] AIR SC 849 992
Golak Nath v State of Punjab [1967] AIR SC 1643 (Supreme Court,
India) 283–7, 290–1, 450

Golaknath v State of Punjab [1967] AIR SC 1643 (Supreme Court,
  India.. 350–1, 448–9
Govind v State of Madhya Pradesh [1975] AIR SC 1378....................................... 814
Gurleen Kaur v State of Punjab CWP No 14859 of 2008, [2009] INPBHC
  21163 (30 May 2009).. 780–1
Himat Lal K Shah v Commissioner of Police [1973] SCR (2) 266 (Supreme
  Court, India)..742, 751–3
Hinsa Virodhak Sangh vs Mirzapur Moti Kuresh Jamat & Ors AIR 2008
  SC 1892 Appeal (Civil) 5469 of 2005 (Supreme Court, India)........................ 873–4
Hiralal Mallick v State of Bihar [1978] 1 SCR 301.. 772
Indira Nehru Ghandhi v Raj Narain [1975] AIR SC 2299 283
J & K National Panthers Party v The Union of India & Ors [2010] INSC 937
  (Supreme Court, India)... 475–7
Jagannath v Union of India (1997) 2 SCC 87.. 1000
Janata Dal (Samajwadi) v The Election Commission of India [1996] AIR 577
  (Supreme Court, India)... 504–5
KA Abbas v The Union of India [1971] AIR 481, [1971] SCR (2) 446............... 650–1
Kameshwar Prasad & Ors v The State of Bihar & Anor [1962] AIR 1166 754
Kesavananda v State of Kerala [1973] AIR SC 1461 (Supreme Court,
  India).. 283, 286–9, 292, 313, 351, 870
Kharak Singh v The State of UP [1964] 1 SCR 332....................................986, 1013
Khatri (II) v State of Bihar [1981] (1) SCC 627.. 1005
Laxmi Mandal v Deen Dayal Harinagar Hospital WP(C) 8853/2008
  (Supreme Court, India).. 1002–4
Life Insurance Corporation v Manubhai [1993] AIR 171, [1992] SCR (3) 595
  (Supreme Court, India)... 665–6
Maneka Gandhi v Union of India [1978] AIR 597, [1978] SCR (2) 621......... 767, 984
Manohar Joshi v Nitin Bhaurao Patil (1996) SCC (1) 169 878
Maru Ram v Union of India & Ors (1981) 1 SCC 107... 154
MC Mehta v Union of India AIR 1988 SC 1037; AIR 1988 SC 1115................... 1014
Minerva Mills Ltd v Union of India [1980] AIR SC 1789 (Supreme Court,
  India)... 283, 288–9, 291–2, 351
Mohd Ahmed Khan v Shah Bano Begum [1985] AIR 945.................................... 872
Mohd Hanif Quareshi v State of Bihar [1958] AR 731 781
Mohinder Singh Gill & Anr v Chief Election Commissioner [1978] AIR
  SC 851 (Supreme Court, India)... 515–16
Mohini Jain v State of Karnataka (1992) 3 SCC 666 1008–9
Muhammad Hanif Qureshi v State of Bihar AIR 1958 SC 731 925
Murli S Deora v Union of India [2002] AIR SC 40 953
Narantakath Avullah v Parakkal Mammu [1923] AIR Mad 171................... 931
Narayanan Nambudripad v Madras [1954] AIR Madras 385............................. 872
Narmada Bachao Andolan v Union of India [1999] AIR SC 3345.................... 1021
Naz Foundation v Government of Delhi & Ors WP(C) No 7455/2001,
  2 Jul 2009 (High Court, Delhi).. 630–2
Niharendu Dutt Majumdar's case [1942] FCR 32.. 604
NP Ponnuswami v Returning Officer [1952] AIR SC 64 (Supreme Court,
  India).. 509–11

Olga Tellis & Ors v Bombay Municipal Council [1985] 2 Supp SCR 51, [1986]
  AIR SC 180 (Supreme Court, India).............................. 985–9, 991–2, 1008, 1013
Paschim Banga Khet Majoor Samiti v State of West Bengal (1996) 4 SCC 37..... 1002
Paschim Banga Khet Mazdoor Samity & Ors v State of West Bengal & Anor
  [1996] AIR SC 2426, [1996] 4 SCC 37 (Supreme Court, India)................... 1004–5
People's Union for Civil Liberties v Union of India & Ors [2009] INSC 811
  (22 April 2009).. 1000
People's Union for Civil Liberties v Union of India & Ors Writ Petition (Civil)
  No 196 of 2001 (Supreme Court, India)...994–1000
People's Union for Democratic Rights v Union of India [1983] AIR SCR (1)
  456 415
PM Bhargava v University [2004] AIR SC 3478... 872
Prakash Mani Sharma v Ministry of Women, Children and Social Welfare,
  SCN, Writ No 2822 of 2062 (28 Nov 2008)... 985
Pt Parmanand Katara v UOI (1989) 4 SCC 286.. 1002
Rabindra Kumar v Forest Officer AIR 1955 Manipur 49....................................... 564
Ram Jethmalani v UOI (2011) 8 SCC 1 814
Ramakrishna Mission [1995] AIR SC 2089.. 877
Ramesh Thapper v State of Madras (1950) SCR 594... 810
Rameshwar Prasad & Ors v Union of India & Anor [2006] AIR SC 980
  (Supreme Court, India)..150, 152–6
Ramjilal Modi v State of UP (1957) SCR 860.. 810
Ranjit D Udeshi v Maharashtra [1965] 1 SCR 65 (Supreme Court, India)......... 725–6
Ratilal Panachand Gandhi v State of Bombay [1954] SCR 1055........................... 809
Rev Stainislaus v State of Madhya Pradesh [1975] AIR MP 163........................... 808
Rural Litigation & Entitlement Kendra v State of UP AIR 1985 SC 652............. 1013
St Xaviers College v State of Gujarat [1974] AIR SC 1389 1009
Sajjan Singh v State of Rajasthan, 1965 AIR, SCR 1965 (1) 933 .... 284, 290
Samatha v State of Andhra Pradesh & Ors [1997] AIR SC 3297 577
Sankari Prasad Singh v Union of India [1951] AIR SC 458.................... 282, 284, 290
Saraswathi Ammal v Rajagopal Ammal [1954] SCR 277 780
Sardar Syena Taher Saifudin Sahib v State of Bombay AIR 1962 SC 853 926
Satya Ranjan Majhi v State of Orissa (2003) 7 SCC 439....................................... 810
Secretary, Ministry of I & B v Cricket Association of Bengal [1995] AIR 1995
  SC 1236 (Supreme Court, India)... 655–8
Shantisar Builder v Narayanan Khumlal Totame [1990] AIR SC 630..................... 984
Shihabuddin Imbichi Koya Thangal v KP Ahammed Koya [1971] AIR Ker 206... 931
Shri Sachidanand Pandy v State of West Bengal AIR 1987 SC 1109 1014
Smt Sarla Mugdal, President v Union of India [1995] AIR 1531 872
SP Gupta v President of India and Ors [1982] AIR SC 149 (Supreme Court,
  India) 378, 381, 383, 385, 411–13, 418, 420–1
SP Mittal v Union of India [1983] AIR 1, (1983) SCR(1) 729............................... 774
SR Bommai v Union of India AIR 1994 SC 1918 ...... 113, 130, 153–4, 210–12, 870–2
Sri Venkataramana Devaru v State of Mysore [1958] AIR SC 255 872
Stanislaus v State of Madya Pradesh [1977] AIR SC 908............................... 810, 821
State of Bombay and Another v FN Balsara [1951] SCR 682.................... 594, 598–9
State of Himachal Pradesh v Umed Ram Sharma AIR 1986 SC 847............985, 1013

State of Uttar Pradesh v Deoman 1960 AIR 1125 SC 553
State of West Bengal vs Anwar Ali Sarkar [1952] AIR 75; [1952] SCR 284
    (Supreme Court of India).. 589–605
Subhash Kumar v State of Bihar [1991] AIR SC 420.. 985
Surendra v Nabakrishma AIR 1958 Orissa 168 696
Synthetics & Chemicals Ltd Etc v State of Uttar Pradesh [1989] AIR SCR
    Supl (1) 623... 426, 429–30
TK Rangarajan v Government of Tamil Nadu [2003] AIR SC 3032.................... 961
Union of India v Rakesh Kumar and Ors [2010] AIR SC 3244 (Supreme Court,
    India).. 494–6
Union Of India vs Sankal Chand Himatlal Sheth and Anr [1977] AIR SC
    2328 (Supreme Court, India)..382–3, 385
Vellore Citizen's Welfare Forum v Union of India AIR 1996 SC 2715.............. 1020
Virendra v The State of Punjab... 677–80
Vishakha v State of Rajasthan [1997] AIR SC 3011 (Supreme Court,
    India) 79, 415, 433, 435–6, 459–60, 985
Yagnapurushdasji v. Muldas AIR 1966 SC 1119.. 877
Yulitha Hyde v State of Orissa [1973] AIR Ori 116.. 808–9

Indonesia

Decision Number 001/PUU-IV/2006 25 Jan 2006 (Constitutional Court,
    Indonesia)... 367–8
Decision Number 005/PUU-IV/2006 23 Aug 2006 (Constitutional Court,
    Indonesia)..372–3, 390, 394–6
Decision Number 010/PUU-IV/2006 25 Jul 2006 (Constitutional Court,
    Indonesia)... 410–11
Decision Number 066/PUU-II/2004 (Constitutional Court of Indonesia)............. 356
Decision of the Constitutional Court on the Blasphemy Law No 140/PUU-
    VII/2009, 19 April 2010 (Constitutional Court, Indonesia)......................... 933–41
Dr Eggi Sudjana, SH, MSi, Pandapotan Lubis 013-022/PUU-IV/2006 [2006]
    IDCC 26, 6 Dec 2006 (Constitutional Court, Indonesia) 684–5
Judicial Review of the Electricity Law (No 20/2002) Case No 001-021-022/
    PUU-I/2003 (Constitutional Court, Indonesia)... 969–77
Judicial Review of the Law of the Republic of Indonesia Number 7 Year 2004
    regarding Water Resources (Law Number 7 Year 2004) Case Number
    058-059-060-063/PUU-II/2004; Case Number 008/PUU-III/2005
    (Constitutional Court, Indonesia)... 978–82
Judicial Review on Regulation No 12 year 2003 concerning General Election of
    House of Representatives, 002/PUU-II/2004... 489
Judicial Review on Regulation No 23 year 2003 Regarding General Election of
    President and Vice President AIR 1954 SC 282... 532
Masykur Abdul Kadir Case Constitutional Court Decision No 013/PUU-I/2003
    (Constitutional Court, Indonesia)... 300–5

Inter-American Commission on Human Rights

Cristián Daniel Sahli Vera v Chile, Case 12.219, Report No 43/05, Inter-Am
CHR, OEA/Ser L/V/II.124 Doc 5 (2005) 846
Yanomani Indians v Brazil Inter-American Commission on Human Rights 7615
OEA/Ser.L.V/II/66 Doc 10 rev 1 (1985).. 1019

Japan

Action for Recognition of the Status as a Member of the House of
Representatives and a Claim for Remuneration 14 Minshū 1206 (Supreme
Court, Japan).. 136–7, 150–2, 402–3
Agreement Concluded Between an Employee and Employer, which Obliges the
Employee Not to Exercise the Right to Withdraw From a Particular Labour
Union, is Contrary to Public Policy, Judgment Concerning Whether the 2004
(Ju) No 1787, 2 Feb 2007 (Sup 758–9
All Agricultural and Forest Workers, Police Office Act Amendment Opposition
Case Saik-o Saibansho [Sup Ct] 25 Apr 1973; Sho 43 (A) no 2780, 27 Saik-o
Saibansho Keiji Hanreishu [Keishu] 547 (Grand Bench)................................. 961
All Postal Workers, Tokyo Central Post Office Case Saik-o Saibansho [Sup Ct]
26 Oct 1966, Sho 39 (A) no 296, 20 Saik-o Saibansho Keiji Hanreishu [Keishu]
901 (Grand Bench).. 961
Anzai v Shiraishi or the Ehime Tamagushi-ryo case 51 Minshūo 1673 (Sup Ct
Apr 2, 1997) 898
Arudou v Earth Cure Judgment of 11 Nov 2002 (Sapporo District Court, Japan)
(2008) 9(2) Asian-Pacific Law & Policy Journal 297 637–9
Bortz v Suzuki, Judgment of October 12, 1999, Hamamatsu Branch, Shizuoka
District Court (2007) 16(3) Pacific Rim Law & Policy Journal 631.................... 639
Case Concerning the National Police Reserve 6 Minsh-u 9 (Supreme Court,
Japan) 344–5
Case of Constitutionality of the Forced Leasing of Land for US Bases in Okinawa
Prefecture 1996(Gyo-Tsu)No 90, 28 Aug 1996 (Supreme Court, Japan)..... 199–201
Case of Defamation 1966(A) No 2472, 25 Jun 1969 (Supreme Court, Japan).... 707–8
Case of Injunctions against Publication In Relation To the Freedom of Expression
40 Minshū 872 (Supreme Court, Japan) 646–7
Case of the so-called 'Sunakawa Case'... 197–8, 236–8
Case of Translation and Publication of Lady Chatterley's Lover and Article
175 of the Penal Code 1953(A) No 1713, 13 Mar 1957 (Supreme Court,
Japan) 723–5, 729
Case Seeking Nullification of an Election 58 Minshū 1 (Supreme Court,
Japan.. 483–4
Case to Seek Damages and Compensation for Non-Pecuniary Damages Caused
by Libel and Damage to Credit 20 Minshū 5 (Tokyo High Court, Japan) 706
Case to Seek Declaration of Eligibility to Become a Candidate for an
Examination for Selecting Management Level Employees, 59 Minshū 1 535

Case to Seek Declaration of Illegality of Deprivation of the Right to Vote
    of Japanese Citizens Residing Abroad 59 Minsh–u 7 (Supreme Court,
    Japan) 409, 522–4, 527–8
Case to Seek Invalidation of Election 65 Minshū 2 (Supreme Court,
    Japan) 468–72, 476
Case to Seek Revocation of the Disposition of Notification to the Effect that
    the Goods to be Imported Fall Within the Category of Prohibited Goods
    2003 (Gyo-Tsu) No 157, 19 Feb 2008 (Supreme Court, Japan)................728–9, 731
Case where a Newspaper Company, when Printing an Article Distributed from
    a News Agency, is Deemed to have Reasonable Grounds for Believing the
    Fact Alleged to be True 2009(Ju) No 2057, 28 Apr 2011 (Supreme
    Court).. 707, 720
Case Where the Dissolution Order on the Grounds Provided by Article 81(1)(1)
    and (2) of the Law on Religious Organizations is Not Against Art 20(1) of the
    Constitution 1996 (ku) 8, Minshū Vol 50, No 1, at 199 (Tokyo High Court).. 833–4
Claim for the Invalidity of an Election, 1999 (Gyo-Tsu) No 8, 10 Nov 1999.......... 489
Constitutionality of the Prefecture's Expenditure from Public Funds to Religious
    Corporations Which Held Ritual Ceremonies (Yasakuni Shrine Case) 1992
    (Gyo-Tsu) No 156, 2 April 1997 (Supreme Court, Japan, Grand Bench).... 898–901
Enshrinement of a Dead SDF Officer to Gokoku Shrine (Self Defence Force
    Officer Enshrinement Case) 1 June 1988, 1982(0) No 902 (Supreme Court,
    Japan) 902–4
Higo v Tsuchiya, 56 Minshū 1204 (Sup Ct July 11 2001).. 898
Japan Communist Party v Sankei Newspaper Inc 875 Hanrei Jih-o 30, 1977
    (Supreme Court, Japan)... 663–4
Japan v Teramae (1975) 29 Keishu 489 (Supreme Court, Japan)........................ 744–6
Judgment Upon Case of Validity of Cabinet Order 1952 (A)No 2868, 27 Jul
    1953 (Supreme Court, Japan).. 231–4
Kakunaga v Sekiguchil (Tsu City Shinto Ground-breaking Ceremony Case)
    31 Minshū 533 (Supreme Court of Japan, 13 July 1977)....................... 774–5, 838,
                                                                                        893–6, 898, 901
Kayano et al v Hokkaido Expropriation Committee (The Nibutani Dam
    Decision) (Sapporo District Court, Civil Division No 3), 27 Mar 1997 (1999)
    38 International Legal Materials 397.. 566–77
Kim v Osaka Electoral Commission 49 Minshū 639 (Supreme Court,
    Japan) 521–2, 527
Kohno v Hiramatsu 56 Minshū 1204 (Sup Ct July 9, 2002)................................... 898
Kurokawa v Chiba Prefecture Election Commission, 30 Minshū 223.................... 476
Matsumoto v Kobayashi 50 Minshū 469, 8 March 1996 (Supreme Court,
    Japan) 836–8
Ogawa v Hokkaido, also known as the Ainu Communal Property (Trust Assets)
    Litigation 577
Oguri v Kageyama 10 Minshū 785 (1956)... 738
Shigeru Asahi v Minister of Health and Welfare Case Number Gyo Tsu
    No 14 of 1964 (Judgment of May 24, 1967).. 949–51

Malaysia

Adong bin Kuwau & Ors v Kerajaan Negeri Johor & Anor [1997] 1 MLJ 418
(Court of Appeal, Malaysia)..560–5, 993
Attorney-General, Malaysia v Manjeet Singh Dhillion [1991] 1 MLJ 167
(Supreme Court, Malaysia).. 693–7
Attorney-General v Arthur Lee Meng Kuang [1987] 1 MLJ 207 699
Bato Bagi & Ors v Government of the State of Sarawak [2008] 5 MLJ 547 578
Bato Bagi v Kerajaan Negeri Sarawak [2011] 6 MLJ 297.................................... 993
Beatrice Fernandez v Sistem Penebrangan Malaysia [2005] 2 CLR 713 79
Che Omar bin Che Soh v PP [1988] 2 MLJ 55 (Federal Court,
Malaysia) 117, 787, 793, 796
Dalip Kaur [1992] 1 MLJ 1 (SC)..784, 789–91
Datuk Haji bin Harun Idris v Public Prosecutor [1977] 2 MLJ 155....................... 606
Daud bin Mamat v Majlis Agama Islam [2001] 2 MLJ 390 (High Court,
Malaysia)... 783–4
Dow Jones Publishing Company (Asia) Inc v Attorney General [1989] 2
MLJ 385... 668
Dr Mohd Nasir Hashim v Menteri Dalam Negeri [2006] 6 MLJ 213 (Court of
Appeal, Malaysia)... 499–500, 766–8
Government of Malaysia v Lim Kit Siang [1988] 2 MLJ 12 (Supreme Court,
Malaysia) 405–6
Government of the State of Kelantan v Government of the Federation of
Malaya [1963] MLJ 355 (Federal Court, Malaysia)..................................... 432
Hjh Halimatussaadiah bte Hj Kamaruddin v Public Services Commission,
Malaysia [1992] 1 MLJ 513; [1994] 3 MLJ 61 776–7
Jalang anak Paran & Anor v Government of the State of Sarawak & Anor
[2007] 1 MLJ 412.. 578
Karpal Singh v Sultan of Selangor [1988] 1 MLJ 64 (High Court, Malaysia).... 397–8
Kerajaan Negeri Selangor & Ors v Sagong bin Tasi & Ors [2005] 6 MLJ 289 577
Latifah Mat Zin v Rosmawati bte Sharibun [2007] 5 MLJ 101.............................. 784
Lau Dak Kee v Public Prosecutor [1976] 2 MLJ 229... 741
Lina Joy v Majlis Agama Islam Wilayah [2004] 2 MLJ 119 (High Court,
Malaysia); [2007] 4 MLJ 585 (Federal Court, Malaysia) 116, 785–92, 794–7
Loh Kooi Choon v Government of Malaysia [1977] 2 MLJ 187 (Federal Court,
Malaysia) 298
Malaysian Bar & Anor v Government of Malaysia [1987] 2 MLJ 165................... 606
Mamat bin Daud v Government of Malaysia [1988] 1 MLJ 199.............................. 789
Meor Atiqulrahman bin Ishak & Ors v Fatimah bte Sihi [2000] 5 MLJ 375,
6 August 1999.. 117
Meor Atiqulrahman bin Ishak v Fatimah bte Sihi [2006] 4 MLJ 605 (Federal
Court, Malaysia)...777–8, 830–2, 906
Nordin bin Salleh v The Kelantan State Assembly [1992] 1 MLJ 697 492
Persatuan Aliran Kesadran Negara v Minister of Home Affairs [1987] 1 MLJ
442 (High Court, Malaysia) 645–6
Phang Chin Hock v PP [1980] 1 MLJ 70 (Federal Court, Malaysia)..................... 298

PP v SRN Palaniappan & Ors [1949] MLJ 246 697
PP v Tengku Mahmood Iskandar & Anor [1973] 1 MLJ 128 550–1
PP v The Straits Times Press Ltd [1949] MLJ 81 696–7
Public Prosecutor v Dato' Tap Peng [1987] 2 MLJ 311 (Supreme Court,
    Malaysia) 450
Public Prosecutor v Oh Keng Seng [1977] 2 MLJ 206 (Federal Court,
    Malaysia) 673–5
Ritz Hotel Casino v Datuk Seri Osu Haji Sukam [2005] 6 MLJ 760 (High Court,
    Kota Kinabalu, Malaysia) 890
Selangor Pilot Association (1946) v Government of Malaysia & Anor [1975]
    2 MLJ 66 564
Shamala Sathiyaseelan v Dr Jeyaganesh Mogarajah [2004] 2 CLJ 416 (High
    Court, Kuala Lumpur) 798
Sivarasa Rasiah v Badan Peguam Malaysia & Anor [2010] 2 MLJ 333 (Federal
    Court, Malaysia) 298, 761–2, 907
Soon Singh v Pertubuhan Kebajikan Malaysia (PERKIM) Kedah [1994]
    1 MLJ 690 .... 783, 786, 790, 797
Stephen Kalong Ningkan v Government of Malaysia [1968] 2 MLJ 238
    (Privy Council, on appeal from Malaysia) 361–2, 364
Subashini Rajasingam v Saravanan Thangathoray [2008] 2 MLJ 147 798
Sulaiman bin Takrib v Kerajaan Negeri Terengganu [2009] 6 MLJ 354
    (Federal Court, Malaysia) 859
Tan Tek Seng v Suruhanjaya Perkhidmatan Pendidikan [1996] 1 MLJ 261 992–3
Teh Cheng Poh v Public Prosecutor [1979] 1 MLJ 50 (Privy Council,
    Malaysia) 207–8
Teoh Eng Huat v Kadhi, Pasir Mas & Anor [1990] 2 MLJ 300 786
Titular Roman Catholic Archbishop of Kuala Lumpur v Menteri Dalam
    Negeri [2010] 2 MLJ 78 (High Court, Malaysia) 905–8
TSC Education Sdn Bhd v Kolej Yayasan Pelajaran Mara & Anor [2002]
    5 MLJ 577 578
Tun Datu Haji Mustapha bin Datu Harun v Tun Datuk Haji Mohamed Adnan
    Robert, Yang di-Pertua Negeri Sabah & Datuk Joseph Pairin Kitigan (No 2)
    [1986] 2 MLJ 420 (High Court, Malaysia) 137–8

Mongolia

Adjudication on the Matters Whether the Interpretation of the Constitution by
    the State Great Hural Breached or Not the Constitution 23 Mar 2001
    (Constitutional Court, Mongolia) 353
Hearing on the matters of whether the amendments to the Constitution breach
    the Constitution Decisions of the Constitutional Court of Mongolia (2012),
    94–100 352

Nepal

Sunil Babu Pant & Ors v Government of Nepal Writ No 917 of 2007 (Supreme
  Court, Nepal).. 632–4

New Zealand

SG v Radio Avon Ltd [1978] 1 NZLR 225.. 696

Pakistan

Ahmed Abdullah v Government of Punjab PLD 2003 Lahore 752..................... 1009
Ameer Bano v SE Highways, PLD 1996 Lahore 592.................................... 1016
Benazir Bhutto v President of Pakistan PLD 1988 Supreme Court 377.............. 1017
Benazir Bhutto v President of Pakistan PLD 1998 SC 607 1017
Chakar Ali Khan Rind v Government of Balochistan, Constitutional Petition
  No 635 of 2009, 2011 CLC 601 992
Dosso v The State [1958] PSCR 180... 248
Employees of the Pakistan Law Commission v Ministry of Works (1994) SCMR
  1548 1009
General Secretary, West Pakistan Salt Miners Labour Union (CBA) Khewara,
  Jhelum v The Director, Industries and Mineral Development (1994) SCMR
  2061 1016
Ghulam Umar Qazi v General Manager & others, 2006 PLC (CS) 1143............. 1016
IA Sherwani v Government of Pakistan [1991] SCMR.................................. 605
Khondker Delwar Hossain, Secretary, BNP Party v Bangladesh Italian
  Marble Works Ltd, Dhaka Civil Petition for Leave to Appeal 1044 and
  1045/2009 .... 110–16, 245–6
Mahmood Khan Achakzai v Federation of Pakistan (PLD 1997 SC 426)............. 253
Majibur Rehman v Federal Government of Pakistan PLD 1985 Federal
  Shariat Court 8 Vol XXXVII 917–20
Mian Najibuddin Oawaisi v Aamir Yar [2011] PLD 1................................. 533
Mst Sajida Bibi v Incharge Chouki No 2 Police Station Saddar, Saihwal, PLD
  1997 Lahore 666.. 1016
Muhammad Ismail Qureshi v Pakistan (1991) 43 PLD 10 921
Muhammad Tariq Abbassi v Defence Housing Authority (2007) CLC 1358
  [Karachi]... 1016
Mujibur Rehman v Federal Government of Pakistan PLD 1985 FSC 8 923
Pakistan Chest Foundation v Government of Pakistan (1997) CLC 1379............. 953
Pakistan v Public at Large PLD 1987 SC 304 927–8
Shehla Zia v WAPDA (Water and Power Development Authority) PLD 1994
  SC 693, 712 (Supreme Court, Pakistan) 1009–17
Sindh High Court Bar Association v Federation of Pakistan 31 Jul 2009
  (Supreme Court, Pakistan).. 212–14

Suo Moto Case No 25 of 2009 (Lahore Canal Bank Case).............................. 1015
Tikamdas v Divisional Evacuee Trust Committee, Karachi, PLD 1968 Kar 703
  (FB) 924
Watan Party v The Chief Executive/President of Pakistan & Anor Constitutional
  Petition No 36 of 2002, 7 Oct 2002 (Supreme Court, Pakistan) 252–4
Zaheeruddin v The State (1993) 26 SCMR 1718 (Supreme Court, Pakistan)... 922–31
Zulfiqar Mehdi v Pakistan International Airlines Corporation (1998 SCMR
  793)... 254

Philippines

ABS-CBN Broadcasting Corporation v Commission on Elections GR
  No 133486, 28 Jan 2000 (Supreme Court, Philippines)................................ 516–18
Aglipay v Ruiz 64 Phil 201 (1937)... 878
Alejandro Estrada v Soledad Escritor AM No P-02-1651 22 June 2006 (En
  Banc) (Supreme Court, Philippines)... 879–89
Ang Bagong Bayani-OFW Labor Party v Commission on Elections GR
  No 147589, 26 Jun 2001 (Supreme Court, Philippines)................................ 486–8
Ang Ladlad LGBT Party v Commission on Elections GR No 190582,
  8 Apr 2010 (Supreme Court, Philippines)... 487–9
ARIS Inc v National Labor Relations Commission GR No 90501 (SC Aug 5,
  1991)... 963
Arnold V Guerrero v Commission on Elections GR No 137004, 26 Jul 2000 520
Arturo De Castro et al v Judicial and Bar Council et al Case GR No 191002,
  17 Mar 2010 (Supreme Court, Philippines).................. 185–6, 190, 269, 377–8, 381
Bagabuyo v COMELEC GR No 176970, 8 Dec 2008 (Supreme Court,
  Philippines).. 474–5, 477
Basco v Pagcor 197 SCRA 52 May 14, 1991 963
Bengzon v Drilon GR No 103524, 15 Apr 1992 (Supreme Court,
  Philippines).. 387–8
Chavez v Presidential Commission on Good Government GR No 130716,
  9 Dec 1998 (Supreme Court, Philippines).. 411, 413–14
De Guzman, et al v Commission on Elections, GR No 129118, 19 Jul 2000,
  336 SCRA 188... 611
Ebralinag v Division Superintendent of Schools of Cebu GR No 95770,
  1 March 1993, 219 SCRA 256 (1993) (Supreme Court, Philippines)........ 852–7, 885
Enrique T Garcia v Commission on Elections 237 SCRA 279 (1994) (Supreme
  Court, Philippines)... 541–3
Fariñas et al v Executive Secretary et al GR No 147387, 10 Dec 2003, 417
  SCRA 503... 608
Ferdinand E Marcos et al v Honorable Raul Manglapus et al 177 SCRA 668
  (1989) (Supreme Court, Philippines)... 158–60, 401–2
G Long and Almeria v Basa GR Nos 134963-64 (27 Sep 2001) 862
Garces v Estenzo GR No 53487, 25 May 1981... 776
German vs Barangan, 135 SCRA 514... 855
Gerona vs Secretary of Education, 106 Phil 2 (1959) 853–4

Habeas Corpus Petition of Benigno S Aquino, Jr et al v Sec Juan Ponce Enrile,
  Gen Romeo Espino & Gen Fidal Ramos 59 SCRA 183; GR No L-35538,
  17 Sep 1974 (Supreme Court, Philippines) 248–50, 252
Iglesia ni Cristo v Court of Appeals, GR No 119673, July 26, 1996 824
Islamic Da'Wah Council of the Philippines Inc v Office of the Executive
  Secretary GR No 153888, 9 July 2003 (Supreme Court, Philippines) 891–2
Javellana v Executive Secretary GR No L-36142 [1973] PHSC 43, 31 Mar 1973
  (Supreme Court, Philippines) 250, 265–9, 351, 400–1
Joya v PCGG GR No 96541, 24 Aug 1993 (Supreme Court, Philippines) 397–9
KiliosBayan Foundation, et al v Eduardo Ermita et al GR No 177721,
  3 Jul 2007 (Supreme Court, Philippines) 376–7, 381
Kilosbayan, Incorporated v Morato 246 SCRA 540 July 17, 1995 963
Laban ng Demokratikong Pilipino v COMELEC, GR No 161265, 24 Feb 2004 ... 507
Macalintal v COMELEC GR No 157013, 10 Jul 2003 (Supreme Court,
  Philippines) 512–13
Manila Prince Hotel v Government Service Insurance System GR No 122156
  (SC 3 Feb 1997) (en banc) 968
Mercado v Manzano 307 SCRA 630 (1999) (Supreme Court, Philippines) 529–30
National Police Commission v De Guzman et al, GR No 106724, 9 Feb 1994,
  229 SCRA 801 610
National Press Club v Commission on Elections, GR No 102653, 5 Mar 1992 668
Oposa et al v Fulgencio S Factoran, Jr et al, GR No 101083 .... 82, 404, 415, 964–8
Pamil v Teleron GR No L-34854 20 Nov 1978 107
Pastor Dionisio Austria v National Labor Relations Commission GR
  No 124382 (16 August 1999) 861
People v Cayat, 68 Phil 12, 18 (1939) 610
People v Lagman 66 Phil 13 (1938) 858
Perfecto V Galido v Commission on Elections GR No 95346, 18 Jan 1991 519–20
Philippine Judges Association et al v Prado et al, GR No 105371, 11 Nov
  1993, 227 SCRA 703 610
Prof Randolf S David et al v Gloria Macapagal-Arroyo GR No 171396,
  3 May 2006 (Supreme Court, Philippines 208–10
Quinto v Commission on Elections GR No 189698, 22 Feb 2010 (Supreme
  Court, Philippines) 607–12
Robert V Tobias Jr v Hon City Mayor Benjamin S Abalos GR No L-114783,
  8 Dec 1994 (Supreme Court, Philippines) 473–4
Senator Aquilino Pimental et al v Ermita, Office of the Executive Secretary
  GR No 158088, 6 Jul 2005 (Supreme Court, Philippines) 163–4
Simon v Commission on Human Rights GR No 100150 (SC 5 Jan 1994) 963
Sixto S Brillantes Jr v Yorac GR No 93867, 18 Dec 1990 (Supreme Court,
  Philippines) 513–14
Sulu Islamic Association of Masjid Lambayong v Malik AM No MTJ-92-691,
  September 10, 1993, 226 SCRA 193 886
Tan Chong v Secretary of Labor, 79 Phil 249 (1941) 609
Tanada v Angara GR No 118295, 2 Ma 1997 963
United States v Balcorta, GR No 8722, 10 Sep 1913 878
Victoriano vs Elizalde Rope Workers' Union, 59 SCRA 54 .... 855, 885

Villanueva, Jr v Court of Appeals, et al, GR No 142947, 19 Mar 2002, 379
    SCRA 463 610

Singapore

Abdul Nasir bin Amer Hamsah v Public Prosecutor [1997] SGCA 38 (Court
    of Appeal, Singapore) 451–2
AG v Wain Barry [1991] 1 SLR(R) 85; [1991] 1 SLR(R) 108 .... 689, 699
Angliss Singapore Pte Ltd v PP [2006] 4 SLR 653 890
Attorney-General v Chee Soon Juan [2006] SGHC 54, 2 SLR 650 (High Court,
    Singapore) 437–8
Attorney-General v Hertzberg Daniel [2008] SGHC 218 (High Court,
    Singapore) 436–7, 440, 699
Attorney-General v Tan Liang Joo John & Ors [2009] SGHC 41 (High
    Court, Singapore) 690–2, 698
AttorneyGeneral v Shadrake Alan [2010] SGHC 327 688
Bermuda Trust (Singapore) Ltd v Richard Wee (2000) 2 SLR 126 802
Chan Hiang Leng Colin v Minister for Information and Arts [1996] 1 SLR 609
    (Court of Appeal, Singapore) 313, 406–7, 834, 836, 848–50
Chee Siok Chin & Ors v Minister for Home Affairs & Anor [2006] 1 SLR(R) 582
    (High Court, Singapore) 746–8
Constitutional Reference No 1 of 1995 [1995] SGCT 1 (Constitution of the
    Republic of Singapore Tribunal, Singapore) 346–7, 427–8
Goh Chok Tong v Chee Soon Juan (No 2) [2005] 1 SLR 573 .... 90, 721
Goh Chok Tong v Jeyaretnam JB [1998] 1 SLR 547 705
JB Jeyaretnam v Lee Kuan Yew [1992] 2 SLR 310 705
Lee Hsien Loong v Singapore Democratic Party [2009] 1 SLR 642 .... 91, 721
Lim Eng Hock Peter v Lin Jian Wei [2010] 4 SLR 357 119
Lim Mey Lee Susan v Singapore Medical Council [2011] 4 SLR 156 (High
    Court, Singapore) 397–8
Lo Pui Sang v Mamata Kapildev [2008] 4 SLR(R) 754 983
Mohammad Faizal bin Sabtu v Public Prosecutor [2012] 4 SLR 974 298
Nappalli Peter Williams v Institute of Technical Education [1992] 2 SLR 569
    (Court of Appeal, Singapore) 771, 798, 851–3
Ng Chye Huay v PP [2006] 1 SLR(R) 157 773
Ong Kian Cheong v PP [2009] SGDC 163 823
PP v Koh Song Huat Benjamin [2005] SGDC 272 824
Public Prosecutor v Koh Song Huat Benjamin [2005] SGDC 272 (District
    Court, Singapore) 676–7
Public Prosecutor v Taw Cheng Kong [1998] 2 SLR 410 606
Review Publishing Co Ltd & Anor v Lee Hsien Loong & Anor [2009] SGCA
    46 (Court of Appeal, Singapore) 712, 716–21
Review Publishing Co Ltd v Lee Hsien Loong [2010] 1 SLR 52 653
Shadrake Alan v A-G [2011] 3 SLR 778 .... 79, 440, 688–90, 698–9
Tan Eng Hong v Attorney-General [2012] SGCA 45 (Court of Appeal,
    Singapore) 405, 407–8

Taw Cheng Kong v Public Prosecutor [1998] 1 SLR 943 (High Court,
    Singapore)..606
Teo Soh Lung v Minister for Home Affairs [1989] 1 SLR(R) 461 (High Court,
    Singapore)..298
Yong Vui Kong v Attorney-General [2011] SGCA 9 (Court of Appeal,
    Singapore)..119, 131–3

South Africa

Harksen v Lane 1998 (1) SA 300 (CC)..632
Mazibuko v City of Johannesburg [2009] ZACC 28..952
National Coalition for Gay and Lesbian Equality v The Minister of Justice, Case
    CCT 11/98 (South Africa)...630
Occupiers of St Olivia Road v City of Johannesburg (2008) 5 BCLR 475 (CC).....987
Prinsloo v Van Der Linde 1997 (3) SA 1012 (CC)...632
Republic of South Africa v Grootboom (2000) (11) BCLR 1169 (CC).................945
Soobramoney v Minister of Health Kwazulu-Natal (CCT 32/97) [1997] ZACC 17,
    1998 (1) SA 765 (CC)...1006

South Korea

Act on the Immigration and Legal Status of Overseas Koreans Case 13-2
    KCCR 714, 99Hun-Ma 494, 29 Nov 2001 (Constitutional Court, South
    Korea)...607, 612–16
Administrative Centre Case 17(B) KCCR 481, 2005 Hun-Ma 579 (consolidated),
    24 Nov 2005...273
Advance Report Duty for Outdoor Assembly Case, 2007 HunBa 22, 28 May
    2009 741
Appointment of Acting Prime Minister Case 98Hun-Ra1, 14 Jul 1998
    (Constitutional Court, South Korea) 182–3
Ban on Civil Servants' Labor Movement 2003 Hun-Ba50 and 2004 Hun-Ba96,
    27 Oct 2005..442
Ban on Fetus Sex Identification Case 20-2(a) KCCR 236, 2004Hun-Ma 1010,
    2005Hun-Ba90, 31 Jul 2008...629
Ban on Improper Communication on the Internet Case, 99 HunMa 480,
    27 Jun 2002..651
Ban on Outdoor Assembly and Demonstration Adjacent to Courthouses
    Case, 2004 HunKa 17, 24 Nov 2005...754
Capital Punishment Case 161 KCCG 452, 2008Hun-Ka23, 25 Feb 2010...............555
Case Prohibition of Censorship and Article 18(1)(5) of the Functional Health
    Foods Act 2006 HunBa 75, Jul 29 2010...649
Compulsory Subscription to the National Pension Plan 13-1 KCCR 301,
    99Hun-Ma 365, 22 Feb 2001 954–7
Conscientious Objection to Military Service Case 16-2(A) KCCR 141
    2002Hun-Ka1, August 26, 2004 (Constitutional Court, South Korea).........839–45

Constitutional Complaint Against Article 8(1) of the Support for Discharged
  Soldiers Act Case, 98Hun-Ma 363, 23 Dec 1999 442
Constitutional Complaint against the Proviso of Trade Union and Labor
  Relations Adjustment Act Article 81 Item 2 17-2 KCCR 392, 2002Hun-Ba
  95·96, 2003Hun-Ba9 (consolidated) 24 Nov 2005 957–60
Constitutional Review of Judgments Case 96 Hun-Ma 172, 24 Dec 1997
  (Constitutional Court, South Korea) 366–7, 444–5
Day and Time of, and Method of Determining the Elect at the Re-election and
  the Vacancy Election for Members of the National Assembly 2003Hun-Ma
  259, 27 Nov 2003 (Constitutional Court, South Korea) 507–9
Disclosure of the Identity of Sex Offenders Convicted of Acquiring Sexual
  Favors from Minors in Exchange for Monetary Compensation 2002 Hun-Ka14,
  6 Jun 2003 (Constitutional Court, South Korea) 439–40
Establishment of Public Employees' Union Case 20-2(B) KCCR 666,
  2005Hun-Ma 971·1193, 2006Hun-Ma 198 (consolidated), 26 Dec 2008 961
Excessive Electoral District Population Disparity Case, 95 Hun-Ma 224,
  27 Dec 1995 476
Extracurricular Lesson Ban Case 12-1 KCCR 427, 98Hun-Ka16, etc
  (consolidated) 27 Apr 2000 (Constitutional Court, South Korea) 84
Impeachment of the President Case 2004Hun-Na1, 14 May 2004
  (Constitutional Court, South Korea) 537–9
Joint and Several Liability of Executive Officers and Oligopolistic Stockholders
  Case 2000 Hun-Ka 5, 29 Aug 2002 (Constitutional Court, South Korea) 445–6
Letter of Condolence for Kim Il-sung Case 97Hun-Ma 265, 24 Jun 1999
  (Constitutional Court, South Korea) 710, 721
Mandatory Employment of Disabled Persons 15-2(A) KCCR 58,
  2001Hun-Ba96, 24 Jul 2003 588
May 18 Incident Non-institution of Prosecution Decision Case 7-2 KCCR 697,
  95Hun-Ma 221, 15 Dec 1995 (Constitutional Court, Korea) 241–2, 359–60
National Assembly Candidacy Deposit Case, 88Hun-Ka6, 8 Sep 1989 534
National Assembly Election Redistricting Plan Case 2000Hun-Ma92, 25 Oct 2001
  (Constitutional Court, South Korea) 472–3, 476–7
National Seat Succession Case 92Hun-Ma 153, 28 Apr 1994 (Constitutional
  Court, South Korea) 491
Nationality Act Case 12-2 KCCR 167, 7Hun-Ka12, 31 Aug 2000 619–20
Night time Outdoor Assembly Ban Case, 2008 HunKa 25, 24 Sep 2009 754
No-smoking Zone and Right to Smoke Cigarette 16-2(A) KCCR 355,
  2003Hun-Ma 457, 26 Aug 2004 (Constitutional Court, Korea) 952–3, 958
Notice of Apology case 89 Hun-Ma 160, 1 Apr 1991 (Constitutional Court,
  South Korea) 733–4
One-Person One-Vote Case 2000Hun-Ma91, 19 Jul 2001 (Constitutional
  Court, South Korea) 484–6
Overseas Citizens Voting Rights Ban Case, 97Hun-Ma 253, 28 Jan 1999 528
Pledge to Abide by the Law Case 14-1 KCCR 351, 98Hun-Ma 425, etc,
  (consolidated), 25 Apr 2002 (Constitutional Court, South Korea) 620–2
Praising and Encouraging under National Security Act Case 89 Hun-Ka 113,
  2 Apr 1990 (Constitutional Court, South Korea) 672, 680

Presidential Decision to Dispatch Korean National Armed Forces to Iraq,
    Concerning the 2006 Hun-Ma 1098, 1116, 1117 (Consolidated) 30 Oct 2006
    (Constitutional Court, South Korea) 165, 202–3
Presidential Impeachment Case 2004 Hun-Na 1, 14 May 2004 (Constitutional
    Court, South Korea) 171–2
President's Proposition for National Confidence Referendum Case
    2003HunMa694, 27 Nov 2003 (Constitutional Court, South Korea) 160
Prohibition of Assembly in the Vicinity of Diplomatic Institutions
    2000HunBa67, 30 Oct 2003 753
Prohibition of Political Party Membership of Primary and Middle School Teachers
    2001Hun-Ma 710, 25 Mar 2004 (Constitutional Court, South Korea) 759–60
Refusal of Collective Bargaining Case 14-2 KCCR 824, 2002Hun-Ba12,
    18 Dec 2002 961
Registration Requirement of Political Parties 2004Hun-Ma 246, 30 Mar 2006
    (Constitutional Court, South Korea) 498–9
Registration Revocation of Obscenity Publishers Case 95 HunKa 16, 30 Apr
    1998 730
Relocation of the Capital City Case 2004 Hun-Ma 554, 21 Oct 2004
    (Constitutional Court, Korea) 65, 271–3
Request for a Corrective Report Case 89 Hun-Ma 165, 16 Sep 1991
    (Constitutional Court, South Korea) 662
Request for Constitutional Review of Article 53 Section 1 of the Military
    Criminal Act 19-2 KCCR 535, 2006Hun-Ka13, 29 Nov 2007 555
Restriction on Prisoner's Right to Vote Case 2007Hun-Ma 1462, 29 Oct 2009
    (Constitutional Court, South Korea) 525–8
Right to Vote of Nationals Residing Abroad Case 2004 Hun-Ma 644 et al,
    28 Jun 2007 (Constitutional Court, South Korea) 448, 453–4
Rules implementing the Certified Judicial Scriveners Act Case 89 Hun-Ma 178,
    15 Oct 1990 (Constitutional Court, South Korea) 358–9
Visually Impaired Massagers Case 20-2(A) KCCR 1089, 2006Hun-Ma
    1098·1116·1117 (consolidated), 30 Oct 2008 (Constitutional Court, South
    Korea) 581–8
Withholding of Video Product Classification Case, 2004 HunKa 18, 30 Oct
    2008 650

Sri Lanka

Ariyapala Gunaratne v The People's Bank [1985] 1 Sri LR 338 (Supreme Court,
    Sri Lanka) 756–7
Dharmadasa Gomes v Commissioner of Elections [2000] SLR 3V207 (Court of
    Appeal, Sri Lanka) 539
Eighteenth Amendment to The Constitution and The Provincial Councils Bill,
    In Re The (2002) 3 Sri Lanka Law Reports 71, 3 Oct 2002 (Supreme Court,
    Sri Lanka) 262–5, 291
Hewamanne v Manik de Silva & Another [1983] 1 Sri LRI (Supreme Court,
    Sri Lanka) 697–8

Liyanage v The Queen [1967] AC 259 .... 298, 313, 650
Mallikarachchi v Shiva Pasupati, Attorney-General (1985) 1 Sri Lanka Reports
    74 (Supreme Court, Sri Lanka) 167–9
Nineteenth Amendment to the Constitution, In Re The (2002) 3 Sri Lanka Law
    Reports 85 (Supreme Court, Sri Lanka) 161–2, 291, 293–5
Prohibition of Forcible Conversion of Religion, Supreme Court Determinations
    Nos 02 to 22/2004 821
Siriwardena v Liyanage SC Application 120/82, 17 Dec 1982 650
Sunila Abeysekera v Ariya Rubesinghe (2000) 1 SLR 314 819
Teaching Sisters of the Holy Cross in Menzingen v Sri Lanka, SC Special
    Determination No 19/2003 (Supreme Court, Sri Lanka) 817
Thirteenth Amendment to the Constitution and the Provincial Councils Bill,
    In Re the (1987) 2 Sri Lanka Law Reports 312 (Supreme Court, Sri Lanka).. 291–3

Taiwan

JY Interpretation No 3, 21 May 1952 (Constitutional Court, Taiwan) 424–6
JY Interpretation No 31, 29 Jan 1954 (Constitutional Court,
    Taiwan) 224–7, 261–2, 264
JY Interpretation No 86, 15 Aug 1960 (Constitutional Court,
    Taiwan) 396, 456–7, 459
JY Interpretation No 105, 7 Oct 1964 (Constitutional Court, Taiwan) 648–9
JY Interpretation No 154, 29 Sep 1978 (Constitutional Court, Taiwan) 365–6
JY Interpretation No 211, 5 Dec 1986 (Constitutional Court, Taiwan) 456–9
JY Interpretation No 216, 19 Jun 1987 (Constitutional Court, Taiwan) 356, 358
JY Interpretation No 251, 19 Jan 1990 (Constitutional Court, Taiwan) 455
JY Interpretation No 261, 21 Jun 1990 (Constitutional Court,
    Taiwan) 217–18, 224–7, 455
JY Interpretation No 290, 24 Jan 1992 (Constitutional Court, Taiwan) 530–1, 533
JY Interpretation No 328, 26 Nov 1993 (Constitutional Court, Taiwan) 403
JY Interpretation No 329, 24 Dec 1993 (Constitutional Court, Taiwan) 355
JY Interpretation No 331, 30 Dec 1993 (Constitutional Court, Taiwan) 297, 490–1
JY Interpretation No 340, 25 Feb 1994 (Constitutional Court, Taiwan) 534
JY Interpretation No 364, 23 Sep 1994 (Constitutional Court, Taiwan) 653, 660–1
JY Interpretation No 371, 20 Jan 1995 (Constitutional Court, Taiwan) 332, 335–7
JY Interpretation No 373, 24 Feb 1995 (Constitutional Court, Taiwan) 760–1
JY Interpretation No 392, 22 Dec 1995 (Constitutional Court, Taiwan) 418–19
JY Interpretation No 407, 5 Jul 1996 (Constitutional Court, Taiwan) 723, 727
JY Interpretation No 414, 8 Nov 1996 (Constitutional Court, Taiwan) 650
JY Interpretation No 419, 31 Dec 1996 (Constitutional Court, Taiwan) 218, 353–4
JY Interpretation No 439, 30 Oct 1997 (Constitutional Court, Taiwan) 458
JY Interpretation No 445, 23 Jan 1998 (Constitutional Court,
    Taiwan) 739–42, 749–51, 753
JY Interpretation No 468, 22 Oct 1998 (Constitutional Court, Taiwan) 534
JY Interpretation No 470, 27 Nov 1998 (Constitutional Court, Taiwan) 381
JY Interpretation No 476, 29 Jan 1999 (Constitutional Court, Taiwan) 619

JY Interpretation No 479, 1 Apr 1999 (Constitutional Court, Taiwan)....... 764–5, 770
JY Interpretation No 490, 1 Oct 1999 (Constitutional Court, Taiwan).............. 846–7
JY Interpretation No 499, 24 Mar 2000 (Constitutional Court,
    Taiwan)... 296, 296–7, 351
JY Interpretation No 509, 7 Jul 2000 (Constitutional Court, Taiwan).................. 709
JY Interpretation No 520, 15 Jan 2001 (Constitutional Court, Taiwan)............. 191–2
JY Interpretation No 530, 5 Oct 2001 (Constitutional Court, Taiwan)....... 389, 391–3
JY Interpretation No 541, 4 Apr 2002 (Constitutional Court, Taiwan)................. 381
JY Interpretation No 543, 3 May 2002 (Constitutional Court, Taiwan).. 206–7, 362–4
JY Interpretation No 549, 2 Aug 2002 (Constitutional Court, Taiwan)................ 441
JY Interpretation No 578, 21 May 2004 (Constitutional Court, Taiwan).... 442, 962–3
JY Interpretation No 582, 23 Jul 2004 (Constitutional Court, Taiwan) 433
JY Interpretation No 585, 15 Dec 2004 (Constitutional Court, Taiwan)............... 447
JY Interpretation No 599, 10 Jun 2005 (Constitutional Court, Taiwan) 460–1
JY Interpretation No 601, 22 Jul 2005 (Constitutional Court, Taiwan) .. 371–3, 386–8
JY Interpretation No 603, 28 Sep 2005 (Constitutional Court, Taiwan). 399, 461, 737
JY Interpretation No 613, 21 Jul 2006 (Constitutional Court,
    Taiwan).. 141–3, 186–90, 455, 658
JY Interpretation No 617, 26 Oct 2006 (Constitutional Court, Taiwan)..... 723, 727–8
JY Interpretation No 618, 3 Nov 2006 (Constitutional Court, Taiwan)................. 617
JY Interpretation No 623, 26 Jan 2007 (Constitutional Court, Taiwan)................ 730
JY Interpretation No 627, 15 Jun 2007 (Constitutional Court,
    Taiwan)... 167, 169–70, 423
JY Interpretation No 632, 15 Aug 2007 (Constitutional Court,
    Taiwan).. 183–4, 190
JY Interpretation No 644, 20 Jun 2008 (Constitutional Court,
    Taiwan).. 641, 755, 763–4, 770
JY Interpretation No 645, 11 Jul 2008 (Constitutional Court, Taiwan) 540
JY Interpretation No 649, 31 Oct 2008 (Constitutional Court, Taiwan) 579–81
JY Interpretation No 656, 3 Apr 2009 (Constitutional Court, Taiwan).............. 736–8
JY Interpretation No 666, 6 Nov 2009 (Constitutional Court, Taiwan)...... 455–6, 617
JY Interpretation No 678, 29 Jul 2010 (Constitutional Court, Taiwan) 654–5, 659

Thailand

Application to the Constitutional Court for the interpretation of s 241 para 4
    and s 264 in conjunction with s 6 of the Constitution, BE 2540 (1997) Ruling
    No 5/2541, 4 Aug 1998 (Constitutional Court, Thailand) 336–7
Attorney-General requested for a Constitutional Court order to dissolve
    Neutral Democratic (Matchima Thippathai) Party, Re The Ruling No 18/2551,
    2 Dec 2008 (Constitutional Court, Thailand).. 502–4
Attorney-General requested for a Constitutional Court order to dissolve People's
    Power (Palang Prachachon) Party, Re The Ruling No 20/2551, Dec 2 2008 216
Constitutional Court Ruling No 15/2549 (22 Aug 2006)... 618
Phra Nakhon Si Ayutthaya Provincial Court referred the objections of the
    defendants to the Constitutional Court for a ruling under s 264 of the

Constitution, BE 2540 (1997), Ruling No 14-15/2543, 4 Apr 2000
(Constitutional Court, Thailand) 357
Political Party Registrar's application for an order to dissolve Patiroop Party
Ruling 2/2542, 4 Mar 1999 (Constitutional Court, Thailand) 500–1
President of the House of Representatives Requests for a Constitutional Court
Ruling that the Enactment of Emergency Decrees were Inconsistent with s 218
of the Constitution, BE 2540 (1997) Ruling No 1/2541, 23 May 1998
(Constitutional Court, T 194
Request of the Attorney-General for dissolution orders against Pattana Chart
Thai Party, Paen Din Thai Party and Thai Rak Thai Party, Re Ruling
No 3-5/2550, 30 May 2007 (Constitutional Court, Thailand) 501–2
Termination of ministerial office of the Prime Minister, Re petition and request
for ruling on Ruling, No 12-13/2551 (2008), Sep 9 2008 216

Trinidad & Tobago

Sumayyah Mohammed v Moraine [1996] 3 LRC 475 (High Court, Trinidad &
Tobago) 827

UN Human Rights Committee

Sister Immaculate Joseph and 80 Teaching Sisters of the Holy Cross of the Third
Order of Saint Francis in Menzingen of Sri Lanka v Sri Lanka, No 1249/2004,
UN Doc CCPR/C/85/D/1249/2004 (2005) 820
Yeo Bum Yoon and Myung Jin Choi v Republic of Korea Communications
Nos 1321/2004 and 1322/2004 845

United Kingdom

Bowman v Secular Society [1917] AC 406 604
Dr Bonham's Case (1610) 8 Co Rep 114 (Court of Common Pleas, England) 311
International Transport Roth GmbH v Secretary of State for the Home
Department [2003] QB 728 946
Pepper (Inspector of Taxes) v Hart [1993] AC 593 427
R (Carson) v Secretary of State for Work and Pensions [2003] 3 All ER 542,
577 946–7
R (on the application of Begum) v Head Teacher and Governors of Denbigh
High School [2005] 2 All ER 487 (HL) 827–8
R (Westminster City Council) v National Asylum Support Service [2002]
1 WLR 2956 947
R v Cambridge Health Authority ex parte B [1995] 1 WLR 898 947
R v Chief Metropolitan Stipendiary Magistrate, ex p Choudhury [1991]
1 QB 429 915
Regina v Hicklin (1868) LR 3 QB 360 722

Reynolds v Times Newspapers Ltd [2001] 2 AC 127 712
Whitehouse v Lemon [1979] 2 WLR 281 915

United States

Abington School District v Schempp 374 US 203 (1963) 880
Abrams v United States 250 US 616 (1919) 641
Adamson v California 332 US 46 (1947) 556
Atchison, Topeka & Santa Fe R Co v Matthews 174 US 96 (1899) 590, 592
Atchison, Topeka & Santa Fe R Co v Matthews 184 US 540 (1891) 591
Bain Peanut Co v Pinson 282 US 499 (1931) 599
Baker v Carr 369 US 186 (1962) 400, 477
Brandenburg v Ohio 395 US 444 (1969) 670
Bridges v California 314 US 252 79
Brown v Board of Education 347 US 483 (1954) 426, 618
Cantwell v Connecticut 310 US 296 .... 885, 923–4, 930
Chamber of Commerce of the USA v New Jersey, 89 NJ 131, 159, 445
    A 2d 353 (1982) 611
Chaplinsky v New Hampshire 315 US 568 (1942) 681
Church of Lukumi Babalu Aye v City of Hialeah 508 US 520 (1993) 782
City of St Louis v Liberman, 547 SW 2d 452 (1977) 611
Commonwealth vs Plaisted (1889) 148 Mass 375 925
Connolly v Union Sewer Pipe Co 184 US 540 (1902) 590–1
Craig v Boren 429 US 190 (1976) 618
Crowley v Christensen 137 US 86 (1890) 596
Davie v Benson 133 US 333, 342 (1890) 771
Engel v O' Malley 219 US 128 (1911) 593
Everson v Board of Education 330 US 1 (1946) 880
First Bank & Trust Co v Board of Governors of Federal Reserve System,
    605 F Supp 555 (1984) 611
Flast v Cohen 392 US 83 (1968) 343, 411
Gertz v Welch 418 US 323, 324 (1974) 704
Greenberg v Kimmelman, 99 NJ 552, 577, 494 A 2d 294 (1985) 611
Gulf, Colorado & Santa Fe Railway Co v Ellis 165 US 150 (1891) 591, 599
Hamilton v Board of Regents of University of California, (1934) 293 US 245 925
Holbrook v Lexmark International Group, Inc, 65 SW 3d 908 (2002) 611
Jacobellis v Ohio 378 US 184 (1964) 731
Joseph Burstyn Inc v Wilson 343 US 495 (1952) 915
Kotch v Pilot Comm'rs 330 US 552 (1947) 591
Lawrence v Texas 539 US 558 (2003) 630
Lemon v Kurtzman 403 US 602 (1971) 838
Linkletter v Walker 381 US 618, 629 (1965) 447–8, 450
Lujan v Defender of Wildlife 504 US 555, 560 (1992) 404
Luther v Borden 48 US 1, 12 L Ed 581 269
McCollum v Board of Education 333 US 203 (1948) 883
Marbury v Madison (1803) 5 US (1 Cranch) 137 .... 307, 311, 313

Meyer v Nebraska, 262 US 390, 67 Led 1042...855
Miami Herald Publishing Co v Tornillo 518 US 241 (1974)......................... 660, 667
Michael M v Sonoma County Superior Court 450 US 464 (1980)........................ 618
Miller v State of California 413 US 15 (1973).. 723, 731
Minersville School District v Gobitis 310 US 586 (1940).................................... 857
Mitchel v United States 34 US 711 (1835)...562
New Jersey State League of Municipalities, et al v State of New Jersey,
    257 NJ Super 509, 608 A 2d 965 (1992)..611
New York ex rel Lieberman v Van De Carr 199 US 552 (1905)...........................593
New York Times v Sullivan 376 US 254 (1964).. 704–5
Newark Superior Officers Ass'n v City of Newark, 98 NJ 212, 227, 486 A 2d
    305 (1985)..611
Old Dearborn Distributing Co v Seagram Distillers Corporation 299 US 183
    (1936)..595
Oregon Department of Human Resources v Smith 494 US 872 (1990).......882–3, 885
Red Lion Broadcasting Co v FCC 395 US 367 (1969) 653
Reynolds v Sims 377 US 533, 562 (1964)...468
Reynolds v United States, 98 US 145 (1878) 886, 924
Richardson v Secretary of Labor, 689 F 2d 632 (1982) 611
Robbiani v Burke, 77 NJ 383, 392–93, 390 A 2d 1149 (1978)............................611
Romer v Evans, 517 US 620 (1996)...630
Rosenblatt v Baer 383 US 75, 92 (1966) 704
Schenck v United States 249 US 47 (1919).. 670
Shelley v Kraemer, 334 US 1, 22 (1948) 630
Sherbert v Berner, 374 US 398, 10 L Ed 2d 965, 970, 83 S Ct
    1790 .... 838, 855, 882, 885
Skinner v Oklahoma 316 US 535 (1942) 596–7
Southern Railway Co v Greene 216 US 400 (1910).. 596
State v Ewing, 518 SW 2d 643 (1975)...611
Sunday Lake Iron Cornparty v Wakefield 247 US 350..597
Sweatt v Painter, 339 US 629, 635 (1950) 630
Taxpayers Ass'n of Weymouth Tp v Weymouth Tp, 80 NJ 6, 40, 364 A 2d 1016
    (1976)..611
Texas v Johnson 491 US 397 (1989) 683
Thomas v Review Board of the Indian Employment Security Division (1981)
    450 US 707..852
Tigner v Texas 310 US 141.. 590–1
Torcaso v Watkins 367 US 488 (1961)...772
Truax v Corrigan 257 US 312 592
United States v Board of Education of School District & Commonwealth
    Philadelphia 911 F 2d 882 (1990) 827
United States v Carolene Products Co 304 US 144 (1938) 556
United States v Cruikshank 92 US 542 (1876) 641
United States v O'Brien 391 US 367 (1968)... 703
United States v Seeger 380 US 163 (1965)... 772
United States v Virginia 518 US 515 (1996) 618
Ward v Flood 17 Am Rep 405 (1874)...590

Werner v Southern California Associated Newspapers, 35 Cal 2d 121, 216
    P 2d 825 (1950)...611
West Virginia v Barnette, 319 US 624 (1943).................................... 852, 854, 857–8
Whitney v California, 274 US 357, 47 S Ct 641, 71 L Ed 1095..............................916
Willis Cox v New Hampshire 312 US 569 (1941)...925
Yick Wo v Hopkins 118 US 356 (1888)... 590, 592, 596
Zorach v Clauson 343 US 306 (1952).. 782, 881, 897

Table of Legislation

Because the whole of this work relates to the constitutions of Asian countries, and to avoid excessively long, unhelpful lists of page numbers, only references to specific provisions (articles, sections and the like) are included for the main countries discussed. The year of a constitution is only cited where this is of particular significance for the development of provisions.

Afghanistan

Constitution
  Art 15 1020

Australia

Aboriginals Ordinance 1918 (NT) 851
Constitution
  s 116 925
National Security (Subversive Associations) Regulations 848–9
Native Title Act 562

Austria

Constitution 308
  Art 139 448
  Art 140 .... 335, 447
  Art 141(1) 335

Bangladesh

Code of Criminal Procedure
  s 99A 910
  s 255K 434
Constitution
  preamble 113–14
  First Amendment 246
  Fourteenth Amendment 247
  Second Amendment 246
  Third Amendment 246

Fourth Amendment..246
Sixth Amendment..247
Seventh Amendment...244–5, 247
  s 3...244–5
Eighth Amendment..247, 390
Ninth Amendment..247
Eleventh Amendment...247
Twelfth Amendment...247
Thirteenth Amendment..180, 247
Fifteenth Amendment..115, 247
Art 2...114
Art 2(A)..110
Art 2A...115, 828, 860, 867
Art 7(2)...308
Art 8...111
Art 8(1)..113–15
Art 8(1A)...867–8
Art 9...113
Art 10...113
Art 12...111, 114–15
Art 14...114
Art 15...113
Art 16...113
Art 18...78, 1001
Art 18A..1020
Art 23A..115
Art 25..111, 113, 115
Art 26..113, 351
Art 26(2)..351
Art 27..550, 556
Art 28(2)..829
Art 28(2) and (3)...625
Art 28(4)..494
Art 29...829
Art 31...1020
Art 32..984, 988, 1020
Art 35(3)..393
Art 38...768
Art 39..652, 687, 704, 829
Art 53B...180
Art 65...493
Art 65(3)..494
Art 94...390–1
Art 95...374
Art 100...390
Art 100(5)...391
Art 101...391

Art 102... 828
Art 102(1)... 416
Art 115... 394
Art 116... 394
Art 116A... 393–4
Art 118(1)... 518
Art 121... 494
Art 122(1)... 494
Art 133... 394
Art 136... 394
Art 142... 351, 390
Art 142(2)... 351
Art 152(1)... 394
Pt II, s 8... 105
Pt III.. 828
Pt IX, Ch I... 394
Constitution 1972... 110–11
Art 38... 110
Constitution 2011.. 115
East Pakistan Government Land and Building (Recovery of Possession)
Ordinance
s 5... 989
Government Servants (Discipline and Appeals) Rules.................................... 829
Industrial Relations (Amendment) Act 1990... 768
s 2... 768
s 5... 768
Industrial Relations Ordinance 1969
s 2(iv).. 769
s 7(2)... 768
s 8... 768
s 11A... 769
s 22... 768
s 22(1)... 769
s 22(12)... 769
s 22(2)-(10)... 769
Penal Code
s 99A... 909
s 295A... 909–10
Proclamation Order No 1 1977.. 113–14
Representation of the People Order 1972.. 518
s 4 518
s 20(1)... 519
s 91(b)... 519
Second Proclamation (Sixth Amendment) Order No III................................ 110
Second Proclamation Order No IV 1978... 113–14
Services (Reorganisation and Conditions) Act 1975...................................... 393

Suppression of Cruelty to Women and Children Act 2000
  s 6(2) 434
Trade Unions Act 1926
  s 28B 769

Belize

Constitution
  s 7 434–5

Bhutan

Constitution
  Art 2 .... 77, 107
  Art 3 803
  Art 3(1) 106, 802
  Art 3(2) 802
  Art 3(3) 106, 803
  Art 3(7) 867
  Art 4(1) 77
  Art 4(3) 77, 104
  Art 4(4) 77
  Art 5 .... 80, 1019
  Art 6 104
  Art 7(15) 802
  Art 7(4) 802
  Art 8 .... 80, 804
  Art 8(2) 80, 104
  Art 8(3) 80, 803
  Art 8(5) 80
  Art 8(6) 80
  Art 9 .... 82, 860, 1001
  Art 9(10) 81
  Art 9(20) 78
  Art 15 .... 103, 550, 556
  Art 15(3) 106
  Art 15(4)(b) 106
  Art 17 625
  Art 18 103
  Art 18(3) 103
  Art 28(6) 81
Penal Code 804
  s 463(A) 804
Religious Organisation Act, s 5(b) 106
Religious Organisations Act 2007 803–4

Brazil, Constitution

Art 5 V.. 660

Brunei

Constitution
  Art 3... 105, 860
  Art 4(1) 135
  Art 4(1A) 135
  Art 4(2) 136
  Art 86.. 309
  Pt II
    s 3 860
Constitution 1959 37

Burma, *see* Myanmar/Burma

Cambodia

Constitution
  preamble 86
  Art 1... 86, 120
  Art 7.. 86
  Art 11.. 56
  Art 31... 78, 431, 625
  Art 39.. 86
  Art 43... 860
  Art 46... 83, 704
  Art 47.. 80
  Art 48.. 79
  Art 51... 56, 86
  Art 53.. 80
  Art 54.. 81
  Art 117... 310
  Art 136... 341
  Art 140... 330
  Art 141... 330, 332, 334
  Art 143... 350
  Art 151... 350
  Art 153.. 56
  Ch X 310
Constitution 1947 50–1

Interim Constitution
  Art 1...464
Paris Peace Accord 466

Canada

Charter of Rights and Freedoms 696
  s 15(1)..632
  s 33...324
Criminal Code
  s 319(2)...680–1

China

Ancestral Injunctions...9
Common Programme 1949 .... 40–1, 43
  Art 1..41
  Art 4..41
  Arts12 and 13..41
Constitution
  preamble 100, 104
  Art 1..173
  Art 2..121
  Art 5... 101, 121
  Art 6..101
  Art 7..101
  Art 11..101
  Art 21..83
  Art 24..101
  Art 26..80
  Art 31.. 228, 315
  Art 33.. 78, 550
  Art 36..865
  Art 36(1) 911
  Art 46(1) 322
  Art 48..625
  Art 49..80
  Art 51..121
  Art 57.. 176, 228, 315
  Art 58.. 228, 315
  Art 59..176
  Art 60..176
  Art 62.. 121, 176
  Art 63..177
  Art 67.. 177, 277, 313, 325

Art 67(4) 319, 321
Art 70 177
Art 80 176
Art 85 177
Art 89 177
Constitution 1914 14
Constitution 1923
Art 5 551
Art 6 419
Constitution 1949
preamble 86–7
Constitution 1954 43–4
Art 29 44
Constitution 1975 44
Constitution 1982 .... 45, 177
preamble 45
Art 11 45
Ch II 45
Criminal Law
Art 300(1) 913
Art 300(2) 913
Art 300(3) 913
Election Law for the House, 1912 13
Election Law for the Senate, 1912 13
General Plan for Organization of the Provisional Government of the Republic of
China 1911 13
Great Ming Code 9
Hong Kong, *see* Hong Kong
Law for Court Organization 1909 418
Macau, *see* Macau
Organic Law 1928 40
Organic Law for the Congress (House and Senate) 1912 13
Organic Law of the Central People's Government of the People's Republic of China
1949 40
Organic Law of the People's Court
Art 33 322
Provisional Constitution for the Period of Political Tutelage 419
Provisional Constitution of the Republic of China, 1912 .... 13, 38, 546
Art 5 547
Art 18 13
Art 53 13
Regulations on Petitions by Letters and Calls
Art 1 543
Resolution on Banning Heretic Cult Organizations, Preventing and Punishing Evil
Cult Activities 1999 912–13
Taiwan, *see* Taiwan
Tribunal Organization Law for Da Li Yuan 1906 418

Cyprus

Constitution 1960 308

Czech Republic

Constitution
  Art 19 431

Denmark

Consolidated Act on Danish Municipal and Regional Elections
  s 1 528

France

Constitution
  Art 7 340
  Art 11 340
  Art 58 340
  Art 60 340
Constitution 1793 1022

Germany

Basic Law 279–80, 338
  Art 1 .... 279, 952
  Art 5(1) 682
  Art 20 .... 279, 952
  Art 21 339
  Art 21(2) 497
  Art 61 338
  Art 79 448
  Art 79(3) 279, 350
  Art 93 335
  Art 98 338
  Art 100 335
Code of Criminal Procedure
  Art 239 433
Constitutional Court Act
  Art 78 448
Weimar Constitution 24, 1022
  Art 109 .... 551, 553

Greece, Constitution

Art 3 801
Art 13 801

Hong Kong

Basic Law.. 178, 227–8, 230, 274–7, 325, 441, 478
  Art 19(1) 228, 315
  Art 19(2) 229
  Art 22.. 229–30
  Art 22(4) 314, 317–19, 321, 428–9
  Art 24.. 317, 320, 429
  Art 24(2) 314, 320, 322, 640
  Art 24(2)(1)... 321–2, 421
  Art 24(2)(3)... 318–21, 423
  Art 24(2)(4) 640
  Art 24(3) 314, 317, 321, 421–2
  Art 25.. 550, 625
  Art 26.. 479
  Art 27.. 693
  Art 28.. 1018
  Art 36.. 946
  Art 39.. 79, 277, 429, 441, 480, 944
  Art 39(2) 743
  Art 43.. 319
  Art 45.. 178
  Art 46.. 178
  Art 48.. 1018
  Art 48(2) 319
  Art 48(4) 946
  Art 62..946, 1018
  Art 73(1)-(9).. 276
  Art 73(10).. 274, 276
  Art 80.. 228, 315
  Art 88.. 374
  Art 103.. 179
  Art 158.. 314, 316–18, 321, 429
  Art 158(1)............................... 229, 313, 315, 318–19, 321, 325
  Art 158(2)... 313, 315–16, 318, 325
  Art 158(3)............................... 316, 318–19, 321–2, 326
  Art 158(4)... 316
  Art 159(4).. 228, 315
  Art 160(1)... 275
  Ch III.. 428–9
  Ann II.. 478

Bill of Rights Ordinance 277, 441, 524, 703, 1017
  Art 2 1018
  Art 2(1) 1018
  Art 16(2) 693
  Art 21 531
  Art 21(a) 525, 531
  Art 21(b) 479
  Art 22 946
  s 8 441
Civil Service (Disciplinary) Regulations 179
Colonial Regulations 179–80
Disability Discrimination Ordinance 735
  s 72(4)(b) 735–6
Disciplinary Proceedings (Colonial Regulations) Regulations 179
Guidelines on Election-related Activities in respect of the Legislative Council
    Election
  Art 3(3) 478
Immigration Ordinance 314, 321, 421, 640
  s 2(4)(a)(vi) 640
Kuk Ordinance 524
Legislative Council (Powers and Privileges) Ordinance
  s 9(2) 274
Letters Patent 179–80
Medical Practitioners Regulations
  s 4(2)(b) 531–2
National Flag and National Emblem Ordinance
  s 7 .... 700, 702
Public Order Ordinance
  s 13A 743
  s 14(1) 743
  s 17A(3)(b)(i) 743
Public Service (Administration) Order 1997 (EO No 1 of 1997) 178–9
Public Service (Disciplinary) Regulation 178–9
Regional Flag and Regional Emblem Ordinance
  s 7 .... 700, 702
Telecommunication Ordinance
  s 33 452

Hungary

Constitution
  Art 7(1) 431

India
Bombay Municipal Corporation Act 986–7

Bombay Police Act 1951 .... 751, 986
  s 33(1)(o) 751–2
Constitution
  preamble 287, 289, 831, 860
  Seventh Amendment 283
  Seventeenth Amendment 283, 285
  Twenty-Fourth Amendment 283
  Thirty-Eighth Amendment 211
  Thirty-Ninth Amendment 288
  Forty-Second Amendment 113, 283, 288–9, 788, 870
  Forty-Fourthth Amendment 211
  Eighty-Sixth Amendment 1009
  Art 1 874
  Art 11 992
  Art 12 .... 590, 665
  Art 13 .... 351, 752
  Art 13(2) 282, 286–7, 811
  Art 14 .... 283, 286, 415, 435, 550, 553–4, 556, 590–1,
           594–6, 598–9, 601, 604–5, 630–1, 767, 810, 815
  Art 15 .... 435, 625, 630–2
  Art 15(1) 631
  Art 15(2) 632
  Art 15(4) 496
  Art 16 631
  Art 16(4) 496
  Art 16(5) 872
  Art 17 872
  Art 19 .... 284, 415, 630, 687, 704, 766, 800, 873
  Art 19(1) 678
  Art 19(1)(a) 645, 655, 666, 679, 725, 755
  Art 19(1)(b) 752
  Art 19(1)(c) 766
  Art 19(1)(d) 752
  Art 19(1)(e) 986
  Art 19(1)(f) 286, 564
  Art 19(1)(g) 435, 679
  Art 19(2) 642, 645, 655–8, 665–6, 725, 810
  Art 19(3) 751
  Art 19(6) 656, 679
  Art 19(f) and (g) 283
  Art 21 .... 415, 435, 630, 810, 984–5, 987, 992, 994,
           997, 1001–4, 1006–8, 1013, 1019, 1021
  Art 21A 1009
  Art 25 .... 286, 781, 788, 799–800, 809–11, 857–8, 872
  Art 25(1) 801, 808–9, 818, 925
  Art 25(2) 860
  Art 25(2)(b) 780, 874

Art 25(b) 872
Art 26 .... 286, 810
Art 26(b) 926
Art 28 510
Art 28(2) 872
Art 29(b) 510
Art 31 .... 286, 564, 992
Art 31A 285
Art 31B 285, 288
Art 32 .... 283, 286, 436, 443, 459–60, 628, 678, 983, 992, 1005
Art 32(2) 286
Art 32(4) 286
Art 33 286
Art 37 .... 983, 986, 989
Art 38 988
Art 39 .... 988, 1001
Art 39(3) 1001
Art 39(a) 986
Art 39(e) and (f) 1007
Art 41 .... 986, 1001, 1006–7
Art 42 1007
Art 43 1001
Art 44 872
Art 45 1006–8
Art 46 .... 988, 1006–7
Art 47 .... 997, 1001, 1021
Art 48 874
Art 48A 1001, 1020
Art 48A(g) 1021
Art 51(c) 435
Art 51A 80, 859
Art 51A(g) 1021
Art 72 211
Art 73 436
Art 74(2) 212
Art 79 146
Art 80 146
Art 83 146
Art 124 374
Art 124(2) 379
Art 124(4) 384
Art 141 .... 436, 460
Art 163(1) 154
Art 217 .... 378–9, 384, 412
Art 217(1) 379–80, 384
Art 222 .... 382–3, 412, 420
Art 222(1) 379–80, 382–5

Art 224.. 378–80, 382, 412
Art 224(1).. 379–80
Art 226...510, 595, 983, 1005
Art 243-D..495
Art 243-M(4)(b) 495–6
Art 244..494
Art 253..436
Art 256..1008
Art 324..515
Art 324(1). 510–11
Art 324(5). 511
Art 327..509–10
Art 328..509–10
Art 329..509
Art 329(b) 509–10, 516
Art 330..467, 493, 559
Art 332..559
Art 334..559
Art 335..559
Art 338A..559
Art 338A(5). 560
Art 343..874
Art 355..154
Art 356... 153–5, 210–11
Art 356(1).. 153–4, 210–11
Art 356(3). 211
Art 361..168
Art 368.. 286–90, 292
Pt III 285, 288, 811, 814, 983, 1005
Pt IV 285, 288, 983
Pt IX 495
Pt XV 510–11
Fifth Schedule...494
Sixth Schedule...495
Seventh Schedule...430, 436, 810
Ninth Schedule..283, 285, 288
Constitution 1950 32
Constitution 1976 113
Criminal Procedure Code 604
Dowry Prohibition Act 1961... 627, 629
East Punjab Public Safety Act 1949
  s 7(1)(c) 644–5
Female Infanticide Prevention Act 1870 627
Gurdwara Act 1925...780
Himachal Pradesh Freedom of Religion Act 2006............................ 810–11, 814–15
  s 4 812, 815
  s 4(2) 813

s 5 813
s 7 813
s 8 812
Hindi Sahitya Sammelan Act.. 765
  s 4(1) 765
Industries (Development Regulation) Act 1951
  s 1S.. 288
  s 18A.. 288
Jharkhand Panchayati Raj Act 2001
  s 21(B).. 495
  s 40(B).. 495
  s 55(B).. 495
Kerala Land Reforms (Amendment) Act 1969.................................... 286
Kerala Land Reforms Act 1963 286
Land Acquisition Act 591
Life Insurance Corporation Act 1956 665
Madhya Pradesh Dharma Swatantraya Adhiniyam 1968........................ 808, 810–14
Orissa Freedom of Religion Act 1967.................................... 807, 811–14
  s 3 810
  s 4 810
Orissa Freedom of Religion Rules 1999 .... 807, 813
Panchayats Extension to the Scheduled Areas Act 1996
  s 4(g) 495
Penal Code
  s 292... 725–6
Penal Code 1860
  s 377.. 630
Pre-Conception and Pre-Natal Diagnostic Techniques (Prohibition of Sex Selection)
    Act 1994.. 627–8
Protection of Human Rights Act 2008.. 1003
  s 2(d) 1003
  s 2(f).. 1003
Punjab Security and Land Tenures Act 1953...................................... 283
Punjab Special Powers (Press) Act 1956 678
  s 2 677
  s 2(1)(a).. 677–8, 680
  s 2(2) 678
  s 3 .... 677, 680
  s 3(1) 678, 680
  s 3(2) 678
  s 4 678
Representation of the People Act 1951 511
  s 36... 510, 875
  s 123.. 875, 877–8
  s 123(3)... 877
  s 123(3A)... 875, 877
Sick Textile Undertakings (Nationalisation) Act 1974 288

Suppression of Immoral Traffic Act 1933 992
Symbols Order 504–5
West Bengal Special Courts Act 1950 .... 589, 594, 599, 605
  s 3 589
  s 5 589–90
  s 5(1) 595, 597
West Bengal Special Courts Ordinance 1949 594

Indonesia

Bill of Rights 304
Blasphemy Law 930, 932, 933–42
  s 1 .... 932, 936–8, 940–1
  s 1(1) 939
  s 1(3) 939
  s 2(1) 932, 941
  s 2(1) and (2) 937
  s 2(2) 933
  s 3 .... 933, 937
  s 4 .... 933, 937–8
Constitution 53–4, 61, 89
  preamble 303, 935–6
  First Amendment 54
  Second Amendment 54, 304, 968
  Third Amendment 54
  Fourth Amendment 54, 969
  Art 1(2) 684
  Art 6A(2) 532
  Art 7A 685
  Art 7B 339
  Art 9(1) 934
  Art 22 311
  Art 24(1) 372, 394
  Art 24(2) 395
  Art 24A 357, 373, 395
  Art 24A(3) 395
  Art 24B 373, 395
  Art 24B(1) 372–3, 390, 395
  Art 24C 311, 331, 334, 339–40, 357, 367–8, 373, 395, 969
  Art 24C(1) 334, 341, 356, 367
  Art 27 .... 625, 684
  Art 28 684
  Art 28(2) 733
  Art 28A 981
  Art 28C 968
  Art 28D 550, 556

Art 28D(1) 685
Art 28E 933
Art 28E(1)(2) 934
Art 28F 685
Art 28H 981
Art 28H(1) 979
Art 28H(1)(3) 969
Art 28I 302, 981
Art 28I(1) 302, 933–4
Art 28J(1) 936
Art 28J(2) 302, 934, 936–7, 940
Art 29 .... 860, 933
Art 29(1) 106, 934–5
Art 29(2) 932, 939
Art 31(3) 934
Art 31(4) 969
Art 33 .... 971–3, 975–7
Art 33(1) 81
Art 33(2) 969–72, 976–7
Art 33(3) 979, 981–2
Art 67(11) 374
Ch IX 394
Ch XA 304, 937, 968
Ch XI 937
Constitution 1949 53
Constitution 1950 53
Constitutional Court Law 356, 410–11
Art 23 373
Art 51(1) 410–11
Art 51(1)(a) 410
Art 51(3) 411
Corruption Eradication Commission Law 411
Criminal Code 305
Art 134 684–5
Art 136bis 684–5
Art 137 684–5
Art 156a 933, 937
Decree 70/1978 on the Guidelines for the Propagation of Religion 823
Interim Law No 1 2002 302
Jakarta Charter 89
Joint Decree of the Minister of Religion, the Attorney-General and the Minister of
   Home Affairs No 3/2008 942
Judicial Authority Law 372–3, 390, 394
Art 34(3) 373
Judicial Commission Law 372–3, 390, 394
Law No 4 of 2003 934
Law No 4 of 2004 .... 372, 394

Law No 7 of 2004
  Art 5...979–80
  Art 9..981
  Art 10..981
  Art 11(3) 981
  Art 14...979–80
  Art 15...979–80
  Art 16..980
  Art 26..981
  Art 26(7) 980
  Art 29(3) 980
  Art 45..981
  Art 46..981
  Art 49(4) 982
  Art 80..981
  Art 80(1) 980
Law No 11 of 2006
  Art 15..868
Law No 14 of 1970 934
Law No 15 of 1985 977
Law No 15 of 2003 301
Law No 19 of 1964 934
Law No 20 of 2002 969–77
  Art 16..976–7
  Art 17..977
  Art 68..977
Law No 22 of 2004 ....372, 394
  Art 20..395
Law No 23 of 2003
  Art 25..532
Law No 24 of 2003 934
  Art 10(1) 368
  Art 47..969
  Art 51(1) 368, 532
  Art 56..969
  Art 60..969
Law No 39 of 1999 on Human Rights
  Art 4...933
  Art 7...301
  Art 22(2) 933
Law No 48 of 2009 934
Law on Constitutional Court
  Art 51...331, 334
  Art 68..340
  Art 74..341
Presidential Decree No 1/PNPS/1965 on the Prevention of the Misuse/Insulting
  of a Religion Made into a Law by Law 5/1969.............................932

Regulation No 12/2003 489
Regulation No 23/2003 532

International

African Convention on Human Rights
  Art 11 739
Agreement on Restoration of Okinawa
  Art 3(1) 201
Agreement on the Status of US Armed Forces 197, 199–200
  Art 2 201
  Art 2(1) 200
  Art 25 200
American Convention on Human Rights (ACHR) 667, 846
  Art 14 667
  Art 14(1) 667
  Art 14(1)(1) 667
  Art 14(2) 667
  Art 15 739
Asian Human Rights Charter 739
Cairo Declaration, 27 November 1943 20
Convention for the Elimination of All Forms of Discrimination Against Women
  (CEDAW) 79, 442, 496, 624–5
  Art 2 624
  Art 4 624
  Art 5 624
  Art 12 1003
  Art 14 1003
Convention on the Elimination of Racial Discrimination (CERD) 638, 681
  Art 4 681
  Art 5 681
  Art 5(f) 638
  Art 6 638
Council of Europe Convention on the Participation of Foreigners in Public Life at
  Local Level
  Art 6(1) 527, 533
Covenant of the League of Nations 623
  Art 21 547
Declaration on Measures to Eliminate International Terrorism 304
Declaration to Supplement the 1994 Declaration on Measures to Eliminate
  International Terrorism 1996 304
European Convention on Human Rights 120, 348, 437, 667
  Art 6(3)(iv) 433
  Art 8 .... 947, 1019
  Art 9 .... 846, 861
  Art 11 .... 108, 739

Protocol 1
Art 3 528–9
ILO Indigenous and Tribal Peoples Convention (No 169) 634–5
International Convention for the Suppression of Terrorist Bombings 1997 304
International Convention for the Suppression of the Financing of
    Terrorism 1999 304
International Covenant on Civil and Political Rights (ICCPR) ....
    79, 277, 303, 429, 441, 521, 531, 567–8, 631–2, 638, 641, 687, 693, 702, 743, 756,
    805, 820, 829, 845, 937, 944, 982, 1003
    Art 2(1) 567, 632
    Art 2(26) 632
    Art 4(2) 650
    Art 14(3)(v) 433
    Art 15 302–3
    Art 15(2) 303
    Art 18 .... 805, 820, 847, 933, 936, 938
    Art 18(3) 845, 937
    Art 19 .... 650, 820
    Arts 19-22 641
    Art 19(2) 818
    Art 19(3) 441, 701, 936
    Art 20(2) 671, 681
    Art 21 .... 739, 742
    Art 22 755
    Art 22(1) 756
    Art 22(2) 756
    Art 25 .... 409, 521
    Art 26 .... 567, 638, 820
    Art 27 .... 567–9, 574, 820
    Art 40 567
International Covenant on Economic, Social and Culture Rights
    (ICESCR) 79, 756, 829, 944, 963,
    982, 1002–3, 1008, 1017–18
    Art 8(a) 756
    Art 10 1002
    Art 12 .... 978, 1002, 1018
    Art 12(1) 978
International Telecommunication Union, Radio Regulations
    Art 18 654
Peace Treaty between the Allied Powers and Japan 198, 231–4, 237
Proclamation Defining Terms for Japanese Surrender (Potsdam Declaration),
    26 July 1945
    Art 10 19
Rio Declaration on Environment and Development 416, 1010, 1020
Rome Statute of the International Criminal Court 163–4, 301
UN Charter 78–9, 431
    preamble 624

UN Convention on the Law of the Sea
  Art 109..654
UN Convention on the Rights of the Child
  Art 24..1003
  Art 27..1003
  Art 34..439
UN Declaration on the Elimination of All Forms of Intolerance and Discrimination
    Based on Religion or Belief 1981 933
UN Declaration on the Rights of Indigenous Peoples....................................634
  Art 3..635
  Art 6..635
  Art 11..635
  Art 12..635
  Art 13..635
  Art 14..635
  Art 15..635
  Art 16..635
  Art 18..635
  Art 19..635
  Art 20..635
  Art 23..635
  Art 24..635
  Art 25..635
  Art 26..635
  Art 29..635
  Art 31..636
  Art 32..636
  Art 33..636
  Art 34..636
  Art 35..636
  Art 37..636
  Art 39..636
  Art 40..636
  Art 41..636
  Art 42..636
UN Declaration on the Rights of Persons Belonging to National or Ethnic,
    Religious and Linguistic Minorities
  Art 1..623
Universal Declaration of Human Rights (UDHR)............................ 78–9, 304, 431,
                                                            433, 442, 681, 829, 937
  Art 1...545–6
  Art 2..546
  Art 7..546, 623
  Art 18..783, 818, 933
  Art 23(2) 623
  Art 25..978, 1002
  Art 29..847

Art 29(2) 303
US-Japan Mutual Security Treaty........................... 196–8, 200–1, 236–8
Vienna Convention on Diplomatic Relations 1961................................. 555
   Art 29.. 555
   Art 30.. 555
WHO Formation Charter 978

Italy

Constitution
   Art 134.. 335
   Art 136.. 335

Japan

Act for Establishment of the Demarcation Council 468, 470
   Art 3.. 469
   Art 3(1).. 472
Act for Partial Revision of the Public Offices Election Act 469
Act for Revision of the Imperial Constitution, 1946................................ 20
Act on State Liability for Compensation.. 728
Basic Law on Education
   Art 3(1).. 837
   Art 9.. 837
Cabinet Order No 325 1950 231–4
Civil Code.. 706
   Art 1... 638, 903
   Art 90... 638, 903
Code of Criminal Procedure
   Art 304.. 433
Commercial Code
   Art 58.. 833
Constitution.................. 13, 19, 63, 205, 231–2, 236, 374, 468, 535, 568, 833, 897, 904
   preamble 198, 200–1, 237, 523
   Art 1... 134, 521, 523, 535, 892
   Art 3(1).. 150
   Art 4.. 136
   Art 7.. 135–7, 150–2, 374
   Art 7(3) 136, 150
   Art 9.. 81, 196–8, 200–1, 234–9, 344
   Art 9(2)... 197, 236–8
   Art 12... 568, 642
   Art 13...84, 200–1, 568, 574
   Art 14.. 201, 550–1, 554, 625, 639
   Art 14(1) 409, 471, 638

Art 15...483
Art 15(1) 409, 521–4, 535
Art 15(3) 409, 523–4
Art 20..139, 837, 860, 893
Art 20(1) 833, 897, 903
Art 20(3) 774, 838, 893–5, 897–9, 902–4
Art 21...................................233, 642, 644, 652, 663–4, 708, 724, 746
Art 21(1) 647
Art 21(2) 233, 646–7
Art 25...950–2
Art 25(a) 950
Art 29(3) 200–1
Art 31...745
Art 37(2) 433
Art 39...232
Art 41..145, 147
Art 42...145
Art 43...409, 468
Art 43(1) 409, 484, 523–4
Art 44...409, 523–4
Art 47...468
Art 59(2) 145
Art 65...147
Art 66..81
Art 67...145
Art 69..136, 145, 148, 150–2
Art 73...147
Art 76(1) 150, 345
Art 77...389
Art 79...374
Art 81..344–5
Art 89...893, 898–9
Art 92...201
Art 93(2) 522
Art 95...201
Art 98(2) 198, 237–8, 567
Ch 3 521
Ch 8 522
Constitution 1889 106
Constitution 1946 106
Court Organization Law
Art 41(1) 345
Criminal Code
Art 199...554
Art 200...554
Customs Tariff Act
Art 21(1)(4) 728

Grand Council of State Decree No 234 896
Grand Council of State Decree No 235 896
Hokkaido Former Aboriginals Protection Act 1899 .... 572, 575
House of Councillors Election Law 484
Imperial Ordinance No 542 1945 232–4
Labour Standards Act 758
Land Expropriation Law 199, 566
  Art 20(3) 566, 577
  Art 36(5) 199
Law for Special Measures Concerning Criminal Cases
  Art 2 236
Law No 81 1952 232–4
Law No 137 1952 .... 232, 234
Law on Religious Organizations 833
  Art 1(2) 833
  Art 49(2) 833
  Art 50 833
  Art 51 833
  Art 81(1)((3)-(5) 833
  Art 81(1)(1) and (2) 833
Livelihood Protection Law 950
  Art 2 950
  Art 3 951
  Art 8(b) 950–1
  Art 9 951
Local Autonomy Law 199
  Art 74 540
  Art 75 543
  Art 76 543
  Art 80 543
  Art 86 543
  Art 124 543
  Art 151 199
Meiji Constitution 12, 19, 63, 546–7, 774, 896
  Art 1 892
  Art 3 892
  Art 4 134
  Art 5 134
  Art 28 893
Penal Code
  Art 175 .... 723–5, 729
  Art 2301 708
  Art 2302 .... 706, 708
Police Law
  Art 71 205
Public Offices Election Law 409, 483, 522–3, 706
  Art 86-3(1) 523

Supplementary Provisions
  Art 8.. 523–4
    Supplementary ProvisionsArt 8...409
Road Traffic Law
  Art 3(3) 745–6
  Art 3(3) and (5) 745
  Art 77(3) 745
  Art 119(1)(13) 745
Shotoku Constitution 9
  Art 3..9
  Art 12..9
Special Measures Concerning Land for US Armed Forces Law............. 197, 199–201
  Art 3..201

Laos

Constitution
  preamble 104
  Art 2... 104, 174
  Art 3... 104, 174
  Art 9... 799, 860
  Art 22.. 101
  Art 23..77
  Art 35... 550, 625
  Art 44.. 652
Constitution 1947 49
Constitution 1991 50
Prime Minister's Decree No 92/PM on Management and Protection of Religious
    Activities... 866
  Art 14... 866

Macau

Basic Law
  Art 25... 550, 625
  Art 40.. 79, 944
  Art 42.. 105

Malaysia

Aboriginal Peoples Act 1939.. 563
  s 11... 563
Administration of Islamic Law (Federal Territories) Act
  s 2 .... 785, 791

s 7(1) 786, 791
Administration of Muslim Law (Negri Sembilan) Enactment 1991
  s 90A... 793
Civil Law Act 1956.. 695, 794
  s 3 694–6
Constitution
  Art 3.. 117, 786, 789, 794, 823, 860, 867
  Art 3(1) 105, 117, 787–9, 793, 796, 905–6, 908
  Art 3(4) 787, 793, 796
  Art 4... 135, 563, 565
  Art 4(1) 450
  Art 5... 992
  Art 5(1) 993
  Art 6(3) 137–8
  Art 8.. 550–1, 556, 795–6
  Art 8(1) 499, 560, 767, 907
  Art 8(2) 625
  Art 8(5)(c) 560, 564
  Art 9(2) 565
  Art 10.. 642, 687, 704, 756, 766, 905, 908
  Art 10(1)(c) 761–2, 766–7
  Art 10(2)(c) 766–7
  Art 11... 794–7, 908
  Art 11(1) 776–7, 783–5, 787–8, 790–1, 796, 830–2, 905–8
  Art 11(3) 789–90, 906
  Art 11(3)(a) 786, 789, 791
  Art 11(4) 786, 788–9, 806, 905–7
  Art 11(5) 786, 830, 832
  Art 12.. 117, 905–6, 908
  Art 12(2) 788–9
  Art 12(4) 798
  Art 13... 564–5, 993
  Art 13(1) 564
  Art 13(2) 565
  Art 32... 134
  Art 40... 558
  Art 42... 397
  Art 42(8) 397
  Art 44... 207
  Art 74... 788
  Art 74(2) 789
  Art 89... 560
  Art 121... 271
  Art 121(1)... 450, 784
  Art 121(1A)..................................... 784–5, 788–9, 791, 795, 797
  Art 149... 362
  Art 150... 362

Art 150(2)..207
Art 150(6)..208
Art 152..674
Art 153...558, 577–8, 674
Art 153(1) and (2)..560
Art 160..788–9, 792
Art 160(2)..560, 792
Art 161A(5)..560
Art 162..794
Art 181..674
Pt III..674
Ninth Schedule..789, 797
Constitutional Amendment 1993
Art 32..135
Art 182..135
Control and Restriction of the Propagation of Non-Islamic Religions Enactment
    1991 (State of Johor)..806
s 2...806
s 5...807
s 6...807
s 7...807
s 8...807
s 9...807
ss 10-11...807
s 15..807
Criminal Procedure Code
s 418A...450
Essential (Security Cases) (Amendment) Regulations 1975..............................207–8
Federation Constitution Ordinance 1957...35
Federation of Malaya Agreement 1957..35
Guardianship of Infants Act 1961...798
Internal Security Act 1960...134, 207, 914
s 57(1)..207
Kelantan Constitution
Art XXXIA...492
Kelantan Enactment on the Administration of Muslim Law
s 69..783
s 102...783, 795
Legal Profession Act 1976
s 46A...761
s 46A(1)...761
National Land Code 1965...565
Ordinance No I..208
Printing Presses and Publications Act 1984..646
s 4...646
s 6(2)...646
s 7...646

s 12(2)... 645
Rukunegara declaration.. 89–92
Sedition Act 1948... 673
   Art 4(1) 671
   s 2 674
   s 3(1) 674
   s 3(1)(a) 675
   s 3(1)(c) 675
   s 3(2) 675
Societies Act 1966.. 847
   s 6 767
   s 7 499
   s 7(1) 499, 767
State of Perak Enactment No 3 of 1939.. 561

Maldives

Constitution
Art 22 1020

Mexico

Constitution 1917 1022

Mongolia

Constitution.. 57, 260, 310, 325, 375
   Art 6(20) 80
   Art 6(3) 81
   Art 7... 76
   Art 9... 860
   Art 14... 550
   Art 14(2) 557, 625
   Art 25... 353
   Art 29... 216
   Art 51(3) 375
   Art 64... 310
   Art 65... 325
   Art 66(1) 330, 332–3
   Art 66(1)(4) 339
   Art 66(2) 330
   Art 66(2)(1) 352, 354
   Art 66(2)(2) 341
   Art 66(4) 353

Art 67.. 330
Art 68.. 350, 352
Art 68(1) 352
Ch 2 78
Ch 5 310
Constitution 1940 52
Constitution 1960 52
  preamble 52
Constitution 1992 .... 52, 58, 328

Myanmar/Burma

Constitution
  Art 22(f)... 309
  Art 28.. 1001
  Art 46.. 309
  Art 74.. 81
  Art 299(d) 374
  Art 322.. 334
  Art 322(f) and (g).. 331
  Art 347... 550, 556
  Art 348.. 625
  Art 361.. 860
  Art 364.. 860
Constitution 1935-1937... 29
Constitution 1947 222
  Art 13.. 552
Constitution 1948 30
Constitution 2008 .... 309, 328
Emergency Measures Act 1950 204

Nepal

Constitution 1990 58
  Art 39(1) 806
Interim Constitution 2008... 58, 61, 109, 464, 1019
  Art 4... 860
  Art 4(1).. 109, 806
  Art 12... 687, 704
  Art 12(3)(1).. 670
  Art 13... 550, 556
  Art 13(2) 625
  Art 13(3) 558
  Art 16...1001, 1019
  Art 23.. 806

Art 33(c).. 464
Art 33(r1)... 103
Pt III 633
Pt IV 633

New Zealand

Bill of Rights Act.. 324

North Korea

Constitution
    preamble 102
    Art 3.. 102
    Art 9.. 102
    Art 26.. 102
    Art 29.. 102
    Art 39.. 102
    Art 40.. 102
    Art 43.. 102
    Art 52.. 102
    Art 63.. 102
    Art 65.. 550
    Art 77.. 625
    Art 81.. 103
    Art 83.. 102
    Art 84.. 102
Constitution 1948 24
Constitution 1972 24
    Art 4.. 25
    Art 37.. 25
Constitution 1992 25
Constitution 1998 25–6

North Vietnam, *see* Vietnam

Pakistan

Conduct of General Elections Order 2002.. 254
Constitution (Amendment) Order 2007 214
Constitution (Second Amendment) Order 2007... 214
Constitution
    5th amendment 108
    8th Amendment 252

13th Amendment 252
Art 2 .... 860, 916
Art 2A 927–8
Art 4(2)(a) 953
Art 9 .... 953, 984, 992, 1009–10, 1013, 1015–17
Art 14 .... 1009, 1013, 1015
Art 15 204
Art 16 204
Art 17 204
Art 18 204
Art 19 .... 204, 687, 704
Art 20 .... 919–20, 922, 924
Art 24 204
Art 25 .... 550, 556, 605
Art 25(2) 625
Art 25A 983
Art 37 78
Art 41(2) 860
Art 51 493
Art 58(2)(b) 252–3
Art 91(3) 860
Art 106 920
Art 160 916
Art 175A 374
Art 177 374
Art 184 1012
Art 184(3) 253–4, 349, 444
Art 203-D 918
Art 203C 866
Art 227 868
Art 239 254
Art 260(3) 860, 916, 919–20
Art 260(3)(a) 924
Art 260(3)(b) 923
Ch 1, Pt II 253
Constitution 1956 .... 33, 112
Constitution 1973 213
High Court Judges (Pensionary Benefits) Order 2007 214
Islamabad High Court (Establishment) Order 2007 214
Legal Framework Order 2002 252–4
Oath of Office (Judges) Order 2007 213–14
Ordinance No XX of 1984 .... 917, 921–2, 924
Penal Code
  s 295-A 931
  s 295-B 921–2
  s 295-C 921, 930
  s 298-A 921

s 298-B...921, 928
s 298-C...919, 921–2, 928
Political Parties Order 2002...253
Provisional Constitution Order No 1 2007..212–14
Representation of the People Act 1976
  s 99(cc)..533
Supreme Court Judges (Pensionary Benefits) Order 2007 214

Philippines

Administrative Code... 166, 854, 879, 966
  s 55..609
Bill of Rights, *see* Philippines, Constitution
  Art III
Civil Code..888
  Art 19..965
  Art 20..965
  Art 21..965
Constitution
  preamble 878
  Art II
    s 2..858
    s 6..891
    s 8...81
    ss 8-24...963
    s 9..56
    s 12..887
    s 14..625
    s 15..967
    s 16..964–5
    s 19...81, 963
    s 22..105
    s12..83
  Art III..854, 889, 964, 966
    s 1..550, 556, 625
    s 4...641, 652
    s 5...878–9, 891
    s 7..414
    s 10..652
  Art IV 530
  Art VI 512
    s 5..475, 482, 487
    s 5(1)..474
    s 17..520
    s 23(2)...209
    s 32...540, 542

Art VII

s 1...158

s 14..185

ss 14-23...159

s 15...184–6, 376–8

s 16..185

s 18..209

s 21..163–4

Art VIII...185, 378

s 1..963

s 1(2)...967

s 2..389

s 3...386–7

s 4(1)...185–6, 378

s 5(5)...964

s 6..389

s 7(1)..375, 377

s 9...185, 374, 378

Art IX(A)

s 1..512, 514

s 7..514

Art IX(C)..468

s 2(2)..515, 519

s 4..660

Art X

s 10...475

Art XII

s 1..82, 965

s 10...82

s 10(2)..968

s 17..209–10

Art XIII

s 14...56

Arts XIII–XV..963

Art XIV

s 3(2)...854

s 14..965

s 17..558

Art XV..268

Art XVI

s 12..559

Art XVII

s 2...536, 540–1

s 3(2)...250

s 16..267

s 165...536

Art XVIII

s 18 687
Constitution 1876 878
Constitution 1935 .... 15, 55, 163
   Art 15 351
   Art X
      s 1 512
   Art XV 400–1
Constitution 1973 .... 55, 163
   Art II
      s 6 55
Constitution 1987 .... 55, 541, 878
Cybercrime Prevention Act 711–12
Emergency (Essential Powers) Act 1964 208
Executive Order No 46 891–2
Executive Order No 192
   s 3 966
   s 4 965–6
Executive Order No 459 164
Executive Order No 697 891
Fair Election Act 608
   s 14 608–9
Family Code
   Art 149 887
General Appropriations Act (GAA) 195, 387
General Order No 2 of the President 248
Judiciary Act 1948
   s 12 513
Local Government Code 1991 .... 475, 542
   s 40 529
   s 120 542
Omnibus Election Code 517, 608–9
   s 66 608–9
   s 67 608–9
Penal Code 886, 888
Presidential Decree No 73 .... 266, 400
Presidential Decree No 1151
   s 3 965
Presidential Proclamation 1021 208
Proclamation 1102 .... 266, 268
Proclamation No 3 on the Provisional Constitution of the Revolutionary
   Government 55
Proclamation No 8, the Law Governing the Constitutional Commission
   of 1986 55
Proclamation No 1081 .... 248–9, 269
Republic Act No 1265 853–4
Republic Act No 1797 387
Republic Act No 6735 542

Republic Act No 7160..530
Republic Act No 7394, Arts 74-85 892
Republic Act No 7675...473–4
Republic Act No 7854..530
Republic Act No 7941..488
Republic Act No 9189..512
   s 19..512–13
   s 25..512–13
Republic Act No 9369
   s 13...608
Republic Act No 9371..474

Poland

Constitution..240

Prussia

Constitution of 1850..12

Russia

Constitution
   Art 17...431

Singapore

Armed Forces Act
   s 17...849
Constitution
   Art 4..309
   Art 5(2A) 346–7, 427
   Art 5A..347
   Art 9..407, 983
   Art 9(1)..408
   Art 12...407–8, 550, 556, 625, 634
   Art 12(1) 408
   Art 14......................................407, 440, 642, 687, 704, 747–8, 756
   Art 14(1) 747
   Art 14(1)(a) 719, 748
   Art 14(1)(b)..748
   Art 14(2) 747–8
   Art 15...407, 773, 848, 850–2
   Art 15(1) 798, 835, 847, 852
   Art 15(4) 834–6, 850, 852

Art 16...851–2
Art 16(3)..851
Art 16(4)..851
Art 20..834
Art 21(1)...131, 133
Art 21(2)..133
Art 22(1)..131
Art 22A..148
Art 22B(7)...148
Art 22C..148
Art 22D(6)...148
Art 22E..148
Art 22H...148, 427
Art 22H(1)...346–7, 428
Art 22P...131–2
Art 22P(2)..133
Art 38..146
Art 39(1)..478
Art 39(1b)..478
Art 46(2)(b)...490
Art 58..146
Art 59(1)..146
Art 93...298, 309
Art 94..382
Art 95..374
Art 100..343
Art 100(4)..343
Art 128..849
Art 131..849
Art 142(2)(b)..82
Art 144..148
Art 144(2)..148
Art 148A..148
Art 148G..148
Art 149...361, 836
Art 151(4)..148
Art 152...559, 578
Art 153..890
Fourth Schedule
  s 3(2)...478
Constitution of the Republic of Singapore (Amendment) Act 1991
  s 4 133
Enlistment Act...847, 850
Interpretation Act
  s 9A...417, 427
Kidnapping Act...451
Maintenance of Religious Harmony Act 1990..........................124, 148, 825

s 8(1)(a) 825
s 12 148
Medical Registration (Amendment) Regulations 2010 398
Medical Registration Act, s70 398
Miscellaneous Offences Act 746–8
Newspaper Printings and Presses Act 668–9
s 10 669
s 24(1) 668
Order 179/72 406
Order 405/94 406
Penal Code
s 294(a) 407
s 298 .... 671, 824
s 298A 671
s 377A 407–8, 634
Prevention of Corruption Act
s 37 606
Public Entertainments and Meetings Act (PEMA) 755
Republic of Singapore Independence Act 1965 36–7
Rules of the Supreme Court (RSC) 406
Sedition Act 677, 823
s 3 .... 671, 676
s 3(1) 823
s 3(1)(e) 676
s 4(1)(a) 676
Societies Act 763, 834, 847–8
s 4(2)(e) 763
s 24(1)(a) 835
State Constitution 1958 36
State of Singapore Constitution 1963 36–7
Supreme Court of Judicature Act
s 7(1) 690
Undesirable Publications Act 835, 847–8
s 3 406

South Africa

Constitution 240, 632
Art 26 988
Art 27 952
Art 27(1) and (2) 1006
Art 27(3) 1006
Art 39(1) 431
Interim Constitution 1993 240
Art 71(2) 350

South Korea

Act on the Election of Public Officials and the Prevention of Election
    Malpractices 507–9
  Art 15 614
  Art 16 614
Act on the Establishment and Operation of Private Teaching Institutes
  Art 3 84
Act on the Immigration and Legal Status of Overseas Koreans 607, 612–16
  Art 2(1) 616
  Art 2(2) 613, 616
Assembly and Demonstration Act 620–1
  Art 10 754
  Art 23 754
Aviation Act
  Art 6 614
Certified Judicial Scriveners Act 359–60
  Art 4 358
  Art 4(1) 359
  Art 4(1)(ii) 359
  Art 4(2) 359
Civil Code
  Art 764 734
Civil Procedure Act
  Art 239 242
Constitution
  preamble 87, 588
  Art 3 85
  Art 4 .... 339, 672
  Art 5 .... 165, 202
  Art 5(2) 840
  Art 6(1) 431
  Art 7(1) 491, 759
  Art 7(2) 760
  Art 8 .... 86, 498
  Art 8(2) 499
  Art 9 76
  Art 10 .... 83–5, 582, 584–5, 952, 954, 956, 958
  Art 11 .... 550, 612, 616
  Art 11(1) 359, 554, 613, 619, 625
  Art 12 649
  Art 14 614
  Art 14(1) 160
  Art 15 .... 359, 581, 586, 614
  Art 17 952
  Art 19 .... 839–40, 843, 845

Art 20..843
Art 20(1) 839
Art 20(2) 860
Art 21..644, 652
Art 21(1) 642, 958
Art 21(2) 754
Art 21(3) 649
Art 21(4) 642
Art 22...160
Art 23..581, 614, 954
Art 23(3) 955
Art 24...614
Art 25..535, 614
Art 26...160
Art 29(2) 614
Art 30...614
Art 31(4) 760
Art 32...588
Art 33(1) 957–8, 960
Art 33(2) 961
Art 34..582, 588
Art 34(1) 581, 953–6
Art 34(2) 587, 954–6
Art 34(5) 581–2, 584–5, 587, 955–6
Art 36(1) 84–5
Art 37(1) 84–5
Art 37(2) 582, 586, 619, 642,
                                                    649, 734, 840, 843, 845, 953
Art 39...839
Art 39(1) 840
Art 41...526
Art 45...491
Art 46(2) 491
Art 49...160
Art 50...160
Art 60(2) 165
Art 65..339, 423
Art 67...526
Art 72...160, 172, 273, 537–9, 614
Art 73...165
Art 74(1) 165
Art 76...204
Art 84..242, 360
Art 89...160
Art 91...160
Art 104...374
Art 106...385

Art 107...357
Art 107(2)..358–9
Art 111...330, 332, 339
Art 111(1)..310
Art 113...444
Art 119...954
Art 119(1)..954
Art 119(2)...588, 954
Art 130...272, 274
Art 130(2)...273, 614
Ch IX..160
Ch VI..310
Ch VIII...160
Constitution 1948..23–4, 63
Constitution 1972 (Yusin Constitution)..23
Constitutional Court Act...217
  Art 23..217
  Art 40..242
  Art 41(1)..332
  Art 41(4) and (5)...332
  Art 49(2)..171
  Art 53(1)..171
  Art 61..330, 334
  Art 68(1)...333, 358–9, 365–6
  Art 68(2)..332
  Art 75(3)..367
Crime Victims Aid Act
  Art 10..614
Criminal Act..554–5
Decree on Civil Service Entrance Examination............................535
Diplomatic Public Officials Act
  Art 9..614
Enforcement Regulation of the Act on the Immigration and Legal Status of
    Overseas Koreans
  Art 2(1)...613
  Art 3(1)...613
Fisheries Act
  Art 5..614
Foreigner's Land Acquisition Act
  Art 3..614
Framework Act on Social Security
  Art 3(1)...955
  Art 3(2)...955
Functional Health Foods Act
  Art 18(1)(5)..649
Governmental Organization Act
  Art 23..183

Immigration Control Act
   Art 7..614
   Art 17..614
Juvenile Sex Protection Act..439
Local Autonomy Act
   Art 15..540
Local Public Officials Act
   Art 9..614
Medical Service Act..629
   Art 61(1) 581
Military Criminal Act
   s 53(1)..555
Military Service Act..839
   Art 3..839
Mutual Savings and Finance Company Act.......................445–6
National Health Promotion Act 952
National Pension Act
   Art 1..956
   Art 75..954
   Art 79..954–5
National Referendum Act...160, 453
   Art 7..614
National Security Act 620–1, 672, 680
   Art 7(1) 672
   Art 7(5) 672
Ordinance for Parole Review
   Art 14..620
Overseas Korea Foundation Act
   Art 2..616
Patent Act
   Art 25..614
Pilotage Act
   Art 6..614
Political Parties Act
   Art 25..498
   Art 27..498
Promotion, etc of Employment of Disabled Persons Act................588–9
Public Election Act
   Art 146(2)..484
   Art 189(1)..484–6
Public Official Election Act...453
   Art 18(1)(2)...525
Registration, etc of Periodicals Act......................................648
   Art 6(iii)..648
   Art 7(1) 648
   Art 7(1)(ix)..649
   Art 16(1) 662

Art 16(3) 662
Art 19(3) 662
Art 22(iii) 648
Registration of Korean Nationals Residing Abroad Act 613
Registration of Publishing Companies and Printers Office Act
Art 52(V) 730
Rules implementing the Certified Judicial Scriveners Act 358, 360
Art 3(1) 359
Special Act Concerning the May 18 Democratisation Movement, Law No 5029
of 1995 .... 241, 243
Special Act on the Establishment of the New Administrative Capital 2004 271–2
State Compensation Act
Art 7 614
State Public Officials Act
Art 35 614
Support for Discharged Soldiers Act
Art 8(1) 442
Supreme Court Rule No 1108
Art 3(1) 358
Telecommunications Business Act
Art 53 651
Trade Union and Labor Relations Adjustment Act 957, 959, 961
Art 81 .... 957–8, 960
Welfare of Disabled Persons Act
Art 8(1) 582
Art 36 583
Art 38 583
Art 41 583
Art 42 583
Art 43 583
Art 44 583
Art 49 583

South Vietnam, *see* Vietnam

Soviet Union

Constitution 1936 43

Spain

Constitution
Art 161 335
Art 163 335

Sri Lanka

Code of Criminal Procedure Act
  s 136.. 822
Companies Act 817
Constitution
  First Amendment... 264
  Second Amendment... 265
  Third Amendment.. 265
  Fourth Amendment.. 265
  Fifth Amendment 265
  Sixth Amendment 265
  Seventh Amendment.. 265
  Eighth Amendment.. 265
  Ninth Amendment... 265
  Tenth Amendment 265
  Eleventh Amendment... 265
  Thirteenth Amendment... 265, 291, 291–3
  Fourteenth Amendment.. 265
  Fifteenth Amendment 265
  Sixteenth Amendment.. 265
  Seventeenth Amendment.. 265
  Eighteenth Amendment 263–4, 291
  Nineteenth Amendment...161–2, 293–5
  Art 1.. 293
  Art 2... 291–2
  Art 3.................................. 161–2, 263–4, 291, 293–5, 823
  Art 4.................................. 161–2, 263–4, 291, 293–5
  Art 4(b)...161–2, 293
  Art 9.............................. 106–7, 291, 817, 819, 823, 860
  Art 10...817–21, 823
  Art 12.. 550, 556
  Art 12(1) 264, 823
  Art 12(2) 167, 625, 823
  Art 14.. 697
  Art 14(1) 817
  Art 14(1)(a).. 670
  Art 14(1)(a)-(d) 167
  Art 14(1)(c) 821
  Art 14(1)(e) 817–20, 823
  Art 14(1)(g) 821
  Art 15.. 670, 687, 704
  Art 15(1) 817
  Art 15(2) 670
  Art 18(1)(f)... 757
  Art 18(2) 757

Art 27..1001
Art 27(14)..1019
Art 27(2)..80
Art 30(1)...161–2
Art 35...168
Art 35(1)...167–8
Art 35(3)...168–9
Art 44(2)...168–9
Art 62(2)...162
Art 70(1)...161–2
Art 70(1)(a)...162
Art 70(1)(d)...161
Art 70A(1)(a)..161–2
Art 82...263, 292
Art 83...162, 263, 291–3, 343, 350
Art 83(a)..293
Art 84(2)...162
Art 85(2)...539
Art 86...539
Art 105(3)..697
Art 120..343, 350
Art 121..343
Art 121(1)..263, 817
Art 122..343
Art 123..263, 343
Art 126..264
Art 129(2)..168
Art 130(a)..168
Constitution 1972..343
Art 23(1)...168
Art 51...292
Constitution 1978...343–4
Art 82...292
Art 82(7)...292
Emergency Regulations..167, 204, 756
Interpretation Ordinance
s 24(1)...539
s 24(2)...539
Public Security Ordinance..167, 204, 265

Taiwan

Act Governing Judicial Personnel
Art 40(3)...372
Act Governing Relations between People of the Taiwan Area and Mainland Area
Art 21-I...617

Act of Special Commission on the Investigation of the Truth in Respect of the
    319 Shooting...447
Act to Prevent Purchase of Sex from Children and Minors 439
Amendment to the Constitution
    Art 1...296, 490
    Art 2...490
    Art 2(3) 206, 363
    Art 4...490
    Art 4(2) 336
    Art 5(1) 372
    Art 5(2) 372
    Art 5(3) 372
    Art 5(4) 372
    Art 5(5) 764
    Art 7(1) and (2) 184
    Art 10...617
Assembly and Parade Act 741, 749, 753
    Art 4...749
    Art 9I...751
    Art 9I(ii)..749
    Art 11...749–50
    Art 15I...749
    Art 26..750–1
    Art 29..742
Budget Act..191
    Art 61...191
    Art 62...191
Civic Organisation Law...22
Civic Organizations Act
    Art 2...763–4
    Art 3...765
    Art 5...765
    Art 8...763
    Art 12...765
    Art 44...763
    Art 46...763
    Art 53...764
Civil Code
    Art 195(1)...737
Civil Organisation Law...22
Code of Criminal Procedure
    Art 230-III 170
    Art 231-III 170
Conscription Act 846
    Art 1...846
Constitution
    preamble 425

Additional Articles
  Art 2..338
  Art 2(3)..204
  Art 4(1)(2)...482
  Art 5..770
  Art 5(5)..339
  Art 5(6)..386
  Art 10(7)...579–80
Art 1...297, 352
Art 1(IX)..173
Art 2...297, 352
Art 4...381, 403
Art 7..................................457, 550, 579, 616–17, 625, 847
Art 8..418
Art 8(2)..419
Art 11..654, 661, 709, 737
Art 13..846–7
Art 14...751, 761, 764–5
Art 15...580, 654–5, 962
Art 16...433, 458
Art 20..846
Art 22..737
Art 23.....................363, 618, 648, 654–5, 737, 740, 742, 749–50, 761, 765, 962
Art 25..296
Art 28(2)..225
Art 34..424
Art 38..355
Art 43...206, 363
Art 52..167, 169–70, 423
Art 53..425
Art 55..354
Art 56..189
Art 57(2)..192
Art 57(2) and (3)...354
Art 58(2)..355
Art 62..425
Art 63..355
Art 64(2)..424
Art 65...224–5
Art 70..191
Art 71..425
Art 77..392, 425, 457
Art 78..336
Art 79(2)...336, 372
Art 80...336, 358
Art 81...335, 371–2, 385–6
Art 82..457

Art 83... 425
Art 87.. 424–5
Art 90... 425
Art 93.. 224–5
Art 130.. 531
Art 133.. 297
Art 134.. 493
Art 153(1).. 761, 962
Art 155.. 579–80
Art 170.. 386
Art 171.. 335
Art 173... 335–6
Art 174.. 296
Constitutional Interpretation Procedure Act 331, 335
Art 5... 330, 333
Art 5-I(iii) 399
Art 5(2) and (3) 336
Art 8(1) 336
Art 13... 417
Control Yuan Organization Act.. 424
Court Organic Act.. 392
Art 25... 365
Art 90... 358
Court Organization Act.. 457
Criminal Code
Art 100 (former)... 670
Art 149.. 741–2
Art 235... 727
Art 309... 710
Art 310... 710
Art 310(2).. 709
Art 310(3).. 709
Customs Smuggling Control Act 457–8
Art 49... 458
Directives for the Operational Procedure of Administrative Court......... 366
Election and Recall Law 22
Grand Justices Council Adjudication Act
Art 4(1) 365
Art 4(1)(2)... 358, 366
Handicapped Welfare Act.. 580
Household Registration Act
Art 8.. 461
Labor Insurance Act.. 962
Labor Standards Act... 962–3
Art 55... 962
Art 56... 962
Labour Union Law 761

Art 4... 760–1
Legislative Yuan Functioning Act
   Art 15(1)-(3)..363
Martial Law Decree...328
NCC Organic Act 2003.. 658–9
   Art 4-II and III 141, 187–8
   Art 4-V..188
Organic Act of the Administrative Court...392
Organic Act of the Commission on the Disciplinary Sanction of
   Functionaries... 392–3
Organic Act of the Judicial Yuan... 376, 392
   Art 4...392
   Art 5(4)...372
Physically and Mentally Disabled Citizens Protection Act
   Art 37(1) 579
Presidential and Vice Presidential Election and Recall Act...................................534
   Art 70..173
Provisional Constitution for the Period of Political Tutelage.......................... 418–19
Public Officials Election and Recall Act..534
   Art 69(2) 490
Public Service Election and Recall Law..531
   Art 32(1) 531
Publication Act... 644, 648
   Art 32(3) 727
   Art 40..648
   Art 41..648
Regulations Governing the Qualifications and Management of Vision-Impaired
   Engaged in Massage Occupation...580
Regulations of the National Assembly Proceedings
   Art 38(2) 296
Social Order Maintenance Act..750
   Art 64-I...741
Standard Act of Central Executive Agencies and Organizations 2004 140
   Art 3(1)...140
   Art 3(1)(2)...140
   Art 21..140
Telecommunications Act
   Art 48(1) 654
   Art 49(1) 655
   Art 58(2) 654–5
   Art 60..654
   Art 67(3) and (4) 655
Temporary Provisions Effective During the Period of Communist
   Rebellion...21–2, 225

Thailand

Civil Procedure Code
s 156..618
s 229..618
Computer Crimes Act...687
Constitution
Art 5..556, 625
Art 9..109, 860
Art 18...341
Art 28...78
Art 30..550, 556, 618
Art 36...78
Art 45...652
Art 46...652
Art 47..653, 669
Art 48...653
Art 49...78
Art 61...83
Art 65..105, 339–40
Art 68...340
Art 77(4)..78
Art 78...106
Art 79..109, 860
Art 79(3)..78
Art 82...81
Art 82(6)..83
Art 83(2)..78
Art 83(6)..81
Art 84...80
Art 91..341, 355
Art 93...482
Art 94(2)..109
Art 95...482
Art 106..340, 490
Art 138...331
Art 141...331
Art 154...331
Art 155..331, 352
Art 158...148
Art 168...355
Art 183...135
Art 184...361
Art 185...361
Art 189...135
Art 190(6)...354

Art 197(3)..382
Art 204..311
Art 204(1)(4)...376
Art 211..332
Art 211(4)..333
Art 212..333
Art 214..334
Art 216..311
Art 218(1)..194
Art 229..511
Art 230..511
Art 232..511
Art 233...341, 355
Art 236..514
Art 237...340, 502
Art 237(2)..502
Art 245..331
Art 257..331
Art 267..216
Art 270..77
Constitution 1932..17
Constitution 1997..58, 222–3, 328, 330, 332, 466
Art 6...336–7
Art 30..357
Art 50..357
Art 60..357
Art 241(4)..336–7
Art 255..311
Art 264...336, 357
Art 264(1)..337
Art 268..311
Constitution 2007...108, 222, 330, 466, 482
Organic Act on Political Parties...340, 500–2, 506
s 29..500, 506
s 65...500–1
s 66(1)-(3)..501–2
s 92...500–1
s 94(1)...501
s 94(1) and ()..502
Penal Code..687
s 112..683

Timor-Leste

Constitution...58
preamble..86

Pt II..944
s 1 86
s 2(4)..77
s 6(c)...86
s 6(e)...78
s 6(f)...80
s 6(g)...76
s 6(i)..81
s 7 86
s 9 431
s 10...86
s 11..86, 860
s 16...550
s 17...625
s 18(2)...944
s 23...79, 431
s 38(1)...83
s 45...836
s 53...83
s 57..1001
s 61...80

United Kingdom

Blasphemy Act 1679 928
British North America Act 426
Ceylon (Constitution and Independence) Orders in Council 1947 31
Ceylon Constitution Order in Council 1946...31
Ceylon Independence Act 1947...31
Contempt of Court Act 1981..437
Federation of Malaya Independence Act 1957..35
    s 1(1)...35
Federation of Malaya Order-in-Council 1948 SI 1948, No 108..........................34
Government of India Act 1919..29
Government of India Act 1935..33
Human Rights Act 1998 ....118, 120, 324, 437, 719, 947
    s 12(4)(a)(ii)..719
Indian Independence Act 1947..31–3
    s 1 32
    s 7(1)...32
    s 8(1)...32
Pakistan (Provisional Constitution) Order 1947..33
Sabah, Sarawak and Singapore (State Constitutions) Order-in-Council, 2 SI 1963,
    No 2656...36
Singapore (Constitution) Order-in-Council 1958, 2 SI 1958, No 1956 36
Singapore Colony Order-in-Council 1955, SI 1955, No 187..............................35

United States

Constitution...3, 15, 39, 60, 83, 155, 181, 282,
424, 426, 545, 551, 590, 594, 656, 884, 902
   First Amendment... 440, 641, 703, 782, 848,
858, 880–6, 897, 902, 915
   Sixth Amendment 433
   Fourteenth Amendment.....................551, 553, 556–7, 590, 592–3, 595–6, 598, 607
   Art 1, s 3(6)..338
   Art 2(1)..143
   Art 3..342, 397
Declaration of Independence 1787.. 83, 219
Espionage Act 1919 670
Hare-Hawes-Cutting Act, 1933..15
Jones Act, 1916... 14–15
Massachusetts Constitution 1780...83
Philippines Independence Act, 1934..15
Statute of Virginia for Religious Freedom (Va Code Ann S 57-1).........................219
Tydings-McDuffie Act, *see* Philippines Independence Act, 1934

Vietnam

Constitution...80, 86, 863
   preamble 100
   Art 2...173
   Art 4... 100, 173
   Art 5...104
   Art 9...100
   Art 12...101
   Art 15...101
   Art 16...78
   Art 21...101
   Art 29...80
   Art 30... 101, 865
   Art 48...101
   Art 50...78
   Art 52...550
   Art 53... 536, 543
   Art 61...1001
   Art 63...625
   Art 64...80
   Art 66...101
   Art 70...865
   Art 77...836
Constitution 1946 (North)...46–7

Constitution 1956 (South)..47
Constitution 1959 (North)..47–8
  preamble..48
Constitution 1965 (South)..47
Constitution 1980..48
  Art 3..48
  Art 67..48
Constitution 1992
  Art 91..313
Decision 83/2001/QD-TTg...866
Decree No 22
  Art 2..865
Decree No 26/1999/ND-CP (19 April 1999) on Religious Activities.....................866
Decree No 26 ND-CP 1999 on Religious Activities
  Art 9..863
Law on Vietnam Fatherland Front...863
Ordinance on Beliefs and Religions (No 21/2004/PL-UBTVQH11)
  Art 14..864
Penal Code
  Art 247..865
Provisional Charters (South)..47
Resolution 24-NQ/TW 1990...864

Introduction

Asia, Constitutions and Constitutionalism

I. CONSTITUTIONALISM IN ASIA: THE LEGACY

Fifty years ago, at a very young law faculty, in a newly-independent republic in Asia, an African-American professor of constitutional law compiled and published the first-ever comparative constitutional law casebook. It was a pioneering work on many fronts. The law faculty was the Faculty of Law of the University of Singapore, established in 1957, and the professor was Harry E Groves,[1] The ground-breaking book was his *Comparative Constitutional Law: Cases and Materials*.[2]

Groves, who had come to Singapore after a distinguished career in the United States, chose the casebook form for his enterprise. While acknowledging that the casebook was a singularly American device developed by Christopher Columbus Langdell at Harvard, he nevertheless justified its more extensive use:

> Libraries seldom have more than one set of a particular series of reports, and the pressure on the library of an entire class if obliged to read specific cases for certain class discussions can be intolerable. Secondly, it is possible to shorten substantially many cases by appropriate editing, without lessening their value as teaching tools, thereby reducing the reading time of students of individual cases and making possible a wider coverage than would otherwise be feasible. Finally a casebook may make available cases not in the school's library. For these reasons and perhaps for others, the casebook method of teaching has spread, and continues to spread, beyond the borders of the United States.
>
> . . . The modern casebook is considerably more than a collection of cases. It is a guide to further reading, especially of articles in legal periodicals; and it frequently, as does this book, poses collateral and additional problems for analysis.[3]

---

[1] Harry E Groves was born in Manitou Springs, Colorado in 1921. He was educated at the University of Colorado (*cum laude*), University of Chicago (JD) and Harvard Law School (where he obtained his LLM as Ford Foundation Fellow). An artillery officer in World War II, he was a member of the Judge Advocate General in the Korean War. He began his academic career as an Associate Professor at the North Carolina College Law School in 1949. Between 1951 to 1956, Groves served as a Captain in the Judge Advocate General's corps and then practised law in Fayetteville, North Carolina. In 1956, he became Dean of the School of Law at Texas Southern University (now Thurgood Marshall School of Law). In 1962, he was appointed Asia Foundation Professor of Constitutional Law at the University of Singapore, and became Dean of the Faculty the next year. He left Singapore in 1964 to become President of the Central State University in Wilberforce, Ohio, a position he held till 1968 when he was appointed Professor at the School of Law, University of Cincinnati. From 1976 to 1981, he was Dean of the North Carolina Central University Law School before leaving to take up the position of Brandis Professor of Law at the University of North Carolina, Chapel Hill, where he has since been made Emeritus Professor.

[2] HE Groves, *Comparative Constitutional Law: Cases and Materials* (Dobbs Ferry, NY: Ocean Publications, 1963).

[3] Ibid at vii.

Explaining his choice of the American casebook form, Groves said that it was useful to 'illustrate the methods by which courts in a number of jurisdictions whose source of fundamental law traces to the Anglo-American concepts have solved problems that arise under such constitutions'.[4]

Groves' collection was arranged in five chapters over 628 pages: (1) Principles of Constitutional Interpretation; (2) Equal Protection of the Laws: (3) Emergency Powers; (4) Aliens and Citizens; and (5) Government Employment. Included in this collection were excerpted cases from Australia (2 cases); Burma (6); Canada (6); the United Kingdom (3); India (23); Ireland (2); Malaya (3); Pakistan (7); Singapore (1); and, of course, the United States (32). This was not only the first casebook to include material from the Asian states, albeit only from India, Pakistan, Burma, Malaya and Singapore, it was, until the appearance of this volume, the only one in which Asian material made up a substantial proportion of the book. In all, 40 out of the 85 cases excerpted by Groves emanated from the five jurisdictions in Asia.

In contrast, the 1968 casebook of Professor Thomas M Franck (1931–2009) of New York University, contained a total of 175 excerpted cases, of which 31 were from three Asian states: India, Ceylon and Pakistan. Franck's collection, *Comparative Constitutional Process: Cases and Materials – Fundamental Rights in the Common Law Nations*,[5] which is rather better known[6] than Groves' earlier effort, focused primarily on cases involving fundamental rights, rather than institutions and covers the following countries: Australia (5 cases); Barbados (1); Buganda (1); Canada (3); Ceylon (13); India (17); Kenya (8); Nigeria (4); Pakistan (1); South Africa (7); Southern Rhodesia (6); Swaziland (1); Tanzania and Tanganyika (12); Uganda (7); the United Kingdom (23); and the United States (66). In its 595 pages, Franck not only organises these cases, but also includes introductions and notes on the various decisions – so useful in contextualising the material – and his work could be said to be the precursor of the modern 'text, cases and materials' books that are now so popular with professors seeking to impart more than pure 'textbook knowledge' to their students, and where students still have to grapple with the original judgments, albeit in truncated form.

In the same year that Groves' book was published – 1963 – a small volume of a dozen essays, entitled *Constitutionalism in Asia*, was published in New Delhi under the editorship of RN Spann.[7] Professor Richard Neville Spann (1916–81), Chairman of the Department of Government and Public Administration at the University of Sydney, had organised a symposium-themed 'Constitutionalism in Asia' seminar at the Australian National University in Canberra in August 1960 that brought together 38 scholars and jurists to 'consider how constitutional government was faring in some Asian countries which had achieved independence under Western-type constitutions since the war'.[8] The 12 papers that were presented – which dealt with various aspects of constitutionalism in Burma, India, Indonesia and Pakistan – were edited and

---

[4] Ibid at viii.

[5] TM Franck, *Comparative Constitutional Process: Cases and Materials – Fundamental Rights in the Common Law Nations* (London: Sweet & Maxwell, 1968).

[6] Indeed, Norman Dorsen, Michel Rosenfeld, András Sajó and Susanne Baer, authors of *Comparative Constitutionalism: Cases and Materials* (St Paul, Minn: West, 2003) at iii, wrote: 'Of course there have been earlier casebooks in this field, going back at least to 1968, when Thomas Franck's notable *Comparative Constitutional Process* appeared.'

[7] RN Spann (ed), *Constitutionalism in Asia* (New Delhi: Asia Publishing House, 1963).

[8] Ibid at vii.

collated in this volume. Spann's volume was the very first collection of essays focusing on constitutions in Asia. It was, however, very much a look at constitutionalism in Asia through Western liberal lenses.

In the next half-century, few scholars attempted the study of constitutions and constitutionalism in Asia as a whole. As a consequence, the literature consists of only a few edited collections of essays and one book. Two collections of essays were published under the hand of Professor Lawrence Ward Beer (b 1932): *Constitutionalism in Asia: Asian Views of the American Influence* (1979);[9] and *Constitutional Systems in Late Twentieth Century Asia* (1992).[10] The 1979 volume, declared Beer (a Japanese law specialist), was 'inspired by the 1976 Bicentennial of the Declaration of Independence of the United States of America'. Comprising just nine chapters, the book features contributions from eight Asian countries: Bangladesh, China, India, Indonesia, Japan, Malaysia, the Philippines and Singapore. The authors were asked to consider the extent of American influence in the development of their respective constitutions. Another collection of this ilk is Joseph Barton Starr's *The United States Constitution: Its Birth, Growth and Influence in Asia*, published in 1988[11] (and inspired by the bicentennial celebration of the American Constitution).

Beer's 1992 volume is slightly less focused on the American experience in Asia and is thus a more valuable collection. This time, the scope was expanded to include contributions from 13 countries: China, Taiwan, Japan, North and South Korea, Vietnam, Brunei, India, Indonesia, Malaysia, Philippines, Singapore and Thailand. The latest collection of essays to join this small selection is one that compares the constitutions of South Asia, *Comparative Constitutionalism in South Asia*.[12]

Thus far, the only effort to explain constitutionalism on an Asia-wide scale has been the brief and wide-ranging *Asia-Pacific Constitutional Systems* by Graham Hassell and Cheryl Saunders,[13] which focuses primarily on the institutional arrangements of constitutional systems in the ASEAN states and a selection of the Pacific islands, including Papua New Guinea, the Solomon Islands, Vanuatu, Fiji and Tonga.[14]

Writers of casebooks in the 1970s were less ambitious in scope and coverage than either Groves or Franck. Almost all of them were American scholars[15] who had only a passing interest in Asia. For example, Walter F Murphy and Joseph Tanehaus's 1977 work, *Comparative Constitutional Law: Cases and Commentaries*,[16] focuses on judicial

---

[9] LW Beer, *Constitutionalism in Asia: Asian Views of the American Influence* (Berkeley, Cal: University of California Press, 1979). A second edition was published in 1988 as LW Beer, 'Constitutionalism in Asia: Asian Views of the American Influence', *Occasional Papers & Reprints in Contemporary Asian Studies*, No 6 – 1988(89) (School of Law, University of Maryland).

[10] LW Beer, *Constitutional Systems in Late Twentieth Century Asia* (Seattle, Wash: University of Washington Press, 1992).

[11] J Barton Starr, *The United States Constitution: Its Birth, Growth and Influence in Asia* (Hong Kong: Hong Kong University Press, 1988); see also GA Billias, *American Constitutionalism Heard Around the World 1976–1989* (New York: New York University Press, 2009).

[12] See S Khinani, V Raghavan and AK Thiruvengadam, *Comparative Constitutionalism in South Asia* (New York: Oxford University Press, 2013).

[13] G Hassall and C Saunders, *Asia-Pacific Constitutional Systems* (New York: Cambridge University Press, 2002).

[14] Ibid at 2.

[15] The exception was Mauro Cappelletti (1927–2004), an Italian scholar who also taught at Stanford University Law School.

[16] WF Murphy and J Tanehaus, *Comparative Constitutional Law: Cases and Commentaries* (New York: St Martin's Press, 1977).

policy-making through case law from six countries, only one of which was Asian: Japan. Mauro Cappelletti and William Cohen concentrate on constitutional adjudication and procedures in Italy, the United Kingdom, the Soviet Union, the United States, Germany and the European Union in general in their casebook *Comparative Constitutional Law: Cases and Materials* (1979).[17] No Asian country is included in this study.

Over the next two decades – the 1980s and 1990s – comparative constitutional law seems to have gone out of style and no casebooks were produced. It was only at the end of the 1990s that the first of two prominent casebooks was published, again by American scholars. This was *Comparative Constitutional Law* by Vicki C Jackson and Mark Tushnet.[18] The second, published four years later in 2003, was *Comparative Constitutionalism: Cases and Materials* by Norman Dorsen, Michel Rosenfeld, András Sajó and Susanne Baer.[19]

Both these works were enormous tomes, weighing in at 1,500 and 1,400 pages respectively. These wide-ranging works were written in the best tradition of the modern American casebook, with useful introductions, primary and secondary readings, and notes and questions to guide the reader along. Of the 15 countries discussed in the Jackson and Tushnet volume, only two Asian countries were featured: India and Japan. The book by Dorsen et al is more consciously comparative and non US- or West-centric in outlook. In their introduction, the authors make the point that '[a]s far as possible, the casebook presents issues generically' and avoids 'characterizations and classifications that present the US position as the norm and other positions as departures'.[20]

The reluctance to include Asian states in comparative constitutional law surveys may be attributed to two factors. First, many comparative constitutional law scholars view constitutionalism as embodying the best in liberal democratic ideals. As such, the kind of 'constitutionalism' practised by many states in Asia may not merit study or inclusion since they are non-liberal or fundamentally 'anti-constitutional' or 'non-constitutional'. States that have no recognisable democratic institutions, independent courts and a robust constitutional culture, would not, in this paradigm, merit inclusion. The second reason is simply the fact that much of the material in Asia has hitherto not been available, much less in the English language. This has changed, and a lot more material has been translated, digitised and freely distributed, and it is upon this resource and the legacy of scholars in the last half century that we hope to build.

---

[17] M Cappelletti and W Cohen, *Comparative Constitutional Law: Cases and Materials* (New York: Bobbs-Merrill, 1979). For a review of this volume and that of Murphy and Tanehaus, see DP Kommers, 'Comparative Constitutional Law: Casebooks for a Developing Discipline' (1981–1982) 57 *Notre Dame Law Review* 642.

[18] VC Jackson and M Tushnet, *Comparative Constitutional Law* (New York: Foundation Press, 1999).

[19] N Dorsen, M Rosenfeld, A Sajó and S Baer, *Comparative Constitutionalism: Cases and Materials* (St Paul, Minn: West, 2003). A second edition of this book was published in 2010. Like the volume by Jackson and Tushnet, it had grown considerably between editions and had a staggering 1,700 pages.

[20] Ibid at iv.

II. AIMS AND AMBIT OF THIS BOOK

This book is ambitious in scope but with modest aims. It is not a book about 'Asian constitutionalism' as there is no singular or monolithic conception or practice which may be described as such. Bearing in mind the difficulties in defining 'Asia', and indeed the range of understandings of what 'constitutionalism' entails, it makes little sense in discussing 'Asian constitutionalism' as though this was something self-evident and recognisable, for this is itself a problematic beast, as much as the idea of 'Asian values' was. It would be more prudent and accurate to say that there is no single Asian constitutionalism but many Asian constitutionalisms; some may reflect the practice of liberal constitutionalism, while others may be better described as non-liberal constitutions with communitarian or theocratic elements for instance; still others may borrow constitutionalist forms while being anti-constitutionalist in ideology and practice. By broadening the palette of experiences in this book, we are providing both raw material and occasion for scholars to reflect upon the contours and concepts of our field. As such, the study of Asian practices will both challenge and confirm how constitutional scholars apprehend 'constitutionalism'.

Neither is this another comparative constitutional law book featuring Asian cases and materials. What this book does is to show how constitutionalism is practised in Asia. It attempts to paint a picture of what is *actually going on*, rather than normatively to suggest what should be done, or if an act or device qualified as 'constitutional'. In a nutshell, we want to take Asia on its own terms, warts and all. Our focus is on a region, its constitutions and how it uses constitutional law to meet its various challenges. Comparisons between the constitutional practices of the various Asian states can certainly be made, but that is not the primary object of this volume. There is nothing prescriptive in the book, even if the reader will often be asked to consider if one constitutional solution or argument might be better than another, or whether it might work better in one circumstance than another.

We often speak of 'Asia' as if it were just another country like China or Indonesia. In ancient times, the Greeks saw the world through their limited topographical lens, as being made up of only three continents: Europe, Asia and Africa. If only life were that simple.[21] At what point does Asia become Europe or the Middle East? Why does Russia, which extends further east than Japan, insist that it is a European state? For that matter, why does Australia claim to be an Asian state every now and then?

For our purposes, we adopt the definition of Asia used by the Association for Asian Studies (AAS), the well-established scholarly association to which so many scholars of Asia belong. Founded in 1941 and headquartered in Ann Arbor, Michigan, the AAS divides the region into China and Inner Asia (including Tibet and Mongolia, as well as the Special Administrative Regions of Hong Kong and Macau); Northeast Asia (Japan, Taiwan and the Koreas); Southeast Asia (Brunei, Cambodia, Indonesia, Laos, Malaysia, Myanmar, the Philippines, Singapore, Thailand, Timor-Leste and Vietnam); and South Asia (India, Pakistan, Bangladesh, Sri Lanka, Nepal and Bhutan). We cover 26 jurisdictions in this volume, even though they are not all analysed in equal depth and measure.

---

[21] For a thoughtful attempt to conceptualise and reconceptualise 'Asia', see P Duara, 'Asia Redux: Conceptualizing a Region for Our Times' (2010) 69(4) *The Journal of Asian Studies* 963.

'Constitutionalism' as Louis Henkin famously wrote, 'is nowhere defined' though 'we speak of it as if its meaning is self-evident, or that we know it when we see it'. Henkin then proceeds to offer seven concepts he considered to be the 'principal demands of constitutionalism'.[22] Henkin's benchmarks, like so many others, are premised on a clear concept of the rule of law, limited government, and democratic representation and values. While Henkin's guidelines are penetrating and helpful, we found them too narrow for our purposes, for in many Asian states may be found a weak tradition of the rule of law and of rights-based thinking. This has manifested itself in the lack of a human rights or rights-orientated culture and recognisably democratic institutions, especially in the socialist states where the rule of the party supersedes the rule of law. It is worth noting that of the five surviving communist states in the world, four of them are in Asia.[23]

'Asia' is a vast region, immensely diverse in its political ideology, culture, economic development, colonial history, legal transplants and autochthonous constitutional experiments. A study of Asian constitutional practice in terms of principles, institution-building and operation within the political process and rights adjudication, yields rich insights and perspectives into how we understand the role of law and government in issues like legitimacy, accountability and the construction of national identity.

Important and often distinctive constitutional developments in many Asian states in the last decade have caught the attention of comparative constitutionalists in Asia and beyond. These include the robust exercise of constitutional review in South Korea and Taiwan with respect to rights and high politics, constitutional instrumentalism and conceptions of the rule of law which undergird economic development in 'Asian tigers' like Singapore and Hong Kong, a range of religion–state arrangements which defy binary 'theocratic' or 'separationist' models, constitutional making and re-making in the aftermath of 'people power' revolutions in new and fragile democracies such as the Philippines and Thailand, and attempts to institutionalise legal pluralism to accommodate ethno-cultural diversity in Indonesia and Malaysia. These constitute important precedents for comparative constitutional studies, in facilitating comparative engagement of constitutional laws and processes beyond dominant understandings of constitutionalism forged by developments in the West.[24] The rich Asian constitutional jurisprudence on civil and political rights, as well as socio-economic rights, also sheds light on the varying conceptions of rights beyond Dworkinian trumps, and how these interact with ideas of duties, competing rights and public goods, in liberal and non-liberal settings.

We begin with the basic proposition that constitutions and constitutional laws are used in a variety of ways to respond to problems in each society. Questions of constitutional importance are posed and the reader is led, by engaging with the primary and secondary materials, through how the various Asian states respond to these questions and challenges. Each section is accompanied by notes, comments and

---

[22] L Henkin, 'A New Birth of Constitutionalism: Genetic Influences and Genetic Defects' in M Rosenfield (ed), *Constitutionalism, Identity, Difference, and Legitimacy: Theoretical Perspectives* (Durham, NC: Duke University Press, 1994) 39, 40–42.

[23] They are: China, Vietnam, Laos and North Korea. The only non-Asian communist state is Cuba.

[24] On the resurgence of interest in comparative constitutional law, see AE Dick Howard, 'A Traveler from an Antique Land: The Modern Renaissance of Comparative Constitutionalism' (2009–2010) 50 *Virginia Journal of International Law* 3.

questions to facilitate critical and comparative analysis, as well as suggestions for further reading.

III. OUR APPROACH

Casebooks, properly constructed, are excellent teaching tools. The need to grapple with primary sources like cases, forces us actively to engage with the material. We are forced to probe the minds of judges, legislators and decision-makers, and to question the philosophical assumptions upon which constitutional theories, institutions and ideas are built. It is through this process that we learn 'to think like lawyers'.

This book is not exhaustive in its coverage. We have tried to organise its chapters around carefully selected themes that cover the central issues in the field of constitutional law and practice in Asia. The organisation of these themes was arrived at after much consultation and deliberation. No single person can hope to put together a book like this. The topic is too vast and the material too prodigious. Only by collaborating and sharing our many years of comparative studies were we able even to agree on how a book like this might appear. We were very anxious that this book be about Asia by those who live in the region. This perspective required us to live imaginatively in the minds of fellow Asians and to have a good intuitive feel of what constitutional subjects were uppermost in the minds of the people living in this vast continent.

We have tried to spend some time in each of the countries covered in this volume, talking to lawyers, academics, judges and civil society actors. Save for Pakistan, Brunei and Timor, at least one of us has spent some time in each of the countries featured here. Such a short exposure does not count as field work by any measure, nor does it allow any one of us to truly *know* what the issues are. But talking to principal actors in each state does give us a good feel of what people are concerned about.

The book is in 10 chapters. The first two chapters – covering the history of constitutional development in Asia and the constitutional culture of the Asian states – are essentially extended essays that we hope will set the context for the rest of the book. These chapters highlight the histories, colonial influences and cultural particularities extant in the region, and provide a provisional orientation towards the major constitutional developments and controversies one encounters in the study of constitutional law in Asia.

Chapters three and four focus on institutional arrangements and constitutional change, while chapter five deals with how judicial review operates in Asia. The remainder of the book deals with the various fundamental rights found in most constitutional orders: democracy and the right to political participation (chapter six); equality and equal protection of the law (chapter seven); free speech and the *res publica* (chapter eight); religious freedom and state-religion orderings (chapter nine) and socio-economic rights (chapter ten). Other than chapters one and two, each chapter is framed by an introductory essay which sets out the issues and succinctly highlights critical perspectives and themes. Aside from the judicious selection of representative materials, each chapter is organised in a way that will speak to the discipline of constitutional law in general, as well as underscore points of dissonance, harmony, convergence/divergence in Asian practice.

We hope that this book will go some way towards filling that gap and provide a useful resource for both teachers and scholars.

Wen-Chen Chang
Li-ann Thio
Kevin YL Tan
Jiunn-rong Yeh
May 2013

1

Constitution Making and State Building

I. INTRODUCTION

In Asia, attempts to set down the structures and rules of government and governance in writing can be traced back to ancient times. One is reminded of King Ashoka's attempt to set out the *Edicts* of his empire in around 3 BCE, wherein the great Mauryan ruler sets out his Buddhist beliefs, his moral and religious precepts, and his social and animal welfare programme.[1] In 604 CE, Crown Prince Shotoku of Japan, acting as Crown Prince Regent in the reign of his childless aunt, the Empress Suiko (554–628 CE) formulated a 17-Article 'Constitution'.[2] Like Ashoka's *Edicts*, this was more a series of moral precepts and injunctions than a blueprint for limited government. That said, the 17-Article Constitution does lay down certain precepts of government. For example, Article 3 requires all subjects to obey imperial commands 'with reverence', while Article 12 prohibits local nobles (*Kuni no miyasuko*) and provincial authorities (*mikotomochi*) from levying taxes or imposing levies on the people.

The founder of China's Ming Dynasty, Zhu Yuanzhang (1328–98) attempted in the fourteenth century completely to re-order and remould China through a serious of pronouncements, codes and regulations. This has been seen by some scholars as an attempt to formulate what might be considered a 'constitution'. Chief among these documents were the *Ancestral Injunctions* or *Huang Ming Zu Xun* (皇明祖训)[3] and the Great Ming Code or *Da Ming Lu* (大明律),[4] which, taken together, form the basis for the operation of Ming government.[5]

These early constitution-makers were primarily concerned with the ordering and organisation of society. They were *not* concerned with curbing the power of sovereign rulers, and their 'constitutions' were primarily designed to enhance and centralise the power of the state. In that respect, few scholars steeped in traditions of liberal democracy recognise these early efforts as constitutions in the modern sense, but rather view

---

[1] See, eg, R Thapar, *Early India: From the Origins to AD 1300* (Berkeley, Cal: University of California Press, 2004) at 174–204; B Stein and D Arnold, *A History of India*, 2nd edn (London: Blackwell, 2010) at 74–75; and K Pletcher (ed), *The History of India* (New York: Britannica Publishing, 2011) at 73–75.

[2] See DJ Lu, *Japan: A Documentary History* (Armonk, New York: ME Sharpe, 1997) at 22–26, where a translation of the 17 Articles is presented.

[3] For an English translation of the *Huang Ming Zu Xun*, see EL Farmer, *Zhu Yuanzhang & Early Ming Legislation: The Reordering of Chinese Society following the End of Mongol Rule* (Leiden: EJ Brill, 1995), App I.

[4] See *The Great Ming Code: Da Ming Lü*, translated and introduced by Jiang Yonglin (Seattle, Wash: University of Washington Press, 2005).

[5] See Wu Yanhong and Jiang Yonglin, 'The Emperor's Four Bodies: Embodied Rulership and Legal Culture in Early Ming China' (2007) 2(1) *Frontiers of History in China* 25.

them as state-centric codes designed to establish the relationship between the rulers and the ruled, and as imposing duties on (rather than according rights to) the latter. Constitution-making of the 'government-limiting' variety occurred in Asia only towards the end of the nineteenth century.

II. EARLY INSPIRATIONS

A. Introduction

Right up till the nineteenth century, most states in Asia were ruled by imperial fiat. For centuries, the largest and most populous states, like China, India and Japan, operated systems of government that might be described as undemocratic and illiberal at best, and despotic and tyrannical at worst. Over the centuries, social intercourse between the peoples of Asia and those of Europe seldom went beyond the traders and sailors who plied the lucrative but dangerous trade routes that linked China with Europe and Asia Minor. While Asia had become increasingly xenophobic after the demise of the Mongol Yuan Dynasty (1271–1368) in China, European traders and governments became increasingly expansive in their search for new produce, markets and territory.

By the 1500s, the West had begun surpassing the East in technological and social terms, and would do so for the next 500 years.[6] In the nineteenth century, the major states in Asia – China, India and Japan – were lagging far behind their European and American counterparts in military and industrial power. An impartial observer would see the West as modern and the East as backward. Concerned reformists in some Asian states were convinced that if their countries were to shake off the mantle of backwardness and rejoin the great community of nations, radical reforms of their government and social systems would be necessary. Among the states in Asia, Japan and China were the first to attempt reforming and modernising their legal and constitutional systems by copying models from the West.

B. Japan

Japan took this modernisation process most seriously. In 1867, Tokugawa Yoshinobu, the fifteenth Tokugawa Shogun, literally surrendered his powers and prerogatives to the Meiji Emperor. This led to a chain of events that saw the restoration of power to the emperor for the first time in over a thousand years. The Meiji Restoration also saw the transformation of feudal Japan into a modern state.[7]

---

[6] See I Morris, *Why the West Rules . . . For Now: The Patterns of History and What They Reveal About the Future* (London: Profile Books, 2010) at 434–89; and WH McNeill, *The Rise of the West: A History of the Human Community* (Chicago, Ill: University of Chicago Press, 1961) at 565–652.

[7] See EH Norman, *Japan's Emergence as a Modern State: Political and Economic Problems of the Meiji Period*, 60th anniversary edition (Toronto: UBC Press, 2000); WG Beaseley, *The Meiji Restoration* (Stanford, Cal: Stanford University Press, 1972); WG Beaseley, *The Rise of Modern Japan: Political, Economic and Social Change Since 1850*, rev edn (New York: St Martin's Press, 2000) at 54–83; Junji Banno, *The Establishment of the Japanese Constitutional System*, JAA Stockwin (trans) (London: Routledge, 1992); *The Cambridge History of Japan, Vol 5: The Nineteenth Century* (Cambridge: Cambridge University Press, 1989) at 651–67.

One of the most important facets of this modernisation was the adoption of a modern constitution entrenched with clear limits on the power of the executive branch and the absolutism of the Emperor. The drafting of the constitution was a pre-emptive response by the conservative ruling Meiji oligarchs[8] to increasing demands for elections and representative government. Leading these calls was Itagaki Taisuke (1837–1919), leader of the Freedom and People's Rights Movement that later became Japan's first political party. Itagaki demanded the immediate establishment of a elected national assembly and a written constitution. The Meiji Government agreed to put in place a Western-style constitution and an elected national assembly by 1890. To stem the tide of the reformists, the Meiji rulers moved quickly to have in place a conservative constitution, and in 1881, a list of minimally accepted provisions was put forward by Iwakura Tomomi (1825–83), the Meiji Government's most senior bureaucrat.

Iwakura Tomomi placed Ito Hirobumi (1841–1909) – the London-educated samurai from Choshu – in charge of the constitution-drafting committee in 1881. Describing the process of constitution-making,[9] Professor William Beasley noted as follows:

WG Beasley, The Rise of Modern Japan: Political, Economic and Social Change Since 1850, rev edn (New York: St Martin's Press, 2000) 76–77

The government's response to the constitutional movement was not wholly negative. In the summer of 1881, Ito and Iwakura had worked out an outline of the constitutional provisions they thought to be acceptable, including a cabinet clearly responsible to the emperor; . . . a bicameral assembly with an elected lower house, having no power to initiate legislation or in the last resort to deny the government money; and an electorate based on a property qualification, such as already existed in the prefectures. The proposals were not published, but the inner council approved them in October.

In March 1882 Ito left for a visit to Europe on a constitutional fact-finding mission which was to last eighteen months. Since he knew broadly what he was looking for he went straight to Berlin and Vienna, where he expected to find it, and only later paid visits to Paris and London, where the political traditions were alien to his purpose. Most of his time was spent seeking advice from Rudolph Gneist and Lorenz von Stein, whose ideas were later injected directly into the drafting of the constitution by two Germans employed by the Meiji government, Alfred Mosse and Hermann Roesler. A brief excursus into the theory of parliamentary government under the guidance of Herbert Spencer did little to change the overall character of the expedition.

For some time after his return to Japan Ito was preoccupied with plans for the peerage, cabinet, and civil service. Once work started on the constitution itself, which was not until 1886, it was carried out in secret under Ito's personal supervision. The pace was leisurely, little affected by public agitation or debate. It is not surprising in these circumstances that the nature of what was done did not differ fundamentally from the principles laid down in 1881. Indeed, the document put before the Privy Council in May 1888, and proclaimed at a short ceremony in the palace on 11 February 1889, might well be described as little more than an amplification of points originally made by Iwakura, who had always been more alert than most of his colleagues to constitutional questions.

[8] The Meiji oligarchy refers to the ruling elite of the Meiji era. Among these were Okubo Toshimichi, Saigo Takamori, Kido Koin, Iwakura Tomomi, and Okuma Shigenbu.
[9] Possibly the most detailed study of the constitutional development of Japan in this early period is G Akita, *Foundations of Constitutional Government in Modern Japan 1868–1900* (Cambridge, Mass: Harvard University Press, 1967).

Although the Meiji Constitution was promulgated in February 1889, it came into effect on 29 November 1890. The model that most heavily influenced the drafters of the Meiji constitution was the Prussian Constitution of 1850,[10] a highly-conservative constitution that focused power in the King, and whose electoral system was based on an elector's ability to pay taxes. Interestingly, in a case of 're-borrowing', Japan's Meiji Constitution acted as the model for Ethiopia's first Constitution of 1931.[11]

C. China

Constitutional development in China was fuelled by the twin pressures brought to bear by the revolutionary forces intent on overthrowing the Qing Dynasty and by the internal reformist elements within the imperial order. Interestingly, it was to Japan that it looked for inspirations on the kind of constitution it would promulgate.

> **Hungdah Chiu, 'Constitutional Development and Reform in the Republic of China on Taiwan' in Bih-Jaw Lin, *Contemporary China and the Changing International Community* (Columbia, SC: University of South Carolina Press, 1994) 3 at 4–6**
>
> With the gradual opening of China after the mid-nineteenth century, many Chinese went abroad as workers, students, or visiting scholars. As a result of this contact between China and the West, the Chinese came to know Western political systems and constitutionalism better. In 1889, Japan adopted a Western-style constitution (usually referred to as the Meiji Constitution) and soon became an important power. This event also significantly influenced Chinese political and constitutional development.
>
> On June 30, 1895, an intellectual named K'ang Yu-wei submitted a memorial to Emperor Kuang-hsu (1875–1908), urging him to take a series of reform measures. Among the proposed reforms were the creation of a parliament, the adoption of a constitution, and the division of power between the executive, the legislature, and the judiciary. In other words, K'ang proposed a constitutional monarchy similar to that of Japan. Emperor Kuang-hsu, K'ang, and his associates tried to implement part of the reform measures (but not the constitutional aspects) that K'ang had suggested between June 11 and September 20, 1898, but this ended only in K'ang's exile abroad and the 'house arrest' of the Emperor himself by Empress Dowager Tz'u-hsi for the rest of his reign.
>
> On June 21, 1900, the Chi'ng government under Empress Dowager Tz'u-his, relying on the superstitious Boxers, declared war on the Western powers. The Western powers retaliated by sending an expeditionary force to invade China and soon occupied Peking, and on September 7, 1901, China was compelled to sign the most humiliating peace treaty it ever concluded. The treaty not only required China to pay a heavy indemnity of 450 million taels of silver, but also allowed foreign countries to station troops in the Chinese capital, Peking. However, this tragedy forced the Ch'ing government to institute some reforms leading toward constitutional government, in order to undercut the revolutionary movement to overthrow the Ch'ing Dynasty.

[10] See 'Constitution of the Kingdom of Prussia, translated and supplied with an Introduction and Notes by James Harvey Robinson' (1894) 5(8) *Annals of the American Academy of Political and Social Science* (Supplement) 1–54, especially the introduction by Robin at 7–25.

[11] See Saheed A Adejumobi, *The History of Ethiopia* (Westport, Conn: Greenwood Publishing, 2007) at 54–55.

In 1905, the tiny constitutional monarchy of Japan defeated the colossal dictatorial Russian Empire. To many Chinese this was proof of the effectiveness of constitutionalism. They also discovered that nearly all leading Western powers were constitutional governments. The famous scholar-turned-industrialist, Chang Chien, commented that 'the victory of Japan and the defeat of Russia are the victory of constitutionalism and the defeat of monarchism.' He urged Yuan Shih-K'ai, then governor-general of Chihli, to assume vigorous leadership in promoting the cause of constitutionalism.

At the same time, revolutionaries led by Dr Sun Yat-sen opposed the idea of a constitutional monarchy and contended that it was essential for China to overthrow the Ch'ing Dynasty and establish a republican form of government, which of course would be based on a democractic constitution.

Finally, in July 1905, the Empress Dowager accepted Yuan Shih-K'ai's recommendation to send high officials abroad to investigate foreign political systems as a prelude to introducing a constitution. A inspection mission was soon sent to Japan, Great Britain, France, Belgium, the United States, Germany, the Austro-Hungarian Empire, and Italy. The mission returned in July 1906.

The mission reported favourable impressions of the British and the German systems of government, but concluded that the Japanese constitution was more suitable to China because of greater similarity between the two countries.[12] On August 27, 1908, the Ch'ing government issues an 'Outline of Constitution,' a parliamentary law, and prescribed a nine-year tutelage period (1908–17) before the constitution became effective.

On October 10, 1911, revolution broke out in Wuchang, resulting in the abdication of the Ch'ing Dynasty on February 12, 1912. On November 2, 1911, in order to thwart the revolutionary movement, the Ch'ing government promulgated the 'Nineteen Articles [on Constitutional Law],' which however, never entered into force. Therefore, no constitution was ever adopted before the downfall of the Ch'ing Dynasty.

. . . The Republic of China (ROC) was established on January 1, 1912. A twenty-one article General Plan for Organization of the Provisional Government of the Republic of China had been adopted on December 2, 1911 by delegates from ten provinces, and after several revisions it was finalized on January 2, 1912 with the approval of delegates from seventeen provinces. Article 21 provides that the General Plan would be effective until the adoption of the Constitution of the Republic of China. This is the first constitution adopted by China. This constitution bore some striking similarities to the original United States Constitution, as it made the provisional President the real chief-executive, and there was no mention of the basic rights and duties of the people.

On March 11, 1912, a Provisional Constitution of the Republic of China was promulgated. It contained fifty-six articles and changed the American-style presidential system established in the General Plan to the cabinet system based on the French model. A unicameral house, the Senate, was appointed by each province, Inner Mongolia, Outer Mongolia, Tibet, and Tsinghai and was to exercise the legislative power (Article 18). Within ten months, however, the Senate was required to enact laws for the organization of the Congress and its election method (Article 53). On August 10, 1912, the Organic Law for the Congress (House and Senate), the Election Law for the House and the Election Law for the Senate were all enacted, and an election was soon held in early 1913. On April 8, 1913, the Congress was inaugurated.

---

[12] For the text of the Report of this Commission in English, see Document 52, 'A Report on Constitutional Governments Abroad, 1906' in Ssu-yu Teng and JK Fairbank, *China's Response to the West: A Documentary Survey, 1939–1923* (Cambridge, Mass: Harvard University Press, 1979) at 208–09.

When formulating a draft for a permanent constitution on October 31, 1913, the Congress retained the cabinet system. However, President Yuan Shih-k'ai opposed this draft constitution, and on November 4, 1913, he illegally dissolved the Congress. Yuan organized a Constitutional Conference to draft a new constitution, which was promulgated on May 1, 1914. This constitution adopted a presidential system with widespread powers.

Up to 1946, the only independent states in Asia were Japan, China, Mongolia, the Philippines and Siam (Thailand). It should therefore come as no surprise that Japan and China were two of the earliest Asian states to attempt to reform their feudal state structures and governments by adopting what was perceived to be more 'modern' forms of government characterised by the constitutional limitation on state authority.

Mongolia had, until the fall of the Qing Dynasty, been part of China. When the last imperial dynasty collapsed in 1911, the Bogd Khan of Mongolia declared independence for Mongolia. However, true independence was not achieved till 26 November 1924, after the Mongolian army, with help from the Soviet Union, expelled the Chinese from their territory. Upon independence, the Mongolians promulgated a Soviet-style socialist constitution.[13] This constitution abolished its traditional monarchical theocracy and, from then on, placed Mongolia within the Soviet sphere of influence till 1989.

D. The Philippines

The United States of America acquired the Philippines[14] in 1898 following the defeat of Spain in the Spanish–American War 'with a bad conscience'.[15] Almost immediately, the US Senate passed a resolution not to annex the Philippines, making it eligible for future statehood.[16] In 1907, elections were introduced into the Philippines. An assembly with limited legislative powers was created, although the governor-general wielded real power. More than any colonial power, America actively took steps to induct Filipinos into administration and to politicise its colony. In March 1912, the Philippines Committee in the United States proposed a law that would immediately give the Islands internal autonomy and promised full independence by 1921, although this was never formally adopted. Unlike other colonial powers, America was prepared to establish and abide by timetables for independence.[17] The 1916 Jones Act's preamble stated that the US proposed to withdraw from the Philippines and recognise its independence 'as soon as a stable government can be established therein'.

---

[13] See AJK Sanders, 'Mongolia's New Constitution: Blueprint for Democracy' (1992) 32(6) *Asian Survey* 506.

[14] On the evolution of the Philippines Constitution, see EM Fernando, 'The American Constitutional Impact on the Philippine Legal System' in L Ward Beer (ed), *Constitutionalism in Asia: Asian Views of the American Influence* (Berkeley, Cal: University of California Press, 1979) 140; and EM Fernando and E Quisiumbing-Fernando, 'The 1987 Constitution of the Philippines: The Impact of American Constitutionalism Revisited' in L Ward Beer (ed), *Constitutional Systems in Late Twentieth Century Asia* (Seattle, Wash and London: University of Washington Press, 1992) 571.

[15] See R von Albertini, *Decolonization: The Administration and Future of the Colonies, 1919–1960* (New York: Doubleday, 1971) [hereinafter 'Albertini'] at 474.

[16] Ibid.

[17] See Albertini, n 15 above, at 476.

The Act introduced important reforms, including elections of both legislative houses on a wider franchise and requiring that senior officials' appointment receive the Senate's assent.[18] Like other colonial powers, local politics acted as a barometer for reform. The Democrats were much more inclined to move the Philippines towards independence, while Republicans emphasised the need for 'stable government' and constantly argued that the Filipinos were not ready for independence. Nonetheless, the Americans were far more progressive than other colonial powers like Britain and France, as their colonial educational policy specifically aimed to prepare Filipinos for political responsibility and nationhood. The induction of Filipinos to all levels of government during the 1920s resulted in an entire administrative structure populated by locals.

However, American decolonisation policy in the Philippines also had unaltruistic economic motives. The Philippines exported the bulk of its cheap produce to America without tariffs, since the Philippines was part of America. This was unfavourable to American farmers and producers competing with lower Philippines labour and product costs.[19] In 1933, Congress overrode President Herbert Hoover's veto and passed the Hare-Hawes-Cutting Act, providing for independence for the Philippines within 10 years. A Philippine Commonwealth Constitution was to be drafted and elections held, while quotas would be imposed on hitherto duty-free Philippine exports to the United States.[20] This legislation was opposed by the Philippines legislature led by Manuel Quezon, who subsequently renegotiated the agreement. Slight modifications were made and it was eventually passed as the Tydings-McDuffie Act, or the Philippines Independence Act, in 1934. Quezon's faction won the 1934 elections to select delegates to the Constitutional Convention, and the transition period commenced in 1935 with a national plebiscite approving the new constitution and the country's first presidential election, which Quezon also won.[21]

The 1935 Constitution gave the executive a dominant position and provided for a unicameral legislature – the National Assembly. The bicameral legislative structure – with its Senate and House of Representatives – came into being only in 1940 following amendments to the Constitution. The power of judicial review was vested in the courts, but the 1935 Constitution required a two-thirds majority vote in the Supreme Court to annul any legislative act or treaty.[22] As the Philippines was an unincorporated territory of the US, its 1935 Constitution operated much along the lines of the American one.[23] On 4 July 1946, following American reoccupation of the Philippines after the capitulation of the Japanese, President Harry Truman proclaimed the Philippines' independence. The 1935 Constitution, with its amendments, remained in force up till 1973.

---

[18] Ibid.

[19] Ibid at 480–81. See generally P Kratoska, 'Nationalist and Modernist Reform' in Nicholas Tarling (ed), *The Cambridge History of Southeast Asia*, vol 2 (Cambridge: Cambridge University Press, 1992) 249 at 263.

[20] Albertini, above n 15.

[21] Kratoska, above n 19.

[22] See Fernando and Quisiumbing-Fernando, above n 14, at 572.

[23] Fernando and Quisiumbing-Fernando observed that 'there was a great deal of truth to the charge that the working of the 1935 Constitution, especially the Bill of Rights, owed much to the first Ten Amendments of the American Constitution – its Bill of Rights – as well as the Thirteenth Amendment prohibiting slavery and the Fourteenth Amendment enshrining the principal guarantees of due process and equal protection' (ibid at 573).

E. Siam (Thailand)

Siam's attempt at modernising its government started at about the same time as Japan's; however, it was not until 1932 that a constitutional monarchy was established:

A Harding and P Leyland, *The Constitutional System of Thailand: A Contextual Analysis* (Oxford: Hart Publishing, 2011) 10–14

In 1887 a memorandum signed by 11 princes urged [King] Chulalongkorn to adopt a democratic system of parliamentary government under a constitutional monarchy. The King, while apparently agreeing with the principles that inspired the memorandum, responded that a parliamentary form of government would be difficult to create when so few of his subjects would be able to perform parliamentary duties; administrative reform had to come first, in any case. Both these arguments left the door of constitutional reform enticingly ajar. A similar position was also held by the foreign advisers who assisted Siam's legal development over four decades from the 1890s to the 1930s. Speaking of constitutional reform, Siam legal adviser, Harvard law professor and US Ambassador, Francis B Sayre, stated in a 1926 memorandum to King Prajadhipok that:

> what works well in Great Britain might work disastrously in Siam. Siam should not slavishly copy the system of any Western nation, but should evolve out of her own experience what seems best adapted to her own genius and conditions.

Reformers, in a failed coup attempt in 1912, near the beginning of the reign of King Vajiravudh, intended to create a republic. The King himself was more interested in advancing the idea of nationalism and in inculcating an almost Victorian sense of personal and sexual morality as a mark of 'siwilai' (civilisation). The foreign advisers, as well as the Chakri kings, at least up to King Prajadhipok, were at any rate clearly of the view that, despite the creation of a free press in Chulalongkorn's later years, an independent Bar in the 1920s and the democratic pressures that led to the 1932 coup, public law reform, unlike private law reform, could wait until the population was broadly literate and well educated.

III. The 1932 Revolution

King Prajadhipok displayed some interest in developing a more democratic form of government, instituting the King's Privy Council in 1927 and considering drafts for a written constitution in 1926 and 1931. His constitutional plans were forestalled by economic and fiscal difficulties stemming from the world depression of 1929–32, by opposition from within the royal family and ultimately by the coup of June 1932. This coup was led in the name of democratic government by the 'People's Party' – a combination of leftist intellectuals such as constitutional law professor Pridi Banomyong and rightist officers such as Field-Marshal Plack Phibunsongkram (Phibun). It was not a popular but, rather, an educated-elite uprising, which resulted in the King being compelled to sign a written constitution (the Interim Constitution of June 1932) drafted by Pridi. The coup leaders' statement, issued in the name of the People's Party, stated that the King 'governs without principle. The country's affairs are left to the mercy of fate, as can be seen from the depression of the economy.' However the People's Party had no wish to snatch the throne. Hence it invites this [*sic*] King to retain the position, but he must be under the law of the constitution for governing the country, and cannot do anything independently without the approval of the assembly of the people's representatives.

Thus the objective of parliamentary democracy was clearly espoused by the People's Party.

In an early rapprochement the coup leaders apologised to the King for their disrespect, using humble language appropriate to his position. At the same time he was prevailed upon to remain in the country and not mount a counter-coup, while granting an amnesty to the coup leaders. However, the King in his response inserted the words 'chua krao' (provisional) at the head of the constitution, thus perhaps inadvertently setting in motion what is now an all too familiar sequence of events around the constitutional change (coup, amnesty, interim constitution). The King did not consider that, under the Interim Constitution, the monarchy was given a status appropriate even to a constitutional monarchy such as that of Britain. The people were said to be sovereign, and the King did not even have the power of appointing the Prime Minister or making any order without a counter-signature; moreover, the language of the document smacked to him of communism. The 'final form' of the Constitution was 'submitted' to the King by an Assembly of the People's Representatives, comprising 70 members, which had been nominated in the wake of the coup. The King was 'graciously pleased' to fix 10 December 1932 as the date for the 'giving' of the Constitution, which took place 'with great public rejoicing'. This 'permanent' Constitution of December 1932 restored some degree of royal prestige. The Preamble asserted that the King had been asked to grant a Constitution and had graciously bestowed it on his subjects, 'so that the Kingdom of Siam may have the same form of government as that of a civilised country.' The Constitution was clearly inspired by the British version of constitutional monarchy, and envisaged the great functions of State as emanating from the throne . . .

. . . The machinery established by this brief Constitution of 68 sections is largely based on the Westminster pattern. This might seem strange in view of the fact that Siam, in reforming its legal system, had ultimately rejected the common law as a pattern of reform in favour of an amalgam of mainly French, but also other European, civil law provisions. However the civil law systems did not offer a tested model of constitutional monarchy comparable with that of Britain.

III. COLONIALISM AND DECOLONISATION[24]

A. The Colonisation of Asia

China, Japan and Siam remained Asia's only independent states up until the end of World War II in 1945. The rest of Asia had, for the preceding century, been under colonial domination. The first Europeans to arrive in Asia were the Portuguese, when Vasco da Gama arrived in Calicut, India in 1498. They were quickly followed by the Dutch, and then the English, and later by the French. Trade and commerce lay at the heart of rivalry between the European powers in Asia. Until about 1800, spices like cloves, mace and nutmeg could only be found in the Moluccas (modern-day Maluku)

[24] See generally, C Geertz (ed), *Old Societies and New States: The Quest for Modernity in Asia and Africa* (New York: Free Press of Glencoe, 1963); M Brecher, *The New States of Asia: A Political Analysis* (London: Oxford University Press, 1963); C Mason, *Asia Emerges* (Sydney: Southern Cross International, 1968); R Emerson, *From Empire to Nation: The Rise to Self-Assertion of Asian and African Peoples* (Boston, Mass: Beacon Press, 1962); and RN Spann, *Constitutionalism in Asia* (New York: Asia Publication House, 1963).

and a group of islands known as the Spice Islands. Because of their scarcity, spices were expensive, and before long, the great European powers began fighting each for control of the spice trade.

For the enormous risks to pay off, a viable sea route to Asia had to be found. For centuries, the sea route between Asia and the Middle East was dominated by Arab traders, but by the fifteenth century the Europeans began building larger and larger ships and sending them further and further afield. The Portuguese, the premier naval power of the 1400s and 1500s, were the first to expand into Asia with the establishment of a fort in Kochi, India in 1503 and the conquest of the ancient city of Melaka in 1511. By 1557, the Portuguese had established a permanent base in Macau.

The conquest of Melaka was significant for two reasons. First, the Portuguese capitalised on its location and used it as a strategic base for Portuguese expansion in the East Indies, including the Spice Islands; and, secondly, it signalled the beginning of trading rivalry between the great European powers – Portuguese, English, Dutch and French – in the region that would lead to the colonisation of Southeast Asia.

The Portuguese had a significant 'first-mover' advantage over the other European powers, and this allowed them to dominate the spice trade for a century. However, the other European powers, most notably the Dutch and the English, were not content to allow Portugal to dominate trade with the East Indies. They too began sending their own expeditions to establish trading ports in the East. By the end of the sixteenth century, Portugal was over-extended and was quickly eclipsed as a naval power by Spain, Holland and England. The Spanish concentrated their expansion in the Philippines and Formosa (modern-day Taiwan), while the Dutch and English battled for supremacy in Southeast Asia.

By the end of the nineteenth century – the height of European colonial expansion –the Dutch controlled the archipelago then known as the Dutch East Indies (modern-day Indonesia), while the English controlled India (including modern-day Pakistan and Bangladesh), Ceylon, Burma, the Malay peninsula (including the island of Singapore), Hong Kong and the northern part of the island of Borneo. The French controlled Indo-China, comprising Cambodia, Laos and Vietnam, while the Spanish occupied the Philippines. Taiwan was a colony of Japan, and Korea would be annexed by Japan in 1910.

B. Japan, Taiwan and Korea[25]

i. Japan[26]

Japan's defeat in World War II and unconditional surrender to the Allied Forces left it open to major changes. Under the Potsdam Declaration, the Allied leaders required

---

[25] Yeh and Chang consider the constitutional development of these three states to have sufficient similarities as to constitute an emergent 'East Asian' model of constitutionalism. See Jiunn-rong Yeh and Wen-Chen Chang, 'The Emergence of East Asian Constitutionalism: Features in Comparison' (2011) LIX(3) *American Journal of Comparative Law* 805; see also Wen-chen Chang, 'East Asian Foundations for Constitutionalism: Three Models Reconstructed' (2008) 3(2) *National Taiwan University Law Review* 111.

[26] The literature on the creation of Japan's post-War Constitution is voluminous. This brief account draws on some of the following: N Ashibe, L Ward Beer and M Ito, 'Japan: The United States Constitution

Japan to 'remove all obstacles to the revival and strengthening of democratic tendencies among the Japanese people', as well as to establish 'freedom of speech, of religion, and of thought'.[27] The Supreme Commander for the Allied Powers (SCAP) was American General Douglas MacArthur, who was initially reluctant to impose a US-style political system on Japan. However, when asked if he had any suggestions on the composition of the new government, he stated in no uncertain terms that he considered constitutional revision and reform crucial. Many elites of the old order were still wielding levers of power and were determined to seize the initiative on constitutional revision. In late 1945, Japanese Prime Minister Kijuro Shidehara established a Committee to Study Constitutional Problems with State Minister Joji Matsumoto as chairman.[28] This Committee – later on commonly referred to as the Matsumoto Committee – had originally been convened to study problems relating to the Meiji Constitution with a view to revising it. However, pressure from the SCAP and other domestic actors compelled the Committee to work on a new draft constitution, known later as the Matsumoto Draft.

The Committee met between 27 October 1945 and 2 February 1946, and presented its 'Outline of Constitution Revision' on 8 February 1946. This draft was rejected outright by MacArthur because it proposed only cosmetic changes to the constitution and left the old system and the inviolability of the Emperor unchanged. MacArthur ordered the Government Section of the SCAP to prepare an alternative draft. Overseeing this drafting procedure was a small Steering Committee comprising Commander Alfred Hussey, Lieutenant-Colonel Milo E Rowell and Lieutenant-Colonel Charles L Kades. Over a remarkable five-day period, this Steering Committee supervised and oversaw the work of seven separate committees to deal with the various subjects under consideration: the legislature, the executive, the judiciary, civil rights, local government, finance, treaties, the emperor and miscellaneous issues. On 8 February, a draft was sent to MacArthur for his approval, and this was shown to the Japanese officials on 13 February. MacArthur was anxious that the draft be accepted by the Japanese people and not seen as a mere foreign imposition. He thus presented his draft to the Japanese leaders with the hope that they would take it to the Japanese people for endorsement. If they refused then he would do so himself.

MacArthur's original idea was that the Japanese Cabinet would present before the Japanese people – and the world – a brand new constitution that would signal a clear

and Japan's Constitutional Law' in Ward Beer (ed), 128–269; Tetsuya Kataoka, *The Price of a Constitution: The Origin of Japan's Post War Politics* (New York: C Russak, 1991); DM Hellegers, *We, the Japanese People: World War II and the Origins of the Japanese Constitution*, 2 vols (Stanford, Cal: Stanford University Press, 2002); Koseki Shoichi, *The Birth of Japan's Postwar Constitution*, RA Moore (trans) (Denver, Col: Westview Press, 1998); Inoue Kyoko, *MacArthur's Constitution: A Linguistic and Cultural Study of Its Making* (Chicago, Ill: University of Chicago Press, 1991); RE Ward, 'The Origins of the Present Japanese Constitution' (1956) 50(4) *American Political Science Review* 980; CL Kades, 'The American Role in Revising Japan's Imperial Constitution' (1989) 104(2) *Political Science Quarterly* 215; and Y Yamada, 'The New Japanese Constitution' (1955) 4(2) *International & Comparative Law Quarterly* 197.

[27] Proclamation Defining Terms for Japanese Surrender (Potsdam Declaration), 26 July 1945, Art 10.

[28] This Committee comprised: Matsumoto Joji (Chairman); Miyazawa Toshiyoshi (Professor, Tokyo University); Kiyomiya Shiro (Professor, Tohoku University); Kawamura Matasuke (Professor, Kyushu University); Ishiguro Takeshige (Chief Secretary, Privy Council); Narahashi Wataru (Director-General, Legislative Bureau); Irie Toshio (Deputy Director, Legislative Bureau); and Sato Tasuo (Councillor, Legislative Bureau). Acting as advisers were: Shimizu Toru (Vice-President of the Privy Council and member of the Imperial Academy); Minobe Tasuikichi (member of the Imperial Academy and Professor Emeritus, Tokyo University); and Nomura Junji (Professor Emeritus, Tokyo University).

break with the past. However, the viability and desirability of this notion was questioned by Matsumoto, when he met up with the Steering Committee on 22 February 1946:

> Is it better to retain our present constitution and then revise it in terms of the basic principles you have set forth? Or, is it better to begin with a completely new document?[29]

It would, he thought, be much better to maintain legal and political continuity than to effect a revolutionary break with the past. After some deliberation, Matsumoto agreed to discuss the matter with the Japanese Cabinet. On 26 February, the Cabinet met and decided to draft a government alternative based on the SCAP draft and submit it to MacArthur by 11 March. Matsumoto undertook to do this himself and assigned Sato Tatsuo (Director of the First Department of the Bureau of Legislation) and Irie Toshio (Vice Director-General of the Bureau of Legislation) to assist him. The Japanese draft would be crafted in the form of an amendment bill rather than as a new constitution. Entitled, the Bill for Revision of the Imperial Constitution, the final version was hammered out between March and June 1946 for formal submission to the Imperial Diet by the Emperor. After minor amendments by both the House of Peers and the House of Representatives, the bill was passed on 6 October 1946. It received the Emperor's assent on 3 November and came into effect six months later on 3 May 1947.

Japan's unconditional surrender on 2 September 1945 brought World War II to a close and sounded the death knell for all European colonial empires as well. Most of the territories that Japan had conquered and occupied up till World War II reverted to their former colonial sovereigns: India, Burma, Malaya, Singapore and the Borneo territories to Britain, Indo-China to the French, and the Dutch East Indies (Indonesia) to the Netherlands. Two other territories were also freed from Japanese domination: Taiwan (Formosa) and Korea. The stage for the return of these territories had been set at the Cairo Conference of November 1943, which had been convened to ascertain the Allied position against Japan. The meeting, which was attended by US President Roosevelt, UK Prime Minister Winston Churchill and Generalissimo Chiang Kai-shek of the Republic of China, resulted in the Cairo Declaration which, among other things, stated that

> all territories Japan has stolen from the Chinese, such as Manchuria, Formosa, and the Pescadores, shall be restored to the Republic of China. Japan will also be expelled from all other territories which she has taken by violence and greed. The aforesaid three great powers, mindful of the enslavement of the people of Korea, are determined that in due course Korea shall become free and independent.[30]

ii. Taiwan[31]

Shortly after the Japanese surrender on 2 September 1945, the Republic of China (ROC) established the Taiwan Provincial Government and Taiwan came under

---

[29] Ellerman Report of Conference between General Whitney and Dr Masomoto of 22 February 1946, available at <http://www.ndl.go.jp/constitution/e/shiryo/ 03/083a_e/083a_etx.html> (accessed 1 February 2010).

[30] Cairo Declaration dated 27 November 1943.

[31] See Jiunn-rong Yeh, 'Constitutional Reform and Democratization in Taiwan 1945–2000' in PCY Chow (ed), *Taiwan's Modernization in Global Perspective* (Westport, Conn: Praeger, 2002) 47.

Kuomintang (KMT) rule. In the meantime, the KMT were fighting a civil war against the Communist Party of China for control over all of China. By the end of the war, the KMT recapitulated and fled to Taiwan, where Chiang Kai-shek established a provisional ROC capital at Taipei. The People's Republic of China (PRC) was established on 31 October 1949.

From 1948, Taiwan was controlled by Chiang's KMT army and its successor governments. The western-style Constitution of the Republic of China[32] – which had been adopted in contentious circumstances by the National Assembly in 1946 – was replaced by a series of what were known as 'Temporary Provisions Effective During the Period of Communist Rebellion' in May 1948, which remained in force until their abolition in 1991.

The creation of the Supplementary Elections in 1972 was the first step in normalising the political process and structures which were tied to the increasingly unlikely prospect of KMT forces recapturing the mainland. The death of Chiang Kai-shek in 1975 and the election of his son Chiang Ching-Kuo to the Presidency in 1978[33] heralded an era of great political change. The ascent of Dr Lee Ting-hui – a native-born Taiwanese, who had been Chiang's Vice-President – to the country's top leadership post following Chiang's death in 1988 marked a major political milestone, and paved the way for many of the reforms that were initiated by Chiang shortly before his death.

Martial law, which had been imposed since 1948, was deemed necessary because the Chinese Communist Government had adopted a policy of using force to 'liberate Taiwan'. However, with the United States' decision to de-recognise Taiwan and to recognise the PRC, this policy was reversed. Indeed, in September 1981, Marshal Yeh Chien-ying, chairman of the NPC Standing Committee, made a nine-point proposal to Taiwan on unification.[34] On 15 July 1987, President Chiang Ching-Kuo lifted martial law and ended the ban on organising new political parties. This was the most significant legal and political development in the last 20 years.

With the lifting of martial law, many of the most draconian measures which had been used to deal with sedition and political protest were abandoned. Under martial law, non-military personnel were subject to military trial if they committed one of four types of crimes: sedition, espionage, theft, and the unauthorised sale or purchase of military equipment and supplies, or theft or damage of public communication equipment and facilities. In 1976, the scope of military trials was expanded to include nine serious offences such as homicide, robbery, murder consequent on rape or robbery, and kidnapping. This expansion was in response to popular demand for swift and severe punishment against a rising trend of violent crime on the island. While most trials in military courts followed the same procedure and rules as civilian courts, the most controversial aspect here was that judgment must be approved by a commanding

---

[32] On the evolution of this Constitution, see See Hungdah Chiu, 'Constitutional Development in the Republic of China in Taiwan' in S Tsang (ed), *In the Shadow of China: Political Developments in Taiwan Since 1949* (London: Hurst & Company, 1993) 17.

[33] Chiang Ching-Kuo served as Prime Minister under his father and shortly before the elder Chiang died. Even though he did not become President till 1978, Chiang wielded actual power in Taiwan during this period, partly through family and personal prestige, but also through his various positions in the army. It was a symbolic mark of respect that the younger Chiang did not take office till the official three years of mourning for the death of his father was over.

[34] See Chiu, above note 32, at 22–23.

officer before delivery.[35] The Temporary Provisions were also abolished in May 1991, although the President's emergency powers were retained in a modified form. A declaration of emergency now had to be submitted to the Legislative Yuan for confirmation within 10 days of its issuance, and if confirmation were withheld, the order would cease to be valid.[36]

While political parties had been banned since 1948, opposition politics were already stirring in the 1970s when opposition politicians began organising themselves into various campaign organisations which were amalgamated into a quasi-party called the *dangwai* (outside the KMT) group.[37] After several futile attempts to dissolve this group, the Government chose to tolerate its existence despite its illegal status. In September 1986, 112 *dangwai* leaders met and founded the Democratic Progressive Party (DPP), the first genuine opposition party in Taiwan, and won 12 out of the 288 seats in the Legislative Yuan. The lifting of martial law in July 1987 led to the mushrooming of new political parties. By March 1988, there were nine new political parties, with at least three others in the process of being organised.[38] The Civil Organisation Law, which authorises the formation of political parties, was amended in 1992 to vest the power to dissolve political parties in the Judicial Yuan rather than the Executive Yuan which previously possessed this authority.

On 23 January 1989, President Lee Teng-hui promulgated the Civic Organisation Law which was adopted by the Legislative Yuan. Among its provisions included rules for the formation of new political parties. Eleven days later, the Election and Recall Law was revised and many restrictions on campaign activities were lifted. In the meantime, steps were taken to rectify the increasingly anachronistic situation in Taiwan's legislative and executive bodies. In February that year, President Lee Teng-hui promulgated a law adopted by the Legislative Yuan to allow for the voluntary retirement of those members of the three elective bodies – the Legislative Yuan, the Control Yuan and the National Assembly – who were formerly elected either on the Chinese mainland in 1948 or on Taiwan in 1969. In June 1990, the Grand Council of Justices of the Judicial Yuan ruled that all members of the three elective bodies elected in 1948 and 1969 must resign their offices by 31 December 1991 and that new elections must be held for these bodies. From 1 January 1992, all members of the National Assembly, the Legislative Yuan and the Control Yuan were periodically elected.[39]

In December 1992, Taiwanese voters went to the polls to elect members to the Legislative Yuan in what has been described as 'the most democratic election in the history of any Chinese society'.[40] For the first time since 1948, the entire membership of the Legislative Yuan was being elected by the people of island of Taiwan.

[35] Ibid at 26–27.

[36] Ibid at 25.

[37] See Lu Ya-li, 'Political Developments in the Republic of China' in TW Robinson (ed), *Democracy and Development in East Asia: Taiwan, South Korea and the Philippines* (Washington, DC: The AEI Press, 1991) at 37.

[38] See JF Copper, *Taiwan's Recent Elections: Fulfilling the Democratic Promise* (Maryland: School of Law, University of Maryland Occasional Papers/Reprints Series in Contemporary Asian Studies, 1990) at 21. The nine new parties were: the China Liberty Party, the Democratic Liberty Party, the Labour Party, the China Democratic Justice Party, the China People's Party, the Neo-Socialist Party, the United Democratic Party, the Chinese Republican Party and the China Unification Party. The three other parties being formed were the China Patriotic Party, the Women's Party and the Farmers' Party.

[39] See Hungdah Chiu, above n 33, at 29.

[40] See AJ Nathan, 'The Legislative Yuan Elections in Taiwan' (1993) XXXIII *Asian Survey* 424.

iii The Korean Peninsula[41]

Between 1910 and 1945, Korea was colonised by the Japanese. After Japan surrendered, the Korean peninsula was divided into two at the 38th parallel north in accordance with a United Nations agreement giving control of the north to the Soviet Union and control over the south to the United States of America. With the onset of the Cold War, the Soviets and the Americans could not agree on how to implement their Joint Trusteeship over Korea and this led to the establishment of two separate governments in 1948; one for each half, but both claiming to be the true legitimate government for the whole. These territories eventually became North Korea and South Korea respectively, following the end of the Korean War.

a. South Korea

In the years that followed, South Korea underwent numerous constitutional changes, alternating between democratic and authoritarian governments. The First Republic was established in 1948 with a Constitution promulgated by the National Assembly. Syngman Rhee was elected the President of South Korea following the general election of 10 May 1948. Although Rhee started his tenure in relatively democratic fashion, he turned increasingly autocratic in his last years in power. In 1960, a student revolt – known as the April Revolution – ended Rhee's rule and led to a revision of the 1948 Constitution and to the creation of the short-lived Second Republic under which Yun Po Sun was elected President.

On 16 May 1961, General Park Chung-hee staged a successful military coup in a bid to curb the increasingly vocal dissidents, fearing the country would become communist. Park ruled South Korea with an iron fist from 1961 to 1979, narrowly winning elections in 1963, 1967 and 1971. After winning the 1971 election, Park declared a state of emergency, and in October 1972 declared a state of martial law and dissolved the National Assembly. In November 1972, a new Constitution – known as the Yusin Constitution (literally, the 'Restoration Constitution') – was promulgated. This gave Park complete control over Parliament and allowed him to promulgate a series of emergency decrees under which hundreds of opponents and dissidents were jailed.

Park's assassination in 1979 sparked off a wave of protests from university students, civil society groups and trade unions. This prompted General Chun Doo-hwan to stage a coup on 12 December 1979 and clamp down on the dissidents. In May 1980, a confrontation broke out between students of Chonnam National University in Gwangju city and government troops. In a citywide riot that lasted nine days, over 200 persons were killed by government troops. Over the next few years, public outrage over the killings in Gwangju, coupled with pent-up frustrations over Chun's autocratic rule, led to the June Democracy Movement in 1987, with mass marches of protest throughout the country. The protests were sparked by a series of incidents, not least of which was Chun's naming of Roh Tae Woo as presidential candidate of the ruling Democratic Justice Party. Roh immediately made a conciliatory gesture by promising a wide range of political and constitutional reforms. In the ensuing elections, Roh won narrowly

---

[41] See generally, Han-Key Lee, 'Constitutional Developments in South Korea' (1974) 4 *Hong Kong Law Journal* 41.

against Kim Young-Sam and Kim Dae-jung (both of whom became presidents after Roh).

The original 1948 Constitution was based on the Weimar Constitution under which the President was indirectly elected. It was amended nine times and almost fully rewritten five times – the last time in 1987 – but it was never abandoned. Legal continuity was never broken. Successive regimes have been content to rely on the 1948 document which was amended according to the democratic or authoritarian proclivities of the President in power.

b. North Korea[42]

The northern half of Korea was inaugurated as the Democratic People's Republic of Korea (DPRK) in 1948 with a Constitution modelled, not surprisingly, on that of the 1936 Constitution of the USSR. This Constitution was adopted at the First Supreme People's Assembly (SPA) in September 1948 and consisted of 10 Chapters and 104 Articles.[43] It remained in force with very few amendments till 1972. Under the 1948 Constitution, the SPA was the highest organ of state, akin to the Supreme Soviet, and like its Soviet counterpart, a smaller group of individuals, known as the Presidium of the SPA, was responsible for initiating action and policymaking.[44]

Through Soviet patronage, Kim Il Sung – a communist leader, guerilla commander and founder of the Korean People's Army – rose to become Prime Minister of North Korea on 9 September 1948 when the DPRK was proclaimed. On 12 October 1948, the Soviet Union recognised the DPRK as the only legitimate government on the Korean peninsula. By 1949, Kim's Worker's Party of Korea (WPK) had consolidated its power throughout North Korea, and Kim began instituting a system of education and propaganda that would edify himself and create a cult of personality that is the hallmark of modern North Korea.

In 1955, Kim introduced *Juche* as state ideology. Though not a religion, it is implemented with religious fervour. *Juche* is heavily influenced by Marxist-Leninist ideology as well as Confucianism.[45] At its core, *Juche* advocates autonomy and self-reliance in all spheres of national life, including foreign affairs and the economy. Kim had initially formulated *Juche* as a response to his party colleagues who favoured adopting a Soviet-style of government and production. In 1972, when a new Constitution was enacted, *Juche* was declared to be North Korea's official state ideology.

The 1948 Constitution was replaced by a new constitution in 1972, especially since the North Korean leadership was now convinced that their country had entered the 'socialist era' and many aspects of the 1948 Constitution, which was designed for the 'bourgeois democratic' stage of its history, were now obsolete.[46] The main aim of

---

[42] See generally, Dae-Kyu Yoon, 'The Constitution of North Korea: Its Changes and Implications' (2003–2004) 27 *Fordham International Law Journal* 1289.

[43] Ibid at 1292.

[44] Ibid at 1293.

[45] See C Hale, 'Multifunctional Juche: A Study of the Changing Dynamic Between Juche and the State Constitution in North Korea' (2002) *Korea Journal* 283; see also P French, *North Korea: The Paranoid Peninsula – A Modern History*, 2nd edn (London: Zed Books, 2007), especially ch 2, 'The Juche State: Political Theory in North Korea'.

[46] Chong-Sik Lee, 'The 1972 Constitution and Top Communist Leaders' in Dae-Sook Suh and Chae-Jin Lee (eds), *Political Leadership in Korea* (Washington, DC: University of Washington Press, 1976) 192.

the new constitution was legally to protect the socialist system and the dictatorship of the proletariat, as well as 'to bring the goals and structure of the state into consonance with those of the Workers' Party of Korea (WPK)'.[47] Most significantly, the new constitution legally reinforced the relationship between party and state. As Korean specialist Professor Chong-Sik Lee put it:

> One of the first items the new constitution deals with is the relationship between the party and the state. Article 4 states that 'the DPRK is guided in its activity by the *chuch'e* [*juche*] (self-identity) idea of the Workers' Party of Korea, which is a creative application of Marxism-Leninism to our country's reality.' The implication here is that the DPRK and the WPK are not only inseparable, but that a hierarchical relationship exists, the party being superior to the state. . . .
>
> With the relationship between the party and state redefined, the North Korean leaders overhauled the political structure of the DPRK in order that the structure of authority would conform to the reality of power distribution. In doing so, the myth of legislative supremacy embodied in the old constitution was discarded, the supreme authority of the leader legitimized, and the enormous power of the inner circle of the ruling elite institutionalized. These purposes were attained by (1) the creation of a presidency, (2) the establishment of the Central People's Committee, and (3) the emasculation of the Supreme People's Assembly and its Presidium.[48]

The Constitution was significantly amended again in 1992. In the intervening two decades communism had fallen, and China, North Korea's long-time ally and supporter, was moving towards a capitalist economy. The most important development in this new constitution was the creation of the National Defence Commission (NDC) as a separate constitutional organ. Hitherto, the NDC had been a subcommittee of the Central People's Committee. As a result, the top military leadership was separated from the political leadership. At the same time, the new Article 37 evinced a more open policy towards foreign investments. Two years after the constitution was amended, Kim Il Sung died and was succeeded by his son, Kim Jong Il.[49]

A new Constitution was promulgated in 1998. It was based on the 1992 Constitution but 'was tailor-made by Kim Jong Il and designed to suit his personality and method of rule'.[50] Kim Jong Il, anxious that the leadership mantle he inherited from his father lacked legitimacy, capitalised on his late father's charismatic leadership by attributing the founding of North Korea to him and elevating him to the position of Eternal President.[51] This Constitution was amended again in 2009 and 2012, but the changes were more hortatory and ideological rather than real.[52] As Professor Dae-Kyu Yoon observed:

> The Constitution of North Korea is no more than a character of the law of North Korea. In North Korea, where the rule of law does not govern, but the directives and words of leaders and administrative directives do, legal grounds for State actions are not sought for their justification. Although the Constitution is the highest law in form, it functions merely as a

---

[47] Ibid at 193.

[48] Ibid at 194–95. On the 1972 Constitution, see Chin Kim and TG Kearley, 'The 1972 Socialist Constitution of North Korea' (1976) 11 *Texas International Law Journal* 113.

[49] See Dae-Kyu Yoon, above n 42, at 1298–1300.

[50] Ibid at 1300.

[51] Ibid at 1300–01.

[52] See DC Zook, 'Reforming North Korea: Law, Politics and the Market Economy' (2012) 48 *Stanford Journal of International Law* 131, at 137–46.

tool of propaganda. In other words, the Constitution in North Korea exists not for the protection of citizens' rights and interests, but merely as a tool to showcase the superiority of the State's system to its citizens and outside observers alike.[53]

C. British Devolution

The British transfer of power from the metropolis to the colonies is typically effected through a number of legal measures. The first step is a negotiated settlement between Britain and the leaders of the erstwhile colony. This is usually hammered out through a series of constitutional conferences.[54] The British were, according to Dennis Austin, 'addicted to committees and conferences' that were mainly attended by 'politicians, civil servants, academics, lawyers and constitutional advisers, not by business men or financiers – only, at best, economists'.[55] Discussions centred around 'constitutional devices, minority safeguards (or what passed for safeguards), electoral procedures, party relations, and the distribution of regional powers – the stuff of lawyers' chambers and party headquarters, not the board room'.[56] Consequently, this probably accounts for the type of constitutions eventually drafted: strict, legal documents, painstakingly enumerating the intricate rules and arrangements.

Once the draft constitution is ready, the second phase is activated. The British Parliament will enact legislation to legally transfer sovereignty over the territory to the new government, alongside an Order in Council which then becomes the new state's constitution. The form of government adopted by the former colonies is typically modelled on the Westminster constitutional model.[57] This pattern can be discerned by an examination of the creation of the Constitutions of Burma, India, Pakistan, Ceylon, Malaysia, Singapore and Brunei. Lapping offers a useful glimpse into the process of power transfer:

B Lapping, *End of Empire* (New York: St Martin's Press, 1985) 1

The end was generally the same. At teatime or thereabouts, in any case conveniently before sundowner time or the need to change for dinner, the flag on the flagpost at Government House was lowered for the last time. For fifty, or a hundred, or even in the case of The Gambia more than three hundred years – since the place had become a British colony – the flag had been lowered at this hour every day. A sergeant-major in the local regiment shouted the order. A soldier paid out the rope hand over hand, brought the flag down, folded it neatly and gave it to the sergeant-major, who gave it to the officer in charge, who gave it to

---

[53]   Dae-Kyu Yoon, above n 42, at 1304.

[54]   For a description of this process, see Yash P Ghai, 'Constitution Making and Decolonisation' in Yash P Ghai (ed), *Law, Government and Politics in the Pacific Island States* (Suva: University of the South Pacific, Institute of Pacific Studies, 1988) at 9. See also D Austin, 'The Transfer of Power: Why and How?' in WH Morris-Jones and G Fischer (eds), *Decolonisation and After: The British and French Experience* (London: Frank Cass, 1980) at 3ff.

[55]   See Austin, above n 54, at 4.

[56]   Ibid.

[57]   See generally, SA de Smith, 'Westminster's Export Models: The Legal Framework of Responsible Government' (1961–63) 1 *Journal of Commonwealth and Political Studies* 2; SA de Smith, *The New Commonwealth and Its Constitutions* (London: Stevens & Sons, 1964); and W Dale, 'The Making and Remaking of Commonwealth Constitutions' (1993) 42 *International and Comparative Law Quarterly* 67.

the Governor, who gave it to the British Sovereign's representative. At the independence ceremony which effectively marked the end of the British Empire – in 1980 in Southern Rhodesia (about to become Zimbabwe) – the Queen's representative was her son, Charles, the Prince of Wales. He handed the neatly folded flag to his aide-de-camp, and immediately turned away, to lead the guests to the garden party.

The garden party was generally the same. It was marked by absences. In the battle for succession, someone always had to lose and the loser often chose not to come to the party . . .

No generalisation covers all the transfers of power. In Palestine in 1948 and Aden in 1967, the British lost control and scuttled to the docks and the airport . . .

. . . Some years before independence the Governor of each colony, with the approval of Westminster, brought a few of 'the better sort of natives' into Legco. Legco (short for legislative council) was to evolve in most colonies into the local parliament – not elected at first, for that would have brought in 'agitators'; no, Legco began as the Governor's sounding board to which he appointed a few selected local whites, the chairmen of the harbour board, the railway company, the chamber of commerce, then a few browns or blacks who were known to be 'responsible'. Where the British established colonies, others flocked in, finding that the enforcement of law made for good business. These others, Chinese in Singapore and Penang, Hindus in Madras and Calcutta, Arabs in Aden and Zanzibar, were soon sending their children to English schools and universities. From this English-educated group the Governor chose a lawyer or two or a wealthy trader to join the legislative council. They helped keep him informed about the concerns of the merchant classes. In Calcutta the first Indians joined the Governor-General's Legco in 1858. In Accra the first Gold Coast African joined in 1861. These were called the 'unofficials' to distinguish them from the dominant group, the 'officials' – the Chief Secretary, the Attorney-General, the Financial Secretary – who mostly found attending Legco a bore because they hated making speeches, which they regarded as a politician's job. In Legco the officials announced what would happen and the unofficials were supposed to express their views and acquiesce.

Above Legco was Exco (short for executive council), the Governor's board of management. Here none but officials could sit. In the ports that were Britain's original and most important colonies, laws concerning trade had to be enforced and Exco was long thought to have responsibilities which neither natives nor British traders could share. The arrival of the first native on Exco – in India in 1909 – marks the beginning of the End of Empire.

The British, in the twilight years of their Empire, were arrogant about many things. Above all they believed that the British system of government was the best in the world. At the apex was the constitutional monarch, nominally in charge, actually impotent: what could be cleverer than that? One step down came the party system, by means of which governments willingly alternated at elections; below that was the civil service, an intellectual and administrative elite, prepared to obey the orders of mostly less clever politicians. Learning to run such a system, like learning to play cricket, took time. Even the Americans, when, in writing their constitution, they tried to copy it, were misled by a Frenchman into getting it wrong. So the British believed they had a duty to teach the colonised peoples not only the complicated rules but also the tricks by which the rules could be bent.

From the date a colony began its slow progress towards 'internal self-government' or 'Dominion status within the Commonwealth' (euphemisms by means of which the British deceived themselves that full independence would not be demanded), the governor and his colleagues behaved as though the last years of British rule were a university course in the British constitution for clever natives. A senior British official might say, 'That chap Eric Williams' (in Trinidad), or 'That chap Julius Nyerere' (in Tanganyika), 'he really understands the principles of British constitutional government better than I do'. Such a sentence would be intended as the sincere praise of a proud teacher, neither patronising nor impertinent.

This education in the Westminster method was willingly administered to willing pupils. It would have been impossible to run the Empire without local co-operation. Consent, a far more efficient way to keep order than coercion, required the active help of the right sort of natives at all levels. Anyway, not enough Britons could be found to do all the administrative jobs, especially the lowlier ones . . .

Many colonial administrators had honourable and convincing reasons for opposing Britain's transfer of power to the nationalist leaders of its colonies. They had become closely attached to the people they governed, the rural peasants and up-country headmen and chiefs. These sturdy people generally grew their countries' food and often felt threatened by the lawyers and journalists, the 'pushy natives', who clustered around the centres of British power and demanded its removal. The rural district commissioner was often convinced that agitators, fuelled with alien ideas from the United States or Ireland or Soviet Russia, did not represent his tribe or region; they were on the make; their claims to speak for a united national will, determined to be rid of the British, were spurious. The district commissioner knew that the sensible majority of the population would not vote for them – his own tribes, when he asked them, always told him so. And of course his tribes would, wouldn't they? They knew what he wanted to hear. Such British officials were repeatedly surprised when radical, anti-nationalist leaders proved able to win elections.

The man on whom the British had set their hopes often lost the election. Onn bin Ja'afar in Malaya, Dr JB Danquah in the Gold Coast, Joshua Nkomo in Rhodesia were each displaced by independence leaders – Tunku Abdul Rahman, Kwame Nkrumah, Robert Mugabe – whom the British had before their election victories considered thoroughly unsuitable. But having laid down the rules of the game the British accepted the results, patiently transferring their educational and administrative help to the winner. If he was prepared to learn – to make the sudden transition from nationalist agitator and speech-maker to head of a complex bureaucratic machine – they gave him all the support they could.

Sometimes this help went further than the British or the nationalist leaders would like to admit. When in 1959 Lee Kuan Yew was about to fight an election in Singapore as leader of the People's Action Party, he had a private meeting with Alan Lennox-Boyd, the Colonial Secretary, at Chequers, the British Prime Minister's country home. Lee and Lennox-Boyd reached an understanding. The British Government would arrest several leading Communists in Singapore, who were Lee's allies in the election campaign; Lee would make speeches bitterly attacking this illiberal, imperialist action; but once he had won the election and released his former allies, he would find grounds to imprison them again. And so he did. In 1962, when Dr Hastings Kamuzu Banda was on the way to assuming power in Nyasaland, his leading radical supporter, Henry Chipembere, was arrested for sedition – on the grounds that he had made bloodthirstily threatening remarks about an English member of the legislative council. It was a case where the Governor, Sir Glyn Jones, could have persuaded his Attorney-General that a prosecution was against the interests of the state. But Dr Banda assured the Governor that he approved of Chipembere's imprisonment. Thus Banda, like Lee, was helped to purge an extremist from his party. Sir Charles Arden-Clarke's partisanship for Kwame Nkrumah in the Gold Coast shows equally strikingly how, once the winner had demonstrated that he had majority support, the Governor would bend the rules to back him. It was all part of the process of graceful handover.

i. Burma[58]

Britain had acquired Burma in parts between 1826 and 1886. Constitutional development of Burma ran parallel to that of India. In 1923 Burma was ruled as a dyarchy,[59] and in 1935–37 it received semi-responsible government under which the Governor continued to have reserve powers although the predominantly Burmese Cabinet was now responsible to an elected parliament.[60] Of Britain's Asian colonies, Burma and Ceylon (now Sri Lanka) led the push for full self-government.

The Burmese House of Representatives passed a motion on 23 February 1940 calling for the immediate recognition of Burma 'as an independent nation entitled to frame its own constitution'.[61] British Prime Minister Winston Churchill was reluctant to grant self-government to the colonies and refused to give Burma greater autonomy. He suggested granting Burma Dominion status, but not before the War's end. The Japanese invasion of Burma provided just the opportunity young Burmese anti-British intellectuals needed. Aung Sang and his comrades joined the Japanese and marched into Burma with a 'Burma Independence Army'.

Realising that the Japanese-backed independence only meant the replacement of one colonial master with another, Aung San and his followers began negotiations with the British Secret Service to attack the Japanese in order to secure full independence for Burma. This gave the Burmese another opportunity to push Britain for an independence deadline. Churchill remained unmoved. Instead, Lord Mountbatten, High Commander for Southeast Asia, assumed the initiative as he wanted Burmese support to help reconquer Burma, which entailed recognising Aung San's Burma National Army as an Allied Force under British high command. A Rangoon victory in June 1945 saw Aung San's Burma National Army march in as independent troops under the Burmese flag.[62] This scuttled the British decolonisation timetable, which had to be dramatically accelerated.

Aung San's Anti-Fascist People's Freedom League (AFPFL) rejected the conditions for independence stipulated by the May 1945 British White Paper on Burma. The proposed scheme provided that the Governor would be in control for the first three years, and thereafter the Constitution of 1935–37 would come into force. Thereafter, the Burmese could work out a new constitution for complete self-government within the British Commonwealth. Aung San instead demanded the election of a national constitutional assembly.[63] The Labour Government sped up negotiations and the new British Governor Sir Hubert Rance reorganised the Executive Council, making Aung San second-in-command with control over defence and foreign policy. In November 1946, the Burmese issued an ultimatum: elections for a constitutional assembly by

---

[58] See generally, FN Trager, *Burma From Kingdom to Republic: A Historical and Political Analysis* (London: Pall Mall Press, 1966); JF Cady, *Political Institutions of Old Burma* (Ithaca, NY: Cornell Southeast Asia Program, 1954); JF Cady, *A History of Modern Burma* (Ithaca, NY: Cornell University Press, 1958); and Maung Maung, *Burma's Constitution*, 2nd edn (The Hague: Martinus Nijhoff, 1961).

[59] A 'dyarchy' refers to a system of dual rule under which government functions are shared between two bodies. It was introduced into India under the Government of India Act 1919 and government functions divided between the provincial legislatures and the Governor's executive council.

[60] Albertini, above n 15, at 196.

[61] Ibid at 197.

[62] Ibid at 201.

[63] Ibid at 203.

April and the granting of full independence to Burma within a year.[64] Elections for the constituent assembly were held in April 1947 and almost all the seats were won by Aung San's AFPFL. When the Assembly convened, Aung San presented his draft constitution for deliberation. However, he never saw the constitution adopted, for he was assassinated during the constitutional deliberations on 19 July 1947. His successor, U Nu, signed the independence treaty with Clement Attlee in October 1947. On 4 January 1948, Burma was proclaimed independent.

The new constitution provided for a republican form of government with three autonomous States: Shan, Kachin and Karenni State. The legislature was bicameral – with a Chamber of Deputies and a Chamber of Nationalities – which would, in a joint session, elect the President. Typically under the Westminster model, the Prime Minister was accorded extensive powers. The Chief Justice and Supreme Court judges were appointed by the President, with Parliament's approval.

ii. Ceylon[65]

The British occupied the island of Ceylon, located at the southern tip of the Indian sub-continent, as a colony from 1796. In 1909, constitutional development began with a partially-elected legislature, but it was only in 1920 that the number of elected representatives outnumbered official nominees. In 1931, universal suffrage was introduced, and the Ceylon National Congress party was founded to agitate for greater autonomy from British control. During the colonial period, large numbers of Tamil Indians from the south of India were brought in by British indentured labourers to work on the productive and lucrative tea estates in the north-eastern part of the island. Before long, the Tamils made up 10 per cent of the island's population. This demographic change sowed the seeds for later ethnic discord between the Tamils and the Sinhalese majority.

The key protagonists in the pro-independence movement came from two distinct camps: the first group of 'constitutionalists', who believed in working with the British for an eventual devolution of power; and the second group, made up of radical groups such as the Colombo Youth League, the Labour Movement of Goonasinghe and the Jaffna Youth Congress. For obvious reasons, the British preferred working more closely with the constitutionalists, led by Don Stephen Senanayake (1884–1952). Negotiations led first to a Constitution crafted by the Donoughmore Commission (1931–47); and then another Constitution drafted in accordance with the Soulbury Commission's recommendations (1944). This Constitution was drafted by the Board of Ministers headed by Senanayake, and had the benefit of having as its key adviser the distinguished British constitutional law scholar, Sir Ivor Jennings.

During World War II, Ceylon was a frontline British base and was used by Lord Louis Mountbatten as the headquarters of his eastern theatre of operations. This fur-

---

[64] Ibid at 204.

[65] An excellent introduction to the legal history of Ceylon is Tambyah Nadaraja, *The Legal System of Ceylon in Its Historical Setting* (Lieden: EJ Brill, 1972). The history of its constitutional development is comprehensively dealt with in LJM Cooray, *Reflections on the Constitution and the Constituent Assembly: An Analysis of the Law, the Underlying Problems, and Concepts of the Constitution, 1796–1971, with Special Reference to 1948–1971 and the Constituent Assembly of Sri Lanka* (Colombo: Hansa Publishers, 1971). See also I Jennings and HW Tambiah, *The Dominion of Ceylon: The Development of its Laws and Constitution* (London: Stevens & Sons, 1952).

ther cemented ties between the British and Senanayake's faction which eventually formed itself into the United National Party in 1946, the same year the British granted Ceylon Dominion status.[66] Independence was granted to Ceylon on 4 February 1948 through the passage of the Ceylon Independence Act 1947[67] along with the Ceylon (Constitution and Independence) Orders in Council 1947,[68] and Senanayake became the first Prime Minister of Ceylon.

iii. India

One of the first British colonies in Asia to be granted independence was India.[69] It was also the largest of all Asian states to achieve independence in the aftermath of World War II. In 1946, British Prime Minister Clement Attlee dispatched a Cabinet Mission to India with the object of formulating plans for India's independence under Dominion status and the transfer of powers from Britain to India. Among the Mission's purposes was to establish a constituent body to draft a new constitution for India. Talks were held between the British team and representatives of the two largest political parties in India: the Indian National Congress and the All India Muslim League. These two political parties had different aspirations for themselves and for India, and it was in large part due to the fear of a Hindu-dominated central Indian government that ultimately led to partition and the creation of Pakistan. The Cabinet Mission – also known as the Cripps Mission after its leader, Sir Stafford Cripps – arrived on 23 March 1946, and by 16 May the Plan was announced. Among other things, a Constituent Assembly would be created to begin work on the drafting of a new constitution.

The Assembly comprised 389 members of whom 292 were drawn from the British Indian Provinces; 93 from the Princely States; and four from the Chief Commissioner's Provinces. The number of members was reduced in June 1947 when the plan to partition India and create the Islamic state of Pakistan was put in effect.[70] A separate Constituent Assembly was thus established for Pakistan and a number of representatives ceased to be members of the Indian Assembly, thus reducing membership to 299.

---

[66] See Ceylon Constitution Order in Council 1946.

[67] 11 Geo 6, ch 7.

[68] These effectively amended the Ceylon Constitution Order in Council 1946.

[69] The brief account of India draws variously on the numerous accounts on the drafting of the Indian Constitution and on the work of the Constituent Assembly. Notable among these works are: A Gledhill, *The Republic of India: The Development of Its Laws and Constitution* (London: Stevens & Sons, 1951); A Granville, *The Indian Constitution: Cornerstone of a Nation* (Bombay: Oxford University Press, 1972); *The Constituent Assembly Debates: Official Reports* (50 vols) (Delhi: Manager of Publications, 1946); Kartikeswar Patra, *History and Debates of the Constituent Assembly of India* (New Delhi: Vikas Publishing House, 1998); Shibani Kinkar Chaube, *The Making and Working of the Indian Constitution* (New Delhi: National Book Trust, 2009); BM Gandhi (ed), *VD Kulshrestha's Landmarks in Indian Legal and Constitutional History*, 6th edn (Lucknow: Eastern Book Company, 1989); M Rama Jois, *Legal and Constitutional History of India*, 2 vols (Bombay: NM Tripathi, 1984); A Chandra Banerjee, *The Constitutional History of India*, 3 vols (Delhi: Macmillan, 1977); A Chandra Banerjee, *The Making of the Indian Constitution, 1939–1947* (Calcutta: A Mukkerjee, 1948); Sri Ram Sharma, *Constitutional History of India*, 3rd rev edn (Bombay: Orient Longman, 1974); B Shiva Rao et al, *The Framing of India's Constitution: A Study* (New Delhi: Indian Institute of Public Administration, 1968); Vidya Dhar Mahajan, *Constitutional History of India*, 7th edn (Delhi: S Chand, 1967); B Shiva Rao (ed), *India's Constitution in the Making* (Bombay: Allied Publishers, 1963); Sri Ram Sharma, *A Constitutional History of India: 1765–1954*, 2nd edn (Bombay: Macmillan, 1955); and N Chandra Roy, *Towards Framing the Constitution of India* (Calcutta: BG Printers & Publishers, 1947).

[70] See Indian Independence Act, 10 & 11 Geo VI, c 30.

Devolution of power was legally executed through the Indian Independence Act 1947. Under this Act, two independent Dominions – India and Pakistan – were created with effect from 15 August 1947.[71] With the creation of the two new territories, the British Government would have no further 'responsibility as respects the government of any of the territories which . . . were included in British India'.[72] More significantly, the legislative powers of each Dominion were to be exercised by the Constituent Assembly of that Dominion in the first instance.[73]

The Constituent Assembly elected many of the most prominent nationalist leaders of India at that time: Jawaharlal Nehru (later first Prime Minister of India), C Rajagopalachari, Rajedra Prasad, Sardar Vallabhbhai, Malaulana Abul Kala Azad, SP Mukherjee, Nalini Rajan Ghosh. Sachidanand Sinha, the oldest and most senior legislator in India, was elected temporary chairman of the Assembly.[74] It met for the first time on 9 December 1946 at the Central Hall of Parliament House. From the outset, members of the Assembly were conscious of the unique circumstances in which they found themselves. Not only was there no precedent in British constitutional law for the creation of a Constituent Assembly, but the Indian Independence Act 1947 also seemed vague as to its purposes. On 21 August 1947, the Assembly appointed the Committee on the Functions of the Constituent Assembly under the Indian Independence Act to determine the proper function of the Assembly. The Committee, chaired by Shri GV Mavalankar, outlined two functions of the Assembly:

(a) to continue and complete the work of constitution making; and
(b) to function as the Dominion legislature until a legislature under the new constitution came into being.

On 15 August 1947, with India becoming independent, the Constituent Assembly became India's legislature. A Drafting Committee[75] was appointed on 29 August 1947, with the noted jurist Dr BR Ambedkar as its Chairman, and it set about preparing a draft to be submitted to the Assembly by 4 November 1947. After the draft was submitted, the Assembly met for sessions for 166 days over almost three years before accepting the draft. Of these, 114 days were spent considering the draft constitution. All sessions were open to the public. On 24 January 1950, the members of the Assembly signed two handwritten copies of the constitution (in Hindi and in English). It became the Constitution of India two days later.

The drafting of India's Constitution was, like that of the United States, an elitist affair even though there was widespread representation and consultation. The Constituent Assembly adopted the parliamentary form of government almost unanimously, believing that 'it promised strength, cohesive action and leadership; yet at the same time it feared Executive power'.[76]

---

[71] Ibid, s 1.
[72] Ibid, s 7(1).
[73] Ibid, s 8(1).
[74] He was replaced by Dr Rajendra Prasad as permanent chairman just two days later. Dr Prasad later became the first President of India.
[75] Members of this Drafting Committee were: Shri Alladi Krishnaswami Ayyar, Shri N Goplaswami Ayyangar, Shri KM Munshi, Saiyid Mohd Saadulla, Sir BL Mitter, Shri DP Khiatan and Dr BR Ambedkar.
[76] See G Austin, *The Indian Constitution: Cornerstone of a Nation* (Bombay: Oxford University Press, 1972) at 126.

India's post-independence Constitution has been successful, despite Indira Gandhi's Emergency Rule from 1975 to 1977. She managed regular elections, and cultivated a strong, independent judiciary. In that sense, India's post-colonial history has been atypical. However, her multi-party, liberal democratic, parliamentary constitution failed to curb the ethnic and political violence that has marred so much of Indian history, even in modern times. Mohandas (Mahatma) Gandhi, founder of modern India and chief architect of its independence movement, was assassinated, as was first Prime Minister Jawaharlal Nehru's daughter, Indira Gandhi herself, who was Prime Minister after him. Her son, Rajiv Gandhi, who succeeded her to the Prime Ministership, was also assassinated in 1991. Between its enactment in 1950 and 2010, the Constitution was amended 94 times, and except during the Emergency of 1975 to 1977, it was never in any danger of being abandoned or replaced.

iv. Pakistan[77]

Originally, the United Kingdom had hoped to relinquish control over British India as a single entity, but the fear of Hindu domination led Mohammed Ali Jinnah and his Muslim League to agitate for a separate Islamic state. By the time the British were ready to depart from India, they realised that the differences between Jinnah and Nehru were irreconcilable, and they agreed to group the Muslim-dominated provinces into two chunks of territories and grant them independence as Pakistan. This was effected by the Indian Independence Act which also granted independence to India. The Act provided for a separate Constituent Assembly to be convened for Pakistan, and its inaugural session took place in Karachi from 10–14 August 1947. There, Jinnah was elected President of the Assembly. Like the Constituent Assembly in India, the Pakistani Constituent Assembly also served as Pakistan's legislature. Since Jinnah – who assumed the post of Governor-General of Pakistan upon the state's independence – was convinced that the drafting of a constitution would take some time, the old Government of India Act 1935 was modified to suit Pakistan's new status and operated as its interim constitution.[78] Pakistan would be a federation comprising the four provinces of East Bengal, West Punjab, Sindh and North-West Frontier Province; Baluchistan; and such Indian states that would accede to the federation.

Jinnah's death on 11 September 1948, just a year after Pakistan's independence, robbed her of a major driving and stabilising force. Jinnah was succeeded by Sir Khawaja Nazimuddin, although the reins of power were now held by his chosen Prime Minister Liaquat Ali Khan. It was nine years before the Constituent Assembly completed its work and produced the first post-independence constitution for Pakistan, the short-lived 1956 Constitution which came into force on 23 March 1956.[79]

---

[77] For a concise and readable account of Pakistan's post-war constitutional and political development, see David Taylor, 'Parties, Elections and Democracy in Pakistan' (1992) 30 *Journal of Commonwealth and Comparative Politics* pp 96–115; and Ardath W Burks, 'Constitution-Making in Pakistan' (1954) 69(4) *Political Science Quarterly* 541–564. The most comprehensive and authoritative treatment of Pakistan's constitutional history is Hamid Khan's monumental, *Constitutional and Political History of Pakistan* (Karachi: Oxford University Press, 2001).

[78] See Pakistan (Provisional Constitution) Order, 1947.

[79] The 1956 Constitution was suspended following the October 1958 coup that brought President Iskander Mirza to power. Mirza imposed martial law and appointed General Muhammad Ayub Khan as Chief Martial Law Administrator.

v. Malaysia, Singapore and Brunei

The British acquired Singapore, Malaysia and Brunei in parts over many years, hence their complex constitutional histories. The earliest of these acquisitions were the Straits Settlements, comprising the island of Penang and Singapore and the ancient coastal trading state of Malacca. Next came the Federated and Unfederated Malay States, and North Borneo (comprising Sabah, Sarawak and Brunei). The Japanese Occupation (1942–45) brought out latent anti-colonial sentiments among the people of Malaya and Singapore, though not as virulently as in India or Burma. The British War Office and Colonial Office had mapped out the region's future, with Singapore as the headquarters of a Dominion territory comprising Malaya, North Borneo and Singapore. This involved the complete reorganisation of British possessions in the region. The British North Borneo Company would give up its rights over North Borneo. A new Crown Colony of North Borneo was created by amalgamating British North Borneo with Labuan. Raja Charles Brooke would cede his jurisdiction over Sarawak, which would become a Crown Colony. The Straits Settlements of Penang, Malacca and Singapore were disbanded, and Singapore became a separate Crown Colony on its own. Penang and Malacca would then be amalgamated with the Federated and Unfederated Malay States to form a new Malayan Union.

Because of Malay opposition, the Malayan Union scheme never really took off. On 1 February 1948, the whole scheme was revoked and replaced by the Federation of Malaya Order-in-Council 1948,[80] establishing the new Federation of Malaya. To do this, the British negotiated new agreements with the Malay Rulers. The new scheme established a federation consisting of the Malay States, Malacca and Penang, with a strong central government. The 1948 Agreement's preamble stated that the UK Government and the Rulers would work towards eventual self-government. In July 1955, elections for 52 seats on the new Federal Legislative Council were held, and the Alliance, led by Tunku Abdul Rahman, won 51 of the 52 seats.

In January 1956, a constitutional conference was held in London[81] between the British and representatives of Malaya. The latter included four representatives of the Malay Rulers, Tunku Abdul Rahman (Chief Minister of the Federation), three ministers, and the British High Commissioner for Malaya and his advisers. At the close of the meeting, it was proposed that an independent commission be appointed to devise a constitution for a fully self-governing and independent Federation of Malaya. The British Government and Malay Rulers jointly appointed a commission headed by Lord Reid and consisting of constitutional experts from the UK, Australia, India and Pakistan.[82]

Between June and October 1956, the Reid Commission met 118 times, during which it received 131 memoranda from members of the public and organisations. On 21 February 1957, the Commission submitted a working draft of the constitution to the Working Committee – comprising the four representatives of the Malay Rulers, four members of the ruling Alliance Government, the British High Commissioner, the Chief Secretary and the Attorney-General. On the basis of the Working Committee's

---

[80] Federation of Malaya Order-in-Council SI 1948, No 108.

[81] The conference lasted from 18 January to 6 February 1956.

[82] The Members of the Commission were: Lord William Reid (Chairman); Sir Ivor Jennings (UK); Sir William McKell (Australia); B Malik (India); and Abdul Hamid (Pakistan). See JM Fernando, 'Sir Ivor Jennings and the Malayan Constitution' (2006) 4 *The Journal of Imperial and Commonwealth History* 577.

recommendations, changes were made to the draft and the new Federal Constitution was passed by the Federal Legislative Council on 15 August 1957, the Constitution coming into force 12 days later. The Federation of Malaya became an independent sovereign state on 31 August 1957.

The legal transfer of power was effected through several instruments. First, there was the Federation of Malaya Independence Act 1957,[83] passed by the British Parliament on 31 July 1957, together with the Orders-in-Council made thereunder. Secondly, a Federation of Malaya Agreement 1957 was concluded between the Governments of the United Kingdom and the Federation of Malaya. Thirdly, the Federation Constitution Ordinance 1957 was passed by the Federation of Malaya; and finally there were the state enactments in each of the Malay States to approve and give force to the Federal Constitution.

The Reid Commission Report was published on 21 February 1957 and the British Government, the Conference of Rulers and the Government of the Federation appointed a Working Party for detailed study. On the basis of their recommendations the new Federal Constitution was promulgated on Merdeka (Independence) Day, 31 August 1957. To effect the transfer of power, the British Parliament passed the Federation of Malaya Independence Act on 31 July 1957, under which the British Parliament was authorised to conclude such agreements as are 'expedient for the establishment of the Federation of Malaya as an independent sovereign country within the Commonwealth'.[84]

In Singapore, constitutional development after 1945 was slow, as the English-educated elite were not anxious to assume the task of self-government. It did not help that few locals thought Singapore could be a viable state due to its small size and lack of natural resources. The first major move toward constitutional reform came through a constitutional commission, appointed in 1953. Headed by Sir George Rendel, it recommended automatic voter registration, transforming the Legislative Council into a mainly elected assembly of 32 members. Of these, 25 would be elected Unofficial Members, three would be ex-officio Official Members holding ministerial posts, and four would be Nominated Unofficial Members. The Commission also recommended creating a Council of Ministers appointed by the Governor on the recommendation of the 'Leader of the House'. These recommendations were implemented by the Singapore Colony Order-in-Council of 1955.[85] By this time, a new nationalism fuelled island-wide left-wing and communist-front activities.

In 1958, following two constitutional conferences in London, a new constitution was drafted and adopted, giving Singapore the right to self-government with its own head of state, the Yang di-Pertuan Negara. Britain retained responsibility for defence and foreign affairs. Internal security was managed by an Internal Security Council, comprising three British and three Singapore representatives and one Malayan representative. This was the prelude to full independence.

In the meantime, the British Government had turned its attentions to the self-government of North Borneo, Brunei and Sarawak. A joint British–Malayan commission – the Cobbold Commission – was established in April 1962 to determine if the

---

[83] 5 & 6 Eliz 2, c 60.
[84] Ibid, s 1(1).
[85] Singapore Colony Order-in-Council SI 1955, No 187.

people of Borneo wanted to join the Federation of Malaysia. As a result of opposition from the Philippines and Indonesia, the UN Secretary-General was invited to send a mission to determine whether the people of these territories truly supported Malaysia. This mission announced on 15 September 1963 that the majority of people in North Borneo and Sarawak supported Malaysia, but this did not still Indonesian and Filipino opposition against Malaysia.

At a September 1961 meeting of the Commonwealth Parliamentary Association, the principle of merger with the Federation of Malaya was approved by representatives from Malaya, Singapore, North Borneo, Brunei and Sarawak. On 31 August 1963, Prime Minister Lee Kuan Yew declared Singapore's independence from Britain, and 16 days later, Singapore became a part of the Federation of Malaya along with North Borneo (Sabah) and Sarawak. Brunei chose to remain a British colony.

Brunei was once a powerful kingdom covering the island of Borneo. However, after Spanish settlement in the Philippines in the sixteenth century, its influence began to wane. In the nineteenth century, Brunei lost most its territories to Sarawak under the 'White Rajas' and North Borneo (Sabah) under the British. In 1906, the British created a 'Residency' in Brunei, establishing a system of indirect rule lasting until self-government was granted in 1959. The 1959 Constitution provided for future elections, and in 1962 the Brunei Peoples' Party (PRB) won a landslide victory. The PRB was thus in an excellent position to stall the merger of Brunei with Malaya. Sultan Omar Ali Saifuddin III delayed convening the Legislative Council and Brunei opted out of the planned merger to form Malaysia. Brunei became independent only in 1984.

Singapore joined the North Borneo states of Sabah and Sarawak and the Federation of Malaya to form Malaysia on 16 September 1963. The effect of this union was the application of the Federation of Malaya Constitution of 1957 to all the new states. State constitutions had to be drafted for Singapore, Sabah and Sarawak,[86] and in the case of Singapore the State Constitution of 1958[87] served as the base for the constitution. Under the terms of the merger, Singapore was given special status, with its own Prime Minister (all other Malaysian states having only Chief Ministers or *Menteri Besars*). More importantly, Singapore had much greater autonomy than the other Malaysian states, retaining control over finance, labour, education and commerce. Singapore citizens would not, however, automatically qualify for Malaysian citizenship, and Singapore would enjoy smaller representation in the Federal Government.

Almost as soon as the union was sealed, disagreements broke out between Singapore and the Federal Government. The internal politics of the Federation and the abortive attempt by Singapore's People's Action Party (PAP) to supplant the Malayan Chinese Association (MCA) as the de facto political party of the Chinese in Malaysia proved fatal to the merger, and ultimately Singapore was expelled from the Federation of Malaysia on 9 August 1965. Immediately after Singapore gained her independence, Prime Minister Lee Kuan Yew promised Singaporeans a new constitution. In the meantime, Singapore's Parliament amended the State of Singapore Constitution 1963,[88] passed the Republic of Singapore Independence Act[89] and got on with the busi-

---

[86] This was done through the UK's Sabah, Sarawak and Singapore (State Constitutions) Order-in-Council, 2 SI 1963, No 2656.

[87] Singapore (Constitution) Order-in-Council 1958, 2 SI 1958, No 1956.

[88] Act No 9 of 1965.

[89] Act No 8 of 1965.

ness of government. The new constitution never came to pass. In 1979, Parliament passed an amendment to the Constitution to authorise the Attorney-General to consolidate and issue a reprint of the Constitution. The first Reprint of the Constitution of the Republic of Singapore was issued in 1980. All the provisions of the State Constitution of 1963, provisions of the Federal Constitution of the Federation of Malaysia imported through the Republic of Singapore Independence Act,[90] and all subsequent amendments were rearranged, rationalised and published in a single document for the first time.

Brunei is Southeast Asia's youngest state. It became independent in 1984 as an absolute monarchy; an anachronism in the age of democratic liberalism.[91] The Constitution in operation was first promulgated in 1959 by the British as a key step in transferring powers from the British Residency to the Brunei people. The Constitution is a simple document with 12 parts. In 1984, it was amended to suspend the Legislative Council. A Constitutional Review Committee was established in 1994, but to date no reports have been issued. The Sultan of Brunei rules with almost absolute power.

IV. REVOLUTIONARY MOMENTS

A. Communist Revolutions

Political revolutions represent the most drastic and significant break with the past. Revolutionary movements are legitimised by their success and continuity, and the framing of a new constitutional order typically follows. In this section, we consider how various Asian states deal with revolutionary breaks with the past. More significantly, revolutions most often occur with mass support riding on a crest of high emotion and mobilised engagement. We examine two distinct types of revolutions – communist and democratic – and consider how legitimacy is sought and gained in each instance. In particular, we consider the role constitutions and constitutionalism play in the process.

The advent of communism represented the biggest break from the past, both politically and legally. The clearest example would be the Soviet Union, which in 1917 became the first world's communist state. The impact of this revolution continues to be felt in many parts of the world, especially with the Soviet support for worldwide revolution. As was noted in section II.C., the earliest Asian communist state to be created was Mongolia, which proclaimed independence in 1911 and achieved it with Soviet help in November 1924. Mongolia remained under Soviet influence till 1989 when communism collapsed.

The Soviet Union was also supportive of the Chinese Communist Party (CCP) which came to power in 1949. The CCP's success inspired many independence fighters

---

[90] The old 1963 State Constitution of Singapore did not provide for a judiciary in Singapore, neither did it make any provisions to guarantee civil liberties to its people. These deficiencies were dealt with by 'importing' the relevant provisions from the Federation of Malaysia Constitution 1957.

[91] See A Ibrahim and VS Winslow, 'Constitution and Monarchy in Brunei' in Ward Beer (ed), above n 14, 365; and R Kershaw, 'Brunei: Malay, Monarchical, Micro-state' in J Funston (ed), *Government and Politics in Southeast Asia* (Singapore: ISEAS, 2001) 1.

in Southeast Asia, and several countries there gained their independence on the back of communism, especially the Indochinese states. Since Marxist thought consigns law to a mere instrument of the state which will wither away – just like all political and legal institutions – with the establishment of a socialist state,[92] communist states have sought legitimacy politically, rather than constitutionally or legally. In this section, we consider the developments in China, Vietnam, Laos and Cambodia.

i. China[93]

From the founding of the Republic of China in 1911 to 1949, China underwent a period of constitutional experimentation and turmoil. Sun Yat-Sen (1866–1925) was replaced by Yuan Shikai (1859–1916) as President in 1912, thus beginning a period of conflict between Yuan's forces in the north (China's only modern army at the time) and the Kuomintang (KMT) forces in the south. The KMT Government promulgated a Provisional Constitution in March 1912, but this was not to be implemented till 1928 when the KMT established control over most of China. In the meantime, the rule of law became a plaything of Yuan Shikai and the generals and warlords who governed China between 1912 and 1928.

In 1913, Yuan Shikai took over the Government, dissolving the national and provincial assemblies, and replaced it with his own Council of State. In January 1914, Parliament was official dissolved. The year before, Charles Eliot – President Emeritus of Harvard University and Trustee of the Carnegie Endowment for International Peace – suggested to Yuan that an expert be appointed to assist the Chinese Government to draft a new constitution. The Carnegie Endowment appointed Professor Frank Johnson Goodnow, an established scholar of political science at Columbia University, on a three-year contract to fulfil that mission.[94] Arriving in Beijing full of ideas and ideals, Goodnow was soon confronted by the internecine fighting between Yuan Shikai and the KMT, and quickly concluded that China was as yet unready for democratic government.

In 1915, Goodnow wrote a private memorandum for Yuan Shikai, entitled 'Monarchy or Republic', in which he opined that China's history, traditions and social and economic conditions made republicanism difficult and that '[i]t is of course not susceptible of doubt that a monarchy is better suited than a republic to China'.[95] Yuan, who for some time had entertained visions of crowning himself Emperor, took this memorandum to heart. In October 1915, he announced that he would accept 'the overwhelming popular demand' to re-establish imperial rule, and fixed the date for his enthronement for 1 January 1916.[96] However, Yuan misjudged anti-imperialist senti-

---

[92] See generally, C Sypnowich, *The Concept of Socialist Law* (Oxford: Oxford University Press, 1990).

[93] For a succinct discussion of modern China's constitutional development, see Qianfan Zhang, *The Constitution of China: A Contextual Analysis* (Oxford: Hart Publishing, 2012) at 1–74.

[94] N Pugach, 'Embarrased Monarchist: Frank J Goodnow and Constituitonal Development in China, 1913–1915' (1973) 42(4) *Pacific Historical Review* 499 at 501–02; see also JJ Kroncke, 'An Early Tragedy of Comparative Constitutionalism: Frank Goodnow and the Chinese Republic' (2012) 21(3) *Pacific Rim Law & Policy Journal* 533.

[95] F Goodnow, 'Monarchy or Republic?' in *Papers Relating to the Foreign Relations of the United States* (Washington DC: Government Printing Office, 1924) 53–58, cited in Kroncke, above n 94, at 570.

[96] See Suisheng Zhao, *Power by Design: Constitution-Making in Nationalist China* (Honolulu: University of Hawaii Press, 1996) at 23.

ments; protests came from all over the country and he was forced to restore republican rule in March 1916. Yuan died three months later. The following year, a Qing loyalist general, Zhang Xun (1854–1923), together with Kang Youwei (1858–1927), a reformist Confucian scholar and political philosopher, attempted to restore the Qing dynasty, but this feeble effort faded away, with both men taking flight.

Yuan's death plunged China into the chaotic period of war-lordism, with no one strong enough to hold the country together. It was not till 1928 that KMT forces, under Generalissimo Chiang Kai-shek, took control of much of China. Describing the constitution-making process and the influence of Sun Yat-sen's philosophical thoughts on constitutional government, Professor Suisheng Zhao notes:

Suisheng Zhao, *Power by Design: Constitution-Making in Nationalist China* (Honolulu: University of Hawaii Press, 1996) 25–26

In his endeavor to develop a system of government that would reflect modern thought, Sun Yat-sen made various attempts to frame the political institutions of the new Republic of China upon the patterns adopted by Western democracies. Indeed, he elaborated a whole set of doctrines in this regard. The key element was the 'five-power constitution' doctrine proposed in his *Jian Guo Da Gang* (Fundamentals of National Reconstruction). Sun Yat-sen distinguished *quan* (power) from *zheng* (function), or sovereignty from governing. *Quan* was 'the right to rule as sovereign'; *zheng* was 'the right to administer as an official'. According to Sun Yat-sen, the people should exercise four sovereign powers – election (*xuanju*), recall (*bamian*), initiative (*chuangzhi*), and referendum (*fujue*) – and the government should exercise five governing powers: administration (*xingzheng*), adjudication (*sifa*), legislation (*lifa*), examination (*kaoshi*), and control (*jiancha*). These two sets of powers were clearly different from each other, he thought, and should therefore be completely separated.

The system of government to be set up according to Sun Yat-sen's five-power constitution doctrine consisted mainly of five *yuan*, or branches: the legislative, the executive, the judicial, the censoring (or control), and the examination. The essential function of the Legislative Yuan was to make laws; the Executive Yuan was to enforce the laws; the Judiciary Yuan was to interpret their meaning and apply them to particular cases,; the Control Yuan to supervise the conduct of government officials; the Examination Yuan was to recruit government officials through a system of public examination. For each of these *yuan* there was a head, later called president, directing the activities of his own *yuan*. Provision was also made for a chief of state: the president. Sun Yat-sen contemplated a National Assembly, as well, consisting of delegates from districts into which the provinces were divided, one delegate from each district. The president of the nation and the presidents of the five *yuan* were all to be elected at the National Assembly, the representative organ of the electorate, and were to be responsible to it. Since the National Assembly was an organ of public opinion through which the popular political powers of election, initiative, referendum and recall were exercised, it was the reservoir of national sovereignty.

The five-power doctrine was obviously an elaboration of the traditional Western democratic theory of three powers long ago enunciated by Aristotle, Cicero, and Polybius, elaborated by Montesquieu at a later time, and adopted by the framers of the US Constitution as a fundamental principle of their government toward the close of the eighteen century. Yet it was also rooted in two native Chinese institutions, centuries old, namely, the civil service examination and the censorial system, which were realized in two of the five *yuan*, the Examination Yuan and the Control Yuan. Examination was separated by Sun Yat-sen from administration because he was fascinated by the examination system of ancient China. For a similar reason, control was separated from legislation: in Chinese history there is a long list of famous officials in charge of impeachment who even admonished the emperors for their misdeeds.

Sun Yat-sen died on March 12, 1925. But the Nationalist government, established soon after his death, followed Sun's doctrine and maintained its form of republic. The five-power structure of government was erected in light of the Organic Law of the Nationalist government in 1928, a provisional constitution was promulgated in 1931, and a permanent draft of a five-power constitution was made in public in 1936.

The Provisional Constitution of 1931 is sometimes referred to as the Provisional Constitution of the Political Tutelage Period, because it was intended to give near absolute power to the KMT to guide China until its people had been sufficiently educated to participate in democratic government. In 1947, following the Second Sino-Japanese War (1937–45) Chiang Kai-shek was pressured into promulgating a more democratic constitution. This constitution became the basis for the Constitution of the Republic of China (ROC) after Chiang Kai-shek's forces were defeated by the communists in 1949 and were forced to flee to the island of Formosa (Taiwan).

The proclamation of the People's Republic of China on 1 October 1949 must rank as one of the most significant historical events of the twentieth century. Not only did this signify the end of a long-running civil war between the Chinese Community Party (CCP) forces and the Chinese Nationalist Party (*Guomindang*) forces, but it ushered in a Communist Government for the world's most populous state. The CCP succeeded on the back of overwhelming support from the masses, and clearly carried the mandate of the majority of the Chinese in the country.

In June 1949, as the tide turned against the *Guomindang* forces, the CCP convened the Chinese People's Political Consultative Conference (CPPCC). The CPPCC, which comprised the CCP and its eight politically aligned parties,[97] operated effectively as a constitutional convention in which the structure of the new Government as well as the name and symbols of state were decided. At the end of the conference, the People's Republic of China was proclaimed on 1 October 1949. Three key documents that would determine the way China would be run – the Common Programme of the Chinese People's Political Consultative Conference (the 'Common Programme') and two sets of the Organic Law of the Central People's Government of the People's Republic of China[98] – were unanimously passed by the CPPCC on 29 September 1949. The Common Programme – containing 60 Articles governing subjects from marriage to land reform to counter-revolutionaries – may be regarded as China's interim constitution from 1949 to 1954, even if it the CPPCC never described it as such.

---

[97] The eight aligned parties were: the Revolutionary Committee of the Guomindang (*Zhongguo Guomindang Geming Weiyuahhui*); the China Democratic League (*Zhonguo Minzhu Tongmeng*); China Democratic; China Democratic National Construction Association (*Zhongguo Minzhu Jianguo Hui*); China Association for Promoting Democracy (*Zhungguo Minzhu Cujin Hui*); Chinese Peasants' and Workers' Democratic Party (*Zhongguo Nonggong Minzhu Dang*); China Zhi Gong Party; the September 3 Society (*Jiu San Xueshe*); and the Taiwan Democratic Self-Government League (*Taiwan Minzhu Zishi Tongmeng*).

[98] These were passed on 27 September and 29 September 1949 respectively. See HA Steiner, 'The People's Democratic Dictatorship in China' (1950) 3(1) *The Western Political Quarterly* 38 at 38.

However, the Articles of the Common Programme do not provide for a detailed government structure – such as the separation of powers or specific guarantees of rights – as one might come to expect from a typical constitutional document. Its preamble arrogated to the CPPCC the right to represent 'the will of the people of the whole country' and to proclaim 'the establishment of the People's Republic of China' and organise 'the people's own central government'. Under the Common Programme, power was vested in the people, but was to be exercised at various levels through elected representatives in the People's Congresses (the highest being the National People's Congress (NPC)) and other government organs. Under Articles 12 and 13 of the Common Programme, the power that was to have been exercised by the NPC would be exercised by the CPPCC until such time as the NPC could be constituted.

There was no plebiscite of any sort, and the CCP and its aligned political parties declared themselves the representatives of the 'People's Democracy' and to rule the country on this basis. Thus, while Article 1 of the Common Programme declared that the CPPCC would carry out 'the people's democratic dictatorship led by the working class, based on the alliance of workers and peasants, and uniting all democratic classes and nationalities', it provided for no mechanism to operationalise the provision. Article 4 provided that the people 'shall have the right to elect and to be elected according to law', but nothing was said about how this would be done or how many representatives would be elected to represent the people.

At no point did the CPPCC declare itself to be a Constituent Assembly, or that the instruments promulgated at its first session were constitutional documents.[99] It simply assumed plenary powers on the basis of Chairman Mao Zedong's concept of the 'People's Democratic Dictatorship':

> Democracy is practised within the ranks of the people, who enjoy the rights of freedom of speech, assembly, association and so on. The right to vote belongs only to the people, not to the reactionaries. The combination of these two aspects, democracy for the people and dictatorship over the reactionaries, is the people's democratic dictatorship.
>
> Why must things be done this way? The reason is quite clear to everybody. If things were not done this way, the revolution would fail, the people would suffer, the country would be conquered.
>
> 'Don't you want to abolish state power?' Yes, we do, but not right now; we cannot do it yet. Why? Because imperialism still exists, because domestic reaction still exists, because classes still exist in our country. Our present task is to strengthen the people's state apparatus – mainly the people's army, the people's police and the people's courts – in order to consolidate national defence and protect the people's interests. Given this condition, China can develop steadily, under the leadership of the working class and the Communist Party, from an agricultural into an industrial country and from a new-democratic into a socialist and communist society, can abolish classes and realize the Great Harmony. The state apparatus, including the army, the police and the courts, is the instrument by which one class oppresses another. It is an instrument for the oppression of antagonistic classes; it is violence and not 'benevolence'. 'You are not benevolent!' Quite so. We definitely do not apply a policy of benevolence to the reactionaries and towards the reactionary activities of the reactionary classes. Our policy of benevolence is applied only within the ranks of the people, not beyond them to the reactionaries or to the reactionary activities of reactionary classes.

[99] Ibid at 41.

The people's state protects the people. Only when the people have such a state can they educate and remould themselves by democratic methods on a country-wide scale, with everyone taking part, and shake off the influence of domestic and foreign reactionaries (which is still very strong, will survive for a long time and cannot be quickly destroyed), rid themselves of the bad habits and ideas acquired in the old society, not allow themselves to be led astray by the reactionaries, and continue to advance – to advance towards a socialist and communist society.[100]

This assumption of plenary powers was based entirely on the success of the CCP in the civil war and on Mao's personal charismatic persona and doctrine. It was an elite assertion of power masquerading as a 'people's dictatorship'.

At the end of the first session of the CPPCC in 1952, the Conference had two choices. It could constitute the NPC and elect members into it, or maintain the status quo by convening a second session of the CPPCC. It opted for the latter option, and this decision was conveyed to Soviet leader Josef Stalin in October 1952.[101] Interestingly, Stalin did not think the CPPCC sufficiently legitimate, and had urged Mao twice – in 1949 and then again in 1950 – to hold elections and adopt a constitution.[102] Mao felt otherwise, arguing that the system worked well and that the promulgation of a constitution should wait till China transited to socialism, when the fundamental change in class relations necessitated this.[103] He hoped to do what Stalin had done in 1936 when he proclaimed the Constitution of the USSR at the same time that he declared the Soviet Union had attained socialism. Stalin repeated his call for elections when Chinese President Liu Shaoqi visited him in Moscow on the occasion of the nineteenth Soviet Party Congress:

Now, with Liu once more before him, Stalin restated his position and buttressed it with several points. First, the government of the PRC had not been elected. This allowed its enemies to question its legitimacy, and to accuse it of being nothing more than a self-proclaimed, military dictatorship. Second, the country had no official constitution. The Common Program offered little consolation here since its legitimacy and the legitimacy of all PRC law were clouded by their origin in the equally unelected CPPCC. Third, the multi-party coalition government established by the Common Program presented a grave security risk to the CCP. Many members of the minor parties had close ties to foreign countries, especially the United States and United Kingdom, and could spy on behalf of those hostile powers.[104] Stalin argued that the CCP could solve these problems and deny its enemies propaganda points simply by holding an election in 1954, which it would surely dominate thanks to its deep reservoir of popular support and experience with mass mobilization. Such an election would allow it to claim a genuine popular mandate and sideline its coalition partners, thereby legitimating at the ballot box a one-party state that could draft a constitution and govern with an essentially free hand.[105]

---

[100] This concept was developed in an important speech Mao delivered on 30 June 1949, the 28th anniversary of the founding of the Chinese Communist Party. See *Selected Works of Mao Tse-tung*, vol 4 (Peking: Foreign Languages Press, 1969) 411–24 at 418.

[101] See GD Tiffert, 'Epistrophy: Chinese Constitutionalism and the 1950s' in S Balme and M Dowdle (eds), *Building Constitutionalism in China* (London: Palgrave Macmillan, 2009) 59 at 65.

[102] See Hua-yu Li, 'The Political Stalinization of China: The Establishment of One-Party Constitutionalism, 1948–1954' (2001) 3(2) *Journal of Cold War Studies* 28 at 39–40.

[103] Tiffert, above n 101, at 65.

[104] As noted by Li, above n 102, at 40, Stalin told Liu: 'Your enemies have two ways to threaten you. First, they can tell the masses that the CCP did not have an election and therefore is not a legitimate government; second, if there is no constitution and the Political Consultative Conference is not elected, your enemies could accuse you of taking power by force. They could say that the government was imposed on the people . . . You should take these weapons away from your enemies.'

[105] Tiffert, above n 101, at 66.

The roots of Stalin's constitutional thinking can be traced to his plan to place all communist countries under single-party rule. His early efforts succeeded in putting in place constitutions based on the Soviet Union's 1936 Constitution in each of the eastern European communist states by 1949.[106] Thus, by the time the Chinese Communist Party came to power, a template had been created. Stalin proposed the same model of constitutionalism for China and, as mentioned above, twice urged Mao to act on it. It was only in the fall of 1952 that Mao began to plan China's transition to socialism, under which he planned to draft a constitution and hold the first NPC elections in 1954, the year previously recommended by Stalin. This did not please Stalin, who insisted that the CCP convene the NPC and draft the new constitution as soon as possible.[107]

Drafting of communist China's first constitution began after the twentieth meeting of the People's Central Government on 13 January 1953 – just two months before Stalin's death – when a 32-member committee, headed by Mao, was established to effect a draft.[108] Mao's leadership of the drafting committee was significant for two reasons: first, he wanted to demonstrate to Stalin that the CCP took the task of drafting a constitution very seriously and that the Party was willing to work with non-Communist Party leaders; and, secondly, he wanted to show Stalin that he gave as much serious attention to the business of drafting a constitution as the Soviet leader, by personally overseeing it.

The constitution-drafting process was a purely elitist exercise, with Mao himself being responsible for its first draft. Indeed, in December 1953, he travelled to Hangzhou, with two bookcases of reference materials and three of his most experienced personal secretaries, to work on the document. This small group constituted what might be called the Constitution Drafting Small Group. Within a month, they had produced a detailed nine-month drafting plan for the constitution.[109]

The draft went through several revisions by members of the CCP Politburo and senior officials. Like Stalin before him, Mao had scheduled a four-month 'national discussion' of the draft so that the views of 'ordinary citizens' could be incorporated in the final document. However, this exercise lasted all of two months. During this time, some 500 Beijing residents and 8,000 citizens from different social groups from all over China were invited to discuss the constitution. Close to 6,000 suggestions were received, but in the end, only 'correct' ones were adopted.[110] The Constitution was finally adopted on 20 September 1954 by the NPC.

The Constitution, comprising 106 Articles in four Chapters,[111] was modelled along the lines of the 1949 Common Programme, with provisions drawn from the 1936 Soviet Constitution. Power was divided among the legislature, with the powerful NPC being

---

[106] Li, above n 102, at 32. These included all the Eastern-bloc countries except for Poland and East Germany.

[107] Ibid at 40.

[108] The Committee included: Mao, Zhu De, Liu Shaoqi, Zhou Enlai, Chen Yun, Peng Dehuai, Dong Biwu, Lin Boqu, Gao Gang, Rao Shushi, Deng Xiaoping, Wu Lan Fu, Sai Fu Ding, Chen Boda, Hu Qiaomu, and 12 individuals from a variety of political parties and some with no party affiliation. See Li, above n 102, at 42.

[109] Tiffert, above n 101, at 66.

[110] Li, above n 102, at 44.

[111] For contemporaneous commentaries on the Constitution, see HA Steiner, 'Constitutionalism in Communist China' (1955) XLIX *The American Political Science Review* 1; and Tao-Tai Hsia, 'The Constitution of Red China' (1955) 4(3) *American Journal of Comparative Law* 425.

the most important organ of government; the executive, comprising the President and the State Council; and the judiciary, made up of courts headed by the Supreme People's Court and a procuratorial system headed by the Supreme People's Procuratorate. Under Article 29, the Constitution was amendable by the NPC by two-thirds majority (a minor inconvenience given the hegemony of the CCP in the Congress.)

The 1954 Constitution did not function according to its own tenets for long. In 1956 Mao launched the Hundred Flowers Campaign, in which he encouraged China's intellectuals to discuss China's problems in order to promote new forms of arts and cultural institutions, as well as to promote socialism. After a slow start, Mao jumped in again and encouraged 'constructive criticism' among the intellectuals, stating that criticism was preferred to inaction. This led to numerous intellectuals voicing concerns and critiques openly, and the Government received millions of critical letters.[112] In respect of the 1954 Constitution, some of its architects – Luo Longji, Qian Duansheng, Wang Tieya and Zhang Bojun – publicly invoked constitutional principles to criticise the CCP for violation of human rights and the rule of law.[113]

By July 1957, the campaign was causing Mao great discomfort, and he launched the anti-Rightist Movement which marked the start of a period of purges against the intellectual class. Many intellectuals and critics were persecuted, placed under arrest and sentenced to long spells of imprisonment. By 1959, the Ministry of Justice had all but shut down. Constitutionalism was dead, and laws were forgotten. Indeed, Mao nonchalantly declared: 'The Civil Law, the Criminal Law, who remembers those texts? I participated in the drafting of the Constitution, but even I don't remember it.'[114] Any pretence of constitutional or legal legitimacy had evaporated. Between 1957 and 1976, power was exercised by Mao or in his name with no regard for legal niceties or legalities. Mao tried to formalise his power by drafting a new Constitution in 1975. This Constitution abolished the position of President as head of state. Power centred around Mao, as Chairman of the CCP, and presidential duties were carried out by the Chairman of the NPC. The 106 Articles of the 1954 Constitution were truncated to just 30 Articles, and many fundamental liberties were curtailed. Constitutional rights that were removed included the rights to property, privacy, freedom from political discrimination, freedom of movement, speech and freedom of artistic expression.

When Mao died in 1976, a new Constitution-making process began. Drafted under the chairmanship of Hua Guofeng (who replaced Mao as Chairman of the CCP), this new Constitution represented a compromise between preserving Mao's legacy and addressing the worst excesses of the leftist campaign that began in the late 1950s. The 1978 Constitution restored the system of government provided for in the 1954 Constitution, although the post of President continued to be omitted. This Constitution was short-lived and was replaced by a new one drafted after Deng Xiaoping consolidated his power base to become China's paramount leader. In August 1980, the Central Committee of the CCP recommended the establishment of a committee to revise the Constitution, and this was approved at the NPC.

---

[112] On the Hundred Flowers Campaign, see generally JD Spence, *The Search for Modern China* (New York: WW Norton, 1990) at 539–43; R MacFarquhar, 'Mao's Last Revolution' (1966–67) 45 *Foreign Affairs* 112; and R Peerenboom, 'Let One Hundred Flowers Bloom, One Hundred Schools Contend: Debating Rule of Law in China' (2001–2002) 23 *Michigan Journal of International Law* 471.

[113] Tiffert, above n 101, at 68.

[114] Quoted ibid at 72.

The 1982 Constitution[115] brought China back full circle. Most elements of the 1954 Constitution that had been expunged from the 1975 Constitution were restored, including the Presidency. Chapter II, on the Fundamental Rights and Duties of Citizens, was noticeably expanded to guarantee a host of civil, political, social and economic rights. More importantly, the Constitution signalled a clear shift away from ideology towards law. Nominally, the Constitution has supreme authority, but it can be amended by the NPC.[116] Despite these changes, the 1982 Constitution remains very much a socialist instrument embodying aspirations of the CCP. It is not a legal charter to curb the control of state power, but rather centralises power in the state.

Between 1982 and 2010, the Constitution underwent four major revisions, none of which drastically altered the philosophical underpinnings of the 1982 version. In 1988, in keeping with China's market economy experiments, the Constitution was amended to make reference to the private sector that would complement the 'socialist public economy'.[117] In 1993, amendments were made to the preamble to introduce the concept of a 'socialist market economy':

> China is at the primary stage of socialism. The basic task of the nation is, according to the theory of building socialism with Chinese characteristics, to concentrate its effort on socialist modernization.[118]

The preamble was amended further in 1999, and then again in 2004. Note how often it is tweaked by the NPC to reflect China's changing perspective of socialism. In 1993, Deng Xiaoping's formulation of a socialist market economy found expression in the document, and in 1999, the recently-deceased Deng himself and the Deng Xiaopeng Theory achieved mention in the preamble, alongside Marx, Lenin and Mao. In 2004, the Three Representations[119] idea of President Jiang Zemin was also incorporated into the preamble.

ii. Vietnam

The experience of Vietnam, Asia's second largest communist state, mirrors that of China to a large extent, except that it went through a further stage of having fought a war against the colonial power – France. Ho Chi Minh established the Indochinese Communist Party (ICP) in Hong Kong in 1930, while Vietnam was still a French colony. In 1941, he established the Vietminh (League for Vietnamese Independence) to work for Vietnamese independence. On 11 March 1945, while under Japanese administration, the

---

[115] See generally, WC Jones, 'The Constitution of the People's Republic of China' (1985) 63 *Washington University Law Quarterly* 707.

[116] The preamble to the Constitution states, inter alia: 'This Constitution . . . is the fundamental law of the state and has supreme legal authority'.

[117] Art 11 (as amended in 1988) states: 'The State permits the private sector of the economy to exist and develop within the limits prescribed by law. The private sector of the economy is a complement to the socialist public economy. The State protects the lawful rights and interests of the private sector of the economy, and exercises guidance, supervision and control over the private sector of the economy.'

[118] Amendment Two, approved by the 8th NPC at its first Session, 29 March 1993.

[119] This theory was introduced by Jiang Zemin on 25 February 2002 during an inspection tour of Guangdong Province. In summarising the history of the CCP, he noted that the Party had always represented: (i) China's developmental needs; (ii) the progressive direction of China's advanced culture; and (iii) the fundamental interests of the broad majority.

Vietnamese Emperor Bao Dai[120] proclaimed Vietnam independent of the French Empire. Five months later, he abdicated and Ho Chi Minh, by now the Chairman of the National Liberation Committee – proclaimed his Provisional Government of the Democratic Republic of Vietnam (DRV) in Hanoi. When France returned to Indochina in 1946, Vietnam was pronounced a 'free state' within the French Union and was promised a referendum to determine whether the territories of Tonkin (northern Vietnam, around Hanoi), Annam (Central Vietnam) and Cochin China (south Vietnam around Saigon and the Mekong delta) should be reunited.

From May to September 1946, Ho Chi Minh negotiated with the French, but only a limited agreement was reached. The French were adamant about holding onto their Indochinese empire, and before long the First Vietnam War broke out. The Vietminh controlled most of the north while the French – now with Bao Dai on their side – controlled the south. In January 1950, Ho declared the DRV the only legal Government of Vietnam, and it immediately received recognition from the Soviet Union and China. To complicate matters, Britain and the United States recognised Bao Dai's pro-French Government less than a month later. China began supplying arms to the Vietminh, while US President Truman approved legislation granting the French $15 million in military aid for their war in Indochina. This led to a full escalation of the war between Ho's Vietminh forces and the French. The defeat of the French in Dien Bien Phu in 1954 immediately led to ceasefire talks and the Geneva Accord, under which Vietnam was partitioned into North and South, along the 17th parallel. By October that year, the French forces left Hanoi.

The Constitution that came into force at this time was the 1946 Constitution drafted when the DRV's control was limited to the northern provinces. This Constitution was approved by the National Assembly in 1946 but not officially promulgated.[121] Vietnam's 1946 Constitution had a limited impact on the country, then embroiled in civil war. At the time of its drafting, the leadership of the DRV controlled only the northern part of the country, and this Constitution was a 'moderate document . . . drafted to appeal to a broad spectrum of the population throughout Vietnam'.[122] However, with the outbreak of the First Vietnam War, constitutional niceties took a back seat, and the 1946 Constitution did not impact society generally.

As a socialist constitution, it was rather mild. There was a political section emphasising democratic freedoms and the need for a coalition of forces to struggle against French rule, and its economic provisions guaranteed the sanctity of private property. There were no references to the ICP's ultimate objective to build a communist society.[123] After the French defeat at Dien Bien Phu in 1954, and immediately following partition, non-communist South Vietnam promulgated a new Constitution while

---

[120] Born in 1913, Bao Dai was the last emperor of Vietnam. He succeeded his father in 1925 at the age of 12, but did not ascend the throne until 1932. During World War II he collaborated with the Japanese, but abdicated to collaborate with the Vietminh in 1945. He then went into exile but was brought back by the French to rule as head of state (1949–55); he was ousted by Ngo Dinh Diem. He died in exile in Paris in 1997. See ME Chamberlain, *The Longman Companion to European Decolonization in the Twentieth Century* (London & New York: Longman, 1998) at 211.

[121] See W Duiker, 'The Constitution of the Socialist Republic of Vietnam' in Beer (ed), above n 14, 331. An English translation of the text can be found in BB Fall, *The Viet-Minh Regime* (Ithaca, NY: Cornell University Southeast Asia Program, 1956).

[122] See Duiker, above n 121, at 331.

[123] Ibid.

North Vietnam continued to rely on the 1946 DRV-drafted Constitution. Five years later, a new Constitution was promulgated on 31 December 1959.

Constitutional development in South Vietnam was chaotic.[124] Ngo Dinh Diem was appointed Prime Minister in 1954. In October 1955, he defeated former Emperor Bao Dai in a heavily rigged referendum to become head of state. Three days later, he proclaimed the Republic of Vietnam with himself as President, and immediately began clamping down on Vietminh supporters in the South. After Diem took office, a long list of emergency decrees was promulgated to control the population and protect the state against insurgents. In all, seven different Constitutions 'were promulgated, suspended, and replaced as a result of a series of coups and counter coups'.[125] Within the first year of his assuming office, Diem promulgated the first of these Constitutions on 26 October 1956. The Constitution provided for the separation of executive and legislative powers, but with no autonomous judiciary. In practice the legislative power was insignificant and the executive, through the Department of Justice, supervised the courts. The President was vested with broad emergency powers to rule by decree between the short sessions of the legislature and, in time of war, internal disturbance, or financial or economic crisis, to exercise extraordinary power to institute any appropriate measures. There were hardly any effective checks against executive abuses of power.[126]

Diem's repressive regime was violently ended when he was assassinated in a coup on 1 November 1963. A provisional charter was quickly drafted, replacing the 1956 Constitution and vesting all legislative and executive power in the Revolutionary Military Council headed by Major-General Duong Van Minh. This was replaced by a second provisional charter on 2 July 1964, and a third on 16 August 1964. Both these charters emphasised the supremacy of the military leadership. This third charter was later withdrawn when subjected to a barrage of criticism about its dictatorial tendencies. In October 1964, a fifth provisional Constitution was enacted, providing for the transfer of authority to a civilian government. The civilian government was ineffective and eventually relinquished authority to the military in June 1965. On 19 June 1965, Air Marshall Nguyen Cao Ky was named Prime Minister, and he promulgated the sixth Constitution.[127]

In September 1966, a national ballot was conducted to elect a Constituent Assembly to draft another Constitution providing for the return to civilian government. In the first serious effort at constitution-making, the drafting committees studied several constitutional models – French, American, Japanese and Korean – and were assisted by the United States. On 1 April 1967, the seventh Constitution – after the American model – was promulgated, which provided for a president, a bicameral legislature and an independent judiciary.[128]

Despite the enactment of this Constitution, many of the emergency decrees promulgated earlier – which were of questionable validity – remained in effect. Furthermore, additional decrees were promulgated, further concentrating power in the executive. On 10 May 1972, President Nguyen van Thieu declared martial law.[129]

---

[124] See generally GS Prugh, *Law at War: Vietnam 1964–1973* (Washington, DC: Department of the Army, 1975) 21–27.
[125] Ibid at 21.
[126] Ibid at 22.
[127] Ibid at 23.
[128] Ibid.
[129] Ibid at 26.

In North Vietnam, the DRV Government promulgated two other Constitutions after 1946. The 1959 Constitution was outwardly communist in character. Its preamble stated that the DRV was a 'people's democratic state led by the working class'. There was a nominal separation of powers between the three government branches, and theoretically the legislative function was carried out by the National Assembly which was empowered to make laws and elect the chief state officials (president, vice-president and cabinet ministers) who formed the Council of Ministers. While the Council of Ministers was technically subject to the National Assembly's supervision, real power lay in the Political Bureau.

With the reunification of North and South Vietnam in 1976 under communist rule, the 1959 Constitution was revised. In keeping with the ideological thrusts of the Fourth National Congress of the Vietnamese Communist Party in 1976, the new Constitution emphasised popular sovereignty, stressing the need for a new political system, a new economy, a new culture and a new socialism. The new constitution-drafting commission presented its draft to a plenary session of the Central Committee of the Party in September 1980, and on 18 December 1980 the National Assembly gave its unanimous approval.[130]

Soviet influence on the 1980 Constitution was evident. Power was concentrated in a newly-established Council of State much like the Presidium of the Supreme Soviet. The executive branch of government was substantially strengthened, with a corresponding decrease in the importance of the National Assembly. The Council of Ministers, while nominally subordinate to the Council of State, remained all-powerful in practice. One interesting innovation of the 1980 Constitution was the concept of 'collective mastery' attributed to the late Party Secretary Le Duan and encapsulated in Article 3:

> In the Socialist Republic of Vietnam, the collective masters are the working people, with the worker-peasant alliance, led by the working class, as the core. The state ensures the continuous perfection and consolidation of the working people's collective mastery in the political, economic, cultural and social fields; collective mastery in the whole country and in each unit; collective mastery over society, over nature, and over oneself.[131]

The 1980 Constitution had 147 Articles in 12 Chapters. Notably, Article 67 guaranteed the citizens' rights to 'freedom of speech, the press, assembly, and association, and the freedom to demonstrate'. However, the same Article provided that 'no one may misuse democratic freedoms to violate the interests of the state and the people'.[132]

iii. Laos

Although part of the French empire, Laos and Cambodia (the latter discussed at section IV.A.iv. below) were often considered the 'poorer cousins' of Vietnam which held far greater economic importance for the French. Political development in these two territories also lagged behind that of Vietnam.[133] The reasons for this are, first, the

---

[130] See Duiker, above n 121, at 333–34.
[131] Ibid at 337.
[132] Ibid at 345.
[133] '[W]hen contrasted with the case of Vietnam, the paucity of pre-1941 Cambodian and Lao "nationalist" activity is striking. It is difficult to point to any organized parties, other than the Vietnamese-initiated ICP [Indochinese Communist Party], and only a handful of individuals emerge as identifiable "nationalist",

French ruled Cambodia and Laos with a relatively light hand, especially since they were economically unimportant; secondly, many Cambodians and Laotians viewed French domination as the lesser of two evils. If the French left, Viet or Thai domination was likely.[134]

However, by 1941, anti-colonial movements began to emerge in the two territories. The Kingdom of Laos was originally a grouping of smaller independent kingdoms centred on Vientiane, Luang Prabang and Champassak. In the nineteenth century, these kingdoms became Thai vassals. The current territory of Laos was the result of French acquisition in the latter part of the nineteenth century.[135] Like Vietnam, Laos experienced Japanese occupation during World War II. Under Japanese pressure, King Sisavangvong declared Laos' independence in April 1945. However, he retracted this pronouncement in August 1945 following Japan's surrender. Prince Phetsarath, the leader of the Lao Issara (Free Laos) nationalist movement, reasserted Laos' independence a month later. The French returned in large numbers and Lao Issara leaders fled to Thailand. The war also threw up radical anti-colonial leaders like Prince Souphanouvong (Prince Phetsarath's half-brother), who refused to accept French reoccupation of Laos. Souphanouvong and his supporters took to the jungles to pursue their goal of independence against the French.[136] The other prominent leader of the anti-colonial forces was Souphanouvong's other half-brother Prince Souvanna Phuoma (younger brother of Prince Phetsarath) who held more neutral political views. A new Constitution was promulgated by King Sisavangvong on 11 May 1947. The French made Laos an independent associate state of the French Union in 1949, and in October 1953 Laos secured full sovereign status as a constitutional monarchy, the Royal Lao Government (RLG).[137]

Immediately after Laos became part of the French Union, anti-colonial forces under Prince Souhanouvong and his Pathet Lao forces, aided by the Vietminh, attacked central Laos. Under the 1954 Geneva Agreements and the 1955 armistice, the two northern provinces were given to the Pathet Lao while the rest of the country went to the royal regime. In 1957, Prince Souvanna Phuoma, the royal premier, and Prince Souphanouvong agreed to re-establish a unified government. However the agreement broke down in 1959, and further armed conflict ensued. The Laotian situation was further complicated when General Phoumi Nosavan, who controlled the royal army, established a pro-Western revolutionary government headed by Prince Boun Gum in the south. Prince Souvanna Phuoma was driven into exile in Cambodia. In 1961, a cease-fire was arranged and the three princes agreed to form a Coalition Government headed by Prince Souvanna Phuoma. In 1975, the Pathet Lao seized power completely. Prince Souphanouvong was installed as President and Kaysone Phomvihane as Prime Minister. On 2 December 1975, the monarchy was abolished and King Sasavang Vatthana abdicated.

---

compared to the scores of prominent figures in histories of the early Vietnamese anti-colonialist and nationalist movements.' See P Kratoska and B Batson, 'Nationalism and Modernist Reform' in N Tarling (ed), *The Cambridge History of Southeast Asia*, vol 2 (Cambridge: Cambridge University Press, 1992) 249 at 282.

[134] Ibid at 283.

[135] See NJ Freeman, 'Laos: Timid Transition' in Funston (ed), above n 91, 120 at 120.

[136] See M Osborne, *Southeast Asia: An Introductory History*, 11th edn (Sydney: Allen & Unwin, 2013) at 205–8.

[137] Ibid at 207–8.

Redrafting a new constitution enjoyed low priority with the new Lao Government.[138] It was only in 1982, at the Lao People's Revolutionary Party (LPRP)'s third Congress, that General Secretary Kaysone Phmovihane declared that the party should 'urgently undertake the major task . . . of preparing a socialist constitution at an early date'.[139] Work on the constitution began under the chairmanship of Sisomphon Lovansay, a Politburo member, aided by East German advisers. However, the pace of constitution-drafting was excruciating slow.[140] In March 1989, elections for the Supreme People's Assembly (SPA) were conducted, and a new 17-member constitutional drafting committee appointed. One of the tasks the new SPA set for itself was completing the new Constitution. In August 1991, the SPA adopted the new Constitution, which dropped all references to socialism. However, the single-party state structure was left intact.

iv. Cambodia

In 1863, Cambodia became a protectorate of France, and in October 1887 it became part of *Union Indochinoise* (Union of Indochina) along with Vietnam. Laos was added in 1893 after the French annexed it from the Siamese. From the time of King Norodom, the French controlled all levers of power in Cambodia, and even determined the accession of monarchs. On 25 April 1941, the French crowned Prince Norodom Sihanouk King of Cambodia in preference to his brother whom they regarded as too independent. Capitalising on the weakness of the French during World War II, Sihanouk unilaterally declared Cambodia's independence from France. However, this was short-lived, and the French returned to Indochina after the War. Due to internal pro-independence pressure, the French introduced multi-party elections in 1946. The Democratic Party, led by Prince Sisowaath Yutevong, won the elections. Prince Yutevong was the main architect of the Khmer Constitution of 1947, which he modelled on that of the French Fourth Republic. On 6 May 1947, King Sihanouk proclaimed the birth of the new Khmer Constitution.

Prince Yutevong did not live to see the fruits of his victory and his handiwork. He died on 17 July 1947 in mysterious circumstances, being only 34 years old at the time of his death. This ushered in a period of instability, with numerous changes in leadership. In 1953, King Sihanouk went to France to demand full independence for Cambodia, but the French demurred, thinking him an alarmist for exaggerating the anti-French sentiment building up in Cambodia. The King increased the stakes by declaring that until the French granted Cambodia independence, he would live in self-imposed exile in Thailand. The Thais did not welcome him and King Sihanouk left for the autonomous zone of Siem Reap, where he collaborated with Lieutenant-Colonel Lon Nol to fight the French. On 3 July 1953, the French backed down and declared themselves ready to discuss independence for Cambodia. The process was swift, and King Sihanouk succeeded in getting all his demands. Khmer Independence Day was

---

[138] See JJ Zasloff, 'The Emergence of the Constitution in Laos' in AP Blaustein and GH Flanz, *Constitutions of the Countries of the World* (New York: Oceana Publications, 1971) at 41.

[139] Ibid.

[140] '[T]here was no manifest demand for a constitution from an aroused Lao public opinion. Perhaps most important, party authorities, accustomed to rule without question, must have assigned low priority, despite their rhetoric to the contrary, to producing a document that might eventually lead to a challenge of their authority.' Ibid at 42.

proclaimed on 9 November 1953. The 1947 Constitution – which gave tremendous powers to the King – was amended in 1957 to guarantee fundamental rights and liberties to the people.

King Norodom Sihanouk (1922–2012) ruled till 1955 when he abdicated in favour of his father to form his own political party, the Sangkhum Reastr Niyum (People's Socialist Community), becoming the Prime Minister. Sihanouk continued to dominate politics in Cambodia until he was overthrown by his armed forces chief, Lon Nol, in a 1970 military coup. Sihanouk left for exile in China. In the meantime, Lon Nol, who was backed by the Americans, presided over an economically ruined and war-torn Cambodia from 1970 to 1975. The American bombing and the Vietnam War had spilled over into Cambodia's territory. In April 1975, the communist anti-government insurgent group, the Khmer Rouge (Red Cambodians), overthrew Lon Nol, and even Sihanouk supported the rebels from his base in China.

The Khmer Rouge, under the genocidal Pol Pot regime, began a programme of social reconstruction, plunging Cambodia into the Dark Ages. Throughout this period, the Cambodian Constitution was suspended, and law and legal institutions scarcely existed. Indeed, part of Pol Pot's pogrom was to execute anyone who was educated, hence the 'Killing Fields'.

On Christmas Day 1978, Vietnamese troops invaded Cambodia and overthrew the Pol Pot regime. A new Government headed by Hun Sen was established and governed with the backing of Vietnamese troops who occupied Cambodia from 1979–89. The Hun Sen regime had to do battle with three resistance groups: the royalist FUNCINPEC, founded by Prince Sihanouk; the Khmer People's National Liberation Front (KPNLF), led by former Prime Minister Son Sann; and the surviving Khmer Rouge army and leadership.[141]

B. Democratic Revolutions

Regime change usually engenders a corresponding change to a state's constitutional structure. Just as communist regimes brought about the transformation of constitutional systems in Asia, democratic revolutions did the same. In many ways, democratic revolutions are far less problematic than communist ones. Each of these revolutions occurred when the masses mobilised against a repressive or an authoritarian regime, thus engendering a break from the past. The break is both political and constitutional, and the legitimacy established is thus a combination of both. In this section, we consider the transformations in Indonesia, South Korea, Philippines, Cambodia and Mongolia. We begin with the cases of Mongolia and Indonesia, which are unique: both states became independent as a result of revolutionary breaks with their colonial past – Mongolia from China, and Indonesia from the Netherlands – and then experienced pro-democracy revolutions in the latter half of the twentieth century.

---

[141] Sorpong Peou, 'Cambodia: After the Killing Fields' in Funston (ed), above n 91, 36 at 38.

i. Mongolia

As noted in section II.C. above, Mongolia became independent in 1924 with the help of Soviet troops. It promulgated a Soviet-style Constitution that year, and this was followed by two other Soviet-inspired Constitutions in 1940 and 1960.[142] The 1940 Constitution explicitly committed Mongolia to a non-capitalist path of development and to state planning. The 1960 Constitution,[143] noted Professor William Butler, was a substantially reworked version of the 1940 Constitution, 'with an extensive preamble [that] placed socio-economic and political developments in Mongolia squarely within the context of developments in the Soviet Union' and that also 'recounted past achievements', evinced 'a renewed commitment to completing the construction of socialism, enunciated a declaration of basic foreign policy aims, and proclaimed the Mongolian People's Revolutionary Party to be the guiding and directing force of society'.[144]

In 1989, with the collapse of the Soviet Union, a populist movement brought down the Political Bureau of the Mongolian People's Republican Party (MPRP). This led to the holding of democratic general elections which the MPRP won. A Constitution Drafting Commission under the chairmanship of President Punsalmaagiin Ochirbat was established. The Commission completed a new Draft Constitution that was released and circulated to the public in June 1991.

Under this Constitution, a new unicameral national assembly, called the Mongolian Great Hural, would be created, with its members elected for six years. Another important innovation under the Constitution was the Constitutional Court. Another draft was produced in November 1991 after some deliberation and rethinking. After much consideration by legislators and the public, the final version of the Constitution was adopted on 13 January 1992.[145] It established a parliamentary-style democracy with guarantees of freedom of religion, rights, travel and expression. The Constitution was amended in 2001 and then again in 2010.[146]

ii. Indonesia[147]

Dutch acquisition of colonies in Southeast Asia began with their claim on Batavia (now Jakarta) in 1602. By the 1820s, their territories in the region comprised two blocs: the Dutch East Indies[148] and the Dutch West Indies.[149] Nascent pro-independence initiatives were accelerated by the Japanese occupation of Indonesia in 1942. Local

---

[142] See generally, WE Butler, *The Mongolian Legal System: Contemporary Legislation and Documentation* (The Hague: Martinus Nijhoff, 1982) at 174–230.

[143] See G Ginsburgs, 'Mongolia's "Socialist" Constitution' (1961) 34 *Pacific Affairs* 141.

[144] WE Butler, 'Mongolia: Introduction' in WB Simons (ed), *The Constitutions of the Communist World* (The Netherlands: Sijthoff & Noordhoff, 1980) 256 at 257.

[145] See AJK Sanders, 'Mongolia's New Constitution: Blueprint for Democracy' (1992) 32(6) *Asian Survey* 506.

[146] See Lhamsuren Munkh-Erdene, 'The Transformation of Mongolia's Political System: From Semi-Parliamentary to Parliamentary?' (2010) 50(2) *Asian Survey* 311.

[147] See generally, S Butt and T Lindsey, *The Constitution of Indonesia: A Contextual Analysis* (Oxford: Hart Publishing, 2012).

[148] The Dutch East Indies included the Indonesian territories of Java, Madura, Sumatra, Rhiau-Lingga Archipelago, Banka and Billiton, Celebes, Moluccas, Timor, Bali and Lombok, Dutch Borneo and Dutch New Guinea.

[149] This included Curacao (including Curacao, Bonaire, Aruba, St Martaans, St Estatius and Saba) and Surinam (Dutch Guiana).

leaders Sukarno and Mohamed Hatta collaborated with the Japanese and headed the Government. Just two days after the Japanese surrendered, Sukarno proclaimed Indonesia a republic on 17 August 1945. A new Constitution was promulgated the very next day.

The Dutch tried unsuccessfully to reassert control over Indonesia, eliciting immediate, fierce opposition from the Indonesians. In July, the Dutch sought to re-establish order by launching a 'police action', which resulted in a two-year battle with nationalist forces. In December 1948, the Dutch captured resistance leaders like Sukarno and Hatta but could not end the resistance put up by the 65,000-strong Japanese-trained military. In December 1949, the Netherlands agreed to 'an unconditional and complete transfer of sovereignty of the entire territory of the former Dutch East Indies (except Western New Guinea) to the Republic of the United States of Indonesia by 30 December 1949 at the latest'.[150] On 27 December 1949, the transfer of sovereignty took place. A few days earlier, Sukarno had been proclaimed President of the United States of Indonesia.

The Dutch decolonisation of Indonesia was considered a failure, 'because economic exploitation and social paternalism completely overshadowed political questions and the colonial powers neither envisaged nor prepared for gradual dissociation'.[151] Albertini argued that 'the Netherlands developed no real imperial concept or ideology and therefore did not feel obliged to consider the possibility of decolonization'.[152] The Constitution of 1949 was intended to be a provisional one and provided a federal state structure. Unfortunately, the federal structure was considered unsuitable given Indonesia's geographical nature, and a unitary state structure was implemented in 1950.[153]

In 1955, Indonesia held its first general elections since independence. However, the country was far from stable. In 1948, the Communists staged the Madiun Rebellion, and from 1950 to 1962, the Darul Islam movement fought for an Islamic state in the provinces of Aceh, West Java and South Sulawesi.[154] By 1956, Vice-President Mohd Hatta had fallen out with President Sukarno, and a number of local army commanders in Sumatra and Sulawesi proclaimed rival governments. By 1958 state institutions were beginning to crumble due to political infighting, and in 1959 Sukarno banned elections and announced that he would preside over a 'guided democracy'. He suspended the 1950 Constitution, established the National Advisory Council and reverted to the 1945 Constitution which provided greater presidential powers. During this period, Sukarno also became increasingly radical. He grew close to the People's Republic of China and the Partai Kommunist Indonesia (PKI, the local communist party), and brooked no opposition.[155]

Sukarno's 'guided democracy' experiment did not bring prosperity or economic growth. The Government was corrupt, and the country nearly collapsed. On 30 September, Sukarno arrested six leading generals and executed them, alleging a coup

---

[150] Ibid.

[151] Ibid at 487.

[152] See Albertini, above n 15, at 491.

[153] See generally, Oemar Seno Adji, 'An Indonesian Perspective on the American Constitutional Infuence' in L Ward Beer (ed), *Constitutionalism in Asia: Asian Views of the American Influence* (Berkeley, Cal: University of California Press, 1979) 102; and Padmo Wahjono, 'Democracy in Indonesia: Pancasila Democracy' in Ward Beer (ed), above n 14, 462.

[154] See AL Smith, 'Indonesia: Transforming the Leviathan' in Funston (ed), above n 91, 74.

[155] Ibid at 77.

plot. Within hours of the coup attempt, General Suharto, a little-known commander of the Kostrad, the military's strategic reserve, assumed control. Suharto blamed the coup on the PKI, and in the next two years allowed PKI supporters in central and east Java and Bali to be massacred by Muslims in a *jihad*. It is estimated that between 500,000 and one million people – many of whom were ethnic Chinese – were murdered. Sukarno was placed under house arrest and Suharto slowly assumed power. He was named Acting President in 1967. Suharto announced his New Order, emphasising 'authoritarian government, economic development and political stability'.[156] Suharto for the most part brought economic prosperity and a heightened living standards for Indonesians. However, corruption, nepotism and the regime's disrespect for human rights brought about Suharto's downfall.

During his many years in office, Suharto refused to consider amending the 1945 Constitution even though Sukarno himself had seen it as a provisional document. What made the Constitution next to impossible to amend were two decrees passed by the People's Consultative Assembly or *Majelis Permusyawaratan Rakyat* (MPR, Indonesia's legislature). The first, in 1983, required a nationwide referendum for any amendment to the Constitution, while the second, in 1985, required that for such a referendum to be valid, a 90 per cent voter turnout was necessary, and that all changes be approved by 90 per cent of those voting in the referendum. In May 1998, after 10 days of student-led anti-Government demonstrations, Suharto resigned and his Vice-President BJ Habibie took over.

Habibie had no choice but to embark upon political reform. He changed the law to allow new political parties to be formed, and early general elections were promised. Hundreds of political prisoners were also released. In June 1999, the first truly democratic elections were held in Indonesia since 1955.[157] In October 1999, the MPR decided to hold annual sessions to amend the Constitution. To that end, the First Amendment to the Constitution was passed in 1999 and the Second Amendment in August 2000. The Third Amendment was passed in 2001 and a Fourth in 2002. In the course of these amendments, the original 1945 Constitution was substantially altered, with a doubling of the number of Articles. More importantly, more than 80 per cent of the substantive content of the Constitution was altered. Among the most important changes effected by these amendments were the limiting of presidential terms to two; reconstituting the MPR to comprise a Regional Representative Council and a People's Consultative Council; direct election of the President; establishment of a Constitutional Court and a Judicial Commission; and 10 new Articles guaranteeing human rights. Interestingly, the democratic revolution of 1998 did not result in the replacement of the 1945 Constitution.

iii. The Philippines

The Philippines' independence from the United States in 1946 ushered in Southeast Asia's first truly democratic regime. From 1946 to 1972, the Philippines enjoyed American-style democracy, with considerable strides made in social-economic reform.

---

[156] See CD Neher, *Southeast Asia: Crossroads of the World* (DeKalb, Ill: Northern Illinois University Center for Southeast Asian Studies, 2000) at 108.

[157] Smith, above n 154, at 79.

Ferdinand Marcos was elected President in 1965 and re-elected in 1969. However, in his second term in office, Marcos was faced with major law-and-order problems. Private armies clashed and the communist-led New People's Army (NPA) gained ground. In the south, the Muslim Moro National Liberation Front (MNLF) was fighting a secessionist war.

In September 1972, Marcos proclaimed martial law. He abrogated the Constitution, repressed civil liberties and imprisoned his political opponents. Marcos argued that he needed to rule by decree in order to curb rising crime and to crush the NPA. He was constitutionally banned from contesting a third term, and his desire to hang onto power undoubtedly influenced his decision to declare martial law. Prior to Marcos's declaration of martial law, a Constitutional Convention elected in November 1970 had reviewed the 1935 Constitution, resulting in the adoption of the 1973 Constitution, which was very similar to the 1935 Constitution. Unique among the changes were the new provisions emphasising social and economic rights.[158]

Marcos called snap elections in 1986 to stem the growing opposition to his corrupt regime, following Benigno Aquino's assassination in 1983. Aquino's widow, Corazon 'Cory' Aquino, won a landslide victory, but Marcos declared himself duly re-elected. A spontaneous popular uprising called 'People Power' brought Marcos down, driving him from Malacanang Palace.

Cory Aquino was sworn in as President and immediately ordered a new Constitution to be drafted. The revolutionary pedigree of this new Constitution is evident, as Aquino governed by decree and through one of these decrees created a Constitutional Commission composed of her appointees. In a statement appended to Proclamation No 3 on the Provisional Constitution of the Revolutionary Government, Aquino declared:

> To hasten the restoration of full normal constitutional government, she shall appoint, within 60 days, men and women of probity and patriotism to a Constitutional Commission which will draft a constitution that will be submitted to the people in a national plebiscite.[159]

The time frame for the drafting of the new Constitution was one year. On 23 April 1986, Aquino issued Proclamation No 8, the Law Governing the Constitutional Commission of 1986, providing that the Commission comprise 'not more than fifty (50) national, regional, and sectoral representatives who shall be appointed by the President'.[160] The draft 1987 Constitution was approved on 12 October 1986, signed on 15 October and ratified on 2 February 1987.

Commentators have noted that the 1987 Constitution took yet another step away from the American model which had influenced both the 1935 and 1973 Constitutions. The American influence is most evident in three areas: the separation of powers; the Bill of Rights; and judicial review. The emphasis on social and economic rights in the 1987 Constitution was unique among Southeast Asian democratic Constitutions. The focus on social justice and protection for labour was taken to new heights. Article

---

[158] Art II Section 6 provides for state management of private property to ensure its equitable diffusion and enjoyment of its profits. Art II Section 7 states: 'The State shall establish, maintain, and ensure adequate social services in the field of education, health, housing, employment, welfare, and social security to guarantee the enjoyment of the people of a decent standard of living.'

[159] See Fernando and Quisiumbing-Fernando, above n 14, at 579.

[160] Ibid.

II Section 9 provides for freedom from poverty 'through policies that provide adequate social services, promote full employment, a rising standard of living, and an improved quality of life for all'. Special provisions were also drafted to promote agrarian and natural resources reform; urban land reform and housing; science and technology; arts and culture; and sports. Women are given special protection under Article XIII Section 14.[161]

The 1987 Filipino Constitution is the first revolutionary Constitution in Southeast Asia with a strong democratic ethos. It is remarkable for including indigenous elements and third-generation rights (in this case, social and economic rights). Aquino served the maximum single term as President, followed by Fidel Ramos who had served as her Vice-President.

iv. Cambodia

In 1991, the warring political factions signed a major peace accord and invited the UN to intervene in Cambodia. The United Nations Transitional Authority in Cambodia (UNTAC) was mandated to create a neutral political environment for free and fair elections. After two years, UNTAC held general elections in May 1993, and FUNCINPEC won 58 of the 120 seats. The Cambodian People's Party (CPP) won 51 seats, the KPNLF 10 seats and the independent Moulinaka one seat. The 120-member Constituent Assembly adopted a new Constitution promulgated by the reinstated King Sihanouk as head of state.

The 1993 Constitution was drafted by a 26-member multi-party committee formed on 30 June 1993, after the general elections. Following a short period of parliamentary debate, the Constitution was adopted by the Constituent Assembly. The Constitution was amended in March 1999 after opposition parties argued that more checks and balances were needed. The main change in 1999 was the creation of a Senate.[162] The 1993 Constitution is replete with democratic aspirations and values,[163] rejecting political authoritarianism. In 1997, Co-Prime Minister Hun Sen staged a successful coup to oust Prince Ranariddh (King Sihanouk's son) as his Co-Prime Minister. Hun Sen, who heads the CPP, then exploited internal strife within FUNCINPEC and emerged as Cambodia's strongman. The CPP won the 1998 elections convincingly, gaining 64 of the 123 seats, and continued to increase its majority in succeeding elections, with 73 seats in the 2003 elections and 90 seats in the 2008 elections, commanding 58 per cent of the votes.

---

[161] 'The State shall protect working women by providing safe and healthful working conditions, taking into account their maternal functions, and such facilities and opportunities that will enhance their welfare and enable them to realise their full potential in the service of the nation.'

[162] Article 11, as amended.

[163] Art 51 of the Constitution actually states that 'Cambodia adopts a policy of liberal democracy and pluralism'. Art 153 forbids any revision or amendment that affects 'the system of liberal and pluralistic democracy and the regime of Constitutional Monarchy'. Ibid at 41–42.

V. CONSTITUTION-MAKING IN ASIA: SOME GENERAL OBSERVATIONS

A. Epochs of Constitution-making and Asia

Professor Said Amir Arjomand summarises the development of constitutions around the world in five stages.[164]

The first stretches from the medieval and pre-modern era to the eighteenth century, 'where the dominant pattern of legal development in many traditions consisted of law-finding and jurisprudence while law-making was confined to administrative law by royal decrees'.[165]

The second stage takes place in the late eighteenth century, when 'political reconstruction' through 'rational design' takes place 'in the age of democratic revolutions'. In this stage, constitutions are made to elaborate 'a rational design for political reconstitution, alongside parliamentary law-making as an expression of national sovereignty and the principle of separation of powers'.[166]

The third stage is what Arjomand calls 'the age of modernization', which occurs in the second half of the nineteenth and early twentieth centuries. During this period, '(authoritarian) constitutions served as instruments of state-building and rationalisation of the centralised bureaucratic *Rechtsstaat*, and law-making by parliaments and administrative organs dominated legal development'.[167]

The fourth stage is the 'era of ideological constitutions as instruments of social transformation' which spans 1917 and 1989. This stage was 'marked by the subservience of narrowly conceived rule of law and legality to the dominant ideology of the regime' and included the period of decolonisation (1947–1970s), 'in which a significant number of new states wedded ideological constitution-making to developmentalism, as the age of ideology spread from the first and the second worlds to the emerging third world'.[168]

Arjomand calls the fifth stage the 'era of new constitutionalism', which starts from 1989, following the end of the Cold War. Constitutions framed in this period are 'marked by a mixture of increasingly judicialised legislation by parliaments and administrative organs and legislative jurisprudence by the constitutional courts and supra-national judiciary organs'.[169]

The earliest modern constitutions in Asia – those of Japan, China and Mongolia – were drafted during the second stage and were clearly attempts to introduce 'modern' and 'rational' forms of government to these states, although it may be added that in the case of Mongolia, it was the overriding influence of the Soviet Union that led to its adoption of a socialist constitution.

---

[164] SA Arjomand, 'Constitutonal Development and Political Reconstruction from Nation-building to New Constitutionalism' in SA Arjomand (ed), *Constitutionalism and Political Reconstruction* (Leiden: Brill, 2007) 3 at 6–7.

[165] Ibid at 6.

[166] Ibid.

[167] Ibid at 7.

[168] Ibid.

[169] Ibid.

Most of the other constitutions in Asia were drafted in the third stage (1947–1970s), following the departure of the European colonial powers and the decolonisation process that took place in its aftermath. The constitutions of the former British colonies (Burma, Sri Lanka, India, Pakistan, Malaysia, Singapore and Brunei) and of Indonesia (the former Dutch East Indies) may be classified in this category. In addition, the defeat of Japan in World War II led to the independence of Korea and Taiwan, and their constitutions were framed in this third stage (even if that of Taiwan was a hold-over from Republican China). The last of these decolonisation constitutions to be crafted was that of Timor Leste. Abandoned by Portugal in 1975, it was invaded by Indonesia. In 1999, following a United Nations-sponsored referendum, Indonesian forces withdrew and a constituent assembly was elected in 2001 to draft a new constitution. The new Constitution was promulgated in 2002.

In the post-1989 era, several states in Asia also embarked on constitution-making exercises: Thailand (1991, 1997, 2006), Cambodia (1993), Mongolia (1992), Nepal (2007), Bhutan (2008), Myanmar (2008) and Timor Leste (2001). Of Thailand's post-1989 Constitutions, only the 1997 Constitution – considered the most democratic ever promulgated, with a full-elected bicameral legislature and a Constitutional Court – is of the variety highlighted by Arjomand. Mongolia abandoned it socialist-style Constitution in 1992, following the 1990 democratic revolution that swept Mongolia after the fall of the Berlin Wall and the collapse of the Soviet Union. This Constitution established a parliamentary democracy and contained a list of guaranteed rights and freedoms. A Constitutional Court was also created.

Nepal promulgated a new Constitution in 1990 and, following the decade-long Maoist rebellion (1996–2006) against the monarchy, put in place an Interim Constitution in 2007. As of the end of 2012, the long-promised new Constitution had not yet been revealed. Starting from 2001, Bhutan's monarchy did the unthinkable – it voluntarily gave up its absolute powers. King Jigme Singye Wangchuck convened a committee comprising the *Lhengye Zhungstchog* (Council of Ministers), the Chief Justice and the Royal Advisory Council to draft a constitution of the kingdom. This eventually passed into law in 2008 and established Bhutan as a democratic constitutional monarchy with power in the hands of elected representatives in the Parliament of Bhutan.

B. Constitutionalism and Legitimacy

Constitution-making may be induced by any of the following factors:

(a) a social or economic crisis;
(b) a revolution;
(c) regime collapse (or fear of regime collapse);
(d) defeat in war;
(e) reconstruction after war;
(f) creation of a new state; and
(g) liberation after colonial rule.[170]

---

[170] See J Elster, 'Forces and Mechanisms in the Constitution-making Process' (1995) 45 *Duke Law Journal* 364 at 371.

In all these cases, framers of constitutions will do their best to achieve two things: first, to create a set of institutions that will work well in the setting in which it is intended to operate; and, secondly, to imbue the constitution with as much legitimacy as possible. Both these objects are highly practical in nature. If a constitution contains rules or institutions that do not sit comfortably with the legal culture of the society in which it is to work, it will soon be marginalised. At the same time, for a constitution to work well, it must command the respect and confidence of society at large. One of the best ways to do this is to engage the widest possible segment of the population in its drafting or creation. The bigger the majority, the great the support, and correspondingly, the greater a constitution's legitimacy.

i. Majoritarian Legitimacy

Legal legitimacy may be attained in two ways. The first is in tracing a line of legal authority linking the present to the past. Legal continuity legitimises changes in legal and political structures through legally-sanctioned amendments to the constitution. However, if such continuities are broken – whether through revolution, secession or a plebiscite – both legality and legitimacy are conferred anew by the overwhelming endorsement of the new constitutional order by 'the people'. This reference back to 'the people' (however defined) is premised on the democratic principles of individual choice, autonomy and political freedom. As Professor Carl J Friedrich pointed out:

> Legitimate rule is rightful rule, and many specific grounds have been believed in the course of the evolution of government. Constitutionalism has been the modern ground: only a regime which is based upon the will of the people is legitimate. To put it another way: the constitution-making power, the constituent power of the people provides legitimate government. By the middle of the twentieth century the prevalent claim to legitimacy is democratic legitmacy.[171]

Two problems of legitimacy arise for consideration here. The first is a legal one arising from the method by which most post-colonial constitutions are drafted. The second concerns the limit of constitutional government in a newly-independent state.

Many new governments lack the necessary constitutional legitimacy to function effectively at independence because of the way their post-independence constitutions were drafted. Very often these constitutions were drafted by the departing colonial powers and were the result of a series of compromises among contending political actors, and more importantly of the desire of the colonial powers to impose their idea of government on the 'natives'. This caused numerous problems when the state eventually succeeded in getting independence. Cultural differences, coupled with a distinct distrust of the former colonial power, served further to undermine the legitimacy of the constitution that was eventually drafted. As McWhinney argued:

> The new post-colonial constitutions were invariably highly derivative, and tended to borrow very heavily from the constitutional institutions and developed practices of the 'parent' European powers involved; . . . Some of the later political and economic problems of this group of 'succession' states . . . undoubtedly stem from this constitutional eclecticism – too-ready application to non-European societies of essentially European constitutional stereotypes, without prior examination of whether the different communities concerned were

---

[171] CJ Friedrich, *Limited Government: A Comparison* (Englewood Cliffs, NJ: Prentice-Hall, 1974) 110.

at the same essential stages of political and economic stages of development, and whether, in consequence, the socio-economic infrastructures that inevitably condition the operation of positive law prescriptions were the same.[172]

One of the most popular majoritarian devices used is the *constituent assembly*.[173] The idea of a constituent assembly as a separate and distinct entity from the legislature, with the sole purpose of drafting or adopting a constitution, gained popularity in eighteenth-century America when the various States used constitutional conventions to draft and adopt constitutions of their own. This led to the Constitutional Convention of Philadelphia in 1787, which drafted the Constitution of the United States of America and remains the most famous and inspirational of such conventions.

There are several reasons why constituent assemblies have been used:[174]

(a) tradition;
(b) inadequacy of existing amendment processes to facilitate a major overhaul of the constitution, especially where radical changes are needed, or where the proverbial legal revolutionary break with the past is required (such as when Ceylon wanted to cease being a dominion of Great Britain in 1972);[175]
(c) where there are no legitimate institutions to undertake the task of constitution-making (such as when the state collapsed in Cambodia in 1993, or when Indonesia withdrew from Timor Leste in 2001); and
(d) the representative and inclusive nature of such assemblies in which 'the people' can participate in the moulding of their constitution.

Today, the constituent assembly is seen as

embodying people's sovereignty, as reflecting diversity, and being linked to the broad social charter character of the ultimate constitution. It is used to develop a consensus in deeply divided societies, and to define the country's identity. This emphasis reflects the nature of many contemporary constitutions – as negotiated documents, a way out of political or ethnic stalemate, an exercise in building and consolidating peace, solving internal conflicts, managing diversity and aiming at inclusiveness. Consequently, the older models of the constituent assembly may not be always useful today. The structure, powers and procedures of the constituent assembly must reflect these changed realities.[176]

Traditionally, the British did not favour constituent assemblies. Indeed, they long resisted Indian demands for a constituent assembly, finally convening one in 1946, after almost two decades of dithering. Constituent assemblies were also convened in Pakistan and Burma in 1947 during the process of decolonisation. Another early Asian constituent assembly was that of the Republic of China, which in 1946 promulgated the KMT-drafted Constitution. In the post-independence era, several other Asian states convened constituent assemblies to redraft their constitutions. The first

---

[172] E McWhinney, *Constitution Making: Principles, Process, Practice* (Toronto: University of Toronto Press, 1981)
[173] On the role of constituent assemblies in Constitution-making, see Y Ghai, *The Role of Constituent Assemblies in Constitution Making* (Institute for Democracy and Electoral Assistance, available at <http//:www.idea.int>); see also RS Kay, 'Constituent Authority' (2011) 59 *American Journal of Comparative Law* 715.
[174] See Ghai, above n 173, at 8–10.
[175] See WA Wiswa Warnapala, 'The New Constitution of Sri Lanka' (1973) 13(12) *Asian Survey* 1179.
[176] Ghai, above n 173, at 10.

was Indonesia, which elected a *Konstituante* in 1955 to draw up a permanent constitution. The *Konstituante* sat between 1956 and 1959, but was dissolved in June 1959 by President Sukarno who restored the 1945 Constitution by decree.[177]

The most recent constituent assembly in Asia is that of Nepal. Following the end of the Nepali Civil War in 2006, and at the insistence of the Communist Party of Nepal, a constituent assembly was convened. A total of 601 members were elected under the terms of the Interim Constitution of Nepal (2007). Of these, 240 were elected through direct elections, while 335 were elected through a proportional election system; the remaining 26 members were nominated. The Assembly, which first convened on 28 May 2008, proclaimed Nepal a republic and abolished the monarchy. It was given four years to draft a new constitution but failed to do so and was dissolved on 28 May 2012. Elections were held on 22 November 2012 to constitute a new constituent assembly to carry on the work of the first Assembly.

This reference back to 'the People' is a necessary legal fiction that lends legitimacy to the constitutional orders that are ascribed to this collective.[178] As Hahm and Kim astutely observe:

> By many accounts, the entire legitimacy and practice of constitutional founding hinge on 'We the People.' Virtually all modern constitutions claim some mandate from the people who gave birth to it at some discrete point in time. The constitution is also seen as always subject to amendment and even abrogation by the same people. In a sort of 'he that giveth, may also taketh away' logic, modern democratic constitutions are destined to have life so long as the people find it pleasing. And a constitution will be pleasing to the people insofar as it is perceived to be faithfully implementing their will. This is the case despite disagreements at the retail level as to how best to implement the people's will. As regards the constitution, 'We the people' is its author and font of legitimacy as well as its master and chief beneficiary.
>
> ... The identity of the people, as such, is assumed to remain constant over time despite the deeply transformative politics entailed in the historic act of constitutional founding. The people are also assumed to have an agency that is nearly omnipotent vis-à-vis the political and constitutional universe they create. If they so choose, 'We the People' are always free to make a new world, a *novus ordo saeclorum*, through another constitutional founding. On this view, the priority of the people over the constitution is not only natural (as a matter of logic) but also necessary (as a matter of normative reasoning).[179]

Attractive as this legal fiction may be, it is nevertheless a fiction. In studying the history of state formation and constitution-making in Asia, it is clear that 'the People' are seldom in the driver's seat and had little, if any, role to play in crafting their own constitutions. As Hahm and Kim found, in their study of the evolution of the Japanese and South Korean constitutions,

> the relationship between the people and the constitution, in both Korea and Japan, was much more complex than meets the eye.

[177] See H Feith, *The Decline of Constitutional Democracy in Indonesia* (Ithaca. NY: Cornell University Press, 1962); and DS Lev, *The Transition to Guided Democracy: Indonesian Politics 1957–1959* (Ithaca, NY: Department of Asian Studies, Cornell University, 1966).

[178] See Z Elkins, T Ginsburg and J Blount, 'The Citizen as Founder: Public Participation in Constitutional Approval' (2008) 81 *Temple Law Review* 361.

[179] See C Hahm and SH Kim, 'To Make "We the People": Constitutional Founding in Postwar Japan and South Korea' (2010) 8(4) *International Journal of Constitutional Law* 800 at 800–02.

The 'people' that authored the constitutions had to be 'constituted' even as they were establishing a new constitutional order. And although both countries had been inhabited by people with discrete political and cultural identities for many centuries, the 'people', as a constituent agent, was a new phenomenon. It emerged in the course of a constitutional politics involving intense interactions with external forces, selective appropriations of the past, and redefinitions of the boundaries of membership.

We believe that both instances of constitution making demonstrate that – neither timeless nor omnipotent – the 'people' is a political and historical construct the identities and boundaries of which are continuously subject to constant redefinition in negotiation with externalities.[180]

The utility of majoritarian legitimacy is thus limited if 'the People' are not really behind the framing of their own constitutions. Where, then, may other sources of legitimacy be found?

ii. *Economic and Legal Legitimacy*

Legal or constitutional legitimacy is insufficient to ensure that a government remains in power. At the same time it fails to provide a satisfactory justification for continued existence when faced with a horde of starving people. Power, once obtained, has to be used effectively to satisfy the demands made on the government – be they economic, social or otherwise. The problem is that while constitutions may provide blueprints for good government in the legal sense, they have had little to say about good government in the political sense.

Even a legitimate government will lose its right to rule unless it continuously reinforces its right to govern. This is done through what Professor Carl J Friedrich calls 'performance legitimacy':

> Success in war, and the maintenance of prosperity, order, and peace are important ingredients. The legitimizing effect of good performance is great, and the decline in legitimacy as a result of failure has been important in the operation of democratic regimes . . . Democratic legitimacy in modern constitutional regimes is subject to continuous performance tests, especially in the economic realm; the original legitimacy of a newly elected government may be broadened or narrowed by the performance achieved in its operation.[181]

This view of legitimacy and constitutional government is also echoed by Lipset:

> The stability of any given democracy depends not only on economic development but also upon the effectiveness and the legitimacy of its political system. Effectiveness means actual performance, the extent to which the system satisfies the basic functions of government as most of the population and such powerful groups within it as big business or the armed forces see them.[182]

The idea of rights, freedom and limited government mean very little to people living on the verge of starvation. Neither does it mean much to those who see their standards of living falling day by day. Abraham Maslow, in his classic book *Motivation and Personality*,[183] postulates that man has several levels of needs, the most crucial and

---

[180] Ibid at 848.
[181] Friedrich, above n 171, at 114.
[182] MS Lipset, *Political Man* (London: Mercury Books, 1961) at 64.
[183] A Maslow, *Motivation and Personality*, 2nd edn (New York: Harper & Row, 1970).

basic of which is physiological in nature. Therefore, unless a government – whether legally or constitutionally legitimate or not – confronts and deals with basic issues such as food, housing, job opportunities and education, its legitimacy will quickly evaporate.[184]

VI. CONCLUSION

What generalisations can we offer from our brief study of constitution-making and the quest for legitimacy in Asia? Three observations may be proffered. The *first* is that constitutions imbued with a combination of both political and legal legitimacy are more likely to endure. The corollary of this observation is that constitutions that are not considered legally or politically legitimate are more likely than not to be abandoned or rewritten. Thus, constitutions that were created through a devolutionary process that kept their legal lineage intact, and which continued to act as the fulcrum of political and state organisation, are most likely to last. Constitutions that endure acquire a patina of legitimacy on account of their age and lineage. The fact of their longevity reinforces the legitimacy that gave them long life.

However, the mere fact that a constitution lasts is no indication of the value it holds for its people. For example, the 1948 South Korean Constitution was never abandoned, but it is doubtful if the Korean people thought too well of its amended form when they were being repressed by the Government of Park Chung-hee. Yet lineage is important in maintaining legitimacy. We saw this in the instance of the debate between the Americans and the Japanese during the drafting of the Japanese Constitution, with the Japanese preferring to amend, rather than discard, the Meiji Constitution. Enduring constitutions do not always enjoy the same level of confidence and legitimacy throughout their existence. In many ways, the constitutional document is an edifice that may at one time be ignored or even scorned, and at another be revered and relied upon. The vicissitudes of political life guarantee that no consistent value can be placed on any particular constitution.

The *second* observation is that clean breaks with the past – ie a break in legal continuity – engendered by cataclysmic events (such as a revolution) actually make Constitutions drafted in the aftermath much more valuable. Perhaps there is wisdom in Thomas Jefferson's injunction to us to engage in a revolution every now and then.[185] The mass mobilisation of the people to act in unison in contemplating their political futures and fates makes for the ideal constitutional moment for cementing the ties that bind them and the constitutions they make. The longevity of the revolutionary constitutions of China and Vietnam suggest that these constitutions are perceived by the people in these countries as legitimate. Yet this need not be the case. It all depends on the people's perception of a constitution. In the case of China and Vietnam, the personal charisma of their early leaders – Mao Zedong and Ho Chi Minh – allowed them to personalise power to the extent that the constitutions themselves do not matter very

---

[184] See KYL Tan, 'Economic Development and the Prospects for Constitutionalism' in A Chin and A Choi (eds), *Law, Social Sciences And Public Policy: Towards A Unified Framework* (Singapore: Singapore University Press, 1998) 187.

[185] Jefferson famously wrote to Madison: 'A little rebellion now and then is a good thing.'

much. Democratic revolutions are another matter, for such revolutions necessarily involve mass mobilisation, and the key democratic instinct will be to subject governments to laws.

Our *third* observation is that constitutions that exist purely on the basis of political legitimacy are inherently problematic and tend to be unstable. Constitutional legitimacy serves to limit government in particular ways – for example, by limiting the power of a president, or by separating powers into the various branches of government. When constitutional legitimacy is lost and where governments are sustained by pure political power alone, the temptation constantly to redraft the constitution or to abandon it will be great. The difficult cases of Thailand, Burma and Pakistan bear testimony to this. The main problem in these three countries is that outside the established constitutional centres of power – the legislature, the executive and the judiciary – there exist other, more powerful centres of power, such as the military and the monarch, who are legitimised in their own ways that may well trump whatever legitimacy the constitution may possess.

Constitutions are often the handiwork of idealists and showpieces of nascent democracies. However, as we have seen in our brief look at constitutional development in Asia, constitutions have also been centres of controversy or the playthings of erstwhile dictators and military strongmen. Constitutions cannot function in the absence of political and social order. Where the rule of law is replaced by anarchy, constitutions fade into oblivion. Ultimately, what makes constitutions work depend on three factors. First, a state where order prevails and where choice is possible for its citizens will allow the constitution to breathe and work. Secondly, a constitution must successfully meet the challenges arising in the state in which it is expected to function. It must be responsive, relevant and provide a suitable framework to allow competing interests and conflicts to be sorted out legally and peacefully. Lastly, the subjects of a constitution must believe in the rule of law and the primacy of law over man. Only then will a constitution be respected and cherished, and over time attain the patina of legitimacy so important in fostering a functional constitutional democracy.

2

Constitutional Cultures in Asia

I. INTRODUCTION

To understand how a constitution really functions, we need to understand how people feel about it; we need to understand the prevailing constitutional culture of that society. Beyond the text ('Big C Constitution') and 'super-statutes' ('small c constitution'),[1] it is imperative that we also understand the important role played by conventions, constitutional custom,[2] or 'soft constitutional law'[3] in maintaining the constitutional order. This is because the rule of law prevails 'not because the courts or police say it should, but because there exists a general acceptance of and confidence in the law'.[4] As Wenzel puts it, these constraints, which are 'captured in the concept of constitutional culture', are 'best understood as a Hayekian mental model' and provide 'a heuristic that people use to make sense of the world and guide their actions'.[5] This accords with the realist perspective of constitutions. Karl Llewellyn, for example, viewed the constitution as a living institution[6] which is 'in first instance a set of ways of living and doing', rather than 'a matter of words or rules'.[7] It rests on people behaving in certain patterns such that 'the working Constitution is in good part utterly extra-Documentary'[8] and is 'a way of doing things'.[9] Llewellyn considered the ways and attitudes of three groups of persons concerned with the working of the constitution:

---

[1] See A King, *Does the United Kingdom still have a Constitution?* (Hamlyn Lectures) (London: Sweet & Maxwell, 2001). In the US context, see WN Eskridge and J Ferejohn, 'Super-Statutes' (2001) 50 *Duke Law Journal* 1215.

[2] The South Korean Constitutional Court inferred from long, continuing practice a 'national consensus' that Seoul was the capital of the nation, and that this was 'a constitutional custom that has traditionally existed since even prior to the establishment of our written Constitution, and a norm that is clear in itself and a premise upon which the Constitution is based although not stated in an express provision in our Constitution.' It was thus part of 'the unwritten constitution established in the form of a constitutional custom'; this had the same effect as that of the written constitution, subject only to change regulated by Art 130 which requires a referendum. *Relocation of the Capital City Case* (16-2(B) KCCR 1, 2004Hun-Ma554, 566 (consolidated), October 21, 2004).

[3] These are interpretive statements issued by the executive which while not legally binding have some legal effect and influence on the behaviour and expectations of constitutional actors. See Li-ann Thio, 'Soft Constitutional Law in Non-liberal Asian Constitutional Democracies' 2010 8(4) *International Journal of Constitutional Law* 766–99.

[4] 'Preface' to DP Franklin and MJ Baun (eds), *Political Culture and Constitutionalism: A Comparative Approach* (Armonk, NY: ME Sharpe, 1995) at vii–viii.

[5] N Wenzel, 'Towards a Research Agenda on the Emergence of (Informal) Constitutional Culture into (Formal) Constitutional Order' (2012) 5 *Studies in Emergent Order* 1, available at <http://docs.sieo.org/SIEO_5_2012_Wenzel.pdf> (accessed 10 February 2013).

[6] K Llewellyn, 'The Constitution as an Institution' (1934) 34 *Columbia Law Review* 1.

[7] Ibid at 17–18.

[8] Llewellyn, ibid at 15, gave the example of a senatorial filibuster which has no textual basis.

[9] M Palmer, 'New Zealand Constitutional Culture' (2007) 22 *New Zealand Universities Law Review* 565.

(a) 'specialists in governing', including office-holders;
(b) interested groups; and
(c) the general public.[10]

Canadian philosopher James Tully described constitutions as 'chains of continual intercultural negotiations' based on mutual recognition and consent,[11] which may comprise structures, processes, principles, rules, conventions and even culture, if they significantly affect the way government power is exercised.[12] Constitutional culture is thus not static but in flux; it speaks to the obligations, expectations and aspirations of constitutional actors and citizens in general.

II. LAW, CULTURE AND THE CONSTITUTION

'Culture' is an inherently problematic concept because of its all-inclusive breadth. The British anthropologist, Sir Edward Burnett Tylor, writing in 1871, defined it as 'that complex whole which includes knowledge, belief, arts, morals, law, custom, and any other capabilities and habits acquired by man as a member of society'.[13] Culture is an intrinsic part of society, and accordingly impacts its laws and legal institutions. The German jurist Frederich Karl von Savigny (1779–1861) argued that law was peculiar to and emerged from the spirit of the people or the *Volk*. Borrowing from the work of Johann Gottfried von Herder (1744–1803), who coined the phrase *Volkgeist* or spirit of the people, he argued that law, just like language, was an expression of the common consciousness of the people.[14] Law, von Savigny said,

> will be found to have . . . a fixed character, peculiar to the *Volk*, like their language, manners and constitution . . . That which binds them into one whole is the common conviction of the *Volk*, the kindred consciousness of an inward necessity, excluding all notion of an accidental and arbitrary origin . . . this organic connection of law with the being and character of the *Volk* . . . may be compared with language. For law, as for language, there is no moment of absolute cessation; it is subject to the same movement and development as every other popular tendency; and this very development remains under the same law of inward necessity . . . the common consciousness of the *Volk* is the peculiar seat of law . . . law is originally formed on the manner in which customary law is said to have been formed: ie, it is first developed by custom and popular faith . . . therefore, by internal silently-operating powers, not by the arbitrary will of a law-giver . . .[15]

The idea that law emerges from a shared past and community led some anthropologists to study how culture and personality might have an impact on 'national character', and

---

[10] Llewellyn, above n 6, at 19, 21.

[11] J Tully, *Strange Multiplicity: Constitutionalism in an Age of Diversity* (Cambridge: Cambridge University Press, 1995) at 5 and 185.

[12] M Palmer, 'Using Constitutional Realism to Identify the Complete Constitution: Lessons from an Unwritten Constitution' (2006) 54(3) *American Journal of Comparative Law* 587 at 595.

[13] E Tylor, *Primitive Culture* (Gloucester, Maine: Smith, 1871) at 1.

[14] FK von Savigny, *On the Vocation of Our Age for Legislation and Jurisprudence*, Abraham Hayward (trans) (New Jersey: The Lawbook Exchange, 2002; orig pub 1841) at 28.

[15] Ibid. This quote is a combination of several passages of von Savigny's work, and quoted directly from M Franklin, 'The Kantian Foundations of the Historical School of Law of Savigny' (1952–1953) 22 *Revista Juridica de la Universidad de Puerto Rico* 64 at 67.

how this in turn might impact various other social phenomena, such as law. In her groundbreaking and highly-influential war-time study of Japanese culture and character, anthropologist Ruth Benedict[16] studied (albeit at a distance) and described the Japanese national character. This spawned a whole series of studies about 'national character'.[17] Such studies are inherently problematic, not least because concepts of society and nation often do not overlap.[18] Moreover, such studies presuppose the existence of *a Volk*, a homogeneous polity or society, which is unrealistic. Furthermore, it is difficult to see how behaviour can properly be imputed to certain actors, or whether the structure of its rules and institutions creates and modifies personality.[19]

Even so, this has not stopped scholars from making nation-based generalisations about society and how these societies respond to law. China-born American anthropologist Francis LK Hsu, for example, observed that Hindu Indians were supernatural-centred; the Chinese were situation-centred and Americans were individual-centred.[20] Two scholars have further suggested that the Chinese conceptions of law have been shaped by the Confucian, Legalist and Buddhist traditions.[21] Japan, it is said, has also been influenced by the Confucian and Buddhist traditions, in addition to Shinto, and by its physical isolation as an island-nation.[22] Korea, too, has been 'greatly influenced by two thousand years of Confucian teachings'.[23] The Sinologist and political scientist Lucian Pye went one step further by generalising about Asians whom he thought desired authority and thus 'respect authority too much to share the Western distrust of authority and power'.[24] More recently, Professor James McHugh, in discussing constitutional traditions, highlights an Eastern Legal Tradition that stresses 'the holistic nature of human activity and the interconnected qualities of all legal, political, social, economic, family and other phenomena'.[25] For McHugh, religion appears to be the most important factor influencing political and constitutional culture in both India and Japan.[26]

Such generalisations, while interesting, are ultimately useless in helping us understand constitutional and legal systems. Greater specificity and thick description[27] will,

---

[16] R Benedict, *The Chrysanthemum and the Sword: Patterns of Japanese Culture* (Boston, Mass: Houghton Mifflin, 1946).

[17] See, eg, M Mead, *And Keep Your Power Dry: An Anthropologist Looks at America* (New York: Morrow, 1965); G Gorer, *The American People: A Study in National Character* (New York: WW Norton, 1948); G Gorer, *Exploring English Character* (New York: Criterion Books, 1955); AJ Barnouw, *The Dutch: A Portrait Study of the People of Holland* (New York: Columbia University Press, 1940); and G Gorer and J Rickman, *The People of Great Russia: A Psychological Study* (New York: WW Norton, 1949).

[18] See E Adamson Hoebel, 'Anthropological Perspectives on National Character' (1967) 370 *Annals of the Amercian Academy of Political and Social Science* 1; and MC Farber, 'The Problem of National Character: A Methodological Analysis' (1950) 30(2) *Journal of Psychology* 307.

[19] Farber, above n 18.

[20] FLK Hsu, *Clan, Class and Club* (Princeton, NJ: D van Nostrand, 1963).

[21] LT Lee and WW Lai, 'The Chinese Conceptions of Law: Confucian, Legalist, and Buddhist' (1977–1978) 29 *Hastings Law Journal* 1307.

[22] See Chin Kim and CM Lawson, 'The Law of the Subtle Mind: The Traditional Japanese Conception of Law' (1979) 28(3) *International & Comparative Law Quarterly* 491.

[23] Dai-Kwon Choi, 'Western Law in a Traditional Society Korea' (1980) 8 *Korean Journal of Comparative Law* 177.

[24] LW Pye, *Asian Power and Politics: The Cultural Dimensions of Authority* (Harvard, Mass: Belknap Press, 1985) at x.

[25] JT McHugh, *Comparative Constitutional Traditions* (New York: Peter Lang, 2002) at 6.

[26] Ibid at 101–16; and 117–32.

[27] See C Geertz, 'Thick Description: Toward an Interpretative Theory of Culture' in C Geertz, *The Interpretation of Cultures* (New York: Basic Books, 1973).

we suggest, lead us closer to the truth. A useful starting point would be the work of Lawrence M Friedman, who coined and popularised the term 'legal culture'.[28] Friedman has used the term to 'describe a number of related phenomena':

> First, it refers to public knowledge of and attitudes and behavior patterns toward the legal system. Do people feel and act as if courts are fair? When are they willing to use courts? What parts of the law do they consider legitimate? What do they know about the law in general? These attitudes differ from person to person, but one can also speak of the legal culture of a country or a group, if there are patterns that distinguish it from the culture of other countries or groups. A specially important kind of group legal culture is that of legal professionals – the values, ideologies, and principles of lawyers, judges, and others who work within the magic circle of the legal system.[29]

Friedman's definition can easily be adapted to our understanding of what might constitute 'constitutional culture': the ideas, values, attitudes and opinions people in a given polity hold with respect to law and the constitution.[30] It is 'a web of interpretive norms, canons, and practices which most members of a particular community accept and employ',[31] and affects a constitution's legitimacy and utility in, for example, vindicating rights.[32] A much narrower definition of 'constitutional culture' would be 'a culture that accepts constitutionalism'[33] through a written instrument that constrains power by establishing parameters for the conduct of ordinary politics. Such a definition necessarily excludes, as a form of 'anti-constitutionalism', the lamentable use of the constitution to give untrammelled and despotic powers to an individual or oligarchic elite, allowing them to rule by *ipse dixit*.[34] Here, the written document becomes a mere handmaiden of the rulers, a constitution bereft of constitutionalism.[35]

More broadly, it encompasses

> the implicit and explicit . . . thoughts, feelings, beliefs, impressions and norms a group holds about the nature, scope and function of constitutional constraints; the thoughts and feelings about balancing political expediency with constitutional principle; and levels of trust and cooperation, within one's community, and also with strangers.[36]

---

[28] For a good overview, see R Cotterell, 'Comparative Law and Legal Culture' in M Reimann and R Zimmermann (eds), *The Oxford Handbook on Comparative Law* (Oxford: Oxford University Press, 2006) 710.

[29] LM Friedman, *The Legal System: A Social Science Perspective* (New York: Russell Sage Foundation, 1975) at 193–94.

[30] See LM Friedman, *The Republic of Choice: Law, Authority and Culture* (Cambridge, Mass: Harvard University Press, 1990) at 4; see also L Friedman, *The Legal System: A Social Science Perspective* (New York: Russell Sage Foundation, 1975) 193–94. For a critique, see R Cotterell, 'The Concept of Legal Culture' in D Nelken (ed), *Comparing Legal Cultures* (Dartmouth, 1997) at 13.

[31] 'Editors' Introduction' in J Ferejohn, JN Rakove and J Riley (eds), *Constitutional Culture and Democratic Rule* (New York: Cambridge University Press, 2001) at 10–11.

[32] RP Pereenboom, 'What's wrong with Chinese Rights? Towards a Theory of Rights with Chinese Characteristics' (1993) 6 *Harvard Human Rights Journal* 29 at 35: '[F]or human rights to be respected, there must be rights consciousness, a culture of rights, an attitude among the people that the government cannot do to them as it wishes. The people must learn to stand up to the government and insist on their rights.'

[33] Wenzel, n 5 above.

[34] G Walker, 'The Idea of Non-liberal Constitutionalism' in I Shapiro and W Kymlicka (eds), *Ethnicity and Group Rights* (New York: NYU Press, 1997) 154 at 166.

[35] HWO Okoth-Ogendo, 'Constitutions without Constitutionalism: Reflections on an African Political Paradox' in D Greenberg et al (eds), *Constitutionalism and Democracy: Transitions in the Contemporary World* (Oxford University Press, 1993), 73 .

[36] Wenzel, n 5 above, at 3. See further Ferejohn et al (eds), above n 31.

This includes the citizens' recognition that they are governed by a written document that creates and limits government institutions; belief that they created this founding text, which, until amended, is binding; and understanding that the constitution unifies society through affirming a common identity.[37]

The Armenian politician and scholar, Gagik Harutyunian describes constitutional culture as 'as an intellectually evolving system of values' with 'deep historical roots', incarnate in 'unwritten constitutions', customs, tradition, spiritual values and canon, statutes and rules of constituting significance.[38] It is 'an important element of the entire intellectual and cultural heritage of a nation, of its collective memory'.[39] As such, it cannot be 'anational'[40] since the constitution is a site for mediating universal values and local particularities; a system of values that live, are reproduced, and provide guidance for public life.[41] Constitutional culture thus composes 'the framework of intangibles within which an interpretive community operates'.[42] It has normative force and shapes community identity, thus reflecting the centrality or marginalisation of the constitution in public life. Indeed, the presence of a constitutional culture is so vital that German philosopher and jurist Bernhard Schlink felt that unless it existed, the instrument of the constitution may be little more than a façade. [43] Wenzel's idea of constitutional culture 'encompasses such things as willingness to sacrifice constitutional procedure for a desired result, philosophical vision of political goods to be delivered by a constitution, the balance between majoritarianism and constitutional constraint'.[44]

The basic idea of legal culture assumes that law (as in rules, practices, institutions, doctrines, etc) must be understood as being embedded in a broader culture. Law is shaped, moulded, affected by the practices, traditions and understandings of the professional lawyers, but equally by the broader society that experiences, reflects, uses or ignores the law. It is understood as being 'cocooned inside a culture'.[45] Law is therefore also particular to the society it operates within.

Constitutions embody the normative architecture of a polity; they contain fundamental values, visions of the common good, institutional structures and processes,

---

[37] J Mazzone, 'The Creation of a Constitutional Culture' (2005) 40 *Tulsa Law Review* 671 at 672.

[38] G Harutyunian *Constitutional Culture: The Lessons of History and the Challenges of Time* (2009, English trans) at 8, available at <http://www.venice.coe.int/CoCentre/Huarytyunyan_Constitutional_Culture.pdf> (accessed 13 February 2013).

[39] Ibid.

[40] Ibid at 25.

[41] D Lessard Levin, *Representing Popular Sovereignty: The Constitution in American Political Culture* (Albany, NY: State University of New York Press, 1999) at 27.

[42] P Legrand, *Fragments on Law-as-Culture* (Deventer: WEJ Tjeenk Willink, 1999) at 27.

[43] B Schlink, 'German Constitutional Culture in Transition' in M Rosenfield (ed), *Constitutionalism, Identity, Difference, and Legitimacy: Theoretical Perspectives* (Durham, NC: Duke University Press, 1994) 197 at 197.

[44] NG Wenzel, 'An Institutional Solution for a Cognitive Problem: Hayek's Sensory Order as Foundation for Hayek's Institutional Order' in WN Butos (ed), *The Social Science of Hayek's 'The Sensory Order'* (Bingley: Emerald Group Publishing, 2010) at 329. In an overt way, a constitution's 'cultural elements' may be found in preambles, declarations of state principles and policies, conceptions of citizenship, and lists of rights and duties. However, not all elements of constitutional culture are expressed in written form. As we shall see, constitutional culture also includes intangible aspects of societal behaviour that are apparent yet empirically difficult to ascertain. How we understand the nature of a constitutional order affects how we locate and understand the constitutional culture within which it is to function.

[45] VG Curran, 'Comparative Law and Language' in Reimann and Zimmermann (eds), above n 28, 675 at 711.

and the rights and duties that shape government–citizen relations. While every polity has a constitution, not everyone practises constitutionalism, which resists absolute power in the form of despotic rulers or dogmatic ideologies, through procedural or substantive restraints.

A country's cultural and political traditions shape the nature and development of constitutionalism – the site where 'national history, custom, religion, social values and assumptions about government meet positive law'.[46] Given Asia's diversity, there is no singular Asian culture either in terms of state religions[47] or political ideologies,[48] not to mention commonalities in economic development or in the various transplanted legal systems. Culture may be valued as central to identity or for its own sake; it can also be constructed by states for instrumental purposes. 'Culture' is both a product and producer of context and is itself influenced by both *endogenous* (tradition, religion, culture) and *exogenous* factors (colonial history, legal transplants, imposed post-war settlement, international intervention, the globalisation of human rights culture). So, while institutional forms and political systems may be imported, they may be greatly modified and transformed in the absence of a supportive culture.

Cultural norms can shape how we view individual–society relations, and this will affect the scope of rights, the role of universal values and the socio-economic foundation necessary for social accord. It further affects how individuals regard constitutional norms (whether rationally or emotionally) and how the community prioritises competing values in balancing political expediency against constitutional principles.

Constitutions typically contain three elements: 'power', expressed through the structuring of decision-making institutions; 'justice', in the form of normative values understood to be of universal applicability; and 'culture', which is *particular* and specific.[49] The cultural element is 'residual human experience in a *pre-political* condition',[50] as culture is used 'to create and sustain societies', remaining 'the fundamental grounding for human social organisation'.[51]

While the constitutional and legal cultures of individual polities and societies are likely to differ in detail as a result of religion, history and social forces, every legal and constitutional system in Asia is now based on models drawn from the West. The imposition of foreign law – whether voluntarily or otherwise – has led to a homogenising effect, leading to common understandings of constitutional principles and edicts. This process has been exacerbated by the increasing globalisation of economics and correspondingly, law. Indeed, Friedman suggests that there is an emergent 'modern legal culture' resulting from the transformation of states into modern states:

---

[46] LW Beer (ed), 'Introduction' in *Constitutional Systems in Late Twentieth Century Asia* (Seattle, Wash: University of Washington Press, 1992) at 2.

[47] Islam is the state religion in Bangladesh and Pakistan and the official religion in Malaysia; Buddhism has the same status in Bhutan, Thailand and Sri Lanka; and Catholicism exerts a strong influence in the Philippines, and Hinduism in India and Nepal.

[48] In Asia, one can find everything from 'eastern liberal democracies' to communitarian democracies and socialism.

[49] D Lutz, 'Thinking about Constitutionalism at the Start of the Twenty-First Century' (2000) 30(4) *Publius* 115 at 127–30.

[50] Ibid at 128.

[51] Ibid.

LM Friedman, 'Is There a Modern Legal Culture?' (1994) 7(2) *Ratio Juris* 117, 120–26

By 'modern,' I refer both to an element of time (contemporary societies), and to another trait which is vaguer and more difficult to define. Among contemporary societies, there is a group of wealthy industrial states, in Europe, North America, and (increasingly) the Far East. This group of states is the primary subject of this essay. The conclusions perhaps apply to other societies as well, but less sharply. The thesis is that the wealthy countries of the developed world share aspects of legal culture. Their legal systems also share traits which reflect modern legal culture. These traits, of legal systems and legal culture, are, as suggested, in principle measurable; but they have not in fact been measured. My discussion, then, should be taken as embodying hypotheses, nothing more.

Six traits strike me as especially characteristic of legal systems in the 1990s. These are not the only characteristics of such legal systems, as we head toward the 21st century; but they are certainly very salient and important. I will briefly describe and explain the six. Each rests on, or implies, or is entwined in some aspect of modern legal culture.

1. *First* of all, these systems, like their societies, are in process of rapid change. Legal systems in the 1990s are legal systems on the move. Very little about modern law is static; every legal system, to be sure, has its tradition, its history, its elements of stability; but, if I am not mistaken, these inherited, historical, stable aspects matter less and less. . . . These are swiftly evolving systems, with little respect for the inherited or the old-fashioned.

. . . The very personality of modern citizens, I believe, differs in fundamental ways from the personality of men and women in traditional societies. Technology is, at least in part, responsible for such changes. . . . The amazing achievements of science and technology lead people to think that anything is possible; they see dreams within their grasp, miracles at their fingertips; the unlimited possibilities stretch their aspirations. This leads, I believe, to a cycle of demand and response, which unsettles the social regimes of every country in the world. The middle class masses of Western societies are, in fact, endlessly demanding – not only of new gadgets and toys, but also new benefits, new programs; they want what is novel in fashion, the arts, and popular culture; but they also expect government to deal, successfully, with its problems; and with theirs.

Legal systems today have become more significant than ever before. We live in a complex, baffling, changing world; a world of enormous populations, and enormous collective and individual demands; enormous states, governments, regimes; enormous systems of law. This is true of the great Western nations, the rich countries of the world; it is also true, more or less, of the states which sprang up out of the graves of colonial empires; more and more, it is true of all the worlds, first, second and third.

There has been, as we said, an inflation of expectations. In open societies – societies not tightly controlled from the top, societies with electorates, pressure groups, lobbies – expectations turn into demands; and demands turn into law. Whatever the cause, it is obvious that government, in the last century or so, has inflated to an enormous degree. Its density and size is its prime characteristic. . . . Since the modern state acts through, by, and with the use of law, this means that legal systems, too, have expanded their scope enormously. They have generated an enormous mass of rules and regulations, statutes, ordinances, decisions, on every conceivable subject of modern life.

Modern legal systems are not merely large and dense; they are also ubiquitous. By this I mean there are fewer 'gaps' in the system – they cover a wider span of social space than before. This is true both of courts and of legislatures, certainly of administrative agencies and tribunals. Each facet of modern life has its corresponding area of law. . . .

3. A *third* trait of modern law is more overtly cultural. It relates to the basis on which the legitimacy of law rests, in the modern world. Every society, and every legal system, presupposes some theory or theories of legitimacy – a ruling idea that justifies the legal order, that makes it right and proper to obey. Legitimacy is a normative question, a philosophical question, much debated by political theorists. But I use 'legitimacy' here in an empirical sense, as a trait of culture, that is, an actual attitude or opinion which people carry around in their heads.

The basic theory of legitimacy, in modern law, is *instrumental*. By this I mean that people, groups, classes, occupations, strata, all conceive of law, and use law, as a weapon, an instrument, a tool for achieving economic and social ends; what is more, they think it is perfectly proper to do so. Interest groups lobby for laws to get them what they want: tax exemptions, less regulation, more regulation of somebody else, better decision-rules, and so on. Nobody thinks that law is (in its totality) timeless, God-given, immutable, beyond the reach of human actors.

In this regard, modern law differs sharply from ancient and medieval law; even from the law of the Enlightenment. Theories of natural law, or theories about the divine origins of law, once dominated conceptions of legal legitimacy. This is no longer the case. Why theories of legitimacy have changed is an interesting and difficult question. Instrumental uses of law are obvious in this day and age; hence an instrumental theory of law seems natural. The machinery of law-making, at least the legislative part, is naked to the world. Everybody can see the wheels turning, as interest groups, lobbyists and ordinary citizens, all try to influence the law. It would be hard to argue that divine inspiration or pure reason lay behind income tax law or environmental law or immigration controls. An instrumental theory, in other words, seems to fit a dense, constantly changing, ubiquitous system of law – which is of course what we have.

4. The *fourth* point may seem somewhat inconsistent with the last point. Instrumental theories of law emerged, roughly, at about the time of the Industrial Revolution, as theory, and as elements of popular legal culture. But there were other strands to popular legal culture; these strands have remained unbroken, indeed, they seem to have gotten stronger over the years. I refer here to the non-instrumental side of law: *the passionate belief in fundamental rights*.

Modern law bristles with rights and entitlements. Some of these rights – the 'basic' or 'fundamental' ones – often come embedded in a written document, a formal constitution, like the 'entrenched' Bill of Rights of Canada, or the German *Grundrechte*. Written constitutions, containing lists of enforceable basic rights, are very much in vogue. 'Constitutionalization' has been a crucial feature of the law of the United States in the 20th century; and of many other nations as well.

. . . It would be only a slight exaggeration to say that constitutionalism, and judicial review, in the period since the end of the second World War, have come to have a fundamentally different character. In this period judicial review has entered the legal history of many nations for the first time: Germany, Japan, and Canada are examples. The use of judicial review to make what is 'sometimes very dramatic public policy . . . is increasingly characteristic of judiciaries around the world'.

5. The link between traits four and five is, in fact, the *fifth* trait, which is this: The basis of modern legal systems, and modern legal culture, is a profound *individualism*, despite the heavy dose of economic regulation, the ponderous bureaucracy of the welfare state and the sheer size of the legal system. Modern law presupposes a society of free-standing, autonomous individuals. Many past legal systems were strongly communal; the unit of legal analysis was the family, the clan, the group. Socialist law, too, had a communal flavor, at least in theory. In the modern West, the individual is the unit of legal analysis. The family

basis of law is in rapid decay. The socialist house of law is crumbling, and has largely vanished in Eastern Europe. Western law and, more and more, the law of most other countries, has swung over radically to the camp of individual rights.

I have written elsewhere about the impact of individualism on the law of the 20th century West (Friedman 1990). At the core of individualism is the notion of right, or entitlement. Every human being should have an opportunity to go beyond mere freedom (meaning absence of restraint) and choose a style of life, or way of life, freely selecting among options, developing a unique personality, a self unlike all other selves.

This form of individualism, in my view, is connected to life in the modern West in a basic, fundamental way; and is different in kind from classic forms of political and economic individualism, the liberalism of Adam Smith or John Locke. It has had a profound effect on legal culture, and hence, on the development of law itself. One of the most striking of these effects is rights consciousness. In country after country-not merely in the United States we hear complaints about a 'litigation explosion' or a 'flood of cases'. Whether these complaints are justified quantitatively is not an easy question to answer. There is not much doubt about the qualitative changes. In these countries, minorities, victim groups, and people in general show a new keenness about injustices against them; a new willingness to take whatever steps are necessary to have justice, as they see it, done.

6. A *sixth* feature of modern legal systems is *globalization*. As the world gets smaller, knit together by the miracles of transportation and communication, the practice of law and, I believe, legal culture, are rapidly internationalizing. National borders means less and less in economic terms. There are no longer any hermit kingdoms. Economic relations bind countries together. Legal relations follow economic relations. Globalized legal relations stimulate plans, schemes, and arrangements to transcend legal boundaries – harmonization of law, uniform and model laws, and structures like the European Community.

More fundamentally, this is an age of convergence in legal cultures. That is, legal systems become more similar as time goes on. The same must be true of legal culture, that is, of public attitudes toward law in various countries. Convergence reflects economic interdependence; but it goes beyond this. In a world bound together by television, satellites, and jetports, there is a certain melting together of world cultures; and legal culture can hardly stay immune. When societies have similar experiences, and are exposed to a single world of transport and communication, their legal systems too necessarily come closer together.

I think the point about convergence rings most true for Western, industrial countries, and for countries developing along similar lines. It is hard to know how much convergence there is in underdeveloped countries. I suspect there is a great deal; but we have much less information about these systems. Clearly, the shock of modernity displaces, erodes, or alters inherited legal traditions. Even indigenous forms of marriage and inheritance find it hard to survive in the modern world.

Notes and Questions

1. On how the transformation of a society leads to new attitudes towards the law in South Korea, see Chan Jim Kim, 'Korean Attitudes Towards Law' (2000–2001) 10 *Pacific Rim Law & Policy Journal* 1.

2. Andrew Harding argues that at a broad level, the trajectory of developments within Asia from the 1950s to the 1990s has resulted in certain commonalities which Asian states share. He calls this the 'new Asian constitutionalism':

A Harding 'Asian Law, Public Law, Comparative Law Stir-Fry: Theory and Methods Considered' in T Groppi, V Piergigli and A Rinella (eds), *Asian Constitutionalism in Transition: A Comparative Perspective* **(Rome: Giuffre Editore, 2009) 19, 28–32**

What exactly is the nature of constitutional transition in Asia? Here I necessarily have to take a broad view, and choose the post-war period for attention. . . .

In the 1950s as a result of post-war reconstruction and decolonizing processes, liberal, parliamentary, constitutionalism briefly flowered across most of East Asia. It was soon eclipsed by the growth of authoritarian government of right and left, and largely personal rule, throughout East Asia in the 1960s and 1970s, which was usually the result of an intensifying cold war. Almost every country in East Asia succumbed to the drastic subversion of constitutional principles. Even in relatively more stable and democratic states such as Japan, Malaysia and Singapore, the exigencies of ethnic tension or economic-growth imperatives resulted in the emergence of a dominant party system and the restriction of a number of elements of constitutionalism is formal law or in the actual practice of government.

This period is referred to as the period of 'Asian Developmental State', in which either capitalist economic development or socialist collectivism was deliberately privileged over democracy and constitutional forms. Constitutional texts existed, and indeed proliferated, but essentially they served to entrench the power of autocratic rulers and military cliques. They were remarkable for what they did not say or what they said but did not mean. Most of East Asia experienced at least some economic growth, and in some cases it was called an 'Asian miracle'. It was plausibly asserted that an Asian version of constitutionalism was in practice based on entirely different principles from those of the democratic states in the West, whose Constitutions were so influential in the post-war wave of Constitution-making. The Asian Developmental State typically embodied all or most of: executive-centred government; uncontrolled administrative discretion; strong or unquestionable personal or party rule; government interference in economic and social affairs; restriction of basic freedoms, the media, elements of political opposition, and judicial and legal professional independence; persistent attacks on or total submergence of the rule of law; and the backing of a powerful military branch. All of these elements are inimical to constitutionalism as we understand it today, which emphasizes the rule of law, the separation or balancing of powers, democratic participation, individual rights, the entrenchment of mechanisms of accountability and the creation of independent supervisory agencies. This definition of constitutionalism is, these days, both well understood and actually demanded across most of Asia, except that in Asia it would also tend to be emphasized that constitutionalism needs to embrace the need for stable government as a firm foundation on which to build all the other desirable aspects of development. Crucial here is the ability of new Asian constitutionalism not only to provide effective checks and balances but also to deliver effective and efficient government and the secure, democratic transfer of political power.

The Asian Developmental State embodied very restricted operation or even suspension of the early liberal-democratic Constitutions under marital law or emergency rule, or even their abandonment or replacement by more executive-friendly or leader-friendly documents. . . .

The present wave of constitutional development which I call 'new Asian constitutionalism' commenced in the mid-1980s, when increasing democratization and globalization, and the resolution of local conflicts, all assisted by the end of the cold war and the emergence of a new factor – 'people power' – propelled forward through the 1990s and 2000s the concept of a liberal and just State based on free and fair elections and operating with a complex and sophisticated array of good-governance mechanisms. This wave has spurred Constitution-builders and reformers to greater and greater fine-tuning of institutions of representation, transparency, accountability, geographical and administrative decentralization, practical law-enforcement and regulation, and compliance with international norms collected together under the mantra of 'good governance' or 'the rule of law'.

The mid-1980s saw the gradual dismantling of the legal support systems of authoritarian government in Philippines, Taiwan and South Korea, in which states there emerged a multi-party democracy, a reformed Parliament and presidential system, and a Constitutional or Supreme Court displaying new or renewed vigour and independence.

Changing notions of Constitutional law and political economy in both the People's Republic of China from 1978 and Vietnam from 1986 have led to a progressively greater adherence, as a matter of constitutional principle, to the rule of law, including the subordination of both party and government to the law, a position previously heretical in communist states, which inveighed against constitutionalism as an instrument of bourgeois exploitation. These 'post-communist' one-party states have gone through several stages of constitutional reform, reflecting different stages of change in political economy. Although it is argued in these states that economic liberalization need not be linked to political liberalization, the potential and actual linkage can be clearly seen in successive stages of liberalization, the potential and actual linkage can be clearly seen in successive stages of constitutional development, as well as in popular demand for more democracy and more rights.

Interestingly enough, the economic crisis which swept across the East Asian region in 1997–1998 seems not to have affected the progress of constitutional reform: in both Thailand and Indonesia, for example, where the economic contagion first struck, a clear linkage was made between the reforms and the prospects for economic recovery. The relationship between constitutional reform and economic development in Asia is indeed an intriguing one about which we need to know more. East Asian experience seems to suggest that economic development drags constitutional development in its wake, but it may well also be the case that constitutional development creates indispensable conditions for further or sustained economic development. This is potentially fruitful area of speculation.

3. Do you agree with Friedman's theory that the socio-economic changes have created in 'modern' states a common legal culture? Does Harding's description of the changes that took place between the 1950s and the 1990s lend support to such a thesis in the case of Asia? See the following works by Kevin YL Tan: 'Economic Development and the Prospects for Constitutionalism' in A Chin and A Choi (eds), *Law, Social Sciences And Public Policy: Towards A Unified Framework* (Singapore: Singapore University Press, 1998) 187; 'The Role of Public Law in a Developing Asia' [2004] *Singapore Journal of Legal Studies* 265; and 'Economic Development and Human Rights in East Asia: Legal Reforms in Singapore and Taiwan' in J Bauer and DA Bell (eds), *The East Asian Challenge For Human Rights* (Cambridge: Cambridge University Press, 1999) 264.

4. Wen-chen Chang has argued that in the constitution-making imperatives of Japan, South Korea and Taiwan in the immediate post-war period were fuelled by several objects, among them: promoting democracy, securing national independence, and inclusion of the various sectors of polity. See Wen-Chen Chang, 'East Asian Foundations for Constitutionalism: Three Models Reconstructed' (2008) 3(2) *National Taiwan University Law Review* 111. It has further been argued that constitutional developments in these three countries reveal four distinctive features:

(a) instrumental constitutional state building;
(b) textual and institutional continuity;
(c) reactive and cautious judicial review; and
(d) a wide range of rights responses to social and political progress.

See Jiunn-rong Yeh and Wen-Chen Chang, 'The Emergence of East Asian Constitutionalism: Features in Comparison' (2011) 59 *American Journal of Comparative Law* 805.

III. CULTURE AND CONSTITUTIONS: A FUNCTIONAL APPROACH

A. Introduction

A state's constitutional culture is often reflected in the values embedded in its constitution. These cultural values are typically found in its preamble, declaration of principles and policies, conceptions of citizenship, and lists of rights and duties. Overt declarations of constitutional values and commitments may signify acceptance of a coherent civic identity and thus form part of the interpretive matrix for judicial review. At the same time, they can influence the design of institutions and preferred modalities of interaction between these institutions. Constitutions may also be used to reflect (as well as reject) cultural values, or even to create or constitute culture through prescription.

A constitution's 'cultural elements' establish the normative orientation of its polity. They may do this by reflecting a pre-political culture that the state is committed to preserve,[52] or by reforming the system by creating a new path that departs from the old regime, adopting a fresh identity or approach.[53] Such moves can also be attempts to harmonise a state's laws with international standards.

In some cases, constitutions directly address the question of culture, so while cultural norms may conflict with general law, the constitution may accommodate them through regimes of exemption. For example, constitutions may protect the rights of indigenous communities even though their 'traditional' lifestyles are at odds with the demands of modernity and development; or they may facilitate the coexistence of customary law (such as *adat*) or religious law with other laws in certain matters. Constitutions may also valorise national culture[54] and assign it a place in the legal hierarchy. Take for example, the Timor-Leste Constitution, which obliges the state to 'value the personality and cultural heritage of the East Timorese people',[55] and 'recog-

---

[52] For example, Art 9 of the South Korean Constitution states: 'The State tries to sustain and develop the cultural heritage and to enhance national culture.'

[53] The constitutional trajectory of independent Singapore after it seceded from the Federation of Malaysia in 1965 reflected a form of aversive constitutionalism in rejecting the privileging of the majority Malays in Malaysia and by adopting equal citizenship as a cardinal tenet of the new polity. The Singapore Constitution is secular, while the Malaysian one confesses Islam, and is consonant with not privileging any class of citizens, and contains more robust religious freedom guarantees, unlike the Malaysian prohibition against propagating other faiths to Muslims: see Thio Li-ann, *A Treatise on Singapore Constitutional Law* (Singapore: Academy Publishing, 2012) at 140–42.

[54] Art 7 of the Mongolian Constitution provides: 'The historical, cultural, scientific and intellectual heritage of the Mongolian people shall be under State protection.'

[55] Sec 6(g), Constitution of the Democratic Republic of Timor-Leste.

nise and value' East Timorese 'norms and customs' that are 'not contrary to the Constitution and to any legislation specifically dealing with customary law'.[56]

Some constitutions express particular views on the culture – about its nature, its preservation or change. Article 23 of the Laos Constitution calls for the 'preservation of the national culture which is representative of the fine tradition of the country and its ethnic people', but also accepts 'selected progressive cultures from around the world'. Article 30 of the Vietnamese Constitution is even more specific, requiring state and society to 'preserve and develop a progressive Vietnamese culture imbued with national identity; and inherit and enhance the values of the multi-ethnic Vietnamese civilisation, Ho Chi Minh's thought, ethics and style' and to 'assimilate the quintessence of human culture; and foster all the creative talents of the people'. At the same time, '[r]eactionary and deprave ideologies and culture are to be banned' and 'superstition is to be driven out'.

While Article (2) of the Bhutan Constitution acknowledges the 'evolving dynamic force' of culture, the state is nonetheless required to 'strengthen and facilitate the continued evolution of traditional values and institutions that are sustainable as a progressive society'. In addition, the Bhutanese state is required to 'preserve, protect and promote the cultural heritage of the country, including monuments, places and objects of artistic or historic interest, Dzongs, Lhakhangs, Goendeys, Ten-sum, Nyes, language, literature, music, visual arts and religion to enrich society and the cultural life of the citizens'.[57] The State is further required to 'conserve and encourage research on local arts, custom, knowledge and culture',[58] and the Bhutanese Parliament is empowered to enact 'such legislation as may be necessary to advance the cause of the cultural enrichment of Bhutanese society'.[59]

B. Culture as Normative Matrix

As supreme law, constitutions publicly articulate a polity's political identity and normative architecture; its values and structural distribution of power; and define its inter-institutional and government–citizen relations. Taken together, this expresses the polity's national identity. The obligations we assume define us. Some Asian constitutions are committed to a 'thick' conception of the good society, which may be quite different from those of western liberal constitutions.

i. Visions of the Common Good

a. The Moral or Virtuous Constitution

Certain Asian constitutions are committed to a vision of a moral society. Among Asian constitutions, the Thai Constitution makes the most references to such a normative aspiration. For example, Article 270 of the Constitution provides that the 'standard of

---

[56] Sec 2(4), Constitution of the Democratic Republic of Timor-Leste.
[57] Art 4(1), Constitution of the Kingdom of Bhutan.
[58] Art 4(3), Constitution of the Kingdom of Bhutan.
[59] Art 4(4), Constitution of the Kingdom of Bhutan.

morality for persons holding political positions, government officials and State officials at all levels shall be in conformity with the established code of morality'. Article 77(4) further requires the state to implement a national administrative policy that focuses on 'the development of quality, ethics, and morals of state officials'. In addition, the state is expected to 'promote the principles of ethics, morals and good governance' in the conduct of business.[60] The Thai state is also required to 'create and indoctrinate the correct perception of morals and ethics' through education.[61] Censorship is permissible in the interests of, among other things, 'good morals',[62] and a person 'can invoke human dignity or exercise his or her rights and liberties in so far as it is not in violation of rights and liberties of other persons or contrary to this Constitution or good morals'.[63] At the same time, a person may enjoy academic freedom, provided that it be 'not contrary to his or her civic duties or good morals'.[64] There are several other references to 'good morals' in the Thai Constitution, but this phrase/concept is nowhere defined in the Constitution. It is interesting to note that in the case of Bhutan, the notion of the 'good' is specifically linked to 'a good and compassionate society rooted in Buddhist ethos and universal human values'.[65]

Both the Timor and Vietnam Constitutions express concern for the material and spiritual welfare and needs of the people. Section 6(e) of the Constitution of Timor-Leste provides that one 'fundamental objective' of the state shall be to 'promote the building of a society based on social justice, by establishing material and spiritual welfare of the citizens'. Article 16 of the Constitution of Vietnam requires its state economic policies 'to build a strong country with prosperous life for its people, and aimed at ever better satisfying the material and spiritual needs of the people'. Sri Lanka's Constitution obliges the state to raise 'the moral and cultural standards of the People' under Article 27. Articles 18 and 37 respectively of the Bangladesh and Pakistan Constitutions identify what falls outside the boundaries of 'good' by constitutionally requiring the state to adopt effective measures to prevent prostitution and gambling, and to curtail alcohol consumption, consonant with promoting the Islamic way of life.

Given that human rights 'has become the lingua franca of moral global thought',[66] it is not surprising to find such language in the newer constitutions, such as those of Indonesia,[67] Vietnam,[68] Mongolia[69] and China.[70] Some other constitutions specifically name human rights instruments like the Universal Declaration of Human Rights (UDHR) and the United Nations Charter, as does Article 31 of the Cambodian

---

[60] Sec 83(2), Constitution of the Kingdom of Thailand 2007.
[61] Sec 79(3), Constitution of the Kingdom of Thailand 2007.
[62] Sec 36, Constitution of the Kingdom of Thailand 2007.
[63] Sec 28, Constitution of the Kingdom of Thailand 2007.
[64] Sec 49, Constitution of the Kingdom of Thailand 2007.
[65] Art 9(20), Constitution of the Kingdom of Bhutan.
[66] M Ignatieff, *Human Rights as Politics and Idolatry* (Princeton, NJ: Princeton University Press, 2001) at 53.
[67] Chapter XA (Human Rights).
[68] Art 50 of the Vietnam Constitution provides: 'In the Socialist Republic of Vietnam, human rights in all respects, political, civic, economic, cultural and social are respected, find their expression in the rights of citizens and are provided for by the Constitution and the law.'
[69] Chapter 2 (human rights and freedoms), Mongolian Constitution.
[70] Art 33 of the Constitution of the People's Republic of China provides: 'The state respects and guarantees human rights.'

Constitution,[71] which also refers to the Convention of the Rights of the Child in Article 48. Article 39 of the Basic Law of Hong Kong and Article 40 of the Basic Law of Macau both provide for the continued enforcement of the International Covenant on Civil and Political Rights, the International Covenant on Economic, Social and Cultural Rights and international labour conventions, after control of these territories reverted to China.

One can also track the degree to which human rights culture has taken root by examining the receptivity of courts to international human right norms in either founding an unenumerated right, or interpreting an enumerated one.[72] Similarly, the manner in which courts deal with foreign precedents is illuminating, whether they sound the chorus of rights-based constitutionalism, or offer dissenting views or divergent approaches. This may manifest a nationalist strain that may either serve as a cynical apology for power, or reflect a 'particularism without parochialism' in affirming the operation of localised values. For example, the Singapore Court of Appeal, in in discussing the test for limits to free speech in relation to contempt of court in the case of *Shadrake Alan v A-G*,[73] rejected the American 'clear and present danger test' which had found support in only 'one apparently solitary Commonwealth decision' in the Ontario Court of Appeal.[74] Put another way, the Singapore court considered the US test an exception that stemmed from its 'unique culture'[75] which valorises free speech.

b. The Good Citizen and the Entrenching of Culture in Social Relations

Liberal states profess 'neutrality' and avoid regulating the private lives of their citizens. That said, the fact that liberal states exalt individual autonomy means that it invariably fosters an experimental, choice-orientated disposition in its citizens. This in turn requires restraining the state from intervening in the choices and activities that fall on the private side of the public–private divide.

In contrast, constitutionally-driven culture often reflects the state's vested interest in a distinct conception of citizenship or of the 'good citizen'. In this respect, certain

[71] 'The Kingdom of Cambodia shall recognize and respect human rights as stipulated in the United Nations Charter, the Universal Declaration of Human Rights, the covenants and conventions related to human rights, women's and children's rights. Every Khmer citizen shall be equal before the law, enjoying the same rights, freedom and fulfilling the same obligations regardless of race, colour, sex, language, religious belief, political tendency, birth origin, social status, wealth or other status. The exercise of personal rights and freedom by any individual shall not adversely affect the rights and freedom of others. The exercise of such rights and freedom shall be in accordance with the law.' Sec 23 of the Timor-Leste Constitution provides that constitutional rights are to be interpreted in accordance with the UDHR.

[72] See, eg, the following cases in which provisions of the Convention for the Elimination of All Forms of Discrimination Against Women (CEDAW) were interpreted: *Vishaka v State of Rajasthan* (1997) 6 SCC 253 (Supreme Court, India); *Bangladesh National Women Lawyers Association (BNWLA) v Govt of Bangladesh*, Writ Petition No 5916 of 2008 (Supreme Court, Bangladesh). CEDAW norms were found not to apply to private actors in the Malaysian Federal Court decision of *Beatrice Fernandez v Sistem Penebrangan Malaysia* [2005] 2 CLR 713 (concerning the dismissal of a pregnant flight stewardess contrary to the collective agreement with the airline).

[73] *Shadrake Alan v A-G* [2011] 3 SLR 778 [43].

[74] *R v Kopyto* (1988) 47 DLR (4th) 213.

[75] *Bridges v California* 314 US 252 (1941). The Singapore Court of Appeal discussed this case in *Shadrake v AG* [2011] 3 SLR 778 [41], and held: 'The concept of freedom of speech has – owing to the unique culture as well as constitutional heritage of the US – been accorded a paramountcy in a manner quite different from other Commonwealth jurisdictions.'

duties may be imposed either 'vertically' by the state on behalf of society, or horizontally, with respect to the right of others. Article 47 of the Cambodia Constitution provides that parents have the duty 'to take care and educate their children to become good citizens', while children are duty bound 'to take good care of their elderly mother and father according to Khmer traditions'. The Chinese[76] and Vietnamese[77] Constitutions contain similar duties within their provisions. These hortatory aspirations reach into the home and hearth, blurring the liberal public–private divide and extending the sphere of legitimate state concern.

Beyond the immediate family, duties may be addressed to the broader community. Article 8 of the Bhutan Constitution lists a set of fundamental duties addressed to Bhutanese citizens, including the responsibility to help victims of accidents or natural calamities.[78] Bhutanese citizens are enjoined not to tolerate or participate in the abuse of women and children, and to take preventive steps[79] to foster a 'spirit of brotherhood' among all peoples, 'transcending religious, linguistic, regional or sectional diversities',[80] and to protect 'the environment, culture and heritage of the nation'.[81] Socialist constitutions seek to foster loyalty by inculcating in their citizens 'patriotism, attachment to the socialist regime'.[82]

At a far more abstract level, Article 51A of the Indian Constitution requires citizens to protect the natural environment and 'to have compassion for living creatures'. The issue of environmental conservation is also embodied in various 'green' norms in the Constitutions of Timor-Leste,[83] Mongolia,[84] Vietnam,[85] Thailand,[86] Bhutan,[87] China[88] and Sri Lanka.[89] Article 5 of the Bhutan Constitution explicitly requires 60 per cent forest cover to be maintained.

c. Constitutions and the Military

Certain constitutions also contain commitments to pacifism and neutrality in foreign policy. For example, Article 53 of the Cambodian Constitution provides:

> The Kingdom of Cambodia adopts a policy of permanent neutrality and non-alignment. The Kingdom of Cambodia follows a policy of peaceful co-existence with its neighbors and with all other countries throughout the world. The Kingdom of Cambodia shall not invade any country, nor interfere in any other country's internal affairs, directly or indirectly, and shall

---

[76] Art 49, Constitution of China: 'Both husband and wife have the duty to practice family planning. Parents have the duty to rear and educate their children who are minors, and children who have come of age have the duty to support and assist their parents.'

[77] Art 64, Constitution of Vietnam: 'Parents are duty bound to bring up and educate their children into useful citizens of society. Children have an obligation to respect and care for their grand-parents and parents. The State and society do not admit any discrimination among children of the same family.'

[78] Art 8(6), Constitution of the Kingdom of Bhutan.

[79] Art 8(5), Constitution of the Kingdom of Bhutan.

[80] Art 8(3), Constitution of the Kingdom of Bhutan.

[81] Art 8(2), Constitution of the Kingdom of Bhutan.

[82] Art 31, Constitution of Vietnam.

[83] Secs 6(f) and 61, Constitution of Timor-Leste.

[84] Art 6(20), Constitution of Mongolia.

[85] Art 29, Constitution of Vietnam.

[86] Art 84, Constitution of Thailand 2007.

[87] Art 5, Constitution of the Kingdom of Bhutan.

[88] Art 26, Constitution of the People's Republic of China.

[89] Art 27(2), Constitution of Sri Lanka.

solve any problems peacefully with due respect for mutual interests. The Kingdom of Cambodia shall not join in any military alliance or military pact which is incompatible with its policy of neutrality. The Kingdom of Cambodia shall not permit any foreign military base on its territory and shall not have its own military base abroad, except within the framework of a Untied Nations request. The Kingdom of Cambodia reserves the right to receive foreign assistance in military equipment, armaments, ammunitions, in training of armed forces, and other assistance for self-defense and to maintain public order and security within its territory.

Prohibitions on the use of nuclear and other weapons can also be found in Article 54 of the Cambodian Constitution and Article II Section 8 of the Philippines Constitution. Most famously, after World War II, Japan was forced to adopt a constitution that renounces war[90] and requires that Cabinet members be civilians.[91] Under Article 28(6) of the Bhutan Constitution, the state 'shall not use military force against a foreign State except in self-defence or for the purpose of maintaining its security, territorial integrity and sovereignty.' Yet other constitutions give an entrenched role to the military in civilian life. Under Article 74 of the Constitution of Myanmar, seats in both houses of the legislature are reserved for 'Defence Services Personnel nominated by the Commander-in-Chief of the Defence Forces'.

d. Constitutions and the Economy

Some constitutions embed principles concerning economic equity and natural resources in their provisions. They may also stipulate the nature of the economy (such as a commitment to market economy) or its organisation.[92] The Constitution of Thailand requires the state to 'promote and support a Philosophy of Sufficiency Economy',[93] while that of Timor-Leste stipulates that one of its state objects is to 'promote the harmonious and integrated development of the sectors and regions and the fair distribution of the national product'.[94]

The state may be obliged to prevent the formation of commercial monopolies and to promote fair market competition.[95] Economic provisions in the constitution may also exhibit a nationalist orientation. For example, Article 6(3) of the Mongolian Constitution states that only citizens may be given private ownership of plots of land. The Constitution of the Philippines has perhaps the most detailed economic provisions privileging its citizens: Article II Section 19 requires the state to develop 'a self-reliant and independent national economy effectively controlled by Filipinos'. At the same time, preferential treatment is given to qualified Filipinos in the grant of rights

---

[90] Art 9 of the Japanese Constitution provides: 'Aspiring sincerely to an international peace based on justice and order, the Japanese people forever renounce war as a sovereign right of the nation and the threat or use of force as means of settling international disputes. / In order to accomplish the aim of the preceding paragraph, land, sea, and air forces, as well as other war potential, will never be maintained. The right of belligerency of the state will not be recognized.'

[91] Art 66, Constitution of Japan.

[92] Art 33(1) of the Indonesian Constitution states that the 'economy shall be organized as a common endeavor based upon the principles of the family system'.

[93] Sec 82, Constitution of the Kingdom of Thailand.

[94] Sec 6(i), Constitution of Timor-Leste.

[95] Art 83(6) of the Thai Constitution requires the state to 'ensure and supervise free and fair competition, prevent direct and indirect monopolies, and protect consumers'; while Art 9(10) of the Bhutan Constitution states that as a matter of state policy, the state 'shall encourage and foster private sector development through fair market competition and prevent commercial monopolies'.

and concessions in relation to the national economy and patrimony.[96] Economic nationalism is further buttressed by state policies under which citizens and corporations in which Filipino citizens hold at least 60 per cent of the capital shall have certain areas of investment reserved for them. The state is further required to protect Filipino enterprises against unfair foreign competition and trade practices.[97]

Constitutions may also contain norms reflecting a commitment to inter-generational equity. For example, the Singapore Constitution requires that 50 per cent of net investment income from Singapore's state investments and capital gains be locked up in the reserves so that a balance between the claims of present and future generations may be achieved.[98] This principle has also been recognised in relation to environmental cases, in granting standing to unborn generations to challenge the grant of timber licences.[99]

e. Beyond Economics: Gross National Happiness

Uniquely, Article 9 of the Constitution of Bhutan provides that the state 'shall strive to promote those conditions that will enable the pursuit of Gross National Happiness (GNH)'. The Constitution carries no definition of what GNH entails, but it clearly establishes an alternative development model to Gross National Product (GNP) in one of the world's poorest countries. The idea was proposed by Jigme Singye Wangchuck – who reigned as King of Bhutan from 1972 to 2006 – shortly after he ascended the Dragon Throne. Such GNH was to be measured by the people's sense of being well-governed, their relationship with the environment, and their satisfaction with the pace of economic development and sense of national belonging.[100] It has been described as a combination of 'Buddhist spirituality and barefoot economics',[101] where the Government seeks the well-being of all sentient beings, and nine key values have been identified: psychological well-being, health, education, time use, cultural diversity and resilience, good governance, community vitality, ecological diversity and resilience, and living standards.[102] The Government established the Gross National Happiness Commission chaired by the Prime Minister to co-ordinate policies and formulate strategies to advance the GNH agenda.[103]

---

[96] Art XII, Section 10, Constitution of the Philippines. See R Pangalangan, 'The Philippine "People Power" Constitution and Rule of Law and the Limits of Liberal Constitutionalism' in R Peerenboom (ed), *Asian Discourses of Rule of Law: Theories and Implementation of Rule of Law in Twelve Asian Countries, France and the US* (London and New York: Routledge, 2004) 365 at 376–78 discussing *Garcia v Board of Investments* GR No 92024, 9 Nov 1990, 191 SCRA 288 and *Manila Prince Hotel Case* GR No 122157 3 Feb 1997, 267 SCRA 408.

[97] Art XII, Secs 1, 10, Constitution of the Philippines.

[98] Art 142(2)(b), Constitution of the Republic of Singapore.

[99] *Oposa et al v Fulgencio S Factoran, Jr et al,* GR No 101083.

[100] 'Bhutan's "Gross National Happiness" Index', *Telegraph* (UK), 2 March 2011 at <http://www.tele-graph.co.uk/news/worldnews/asia/bhutan/8355028/Bhutans-Gross-National-Happiness-index.html>. See also A Simoni and R Whitecross, 'Gross National Happiness and the Heavenly Stream of Justice: Modernization and Dispute Resolution in the Kingdom of Bhutan' (2007) *American Journal of Comparative Law* 165.

[101] 'The UN Happiness Project', *New York Times*, 28 March 2012. For a less felicitous assessment of GNH in a country where many women think their husbands have a right to beat them for refusing sex or burning dinner, see V Arora, 'Wife beating study shocks Buddhist Bhutan's happiness chief', 2 October 2011, *USA Today* at <http://usatoday30.usatoday.com/news/religion/2011-02-11-wife_beating_buddhism_10_ST_N.htm>.

[102] 'Bhutan GNH Index' at <http://www.grossnationalhappiness.com/articles/>.

[103] Gross National Happiness Commission at <http://www.gnhc.gov.bt/mandate/>.

ii. Novel or Unique Rights

To constitutionalise a norm is to give it an elevated position in the hierarchy of legal-political values. Constitutions drafted in the twenty-first century in Asia manifest unique or rare provisions reflecting particular concerns. Section 38(1) of the Timor-Leste Constitution gives citizens the right to access personal data about themselves stored 'in a computer system' or manual records. The Timor and Thai Constitutions constitutionalise consumer rights,[104] while Article 21 of the Constitution of China provides that the state shall promote both modern and traditional Chinese medicine. In Cambodia, where female trafficking is endemic, Article 46 of the Constitution prohibits the 'commerce of human beings, exploitation of women by prostitution and obscenity' affecting the reputation of women. Reflecting the sensibilities of the Catholic majority, Article 2 Section 12 of the Philippines Constitution protects the life of the mother 'and the life of the unborn from conception'.

A distinctive feature is the incorporation of the 'right to pursue happiness' in the Constitutions of Japan and South Korea.[105] This felicitous phrase, penned by Thomas Jefferson in the drafting of the 1787 American Declaration of Independence, does not feature in the eventual US Constitution but is contained in the 1780 Massachusetts Constitution. 'Happiness' is an open-ended term which could mean anything conducive to a subjective emotional state, including hedonistic narcissism; however, that was not how it was understood then. It certainly had connotations of material well-being, but transcended that to include a spiritual, moral and religious dimension,[106] and is better apprehended as a form of virtuous felicity[107] and concern for overall well-being; in the Vattelian sense,[108] it entailed the rigorous state instruction of the people

> in good citizenship and the arts and sciences, both practical and polite, and the cultivation of religious piety within the limits of the right to liberty of conscience. On the part of the individual, it entailed love of country and rigorous attention to the duty of making oneself as virtuous, moral and useful a member of society as possible.[109]

Article 10 of the South Korean Constitution states:

> All citizens shall be assured of human dignity and worth and have the right to pursue happiness. It shall be the duty of the State to confirm and guarantee the fundamental and inviolable human rights of individuals.[110]

---

[104] Arts 61 and 82(6), Thai Constitution and Art 53, Timor-Leste Constitution ('Consumers have the right to goods and services of good quality, to truthful information and protection of their health, safety and economic interests, and to reparation for damages.').

[105] See 'Brazil Considers adding Happiness to Constitution,' *ABC News*, 2 February 2011, at <http://article.wn.com/view/2011/02/02/Brazil_Looks_at_Adding_Happiness_to_Constitution_m/>.

[106] The Massachusetts Constitution of 1780 affirms that 'the happiness of a people and the good order and preservation of civil government essentially depend upon piety, religion and morality, and . . . these cannot be generally diffused through a community but by the institution of the public worship of God and of public instructions in piety, religion and morality'. Art 3 of the Northwest Ordinance of 1787 affirms that 'religion, morality, and knowledge' are 'essential to the happiness of mankind'.

[107] JR Rogers, 'The Meaning of the 'Pursuit of Happiness', *First Things*, 19 June 2012 at <http://www.firstthings.com/onthesquare/2012/06/the-meaning-of-the-ldquopursuit-of-happinessrdquo>.

[108] E Vattel, *Law of Nations* (London, 1758) vol I, ch 11, paras 110–24.

[109] See Fo McDonald, *Alexander Hamilton* (New York: WW Norton, 1979) at 53–57.

[110] See Jibong Lim, 'Pursuit of Happiness Clause in the Korean Constitution' (2001) 1(2) *Journal of Korean Law* 71.

The American influence is also apparent in Article 13 of the Constitution of Japan:

> All of the people shall be respected as individuals. Their right to life, liberty, and the pursuit of happiness shall, to the extent that it does not interfere with the public welfare, be the supreme consideration in legislation and in other governmental affairs.

This is framed more as a government objective than as a justiciable right, though it has been found to be justiciable in the South Korean context, as in the following case:

Extracurricular Lesson Ban Case
12-1 KCCR 427, 98Hun-Ka16, etc (consolidated) 27 Apr 2000 (Constitutional Court, South Korea)

Facts

Article 3 of the Act on the Establishment and Operation of Private Teaching Institutes forbids any person from providing 'extracurricular lessons' except in certain very restricted circumstances. The defendants in these two cases (consolidated in this review) were charged with a violation of Article 3 of the Act and, if convicted, faced the possibility of being fined up to three million Korean *won* or sentenced to a term of imprisonment of up to one year. They challenged the constitutionality of Article 3 of the Act, inter alia, on the ground that it violated Article 10 of the South Korean Constitution, which guaranteed all citizens 'the right to pursue happiness'.

Held

(a) Parents' Right to Educate Children

. . . 'Parents' right to educate children' is not stated in the Constitution. It, however, arises out of the Article 36(1) guarantee of all people's inviolable human rights concerning marriage and family life, the Article 10 guarantee of the right to pursue happiness, and Article 37(1) provides that 'people's liberties and rights shall not be disrespected for not being enumerated in the Constitution.' The Constitutional Court has already ruled . . . that 'parents have rights to educate their children in elementary, middle, and high schools who have yet to achieve maturity and work on their personalities, and the right includes one to choose the schools for their children' (7-1 KCCR 274, 91Hun-Ma204, February 23, 1995) . . .

Parents' right to educate children are [*sic*] different from other basic rights in that the agent of basic rights, parents, do not enjoy it as one of the rights of self-determination. It is a right granted for the purpose of protection and development of personality of children. In other words, parents' right to educate children is protected for children's happiness. Children's happiness becomes the criterion for setting the direction of parental education.

Parents have rights to make an overall plan on their children's education and configure the education according to their own view of life, society, and education, and parents' right of education take precedence over other providers of education in principle. On the other hand, parents' right to educate children and the duty thereof are inseparable from each other. The duty forms the characteristic component of parents' right to educate children. Parents' right to educate children can be described as 'parents' duty to educate children.' Parents' right to educate children means the right to decide freely how they will discharge their duty to educate children. Therefore, it includes the right to decide on the objectives and methods of the education. In other words, parents have the right to set the objectives as to how their children's personalities should be developed, and choose the appropriate means to achieve the objectives in light of the child's individual favor, merits, and mental and physical level of growth. Parents have the primary right to decide on these matters because they, better than any other, can protect children's interests. . . .

(3) Constitutionality of the Instant Statutory Provision

(A) Basic Rights Restricted by Article 3

. . .

3) Article 3 directly bans only the giving of extracurricular lessons by those wishing to give them. However, it practically restricts elementary, middle, and high school students' acts of learning outside schools freely, limiting their rights to pursue happiness. The right to pursue happiness includes the general freedom of action and the right to free development of personality. The ban on extracurricular lessons restricts the student's right to free development of personality.

   Children and adolescents as the learners have the right to develop their personalities, especially their attributes and merits, without the State's intervention. Children and adolescents are immature persons who require the decisions of others such as teachers and parents for the development of their personalities. They are, however, not mere objects of the education given by parents and the State. They are independent persons whose rights to personalities are protected as adults by Article 10 of the Constitution, which protects the human dignity and the right to pursue happiness. Therefore, the Constitution grants children the right to make decisions about their own education or equivalently to receive education freely within the boundaries of the State's power of education and the parents' right of education.

   Children therefore have the right to decide freely of the State's intervention whether to receive separate extracurricular lessons outside school education and from whom and in what format they will receive extracurricular lessons.

4) The basic right limited by Article 3 is parents' right to educate children. We already established above that parents should be given an autonomous area within which they can decide what in terms of education is important and needed for their children's development of personality. Parents' right to educate children as such is a god-given right derived from Articles 36(1), 10, and 37(1) of the Constitution. Therefore, the Article 3 ban on extracurricular lessons restricts parents' right to make decisions on their children's education.

5) Therefore, the basic rights restricted by Article 3 is the right to free development of personality of the children and adolescents wishing to learn, parents' right to educate children, and the freedom to choose occupation and pursue happiness of those wishing to give extracurricular lessons.

C. Constitutional Culture and Instrumentalism

i. Constitution and National Identity: History, Constitutional Patriotism and Cosmopolitanism

'Culture' forms part of what Harold Berman calls 'the religious dimension of law' due to its 'emotional elements, sacred elements, that are intended, at least, to help people believe in inherent rightness'.[111] Constitutional culture may play a unifying role in forging a common national identity in at least two ways. First, by commemorating history or momentous 'founding events', such as resistance against an enemy oppressor or revolution,[112] as well as the role various actors played in this process.[113] Secondly, it does so through the love of *patria* flowing from a shared history or common culture. Where such events or emotions are missing, constitutions may be used to cultivate identity through a common affective commitment to certain political and social ideals. In such instances, one is reminded of Habermas's idea of 'constitutional patriotism'[114] that advocates loyalty to liberal democratic constitutional values instead of ethnos or a vague cosmopolitanism, in an 'always open and incomplete' political system.[115] This is different from constitutional provisions that demand that citizens be patriotic to the state, such as in socialist systems.

For example, Articles 1 and 51 of the Constitution of Cambodia state that the kingdom shall be ruled according to principles of 'liberal democracy and pluralism', while the Constitution of Myanmar seeks 'to adopt multi-party democracy and market economy'[116] in signalling a formal shift away from military government. The Constitutions of Timor-Leste[117] and South Korea[118] contain express commitments to multi-party participatory democracy, while the right to petition government bodies – to protect rights, denounce breach of the law or public duty, or raise general interest issues – is found in the Constitutions of Timor-Leste, Vietnam, Thailand, China, Cambodia and Lao.

The articulation of constitutional values also shows a commitment to 'global values', where states emerging from authoritarian rule or foreign control seek to show a shift towards 'the rule of law, the will of the people, and the respect for the dignity of the human person'[119] and to affirm their participation in the civilised family of liberal states. Solidarity with other nations is also demonstrated through declarations of resistance against 'imperialism, hegemonism and colonialism'[120] and support for national liberation movements.[121]

Solidarity with other states may also be expressed on the basis of faith. For example, Article 25(2) of the Bangladesh constitutional state policy requires the state to 'consolidate, preserve and strengthen fraternal relations among Muslim countries based on Islamic solidarity'. Where political identity is fundamental, as in the case of

---

[111] H Berman, 'Law and Logos' (1994) 44 *De Paul Law Review* 143 at 159.

[112] The Bangladesh Constitution recalls 'a historic war for national independence' proclaimed on 26 March 1971, while the Vietnam Constitution (1991) commemorates in its preamble 'the historic Dien Bien Phu and Ho Chi Minh campaigns, defeating the two colonialist and imperialist wars of aggression, liberating and reunifying their homeland, and completing the people's national democratic revolution'.

[113] Eg, the preamble to the Timor-Leste Constitution recalls the Constitution as 'the culmination of the historical resistance of the Timorese People intensified following the invasion of the 7th of December 1975', and Section 11 valorises those involved in the national liberation movement and the role of the Catholic Church in siding with the People's suffering.

[114] J-W Müller, 'On the Origins of Constitutional Patriotism' (2006) 5 *Contemporary Political Theory* 278.

[115] J-W Müller, *Constitutional Patriotism* (Princeton, NJ: Princeton University Press, 2007) at 61.

[116] Preamble, Arts 7 and 39, Constitution of the Kingdom of Cambodia.

[117] Secs 6(c) and 7, Constitution of Timor-Leste.

[118] Sec 8, Constitution of South Korea.

[119] Part I, Sec 1, Constitution of Timor-Leste (2002).

[120] Preamble, Constitution of China (1949).

[121] Sec 10, Constitution of Timor-Leste (2002).

Taiwan in relation to China[122] or North and South Korea,[123] a commitment to reunification may also be constitutionally expressed.

Where constitutional orders contain non-liberal elements, a modified version of constitutional patriotism may apply in the forging of solidarity and a national ideology. For example, the dominant political philosophy may be communitarian, with the state actively promoting a conception of human flourishing based on non-liberal theories of the good, that draws from tradition, culture and religion. On the one hand, this heightens the illiberal danger of top-down managed collective identity. On the other hand, constitutional patriotism may serve to unite ethnically and religiously divided societies by diverting communal or tribal attachments towards constitutionally entrenched normative commitments. This will in turn feed civic trust and provide a common reference point for all citizens. Below are accounts of how three constitutional cultures have been *constructed*.

A Schwarz, *A Nation in Waiting: Indonesia's Search for Stability* (Singapore: Talisman, 2004) 8–10

The two most important periods of constitutional debates took place in mid-1945 and during the *Konstituante*. The debates ranged from the specific – the national flag – to the broad – the proper relationship between the organs of state. By far the most contentious issue running through all the debates concerned ideology or, more concretely, the ideological basis of the state. There were three main schools of thought which can be called integralists (also known as authoritarians, traditionalists or, to some, Pancasila-ists), Islamists and, for want of a better term, constitutionalists.

In the mid-1940s, the notion of the integralist state was pushed most strongly by Supomo, then a senior judge in the Japanese occupation government. Borrowing from European philosophers Hegel and Spinoza and admiring of governments in Nazi Germany and wartime Japan, the integralists rejected the idea of a separation between rulers and ruled. They specifically rejected the individual-oriented systems of government current in Europe and the United States. 'The traditionalists rejected individualism as the root of colonialism and imperialism. They preferred instead the stylised collectivism of the ancient Javanese kingdom, the mystical sublimation of subject, ruler and realm.'[124]

Supomo likened the state to a large family in which the members of the society were integrated into the whole. In a 31 May 1945 speech to a committee set up in Jakarta to prepare a constitution, Supomo said 'the individual cannot be segregated from the others. Nor can he be separated from the outside world, from groups of humans, not even from other creatures. Everything mixes with other things, every living thing depends on all other forms of life. This is the totalitarian idea, the integralist idea of the Indonesian nation.'

For the integralists, sovereignty was to be held by 'the people', not by individuals. Individualism was seen as the source of conflict between the government and the people. In an integral state, there was no need for specific guarantees for human rights, as these would imply separation between the state and individuals. In an ideal family, Supomo maintained,

---

[122] 'Taiwan is part of the sacred territory of the People's Republic of China. It is the inviolable duty of all Chinese people, including our compatriots in Taiwan, to accomplish the great task of reunifying the motherland.' (Preamble, Constitution of China, 1949)

[123] The preamble to the South Korean Constitution speaks of the 'mission of democratic reform and peaceful unification of our homeland' consonant with justice, humanitarianism and brotherly love (Art 4), while the North Korean one speaks in terms of the 'fatherland's reunification'.

[124] *Indonesian Observer*, 5 Dec 1990, at 3.

children are taken care of and are protected by loving parents: they do not need their 'human rights' protected from the whims of their parents. 'It could not be envisaged,' said lawyer Adnan Buyung Nasution of the integralists, 'that state power wielded by the state's functionaries might also be used to serve the particularistic interests of the rulers, that it might be used against the interests of the people and that it might take the form of repression.'

Two practical consequences of the integralist view were a large role for the state in the economy, particularly as it concerns ownership of land and natural resources, and a strong commitment to cooperatives as a primary pillar of the economy. The integralist state, said its proponents, was concerned primarily with 'social justice' whereas individualism led to capitalism which in turn was linked with colonialism and this, of course, was to be rejected. Consequently, Supomo's views proved popular with advocates of economic socialism.

In contrast, for many Muslim representatives to the constitutional talks, the overriding goal was to ensure that Indonesia would become an Islamic state. Of all the world's great religions, Islam is most committed to the idea of unity between government and religion and Indonesian Muslims, represented by the umbrella party Masyumi, wanted the new republic to formally espouse Islam as the state religion. With some 85 per cent of Indonesians professing Islam as their faith, Muslim constitutional delegates claimed that an Islamic state was a necessary political embodiment of the nation's Islamic community.

On many other constitutional issues – like, for example, human rights – Indonesia's Islamic parties would prove to hold strikingly different opinions. But on the issue of an Islamic state, all Islamic parties responded to the 'call of the Faith' and maintained a unified bloc. . . .

The constitutionalists formed a third lobbying group, but one concerned less with ideology per se than with the proper forms of the state. The essence of the constitutional state, says Nasution, includes 'procedures for the effective participation of the people in government, limitation of the government power, and accountability of the government to the people'. A constitutional government, he says, is based on 'an ethic of means rather than of ends, however noble and just these may be'. Leading the constitutionalist camp in the mid-1940s were several prominent nationalist leaders: Mohammad Hatta, Sutan Sjahrir and Mohammad Yamin.

A chief concern of the constitutionalists was what Nasution calls the 'problem of power'. Hatta, for example, while vigorously defending himself against the charge of individualism, maintained that individual rights needed protection to prevent the new Indonesian state from becoming a state based merely on power. Even in a family, Hatta said, the members still must have the right to express their feelings in order to take good care of the collectivity.

In the constitutional debates preceding independence, the arguments of the constitutionalist lobby fell mostly on deaf ears. In the heady days of mid-1945, flush with the revolutionary spirit, most participants in the constitutional debates were prepared to assume the best of Indonesians as leaders, and consequently focused more on ideological issues than on the relationship between the government's controlling institutions.

Constitutional delegates from the non-Muslim parties viewed the prospect of an Islamic state with horror. In their view, a victory by the Muslims would destroy their hopes for a unified Indonesia. They felt, and probably rightly, that an overly Islamic constitution would lead to immediate revolts by Indonesia's non-Islamic communities, especially those located on the more remote islands.

Sukarno, sympathetic to the integralist view as an ideology but above all a nationalist, offered a way out. On 1 June 1945, Sukarno spelled out his views on Indonesian nationhood. He called for a nation based on Pancasila, or five principles. They are: belief in one supreme God; justice and civility among peoples; the unity of Indonesia; democracy through deliberation and consensus among representatives; social justice for all. The primary objective of this fuzzy doctrine is rooted in its first principle which aimed to undercut demands from the Muslim community for an Islamic state.

'More generally,' says American political scientist Bill Liddle, 'they represent a search . . . for broadly inclusive principles to bind together the diverse groups of an extremely pluralistic society.' Pancasila has proven to be an ideology of remarkable longevity and flexibility. It has been at times – and often at the same time – both a forceful binding agent for a young nation and a powerful tool of repression.

When first announced, says Nasution, Pancasila was seen as 'a meeting point for all the different parties and groups, a common denominator of all ideologies and streams of thought existing in Indonesia.' The principles it espoused were not seen as favouring any particular political system over another. But later, as the nature of Indonesia's government changed, Pancasila began to take on a more specifically political connotation. As the parliamentary democracy period came to an end, it was put forward as the 'only political ideology guaranteeing national unity and suitable to the Indonesian personality and, therefore, the only appropriate basis of state for Indonesia'. Under Soeharto's New Order rule, Pancasila has been seen as synonymous with and justification for an integralist view of the state.

In its original formulation, however, Pancasila did not quite succeed in overcoming Muslim demands for an Islamic state. Pancasila was distrusted by Muslim parties who saw in its religious tolerance a loophole for the atheist Indonesian Communist Party to exploit. Consequently, a few weeks after Sukarno's speech, a constitutional committee agreed to a short addition to the Pancasila doctrine. The first principle became: 'Belief in One God, with the obligation for adherents of Islam to implement the Islamic law (Shariah).'

Known as the Jakarta Charter, it was meant to be included in the preamble of the 1945 Constitution but, after a change of heart by the nationalist and non-Muslim parties, the passage was dropped just before the constitution was proclaimed on 18 August 1945. Its omission engendered deep distrust in parts of the Islamic community against the secular nationalists who would emerge from the revolutionary struggle in charge of the government. Isa Anshary, a Masyumi firebrand, called the omission a 'magic trick . . . an embezzlement against the Muslim stance'. Islamic resentment over the exclusion of the Jakarta Charter would colour the political debate almost continuously for the next fifteen years.

Li-ann Thio, 'Soft Constitutional Law in Non-liberal Asian Constitutional Democracies' (2010) 8(4) I•CON 766, 776–80

Malaysia's Rukunegara declaration of 1971

In 1971, Malaysia's *Rukunegara* ('National Principles') was adopted by royal proclamation. It was drafted by the government-created National Consultative Committee, which co-opted representatives from various ethnic communities, in response to the traumatic race riots of May 13, 1969, which left 'in tatters' the social contract for a multiracial Malaysia. Its chief purpose was to promote nation building through programs that would unify a society of 'diverse races, religions and cultures,' fragmented along the lines of the dominant indigenous Malay community who were primarily Muslim and the immigrant Chinese and Indian minority groups, affirming that the 'task of national consolidation' was 'the responsibility of every one.'

The *Rukunegara* set out 'certain principles' evolving from a 'common history' that were 'enshrined in our Constitution' and 'acceptable' and 'applicable' to all; these principles would 'serve as the nexus which will bind us together.' The declaration contained five objectives: to secure 'a greater unity of all her peoples,' to maintain 'a democratic way of life,' to create 'a just society in which the wealth of the nation shall be equitably shared,' to ensure a 'liberal approach to her rich and diverse cultural traditions,' and to build a 'progressive society' based on modern science and technology. The pursuit of these ends were to be guided by five principles: (1) belief in God, (2) loyalty to king and country, (3) upholding the constitution, (4) rule of law, and (5) good behavior and morality.

Notably the idea of distributive economic justice based on a 'just society,' where wealth is 'equitably shared,' is the rationale and justification for the National Economic Policy (NEP). The NEP is a race-based affirmative action program which arguably exceeds the constitutional recognition of special privileges for Malays and other natives, in the form of reserved public sector jobs, scholarships, and business licenses. The NEP sought to uplift economically disadvantaged Malays and natives to ensure parity with other ethnic communities, particularly, the economically dominant Chinese immigrant community; its subsequent incarnations have received some judicial support and defined the practice of certain government agencies . . .

Singapore's Shared Values

The government-authored shared-values white paper was debated in parliament and adopted in 1991 as a 'national ideology,' an attempt to constitute a 'coherent Singaporean identity' distinct from Western societies, which manifested a more 'individualistic and self-centred outlook on life,' contrary to '[t]raditional Asian ideas of morality, duty and society.' While positive 'values from European and American civilizations,' such as parliamentary democracy and the rule of law, had been adopted, the negative influence of Western individualism was to be countered by inculcating 'a few key values' shared by all major religious and cultural groups, since proposals conflicting with 'the teachings of Islam, Christianity, Hinduism, Taoism or Buddhism' were unlikely to gain general acceptance.

The five shared values are: (1) 'Nation before community and society above self,' (2) family as the basic unit of society, (3) regard and community support for the individual, (4) consensus instead of contention, and (5) racial and religious harmony. The ideology did not merely reflect but was meant to constitute the culture by reinforcing communitarian or neo-Confucian values in order to arrest excessive individualism. This was to be achieved through prioritizing community concerns over individual rights in the interests of social cohesion. Notably, in rejecting the Madisonian distrust of human nature and the view that governors should 'always be treated with suspicion unless proven otherwise,' the white paper heralded the Confucian ideal of the concept of 'government by honourable men [*junzi*] . . . who have a duty to do right for the people, and who have the trust and respect of the population.' It also emphasizes having the 'right political values,' including 'high standards of personal and public conduct' among political leaders.

This view of governors as honorable gentleman with internalized standards of moral integrity appears to have influenced the judiciary in shaping the normative assumptions underlying the law on political defamation. The courts, in defining the scope of free speech, have not accepted the concept of the public figure who is subject to wider limits of acceptable criticism than a private individual. Instead, one's status as a 'prominent public figure' translates into higher damages, as in *Goh Chok Tong v Chee Soon Juan* (No 2), where an opposition politician libeled a former prime minister in alleging mismanagement of national funds. The robust judicial protection of high ministerial office resides in the premium given to their good reputation, as false allegations would undermine their personal lives, public reputations, and the extent to which they sustain public trust. Justice Ang in

Lee Hsien Loong v Singapore Democratic Party considered that without public vindication, lasting damage would redound 'on their political reputation and their moral authority as leaders.' She approved the observations of the Greek rhetorician Isocrates that an individual's good reputation – his character – was of utmost importance to his personal and professional life 'for human proclivity is such that people are apt to listen to those whom they trust.' This accords with the government perspective that Singaporeans expect a government leader to be a 'Confucian gentleman,' 'a superior man . . . of ability and integrity who can set things right and ensure good government.' Prime Minister Goh noted in court that as *junzi*, government leaders would defend their integrity when impugned.

Arguably, the white paper has functioned as 'a quasi-Constitutional hermeneutical tool' insofar as its communitarian orientation has been judicially endorsed and applied. The white paper as SCL [soft constitutional law] – framing the interpretive matrix through which the balance between competing rights and public goods are struck – helps make sense of the contemporary adjudicatory approach toward fundamental liberties. Despite the Privy Council's exhortation to give a 'generous interpretation' to ensure individuals enjoyed the 'full measure' of their fundamental rights in *Ong Ah Chuan v Public Prosecutor*, a decision from Singapore, one may argue that the parsimony in treating rights as defeasible interests, rather than as trumps, is motivated by communitarian values which prioritize community goods like public order. For example, the blanket ban on the religious publications of the Jehovah's Witnesses, an organization which opposes military service, was unsuccessfully challenged in *Colin Chan v Public Prosecutor*. Religious freedom was trumped by unwritten statist values where Chief Justice Yong declared that the 'sovereignty, integrity and unity of Singapore' as 'the paramount mandate of the Constitution' such that anything, including rights of religious freedom, 'which tend to run counter to these objectives must be restrained.' The High Court subsequently reiterated this mantra in *Nappalli Institute of Technical Education* to justify dismissing a teacher who refused to take the national pledge or salute the flag during school assembly because this violated his faith as a Jehovah's Witness. This was treated as an implied contractual breach, with Justice Tan observing that Singapore's success lay in maintaining the unity of its multiracial and religious population which entitled the government to take reasonable steps to ensure that future generations understood the importance of preserving 'the sovereignty, integrity and unity of Singapore.' Thus, the defense of the nation, whether through prohibiting conscientious objections to compulsory military service or dismissing teachers who refused to participate in 'idolatrous' flag ceremonies, trumped the individual's religious freedom, reflecting a weak rights culture.

Notes and Questions

1. On the drafting and impact of Pancasila, see E Darmaputera, *Pacasila and the Search for Identity and Modernity in Indonesian Society* (Leiden: EJ Brill, 1988); Seung-won Song, *Back to Basics in Indonesia? Reassessing the Pancasila and Pancasila State and Society: 1945–2007*, unpublished PhD thesis (Ohio University, 2008); B Fleming Intan, '*Public Religion' and the Pancasila-Based State of Indonesia: An Ethical and Sociological Analysis* (New York: Peter Lang, 2008); M Morfit, 'Pacasila: The Indonesian State Ideology According to the New Order Government' (1981) 21(8) *Asian Survey* 838; and DE Ramage, *Politics in Indonesia: Democracy, Islam and the Ideology of Tolerance* (London: Routledge: 1995).

2. For a background to the drafting of the *Rukunegara* and the constitutional amendments that followed its promulgation, see A Harding, 'The Rukunegara Amendments

of 1971' in A Harding and HP Lee (eds), *Constitutional Landmarks in Malaysia: The First 50 Years 1957–2007* (Kuala Lumpur: LexisNexis, 2007) 115. See also CW Watson, 'The Construction of the Post-Colonial Subject in Malaysia' in S Tønnesson and H Antlöv (eds), *Asian Forms of the Nation* (London: Curzon, 1998) 297.

3. In relation to the Pancasila, *Rukunegara* and Shared Values, it was observed by Michael RJ Vatikiotis, in his *Indonesian Politics Under Suharto: The Rise and Fall of New Order*, 3rd edn (London: Routledge, 1998) at 145, that:

> Having overcome the imperialist overlords, these [Southeast Asian] states redefined nationalism in terms of the resilience drawn from economic development and the fostering of traditional values. It was agreed that to achieve the goals of development and preserve the fabric of society and its traditional values, some of the aspects of western government had to be adapted, or suspended 'temporarily'. In their place indigenous quasi-ideologies were developed: *Pancasila* in Indonesia; the *Rukun Negara* in Malaysia, and more recently, Singapore' 'Core Principles' [*sic*]. By this process the leadership of each country acquired more power, and the political enfranchisement of ordinary people, indeed their involvement in politics, was diluted. The legitimacy of this power was justified more and more in terms of traditional values, rather than through the ballot box.

Do you agree with Vatikiotis' analysis? Why?

Chinese thinkers have long felt that it would be unwise to clone Western forms of government in China, as the problems of governing a polity like China were vastly different from those of European states. Many thinkers felt that it would be much wiser to draw on traditional forms of government and ideology to craft a constitutional order suitable to China's needs. One of the first modernist thinkers along this line was Kang Youwei (康有为 1858–1927), a Confucian scholar who led movements to establish a constitutional monarchy in the dying days of the Qing dynasty. Kang, and his famous student Liang Qichao (梁启超 1873–1929), as leaders of the *Wuxu Reform* or Hundred Days' Reform, argued for a transition towards a constitutional democracy underpinned by Confucian humanitarian thought. More radical was Sun Yat-sen, founder of Republican China, who wanted a republican state built on a mix of western and Chinese notions of power. Sun's Five-Power Constitution idea has been made manifest in Taiwan's 1947 Constitution, in which power is divided between the legislative, executive, judicial, control and examination branches or *yuan*s. More recently, Chinese intellectual Jiang Qing has argued that Western forms of democracy are inherently unsuitable for China and that a new constitutional order based on Confucian ideology should be established.

E Ip, 'Building Constitutional Democracy on Oriental Foundations: An Anatomy of Sun Yat-Sen's Constitutionalism' (2008) 9 *Historia Constitucional* 373

III. An Overview of the Model

11. A superficial glance at the constitutional model of Sun Yat-sen might be misleading. Rhetoric like the separation of the executive, legislative and judicial powers, the talk of republicanism and representative assemblies, the discussion of regional autonomy

and party politics might deceive the lay reader that Sun's theory was foreign to traditional Chinese political theory, or at least, heavily influenced by Western ideas. Sun compared his Three Principles of the People with the French revolutionary slogan of 'liberty, equality and fraternity', as well as Abraham Lincoln's 'Government of the people, by the people and for the people.' But it must be noted that Sun's philosophy was actually highly regionalized both in form and substance. Sun deployed Western terminologies and concepts to refine the pitfalls of the Chinese political tradition.

12. Sun was without doubt one of the foremost thinkers in modern China to give a predominant position to constitutional law and the legal system as a whole in the political establishment. He adopted a mechanical metaphor for the constitution – it is like a machine that strikes a balance between the apparent conflicting values of liberty and rulership. The pursuit of the rule of law is at the heart of his thought. Sun observed that the law is fundamental to the survival of democratic politics, and it is essential to protect human rights, prohibit bandits, and resolve conflicts. Since these ideas were virtually non-existent at that time, his contemporaries could not really see how significant it is. The following metaphor was also central to Sun Yat-sen's political theory. Sun believed that the shareholders of a factory should hold the power, but they lack administrative techniques. Thus, administrative power should be vested in the administrative talents, who do not possess power but are able to run the factory expeditiously. Sun applied this analogy to the concept between the people and the public administration. Some significant strands of thoughts flowing through the writings of Sun included the classification of political force into the force of liberty and the force of order maintenance. While the people ought to possess political power, administrative power is to be given to a 'Five-Power Government'.

13. The five powers refer to the additions of the independent branches of *public examination* and *supervisory impeachment* to the executive, legislative and judicial. Sun briefly expressed the working mechanisms of the center-piece of his constitutional ideology, the 'Five-Power Constitution' in an essay so named, that 'after the enactment of the constitution, the people from each prefecture should directly vote for a president in order to form the Executive Council (yuan), which exercises the executive powers of the government. They should also elect their representatives to form the Legislative Council. The heads of the Judicial, Examination and Supervision Councils should be appointed by the president with consent of the Legislative Council.'

14. All of the five Councils should be responsible to the state sovereign authority, the National Assembly. According to Sun, 'the Supervision Council should have the power to advice the National Assembly to recall any government officials on the basis of misconduct. The major responsibilities of the National Assembly are to amend the Constitution and adjudicate the misconduct of public servants. All members of the National Assembly and the five councils should be separately examined by the Examination Council in order to be qualified for their posts.'

15. It is Sun's belief that only the introduction of a Five-Power Constitution could eliminate the shortcomings of the three powers within the Western doctrine of separation of powers. In his view, the separation of executive, judicial and legislative powers are incomplete in two respects, firstly, the executive appointment of bureaucrats and mere election of lawmakers lack a serious and transparent examination system, which limits the possibility of having the most talented to serve for the state. This is largely an elitist meritocracy viewpoint having roots in the traditional Chinese political system . . .

16. He was particularly resisting the American example where the right to be elected is often constrained by factors like financial disparity among candidates, and corruption

in election. He argued that the United States congress was 'full of unwise and ignorant people', and the appointment in the executive wing was often determined by connections and personal will of the serving president. Sun believed that this would result in bribery and bias in the selection of government officials. He believed that government ministers should aim at serving the people instead of agreeing with certain vested political interests. Since state examinations were not independent from the executive, selections and appointments of the public servants would be subjected to the arbitrariness of ruling political parties. In his view, this would lead to the production of unsatisfactory bureaucrats, who would only serve the party they are loyal to.

17. On the other hand, Sun regarded the legislature's possession of impeachment powers, that is, the powers to recall government officials, a cause of legislative hegemony over the executive government. Since the functions of recalling and supervising state officials were both installed in the legislature, lawmakers could easily abuse their extensive powers. Both these shortcomings could severely hamper the quality and efficiency of public administrative services. The power to adjudicate upon officials should rest with an institution independent from others, including the legislature. This led to his formulation of an independent impeachment organ, the Supervision Council. The Supervision Council should not only check misconduct and misbehavior in national politics, rectify mistakes, but also improve the incapacities of the republican polity.

18. The entire notion of a Five-Power Constitution is based on the idea of dividing national power into 'political power' (*zhengquan*) and 'administrative power' (*zhiquan*). Although this concept is in many ways original, especially in modern Asian political thought, it is in effect, quite similar with the American theory of identifying a dichotomy between politics and public administration. 'Political power' means the citizenship's power to control the government, through the channel of the four powers of election, recall, initiation of laws and referendum. In contrast, 'administrative power' refers to the power of the government. This power ought to be exercised through the five organs of executive, legislature, judiciary, examination and supervision. To sum up, the dichotomy of 'political power' and 'administrative power' was elaborated as the division between 'quan' (people's power and rights) and 'neng' (government's capacity). To distinguish these two powers is the first task to building a state where the people are in power, and where the government is capable. It is Sun's ambition to strike a balance between the two . . .

IV. *An Oriental Constitutionalism?*

1. Traditional Chinese Philosophy

22. Sun's constitutionalism reflected many core elements of Chinese philosophy. One of his highest principles, 'public justice for all in the world' (*tianxia weigong*) was originated in the teachings of Confucius, in which he praised as recognizing certain civil rights. His theories embodied a 'pervasive humanness' which was quite similar with the Confucian concept of 'ren' (仁). But he believed that a restoration of Chinese traditional virtues and wisdom would not be sufficient, not until the Chinese people could catch up and surpass the West in scientific development. One of his famous analogies was that were democracy implemented, the 4 billion of populace would all be as powerful as the previous emperors. Apparently this was targeted to an audience who had been so used to the concept of having an imperial authoritarian ruler over the country.

23. However, at the same time, he advocated that the ability of the collective population, were nothing more than Liu Chan/Ya Dou, the incapable emperor of the Shu Han

State in the Three Kingdoms period (220–280 AD). The republican government, however, was compared with Zhuge Liang, the mystically wise prime minister and genius military strategist of Shu Han. Zhuge Liang represented a category of elites who 'knows and understands in advance'. This may imply that while the sovereignty of the people and their residual four powers ought to be upheld and protected, in practice, the position of the people is actually similar to that of a ceremonial head of state in a constitutional monarchy or parliamentary republic. True power was intended to be wielded by experts on behalf of the populace.

24. Sun classified people into those who are alert and sensitive (to national affairs); those who are less alert and less sensitive; and the majority of those who are never alert and never sensitive. Thus, he believed that constitutional democracy could never be possible unless the stages of 'military administration', 'political tutelage' have been successfully endured, which were supposed to educate the people with democratic doctrines and teaching them how to exercise their rights and powers. Therefore, in Sun's vision, the sovereign (the people) should not directly manage state affairs, which should instead be placed in the hands of the government. It is arguable that this vision echoed with some portions of the ancient Legalist philosopher Han Feizi's (280–233 BCE) political theory, who advocated that while the sovereign should retain the powers of enacting laws and appointment and dismissals of officials, he should not rule the population directly. Instead, the best statecraft refers to administering ministers effectively.

25. In Sun's analysis of the five powers, emphasis was placed on how the examination and supervisory powers ought to be separated as independent branches of government to check and balance the other powers. However, Sun did not sufficiently discourse on how the executive, legislative and judiciary should interact with each other. But it was evident that these three branches were actually designated to be three specialized departments within one organization (the central government) and dependent on each other. Sun's understandings of the role of the judiciary link with his ideas about the role of law in society. He believed that the social instability present in the country was a result of internal and external impacts on the old imperial political structure, which led to the weakening of the Confucian social order of moral virtues. As we know, these virtues and rituals, the li, were the building blocks of social norms that controlled nearly all aspects of social life in traditional China. Law has always been a politicized instrument manipulated to supplement this social order, and Sun believed that it was useful to restore stability to the Chinese state.

26. The 'examination power' as he referred to, was a long established institution in the imperial Chinese government, dating back to at least the Sui Dynasty (581–618 AD) where open examinations on Confucian texts were held in order to select a professional and relatively independent bureaucracy. Moreover, the 'impeachment power' was also inspired by the the imperial agency called the Censorate, established as early as in the Qin Dynasty (221–207 BCE), which advises, checks and recalls government bureaucrats and sometimes even the emperor. Sun believed that these are the precious treasures of ancient Chinese legal-political philosophy and they were nevertheless invaluable to China even in modern times.

27. He praised the members of the Censorate, 'even [though] their ranks were low, their jurisdiction still encompassed the wide array of officials ranging from the Prime Minister to the smallest officers, making them fear of the consequences of breaking the law. No matter what physical penalty or criticisms they face, these brave and courageous men will always endure.' The supervisory institutions of the imperial past could to a certain extent, be considered as an embodiment of the intellectual class'

defense of imperial morality. Probably this could have enlightened Sun to believe that an independent impeachment branch could represent a sense of justice in the republic.

28.   Many strands of thought of Sun revealed patterns of the ancient Chinese concept of yin and yang, which formed the cosmological basis of mainstream philosophies like Confucianism and Daoism. The ancient Chinese believed that a balance must be stroke between the yin (literally 'brightness'') and yang (literally 'darkness'), otherwise, prevalence of either side will cause undesirable events. However, they are not simplistically against each other, for their competition forms the basis of their cooperation, and either the yin or the yang could not survive without each other. In Sun's theories, notable examples include the balance between the political and governing powers, liberty and rulership and people's rights and government influence. Indeed, political and administrative powers must not only be separated but must also be kept in equilibrium. With the four powers and rights of the people and the five powers of the government effectively exercised and maintained on equal weight, democratic problems may truly be resolved and the public administration will have a clearer agenda to follow. The objective of the Five-Power Constitution is to maintain a balanced harmony between the people and their government, so as to establish a powerful and efficient democratic system which realizes its full potential.

DA Bell, 'Introduction' in Jian Qing, *A Confucian Constitutional Order: How China's Ancient Past Can Shape Its Political Future* (Princeton, NJ: Princeton University Press, 2013) 1, 5–10

Although democracy – more specifically, a form of government that grants ultimate controlling power to democratically elected representatives – is built on the separation of powers, the separation, Jiang argues, is a matter of implementation rather than legitimization. In a democracy, legitimacy is based on the sovereignty of the people. But Jiang objects to the idea that there is only one source of legitimacy. He claims that the modern notion of sovereignty of the people is similar in form to the medieval notion of the sovereignty of God, but with the content changed from God to the people: 'In fact, the sovereignty of the people is simply the secular equivalent of the sovereignty of God.'

   In political practice, the overemphasis on popular sovereignty translates into the politics of desire: '[I]n a democracy, political choices are always down to the desires and interests of the electorate.' This leads to two problems. First, the will of the people may not be moral: it could endorse racism, imperialism, or fascism. Second, when there is a clash between the short-term interests of the populace and their long-term interests or the common interests of all mankind, the former have political priority. Jiang specifically worries about the ecological crisis. It is difficult if not impossible for democratically elected governments to implement policies that curb energy usage in the interests of future generations and foreigners. If China were to follow the American model in terms of per capita carbon emissions, for example, the world would be damaged beyond repair. But 'it is impossible for Green Parties to fully – through legitimization and implementation – realize ecological values in a Western democracy, without radical change in both the theory and structure of Western democracy.' Hence, a political system must place more emphasis on what Jiang calls 'sacred values' that are concerned with the well-being of the environment, the welfare of future generations, and humanity as a whole.

   Jiang's political alternative is the Confucian *Way of the Humane Authority*. The question of political legitimacy, he argues, is central to Confucian constitutionalism. He defines legitimacy as 'the deciding factor in determining whether a ruler has the right to rule.' But unlike Western-style democracy, there is more than one source of legitimacy. According to the *Gongyang Commentary*, political power must have three kinds of legitimacy – that of heaven, earth, and the human – for it to be justified. The legitimacy of heaven refers to a transcendent ruling will and a sacred sense of natural morality. The legitimacy of earth refers to a legitimacy that comes from history and culture. And the legitimacy of the human refers to the will of the people that determines whether or not the people will obey political authorities. All three forms of legitimacy must be in equilibrium, but Jiang notes that the equilibrium is not one of equality. According to the *Book of Changes*, the multiplicity of things comes from the one principle of heaven, hence the sacred legitimacy of the way of heaven is prior to both the cultural legitimacy of the way of earth and that of the popular will of the human way.

In ancient times, the Way of the Humane Authority was implemented by the monarchical rule of the sage kings of the three dynasties (Xia/Shang/Zhou). But changes in historical circumstances necessitate changes in the form of rule. Today, the will of the people must be given an institutional form that was lacking in the past, though it should be constrained and balanced by institutional arrangements meant to implement the other two forms of legitimacy. Hence, Jiang argues that the Way of the Humane Authority should be implemented by means of a tricameral legislature that corresponds to the three forms of legitimacy: a House of the People that represents popular legitimacy, a House of Ru that represents sacred legitimacy, and a House of the Nation that represents cultural legitimacy.

Jiang goes into more institutional detail. The members of the House of the People 'are chosen according to the norms and processes of Western democratic parliaments,' including universal suffrage and election from functional constituencies. The leader of the House of Ru (儒) is a great scholar proposed by the Confucian scholars. The candidates for membership are nominated by the scholars, and then they are examined on their knowledge of the Confucian classics and assessed following a trial period of administration at lower levels of government, similar to the examination and recommendation systems used in China in the past. The leader of the House of the Nation should be a direct descendant of Confucius, who would select from 'among the descendants of great sages of the past, descendants of the rulers, descendants of famous people, of patriots, university professors of Chinese history, retired top officials, judges, and diplomats, worthy people from society as well as representatives of Daoism, Buddhism, Islam, Tibetan Buddhism, and Christianity.'

Each house deliberates in its own way and may not interfere in the running of the others. Jiang addresses the key issue of how to deal with political gridlock that may arise as a result of conflicts between the three houses of parliament. He says that a bill must pass at least two of the houses to become law. The priority of sacred legitimacy is expressed in the veto power exercised by the House of Ru. However, Jiang notes that the power of the Ru is restrained by the other two houses: for example, 'if they propose a bill restricting religious freedom, the People and the Nation will oppose it and it cannot become law.' In that sense, it differs from the Council of Guardians in theocratic Iran, where the sacred is the only form of legitimacy and 'and so the council of guardians has power over the assembly and is not subject to its restraint.'

In chapter 2, Jiang puts forward a proposal for another institution – the Academy – that is meant to further restrain the power of parliamentarians. In Western constitutionalism, power is limited by means of rights. In Confucian constitutionalism, power is limited primarily by means of morality (Jiang is not against the protection of rights per se, but he says that it cannot be the sole aim of a constitution; put differently, the protection of rights will not be effective unless the power holders are primarily regulated by morality). Again, however, new historical circumstances dictate new institutions and practices: 'Now that China has ended monarchical rule and begun republican rule, Confucian constitutionalism must create a new structure adapted to the times.' The key institution designed to limit power today is what Jiang calls the 'Academy,' an institution that continues China's tradition and spirit of rule by scholarship.

Jiang explicitly invokes the seventeenth-century Confucian scholar Huang Zongxi's (黄宗羲) proposal for an Academy composed of scholar-officials who could question the emperor and appraise and adjudicate the rights and wrongs of his policies (Huang's proposal was too radical for his own day: it circulated samizdat-style for over 250 years, surfacing only in the late Qing period, with the dynasty in disarray). An Academy adapted to the present, Jiang argues, would have six functions. First, it would supervise all levels and organs of government by means of a Historical Records Office that would record the words and deeds of the highest decision makers so that they would be answerable to their own time, to history, and to future generations, and a Modern System of Posthumous Titles that would help to restrain the actions of the living. Second, it would set the examinations to ensure that people in all state institutions have the basic qualifications for governing as well as train parliamentarians for the House of Ru. Third, it would preside at state ceremonies of a religious nature, sacrifices to heaven, to sages of the past, and to the natural world, and at the investiture of a new head of state. Fourth, it would have the supreme power of recall of all top leaders of state institutions in the event of dereliction of duty. Fifth, it would have the power to undertake mediation and issue final verdicts in the event of serious conflicts among state bodies. And sixth, it would have the power to uphold religion. Jiang is careful to note that 'the Academy supervises, but does not run the state. Subordinate bodies exercise their own authority according to the principle of balance of powers and independence.' The Academy does not interfere in these operations and hence its maintenance of religion and morality is different from that of a Taliban-style theocracy. Ordinarily, the members of the Academy spend their time on the study of the Confucian classics, and only rarely intervene in the affairs of the state. Such work has special importance because Jiang argues that Confucian constitutionalism cannot be realized without a substantial body of scholars who keep to Confucian beliefs and practices.

In chapter 3, Jiang turns to the third feature of Confucian constitutionalism: the symbolic monarch. Kang Youwei (康有为) had put forth a similar proposal a century ago, but Jiang defends it in unprecedented detail. According to Jiang, the state is a mysterious body from a distant past, and present-day people have an obligation to maintain it and hand it down to future generations. A leader chosen by the current generation such as an elected president cannot express the state's historical legitimacy because the state also belongs to past and future generations. Hence, a hereditary monarch descended from a noble and ancient lineage is most likely to embody the historical and trans-generational identity of a state: 'Inheritance alone bears the hallmarks of status and tradition demanded by the continuity of the state.' But Jiang is not calling for the restoration of the imperial system. In traditional China, the monarch represented 'both state and government, which means that the structure of the state and that of the government are confused and not very clearly separated.' In modern-day Confucian constitutionalism, by contrast, the tricameral legislature would exercise real political (legislative) power, the Academy would exercise supervisory power, and the monarch would exercise symbolic power.

Symbolic power, however, is not really 'nothing.' The monarch will head the House of the Nation and influence the life of the nation by mediating conflicts between power holders and by 'signing and concluding international treaties, proclaiming the law, naming civil and military officials, proclaiming amnesties and pardons, distributing honors, and the like.' The monarch can also exercise moral power by speaking out on such issues as environmental degradation that affect future generations. Most important, the symbolic monarch contributes to the legitimacy of political power by instantiating the historical legitimacy of the state. The state is more likely to be legitimate in the eyes of the people if it is headed by a symbolic monarch who commands awe and respect. Jiang emphasizes that loyalty to the state – which underpins its legitimacy, hence the unity and stability of the state – is not purely rational, and it is better for people to project their psychological sense of belonging onto a symbolic monarch than onto those who hold real (legislative) power.

But who exactly should be the symbolic monarch? In today's China, Jiang argues, 'the symbolic monarch will have to meet five conditions to be acceptable: (1) the monarch must have a noble and ancient blood lineage; (2) this lineage must be political in nature; (3) it must be clearly shown that the lineage is direct and unbroken; (4) the lineage must be so unique as to exclude competition from any other lineages; and (5) the citizens must universally respect and accept the person with this noble political lineage.' Jiang shows that descendants of past emperors cannot meet those conditions. He then goes through each condition and argues that only one person qualifies to be the symbolic monarch in today's China: 'the direct heir of Confucius.'

Notes and Questions

1. Do you think that a constitutional order founded on traditional elements is more likely to more legitimate and therefore more effective than one which is borrowed from a foreign source? Why?

2. The inadequacy of the standard Montesquieu iteration of the separation of powers doctrine is particularly evident in some polities. Kevin YL Tan made the following observation with respect to the study of constitutions in Asia, and in particular in Thailand:

    Constitutions based purely on political or sociological legitimacy are inherently problematic and there is this constant seeking of legitimacy through the remaking of constitutions. The difficulty that hinders our constitutional thinking is we were taught that there are only three powers that need to be separated, respectively the legislative, executive and judiciary. This is the standard theory constructed by John Stuart Mill and Montesquieu. However we tend to forget that there may be real substantial powers outside these three institutions that continue to influence how the state is run, such as the military and the monarchy. In other words, the constitution must be practical; it must take into account these various facets of state power if it is to be taken seriously. Otherwise the constitution could easily be subverted by one of them. I have observed this phenomenon in countries like Thailand and Burma. Thailand is a classic case, because every now and then the military comes out of the barracks and takes power. After the elections are held, they go back to the barracks.

    Besides the military, there are also rather odd institutions such as the Privy Council with ex-military men like Prem Tinsulanonda who are up there and very influential. Another cause of concern is the revered King who has amassed a huge political influence. These alternative and legitimate sources of power must be counted and constitutionally limited, otherwise the constitution is going to be subverted once again.

    See KYL Tan, 'Constitutionalism and the Search for Legal and Political Legitimacy in the Asian States' (2012) 7(2) *National Taiwan University Law Review*

503, 518. Tan's observations were first made in a symposium on the Thai Constitution in 2006. See A Harding and P Leyland, *The Constitutional System of Thailand: A Contextual Analysis* (Oxford: Hart Publishing, 2011) at 30.

3.   On Sun Yat-sen's Five Power Government, see: Suisheng Zhao, *Power by Design: Constitution-Making in Nationalist China* (Honolulu: University of Hawaii Press, 1996); and RL Walker, 'The Control System of the Chinese Government' (1947) 7(1) *The Far Eastern Quarterly* 2. See also generally Xiaohong Xiao-Planes, 'Of Constitutions and Constitutionalism: Trying to Build a New Political Order in China, 1908–1949' in S Balme and MW Dowdle (eds), *Building Constitutionalism in China* (New York: Palgrave Macmillan, 2009) at 37–58.

4.   On the reforms of Kang Youwei and his acolytes, see P Zarrow, 'The Reform Movement, the Monarchy and Political Modernity' in RE Karl and P Zarrow (eds), *Rethinking the 1898 Reform Period: Political and Cultural Change in Late Qing China* (Cambridge, Mass: Harvard University Press, 2002) at 17; RR Thompson, *China's Local Councils in the Age of Constitutional Reform: 1898–1911* (Cambridge, Mass: Harvard University Press, 1995); and P Zarrow, *After Empire: The Conceptual Transformation of the Chinese State, 1885–1924* (Stanford, Cal: Stanford University Press, 2012). See also Tay Wei Leong, *Saving the Chinese Nation and the World: Religion and Confucian Reformation, 1880s–1937*, MA thesis (National University of Singapore: Department of History 2012).

5.   On the continuing influence of Confucian thought in constitution-making, see Ruiping Fan (ed), *The Renaissance of Confucianism in Contemporary China* (New York: Springer, 2011); SC Angle, *Contemporary Confucian Political Philosophy* (Cambridge: Polity Press, 2012); and DA Bell and Hahm Chaibong, *Confucianism for the Modern World* (Cambridge: Cambridge University Press, 2003).

ii. Culture as a Platform for Political Ideology

A constitution may serve as an instrument for creating a new culture when it underwrites a political system that breaks radically with the past. Socialist constitutions often project themselves as products of revolutionary struggle, thus forming a blueprint to promote and sustain a specific socialist ideology. They signify a radical departure from the old regime and a *new ideological orientation* of the state. The constitutions are embedded with a overarching meta-ideology, as can be seen in the preambles to the Constitutions of Vietnam and China. Both preambles pay tribute to Marxist-Leninism and to the political thought of Ho Chi Minh and Mao Zedong respectively.

Central to the new regime is the constitutional recognition of the Communist Party's leading role: the Communist Party of Vietnam,[125] Communist Party of China and the Lao People's Revolutionary Party as the 'leading nucleus'. These are facilitated by various patriotic grassroots organisations.[126]

---

[125] Art 4: 'The Communist Party of Vietnam, the vanguard of the Vietnamese working class and loyal representative of the interests of the working class, the working people and the whole nation, who adheres to Marxism-Leninism and Ho Chi Minh's thought, is the force assuming leadership of the State and society. All organisations of the Party shall operate within the framework of the Constitution and the law.'

[126] Art 9: 'The Vietnam Fatherland Front is the political allied organization and voluntary union of political organizations, social-political organizations, social organizations and representative individuals of social strata and classes, of ethnic groups, of religions and of Vietnamese people residing abroad.'

The socialist state actively fosters 'the people's patriotism and revolutionary heroism', and seeks to instill in the youth 'the sense of civic responsibility, Ho Chi Minh's thought, ethics, style' and 'the socialist ideal'[127] in relation to military service and defence. Socialist states are deeply committed to moulding their citizenry, through education, to build 'good citizens with revolutionary competence, knowledge and abilities'.[128] Article 24 of China's Constitution requires the state to provide education 'in patriotism and collectivism, in internationalism and communism and in dialectical and historical materialism, to combat capitalist, feudalist and other decadent ideas', in order to build 'socialist spiritual civilization' and 'civic virtues of love for the motherland, for the people, for labour, for science and for socialism'.

Constitutions are also used as instruments of evolutionary change within the socialist framework. These changes relate to the needs of the market economy and, correspondingly, the need to respect the rule of law to facilitate business and investment, even if this is to function in a milieu where 'law' is more an instrument of state control then to protect individual autonomy. Article 5 of the Constitution of China describes the state as 'a socialist country ruled by law', and states that all state functionaries will abide by the Constitution and law, and any violation will be investigated. At the same time, its preamble enjoins the 'Chinese people of all ethnic groups' to 'continue to adhere to the people's democratic dictatorship and the socialist road, persevere in reform and opening to the outside world' under the 'guidance of Marxism-Leninism, Mao Zedong Thought, Deng Xiaoping Theory and the Important Thought of the "Three Represents"'.[129]

The Vietnam Constitution constitutes culture by charting out a path for future national development. Article 12 commits the state to governance 'by rule of law' and to strengthening socialist legislation. At the same time, Article 15 requires the state to adopt 'consistent policies on development of a socialist-oriented market economy'. This represents a departure from the Marxist vision of law 'as a tool used by the ruling classes to exploit the working class'.[130] Furthermore, Article 21 permits the establishment of 'individual economic entities, small-holders and the private capitalist economic sector' where these are 'beneficial to the well-being of the nation and its people'.

Articles 6 and 7 of China's Constitution identify socialist public ownership and the state-owned economy as the basis of China's socialist economic system, but it is recognised in Article 11 that individual, private and non-public sectors of the economy are 'major components', existing within the law, which the state guides and supervises, and whose lawful interests it protects.

Thus the rule of law culture in these two states is limited to supporting economic development, trade and investment, and harmonising with Western-based commercial

---

[127] See Arts 30, 48, 66, Vietnam Constitution.

[128] See Art 22, Laos Constitution.

[129] See R Pereenboom (ed), *Asian Discourses of Rule of Law: Theories and Implementation of Rule of Law in Twelve Asian Countries, France and the US*, (London and New York: Routledge 2004); and L Cata Backer, The Rule of Law, the Chinese Communist Party, and Ideological Campaigns: Sange Daibiao (the "Three Represents"), Socialist Rule of Law, and Modern Chinese Constitutionalism' (2006) 16 *Journal of Transnational & Contemporary Problems* 29; B Sheehy, 'Fundamentally Conflicting Views of the Rule of Law in China and the West and the Implications for Commercial Disputes' (2005–2006) 26 *Northwestern Journal of International Law & Business* 225.

[130] Pham Duy Nghia, 'Confucianism and the conception of the law in Vietnam' in J Gillespie and P Nicholson (eds), *Asian Socialism and Legal Change* (Canberra: ANU Press, 2005) 76 at 77 (whole book available at <http://epress.anu.edu.au/titles/as_citation>).

laws. It is not intended to act as a limit on state power, and thus diverges from the liberal conception of the rule of law.[131]

iii. Constitutional Cultism: North Korea

The Constitution of the Democratic People's Republic of Korea (North Korea) embodies the personality-driven *juche* or *chuch'e*-based socialist ideology ('self-reliance') centred around the charismatic personality of 'great leader Comrade Kim Il Sung' and his familial successors.[132] It reads like a paean to the state's founding father, who 'devoted his whole life' to serving the people 'with his noble politics of bene-volence', transforming society 'into one big single-heartedly united family', being 'the sun of the nation and the lodestar of the fatherland's reunification'. The preamble proclaims Comrade Kim as 'a genius in ideology and theory and in the art of leader-ship, an ever-victorious, iron-willed brilliant commander, a great revolutionary and politician, and a great human being'.

A 'constitutional totalitarianism' is thus created, and ideology permeates all of life and the hereditary dictatorship. Article 3 declares that the state will be 'guided in its activities by the Juche idea'. Collectivism undergirds society and its understanding of rights and responsibilities.[133] To achieve 'the complete victory of socialism' and reuni-fication of North and South Korea, three revolutions are to be waged: 'ideological, cultural and technical'.[134] The 'self-supporting national economy' was to be a 'highly developed Juche-oriented' economy befitting 'a completely socialist society';[135] the state would develop 'Juche-oriented and revolutionary literature and art, which are national in form and socialist in content',[136] to meet the 'sound cultural and aesthetic demands' of the working people.[137] The use of emotional terms is evident in the obli-gation of the state to make the labour of the working people 'more joyful and worth-while' to promote 'voluntary enthusiasm and initiative for the society, the collective and themselves',[138] as well as 'sincerity' in labour.[139] The young are to be raised as 'resolute revolutionaries' steeped in *juche* knowledge, virtue and physical health,[140] while all people would be trained 'as builders of socialism' in an effort to 'intellectual-ise' the whole of society.[141] Citizens are to 'value and love' state property,[142] and 'must demonstrate the spirit of devoting themselves to the work for the society and the

---

[131] For a discussion of the stark differences between Western and Chinese conceptions of the rule of law, see Sheehy, above n 129.

[132] G Lee, 'The Political Philosophy of Juche' (2003) 3(1) *Stanford Journal of East Asian Affairs* 106, at <http://www.stanford.edu/group/sjeaa/journal3/korea1.pdf> (primary tenets of *juche* include economic independence and military self-defence, a Koreanisation of Stalinist principles, Confucian values and nationalism).

[133] Art 63 of the Constitution provides that 'the rights and duties of citizens are based on the collectivist principle, One for all and all for one.'

[134] Art 9, Constitution of the Democratic People's Republic of Korea.

[135] Art 26, Constitution of the Democratic People's Republic of Korea.

[136] Art 52, Constitution of the Democratic People's Republic of Korea.

[137] Art 39, Constitution of the Democratic People's Republic of Korea.

[138] Art 29, Constitution of the Democratic People's Republic of Korea.

[139] Art 83, Constitution of the Democratic People's Republic of Korea.

[140] Art 43, Constitution of the Democratic People's Republic of Korea.

[141] Art 40, Constitution of the Democratic People's Republic of Korea.

[142] Art 84, Constitution of the Democratic People's Republic of Korea.

people' while safeguarding 'the political and ideological unity and solidarity of the people'.[143]

The extent to which this kind of cultism has permeated North Korean society can be seen in the instance of an official report from the Korean Central News Agency after a munitions train exploded in Ryongchon in April 2004. The report stated that citizens displayed the 'spirit of guarding the leader with their very lives' by rushing into burning buildings to save portraits of Kim 'before searching for their family members or saving their household goods'.[144] In serving as an instrument to support a dictatorship, constitutionalism is thwarted rather than fostered.

D. Culture and Paths of Institutional Interaction

i. Governing Institutional Interactions Through Culture

Article 15 of the Bhutan Constitution requires political parties to promote nationality and progressive economic development to ensure the well-being of the nation. The Opposition is required to play a 'constructive role' to ensure the Government provides good governance and promotes the national interest,[145] in the interests of securing government responsibility, accountability and transparency. Party interests should not supercede national interests, and the Opposition is required to 'promote and engage in constructive and responsible debate in Parliament while providing healthy and dignified opposition to the Government'.[146] Article 33(r1) of the Interim Nepal Constitution (2008) also prescribes the development of a culture 'of resolving major political problems of the country with understanding, consensus and cooperation among the major political parties'.

An institutional culture with respect to the working practices of government bodies may evolve out of experience. This can be seen in the case of Singapore's elected presidency. Under Singapore's Constitution, the President has limited 'veto' powers over certain financial decisions taken by the Cabinet. At the end of his tenure, President Ong Teng Cheong held a press conference where he aired various difficulties he encountered in the course of discharging his duties, such as uncooperative civil servants. This 'adversarial' outburst sparked a parliamentary debate as well as two ministerial rebuttals, leading to the adoption of a non-binding white paper. This document has been described as a consensus 'convention of agreed rules' to which both parties would adhere until one side gave the other notice to the contrary. These soft constitutional law norms, which were created afresh rather than being a product of past practice, were designed prevent a public confrontation between the President and the Cabinet. This evinced a clear preference for 'quiet diplomacy' that would flow from the parties' declared goal of a maintaining a 'harmonious working relationship'.[147] This

---

[143] Art 81, Constitution of the Democratic People's Republic of Korea.

[144] Committee to Protect Journalists, '10 most censored countries', 2 May 2006, at <http://cpj.org/reports/2006/05/10-most-censored-countries.php>.

[145] Art 18, Constitution of the Kingdom of Bhutan.

[146] Art 18(3), Constitution of the Kingdom of Bhutan.

[147] Principles for Determining and Safeguarding the Accumulated Reserves of the Government and the Fifth Schedule Statutory Boards and Government Companies (Cmd 5 of 1999); see Thio Li-ann, above n 53, at 78–80.

white paper reflects Singapore's national ideology which urges 'consensus over contention', that is found in the 'shared-values white paper' (mentioned in the extract from Li-ann Thio in section III.C.i. above) which has influenced the practical operation of government.

IV. CONSTITUTIONAL CULTURE AND THE CHARACTER OF THE POLITY (DEFINING THE 'WE')

A. Cultures and Frameworks for Co-existence

As Lutz[148] points out, constitutional cultures may encompass several nationalities (multi-cultural), or identify with a particular national culture (mono-cultural). Culture may also be classified between a national or mainstream modern culture and a 'traditional' 'backward' culture of indigenous peoples. The socialist constitutions of China,[149] Vietnam[150] and Laos[151] present themselves as being multi-ethnic or multinational in composition, but united in terms of socialist ideology.

The conservationist approach towards culture is evident in Article 4(3) of the Bhutan Constitution, which makes it a state duty to 'conserve and encourage research on local arts, custom, knowledge and culture'. Citizens are also required to protect Bhutan's cultural heritage.[152] These provisions are an attempt to thwart the decreasing influence of religion (Buddhism) and the potential rise in consumerism and crime rates.[153] The Constitution is unequivocal about its commitment to Bhutanese culture. For example, Article 6 of the Bhutan Constitution requires citizens to be able 'to speak and write Dzongkha' and to have 'a good knowledge of the culture, customs, traditions and history of Bhutan'. The attempt to ward off cultural invasion from

---

[148] Lutz, above n 49, at 127.

[149] The preamble to the Constitution of China notes that China is 'a unitary multi-ethnic state created jointly by the people of all its ethnic groups', noting the importance of combatting 'big-ethnic chauvinism, mainly Han chauvinism' to ensure the unity of all. Art 4 declares the equality of all ethnic groups. Notably the PRC Government fears 'splittism' or separatist attempts, particularly from, say, the restive Uighur Muslim minority in Xinjiang province. 'History and Development of Xinjiang', White Paper, Information Office of the State Council of the PRC (Beijing May 2003), at <http://www.china.org.cn/e-white/20030526/>; 'No Room for Splittists in Xinjiang', 16 September 2004, at <http://www.china.org.cn/english/2004/Sep/107307.htm>.

[150] Art 5: 'The State of the Socialist Republic of Vietnam is the unified State of the various ethnic communities cohabiting on the Vietnamese land.'

[151] Preamble, Laos Constitution: 'Since the 1930s, under the correct leadership of the former Indochinese Communist Party and the present Lao People's Revolutionary Party, the multi-ethnic Lao people have carried out difficult and arduous struggles full of great sacrifices until they managed to crush the yokes of domination and oppression of the colonial and feudal regimes, completely liberate the country and establish the Laos People's Democratic Republic on 2 December 1975.' Art 2 refers to the 'multi-ethnic people of all social strata with the workers, farmers and intelligentsia as key components', while Art 3 affirms that 'the multi-ethnic people are the masters of the country', with the Lao People's Revolutionary Party as its 'leading nucleus'.

[152] Art 8(2), Constitution of the Kingdom of Bhutan.

[153] T Mathou, 'The Politics of Bhutan: Change in Continuity' (2000) 3 *Journal of Bhutan Studies* 228 at 247. For example, the Bhutanese believe that anti-social criminal behaviour arrived in their country due to the influence of other cultures, primarily due to the action-packed 'blood and guts' plots portrayed in Hindi movies imported from Bombay.

Nepali-speaking Hindus manifests itself in the legislative enforcement of traditional national Drukpa clothing and a mandatory code of etiquette (*driglam namzha*) in advancing a state-sponsored form of national identity,[154] which detractors deem racist.[155]

Constitutions may recognise obligations to protect the culture of minorities and other groups, as distinct from national culture. Article 42 of the Basic Law of Macau provides that the 'customs and cultural traditions' of residents of Portuguese descent shall be protected. Constitutions may also protect indigenous groups and exempt them from the operation of general law, or such groups may attract special protective state measures. Article 2 Section 22 of the Philippines Constitution 'recognises and promotes the rights of indigenous cultural communities within the framework of national unity and development'.

Indigeneity is often a code word for 'backward', and a constitution may exempt such groups from general law and require their special protection. Section 65 of the Thai Constitution provides that members of 'a traditional community' have the

> right to conserve or restore their customs, local knowledge, arts or good culture of their community and of the nation and participate in management, maintenance, preservation and exploitation of natural resources and environment in a balanced and sustainable manner and persistently.

This assumes a tension between indigenous lifestyles and the imperatives of modernity and development.

B. Religion and Constitutional Identity

A key facet of constitutional identity is its treatment of religion(s) in potential competition with secular politics. Constitutions may create a regime of exemption for religious laws in certain circumstances, or a religious system may form part of the general law and direct state policy, as in the case of Islam in Bangladesh.[156] Many Asian states take religion seriously and recognise its public role through constitutional enactments. Confessional constitutions may stipulate an official religion while guaranteeing the peaceful co-existence and practice of other faiths, which is important in a multi-faith society.[157] Other constitutions may not have an official religion but accord pre-eminence or patronage to a specific religion. Such is the case with Buddhism in

---

[154] Tashi Deki, 'Forty-four teachers trained on Driglam Namzha', *The Bhutanese* 16 May 2012, at <http://www.thebhutanese.bt/forty-four-teachers-trained-on-driglam-namzha/>.

[155] SJ Thapa, 'Bhutan's Hoax: Of Gross National Happiness', *Wave Magazine*, 13 July 2011, at <http://fletcher.tufts.edu/News-and-Media/2011/07/13/Thapa-Jul13>.

[156] Pt II Sec 8: '(1) The principles of absolute trust and faith in the Almighty Allah, nationalism, democracy and socialism meaning economic and social justice, together with the principles derived from them as set out in this Part, shall constitute the fundamental principles of state policy. (1A) Absolute trust and faith in the Almighty Allah shall be the basis of all actions.'

[157] Art 3(1), Constitution of Malaysia: 'Islam is the religion of the Federation; but other religions may be practised in peace and harmony in any part of the Federation.' Art 3 of the Brunei Constitution is similar, except it identifies the Shafeite sect of Islam as the national religion.

the Thai,[158] Myanmar, Laos, Vietnam, Sri Lanka[159] and Bhutan[160] Constitutions. The Indonesian Constitution – in accordance with its Pancasila commitment – states that 'The State shall be based upon the belief in the One and Only God.'[161]

The decision of whether or not to include a religion in a constitution (and its attendant debates) can go to the heart of a nation's self-identity and remain a sore point for those whose religions are excluded. This is exacerbated where religious law has been displaced by a secular legal system, introduced by colonial or conquering powers. Such was the case in Malaysia, and also where the victorious Americans dictated the terms of Japan's 1946 Constitution which omitted provisions relating to state shintoism and Emperor worship contained in the 1889 Constitution.

Notes and Questions

1. While most Buddhist clergy steer clear of politics, this is not always the case. In 1981, Major General Chamlong Srimuang, a member of the Santi Asoke Buddhist movement, successfully mobilised a religious coalition against amendments to liberalise laws regulating abortion. The sect's founder, Phra Phothirak, believed that monks had a duty to oppose abortion as a sin in killing human life; his followers considering abortion to be linked to the influence of Western promiscuity and 'un-Buddhist, anti-religious and therefore un-Thai': 'Abortion reform is up against Buddhism in Thailand', *Guardian* (UK), 25 November 2010.

2. When Bhutan, which originated as a Buddhist theocracy in the fifteenth century, received its first written constitution in 2008, transforming it into a constitutional monarchy, the constitutional drafting committee decided not to make Buddhism the official religion but described it as 'the spiritual heritage of Bhutan' (Article 3(1)). Religion is to remain 'separate from politics' and '[r]eligious institutions and personalities shall remain above politics' (Article 3(3)). The Chairman of the Constitution Drafting Committee explained Article 3(3) by pointing out that 'Lord Buddha was the first to separate religion from politics by renouncing His Kingdom to pursue enlightenment'.[162] Article 15(3) requires political parties not to resort to regionalism, ethnicity and religion for electoral gain; their membership cannot be based, inter alia, on religion (Article 15(4)(b)).

3. In February 2007, it was announced that all monks, nuns, and *gomchen* (lay practitioners) who receive support from the Bhutanese state will not be permitted to vote in the elections on the grounds that religion and politics should be separated, under section 5(b) of the Religious Organisation Act.[163] The Constitution removed

---

[158] Thai Constitution, Sec 78: 'The state shall patronize and protect Buddhism and other religions, promote good understanding and harmony among followers of all religions as well as encourage the application of religious principles to promote virtues and develop quality of life.'

[159] Art 9, Sri Lanka Constitution: 'The Republic of Sri Lanka shall give to Buddhism the foremost place and accordingly it shall be the duty of the State to protect and foster the Buddha Sasana, while assuring to all religions the rights granted by Articles 10 and 14(1)(e).'

[160] Art 3(1), Bhutan Constitution: Buddhism is the spiritual heritage of Bhutan, which promotes the principles and values of peace, non-violence, compassion and tolerance

[161] Art 29(1), Constitution of the Republic of Indonesia.

[162] Bhutan, *1st Session of the First Parliament* at 102 (14 May 2008), National Assembly of Bhutan, at <http://www.nab.gov.bt/downloads/851st%20sessionofFirstParliamentresolutionE.doc>.

[163] RW Whitecross, 'Separation of Religion and Law?: Buddhism, Secularism and the Constitution of Bhutan' (2007–2008) 55 *Buffalo Law Review* 707.

the Central Monk Body (*Dratshang Lhentshog*) from having any formal role in the new legislature, where it had previously been represented in the National Assembly. Nonetheless, the privileged treatment of Buddhism is evident in other constitutional provisions, such as the requirement that the King (*Druk Gyalpo*) as head of state is a Buddhist who will uphold the dual system of religion and politics which is unified in his person (Article 2).

4. From 1616–1907, Bhutan had a dual administrative system composed of the religious branch (*Je Khenpo*), led by the Lord Abbot, and a civil branch headed by the *Druk Desi* elected by the Privy Council from amongst the head of state's (Shabdrung's) confidants.[164] Further, state-produced educational materials are filled with stories of Buddhist saints, reflecting the intertwining of religion and state.[165] It is common for Ministers and parliamentarians to make arguments on the basis of religious beliefs and secular argument, such as calls for tobacco control as being bad for health and contrary to Bhutanese religious beliefs,[166] and for alcohol control, as it caused social problems and was considered a sin.[167]

5. The Catholic Church in the Philippines also speaks out in public on issues such as abortion and contraception, despite having no formal constitutional status. The Catholic Church mobilised support against dictator Ferdinand Marcos in 1986, and against Joseph Estrada for alleged corruption in 2001 ('Philippine church hits president on contraception', Associated Press, 28 September 2010). The historical experience of the friars during the Spanish regime, wielding power to abuse the people, especially through expropriating land, gave rise to a ban preventing Filipino ecclesiastics from seeking public office. In *Pamil v Teleron* GR No L-34854 20 Nov 1978, the Supreme Court upheld a law barring a Catholic priest from contesting an elective municipal position. Teehankee J, dissenting, argued that the friars' abusive acts took place 'due to the union of the State and the Church then'. Just as the 'no religion test' clause bars the state from disqualifying an atheist from running for political office, as this would compel profession of belief in God, it was equally to 'exact a religious test' to require ecclesiastics to quit their religious calling to run for political office. Further, while the friars grabbed land by exploiting the masses, 'the priests of today' were at the forefront of social justice struggles, and where the state 'fails or falters, the priest must needs help minister to this temporal power'. Moreover, 'it is to be presumed that no responsible person would seek public office knowing that his ecclesiastical duties would be a hindrance to his rendering just and efficient public service'. Is this persuasive?

6. Contrast Thailand with Sri Lanka (another Buddhist majority Asian state). Article 9 of the Sri Lanka Constitution provides that Buddhism is given the 'foremost place' and obliges the state to 'protect and foster the Buddha Sasana'. Here, Buddhist monks have been elected to Parliament, and even formed a political

---

[164] 'Democracy in Bhutan: An Analysis of Constitutional Change in a Buddhist Monarchy' (March 2010), 24 *IPCS Research Papers*, at <http://www.ipcs.org/pdf_file/issue/RP24-Marian-Bhutan.pdf>.

[165] Whitecross, above n 162, at 710–11.

[166] Bhutan, *8th Session of the First Parliament (Bill)* at 26 (17 January 2012), National Assembly of Bhutan, at <http://www.nab.gov.bt/downloads/97Eng_bill_resolution.pdf>.

[167] Bhutan, *7th Session of the First Parliament* at 13 (31 May 2012), National Assembly of Bhutan, at <http://www.nab.gov.bt/downloads/95engres.pdf>.

party, the *Jatila Hela Urumaya* (JHU). This has been controversial amongst those who do not believe that Buddhist teachings warrant the engagement of monks in political activities and that monks should pursue their real duties in preaching Buddhist teachings on '*maithree*' (loving kindness) and observing '*vinaya*' (the code of conduct for monks) (letter, 'Monks should leave politics to the politicians', *Sunday Times* (Sri Lanka), 21 March 2010; see M Deegalle, 'Politics of the Jathika Hela Urumaya Monks: Buddhism and Ethnicity in Contemporary Sri Lanka' (2004) 5(4) *Contemporary Buddhism* 83). Unsurprisingly, JHU leader Dr Omalpe Sobitha Thero opposed a private bill by Member of Parliament Wijedasa Rajapaksa (UNP) seeking to prevent political parties from fielding clergy from any religion at parliamentary elections, alleging a hidden agenda:

> This particular bill was presented not to safeguard our religion but for their survival since they know we have become so powerful in parliament. There is an unforeseen hand behind all these elements such as tobacco businessmen, liquor shop owners and the LTTE [Liberation Tigers of Tamil Eelam] sympathisers. The UNP is in forefront amongst the LTTE sympathisers who have openly agitated against the war. It was the UNP that once branded us as 'war' monks and wanted the government to go back to peace talks in order to safeguard the LTTE leaders.

See Nirmala Kannangara, 'JHU Slams move to keep monks away from Parliament', *Sunday Leader* (Sri Lanka), 2 October 2012.

7. In 2010, the Pakistan Supreme Court got rid of most of its Fifth Amendment which was seen as legitimising military dictatorship and facilitating the spread of religious political parties. It also banned political parties that propagated Islamic ideology. However, the Prime Minister stated that her government did not intend to ban religion-based political parties as this would only force them underground, fuelling militancy ('Religion-based political parties: Not banning them exhibits PM's robust sense of realism', *The Daily Star* (Pakistan), 4 August 2010). Notably, the European Court of Human Rights upheld the banning of a Islamic political party in Turkey which sought to impose syariah law, as not violating Article 11 ECHR, as the ban was incompatible with democracy.[168]

i. The Non-recognition of Buddhism as Official Religion in the 2007 Thai Constitution

The Constituent Drafting Assembly (CDA) decided against officially recognising Buddhism as Thailand's national religion in the 2007 Thai Constitution, even though 95 per cent of Thais profess Buddhism. Buddhist monks opposed this move as they felt that Buddhism was threatened by an Islamic separatist insurgency in the Muslim-dominated southern provinces. The monks felt that official recognition was necessary to ensure that Buddhism continued to be the country's main religion.

The Chairman of the CDA, Prasong Soonsiri, felt that official recognition would not affect Buddhism's popularity and that it would be undemocratic by privileging Buddhists. Further, its inclusion could be seen as an oppressive assimilationist measure by the under-developed Muslim-majority south which has experienced an insurgency since 2005, and where the state provides funding for Buddhist and Muslim

---

[168] *Refah Partisi v Turkey* App no 41340/98 (ECtHR, 13 February 2003).

religious institutions in an effort to integrate Muslim minorities.[169] Such a clause could well provoke greater inter-religious violence should religious fanatics try to 'cleanse' society.[170]

Nonetheless, Buddhism still has a special position in the Thai Constitution. Section 79 provides for state patronage of Buddhism and obliges the state to 'encourage the application of religious principles to create virtue and develop the quality of life'. The King is a Buddhist and Upholder of religions, under Section 9. Notably Section 94(2) provides that a 'Buddhist priest, novice, monk or clergy' is disenfranchised on election day. While this may seem discriminatory, this provision reflects the special position of Buddhism within the Thai constitutional order. The Constitution gives effect to Buddhist tenets that its adherents should not be politically partisan, thereby trumping constitutional guarantees of religious freedom and non-discrimination on the basis of religion.

ii. Nepal: From Hindu Kingdom to Secular State

Since its creation in 1768, Nepal was a Hindu monarchy where law was part of religion and closely linked to national identity. The dominant faith was Hinduism, and Nepal's 1990 Constitution proclaimed the state to be the world's sole Hindu Kingdom. In 2006, Parliament declared Nepal a democratic secular state, dismantling the Hindu monarchy and dissolving the *Rajparishad* (Royal Privy Council).[171] The long-standing demand of ethnic and religious minorities for a secular state was met by Article 4(1) of the Interim Constitution (2007), which provides that 'Nepal is an independent, indivisible, sovereign, secular, inclusive and a fully democratic State'. Minorities considered secularism necessary to guarantee religious freedom and to end religious discrimination which made them second-class citizens. This was and continues to be opposed by Hindu groups, who fear a loss of global identity.[172] Of secularism in Nepal, it has been written:

> Although constitutionally Nepal is a multicultural and multi-religious secular country, the separation of religion from the state-professed philosophy of secularism is not evident. Nepalese social structure is still based on and guided by the old values, norms, customs, and rituals of the Hindu religion. Although the overwhelming majority (80.6%) of people in Nepal professes to be Hindu, the Interim Constitution of Nepal fails to establish a wall or partition between religion and state. Thus, Nepal is not a secular state (with complete separation of religion from the state) as understood in the West. Nepal is not, however, a theocratic country because none of the essential characteristics of theocracy are found in Nepal.
>
> Democracy in Nepal, as structured by the Interim Constitution, incorporates the philosophy of secularism and a secular state. Yet, the ideology of secularism or the secular state in the Constitution is influenced by the historical and social background of Nepal, which is largely different from the western world. The Interim Constitution is not anti-god or

---

[169] Li-ann Thio, 'Constitutional Accommodation of the Rights of Ethnic and Religious Minorities in Plural Democracies: Lessons and Cautionary Tales from South-East Asia' (2010) 22 *Pace International Law Review* 43.

[170] Pravit Rojanaphruk, 'State Religion Rejected', *The Nation* (Thailand), 29 June 2007, at <http://www.siawi.org/article132.html>.

[171] Kanak Bikram Thapa, 'Religion and Law in Nepal' (2010) 3 *Brigham Young University Law Review* 921.

[172] 'Nepal Hindu fundamentalists plan to restore a theocratic monarchy', *AsianNews.it*, 24 May 2010, available at http://www.asianews.it/news-en/Hindu-fundamentalists-plan-to-restore-a-theocratic-monarchy-18493.html.

antireligious. Rather, it recognizes that religion has relevance and validity in the lives of many, though not necessarily all, citizens. Furthermore, it also emphasizes that while religion may be relevant in life, it cannot frustrate the progress of democracy in its allotted task of creating a new secular order in Nepal. Yet, a doctrine of secularism dedicated to creating a new social order founded on justice is currently limited in Nepal by the restrictions imposed upon the exercise of the right to freedom of religion.[173]

iii. Bangladesh: From Secular to Islamic Republic and Back: The Fifth Amendment Case of 2010

When Bangladesh became independent after seceding from Pakistan in 1972, its Constitution – which was drafted by the Awami League – was based on four pillars: secularism, democracy, socialism and nationalism. In 1979, General Ziaur Rahman adopted the Fifth Amendment and reversed the earlier constitutional ban on religion-based political parties.[174] At the same time, the preamble was amended to replace the former commitment to secularism with one to Islam. See further Table 2.1.

In 1988, Islam was declared the state religion under Article 2(A). Many political parties viewed secularism as synonymous with ideologies based on atheism, blasphemy, scepticism and anti-Islamisation. In 2010, the Bangladesh Supreme Court upheld an earlier High Court decision and declared the Fifth Amendment illegal, in *Khondker Delwar Hossain, Secretary, BNP Party v Bangladesh Italian Marble Works Ltd, Dhaka* (below). This nullified the legality and constitutionality of the martial law regime during 1975–79, noting that the basic character of the Constitution had been changed by, inter alia, removing its secular character. Thus, a martial law regulation that annulled a judgment directing that a hall which had forcibly been dispossessed be returned to its owner, was invalidated. The following excerpts shed light on the constitutional history in relation to religion, Pakistan and the war of independence.

Table 2.1 Fifth Amendment of the Bangladesh Constitution

Original 1972 Constitution	Fifth Amendment (1979)
Second Preambular Paragraph Pledging that the high ideals of nationalism, socialism, democracy and secularism, which inspired our heroic people to dedicate themselves to, and our brave martyrs to sacrifice their lives in, the national liberation struggle, shall be the fundamental principles of the constitution;	Pledging that the high ideals of absolute trust and faith in the almighty Allah, nationalism, democracy and socialism, meaning economic and social justice, which inspired our heroic people to dedicate themselves to, and our brave martyrs to sacrifice their lives in, the war for national independence, shall be the fundamental principles of the Constitution;

[173] Kanak Bikram Thapa, above n 171, at 929–30. Art 23 of the 2007 Interim Constitution guarantees the right of every person 'to profess, practise and preserve his/her own religion as handed down to him/her from ancient times having due regard to the social and cultural traditional practices. Provided that no person shall be entitled to convert another person from one religion to another, and shall not act or behave in a manner which may jeopardize the religion of others.'

[174] Second Proclamation (Sixth Amendment) Order No III of 1976 omitted the proviso to Art 38 in the 1972 Constitution which read: 'Provided that no person shall have the right to form, of be a member or otherwise take part in the activities of, any communal or other association or union which in the name or on the basis of any religion has for its object, or pursues, a political purpose.'

Original 1972 Constitution	Fifth Amendment (1979)
Article 8 (1) The principles of nationalism, socialism, democracy and secularism, together with the principles derived from them as set out in this Part, shall constitute the fundamental principles of state policy. (2) The principles set out in this Part shall be fundamental to the governance of Bangladesh, shall be applied by the State in the making of laws, shall be a guide to the interpretation of the Constitution and of the other laws of Bangladesh and shall form the basis of the work of the State and of its citizens, but shall not be judicially enforceable.	(1) The principles of absolute trust and faith in the almighty Allah nationalism, democracy and socialism meaning economic and social justice, together with the principles derived from them as set out in this Part, shall constitute the fundamental principles of state policy. (1A) Absolute trust and faith in the Almighty Allah shall be the basis of all actions. (2) The principles set out in this Part shall be fundamental to the governance of Bangladesh, shall be applied by the State in the making of laws, shall be a guide to the interpretation of the Constitution and of the other laws of Bangladesh, and shall form the basis of the work of the State and of its citizens, but shall not be judicially enforceable.
Article 12 The principle of secularism shall be realized by the elimination of – (a) communalism in all its forms; (b) the granting by the State of political status in favour of any religion; (c) the abuse of religion for political purposes; (d) any discrimination against, or persecution of, persons practicing a particular religion.	Deleted
Article-25: Did not exist.	Article-25: [(2) The State shall endeavour to consolidate, preserve and strengthen fraternal relations among Muslim countries

***Khondker Delwar Hossain, Secretary, BNP Party v Bangladesh Italian Marble Works Ltd, Dhaka* Civil Petition for Leave to Appeal 1044 and 1045/2009 (the 'Fifth Amendment Case')**

The Dominion of Pakistan formally came into existence on August 14, 1947 and MA Jinnah, was elected the first President of the Constituent Assembly of Pakistan. In his inaugural address on September 11, 1947 he outlined basic ideals on which the State of Pakistan was going to flourish which are as follows:

> . . . If you change your past and work together in a spirit that everyone of you, no matter to what community he belongs, no matter what relations he had with you in the past,

no matter what is his colour, caste or creed, is first second and last a citizen of this State with equal rights, privileges and obligations, there will be no end to the progress you will make. . . . Now, I think we should keep that in front of us as our ideal and you will find that in course of time Hindus would cease to be Hindus and Muslims would cease to be Muslims, not in the religious sense, because that is the personal faith of each individual, but in the political sense as citizens of the State.

. . . You are free; you are free to go to your temples, you are free to go to your mosques or to any other places or worship in this State of Pakistan. You may belong to any religion or caste or creed – that has nothing to do with the business of the State.

As it appears the above speech echoed Secular State . . . However, as we have experienced, the dreams of the people of the then East Pakistan were soon shattered in no time and the history of Pakistan was ridden with palace clique, deception and disappointment. The people of the then East Pakistan discovered that they were reduced to second class citizens, creation of Pakistan brought them only a change of rulers and for all practical purposes the then East Pakistan became a colony of the then West Pakistan . . .

[The Court then discussed the Fifth Amendment and the High Court's finding that the removal of 'secularism' from the original second preambular paragraph wrought a basic change in the Constitution as 'secularism' was a fundamental principle in the original but omitted by the Fifth Amendment change its treatment by the High Court.]

. . . The High Court Division then quoting the provisions of original Article 8(1) and its amended version and sub Article (1A) of the same as shown in the above chart [Table 2.1], held as follows:

It is true that partition was made, more or less on the basis of religion but India declared itself as a secular nation. Mr Mohammad Ali Jinnah, the first Governor General of Pakistan, although in his first speech made on September 11, 1947, hinted that in Pakistan, people of all religion would be equal without any religious discrimination but its first Constitution, made in 1956, declared the country as the Islamic Republic of Pakistan. The Constitution of 1962 made no difference. Pakistan, since the death of its first Governor General, reduced itself into a theocratic nation as happened in medieval Europe.

But the high ideals of equality and fraternity so very gloriously enshrined in Islam could not spare the majority population of the erstwhile East Pakistan from total discrimination in all spheres of the State without any exception. The erstwhile East Pakistan was treated as a colony of West Pakistan and when voice was raised praying for at least near equal treatment, steam roller of oppression was perpetrated on the people of the Eastern wing. After a long 23 years, the first general election in Pakistan was held in 1970 with one of the objects, to frame a Constitution. The National Assembly was scheduled to be convened at Dhaka on March 3, 1971, but General Yahya Khan, the President and CMLA postponed the Assembly, forcing the country into turmoil. Thereafter, on the night following March 25, 1971, General Yahya Khan and his military government unleashed the worst genocide in the history of mankind on the unarmed people of the erstwhile East Pakistan, and the 'valient' [*sic*] armed forces of Pakistan brutally killed millions. The vast majority of the people of this part of the world are God-fearing Muslims but their religion could not even save the fellow Muslims from being persecuted, killed and raped and their belongings being plundered and all ironically in the name of Islam.

Of necessity and being forced, the unarmed simple minded Bangalees of the then East Pakistan took up arms and rose against the tyranny for their survival. After liberation, such oppression and persecution on the Bangalee population was very much fresh in their minds. They were determined to establish an independent sovereign nation based on the democratic principles of equality and social justice where nobody will be discriminated on the ground of religion.

As such, the framers of the Constitution, from their earlier bitter experience during the liberation war, gave effect to the above lofty ideals of our martyrs which were reflected in the Preamble and Article 8(1) and other provisions of our Constitution. Those are the basic structures of the Constitution which were changed on replacement of the provisions of the original Preamble and Article 8(1) by the Proclamation Order No 1 of 1977 and Second Proclamation Order No IV of 1978, but such replacements changed the secular character of the Republic of Bangladesh into a theocratic State. . . .

Then regarding Articles 9 and 10 the High Court Division held as follows:

. . . In this connection it should be remembered that the purpose of a Constitution is not to describe the tenets of a particular religion but is an Instrument creating the high institutions of the Republic and its relationship with its people . . . The Constitution of such a Republic would never contain or refer to a particular faith but would leave such faculties with the people themselves. Bangladesh was dreamt of as a secular country and came into being as a secular country, as such, its Constitution was framed on that ideal, but any change from such a basis would constitute a change of the basic structure of the Constitution

Such belief would reside with the people in accordance with their free will and shall never be interfered with, either by the State or any section of the population, however majority they may be. Such a secular concept would be inhibited in a modern democratic Constitution unless, of course, it is a theocratic State. . . .

The High Court Division also referred the case of *SR Bommai v Union of India* AIR 1994 SC 1918 wherein the addition of 'Socialist' and 'Secularism' the Constitution of India in the year 1976 was considered. Ahmedi J (as his Lordship then was) in considering secularism as one of the basic structures of the Constitution observed at para 28:

Notwithstanding the fact that the words 'Socialist', and 'Secular' were added in the Preamble of the Constitution in 1976 by the 42nd Amendment, the concept of Secularism was very much embedded in our Constitutional philosophy. . . . By this amendment what was implicit was made explicit. The Preamble itself spoke of liberty of thought, expression, belief, faith and worship. While granting this liberty the Preamble promised equality of status and opportunity. It also spoke of promoting fraternity, thereby assuring the dignity of the individual and the unity and integrity of the Nation. While granting to its citizens liberty of belief, faith and worship, the Constitution abhorred discrimination on grounds of religion etc, but permitted special treatment for Scheduled Castes and Tribes, vide Arts 15 and 16. Art 25 next provided, subject to public order, morality and health, that all persons shall be entitled to freedom of conscience and the right to profess, practice and propagate religion. Art 26 grants to every religious denomination or any section thereof, the right to establish and maintain institutions for religious purposes and to manage its own affairs in matters of religion. These two articles clearly confer a right to freedom of religion . . . State's revenue cannot be utilised for the promotion and maintenance of any religion or religious group that secularism is a basic feature of our Constitution . . . (pages 1951–52).

In considering the concept of secularism, Sawant, J, held at para 88:

> These contention inevitably invite us to discuss the concept of secularism as accepted by our Constitution. Our Constitution does not prohibit the practice of any religion either privately or publicly . . . under Articles 14, 15 and 16, the Constitution prohibits discrimination against any citizen on the ground of his religion and guarantees equal protection of law and equal opportunity of public employment. (Page 2000) . . . These provisions by implication prohibit the establishment of a theocratic State and prevent the State either identifying itself with of favouring any particular religion or religious sect or denomination. The State is enjoined to accord equal treatment to all religions and religious sects and denominations. (Page 2000) . . .
>
> K Ramaswamy J, quoting Dr S Radhakrishnan and Mahtma Gandhi, explained the concept of secularism as a basic feature of Constitution of India, at para 124:
>
> > The Constitution has chosen secularism as its vehicle to establish an egalitarian social order . . . Secularism, therefore, is part of the fundamental law and basic structure of the Indian political system to secure all its people socioeconomic needs essential for man's excellence and of moral well being, fulfillment of material prosperity and political justice. (Pages 2019–20) . . .

Shahabuddin Ahmed J in *Anwar Hossain Chowdhury's* case evaluates Constitution in this manner at para-272, page 118:

On the one hand, it gives out-lines of the state apparatus, and aspirations of the people; it gives guarantees of fundamental rights of a citizen and also makes him aware of his solemn duty to himself, to his fellow citizen and to his country.

> No wonder his Lordship did not see any role of religion in the Constitution itself [affirming that omitting secularism from the Constitution changed the basic character of the Republic, as enshrined in the Preamble and art 8(1)].

. . . The High Court Division then quoting the original provision of Article 12 of the Constitution as shown in the above chart [Table 2.1], which was omitted from the Constitution by the Proclamation Order No 1 of 1977, held as follows:

> This provision of secularism explained and expounded in Article 12, is one of the most important and unique basic features of the Constitution. Secularism means both religious tolerance as well as religious freedom. It envisages equal treatment to all irrespective of caste, creed or religion but the State must not show any form of tilt or leaning towards any particular religion either directly or even remotely. It requires maintenance of strict neutrality on the part of the State in the matters of different religions professed by various communities in the State. The State must not seen to be favouring any particular religion, rather, ensure protection to the followers of all faiths without any discrimination including even to an atheist. This is what it means by the principle of secularism.
>
> Secularism was one of the ideals for which the struggle for liberation was fought and won and the framers of the Constitution in their wisdom in order to dispel any confusion, upheld and protect the said ideal of secularism as spelt it out in Article 2 of the Constitution as one of the fundamental principles of State Policy. Indeed this was one of the most important basic features of the Constitution. But the said basic feature of the Constitution was deleted by the Proclamation Order No 1 of 1977 and the Second Proclamation Order No IV of 1978 and thereby sought to change the secular character of the Republic of Bangladesh as enshrined in the original Constitution.

The High Court Division then quoting the provision of original Article 25 of the Constitution and its amended version as shown in the above chart [Table 2.1] held as follows:

> This clause 2 is redundant. The original Article 25 itself provides for promotion of international peace, security and solidarity amongst all the nations including of course, the Muslim countries, in accordance with the charter of the United Nations. As such, its endeavor to foster further relations amongst only with the Muslim countries based on Islamic solidarity, as stated in the added clause 2, can only be explained by its leaning towards becoming an Islamic Republic from a Secular Republic and thereby destroying its one of the most important and significant basic feature of our Constitution, namely, secularism. . . .

The High Court Division then concluded [that Martial Law Proclamations altered the basic features of the Constitution and were illegal] . . .

Notes and Questions

1. The Appellate Division of the Supreme Court confirmed the illegality of the Fifth Amendment Act. Did the Court effectively restore the character and spirit of the original 1972 Constitution by banning religion-based political parties?

2. Has the principle of secularism been compromised by the retention of Islam as the state religion? Is the Fifteenth Amendment a workable fusion of Islam and secularism, to produce a 'moderate' Muslim country through a hybrid polity, or an unruly, ideological hodgepodge?

3. Despite pledges by Prime Minister Sheikh Hasina to restore secularism as the constitutional cornerstone, the Fifteenth Amendment (Act XIV of 2011), adopted on 30 June 2011, retained Islam as the state religion[175] (introduced by the Eighth Amendment) and made the Arabic phrase '*Bismillahir Rahmanir Rahim*', with its translation 'In the name of Allah, the Beneficent, the Merciful/In the name of the Creator, the Merciful', a part of the Constitution. It also allowed religion-based politics that the cancellation of the Fifth Amendment had banned. Secularism has been restored as one of four fundamental principle of state policy under Article 8(1), and Article 12 of the 1972 Constitution has been revived. Additionally, 'Absolute faith and trust in Allah' has been removed from the Constitution pre-amble. A new clause, Article 23A, was added stating: 'The state shall take steps to protect and develop the unique local culture and tradition of the tribes, minor races, ethnic sects, and communities.'[176]

4. It has been suggested that secularism in Bangladesh is 'endogenous' and 'While the western notion of secularism insists upon a complete separation between the state and religion, the sub-continental concept implies a role of the state in religious

[175] Art 2A: 'The state religion of the Republic is Islam, but the State shall ensure equal status and equal right in the practice of the Hindu, Buddhist, Christian and other religions.' Text of 2011 Constitution of Bangladesh, at <http://www.supremecourt.gov.bd/scweb/constitution/pdf/04_part1-4.pdf>.

[176] 'Caretaker system abolished', *The Daily Star* (Bangladesh), 1 July 2011, at <http://www.thedailystar.net/newDesign/news-details.php?nid=192303>; see also 'Salient features of 15th Amendment of Constitution', *The Daily Star* (Bangladesh), 30 June 2011, at <http://www.thedailystar.net/newDesign/latest_news.php?nid=30610>.

affairs.'[177] In addition, 'secularism' may not capture the Bengali word '*dharmanira-pekhata*', which means that a state remains neutral in matters of religious theory, doctrine and practice. Neutrality is 'distinguished from non-involvement with religion', implying 'governmental engagement with religion for the purpose of treating all religious groups fairly, equally and equitably, while non-involvement implies governmental isolation from matters of religion. Neutrality in religion, in other words, is religious pluralism.'[178]

5.   Can a minimum core of secularism be identified?

iv.   Malaysia: 'Islam' – The No Longer Innocuous Clause?

One of the issues raised during the Anglo-Malayan drafting of the 1957 Federal Constitution of Malaysia was whether to include a reference to 'Islam' as the Federation's religion. The British colonial authorities considered that Malaya should be an experiment in a 'new form of secular state' where ethnically distinct communities living largely separate existences could 'develop a common political loyalty'[179] rather than a shared past, as non-Malays did not identify with the constructed history of a glorious Islamic-Malay sultanate.[180] The Sultans, who in the pre-colonial era had been both the political and religious leaders of their states and who ruled over Muslim subjects, were wary that such inclusion would diminish their positions as heads of Islam within their states,[181] and the Reid Constitutional Commission was discomfited as the state was supposed to be 'secular'. The local Alliance political coalition issued a Memorandum stating that such a clause[182] 'shall not imply that the State is not a secular State',[183] assuring the Colonial Office that they 'had no intention of creating a Muslim theocracy and that Malaya would be a secular state'.[184] The sole Muslim mem-

---

[177]   A Riyaja, '"God Willing": The Politics and Ideology of Islamism in Bangladesh' (2003) 23 *Comparative Studies of South Asia, Africa and the Middle East* 301 at 303.

[178]   Harun ur Rashid (former Bangladesh Ambassador to UN, Geneva), 'Religion-based political parties', *The Daily Star* (Bangladesh), 18 August 2010.

[179]   ADC Peterson, 'The Birth of the Malayan nation' (1955) 31(3) *International Affairs* 311 at 314.

[180]   Thamby Chik J in *Lina Joy v Majlis Agama Islam Wilayah* [2004] 2 MLJ 119 [15]. As Farish A Noor has pointed out: 'We were Hindus and Buddhists before, and before that we were pagan animists who lived at peace with nature. The coming of the great religions – Hinduism, Buddhism and Islam – and the arrival of new modernist schools of thought should not be seen as distinct episodes that keep our histories apart. Instead they should be seen as layers of civilization acculturation that have added depth to our collective sense of identity . . .' (FA Noor, *The Other Malaysia: Writing on Malaysia's Subaltern History* (Kuala Lumpur: Silverfish Books, 2002) at 230).

[181]   A Ibrahim, 'The Position of Islam in the Constitution of Malaysia' in Mohd Suffian et al (eds), *The Constitution of Malaysia: Its Development: 1957–1977* (Oxford, Oxford University Press, 1978), 44–68, at 49.

[182]   The Alliance recommended the insertion of the following clause: 'Islam shall be the religion of the State of Malaya, but nothing in this article shall prevent any citizen professing any religion other than Islam to profess, practice and propagate that religion, nor shall any citizen be under any disability by reason of his being not a Muslim.' (Para 11, Note of Dissent by Justice Abdul Hamid, *Report of the Federation of Malaya Constitutional Commission* (Kuala Lumpur: HMSO, 1957)1; KYL Tan and LA Thio, *Constitutional Law in Malaysia and Singapore*, 2nd edn (Butterworths, 1997) at 982.

[183]   See also para 57, Federation of Malaya Constitutional Proposals, though noting that propagation 'is subject to any restrictions imposed by State law relating to the propagation of any religious doctrine or belief among persons professing the Muslim religion.' Imam argues that 'secular' may be understood in a limited sense as meaning 'it does not derogate from the freedom to profess and practice religion of the non-Muslims': M Imam, 'Freedom of Religion under Federal Constitution of Malaysia – A Reappraisal [1994] 2 *CLJ* lvii at lxvi.

[184]   Ibid at 162–63.

ber of the Commission, Judge Abdul Hamid of Pakistan, wrote in his minority report that the Alliance's proposal was 'innocuous',[185] noting that state constitutions already had this clause, and that it was only necessary to 'transplant it from the State Constitutions and to embed it in the Federal'.[186] The Sultans finally gave their support after being assured that their positions and the religious rights of minorities would be unaffected. Article 3(1) therefore reads: 'Islam is the religion of the Federation; but other religions may be practised in peace and harmony in any part of the Federation.'

'Islam' in Article 3 was to be understood in ceremonial, rather than substantive, terms and constitutional supremacy was affirmed in Article 4. The Constitution recognised the status of the Muslim rulers, and Article 12 authorised the provision of federal or state funds to establish and maintain Islamic institutions or underwrite instruction in Islam. What colonialism did was to remove Islam from the realm of public law; by severing 'the divine source of legal validity', the British 'turned the system into a secular institution'. Islamic law no longer holistically applied to human affairs but became the particular rather than general law, divided into its public and private aspects and confined to limited topics. Even the instruments providing for the administration of Islamic law were validated 'through a secular fiat'.[187] Thus, 'Malaysia is not an Islamic state but a secular state with Islamic characteristics and bias'.[188]

However, with the growing Islamisation of society after the 1979 Iranian revolution, Malay political leaders in the 2000s began arguing that Malaysia was an Islamic state, and some courts began delivering revisionist visions of 'Islam'[189] as a source of substantive law and primacy, a reflection of the merger of Islamic identity and Malay nationalism.[190] This trend disquieted the religious minorities who had entered the Federation on the understanding that the Constitution, as a pre-commitment strategy, would establish a secular, multi-religious order. It reflects the discontent certain Malay factions have towards 'secularism' as a diminishing of Malay ethno-religious identity, representing the 'largest single remaining grievance in connection with the imposition of colonial law' in Southeast Asia and 'the failure of Islamic law to attain the status of global doctrine.[191] Article 3 is no longer an innocuous clause but at the heart of political and legal debates as to the character of the Malayan polity.

---

[185] Above n 182.

[186] Ibid, at [12].

[187] *Che Omar bin Che Soh v PP* [1988] 2 MLJ 55 (Federal Court, Malaysia). See generally JM Fernando, *The Making of the Malayan Constitution* (Kuala Lumpur: MBRAS, 2002) at 162.

[188] Wu Min Aun, *The Malaysian Legal System*, 2nd edn (Singapore: Longman, 1999) at 154.

[189] For example, in *Meor Atiqulrahman bin Ishak & Ors v Fatimah bte Sihi* [2000] 5 MLJ 375, 6 August 1999, High Court Judge stated that Article 3 meant that Islam was the main religion superior to other religions practised in the country: 'Islam is not of the same status as the other religions; it does not sit side by side nor stand side by side. Rather, Islam sits at the top, it walks first, and is placed on a mantle with its voice loud and clear. Islam is like a "jati" tree – tall, firm and able. Otherwise, Islam will not be the religion of the Federation but just another of the many religions embraced in the country and everybody would be equally free to embrace religions, with none better or more than any other.'

[190] Li-ann Thio and J Ling-Chen Neo, 'Religious Dress in Schools: The Serban Controversy in Malaysia (2006) 55(3) *International & Comparative Law Quarterly* 871.

[191] A Harding, 'Global Doctrine and Local Knowledge: Law in South East Asia' (2002) 51(1) *International & Comparative Law Quarterly* 35 at 40.

V. THE INFLUENCE OF CONSTITUTIONAL CULTURE ON
THE STYLE OF CONSTITUTIONALISM: BEFORE AND BEYOND
THE COURTS

A. Introduction

Constitutional cultures affect a polity's conception of 'law' and the function and strength of the 'rule of law' as a constraint on government power. They also affect the primary forum and manner through which constitutionally-related disputes are resolved, inside and outside the courts, reflecting orientations towards legal or political constitutionalism. This flows from a vision of man in society, the relative importance of individual autonomy, social harmony and the common good. The degree of trust to be accorded a state's rulers is also an influential factor, affecting the degree to which external regulation, co-regulation and self-regulation (internal restraint) are adopted.[192]

The deep Madisonian distrust of the corruptibility of human nature[193] and the danger of the abuse of public powers has, in the United States and jurisdictions with constitutional courts, been translated into a predilection for legal constitutionalism and a heightened judicialisation,[194] with courts as the primary institution for controlling power. This may be contrasted with the British 'Government–Parliament Oriented Model for Protecting Human Rights'.[195] It has been argued that the British do not 'possess an inherent suspicion of the political authorities',[196] in so far as Parliament may be trusted to act reasonably and with self-restraint, in relation to individual rights, to safeguard common morality and to play fairly by the rules of the game.[197] Thus, there has been no 'public outcry' for 'increased judicial review of primary legislation',[198] although judicial powers have been heightened under the Human Rights Act.[199] This veers towards political constitutionalism, where the chief method of controlling power resides in political checks like elections, parliamentary processes, a free press and other non-judicial institutions such as ombudsmen or national human rights institutions.

Asian countries like Singapore have evidenced in their constitutional development a mixed trust and distrust towards governors. In the 1990s, the Confucian idea of the trustworthy ruler was invoked as the preferred national ideology:

> Many Confucian ideals are relevant to Singapore. For example, the importance of human relationships and of placing society above self are key ideas in the Shared Values. The concept of government by honourable men '君子' (*junzi*), who have a duty to do right for the people, and who have the trust and respect of the population, fits us better than the Western idea that

---

[192] See R Sidelsky, 'In regulation we trust? 18 December 2009, Project Syndicate at <http://www.project-syndicate.org/commentary/in-regulation-we-trust->.

[193] J Madison, *Federalist No 51*, J Cooke (ed) (Middletown, Conn: Wesleyan University Press, 1961) at 347.

[194] See A-M Slaughter, 'Judicial Globalisation' (2000) 40 *Virginia Journal of International Law* 1103.

[195] AL Bendor and Z Segal, 'Constitutionalism and Trust in Britain: An Ancient Constitutional Culture, a New Judicial Review Model' (2002) 17 *American University International Law Review* 683 at 705.

[196] Ibid at 686.

[197] Ibid at 700–02.

[198] Ibid at 686.

[199] D McGoldrick, 'The United Kingdom's HRA 1998 in Theory and Practice' (2001) 50(4) *International & Comparative Law Quarterly* 901.

a government should be given as limited powers as possible, and should always be treated with suspicion unless proven otherwise.[200]

This may be contrasted with the creation of the elected presidency in 1991, which was designed to check the untrammelled powers of a dominant party state with over-whelming control of Parliament,[201] primarily in relation to certain financial decisions. This was predicated on an adversarial vision of institutional oversight, though in practice this has been modulated to work more along the lines of a harmonious brand of consultation and recommendation.

The 'Confucian *junzi*' model appears to requires trust in the inherent quality of governors,[202] something no legal system can guarantee. This is different from the British, who trust that their elected representatives will not blatantly act against the popular will. More recently, a senior Singapore Government Minister stated, in a 2010 speech entitled 'Increasing Public Trust in Leaders of a Harmonious Society', that public trust could not be demanded of citizens but had to be earned through the 'track record' of the Government, in terms of delivering economic development while main-taining moral integrity.[203]

The starting point of trust rather than distrust also operates with respect to the exercise of public powers by high constitutional officers like the Attorney-General in exercising prosecutorial discretion or with respect to the grant of clemency. The Singapore courts, in upholding a vision of separation of powers, apply the presump-tion of legality (*omnia praesumuntur rite esse acta*),[204] where 'all things are presumed to have been done rightly and regularly, *ie*, in conformity with the law'. This presump-tion weeds out 'fanciful hypotheses' that a holder of high constitutional office would act spitefully. Presumptions about how governors should act may of course be rebut-ted. Courts have a role, but not as 'the first line of defence against administrative abuses of power'. Instead, the political process should be considered the first line of resort for redressing bad government, with the courts playing 'a supporting role by articulating clear rules and principles by which the Government may abide by and conform to the rule of law'.[205]

---

[200] Para 41, shared-values white paper (Cmd 1 of 1990) and see see section III.C.i. above.

[201] 'Overwhelming' might be gauged in terms of commanding a two-thirds majority necessary to amend the Constitution, which the People's Action Party (PAP) had comfortably retained since Independence in 1965.

[202] The idea of 'honourable' leaders is reflected in the greater quantum of damages awarded to this cate-gory for political libel in Singapore case law, which reflects a view of reputation as 'honour': *Lim Eng Hock Peter v Lin Jian Wei* [2010] 4 SLR 357.

[203] 'Trust cannot be compelled. It cannot be based on fear. It has first to be earned and then nurtured based on integrity, dedication, fairness and the ability to produce results for the people. Many governments around the world face a trust deficit. The response in some countries has been to develop institutional checks on government. These may have their place in certain contexts. Some take an adversarial approach because their starting premise is that governments are fundamentally not to be trusted. In the United States, many Americans believe that the less power the government has, the better it is for private citizens. In Singapore, our starting premise is that given our unique characteristics and vulnerabilities as a little nation, a strong, competent and morally upright government is essential to Singapore's survival. This does not mean that government has to be everywhere, but that government has a critical and leading role to play in nation building.' Paras 25–26, Senior Minister Goh Chok Tong, Singapore–China Forum on Leadership, 16 April 2010, archived at <http://www.news.gov.sg/public/sgpc/en/media_releases/agencies/micacsd/speech/S-20100416-1.print.html?AuthKey=>.

[204] *Yong Vui Kong v Attorney-General* [2011] 2 SLR 1189 [45].

[205] This vision of a 'green light' approach towards judicial review was suggested in an extra-judicial lecture by Chief Justice Chan Sek Keong: 'Judicial Review – From Angst to Empathy' (2010) 22 *Singapore Academy of Law Journal* 469 [29].

Beyond the dominant Western liberal paradigm of judicially enforceable, rights-based constitutionalism,[206] a range of means may be deployed to regulate public power and to both empower and constrain government. American constitutional culture emphasises rights over duties, underscores the judicial protection of rights and views the Constitution as a living document.[207] This brand of *liberal constitutionalism* forms an autonomist, experimental choice-orientated disposition in citizens, which is unable to sustain group identity or social solidarity. Traditionally, British constitutionalism – exported via colonialism to Commonwealth jurisdictions – rests on the foundation of parliamentary sovereignty, where trust is reposed in Parliament as an expression of the political will and where aristocratic judges are distrusted.[208] This brand of *political constitutionalism*, which relies primarily on political methods of accountability, is distinct from American-style judicial review which can invalidate legislation on grounds of constitutionality. British constitutional culture is evolutionary rather than revolutionary,[209] and develops unconsciously and incrementally through the common law, custom and convention. This traditional constitution is 'a partnership not only between those who are living but between those who are dead and those who are to be born',[210] producing a historically-shaped system of constitutional values.

A third broad continental model is the Kelsenian compromise, where a constitutional court with partial powers of constitutional review tempers parliamentary supremacy. In this context, Asian constitutional courts in Japan, South Korea and Taiwan may have evolved a distinctive style of review, reflecting Confucianist overtones where the courts remonstrate with the political branches, by engaging in dialogue and advice rather than overt confrontation.[211] Traditional Confucian culture was a 'no law society', given that legalism was considered contrary to Confucian principles which prioritised social harmony.[212] 'Remonstrance' is a less aggressive method of engaging with the political branches.

An examination of Asian practice yields both constitutional commitments to plural, 'Eastern' liberal democracy,[213] as well as alternative, non-liberal and non court-centric

---

[206] Klarman, for example, focuses on the judicially enforceable variety of constitutionalism without denying the possibility of constitutionalism without judicial review: MJ Klarman, 'What's so Great About Constitutionalism?' (1998) 93 *Northwestern University Law Review* 145. See generally Li-ann Thio, 'Constitutionalism in Illiberal Polities' in A Sajó and M Rosenfeld (eds), *Oxford Handbook on Comparative Constitutionalism* (New York: Oxford University Press, 2012) 133–52; G Walker, 'The Idea of Nonliberal Constitutionalism' in I Shapiro and W Kymlicka (eds), *Ethnicity and Group Rights* (New York: New York University Press, 1997) at 154.

[207] R Goldman, 'The Protection of Individual Rights as the Fundamental Element of the United States Constitutional Culture' in M Wyrzykowski (ed), *Constitutional Cultures* (Warsaw: ISP, 2000) at 25.

[208] This has been modified, given the enlarged judicial role under the Human Rights Act, under which the courts can declare a provision incompatible with norms under the ECHR: see Bendor and Segal, above n 194.

[209] C Saunders, 'Constitutional Culture in Tradition' in Wyrzykowski (ed), above n 206, at 41.

[210] E Burke, *Reflections on the Revolution in France* (1790), F Turner (ed) (New Haven, Conn: Yale University Press, 2003) at 82.

[211] Wen-Chen Chang, 'The Emergence of East Asian Constitutionalism: Features in Comparison' (2011) 59 *American Journal of Comparative Law* 805; T Ginsburg, 'Confucian Constitutionalism? The Emergence of Constitutional Review in Korea and Taiwan' (2002) 27(4) *Law & Social Inquiry* 763.

[212] Pham Duy Nghia, 'Confucianism and the Conception of the Law in Vietnam' in J Gillespie and P Nicholson (eds), *Asian Socialism and Legal Change* (Canberra, Australian National University Press, 2005) 76 at 82.

[213] Art 1, Constitution of Cambodia (1993) states that Cambodia is a kingdom adhering to the principles of liberal democracy and pluralism.

varieties of constitutionalism.[214] The dominant political philosophy may not valorise individual autonomy or espouse a brand of 'state neutrality'; rather, it may take the common good seriously as a means for structuring rights discourse and adjudication, or articulate a robust vision of the common good, drawing from culture or religion as a resource for a constitutional identity. Constitutionalism may thus be theocratic or communitarian in nature, and may even espouse a (modified) socialist commitment to a one-party state.

Four trajectories related to the constitution beyond the court may be identified.

B. Intra-Party Democracy in Socialist States

Within socialist states like China, where the Chinese Communist Party (CCP) is the driving force, the rise of a form of 'intra-party democracy'[215] (党内民主 *dangnei minzhu*) may lead to the evolution of a brand of Chinese-style democracy. Such a system may have a modicum of representation and accountability within 'a socialist country ruled by law',[216] anchored by the National People's Congress (NPC) as the organ through which the people exercise state power.[217] The revolutionary nature of the CCP as the worker's party, which has some 76 million members, has been mitigated by the idea of *sange daibiao*[218] (三个代表 'three represents'), advanced by Jiang Zemin in 2000 in a bid to reform elite politics and prevent individual dictatorial actions. This move is to curtail the rule of personality or strongman politics and promote a form of collective leadership where rival factions compete for influence but need to coalesce to preserve one-party rule.[219] The CCP presents itself as representing the entirety of Chinese people and serving the requirements of the most advanced form of production and culture.[220] In this context, a strong, independent judiciary is not envisaged, as the NPC is constitutionally empowered to supervise the enforcement of the Constitution.[221] The idea that rights can limit state power is undercut, however, by the extensive discretion conferred upon the state by Article 51, which provides:

---

[214] This may be seen when we look at ancient and medieval constitutionalism in Europe. See CH McIlwain, *Constitutionalism: Ancient and Modern* (Ithaca, NY, Cornell University Press, 1958).

[215] This is not without its sceptics: see Cheng Li, 'Intra-Party Democracy in China: Should we take it seriously?' Fall (2009), *China Leadership Monitor*, Brookings, available at <http://www.brookings.edu/~/media/research/files/papers/2009/11/fall%20china%20democracy%20li/fall_china_democracy_li>. He writes of two informal coalitions within the CCP: the populists and the princelings engaged in political competition within the Party-State.

[216] Art 5, Constitution of China (1949): 'The People's Republic of China governs the country according to law and makes it a socialist country ruled by law.'

[217] Art 2, Constitution of China (1949).

[218] L Cata Backer, 'The Rule of Law, the Chinese Communist Party and Ideological Campaigns: *Sange Daibiao* (The Three Represents), Socialist Rule of Law and Modern Chinese Constitutionalism' (2006) 16(1) *Journal of Transnational Law & Contemporary Problems* 29.

[219] W Lam, 'Intra-Party Democracy with Chinese Characteristics' in JYS Cheng (ed), *Whither China's Democracy: Democratization in China Since the Tiananmen Incident* (Hong Kong: City University of Hong Kong Press, 2011) at 41–42.

[220] He Baogang, 'Intra-party democracy: A revisionist perspective from below' in KE Brodsgaard and Y Zheng (eds), *The Chinese Communist Party in Reform* (New York: Routledge, 2006).

[221] Art 62, Constitution of the People's Republic of China (1949).

The exercise by citizens of the People's Republic of China of their freedoms and rights may not infringe upon the interests of the state, of society and of the collective, or upon the lawful freedoms and rights of other citizens.[222]

Furthermore, the Constitution is non-justiciable. Attempts to enforce constitutional rights through constitutional litigation have been thwarted, with the withdrawal of the interpretation of the *Qu Yuling* case, which optimists had earlier lauded as China's first *Marbury v Madison*.[223] The law in socialist legal thought serves the Party, not individuals.

In Vietnam, the Communist Party selected its top leaders through competitive elections, and holds elections to its National Assembly where 10 per cent of legislators are allowed to be non-party members, although these candidates, self-nominated or put forward by or organisations such as official womens' or veterans' groups are still screened by the Fatherland Front which links the party and the people.[224] This demonstrates that socialist constitutional orders are not monolithic.

C. Culture, Propriety and Persuasion: Virtuous Rulers and Internal Restraint of Leaders

Cultural norms that exert social traction may fashion the working practices of government actors, and may even be institutionalised. A civic virtue norm such as the role of '*li*' (礼), or ritual propriety, in Confucianist East Asia not only educates citizens but disciplines governors, operating as it did within a stratified, status-based society. Chaihark Hahm noted that during the Korean Choson dynasty, court historians, in recording all that the King said or did as a 'rites-bearer', exercised a form of continuous surveillance which checked the ruler, buttressing the *internal restraint* of '*li*' and the social expectations of what was required of a virtuous ruler, as embodied in ritual regulations backed by the normative force of tradition.[225] Hahm's understanding of constitutionalism encompasses legal and political institutions and practices, including conventions and soft moral norms about what is proper in matters of government, which discipline political power.[226] In the contemporary context, the Confucian practice of scholar-officials remonstrating with errant leaders may be translated into a

---

[222] RP Pereenboom, 'What's Wrong with Chinese Rights? Towards a Theory of Rights with Chinese Characteristics' (1993) 6 *Harvard Human Rights Journal* 29.

[223] TE Kellogg, 'The Death of Constitutional Litigation in China?' (2009) 9(7) *China Brief* 4; see also RJ Morris, 'China's *Marbury v Madison*: *Qi Yuling v Chen Xiaoqi* – The Once and Future Trial of Both Education and Constitutionalization' (2010) 2(2) *Tsinghua China Law Review* 273.

[224] 'One-party Vietnam votes in national elections' AFP, 21 May 2011.

[225] C Hahm, 'Constitutionalism, Confucian Civic Virtue and Ritual Propriety' in DA Bell and C Hahm (eds), *Confucianism for the Modern World* (Cambridge: Cambridge University Press, 2003) 31, 35. Brian Tamanaha, in discussing pre-liberal conceptions of the rule of law, noted that while they lacked effective legal remedies, there were three ways by which restraints imposed by law were realised: through acceptance, common understanding, as in the workings of German customary law, and as a matter of routine conduct in the conduct of ordinary activities like the King borrowing money. Breach of these norms entailed political consequences, where violations of the law provided a symbolic resource for those resisting such action, in the name of fidelity to law: BZ Tamanaha, *The Rule of Law for Everyone?*, St John's Legal Studies Research Paper, available at SSRN, <http://ssrn.com/abstract=312622 or http://dx.doi.org/10.2139/ssrn.312622>.

[226] C Hahm, 'Conceptualizing Korean Constitutionalism: Foreign Transplant or Indigenous Tradition?' (2001) 1(2) *Journal of Korean Law* 151–96.

dialogue form of 'judicial review'. Recommendations are made rather than action or restraint demanded[227] in a manner consonant with the Chinese tradition of being 'ruled by the learned'.[228]

D. Popular Petition and Populist Constitutionalism

While socialist constitutions contain lists of rights, these are not judicially enforceable. A form of 'constitutional consciousness' may be discerned from the invocation of constitutional norms and arguments in the court of public opinion. Aided by media and the Internet, this acts as a form of pressure against state officials in countries where the constitution is non-justiciable. For example, Vietnamese citizens in Hanoi objected to an unpopular police regulation, limiting each citizen to one motorcycle each, as being 'unconstitutional'. This action was thought to violate constitutional rights to property. The National Assembly eventually agreed to annul the regulation, given the public pressure. In essence, the legislature is a venue for the practice of 'safe constitutionalism' since the existing political status quo was not threatened.[229] The resort to informal petition via the Internet has also arisen as a forum where individuals seek interpretations of extant constitutional provisions, such as the scope of free expression and the legality of anti-subversion legislation.[230]

In China, this brand of citizen legal activism occurred in a 2004 petition from residents of Anyuan for economic justice. A petition was sent to the Pingxiang Mining Company and its Communist Party Committee to raise wages, and if this was not granted, for permission to stage a large-scale protest demonstration as a constitutionally-given right. This posture does not challenge state power and manifests a vision of rights not as limits against state power but as 'state-authorised channels to enhance national unity and prosperity'.[231]

In 2006, a professor issued two open letters (including one which was signed by hundreds of scholars) arguing that the proposed Property Rights Law violated Article 12 of the Constitution ('socialist public property is inviolable'). This elicited a strong response from the Government: the NPC Standing Committee amended the draft law and issued an extensive defence of the law, confirming its constitutionality, with the support of state-run media and scholarly articles, thus underscoring the point that legislation had to have a constitutional basis.[232] This brand of populism and grassroots

---

[227] T Ginsburg, 'Confucian Constitutionalism? The Emergence of Constitutional Review in Korea and Taiwan' (2002) 27(4) *Law & Social Inquiry* 763.

[228] Ibid at 795.

[229] M Sidel, 'Motorbike Constitutionalism: The Emergence of Constitutional Claims in Vietnam' in M Sidel, *Law and Society in Vietnam: The Transition from Socialism in Comparative Perspective* (Cambridge: Cambridge University Press, 2008) at 86.

[230] 'Chinese reformers petition for review of subversion law', *New York Times*, 1 February 2004; see also 'China's ancient petition system goes online', available at <http//:www.FT.com>, 30 September 2011. See further K Hand, 'Resolving Constitutional Disputes in Contemporary China' (2011) 7 *University of Pennsylvania East Asia Law Review* 51.

[231] EJ Perry, 'Chinese Conception of "Rights": From Mencius to Mao – and Now' (2008) 6(1) *Perspectives on Politics* 37.

[232] K Hand, 'Can Citizens Vitalize China's Constitution', *Far Eastern Economic Review*, May 2007, 15, available at <http://www.law.yale.edu/images/IntellectualLife/Hand_-_Can_Citizens_Vitalize_the_Constitution.pdf>.

awareness of the Constitution, demonstrates the Constitution's significance beyond the courtroom. It acts as a more conciliatory approach to resolving disputes, as can be seen in the Wukan Incident, where land was seized without adequate compensation. Cast as property rights violations, this dispute was resolved by a compromise settlement. Here, the Constitution was cited not to win a case but to advance public discourse. This is important, since the Constitution is not judicially enforceable but is capable of influencing the behaviour of government actors.[233]

E. Relational Constitutionalism: Beyond Sanctions and Rights to Solidarity and Reconciliation

In countries where social harmony is a priority – especially if their societies are divided along the fault-lines of race and religion – legalistic solutions to certain conflicts may be considered inappropriate. Solutions that provoke adversarial behavior and alienation are considered harmful to the objectives of what may be described as 'relational constitutionalism'. Chief among its goals is to ensure the sustainability and durability of relationships in cultivating social solidarity and harmonious co-existence.

Constitutional or soft constitutional norms may promote reconciliation through creating institutional structures[234] that promote dialogue between parties who may come into conflict, or espouse hortatory norms pointing to a common set of responsibilities and share in the common good. For example, in Singapore, 'racial and religious harmony' has the status of a quasi-constitutional trump, and has been underscored in numerous ministerial statements and treated in detail in the 1989 White Paper on the Maintenance of Religious Harmony.[235] 'Harmony' is distinct from 'public order' and speaks to the quality of relationship rather than the mere absence of disorder. While the right to religious propagation is constitutionally entrenched, conflicts – whether between religious groups or where hostility is directed against one religious group – have arisen. The Singapore Government, which enjoys a overwhelming majority in Parliament, can certainly wield legal sanctions against those perceived to breach the public order, but has chosen instead to rebuke (where religious ministers receive warnings) or promote reconciliation between disputing parties by taking a backseat while maintaining a watchful eye. While it has consistently affirmed the right to evangelise, it has urged that this be done in a sensitive manner, without denigrating any sect. Such norms are contained in non-binding instruments such as the White Paper on the

---

[233] K Hand, 'Constitutionalizing Wukan: The Value of the Constitution Outside the Courtroom' (2012) 12(3) *China Brief* 5; see also Zhang Qianfan, 'A Constitution without Constitutionalism? The Paths of Constitutional Development in China' (2010) 8(4) *I•CON* 950; Cai Dingjian, 'The Development of Constitutionalism in the Transition of Chinese Society' (2005) 19(1) *Columbia Journal of Asian Law* 28.

[234] For example, 'harmony boards' comprising representatives of different racial or religious groups who are able to build relations and trust before a crisis, and so be better equipped to diffuse a crisis. See Singapore's Presidential Council for Religious Harmony established under the Maintenance of Religious Harmony Act (Cap 167A). See also F Farooq, 'Rehman Malik says government to create interfaith council for religious harmony', *NewsPakistan*, 24 August 2012, at <http://www.newspakistan.pk/2012/08/24/rehman-malik-government-create-interfaith-council-religious-harmony/>.

[235] Cmd 21 of 1989; see further below, n 235.

Maintenance of Religious Harmony (1989),[236] the 2004 Declaration on Religious Harmony[237] and conciliatory ministerial reminders.[238] While these are not justiciable norms, they create expectations of appropriate behaviour which influence conduct, pointing towards the shared interests in a common polity which requires forgiveness, tolerance and understanding, which litigation does little to foster. A harmony-orientated, reconciliatory ethos directed by constitutional culture does serve the instrumental value of peace and the intrinsic one of solidarity, in the interests of state survivability.

[236] Para 13 of the White Paper notes the importance of 'respect and tolerance for other faiths' to ensure that 'harmony should prevail', given the fragility of religious harmony which may be disrupted by religious groups 'denigrating other faiths or by insensitively trying to convert those belonging to other religions'.

[237] 'We, the people in Singapore, declare that religious harmony is vital for peace, progress and prosperity in our multi-racial and multi-religious Nation. We resolve to strengthen religious harmony through mutual tolerance, confidence, respect, and understanding. We shall always Recognise the secular nature of our State, Promote cohesion within our society, Respect each other's freedom of religion, Grow our common space while respecting our diversity, Foster inter-religious communications, and thereby ensure that religion will not be abused to create conflict and disharmony in Singapore.' See Thio Li-ann, 'Constitutional "Soft" Law and the Management of Religious Liberty and Order: The 2003 Declaration on Religious Harmony' (2004) *Singapore Journal of Legal Studies* 414.

[238] The Deputy Prime Minister, in relation to a conflict between a Christian pastor and some insulted Buddhists, reiterated the norm that 'Mutual respect, tolerance and restraint are critical to maintaining communal peace and harmony in our multi-ethnic, multi-religious society. Religious leaders especially, must lead and set the right example in this regard. While each of us is free to propagate our religious beliefs, it must never be by way of insulting or denigrating the religious beliefs of others. This is a fundamental OB marker that we must all steer by in Singapore.' ('Statement from DPM Wong Kan Seng', *Straits Times*, 10 February 2010) See also Li-ann Thio, 'Relational Constitutionalism and the Management of Inter-Religious Disputes: The Singapore "Secularism with a Soul" Model' (2012) 2 *Oxford Journal of Law and Religion* 1.

3

Government System and Structures

I. INTRODUCTION

Traditionally, the key function of constitutionalism is to limit government power, through its diffusion and protecting individual rights after the liberal tradition. In Asia, the primary function of constitutions has been to establish a basic structure of government to facilitate effective governance and the provision of public services, especially in the many states that emerged in the aftermath of World War II and decolonisation. In that sense, constitutions have been facilitative, rather than limiting.

As countries build states, the process of choosing and creating a workable government system has been critical. Even today, for example, those engaged in drafting a new constitution for Nepal – a process that has been underway since 2007 – have been divided on which government system to choose. While recognising that no perfect form of government exists, foreign scholars and consultants nevertheless have offered their thoughts on the virtues and vices of presidential or parliamentary systems, in consultations during the Nepali constitution-making process.[1]

The two major forms of government – parliamentary and presidential – can be found in Asia. States like Japan, Thailand, Singapore, Malaysia and India have adopted a version of the parliamentary system of government, in part – at least in the case of the last three countries – because of their colonial legacy. The presidential system is practised in South Korea, Taiwan, Indonesia and the Philippines. There is also evidence of hybridised developments mixing elements of presidentialism and parliamentarianism. The most potent example of this has been Sri Lanka,[2] which in 1978 adopted a Gaullist system of government similar to that of France. Both South Korea and Taiwan have strong elected presidencies, but have also retained a premier who is accountable to the legislature. Often, these mixed elements become the source of constitutional conflicts among government branches, requiring judicial resolution.

Constitutional engineering requires the skilful weaving of powers and interests to produce optimal co-ordination among political branches and other powerful state agents like the bureaucracy. On paper, all constitutions in Asia govern the proper power relations between *all* branches of government. However, this is deceptive, for in some Asian states these power relations are not so clearly demarcated. The *real* power of two institutions – the monarchy and the bureaucracy – is often not accurately reflected in the constitution. Monarchies exist in Cambodia, Thailand, Malaysia,

---

[1] See Bipin Adhikari (ed), *Nepal: Design Options for the New Constitution* (Kathmandu: Nepal Constitution Foundation, 2010).

[2] See A Jeyaratnam Wilson, *The Gaullist System in Asia: The Constitution of Sri Lanka* (London: Macmillan, 1978).

Brunei, Japan, and Bhutan. On paper, these modern monarchs exercise only ceremonial functions, but because of their prestige, popularity and legitimacy, they may sometimes intervene in the operations of government. Naturally, such interventions are highly controversial. Strong bureaucracies also play an important role in the governance of countries like Japan and Singapore. The relationship between these bureaucrats and elected politicians often results in tensions that complicate the constitutional principle of separation of powers and the functioning of checks and balances among government branches.

In this chapter, we first examine the organisation of the state by identifying the head of government and head of state in the Asian constitutional context. We then discuss the concept of separation of powers and how this is realised through different institutional arrangements. This chapter concludes with a general examination of how courts have resolved institutional conflicts among government branches.

II. ORGANISATIONS OF STATE

Modern constitutions typically divide government powers into three branches: the executive, the legislature and the judiciary. The head of the government is usually the prime minister or the president, supported by political appointees and career bureaucrats. In many cases, the head of government is also the head of state; however, in some Asian states, the monarch is the head of state and symbol of sovereignty. The Japanese Emperor and Thai King are the most renowned examples. Modern government cannot function well without the support of bureaucracy. This section addresses the function and role of the head of state and its symbolic powers, followed by a general discussion of the head of government and its control over bureaucracy in modern Asian states.

A. The Head of State and Symbolic Powers

Depending on the government system and constitutional design, the head of state could be the monarch, president or hold an equivalent title. The head of state is a symbol of the state's power and authority and holds the highest office within the country. He represents the nation and serves as a focal point for citizen loyalty and patriotism.

Table 3.1 shows the selection method and tenure of the heads of state of the various Asian states. Japan, Thailand, Malaysia, Cambodia, Brunei and Bhutan still maintain monarchies, most of which are for the monarch's life. Others, such as Mongolia, South Korea, Taiwan, the Philippines, Singapore, Sri Lanka, Indonesia, India, East Timor, Lao, Bangladesh and Nepal, have a president as the head of state. Most presidents are elected by popular direct election, with tenure ranging from four to six years; but in Mongolia, Lao, India and Bangladesh the president is chosen through indirect election. The presidents of socialist countries such as China and Vietnam are elected by their respective National People's Congresses or National Assemblies.

Table 3.1 The Selection and Tenure of the Head of State in Asian Countries

States	Head of State	Method of Selection	Tenure
Bangladesh	President	Elected by Parliament	5 years
Bhutan	Monarch	Heredity (eldest male)	Until the age of 65
Brunei	Monarch	Heredity	Life
Cambodia	Monarch	Heredity	Life
China	President of the People's Republic of China	Elected by National People's Congress of China	5 years
East Timor	President	Elected by Popular Election	5 years
India	President	Elected by Electoral College	5 years
Indonesia	President	Elected by Popular Election	5 years
Japan	Monarch	Heredity (eldest male)	Life
Lao	President	Elected by Parliament	5 years
Malaysia	Monarch	Election by Conference of Rulers	5 years
Mongolia	President	Direct Popular Election by two-round system	4 years
Nepal	President	Elected by Electoral College	5 years
Philippines	President	Elected by Popular Election	6 years
Singapore	President	Elected by Popular Election	6 years
South Korea	President	Elected by Popular Election	5 years
Sri Lanka	President	Elected by Popular Election	6 years
Taiwan	President	Elected by Popular Election	4 years
Thailand	Monarch	Heredity	Life
Vietnam	The President of the Socialist Republic	National Assembly of Vietnam	5 years

In the Westminster tradition, the head of the state often exercises symbolic power while real political power resides in the hands of a government Cabinet, led by the prime minister who is the head of government. Heads of state perform not only ceremonial functions, but also the duties of awarding honours and promulgating amendments to the constitution, laws, Cabinet orders and treaties on the advice of the Cabinet.[3] In Asian states with a presidential system of government, the president simultaneously functions as both the head of state and the head of government. In these states, the president also performs ceremonial functions in the capacity of the head of the state.

The president in the parliamentary system usually does not have clearly defined constitutional powers. This frequently gives rise to clashes with the prime minister

---

[3] A Heywood, *Politics* (New York: Palgrave, 2002) at 359.

over matters not specifically provided for under the constitution. In fact, the president may exercise powers beyond the formal powers of that office, where he is constitutionally described as the protector of the state. This may lead to the assumption that the president has some powers to lead the country. However, the issue of how power is allocated between the president and the prime minster in a parliamentary system was addressed by the Indian Supreme Court in *SR Bommai v Union of India*:

> [T]he President in the parliamentary system has acted with the aid and advice of the Council of Ministers with the Prime Minister. The Constitution of India has introduced parliamentary democracy; the real power of governance is thus placed in the Prime Minister and Council of his Ministers who are very often drawn from the majority party in Parliament. Some jurists indeed refer to it derisively as Prime-ministerial form of Government. In such a democracy, the head of the state, be he the King or the President, remains a constitutional head of the state. He acts in accordance with the aid and advice tendered to him by the Council of Ministers with the Prime Minister at its head ... The advice tendered on such reconsideration is made binding upon the President ... Any and every action taken by the President is really the action of his Ministers and subordinates. It is they who have to answer for, defend and justify any and every action taken by them in the name of the President, if such action is questioned in a court of law. The President cannot be called upon to answer for or justify the action. It is for the Council of Ministers to do so ...
>
> Even where he acts directly, the President has to act on the aid and advice of the Council of Ministers or the Minister concerned, as the case may be.[4]

We noted earlier that heads of state may sometimes exercise powers beyond mere symbolism either because of constitutional design or because of entrenched cultural norms. This may in turn lead to political controversies requiring judicial resolution. Two issues of concern are:

(a) the extension of the president's powers as the head of the state through constitutional revision; and
(b) controversial exercise of power by the monarch.

We begin our analysis with a case study on Singapore, where the President is the head of state, and examine the extent to which the powers of the presidency transcend ceremonial functions.

The President is constitutionally designated Singapore's head of state and thus serves as a unifying symbol within the multi-racial and multi-religious society. Prior to constitutional amendments in 1991, the presidential powers were largely ceremonial, save for residual powers to appoint as Prime Minister the person who commanded the 'confidence of the majority' of Parliament and to dissolve Parliament at the request and advice of the Prime Minister. The 1991 amendments transformed the office of President into a popularly elected one with discretionary powers to '[protect] the Republic's financial assets, and [preserve] the integrity of the public services'.[5] For example, the President may withhold assent to certain financial decisions, such as the supply budget under Article 148A, though this action may be overridden by a resolution supported by a two-thirds parliamentary majority.

---

[4] *SR Bommai v Union of India* [1994] 2 SCR 644.
[5] Constitutional Amendments to Safeguard Financial Assets and the Integrity of the Public Services, Cmd 10 of 1988.

Although the elected President exercises substantial powers in certain matters, he still functions as a titular chief executive in many matters. Under the Singapore Constitution, the President's powers are negatively or reactively couched.[6] For example, the President may refuse to give his assent to the appointment of key public officials like Judges or the Attorney-General under Article 22(1). However, he has no powers to initiate or implement his own policies. Nonetheless, the President may employ his 'soft powers' to promote charities, or to champion worthy projects and other community-bonding functions. For example, former President Wee Kim Wee has tried privately to influence the Government by offering his own views and experiences,[7] though this is consonant with Westminster practice, where the monarch has the right to be consulted, to encourage and to warn.

Article 22P[8] vests the power of clemency in the President, but the power to pardon is not one of the President's powers that can be exercised under a personal discretion.[9] This power traditionally inheres in the Cabinet, which is responsible for 'advising' the President on the application of such powers. Under Article 21(1) of the Constitution, 'the President shall ... act in accordance with the advice of the Cabinet or of a Minister acting under the general authority of the Cabinet'.

The following case discusses whether the power of clemency of the President is subject to judicial review, and whether the President as the head of state has discretion in exercising the power of clemency. The Court of Appeal dismissed the claim on the ground that the President had no personal discretion in exercising the power of clemency, but held that the power is, nonetheless, subject to judicial review. The Court characterised the power of clemency as a legal power of an extraordinary character.

Yong Vui Kong v Attorney-General [2011] SGCA 9 (Court of Appeal, Singapore)

Facts

In 2008, the appellant was convicted of a capital drug trafficking offence and sentenced to death. He appealed but then withdrew his appeal. The Court of Appeal formally dismissed the appeal in April 2009. On 11 August 2009, the appellant submitted a petition

---

[6] KYL Tan and Thio Li-ann, *Constitutional Law in Malaysia and Singapore* (Singapore: LexisNexis, 2009) at 421.

[7] Thio Li-ann, *A Treatise on Singapore Constitutional Law* (Singapore: Singapore Academy of Law, 2012) at 393.

[8] Art 22P, which is set out in full below, makes it clear that these procedural safeguards apply only to death sentence cases, and are inapplicable to non-death sentence cases: '22P–(1) The President, as occasion shall arise, may, on the advice of the Cabinet – (a) grant a pardon to any accomplice in any offence who gives information which leads to the conviction of the principal offender or any one of the principal offenders, if more than one; (b) grant to any offender convicted of any offence in any court in Singapore, a pardon, free or subject to lawful conditions, or any reprieve or respite, either indefinite or for such period as the President may think fit, of the execution of any sentence pronounced on such offender; or (c) remit the whole or any part of such sentence or of any penalty or forfeiture imposed by law. (2) Where any offender has been condemned to death by the sentence of any court and in the event of an appeal such sentence has been confirmed by the appellate court, the President shall cause the reports which are made to him by the Judge who tried the case and the Chief Justice or other presiding Judge of the appellate court to be forwarded to the Attorney-General with instructions that, after the Attorney-General has given his opinion thereon, the reports shall be sent, together with the Attorney-General's opinion, to the Cabinet so that the Cabinet may advise the President on the exercise of the power conferred on him by clause (1).'

[9] See Art 22P, Constitution of the Republic of Singapore.

to the President for clemency under Article 22P of the Constitution, but this was turned down. The appellant subsequently applied for leave to commence judicial review proceedings in the High Court, seeking declarations that under Article 22P of the Singapore Constitution the power of clemency was exercisable by the President *personally*. The High Court dismissed the Appellant's application for leave to commence judicial review proceedings under Order 53 of the Rules of Court. The appellant appealed again. The appellant's counsel, Mr Ravi, made an oral application for the Chief Justice, Chan Sek Keong, to recuse himself from hearing the appeal on the ground that he must, while serving as Attorney-General from 1992 to 2006, have advised the President that he had no discretion in exercising the power of clemency under Article 22P. This application was dismissed.

Chan Sek Keong CJ

I start by stating that the clemency power is a legal power of an extraordinary character. It is unlike all other legal powers in that:

(a) It is an executive power which is exercised as an act of executive grace and not as a matter of legal right . . .

(b) A decision to grant clemency is '[a] determination of the ultimate authority that the public welfare will be better served by inflicting less [punishment] than what the judgment fixed' . . . Conversely, a decision not to grant clemency represents a determination by the ultimate authority that the public welfare is better served by allowing the law to take its course, ie, by carrying out the punishment prescribed by the law.

(c) Ordinarily, the law should be allowed to take its course. However, when the clemency power is exercised in favour of an offender, it will 'involve a departure from the law' . . . in that, in the interests of the public welfare, the law (in terms of the punishment mandated by the law) is prevented from taking its course.

(d) The considerations of public welfare that the ultimate authority deems relevant in making a clemency decision are entirely a matter of policy for it to decide. As was said by SH Kapadia J . . ., '[t]he President and the Governor [viz, the ultimate authority in the context of India's clemency regime] are the sole judges of the sufficiency of facts and of the appropriateness of granting . . . pardons and reprieves'.

(e) In the specific context of a death sentence case (which is also the context of the present appeal), the grant of clemency to the offender confers a gift of life on him. This is because the offender has effectively already been deprived of his life by the law due to his conviction for a capital offence . . .

Given that the clemency power is a constitutional power vested exclusively in the Executive, it is not justiciable on the merits, firstly, on the basis of the doctrine of separation of powers. In our local context, this entails that, assuming the clemency power is exercised in accordance with law, the merits of the clemency decision made will fall outside the purview of our courts. Our courts cannot look into whether a clemency decision is wise or foolish, harsh or kind; neither can they substitute their own decision for the clemency decision made by the President simply because they disagree with the President's view on the matter. This principle is common ground between the parties in the present appeal.

However, this conclusion – viz, that the merits of a clemency decision are not reviewable by our courts – does not, in my view, entail that the clemency power in our constitutional context is therefore an 'extra-legal' power in the sense of being a power beyond any legal constraints or restraints . . .

A further reason (apart from the *Chng Suan Tze* principle) for holding that the clemency power is amenable to judicial review lies in the specific procedural safeguards prescribed by Art 22P for the conduct of the clemency process in death sentence cases . . .

Unlike the position in non-death sentence cases, in a death sentence case, the President is required under Art 22P(2) to cause the report of the trial judge and (where there is an appeal from the trial judge's decision) the report of the presiding judge of the appellate court to be sent to the Attorney-General, who must give his opinion thereon. The Attorney-General's opinion and the aforesaid report(s), which collectively form the Art 22P(2) materials in a death sentence case, must then be sent to the Cabinet so that the Cabinet may advise the President on the exercise of the clemency power. In my view, the requirement that the trial judge's report, the report of the presiding judge of the appellate court (where there is an appeal) and the Attorney-General's opinion on the report(s) must be sent to the Cabinet for its consideration necessarily implies a constitutional duty on the Cabinet's part to consider those materials impartially and in good faith before it advises the President on the exercise of the clemency power.

It therefore follows that if, hypothetically speaking, conclusive evidence is produced to the court to show that the Cabinet never met to consider the offender's case at all, or that the Cabinet did not consider the Art 22P(2) materials placed before it and merely tossed a coin to determine what advice to give to the President . . ., the Cabinet would have acted in breach of Art 22P(2). If the courts cannot intervene to correct a breach of Art 22P of this nature, the rule of law would be rendered nugatory. In this regard, it should be noted that in Singapore (just as in many other common law jurisdictions which have elevated the clemency power from a common law prerogative power to a constitutional power under a written Constitution), the making of a clemency decision pursuant to Art 22P is now 'not a private act of grace from an individual happening to possess power . . . [but] a part of the [c]onstitutional scheme' . . .

Andrew Phang Boon Leong & VK Rajah JJA

. . . Prior to the establishment of the elected Presidency via s 4 of the Constitution of the Republic of Singapore (Amendment) Act 1991 (Act 5 of 1991), which came into effect on 30 November 1991, the position under our constitutional framework was that '[t]he President was a constitutional Head of State with very little discretionary [power], save in the appointment of the Prime Minister and the dissolution of Parliament at the request of the Prime Minister'. . . . In contrast, after the establishment of the elected Presidency, the President was vested with certain additional discretionary powers ('the additional discretionary powers'). These are now specified in Art 21(2) of the Singapore Constitution . . ., which explicitly declares that the President '*may act in his discretion*' [emphasis added] in exercising such powers. These words clearly serve to distinguish the additional discretionary powers from the President's traditional pre-existing powers prior to the establishment of the elected Presidency, the latter powers being exercisable by the President only 'in accordance with the advice of the Cabinet or of a Minister acting under the general authority of the Cabinet' (see Art 21(1)).

According to Constitutional Amendments to Safeguard Financial Assets and the Integrity of the Public Services (White Paper, Cmd 10 of 1988, 29 July 1988), the purpose of conferring the additional discretionary powers on the President was to enable him to '[protect] the Republic's financial assets, and [preserve] the integrity of the public services' (at para 20). In a subsequent White Paper explaining the proposed constitutional amendments to provide for the elected Presidency, Safeguarding Financial Assets and the Integrity of the Public Services . . . the additional discretionary powers were summarised as follows:

Summary of Discretionary Powers

The President will have the discretion to withhold concurrence to:

a. the budgets of the Government, and of key Government companies and statutory boards;
b. any debt, guarantee or loan to be incurred, given or raised by the Government;
c. certain appointments to office;
d. requests to issue a Proclamation of Emergency;
e. detentions under the Internal Security Act, contrary to the recommendations of the Advisory Board; and
f. decisions by a Minister under the Maintenance of Religious Harmony Bill, contrary to the recommendations of the Presidential Council for Religious Harmony.

The President can also authorise Director CPIB [Corrupt Practices Investigation Bureau] to carry out any inquiries or investigations into a Minister if the Prime Minister had withheld consent to such investigations.

The power to pardon is conspicuously absent from this list of personal discretionary powers. This is manifestly understandable, given that that power is not a power or function which is related to the President's ultimate duty of protecting Singapore's financial assets and preserving the integrity of the public services.

Singapore's system of having a directly elected president within a parliamentary system is exceptional. In most Asian states with a Cabinet system, the monarch remains the head of state.[10] Historically, a monarch was considered sacred, embodying not only state sovereignty but also the government itself. For example, Article 4 of the Constitution of the Empire of Japan (Meiji Constitution) of 1890 provided that the Emperor was the head of the Empire, combining in Himself the rights of sovereignty, and exercised them according to the provisions of the present Constitution. Article 5 further stipulated that the Japanese Emperor exercised the legislative power with the consent of the Imperial Diet.[11]

Monarchies were common in Asia prior to the two great wars. However, in the wake of decolonisation, democratisation and nationalism, states like Laos, Myanmar and more recently Nepal abolished the monarchical system.[12] Democratisation has, however, substantially transformed the power and role of the remaining Asian monarchs. Modern constitutions have substantially limited the powers of monarchs as heads of state, who are now largely symbolic national figures.[13] For example, Japan's post-War constitution retained the Emperor as the symbol of the state to secure the stability of the polity.[14] Under Article 32 of the Constitution of Malaysia, the *Yang di-Pertuan Agong* – Malaysia's constitutional monarch who is elected for a five-year term – is the

---

[10] G Hassall and C Saunders, *Asia-Pacific Constitutional Systems* (New York: Cambridge University Press, 2002) 120.

[11] The Constitution of the Empire of Japan (Ito Miyoji, trans), 1890, at <http://www.ndl.go.jp/constitution/e/etc/c02.html>.

[12] Nepal abolished its monarch in 2007. See D Pimentel, 'Constitutional Concepts for the Rule of Law: A Vision for the Post-Monarchy Judiciary in Nepal,' (2009) 9 *Washington University Global Studies Law Review* 290.

[13] Heywood, above n 3, at 366.

[14] Art 1, Constitution of Japan. See Hiroyuki Hata and Go Nakagawa, *Constitution Law of Japan* (Boston, Mass: Kluwer Law International, 1997) at 50.

head of state in whom the executive authority of the Federation is vested. The *Agong*, who is elected from among the nine hereditary rulers, must act on the advice of the Cabinet.[15] However, the *Agong* still enjoys discretionary powers in some matters, although various amendments have whittled these down over the years.[16]

Although monarchs may not be vested with substantive powers, their royal influence can, in some cases, still be significant during transitional situations or in times of political crisis. For example, the King of Thailand often exerts his influence over Thai politics. The concept of kingship in Thailand, a constitutional monarchy, is a particularly strong one.[17] The collapse of Thaksin Shinawatra's Government amply demonstrated the royal influence of King Bhumibol in Thai politics. During the conflict between Thaksin Government and the People's Alliance for Democracy, it is believed that King Bhumibol played a significant role.[18] Between March and June 2006, conflict intensified and the elections were boycotted. The King's intervention made a difference; after meeting with Prime Minister Thaksin, Thaksin announced that he would not remain as Prime Minister in the newly elected parliament. Subsequently, the King informed newly appointed judges that the one-party election had not been democratic. While he refrained from direct royal intervention, the King called on the judiciary to find a solution to resolve the political mess. King Bhumibol's intervention not only legitimised the coup, but also served to safeguard national interests in the midst of the political clash, all in the exercise of an extra-constitutional power.[19]

More typically, modern constitutions vest largely ceremonial powers in the monarch. For example, the Emperor of Japan can promulgate constitutional amendments, dissolve the House of Representatives, appoint or dismiss the Ministers, and grant general and special amnesty, but only with the advice and approval of the Cabinet.[20] Likewise, the King of Thailand has the prerogative to remove a Minister from his or her office upon the advice of the Prime Minister[21] and to declare war with the approval of the National Assembly.[22] In contrast, the Sultan of Brunei enjoys substantial executive powers. Article 4(1) of Brunei Constitution vests supreme executive authority of Brunei Darussalam in His Majesty the Sultan and the *Yang Di-Pertuan* who, under Article 4(1A), is the Prime Minister. Further, the *Yang Di-Pertuan* has the power to appoint from among citizens of Brunei Darussalam any number of Ministers and Deputy Ministers who shall be responsible solely to the *Yang Di-Pertuan* for the exercise of

---

[15] Art 4, Constitution of the Federation of Malaysia, 1957.

[16] For example, Art 32 and Art 182 of the 1993 Constitutional Amendment removed the legal immunity of the *Agong*. Art 32(1) provided that there shall be a Supreme Head of the Federation, to be called the Yang di-Pertuan Agong, who shall take precedence over all persons in the Federation and shall not be liable to any proceedings whatsoever in any court except in the Special Court established under Part XV. Art 182 stipulated that 'the Special Court shall have exclusive jurisdiction to try all offences committed in the Federation by the Yang di-Pertuan Agong or the Ruler of a State and all civil cases by or against the Yang di-Pertuan Agong or the Ruler of a State notwithstanding where the cause of action arose'. See Hassall and Saunders, above n 10, at 120; Tan and Thio, above n 6, at 361.

[17] J Ockey, 'Monarch, Monarchy, Succession and Stability in Thailand,' (2005) 46(2) *Asia Pacific Viewpoint* 115.

[18] M Peleggi, *Thailand: The Worldly Kingdom* (London: Reaktion, 2007) at 103.

[19] MH Nelson, 'Political Turmoil in Thailand: Thaksin, Protests, Elections, and the King,' (2006) 5(1) *Eastasia.* at 1.

[20] Art 7, Constitution of Japan.

[21] Sec 183, Constitution of the Kingdom of Thailand.

[22] Sec 189, Constitution of the Kingdom of Thailand.

executive authority, and who shall assist and advise him in the discharge of his executive authority, under Article 4(2).

The discretionary powers of monarchs have long been the subject of controversy. In this connection, we examine two cases. The first is *Action for Recognition of the Status as a Member of the House of Representatives and a Claim for Remuneration*, where the Supreme Court of Japan had to consider the constitutionality of the dissolution of the Japanese House of Representatives, a power exercisable by the Emperor under Article 7(3) of the Constitution. In determining the constitutionality of the dissolution, the Court was confronted with the question of how to interpret the power of the Emperor. The second case concerns the constitutionality of the appointment of the Sabah Chief Minister by the Governor, the *Yang di-Pertua Negeri*. The High Court of Malaysia held that the swearing-in of the former Chief Minister was null and void on the ground that Yang di-Pertua Negeri had not exercised his discretion on this appointment.

Action for Recognition of the Status as a Member of the House of Representatives and a Claim for Remuneration 14 Minshū 1206 (Supreme Court, Japan)

Facts

On August 28, 1952, the House of Representatives was dissolved by the Cabinet. A politician who was a member of the House of Representatives at that time filed a suit and claimed that he had not lost the status as a member of the House of Representatives since the dissolution of the House under Article 7 of the Constitution was unconstitutional.

Justices Kotani Katsushige & Okuno Kenichi (concurring opinion)

Dissolution of the House of Representatives, including dissolution under Article 69, is effected by the emperor with the advice and approval of the cabinet as an act of [a] matter of state in accordance with Article 7. Dissolution by the emperor is effected with the advice and approval of the cabinet and the emperor formally and ceremoniously performs it, and therefore, the power to decide the dissolution of the House of Representatives rests with the cabinet. Since the dissolution by the emperor is effected with the advice and approval of the cabinet and the emperor formally and ceremoniously performs it, this does not make the power of the emperor unnecessarily strong, and the criticism that the fact that the cabinet has the power to decide dissolution makes the cabinet superior to the parliament and gives excessive power to the cabinet is not justifiable . . .

Advice and approval by the cabinet as provided by Article 7 of the Constitution should not be separated as in the judgment of the first instance court, but in summary, should be construed so that regarding acts of state matters by the emperor, the cabinet has the real decision-making power and the emperor follows the decision of the cabinet and dissolves the House of Representatives formally and ceremoniously.

Kawamura Daisuke (concurring opinion)

Article 7, subpara 3 of the Constitution attributes the power to dissolve the House of Representatives to the emperor, but since the emperor does not have the power related to government (Article 4), dissolution as an act in matters of state by the emperor is based upon the decision of dissolution by another body and merely functions as a declaration to the outside, ie a formal and declaratory act. The cabinet is to give advice and approval on this formal act of the emperor, and therefore, the decision of dissolution in substance precedes the above advice and approval. 'Advice and approval' as provided in Article 7 seems to mean that it is necessary to consider both words separately. The reason why this provision requires the advice and approval of the cabinet for the act on the matters of state by the emperor is merely because the emperor is not supposed to effect such acts on his own, but must perform such acts on the basis of the opinion of the cabinet, ie the will of the cabinet, so there is no need particularly to separate advice and approval, and thus, they should be understood legally as a single concept. Merely on the basis of this evidence, it is appropriate to find that it was proved that the declaration of dissolution by the emperor was based upon the will of the cabinet, and thus the requirement of the Constitution has been sufficiently met. Therefore, the arguments in the grounds of *jokoku* appeal are not acceptable . . .

Tun Datu Haji Mustapha bin Datu Harun v Tun Datuk Haji Mohamed Adnan Robert, Yang di-Pertua Negeri Sabah & Datuk Joseph Pairin Kitigan (No 2) [1986] 2 MLJ 420 (High Court, Malaysia)

Facts

At about 5.30 am on the morning of 22 April 1985, after the state elections in Sabah, the plaintiff took the prescribed oath of Chief Minister before the first defendant, who was Governor of the Malaysian state of Sabah. The same day the first defendant purported to revoke the plaintiff's appointment as Chief Minister. At about 8.00 pm the same day, the Governor appointed and swore in the second defendant as Chief Minister. The plaintiff sued for a declaration that the Governor's revocation of his appointment as Chief Minister and the appointment of the second defendant as Chief Minister were ultra vires the Sabah Constitution. The plaintiff also sought an injunction to restrain the second defendant from exercising the powers of the Chief Minister.

Tan Chiaw Thong J

It is common ground that the State of Sabah operates under a party system of government, and the general election concerned here was held under the same system. The Head of State therefore cannot constitutionally exercise or make his judgment on the appointment of a Chief Minister without taking into account the number of elected seats secured by each and every political party and, for that matter, by the independent candidates, in the election. It is clear that, if he omits to take into account the number of seats obtained by any particular political party which participated in the election, it cannot be said that he had exercised or made his judgment under Article 6(3), for, if he did so, he would be acting unlawfully and unconstitutionally by ignoring or not complying with the requirement, in particular of Article 6(3). In such circumstances, it is equally clear, in my view, that he has made no judgment under Article 6(3). In this connection, I see no difference between this situation and the case where the Head of State appoints as Chief Minister a person who is not a member of the Legislative Assembly, contrary to the express requirement of Article 6(3) . . .

Here, I have found as a fact on the evidence as accepted by me and for the reasons given, that, in swearing in [the] plaintiff, DW1 as Head of State had not taken into account the number of seats secured by PBS, particularly since he was still waiting for the official results to be announced when he swore in [the] plaintiff. Even if it can be said that, at some stage before the swearing in, the number of seats secured by PBS were made known to him, the evidence indicates that this left no impression on his mind so as to cause him to take this factor into consideration when he decided to swear in [the] plaintiff . . .

For the reasons given therefore, I find that the swearing in of [the] plaintiff by [the] first defendant is null and void and has no legal effect on this ground . . .

As to the second ground for my conclusion that [the] first defendant did not make or exercise a judgment under Article 6(3) of the Constitution, because the swearing in of [the] plaintiff was made solely as a result, cumulatively, of the pressure and threat contained in the words in the 'paper' as understood by [the] first defendant, operating on his mind, and when he was frightened and confused in mind and tired physically, and when he was unable to think properly, it would be a remarkable and dangerous situation were I to accept the view that, in such circumstances, the swearing in of [the] plaintiff is legal, constitutional and valid. If such be the legal position, the same will have to be the position, if, for instance (this is an illustration only, with no disrespect meant to His Majesty or anyone else), an elected leader of a party who claims to be qualified to be the Prime Minister after a general election, adopts the same methods of persuasion on His Majesty the Yang di-Pertuan Agong, and as a result of such persuasion, His Majesty appoints him to be the Prime Minister. Such a situation would be so ridiculous that it hardly needs any elaboration . . .

In my view, the Constitution envisages that the Head of State should be allowed to make his judgment quietly, freely, independently and impartially, without any influence, pressure, threat or other factors not sought by him which might influence his judgment. Hence, I find that, in swearing in [the] plaintiff under the circumstances as found by me, [the] first defendant has made no judgment under Article 6(3) of the Constitution. Accordingly, such swearing in is null, void and of no legal effect . . .

Notes and Questions

1. Asian constitutional systems often contain mixed elements warranting special attention. Some states have transformed their parliamentary system to a semi-presidential system, while others have grafted additional presidential powers to a parliamentary system. Both reflect a trend towards expanding the powers of the head of state. Do you see this trend as a manifestation of traditions in Asia where there is a long history of powerful monarchs and authoritarian rule? Or do you think this might be a result of special needs unique to the Asian political context? Consider the cases of Taiwan, South Korea and Indonesia; do the diverse group identities and unstable politics call for a strong leader to represent the unified voice of the people? Consider also the case of Singapore: are the reasons cited, namely, to '[protect] the Republic's financial assets and [preserve] the integrity of the public services', the real reasons for empowering the President, given arguments that subsequent amendments have hampered the efficacy of the institution? See YCL Lee, 'Under Lock and Key: The Evolving Role of the Elected President as Fiscal Guardian' (2007) *Singapore Journal of Legal Studies* 290; and Yusaku Horiuchi and Seungjoo Lee, 'The Presidency, Regionalism, and Distributive Politics in South Korea' (2008) 41(6) *Comparative Politics Studies* 861. Observers have also noted the expansive authority of the president in Latin America; see, eg, C Grossman, 'States of Emergency: Latin American and the United States' in L Henkin and AJ Rosenthal (eds), *Constitutionalism and Rights: The Influence of the United States Constitution Abroad* (New York: Columbia University Press, 1990) at 185.

2. While most modern Asian states have adopted a form of constitutional democracy, some still maintain a monarchy. The longevity of the monarchy in Asia, however, cannot be guaranteed. Revolutions, wars or dramatic transitions have triggered debates over the continuation of imperial functions. The last Emperor of China was dethroned by the republican revolution against Manchurian rule in the early twentieth century. See ICY Hsu, *The Rise of Modern China* (New York: Oxford University Press, 2000) at 408–12 and 452–83. The Japanese Emperor was nevertheless saved to symbolise the state and the unity of the people, provided he honoured democratisation and denied being a deity. See Shigenori Matsui, *The Constitution of Japan: A Contextual Analysis* (Oxford: Hart Publishing, 2012) at 58–61; Katsutoshi Takami, 'From Divine Legitimacy to Myth of Consensus: The Emperor System and Popular Sovereignty' in Yoichi Higuchi (ed), *Five Decades of Constitutionalism in Japanese Society* (Tokyo: University of Tokyo Press, 2001) at 1–26. Post-World War II Japanese scholarship has actively debated the abolition of the Emperor's office. See, for examples, SBen-Rafael Galanti, 'The Emperor in the Constitutional Debate' in B-A Shillony (ed), *The Emperors of Modern Japan* (Boston, Mass: Brill, 2008) at 299. Why do you think China abolished its monarchy, while Japan retained her Emperor?

3. While the Japanese Emperor lost some popularity after the War, the imperial family regained acclaim as Japan recovered its economy in the 1960s and 1970s. Regardless of popularity, the Emperor is obliged to uphold the Constitution and serves only ceremonial functions. However, scholars argue that the actual influence that the Japanese Emperor exerts far exceeds constitutional limitations. See Hiroyuki Hata and Go Nakagawa, *Constitution Law of Japan* (Boston, Mass: Kluwer Law International, 1997) at 50. See also N Berlin, 'Constitutional Conflict with the Japanese Imperial Role: Accession, Yasukuni Shrine, and Obligatory Reformation' (1998) 1(2) *University of Pennsylvania Journal of Constitutional Law* 383 (arguing that the current role of Emperor, as chief shaman-priest of the Shinto religion and the mandated symbol of the State, may violate Article 20 of the Japanese Constitution; in order to accommodate the role of the Emperor, the Constitution must be amended to harmonise the principle of separation of religion and state).

4. Notwithstanding decades of constitutional governance, do most Asian people still expect a Weberian charismatic leader to provide guidance in political and personal lives? In modern Asia, do the words of the emperor, the king or a ruler still override rules of law? Consider the Thai political crisis in 2005–06, when the elected Thaksin Government was ousted by a military coup led by General Sonthi Boonyaratglin and the King intervened. See J Ockey, 'Monarch, Monarchy, Succession and Stability in Thailand' (2005) 46(2) *Asia Pacific Viewpoint* 115; MJ Montesano, 'Political Contexts in the Advent of Bangkok's 19 September Putsch' in J Funston (ed), *Divided over Thaksin: Thailand's Coup and Problematic Transition* (Chiang Mai: Silkworm Books, 2009) at 1–26. It is noteworthy that veteran American journalist Harrison Salisbury entitled his book about Mao Zedong and Deng Xiaoping, *The New Emperors: Mao and Deng* (New York: HarperCollins, 1993).

5. When the people of Nepal were recently presented with the opportunity to con-
    sider whether to keep their King, they decided to abolish the monarchy. See
    D Pimentel, 'Constitutional Concepts for the Rule of Law: A Vision for the Post-
    monarchy Judiciary in Nepal' (2009) 9 *Washington University of Global Studies LR*
    283. Sandwiched between China and India, Nepal must deal with national inter-
    ests and identity concerns in drafting its new constitution, including the choice of
    a government system beyond partisan patronage. See Jiunn-rong Yeh, 'Strategies
    of Preservation of National Interest through a New Constitution: Institutional
    Capacity Building for Nepal' in Bipin Adhikari (ed), *Nepal: Design Options for the
    New Constitution* (Kathmandu: Nepal Constitution Foundation, 2010) at 387.
    Shorn of a monarchy, how would Nepal consolidate the will of people and ensure
    it is entrenched in the state's constitutional foundations?

B. The Head of Government and Administrative Unity

Under the principle of administrative unity, the head of government ensures that the
machinery of government works coherently and effectively. What happens if you
establish an independent regulatory commission aimed at insulating the adjudicatory
process from the command or influence of the president or premier? Would this not
pose a major challenge to the principle of administrative unity? Two issues are worth
noting:

(a) whether the creation of the independent regulatory commission is constitutional;
     and
(b) whether the head of government should retain the power to appoint commission
     members.

In the following extract, the Grand Justices of Taiwan had to consider these two
constitutional issues in a case concerning the creation of the National Communications
Commission (NCC). The NCC was first independent regulatory commission to be
established under the Standard Act of Central Executive Agencies and Organizations,
2004. Under the Act, an independent regulatory commission is 'a collegial commission that acts independently in accordance with the law and without being subject to
supervisions of other organs'.[23] It consists of five to seven full-time commissioners
with fixed terms, appointed by the Premier with legislative approval.[24] The number of
commissioners from the same political party shall not exceed the number provided by
organic laws.[25] The NCC was created amidst contentious partisan fights in the legislature, and in an effort to entrench its dominance in the NCC, the KMT political party
defied Article 21 of the Standard of Central Executive Agencies and Organizations
Act, 2004. The appointments were made in such a manner as to leave the Premier
merely with ceremonial power in appointing the NCC commissioners. The Democratic

---

[23] Art 3(1)(2), Standard Act of Central Executive Agencies and Organizations, 2004.
[24] Art 3(1), Additional Article 1997.
[25] Art 21, Standard Act of Central Executive Agencies and Organizations, 2004. See Jiunn-rong Yeh,
'Experimenting with Independent Commissions in a New Democracy with a Civil Law Tradition: The Case
of Taiwan' in S Rose-Ackerman and P Lindseth (eds), *Comparative Administrative Law* (Northampton:
Edward Elgar, 2010) at 251.

Progressive Party (DPP), unable to stop the KMT's partisan formula, petitioned to the Council of Grand Justices for resolution.[26]

JY Interpretation No 613 21 Jul 2006 (Constitutional Court, Taiwan)

Facts

As a policy response to digital convergence, Taiwan moved to establish an independent commission, the National Communications Commission, to reduce political interference with the mass media and the press. In 2003, the Bill of the Organic Act of the National Communications Commission ('NCC Organic Act') was delivered to the Legislative Yuan for approval. However, the debates occurred at the time of renewal of the licences of some broadcast and television organisations, and thus triggered political confrontation between parties. Dominant parties, including Kuomintang (KMT) and its alliance People First Party (PFP), proposed to organise the NCC along party lines in the Legislative Yuan. The Executive Yuan and the opposition party (DPP) brought the case before the Court and claimed that the design would lead to political manipulation and deprive the the Executive Yuan of its power. The Court declared the NCC Organic Act unconstitutional on the basis of the principle of administrative unity.

Held

The Executive Yuan shall be the highest administrative organ of the state. Under the principle of administrative unity, the Executive Yuan must be held responsible for the overall performance of all the agencies subordinate to the said Yuan, including the National Communications Commission (hereinafter referred to as the 'NCC'), and shall have the power to decide on personnel affairs in respect of members of the NCC because the success or failure of the NCC will hinge closely on the candidates for membership in the NCC.

. . . [S]ince the existence of an independent agency will diminish the administrative unity and the politics of accountability, its establishment should be an exception. The constitutionality of establishing an independent agency will be upheld only if the purpose of its establishment is indeed to pursue constitutional public interests, if the particularity of the mission justifies the necessity of its establishment, if important matters are determined by means of hearings, if the performance of the execution of its mission is made transparent and public for purpose of public supervision, and if, owing to the vested authority of the Legislative Yuan to supervise the operation of the independent agency through legislation and budget review and having considered any and all factors on the whole, a certain degree of democratic legitimacy can be sufficiently preserved to compensate for the diminished administrative unity and politics of accountability . . .

According to Article 4-II and –III of the NCC Organic Act, however, a total of fifteen members of the NCC will be recommended based on the percentages of the numbers of seats of the respective parties (groups) in the Legislative Yuan, and, together with the three members to be recommended by the Premier, shall be reviewed by the NRC, which is composed of eleven scholars and experts as recommended by the various political parties (groups) based on the percentages of the numbers of seats of the respective parties (groups) in the Legislative Yuan, via a two-round majority review by more than three-fifths and one-half of its total members, respectively. And, upon completion of the review, the Premier shall nominate those who appear on the list as approved by the NRC

---

[26] Jiunn-rong Yeh, above n 25, at 253.

within seven (7) days and appoint same upon confirmation by the Legislative Yuan. Given the fact that the Premier can recommend only three out of the eighteen candidates for membership in the NCC, that he has no say in the personnel affairs during the review, that he is bound by the list as approved by the NRC, which is formed according to the percentages of the numbers of seats of the respective parties (groups) in the Legislative Yuan, and that he is obligated to nominate those appearing on the said list, to send the nominations to the Legislative Yuan for the latter's confirmation, and to appoint those candidates confirmed by the Legislative Yuan as members of the NCC, it is very clear that the Executive Yuan, in fact, has mere nominal authority to nominate and appoint and substantially limited power to recommend only one-sixth of the candidates for members of the NCC during the entire selection procedure. In essence, the Premier is deprived of virtually all of his power to decide on personnel affairs. In addition, the executive is in charge of the enforcement of the laws whereas the enforcement depends on the personnel. There is no administration without the personnel. Therefore, it is only natural that the executive should have the authority by law to decide on specific personnel matters, irrespective of whether such matters concern general government employees or political appointees, and such authority should be an indispensable prerequisite for the executive power of a democratic rule-of-law nation to perform its functions to the utmost extent. Accordingly, the aforesaid provisions, in substantially depriving the Executive Yuan of virtually all of its power to decide on specific personnel affairs in respect of the members of the NCC, are in conflict with the constitutional principle of politics of accountability, and are contrary to the principle of separation of powers since they lead to apparent imbalance between the executive and legislative powers . . .

As for the issue of whether the provisions are unconstitutional that empower the various political parties (groups) to recommend candidates for membership in the NCC based on the percentages of the numbers of seats of the respective parties (groups) in the Legislative Yuan, and to recommend scholars and experts to form the NRC based on such percentages, it depends on whether such participation provisions substantially deprive the Executive Yuan of its power to decide on personnel affairs. The aforesaid provisions have, in essence, transferred the power to decide on personnel affairs from the Executive Yuan to the various political parties (groups) of the Legislative Yuan and the NRC, which is composed of members recommended by such political parties (groups) based on the percentages of the numbers of their seats in the Legislative Yuan, and which obviously oversteps the limits of participation and runs counter to the checks and balances in restricting the executive power to decide on personnel affairs. Besides, since the purpose of the aforesaid provisions is to reduce the political clout on the exercise of the NCC's functions and duties and to further promote the public confidence in the NCC's fair enforcement of the law, it is questionable whether the means serve the said purpose. Although the lawmakers have certain legislative discretion to decide how to reduce the political influence on the exercise of the NCC's authorities and to further build up the people's confidence in the NCC's fair enforcement of the law, the design of the system should move in the direction of less partisan interference and more public confidence in the fairness of the said agency. Nevertheless, the aforesaid provisions have accomplished exactly the opposite by inviting active intervention from political parties and granting them a special status to recommend and, in essence, nominate, members of the NCC based on the percentages of the numbers of their seats, thus affecting the impartiality and reliability of the NCC in the eyes of the people who believe that it shall function above politics. As such, the purpose of establishing the NCC as an independent agency is defeated, and the constitutional intent of safeguarding the freedom of communications is not complied with . . .

Notes and Questions

1. The NCC controversy in Taiwan occurred in the context of a government divided between different political parties, but was also concerned with aspects of the regulatory sector, particularly those concerning information, the media and tele-communications. The need for the Commission's independence was paramount when it was established; it has proven difficult for the courts to navigate a politi-cally contentious field in a maturing democracy. The social context for creating an independent regulatory commission varies from state to state. In America, an independent regulatory commission is designed to be insulated from presidential control. However, in states undergoing democratic transition, the underlying motive for creating such commissions is different. In Eastern and Central Europe, independent regulatory commissions were established to gain trust in the midst of political flux. See A Sajó, 'Neutral Institutions: Implications for Government Trustworthiness in East European Democracies' in J Kornai and S Rose-Ackerman (eds), *Building a Trustworthy State in Post-Socialist Transition* (New York: Palgrave Macmillan, 2004) at 29. In Taiwan, the real motivation behind the NCC's creation was the buying of 'political insurance', since both major political parties were unsure if either of them would convincingly win the next presidential election.

2. In *JY Interpretation No 613*, the Court upheld the integrity of administrative unity against political transitions. It follows that the constitutionality of the NCC depends on a substantive power of appointment to be exercised by the head of government. Interestingly, the Court derived the principle of administrative unity from Article 53 of the Constitution, which states that 'the Executive Yuan shall be the highest administrative organ of the state'. Similar wording may be found in Article 2(1) of the US Constitution, which provides that 'the executive power shall be vested in a President of the United States of America'. However, the US Supreme Court prefers to use the principle of checks and balances as the basis for constitutional scrutiny, rather than the principle of administrative unity. In his concurring opinion in *JY Interpretation No 613*, Justice Tzu-Yi Lin suggested that the principle of checks and balances should be employed to examine the constitutionality of the independent agency. He further opined that one should examine whether a branch expands its power at the expense of other constitutional branches. Do you think this level of judicial endorsement of administrative unity cuts across civil law/common law and presidential system/parliamentary system divides?

III. SEPARATION OF POWERS AND GOVERNMENT SYSTEMS

The separation of powers is widely accepted as a core constitutional doctrine, and is premised on the divisibility of power. The doctrine has two aspects: a *horizontal* separation between the legislative, executive and judicial branches of the central government; and a *vertical* separation among levels of the government, in either a federal or a unitary system. This section addresses the horizontal aspect of the doctrine.

The principle of the separation of powers originated from the work of European philosophers like John Locke and Baron de Montesquieu, who stated that

> when the legislature and the executive powers are united in the same person, or in the same body of magistrates, there can be no liberty; because apprehensions may arise, lest the same monarch or senate should enact tyrannical laws, to execute them in a tyrannical manner. Again, there is no liberty, if the power of judging be not separated from the legislative and executive powers.[27]

This notion of government was adopted during the founding era of the United States. *Federalist No 47* noted that the accumulation of all powers in one hand constituted 'the very definition of tyranny'.[28] Despite its Western origin, the separation of powers principle finds expression in many contemporary Asian constitutions. Asian states with a strong parliamentary tradition may modify their system by enhancing the powers of a formerly ceremonial presidency, as in Singapore. Others with robust presidential systems may retain a premier to co-ordinate with the president. For example, both South Korea and Taiwan have directly elected presidencies, but they have also retained a premier who is answerable to parliament in respect of daily operations. These mixed elements within modified parliamentary or presidential systems have given rise to constitutional conflicts between or among political branches, which may call for judicial resolution or, *in extremis*, military intervention.

For comparative purposes, this chapter is organised using the traditional categories of parliamentary and presidential systems. Jurisdictions where the president commands significant executive power and serves as the head of state, including presidential and so-called presidential systems, are discussed under the category 'Presidential System'. Table 3.2 shows the different categories of government systems in Asia.

However, the dichotomy of parliamentary and presidential systems cannot capture the complexity and dynamics of how the separation of powers operates within Asian constitutions. Cognisant of this, this section examines the institutionalisation and operation of the separation of powers in Asia in three types of government systems – parliamentary, presidential and unique systems.

Table 3.2 Government Systems in Asia

Systems	Parliamentary System	Presidential/Semi-Presidential System	Unique System
States	Japan, Thailand, Malaysia, India, Singapore, Mongolia, Cambodia, Bangladesh	Philippines, Indonesia, South Korea, Taiwan, Pakistan, Sri Lanka	China, Myanmar, Brunei, Vietnam, Hong Kong

---

[27] Baron de Montesquieu, *The Spirit of the Laws, vol 1*, Thomas Nugent (trans) (New York: Hafner, c1949) at 221–73.

[28] A Hamilton, J Madison and J Jay, *Federalist No 47*, BF Wright (ed) (Cambridge: Belknap Press, 1961) at 336.

A. Parliamentary System

About half of the Asian states adopt the parliamentary system of government, including India, Malaysia, Singapore, Japan, Thailand, Mongolia, Cambodia and Bangladesh. Many of them were influenced by their colonial history. In the parliamentary system, the legitimacy of the executive branch is built on the confidence it enjoys in the legislature. Two issues are germane: first, the extent of executive autonomy within the parliamentary system; and, secondly, the resolution of gridlocks between the executive and legislative branches.

i. The Legislative Power in the Parliamentary System

In a parliamentary democracy, the legislature is the symbol of popular sovereignty, deriving legitimacy from its representative nature. As John Locke observed:

> [I]t is in their legislative, that the members of a commonwealth are united, and combined together into one coherent living body. This is the soul that gives form, life, and unity, to the common-wealth: from hence the several members have their mutual influence, sympathy, and connexion: and therefore, when the legislative is broken, or dissolved, dissolution and death follows: for the essence and union of the society consisting in having one will, the legislative, when once established by the majority, has the declaring, and as it were keeping of that will. The constitution of the legislative is the first and fundamental act of society, whereby provision is made for the continuation of their union, under the direction of persons, and bonds of laws, made by persons authorized thereunto, by the consent and appointment of the people, without which no one man, or number of men, amongst them, can have authority of making laws that shall be binding to the rest.[29]

The main functions of the legislature generally include representation, deliberation, legislation, authorising expenditure and the formation of governments. In most parliamentary democracies, the executive government is made up of members of the legislature. Its power varies, depending on:

(a) whether the legislature is unicameral or bicameral;
(b) the extent to which it shares its power with the executive;
(c) the party system; and
(d) electoral rules.

Consider the following examples. Japan's legislature is bicameral. Articles 41 and 42 of the Japan Constitution give the Diet exclusive power to make laws, establishing two houses: the House of Representatives and the House of Councillors. The superior House of Representatives is vested with the power to propose a budget without the consent of the House of Councillors,[30] appoint the Prime Minster without the approval of the House of Councillors,[31] and override a rejection of legislation by the House of Councillors by a two-thirds vote.[32] The power of the House of Councillors is much

---

[29] J Locke, *Second Treatise of Civil Government* (Oxford: Basil Blackwell, 1690), § 212.
[30] Art 69, Constitution of Japan.
[31] Art 67, Constitution of Japan.
[32] Art 59(2), Constitution of Japan.

more limited, but its two-third majority is needed alongside that of the House of Representatives if the Constitution is to be amended.[33]

In contrast, Singapore has a unicameral legislature consisting of 87 elected seats and up to 18 non-elected seats.[34] Article 38 of the Constitution vests legislative power in both the President and Parliament, even though the powers of the former are nominal. In line with the Westminster convention, Article 58 stipulates that law-making power is exercised by 'bills passed by Parliament and assented to by the President'. Although most bills are Government initiated, Article 59(1) provides that any Member of Parliament (MP) may introduce a bill before Parliament. The non-elected MPs, namely the Non-Constituency MPs (NCMPs) and the Nominated MPs (NMPs), provided for under Article 39, have truncated powers, compared to elected MPs, and may not bring any bill to amend the Constitution or vote on a non-confidence motion against the Government. The rationale for having NCMPs was to guarantee opposition political parties a minimum number of seats in Parliament. As for NMPs, a Special Select Committee is charged with selecting persons who have rendered 'distinguished public service, or who have brought honour to the Republic, or who have distinguished themselves in the field of arts and letters, culture, the sciences, business, industry, the professions, social or community service or the labour movement'.[35] These individuals are appointed to bring independent, non-partisan perspectives into Parliament. Critics have, however, characterised this as creating an ersatz opposition, to manage public demands for a two- or multi-party system.

Like Japan, India has a bicameral legislature: the Council of States (*Rajya Sabha*) and the House of the People (*Lok Sabha*).[36] Article 80 of the Constitution provides that the *Rajya Sabha* should have a maximum of 250 seats. Of these, 238 members are chosen by the States and the two Union Territories (Delhi and Puducherry), while the remaining 12 members are nominated by the President. Members nominated by the President are persons having special knowledge or practical experience in respect of such matters as literature, science, art and social service. The maximum number of seats of the *Lok Sabha* is 530, all of whom are elected directly by the territorial constituencies in the States. The President shall from time to time summon each House of Parliament to meet. He may prorogue either House or both Houses. However, the *Rajya Sabha* cannot be dissolved. Instead, a third of its members will retire at the expiration of every second year.[37] The *Lok Sabha*, unless dissolved sooner by the President, shall continue for five years from the date appointed for its first meeting.

ii. *Executive Power in a Parliamentary System*

In Westminster-style parliamentary systems, the two political branches of government are the Cabinet and parliament. The Cabinet is typically formed by the party holding the majority of seats in parliament, or by a coalition of parties where there is no major-

---

[33] Art 33, ibid. See CF Goodman, *The Rule of Law in Japan: A Comparative Analysis* (Frederick: Aspen Pub, 2008) at 38.

[34] Thio, above n 7, at 369–72.

[35] Fourth Schedule, Constitution of the Republic of Singapore.

[36] Art 79, Constitution of India.

[37] Art 83, Constitution of India.

ity government. The leader of the majority party serves as the prime minister and he appoints his Cabinet ministers. Following the principle of parliamentary sovereignty, the parliament has the power to determine all matters concerning its function, although it may delegate part of the power to executive agencies. In reality, the Cabinet wields tremendous powers and determines state policy, despite being formally answerable to the Parliament under the doctrine of ministerial responsibility. This phenomenon is evident in all jurisdictions where the parliamentary system is practised.

Japan is a prime example. Article 65 of the Constitution allocates executive power to the Cabinet headed by a Prime Minister, who is responsible to the Diet. During Diet sessions, the Prime Minister is questioned by legislators, but the Diet normally accepts the Cabinet's policies even though it can reject or amend them.[38] The Cabinet is responsible for preparing and proposing the annual budget, managing foreign and domestic policy, supervising the civil service, administering the branches of the government, and proposing bills to the Diet.[39] Despite the principle of parliamentary supervision of executive action, the executive dominates within the parliamentary system. In Japan, the Liberal Democratic Party (LDP) held power for almost 60 years.[40]

Although Article 41 of the Japanese Constitution makes the Diet the sole law-making body, most legislation is actually introduced and promoted by the Cabinet. Diet members have relatively small staffs and must rely on the Cabinet to submit legislative proposals. Moreover, the elected executive officials do not have legislative staff of their own to draft legislation for Diet action, so they rely on state departments and agencies. Consequently, any bill emerging from the Cabinet will be highly influenced by the bureaucracy.[41]

The main check against a strong Cabinet and bureaucracy is the existence of the dissenting factions within the political party. In Japan, the Cabinet is made up of representatives of different factions within the LDP. These factional representatives are not beholden to the Prime Minister for their position but to the leaders of their respective factions. Accordingly, disputes between faction leaders are the cause of most arguments in Cabinet, but the public seldom see this.[42] Once the Government settles its internal disputes over legislation and policy, it must then negotiate with the minority party. This was especially the case in recent years, when the LDP had to lead a coalition government involving other political parties. A two-stage coalition consensus process takes place: the LDP coalition must first agree on a common position, before negotiating with its coalition partners to secure their agreement.

The description of Japan's system is equally applicable to Singapore, where the ruling People's Action Party (PAP) has been in power continuously since 1959. The PAP has been so dominant in Parliament, and so strict in terms of party discipline, that it has never had to negotiate legislation or policy with anyone. Strict party discipline compels party members to vote according to the party's line and, as a result, no legislation has ever been defeated. The number of opposition party members in Singapore's Parliament

---

[38] Goodman, above n 33, at 43.

[39] Art 73, Constitution of Japan.

[40] The LDP has been in power since 1955. It lost power between 1993 and 1994; and then again between 2009 and 2012.

[41] Goodman, above n 33, at 36.

[42] Harumi Hori, *The Changing Japanese Political System: the Liberal Democratic Party and the Ministry of Finance* (New York: Routledge, 2005) at 48–49.

is too negligible for them to act as a check on the **PAP** Cabinet. However, the transformation of the office of the President into an elected one has instituted some checks on the legislature.

Since 1991, the President is empowered to exercise a personal discretion in relation to specific matters, including:

(a) withholding assent to any Bill under Articles 22E, 22H, 144(2) or 148A;
(b) withholding concurrence to any guarantee or loan to be given or raised by the Government;[43]
(c) withholding concurrence and approval to appointments and budgets of the statutory boards and Government companies under Articles 22A and 22C;
(d) disapproving of transactions referred to in Articles 22B(7), 22D(6) or 148G;
(e) withholding concurrence under Article 151(4) in relation to the detention or further detention of any person under any law or ordinance made or promulgated in pursuance of Part XII (Special Powers Against Subversion and Emergency Powers);
(f) the exercise of his functions under section 12 of the Maintenance of Religious Harmony Act 1990; and
(g) any other constitutionally mandated exercise of discretion.[44]

The President is also authorised to have access to any information concerning the Government which is available to the Cabinet and any statutory board or government company under his purview, and under the discretion, he may also withhold his assent to any Bill which 'provides, directly or indirectly, for the circumvention or curtailment of the discretionary powers conferred upon him by this Constitution'.[45]

iii. *Vote of No Confidence and Dissolution of the Parliament*

The Cabinet in a parliamentary democracy depends on legislative support for its legitimacy. If the legislative support wanes, the Cabinet may face a no-confidence motion. This motion might be met by a counter-motion to dissolve parliament and call general elections. This is a distinctive feature of parliamentary systems. Most parliamentary democracies in Asia adopt a system of collective ministerial responsibility under which a no-confidence motion would affect the whole Cabinet.[46] There are, of course, exceptions. For example, Section 158 of the Thai Constitution stipulates that any no-confidence motion can only be directed against individual members of Cabinet. In Asia, political parties have successfully used the no-confidence motion to wrest executive power from the incumbent government.

No-confidence motions in Japan were generally a strategy manipulated by opposition parties, who knew that such motions were unlikely to succeed in the lower House. From 1948 to 1993, four resolutions of no confidence were passed on the Cabinets of Yoshida (1948 and 1953), Ohira (1980) and Miyazawa (1993). Although none of these resulted in the resignation of the Cabinet, the opposition succeeded in

[43] Art 144, Constitution of the Republic of Singapore.
[44] Tan and Thio, above n 6, at 420–24.
[45] Art 22H, Constitution of the Republic of Singapore. See also Tan and Thio, above n 6, at 420–30.
[46] See, eg, Art 69, Constitution of Japan.

getting the Cabinet to propose the dissolution of the lower House and call early elections.[47]

In Nepal, the strategic use of no-confidence motions led to a complete paralysis of the legislature. In November 1994, Mana Mohan Adhikari, leader of the Communist Party of Nepal-United Marxist Leninist, was appointed Prime Minister after his party won the majority of seats in Parliament.[48] In June 1995, as a result of a dispute over a World Bank project, the opposition proposed a motion of no confidence against Adhikari's Government. Seventy Nepali Congress MPs requested King Birenda to hold a special session of Parliament on 15 June. Under pressure, and pursuant to the Prime Minister's recommendation, the King summoned a special parliamentary session, dissolved Parliament and called fresh elections. The King agreed to the Prime Minister's resignation, but requested that he be caretaker Prime Minister and supervise the election.

The opposition parties successfully challenged the legality of the dissolution in the Supreme Court, and this allowed them a second chance to put their no-confidence motion before Parliament.[49] This time, the no-confidence motion succeeded, and in September 1995 the King appointed Sher Bahadur Deuba as Prime Minister, and he formed a coalition government. However, in March 1996, Deuba's Government was challenged by another no-confidence motion filed by the Communist Party of Nepal-Unified Marxist-Leninist.[50] The motion succeeded and Deuba was replaced by Girija Prasad Koirala as Prime Minister. This ushered in a decade of great instability, with changes of Prime Minister practically every year till 2006.

In Thailand, the allegations of corruption against members of Prime Minister Banharn Silipa-archa's Cabinet appeared in the daily newspapers in 1996. By mid-September, the opposition party decided to file a no-confidence motion against the Prime Minister. This motion failed, but partners of the coalition Cabinet forced Banharn to resign, in return for their withdrawing support for the vote of no confidence. Barharn responded by dissolving Parliament after five days of political manipulation, and called for new elections on 17 November. A six-party coalition government was subsequently formed by Chavalit Yongchaiyudh, leader of the National Action Party.[51]

As we have seen, one counterweight to a no-confidence motion is to ask for Parliament to be dissolved and fresh elections held. Generally, in a parliamentary system where the Cabinet fails to command the confidence of the majority in Parliament, those in the leadership of the majority party may respond by forming a new government with a new leader, or ask the head of state to dissolve Parliament and call for fresh elections, causing parliamentarians to face the threat of polls.[52] The dissolution

[47] Mikitaka Masutama and B Nyblade, 'Japan: The Prime Minister and the Japanese Diet' (2004) 10(2–3) *Journal of Legislative Studies* 252; Harumi Hori, *The Changing Japanese Political System: The Liberal Democratic Party and the Ministry of Finance* (New York: Routledge, 2005) at 20–76.

[48] AR Poudyal, 'Nepal in 1995: The Communist-Rule Experiment' (1996) 36(2) *Asian Survey* 212.

[49] Hassall and Saunders, above n 10, at 83; Poudyal, above n 48, at 212.

[50] K Hachhethu, 'Nepal in 1996: Experimenting With A Coalition Government' (1997) 37(2) *Asian Survey* 150.

[51] Hassall and Saunders, above n 10, at 83; DE King, 'Thailand in 1996: Economic Slowdown Clouds Year' (1997) 37(2) *Asian Survey* 160.

[52] A Sajó, *Limiting Government: An Introduction to Constitutionalism* (New York: Central European University Press, 1999) 126.

of Parliament sometimes raises constitutional issues which require judicial resolution. Two cases serve to illustrate the difficulties confronted by the courts, given the highly political nature of these situations.

In the Japanese case of *Action for Recognition of the Status as a Member of the House of Representatives and a Claim for Remuneration*, the Supreme Court was asked to consider the legality of a dissolution. Under Article 7(3) of the Constitution of Japan, the Emperor may dissolve the House of Representatives on the Cabinet's advice and with its approval. However, if the House of Representatives passes a no-confidence resolution or rejects a confidence motion, the Cabinet must resign *en masse* unless the House is itself dissolved within 10 days.[53] The Supreme Court had to rule on whether the House could be dissolved only under the conditions of Article 69. In *Rameshwar Prasad & Ors v Union of India & Anor*, the Supreme Court of India had to consider whether the notification of dissolution of the Bihar Legislative Assembly was unconditional.

Action for Recognition of the Status as a Member of the House of Representatives and a Claim for Remuneration
14 Minshū 1206 (Supreme Court, Japan)

Facts

On 28 August 1952, the House of Representatives was dissolved by the Cabinet. A politician who was a member of the House of Representatives filed a suit claiming that he had not lost the seat in the House of Representatives since the dissolution of the House under Article 7 of the Constitution was unconstitutional.

Held

As is evident in these arguments, the primary points of dispute concerning the voidness of the dissolution are obviously whether the dissolution in the present case should be found to be void since it did not fulfil the requirements of Article 69, but was based upon Article 7 of the Constitution, and whether the cabinet's advice and approval had been lawfully given regarding the dissolution as provided by Article 7 of the Constitution.

However, whether the dissolution of the House of Representatives which had actually taken place was void by law because of the wrongful application of the chapters and provisions of the Constitution on which the dissolution was based or whether it was void for the lack of advice and approval of the cabinet which are required by the Constitution should be regarded as beyond the power of review by the court.

The Constitution established the separation of the legislative, administrative and judicial powers and provided that the entire judicial power is to be exercised by the court (Article 76, para 1 of the Constitution), and the Law on Courts provides that the court handles all judicial disputes (Article 3, para 1), thus, not only civil and criminal cases, but also administrative cases, without limiting the matters, universally fall within the jurisdiction of the judicial court . . .

However, even under the system of separation of powers under the Constitution, the exercise of judicial power is not immune from a certain limit, and it should not be hastily concluded that all acts are subject to judicial review without a limit. Acts such as a highly

---

[53] Art 69, Constitution of Japan.

political act of the state which is directly related to the ruling of the nation are outside the scope of judicial review even if they are disputes in law and the determination of their validity is legally possible, and the determination shall be left to the political section such as the cabinet and Parliament which bears political responsibility vis à vis the people who are the sovereigns, and shall be left ultimately to the political will of the people . . .

Dissolution of the House of Representatives deprives the members of their status as members of the House against their will and suspends the functioning of the House which is an essential part of the Parliament which is the supreme body of the nation, and by the subsequent general election, triggers the creation of a new House of Representatives and a cabinet, and therefore, its significance under the law of the nation is undeniable. Furthermore, dissolution takes place mostly when the cabinet intends to find out the general view of the people concerning the cabinet's important policies and subsequently, the continuation of the cabinet, and therefore, its political significance is extremely grave. Thus, the dissolution of the House of Representatives is a highly political act of the state involving the basis of ruling the nation and as explained above, it is evident that reviewing the legal validity of such an act is beyond the power of the court. The same applies when, as is in the present case, the dissolution of the House of Representatives is the preliminary issue in a litigation; in both instances, the matter is beyond judicial review.

There is no dispute that the dissolution in question has taken place on the basis of Article 7 of the Constitution, and the view of the cabinet is that even in cases where Article 69 of the Constitution is not applicable, the House of Representatives can be dissolved constitutionally lawfully and effectively by Article 7. It is evident that [since] the dissolution in the present case has been effected on the basis of Article 7 of the Constitution with the advice and approval of the cabinet, the court is unable to deny this view of the cabinet and find the dissolution in the present case to be void under the Constitution . . .

Justices Kotani Katsushige & Okuno Kenichi (concurring opinion)

Under the system of a parliamentary government, the existence and continuation of the cabinet is conditional on the trust of the House of Representatives, and if the cabinet loses this trust, in principle, it has to resign as a matter of course, but the Constitution allows an exceptional counter-measure to the cabinet by way of dissolving the House of Representatives and putting the question of confidence to the people as sovereigns – this is Article 69 of the Constitution. In such cases, the cabinet has to choose between dissolution and resignation. As indicated above, the dissolution of the House of Representatives is a system by which the cabinet appeals to the people and asks for their views. There are many instances other than the adoption of a vote of no-confidence or the rejection of a vote of confidence in the cabinet, such as where an important bill which is submitted by the cabinet or a budget is rejected, where the cabinet needs to ask for the views of the people, there is a doubt as to whether the House of Representatives truly reflects the view of the people in cases where there were changes in the number of members of the political parties, or a new and important situation has emerged inside or outside Japan so that there is a necessity to ask for the views of the people afresh, which would require dissolution other than the instances provided under Article 69. If dissolution is only possible in the cases provided under Article 69, in all of the above instances, dissolution is not available, particularly since under the system of parliamentary government, under which it is customary for the majority party to set up the cabinet, there is no real possibility of a vote of no-confidence to be adopted, and thus, in reality, there will be no dissolution of the House of Representatives on the occasions mentioned above.

According to the Constitution, dissolution of the House of Representatives takes place in accordance with Article 7 of the Constitution, but this provision does not limit the occasion of dissolution. Therefore, Article 69 provides for one of the instances where dissolution of the House of Representatives is available, and should not be construed as not allowing dissolution on other occasions . . .

Kawamura Daisuke (concurring opinion)

In the grounds of appeal, it is argued that the House of Representatives should be dissolved only in the cases provided by Article 69 of the Constitution and that dissolution such as the present one merely based upon Article 7 is unconstitutional and therefore void. However, Article 69 provides for the resignation of the cabinet in cases of no-confidence of the parliament. Since there is a clause stating 'unless the House of Representatives is dissolved' in this provision, it can be said that it presupposes dissolution, but it is obvious that it does not contain a meaning that dissolution unrelated to this provision is generally impermissible. . . .

Moreover, since the Constitution is understood not to allow voluntary dissolution, it is evident at least that the power of dissolution does not belong to the legislature or the judiciary. Also from this viewpoint, it cannot be understood otherwise than that the Constitution has left the decision of dissolution to the cabinet. It is argued that under the system of the parliamentary government in which the existence and continuation of the cabinet is based upon the trust of the parliament, it is an extreme contradiction to grant a general power of dissolution, since it means that the status of the parliament as the supreme organ of the nation is eroded. However, it is the requirement of the principle of the separation of powers that the balance and control of the powers of the legislature and administration are maintained, and the aim of the system in which the administration puts the issue to the people in a general election in order to constrain the abuse or excess of the legislature is not necessarily against the idea of the supremacy of the legislature. In fact, in the case of Article 69, the fact that the cabinet is granted the power to dissolve the House of Representatives as a countermeasure against the vote of no-confidence also demonstrates that the cabinet is granted an independent power. Furthermore, dissolution results not only in the curtailment of the term of the members of the House of Representatives, but also in the resignation of the cabinet after the general election, and in the end, the balance between the two powers is maintained, since on the one hand, the House of Representatives is dissolved, and on the other hand, the cabinet resigns. Therefore, the criticism of the supremacy of the administration or disrespect for the legislature is not justifiable.

Thus, in sum, the dissolution in the present case which took place in accordance with the method of Article 7 of the Constitution is not unlawful as argued.

Rameshwar Prasad & Ors v Union of India & Anor
[2006] AIR SC 980 (Supreme Court, India)

Facts

The Bihar Legislative Assembly comprises 243 members, and 122 members are required to secure an absolute majority. In the 2005 election in the State of Bihar, two major alliances each obtained 92 seats. In normal circumstances the Governor should be the leader of majority party in the Legislative Assembly. However, no political party or coalition had the sufficient majority to form the Government. A notification was issued on 7 March 2005 under Article 356 of the Constitution empowering the President to govern Bihar, and its Assembly was kept in suspended animation. On 23 May 2005, the President issued a notification to dissolve the Bihar Assembly to prevent further political turbulence. However, the petitioners believed the dissolution to be a fraud since it was issued just at the point when one political alliance, the National Democratic Alliance, had the support of over 135 Legislative Assembly members and the Government was about to be formed. One question of far-reaching consequence was whether the dissolution of Assembly under Article 356(1) could be ordered to prevent a majority from staking a claim to government, on the ground that the majority had been obtained by illegal means.

YK Sabharwal CJI

Under Article 356 of the Constitution, the dissolution of an Assembly can be ordered on the satisfaction that a situation has arisen in which the Government of the State cannot be carried on in accordance with the Constitution. Such a satisfaction can be reached by the President on receipt of report from the Governor of a State or otherwise. It is permissible to arrive at the satisfaction on receipt of the report from Governor and on other material. Such a satisfaction can also be reached only on the report of the Governor. It is also permissible to reach such a conclusion even without the report of the Governor in case the President has other relevant material for reaching the satisfaction contemplated by Article 356. The expression 'or otherwise' is of wide amplitude.

In the present case, it is not in dispute that the satisfaction that a situation has arisen in which the Government of State cannot be carried on in accordance with the provisions of the Constitution has been arrived at only on the basis of the reports of the Governor. It is not the case of the Union of India that it has relied upon any material other than the reports of the Governor which have been earlier reproduced in extenso. The Governor in the report dated 6th March, 2005 has referred to *Bommai's* case as also to the recommendations of Sarkaria Commission. Sarkaria Commission Report in Chapter IV deals extensively with the role of the Governors. Since in this case, the dissolution of the Assembly is based solely on the reports of the Governor and the issue also is as to the role played by the Governor and submissions also having been made on [the] role which is expected from a high constitutional functionary like Governor, it would be useful to first examine that aspect . . .

The role of the Governor has been a key issue in the matters of Central–State relations. The Constitution of India envisages three tiers of Government the Union, State and the Local Self-Government . . .

Referring to Article 356 of the Constitution, the Court reasoned that 'one highly significant role which he (Governor) has to play under the Constitution is of making a report where he finds that a situation has arisen in which the Government of the State cannot be carried on in accordance with the provisions of the Constitution' and further added that the Governor 'is not amenable to the directions of the Government of India, nor is he accountable to them for the manner in which he carries out his functions and duties. He is an independent constitutional office which is not subject to the control of the Government of India.' . . .

Querying as to what could be an objective and representative body which will fit into our Constitutional framework to facilitate the appointment of Governors on meritorious basis, the Sarkaria Commission has observed that 'There is no gainsaying that a procedure must be devised which can ensure objectivity in selection and adherence to the criteria for selection and insulate the system from political pressures. Also, the new procedure must not only be fair but should be seen to be fair.' . . .

The expression 'required' found in Article 163(1) is stated to signify that the Governor can exercise his discretionary powers only if there is a compelling necessity to do so. It has been reasoned that the expression 'by or under the Constitution' means that the necessity to exercise such powers may arise from any express provision of the Constitution or by necessary implication. The Sarkaria Commission Report further adds that such necessity may arise even from rules and orders made 'under' the Constitution. Observing that the Governor needs to discharge 'dual responsibility' – to the Union and the State – the Sarkaria Commission has sought to evaluate the role of the Governors in certain controversial circumstances, such as, in appointing the Chief Minister, in ascertaining the majority, in dismissal of the Chief Minister, in dissolving the Legislative Assembly, in recommending President's Rule and in reserving Bills for [the] President's consideration . . .

Despite best efforts, if ultimately a viable Ministry fails to emerge, a Governor is faced with two alternatives he may either dissolve the Assembly or recommend President's rule under Article 356, leaving it to the Union Government to decide the question of dissolution. The Commission expressed its firm view that the proper course would be 'to allow the people of the State to settle matters themselves'. The Commission recommended that 'the Governor should first consider dissolving the Assembly and arranging for a fresh election and before taking a decision, he should consult the leaders of the political parties concerned and the Chief Election Commissioner.'

. . . It is in this context that the Governor says that instead of installing a Government based on a majority achieved by a distortion of the system, it would be preferable that the people/electorate could be provided with one more opportunity to seek the mandate of the people. This approach makes it evident that the object was to prevent a particular political party from staking a claim and not the professed object of anxiety not to permit the distortion of the political system, as sought to be urged. Such a course is nothing but wholly illegal and irregular and has to be described as mala fide. The recommendation for dissolution of the Assembly to prevent the staking of claim to form the Government purportedly on the ground that the majority was achieved by distortion of system by allurement, corruption and bribery was based on such general assumptions without any material which are quite easy to be made if any political party not gaining absolute majority is to be kept out of governance . . .

The constitutionalism or constitutional system of Government abhors absolutism it is premised on the Rule of Law in which subjective satisfaction is substituted by objectivity provided by the provisions of the Constitution itself. This line is clear also from *Maru Ram v Union of India & Ors* [(1981) 1 SCC 107]. It would also be clear on in depth examination of *Bommai* that declared the dissolution of three Assemblies illegal[,] but before we further revert to that decision, a brief historical background including the apprehension of its abuse expressed by our founding fathers may be noted. Articles 355 and 356 of the Constitution set the tenor for the precedence of the Union over the States. It has been explained that the rationale for introducing Article 355 was to distinctly demarcate the functioning of the State and Union governments and to prevent any form of unprincipled invasions by the Union into the affairs of the State. It was felt that through the unambiguous language of Articles 355 and 356, the Union shall be constitutionally obliged to interfere only under certain limited circumstances as laid down in the provisions . . .

The language of Article 356(1) is very wide. It is desirable that conventions are developed channelizing the exercise of this power. The Court can interfere only when the power is used in a grossly perverse and unreasonable manner so as to constitute patent misuse of the provisions [or an] abuse of power. The same idea is expressed at another place saying that if 'a constitutionally or legally prohibited or extraneous or collateral purpose is sought to be achieved' by the proclamation, it would be liable to be struck down. The question whether the majority party in the Legislative Assembly of a State has become totally estranged from the electorate is not a matter for the Court to determine.

The assessment of the Central Government that a fresh chance should be given to the electorate in certain States as well as the question when to dissolve the Legislative Assemblies are not matters alien to Article 356. It cannot be said that the reasons assigned by the Central Government for the steps taken by them are not relevant to the purposes underlying Article 356 . . .

Notes and Questions

1. The decision to choose between presidential or parliamentary systems of government is one some Asian states have had to make in the aftermath of democratic transition. In his article 'The New Separation of Powers' (2000) 113 *Harvard Law Review* 633, Bruce Ackerman argues that new democracies tend to adopt the German-style constrained parliamentary system rather than the US presidential system, because the competition between the US President and Congress for control over the administrative apparatus makes for an excessively politicised style of bureaucratic government that casts the executive power as an enemy of the rule of law. In rebuttal, Steven Calabresi cited 10 reasons why the presidential system ('US model') is more democratic, stable, protective of judicial review and libertarian than parliamentary regimes ('German model of constrained parliamentarianism'). In sum, the 10 reasons are:

    (a) the US style of separation of powers is more democratic since it has a dual election system;
    (b) the US model is more stable since both executive and legislative branches are elected to serve a fixed term;
    (c) the presidential system is more legitimate since the head of government is indirectly elected by open election rather than by the elites in the political party;
    (d) the American model is preferred over the German model as it can enhance democratic control of the Cabinet and of bureaucracy;
    (e) the US model is preferred because presidentialism gave rise to a flourishing, stable and democracy-enhancing two-party system;
    (f) the US model is preferable because it is less ideological than the German model;
    (g) the US model is more compatible with a strong system of judicial review;
    (h) the US model is more compatible with bicameralism and a federal system;
    (i) presidential regimes may be better at fighting and winning wars than parliamentary systems; and
    (j) presidential systems of government have a greater capacity to preserve liberty and the status quo.

    See SG Calabresi, 'Virtues of Presidential Government: Why Professor Ackerman is Wrong to Prefer the German to the US Constitution' (2001) 18 *Constitutional Commentary* 51. Consider and compare their arguments.

2. One view in support of a parliamentary system is that it is more stable since powers are shared in proportion to seats in lieu of a 'winner-takes-all' model in a presidential system. However, as we noted above, the experiences of Japan and Thailand in recent decades buck the trend. The fate of former Thai Prime Minister Samak Sundaravej is instructive. For more than seven years, Samak hosted the popular television show 'Tasting-Grumbling'. He stopped appearing on the show in April 2008, two months after he became Prime Minister. However, the few shows he participated in during that period prompted a group of senators to bring a complaint before the Counter Corruption Commission in Thailand, which eventually forwarded the matter to the Constitutional Court. The nine-member Court unanimously held that Samak had breached a conflict-of-interest law by hosting the cooking shows while in office. While Samak was not paid for his appearances, he did receive 2,350 Baht (about US$80) for transport and purchase of ingredients for each of the four shows. The Court deemed these payments to constitute the cultivation of a business interest. After initial hesitation, the Samak stepped down and paved the way for his deputy, Somchai Wongsawat, to replace him. The Constitutional Court decision came just two weeks after anti-government protesters blockaded the Prime Minister's office, and it appeared that Samak was losing control of the capital. The confrontation also impacted financial markets and the tourism industry, raising fears of violence or a possible military coup.

3. The other argument in favour of a parliamentary system is that it is less likely to be captive to strong leaders, whereas the all-or-nothing nature of presidential elections tends to polarise the polity, such as in South Korea and Taiwan. However, for present purposes, consider Singapore's first Prime Minister Lee Kuan Yew, former Malaysian Prime Minister Mahathir Mohamed and former Thai Prime Minister Thaksin Shinawata. Their personalities and parliamentary majorities made them very 'strong leaders' while in office. Do you think they would have been even stronger under a presidential system?

4. One scholar characterised modern Japan as a dual state: one nominally run by elected ministers and politicians, and the other controlled by the strong bureaucracy. Although the Liberal Democratic Party (LDP) has dominated the parliaments and Cabinets of Japan since 1955, intra-party factional politics has, from time to time, weakened the LDP's governing capacity. This political weakness has in turn led to the increase in the bureaucracy's powers, especially since the latter has always enjoyed a very high degree of autonomy in policy-making process. See E Kawabata, *Contemporary Government Reform in Japan: the Dual State in Flux* (New York: Palgrave Macmillan, 2006) 36.

5. In *Rameshwar Prasad v Union of India* (above), it was argued that the dissolution of the Bihar Legislative Assembly 'was achieved by distortion of system by allurement, corruption and bribery'. The use of dissolution to combat corruption is a far cry from the original idea of using dissolution to resolve political deadlocks and to ensure inter-branch checks and balances. Do you think the power of dissolution was misused in this case? Anti-corruption laws are designed to promote the integrity of individual officials. Yet the dissolution process in India was used to hold members of assembly collectively accountable to the people. Why do you think the Indian Supreme Court resorted to a higher constitutional mechanism of

collective responsibility? See, for example, C Raj Kumar, 'Corruption, Development and Good Governance: Challenges for Promoting Access to Justice in Asia,' (2008) 16 *Michigan State Journal of International Law* 475; A Verma, 'Cultural Roots of Police Corruption in India' (1999) 22 *Policing: An International Journal of Police Strategies & Management* 264.

B. Presidential System

In a typical presidential system, the president and the legislature are elected directly by the people for fixed terms. The president serves as head of state and head of government, commanding and overseeing the operation of the executive government, and has power to appoint ministers and senior government officers. These appointees cannot be members of the legislature at the same time, and legislative members wishing to serve in government must resign their seats in the legislature.[54]

The American presidential system is the prototype of this political system. The US President wields tremendous powers, including the power, as Army and Navy Commander-in-Chief, to declare war; to make treaties with the advice and consent of the Senate; to grant pardons; appoint Supreme Court Judges; and ensure that laws are executed.

Many Asian states adopted a presidential system either at the beginning of the state-building process, or in the midst of political change and constitutional reform. The presidents of Indonesia, the Philippines, South Korea, Taiwan, the Executive President of Sri Lanka and the Chief Executive Official of Hong Kong Special Administrative Region are examples of such presidencies. This section explores the operation and controversies in relation to presidential systems in Asia. It first discusses presidential powers in relation to foreign and domestic affairs, and then proceeds to examine presidential immunity, followed by the institution and process of presidential impeachment.

i. Domestic Affairs

Among the powers Asian constitutions confer on their presidents are powers relating to commanding armed forces, declaring war, issuing emergency decrees, and granting amnesty and pardons. Only the President of Taiwan enjoys the power to dissolve the legislature after consultation with the President of the Congress. Table 3.3 sets out a comparison of presidential powers in Asian states.

The exercise of presidential power in these presidential systems has often given rise to political controversies, which sometimes require judicial resolution. For example, in the Philippines, the Constitution gives the President tremendous executive power, but does this include the power to oppose the return of deposed dictator Ferdinand Marcos? This was the question before the Philippines Supreme Court in the following case.

---

[54] R Hague and M Harrop, *Political Science: A Comparative Introduction* (New York: Palgrave Macmillan, 2010) at 321.

Table 3.3 Powers of the President in South Korea, Taiwan, the Philippines, Indonesia and Sri Lanka

Presidential powers	South Korea	Taiwan	Philippines	Indonesia	Sri Lanka
Appoint important officials	✓	✓	✓	✓	✓
Issue emergency decree	✓	✓	✓	✓	✓
Return bill to Parliament upon objection	✓	✓			
Commander-in Chief of all armed forces	✓	✓	✓	✓	✓
Declare martial law	✓	✓	✓		
Declare war	✓	✓	✓	✓	✓
Grant amnesty and pardon	✓	✓	✓	✓	✓
Dissolve legislature after consulting with the leader of the legislature		✓			
Attend and address the legislature	✓		✓		✓

Ferdinand E Marcos et al v Honorable Raul Manglapus et al
177 SCRA 668 (1989) (Supreme Court, Philippines)

Facts

In February 1986, President Ferdinand E Marcos was deposed from the presidency via the non-violent 'people power' revolution and forced into exile in Hawaii. In his stead, Corazon C Aquino was declared President of the Republic under a revolutionary government. The Philippines, however, suffered from both political and economic crisis. Rabid followers of Marcos created armed threats, and the communists set up a parallel government in areas they effectively controlled, while the separatists in the south were virtually free to move about in armed bands. In addition, crushing foreign debt and empty coffers caused by the plundering of Marcos and his cronies left the economy devastated. Efforts by the Aquino Government to resuscitate the economy had yet to show concrete results after three years. In 1989, Marcos was desperately ill and expressed a wish to return to the Philippines to die. Aquino, considering the dire consequences of his return at such a time, stood firm on the decision to bar Marcos and his family from returning. Marcos questioned the constitutionality of Aquino's decision.

Cortes J

As stated above, the Constitution provides that '[t]he executive power shall be vested in the President of the Philippines.' [Art VII, Sec 1] However, it does not define what is meant by executive power' although in the same article it touches on the exercise of certain powers by the President, ie, the power of control over all executive departments, bureaus and offices, the power to execute the laws, the appointing power, the powers under the commander-in-chief clause, the power to grant reprieves, commutations and pardons, the power to grant amnesty with the concurrence of Congress, the power to contract or guarantee foreign loans, the power to enter into treaties or international agreements, the power to submit the budget to Congress, and the power to address Congress [Art VII, Sec 14–23].

The inevitable question then arises: by enumerating certain powers of the President did the framers of the Constitution intend that the President shall exercise those specific powers and no other? Are these enumerated powers the breadth and scope of 'executive power'? . . .

We do not say that the presidency is what Mrs Aquino says it is or what she does but, rather, that the consideration of tradition and the development of presidential power under the different constitutions are essential for a complete understanding of the extent of and limitations to the President's powers under the 1987 Constitution . . .

It would not be accurate, however, to state that 'executive power' is the power to enforce the laws, for the President is head of state as well as head of government and whatever powers [in here] in such positions pertain to the office unless the Constitution itself withholds it. Furthermore, the Constitution itself provides that the execution of the laws is only one of the powers of the President. It also grants the President other powers that do not involve the execution of any provision of law, eg, his power over the country's foreign relations.

On these premises, we hold the view that although the 1987 Constitution imposes limitations on the exercise of specific powers of the President, it maintains intact what is traditionally considered as within the scope of 'executive power.' Corollarily, the powers of the President cannot be said to be limited only to the specific powers enumerated in the Constitution. In other words, executive power is more than the sum of specific powers so enumerated . . .

Faced with the problem of whether or not the time is right to allow the Marcoses to return to the Philippines, the President is, under the Constitution, constrained to consider these basic principles in arriving at a decision. More than that, having sworn to defend and uphold the Constitution, the President has the obligation under the Constitution to protect the people, promote their welfare and advance the national interest . . .

To the President, the problem is one of balancing the general welfare and the common good against the exercise of rights of certain individuals. The power involved is the President's residual power to protect the general welfare of the people. It is founded on the duty of the President, as steward of the people . . .

That the President has the power under the Constitution to bar the Marcoses from returning has been recognized by members of the Legislature, and is manifested by the Resolution proposed in the House of Representatives and signed by 103 of its members urging the President to allow Mr Marcos to return to the Philippines 'as a genuine unselfish gesture for true national reconciliation and as irrevocable proof of our collective adherence to uncompromising respect for human rights under the Constitution and our laws.'

. . . What we are saying in effect is that the request or demand of the Marcoses to be allowed to return to the Philippines cannot be considered in the light solely of the constitutional provisions guaranteeing liberty of abode and the right to travel, subject to certain exceptions, or of case law which clearly never contemplated situations even remotely similar to the present one. It must be treated as a matter that is appropriately addressed to those residual unstated powers of the President which are implicit in and correlative to the paramount duty residing in that office to safeguard and protect general welfare. In that context, such request or demand should submit to the exercise of a broader discretion on the part of the President to determine whether it must be granted or denied . . .

A similar controversy arose in South Korea when President Roh Moo-hyun advocated a proposition for a national confidence referendum. The proposition was politically contentious and was challenged in court. The Constitutional Court of Korea dismissed the claim on the basis that the President's statement by and in itself might not be deemed a legally binding decision or measure taken concerning the implementation of a national referendum, nor did such a statement affect the legal status of the citizens.

President's Proposition for National Confidence Referendum Case
2003Hun-Ma694, 27 Nov 2003 (Constitutional Court, South Korea)

Facts

In a speech delivered at the 243rd plenary session of the National Assembly on 13 October 2003, President Roh Moo-hyn stated that he intended to call a national referendum on or around 15 December 2003 to seek a nationwide endorsement of his presidency. The complainants argued that President Roh's statement was unconstitutional since the referendum was not associated with any important policy and thus violated Article 72 of the Constitution and infringed upon their right to pursue happiness, freedom of conscience, right to vote, property right and certain other rights.

Held

A process of national referendum may be legally initiated only when the President publicly announces the national referendum by identifying a specific subject matter. Under the current National Referendum Act, a national referendum is to proceed in the order of the public announcement of the proposal of a national referendum (Article 49), the notice upon the proposal of national referendum (Article 22), the campaign on national referendum (Article 26), the preparation of poll books (Article 14(1)), voting (Article 50), ballot counting and final decision (Chapters VIII and IX), the publication of the result and the notification thereof to the President and the Speaker of the National Assembly by the National Election Commission (Article 89), and the promulgation of the final decision by the president (Article 91). Therefore, either under the current National Referendum Act or under any statute that may separately be enacted or revised concerning the national referendum, public power is exercised with legal effect only upon an act that may be deemed to legally initiate the national referendum process such as a public announcement. A political proposal or an advance review upon an internal plan for the implementation of a national referendum prior to any such legal act is merely an act of preparation for a matter that has yet to be officially determined, and the plan therefor or the content thereof may always be subject to a change or abrogation. The act of the respondent that is the subject matter in this case is one of such acts. As such, the statement of the respondent, by and in itself, without further, may not be deemed as a legally binding decision or measure taken concerning the implementation of a national referendum, nor does such statement affect the legal status of the citizens . . .

The Executive Presidency was introduced to supplement the parliamentary system in Sri Lanka under the 1972 Constitution. However, in 2002, attempts were made to amend this provision to curtail the President's powers of dissolution. The Sri Lanka Supreme Court was asked to consider the nature of the dissolution power under the Constitution.

In Re The Nineteenth Amendment to the Constitution
(2002) 3 *Sri Lanka Law Reports* 85 (Supreme Court, Sri Lanka)

Facts

On 19 September 2002, a Bill bearing the title '19th Amendment to the Constitution' was proposed. The Amendment dealt broadly with four matters: (a) the appointment of the Prime Minister; (b) the dissolution of the Cabinet of Ministers; (c) the dissolution of Parliament; and (d) the conferment of certain immunities on Members of Parliament. Twenty-four petitions were filed, requesting the Court to rule on the constitutionality of the Amendment. This excerpt deals only with the Supreme Court's holding on the power to dissolve Parliament.

Held

It is clear that according to the framework of our Constitution, the power of dissolution of Parliament is attributed to the President, as a check to sustain and preserve the balance of power that is struck by the Constitution. This power attributed to the President in broad terms in Article 70(1) is subject in its exercise to specifically defined situations as set out in provisos (a) to (c) referred to above. Even in these situations, the final say in the matter of dissolution remains with the President. The only instance, in which dissolution is mandatory, is contained in proviso (of), in terms of which, if the Appropriation Bill (the Budget) has been rejected by Parliament and the President has not dissolved Parliament, when the next Appropriation Bill is also rejected, the President shall dissolve Parliament. This is a situation of a total breakdown of the government machinery, there being no money voted by Parliament for the government to function. This demonstrates the manner in which the Constitution has carefully delineated the power of dissolution of Parliament. The People in whom sovereignty is reposed have entrusted the organs of government, being the custodians of the exercise of the power, as delineated in the Constitution. It is in this context that we arrived at the conclusion that any transfer, relinquishment or removal of a power attributed to an organ of government would be inconsistent with Article 3 read with Article 4 of the Constitution. The amendments contained in clauses 4 and 5 of the Bill vest the Parliament with the power, to finally decide on the matter of dissolution by passing resolutions to that effect in the manner provided in the respective sub clauses set out above. The residuary discretion that is now attributed to the President (except in Article 70(1)(d) – Appropriation Bill being rejected for the second time) – is removed and it becomes mandatory on the part of the President to dissolve Parliament within four days of the receipt of the communication of the Speaker notifying such resolution.

The provision which attracted most of the submissions of the petitioners who opposed the Bill, is the proposed Article 70A(1)(a) referred to above, which totally removes the power of the President to dissolve Parliament, if the majority of the members of Parliament belong to a political party or independent group of which the President is not a member. In such event the President shall not dissolve Parliament unless upon a resolution passed by Parliament by a two-thirds majority. Significantly, there were no submissions in support of this provision. Article 4(b) of the Constitution provides that the executive power of the People shall be exercised by the President of the Republic, elected by [the] People. Thus, upon election the incumbent becomes the 'President of the Republic', who in terms of Article 30(1) is 'the Head of the State, the Head of the Executive and of the Government, and the Commander-in-Chief of the Armed Forces.' The power attributed to such an office cannot possibly be different, dependent on the absence of membership of a political party or group. The Constitution conceives of a President, who is the 'Head of the State', and who would stand above party politics. This provision moves in the opposite direction. There may be practical considerations that led to this provision being conceived, of which we cannot be unmindful . . .

We would now consider the amendment suggested by the Attorney-General according to which the proposed Article 70A(1)(a) is replaced with a provision stating that after the lapse of one year from a General Election, the President shall not dissolve Parliament unless upon a resolution passed by not less than one-half of the whole number of members of Parliament, including those not present. It has to be noted that this amendment does not address the inconsistency with Articles 3 and 4, dealt with in the preceding sections of this determination. We have stated clearly, on the basis of a comprehensive process of reasoning, that the dissolution of Parliament is a component of the executive power of the People, attributed to the President, to be exercised in trust for the People and that it cannot be alienated in the sense of being transferred, relinquished or removed from where it lies in terms of Article 70(1) of the Constitution. Therefore, the amendments contained in clauses 4 and 5 of the Bill, even as further amended, as suggested by the Attorney-General, constitute in our view such an alienation of executive power, inconsistent with Article 3 read with Article 4 of the Constitution and require to be passed by the special majority required under Article 84(2) and approved by the People at a Referendum, by virtue of the provisions of Article 83 . . .

It is obvious that the proposed amendment has been conceived due to certain difficulties that are envisaged. Although, those who framed the Constitution are presumed to have looked to the future, it may be that they did not fully visualize the stress on the machinery of State that would build up, when there is a divergence in policies between the President who exercises executive power on a mandate of the People, and the majority in the Parliament exercising legislative power also on a mandate of the People. Article 70(1)(a) is intended to provide for such a situation in terms of which during the first year after a General Election held pursuant to a dissolution of Parliament by the President, Parliament could be dissolved only if there is a resolution requesting such dissolution. Thus, in effect during this period the matter of deciding on the dissolution of Parliament becomes a responsibility shared by the President with Parliament. There is no alienation of the power of dissolution attributed to the President. Any extension of this period of one year may be seen as a reduction or as contended by Mr HL de Silva an erosion of that power. However, we are of the view that on an examination of the relevant provisions in the different contexts in which they have to operate, that every extension of such period would not amount to an alienation, relinquishment or removal of that power. That would depend on the period for which it is extended. If the period is too long, it may be contended that thereby the power of dissolution attributed to the President to operate as a check to sustain the balance of power, as noted above, is by a side wind, as it were, denuded of its efficacy. But, if we strike middle ground, the balance of power itself being the overall objective would be strengthened especially in a situation of a divergence of policy, noted above. We are of the view that if Clauses 4 and 5 of the Bill, dealt with in the preceding portion of this determination are removed and replaced with a clear amendment to proviso (a) of Article 70(1), whereby the period of one year referred to therein is extended to a period to be specified not exceeding three years (being one half of the period of Parliament as stated in Article 62(2)) that would not amount to an alienation, relinquishment or removal of the executive power attributed to the President. The inconsistency with Article 3 read with Article 4(b) would thereby cease. The substituted clause should be passed by the special majority provided in Article 84(2) and not require approval by the People at a Referendum . . .

ii. Foreign Affairs

In presidential systems, the President plays a principal role in the conduct of foreign relations, in activities such as the negotiation of treaties and international agreements, the appointment of ambassadors and other public officials, and receiving ambassadors from other countries with the advice and consent of parliament. He has the power to contract and guarantee foreign loans on behalf of his country, as well as to declare war on other countries, sometimes conditioned by requiring legislative consent.

The following cases illustrate the role of presidents in handling these foreign relations powers, as provided by different constitutions. The first case deals with the nature of the Filipino President's power to enter treaties, while the second case deals with the South Korean President's decision to dispatch troops to Iraq.

Senator Aquilino Pimental et al v Ermita, Office of the Executive Secretary GR No 158088, 6 Jul 2005 (Supreme Court, Philippines)

Facts

The Philippines signed the Rome Statute of the International Criminal Court on 28 December 2000 through Chargé d'Affaires Enrique A Manalo of the Philippine Mission to the United Nations. The provisions require that this treaty be subject to ratification, acceptance or approval of the signatory states. The petitioners filed the petition to compel the Office of the Executive Secretary and the Department of Foreign Affairs to transmit the signed text of the treaty to the Senate of the Philippines for ratification. One core issue in this case is whether the Office of the Executive Secretary and the Department of Foreign Affairs are legally obliged to transmit a copy of any treaty to the Senate even if it does not carry the signature of the President.

Puno J

In our system of government, the President, being the head of state, is regarded as the sole organ and authority in external relations and is the country's sole representative with foreign nations. As the chief architect of foreign policy, the President acts as the country's mouthpiece with respect to international affairs. Hence, the President is vested with the authority to deal with foreign states and governments, extend or withhold recognition, maintain diplomatic relations, enter into treaties, and otherwise transact the business of foreign relations. In the realm of treaty-making, the President has the sole authority to negotiate with other states.

Nonetheless, while the President has the sole authority to negotiate and enter into treaties, the Constitution provides a limitation to his power by requiring the concurrence of 2/3 of all the members of the Senate for the validity of the treaty entered into by him. Section 21, Article VII of the 1987 Constitution provides that 'no treaty or international agreement shall be valid and effective unless concurred in by at least two-thirds of all the Members of the Senate.' The 1935 and the 1973 Constitution also required the concurrence by the legislature to the treaties entered into by the executive . . .

The participation of the legislative branch in the treaty-making process was deemed essential to provide a check on the executive in the field of foreign relations. By requiring the concurrence of the legislature in the treaties entered into by the President, the Constitution ensures a healthy system of checks and balance necessary in the nation's pursuit of political maturity and growth.

In filing this petition, the petitioners interpret Section 21, Article VII of the 1987 Constitution to mean that the power to ratify treaties belongs to the Senate.

We disagree . . .

Petitioners' arguments equate the signing of the treaty by the Philippine representative with ratification. It should be underscored that the signing of the treaty and the ratification are two separate and distinct steps in the treaty-making process. As earlier discussed, the signature is primarily intended as a means of authenticating the instrument and as a symbol of the good faith of the parties. It is usually performed by the state's authorized representative in the diplomatic mission. Ratification, on the other hand, is the formal act by which a state confirms and accepts the provisions of a treaty concluded by its representative. It is generally held to be an executive act, undertaken by the head of the state or of the government. Thus, Executive Order No 459 issued by President Fidel V Ramos on November 25, 1997 provides the guidelines in the negotiation of international agreements and its ratification. It mandates that after the treaty has been signed by the Philippine representative, the same shall be transmitted to the Department of Foreign Affairs. The Department of Foreign Affairs shall then prepare the ratification papers and forward the signed copy of the treaty to the President for ratification. After the President has ratified the treaty, the Department of Foreign Affairs shall submit the same to the Senate for concurrence. Upon receipt of the concurrence of the Senate, the Department of Foreign Affairs shall comply with the provisions of the treaty to render it effective . . .

Petitioners' submission that the Philippines is bound under treaty law and international law to ratify the treaty which it has signed is without basis. The signature does not signify the final consent of the state to the treaty. It is the ratification that binds the state to the provisions thereof. In fact, the Rome Statute itself requires that the signature of the representatives of the states be subject to ratification, acceptance or approval of the signatory states. Ratification is the act by which the provisions of a treaty are formally confirmed and approved by a State. By ratifying a treaty signed in its behalf, a state expresses its willingness to be bound by the provisions of such treaty. After the treaty is signed by the state's representative, the President, being accountable to the people, is burdened with the responsibility and the duty to carefully study the contents of the treaty and ensure that they are not inimical to the interest of the state and its people. Thus, the President has the discretion even after the signing of the treaty by the Philippine representative whether or not to ratify the same . . .

It should be emphasized that under our Constitution, the power to ratify is vested in the President, subject to the concurrence of the Senate. The role of the Senate, however, is limited only to giving or withholding its consent, or concurrence, to the ratification. Hence, it is within the authority of the President to refuse to submit a treaty to the Senate or, having secured its consent for its ratification, refuse to ratify it. Although the refusal of a state to ratify a treaty which has been signed in its behalf is a serious step that should not be taken lightly, such decision is within the competence of the President alone, which cannot be encroached by this Court via a writ of mandamus. This Court has no jurisdiction over actions seeking to enjoin the President in the performance of his official duties. The Court, therefore, cannot issue the writ of mandamus prayed for by the petitioners as it is beyond its jurisdiction to compel the executive branch of the government to transmit the signed text of Rome Statute to the Senate . . .

Concerning the Presidential Decision to Dispatch Korean National Armed Forces to Iraq **2006Hun-Ma1098, 1116, 1117 (Consolidated) 30 Oct 2006 (Constitutional Court, South Korea)**

Facts

On 18 October 2003, the President of South Korea decided to dispatch Korean National Armed Forces troops to Iraq. He did so after consulting the National Security Council, the body in charge of policies concerning national security. The complainant, a Korean national, argued that the President's decision was unconstitutional as it violated Article 5 of the Constitution which renounces all aggressive wars.

Held

The Constitution endows the President with the authority to declare war and conclude peace along with the authority concerning the diplomatic relationship with foreign nations (Article 73), and also with the authority to command the Korean National Armed Forces pursuant to the Constitution and the applicable laws (Article 74, Section 1). At the same time, however, the Constitution prevents arbitrary warfare or dispatch of Armed Forces by mandating prudence in exercising the prerogative of supreme command of military by the President, by requiring the consent of the National Assembly in case of the declaration of war or the dispatch of National Armed Forces (Article 60, Section 2). A decision to dispatch Armed Forces requires a resolution of highly political nature based upon the consideration of total circumstances concerning domestic and international political relations, and upon the presupposition of the future and the establishment of the goals concerning a desirable stance of the nation in the future and the direction in which the nation should move forward . . .

The Constitution in this vein endows such authority onto the President who is directly elected by the constituents and is responsible directly for the constituents, while authorizing the National Assembly to determine whether or not to consent to a decision to dispatch the Armed Forces, in order to ensure prudence in the President's exercise of such authority. Under the government structure of representative democracy adopted by the current Constitution, an utmost deference should be given to such a decision of highly political nature as this one rendered by the representative institutions of the President and the National Assembly.

Therefore, whether or not the dispatch decision at issue in this case is in violation of the Constitution, that is, whether such decision contributes to the world peace and human prosperity, whether such decision will ultimately benefit the interest of the citizenry and the nation by enhancing national security, and whether the war in Iraq is a war of aggression that is in violation of international norms, should be judged by the representative institutions of the President and the National Assembly, and may not be appropriately judged by this Court that is by nature in possession of no more than limited materials and information . . .

Notes and Questions

1. Some observers believe that presidentialism might not be good choice for new and unstable democracies. Francis Fukuyama, Bjorn Dressel & Boo-Seung Chang in their article 'Facing the Perils of Presidentialism?' (2005) 16(2) *Journal of Democracy*, 102, summarised four major 'perils':

'(a) the inherent 'winner-takes-all' nature of presidential elections can too readily produce a president who enjoys the support of only a minority of the electorate and hence suffers from a legitimacy gap;

(b) the rigidity of presidential terms and the difficulties in removing an incumbent president make changes to the executive excessively difficult, and term limits may turn even popular and effective incumbents into lame ducks;

(c) the 'dual legitimacy' of elected executives and legislatures often leads to policy gridlock when the two branches are captured by different parties or when presidents fail to muster solid legislative majorities to support their agendas;

(d) presidentialism can foster 'personality politics' and make it possible for inexperienced outsiders to rise to the top.'

See also J Linz, 'The Perils of Presidentialism', (1990) 1(1) *Journal of Democracy* 51. Are these perils of presidentialism evident in the states of Asia?

2. In the Philippines, executive power is 'vested in the President of the Philippines' who is 'elected by direct vote of the people for a term of six years' and is ineligible for re-election. The Philippine President's quasi-legislative authority has statutory and constitutional dimensions. The 1987 Revised Administrative Code categorises the President's Ordinance Powers into five categories:

(a) executive orders of a general or permanent character that implement or execute constitutional or statutory powers;

(b) administrative orders that relate to governmental operations;

(c) proclamations that fix a date or declare a status or condition of public interest;

(d) memorandum orders and circulars that relate to administrative details; and

(e) orders issued by the President in his or her capacity as Commander-in-Chief of the Armed Forces of the Philippines.

Are these constitutional arrangements concerning the powers of the President problematic in the sense that they tend to lead to an abuse of power?

3. Both Korea and Taiwan consolidated the powers of the president in the course of constitutional reform during their democratic transitions. One feature of this development is the keen contest in each presidential election, manifesting itself in heightened tension, polarisation and widespread political bickering. Why is it that presidents, who function as heads of state and serve as symbols of the people and the nation, cannot act as a constructive force to promote political integration but instead become divisive figures? What are the underlying institutional, structural or political explanations for this? More importantly, what would be the proper role for courts, particularly constitutional courts, when called upon to resolve such disputes that may bring them into direct confrontation with various political actors, including presidents, who typically possess the power of judicial appointment? Can courts help resolve these disputes while protecting themselves from a political backlash?

4. The question of how courts can help ease political tensions in still-fledgling democracies is an important issue in the study of comparative constitutionalism. Taiwan and South Korea present two interesting case studies in how and why presidents become involved in divisive constitutional disputes. See Juinn-rong Yeh, 'Presidential Politics and the Judicial Facilitation of Dialogue between

Political Actors in New Asian Democracies: Comparing the South Korean and Taiwanese Experiences' (2010) 4 *I•CON* 911.

iii. Presidential Immunity

Many presidents in Asia have faced criminal charges after they leave office: Presidents Roh Tei-yu and Chun Do-huan of South Korea; President Chen Sui-bian of Taiwan; and more recently President Gloria Macapagal-Arroyo of the Philippines, for example. Presidents enjoy constitutional immunity while in office so that their functions are not impeded and undermined by obstructive law suits. Presidential immunity also protects the president from unfounded accusations that may nevertheless undermine the office of the president. Article 35(1) of the Sri Lankan Constitution confers on the President immunity from legal proceedings while in office, in respect of any acts done or omitted to be done by him in both his official and his private capacity. In other words, the President has blanket immunity from proceedings against him or her. Article 52 of the Taiwanese Constitution limits presidential immunity to criminal charges other than rebellion and treason, but only during the term of office.

Constitutional provisions on presidential immunity, however, often require judicial adjudication, as the following cases indicate. The first case – *Mallikarachchi v Attorney-General of Sri Lanka* – addressed the range of presidential immunities, with a focus on charges against the Attorney-General in lieu of the President. The second case is from the Taiwanese Constitutional Court, *JY Interpretation No 627*. While in office, President Chen Shui-bian of Taiwan was charged with misallocation of public funds. His wife was also allegedly involved. The case dealt with the scope of presidential immunity issues, and permitted limited criminal investigation to be carried out regarding the President, provided his presidential functions were not hindered.

Mallikarachchi v Shiva Pasupati, Attorney-General
(1985) 1 *Sri Lanka Reports* 74 (Supreme Court, Sri Lanka)

Facts

The petitioner was a member of the Politburo of the Jathika Vimukthi Peramuna (JVP) political party and was elected a member of the District Development Council of Colombo as its candidate. On 30 July 1983, the President proscribed him under the provisions of the Emergency Regulations made under the Public Security Ordinance. The petitioner alleged that the President's actions were targeted at eliminating opposition and that the proscription orders infringed his fundamental rights under Article 14(1)(a), (b), (c) and (d) and Article 12(2) of the Constitution. The petitioner cited the Attorney-General as the respondent. Although the Court held that the President's actions in certain matters might be questioned in proceedings brought against the Attorney-General, in the present case the Attorney-General was not competent to represent the President and that the application was improperly constituted.

Sharvananda CJ

[T]he allegations in the petition involved Constitutional questions regarding the legal immunity of His Excellency the President, the court invited ... Article 35 of the Constitution which confers personal immunity, on the President provides as follows:

35(1)   While any person holds office as President, no proceedings shall be instituted or continued against him in any court or tribunal in respect of anything done or omitted to be done by him either in his official or private capacity.

(2)   Where provision is made by law limiting the time within which proceedings of any description may be brought against any person, the period of time during which such person holds the office of President shall not be taken into account in calculating any period of time prescribed by that law.

(3)   The immunity conferred by the provisions of paragraph (1) of this Article shall not apply to any proceedings in any court in relation to the exercise of any power pertaining to any subject or function assigned to the President or remaining in his charge under paragraph (2) of Article 44 or to proceedings in the Supreme Court under paragraph (2) of Article 129 or to proceedings in the Supreme Court under Article 130 (a) relating to the election of the President. Provided that any such proceedings in relation to the exercise of any power pertaining to any such subject or function shall be instituted against the Attorney-General.

Article 35(1) confers on the President during his tenure of office an absolute immunity in legal proceedings in regard to his official acts or omissions and also in respect of his acts or omissions in his private capacity. The object of the article is to protect from harassment the person holding the High Office of the Executive Head of the State in regard to his acts or omissions either in his official or private capacity during his tenure of the office of President. Such a provision as Article 35(1) is not something unique to the Constitution of the Democratic Socialist Republic of Sri Lanka of 1978 ...

There was a similar provision in the Article 23(1) of the Constitution of Sri Lanka of 1972. The corresponding provision in the Indian Constitution is Article 361. The principle upon which the President is endowed with this immunity is not based upon any idea that, as in the case of the King of Great Britain, he can do no wrong. The rationale of this principle is that persons occupying such a high office should not be amenable to the jurisdiction of any but the representatives of the people, by whom he might be impeached and be removed from office and that once he has ceased to hold office, he may be held to account in proceedings in the ordinary court of law ...

It is very necessary that when the Executive Head of the State is vested with paramount power and duties, he should be given immunity in the discharge of his functions. It will thus be seen that the President is not above the law. He is a person elected by the People and holds office for a term of six years. The process of election ensures in the holder of the office correct conduct and full sense of responsibility for discharging properly the functions entrusted to him. It is therefore essential that special immunity must be conferred on the person holding such high executive office from being subject to legal process or legal action and from being harassed by frivolous actions. If such immunity is not conferred, not only the prestige, dignity and status of the high office will be adversely affected but the smooth and efficient working of the Government of which he is the head will be impeded. That is the rationale for the immunity cover afforded for the President's actions, both official and private.

The immunity afforded by Article 35(1) is personal to the President. Article 35(3) however provides that the said immunity shall not apply to any proceedings in court in relation to the exercise of any power pertaining to any subject or function assigned to the President, or remaining in his charge under paragraph (2) of Article 44 and that in relation to the exercise of any power, pertaining to any such subject or function, it is competent to institute any such proceeding against the Attorney-General . . .

Thus though the President is personally immune from legal proceedings in a court in respect of anything done or omitted to be done by him in his official or private capacity, his acts or omissions in relation to the category of matters referred to in Article 35(3) can be questioned in court in proceedings instituted against the Attorney-General.

JY Interpretation No 627
15 Jun 2007 (Constitutional Court, Taiwan)

Facts

In September 2006, the self-proclaimed Red-shirt Army occupied the boulevard in front of the presidential palace in Taipei, demanding that President Chen Shui-bian resign for various corrupt acts. The protest went on for months. Meanwhile, prosecutors in the Taipei District Court began investigating the allegations of corruption against the President. Given that President Chen had criminal immunity under Article 52 of the Constitution, it was argued that these investigations were unconstitutional. The prosecutors argued that the first lady, Ms Wu Shu-Chen, was suspected of embezzlement with respect to a presidential special fund and that the investigation was directed at her and not at the President. In November, Wu was charged with embezzlement. Although President Chen was not formally charged, he was indicted as an accomplice and cited throughout the prosecutorial motion. Motions for presidential impeachment and recall were placed on the Legislative Yuan's agenda. President Chen argued that the prosecution against his wife should have been barred by his constitutional immunity, and that the disclosure of details in the special fund violated presidential privileges and was a grave encroachment on the separation of powers.

Held

The immunity or privilege from criminal prosecution for heads of states originated from the concept of a divine and inviolable kingship during the autocratic era. Modern democracies differ on the provisions regarding presidential criminal immunity. The existence, contents and scope of presidential criminal immunity do not have any direct connection with the institution of the central government. Furthermore, it is not an essential idea of constitutional law, but rather a decision of constitutional policy made by the respective states . . .

In light of the intent of *JY Interpretation No 388*, presidential immunity from criminal prosecution is merely a temporary procedural barrier, rather than a substantive immunity from any criminal liability on the part of the President. As such, the phrase 'not . . . subject to criminal prosecution' provided for under Article 52 of the Constitution should be so interpreted as to mean that the criminal investigation authorities and the trial courts may not treat the President as a suspect or defendant and proceed with any investigation, prosecution or trial against the President during his presidency for any criminal offense committed by him other than rebellion or treason. Therefore, no criminal investigation or trial shall begin after a President takes office if such investigation or trial has treated him as a suspect or defendant but has not begun prior to his inauguration. And, if such criminal investigation or trial has begun prior to the inauguration of the President and has treated him as a suspect or defendant, it shall be suspended as of the day when he takes the office. However, in order to also maintain the essence of presidential criminal immunity, which would still subject the President to criminal prosecution upon his recall, dismissal or expiry of term, any measure not directly concerning the esteemed status of the presidency and exercise of the presidential authorities, or prompt inspection and investigation of a crime scene may still be conducted by the criminal investigation authorities or the trial courts in a case where the President is considered as a suspect or defendant. For instance, the prosecutor may accept and register a case filed under criminal complaint, information, or transfer, and the court may do the same for a case filed under private prosecution. In respect of the criminal investigation procedure already initiated against the President as a suspect or defendant prior to his inauguration, it should be suspended as of the day when he takes office; and with respect to the criminal trial procedure already initiated against the President as a defendant prior to his inauguration, a ruling to stay the trial should be made. Such investigation or trial procedure may resume only upon the President's recall, dismissal or expiry of term.

Presidential criminal immunity is merely a procedural barrier that temporarily prevents criminal prosecution. If the President is suspected of having committed a crime, prosecution may still be conducted against him according to law upon his recall, dismissal or expiry of term. Therefore, although the criminal investigation authorities and the trial courts may not treat the President as a suspect or defendant and proceed with any investigation, prosecution or trial against him during his presidency for any criminal offense committed by him other than rebellion or treason, prompt inspection and investigation of a crime scene may still be conducted. (See Article 230-III and 231-III of the Code of Criminal Procedure.) Presidential criminal immunity merely refers to a temporary stay of prosecution for a President who has acted alone in the commission of a crime, but does not extend to the evidentiary investigation and preservation directed at him during the investigation or trial for a criminal case involving another person. However, if, as a result, the President is suspected of having committed a crime, necessary evidentiary preservation may still be conducted pursuant to the intent of this Interpretation so as to avoid any cover-up of evidence that may render the prosecution and trial against the President upon his recall, dismissal or expiry of term unlikely, although no investigation may be commenced against the President regarding him as a suspect or defendant. For instance, such evidentiary preservation may include the inspection of objects or electronic records, investigation of crime scene(s), review of documents and objects, and collection of samples to be examined from persons other than the President. However, in light of the esteemed status of the presidency and the protection of the exercise of the presidential authorities provided for under Article 52 of the Constitution, the President's person may not be restrained when any measure and evidentiary preservation is conducted that is not subject to presidential criminal immunity . . .

iv. The Impeachment of the President

Many Asian presidencies have operated in rather contentious polities, including South Korea, Taiwan and Indonesia. It is unsurprising to find frequent motions to impeach the president. Under a governmental system in which the president has more power than any other governmental branch, the impeachment process is an important means to remove a president who violates the constitution or other laws while in office. The impeachment procedure of presidents in Asia takes two forms. The impeachment motion can be initiated by the legislature and adjudicated upon by the Constitutional

Court or Supreme Court (like in Taiwan, Singapore, South Korea and Sri Lanka); or it can be proposed by the lower chamber of the legislature and decided by the higher chamber (as in the Philippines and Indonesia).

The following case addresses the impeachment of former South Korean President Roh Moon-Hyun with respect to his proposal for a national confidence referendum. The Court rejected the impeachment on the ground that his acts did not constitute an affirmative violation of law against the fundamental rules of the constitution, and also there was no serious negative impact on the constitutional order.

Presidential Impeachment Case
2004Hun-Na1, 14 May 2004 (Constitutional Court, South Korea)

Facts

On 12 March 2004, the National Assembly of South Korea proposed to impeach President Roh Moo-hyun. The motion was passed by a majority of 193 votes out of 271. The Chair of the National Assembly Legislation and Judiciary Committee, Kim Ki-chun, acting ex officio as petitioner, requested an impeachment adjudication against Roh pursuant to Article 49(2) of the Constitutional Court Act.

Held

Under such interpretation, the Constitutional Court is bound to order removal from public office upon finding any act of the respondent in violation of law without regard to the gravity of illegality. Should the respondent be removed from his office for any and all miscellaneous violations of law committed in the course of performing his official duties, this would be against the principle of proportionality that requests constitutional punishment that corresponds to the responsibility given to the respondent.

Therefore, the existence of the 'valid ground for the petition for impeachment adjudication' in Article 53(1) of the Constitutional Court Act means the existence of a 'grave' violation of law sufficient to justify removal of a public official from his or her office and not merely any violation of law . . .

The question of whether there was a 'grave violation of law' or whether the 'removal is justifiable' cannot be conceived by itself. Thus, whether or not to remove a public official from office should be determined by balancing the 'gravity of the violation of law' by the public official against the 'impact of the decision to remove.' As the essential nature of the impeachment adjudication process lies in the protection and the preservation of the Constitution, the 'gravity of the violation of law' means the 'gravity in terms of the protection of the constitutional order . . .

Therefore, in the case of the President, the 'directly delegated democratic legitimacy' vested through a national election and the 'public interest in continuity of performance of presidential duties' should be considered as important elements in determining whether to remove the President from office. Therefore in light of the gravity of the effect to be caused by the removal of the President from office, the ground to justify a decision of removal should also possess corresponding gravity. As a result, a grave violation of law is required for a decision to remove the President from office that can overwhelmingly outweigh the extremely significant impact of such decision of removal, whereas even a relatively minor violation of law may justify the removal from office of public officials other than the President as the impact of removal is generally light . . .

Accordingly, a 'violation of law significant from the standpoint of protection of the Constitution' requiring the removal of the President from office means an act threatening the basic order of free democracy that is an affirmative act against the fundamental principles constituting the principles of the rule of law and a democratic state. An 'act of betrayal of the public's trust' is inclusive of other patterns of act than a 'violation of law significant from the standpoint of protection of the Constitution,' and, as such, typical examples thereof include bribery, corruption and an act manifestly prejudicing state interest, besides an act threatening the basic order of free democracy . . .

The acts of the President intending to seek sanctuary in direct democracy through directly appealing to the public by proposing a confidence referendum in the state of minority ruling party and majority opposing party rather than administering state affairs in conformity with the spirit of the presidential system and parliamentary system of the Constitution, were not only in violation of Article 72 of the Constitution, but also against the principle of the rule of law. Also, however, in this regard, the above acts of the President did not constitute an affirmative violation of law against the fundamental rules of the Constitution forming the principle of democracy and accordingly, there was no grave negative impact upon the constitutional order, considering that the President merely proposed an unconstitutional confidence referendum and did not attempt to enforce such and that the interpretation as to whether the 'important policy concerning national security' of Article 72 of the Constitution includes the issue of confidence in the President has been subject to academic debates . . .

Notes and Questions

1. Several presidents in Asia have also been subject to impeachment motions. Former Indonesia President, Abdurrahman Wahid was charged with alleged involvement in an improper transfer of state funds and his contradictory statements about donations from the Sultan of Brunei. Abdurrahman Wahid, who became Indonesia's first democratically elected president after the collapse the authoritarian Suharto regime, was head of a coalition of all major parties in Indonesia's Parliament, the People's Representative Assembly (DPR). Dissention in the party grew after he dismissed two Cabinet ministers and after an investigation by the People's Consultative Assembly (MPR) in August 2000. After a long debate in the MPR, Abdurrahman Wahid was impeached in July 2001. See G Barton, *Abdurrahman Wahid: Muslim Democrat, Indonesian President* (Sydney: University of New South Wales Press, 2002) 302–45; and MS Malley, 'Indonesia in 2001: Restoring Stability in Jakarta' (2002) 42(1) *Asian Survey* 125.

2. There was another failed attempt to impeach Taiwan President Chen Shui-bian. Chen's victory in the 2000 presidential elections resulted in a politically divided Government: his DPP controlled the executive power, while the opposition KMT party held the legislative majority. Unsurprisingly, most disputes concerning separation of powers issues within this Government occurred between the President and the legislature. The first controversy arose when the Government suspended the construction of the Fourth Nuclear Power Plant, which was a project initiated during the KMT administration. Chen made an election campaign promise to do so, and made good on this promise about six months after his inauguration in May 2000. Infuriated, the KMT legislative caucus launched filibusters on nearly

every government budget and government bills. The KMT argued that the decision on the nuclear power plant construction was within the legislature's powers, to which the premier was politically accountable. The KMT accused President Chen of violating the constitution and called for his impeachment and recall. Although this impeachment was not passed in the Legislative Yuan dominated by a KMT majority-led campaign, President Chen's authority as a state leader suffered and his legitimacy was repeatedly challenged by the KMT campaign during his term of office. See Wen-Chen Chang, 'Strategic Judicial Responses in Highly Politically Charged Cases: East Asian Experiences' (2010) 8(4) *I•CON* 885.

3. Most Asian states with a presidential system of government have processes for impeaching the president. Impeachment is a very serious procedure and is resorted to only in extreme cases when the president is accused of some unlawful act or violation of the constitution. Another process that is occasionally used is that of a 'recall election' or a 'recall referendum'. This procedure, which dates back to ancient Greece, allows voters to remove the president from office by a direct vote any time before his or her term ends. In cases of recall, the president has not breached any law but instead has lost the confidence of his supporters and voters. A president's recall will invariably lead to fresh presidential elections. Do you think that having a recall procedure in the constitution is a good thing? Why?

4. Article 1 IX of the Constitution of Taiwan allows one-quarter of the legislature to propose a motion to recall the president. This is subject to a two-thirds approval of the legislature and a majority vote of all legitimate citizens. Given the peculiar presidential politics in Taiwan, this recall system is vulnerable to political manipulation. This is why Article 70 of the Presidential and Vice Presidential Election and Recall Act in Taiwan specifically provides a year-long period of grace, during which no motion of recall of an elected president may be initiated.

C. Other Unique Systems

In Asia, the socialist states – China, Vietnam and Laos – have adopted government systems that are unique. The most unusual aspect of these socialist systems is the primacy of the Communist Party, which supervises and controls all other government branches. The ideology of such Communist Party states is reflected in their constitutions. For example, China's Constitution affirms four fundamental principles:

(a) the people's dictatorship;
(b) Marxism-Leninism and Mao's thought;
(c) the socialist road; and
(d) the supreme leadership of the Chinese Communist Party (CCP).[55]

   Article 2 of the Vietnam Constitution pronounces Vietnam 'a state of the people, by the people, for the people' and that 'all state power belongs to the people whose foundation is the alliance between the working class and the peasantry and the intelligentsia'. Article 4 further states that the Communist Party of Vietnam is 'the vanguard of

---

[55] Art 1, Constitution of the People's Republic of China.

the Vietnamese working class' and 'the force assuming leadership of the State and society'. Article 2 of the Laos Constitution declares Laos to be 'a people's democratic state' with all power belonging to the people. Power is to be exercised 'by the people and for the interests of the multi-ethnic people of all social strata with the workers, farmers and intelligentsia as key components'. Article 3 further states that the rights of the people 'to be the masters of the country are exercised and ensured through the functioning of the political system with the Lao People's Revolutionary Party as its leading nucleus'.

In this section, we examine the workings of the socialist system of government, using China as an example, as well as two other oddities. The first is the unique 'one country two systems' model in Hong Kong; and the second, the caretaker government system that emerged in Bangladesh to counter manipulation during the elections.

i. The Chinese Communist Party and Government

In China, the Chinese Communist Party (CCP) is not only the dominant political party but its primary political organ. Over the years, the CCP has evolved into a highly complex, adaptable, autonomous and coherent organisation. It is run by an elite cadre system and can mobilise members across an extremely large society.[56] Since 1978, the Party has developed a collective leadership system that observes term limits and vests power in the Standing Committee of the Politburo. Like all Leninist parties, the CCP has an elite structure that can transmit instructions from the top, right down to the neighbourhood level. Its ability to enforce rules is much stronger than that of other authoritarian regimes.[57] Table 3.4 sets out the central organisation and composition of the CCP.

Like all communist regimes, China also faces the problem of having the ruling party engaged in government operations. The ruling policy of the CCP is to install its top leaders in leading government positions, while its members are posted throughout the government apparatus.

Table 3.4 Central Organisation of the CCP

National Party Congress of CCP			
Central Committee of CCP (205 full delegates and 171 alternative delegates)			Central Commission for Inspecting Discipline of CCP (130 delegates)
Standing Committee of the Politburo (7 members)	Politburo of the Central Committee (25 members)	Secretariat of the Central Committee (7 members)	

[56] F Fukuyama, 'China and East Asian Democracy – The Patterns of History' (2012) 23(1) *Journal of Democracy* 20.
[57] Ibid.

When the CCP exercises power through the government apparatus as provided in the Constitution, it also exercises legitimate power.[58] Under the current political system, the state structure and the CCP structure are not only very closely connected and integrated, but actually fused at various junctures. This system has been in place since 1949. Government agencies are required to report upwards (vertically) to their superior agencies and subject themselves to horizontal control by Party committees operating at the same level. Although the 1982 Constitution and CCP Party Charter downplayed the power of the CCP in the text, the Party's manipulation of state affairs persists at every level.[59] For example, the President, leading members of the State Council and the National Party Congress (NPC) Standing Committee also serve as members of the Politburo, a group of about 20 persons who meet weekly to discuss operational issues. Further, governors of provinces are usually vice-secretaries of provincial party committees, and an increasing number of directors of the standing committees of provincial people's congresses are first secretaries of the relevant provincial party committee.[60] It is also common to find powerful party cadres holding important posts within government agencies at national or local levels.

Management of the party–state relationship is difficult. Under pressure for economic reform in the late 1970s, the post-Mao leaders decided to establish a template for party–state relations. In a speech on political reform in August 1980, Premier Deng Xiaoping stated that the party leadership should be limited;[61] authorised the removal of all party groups from government and administrative bodies; and ordered that party secretaries no longer be empowered to take charge of government work.[62] Since the early 1980s, numerous measures were taken to reform the political system, including adopting a new constitution and party statutes, downsizing the bureaucracy and enhancing citizen participation.[63] At the highest level of the party, Deng took the important but symbolic step of abolishing the post of CCP Chairman, and increasing the powers of the NPC and the Central Committee in relation to the Politburo and the Central Politburo Standing Committee (PSC) respectively.[64]

Despite operating in the shadow of party dominance, China's Government is nevertheless organised to reflect the trichotomy of government branches: legislature, executive and judiciary. The main organs of Chinese government include the NPC (legislature), State Council (executive) and the Supreme People's Court (judiciary).

a. The President as Head of the State

China's President is its head of state and main representative in both foreign and domestic matters. The President's powers include the power to:

---

[58] A Chen, *An Introduction to the Legal System of the People's Republic of China*, 3rd edn (Hong Kong: LexisNexis, 2004) at 43.

[59] See Shiping Zheng, *Party vs State in Post-1949 China: The Institutional Dilemma* (New York: Cambridge University Press, 1997) at 83; and T Saich, *Governance and Politics of China* (New York: Palgrave, 2001) at 111.

[60] Chen, above n 58, at 91.

[61] Saich, above n 59, at 99.

[62] R Weatherley, *Politics in China since 1949* (New York: Routledge, 2006) at 115.

[63] Saich, above n 59, at 99.

[64] Ibid at 116.

(a) promulgate statutes adopted by the NPC;

(b) appoint and remove members of the State Council;

(c) confer state medals and titles of honour as decided by the NPC and its Standing Committee;

(d) issue orders for special pardons;

(e) proclaim martial law;

(f) declare war and issue orders of mobilisation;

(g) accept letters of credentials offered by foreign diplomatic representatives on behalf of the state; and

(h) appoint and recall diplomatic envoys, and to ratify and abrogate treaties and important agreements signed with foreign states.[65]

In practice, however, China's system of the head of state is a system of collective leadership. The President is subordinate to the NPC and directly receives instructions from higher state organs.[66]

b. The National People's Congress

Since its creation in 1954, the NPC has been the highest organ of state power. It comprises deputies elected by provinces, autonomous regions and municipalities directly under the central government, and by the armed forces. The NPC is elected for a term of five years and meets once a year. It is empowered to amend the Constitution, make fundamental laws, elect and remove top officials, to consider and approve the state budget, to make plans for national economic and social development and report on their implementation, and generally to supervise the implementation of the Constitution.[67]

Although these powers are extensive, they are largely shared with the CCP. The CCP's legal and political groups or a special drafting committee will assess proposed legislation and forward their opinions to the CCP and the NPC. The NPC's power to supervise the State Council, ministers or courts is, however, relatively limited. During the political reform of the late 1980s, the NPC was strengthened.[68] Its decision-making procedure became more institutionalised and there was an increase in the number of dissenting votes on legislation and appointments.[69]

As the full NPC is large, unwieldy and inefficient, it elects a Standing Committee to act on its behalf when it is not in session.[70] The Standing Committee meets every two months, and each session lasts for between seven and 10 days. The NPC's powers includes:

(a) law-making;

(b) interpreting the Constitution and laws;

(c) supervising the implementation of the Constitution and the work of various state organs;

(d) deciding on the appointment and removal of some state personnel; and

---

[65] Art 80, Constitution of the People's Republic of China.

[66] Chen, above n 58, at 47.

[67] Arts 57, 59, 60 and 62, Constitution of the People's Republic of China.

[68] Chen, above n 58, at 66.

[69] Saich, above n 59, at 125–27.

[70] Ibid.

(e) the annulment of administrative regulations or local regulations which contravene norms of a higher level in the hierarchy of legal norms.[71]

When the NPC is not in session, the Standing Committee can also examine and approve adjustments to state plans and the budget. The NPC also set up special committees under Article 70 of the Constitution, to examine, discuss and draw up relevant bills and draft resolutions under the direction of the NPC and its Standing Committee. These include committees on: Nationalities, Law, Finance and Economics, Education, Science, Culture and Public Health, Foreign Affairs and Overseas Chinese.

The function and role of the NPC Standing Committee and the Central Military Affairs Commission are unique since they enjoy more real power than any other legislative body. Under Article 63 of the Constitution, the Chairman of the Central Military Commission is elected by the NPC, while the Commission's other members are nominated by the Chairman but chosen by the NPC and its Standing Committee. Members of the State Central Military Commission are often also members of the Communist Party's Central Military Commission. As such, the national armed forces are indirectly under the control of the CCP.

c. State Council

To ensure more effective and efficient administration, the 1982 Constitution reconfirmed the legal status of the State Council as the highest executive branch of the Government.[72] The State Council is responsible to the NPC and can supervise the non-central levels of administration and implement the national policy and budget.[73] The State Council also has law-making power in that it can submit proposals on laws and administrative measures to the NPC. In such cases, the Standing Committee may enact administrative regulations or vary inappropriate orders, directions, rules, decisions or orders of state departments.[74]

Notes and Questions

1. Compare the bureaucracy in the party–state regime and the developmental state. A developmental state operates at two levels: institutional and operational. Institutionally, it favours technocrats for public governance and finds the legal regime and its main players – lawyers – hostile, or at least unfriendly. Courts, bar associations and other legal institutions are not at the centre of policy-making or management in a developmental state. At the operational level, a developmental state focuses on economic development as the primary goal of state policy. It emphasises public construction and moving up the technological ladder over goals of social welfare and equal distribution. Hardware expenditure is disproportionately higher than its software counterpart. See Jiunn-rong Yeh, 'Democracy-Driven Transformation to Regulatory State: The Case of Taiwan' (2008) 3(2) *National Taiwan University Law Review* 312.

---

[71] Art 67, Constitution of the People's Republic of China.
[72] Art 85, Constitution of the People's Republic of China.
[73] Art 89, Constitution of the People's Republic of China.
[74] Saich, above n 59, at 119.

2. The bureaucracy in China is largely controlled by the CCP. As with other communist states, the ultimate functions of bureaucracy are to adhere to the political course set by the Communist Party and implement the state's policies. Although the CCP remains in control, the bureaucracy is undergoing change. Following economic reforms from 1978, Chinese leaders launched a parallel series of administrative reforms to improve the quality of the Chinese bureaucracy, which was criticised for problems such as overstaffing, inefficiency and corruption. The main goals of the administrative reforms focused on decentralising decision-making power, separating economic enterprises from government, recreating the civil service system, reducing the number of administrative agencies and improving the quality of public administration. See Xueguang Zhou, 'Partial Reform and the Chinese Bureaucracy in the Post-Mao Era' (1995) 28 *Comparative Political Studies* 440.

ii. Hong Kong: One Country Two Systems

When the British surrendered Hong Kong to China in 1997, the former colony became the Hong Kong Special Administrative Region (HKSAR) under the 'one country two systems' principle specified under its new constitution, the Basic Law. This structure is unique as two different political systems operate simultaneously within one polity. Under the Basic Law, government is organized into three main organs: the Chief Executive and his secretaries, forming the executive; the Legislative Council making up the legislature; and the Court of Final Appeal, which is the apex of the judiciary. However, this is no typical parliamentary or presidential system.

Under Article 45 of the Basic Law, Hong Kong's Chief Executive (CE) is 'selected by election or through consultations held locally and is appointed by the Central People's Government'. The term of office is five years and no CE may serve for more than two consecutive terms. The CE is accountable to the Central People's Government and the HKSAR,[75] and has a wide variety of powers, both legislative and non-legislative. The CE's legislative powers include the introduction of legislation, budgetary powers, package veto (override) and decree powers, while his non-legislative powers include deciding government policies, issuing executive orders, conducting external affairs, and other matters authorised by the Central Authorities. The CE plays a role in Cabinet formation and dismissal, the in the appointment of public officials and the dissolution of the legislature. The exercise of some of the CE's constitutional powers may require the approval or endorsement of the Legislative Council.[76]

Interestingly, when the policy of 'one country two systems' was first implemented in 1997, the CE promulgated a Public Service (Administration) Order 1997 (EO No 1 of 1997) and a Public Service (Disciplinary) Regulation to ensure continuity in the public service after 1 July 1997. The Executive Order provided for the appointment, dismissal, suspension and discipline of public servants; the Regulation established a disciplinary procedure for the investigation and adjudication of disciplinary breaches by public servants. These instruments raised constitutional concerns, since the Basic Law embedded

---

[75] Art 46, Hong Kong Basic Law.

[76] PY Lo, *The Hong Kong Basic Law* (Hong Kong: LexisNexis, 2011) 293–350. Yash Ghai, *Hong Kong's New Constitutional Order: The Resumption of Chinese Sovereignty and the Basic Law* (Hong Kong: Hong Kong University Press, 1999) 368–78.

the separation of power between the CE and the Legislative Council. This resulted in the following case, which was decided by the Court of First Instance which held that the CE enjoys some legislative power in the recruitment and discipline of the public service.

The Association of Expatriate Civil Servants of Hong Kong v The Chief Executive of HKSAR 1 HKLRD 615 (CFI) (Court of First Instance, Hong Kong)

Facts

After Hong Kong's return to China in 1997, the Chief Executive promulgated the Public Service (Administration) Order 1997 (EO No 1 of 1997) and Public Service (Disciplinary) Regulation to replace the previous colonial instruments dealing with administration of the public service and ensure continuity in the public service after 1 July 1997. The Association of Expatriate Civil Servants of Hong Kong (AECS) applied for judicial review of the Executive Order and the Regulation.

Keith J

In order to evaluate the AECS's argument on art 103, it is necessary to identify the instruments by which 'Hong Kong's previous system of recruitment [and] . . . discipline . . . for the public service' was established and their legal status. Those instruments were: (a) the Letters Patent, (b) the Colonial Regulations, (c) the Disciplinary Proceedings (Colonial Regulations) Regulations and directions given by the Governor under them, and (d) the Civil Service (Disciplinary) Regulations.

The Letters Patent were the principal instrument by which the prerogative powers of the Crown over Hong Kong were delegated to the Governor of Hong Kong. Thus, arts XIV and XVI of the Letters Patent gave the Governor of Hong Kong the power to appoint, dismiss, suspend and discipline public servants. However, the Letters Patent did not identify how these powers should be exercised or what procedure for their exercise should be adopted. The principal instrument which established the manner in which these powers should be exercised and the procedures which should be adopted were the Colonial Regulations. The Colonial Regulations were directions to colonial governors given by the Crown, again by virtue of its prerogative, through the Secretary of State for Foreign and Commonwealth Affairs. The Court of Appeal in *Lam Yuk Ming v AG* [1980] HKLR 815 held that the Governor of Hong Kong was obliged to give effect to them. The relevant articles of the Letters Patent and relevant provisions in the Colonial Regulations have been reproduced in the executive order.

The Disciplinary Proceedings (Colonial Regulations) Regulations and the Civil Service (Disciplinary) Regulations were made by the Governor. The former required the approval of the secretary of state. The latter did not. The power of the Governor to make both sets of regulations derived from those of the Colonial Regulations which applied to Hong Kong. The power to make the former was given to the Governor by regs 56(1) and 57(1) of the Colonial Regulations. The power to make the latter was given to him by reg 54(2) of the Colonial Regulations. The relevant provisions of these regulations, and the directions made by the Governor under the former, have been reproduced in the regulation.

This analysis shows that 'Hong Kong's previous system of recruitment [and] . . . discipline . . . for the public service' was established neither by the legislature nor with legislative approval. It was established by the Crown under the Letters Patent and the Colonial Regulations in the exercise of its prerogative, and by the Governor in the exercise of powers expressly conferred upon him by the Colonial Regulations. The suggestion, therefore, that

Hong Kong's previous system could only be maintained if the system which replaced it had the approval of the legislature is not borne out. I note that in *Lam Yuk Ming v AG* [1980] HKLR 815 the Letters Patent were described as an exercise of the Crown's *legislative* power, and the Colonial Regulations were said to constitute a form of subordinate *legislation*, but since the Letters Patent and the Colonial Regulations were prerogative instruments, these descriptions did not mean that the approval of the legislature was required for them. Indeed, none of the instruments by which the previous system was established in Hong Kong required the approval of either Parliament in the UK or the Legislative Council in Hong Kong.

In summary, while there are undoubtedly constitutional differences between 'Hong Kong's previous system of recruitment [and] . . . discipline . . . for the public service' and the current system established by the executive order and the regulation, the maintenance of the previous system did not require the current system to have the approval of the legislature. The hallmark of the previous system was that, where procedures were to be established locally, they were established by the Governor by executive action. It follows that art 103 of the Basic Law did not require any system which replaced the previous system to have the approval of the Legislative Council . . .

iii. Bangladesh: The Caretaker Government

Following a bloody war, Bangladesh seceded from Pakistan in 1971. In heightened recognition of the need for free, fair and credible elections in a fragile polity, the Constitution (Thirteenth Amendment) Act of 1996 introduced the concept of a non-party caretaker government. This amendment was based on the assumption that a non-party neutral caretaker government would have no motivation to manipulate the electoral process since its members would be barred from contesting elections. The Constitution required all future general elections in Bangladesh to be held in compliance with this amendment.

Under Article 53B of the Constitution, the President of Bangladesh is required to invite the immediate past Chief Justice to become Chief Adviser (CA) or head of the caretaker government in the period between the dissolution of Parliament and the conduct of general elections. The non-political caretaker government functions as the Government, with the CA enjoying the status and privileges of the Prime Minister. Article 58C(1) stipulates that the 'Non-Party Care-taker Government shall consist of the Chief Adviser at its head and not more than ten other Advisers'. The advisers are to be appointed by the President on the advice of the CA. The CA then exercises the executive power of the republic during the tenure of the caretaker government. The CA's tenure commences from the moment of taking the oath of office and ends when a new prime minister is sworn in after the general elections. The amendment makes it mandatory for general election to be held within 90 days.[77]

---

[77]   AKM Masudul Haque, 'Emergency Powers and Caretaker Government in Bangladesh' (2008) 1(1) *Journal of the Australasian Law Teacher Association* 79–94.

Notes and Questions

1. Isolating partisan interests from government is not new. The framers of the American Constitution, such as James Madison, famously equated political parties with factions and attempted to design a 'Constitution against Parties'. See G Leonard, *The Invention of Party Politics: Federalism, Popular Sovereignty, and Constitutional Development in Jacksonian Illinois* (Chapel Hill, NC: University of North Carolina Press, 2002) 18–50; A Hamilton, J Madison and J Jay, *Federalist No 10*, B Fletcher Wright (ed) (Cambridge, Mass: Belknap Press, 1961). However, partisan politics have proved to be inevitable in healthy democratic politics. See, eg, B Ackerman, *The Failure of the Founding Fathers* (Cambridge, Mass: Belknap Press, 2005) 16–26.

2. Consider the vibrant partisan politics in Asian countries. Do you think a non-party caretaker system would be able successfully to isolate partisan interests from government? Also consider whether the caretaker government in Bangladesh would be able satisfactorily to fulfil the core constitutionalist requirements of accountability and the separation of powers.

IV. POLITICAL BRANCHES: CONFLICT AND CONCILIATION

The separation of powers doctrine restrains governments by institutionalising a system of checks and balances. It may also act as a mechanism to stabilise social turbulence and conciliate political conflicts. Through democratic elections and institutional checks, social discontent and power struggles can be channelled away from the streets and mediated through constitutional institutions. When political confrontations are reshaped as constitutional controversies between branches, courts invariably turn to the separation of powers doctrine. Being as abstract as they are, these principles do not always offer useful and effective solutions to power disputes among constitutional institutions. In Asia, conflicts over separation of powers issues are especially thorny. On the one hand, various 'atypical' constitutional systems complicate the dynamics between institutions; and on the other, strong social distrust and political confrontation may lead to constitutional crisis in the form of conflicts between branches. In this section, we examine how political conflicts are reshaped as institutional controversies and how courts deal with these conflicts. Issues pertaining to appointments, budget policy, war and foreign affairs, and emergency powers have triggered conflicts between political branches, since jurisdiction over these areas is shared between the executive and legislative branches.

A. Appointment

The process of filling various high government offices is often embedded in the constitution, with key constitutional actors empowered to make such appointments. This process often becomes a battlefield for conflicting political parties, and as such, the appointment system and process may well reflect the nature of political confrontation and determine the degree and pattern of such conflicts. The appointment of key officials, such as the prime minister or a superior court judge, often involves a two-step process of executive nomination and legislative confirmation. In states where the government is politically divided, this process can often become a surrogate war zone.

In Korea and Taiwan, the power-sharing appointment mechanism has often invited political boycott, resulting in institutional paralysis, leading to a constitutional crisis. The following two cases, from South Korea and Taiwan, exemplify this type of controversy. The issue in both cases was similar: Was the legislature duty-bound to act constitutionally and faithfully in the appointment process? In the Korean case, the Constitutional Court avoided the issue by dismissing the complaint, while in the Taiwanese case the Court upheld this constitutional duty, requiring the legislature to act.

The Korean case was decided during a period of early democratic transition. Kim Dae-jung's victory in the 1998 presidential campaign marked the first peaceful and democratic regime change in Korean history. However, the majority opposition party, the Grand National Party (GNP), attempted to resist the President by turning the process of appointing the Prime Minister into a political battle. Members of the GNP tried to sabotage the confirmation of the appointment of Kim Jong-pil as Prime Minister by absenting themselves from the voting process. President Kim Dae-jung nonetheless bypassed the legislature to make the appointment. All 156 GNP representatives submitted a competence dispute to the Court. Four Justices held the appointment to be unconstitutional, while the other five voted to dismiss the case.

Appointment of Acting Prime Minister Case
98Hun-Ra1, 14 Jul 1998 (Constitutional Court, South Korea)

Facts

President Kim Dae-jung took office on 25 February 1998 and appointed Kim Jong-pil as Prime Minister. This appointment required the consent of the National Assembly. That same day, the Speaker of the National Assembly tried to convene the 189th Extraordinary Session, but failed to do so because of the overwhelming abstention of the opposition Grand National Party (GNP) members. On 2 March 1998, the 189th Extraordinary Session began and the representatives proceeded to vote anonymously on the confirmation of the Prime Minister. Members of the National Congress for New Politics (NCNP) and the United Liberal Democrats (ULD) interrupted the vote, accusing the GNP of casting blank votes, by blocking access to the ballot dispensers and the poll boxes. The Speaker suspended the proceedings and voting stopped. Even though the ratification process failed, President Kim proceeded to appoint all the Cabinet members based on outgoing Prime Minister Ko-kun's recommendations. He also appointed Kim Jong-pil as Acting Prime Minister on 2 March 1998. The applicants submitted this competence dispute before the Court, arguing that the President infringed upon the National Assembly's power, or alternatively the Assembly's power to review and vote on the same issue. They sought to invalidate the appointment of the Acting Prime Minister. The Court dismissed the complaint on the ground of justiciability requirements.

Justice Kim Yong-joon

The power to ratify appointment of the Prime Minister belongs to the National Assembly, which, therefore, must be a party to this competence dispute. Only when the majority in the

National Assembly does not consent to becoming a party, [may the Court grant] a third party standing to partial components of the National Assembly in order to protect the minority. In this case, the plaintiffs account for a majority in the National Assembly, which therefore can contemplate venues to restore the power of the legislature through its resolution. Therefore, it is not necessary to commandeer for this case a third party standing, which is not statutorily sanctioned anyway. As to the claim [of] prospective infringement, the power to review and vote concerns a legal relationship among the representatives themselves or between them and the speaker, and does not concern the relationship between the President and the representatives. His appointment is not likely to infringe upon the representatives' power. . . .

Justices Cho Seung-hyung & Koh Joong-suk

The President neither refused to submit the appointment for ratification nor finalized it against the legislature's disapproval. His action amounts to merely appointing a temporary substitute to the Prime Minister as authorized by Article 23 of the Governmental Organization Act. Even if there had been any procedural fault in his action, it does not and is not likely to infringe upon the power of the legislature or its members. The National Assembly can still vote on the appointment, and the plaintiffs who form the majority in there can influence the outcome of such vote and resolve the dispute thereby. There is no legally protectable interest in this case . . .

Justices Kim Moon-hee, Lee Jae-hwa & Han Dae-hyun

The legislature is a conferential body. Its position is the aggregate of individual representatives' [positions] expressed through their votes. The plaintiffs can file a competence dispute alleging simultaneous infringement on the ratification powers of the legislature and on their own power to review and vote. Also, even if the legislature still can disapprove the appointment in the future, there is [a] legal interest subject to [the] competence dispute in the meantime. They continued, ratification by the Assembly is an indispensable substantive prerequisite to appointment of [the] Prime Minister. Appointing one without ratification clearly violates the Constitution and cannot be justified by [the] existence of such custom in the past. Custom does not take precedence over the Constitution just because it has been repeated. Neither can it be justified as a measure to prevent [a] vacuum in administration when a system of stand-ins is already in place . . .

As in the Korean case, the following Taiwanese case illustrates how the President's powers of appointment were undermined. But unlike the Korean Constitutional Court, the Grand Justices of Taiwan denounced the political manipulation and upheld the legislature's constitutional duty to act faithfully according to its constitutional mandate.

JY Interpretation No 632
15 Aug 2007 (Constitutional Court, Taiwan)

Facts

The third term of the Control Yuan Commissioners of Taiwan expired at the end of January 2005. President Chen Shui-bian submitted a list of nominated individuals for legislative confirmation by the end of 2004. However, the KMT legislative majority blocked it from discussion for an entire year. In February 2005, a new legislature, in which the KMT still enjoyed a majority, was inaugurated. President Chen submitted the list again, but the KMT continued to boycott the confirmation process for another three years.

Held

Article 7, Paragraphs 1 and 2 of the Constitutional Amendments stipulate that '[t]here shall be a Control Yuan as the highest authority for the exercise of impeachment, censure and audit power,' and that '[t]he Control Yuan shall consist of 29 Commissioners, among whom one shall be appointed as Chief Commissioner and one as Deputy-Chief Commissioner for a term of six years by the President and with the consent of the Legislative Yuan.' As such, the Control Yuan is an integral and indispensable national agency for the normal operations of the constitutional system with its specific power bestowed by the Constitution. Given that the Chief Commissioner, Deputy-Chief Commissioner and Commissioners are all legal positions preserved by the Constitution, it behoves all constitutional agencies, as regards their respective duties, to maintain the functional existence and normal operations of the Control Yuan. In accordance with Article 7, Paragraph 2, of the Constitutional Amendments, the Chief Commissioner, Deputy-Chief Commissioner and Commissioners shall be nominated by the President and consented to or approved by the Legislative Yuan before they can be appointed. This design is based upon the consideration of separation of powers as well as checks and balances. While the President is empowered to initiate decisions regarding the Control Yuan's personnel, such decisions are subject to the checks and balances of review by the Legislative Yuan. In order that the Control Yuan may exercise its power without interruption, the President should nominate successors [to fill the positions] of Chief Commissioner, Deputy-Chief Commissioner and Commissioners in a timely manner before the term of these incumbents expires and seek approval from the Legislative Yuan. The Legislative Yuan, in turn, should also exercise its consent power in a timely manner to ensure the normal operations of the Control Yuan. Regardless of its decision to approve or disapprove, the Legislative Yuan shall have fulfilled its constitutional duty once such a decision is actively made. As their respective constitutional obligation, if the Legislative Yuan should disapprove of the nominees so that the Control Yuan temporarily cannot carry out its normal functions, the President should nevertheless nominate [other] suitable candidates and submit the list [in a new bill] to the Legislative Yuan for approval, and the Legislative Yuan should also actively engage in the exercise of its consent power. The Constitution does not allow for the event in which either the President or the Legislative Yuan fails to nominate or consent to the nomination of candidates so that the Control Yuan cannot exercise its power or function, thereby jeopardizing the integrity of the constitutional system . . .

In some other situations, presidential appointments become problematic during a time of transition of power. The following Filipino case concerns the constitutionality of President Gloria Arroyo-Macapagal's 'midnight' appointment of Renata Corona as Chief Justice, barely a month before her own presidential term ended, even though Article VII Section 15 of the Philippines Constitution prohibits any appointment to any executive positions during the 'two months immediately before the next presidential elections'.

Arturo De Castro et al v Judicial and Bar Council et al Case
GR No 191002, 17 Mar 2010 (Supreme Court, Philippines)

Facts

Chief Justice Reynato S Puno of the Philippines Supreme Court was required to retire by 17 May 2010 when he attained the age of 70. President Gloria Arroyo-Macapagal proceeded to appoint Associate Justice Renato Corona as Puno's successor on the eve of her departure from office. Article VII, Section 15 of the Constitution prohibits the President or Acting President from making appointments within the 'two months immediately before the next presidential elections and up to the end of his term', except temporary appointments to executive positions when continued vacancies will prejudice public service or endanger public safety. The issue was whether Arroyo-Macapagal's appointment of Corona violated the Constitution.

Bersamin J

The first, Section 15, Article VII (Executive Department), provides:

> Two months immediately before the next presidential elections and up to the end of his term, a President or Acting President shall not make appointments, except temporary appointments to executive positions when continued vacancies therein will prejudice public service or endanger public safety.

The other, Section 4(1), Article VIII (Judicial Department), states:

> The Supreme Court shall be composed of a Chief Justice and fourteen Associate Justices. It may sit en banc or in its discretion, in [divisions] of three, five, or seven Members. Any vacancy shall be filled within ninety days from the occurrence thereof.

As can be seen, Article VII is devoted to the Executive Department, and, among others, it lists the powers vested by the Constitution in the President. The presidential power of appointment is dealt with in Sections 14, 15 and 16 of the Article.

Article VIII is dedicated to the Judicial Department and defines the duties and qualifications of Members of the Supreme Court, among others. Section 4(1) and Section 9 of this Article are the provisions specifically providing for the appointment of Supreme Court Justices. In particular, Section 9 states that the appointment of Supreme Court Justices can only be made by the President upon the submission of a list of at least three nominees by the JBC [Judicial and Bar Council]; Section 4(1) of the Article mandates the President to fill the vacancy within 90 days from the occurrence of the vacancy.

Had the framers intended to extend the prohibition contained in Section 15, Article VII to the appointment of Members of the Supreme Court, they could have explicitly done so. They could not have ignored the meticulous ordering of the provisions. They would have easily and surely written the prohibition made explicit in Section 15, Article VII as being equally applicable to the appointment of Members of the Supreme Court in Article VIII itself, most likely in Section 4(1), Article VIII. That such specification was not done only reveals that the prohibition against the President or Acting President making appointments within two months before the next presidential elections and up to the end of the President's or Acting President's term does not refer to the Members of the Supreme Court . . .

Moreover, the usage in Section 4(1), Article VIII of the word shall – an imperative, operating to impose a duty that may be enforced – should not be disregarded. Thereby, Section 4(1) imposes on the President the imperative duty to make an appointment of a Member of the Supreme Court within 90 days from the occurrence of the vacancy. The failure by the President to do so will be a clear disobedience to the Constitution.

The 90-day limitation fixed in Section 4(1), Article VIII for the President to fill the vacancy in the Supreme Court was undoubtedly a special provision to establish a definite mandate for the President as the appointing power, and cannot be defeated by mere judicial interpretation in Valenzuela to the effect that Section 15, Article VII prevailed because it was 'couched in stronger negative language.' Such interpretation even turned out to be conjectural, in light of the records of the Constitutional Commission's deliberations on Section 4(1), Article VIII . . .

Consequently, prohibiting the incumbent President from appointing a Chief Justice on the premise that Section 15, Article VII extends to appointments in the Judiciary cannot be sustained . . .

Conflicts between the branches of government have also arisen from the creation of independent regulatory commissions. In a transitional situation, the creation of independent agencies represents a rearrangement of political control to cultivate social trust. The following Taiwanese case shows how political confrontation may undermine public trust in independent agencies. In Taiwan, the first independent agency was the National Communication Commission (NCC). The majority Pan-Blue Coalition in the legislature was determined to change the organic law of the NCC to allow partisan representation in appointing commissioners. The Pan-Blue Coalition – comprising the KMT, the People First Party and the New Party – argued that partisan representation was the most democratic means of reflecting popular opinion and protecting the NCC from undue political influence. However, the Executive Yuan saw this proposal as nothing more than politic manipulation by the Pan-Blue Coalition to consolidate its political influence over the NCC, and the matter was referred to the Constitutional Court for adjudication.

JY Interpretation No 613
21 Jul 2006 (Constitutional Court, Taiwan)

Facts

The creation of independent regulatory commissions was part of the DPP's reform agenda. In creating the first independent commission, the NCC, the majority Pan-Blue Coalition tried very hard to influence the appointment of commissioners to that body. To this end, it enacted a law under which independent commissioners were appointed directly by a legislative appointment committee whose membership was to be allocated in proportion to the seats the different parties held in the legislature. The question before the Court was whether this law violated the executive power of the Executive Yuan.

Held

The Executive Yuan, as the highest administrative organ of the state, must be held responsible for the overall performance of all the agencies subordinate to the said Yuan, including the NCC, under the principle of administrative unity, and shall have the power to decide on personnel affairs in respect of members of the NCC because the success or failure of the NCC will hinge closely on the candidates appointed to be members of the NCC.

Nevertheless, the Legislative Yuan, which exercises the legislative power, is not precluded from imposing certain restrictions on the Executive Yuan's power to decide on personnel affairs in respect of members of the NCC for purposes of checks and balances so as to prevent the Executive Yuan from arbitrarily exercising the power to appoint personnel, thus jeopardizing the independence of the NCC. The principle of separation of powers, as a fundamental constitutional principle, signifies not only the division of powers whereby all state affairs are assigned to various state organs with the right organizations, systems and functions so as to enable state decisions to be made more appropriately, but also suggests the checks and balances of powers whereby powers are mutually containing and restraining so as to avoid infringement upon the people's freedoms and rights due to unrestrained misuse of the powers. However, there are still some limits on the checks and balances of powers. There should be no violation of an unambiguous constitutional provision, nor should there be any encroachment upon the core areas of the powers of various constitutional organs or restriction of the exercise of powers by other constitutional organs or breach of the politics of accountability . . .

The checks and balances as imposed by the legislative power on the executive power in respect of the power to decide on the personnel affairs for an independent agency, in general, are manifested in the restrictions on the personnel's qualifications, which are intended to ensure the specialization of the independent agency, and also in the formulation of conditions such as a guaranteed term of office and statutory grounds for removal from office, which are designed to maintain the independence of the independent agency with a view to shielding the members of such agency from external interference and enabling them to exercise their functions and duties independently. However, in light of the fact that the mass media under the supervision of the NCC serve such function as shaping public opinions to supervise the government and political parties, the freedom of communications necessitates strong demand for an NCC that is free of political considerations and interferences. As such, if the legislative power intends to further reduce the political influence of the Executive Yuan on the composition of the NCC to promote the public confidence in the NCC's fair enforcement of the law by means of setting forth a ceiling on the number of the NCC members who come from the same political party, or adding a provision in respect of overlapping terms of office, or even empowering the Legislative Yuan or diversified civil associations to participate in the decision-making process with the Executive Yuan regarding the candidates for membership in the NCC, it is permissible under the freedom of communications as guaranteed by the Constitution as long as the design of the checks and balances at issue may indeed help reduce or eliminate the political influence to promote the independence of the NCC and to further build up the public confidence in the NCC's freedom from considerations and influence of partisan interests and its fair enforcement of the law. As to the question of how the Legislative Yuan or other diversified civil associations will participate in the decision-making process with the Executive Yuan regarding the candidates for membership in the NCC, the legislators are free to a certain extent to formulate the rules. Yet there should be no encroachment upon the core areas of the executive power, nor any restriction of the exercise of the Executive Yuan's power.

According to Article 4-II and -III of the NCC Organic Act, however, a total of fifteen members of the NCC will be recommended based on the percentages of the numbers of seats of the respective parties (groups) in the Legislative Yuan, and, together with the three members to be recommended by the Premier, shall be reviewed by the NRC, which is composed of eleven scholars and experts as recommended by the various political parties (groups) based on the percentages of the numbers of seats of the respective parties (groups) in the Legislative Yuan, via a two-round majority review by more than three-fifths and one-half of its total members, respectively. And, upon completion of the review, the Premier shall nominate those who appear on the list as approved by the NRC within seven (7) days and appoint same upon confirmation by the Legislative Yuan. Given the fact that the Premier can recommend only three out of the eighteen candidates for membership in the NCC, that he has no say in the personnel affairs during the review, that he is bound by the list as approved by the NRC, which is formed according to the percentages of the numbers of seats of the respective parties (groups) in the Legislative Yuan, and that he is obligated to nominate those appearing on the said list, to send the nominations to the Legislative Yuan for the latter's confirmation, and to appoint those candidates confirmed by the Legislative Yuan as members of the NCC, it is very clear that the Executive Yuan, in fact, has mere nominal authority to nominate and appoint and substantially limited power to recommend only one-sixth of the candidates for members of the NCC during the entire selection procedure. In essence, the Premier is deprived of virtually all of his power to decide on personnel affairs. In addition, the executive is in charge of the enforcement of the laws whereas the enforcement depends on the personnel. There is no administration without the personnel. . . .

Accordingly, the aforesaid provisions, in substantially depriving the Executive Yuan of virtually all of its power to decide on specific personnel affairs in respect of the members of the NCC, are in conflict with the constitutional principle of politics of accountability, and are contrary to the principle of separation of powers since they lead to apparent imbalance between the executive and legislative powers.

As for the issue of whether the provisions are unconstitutional that empower the various political parties (groups) to recommend candidates for membership in the NCC based on the percentages of the numbers of seats of the respective parties (groups) in the Legislative Yuan, and to recommend scholars and experts to form the NRC based on such percentages, it depends on whether such participation provisions substantially deprive the Executive Yuan of its power to decide on personnel affairs. The aforesaid provisions have, in essence, transferred the power to decide on personnel affairs from the Executive Yuan to the various political parties (groups) of the Legislative Yuan and the NRC, which is composed of members recommended by such political parties (groups) based on the percentages of the numbers of their seats in the Legislative Yuan, and which obviously oversteps the limits of participation and runs counter to the checks and balances in restricting the executive power to decide on personnel affairs. Besides, since the purpose of the aforesaid provisions is to reduce the political clout on the exercise of the NCC's functions and duties and to further promote the public confidence in the NCC's fair enforcement of the law, it is questionable whether the means serve the said purpose. Although the lawmakers have certain legislative discretion to decide how to reduce the political influence on the exercise of the NCC's authorities and to further build up the people's confidence in the NCC's fair enforcement of the law, the design of the system should move in the direction of less partisan interference and more public confidence in the fairness of the said agency. Nevertheless, the aforesaid provisions have accomplished exactly the opposite by inviting active intervention from political parties and granting them a special status to recommend and, in essence, nominate, members of the NCC based on the percentages of the numbers of their seats, thus affecting the impartiality and reliability of the NCC in the eyes of the people who believe that it shall function above politics. As such, the purpose of establishing the NCC as an independent agency is defeated, and the constitutional intent of safeguarding the freedom of communications is not complied with.

As for the provisions of Article 4-III of the NCC Organic Act regarding the appointment of members of the NCC by the Premier, as well as Paragraph V thereof, which provides that the Chairperson and Vice-Chairperson will be elected by and from among the members before their appointment by the Premier, there is some doubt as to whether

Article 56 of the Constitution is violated. . . . [A]s long as the Executive Yuan is not substantially deprived of its power to decide on the personnel affairs in respect of members of the NCC, there will be no violation of the principles of separation of powers and politics of accountability even if the Chairperson and Vice-Chairperson are elected by and from among the members themselves. Furthermore, as the NCC is an independent agency which, in nature, differs from the general ministries and commissions, it goes without saying that Article 56 of the Constitution, which provides that the Vice Premier, Ministers and Chairpersons of various Commissions, and Ministers without Portfolio shall be appointed by the President of the Republic upon the recommendation of the Premier, will remain unaffected by the fact that the Legislative Yuan or other diversified civil associations are allowed to participate in the selection of members of the NCC . . .

Notes and Questions

1. Different appointment mechanisms reflect different ideas of power sharing and political control. For example, there are at least three models for the appointment of constitutional court justices in Asia: co-operative, representative and dynamic. All three models involve more than one government branch. Under the co-operative model, the appointment of a constitutional court justice requires two government bodies. The Taiwanese system embodies this model. The appointment of each justice requires the nomination of the President as well as the consent of the Legislative Yuan. The representative model emphasises the need to represent the different interests fairly. South Korea, Indonesia, Mongolia and Cambodia embody the representative model, in which the executive, legislature and the judiciary may appoint a number of justices without the concurrence of the other. An example of the dynamic model is Thailand, where the constitutional justices are appointed by the King upon the advice of the Senate. However, the King's appointment is only nominal and the power of appointment lies in the hands of other government bodies. Of the nine members of the court, five are selected by the judiciary and the remaining four are elected by the Senate from a list submitted by the Selection Committee for Judges of the Constitutional Courts. The requirement of a supermajority and the co-operative model emphasises the need for democratic consensus, the representative model considers the importance of diversity, while the dynamic model aims to enhance deliberation. See T Ginsburg, *Judicial Review in New Democracies: Constitutional Courts in Asian Cases* (New York: Cambridge University Press, 2003) 42–46.

2. Consider the different rationales behind the design of appointment mechanisms. Judicial independence is usually a key value in the appointment process, especially for judges and independent agency commissioners. For example, Shimon Shetreet argues that the independence of the judiciary is closely linked with judicial appointment because the appointment system has a direct bearing on the impartiality, integrity and independence of judges. In Asia, most constitutional justices are political appointees who are emplaced through power-sharing mechanisms. Some scholars argue that political appointment systems lean toward accountability rather than independence. In other words, political appointments may have the virtue of ensuring political support for the institution but bear the risk of politicisation. See

S Shetreet, *Judges on Trial* (New York: North-Holland Publications, 1976) at 46; see also N Garopa and T Ginsburg, 'Guarding the Guardians: Judicial Councils and Judicial Independence' (2009) 57(1) *American Journal of Comparative Law* 103, at 111–21.

3.   What is the proper role of courts, particularly constitutional courts, when they are requested to resolve disputes that may bring them into direct confrontation with other political actors? Should the courts insist on only interpreting constitutional provisions, or should they take on a more active role in resolving the conflict? Compare *J Y Interpretation No 613* (Taiwan) with *De Castro et al v Judicial and Bar Council et al* (the Philippines). The Taiwanese Constitutional Court judges looked into the political confrontation and stressed that 'the design of the system should move in the direction of less partisan interference and more public confidence in the fairness of the said agency'. However, the Supreme Court of the Philippines insisted that the constitutional ban against 'midnight' appointments did not extend to Supreme Court judges simply because the office was not specified in the Constitution. Furthermore, while all these cases were decided on the basis of the separation of powers, they had different focal points. For example, the Court in *J Y Interpretation No 632* emphasised the constitutional obligation of the appointment process, and in *J Y Interpretation No 613* stressed the doctrine of administrative unity.

B. Policy and Budget

In most systems, the executive branch of government is empowered to decide and implement policies and enforce the law, while the power of the purse lies with the legislature. The legislature authorises revenues and ensures that the national budget is implemented properly. At the same time, legislators may endeavour to please voters through generous spending. Consequently, the legislature's budget power may also be subject to some constraints as well. Budgets are not only about money but also about policy. How a government spends money also determines its state policy. Checks and balances over the power of the purse may thus give rise to tensions between the legislative and the executive.

The controversies about budget vary, depending on government systems and the political context. In a presidential system like that of the United States, Congress can cut the budget or demand that the President support a balanced budget, while the President can impound appropriate funds[78] to address dissatisfaction with regular appropriations outcomes.[79] In the Philippines, where the President has enormous power, the issue is how the constitution can limit the President's powers in relation to the budget. In this section, we discuss two cases dealing with budget controversies, from Taiwan and Korea.

The first Taiwanese nuclear case concerned the issue of peace-time budget control. The executive is empowered to propose the budget, while the Legislative Yuan has

---

[78] The power of impoundment is the power of the President not to spend the money that had previously been appropriated or allocated by Congress.

[79] RS Abascal and JR Kramer, 'Presidential Impoundments, Part 1: Historical Genesis and Constitutional Framework' (1973–1974) 62 *Georgetown Law Journal* 1549.

power to scrutinise the budget and to pass it. The Legislative Yuan has no power to propose any increase in the budget estimates submitted by the Executive Yuan.[80] The case arose in 2000 when President Chen Shui-bian, fresh from his electoral victory, sought to fulfil his campaign promise of a no-nuclear homeland by suspending the construction of the fourth nuclear power plant on the island.

JY Interpretation No 520
15 Jan 2001 (Constitutional Court, Taiwan)

Facts

Soon after the regime change in 2000, the DPP Government announced the termination of the Fourth Nuclear Power Plant installation. This decision led to political turmoil. The Legislative Yuan, which was still controlled by the former ruling party, the KMT, refused to receive the Premier and threatened to recall the President. Opponents also filed a suit before the Court to determine whether President Chen's decision to cancel the installation was constitutional.

Held

For funds under the statutory budget designated for the maintenance of an agency's normal operations and exercising its legally authorized duties, since the withholding of those funds would affect the existence of that agency, the law does not permit [the spending] to be left to the administrative agency's random discretion. For withholding of statutory budget [funds] that has the functional effect of changing administrative or critical national policies, it is contrary to the constitutional purpose of having the Legislative Yuan participate in the decision-making process of critical national issues if such withholding does not indeed involve the Legislative Yuan's participation. Hence, the abovementioned flexibility of budget execution does not mean that an authorized administrative agency may pick and choose items by itself in administering [the budget] without regard to the fact that the statutory budget is one that is passed by the Legislative Yuan and has the effect of a mandatory statute. Under the Budget Act, the status of appropriation and distribution of annual expenditures must be reviewed period-by-period and level-by-level, and the review reports must be submitted to the Legislative Yuan for further examination (Article 61); there is an express prohibition against commingling of funds among individual agencies, divisions, projects or budgetary items in administering the budget (see Article 62); moreover, the supervising personnel shall be subject to disciplinary actions in accordance with the regulations if the discharging agency does not achieve 90% of the planned annual budget . . .

It follows that if the Executive Yuan should consider a budgetary bill passed by the Legislative Yuan difficult and not intend to execute in accordance with its contents, it should indeed follow the above-indicated reconsideration process before a budgetary bill is promulgated to become a statutory budget. If the petition agency's argument is correct that carrying out the statutory budget is the core area of the executive power, and that there is room for the administrative agency to decide in its liberty whether to carry that out, then whenever a budgetary bill passed by the Legislative Yuan does not meet [the Executive Yuan's] satisfaction or there is difficulty in carrying it out, it can indeed simply decide not to execute or exercise some other discretions, and there is no need for

---

[80]   Art 70, Constitution of the Republic of China, 1947.

the installation of the reconsideration process regarding a budgetary bill under the Constitution.

In addition to specifying the concrete figures of the needed funding for the normal operations of national agencies and carrying out legally authorized duties, the budgetary bill also includes the necessary financial resources for the promotion of all kinds of policies. In accordance with modern financial economic theory, the budget [also] carries the function of guiding the economic development and affecting the cycles of prosperity. Under the system of representation through constitutional democracy, the legislature has the authority to review and resolve the budget. This is not only supervision, as the representative of public opinion, over the financial expenditures and relief of the citizens' taxation, but also the realization of national policies and formation of projects in carrying out those policies through the review of the budget, academically known as the parliamentary power of decision-making participation. In the present petition, having [first] passed the related budget concerning the fourth nuclear power plant, the Third Legislative Yuan in its 15th Meeting of the First Session on May 24, 1996, and in accordance with the then applicable Article 57, Subparagraph 2, of the Constitution, resolved to change the Executive Yuan's critical policy by abolishing the construction scheme of the nuclear power plant. All [related] projects in progress had to be stopped immediately and thus could not take expenditure from the budget. Subsequently, the Executive Yuan, on the ground of disagreeing with [this] critical policy change, submitted [the resolution] to the Legislative Yuan for reconsideration on June 20 of the same year. It is apparent, therefore, that based upon the effect the construction of a nuclear power plant has on energy reserves, the environment, and related industries, together with the massive budget expenses and the complexity in the disposition of the aftermath in the event such withholding should be carried out, [the present withholding] should indeed be considered a change of a critical national policy, which was not disputed during the oral argument by representatives from either the Executive or Legislative Yuan. Consequently, since the Legislative Yuan participated in and resolved the budgetary bill concerning the construction of the nuclear power plant from its initiation, through its previous suspension or withholding, to reconsideration of the administration of [the budget], the Legislative Yuan should naturally be given the same opportunity to participate in or resolve the issue of further withholding [of funds]. Since this statutory budget touches upon a critical policy, its revision is obviously different from a simple adjustment of a budgetary item concerning non-critical national policies. Thus, the petitioning [administrative] agency does not have the discretionary leeway to decide and implement [the withholding] arbitrarily, on the ground that the so-called statutory budget is [in fact] a substantive administrative act, or [alternatively] relying on its self-imposed regulation, yet to be submitted to and reviewed by the Legislative Yuan, the Guidelines on the Execution of the Budget by the Central [Government] Agencies and Their Affiliated Units. It is not without merits for the Related Institution, the Legislative Yuan, to consider this [argument] to be unilateral decision-making . . .

Dramatic social change can also reshape budgetary issues. The Asian financial crisis of 1997–99 came as a shock to the international community. In response to the crisis, some Asian countries took extraordinary measures, such as the reallocation of state budgets and financial reform. These arrangements can significantly reshape the power structures set out in the constitution.

In 1997, South Korea went through a severe financial crisis during which 17,168 firms went bankrupt. To deal with the crisis, President Kim Young Sam launched a series of financial reforms, including the setting up of a financial reform commission.[81] In addition, the International Monetary Fund (IMF) also approved a US$21 billion financial package and delivered guidelines to the Government on 4 December 1997.[82] To meet the IMF's expectations, President Kim Dae Jung (who succeeded Kim Young Sam) undertook many reform measures. He did not only rely on legislation, but also created corporatist arrangements that permitted negotiation with business and labour.

An important feature of this reform legislation was the creation of a new supervisory agency, the Financial Supervisory Commission (FSC), with substantial powers to manage the crisis. Existing supervisory bodies were consolidated into the Financial Supervisory Service (FSS) under the FSC, which is responsible for supervising all banks. This new arrangement placed the FSC and FSS under the Prime Minister's office.[83] President Kim Dae Jung also embarked on administrative reform to create a small but efficient government. The Ministry of Finance and Economy was a target of this reform, and its budget power was given over to a Planning and Budget Commission directly controlled by the President and an independent office of the national budget. At the same time, the bulk of the Ministry's financial supervisory functions were transferred to the FSC.[84]

In response to the 1997 financial crisis, the Thai Government sought a US$17 billion financial rescue package from the IMF and pledged to take certain actions in the form of Letters of Intent. During the transition from the Chavalit Government (1998–2000) to Chuan Leekpai's administration (1997–2001), the Thai Government signed six Letters of Intent with the IMF.[85] The Chuan Government initiated a number of measures to resolve the crisis, including issuing six royal ordinances and emergency decrees.

In normal circumstance, legislative power was in the hands of the National Assembly and the King. However, in cases of emergency and unavoidable necessary urgency, the King might, upon the advice of the Council of Ministers, issue a royal ordinance or an emergency decree, having the force of law. The Council of Ministers must forthwith submit any such ordinance to the House of Representatives and the Senate for their approval. If not approved, the ordinance would lapse. However, the lack of parliamentary disapproval did not affect any act done whilst the ordinance was in force.

On 21 May 1998, the President of the House of Representatives referred an opinion of 90 members of the House of Representatives – that four of the decrees passed were not in fact emergency decrees – to the Constitutional Court for an opinion.

[81] S Haggard, *The Political Economy of the Asian Financial Crisis* (Washington, DC: Institute for International Economics, 2000) 47–162.
[82] Ibid.
[83] Ibid.
[84] Ibid.
[85] Borwornsak Uwanno, 'Economic Crisis and Political Crisis in Thailand' (2009) 4(3) *National Taiwan University Law Review* 143.

The President of the House of Representatives Requests for a Constitutional Court Ruling that the Enactment of Emergency Decrees were Inconsistent with Section 218 of the Constitution of the Kingdom of Thailand, BE 2540 (1997)
Ruling No 1/2541, 23 May 1998 (Constitutional Court, Thailand)

Facts

The President of the House of Representatives referred to the Constitutional Court the opinion of 90 members of the House of Representatives on 21 May BE 2541 (1998). The opinion stated that four Emergency Decrees – (a) Emergency Decree Conferring Powers on the Ministry of Finance to Incur Foreign Debts in Order to Revive the Economy; (b) Emergency Decree Conferring Powers on the Ministry of Finance to Borrow and Manage Borrowings in order to Assist the Fund for Rehabilitation and Development of Financial Institutions; (c) Emergency Decree Amending the Emergency Decree Amending the Bank of Thailand Act; and (d) Emergency Decree on Financial Institution Asset Management Corporation – were not urgent laws.

Held (unanimously)

The reasons for enacting the four such Emergency Decrees could be summarized as follows. Thailand has suffered a severe economic slump caused by persistent financial crises. The State found it necessary to implement numerous measures in order to remedy such an economic problem, such as by acceptance of obligations prescribed by the International Monetary Fund, the suspension of two-thirds the licensed and operating financial institutions in the category of securities companies, the enactment of the law on reform of financial institutions to remedy the problem of financial institutions, the assistance of the fund for Rehabilitation and Development of Financial Institutions which offered financial assistance for enhancing the liquidity of financial institutions and the establishment of the Financial Institution Asset Management Corporation to manage the low quality debts of financial institutions facing problems in their management.

Such facts stated above were evident to the public. Moreover, the provisions in all four Emergency Decrees related to the remedy of the economic crisis. The first two Emergency Decrees conferred powers on the Ministry of Finance, with the approval of the Council of Ministers, to borrow for the Government of the Kingdom of Thailand from domestic and foreign sources to utilize in the rehabilitation of the national economy, enhance the liquidity of the problematic economy and restructure the sources of capital. As for the third Emergency Decree, protection and securities were given to the Fund for the Rehabilitation and Development of the Financial Institution System. The fourth Emergency Decree increased the capital and enabled the Fund to give financial assistance to suspend financial institutions. Implementation under all such measures above could be deemed as cases for the benefit of preserving the economic security of country, being cases for the enactment of an Emergency Decree under section 218 paragraph one of the Constitution of the Kingdom of Thailand, BE 2540 (1997) . . .

Notes and Questions

1. According to a World Bank study, more than a quarter of the world's states revised their constitutions during the 1990s to expand the role of their legislatures. In most cases, the role of the legislature to scrutinise and authorise revenues and

expenditures was strengthened. See R Stapenhurst, 'The Legislature and the Budget' (2004) *World Bank* 1–15.

2. The great variation in the pattern of budget processes may stem from differences in government systems. Thus, where the legislature has a strong role in the presidential system, the executive generally dominates budget decisions in parliamentary systems. However, Joachim Wehner disagrees. In his study of 43 countries, he explains that the role played in budgetary processes is not determined by the type of government system but rather depends on factors such as access to information, federalist structures and constitutional provisions affected by colonial rule. See J Wehner, 'Legislative Arrangements for Financial Scrutiny: Explaining Cross-National Variation' in R Pelizzo, R Stapenhurst and D Olson (eds), *The Role of Parliaments in the Budget Process* (Washington DC: World Bank, 2005) 2–17.

3. A study suggests that the role of legislature in the budget process is becoming important again. See P Posner and Chung-Keun Park, 'Role of the Legislature in the Budget Process: Recent Trends and Innovations' (2007) 7(3) *OECD Journal on Budgeting* 2–4.

4. While most countries delegate the power of budgetary control to the legislature, the reverse is true in a few exceptions. For example, the transformation of Singapore's formerly ceremonial presidency into an elected institution was predicated on assigning the constitutional power of 'withholding concurrence and approval to appointments and budgets of the statutory boards and Government companies'. See YCL Lee, 'Under Lock and Key: The Evolving Role of the Elected President as a Fiscal Guardian' (2007) *Singapore Journal of Legal Studies* 290–322; and KYL Tan and Lam Peng Er (eds), *Managing Political Change in Singapore: The Elected Presidency* (London: Routledge, 1997).

5. The 1987 Philippines Constitution authorises the President to propose the annual budget for congressional approval. The President can veto 'any particular item or items in an appropriation, revenue, or Tariff bill', including the General Appropriations Act (GAA) which outlines the annual government budget. However, each GAA since 1996 has authorised the President to augment items in the general appropriations law with savings from other appropriated items within the Executive branch, even though the Constitution requires that the legislature authorises transfers of appropriations in the budget bill. The President can realign its budget only subject to prior statutory authorisation. In recent years, President Gloria Arroyo-Macapagal did not appear to pay sufficient attention to the specificity and accountability mandated under the Administrative Code. According to her critics, there has been a profusion of budget increases for some government projects, with limited, if any, description of their use. In 2008, the Alternative Budget Initiative, a budget reform advocacy NGO consortium, claimed that the 'economic stimulus fund' signed into law in 2009 would be used as an 'election-stimulus fund' to aid the President's political allies. It also worried that discretionary funds invited corruption. A recent audit report showed that in 2009, the President funded some of her foreign travel with the Government's emergency fund earmarked for calamities. She used almost all the $16.6 million in the fund,

leaving the Government with few resources to respond to numerous natural disasters and massive flooding which occurred that same year. Budget impounding 'when revenues are scarce' creates a lack of transparency in the administration of the national budget. See S Rose-Ackerman, D Disierto and N Volosin, 'Hyper-Presidentialism: Separation of Powers without Checks and Balances in Argentina and the Philippines' (2011) 29 *Berkeley Journal of International Law* 246.

6.   Consider the cases of Singapore and the Philippines, where the presidents possess budget powers. What are the consequences if the president abuses his or her budgetary powers? Are there any constitutional mechanisms available to maintain checks and balances?

C. Foreign Policy and War

The executive branch of government is in the best position to deal with matters relating to foreign policy and national security. Perceived advantages such as secrecy, dispatch and access to broad sources of information are often mentioned in this connection. In the case of foreign policy and war, courts typically assume a highly deferential attitude in reviewing government decisions of this nature. Courts may also employ the political question doctrine when called upon to review the powers of the executive pertaining to foreign affairs and war, and hold these powers to be non-justiciable.

Issues relating to war powers are complex in Asia. On one hand, the history of imperialism, colonialism and numerous wars complicates foreign relations between Asian countries. The involvement of the United States in the World War II, the Korean War as well as the Vietnam War ushered foreign power intervention into the domestic affairs of Asian states. Moreover, some territories, such as Ieodo Island, Dokdo and Aksai Chin, have been the subject of territorial disputes between states, raising security concerns. The historical and geographical complexities not only trigger international tensions from time to time, but also become part of the constitutional mandates in some countries. As a result, war and foreign policy issues in Asia involve not only the separation of powers, but also international relations and constitutional mandates.

Japan presents a felicitous example. Its post-war Constitution prohibits the act of war by the state. Under Article 9, the Japanese state is said to be 'aspiring sincerely to an international peace based on order' and 'the Japanese people forever renounce war as a sovereign right of the nation and the threat or use of force as means of settling international disputes'. However, in light of concerns relating to the security of post-war Japan, especially the growing threat of communism, the US–Japan Security Treaty was signed. Under the Treaty, the American military is permitted to continue to use important bases in Japan for the defence of the Far East, and to intervene in Japan to put down internal disturbances if requested by the Japanese Government. Although Japan retains an interest in having US armed force stationed on Japanese soil, it is often confronted with the question as to whether the US–Japan Mutual Treaty violates Article 9 of the Constitution. Beyond the legalities, the presence of large numbers of American troops in Okinawa presents social and cultural problems as well. Some 20 per cent of Okinawa is occupied by US forces, and land was forcibly taken from thousands of Japanese for military use.

The first challenge came to the court in 1959, when the people of Okinawa questioned the constitutionality of the Treaty. In the second case, the power of judicial supremacy of the United States over these military bases was challenged after a 12-year-old girl was abducted and raped by three American servicemen in September 1995. In the meantime, the terms of leases for the land to be used for US armed forces in Okinawa were about to expire, and landowners refused to renew their leases. Under the US-Japan Mutual Security Treaty, the Japanese government is obligated to supply American forces with land and facilities, and thus the Prime Minister approved the expropriation proceeding. Landowners, mayors of the cities, towns, as well as the governor of Okinawa refused to comply with the necessary measures for expropriation. The case was brought to the Court by the Japanese Prime Minister. The Court suggested that expropriation is lawful unless the US Security Treaty and the Agreement on the Status of US Armed Forces are unconstitutional. The Court then went on to uphold the constitutionality of the Special Measures concerning Land for US Armed Force Law.

Judgment upon Case of the so-called 'Sunakawa Case' [Violation of the Special Criminal Law Enacted in Consequence of the Administrative Agreement under Article III of the Security Treaty between Japan and the United States of America] 1959(A)No 710, 16 Dec 1959 (Supreme Court, Japan)

Facts

Some protestors entered the US Air Force base and were prosecuted before the Tokyo District Court. The lower court held that the stationing of armed forces on Okinawa was unconstitutional, as was the special criminal law governing Okinawa. The procurator's office appealed to the Supreme Court.

Held

We, the people of Japan, do not maintain the so-called war potential provided in paragraph 2, Article 9 of the Constitution, but we have determined to supplement the shortcomings in our national defense resulting therefrom by trusting in the justice and faith of the peace loving people of the world, and thereby preserve our peace and existence.

This, however, does not necessarily mean that our recourse is limited to such military security measures as may be undertaken by an organ of the United Nations, such as the Security Council, as stated in the original decision. It is needless to say that we are free to choose whatever method or means deemed appropriate to accomplish our objectives in the light of the actual international situation, as long as such measures are for the purpose of preserving the peace and security of our country. Article 9 of the Constitution does not at all prohibit our country from seeking a guarantee from another country in order to maintain the peace and security of the country.

Now, therefore, let us consider the legal intent of paragraph 2 in the light of the purport of Article 9 elucidated above. It is entirely proper to interpret that the prohibition of the maintenance of war potential contained in this paragraph was intended for the purpose of preventing Japan from maintaining the so-called war potential of its own, exercising its own control and command over the same, and thereby instigating a war of aggression renounced forever in the first paragraph of the Article . . .

The Security Treaty is a treaty concluded between Japan and the United States regarding stationing of the United States armed forces, the foreign armed forces recognized in the above provision of the Treaty of Peace. This provision was approved and signed by a majority of forty countries out of sixty United Nations countries.

According to the Preamble of the Japan–United States Security Treaty, the Treaty of Peace recognizes that in consideration of the fact that Japan will not have the effective means to exercise its inherent right of self-defense at the time of coming into force of the Treaty of Peace, and since there is a necessity of coping with the danger of irresponsible militarism, that Japan, as a sovereign nation, has the right to enter into collective security arrangements. It is clear, therefore, that the purpose of the Japan–United States Security Treaty is to provide, as a provisional arrangement, for the defense of Japan, and to stipulate matters necessary to insure the safety and defense of our country, such as granting of the right to the United States to deploy its armed forces in and about Japan to guard against armed attack upon the country. Consequently, it must be stated that the Security Treaty, in its essence, bears a vital relationship with peace and security and also with the very existence of our sovereign country . . .

The Security Treaty, therefore, as stated before, is featured with an extremely high degree of political consideration, having bearing upon the very existence of our country as a sovereign power, and any legal determination as to whether the content of the treaty is constitutional or not is in many respects inseparably related to the high degree of political consideration or discretionary power on the part of the Cabinet which concluded the treaty and on the part of the Diet which approved it. Consequently, as a rule, there is a certain element of incompatibility in the process of judicial determination of its constitutionality by a court of law which has as its mission the exercise of the purely judicial function. Accordingly, unless the said treaty is obviously unconstitutional and void, it falls outside the purview of the power of judicial review granted to the court . . .

Accordingly, the Court in proceeding to deliberate over the Security Treaty relating to the stationing of the United States armed forces and the provisions of the Administrative Agreement based on Article 3 of the said treaty, finds that these Security Forces are foreign troops, and naturally they are not a war potential of our country. All command and supervisory authorities are vested in the United States, and furthermore, it is clear that our country has no right to command or supervise such armed forces as we do over our own armed forces. These armed forces are stationed here in accordance with the principle set forth in the Preamble to the Security Treaty, and as stated in Article I of the Treaty, these forces are to be utilized to contribute to the maintenance of international peace and security in the Far East and to the security of Japan against armed attack from without, including assistance given at the express request of the Japanese Government to put down large-scale internal riots and disturbances in Japan caused through instigation of, or intervention by, an outside power or power . . .

If such be the case, it cannot be acknowledged that the stationing of the United States armed forces is immediately, clearly unconstitutional and void, contravening the purport of Article 9, paragraph 2 of Article 98, and the Preamble of the Constitution. On the contrary, it must be held that it is in accord with the intent and purpose of these constitutional provisions . . .

Judgment upon Case of Constitutionality of the Forced Leasing of Land for US Bases in Okinawa Prefecture
1996(Gyo-Tsu)No 90, 28 Aug 1996 (Supreme Court, Japan)

Facts

The land leases used by US armed forces in Okinawa were expected to expire on 31 March 1996 and 14 May 1997 respectively. The land owners refused to renew the leases and comply with expropriation proceedings. The director of the Naha Defense Facilities Administration Agency then requested the Governor of Okinawa Prefecture to sign the documents and attend the process on the basis of Article 14 of the Special Measures for US Armed Forces Law and Article 36(5) of the Land Expropriation Law. The Governor rejected this request. Accordingly, the Prime Minister issued a mandate on the basis of the Local Autonomy Law. Again, the Governor rejected this mandate. The Prime Minister filed a suit against the Governor requesting a judgment ordering the execution of the assigned duty on the basis of Article 151-2(3) of the law. On 25 March 1996, Naha Branch of Fukuoka High Court, the court of first instance in this special proceeding, held that the Governor's refusal significantly undermined the public interest and ordered the Governor to carry out the assigned duty. The Supreme Court ruled that Article 14 of the Special Measures for US Armed Forces Law and Article 36(5) of the Land Expropriation Law are constitutional.

Held

The purpose of the Special Measures Concerning Land for US Armed Forces Law is to implement the Agreement on the Status of US Armed Forces in terms of the expropriation and utilization of land for US armed forces (Article 1). From this purpose, it follows that the administration concerning the expropriation and utilization of land regulated by the Special Measures Concerning Land for US Armed Forces Law is a duty relating to the security of Japan and the peace and security of the Far East region, which relate closely to each other, and to the duty of Japan to the United States to provide facilities and areas under the Japan-US Security Treaty . . .

Then, the reason why the article involves courts is that the court shall make the decision whether or not the mandate made to the governor of a prefecture by a competent minister of state is lawful, and the minister of state can directly manage the affairs instead of the prefectural governor as long as the court decides that it is lawful. This helps the aforesaid harmonization.

After considering from the above perspective, the court in mandamus proceedings should not judge whether the governor of a prefecture must obey the mandate on the premise that the order by the competent minister of state has superiority but should judge objectively whether the mandate by the competent minister of state in meets the conditions or not . . .

The examination of the lawfulness of the mandate, except for the examination of the requirements provided by Article 151-2 of the Local Autonomy Law, means [an] examination of whether or not the governor of a prefecture has an obligation to administer the affairs ordered by the mandate. The governor of the prefecture shall examine whether the conditions for the administration are met within the purview of the power that is permitted by laws and regulations and shall have the obligation to administer the affairs of the State when he or she decides that the requirements are met. Therefore, the courts, which also shall examine whether or not the governor of a prefecture has the obligation, are not able to examine matters beyond the purview of the power permitted by the laws and regulations.

However, if the laws and regulations that are legal grounds for the administration by the governor of the prefecture are unconstitutional, it can be said that the executing order is unlawful and lacks legal ground, even though it is not permitted from the viewpoint of the general rule of the government organization for the governor of a prefecture to refuse to administer affairs on account of their unconstitutionality [.] Thus, an order to administer affairs is not always lawful just because the governor of a prefecture has an obligation to administer it. Therefore, the judgment that the examination of the lawfulness of the mandate means an examination of whether or not the governor of a prefecture has an obligation to administer the affairs ordered by the mandate is not proper . . .

[T]he question of whether or not the Special Measures Concerning Land for US Armed Forces Law, which is the legal ground for the aforesaid mandate, is constitutional is within the purview of the power of judicial review in this lawsuit, in which the court should judge whether the aforesaid mandate meets the conditions or not. On the other hand, the appellant contends on this issue that it violates the right to live in peace, which is guaranteed by the Preamble and Articles 9 and 13 of the Constitution, and infringes Article 29(3) of the Constitution, even though the stationing of armed forces authorized by the Japan–US Security Treaty and the Agreement on the Status of US Armed Forces itself does not violate the Constitution.

Article 6 of the Japan–US Security Treaty and Article 2(1) of the Agreement on the Status of US Armed Forces provide that Japan has the obligation by the treaties to grant the use by US armed forces of facilities and areas provided that it is agreed between the two governments though the Joint Committee under Article 25 of the Agreement on the Status of US Armed Forces . . .

When land cannot be acquired through agreement, it is held to be necessary and reasonable to use force or expropriate the land in the case in which the conditions (it is proper and rational to use the land for the stationing of US armed forces) are met. This means that private property is taken for public use (Article 29(3) of the Constitution). If the appellant contends that it infringes the Preamble and Articles 9 and 13 of the Constitution if the government does something necessary and reasonable to observe the treaties, then it is the same as saying that the treaties themselves are unconstitutional. However, unless the Japan–US Security Treaty and the Agreement on the Status of US Armed Forces are obviously unconstitutional and void, the courts should examine whether the Special Measures concerning Land for US Armed Forces Law is constitutional or not on the premise that the treaties are constitutional. The appellant also states clearly that he does not contend that the treaties are unconstitutional. Accordingly, the Special Measures concerning Land for US Armed Forces Law does not violate the Preamble and Articles 9, 13, and 29(3) of the Constitution . . .

What is required in issuing the approval is not only a political and diplomatic decision through the comprehensive consideration of various factors, including the international situation that is crucial to Japan's security and international peace and security in the Far East, the necessity of the land for the US armed forces and its scale, the degree of burden and damage to the landowners and residents around the land incurred by the supply of the land to the US armed forces, and the possibility of supplying alternative land, but also a specialized technical decision concerning the US military bases, so it should be said that the decision is within the political and technical discretion of the appellee . . .

In accordance with the above analysis, in spite of the present situation of US military bases in Okinawa Prefecture and the various problems allegedly incurred by this situation, it cannot be said that it is always clearly inappropriate and unreasonable to supply the US armed forces with land in the prefecture and that the application of the Special Measures Concerning Land for US Armed Forces Law in the prefecture through the lawful discretion made by the appellee must always be prohibited. So the appeal, which claims that the application of the above law to Okinawa Prefecture is in violation of the Preamble and Articles 9, 13, 14, 29(3), 92, and 95 of the Constitution, cannot be accepted. In addition, since the Special Measures Concerning Land for US Armed Forces Law is not a special law only for Okinawa Prefecture, [the appeal] which claims that the application of the above law to Okinawa Prefecture is in violation of Article 95 of the Constitution, lacks a valid premise . . .

Justices Masao Ono, Hisako Takahashi, Yukinobu Ozaki, Shinichi Kawai, Mitsuo Endo & Justice Masao Fujii

According to these facts ascertained by the court, we agree that Okinawa Prefecture and citizens there have a great burden because of the US military bases in Okinawa. At the same time, however, the easing of the burden on Okinawa due to the concentration of bases needs an agreement between the governments of Japan and the United States of America and various administrative measures inside Japan, since the existence of the bases of US armed forces is based on international agreements that is, Article 3(1) of the Agreement on Restoration of Okinawa, Article 6 of the Japan–US Security Treaty, and Article 2 of the Agreement on Status of US Armed Forces. In other words, it needs an appropriate exercise of diplomatic and administrative power. This power ought to be used by the administrative government at its discretion and under its responsibility, achieving a balance between easing of the burden on Okinawa Prefecture and its people on the one hand and the necessity of the bases on the other. Therefore, apart from the extreme case in which there is no leeway to consider a balance, it cannot be said that the application of the Special Measures Concerning Land for US Armed Forces Law to Okinawa Prefecture and the approval of utilization on the basis of this law are clearly unconstitutional and illegal. If, as the appeal claims, we declared that the application of the Special Measures Concerning Land for US Armed Forces Law to Okinawa Prefecture were unconstitutional and invalid and declared all the authorization of utilization based on this law to be void, then the existence of US military bases in Okinawa Prefecture would be legally overturned without any international agreement or administrative measure. Such a decision would be beyond the power of a judicial branch.

From the beginning, providing US armed forces with bases in Okinawa is not based only on administrative and diplomatic considerations. Regarding approval of the utilization of individual plots of land, it is necessary to satisfy the condition of 'proper and rational' in Article 3 of the Special Measures Concerning Land for US Armed Forces Law. Therefore, even if the approval of utilization is not definitely unconstitutional or illegal, a person whose rights or legitimate interests are allegedly violated is entitled to insist on the defect of the approval of utilization in cancel litigation against the approval of utilization or the decision by the Expropriation Committee. This was the opinion of the court ruling. However, in determining the unconstitutionality of the application of the Special Measures Concerning Land for US Armed Forces Law to Okinawa Prefecture and the invalidity of the approval utilization for the reason of concentration of US military bases in Okinawa, many administrative and diplomatic factors should be considered. So this issue is not suitable for the court to decide definitely. Therefore, we think it proper that the court should examine only whether there exists a clear reason for unconstitutionality or illegality.

The case of South Korea is another interesting example. After the UN Security Council declared that by invading Kuwait in 1990, Iraq had committed 'a breach of international peace and security', this declaration was followed by a number of international measures, including economic sanctions against Iraq. South Korea's President Roh Tae-woo decided to send Korean National Armed Forces troops to Iraq. A Korean national brought the case before the Constitutional Court, arguing that the President's decision was unconstitutional since the Article 5 of the Constitution renounced all aggressive wars.

Case Concerning the Presidential Decision to Dispatch Korean National Armed Forces to Iraq
2003Hun-Ma814, 29 Apr 2004 (Constitutional Court, South Korea)

Held

A decision to dispatch Armed Forces to a foreign nation as at issue in this case is a complex and significant matter not only affecting the life and the bodily safety of the individual soldiers who are dispatched, but ultimately affecting the interest of the citizenry and the nation, including the status and the role of the nation in the international community, the nation's relationship with the allies, and the national security issues. As such, a decision to dispatch Armed Forces requires a resolution of highly political nature based upon the consideration of total circumstances concerning domestic and international political relations, and upon the presupposition of the future and the establishment of the goals concerning a desirable stance of the nation in the future and the direction in which the nation should move forward.

Therefore, it is desirable that such a decision is to be made by the institution representative of the constituents that can be held politically responsible toward the constituents thereof, by way of prudent decision-making through an expansive and extensive deliberation with the experts in the relevant fields. The Constitution in this vein [endows the President with such authority]who is directly elected by the constituents and is responsible directly for the constituents, while authorizing the National Assembly to determine whether or not to consent to a decision to dispatch the Armed Forces, in order to ensure prudence in the President's exercise of such authority. Under the government structure of representative democracy adopted by the current Constitution, utmost deference should be given to such a decision of highly political nature as this one rendered by the representative institutions of the President and the National Assembly.

Therefore, whether or not the dispatch decision at issue in this case is in violation of the Constitution, that is, whether such decision contributes to the world peace and human prosperity, whether such decision will ultimately benefit the interest of the citizenry and the nation by enhancing national security, and whether the war in Iraq is a war of aggression that is in violation of international norms, should be judged by the representative institutions of the President and the National Assembly, and may not be appropriately judged by this Court that is by nature in possession of no more than limited materials and information ... The record indicates that the dispatch at issue in this case was determined by the President after consultation with the National Security Council with respect to the nature and the size of the detachment and the duration of the station, based on the consideration not only of the justifiability of the dispatch but also of various elements concerning [the national interest] such as the relationship with the allies for amicable settlement of the nuclear situation in North Korea, our national security, and the domestic and foreign political relationships; and subsequently that the dispatch decision at issue in this case was rendered with the consent of the National Assembly following the deliberation and the resolution of the State Council, thereby securing procedural justification pursuant to the Constitution and the relevant statutes. The detachment decision at issue in this case is by its own nature a matter requiring a determination of highly political nature concerning national defense and diplomacy. As this decision has clearly been rendered following the procedures established by the Constitution and the relevant laws, the judgment of the President and the National Assembly upon this matter should be respected, while this Court should refrain from passing judgment upon this matter solely under judicial standards . . .

Notes

1. Certain historical events enabled Japan to develop its substantial military power after World War II. These include the establishment of the Self-Defence Forces in the 1950s, the ratification and renewal of the Mutual Security Treaty with American governments, and Japanese participation in UN peacekeeping missions. In cases involving the dispatch of troops, the Japanese judiciary has often avoided dealing squarely with issues or has simply deferred to the political branches. Japanese courts have given the political branches a wide berth as regards the implementation of Japan's military policy. Under Article 9 of the Constitution, the Diet (legislature) is constitutionally responsible for checking the Cabinet's military decisions and has done so in the past. See L Fisler Damrosch, 'Constitutional Control over War Powers: a Common Core of Accountability in Democratic Societies?' (1995) 50 *University of Miami Law Review* 181, 194–95.

D. Emergency Power[86]

War, economic crisis, civil unrest, terrorist attacks, natural disasters and epidemics are some of the events that necessitate extraordinary measures and even the temporary suspension of certain fundamental rights. Most Asian countries do not have provisions for the making of emergency legislation in their constitutions. Interestingly, some countries make a distinction between different kinds of emergencies. For example, Pakistan's Constitution authorises the President to declare three types of emergencies:

(a) war;
(b) external aggression; and
(c) internal disturbance.

The Constitutions of Thailand, Singapore[87] and Bangladesh stipulate that an emergency may be declared in the interests of national economic security. The Constitutions of Taiwan and South Korea provide that an emergency may be declared in circumstances of financial or natural disaster. For example, Article 76 of the Constitution of South Korea empowers the President to take urgent measures in emergencies such as internal turmoil, external menace, natural calamity, or a grave financial or economic

[86] On emergency powers in Southeast Asia generally, see KYL Tan, 'From Myanmar to Manila: A Brief Study of Emergency Powers in Southeast Asia' in V Ramraj and A Thiruvengadam (eds), *Emergency Powers in Asia: Exploring the Limits of Legality* (Cambridge: Cambridge University Press, 2010) 148.

[87] See KYL Tan, 'Constitutionalism in Times of Economic Strife: Developments in Singapore' (2009) 4(3) *National Taiwan University Law Review* 115.

crisis.[88] Article 2(3) of Additional Articles of the Constitution of the Republic of China stipulates that the President may, by resolution of the Executive Yuan Council, issue emergency decrees and take all measures necessary to avert imminent danger affecting the security of the State or of the people, or to cope with any serious financial or economic crisis.

The state of emergency may lead to the suspension of constitutional liberties. For example, the Public Security Ordinance in Sri Lanka authorises the overriding of any legislation by emergency regulations. Moreover, certain fundamental rights in the 1978 Constitution are subject to restriction in the interests of national security, including equal treatment before the law; freedom of association, assembly, movement, and cultural and religious expression; and procedural requirements regarding arrest and detention.[89] In the Philippines, the State may, during an emergency and under reasonable terms prescribed by it, temporarily take over or direct the operation of any privately-owned public utility or business affected with the public interest. While a Proclamation of Emergency is in operation, the President of Bangladesh can, with the Prime Minister's written advice, suspend the enforcement of fundamental rights in the Constitution. The President of Pakistan is also entrusted with the additional power to take any decision in contravention of the fundamental rights of the citizens contained in Articles 15, 16, 17, 18, 19 and 24 of the Constitution relating to rights of freedom of movement, assembly, association, of trade, business or profession, of speech and of protection of property.

Such a draconian power needs to be constrained, and in most instances this is done in two ways: first, through time limits; and, secondly, through institutional or procedural mechanisms. The restriction on the duration of states of emergency shows great similarity across jurisdictions. In Malaysia, a state of emergency may be declared for a period of six months, and any extension must be laid before both Houses of Parliament. In India, states of emergency may be declared for one month and extensions are subject to the approval of both houses of Parliament for six months at a time. In Pakistan, states of emergency may last initially for two months, unless approved by the National Assembly. In South Korea, a state of emergency ceases immediately if it is not approved by the National Assembly.

Some countries have experienced emergency conditions lasting for much longer. Martial law in Taiwan lasted for 38 years, from 20 May 1949 to 15 July 1987. The Emergency Measures Act of 1950 enacted on 9 March 1950 still has legal effect in Burma/Myanmar. Indeed, the Parliament of Burma/Myanmar rejected an attempt to abolish this law in August 2011.[90]

Another mechanism to restrict emergency powers is institutional and procedural in nature. Under most constitutional arrangements, the authority to declare the state of

---

[88] Art 76 of the Constitution of South Korea provides in time of internal turmoil, external menace, natural calamity, or a grave financial or economic crisis, the President may take in respect of them the minimum necessary financial and economic actions or issue orders having the effect of law, only when it is required to take urgent measures for the maintenance of national security or public peace and order, and there is no time to await the convocation of the National Assembly.

[89] Ramraj and Thiruvengadam (eds), above n 86, 21–80.

[90] MIZZIMA, 'Burmese Parliament rejects motion to repeal Emergency Provisions Act', at <http://www.mizzima.com/news/inside-burma/5858-burmese-parliament-rejects-motion-to-repeal-emergency-provisions-act.html>.

emergency is shared by the executive and legislative powers.[91] In Asia, most modern constitutions vest the primary power to declare the emergency in the President, requiring the prior authorisation of or subsequent ratification by the legislature. For example, the President of East Timor issues emergency decrees only after authorisation by the National Parliament and consulting the Council of State, and the Government and the Supreme Council of Defence and Security. In the Philippines, the President can declare the state of emergency for up to 60 days, but such a declaration must be presented to Congress for approval within 48 hours. In South Korea, the President must notify the National Assembly and obtain its approval after the declaration of an emergency.

Other countries may confer the power to declare an emergency on the head of state, acting on the advice of the Cabinet or the Government. In Thailand and Cambodia, the respective kings may make an emergency proclamation with the concurrence of the Cabinet or the agreement of other forms of power-sharing mechanisms. Exceptionally, Brunei's Sultan can declare a state of emergency without needing parliamentary approval.

Yet other countries vest the authority to declare a state of emergency in the legislature. The State Ikh Khural of Mongolia is one example. In China and Vietnam, the Standing Committee of the NPC has the power to declare the emergency, and to decide on the enforcement of martial law throughout the whole country or in particular provinces. Table 3.5 shows where authority lies to declare a state of emergency.

Table 3.5 The Authority to Declare a State of Emergency

King	President	Cabinet (Prime Minister)	Parliament	The Standing Committee of the National People's Congress
Brunei, Thailand (with the opinion of the Cabinet), Cambodia (after agreement with the Prime Minster, the president of Assembly and the president of the Senate) Malaysia (authorisation by the Parliament)	Sri Lanka, East Timor, Indonesia, Lao, South Korea, Bangladesh Pakistan, Taiwan, Hong Kong (Chief Executive)	Nepal (Council of Ministers of the Government), Japan*	Mongolia (State Ikh Khural)	China, Vietnam

* The Japanese Constitution does not contain emergency provisions or any provision dealing with the acts of war. However, Article 71 of the Police Law provides that the Prime Minister has the authority to declare a state of emergency.

[91] O Gross, 'Constitutions and Emergency Regimes' in T Ginsburg and R Dixon (eds), *Comparative Constitutional Law* (Northampton: Edward Elgar, 2010) at 339.

The following section focuses on the institutional and procedural arrangements governing the emergency regime and the limits of the exercise of its power.

i. Taiwan

Soon after the earthquake in central Taiwan on 21 September 1999, the authorities adopted many extraordinary measures under the emergency decree issued by the President. The question before the Court was whether the decrees issued by the President were constitutional.

JY Interpretation No 543
3 May 2002 (Constitutional Court, Taiwan)

Facts

A rare major earthquake hit Taiwan on 21 September 1999, which prompted the President to issue an emergency degree four days later. The Executive Yuan drafted the 'Emergency Decree Execution Outline of September, 1999' and submitted it to the Legislature Yuan, which referred it to the Court for an opinion on whether the Legislative Yuan had authority to review this outline and whether it complied with the Constitution.

Held

The issuance of emergency decrees under the Constitution is an endeavor to maintain the Nation's existence and restore its constitutional structure in the event of national emergency when the existing legal system is insufficient to eliminate danger or handle a major crisis . . . Article 2, Paragraph 3, of the Amendment to the Constitution provides that 'The President may, in order to avert imminent danger affecting the national security or of the people or to cope with any major financial or economic crisis, issue emergency decrees and take all necessary measures through resolution of the Cabinet meeting, and is not subject to the restriction specified in Article 43 of the Constitution. However, such decrees shall, within ten days of issuance, be submitted to the Legislature for ratification. Where ratification is denied by the Legislature, the said emergency decrees shall cease to be valid.' Accordingly, emergency decrees are proclamations made by the President pursuant to resolution of the Cabinet, in order to avert imminent dangers to the State or the people or to deal with a major crisis, when the existing legal system and legislative process are unable to provide countermeasures. The effectiveness of such decree is restricted to a definite emergency period and location and has the effect of temporarily replacing or altering existing laws. Therefore, emergency decrees are an exception to the constitutional rules that the Legislature is to legislate on behalf of the people while the Executive Yuan is responsible for the execution of laws. As a principle, their content should be thorough and detailed so they can be executed forthwith without the need of supplementary regulations. In case of time constraint where provisions for detail and technicality are impracticable and supplementary regulations by the executive authorities are required to achieve objectives of emergency decrees, then the decrees must contain a provision expressing their objectives and be proclaimed only after ratification by the Legislature. To adhere to the constitutional structure, supplementary regulations (or by whatever term it is named) should be reviewed by the Legislature in accordance with the review procedures set out in the administrative orders. The issuance of emergency decrees, though not restricted by the principle of legal reservation stipulated in Article 23 of the Constitution, should observe the principle of proportionality. The requirement of ratification by the Legislature, within 10 days of issuance of emergency decrees, stipulated in the said Amendment to the Constitution is a representative review mechanism for the emergency measure. The Legislature, upon exercising its power of ratification, may only resolve as to the appropriateness of emergency decrees but not alter their contents. Where some parts of an emergency decree are considered to be inappropriate, partial ratification is available if the remainder of the decree has no impact on and is necessary to the entirety of the emergency measure . . .

ii. Malaysia

In 1948, a state of emergency was proclaimed throughout Malaysia as a result of a communist armed insurgency led by the Communist Party of Malaya (CPM). In 1960, with the emergency at an end, Parliament passed the Internal Security Act 1960 (ISA) to enable necessary measures to be taken to counter terrorism. In the following case, which went on appeal all the way to the Judicial Committee of the Privy Council (when it was still Malaysia's highest court), it was held that the Malaysian King, the Yang di-Pertuan Agong, no longer had any power to make Essential Regulations having the force of law.

Teh Cheng Poh v Public Prosecutor
[1979] 1 MLJ 50 (Privy Council, Malaysia)

Facts

The appellant is charged under the Internal Security Act 1960 for possession of a revolver and ammunition in a security area. He was tried under the special procedure laid down by the Essential Regulations 1975, found guilty and sentenced to death. The appellant challenged the validity of (1) the Essential (Security Cases) (Amendment) Regulations 1975; (2) the Proclamation of the Yang di-Pertuan Agong on 15 May 1969 declaring Malaysia a security area; and (3) the Attorney-General's decision to prosecute him under section 57(1) of the Internal Security Act 1960.

Held

There are only two sources from which the Yang di-Pertuan Agong as such can acquire power to make written law, whatever label be attached to it: one is by a provision of the Constitution itself; the other is by the grant to him of subordinate legislative power by an Act passed by the Parliament of Malaysia in whom by Article 44 of the Constitution the legislative authority of the Federation is vested. So far as his power to make written laws is derived from Article 150(2) of the Constitution itself, in which they are described as 'ordinances', it comes to an end as soon as Parliament first sits after the Proclamation of an Emergency; he cannot prolong it, of his own volition, by purporting to empower himself to go on making written laws, whatever description he may apply to them. That would be tantamount to the Cabinet's lifting itself up by its own boot straps. If it be thought expedient that after Parliament has first sat the Yang di-Pertuan Agong should continue to exercise a power to make written laws equivalent to that to which he was entitled during the previous period to exercise under Article 150(2) of the Constitution, the only source from which he could derive such powers would be an Act of Parliament delegating them to him.

This is what had been done in the previous emergency which had been proclaimed on 18 September 1964 the Emergency (Essential Powers) Act, 1964. In compliance with Article 150(6) of the Constitution it contained the declaration that the Act appeared to Parliament to be required by reason of the emergency . . .

Because, unlike the No I Ordinance, the Emergency (Essential Powers) Act, 1964, was an Act of Parliament it was effective under the Constitution to delegate to the Yang di-Pertuan Agong wide powers exercisable throughout the duration of the emergency proclaimed on 3 September 1964 to continue to make regulations having the force of law notwithstanding that Parliament had previously sat, as was held by this Board in Osman & Anor v Public Prosecutor. To the extent, however, that the No 1 Ordinance purports to authorize the Yang di-Pertuan Agong to continue to make instruments having the force of law notwithstanding that Parliament has sat, it suffers from the fatal constitutional flaw that such exercise of legislative power by the Ruler after Parliament has sat, is not authorized by the Constitution itself nor has it been delegated to him by Parliament in whom the legislative authority of the Federation is vested . . .

Once Parliament had sat on 20 February 1971, the Yang di-Pertuan Agong no longer had any power to make Essential Regulations having the force of law. The Essential (Security Cases) (Amendment) Regulations, 1975, purport to alter in respect of security cases the mode of trial laid down by the Criminal Procedure Code. They are ultra vires the Constitution and for that reason void . . .

iii. The Philippines

The Supreme Court of the Philippines demonstrated a similar degree of judicial scrutiny in considering the wide-ranging administrative powers exercisable during an emergency. On 24 February 2006, President Gloria Macapagal-Arroyo issued Presidential Proclamation No 1017 (PP 1017) declaring a state of national emergency. The Proclamation ordered the armed and police forces immediately to take necessary and appropriate measures to suppress and prevent acts of terrorism and lawless violence by the National Democratic Front-Communist Party of the Philippines-New People's Army (NDF-CPP-NPA) and other military adventurists. In the case that follows, the Supreme Court reviewed the constitutionality of PP 1017.

Prof Randolf S David et al v Gloria Macapagal-Arroyo
GR No 171396, 3 May 2006 (Supreme Court, Philippines)

Facts

While the nation celebrated its 20th anniversary, President Gloris Macapagal-Arroyo issued Presidential Proclamation No 1017 (PP 1017) to declare a state of national emergency, which commanded the Armed Forces of the Philippines and Philippine National Police to immediately take necessary and appropriate measures to suppress and prevent acts of terrorism and lawless violence led by the extreme Left and military adventurist extreme Right. All programmes and activities were cancelled. Along with the dispersal, the petitioner was arrested without warrant. A week after PP 1017, President Arroyo announced PP1021 lifting the state of emergency. The petitioner challenged the constitutionality of PP 1017.

Sandoval-Gutierrez J

It may be pointed out that the second paragraph of the above provision refers not only to war but also to 'other national emergency.' If the intention of the Framers of our Constitution was to withhold from the President the authority to declare a 'state of national emergency' pursuant to Section 18, Article VII (calling-out power) and grant it to Congress (like the declaration of the existence of a state of war), then the Framers could have provided so. Clearly, they did not intend that Congress should first authorize the President before he can declare a 'state of national emergency.' The logical conclusion then is that President Arroyo could validly declare the existence of a state of national emergency even in the absence of a Congressional enactment.

But the exercise of emergency powers, such as the taking over of privately owned public utility or business affected with public interest, is a different matter. This requires a delegation from Congress . . .

Generally, Congress is the repository of emergency powers. This is evident in the tenor of Section 23 (2), Article VI authorizing it to delegate such powers to the President. Certainly, a body cannot delegate a power not reposed upon it. However, knowing that during grave emergencies, it may not be possible or practicable for Congress to meet and exercise its powers, the Framers of our Constitution deemed it wise to allow Congress to grant emergency powers to the President, subject to certain conditions, thus:

(1) There must be a war or other emergency.
(2) The delegation must be for a limited period only.
(3) The delegation must be subject to such restrictions as the Congress may prescribe.
(4) The emergency powers must be exercised to carry out a national policy declared by Congress.

Section 17, Article XII must be understood as an aspect of the emergency powers clause. The taking over of private business affected with public interest is just another facet of the emergency powers generally reposed upon Congress. Thus, when Section 17 states that the 'the State may, during the emergency and under reasonable terms prescribed by it, temporarily take over or direct the operation of any privately owned public utility or business affected with public interest,' it refers to Congress, not the President. Now, whether or not the President may exercise such power is dependent on whether Congress may delegate it to him pursuant to a law prescribing the reasonable terms thereof . . .

In *Araneta v Dinglasan*, this Court emphasized that legislative power, through which extraordinary measures are exercised, remains in Congress even in times of crisis:

> After all the criticisms that have been made against the efficiency of the system of the separation of powers, the fact remains that the Constitution has set up this form of government, with all its defects and shortcomings, in preference to the commingling of powers in one man or group of men. The Filipino people by adopting parliamentary government have given notice that they share the faith of other democracy-loving peoples in this system, with all its faults, as the ideal. The point is, under this framework of government, legislation is preserved for Congress all the time, not excepting periods of crisis no matter how serious. Never in the history of the United States, the basic features of whose Constitution have been copied in ours, have specific functions of the legislative branch of enacting laws been surrendered to another department – unless we regard as legislating the carrying out of a legislative policy according to prescribed standards; no, not even when that Republic was fighting a total war, or when it was engaged in a life-and-death struggle to preserve the Union. The truth is that under our concept of constitutional government, in times of extreme perils more than in normal circumstances 'the

various branches, executive, legislative, and judicial,' given the ability to act, are called upon 'to perform the duties and discharge the responsibilities committed to them respectively.'

Following our interpretation of Section 17, Article XII, invoked by President Arroyo in issuing PP 1017, this Court rules that such Proclamation does not authorize her during the emergency to temporarily take over or direct the operation of any privately owned public utility or business affected with public interest without authority from Congress.

Let it be emphasized that while the President alone can declare a state of national emergency, however, without legislation, he has no power to take over privately-owned public utility or business affected with public interest. The President cannot decide whether exceptional circumstances exist warranting the take-over of privately-owned public utility or business affected with public interest. Nor can he determine when such exceptional circumstances have ceased. Likewise, without legislation, the President has no power to point out the types of businesses affected with public interest that should be taken over. In short, the President has no absolute authority to exercise all the powers of the State under Section 17, Article VII in the absence of an emergency powers act passed by Congress . . .

iv. India

The Supreme Court of India had occasion to review the constitutionality of an emergency proclamation declared in the States of Madhya Pradesh, Rajasthan and Himachal Pradesh by the President and the Union Council of Ministers of India. In its decision, the Court reiterated that even though the power was granted by the Constitution, the proclamation was not immune from judicial review.

SR Bommai v Union of India
[1994] 2 SCR 644 (Supreme Court, India)

Ahmadi J

In a country geographically vast, inhabited by over 850 million people belonging to different religions, castes and creeds, [the] majority of them living in villages under different social orders and in abject poverty, with a constant tug of war between the organised and the unorganised sectors . . . [t]o deal with such extraordinarily difficult situations exercise of emergency powers becomes an imperative . . .

Since it is not disputed by the counsel for the Union of India and other respondents that the Proclamation under Article 356 is amenable to judicial review, it is not necessary for us to dilate on that aspect. The power 247 under Article 356(1) is a conditional power. In exercise of the power of judicial review, the court is entitled to examine whether the condition has been satisfied or not. In what circumstances the court would interfere is a different matter but the amenability of the action to judicial review is beyond dispute. It would be sufficient to quote a passage from *State of Rajasthan* . . .

So long as a question arises whether an authority under the Constitution has acted within the limits of its power or exceeded it, it can certainly be decided by the court. Indeed it would be its constitutional obligation to do so . . . this Court is the ultimate interpreter of the Constitution and to this Court is assigned the delicate task of determining what is the power conferred on each branch of Government, whether it is limited, and if so, what are the limits and whether any action of that branch transgresses such limits. It is for this Court to uphold the constitutional values and to enforce the constitutional limitations. That is the essence of the rule of law.

The controversy really pertains to the scope, reach and extent of the judicial review . . .

It is necessary to reiterate that the court must be conscious while examining the validity of the Proclamation that it is a power vested in the highest constitutional functionary of the Nation. The court will not lightly presume abuse or misuse. The court would, as it should, tread wearily, making allowance for the fact that the President and the Union Council of Ministers are the best judges of the situation, that they alone are in possession of information and material sensitive in nature sometimes and that the Constitution has trusted their judgment in the matter . . . But all this does not mean that the President and the Union Council of Ministers are the final arbiters in the matter or that their opinion is conclusive. The very fact that the Founding Fathers have chosen to provide for approval of the Proclamation by Parliament is, itself a proof of the fact that the opinion or satisfaction of the President (which always means the Union Council of Ministers with the Prime Minister at its head) is not final or conclusive. It is well-known that in the parliamentary form of Government, where the party in power commands a majority in Parliament more often than not, approval of Parliament by a simple majority is not difficult to obtain. Probably, it is for this reason that the check created by clause (3) of Article 356 has not proved to be as effective in practice as it ought to have been. The very fact that even in cases like Meghalaya and Karnataka, both Houses of Parliament approved the Proclamations shows the enervation of this check. Even the proponents of the finality of the decision of the President in this matter could not but concede that the said check has not proved to be an effective one. Nor could they say with any conviction that judicial review is excluded in this behalf. If judicial review is not excluded in matters of pardon and remission of sentence under Article 72 a seemingly absolute and unconditional power it is difficult to see on what principle can it be said that it is excluded in the case of a conditional power like the one under Article 356 . . .

Article 356 of the Constitution confers a power upon the President to be exercised only where he is satisfied that a situation has arisen where the Government of a State cannot be carried on in accordance with the provisions of the Constitution. Under our Constitution, the power is really that of the Union Council of Ministers with the Prime Minister at its head. The satisfaction contemplated by the article is subjective in nature.

The power conferred by Article 356 upon the President is a conditioned power. It is not an absolute power. The existence of material which may comprise of or include the report(s) of the Governor is a pre-condition. The satisfaction must be formed on relevant material. The recommendations of the Sarkaria Commission with respect to the exercise of power under Article 356 do merit serious consideration at the hands of all concerned.

Though the power of dissolving of the Legislative Assembly can be said to be implicit in clause (1) of Article 356, it must be held, having regard to the overall constitutional scheme that the President shall exercise it only after the Proclamation is approved by both Houses of Parliament under clause (3) and not before . . .

The Proclamation under Article 356(1) is not immune from judicial review. The Supreme Court or the High Court can strike down the Proclamation if it is found to be mala fide or based on wholly irrelevant or extraneous grounds. The deletion of clause (5) [which was introduced by 38th (Amendment) Act] by the 44th (Amendment) Act, removes the cloud on the reviewability of the action. When called upon, the Union of India has to produce the material on the basis of which action was taken. It cannot refuse to do so, if it seeks to defend the action. The court will not go into the correctness of the material or its adequacy. Its enquiry is limited to see whether the material was relevant to the action. Even if part of the material is irrelevant, the court cannot interfere so long as there is some material which is relevant to the action taken.

If the court strikes down the Proclamation, it has the power to restore the dismissed Government to office and revive and reactivate the Legislative Assembly wherever it may have been dissolved or kept under suspension. In such a case, the court has the power to declare that acts done, orders passed and laws made during the period the Proclamation was in force shall remain unaffected and be treated as valid. Such declaration, however, shall not preclude the Government/Legislative Assembly or other competent authority to review, repeal or modify such acts, orders and laws . . .

The Proclamation dated April 21, 1989 in respect of Karnataka (Civil Appeal No 3645 of 1989) and the Proclamation dated October 11, 1991 in respect of Meghalaya (Transferred Case Nos 5 and 7 of 1992) are unconstitutional. But for the fact that fresh elections have since taken place in both the States and new Legislative Assemblies and Governments have come into existence we would have formally struck down the Proclamations and directed the revival and restoration of the respective Governments and Legislative Assemblies. The Civil Appeal No 3645 of 1989 and Transferred Cases Nos 5 and 7 of 1992 are allowed accordingly. Civil Appeal Nos 193 and 194 of 1989 relating to Nagaland are disposed of in terms of the opinion expressed by us on the meaning and purport of Article 74(2) of the Constitution.

The Proclamations dated January 15, 1993 in respect of Madhya Pradesh, Rajasthan and Himachal Pradesh concerned in Civil Appeal Nos 1692,1692-A to 1692-C of 1993, 4627–4630 of 1993, Transferred Case (C) No 9 of 1993 and Transferred Case No 8 of 1993 respectively are not unconstitutional. The Civil Appeals are allowed and the judgment of the High Court of Madhya Pradesh in MP (C) No 237 of 1993 is set aside. The transferred cases are dismissed . . .

v. Pakistan

There was also judicial intervention by the Supreme Court of Pakistan in emergency power when it ruled that President Pervez Musharraf was a usurper of emergency powers under the Constitution and, as such, all amendments introduced in the Constitution and other statutes during the period of emergency were void. The Court also held the state of emergency declared on 3 November 2007 to be unconstitutional.

Sindh High Court Bar Association v Federation of Pakistan
31 Jul 2009 (Supreme Court, Pakistan)

Facts

On 3 November 2007, General Pervez Musharraf, Chief of Army Staff and the President of the country, issued a Proclamation of Emergency. He also issued Provisional Constitution Order No 1 of 2007, making as many as 61 judges of the superior judiciary, including the Chief Justice of Pakistan and the Chief Justices of three Provinces, disqualified, since many of them either did not agree to take or were not administered the oath. The constitutional validity of the Proclamation of Emergency, Provisional Constitution Order No 1 of 2007, the Oath Order and other relevant orders was challenged in this case.

Held

An independent and strong judiciary is a back bone of viable democratic system all over the world. The time tested experience has proved that independent and strong judiciary provides strength to the institutions running government particularly, those who roll on the wheels of democracy. Equally the independent and strong judiciary acts as an arbiter striking balance among various segments of Democratic system. It helps State organs, such as Legislature, Executive and the judiciary itself to function smoothly maintaining balance inter se. The Constitution of Pakistan, of 1973, too, provides the judiciary guarantees enshrined in it and states that the judiciary shall be fully secured, but, unfortunately, to its great dismay, this organ of State has all along been under the wrath of adventurers imposing their dictatorial terms obviously for their ulterior designs. The history of this country witnessed that in a set up of one government tenure of a Chief Justice of Pakistan was curtailed with ulterior motives and was restored to its original position when the designs were stood achieved. Likewise, through various instruments, the favourites and pliant members of superior judiciary were out rightly given underserved benefits while the others were shown doors. This happened during the era of the then Martial Law Administrator General Zia-ul-Haq and following the same foot steps, General Pervez Musharraf (Rtd) did the same in the year 2000. Many judges of superior judiciary who declined to toe his line of action were unceremoniously sacked.

General Pervez Musharraf (Rtd) through his 1999/2000 action declared that the National Assembly, the Provincial Assemblies, Senate, Chairman and Deputy Chairman of Senate, Speaker of National Assembly and the Provincial Assemblies were suspended and the Prime Minister, Federal Ministers, Parliamentary Secretaries, the Provincial Governors and the provincial Chief Ministers and the Advisors to the Chief Ministers, to have ceased to hold offices. However, his November 2007 action was a singular in nature, in that the onslaught was on judiciary alone. All other institutions were intact. The independence of judiciary was given a serious blow. In order to save the judiciary from being destroyed, for the first time in the history of this Country, a seven member bench of this Court headed by the de jure Chief Justice of Pakistan passed an order, inter-alia, restraining the President and Prime Minister of Pakistan from undertaking any such action, which was contrary to the Independence of Judiciary. So also the Judges of this Court and that of the High Courts including Chief Justice(s) were required not to take oath under the Provisional Constitution Order or any other extra-Constitutional step and on the same day viz 3 November 2007, the order was served on the members of superior judiciary through the respective Registrars of the Courts by way of Fax. It was also sent to all the relevant Executive functionaries.

The action of General Pervez Musharraf (Rtd) was, undeniably, taken to prevent the 11 member Bench of this Court which was hearing the Petition No. 73 of 2007 filed by Mr Justice (Rtd) Wajihuddin Ahmad and others in which the qualification of the General was in question, and perhaps, he was not expecting a favourable decision. The reasons shall, in that behalf be found in the detailed judgment. Be that as it may, Justice Abdul Hameed Dogar, as then he was called, along with four other Judges of this Court took oath in pursuance of unconstitutional Provisional Constitution Order and the Oath of Office (Judges) Order, 2007, and by that he also violated the order of seven member Bench of this Court which was headed by de jure Chief Justice of Pakistan. Mr Justice Abdul Hameed Dogar took the oath of Chief Justice of Pakistan, although, the office was not vacant. Some of High Courts Judges too took oath likewise violating the constitution and the order of seven member Bench, legally and lawfully passed. Besides, many other Judges in this Court and in the High Courts were appointed and they took oath in violation of constitutional provisions and the order of seven member Bench of this Court . . .

It may be noted that the chosen representative of the time, too, did not extend validation to the unconstitutional acts taken up to 3rd November, 2007, as is universally known. It is, however, quite heartening that, for the first time in the history of our beloved country, the chosen representative of people, who took their offices as a result of election taking place on 18th February, 2008, have, commendably, stayed their hands off and have not sanctified the unconstitutional acts, such as, the Declaration of Emergency, the Provisional Constitution Order No 1, the Oath of Office (Judges), Order, 2007, the Constitution (Amendment) Order, 2007 (President's Order No 5 of 2007), the Constitution (Second Amendment) Order of 2007 (President's Order No 6 of 2007) and many other instruments made and declared by General Pervez Musharraf (Rtd). In this, their restraint not extending validity to all these unconstitutional and illegal instruments and other steps taken by retired General are laudable. Evidently, this was done by the present representatives of people believing firmly that the prosperity of the country lies in the strong and independent democratic system which can alone flourish and survive with democratic steps to be taken in the better interest of people always apt and keen to choose them in such a viable system of governance. We are sanguine that the current democratic dispensation comprising of the President, the Prime Minister, Ministers and the Parliament shall continue to uphold the Constitution, its institutions and sacred values . . .

The Proclamation of Emergency issued by General Pervez Musharraf as the Chief of Army Staff (as he then was) on November 3, 2007; the Provisional Constitution Order No 1 of 2007 issued by him on the same date in his said capacity; the Oath of Office (Judges) Order of 2007 issued by him also on the same date though as the President of Pakistan but in exercise of powers under the aforesaid Proclamation of Emergency and the Provisional Constitution Order No 1 of 2007; The Provisional Constitution (Amendment) Order, 2007, issued by him likewise on 15 November 2007; the Constitution (Amendment) Order, 2007, being President's Order No 5 of 2007 issued on November 20, 2007; the Constitution (Second Amendment) Order, 2007, being the President's Order No 6 of 2007 issued on 14th December, 2007; the Islamabad High Court (Establishment) Order 2007 dated 14th December 2007 being the President's Order No 7 of 2007; the High Court Judges (Pensionary Benefits) Order, 2007, being President's Order No 8 of 2007; the Supreme Court Judges (Pensionary Benefits) Order, 2007, being President's Order No 9 of 2007 dated 14th December, 2007, are hereby declared to be unconstitutional, *ultra-vires* of the Constitution and consequently being illegal and of no legal [force] . . .

Notes and Questions

1. In many of the cases above, the courts reiterated the need for and the legitimacy of judicial review over the emergency powers conferred upon the president by the constitution. Bruce Ackerman, however, questions the suitability of having judges review decisions of president or parliament to declare a state of emergency. He questions the wisdom of immediate judicial intervention, especially when the country has experienced a sudden terrorist attack. Presumably, if the president can persuade the majority of Congress to approve a declaration of emergency, legitimacy is secured. The legislature, not the judiciary, would thus be the best branch of government to prevent the abuse of emergency power. This framework would prevent reasonable emergency measures from becoming permanent restrictions on freedoms, and should impose strict limits on unilateral exercises of presidential power. Presidents should be allowed to declare an emergency on their own

authority only for a limited period of time, such as a week or two, while Congress considers the matter. Emergency powers should then lapse unless a majority of both Houses votes to continue them, but even this vote should be valid for only two months. The president must then return to Congress for reauthorisation, and this time, a supermajority of 60 per cent should be required; after another two months, the majority should be set at 70 per cent; and then at 80 per cent for every subsequent two-month extension. Except for the worst terrorist onslaughts, this 'supermajoritarian escalator' will terminate the use of emergency powers within a relatively short period. See BA Ackerman, 'The Emergency Constitution' (2004) 113 *Yale Law Journal* 1047 at 1066.

2. The exercise of emergency power may potentially infringe upon human rights and the regime may eventually descend into a dictatorship. Constitutions thus attempt to restrain such exercise of emergency powers. In most cases, the restraints are in institutional and procedural forms. However, even in cases where these procedural and institutional requirements are met, the potential threat posed to fundamental rights still raises constitutional issues. Two models of constitutional framework responding to emergency powers can be discerned. The *first* is the 'Business as Usual' model, which is based on the idea of constitutional absolutism and perfection. Under this model, ordinary legal rules and norms still apply during times of emergency and crisis. No special 'emergency' powers are introduced either on an ad hoc basis or for a permanent purpose, since the model is premised on the assumption that the ordinary legal system already provides the necessary framework and solutions to deal with any crisis, without requiring legislative or executive assertion of new or additional governmental powers. This model has been criticised as manifesting a naive idealism which disregards context. The *second* has collectively been called 'models of accommodation'. It consists of several constitutional models:

    (a) forging a new understanding of existing legal rules through the context-based interpretation;
    (b) accommodating security in times of crisis through legislative amendments and modifications to the existing ordinary legal system; and
    (c) enforcement of the president's inherent executive powers, allowing him or her to act legally and constitutionally to respond to the needs of an emergency situation.

    The strength of the 'models of accommodation' approach is that it is flexible and can accommodate or respond to the expansive powers needed to meet varying types of such crises. However, the models of accommodation have been criticised for being unprincipled, enabling the authorities to manipulate the legal system to their purposes.

    Oren Gross argues that the two traditional models may not always be adequate in times of emergency and has proposed an alternative model, the 'Extra-Legal Measures' model. This model informs the public that officials may act extra-legally when they believe that such action is necessary to protect the country and safeguard public security in a time of calamity, provided they openly and publicly acknowledge the nature of their actions. It is then left to the people to decide how to respond ex-post facto to such extra-legal actions through direct or indirect channels. They demonstrate a strict commitment to the violated principles and values and hold the official in question to account for the wrongfulness of his actions. That official has to make legal and/or political reparations for his wrongful actions. Alternatively, the people may give retrospective approval to the actions of the public official. See O Gross, 'Chaos and Rules: Should Responses to Violent Crisis Always Be Constitutional?' (2003) 112 *Yale Law Journal* 1011.

E. The Court's Role in Mediating Political Conflicts

Courts are often called upon to resolve political conflicts arising from ambiguous constitutional power-sharing schemes or political divisions. In doing so, a court may be active and aggressive, or reactive and cautious. The Constitutional Courts of Thailand and Mongolia seem to be examples of the active and aggressive model. In a number of cases, the Mongolian Constitutional Court became embroiled in the political conflict instead of resolving it. For example, in the controversy over whether State Great Hural members could serve in Cabinet positions, the Court relied on Article 29 of the Constitution, under which 'Members of Parliament shall have no other employment', to declare the practice unconstitutional. This decision triggered constitutional chaos in Mongolia. The coalition's leadership accused the Court of being politically motivated, and subsequently enacted a new law to allow Members of Parliament to serve in the Cabinet. The Court declared the new law unconstitutional. Parliament then amended the Constitution to allow Members of Parliament to serve as Prime Minister. The decisions of the Mongolian Constitutional Court invited serious criticism and triggered constitutional turbulence.[92] The Court appeared to perceive itself as another political branch with its own political goal, participating in the nexus of politics and competing with other actors.

The Constitutional Court of Thailand operates in a similarly active way. In September 2008, it ruled that Prime Minister Samak Sundaravej violated Thai law by serving as the host of a television cooking programme. Samak had to resign the premiership.[93] The Court held that by appearing on the show, Samak was an 'employee' within the scope of Article 267 of the Constitution, which forbids any public officeholder from holding 'any position in . . . an organization carrying out business . . . or be[ing] an employee of any person'. Several months later, the Court dissolved the People's Power Party and two of its political allies on the grounds that party leader Yongyut Tiyapairat was convicted of buying votes in the December 2007 general elections.[94] These decisions triggered a string of political protests and led to the declaration of a state of emergency.

---

[92] For a detailed discussion, see T Ginsburg and Gombosuren Ganzorig, 'When Courts and Politics Collide: Mongolia's Constitutional Crisis' (2001) 14 *Columbia Journal of Asian Law* 309.

[93] Re: The President of the Senate referred a petition submitted by senators to the Constitutional Court for a ruling on the termination of ministerial office of the Prime Minister; Re: The Election Commission requested for a Constitutional Court ruling on the termination of ministerial office of the Prime Minister. Ruling, No 12-13/2551 (2008), Sep 9 2008.

[94] Re: The Attorney-General requested for a Constitutional Court order to dissolve People's Power (Palang Prachachon) Party Ruling No 20/2551, Dec 2 2008.

In contrast to Mongolia and Thailand, the courts of Japan, South Korea and Taiwan represent a reactive and cautious model. They are 'reactive' because they do not promote any social or political agendas of their own, unlike the South Africa Constitutional Court or Indian Supreme Court. They are 'cautious' because none of them goes directly against the majoritarian preferences of the public, and they do not attract criticisms of democratic illegitimacy or juristocracy.

Although the South Korean Constitutional Court is perceived to be an aggressive court, it rarely rules against the preferences or sentiments of the political majority, especially in relation to some of the most hotly-contested issues. For example, in 1995, the Constitutional Court affirmed a prosecutor's decision not to prosecute two former presidents, Chun Doo-Hwan and Roh Tae-Woo, and other military officials who were responsible for systematic human rights abuses in the early 1980s. Although the Constitutional Court disagreed with the prosecutor on statutory limits and took the view that certain charges had yet to expire, it nevertheless held that the decision not to prosecute was not arbitrary. One further example is a case that was brought by several prominent human rights activists, including Kim Dae-Jung (who later became the President). As he was concerned about the statute of limitations, Kim decided to withdraw the case and sought legislative solutions. The Court quickly dismissed the case upon Kim's withdrawal, indicating that a political compromise might be reached soon. After a Special Act was passed to allow the prosecution of former presidents and military officials, the Court upheld the Act, albeit by a narrow 5:4 margin. The Court did so despite concerns about the retroactive nature of the law. The majority held that that the rule of law prohibited ex post facto criminal legislation and, as such, part of the Act allowing for the prosecution of crimes beyond statutory limitations was unconstitutional. However, as Article 23 of the Constitutional Court Act required a quorum of six votes to uphold the constitutionality of statutes, the Court could not run counter to the political majority's will to prosecute former presidents. Even though the Court had a different view on the rule of law and transitional justice from the public, it chose not to go against the political majority and self-consciously constrained itself by relying on the procedural requirements of the Constitutional Court Act.

Much like its counterparts in Japan and South Korea, the Taiwanese Constitutional Court has also adopted a reactive and cautious style of judicial reasoning. Most of the Court's decisions generally reinforce public opinion and endorse policies of key political alliances in the democratisation process. Given the contentious nature of democratising politics, it is not surprising that the Taiwanese Constitutional Court has had to handle politically-charged cases. While the Court has never declined to hear such cases, it has developed two sharply contrasting approaches in dealing with them.

First, if actual or potential political consensus were possible, the Court would clearly state what the political majority expected in constitutional terms. For example, the Court ordered senior representatives to leave office and set the deadline for re-election in a milestone decision, *Interpretation No 261*. Although this was drastic, a national consensus to undergo democratisation and to suspend the old Parliament had already been reached in the National Affairs Conference amidst unprecedented street protests and student demonstrations in March 1990, three months before the Court's decision. In this context, few were willing to hold that assemblymen who had been elected some four decades earlier should continue to retain their seats. It was against this profound social and political consensus that the Court's ground-breaking ruling in *JY Interpretation No 261* must be understood. The Court was prepared to act more aggressively where there was clear social consensus.

Secondly, in a situation where politics were divisive, the Court issued decisions that were vague, deliberately ambiguous or obscure. For example, in *JY Interpretation No 419*, the Court was asked to decide whether an elected Vice-President could simultaneously be Premier as well. Despite strong protests from the opposition party, public opinion was ambivalent. The Court acknowledged this state of affairs and held that while the Constitution did not contemplate the same person assuming both offices, the practice did not directly contravene the Constitution, especially since it did not create any genuine difficulty in its practical functioning. See Wen-Chen Chang, 'Strategic Judicial Responses in Highly Politically Charged Cases: East Asian Experiences' (2010) 8(4) *International Journal of Constitutional Law* 885; Jiunn-rong Yeh, 'Presidential Politics and Judicial Facilitation of Political Dialogue between Political Actors in New Asian Democracies: Comparing the South Korean and Taiwanese Experiences' (2010) 8(4) *I•CON* 911.

4

Constitutional Change
and Amendments

I. INTRODUCTION

The first systematic discussion on constitutional change was by Georg Jellinek in 1906.[1] According to Jellinek, constitutional change can occur in two ways:

(a) constitutional amendment; and
(b) constitutional transformation.

'Amendment' refers to change effected through the formal constitutional amendment procedure; it is intentional and deliberate. In contrast, 'transformation' occurs through means other than formal amendment procedures.[2] Chinese legalist Hsu Dau-lin (徐道鄰 1907–73) identified four modes of constitutional change in his *Die Verfassungswandlung.*[3]

To constitutional scholars, constitutional amendment is only one way to change the constitution; the theory of constitutional change views this phenomenon against a broader context. Certain prominent issues arise in the investigation of constitutional change. The first is the inevitability and desirability of constitutional change. While the constitution is intended to endure over the long term as the ultimate legal order, it is not writ in stone. It changes with the generations and when a polity faces issues never contemplated or provided for by the constitution's drafters. Thomas Jefferson, principal author of the US Declaration of Independence, espoused a populist view of constitutionalism by advocating that the constitution should be amended by each generation so that the intentions of past generations do not unduly constrain future generations. However, Jefferson also endorsed the idea of immutable natural rights.[4] In contrast, James Madison argued that 'a constitution subject to frequent amendment would promote factionalism and provide no firm basis for republican

---

[1] G Jellinek, *Verfassungsaenderung und Verfassungswandlung* (Berlin: Haering, 1906). This classic has been translated into English. See, eg, G Jellinek, *Constitutional Amendment and Constitutional Transformation* (1906), reprinted in A Jacobson and B Schlink (eds), *Weimar: A Jurisprudence of Crisis* (Berkeley, Cal: University of California Press, 2000)

[2] G Jellinek, *Constitutional Amendment and Constitutional Transformation* (1906), reprinted in A Jacobson and B Schlink (eds), *Weimar: A Jurisprudence of Crisis* (Berkeley, Cal: University of California Press, 2000) at 54.

[3] Hsu Dau-lin, *Die Verfassungswandlung* (Berlin und Leipzig: Walter de Gruyter, 1932).

[4] *The Statute of Virginia for Religious Freedom* (Va Code Ann S 57-1 (Michie 1995), drafted by Thomas Jefferson in 1777 and adopted by the General Assembly in 1786).

self-government'.[5] Thus, the paradox of constitutionalism lies in its commitment to uphold a set of fundamental values while accommodating the need for change, and continues to be a key subject of contemporary constitutional enquiry.

Secondly, it is important to appreciate the diverse and distinctive methods of constitutional change. Aside from constitutional amendment procedures, the constitution may be changed without formal amendment through judicial interpretation, or changes that occur in the aftermath of significant political events, such as a revolution or an emergency. These different routes to constitutional changes impact the constitutional order and constitutionalism differently.

Thirdly, the scope and limits of constitutional change have been issues for continuous debate. A democracy based on popular sovereignty would find it difficult to embrace the concept of an 'unconstitutional constitutional amendment'. This requires the court to serve as the constitution's guardian, and in that capacity to declare unconstitutional and strike down a constitutional amendment instituted by popular vote. However, it is not uncommon for modern constitutions to resort to self-protective measures and to limit the constitution's amendment power through express or implied restrictions.

The issue of legitimacy arises in relation to these three types of constitutional change. Does the imposition of substantive limits on the amendment process furnish the basis for an evaluation of the legitimacy of proposed amendments?

In this chapter we explore the theory of constitutional change and amendments through the lens of Asian experiences and the prevailing social-political contexts. We have divided this chapter broadly into three further parts. In section II., we consider constitutional changes, taking note of what drives constitutional change and contributes to the durability (or fragility) of constitutions. In section III., we look at the various methods of constitutional change, including constitutional amendment and procedures, political actions and referenda, judicial decisions, soft constitutional law and customs. In section IV., we explore the scope of and limits to constitutional change, including implied limits to legislative power, eternity clauses and international legal limits.

II. CONSTITUTIONAL DURABILITY AND ADAPTABILITY

A. Some Observations on the Durability of Constitutions in Asia

Aristotle argued in the *Politics* that the instability of the law could weaken the notion of law itself. The nature of the constitution – as fundamental law – thus requires it to be stable. It should be fairly permanent and not be changed too often. To this end, drafters of constitutions take a long-term view of their handiwork and effectively legislate for future generations. Yet, despite the best of intentions, many constitutions do

---

[5] A Hamilton, J Jay and J Madison, *Federalist No 49* (1788; reprinted with an introduction and commentary by G Wills, New York: Bantam, 1982); see also S Levinson, 'Veneration and Constitutional Change: James Madison confronts the Possibility of Constitutional Amendment' (1990) 21 *Texas Tech Law Review* 2443–61.

not endure. Research shows that most constitutions are relatively short-lived. Zachary, Ginsburg and Melton have found that the average lifespan of the constitutions of all countries is 19 years, with the most enduring constitutions found in either North American or Europe. In Latin America and Eastern Europe, the average constitutional lifespan is some eight years. In any given year, four or five constitutions will be replaced, 10 to 15 will be amended, and about 20 proposals for revision will be under consideration.[6] Naturally, this is a quantitative rather than a qualitative study, and fails to account for the extent to which substantial changes were made by one constitution replacing another.

In contrast to this general finding, textual and institutional continuity has been identified as one feature of constitutionalism in Asia, at least where Korea, Japan and Taiwan are concerned.[7] A more comprehensive investigation into Asian constitutions reveals that constitutions in East Asia are comparatively durable, though quite a few of them were drafted recently. The oldest constitutions claim lifespans of 68 years (Indonesia) and 67 years Japan respectively. Based on Table 4.1, the average lifespan of a constitution in East Asia is 36 years.

Table 4.1 Constitutional Durability in Asia (as of 2013)

Constitutions	Year of Enactment	Years in Continuous Operation
Indonesia	1945	68
Japan	1946	67
Taiwan	1947	66
India	1950	63
Malaysia	1957	56
Singapore	1965	48
Pakistan	1973	40
China	1982	31
Brunei	1984	29
South Korea	1987	26
Philippines	1987	26
Laos	1991	22
Mongolia	1992	21
Vietnam	1992	21
Cambodia	1993	20
Thailand	2007	6
Myanmar	2008	5

[6] Z Elkins, T Ginsburg and J Melton, *The Endurance of National Constitutions* (New York: Cambridge University Press, 2009).

[7] Jiunn-rong Yeh and Wen-Chen Chang, 'The Emergence of East Asian Constitutionalism: Features in Comparison' (2011) 59 *American Journal of Comparative Law* 805, 820–23.

At the beginning of the twentieth century, many Asian polities were under colonial rule. The first wave of constitution-making started after the end of World War II, when Japan, the Republic of China (Taiwan), Vietnam, India, Pakistan, Ceylon and Burma/Myanmar embarked on the process which produced constitutions lasting for more than 60 years until the present day.[8] The second wave began with decolonisation in the 1950s and accelerated during the 1960s, when states such as Singapore, Malaya and North Borneo attained independence. These constitutions have endured for almost 50 years. The third wave of constitution-making was impelled by the economic and political transitions of the 1980s, where states such as Korea, Mongolia and the Philippines underwent democratic transitions; socialist states like the China, Laos and Cambodia embraced economic reform which translated into constitutional changes to allow for some degree of free market competition.

Thailand stands in sharp contrast to the general durability of Asian constitutions, having undergone numerous military coups, each resulting in a new constitution. Since its transition from an absolute to constitutional monarchy in 1932, Thailand has had some 17 constitutions. The latest 2007 constitution – which replaced the 1997 Constitution – was promulgated after a coup that toppled the government of Prime Minister Thaksin Shinawatra.

Constitutions can survive many challenges through constitutional change, allowing them to adapt to dynamic social-political and economic contexts. A few factors may be identified as undergirding the three waves of constitution-making, resulting in the distinctive features of constitutions in Asia. First, constitutional change may be seen as a way to preserve the continuation of state sovereignty and to defend regime legitimacy. Secondly, constitutional change may take place in situations where the constitution was externally imposed (as in the case of Japan) and subsequently subject to challenges demanded by an autonomous polity. Thirdly, constitutional change plays an important role in democratic transition, which not only motivates constitutional change but is also a primary objective.

Notes and Questions

1. The idea of constitutional change was developed to theorise constitutional development beyond formal revisions. So, what exactly is a 'constitutional change'? Must a change take place within the context of an existing constitutional order to be 'constitutional'? Would replacing a constitution with a new one after a military coup constitute a kind of constitutional change?

2. Richard Albert ('Nonconstitutional Amendments' (2009) 22 *Canadian Journal of Law and Jurisprudence* 5) proposes a broad taxonomy that includes:

   (a) constitutional change;
   (b) unconstitutional change;
   (c) extra-constitutional change; and
   (d) anti-constitutional constitutional change.

---

[8] Although the current constitution of Myanmar dates from 2008, its 1947 Constitution survived till 2008, over 61 years.

He argues that the purpose of an anti-constitutional action is to undermine the constitutional order and that it is qualitatively different from an unconstitutional action on at least two grounds. First, an anti-constitutional action is decidedly antagonistic to the state, whereas an unconstitutional action is not necessarily hostile towards the state. Secondly, anti-constitutionality often entails some form of violent conduct that may escalate into a revolution. Unconstitutionality does not reach this level of subversion because those who act unconstitutionally do not contemplate altering the existing constitutional order but seek change within its parameters.

3. Tom Ginsburg argues that the notion of a 'constitutional afterlife' – the impact of a text beyond the constitution's formal survival – provides us with a novel way of thinking about the impact constitutions have. See his 'Constitutional Afterlife: The Continuing Impact of Thailand's Post-Political Constitution' (2009) 7(1) *I•CON* 83. He offers, as an example, the defunct 1997 Thai Constitution, which he argues, continued to exert an influence before 2007 Constitution was adopted; many of the pre-2007 institutions continued to function after the 2006 military coup, notwithstanding the lack of a formal legal basis for their authority:

> Traditionally, we think about the impact of constitutions in terms of the efficacy of their formal provisions. We imagine that constitutions matter when there is congruence between text and practice, and do not matter when such congruence is lacking. We might ask, for example, whether rights promised in the text are actually observed, or whether institutions set up by a constitution operate within its constraints. Another criterion for the success or failure might be the endurance of the formal text, or the ability of a constitutional regime to deliver social goods such as economic growth and democratic stability. The Thai example suggests that constitutions might also matter for their enduring institutional innovations. Constitutional afterlife may be particularly important for the study of constitutionalism in unstable political environments. While modern Thai history does not bode well for the long-term survival of the current constitutional document, institutional endurance alone marks a significant step toward stability, and the legacy of 1997 may continue to make a difference for Thai governance.

Should we view the phenomenon of a 'constitutional afterlife' as a continuation of the previous constitutional regime and assess its endurance accordingly? Should the adoption of institutions established by a prior constitutional order be regarded as a form of constitutional change, or should it be viewed as a form of constitutional continuity?

B. Constitutional Change, Sovereignty and Legitimacy

Constitutional change may be necessary to safeguard and defend a state's sovereignty and legitimacy. It may affirm sovereignty and resolve a crisis of legitimacy. Take the case of Taiwan, for example, where the constitution was amended to address a crisis of legitimacy within the domestic polity.

The Republic of China (ROC) Constitution was drafted and promulgated on the Mainland in 1947 after decades of political conflicts and negotiation. No sooner had it entered into force when civil war broke out between the Nationalists and Communists.

In 1949, the Nationalists fled to Taiwan after losing the war, carrying along with them the 1947 Constitution. Shortly thereafter, representatives were elected under the terms of this Constitution. Ironically, a constitution that was designed for China was instead applied in Taiwan (which China considers a renegade province). However, it was soon placed under the shadow of martial law rule that lasted three decades.

The civil war of the 1940s was only officially declared over in the 1990s after martial law was lifted. The ROC Constitution then began to apply normally in Taiwan, but its legitimacy was soon challenged. The main criticism was that this constitution was unsuitable for Taiwan, given its size and contemporary needs, not least because the ROC Constitution still claimed to represent the sovereign state of China as it was in the 1940s. Taiwan's journey toward democratic transition thus began with a series of constitutional amendments. In the early 1990s, seven rounds of constitutional revisions were made, thereby effecting substantial changes to suffrage, government institutions and the electoral system. Taiwan chose to amend the ROC Constitution gradually rather than replace it with a new one. So, while constitutional change in Taiwan largely resolved the problem of legitimacy, the matter of sovereignty was left unresolved,[9] given that the international community does not recognise Taiwan as an independent state.

On two critical occasions, the Constitutional Court played a significant role in securing the continuation and legitimacy of the regime in Taiwan. In *JY Interpretation No 31 of 1954*, the Court ruled in favour of the Nationalist regime which refused to hold elections in Taiwan for representatives whose term had expired even though this was required under the constitution. By this stroke of judicial constitution-making, the Court endorsed the policy of tenured national representatives and secured the legitimacy of Nationalist rule in Taiwan. In the second case, *JY Interpretation No 261 of 1990*, which was decided after 40 years of authoritarian martial rule under the Nationalist Government, the Court – sensing the rising tide of democratisation in Taiwan – did a *volte face* by demanding that tenured national representatives step down and be replaced in a national election.

JY Interpretation No 31
29 Jan 1954 (Constitutional Court, Taiwan)

Facts

The Constitution of Republic of China was promulgated in 1947, and in the same year the Members of both the Legislative and Control Yuans were elected to represent the people throughout the whole of China. Soon after, a civil war broke out between the Nationalists and the Communists. The defeated Nationalists gave up the mainland and retreated to Taiwan in 1949. By 1954, when the term of the first members of the Legislative and Control Yuans lapsed, the ROC Constitution faced a crisis of legitimacy, since it was impossible for new Members of both the Legislative and Control Yuans to be elected in mainland China under the terms of the Constitution. The Court was asked to decide whether, in the case where electing Members to both the Legislative and Control Yuans was impossible, the incumbent Members should be allowed to remain in office after the expiration of their respective terms under Articles 65 and 93 of the Constitution.

---

[9] Jiunn-rong Yeh, 'Constitutional Reform and Democratization in Taiwan: 1945–2000' in P Chow (ed), *Taiwan's Modernization in Global Perspective* (Westport, Conn: Praeger, 2002) 47.

Held

Article 65 of Constitution provides that Members of the Legislative Yuan shall serve a term of three years; and Article 93 provides that Members of the Control Yuan shall serve a term of six years. Terms shall start from the date when those Members take office, and expire at the end of the term as provided in the Constitution. However, our state has been undergoing a severe calamity, which makes re-election of the second term of both Yuans de facto impossible. It would contradict the purpose of the Five-Yuan system as established by the Constitution, if both the Legislative and Control Yuans ceased to exercise their respective powers. Therefore, before the second-term Members are elected, convene and are convoked in accordance with the laws, all of the first-term Members of both the Legislative and Control Yuans shall continue to exercise their respective powers.

JY Interpretation No 261
21 Jun 1990 (Constitutional Court, Taiwan)

Facts

The lifting of the martial law in 1987 marked the end of the Kuomingtang (KMT) regime's authoritarian rule and ushered in a period of dramatic transition towards democracy. Consequently, the legitimacy of the first-term Members of both the Legislative and Control Yuan, who had served for almost 40 years – courtesy of *JY Interpretation No 31* – was again challenged. The same issue was raised again: Whether the first-term national representatives should be allowed to exercise their powers indefinitely without periodic re-election. This time, the Court came to a completely different decision.

Held

The terms of office of the national representatives are expressly provided in the Constitution. Since the first-term national representatives were elected and took office, our nation has suffered severe calamities. As a result, re-election of the national representatives has been infeasible and all of the first-term national representatives have continued to exercise their powers. Such results were necessary for the maintenance of our constitutional system. . . .

However, periodical re-election of representatives is crucial for reflection of the will of the people and for implementation of constitutional democracy . . .

Neither *JY Interpretation No 31*, nor Article 28, Paragraph 2, of the Constitution, nor Paragraph 6, Subparagraphs 2 and 3, of the Temporary Provisions Effective during the Period of National Mobilization for the Suppression of the Communist Rebellion were intended to allow the first-term national representatives to continue exercising their powers indefinitely. None of these provisions were intended to change their terms of office. . . .

Nor did they prohibit the election of the next-term national representatives from being held. In fact, since 1969, the Central Government has been holding regular elections of the national representatives in the Free Area, in order to reinforce our national representative bodies incrementally. *To cope with the present situations* (emphasis added), those first-term national representatives who have not been reelected on a periodical basis shall cease the exercise of their powers no later than December 31, 1991. Among them, those who have been de facto incapable of exercising or constantly failed to exercise their powers shall be immediately dismissed, after thorough investigation, from their offices. The Central Government is further mandated to hold, in due course, a nationwide second-term election of the national representatives, in accordance with the spirit of the Constitution, the essence of this Interpretation and the relevant regulations, so that the constitutional system will function properly.

Notes and Questions

1. *JY Interpretations No 31* and *No 261* were decisions rendered by the same court (Constitutional Court) on the same issue (the legitimacy of the representatives not subject to re-election) in relation to the same group of persons (national representatives elected on the Mainland), albeit 46 years apart. In *Interpretation No 261*, the Court declared the need to 'to cope with the present situation (emphasis added)'. How did this 'present situation' differ from the state of affairs in 1954? What do you think prompted the Court to change its mind so radically?

2. Following *JY Interpretation No 31*, the national representatives elected in China continued to serve as the Taiwanese people's representatives for more than 40 years. This is a notorious example of how the Court supported a form of 'representational manipulation' under which these representatives could continue in office without being re-elected. By the 1990s, most of these representatives had either passed away or were very old. This presented a major challenge to the legitimacy of the judicially-endorsed tenured representatives. See Jiunn-rong Yeh, 'The Cult of *Fatung*, Representational Manipulation and Reconstruction in Taiwan' in G Hassall and C Saunders (eds), *The People's Representatives: Electoral Systems in the Asia-Pacific Region* (Sydney: Allen and Unwin, 1997) 23.

3. Did *JY Interpretation No 261* contribute to Taiwan's democratic transition? Was the decision a significant factor in accelerating the end of authoritarian rule, or did the Court conveniently align itself with the shifting political tide? Yeh and Chang point out that much like its counterparts in Japan and South Korea, Taiwan's Constitutional Court exhibited a reactive and cautious style of judicial reasoning. Most of the Court's decisions merely reinforced public opinion and endorsed policies of key political alliances. The process of democratisation led to the hearing of many highly-contested disputes. While the Court has never refused to hear such cases, it developed two sharply contrasting patterns in dealing with them. If an actual or potential political consensus was in sight, the Court would clearly state what the political majority expected in constitutional terms. As in *JY Interpretation No 261*, for example, a national consensus to democratise and suspend the old legislature had already been reached at the National Affairs Conference. This Conference involved all major political alliances and civil organisations, and was held amidst unprecedented street protests and student demonstrations in March 1990, three months before the Court's decision. Given this context, few were willing to support the position that geriatric assemblymen should continue to retain their legislative seats, having been elected some four decades earlier. However, where there was a lack of political consensus, the Court tended to issue decisions that were ambiguous in content and tone. See Jiunn-rong Yeh and Wen-Chen Chang, 'The Emergence of East Asian Constitutionalism: Features in Comparison' (2011) 59 *American Journal of Comparative Law* 805, 829–31.

A change in sovereignty may necessitate constitutional change to allow the existing constitutional order to meet the exigencies of the next stage of constitutional development. In *JY Interpretations No 31 and No 261*, the Taiwanese Court sought, on two occasions, to secure the legitimacy of a regime in the aftermath of a civil war and during a period of democratic transition.

In contrast, developments in Hong Kong – which had been a British colony from 1842 to 1997 – demonstrate how the Courts sought to reaffirm self-rule and buttress the rule of law after 1997 when control over Hong Kong reverted to the People's Republic of China (PRC) Government. Under the 'One Country, Two Systems' rule, Hong Kong is a Special Administrative Region (SAR) of the PRC. Its constitution, the Basic Law, secures some autonomy for Hong Kong. However, it remains unclear how and to what extent Hong Kong can extend or perpetuate the mode of government and the freedoms it enjoyed under the British to the new legal framework under the PRC. It was also unclear whether and how the British-style system of judicial review in Hong Kong would be allowed to function under the Basic Law.

This constitutional question was addressed in *Ng Ka Ling v Director of Immigration*. In a unanimous judgment, the Court of Final Appeal preserved Hong Kong's legacy of the rule of law and reconciled it with the Basic Law. Specifically, the issue of who has the right of abode in Hong Kong prompted a fierce debate and tested the 'One Country, Two Systems' policy of the PRC.

Ng Ka Ling v Director of Immigration
[1999] 1 HKLRD 315 (Court of Final Appeal, Hong Kong)

Facts

There was no immigration restriction into Hong Kong until 1950. People were free to travel across the Hong Kong-Chinese border. With the establishment of the People's Republic of China in 1949, the Hong Kong Government decided to close the border and implement immigration control in an attempt to stem waves of immigrants and refugees. The immigration boom intensified throughout the 1950s and 1960s with the onset of Cultural Revolution. The Government adopted the Touch Base Policy in 1974 and began repatriating immigrants intercepted at the border. The Government abolished the policy by 1980 and began repatriating all illegal immigrants once they were apprehended. Even though the PRC maintained that ethnic Chinese of Hong Kong were Chinese nationals, Hong Kong residents were subject to immigration control when entering China and had no right of abode on the mainland. There was also a quota for mainland residents wishing to apply for a One-way Permit to immigrate to Hong Kong. The debate of the right of abode erupted on 29 January 1999, when the Hong Kong Court of Final Appeal ruled that the children of parents who have the right of abode in Hong Kong also have the right of abode, irrespective of whether their parents were permanent residents at the time of their birth. The Applicants were Chinese nationals born on the Mainland. They each had a parent who was a Hong Kong permanent resident.

Andrew Li CJ

Questions involving the proper interpretation of the Basic Law are before us for the first time. These are questions of momentous importance for both the future of the people involved as well as the development of constitutional jurisprudence in the new order. . . .

Before turning to the issues, it is important for us first, to state the position as to the constitutional jurisdiction of the courts in the Hong Kong Special Administrative Region and, secondly, to lay down the proper approach to the interpretation of the Basic Law. The Region is vested with independent judicial power, including that of final adjudication (art 19(1)). The courts of the Region at all levels shall be the judiciary of the Region exercising the judicial power of the Region (art 80). In exercising their judicial power conferred by the Basic Law, the courts of the Region have a duty to enforce and interpret that law. They undoubtedly have the jurisdiction to examine whether legislation enacted by the legislature of the Region or acts of the executive authorities of the Region are consistent with the Basic Law and, if found to be inconsistent, to hold them to be invalid. The exercise of this jurisdiction is a matter of obligation, not of discretion so that if inconsistency is established, the courts are bound to hold that a law or executive act is invalid at least to the extent of the inconsistency. Although this has not been questioned, it is right that we should take this opportunity of stating it unequivocally. In exercising this jurisdiction, the courts perform their constitutional role under the Basic Law of acting as a constitutional check on the executive and legislative branches of government to ensure that they act in accordance with the Basic Law. What has been controversial is the jurisdiction of the courts of the Region to examine whether any legislative acts of the National People's Congress or its Standing Committee (which we shall refer to simply as 'acts') are consistent with the Basic Law and to declare them to be invalid if found to be inconsistent. In our view, the courts of the Region do have this jurisdiction and indeed the duty to declare invalidity if inconsistency is found. It is right that we should take this opportunity of stating so unequivocally.

Under the Chinese Constitution (arts 57 and 58), the National People's Congress is the highest organ of state power and its permanent body is the Standing Committee and they exercise the legislative powers of the state. So their acts are acts of the sovereign. The jurisdiction of the Region's courts to examine their acts to ensure consistency with the Basic Law is derived from the sovereign in that the National People's Congress had enacted pursuant to art 31 of the Chinese Constitution the Basic Law for the Region. The Basic Law is a national law and is the constitution of the Region. Like other constitutions, it distributes and delimits powers, as well as providing for fundamental rights and freedoms. As with other constitutions, laws which are inconsistent with the Basic Law are of no effect and are invalid. Under it, the courts of the Region have independent judicial power within the high degree of autonomy conferred on the Region. It is for the courts of the Region to determine questions of inconsistency and invalidity when they arise. It is therefore for the courts of the Region to determine whether an act of the National People's Congress or its Standing Committee is inconsistent with the Basic Law, subject of course to the provisions of the Basic Law itself. This proposition gains added strength from the circumstance that the Basic Law was enacted to implement China's basic policies regarding Hong Kong to remain unchanged for 50 years as declared and elaborated in the Joint Declaration. Article 159(4) of the Basic Law provides that no amendment thereto shall contravene the established basic policies. The jurisdiction to enforce and interpret the Basic Law necessarily entails the jurisdiction stated above over acts of the National People's Congress and its Standing Committee to ensure their consistency with the Basic Law. In *HKSAR v Ma Wai Kwan David* [1997] HKLRD 761, [1997] 2 HKC 315, which concerned the survival of the common law in the new order and the legality of the Provisional Legislative Council, the Court of Appeal (Chan CJHC, Nazareth and Mortimer V-PP) held, accepting the Government's submission, that the Region's courts have no jurisdiction to query the validity of any acts of the National People's Congress since they are acts of the sovereign. It was held that the jurisdiction of the Region's courts is a limited one to examine the existence (as opposed to the validity) of the acts of the sovereign or its delegate. In our view, this conclusion of the

Court of Appeal as to the jurisdiction of the Region's courts is wrong. The correct position is as stated above. . . .

The courts of the Hong Kong Special Administrative Region shall have jurisdiction over all cases in the Region, except that the restrictions on their jurisdiction imposed by the legal system and principles previously in force in Hong Kong shall be maintained. The Government submitted in that case that prior to 1 July 1997 Hong Kong courts could not have questioned the constitutionality of legislation of the United Kingdom Parliament vis-à-vis that country's unwritten constitution or the Hong Kong Letters Patent, which was Hong Kong's constitutional document as a British colony. So, this was a restriction on the jurisdiction of the Hong Kong courts 'imposed by the legal system and principles previously in force ' envisaged by art 19(2). After 1 July 1997, it applied equivalently to acts of the National People's Congress, so the Government argued. That submission was accepted by the Court of Appeal. The analogy drawn with the old order was misconceived. Prior to 1 July 1997, Hong Kong was a British colony. According to the common law, the United Kingdom Parliament had the supreme authority to legislate for Hong Kong and the courts in Hong Kong could not have questioned that authority. For the reasons already explained, the position in the new order is fundamentally different. Article 19(2) of the Basic Law provides for the limitation on the constitutional jurisdiction of the courts 'imposed by the legal system and principles previously in force in Hong Kong'. This cannot bring to the new order restrictions only relevant to legislation of the United Kingdom Parliament imposed under the old order. . . .

As far as the Court of Final Appeal is concerned, it has a duty to make a reference to the Standing Committee if two conditions are satisfied: (1) First, the provisions of the Basic Law in question: (a) concern affairs which are the responsibility of the Central People's Government; or (b) concern the relationship between the Central Authorities and the Region. That is, the excluded provisions. We shall refer to this as 'the classification condition'. (2) Secondly, the Court of Final Appeal in adjudicating the case needs to interpret such provisions (that is the excluded provisions) and such interpretation will affect the judgment on the case. We shall refer to this as 'the necessity condition.' In our view, it is for the Court of Final Appeal and for it alone to decide, in adjudicating a case, whether both conditions are satisfied. It is for the Court, not the National People's Congress, to decide whether the classification condition is satisfied, that is, whether the provision is an excluded provision. If the Court of Final Appeal is satisfied of both conditions, it would be obliged to seek an interpretation of the relevant excluded provisions from the Standing Committee. It is significant that what has to be referred to the Standing Committee is not the question of interpretation involved generally, but the interpretation of the specific excluded provisions.

Notes and Questions

1. Following the *Ng Ka Ling* decision, the Hong Kong Government estimated that the number of permanent residents residing in China eligible for the right of abode would overwhelm Hong Kong if they migrated, resulting in very severe social and economic problems. The Hong Kong Government sought an interpretation of the Basic Law by the National People's Congress Standing Committee (NPCSC). Notably, Article 158(1) requires the Court of Final Appeal to seek an interpretation only when interpreting 'an excluded provision'; the Government had no explicit obligation or power to refer Article 22 of the Basic Law to the NPCSC. On 26 June 1999, the NPCSC overturned *Ng Ka Ling*. This was the first

time since 1997 that the NPCSC wielded its exclusive power to interpret the Basic Law. In its interpretation, the NPCSC stated that children born outside Hong Kong were eligible for the right of abode only if at least one of their parents had already acquired permanent residence status at the time of their birth. Legislation concerning their right to enter Hong Kong was to comply with Article 22 of the Basic Law, such that they needed the approval of relevant Mainland authorities before entering Hong Kong. Nonetheless, the Court in subsequent cases did not retreat from exercising judicial review. See Yash Ghai, 'The NPC Interpretation and its Consequences' in JMM Chan, HL Fu and Yash Ghai (eds), *Hong Kong's Constitutional Debate: Conflict Over Interpretation* (Hong Kong: Hong Kong University Press, 2000) 199–215; and *Cheung Lai Wah & Ors v Director of Immigration*.[10]

2. The *Ng Ka Ling* case has profound constitutional significance for Hong Kong. Through this ruling, the Court of Final Appeal affirmed not only the validity of the law previously in force, but also the legitimacy of the Court in interpreting the Basic Law. Do you think the Court was aware of the constitutional significance and chose to do so? The Court proclaimed:

> Questions involving the proper interpretation of the Basic Law are before us for the first time. These are questions of momentous importance for both the future of the people involved as well as the development of constitutional jurisprudence in the new order.[11]

3. The health of constitutionalism in Hong Kong under the 'One Country, Two Systems' policy continues to concern constitutional scholars. While the judicial system has contributed greatly to preserving the rule of law, the spectre of political interference from the central government remains. As Johannes Chan indicates,

> by and large, fundamental rights have been upheld in the last decade. The promise of a high degree of autonomy has largely been kept as the Central Government has exercised great restraint in not interfering with the domestic affairs of Hong Kong, save in the area of democratic development. Nonetheless, many cases with political overtones are increasingly brought before the Courts. If this trend continues and if the judiciary is unable to meet the expectations of the people, the rule of law in Hong Kong will be undermined.[12]

C. Imposed and Autonomous Constitutional Change

One prominent aspect of constitutional history in Asia is its colonial past and the dynamism of its post-colonial constitution-making.[13] Colonialism introduced into Asia foreign legal systems that were primarily designed to facilitate and consolidate foreign rule. Upon independence, different Asian states reacted differently to the colonial legal order. Certain states embraced the legacy of colonial rule and adopted it to

---

[10] *Cheung Lai Wah & Ors v Director of Immigration* [1997] HKLRD 1081, [1997] 3 HKC 64.

[11] *Ng Ka Ling v Director of Immigration* [1999] 1 HKLRD 315, at 323.

[12] J Chan SC, 'Basic Law and Constitutional Review: The First Decade' (2007) 37 *Hong Kong Law Journal* 407.

[13] See KYL Tan, 'The Making and Remaking of Constitutions in Southeast Asia: An Overview' (2002) 6 *Singapore Journal of International and Comparative Law* 1.

frame the new autochthonous local order; other states sought to remove every trace of their colonial legacy and to create a new constitutional system of their own.

For states with imposed constitutions, the issue of how these should be adapted to accommodate local needs persists. States seeking to create their own indigenous constitutional orders have to deal with the colonial legacy whose influence remains palpable. As the experiences of Japan, Iraq and other 'occupation constitutions' show, constitutions received during occupation bear some similarity to those of the principal occupying nation. In other jurisdictions, options from a range of influences were freely borrowed and adapted to the local setting.[14] Consequently, such constitutions have mixed origins.[15]

There is no clear evidence whether imposed or home-grown constitutions fare better. The usual argument advanced in favour of autochthonous constitutions is that self-determination is indispensable to the development of constitutionalism, and that autonomy and self-determination are integral to democratic constitutionalism.[16] For imposed constitutions, it has been argued that some degree of local participation in the constitution-making process is crucial to their success and longevity.[17]

In Japan, the Supreme Court reviewed and redefined the imposed constitutional order while asserting Japan's national identity and establishing the rule of law. As a defeated nation after World War II, Japan had to deal with a legal order imposed by the Supreme Commander for the Allied Powers (SCAP). In the *Judgment Upon Case of Validity of Cabinet Order 1952*, the Court reviewed the constitutionality of a Cabinet Order promulgated to effectuate the SCAP's rule. The Court unanimously upheld the Japanese Constitution as the supreme law of the land, and further held that Japan was, upon the signing of the peace treaty, a sovereign state with a self-operating legal order. At this point, it was no longer under the SCAP's control, nor that of any foreign force. However, the opinions of 14 Supreme Court Justices differed in their approaches in defining and reviewing the disputed Cabinet Order. This phenomenon was not commonly seen in later Supreme Court decisions which were much more consensual.

Judgment upon Case of Validity of Cabinet Order No 325 of 1950
1952(A)No 2868, 22 Jul 1953 (Supreme Court, Japan)

Facts

Following defeat in World War II, Japan had accepted the Potsdam Declaration, signed the Instrument of Surrender and proclaimed unconditional surrender to the Allied Powers. In consequence thereof, the SCAP acquired the authority to take such measures as he deemed proper to effectuate the terms of surrender, and to that extent the power of the Japanese

---

[14] Z Elkins, T Ginsburg and J Melton, 'Baghdad, Tokyo, Kabul . . .? Constitution-making in Occupied States' (2007) 49 *William and Mary Law Review* 1139. This article surveyed 42 instances of constitutions adopted under occupation or shortly thereafter, and developed an index of similarity to compare constitutional dyads.

[15] For example, the Constitution of the Philippines is famous for its amalgamation of concepts and principles drawn from three of the world's legal systems – the civil law, the common law and Islamic law. See E Daenecke, 'Constitutional Law in the Philippines' (1966) 52 *American Bar Association Journal* 161.

[16] N Feldman, 'Imposed Constitutionalism' (2005) 37 *Connecticut Law Review* 857.

[17] A Hadenius, 'Democracy's Victory and Crisis' in J Elster (ed), *Ways of constitution-making* (Cambridge: Cambridge University Press, 1997) 123.

Government to rule the country was made subject to the prerogatives of the SCAP. Imperial Ordinance No 542 of 1945 was enacted in implementation of the occupation administration by the Allied Powers in consequence of the unconditional surrender of Japan. The language of the Cabinet Order was abstract and the SCAP was thus given an entirely free hand in taking any measures deemed by him to be proper. The issue in this case was whether the criminals charged according to the Cabinet Order back in the time of occupation should be exempted from punishment. In this ruling, the Court recognised that Japan was really in a state of law as to subject itself to the authority of the SCAP in so far as it was deemed by him to be proper to effectuate the terms of surrender. It held that Cabinet Order No 325 of 1950 had lost its effect on April 28 of 1952, simultaneous with the enforcement of the Peace Treaty. Separate opinions differed from the Court's opinion in the approaches of reasoning.

Justices Tsuyoshi Mano, Katsushige Kotani, Tamotsu Shima, Hachiro Fujita, Tadaichiro Tanimura & Toshio Irie

In view of the fact that the Ordinance was formulated upon the aforesaid fundamental relations from the necessity of effectuating requirements set by the SCAP, it must be admitted that the Ordinance had legal effect beyond the Constitution of Japan, irrespective of the provisions of the Constitution . . .

As described in detail before, since they are only to punish as a crime violation of directives issued by the SCAP, they necessarily lose their effect because of their very nature, simultaneously with the enforcement of the Peace Treaty. To give Cabinet Order No 325 the effect of a statute at the time the Peace Treaty has come into force without giving similar force and effect to each one of the existing directives, which substantiate the substance of the Order, and to prescribe simply for the punishment of violation of directives as crimes, is tantamount to stipulating matters which are practically impossible, thus eventually resulting in a contradiction of the Constitution. Therefore, the enactment of Law No 81 mentioned above does not prevent Cabinet Order No 325 from losing its effect as a matter of course simultaneously with the enforcement of the Peace Treaty. (If the enactment of Law No 81 was to give the effect of law to the substance of each of the existing directives; there would have arisen the necessity of determining the constitutionality of those directives, but this Law merely gave the effect of law to Cabinet Order No 325, that is, it merely made the act of violation of the directives a punishable offense as in the case of other Potsdam Ordinances in general. Since it was not the intention of the Law to give the force and effect to each one of the directives, there is no need to examine each one of them to determine whether they are constitutional. As stated heretofore, the above-mentioned Law No 81 is null and void and is unconstitutional so far as it purports to punish violation of directives, regardless of whether the substance of the directives in question was in conformity with the Constitution.) Thus, Cabinet Order No 325 had lost its effect on April 28 of 1952 simultaneous with the enforcement of the Peace Treaty. Consequently, if it were intended for the above-mentioned Law No 137, enforced on May 7 of 1952 after the invalidation of the said Cabinet Order, to prescribe that the application of the penal provisions to the acts done prior to invalidation shall be punished as heretofore, such a law must be admitted to be null and void inasmuch as it violates the purport of Article 39 of the Constitution, in that the Law will become so-called ex post facto legislation in reviving anew the penal provisions of Cabinet Order No 325 which was once invalidated . . .

Justices Nobori Inoue, Shigeru Kuriyama, Matasuke Kawamura & Shunzo Kobayashi

Even if the occupation is terminated and the position of the SCAP is dissolved, and thereby his directives as well as our obligation to obey them ceased to exist, it does not necessarily follow that the Cabinet Order in question has completely lost its force and effect as a law of our country subsequent to the Peace Treaty. The directives which constitute the substance of Cabinet Order No 325 contained many elements which were designed, not only for the benefits of the Occupation, but also for maintaining peace in our country and for the promotion of public welfare. One cannot assert that Cabinet Order No 325, embodying the substance as described above, is not entitled to become a legitimate law of our state simply because the directives were issued by the SCAP. Our country is at liberty to continue the validity of the said Cabinet Order as a law of our land insofar as it concerned directives having elements compatible with the Constitution, even after the Peace Treaty had come into force. Law No 81 of 1952 provided that the orders or ordinances issued under Imperial Ordinance No 542 shall, unless measures for their abolition or continued existence are taken by special legislation, remain effective as laws for not more than one hundred and eighty (180) days commencing on the day of the enforcement of the Peace Treaty. As a result Cabinet Order No 325, which is one of the Orders within the meaning of Law No 81, was also preserved to remain effective as a law so far as its substance met the constitutional requirements. The penal provisions of the Cabinet Order in question do not in themselves clearly define or fix the substance of the crime, but it is dependent upon the directives which might be issued by the SCAP from time to time as circumstances would require. Therefore, so long as there existed continuously such an uncertainty, it is open to much question as to whether such provisions should be made a statute of the state. However, the directives already issued have become clearly fixed simultaneously with the enforcement of the Peace Treaty, and the vacuum in the said Order has already been filled even though it was then of a nature of an empty statute. Consequently, as long as the directives are constitutional, there should be no reason why they should be precluded from remaining effective as laws of our country . . .

This leads to the consideration of whether the substance of the said directives which the accused was found to have violated is in conformity with the Constitution. Article 21 of the Constitution guarantees freedom of speech as one of the fundamental human rights. In particular, the provision of Paragraph 2 of the same article expressly prohibits censorship. It is obvious that the directives in question deprived the people of their freedom of speech more drastically than would an ordinary censorship. They are clearly contrary to Article 21 of the Constitution. It therefore naturally follows that Cabinet Order No 325 must also be admitted to be unconstitutional insofar as it is to punish violation of these directives. Therefore it must be concluded, despite any special legislation (to wit: Law No 81), that the effect of such directives is no longer valid after the promulgation of the Peace Treaty.

Justices Kotaro Tanaka, Seiichi Shimoyama, Yusuke Saito & Zentaro Motomura (dissenting)

For in a country governed by law adopting the principle of punishment by law, it is an inevitable premise that an offender should be punished in accordance with the law in force at the time of the commission of the crime. It is natural that the penalty once invoked in accordance with the penal laws, which were already in existence at the time of the commission of the offense, should remain effective unless the same penalty has been specifically cancelled or abolished by a subsequent general amnesty, law, or ordinance. Abolishment of a crime is a waiver of the right to punish which had already been exercised with respect to an offense committed when the law was still in force. Consequently, there is no reason why the legal effect itself of a law should become extinguished as a matter of course, even if the statute which gave rise to the penal provisions has been abolished or rescinded, merely losing its force in the future, unless there has been a clear manifestation of the will of the state to waive and abolish the pre-existing, consummated legal effects of the law. There are certain situations in which, after the commission of an offense, the law which gave rise to the prohibition is abolished or rescinded, and the reason for abolishment is such as to indicate that the legislators have also tacitly waived even the consummated act of punishment. In particular, where a certain penal law has been rescinded by a special legislation after the commission of the prohibited act for the reason that there has been a change in the legal concept or in the evaluation of the criminal law estimation, giving rise to a conclusion that such an act should not be punished, then, it may be assumed that the right to punish a consummated act is waived at the same time the law is abolished. On the other hand, there are some cases involving so-called 'prescription law', particularly those cases in which a saving clause is provided to continue the application of the penal provisions to the acts of violation committed prior to the invalidation of the statute. In those cases abolition or cancellation of the statute is not predicated upon any change in the legal concept or in re-evaluation of criminal concept on the part of the legislators. It is nothing more than a change in the circumstances or a lapse of time. In those cases, it should be interpreted that the will of the state was rather that the consummated legal effect shall not be waived even after the abolition or cancellation of the statute. It is beyond doubt that Cabinet Order No 325 at issue, the Order for the Punishment of Acts Prejudicial to the Occupation Objectives, was intended, from its very nature, to hold good only during the period of occupation as indicated by its appellation, and to lose its effect simultaneously with the termination of the occupation. Therefore, it is needless to dwell upon the correctness of our interpretation that the Cabinet Order was in the nature of a so-called 'prescription law'.

In view of the foregoing reasoning, it follows that even if Imperial Ordinance No 542 of 1945 and Cabinet Order No 325 enacted thereunder are conceived to have lost their validity after the rendition of the original judgment, simultaneously with the enforcement of the Peace Treaty between the Allied Powers and Japan at 10.30 pm on April 28, 1952 (judgment pronounced on the same day), there can be seen no manifestation of the will of the state explicit or implicit by law or ordinance, purporting to nullify the consummated effect of the punishment invoked under Article 2, Paragraph 1, of the above-mentioned Cabinet Order. Furthermore, as pointed out heretofore, because of the very nature of the Order, having the prescriptive effect, it cannot be said that the penalty has been abolished. On the contrary, a series of laws, including Laws No 81 and No 137 of 1952 (apart from judgment whether Law No 81 of 1952 is effective as a new domestic law or not) express a clearly defined will of the state to the effect that the penalty concerned shall not be abolished . . .

Notes and Questions

1. This case was decided on 22 July 1953 and reflected the dynamic and tangled political context of post-war Japan. At that time, the ruling party was the Liberal Democratic Party (LDP) led by Shigeru Yoshida, while the biggest opposition parties were the Social Party and the Democratic Party led by Ichirō Hatoyama. The most controversial issue between them was the issue of comprehensive peace. While Yoshida insisted on enhancing self-defence forces within the Japan–US security system, Hatoyama advocated amending Article 9 of the Constitution. This case affected domestic party politics as well as the equilibrium between Japan and the United States, and the normalisation of Japan–Soviet relationships.

2. The three separate opinions accompanying this decision demonstrated different approaches in dealing with legal continuity of the constitutional order. The majority considered the legal order to have been disrupted before and after the signing

of the Treaty. This meant that the impugned Cabinet Order had nullified all rules promulgated by the SCAP. The concurring separate opinion recognised the effect of occupation rules, but subjected the Cabinet Order to judicial review and found it unconstitutional in substance. The dissenting opinion sided with the view of legal continuity, but upheld the Order from the perspective of the current constitutional order. To what extent do these opinions reflect the view that the Ordinance was 'imposed'?

3. How do we define 'the People' in relation to a constitutional founding? Did 'We, the People' give themselves a constitution? Chaihark Hahm and Sung Ho Kim, in exploring the process of constitution-making in Japan and Korea, challenge the commonly-held notion that constituent power represented 'We, the People'. They argue that the legitimacy and practice of constitutional founding hinges on 'We the People'. Virtually all modern constitutions claim some mandate from the people, in whom is rooted the authority of the constitution. The constitution is thus subject to amendment and even abrogation by the People. It is frequently argued that the relationship between the People and the constitution is one of creation and mastery. This view of the People's authorship of the constitution tends to endow the People with a timeless quality as the constituent agent. However, it may be argued that the actual relationship between the People and the constitution is more complex and multifaceted. In the cases of post-war Japan and post-colonial Korea, the state was for the first time reorganised according to the principle of popular sovereignty, and the new constitutions were drafted and promulgated in the name of 'We[,] the People'. The 'People' that authored the constitutions had to be 'constituted' even as they were establishing a new constitutional order. Although both countries were inhabited by people with discrete political and cultural identities for many centuries, the 'People' as a constituent agent was a new phenomenon. Hahm and Sung argued that the idea of 'We[,] the People' 'emerged in the course of a constitutional politics involving intense interactions with external forces, selective appropriations of the past, and redefinitions of the boundaries of membership'. See C Hahm and Sung Ho Kim, 'To Make 'We the People': Constitutional Founding in Postwar Japan and South Korea' (2010) 8 *I•CON* 800.

4. Constitutions, however, may come into being without reference to popular will, as in the case of the Constitution of Singapore which was ratified by Parliament upon secession from Malaysia, without involving the broader populace in a constituent assembly or referendum. See KYL Tan, 'The Evolution of Singapore's Modern Constitution: Developments from 1945 to Date' (1989) 1 *Singapore Academy of Law Journal* 1.

5. May 'a People' be constructed through the process of constitution making, or should this entity precede the making of the constitution and so constitute the basis for founding a constitution? What insight does the Japanese Cabinet Order case throw on this question?

Another controversial issue concerning Japan's sovereignty and national identity is the 'war renunciation' clause, especially when associated with the stationing American troops in Japan. In light of Japan's role in World War II as a militarist intruder, Article 9 of the SCAP-drafted Constitution dedicated Japan to eternal peace by officially renouncing war as a sovereign right and by banning settlement of international disputes through the use of force. The article also states that armed forces with the potential for war will not be maintained.

For the purpose of national defence, Japan maintains only Self-Defence Forces and allows US armed forces to be stationed in its territory. The latter continues to fan heated debate, as right-wing activists argue that continued American presence in Japan encroaches its sovereignty. In the *Sunkanawa Case*, the Supreme Court of Japan had to consider the constitutionality of Article 9 and the treaty allowing America to station troops in Japan.

Judgment upon the so-called Sunakawa Case [Violation of the Special Criminal Law Enacted in Consequence of the Administrative Agreement under Article III of the Security Treaty between Japan and the United States of America]
1959 (A) No 710, 16 Dec 1959 (Supreme Court, Japan)

Facts

To extend a runway on the United States air force base at Sunakawa, an agreement was made by between the United States forces and the Japanese Government to purchase additional private land. In July 1957, on the occasion of a survey of the land, more than a thousand demonstrators gathered early in the morning in front of the fence of the air base and loudly protested against the survey. Some of the demonstrators were indicted for violation of Article 2 of the Law for Special Measures Concerning Criminal Cases. This law was enacted to implement the Administrative Agreement between the United States and Japan, which essentially constitutes a status of forces agreement under the Security Treaty between the two nations. In March 1959, the Tokyo District Court acquitted seven defendants of the charge of trespassing on the American air base, upholding that the 'war renunciation' clause in the Constitution and that the law providing special protection to their bases was invalid. This verdict caused a public uproar, inasmuch as it was diametrically opposed to the position of the Kishi Government. The state, through its public procurators, appealed to the Supreme Court. On 16 December 1959, the Supreme Court reversed the judgment and remanded the case to the District Court for retrial, holding that the stationing of the United States forces was consistent with the Constitution of Japan.

Held

As it is clear from the Preamble of the Constitution, we, the people of Japan, desire to occupy an honored place in international society, which is striving for the preservation of peace and the banishment of tyranny and slavery, oppression and intolerance for all time from the earth, and affirm that we have the right, along with and in the same manner as all the people of the world, to live in peace, free from fear and want. In view of this it is only natural for our country, in the exercise of powers inherent in a state, to maintain peace and security, to take whatever measures may be necessary for self-defense, and to preserve its very existence. We, the people of Japan, do not maintain the so-called war potential provided in paragraph 2, Article 9 of the Constitution, but we have determined to supplement the shortcomings in our national defense resulting therefrom by trusting in the justice and faith of the peace loving people of the world, and thereby preserve our peace and existence. This, however, does not necessarily mean that our recourse is limited to such military security measures as may be undertaken by an organ of the United Nations, such as the Security Council, as stated in the original decision. It is needless to say that we are free to choose whatever method or means deemed appropriate to accomplish our objectives in the light of the actual international situation, as long as such measures are for the purpose of preserving the peace and security of our country. Article 9 of the Constitution does not at all prohibit our country from seeking a guarantee from another country in order to maintain the peace and security of the country. Now, therefore, let us consider the legal intent of paragraph 2 in the light of the purport of Article 9 elucidated above. It is entirely proper to interpret that the prohibition of the maintenance of war potential contained in this paragraph was intended for the purpose of preventing Japan from maintaining the so-called war potential of its own, exercising its own control and command over the same, and thereby instigating a war of aggression renounced forever in the first paragraph of the Article. . . .

In final analysis, it means the war potential of our country; and consequently, it may be properly construed that the provision of paragraph 2 does not include foreign armed forces even if they are to be stationed in our country.

The next point in issue is whether the stationing of the United States armed forces in Japan is contrary to the purport of Article 9; paragraph 2, Article 98; and the Preamble of the Constitution. Inasmuch as the stationing of the United States troops in Japan is predicated upon the Security Treaty between Japan and the United States, now under consideration, determination of the constitutionality of this treaty must of necessity precede the determination of this point. . . .

The Security Treaty is a treaty concluded between Japan and the United States regarding stationing of the United States armed forces, the foreign armed forces recognized in the above provision of the Treaty of Peace. This provision was approved and signed by a majority of forty countries out of sixty United Nations countries. According to the Preamble of the Japan-United States Security Treaty, the Treaty of Peace recognizes that in consideration of the fact that Japan will not have the effective means to exercise its inherent right of self-defense at the time of coming into force of the Treaty of Peace, and since there is a necessity of coping with the danger of irresponsible militarism, that Japan, as a sovereign nation, has the right to enter into collective security arrangements. Further, the Charter of the United Nations recognizes that all nations possess an inherent right of individual and collective self-defense. It is clear, therefore, that the purpose of the Japan-United States Security Treaty is to provide, as a provisional arrangement, for the defense of Japan, and to stipulate matters necessary to insure the safety and defense of our country, such as granting of the right to the United States to deploy its armed forces in and about Japan to guard against armed attack upon the country. Consequently, it must be stated that the Security Treaty, in its essence, bears a vital relationship with peace and security and also with the very existence of our sovereign country.

In the formulation of the treaty, the Cabinet of the Japanese Government then in power, negotiated with the United States on a number of occasions in accordance with the Constitutional provisions, and finally concluded the same as one of the most important national policies. It is also a well-accepted public knowledge that, subsequent thereto, the question of whether the treaty was in accord with the Constitution was carefully discussed by both Houses and finally ratified by the Diet as being a legal and proper treaty. The Security Treaty, therefore, as stated before, is featured with an extremely high degree of political consideration, having bearing upon the very existence of our country as a sovereign power, and any legal determination as to whether the content of the treaty is constitutional or not is in many respects inseparably related to the high degree of political consideration or discretionary power on the part of the Cabinet which concluded the treaty and on the part of the Diet which approved it. Consequently, as a rule, there is a certain element of incompatibility in the process of judicial determination of its constitutionality by a court of law which has as its mission the exercise of the purely judicial function. Accordingly, unless the said treaty is obviously unconstitutional and void, it falls outside the purview of the power of judicial review granted to the court. It is proper to construe that the question of the determination of its constitutionality should be left primarily to the Cabinet which has the power to conclude treaties and the Diet which has the power to ratify them; and ultimately to the political consideration of the people with whom rests the sovereign power of the nation. . . .

Accordingly, the Court in proceeding to deliberate over the Security Treaty relating to the stationing of the United States armed forces and the provisions of the Administrative Agreement based on Article 3 of the said treaty, finds that these Security Forces are foreign troops, and naturally they are not a war potential of our country. All command and supervisory authorities are vested in the United States, and furthermore, it is clear that our country has no right to command or supervise such armed forces as we do over our own armed forces. These armed forces are stationed here in accordance with the principle set forth in the Preamble to the Security Treaty, and as stated in Article I of the Treaty, these forces are to be utilized to contribute to the maintenance of international peace and security in the Far East and to the security of Japan against armed attack from without, including assistance given at the express request of the Japanese Government to put down large-scale internal riots and disturbances in Japan caused through instigation of, or intervention by, an outside power or powers. Its objective is to maintain the peace and security of Japan and the Far East, including Japan, and to insure that never again shall we be visited by the horrors of war. It can readily be seen that the reason for permitting the stationing of these forces was none other than to supplement the lack of our own defense power, by trusting in the justice and faith of the peace loving people of the world. If such be the case, it cannot be acknowledged that the stationing of the United States armed forces is immediately, clearly unconstitutional and void, contravening the purport of Article 9, paragraph 2 of Article 98, and the Preamble of the Constitution. On the contrary, it must be held that it is in accord with the intent and purpose of these constitutional provisions. This is true, regardless of whether the provisions of paragraph 2 of Article 9 were intended to prohibit the maintenance of war potential even for self-defense.

Notes and Questions

1. In *Sunakawa*, the Japanese Supreme Court had to deal with a politically explosive issue in the midst of the Cold War, when the 'Free World' saw Japan as a major bulwark against communism. The Tokyo District Court decision was delivered about the time the Security Treaty was signed, which explains the explosive nature of its impact on Japan's foreign relations policy and domestic politics. The Supreme Court's decision thus served the much-needed legal foundation for current Japan–US security arrangements and beyond.

2. Since 1947, the Japanese courts have decided at least two dozen cases relating to the constitutionality of various measures under Article 9, including direct challenges to the US–Japan Security Treaty; presence of US military bases; and the Self-Defence Forces. At least seven of these were appellate decisions. The Court's decision in *Sunakawa* is regarded as the principal Grand Bench decision on Article 9 of the Constitution. Two other Grand Bench decisions on Article 9 – which also involved the constitutionality of US–Japan security and US military bases – reaffirmed *Sunakawa*.

3. The constitutionality of Article 9, the re-militarisation of Japan and US–Japan relations have long been the subject of public debate. See DB Gibbs, 'Future Relations between the United States and Japan: Article 9 And the Remilitarization of Japan' (2010) 33 *Houston Journal of International Law* 137. Indeed, there has been increasing pressure to amend this 'imposed' article, a move which some characterise as a challenge to Japan's existing liberal constitution. See, for example, A Mendenhall, 'America Giveth, and America Taketh Away: the Fate of Article 9 After the Futenma Base Dispute' (2011) 20 *Michigan State International Law Review* 83 (discussing the legislative and judicial history concerning Article 9 against the backdrop of current pacific regional politics); and MA Panton, 'Japan's Article 9: Rule of Law v Flexible Interpretation' (2010) 24 *Temple International and Comparative Law Journal* 129 (exploring the current socio-political climate for revising Article 9).

D. Constitutional Change in a Transitional Context

Another characteristic of East Asian constitutionalism is the growing momentum towards democratisation. Like states in East and Central Europe in the late 1980s and early 1990s, several Asian states began to break free of former authoritarian or communist regimes and move towards greater liberalisation and democracy.[18] One notable feature of this transition is the wide acceptance of constitutional principles and judicial review through various forms of constitutional change.

However, the dynamics of constitutional change in Asia are varied and diverse. Jiunn-rong Yeh and Wen-Chen Chang, using the *pace* of constitutional change and constitutional *identity* as two variables, identified four patterns of constitutional change in transitional democracies:

(a) constitution-making;
(b) grand constitution revision;
(c) incremental constitution-making; and
(d) incremental constitutional revision.

See Table 4.2.

States that adopted the constitution-making model took the opportunity to draft new constitutions at the initial stages of democratic transition, marking a clear departure from the past. We saw this in countries like Romania, Bulgaria, Latvia and Estonia in Eastern and Central Europe. In Asia, the Philippines and Mongolia would fall into this category.

States that opted for a grand constitutional revision retained the original constitution but made comprehensive revisions to it at the initial stages of democratic transition. This was done in the case of Argentina in 1994. In Asia, the best example is South Korea. Since the grand revision to its Constitution in 1987, there has been no further revision.

---

[18] SP Huntington, *The Third Wave: Democratization in the Late Twentieth Century*, (Norman, Okla: University of Oklahoma Press, 1992).

Table 4.2 Types of Constitutional Change During Democratic Transition of States in Asia[19]

		Pace of Change	
		Low	High
Constitutional Identity	Low	Incremental constitution-making (eg Thailand)	Constitution-making (eg the Philippines and Mongolia)
	High	Incremental constitutional revision (eg Taiwan and Indonesia)	Grand constitution revision (eg South Korea)

Some states choose to make limited constitutional revisions to address and resolve immediate political problems. Less pressing issues are left to subsequent revisions. This results in a series of incremental constitutional revisions. This is what happened in in Hungary in Europe. In Asia, both Indonesia and Taiwan embarked on several rounds of incremental constitutional revisions.

Lastly, there are states that adopted interim constitutional arrangements while anticipating the final delivery of a new constitution. The best example of this was the South Africa Constitution of 1996, which was finalised through some interim measures including 34 constitutional principles and the Interim Constitution. Before the final promulgation of the 1997 Constitution of Poland, the so-called Small Constitution was introduced as an interim mechanism. There is no Asian example of this practice as yet, although it may be argued that Thailand, with its numerous constitutions since 1932, may fall into this category.

The typology of constitutional change set forth above indicates a spectrum of constitutional change along the line separating constitutional making and revision. Indeed, even for constitutional revisions, practices range from a one-time grand comprehensive revision (South Korea), to many rounds of separate amendments, as in Indonesia and Taiwan.

The adoption of a particular type of constitutional change depends on a variety of factors, including the assumption of sovereignty by the new state; regime change; constitutional traditions; international intervention; and collective choices as expressed formally by the popular will.[20]

The new regime in a transitional state needs to deal with a range of issues peculiar to such transition, especially those of transitional justice. This refers to the need to formalise institutional responses to deal systematically with the wrongs committed by the prior regime, or which occurred during the political conflict that led to the creation of the new regime. The constitution of a new regime may downplay or ignore such issues, especially if an over-emphasis on revisiting past acts of injustice might impede a more forward-looking constitutional process.[21] Constitutions of transitional states

---

[19] This table is adapted from Jiunn-rong Yeh and Wen-Chen Chang, 'Path Dependence or Collective Institutional Choice? Modeling Constitutional Changes in the Context of Democratic Transition' (2006) 45(6) *Issues and Studies* 1 (in Chinese).

[20] Ibid.

[21] R Teitel, 'Transitional Justice and the Transformation of Constitutionalism' in T Ginsburg and R Dixon (eds), *Comparative Constitutional Law* (Northampton, Mass: Edward Elgar, 2011) 57 at 60.

that came about in the third wave of democratisation in the 1990s have been shaped by political negotiation and compromises in dealing with issues of transitional justice. The experiences of South Africa and former communist states in Eastern Europe bear testimony to this.[22] Consequently, a transitional constitution would often shape the course of transitional politics, and may present challenges to how a new democratic regime can deal with its past in a manner that does not sacrifice future efforts to build a stable democracy.

In many Asian states, constitutions were generally created or revised during or shortly after periods of transition. Such new constitutions must thus oftentimes address transitional justice issues. In the *May 18 Incident Non-institution of Prosecution Decision Case*, the Constitutional Court of Korea dealt with the constitutionality of criminal prosecutions against the main actors of a successful coup. Although the Court did not pronounce on the merits – since the complainants withdrew the complaint right before the final decision – it made an important statement that actors involved in a successful coup d'état may be subject to criminal prosecution. In unfurling its rationale concerning the punishability of a successful coup, the Court in effect made it impossible to prosecute a President who came to power through a successful coup, during his term of office. This finding supports the legislative intent of the special law that suspended the application of the statute of limitation, during the terms of Presidents Chun and Roh.[23]

May 18 Incident Non-institution of Prosecution Decision Case
7-2 KCCR 697, 95Hun-Ma221, 15 Dec 1995
(Constitutional Court, Korea)

Facts

President Park Chung Hee of South Korea was assassinated by Kim Chae-kyu, Director of the Korean Central Intelligence Agency, in October 1979. This resulted in a power vacuum which ended with a coup d'état led by Chun Doo Hwan in December 1979. Students and civilians demonstrated and resisted the military regime in the city of Kwangju in southwest Korea on 18 May 1980. The demonstrations were peaceful, but the Special Warfare Commando, which was dispatched to Kwangju, attacked the citizens on the streets randomly and ruthlessly, turning the streets of Kwangju into a battlefield. The conflict resulted in 161 dead, 64 missing, 2,948 wounded and 1,364 arrested or detained. The attack at Kwangju was led by General Roh Tae Woo, who succeeded Chun as President in 1988. This case arose out of three different criminal complaints against the main actors of the 'May 18 Incident'. After investigations, the Seoul District Public Prosecutor decided against prosecuting Chun Doo Hwan and all others named in 70 complaints, on the ground that the accused succeeded in the coup and formed a new constitutional order. The complainants filed a constitutional complaint to nullify the Prosecutor's decision on grounds that that it was an arbitrary exercise of his prosecutorial power.

---

[22] R Teitel, 'Transitional Jurisprudence: The Role of Law in Political Transformation' (1997) 106 *Yale Law Journal* 2009.

[23] *5.18 Kwangju minjuhwa undong deung e kwanhan teukbyeolbeop* [The Special Act Concerning the May 18 Democratisation Movement], Statutes of S Korea, Law No 5029 of 1995. See also, Kuk Cho, 'Transitional Justice in Korea: Legally Coping with Past Wrong After Democratization' (2007) 16 *Pacific Rim Law & Policy Journal* 585.

Held

The majority of five justices declared the case closed upon the complainants' withdrawal pursuant to Article 40 of the Constitutional Court Act interpreted in light of Article 239 of the Civil Procedure Act, forming the Court's opinion. Justices Shin Chang-on, Kim Chin-woo, Lee Jae-hwa and Cho Seung-hyung posited that the Court could proceed to a final ruling even if the complainants had withdrawn. Justice Shin emphasized the objective function of the constitutional complaint process and opined that the Court should publish the opinion as the Justices have previously agreed. Justices Kim Chin-woo, Lee Jae-hwa and Cho Seung-hyung reasoned that, if the complainants withdraw, the case should be closed with respect to its subjective portion, namely giving relief to claims of rights. But, the objective function of the constitutional complaint process demands that it should continue on to a final decision with respect to those issues resolution of which are vital to defense of the constitutional order, if there are such issues. In this case, the question of punishability of a successful coup calls for a constitutional answer because it affects the fate of this nation and the basic rights of all people, and demands a final decision irrespective of the complainants' withdrawal.

Before the withdrawal, a super-majority of the justices had agreed that a successful coup is punishable during the deliberation. The new majority that declared the case closed acquiesced with the minority's publication of a part of the previously agreed-upon final decision, while leaving out the part about expiration of the statute. Thusly, the justices' prevailing view in the deliberation room saw the light of the day: a successful coup is punishable. The following is the summary of the opinion of the three Justices who were in the minority: The constitutional order protected by penalties against treason is one based on people's sovereignty and the basic order of free democracy, not the incumbent power or the order maintained by it. In addition, Article 84 of the Constitution, which stipulates 'the President shall not be prosecuted during the term except on crimes of treason internal or external', stands as an unequivocal expression of a constitutional resolve that treason can be punished at all times regardless of its outcome. Therefore, even if a successful coup makes it practically impossible to punish the perpetrators during their incumbency, they can always be punished whenever the constitutional institutions recover their proper function and thereby regain de facto power to punish them. However, if treasonous activities were the means to create a democratic civil state and to restore the people's sovereignty previously suppressed and excluded under a feudal monarchy or despotism, they can be justified before or after the fact by the will of all the people. Therefore, a successful treason becomes not punishable under the exceptional circumstances that the people have ratified it through free expressions of their sovereign wills. In this case, the treasonous acts of the two former Presidents were neither justified by the circumstances nor were ratified by free expressions of the people (denying legitimacy of the treasonous government does not mean denying the legal effects of all of its acts). The prosecutor's non-institution of prosecution decision for reason of immunity of a successful coup engenders misunderstanding of the ideals of the Constitution and the criminal jurisprudence of treason.

Notes and Questions

1. The Korean National Assembly reacted to the Constitutional Court decision by passing a special law on the Kwangju massacre. The public were not satisfied with this decision and pressured the Government to enact a special law to punish the military leaders responsible for the massacre. Students demonstrated on the streets

demanding the punishment of both Chun and Roh. Scandalous revelations that the two former presidents amassed huge fortunes during their corrupt presidencies further infuriated the people. It became clear that the Korean people did not want to leave their crimes to the judgement of history but wanted an immediate legal response. President Kim Young-Sam ordered his ruling party to enact new legislation. On 21 December 1995, the Korean National Assembly passed a special law, 'the May 18 Act', which disclosed the facts of the Kwangju incident. It suspended the statute of limitations for crimes against the constitutional order committed between 12 December 1979 and 18 May 1980, as this limit would make it 'practically impossible to punish the perpetrators during their incumbency'.

2. The 'May 18 Act' stipulated that the statute of limitations ceased to operate during the presidencies of Chun and Roh in which 'there existed obstacles for the State to institute prosecution'. It allowed courts to review cases in which the prosecutor declined to prosecute. The Act also provided for a special retrial for those who had been punished because of their engagement in the 18 May Massacre or because of their opposition to crimes against the constitutional order. The Seoul District Prosecutor's office prosecuted the two former presidents and former high-ranking officials who led the 1979 military coup and suppressed the 18 May uprising of 1980. Although critics of the Act asserted that it was unconstitutional because it was retroactive, and even filed a petition to the Constitutional Court to challenge it, the Court nevertheless upheld its constitutionality.[24] As a result, former President Chun Doo Hwan was sentenced to life imprisonment, and ex-President Roh Tae-woo was imprisoned for 17 years. The Court also declared that military coups and dictatorships will never be tolerated in South Korea. This ruling is regarded as a milestone for the democratic movement in South Korea.

3. How does one evaluate the wisdom of the Korean Constitutional Court in this case? Though the Court has been seen as fairly active since its establishment in 1988, a careful examination reveals a reactive and cautious judicial attitude, similar to that of Japan's Supreme Court. The Korean Constitutional Court rarely renders decisions that are contrary to the political majority's preferences or sentiments, especially when a case involves politically controversial issues, such as issues of transitional justice. Although the Court disagreed with the prosecutor on the issue of statutory limitations, it held that the decision not to prosecute was not arbitrary. After the Special Act authorising the prosecution of former presidents and military officials was passed, the Court upheld its constitutionality, despite concerns about retroactivity, by just one vote. While the Court held a different view on the rule of law and transitional justice, it chose not to go against the political will of the majority. See Jiunn-rong Yeh and Wen-Chen Chang, 'The Emergence of East Asian Constitutionalism: Features in Comparison' (2011) 59 *American Journal of Comparative Law* 805.

With its history of military uprising and coups, Bangladesh has frequently had to confront the issue of transitional justice. Though the democratic constitutional order is usually restored with the end of military rule, the legacies of the latter need to be addressed.

---

[24] *The Special Act on the May Democratisation Movement Case*, 1996Hun-Ka2, 16 Feb 1996.

In the *7th Amendment Case*, the Supreme Court of Bangladesh reviewed this nation's past history of military rulings with the purpose of enabling the new constitutional order to move on. The *7th Amendment Case* concerns the martial law decree issued by General Hussain Mohammed Ershad upon his assumption of power in 1982 and all other instruments promulgated during his authoritarian rule when he exercised de facto absolute power. In this case, the Court denied the legitimacy of the past militant regimes, and declared unconstitutional all the undemocratic constitutional measures past regimes issued to facilitate their oppressive rule.

Siddique Ahmed v Bangladesh (7th Amendment Case)
Writ Petition 696/2010, 26 Aug 2010 (Supreme Court, Bangladesh)

Facts

After the assassination of President Ziaur Rahman, General Ershad institute martial law in 1982, thus dramatically changing Bangladesh's constitutional order. Ershad assumed power in a bloodless coup and, like his predecessors, suspended the constitution and declared martial law in accordance with the existing constitution, on grounds of pervasive corruption, ineffectual government and economic mismanagement. During the 1980s, following his false promise to lift martial law, the Ershad regime successfully mustered the necessary two-thirds majority in the National Assembly to amend the constitution and legitimise his martial law rule.

The petitioner sought to have his conviction and sentence by a special martial law court on 20 March 2006 set aside. In the course of his arguments, he challenged the validity of all martial law instruments, including the proclamation of martial law itself, and all other instruments emanating from Ershad's rule. In particular, he challenged the constitutionality of the Constitution (Seventh Amendment) Act 1986 under which the Constitution was purportedly amended to accommodate all the aforementioned instruments. The petitioner claimed that the court was in fact a '*coram non judice*' as it was the offspring of an illegal martial law instrument. He further argued that the proclamation of 24 March 1982 and all other instruments, were void *ab initio* as they violated the basic structures of the Constitution. As such, Parliament's attempt to confer legality on the regime through section 3 of the Constitution (Seventh Amendment) Act 1986 was unconstitutional.

AHM Shamsuddin Chowdhury J

The averments and submissions the learned counsels tabled, gave rise to a number of questions that we are enjoined to address in order to meticulously dispose of this petition. They are:

1 whether our Constitution knows or recognizes anything called martial law;
2 whether the proclamation of 24th March 1982 was in concord with any provision of our Constitution;
3 whether such instruments as martial regulations, orders, directions, rules, made under the purported authority of martial law proclamation had any validity in the vision of law;
4 whether courts created under such instruments had any existence de jure;
5 whether the Parliament was within its competence to enact Section 3 of the Constitution (Seventh Amendment) Act 1986;

6 whether this Court is equipped with necessary power to judicially review any Act of Parliament in general and Section 3 of the said Act in particular and strike it off;

7 what relief, if any the petitioner can obtain;

8 how to infernally annihilate the curse of extra-Constitutional take over; and

9 whether and under what provisions of law the perpetrators of the 24th March 1982 coup d'état should be brought to the book . . .

Our judgment may be summed up in following terms:

1 Martial Law is totally alien a concept to our Constitution and hence, what Dicey commented about it, is squarely applicable to us as well.

2 A fortiori, usurpation of power by General Mohammad Ershad, flexing his arms, was void ab-initio, as was the autocratic rule by Mushtaque-Zia Duo, before Ershad, and shall remain so through eternity. All martial law instruments were void ab-initio. As a corollary, action purportedly shedding validity through the Constitution (Seventh Amendment) Act 1986 was a stale, moribund attempt, having no effect through the vision of law, and must be cremated without delay.

3 The killing of the Father of the Nation, which was followed by successive military rules, with a few years of intermission, was not an spontaneous act – it resulted from a well intrigued plot, harboured over a long period of time which was aimed not only to kill the Father of the Nation and his family, but also to wipe out the principles on which the Liberation War was fought.

4 During the autocratic rule of Khandaker Mushtaque and General Ziaur Rahman, every efforts were made to erase the memory of the Liberation War against Pakistan.

5 Two military regimes, the first being with effect from 15th August, 1975, and the second one being between 24th March 1982, and 10th November 1986, put the country miles backward. Both the martial laws devastated the democratic fabric, as well as the patriotic aspiration of the country. During Ziaur Rahman's martial law, the slogan of the Liberation War, 'Joy Bangla' was hacked to death. Many other Bengali words such as Bangladesh Betar, Bangladesh Biman were also erased from our vocabulary. Suhrawarddi Uddyan, which stands as a relic of Pakistani troops' surrender, was converted into a childrens' park. Top Pakistani collaborator Shah Azizur Rahman was given the second highest political post of the Republic, while other condemned collaborators like Col Mustafiz, Suleiman etc were installed in Zia's cabinet. Many collaborators, who fled the country towards the end of the Liberation War, were allowed, not only to return to Bangladesh, but were also blessed with safe heaven, were deployed in important national positions. Self confessed killers of Bangabanduu were given immunity from indictment through a notorious piece of purported legislation. They were also assigned with important diplomatic jobs abroad. The original constitution of the Republic of 1972 was mercilessly ravaged by General Ziaur Rahman who erased from it, one of the basic features, 'Secularism' and allowed communal politics, proscribed by Bangabandhu, to stage a comeback.

6 During General Ershad's martial law also democracy suffered devastating havoc. The Constitution was kept in abeyance. Doors of communal politics, wide opened by General Zia, were remained so during his period. Substitution of Bengali Nationalism by [the] communally oriented concept of Bangladeshi Nationalism, was also allowed longevity during Ershad's martial law.

7 By the judgment in the Fifth Amendment Case all the misdeeds perpetrated by Mushtaque-Zia duo have been eradicated and the Constitution has been restored to its original position as it was, when promulgated in 1972. 8) It is about time that the relics left behind by martial law perpetrators be completely swept away for good. . . .

During the hearing of this petition Mr M Amir-ul-Islam, who is one of the framers of the Constitution, submitting that one of the most ruthless [casualties] of successive martial laws, was the guillotining of the aspiration of our liberation war, pointed out that General Zia pathetically banished, after illegally assuming power, the [words] 'Bangalee Nationalism' from our Constitution, ostensibly with communal consideration although, said Mr Islam, the Liberation War was fought to secure the recognition of 'Bangalee Nationalism' and an independent country for Bangalee Nation. Mr Islam further contended that the phrase Bangalee Nationalism was [figured] in the Constitution of 1972, because the entire population of the country wanted the victory to 'Bangalee Nationalism' and as such, inscription of this phrase in their sacred Constitution reflected the overwhelming will of the people. Mr Islam contended that although it was Zia who ejected this phrase from our Constitution, General Ershad is no less to blame as he continued with it, We could not agree more. The whole world knows that we fought our War of Liberation to hold the flag of 'Bangalee Nationalism' high. It is also true that everyone in Bangladesh, including all ethnic people, who also speak in Bangla, fought valiantly for the liberation of Bangladesh. They are Bangalees too. Mr Islam thought a clear message should be transmitted from this Court in this respect. This question [found a place for consideration] in the Appellate Division at the time the Fifth Amendment Case was being considered. It was viewed by the Appellate Division that return to 'Bangalee Nationalism,' now, would involve huge expenditure and changes have to be recorded in all the passports and other official documents, [at] home and abroad. There is no doubt, and keeping in mind the question of expenses as viewed by the Appellate Division, we can nevertheless gradually, proceed to eventually bring back Bangalee Nationalism' in our Constitution, which was the commitment of the historic War of Liberation and the cherished desire of the people and Bangabandhu himself. Mr Khasru, [with all earnestness] supplied copies of [the] Argentine and Mexican Constitution to depict the measures these countries have taken in order to insulate their Constitution. This would definitely be a commendable action on the part our legislators to follow such move, Pakistan has also taken similar steps. After all, nobody wants to see any more martial law. This outlaw and abhorrent [demon] must find a perpetual exit from our land . . .

Notes and Questions

1. The *7th Amendment Case* was heard against the backdrop of frequent constitutional revisions in Bangladesh. The Seventh Amendment was adopted in 1986 and the Court ruling was in 2010. From 1973 to 2011, the Constitution of Bangladesh was amended 15 times. This stream of constitutional revisions covered a wide range of issues, summarised below:

    (a) First Amendment (1973): providing that war criminals are suspended from the enjoyment of certain fundamental rights.
    (b) Second Amendment (1973): providing for preventive detention and to regulate the promulgation of a state of emergency.
    (c) Third Amendment (1974): giving effect to the agreement with India giving up claims with respect to disputed territories.
    (d) Fourth Amendment (1975): introducing the presidential form of government and a one-party system.
    (e) Fifth Amendment (1979): ratifying all actions, including martial law proclamations and orders, as well as changes in the basic structure of the Constitution brought about between 15 August 1975 and 9 April 1979.

(f) Sixth Amendment (1981): providing that if the Vice-President is elected as President, he shall be deemed to have vacated his office on the date he enters the office of President.

(g) Seventh Amendment (1986): ratifying all martial law proclamations and orders, and the constitutional amendments made by such proclamations and orders.

(h) Eighth Amendment (1988): amending Article 100 of the Constitution and thereby setting up six permanent Benches of the High Court Division outside the capital. By the same amendment, Islam was made the state religion of Bangladesh.

(i) Ninth Amendment (1989): providing for the direct election of the Vice-President.

(j) Tenth Amendment (1990): providing for the reservation of 30 seats for the next 10 years exclusively for women members.

(k) Eleventh Amendment (1991): ratifying all actions taken by the caretaker government. It also ratified the appointment of a Chief Justice as the Vice-President who later became Acting President. In addition, the amendment also confirmed the return of an Acting President to his previous position as Chief Justice.

(l) Twelfth Amendment (1991): reintroducing the parliamentary form of government; the President became the constitutional head of state; the Prime Minister became the executive head of government.

(m) Thirteenth Amendment (1996): providing for a non-party caretaker government.

(n) Fourteenth Amendment (2004): providing for increasing the number of reserved seats from 30 to 45 for women and raising the retirement age of Supreme Court Judges from 65 to 67.

(o) Fifteenth Amendment (2011) scrapping the caretaker government system so that polls could be held, and restoring secularism but retaining Islam as the state religion.

It is interesting to compare the frequent constitutional revisions in Bangladesh with the relative constitutional stability in Japan in terms of there being no revisions. Are there identifiable social or political conditions that may explain this divergence? How significant a factor is military rule in fomenting changes?

2. The Court recognised that the case 'invokes an issue of immense constitutional importance'. However, in contrast to the strategic rulings of the South Korean courts in politically sensitive cases, the Bangladesh Court was very assertive in defending democracy. What do you think accounts for this different judicial strategy?

E. Constitutional Change during Revolutions and Emergencies

Constitutional change may take place during a revolution or state of emergency, especially in Asian states plagued by political turmoil. When the political order begins to disintegrate during revolutions and emergencies, the stability of the constitution is tested. While peace-time disputes are usually resolved through legal or political channels under the constitution, these methods of adjudication or negotiation are unlikely to work in revolutions or emergencies. If a constitution is not abrogated or abolished by a revolution or emergency, it may struggle to accommodate these drastic events. For example, in *Dosso v The State*,[25] the Pakistan Supreme Court had to consider the legality of the declaration of martial law by President Iskander Mirza under which the Central and Provincial Cabinets and Assemblies were dissolved and General Ayub Khan was appointed Chief Martial Law Administrator. The issue was whether the prerogative writs issues by various Pakistani High Courts would abate upon the declaration of martial law. Munnir CJ held, applying Hans Kelsen's theory of revolutionary legality, that following a successful revolution, a new *grundnorm* had arisen:

> It sometimes happens, however, that a Constitution and the national legal order under it is disrupted by an abrupt political change not within the contemplation of the Constitution. Any such change is called a revolution, and its legal effect is not only the destruction of the existing Constitution but also the validity of the national legal order.[26]

The motive behind the revolution is totally irrelevant. What is important is the efficacy of the change in regimes. This decision was much criticised as it appeared to endorse unconstitutional acts and confer legality on erstwhile usurpers of power.[27]

A notable feature in some Asian states is the occurrence of military coups championing the cause of 'good governance' or 'opposing corruption'. In *Habeas Corpus Petition of Benigno S Aquino, Jr et al v Sec Juan Ponce Enrile, Gen Romeo Espino & Gen Fidal Ramos*, the Philippines Supreme Court had to decide whether to review a General Order issued during a state of emergency under which various dissidents were detained. While the judges reached a consensus on dismissing the petitions, they were highly divided in terms of their reasons and views for doing so. Their caution is evident from the fact that the Court did not produce a collective opinion, and the Justices each issued separate opinions.

Habeas Corpus Petition of Benigno S Aquino, Jr et al v Sec Juan Ponce Enrile, Gen Romeo Espino & Gen Fidel Ramos
59 SCRA 183; GR No L-35538, 17 Sep 1974 (Supreme Court, Philippines)

Facts

The petitioners were arrested and held pursuant to General Order No 2 of the President, for participating in or giving aid and comfort in the conspiracy to seize political and state power and to take over the Government by force. General Order No 2 was issued by the President under powers he assumed by virtue of Proclamation No 1081 which placed the entire country under martial law. The main issue was whether the Court could inquire into the validity of Proclamation No 1081. Notably, as the Chief Justice's opinion indicated, the Court was divided as to the manner in which the issues should be treated and developed.

---

[25] *Dosso v The State* [1958] PSCR 180.
[26] Ibid at 184.
[27] For studies of the impact of the *Dosso* case, see T Mahmud, 'Jurisprudence of Successful Treason: Coup d'Etat &(and) Common Law' (1994) 27 *Cornell International Law Journal* 49; as well as TKK Iyer, 'Constitutional Law in Pakistan: Kelsen in the Courts' (1973) 21(4) *American Journal of Comparative Law* 759; MM Stavsky, 'Doctrine of State Necessity in Pakistan' (1983); 16 *Cornell International Law Journal* 341; SA de Smith, 'Constitutional Lawyers in Revolutionary Situations' (1968) 7 *West Ontario Law Review* 93; L Wolf-Phillips, 'Constitutional Legtimacy: A Study of the Doctrine of Necessity' (1979) 1(4) *Third World Quarterly* 97; and JW Harris, 'When and Why Does the Grundnorm Change?' (1971) 29 *CLJ* 103.

Querube Makalintal CJ

The first major issue raised by the parties is whether this Court may inquire into the validity of Proclamation No 1081. Stated more concretely, is the existence of conditions claimed to justify the exercise of the power to declare martial law subject to judicial inquiry? Is the question political or justiciable in character? Justices Makasiar, Antonio, Esguerra, Fernandez and Aquino hold that the question is political and therefore its determination is beyond the jurisdiction of this Court. Justice Antonio, with whom Justices Makasiar, Fernandez and Aquino concur, finds that there is no dispute as to the existence of a state of rebellion in the country, and on that premise emphasizes the factor of necessity for the exercise by the President of his power under the Constitution to declare martial law, holding that the decision as to whether or not there is such necessity is wholly confided to him and therefore is not subject to judicial inquiry, his responsibility being directly to the people.

Arrayed on the side of justiciability are Justices Castro, Fernando, Teehankee and Muñoz Palma. They hold that the constitutional sufficiency of the proclamation may be inquired into by the Court, and would thus apply the principle laid down in Lansang although that case refers to the power of the President to suspend the privilege of the writ of *habeas corpus*. The recognition of justiciability accorded to the question in Lansang, it should be emphasized, is there expressly distinguished from the power of judicial review in ordinary civil or criminal cases, and is limited to ascertaining 'merely whether he (the President) has gone beyond the constitutional limits of his jurisdiction, not to exercise the power vested in him or to determine the wisdom of his act.' The test is not whether the President's decision is correct but whether, in suspending the writ, he did or did not act *arbitrarily*. Applying this test, the finding by the Justices just mentioned is that there was no arbitrariness in the President's proclamation of martial law pursuant to the 1935 Constitution; and I concur with them in that finding. The factual bases for the suspension of the privilege of the writ of *habeas corpus, particularly* in regard to the existence of a state of rebellion in the country, had not disappeared, indeed had been exacerbated, as events shortly before said proclamation clearly demonstrated. On this Point the Court is practically unanimous; Justice Teehankee merely refrained from discussing it.

. . . In the first place I am convinced (as are the other Justices), without need of receiving evidence as in an ordinary adversary court proceeding, that a state of rebellion existed in the country when Proclamation No 1081 was issued. It was a matter of contemporary history within the cognizance not only of the courts but of all observant people residing here at the time. Many of the facts and events recited in detail in the different 'Whereases' of the proclamation are of common knowledge. The state of rebellion continues up to the present. The argument that while armed hostilities go on in several provinces in Mindanao there are none in other regions except in isolated pockets in Luzon, and that therefore there is no need to maintain martial law all over the country, ignores the sophisticated nature and ramifications of rebellion in a modern setting. It does not consist simply of armed clashes between organized and identifiable groups on fields of their own choosing. It includes subversion of the most subtle kind, necessarily clandestine and operating precisely where there is no actual fighting. Underground propaganda, through printed news sheets or rumors disseminated in whispers; recruitment of armed and ideological adherents, raising of funds, procurement of arms and material, fifth-column activities including sabotage and intelligence – all these are part of the rebellion which by their nature are usually conducted far from the battle fronts. They cannot be counteracted effectively unless recognized and dealt with in that context.

Secondly, my view, which coincides with that of other members of the Court as stated in their opinions, is that the question of validity of Proclamation No 1081 has been foreclosed by the transitory provision of the 1973 Constitution [Art XVII, Sec 3(2)] that 'all proclamations, orders, decrees, instructions, and acts promulgated, issued, or done by the incumbent President shall be part of the law of the land and shall remain valid, legal, binding and effective even after . . . the ratification of this Constitution . . .' To be sure, there is an attempt in these cases to resuscitate the issue of the effectivity of the new Constitution. All that, however, is behind us now. The question has been laid to rest by our decision in *Javellana v Executive Secretary* (L-36142, 50 SCRA 30, 31 March 1973), and of course by the existing political realities both in the conduct of national affairs and in our relations with other countries. On the effect of the transitory provision Justice Muñoz Palma withholds her assent to any sweeping statement that the same in effect validated, in the constitutional sense, all 'such proclamations, decrees, instructions, and acts promulgated, issued, or done by the incumbent President.' All that she concedes is that the transitory provision merely gives them 'the *imprimatur* of a law but not of a constitutional mandate,' and as such therefore 'are subject to judicial review when proper under the Constitution. Finally, the political-or-justiciable question controversy indeed, any inquiry by this Court in the present cases into the constitutional sufficiency of the factual bases for the proclamation of martial law – has become moot and purposeless as a consequence of the general referendum of July 27–28, 1973. The question propounded to the voters was:

> Under the (1973) Constitution, the President, if he so desires, can continue in office beyond 1973. Do you want President Marcos to continue beyond 1973 and finish the reforms he initiated under Martial Law?

The overwhelming majority of those who cast their ballots, including citizens between 15 and 18 years, voted affirmatively on the proposal. The question was thereby removed from the area of presidential power under the Constitution and transferred to the seat of sovereignty itself. Whatever may be the nature of the exercise of that power by the President in the beginning – whether or not purely political and therefore non-justiciable – this Court is precluded from applying its judicial yardstick to the act of the sovereign.

With respect to the petitioners who have been released from detention but have not withdrawn their petitions because they are still subject to certain restrictions, the ruling of the Court is that the petitions should be dismissed. The power to detain persons even without charges for acts related to the situation which justifies the proclamation of martial law, such as the existence of a state of rebellion, necessarily implies the power (subject, in the opinion of the Justices who consider Lansang applicable, to the same test of arbitrariness laid down therein), to impose upon the released detainees conditions or restrictions which are germane to and necessary to carry out the purposes of the proclamation. Justice Fernando, however, 'is for easing the restrictions on the right to travel of petitioner Rodrigo' and others similarly situated and so to this extent dissents from the ruling of the majority; while Justice Teehankee believes that those restrictions do not constitute deprivation of physical liberty within the meaning of the constitutional provision on the privilege of the writ of *habeas corpus*. It need only be added that, to my mind, implicit in a state of martial law is the suspension of the said privilege with respect to persons arrested or detained for acts related to the basic objective of the proclamation, which is to suppress invasion, insurrection, or rebellion, or to safeguard public safety against imminent danger thereof. The preservation of society and national survival take precedence. On this particular point, that is, that the proclamation of martial law automatically suspends the privilege of the writ as to the persons referred to, the Court is practically unanimous. Justice Fernando, however, says that to him that is still an open question; and Justice Muñoz Palma qualifiedly dissents from the majority in her separate opinion, but for the reasons she discusses therein votes for the dismissal of the petitions.

Notes and Questions

1. After declaring martial law in 1972, the authoritarian Marcos regime assumed full control of the Philippines Government, including the judiciary. Judicial independence was restored and strengthened only after Marcos was overthrown by a 'People's Power' movement in 1986, when democratic government under President Cory Aquino was established. In the intervening period, the Court was used to legitimate the Marcos dictatorship and to expand Marcos's executive and legislative powers. The Court frequently invoked the political question doctrine to bar judicial review of many of Marcos's acts. A historical text authorised by the Philippine Supreme Court characterises this strategy as one among several forms of judicial accommodation made within the context of an authoritarian regime:

    > [T]he courts gave their cooperation and support to the dictatorship and to its program for a New Society under a new constitutional order. That was their best choice. Supposing that, because of their attachment to constitutionalism, they had resisted the dictatorship, the courts would simply have been replaced by military tribunals. The judges of the period had the sagacity and the foresight to trust the political leadership, and despite their misgivings, follow its path toward a promised constitutional order. It was by such faith and hope that we can justify their collaboration in strategies and measures which, in the fateful months of late 1972 and early 1973, were antithetical and destructive of republicanism. Indeed, looking at the period as a whole, the Judiciary as an institution was basically preserved and functioning all throughout, without disruption or disturbance.[28]

2. In Bangladesh, Pakistan, and Thailand, the corruption of democratically-elected leaders has been used as a primary justification for military-led 'good governance' coups which backed the takeover of government by other forces, and as an instrument for sustaining it. Often the military-backed governments claim that corruption had to be eliminated before civilian democratic rule could successfully take root and flourish. Anti-corruption commissions were revitalised or created, and attempts were made to 'cleanse' the political landscape by levying corruption charges to imprison, exile or marginalise political leaders, frequently with the complicity of the judiciary and international community. The military-backed governments passed laws and created other institutions, ostensibly to promote 'good governance' and to lay the groundwork for more 'anti-corruption campaigns'. Though portrayed as politically neutral, these campaigns do in fact serve politicised agendas. Both national anti-corruption advocates and the international community are severely constrained in addressing corruption within the military, or the military's own potential political biases when it prosecutes acts of corruption by civilians. The military's revered status as the protector of the country and its sovereignty make it difficult either to bring these charges or remind the public of the military's past malfeasance. The result is that the public are presented with a one-sided picture of corrupt and incompetent politicians versus a disciplined and incorruptible military, which strengthens the political clout of the military. See N Robinson and N Sattar, 'When Corruption is an Emergency: "Good Governance" Coups and Bangladesh' (2012) 35 *Fordham International Law Journal* 737.

---

[28] See *The History of the Philippines Judiciary* (Manila: The Philippine Judiciary Foundation, 1998) at 578–79, quoted in DA Desierto, 'Justiciability of Socio-economic Rights: Comparative Powers, Roles, and Practices in the Philippines and South Africa' (2010) 11 *Asian-Pacific Law and Policy Journal* 114, 118–19.

In contrast to the highly divided opinion of the Philippines Supreme Court in *Habeas Corpus Petition of Benigno S Aquino, Jr et al v Sec Juan Ponce Enrile, Gen Romeo Espino & Gen Fidel Ramos*, the Supreme Court of Pakistan held firm in securing political order during a state of emergency by upholding a constitutional revision which was the foundation of General Musharraf's military rule.

Watan Party v The Chief Executive/President of Pakistan & Anor
Constitutional Petition No 36 of 2002, 7 Oct 2002
(Supreme Court, Pakistan)

Facts

In October 1999, General Musharraf issued the Proclamation of Emergency by which Constitution of Pakistan 1973 was suspended and the whole country brought under the armed forces' control. Seven Constitution Petitions were filed by various persons challenging the validity of these extra-constitutional measures. However, the Court validated them on the basis of the doctrine of state necessity. This Court concluded that there were sufficient grounds to justify intervention by the armed forces. Though the Court upheld the 1973 Constitution as the supreme law of the land, it held that Musharraf was entitled act executively and promulgate all necessary legislative measures. It further required the Chief Executive to hold general elections for the National and Provincial Assemblies as well as the Senate, on a date not later than 90 days before the expiry of the period of three years. Musharraf then proceeded to set up various institutions to help and guide him, and several constitutional amendments were announced. One of these was Legal Framework Order 2002, which revived Article 58(2)(b) of the Constitution, which was incorporated in the Constitution in 1985 through the well-known 8th Amendment of the Constitution. This provision empowered the President to dissolve the National Assembly if the Government was not being run in accordance with the Constitution, and appeal to the electorate if necessary. The present petition sought to set aside the amendments made in the Constitution through Legal Framework Order 2002 on the ground that the Order was illegal and unconstitutional.

Sheikh Riaz Ahmed CJ

Article 58(2)(b) of the Constitution conferred powers on the President to dissolve the National Assembly if the government was not being run in accordance with the Constitution and appeal to the electorate was necessary. This power was resorted to four times in this country; firstly by General Ziaul Haq dissolving the National Assembly and dismissing the government of Mr Muhammad Khan Junejo, secondly by Mr Ghulam Ishaq Khan while dissolving the National Assembly and dismissing the government of Mohtarama Benazir Bhutto in 1990 and thirdly again by Mr Ghulam Ishaq Khan while dissolving the National Assembly and dismissing the government of Mian Nawaz Sharif. Although the dismissal of the government of Mian Nawaz Sharif in 1993 was declared by this Court to be unconstitutional but subsequently both the President and the Prime Minister had to resign and as a result of the general election held in 1993, Mohtarama Benazir Bhutto formed the government. Her second government was also dismissed and the National Assembly dissolved in 1996 by Sardar Farooq Khan Leghari, the then President of Pakistan. Consequently, fresh elections were held and Mian Nawaz Sharif for the second time formed the government and became the Prime Minister. Article 58(2)(b) was repealed by Mian Nawaz Sharif through the 13th Amendment of the Constitution. At this juncture, it would be necessary to refer to the validity of the 8th Amendment and Article 58(2)(b) of the Constitution, which was debated in this Court in *Mahmood Khan Achakzai v Federation of Pakistan* (PLD 1997 SC 426). While referring to Article 58(2)(b) and its utility in the background of the political culture of this country, this Court made the following illuminating observations:

> Much has been said against Article 58(2)(b) of the Constitution that it has changed the shape of the Constitution from Parliamentary to Presidential and has concentrated powers in the hands of the President who is not directly elected as is Prime Minister. Perusal of the Constitution, as it is, shows that it is not so and the apprehension is unfounded for the reason that this provision has only brought about balance between the powers of the President and the Prime Minister in Parliamentary Form of Government as is contemplated under Parliamentary Democracy. There is nothing unusual about it and such provisions enabling the President to exercise such power can be found in various Parliamentary and Democratic Constitutions like Australia, Italy, India, France and Portugal. In fact Article 58(2)(b) has shut the door on Martial Law for ever, which has not visited as after 1977.

We can only wish that the then legislators and Mian Nawaz Sharif at the helm of affairs had realized the implications of such repeal. Article 58(2)(b) was described as a safety valve against imposition of martial law/military takeover.

Adverting to the Legal Framework Order, as discussed above, Article 58(2)(b) has now been reincorporated in the Constitution. Mr Zafarullah Khan, learned ASC for the petitioner criticized such incorporation and we drew his attention to the observations made by this Court in Mahmood Khan Achakzai's case and also apprised him of the grave consequences of the repeated military takeovers. However, we are constrained to judge the maintainability of this petition under Article 184(3) of the Constitution filed by Watan Party. We confronted the learned counsel with this aspect of the case and the learned counsel submitted that Watan Party had filed this petition through the Punjab President of the Ladies Wing, namely, Tasneem Shaukat Khan. We have noted the following paragraph in the body of the petition:

> That the petitioner's party has boycotted the general elections, which are undemocratic.

Admittedly, no list of members or office bearers at the national, provincial or local levels has been filed. There is nothing on record to indicate that the party has ever had any representation in the Parliament or in any Provincial Assembly. It was also admitted that the party had not held the intra-party election mandated by the Political Parties Order, 2002 (Chief Executive's Order No 18 of 2002). We asked the learned counsel to name the office bearers of the party in Balochistan but the learned counsel could not give any definite name. In this background, the crucial question seeking an answer is the *locus standi* and bona fides of the petitioner to invoke the jurisdiction of this Court under Article 184(3) of the Constitution. In our view, answer to this question is in negative as the petitioner has no *locus standi* to file this petition. Although as held in *Manzoor Elahi v Federation of Pakistan* (PLD 1975 SC 66) the question raised before the Court under Article 184(3) must be one of public importance with reference to the enforcement of Fundamental Rights contained in Chapter 1, Part II of the Constitution. It is true that as held in *Benazir Bhutto's case* (PLD 1988 SC 416) and *Asad Ali's case* (PLD 1998 SC 161) the person desiring to invoke the jurisdiction of this Court under Article 184(3) of the Constitution need not necessarily be an aggrieved person, nevertheless the person approaching this Court under the aforesaid provision has to demonstrate that the question raised concerns the public at large. It may be appropriate to reproduce observations of this Court in *Zulfiqar*

Mehdi v Pakistan International Airlines Corporation (1998 SCMR 793), which run as under:

> The issues arising in a case, cannot be considered as a question of public importance, if the decision of the issues affects only the rights of an individual or a group of individuals. The issue in order to assume the character of public importance must be such that its decision affects the rights and liberties of people at large. The objective 'public' necessarily implies a thing belonging to people at large, the nation, the State or a community as a whole. Therefore, if a controversy is raised in which only a particular group of people is interested and the body of the people as a whole or the entire community has no interest, it cannot be treated as a case of public importance.

It is worthwhile to mention that all the major political parties have fielded their candidates to contest the General Election 2002 under the Conduct of General Elections Order, 2002 (Chief Executive's Order No 7 of 2002) and none of them has come forward with a petition to question any provision of the Legal Framework Order. It is well-known now that after the election the National and the Provincial Assemblies will meet. The members will elect Speakers, Deputy Speakers, Prime Minister, Chief Ministers and the Senators. The elected Parliament is in immediate sight and obviously the Parliament and not this Court is the appropriate forum to consider all these amendments. We may further observe that procedure to amend the Constitution as enshrined in Article 239, Part XI remains unaltered. The Parliament retains same power to amend the Constitution as it did before the promulgation of the Legal Framework Order. The upshot of the above discussion is that this petition must be dismissed because the petitioner has no *locus standi* to invoke the jurisdiction of this Court under Article 184(3) of the Constitution.

Notes and Questions

1. The Supreme Court of Pakistan upheld the validity of the constitutional revision as being fundamental to the legitimacy of Musharraf's rule on grounds that the petitioner Watan Party lacked *locus standi* since it never had any representation in Parliament or any Provincial Assembly.

2. Pakistan's 1973 Constitution was drafted by a Constituent Assembly elected directly by the people. Since all the political parties in the Constituent Assembly voted for this Constitution, it can be said to have been unanimously endorsed. As the political parties who were represented in all four provinces agreed to the Constitution, it could also be characterised as a federal contract. However, since 1973, the Constitution has been suspended or held in abeyance on two occasions: first, when martial law was imposed on 5 July 1977; and, secondly, when a fourth military coup took place on 12 October 1999.

3. Since 1973, 17 attempts have been made to amend the Constitution. Three of these (the ninth, the eleventh, and the fifteenth amendment bills) failed for a complicated variety of reasons. A total of 14 amendments were thus made to the Constitution. These amendments drastically changed the original character of the fundamental law.

4. The constitutional history of Pakistan after 1973 reveals various recurrent issues. The first concerned the centre–province relationship. It was expected that over time, greater autonomy and rights would be given to the provinces, but this did not happen. Second is the balance of power between the President and Prime Minister; and third, the inviolability of the Constitution. As Pakistan's political system has broken down repeatedly, the Constitution itself has fallen victim to the ambitions of extra-political forces. See S Jaffar Ahmed, Overview of the Constitution of Pakistan, Pakistan Institute of Legislative Development and Transparency, Pakistan Institute of Legislative Development and Transparency, Briefing Paper No 17, August 2004.

5. How should these issues be evaluated, given Pakistan's social-political context? From its performance in adjudicating these cases, is Pakistan's Supreme Court competent or able to address these issues effectively? Is the Court the proper forum for the ventilation and resolution of such disputes?

III. CONSTITUTIONAL MOMENTS AND METHODS OF CONSTITUTIONAL CHANGE

Constitutional change takes place through various channels. First, when a constitution is founded, the framers set the provisions prescribing procedures of constitutional revision, admitting constitutional amendment as the formal and foremost method of constitutional change. Nevertheless, certain constitutional scholars consider there to be alternative approaches to constitutional change, apart from through formal procedure. While there may be no clear line separating one approach from another in certain circumstances,[29] constitutional change may be brought about through formal amendment, political practice or convention,[30] and via judicial interpretation.[31]

Other analytical approaches seek to evaluate constitutional changes in a manner which transcends identification of these avenues of change. Bruce Ackerman, for example, in analysing American constitutional history, proposes that constitutional change takes place from the moment when exceptional 'higher' law-making takes place. This happens when we see higher levels of popular mobilisation and inter-branch collaboration, in contrast to ordinary forms of legislative, judicial and executive action. According to Ackerman, 'the people' speak only during rare moments of 'constitutional politics', while ordinary legislation is the work of mere political agents, who operate during times of 'normal politics'.[32] Under this theory of a 'constitutional moment', the various methods of constitutional change described above may or may

---

[29] S Levinson, 'How many times has the United States Constitution been Amended? (A) < 26, (B) 26, (C) 27, (D) >27: Accounting for Constitutional change' in S Levinson (ed), *Responding to Imperfection: The Theory and Practice of Constitutional Amendment* (Princeton, NJ: Princeton University Press, 1995) 13.

[30] E Young, 'The Constitution Outside the Constitution' (2007) 117 *Yale Law Journal* 408.

[31] D Strauss, 'Common Law Constitutional Interpretation' (1996) 63 *University of Chicago Law Review* 877.

[32] B Ackerman, *We the People: Foundations* (Cambridge, Mass: Harvard University Press, 1991); B Ackerman, *We the People: Transformations* (Cambridge, Mass: Harvard University Press, 1998).

not reflect a *genuine* constitutional change. Constitutional amendment, political actions and judicial interpretations could very well be born out of the day-to-day ordinary forms of law-making, instead of a more concerted expression of the popular will which justifies an episode of higher law-making.

Constitutional change through constitutional amendment, however, may be accompanied by problems arising from procedural defects or substantial limits to legislative powers.[33] Political actions or referenda that shape constitutional change may trigger problems of political mobilisation against the existing constitutional order, which may prove destabilising. Constitutional change through judicial interpretation could raise the problem of judicialisation of politics and juristocracy. In this section, we look at relevant practices of the Asian states, and evaluate these different methods of constitutional change and the problems they engender.

A. Constitutional Amendment and Procedure

Formal provisions for constitutional amendment are a general feature of national constitutions.[34] A written constitution may prescribe a process of constitutional amendment designed to allow later generations to correct or improve upon the existing constitutional provisions, in the light of changing circumstances.[35] This method of amending the constitution is distinct from others in that:

(a) it is the only method that makes changes to the constitutional text; and
(b) it usually prescribes more stringent procedures than those applicable to ordinary legislation, such that a constitutional amendment bill becomes a type of super-statute.

The availability, frequency and degree of change effected by a constitutional amendment depend largely on how the procedure for revision is designed. Flexibility and rigidity are two concerns, as a constitution that will not bend will break. Conversely, an over-flexible constitution may compromise the effective functioning of the constitution itself. The constitution is intended and executed to provide stability for the political order in which the rights and prosperity of the people may be secured; an overly flexible process for amendment might create a situation of endless uncertainty and chaos. However, an over-rigid procedure could render the constitution hard to adjust, such that parts of it become obsolete or ill-suited to contemporary exigencies. Where constitutional amendment is not a viable practical option, this might necessitate resort to extra-constitutional methods for constitutional change.

The procedures for constitutional amendment vary between states, though most require a super-majoritarian procedure that takes the process out of the realm of ordinary law-making. Asian states adopt various kinds of procedures for constitutional amendment as listed in Table 4.3.

---

[33] We discuss only the issue of procedural problems in this section; substantial limits to constitutional change are left to section IV. below.

[34] DS Lutz, 'Toward a Theory of Constitutional Amendment' in Levinson (ed), above n 28, 237.

[35] BP Denning and JR Vile, 'The Relevance of Constitutional Amendments: A Response to David Strauss' (2002) 77 *Tulane Law Review* 247.

As can be seen from Table 4.3, most states in Asia adopt a stricter procedure for constitutional amendments than for ordinary legislation. Some have adopted a simple procedure in the form of requiring that a constitutional amendment be passed by the legislature with the support of a two-thirds majority; this is typical of constitutions such as those of India and Japan, which established a bicameral parliamentary Cabinet system.

Table 4.3 Amendment Procedure in the Constitutions of Asian States

Country	Constitutional Amendment Procedure
Bangladesh	The votes of not less than two-thirds of the total number of Members of Parliament, plus the President's assent (President can refer the bill for a referendum).
Brunei	His Majesty the Sultan and Yang Di-Pertuan can make proposals to amend the Constitution, provided it is placed before the Legislative Council by the Privy Council for deliberation; the Sultan shall consult (but is not bound by) the Privy Council before he decides to proclaim the amendment.
Cambodia	The initiative to review or amend the Constitution shall be the prerogative of the King, the Prime Minister or the Chairman of the National Assembly at the suggestion of one-quarter of all the assembly members. Revision or amendments shall be enacted by a constitutional law passed by the National Assembly with a two-thirds majority vote.
China	Amendments to the Constitution are to be proposed by the Standing Committee of the National People's Congress or by more than one-fifth of the deputies to the National People's Congress, and adopted by a vote of more than two-thirds of all the deputies to the Congress.
East Timor	Members of Parliament and Parliamentary Groups can initiate constitutional revision. The National Parliament may take on powers to revise the Constitution by a majority of four-fifths of the Members of Parliament. Amendments to the Constitution shall be approved by a majority of two-thirds of the Members of Parliament in full exercise of their functions.
Hong Kong	The power of amendment of the Basic Law shall be vested in the National People's Congress. The power to propose bills for amendments to this Law shall be vested in the Standing Committee of the National People's Congress, the State Council and the Hong Kong Special Administrative Region. Amendment bills from the Hong Kong Special Administrative Region shall be submitted to the National People's Congress by the delegation of the Region to the National People's Congress after obtaining the consent of two-thirds of the deputies of the Region to the National People's Congress, two-thirds of all the members of the Legislative Council of the Region, and the Chief Executive of the Region.
India	A bill to amend the Constitution may be initiated only by either House of Parliament; when the Bill is passed in each House by a majority of the total membership of that House and by a majority of not less than two-thirds of the members of that House present and voting, it shall be presented to the President who shall give his assent to the Bill.

Table 4.3 (*cont*)

Country	Constitutional Amendment Procedure
Indonesia	A proposal to amend a constitutional provision may be included in the agenda of an MPR [*Majelis Permusyawaratan Rakyat* – People's Consultative Assembly] session if it is submitted by at least one-third of the total MPR membership. To amend the Articles of this Constitution, at least two-thirds of the total membership of the MPR should be present for that session. Any decision to amend the Articles of this Constitution shall be made with the agreement of at least 50 per cent plus one member of the total MPR membership.
Japan	Amendments to this Constitution shall be initiated by the Diet, through a concurring vote of two-thirds or more of all the members of each House and shall then be submitted to the people for ratification, which shall require the affirmative vote of a majority of all votes cast at a special referendum or such election as the Diet shall specify.
Korea	A proposal to amend the Constitution shall be introduced either by a majority of the total members of the National Assembly or by the President. The National Assembly shall decide upon the proposed amendments within 60 days of the public announcement, and passage by the National Assembly shall require the concurrent vote of two-thirds or more of the total members of the National Assembly. The proposed amendments to the Constitution shall be submitted to a national referendum not later than 30 days after passage by the National Assembly, and shall be determined by more than one half of all votes cast by more than one half of voters eligible to vote in elections for members of the National Assembly.
Lao	Only the National Assembly session of the Lao People's Democratic Republic has the right to amend the Constitution, which requires the affirmative votes of at least two-thirds of the total number of the National Assembly members.
Malaysia	A Bill for to amend the Constitution shall not be passed by the Legislative Assembly unless it has been supported on Second and Third Readings by the votes of not less than two-thirds of the total number of members thereof.
Mongolia	Amendments to the Constitution shall be initiated by the organisation and officials enjoying the right to legislative initiative and could be submitted by the Constitutional Court to the State Ikh Khural. A national referendum on a proposed constitutional amendment may be held with the concurrence of not less than two-thirds of the members of the State Ikh Khural. An amendment to the Constitution shall be adopted by not less than three-quarters of votes of all members of the State Ikh Khural.
Nepal	A Bill regarding the amendment or repeal of any Article of the Constitution may be presented at the Legislature-Parliament. The Bill shall be deemed to be passed where it is approved by at least a two-thirds majority of the Legislature-Parliament of the total number of members present.
The Philippines	Any amendment to, or revision of, this Constitution may be proposed by Congress, upon a vote of three-fourths of all its Members; or a constitutional convention. Amendments to this Constitution may likewise be directly proposed by the people through initiative upon a petition of at least 12 per cent of the total number of registered voters, of which every legislative district must be represented by at least 3 per cent of the registered voters therein. The Congress may, by a vote of two-thirds of all its Members, call a constitutional convention, or by a majority vote of all its Members, submit to the electorate the question of

Country	Constitutional Amendment Procedure
Philippines (*cont*)	calling such a convention. Any amendment to, or revision of, this Constitution shall be valid when ratified by a majority of the votes cast in a plebiscite.
Singapore	The general procedure for amending the Constitution requires the support of a two-thirds parliamentary majority. Certain provisions pertaining to state sovereignty are subject to a two-thirds majority at a popular referendum while other stipulated sections will be referred to a referendum unless the President acting in his discretion otherwise directs the Speaker in writing.
Sri Lanka	A Bill to amend, replace or repeal a constitutional provision shall become law if the number of votes cast in favour thereof amounts to not less than two-thirds of the whole number of Members (including those not present) and upon a certificate by the President or the Speaker. Certain Bills must be subject to a Referendum for approval.
Taiwan	Amendment of the Constitution shall be initiated upon the proposal of one-fourth of the total members of the Legislative Yuan, passed by at least three-quarters of the members present at a meeting attended by at least three-quarters of the total members of the Legislative Yuan. It must be sanctioned by electors in the free area of the Republic of China at a referendum held upon expiration of a six-month period of public announcement of the proposal, wherein the number of valid votes in favour exceeds one-half of the total number of legitimate voters.
Thailand	A motion for amendment must be proposed by the Council of Ministers, members of the House of Representatives of not less than one-fifth of the total number of the existing members of the House of Representatives, or members of both Houses of not less than one-fifth of the total number of the existing members thereof or persons having the right to vote of not less than 50,000 in number under the law on lodging a petition for introducing the law. A motion for amendment must be proposed in the form of a draft Constitution Amendment and the National Assembly shall consider it in three readings. The voting in the first reading for acceptance in principle shall be by roll call and open voting, and the amendment must be approved by votes of not less than one-half of the total number of the existing members of both Houses. The consideration in the second reading section by section shall also be subject to a public hearing participated by persons having the right to vote, who have proposed the draft Constitution Amendment; the voting in the second reading for consideration section by section shall be decided by a simple majority of votes. At the conclusion of the second reading, there shall be an interval of 15 days after which the National Assembly shall proceed with its third reading. The voting in the third and final reading shall be by roll call and open voting, and its promulgation as the Constitution must be approved by votes of more than one-half of the total number of the existing members of both Houses. After the resolution has been passed in accordance with the rules and procedures hitherto specified, the draft Constitution Amendment shall be presented to the King, and the provisions of section 150 and section 151 shall apply mutatis mutandis.
Vietnam	Only the National Assembly has the power to amend the Constitution. Any amendments to the Constitution shall require a majority vote of not less than two-thirds of the total number of deputies to the National Assembly.

More complex amendment procedures tend to be required where the process of constitutional amendment is entrusted to more than one political player. For example, the Thai Constitution requires that a motion for amendment be proposed by the Council of Ministers, or members of the House of Representatives or the National Assembly. The power is distributed among multiple agents, and that may facilitate constitutional amendment. Other constitutions may require the vote of a supermajority to initiate the process of constitutional amendment. For example, the Philippine Constitution requires a vote of three-quarters of all the Members of the Congress, or a constitutional convention to propose a constitutional amendment, before it can subject it to the people. In so doing, it ensures that for a constitutional amendment to be passed, it must enjoy sufficient political consensus.

Holding referenda is another measure widely adopted in Asian constitutions, reflecting a populist brand of popular sovereignty. As Table 4.4 shows, approximately half of the states surveyed in Asia resort to referenda as part of their procedural mechanisms for constitutional revision. Some constitutions make this mandatory, including those of Japan, Korea, Taiwan and the Philippines; it is optional in the Mongolian and Bangladesh Constitutions. Yet other states treat it as a special requirement which applies only to certain constitutional provisions, such as Singapore, East Timor and Sri Lanka. Other Asian states from a diversity of socio-economic backgrounds do not contain referenda-orientated procedures in their constitutions. This includes democratic states such as Thailand, Indonesia, India, Nepal, Cambodia and Malaysia, as well as socialist states (China, Vietnam, Lao) and the absolute monarchy of Brunei.

Given the dynamic and complicated range of constitutional amendment procedures, scholarly studies have reached different conclusions with respect to which procedure makes the constitution most difficult to amend. John Ferejohn found in a regression study that states with super or double majority requirements for constitutional amendments and legislative bicameralism are statistically significant with respect to the success rate of amendments.[36] Björn Rasch and Roger Congleton, in a cross-national study of 19 OECD countries, found that the key determinant for the success of amendments across countries was whether a constitution required an amendment to be ratified by multiple different bodies, and in particular by voters at a referendum, rather than whether a legislative supermajority is required for an amendment.[37] Rosalind Dixon

Table 4.4 Constitutional Amendment Procedures Involving Referenda

Constitutional Amendment Procedures Including Referenda	Constitutional Amendment Procedures Excluding Referenda
Taiwan, Japan, Korea, the Philippines (ordinary requirement) Mongolia, Bangladesh (optional) Singapore, East Timor, Sri Lanka (extraordinary requirement)	Thailand, Indonesia, India, Nepal, Cambodia, Malaysia (democratic states) China, Vietnam, Lao (socialist states) Brunei (absolute monarchy)

---

[36] J Ferejohn, 'The Politics of Imperfection: the Amendment of Constitutions' (1997) 22 *Law and Social Inquiry* 501.

[37] BE Rasch and RD Congleton, 'Amendment Procedures and Constitutional Stability,' in RD Congleton and B Swedenberg (eds), *Democratic Constitutional Change and Public Policy: Analysis and Evidence* (Cambridge, Mass: MIT University Press, 2006) 319.

points out that formal amendment rules are not the exclusive determinants of the success rate of constitutional amendment. Instead, multiple factors include the party system and popular attitudes toward the constitution, which contribute to influencing the rate of successfully adopting amendments. However, formal constitutional amendment rules remain the most direct relevant and determinative factor.[38]

Notes and Questions

1. Which Asian constitution provides for the most stringent constitutional amendment procedure? How do we evaluate 'stringency'?

2. In a study of amendment procedures in four Eastern European states – Bulgaria, Romania, Poland and Hungary – Stephen Holmes and Cass Sunstein found that the Hungarian Parliament and the Polish Sejm enjoyed a great deal of freedom in amending the constitution. These two assemblies are subject only to procedural constraints such as two-thirds supermajorities and an attendance requirement. On the other hand, the Bulgarian and Romanian assemblies are far more limited in their authority, as they both face subject-matter restrictions. In addition, the Romanian Parliament must rely on a referendum. Holmes and Sunstein concluded that the procedure for constitutional modification within Eastern European constitutions today sets relatively relaxed conditions for amendment, with non-amendable provisions kept to a minimal core of basic rights and institutions. Typically, parliament monopolises this process, without any obligatory recourse to popular referenda. This calibrated arrangement makes it possible for these states to respond swiftly to changing circumstances without undermining the already-weak legitimacy of democratically accountable assemblies. See S Holmes and CR Sunstein, 'The Politics of Constitutional Revision in Eastern Europe' in Sanford Levinson (ed), *Responding to Imperfection: The Theory and Practice of Constitutional Amendment* (Princeton, NJ: Princeton University Press, 1995) 275.

Judiciaries throughout Asia have been called upon to decide on the legality of constitutional amendments, and generally the courts have not been reluctant to strike down amendments undertaken in violation of procedural rules. For example, the Supreme Court of the Philippines ended an initiative to amend the Constitution in 2006 because the proponents of change failed to follow the proper procedures.[39]

Controversies over constitutional amendments tend to spike during a transitional period, when politics is in flux. Courts in transitional states need to be conscious of how such cases are handled since they can advance or thwart prospects for social-political renewal or reform. In *JY Interpretation No 314*, the Constitutional Court of Taiwan pronounced on the constitutional amendment process at a critical moment, just when the wave of constitutional revisions was about to begin, setting the tone that would underscore procedural requirements in Taiwan's democratic transition.

---

[38] R Dixon, 'Constitutional Amendment Rules: A Comparative Perspective' in Ginsburg and Dixon (eds), above n 20, 96.

[39] See D Gatmaytan-Magno, 'Changing Constitutions: Judicial Review and Redemption in the Philippines' (2007) 25 *UCLA Pacific Basin Law Journal* 1.

JY Interpretation No 314
25 Feb 1993 (Constitutional Court, Taiwan)

Facts

Taiwan embraced the end of martial rule and embarked on democratisation starting at the end of 1980s. Instead of resorting to a drastic revolution and starting anew, it opted for a more moderate route by amending the ROC Constitution it inherited. A series of constitutional amendments took place in the 1990s that would complete Taiwan's 'peaceful revolution'. During its initial stages, controversies arose as a result of procedural defects caused by political expediency. In this case, the issue was whether the National Assembly, in any extraordinary session that was not convened for the purpose of amending the Constitution, could nevertheless amend the Constitution.

Held

Given that the Constitution is the fundamental basis and supreme law of the country, any amendment thereof greatly affects the stability of constitutional order and the well-being of all the people. Consequently, the people should be provided with an opportunity to know the purpose of any amendment to the Constitution and have the opportunity to express their opinions prior to such amendment to the Constitution. Extraordinary sessions of the National Assembly are convened pursuant to different requirements and procedures; hence, the National Assembly, during any extraordinary session not convened for the purpose of amending the Constitution, may nevertheless not exercise the power to amend the Constitution. *Interpretation No 29* of this Yuan should thus be further supplemented.

Except for improper procedural defects which should in the eyes of the court render questionable the effect of constitutional amendment, controversies could arise on the special rules specified in the constitution for amending crucial constitutional provisions. The Constitution of Sri Lanka prescribes that a bill for the amendment or for the repeal and replacement [of the Constitution] that is inconsistent with certain fundamental Articles, should, besides going through the designated normal procedure for amendment, also be approved by the People at a Referendum before it could become law. Understandably, the problem of whether a proposed bill involves the matters the Constitution confers special protection upon, and whether it is consistent with the fundamental provisions at times often invite controversy. The constitutionalism of Sri Lanka featurs a dynamic history of constitutional change marked by one amendment after the other. Frequent regime change and turbulent party politics usually resulted in seeking legality and legitimacy through amending the constitution, and hence constitutional amendment became the major means of political competition and resolution for political conflict. The reign of the winner or the result of political compromise takes form through a constitutional amendment through which political conflicts were wrapped up until replaced by the next constitutional amendment, and the court is usually required to play the role of the arbitrator once a controversy arises.

While mediating these cases, the court is expected to safeguard the integrity of the Constitution while at the same time maintain the impartiality of the judicial system. In the following '*Eighteenth Amendment Case*', on a severe constitutional crisis concerning the survival of democracy, the Court took a strict approach in reviewing the constitutionality of the amendment, and rendered the amendment at issue unconstitutional.

In Re The Eighteenth Amendment to The Constitution and The Provincial Councils Bill
(2002) 3 Sri Lanka Law Reports 71, 3 Oct 2002 (Supreme Court, Sri Lanka)

Facts

In 1977, the United National Party (UNP) came to power with a huge five-sixths majority and amended the 1972 Constitution to establish an executive presidency. Shortly afterwards, in 1978, the UNP promulgated a new constitution that provided for a unicameral parliament and an executive president, both of whose term of office was six years. Over the decades, the confrontational politics of Sri Lanka led to a series of constitutional amendments which served to make adjustments to the power of the President, the Cabinet and the judiciary. The Eighteenth Amendment, which was presented to Parliament on 18 September 2002, was designed to expand the Government's power by removing the limit on the re-election of the President, and by creating a parliamentary council to decide on the appointment of independent posts like Commissioners of Human Rights and Supreme Court judges. The Court was asked to decide if the procedures for amendment under Articles 82 and 83 of the Constitution had been satisfied.

Held

A Bill titled the 'Eighteenth Amendment to the Constitution' was placed on the Order Paper of Parliament for 18th September 2002. Seven petitions were presented invoking the jurisdiction of the Supreme Court in terms of Article 121(1) for a determination in terms of Article 123 of the Constitution, in respect of the Bill. The Bill provides, inter alia, for the following:

(1) A provision conferring power on the Council to make rules – Clause 2.
(2) A provision enabling the payment of emoluments to the members of the Council – Clause 3.
(3) A provision conferring total immunity from judicial review of the decisions of the Council – Clause 4.
(4) A provision providing immunity from suit against the Council, its members and officers – Clause 5.
(5) A provision for punishment for interference with the Council – Clause 5 . . .

The petitioners contended that Clauses 2, 4 and 5 of the Bill are inconsistent with Article 3 read with Article 4 of the Constitution and that if they require to become law, they must be passed by a two-thirds (2/3) majority in Parliament and thereafter be approved by the People at a Referendum, in terms of Article 83 of the Constitution . . . Article 83 of the Constitution refers to the approval of certain Bills at a Referendum. This Article reads as follows:

Notwithstanding anything to the contrary in the provisions of Article 82 – (a) a Bill for the amendment or for the repeal and replacement of or which is inconsistent with any of the provisions of Articles 1, 2, 3, 6, 7, 8, 9, 10 and 11, or of this Article, and (b) a Bill for the amendment or for the repeal and replacement of or which is inconsistent with the provisions of paragraph (2) of Article 30 or of paragraph (2) of Article 62 which would extend the term of office of the President or the duration of Parliament, as the case may be, to over 6 years, shall become law if the number of votes cast in favour thereof amount to not less than two-thirds of the whole number of Members (including those not present), is approved by the People at a Referendum and a certificate is endorsed thereon by the President in accordance with Article 80.

... By the envisaged 18th amendment, the Constitutional Council is clothed with unlimited and unfettered immunity on their decisions, recommendations and approvals. If such immunity is given to the Constitutional Council, it would in effect be elevated to a body that is not subject to law, which is inconsistent with the Rule of Law. The Rule of Law, means briefly the exclusion of the existence of arbitrariness and maintaining equality before the Law (AV Dicey, Law of the Constitution, p 120). Hitherto, without exception, executive and administrative actions have been subjected to the jurisdiction enshrined in Article 126 of the Constitution. The total immunity expected in terms of the proposed amendment to the Constitution would effectively shut out the justiciability of actions of the Constitutional Council in the exercise of the fundamental rights jurisdiction by the Supreme Court ... The proposed Article 41J referred to above, which grants an immunity to the Constitutional Council, the Chairman, a Member, the Secretary or an officer, from judicial proceedings in respect of anything done or omitted to be done, attracts both objections dealt with, in the preceding paragraphs of this determination. They are: (1) that it would alienate the judicial power from the people; (2) that it creates a special class of people in violation of Article 12 (1) of the Constitution, who would not be subjected to judicial review. For the reasons stated above we determine that there is merit on both grounds of objections and the proposed Article 41J is therefore inconsistent with Article 3 read with Article 4 of the Constitution. For the reasons stated above, the Bill, in its present form, requires approval by People at a Referendum in addition to a two-thirds majority vote (including those not present) in terms of Article 83 of the Constitution ...

Notes and Questions

1. Despite their different contexts, both the courts of Taiwan and Sri Lanka have highlighted procedural flaws in the constitutional amending process that may have inhibited frequent incremental constitutional revisions. While the Taiwanese Court insisted on a citizen's rights to know of a constitutional revision in advance and to participate in the amendment process, the Sri Lankan court required a referendum in addition to the two-thirds majority vote of the Congress. The referendum dispute reflects the problem of ambiguity regarding the extraordinary requirements of referendum in the Constitution of Sri Lanka.

2. Before the 2005 constitutional revision in Taiwan, the National Assembly was vested with exclusive power to amend the Constitution. Through frequent constitutional revisions, the National Assembly gradually expanded its power. *JY Interpretation No 314* was a judicial check against the self-aggrandising efforts of the National Assembly. By insisting on compliance with constitutional procedural requirements, the Constitutional Court offered a judicial articulation of the due process requirement under the Constitution.

3. The history of constitutional amendments in Sri Lanka demonstrates how the constitution served as a political weapon. Both the 1946 and 1978 Sri Lankan Constitutions were subjected to numerous amendments. The amendments to the 1978 Constitution, necessitated by the highly contentious and volatile political climate that emerged in Sri Lanka after its adoption, are listed thus:

    (a) the First Amendment of 20 November 1978 dealt with the jurisdiction of the Court of Appeal;

(b) the Second Amendment of 26 February 1979 dealt with resignations and the expulsion of Members of the First Parliament;

(c) the Third Amendment of 27 August 1982 enabled the President to seek re-election after four years;

(d) the Fourth Amendment, passed on 23 December 1982, extended the term of first Parliament;

(e) the Fifth Amendment, passed on 25 February 1983, provided for by-elections when a vacancy is not filled;

(f) the Sixth Amendment of 8th August, 1983, prohibited any person or policial party to advocate against territorial integrity of Sri Lanka;

(g) the Seventh Amendment, passed on 4 October 1983, dealt with Commissioners of the High Court and the creation of Kilinochchi District;

(h) the Eighth Amendment, passed on 6 March 1984, concerned the appointment of President's Counsel;

(i) the Ninth Amendment, passed on 24 August 1984, concerned the qualification of public officers to contest elections;

(j) the Tenth Amendment, passed on 6 August 1986, repealed section requiring two-thirds majority for Proclamation under Public Security Ordinance;

(k) the Eleventh Constitutional Amendment, passed 5 June 1987, provided a fiscal for the whole Island and the appointment and transfer of the Court of Appeal;

(l) the Twelfth Amendment was not enacted;

(m) the Thirteenth Amendment, passed on 14 November 1987, established Provincial Councils;

(n) the Fourteenth Amendment, passed on 24 May 1988, extended the immunity of the President and increased the number of Members of Parliament;

(o) the Fifteenth Amendment, passed on 17 December 1988, repealed Article 96A to eliminate zones and to reduce the cut-off point to 1/20th;

(p) the Sixteenth Amendment, passed on 17 December 1988, made provision for Sinhala and Tamil to be Languages of Administration and Legislation;

(q) the Seventeenth Amendment, passed on 3 October 2001, made provision for the Constitutional Council and Independent Commissions.

See the official website of the Government of Sri Lanka at <http://www.priu.gov.lk/Cons/1978Constitution/Introduction.htm>. After the *Eighteenth Amendment Case* in 2002, the Supreme Court of Sri Lanka continued to receive requests to adjudicate controversial constitutional amendments dealing with politically sensitive matters.

B. Political Actions and Referenda

Constitutional change may take place through political actions, whether through the adoption of fundamental governmental policies, the holding of referenda on important political issues, or as the result of coups or revolutions. Constitutional change that takes place after a drastic political event may allow for the continuity of the constitutional order in the next stage of normal politics. However, constitutions can also become instruments in the service of rulers. The 1973 Filipino case of *Josue Javellana v The Executive Secretary* ('*The Ratification Case*') deals with a constitutional change resulting from one of the most critical constitutional moments in Philippine history, and how it dramatically shaped Philippine politics for more than a decade.

In coming face-to-face with President Marcos's control of the on-going constitutional convention, the Supreme Court was caught between the un-born democratic constitution and the impending martial rule. What made this case complex was that after Marcos declared martial law in September 1972, he boldly and confidently sought popular support by subjecting the proposed constitutional amendment to a referendum for ratification or rejection. The Court faced the dilemma of whether to recognise the President's proclamation that confirmed the result of the people's assent, thereby upholding the validity of the new 1973 Constitution that replaced the 1935 Constitution. By upholding the new Constitution, the Court would simultaneously recognise the legitimacy of the Marcos regime. If the Court decided otherwise, it would deny the Philippine people a democratic constitution that received clear support from the majority. In a highly divided decision, the Court recognised the 1973 Constitution and, correspondingly, the legality of the Marcos regime, allowing Marcos to wield absolute power until he was forced out by the 1986 People Power Revolution.

Josue Javellana v The Executive Secretary & Ors
GR No L-36142 [1973] PHSC 43, 31 Mar 1973 (Supreme Court, Philippines)

Facts

On the pretext of preventing chaos and anarchy from erupting, following a staged attempted assassination of former Defence Minister Juan Ponce Enrile and an ensuing communist insurgency, President Ferdinand Marcos declared martial law on 22 September 1972. At the time, the Constitutional Convention was working to draft a new constitution. On 29 November 1972, the Convention approved the new constitution. The next day, Marcos issued Presidential Decree 73, 'submitting to the Filipino people for ratification or rejection the Constitution of the Republic of the Philippines proposed by the 1971 Constitutional Convention, and appropriating funds therefore'. On 15 January 1973, Marcos signed Proclamation 1102, which stated that the 1973 Constitution was 'ratified by an overwhelming majority of all the votes cast by the members of all the Barangays (Citizens Assemblies) throughout the Philippines'. A number of cases had earlier been brought, challenging the constitutionality of the Constitutional Convention, but these were dismissed as moot and academic on account of Proclamation 1102. However, the Supreme Court did not foreclose the possibility of a constitutional challenge to the Proclamation. A series of cases were instituted – known collectively as the 'Ratification cases' – questioning the validity of Proclamation 1102. By a majority of 6:4, the Supreme Court dismissed all the cases. By this decision, the 1973 Constitution came into operation.

Barredo J (concurring)

In my opinion in those cases, the most important point I took into account was that in the face of the Presidential certification through Proclamation 1102 itself that the New Constitution has been approved by a majority of the people and having in mind facts of general knowledge which I have judicial notice of, I am in no position to deny that the result of the referendum was as the President had stated. I can believe that the figures referred to in the proclamation may not accurate, but I cannot say in conscience that all of them are manufactured or prefabricated, simply because I saw with own eyes that people did actually gather and listen [to] discussions, if brief and inadequate for those who are abreast of current events and general occurrences, and that they did vote.

It is contended, however, that the understanding was that the referendum among the Citizens Assemblies was to be in the nature merely of a loose consultation and not an outright submission for purposes of ratification. I can see that at the outset, when the first set of questions was released, such may have been the idea. It must not be lost sight of, however, that if the newspaper reports are to be believed, and I say this only because petitioners would consider the newspapers as the official gazettes of the administration, the last set of six questions were included precisely because the reaction to the idea of mere consultation was that the people wanted greater direct participation, thru the Citizens Assemblies, in decision-making regarding matters of vital national interest . . . Accordingly, I take it that if the majority had expressed disapproval of the new Constitution, the logical consequence would have been the complete abandonment of the idea of holding any plebiscite at all. On the other hand, it is very plain to see that since the majority has already approved the new Constitution, a plebiscite would be superfluous. Clear as these rationalizations may be, it must have been thought that if the holding of a plebiscite was to be abandoned, there should be a direct and expressed desire of the people to such effect in order to forestall as much as possible any serious controversy regarding the non-holding of the plebiscite required by the letter of Section 16 of Article XVII, the effectivity clause, of the new Constitution.

. . . I must confess that the fact that the referendum was held during martial law detracts somehow from the value that the referendum would otherwise have had. As I intimated, however, in my former opinion, it is not fair to condemn and disregard the result of the referendum barely because of martial law per se. For one thing, many of the objectionable features of martial law have not actually materialized, if only because the implementation of martial law since its inception has been generally characterized by restraint and consideration, thanks to the expressed wishes of the President that the same be made 'Philippine style', which means without the rigor that has attended it in other lands and other times. Moreover, although the restrictions on the freedom of speech, the press and movement during martial law do have their corresponding adverse effects on the area of information which should be open to a voter, in its real sense what 'chills' his freedom of choice and mars his exercise of discretion is suspension of the privilege of the writ of habeas corpus. The reason is simply that a man may freely and correctly vote even if the needed information he possesses as to the candidates or issues being voted upon is more or less incomplete, but when he is subject to arrest and detention without investigation and without being informed of the cause thereof, that is something else which may actually cause him to cast a captive vote. Thus it is the suspension of the writ of habeas corpus accompanying martial law that can cause possible restraint on the freedom choice in an election held during martial law. It is a fact, however, borne by history and actual experience, that in the Philippines, the suspension of the privilege of the writ habeas corpus has never produced any chilling effect upon the voters, since it is known by all that only those who run afoul the law, saving inconsequential instances, have any cause for apprehension in regard to the conduct by them of the normal activities of life. And so it is recorded that in the elections 1951 and 1971, held while the privilege of writ of habeas corpus was under suspension, the Filipino voters gave the then opposition parties overwhelming if not sweeping victories, in defiance of the respective administrations that ordered the suspensions.

At this juncture, I think it is fit to make it clear that I am not trying to show that the result of the referendum may [be] considered as sufficient basis for declaring that the New Constitution has been ratified in accordance with the amending clause of the 1935

Constitution. I reiterate that in point of law, I find neither strict nor substantial compliance. The foregoing discussion is only to counter, if I may, certain [impressions] regarding the general conditions obtaining during and in relation to the referendum which could have in one way or another affected the exercise of the freedom of choice and the use of discretion by the members of the Citizens Assemblies, to the end that as far as the same conditions may be relevant in my subsequent discussions of the acceptance by the people of the New Constitution they may also be considered. . . .

Concepcion CJ (dissenting)

Referring now more specifically to the issue on whether the new Constitution proposed by the 1971 Constitutional Convention has been ratified in accordance with the provisions of Article XV of the 1935 Constitution is a political question or not, I do not hesitate to state that the answer must be in the negative. Indeed, such is the position taken by this Court, 17 in an endless line of decisions, too long to leave any room for possible doubt that said issue is inherently and essentially justiciable . . . The reason why the issue under consideration and other issues of similar character are justiciable, not political, is plain and simple . . . This principle of separation of powers under the presidential system goes hand in hand with the system of checks and balances, under which each department is vested by the Fundamental Law with some powers to forestall, restrain or arrest a possible or actual misuse or abuse of powers by the other departments. Upon the other hand, under the judicial power vested by the Constitution, the 'Supreme Court and . . . such inferior courts as may be established by law,' may settle or decide with finality, not only justiciable controversies between private individuals or entities, but, also, disputes or conflicts between a private individual or entity, on the one hand, and an officer or branch of the government, on the other, or between two (2) officers or branches of service, when the latter officer or branch is charged with acting without jurisdiction or in excess thereof or in violation of law.

   . . . Indeed, I cannot, in good conscience, declare that the proposed Constitution has been approved or adopted by the people in the citizens' assemblies all over the Philippines, when it is, to my mind, a matter of judicial knowledge that there have been no such citizens' assemblies in many parts of Manila and suburbs, not to say, also, in other parts of the Philippines. . . . It is urged that the present Government of the Philippines is now and has been run, since January 17, 1971, under the Constitution drafted by the 1971 Constitutional Convention; that the political department of the Government has recognized said revised Constitution; that our foreign relations are being conducted under such new or revised Constitution; that the Legislative Department has recognized the same; and that the people, in general, have, by their acts or omissions, indicated their conformity thereto. . . . This, notwithstanding, the political organ of a government that purports to be republican is essentially the Congress or Legislative Department. Whatever may be the functions allocated to the Executive Department – specially under a written, rigid Constitution with a republican system of Government like ours – the role of that Department is inherently, basically and fundamentally executive in nature – to 'take care that the laws be faithfully executed,' in the language of our 1935 Constitution.

   Consequently, I am not prepared to concede that the acts the officers and offices of the Executive Department, in line with Proclamation No 1102, connote a recognition thereof an acquiescence thereto. Whether they recognized the proposed Constitution or acquiesce thereto or *not* is something that cannot legally, much less necessarily or even normally, be deduced from their acts in accordance therewith, because they are *bound* to obey and act in conformity with the orders of the President, under whose 'control' they are, *pursuant to the*

1935 Constitution. They have absolutely *no other choice*, especially in view of Proclamation No 1081 placing the Philippines under Martial Law.

... Perhaps others would feel that my position in these cases overlooks what they might consider to be the demands of 'judicial statesmanship,' whatever may be the meaning of such phrase. I am aware of this possibility, if not probability; but 'judicial statesmanship,' though *consistent* with Rule of Law, *cannot prevail* over the latter. Among consistent ends or consistent values, there always is a hierarchy, a rule of priority. We must realize that the New Society has many achievements which would have been very difficult, if not impossible, to accomplish under the old dispensation. But, *in and for the judiciary, statesmanship* should not prevail over the Rule of Law. Indeed, *the primacy of the law or of the Rule of Law and faithful adherence thereto are basic, fundamental and essential parts of statesmanship itself.*

Notes and Questions

1. It has been argued that the Court acted politically in this case. At the time of this ruling, the Supreme Court consisted of Chief Justice Roberto Concepcion and Associate Justices Querube Makalintal, Calixto Zaldivar, Fred Ruiz Castro, Enrique Fernando, Claudio Teehankee, Antonio Barredo, Felix Makasiar, Felix Antonio and Salvador Esguerra. Of these judges, Concepcion, Makalintal and Zaldivar were not appointed by Marcos. Chief Justice Roberto Concepcion, as in the *Plebiscite Cases*, wrote the decision. In this decision, he summarised the facts, then authored his own dissenting opinion (stating that the 1973 Constitution had not been properly ratified according to law), before proceeding to summarise the votes of the members of the Court. The Court was severely divided on the issues raised in the petition, but when the crucial question of whether the petitioners were entitled to relief was raised, six members of the court (Justices Makalintal, Castro, Barredo, Makasiar, Antonio and Esguerra) voted to dismiss the petition. Six members of the court (the Chief Justice, and Justices Makalintal, Zaldivar, Castro, Fernando and Teehankee) held that the 1973 Constitution had not been validly ratified. It is unusual that of those who said that the Constitution was not validly ratified, Querube Makalintal and Fred Ruiz Castro voted to dismiss the petitions. Makalintal and Castro, in a joint opinion, justified their non-granting of relief on the basis that it was a political question, citing *Luther v Borden*[40] as authority.

2. *The Ratification Case* is still studied by students of Philippine constitutional law for its holding on the proper ratification and approval procedure for a new Constitution. It also serves as a reminder of the Marcos regime and its negative effects on the Filipino people. It also shows that the human failings of the Supreme Court bench. In the words of Justice Isagani Cruz, the Court

    is not an ivory tower occupied by demigods but not an infallible institution composed of persons slightly higher than their fellowmen, perhaps, but also showing their foibles and failings.[41]

---

[40] *Luther v Borden* 48 US 1, 12 L Ed 581 (1849).
[41] *Josue Javellana v The Executive Secretary & Ors* GR No L-36142 [1973] PHSC 43, 31 Mar 1973.

Chief Justice Concepcion took leave 18 days after the decision became public (50 days ahead of his scheduled retirement), supposedly because he was disappointed over the outcome of the decision. He later became a member of the Constitutional Commission that drafted the 1987 Philippine Constitution. Drawing from his experiences during the martial law years, he introduced several new innovations designed to protect the independence of the Supreme Court, such as the Judicial and Bar Council and the express conferment on the Court of the power to review any acts of government. It was aptly observed that while the *Ratification Case* was resolved in a matter of months, the other cases involving Marcos's imprisoned critics were not decided until a year or two later. In fact, some critics withdrew their petitions, mostly for the writ of *habeas corpus*, due to the lack of confidence that the Supreme Court would grant them relief. See P Mijares, *The Conjugal Dictatorship of Ferdinand Marcos and Imelda Marcos* (San Francisco, Cal: Union Square Publishing, 1986) at 499.

C. Judicial Decisions, Soft Constitutional Law and Custom

Judicial decisions can also bring about constitutional change. Resort to this avenue may be had where it is unlikely that a proposed amendment will satisfy the amendment procedure requirements due to the lack of political support. Courts in an age of modern constitutionalism not only resolve disputes, but also interpret and thus make law. In some cases, courts may attempt to make up for a democracy deficit by creating controversial new 'rights', opening them to criticism that judges are imposing their subjective preferences on the law and thus politicising the judiciary.

Many countries have written constitutions creating strong constitutional courts with the power of judicial review.[42] More than three-quarters of the world's states have enshrined some form of judicial review in their constitutions,[43] leading some to view courts as agents of constitutional change and thus beneficial to democracy. For example, in post-communist regimes, constitutional courts are seen to enforce post-communist constitutions, uphold democratic values, protect individual rights and serve as a safeguard against the return to the totalitarian past.[44]

In Asia, courts in some jurisdictions have been effective in guiding democratisation.[45] However, the court's role and its function depends on whether it can not only preserve constitutional values in the face of the pressures of normal politics, but also identify and declare from past constitutional moments, principles of greater generality than those consciously embraced before. In Asia, where the judicial branch does not traditionally enjoy popular confidence nor possess a strong reputation for impartiality, courts must be sensitive to the social context and be cautious of public reaction in

---

[42] B Ackerman, 'The Rise of World Constitutionalism' (1997) 83 *Virginia Law Review* 771.

[43] DL Horowitz, 'Constitutional Courts: A Primer for Decision Makers' (2006) 17 *Journal of Democracy* 125.

[44] A Trochev, 'Less Democracy, More Courts: A Puzzle of Judicial Review in Russia' (2004) 38 *Law and Society Review* 513.

[45] Kun Yang, 'Judicial Review and Social Change in the Korean Democratizing Process' (1993) 41 *The American Journal of Comparative Law* 1.

delivering a judicial decision so that they can avoid being tangled in disputes that could severely damage institutional reputation. In addition, courts in developing countries may find their jurisdictions and powers pared down through constitutional amendments initiated by a strong and disgruntled executive. For example, in Malaysia, after the courts issued a number of decisions against the Mahathir Government in the late 1980s, the country's higher judiciary effectively was decimated when the Lord President (the country's highest ranking judge) and two of his brethren were sacked for 'misconduct'. Article 121 of the Federal Constitution, which vested judicial power in the courts, was amended to limit severely the courts' powers of judicial review.[46]

Besides the written constitution, there are unwritten laws forming part of the constitutional order, in the form of 'soft constitutional law'[47] and constitutional custom. These shape the scope of obligations and expectations of various constitutional actors. The *Relocation of the Capital City Case* of South Korea, for example, reveals how the judicial recognition and creation of norms such as constitutional custom play a determinative role when the court adjudicates controversial constitutional disputes.

At the centre of the debate in this case was the Korean President Roh Moo-Hyun's plan to relocate the state's national capital (from Seoul to Sejong City in Chungcheong). While the constitution remains silent on the location of the national capital, petitioners challenged the President's policy on the ground that the location of the capital is so crucial an issue that its change should be subject to referendum. What lies beneath this seemingly trivial political disagreement is the context of Korea's national identity and domestic regional politics. This case is but one flashpoint in South Korea's deeply divisive politics and its brand of hyper-dynamic politics. The Court strategically referred to constitutional custom as a means by which the decision could be deferred to popular opinion.

Relocation of the Capital City Case
2004Hun-Ma554, 21 Oct 2004 (Constitutional Court, Korea)

Facts

During the presidential election campaign, Roh Moo-Hyun, a member of the New Millennium Democratic Party, promised to relocate South Korea's administrative capital, and that 'the Blue House and the governmental ministries will be moved to Sejong City in the Chungcheong area as a curb on the concentration and overpopulation at the capital and a solution for the lagging local economy'. Roh was elected President 19 December 2002. Subsequently, the bill for the Special Act on the Establishment of the New Administrative Capital was proposed and enacted by the National Assembly. The Special Act on the Establishment of the New Administrative Capital was then promulgated on 16 January 2004. The complainants, who were Korean citizens from across the nation, filed the constitutional complaint on the grounds that the above Act was unconstitutional in its

---

[46] On the Malaysian judicial crisis, see: A Harding, 'The 1988 Constitutional Crisis in Malaysia' (1990) 39 *ICLQ* 57; FA Trindade, 'The Removal of the Malaysian Judges' (1990) 106 *LQR* 51; RH Hickling, 'The Malaysian Judiciary in Crisis' [1990] *Public Law* 20; and AJ Harding, 'The Malaysian Judiciary Crisis' (1989) 8 *Commonwealth Judiciary Journal* 3.

[47] These are statements contained in non-binding documents like white papers and declarations which constitute executive interpretations of constitutional norms. See Li-ann Thio, 'Soft Constitutional Law in Non-liberal Asian Constitutional Democracies' (2010) 8(4) *I•CON* 766.

entirety as it was an attempt to relocate the nation's capital without revising the Constitution, and that the Act violated the right to vote at a referendum and taxpayers' rights as well. The Constitutional Court held (8:1) that the Act was unconstitutional, with a separate dissenting opinion of one Justice.

Majority Opinion of Seven Justices

The Act at issue in this case determines the transfer of the capital of the nation, which falls within the meaning of the capital under the Constitution as the location of national institutions that perform pivotal functions of politics and administration of the nation. As such, the transfer of a new administrative capital pursuant to the Act at issue in this case means the transfer of the capital of the Republic of Korea. The establishment or relocation of the capital is the geographical placement of the basis of the nation's organization and structure through determination of the location of the highest constitutional institutions such as the National Assembly and the President, and is thus a fundamental decision by the citizens concerning the nation, and, at the same time, a core constitutional matter that forms the basis for the establishment of a nation. There is no express provision in our Constitution that states 'Seoul is the capital.' However, that Seoul is the capital of our nation is a continuing practice concerning the life in the national realm of our nation for a period of over six-hundred years since the Chosun Dynasty period. Such practice should be deemed to be a fundamental matter in the nation that has achieved national consensus from its uninterrupted continuance over a long period of time. Therefore, that Seoul is the capital is a constitutional custom that has traditionally existed since even prior to the establishment of our written Constitution, and a norm that is clear in itself and a premise upon which the Constitution is based although not stated in an express provision in our Constitution. As such, it is part of the unwritten constitution established in the form of a constitutional custom. Constitutional custom is also part of the constitution and is endowed with the same effect as that of the written constitution. Thus, such legal norm may at the least be revised only by way of constitutional revision pursuant to Article 130 of the Constitution. That Seoul is the capital of our nation is unwritten constitutional custom, and, therefore, retains its effect as constitutional law unless invalidated by establishment of a new constitutional provision ordaining a new capital through the constitutional revision procedure. On the other hand, other than through formal constitutional revision, a constitutional custom may lose its legal effect by loss of the national consensus that supports it. However, in this case, such circumstance is not found. Pursuant to Article 130 of the Constitution, national referendum is mandatory for the constitutional revision. Therefore, the citizenry has the right to express its opinion with respect to the constitutional revision through a binary pro-and-con vote. Here, the Act at issue in this case realizes the transfer of the capital, which is a matter to be undertaken by the constitutional revision, merely in the form of a simple statute without following the constitutional revision procedure. Thus, the Act is in violation of the Constitution as it excludes the exercise of the right to vote on referendum, thereby violating such right, which is a fundamental right to participate in politics retained by the people at the constitutional revision pursuant to Article 130 of the Constitution.

Dissenting Opinion of One Justice

In a legal system under a written constitution, customary constitutional law may not be established or maintained apart from the written constitution, and, instead, is always given no more than supplementary effect as it may be established and maintained only when harmonized with various principles of the written constitution. Also, the constitutional revision is a concept that pertains to the constitution in the formal sense, ie, the written constitution. Therefore, the change of the customary constitutional law does not belong to constitutional revision, and may occur through the enactment or the revision of the statute that is the procedure for representative democracy established by the Constitution. In the case of a change in constitutional custom such as the transfer of the capital, as there is no particular constitutional provision that prohibits this, it may be done by the enactment of the statute by the National Assembly. Therefore, there is no possibility that the Act at issue in this case violates the right to vote on referendum under Article 130, Section 2, of the Constitution. On the other hand, Article 72 of the Constitution endows the President with the discretion of whether or not to submit an 'important policy concerning the national security' to the referendum, which may not be interpreted to the effect that such discretion varies according to the significance of the matter. Further, such discretion is endowed directly by the Constitution. Thus, the legal principle of deviation and abuse of discretion of the administrative law may not apply. Therefore, there is no possibility that the right to vote on referendum of Article 72 of the Constitution is violated in this case. To conclude, the assertion of the complainants of the violation of the right to vote on referendum is unjustified, as the possibility of violation of the asserted right itself is lacking.

Notes and Questions

1. A year after the court decision, President Roh tried again and avoided the constitutional issue by characterising his plan as one of building an alternative administrative centre in the south. A law was passed to relocate six ministries, including the ministries of Justice, Defence, Gender Equality, National Unification, Government and Home Affairs, and Foreign Affairs and Trade, to the south. Another constitutional challenge was made but dismissed by a seven-vote majority opinion.[48] Four justices indicated that because the law dealt with an administrative centre rather than the national capital, the passage of the law itself was sufficient and no constitutional amendment was necessary. Three justices even hinted in their opinion that they no longer held the view that the location of the national capital in Seoul formed part of the unwritten constitution.

2. After nearly two years of constitutional disputes, President Roh finally succeeded in implementing his campaign promise to move the capital or the administrative centre to the relatively poorer south in order to realise a more balanced regional distribution of power in the peninsula. The Sejong City plan was a US$20 billion project that proved a major vote-getter. While Seoul remains the capital of South Korea, the Prime Minister's office and 12 ministries moved to Sejong City as from September 2012. It is expected that by the end of 2014, all 36 ministries and government departments and some 10,000 civil servants will relocate to Sejong City. See Juinn-rong Yeh, 'Presidential Politics and the Judicial Facilitation of Dialogue between Political Actors in New Asian Democracies: Comparing the South Korean and Taiwanese Experiences' (2010) 8(4) *I•CON* 911.

---

[48] *The Administrative Centre Case*, 17(B) KCCR 481, 2005Hun-Ma579 (consolidated), 24 Nov 2005.

3. The Korean Constitutional Court found that the siting of the national capital at Seoul was a matter of national consensus, having been a matter of practice for over 600 years, pre-dating the written constitution. Was the Court simply making a factual statement, or was it insisting that any change to the location of the national capital should follow the process of constitutional revision set out in Article 130 of the Constitution?

Contrary to the activism of the Constitutional Court of Korea in referring to constitutional custom and deferring to the President and the people, the High Court of Hong Kong took a rather more constrained approach in the *Cheng v Li* case when reviewing the internal working of the legislature. The Court took a calibrated approach in combining reasoning that was respectful of history but adapted to contemporary needs. To explain why and how the legislature should be allowed more discretion in procedural matters, the Court not only looked into the relevant rules and customs of the colonial era to find support, but also considered the future development of Hong Kong. This case is significant in that it demonstrates how the High Court of Hong Kong sought to sustain the strength of the Hong Kong legislature under the Basic Law, by resorting to constitutional traditions, practices and conventions developed under British rule. This was done, notwithstanding the fact that the Chinese Government intended to subject Hong Kong to centralised control and monitoring under the Basic Law. To some extent, Hong Kong's past constitutional traditions inherited from its colonial past continued to shape its post-colonial political system.[49]

Cheng v Li
[2009] HKEC 1587 (High Court, Hong Kong)

Facts

The Legislative Council resolved on 10 December 2008 to appoint a Select Committee to inquire into the post-service work of one Leung Chin-man (Mr Leung) and related matters. The Committee held two rounds of hearings to obtain evidence from witnesses, with each round focusing on one major area of investigation. It was decided that witnesses would be summoned to attend the hearings according to the order of study, and they would be ordered to produce relevant documents, and provide, on a voluntary basis, written statements in advance to facilitate the taking of evidence at the hearings. On 10 July 2009, the applicants applied for leave to apply for judicial review against the Select Committee's order requiring them to appear before it at the hearing scheduled for 15 July 2009 to give evidence and to produce documents.

    On 14 July 2009, the Court of First Instance granted leave on two grounds. The first was based on the proper interpretation of the Select Committee's power to make relevant orders upon a proper interpretation of the Article 73(10) of the Basic Law of the HKSAR (which stated that one of the powers and functions of the Legislative Council was to summon, as required when exercising the other powers and functions set out in the article, persons concerned to testify or to give evidence) and the constitutionality of section 9(2) of the Legislative Council (Powers and Privileges) Ordinance. The second ground was on the

---

[49] S Shiu Hing-Lo, 'The Emergence of Constitutional Conventions in the Hong Kong Special Administrative Region' (2005) 35 *Hong Kong Law Journal* 103.

question of whether the Select Committee had acted outside its remit under the resolution that established the Select Committee by going into the matters which it said it would go into at the scheduled hearing.

In deciding the constitutionality of the provisions of the Legislative Council Ordinance, the Court held that the courts of the HKSAR did not, as a rule, interfere with the internal working of the legislature. However, in questions of whether the Legislative Council had acted in contravention of the Basic Law of the HKSAR, the courts had jurisdiction to intervene. Even so, the jurisdiction must be exercised with great restraint, having regard to the different constitutional roles assigned under the Basic Law to different arms of the government.

Andrew Cheung J

The Basic Law must not be read with a literal, technical, narrow or rigid approach. It must be given a purposive interpretation, which fully takes into account the context and purpose of the relevant provisions. The context and purpose of the relevant provisions, and indeed that of the Basic Law, should be considered in the light of the internal, as well as the external, aids to interpretation already described . . . [I]t must be remembered that the Basic Law does not create a new legislature out of nowhere. Although it would be simplistic to suggest that the Legislative Council of the Hong Kong Special Administrative Region is simply a continuation of the colonial legislature prior to 1997, the relevant provisions in the Basic Law establishing the new legislature do not intend a complete break from the past, nor is that the contention of any party. Like what was done in colonial days, budgets, taxation and public expenditure have continued to be discussed by the Legislative Council at its committee level as before, although, as I have said, insofar as they require legislation, that must be done in a plenary meeting of the Legislative Council, just as in the colonial days. . . . The committee system had been around for a long time and was still under development in 1990 when the Basic Law was promulgated. The Basic Law expressly leaves it to the new Legislative Council to make its own Rules of Procedure. Both as a matter of history and development as well as a matter of the nature of the substantive powers and functions to be performed, that at least some of the powers and functions described in art 73(1) to (9) may be exercised at committee level must have been something fully envisaged by the drafters of the Basic Law . . . Moving to the context of these provisions in the Basic Law, it must be remembered that when the Basic Law was drafted in the second half of the 1980s and eventually promulgated in 1990, the Ordinance had already become law. It expressly and specifically gave both the Legislative Council and its committees the power to summon witnesses under prescribed circumstances. Although it was never exercised until 1994 (by a panel), the power to do so was clearly in the statute book. Furthermore, as mentioned, the enactment of the Ordinance in 1985 was not a matter without controversy, and the power to summon witnesses by the Legislative Council and its committees was not a mere power existing in theory which nobody expected the Legislative Council or its committees to exercise – if it were thought otherwise, it would not have raised so much concern in the society in the first place. In short, the power to summon witnesses to appear before the Legislative Council or its committees must be regarded as a pre-existing power of the colonial legislature. The power was defined with great care under the Ordinance, and the Ordinance was not amongst those declared by the Standing Committee of the National People's Congress to be in contravention of the Basic Law pursuant to art 160(1). All this forms an important part of the context.

. . . It is true that the power to compel witnesses to appear to testify is a coercive power, affecting individuals' fundamental rights. There is also no dispute that the courts possess such a power for the purposes of adjudication of disputes. However, at least in the Hong Kong context, on many occasions both before and after 1997, such a coercive power has been bestowed on various bodies and tribunals, which do not form part of the judiciary, to enable them to carry out their functions properly. Thus, disciplinary tribunals, such as a solicitors disciplinary tribunal and a barristers disciplinary tribunal, are given powers to compel witnesses to appear in disciplinary proceedings to give evidence. . . . That leaves the question of interpreting the Basic Law and its provisions as a 'living instrument'. One important matter to bear in mind is that the Basic Law is meant to operate and function for 50 years. It is a living instrument and like an Act of Parliament, is to be treated as 'always speaking'. *Bennion on Statutory Interpretation* (5th Ed), 889–912 (on interpreting Acts of Parliament). To that extent, it should be given an 'updating construction' to the extent that its language can bear. In other words, one is not wholly concerned with what the position was in 1990; what that position was is, of course, relevant in finding out the original intent of the drafters. One should also be alive to what the present circumstances are. For the Basic Law is not only meant to apply to the circumstances prevailing at the time of its promulgation in 1990 or in 1997; but it was also meant to apply, by the original drafters, for 50 years up to 2047. . . .

In the proper interpretation of the Basic Law as a living instrument that has been designed to speak for 50 years, all these realities cannot be ignored lightly. The Basic Law must be interpreted flexibly to meet the challenge of the time. Expressing it in terms of the original intent of the drafters as expressed in the language they used, this approach must also have been part of the original intent of the drafters of the Basic Law, who knew fully well that what they drafted has to endure for 50 years. The Basic Law's use of ample and general language bears evidence to that intent. Ultimately, the relevant provisions must be given a purposive interpretation. The advantages of giving a select committee the power to summon witnesses are obvious and hardly require repetition. Criticisms such as the power is a coercive power and an interference with fundamental human rights, the composition of the committee may not be representative enough, the power is susceptible to abuse or misuse, and so on, are more apparent than real. After all, it must be remembered that a select committee is formed by the full body of the Legislative Council in the first place. Whether it is appropriate to give the committee the power to summon witnesses is again a matter to be resolved by the Legislative Council sitting as a full body. . . . Ultimately, the legislature is accountable to the people of Hong Kong, whether directly or indirectly. Moreover, the courts also play a supervisory role in appropriate circumstances . . .

So for all these reasons, I have come to the firm conclusion that the interpretation of the applicants of art 73(10) must be rejected. On its proper interpretation, art 73(10) provides for the exercise by the Legislative Council, whether sitting as a full body, or, functioning through a select committee in accordance with its Rules of Procedure, the power to summon, as required when exercising the powers and functions set out in art 73(1) to (9), persons concerned to testify or to give evidence before the full body, or (as the case may be) the committee, of the Legislative Council. The exercise of that power must also be in accordance with the provisions of the Ordinance, which forms part of the laws in force in Hong Kong. . . . [T]he courts of the Hong Kong Special Administrative Region do not, as a rule, interfere with the internal working of the legislature. Exceptionally, where questions of whether the Legislative Council, in going about its business, has acted in contravention of the provisions in the Basic Law arise, the courts do have jurisdiction to intervene. But the jurisdiction must be exercised with great restraint, having regard to the different constitutional roles assigned under the Basic Law to different arms of the government.

Notes and Questions

1. It is apparent from an examination of Hong Kong's judicial decisions made after 1997 that the courts have a conscious or unconscious tendency to preserve the common law system, as a bulwark of liberty. Under a common law system, the courts interpret the written law and declare the unwritten law. Given that the power of final interpretation is vested in the NPCSC (Article 67, Constitution of the People's Republic of China), a body with little knowledge of the common law, this raises the problem of whether it is appropriate for the courts to apply exclusively common law principles of interpretation in construing the Basic Law, and whether the courts should take into consideration the possible response of the NPCSC in interpreting the Basic Law. These questions, which go to the heart of the issue of judicial independence, were engaged in *Chong Fong Yuen v Director of Immigration*.[50] Here, contrary to the common law system under which the power of interpretation of legislation is vested exclusively in the judiciary, the power to interpret laws is vested in different organs in the Mainland socialist legal system. Under the Constitution of the PRC, the NPCSC is mainly defined as a legislative organ. As such, an interpretation by the NPCSC is, under Chinese law, legislative in nature. Therefore, the position of the NPCSC vis-à-vis the Hong Kong courts is akin to that between the legislature and the judiciary. This characterisation of the NPCSC's interpretation as a legislative process provides a theoretical justification for the court to reconcile the primacy of the common law in the HKSAR and the respect for the sovereign power. In exercising this power of interpretation, the courts will not take into account how the NPCSC would interpret the Basic Law under Chinese law, neither will the courts consider how the NPCSC would respond to their interpretation. A common law court in any other jurisdiction will not consider how the legislature will respond to its interpretation of a particular statutory provision, since the interpretation of laws is a matter exclusively for the courts. On the other hand, once a judicial interpretation has been issued, the legislature, or in this particular situation, the NPCSC, can always intervene through an exercise of its legislative power to reverse the judgment of the courts. See J Chan SC, 'Basic Law and Constitutional Review: The First Decade' (2007) 37 *Hong Kong Law Journal* 407, 416–17.

2. In construing the Basic Law in the common law tradition, the Hong Kong Court has resorted to international and comparative materials as available legal sources when exercising judicial review. The International Covenant on Civil and Political Rights (ICCPR) has been incorporated into domestic law through the Bill of Rights Ordinance and entrenched by Article 39 of the Basic Law. This has provided a convenient basis for the domestic reception of international and comparative jurisprudence. Apart from foreign cases, the courts have freely referred to decisions from the European Court of Human Rights, Human Rights Committee, Inter-American Court of Human Rights and International Court of Justice. The courts are also receptive to soft international law found in the non-binding General Comments and Concluding Observations of various United Nations Human

---

[50] *Chong Fong Yuen v Director of Immigration*, FACV No 26 of 2000.

Rights treaty bodies, Siracusa Principles, as well as United States' State Department Country Reports on Human Rights Practices, which relate primarily to civil-political rights. The courts have been more cautious and conservative in relation to economic, social and cultural rights. While there are some differences between these two sets of rights, the differences are more apparent than real in most cases, especially when the relevant right has been incorporated into domestic law. See Johannes Chan SC, 'Basic Law and Constitutional Review: The First Decade' (2007) 37 *Hong Kong Law Journal* 407, 410–11. Is this another way through which court rulings can bring about substantive constitutional change which affects societal changes?

IV. LIMITS TO CONSTITUTIONAL CHANGE

A constitution may provide for express limits to the power to change the constitution, whether these be procedural and/or substantive. Once a constitutional amendment bill is passed following the stipulated procedure, it becomes part of the constitution and is constitutional. However, it remains an open question whether substantive limits may be implied to condition the exercise of legislative power (reflecting the tenet of popular sovereignty) to change constitutions.

History teaches us that the expression of popular sovereignty without substantial limits could destroy constitutionalism itself. This is predicated on the argument that there are indispensable features of a modern constitutional democracy, such as the rule of law, protection of human rights, separation of power, and checks and balances. If these may be amended out of existence as an expression of popular will, this could pave the way for an anti-constitutionalist state. Constitutionalism implies 'pre-existing restraints on the range of choices available to governing majorities'.[51] This is why constitutionalism is said to be in tension with democracy. The issue thus arises, whether certain constitutional or fundamental values are immutable.

There is a diversity of scholarly opinion on the forms of constitutional change and whether these are normatively desirable. Walter F Murphy argued that through the exploration of the constitutional text, context and legal theory, limitations on valid constitutional change do exist, and that their justification depends on the multiple forms these take.[52] He argues that limits to constitutional change include:

(a) express textual prohibitions;
(b) textual distinctions drawn between amending, revising and transforming;
(c) prohibitions embedded in the structure of the text;
(d) prohibitions imposed by the normative theory in the constitution;
(e) prohibitions imposed by natural law, justice and rights.[53]

---

[51] S Issacharoff, 'Constitutionalizing Democracy in Fractured Societies' (2004) 82 *Texas Law Review* 1861.

[52] WF Murphy, 'Merlin's Memory: The Past and Future Imperfect of the One and Future Polity' in Levinson (ed), above n 28, 163.

[53] Ibid at 172–81.

Constitutional practices indicate that the substantial limits to constitutional change may assume various forms. This could include judicial interpretation of the constitution where certain fundamental values are proclaimed to comprise the 'basic structure' of the constitution, or express 'eternity clauses' which identify what lies beyond constitutional amendment, such as Article 1 of the German Basic Law.[54] Lastly, limits to constitutional change may also be derived from international law that prescribes universal obligation for states.

An examination of relevant practice shows that Asian constitutional orders contain substantive limits to constitutional change. Though having relatively more youthful constitutionalist traditions, many Asian states have exhibited a tendency strongly to defend constitutional fundamentals where these come under attack. Particularly worthy of our attention is the fact that constitutional orders in Asia generally embrace the idea of limited popular sovereignty and see merit in limiting the ability to change a constitution.

This section explores Asian experiences in limiting the power to change a constitution through substantive restrictions to the law-making power. It begins with a general survey of written constitutional eternity clauses, followed by judicially declared implied limits on the power to amend constitutions. Lastly, limits to constitutional change derived from international law and transnational constitutionalism will be examined.

A. Eternity Clauses

A few Asian constitutions provide substantive limits to constitutional amendments. The origins of the device of the 'eternity clauses' may be traced back to the German Basic Law. After World War II, when the Germans drafted a new constitution, it was agreed that fundamental constitutional principles should be entrenched so that in future, atrocities could no longer be carried out under the guise of formal legality. As a result, a number of 'militant democracy' measures were embedded in the Basic Law, including explicit limits on the power of constitutional amendment. Article 79(3) of the Basic Law of the Federal Republic of Germany, the so-called 'eternity clause' (*Ewigkeitsklausel*), reads:

> An amendment of this Basic Law affecting the division of the Federation into Länder, the participation in principle of the Länder in legislation, or the basic principles laid down in Articles 1 and 20, is inadmissible.

The protected provisions seek to commit 'all state authority' to respect and protect human dignity, the state's federal structure and commitment to the welfare state. Notably, the common description of Article 79(3) as the 'eternity clause' is not contained in the text itself but is a colloquial description of it, arising out of the consensus of constitutional theorists with respect to the universality of human dignity, freedom,

---

[54] Art 1 of the German Basic Law prescribes as follows: '(1) Human dignity shall be inviolable. To respect and protect it shall be the duty of all state authority. (2) The German people therefore acknowledge inviolable and inalienable human rights as the basis of every community, of peace and of justice in the world. (3) The following basic rights shall bind the legislature, the executive and the judiciary as directly applicable law.'

equality and rule of law. It limits the legislative power of Parliament with respect to constitutional amendments.

Today, eternity clauses may be found in constitutions around the world. Generally, these 'eternity clauses' come in two kinds:

(a) clauses protecting the 'spirit' of a constitution, ie its fundamental principles; and
(b) clauses protecting certain specified principles (for instance, the republican form of government, human rights, the separation of powers or federalism).

Similar to the normative commitments in the German Basic Law, democracy, human dignity and human rights are commonly regarded as foundational to constitutionalism, and may not be altered.[55]

A few Asian constitutions have eternity clauses which secure constitutional provisions from the amendment procedures. Eternity clauses are contained in the Constitutions of Cambodia, East Timor, Hong Kong, Indonesia, Malaysia and Thailand, as set out in Table 4.5.

A survey of the eternity clauses in Asian constitutions shows that constitutionally-designated limits to constitutional amendment cover a wide range of subjects, including the system of liberal democracy, the form of government, protection of human rights and the rule of law. Nevertheless, there are also constitutions that provide that various provisions may not be changed which relate to state symbols such as the monarch, the national flag or even Independence Day. Certain constitutions prohibit certain constitutional amendments during a state of emergency, such as those of Cambodia and East Timor, as shown in Table 4.5. Generally, eternity clauses in Asia not only serve to protect democracy or a republican form of government, but also shoulder many other functions designed to protect the basic character and identity of a political community.

B. Implied Limits ('Basic Structure' or 'Basic Features')

Even when constitutions are silent and do not place substantive limits on amendment powers, it does not follow that there are no limits to amending the constitution. Various theories limiting powers of constitutional amendment have been articulated. John Rawls opposed amendments that repeal core constitutional freedoms or violate core human rights and deny the basis of equality that he argues is the foundation of equal liberties.[56] Other possible substantive limits on the legislative power to amend constitutions include limitations derived from 'universal' agreements or *jus cogens* principles under international law, including human rights law,[57] and emerging international legal norms that address the separation of powers and constitutional amendment.[58]

---

[55] B Fassbender, 'The United Nations Charter as Constitution of the International Community' (1998) 36 *Columbia Journal Transnational Law* 529, 602.

[56] CL Kelbley, 'Are There Limits to Constitutional Change? Rawls on Comprehensive Doctrines, Unconstitutional Amendments, and the Basis of Equality' (2004) 72 *Fordham Law Review* 1535.

[57] VJ Samar, 'Can a Constitutional Amendment be Unconstitutional?' (2008) 33 *Oklahoma City University Law Review* 668.

[58] SJ Schnably, 'Emerging International Law Constraints on Constitutional Structure and Revision: A Preliminary Appraisal' (2008) 62 *University of Miami Law Review* 417.

Table 4.5 Eternity Clauses in Asian Constitutions

Country	Eternity Clauses in Constitutions
Cambodia	Revisions or amendments shall be prohibited when the country is in a state of emergency. Revision or amendment affecting the system of liberal and pluralistic democracy and the regime of Constitutional Monarchy shall be prohibited.
East Timor	Laws revising the Constitution shall respect: a) National independence and the unity of the State; b) The rights, freedoms and guarantees of citizens; c) The republican form of government; d) The separation of powers; e) The independence of the courts; f) The multi-party system and the right of democratic opposition; g) The free, universal, direct, secret and regular suffrage of the office holders of the organs of sovereignty, as well as the system of proportional representation; h) The principle of administrative deconcentration and decentralization; i) The National Flag; j) The date of proclamation of national independence. Paragraphs c) and i) may be reviewed through a national referendum, in accordance with the law. No action may be taken to revise the Constitution during a state of siege or a state of emergency.
Hong Kong	No amendment to this Law shall contravene the established basic policies of the People's Republic of China regarding Hong Kong.
Indonesia	Provisions relating to the form of the unitary state of the Republic of Indonesia may not be amended.

Malaysia	(2) The provisions affecting succession to the throne and the position of the Ruling Chiefs and similar Malay customary dignitaries may not be amended by the State Legislature.
	(6) This section (constitutional amendment) does not invalidate any provision of the Constitution of this State requiring the consent of any body of persons to any amendment affecting –
	  (a) the appointment and attributes of an heir or heirs to the throne, of the Ruler's Consort or of the Regent or Members of the Council of Regency of the State,
	  (b) the removal, withdrawal, or abdication of the Ruler or his heir or heirs,
	  (c) the appointment and attributes of the Ruling Chiefs or similar Malay customary dignitaries and of members of religious or customary Advisory Councils or similar bodies,
	  (d) the establishment, regulation, confirmation and deprivation of Malay customary ranks, titles, honours, dignities and awards and the attributes of the holders thereof and the regulation of the royal courts and repeal.

Thailand	A motion for amendment which has the effect of changing the democratic regime of government with the King as Head of the State or changing the form of the State shall be prohibited.

In practice, implied limits to constitutional change have been accepted in various jurisdictions. Besides Germany, India and South Africa are said to recognise unconstitutional constitutional change, where courts have the power to declare a constitutional amendment unconstitutional – even if that constitutional amendment complies with constitutionally stipulated procedures – if the amendment violates the 'spirit' of the constitution.[59] However, constitutional scholars also warn against the danger of an overly assertive court assuming the power to infer limits to constitutional amendment as it pleases. John R Vile, in discussing the US Constitution, argued against implicit limits on the constitutional amending process, as the danger of increasing judicial activism might demolish checks and balances among the three branches.[60] Nevertheless Dante B Gatmaytan referred to a general trend in the cases of certain courts endorsing substantive limits to constitutional amendment, arguing that the demands of constitutionalism also require that the power to amend constitutions be limited, and that the courts are arguably the best institution to be entrusted with this task.[61]

In Asia, the problem of a constitutional amendment contravening implicit basic constitutional norms and principles may occur especially during times of transition, when the old constitutional order is gradually being replaced with a new one. Constitutional changes driven by political negotiation, which includes the engagement of civil society, may reflect a political consensus but still contravene the fundamental normative requirements of the constitution. Once disputes of this nature arise, the court must adjudicate. In such cases, the court may be concerned with how best to position itself within the fiercely contested transitional politics. It may also struggle to find the appropriate standard of review, not only to ensure that it preserves fundamental constitutional values it is obliged to safeguard, but also to avoid becoming embroiled in political thickets or making political decisions that stifle the civil society initiatives.

The Supreme Court of India was the first constitutional court in the world to deal with the unconstitutionality of constitution amendments. It took the Supreme Court some 30 years to develop a jurisprudence which gave it the power to hold a constitutional amendment to be unconstitutional, to create the 'basic structure' or 'basic features' doctrine and to find sufficient support for the assumption of the Court's power to strike down an unconstitutional constitutional amendment.

The story began in 1951 when the Court, in *Sankari Prasad Singh v Union of India*,[62] held that it had no power to review constitutional amendments, much less pronounce on unconstitutional constitutional amendments. In that case, the petitioner argued that the constitutional amendment act ran foul of Article 13(2) of the Constitution. The Court found that despite the fact that a constitutional amendment was law, a clear distinction existed between legislative and constituent power, such that 'law' under Article 13(2) of the Constitution of India, did not include a constitutional amendment.

---

[59]   R Albert, 'Nonconstitutional Amendments' (2009) 22 *Canadian Journal of Law and Jurisprudence* 5.
[60]   JR Vile, 'The Case against Implicit Limits on the Constitutional Amending Process' in Levinson (ed), above n 28, 191–213.
[61]   DB Gatmaytan, 'Can Constitutionalism Constrain Constitutional Change' (2010) 3 *North Western Interdisciplinary Law Review* 22.
[62]   *Sankari Prasad Singh v Union of India* [1951] AIR SC 458.

In 1967, when the Seventh Amendment was challenged in *Golak Nath v State of Punjab*,[63] the Supreme Court held that no difference existed between legislation and constitutional amendment with respect to the meaning of 'law', and that Parliament had no power to amend fundamental rights. In response, Parliament passed the Twenty-Fourth Amendment in 1971 to grant itself power to amend any constitutional provision. Three Amendments followed to abridge or take away fundamental rights in the Constitution.

The constitutionality of these three Amendments was challenged in the seminal 1973 decision of *Kesavanana Bharati v State of Kerala*.[64] The Supreme Court over-ruled *Golak Nath* and declared that Parliament had the power to amend any constitutional provision. However, seven judges held that the amending power was not to affect the 'basic structure' or framework of the Constitution. In *Indira Nehru Ghandhi v Raj Narain*,[65] the Court applied the basic structure doctrine. However, Parliament continued to pass constitutional amendments that challenged this doctrine. The Forty-Second Amendment was passed to provide that no amendments shall be called into question in any court on any ground. Finally, in *Minerva Mill Ltd v Union of India*,[66] the Court invalidated the Forth-Second Amendment and affirmed that Parliament had no power to destroy the basic structure of the Constitution. Notably, these cases all involved attempts by Parliament to amend the Constitution for social reforms in matters relating to land reform disputes and government take-over of certain industries.

Golak Nath v Punjab
[1967] AIR SC 1643 (Supreme Court, India)

Facts

Due to the British-implemented taxation and regulation system, independent India inherited a semi-feudal agrarian system, with ownership of land concentrated in the hands of a few individual landlords (Zamindars, Zamindari System). Following the passage of the 1953 Punjab Security and Land Tenures Act, the state government held that landowners could keep only 30 acres each; a few acres would go to tenants and the rest was declared 'surplus'. The Golak Nath family challenged this ruling in the courts and the case was referred to the Supreme Court in 1965. The family filed a petition under Article 32 challenging the 1953 Punjab Act on the ground that it denied them their constitutional rights to acquire and hold property and practise any profession (Articles 19(f) and (g)), and to equality before and equal protection of the law (Article 14). They also sought to have the Seventeenth Amendment – which placed the Punjab Act in the Ninth Schedule – declared ultra vires. In the course of its judgment, the Court ruled that Parliament could not curtail any of the fundamental rights in the Constitution. The Court developed jurisprudence around what was known as the 'basic structure doctrine'. According to this doctrine, the Court was in charge of 'preventing the erosion of those enduring values that constitute the essence of constitutionalism'.

---

[63] *Golak Nath v State of Punjab* [1967] AIR SC 1643.
[64] *Kesavanana Bharati v State of Kerala* [1973] AIR SC 1461.
[65] *Indira Nehru Ghandhi v Raj Narain* [1975] AIR SC 2299.
[66] *Minerva Mill Ltd v Union of India* [1980] AIR SC 1789.

Koka Subba Rao CJ

The duty of reconciling fundamental rights in Art 19 and the laws of social control is cast upon the courts and the touchstone or the standard is contained in the said two expressions. The standard is an elastic one; it varies with time, space and condition. What is reasonable under certain circumstances may not be so under different circumstances . . . It recognizes the social reality and tries to adjust itself to it from time to time avoiding the authoritarian path . . . Now, what are the fundamental rights? . . . They are the rights of the people preserved by our Constitution. 'Fundamental rights' are the modern name for what have been traditionally known as 'natural rights'. As one author puts [it]: 'they are moral rights which every human being everywhere at all times ought to have simply because of the fact that in contradistinction with other beings, he is rational and moral'. . . . Briefly stated, the Constitution declares certain rights as fundamental rights, makes all the laws infringing the said rights void, preserves only the laws of social control infringing the said rights and expressly confers power on Parliament and the President to amend or suspend them in specified circumstances . . . While articles of less significance would require consent of the majority of the States, fundamental rights can be dropped without such consent. While a single fundamental right cannot be abridged or taken away by the entire Parliament unanimously voting to that effect, a two-thirds' majority can do away with all the fundamental rights. The entire super structure built with precision and high ideals may crumble at one false step. Such a conclusion would attribute unreasonableness to the makers of the Constitution, for, in that event [they] would be speaking in two voices. Such an intention cannot be attributed to the makers of the Constitution unless the provisions of the Constitution compel us to do so . . .

. . . The next question is whether our decision should be given retrospective operation. During the period between 1950 and 1967 ie, 17 years, as many as 20 amendments were made in our Constitution. But in the context of the present petitions it would be enough if we notice the amendments affecting fundamental right to property . . . Between 1950 and 1967 the Legislatures of various States made laws bringing about an agrarian revolution in our country – zamindaries, inams and other intermediary estates were abolished, vested rights were created in tenants, consolidation of holdings of villages was made, ceilings were fixed and the surplus lands transferred to tenants. All these were done on the basis of the correctness of the decisions in *Sankari Prasad's* case ([1952] SCR 89) and *Sajjan Singh's* case ([1965] 1 SCR 933), namely, that Parliament had the power to amend the fundamental rights and that Acts in regard to estates were outside judicial scrutiny on the ground they infringed the said rights. The agrarian structure of our country has been revolutionised on the basis of the said laws. Should we now give retrospectivity to our decision, it would introduce chaos and unsettle the conditions in our country. Should we hold that because of the said consequences Parliament had power to take away fundamental rights, a time might come when we would gradually and imperceptibly pass under a totalitarian rule. Learned counsel for the petitioners as well as those for the respondents placed us on the horns of this dilemma, for they have taken extreme positions – learned counsel for the petitioners want us to reach the logical position by holding that all the said laws are void and the learned counsel for the respondents persuade us to hold that Parliament has unlimited power and, if it chooses, it can do away with fundamental rights . . . In the constitutional field therefore, to meet the present extraordinary situation that may be caused by our decision, we must evolve some doctrine which has roots in reason and precedents so that the past may be preserved and the future protected . . .

. . . We have arrived at two conclusions, namely, (1) Parliament has no power to amend Part III of the Constitution so as to take away or abridge the fundamental rights; and

(2) this is a fit case to invoke and apply the doctrine of prospective overruling. What then is the effect of our conclusion on the instant case? Having regard to the history of the amendments, their impact on the social and economic affairs of our country and the chaotic situation that may be brought about by the sudden withdrawal at this stage of the amendments from the Constitution, we think that considerable judicial restraint is called for. We, therefore, declare that our decisions will not affect the validity of the [C]onstitution (Seventeenth Amendment) Act, 1964, or other amendments made to the Constitution taking away or abridging the fundamental rights. We further declare that in future Parliament will have no power to amend Part III of the Constitution so as to take away or abridge the fundamental rights. In this case we do not propose to express our opinion on the question of the scope of the amendability of the provisions of the Constitution other than the fundamental rights, as it does not arise for consideration before us. Nor are we called upon to express our opinion on the question regarding the scope of the amendability of Part III of the Constitution otherwise than by taking away or abridging the fundamental rights. We will not also indicate our view one way or other whether any of the Acts questioned can be sustained under the provisions of the Constitution without the aid of Arts 31A, 31B and the 9th Schedule . . .

Before we close, it would be necessary to advert to an argument advanced on [an] emotional plane. It was said that if the provisions of the Constitution could not be amended it would lead to revolution. We have not said that the provisions of the Constitution cannot be amended but what we have said is that they cannot be amended so as to take away or abridge the fundamental rights. Nor can we appreciate the argument that all the agrarian reforms which the Parliament in power wants to effectuate cannot be brought about without amending the fundamental rights. It was exactly to prevent this attitude and to project the rights of the people that the fundamental rights were inserted in the Constitution. If it is the duty of the Parliament to enforce the directive principles, it is equally its duty to enforce them without infringing the fundamental rights. The Constitution-makers thought that it could be done and we also think that the directive principles can reasonably be enforced with the self-regulatory machinery provided by Part III. Indeed both Parts III and IV of the Constitution form an integrated scheme [and it is elastic] enough to respond to the changing needs of the society. The verdict of the Parliament on the scope of the law of social control of fundamental rights is not final, but justiciable. If not so, the whole scheme of the Constitution will break. What we cannot understand is how the enforcement of the provisions of the Constitution can bring about a revolution. History shows that revolutions are brought about not by the majorities but by the minorities and [sometimes] by military coups. The existence of an all comprehensive amending power cannot prevent revolutions, if there is chaos in the country brought about by misrule or abuse of power. On the other hand, such a restrictive power gives stability to the country and prevents it from passing under a totalitarian or dictatorial regime. We cannot obviously base our decision on such hypothetical or extraordinary situations which may be brought about with or without amendments. Indeed, a Constitution is only permanent and not eternal. There is nothing to choose between destruction by amendment or by revolution, the former is brought about by totalitarian rule, which cannot brook constitutional checks and the other by the discontentment brought about by misrule. If either happens, the constitution will be a scrap of paper. Such considerations are out of place in construing the provisions of the Constitution by a court of law. Nor are we impressed by the argument that if the power of amendment is not all comprehensive there will be no way to change the structure of our Constitution or abridge the fundamental rights even if the whole country demands such a change . . .

Kesavananda v State of Kerala
[1973] AIR SC 1461 (Supreme Court, India)

Facts

The petitioner filed petitions under Article 32 of the Constitution for enforcement of his fundamental rights under Articles 25, 26, 14, 19(1)(f) and 31 of the Constitution. He prayed that the provisions of the Kerala Land Reforms Act 1963 (Act 1 of 1964), as amended by the Kerala Land Reforms (Amendment) Act 1969 (Act 35 of 1969), be declared unconstitutional, ultra vires and void. He further prayed for an appropriate writ or order to issue during the pendency of the petition. The issue was: What is the extent of the amending power conferred by Article 368 of the Constitution, apart from Article 13(2), on Parliament?

Sikri CJ

Before proceeding with the main task, it is necessary to ask: What was decided in *IC Golak Nath v State of Punjab* [1967] 2 SCR 762?
    . . . It must be borne in mind that these conclusions [in *Golak Nath v State of Punjab*] were given in the light of the Constitution as it stood then ie while Article 13(2) subsisted in the Constitution. It was then not necessary to decide the ambit of Article 368 with respect to the powers of Parliament to amend Article 13(2) or to amend Article 368 itself. It is these points that have now to be decided. It may further be observed that the Chief Justice refused to express an opinion on the contention that, in exercise of the power of amendment, Parliament cannot destroy the fundamental structure of the Constitution but can only modify the provision thereof within the framework of the original instrument for its better effectuation . . .
    It will be noticed that Article 368 is contained in a separate part and the heading is 'Amendment of the Constitution', but the marginal note reads 'Procedure for amendment of the Constitution'. The expression 'amendment of the Constitution' is not defined or expanded in any manner, although in other parts of the Constitution, the word 'Amend' or 'Amendment' has, as will be pointed out later, been expanded. In some parts they have clearly a narrow meaning . . . The proviso throws some light on the problem. First, it uses the expression 'if such amendment seeks to make any change in'; it does not add the words 'change of ', or omit 'in', and say 'seeks to change' instead of the expression 'seeks to make any change in' . . .
    The fundamental rights were considered of such importance that right was given to an aggrieved person to move the highest court of the land, ie, the Supreme Court, by appropriate proceedings for the enforcement of the rights conferred by this part, and this right was guaranteed. Article 32(2) confers very wide powers on the Supreme Court, to issue directions or orders or writs including writs in the nature of habeas corpus, mandamus, prohibition, quo warranto and certiorari, whichever may be appropriate, for the enforcement of any of the rights conferred by this Part. Article 32(4) further provides that 'the right guaranteed by this article shall not be suspended except as otherwise provided for by this Constitution[']. Article 33 enables Parliament by law to 'determine to what extent any of the rights conferred by this Part shall, in their application to the members of the Armed Forces or the Forces charged with the maintenance of public order, be restricted or abrogated so as to ensure the proper discharge of their duties and the maintenance of discipline among them[']. This article shows the care with which, the circumstances in which, fundamental rights can be restricted or abrogated were contemplated and precisely described. . . .

It was the common understanding that fundamental rights would remain in substance as they are and they would not be amended out of existence. It seems also to have been a common understanding that the fundamental features of the Constitution, namely, secularism, democracy and the freedom of the individual would always subsist in the welfare state. In view of the above reasons, a necessary implication arises that there are implied limitations on the power of Parliament that the expression 'amendment of this Constitution' has consequently a limited meaning in our Constitution and not the meaning suggested by the respondents. This conclusion is reinforced if I consider the consequences of the contentions of both sides. The respondents, who appeal fervently to democratic principles, urge that there is no limit to the powers of Parliament to amend the Constitution. Article 368 can itself be amended to make the Constitution completely flexible or extremely rigid and unamendable. If this is so, a political party with a two-third majority in Parliament for a few years could so amend the Constitution as to debar any other party from functioning, establish totalitarianism, enslave the people, and after having effected these purposes make the Constitution unamendable or extremely rigid. This would no doubt invite extra-Constitutional revolution. Therefore, the appeal by the respondents to democratic principles and the necessity of having absolute amending power to prevent a revolution to buttress their contention is rather fruitless, because if their contention is accepted the very democratic principles, which they appeal to, would disappear and a revolution would also become a possibility. However, if the meaning I have suggested is accepted a social and economic revolution can gradually take place while preserving the freedom and dignity of every citizen. For the aforesaid reasons, I am driven to the conclusion that the expression 'amendment of this Constitution' in Article 368 means any addition or change in any of the provisions of the Constitution within the broad contours of the Preamble and the Constitution to carry out the objectives in the Preamble and the Directive Principles. Applied to fundamental rights, it would mean that, while fundamental rights cannot be abrogated reasonable abridgements of fundamental rights can be effected in the public interest. It is of course for Parliament to decide whether an amendment is necessary. The Courts will not be concerned with wisdom of the amendment. If this meaning is given it would enable Parliament to adjust fundamental rights in order to secure what the Directive Principles direct to be accomplished, while maintaining the freedom and dignity of every citizen.

Shelat and Grover JJ

. . . It was considered, when the larger bench was constituted, that the decision of the questions before us would hinge largely on the correctness or otherwise of the decision of this court in *IC Golak Nath and Ors v State of Punjab and Anor* [1967] 2 SCR 762, according to which it was held, by majority, that Article 13(2) of the Constitution was applicable to Constitutional amendments made under Article 368 and that for that reason the fundamental rights in Part III could not be abridged in any manner or taken away. The decision in *Golak Nath* has become academic, for even on the assumption that the majority decision in that case was not correct, the result on the questions now raised before us, in our opinion, would just be the same . . .

The argument that the Nation cannot grow and that the objectives set out in the Preamble cannot be achieved unless the amending power has the ambit and the width of the power of a Constituent Assembly itself or the People themselves appears to be based on grounds which do not have a solid [basis]. The Constitution makers provided for development of the country in all the fields social, economic and political. The structure of the Constitution has been erected on the concept of an egalitarian society. But the Constitution makers did not desire that it should be a society where the citizen will not enjoy the various freedoms and such rights as are the basic elements of those freedoms, eg, the right to equality, freedom of religion etc, so that his dignity as an individual may be maintained. It has been strongly urged on behalf of the respondents that a citizen cannot have any dignity if he is economically or socially backward. No one can dispute such a statement but the whole scheme underlying the Constitution is to bring about economic and social changes without taking away the dignity of the individual. Indeed, the same has been placed on such a high pedestal that to ensure the freedoms etc their infringement has been made justiciable by the highest court in the land. . . .

The basic structure of the Constitution is not a vague concept and the apprehensions expressed on behalf of the respondents that neither the citizen nor the Parliament would be able to understand it are unfounded. If the historical background, the Preamble, the entire scheme of the Constitution, the relevant provisions thereof including Article 368 are kept in mind there can be no difficulty in discerning that the following can be regarded as the basic elements of the Constitutional structure. (These cannot be catalogued but can only be illustrated): (1) The supremacy of the Constitution; (2) Republican and Democratic form of Government and sovereignty of the country; (3) Secular and federal character of the Constitution; (4) Demarcation of power between the legislature, the executive and the judiciary; (5) The dignity of the individual (secured by the various freedoms and basic rights in Part III and the mandate to build a welfare State contained in Part IV; (6) The unity and the integrity of the nation.

Minerva Mills Ltd v Union of India
[1980] AIR SC 1789 (Supreme Court, India)

Facts

Minerva Mills Ltd was a limited company dealing in textiles. On 20 August 1970 the Central Government appointed a committee under section IS of the Industries (Development Regulation) Act, 1951 to make a full and complete investigation of the affairs of the company, as it was of the opinion that there had been or was likely to be substantial fall in the volume of its production. The committee submitted its report to the Central Government in January 1971, and on that basis the Central Government passed an order dated 19 October 1971 pursuant to section 18A of the 1951 Act, authorising the National Textile Corporation Ltd to take over the management of Minerva Mills on the ground that their affairs were being managed in a manner highly detrimental to the public interest. This undertaking was nationalised and taken over by the Central Government under the provisions of the Sick Textile Undertakings (Nationalisation) Act, 1974.

The petitioners challenged the constitutional validity of certain provisions of the Sick Textile Undertakings (Nationalisation) Act, 1974 and of the order of 19 October 1971; the constitutionality of the Constitution (Thirty-Ninth Amendment) Act which inserted the impugned Nationalisation Act as Entry 105 in the Ninth Schedule to the Constitution; the validity of Article 31B of the Constitution; and the constitutionality of sections 4 and 55 of the Constitution (Forty Second Amendment) Act, 1976. The petitioners relied on the ratio of the majority judgment in *Kesavananda Bharati's* case and argued that though Article 368 of the Constitution empowered Parliament to amend the Constitution, that power could not be exercised so as to damage the basic features of the Constitution or so as to destroy its basic structure.

YV Chandrachud CJ

The theme song of the majority decision in *Kesavananda Bharati* is: 'Amend as you may even the solemn document which the founding fathers have committed to your care, for you know best the needs of your generation. But, the Constitution is a precious heritage; therefore, you cannot destroy its identity'. The majority conceded to the Parliament the right to make alterations in the Constitution so long as they are within its basic framework. And what fears can that judgment raise or misgivings generate if it only means this and no more: The Preamble assures to the people of India a polity whose basic structure is described therein as a Sovereign Democratic Republic; Parliament may make any amendments to the Constitution as it deems expedient so long as they do not damage or destroy India's sovereignty and its democratic, republican character. Democracy is not an empty dream. It is a meaningful concept whose essential attributes are recited in the preamble itself: Justice, social, economic and political; Liberty of thought, expression, belief, faith and worship, and Equality of status and opportunity. Its aim, again as set out in the preamble, is to promote among the people an abiding sense of Fraternity assuring the dignity of the individual and the unity of the Nation'. The newly introduced clause S of Article 368 demolishes the very pillars on which the preamble rests by empowering the Parliament to exercise its constituent power without any 'limitation whatever'. No constituent power can conceivably go higher than the sky-high power conferred by clause (S), for it even empowers the Parliament to 'repeal the provisions of this Constitution', that is to say, to abrogate the democracy and substitute for it a totally antithetical form of Government. That can most effectively be achieved, without calling a democracy by any other name, by a total denial of social, economic and political justice to the people, by emasculating liberty of thought, expression, belief, faith and worship and by abjuring commitment to the magnificent ideal of a society of equals. The power to destroy is not a power to amend. Since the Constitution had conferred a limited amending power on the Parliament, the Parliament cannot under the exercise of that limited power enlarge that very power into an absolute power. Indeed, a limited amending power is one of the basic features of our Constitution and therefore, the limitations on that power cannot be destroyed. In other words, Parliament cannot, under Article 368, expand its amending power so as to acquire for itself the right to repeal or abrogate the Constitution or to destroy its basic and essential features. The donee of a limited power cannot by the exercise of that power convert the limited power into an unlimited one.

The very 42nd Amendment which introduced clauses 4 and 5 in Article 368 made amendments to the preamble to which no exception can be taken. Those amendments are not only within the framework of the Constitution but they give vitality to its philosophy [and] they afford strength and succor to its foundation. By the aforesaid amendments, what was originally described as a 'Sovereign Democratic Republic' became a 'Sovereign Socialist Secular Democratic Republic' and the resolution to promote the 'unity of the Nation' was elevated into a promise to promote the 'unity and integrity of the Nation'. These amendments furnish the most eloquent example of how the amending power can be exercised consistently with the creed of the Constitution. They offer promise of more, they do not scuttle a precious heritage.

Notes and Questions

1.   Land reform has always been a controversial issue in India. The world's worst recorded food disaster happened in 1943 in British-ruled India. Known as the Bengal Famine, an estimated four million people died of hunger that year in eastern

India (including Bangladesh) alone. As an independent nation in 1947, India continued to be haunted by memories of the Bengal Famine. Thus, food security was a primary item on independent India's social agenda. This led to the 'Green Revolution' in India and legislative measures to ensure that businessmen would never again hoard food to engage in profiteering. However, efforts until 1967 largely concentrated on expanding the farming areas, while the population was growing at a much faster rate than food production. The Green Revolution advanced three measures: the continued expansion of farming areas, double-cropping of existing farmland and using seeds with improved genetics.

2. Against this backdrop, consider whether the role of the Court is to act as the protector of the people. Is the right to private property a fundamental right, or should this be subject to the priority of land reform conducted to promote social welfare? Did the Court represent the interests of landowners but not the people? What role can courts play given the needs of a changing society? Should the courts have taken into consideration the fact that in India, the procedure for law-making and constitution-amending is the same? In the battle between the court and the Parliament, was there a third party who should have had the final say, such as the people, as opposed to the people's representatives? Did the Court fail to pay enough attention to the economic crisis India was undergoing, so as to leave too little space for Parliament and the local governments to discharge their tasks of promoting social welfare?

3. After *Golak Nath v Punjab*, the Indian Supreme Court invoked the basic structure doctrine four more times.[67] Today, it is generally agreed that there is a list of basic features which may not be amended out of existence. This may include the supremacy of the Constitution, the rule of law, the principle of separation of powers, judicial review, freedom and dignity of the individual, unity and integrity of the nation, the principle of free and fair elections, federalism and secularism.[68] However, prior to *Golak Nath v Punjab*, there were two Amendments and two judicial rulings which held that Parliament could curtail fundamental rights by means of Constitutional Amendment based on Article 368 of the Constitution: *Shankari Prasad v Union of India* (1952)[69] related to the First Amendment (1951), and *Sajjan Singh v State of Rajasthan* (1965)[70] related to the Seventeenth Amendment (1964).

4. In *Golak Nath v Punjab*, the Court invented the 'basic structure' doctrine, and in so doing granted itself the power to define the scope and content of the basic structure from the Constitution. In later cases the Court affirmed this doctrine. Should courts have the final say with respect to deciding on the limits attending the power to amend a constitution? The Court in *Golak Nath v Punjab* had applied the doctrine of prospective overruling, so as to confine its ruling to future cases, leaving intact all prior measures taken by the Parliament. Why do you think the Court adopted this approach, and do you agree with it? One might argue that

---

[67] Po Jen Yap, 'Rethinking Constitutional Review in America and the Commonwealth: Judicial Protection of Human Rights in the Common Law World' (2006) 35 *Georgia Journal of International and Comparative Law* 99, 108–09.

[68] GJ Jacobsohn, 'The Permeability of Constitutional Borders' (2004) 82 *Texas Law Review* 1763, 1795.

[69] *Shankari Prasad v Union Of India*, 1951 AIR, SC 458 (4)

[70] *Sajjan Singh v State of Rajasthan*, 1965 AIR, SCR 1965 (1) 933.

there can be only two options: either invalidating an amendment as null and void, or sustaining it completely. Was the Court acting strategically to assert its power over adjudicating political conflicts?

5.   The two major issues in *Golak Nath v Punjab* were the nationalisation of property in response to economic crisis, and the legislative power to amend the Constitution. The Court upheld this exercise in judicial activism which not only declared unconstitutional the constitutional amendment, but interfered with and even mandated the limits of land reform policy. However, despite the Court's strong determination to protect fundamental rights and confidence in its own competence to engage in policy-making, many considered that the Court had crossed a line and abused the idea of the 'basic structure' to increase its power. As the Attorney-General, LN Sinha, who defended the Forty-Second Amendment in *Minerva Mills v Union of India*, argued:

> The State is under an obligation to take steps for promoting the welfare of the people by bringing about a social order in which social, economic and political justice shall inform all the institutions of the national life. . . . [T]he deprivation of some of the fundamental rights for the purpose of achieving this goal cannot possibly amount to a destruction of the basic structure of the Constitution.

When the Sri Lanka Supreme Court faced the issue of an unconstitutional constitutional amendment in *Re the Thirteenth Amendment to the Constitution*, it held that the Indian basic structure doctrine did not apply to the Sri Lanka Constitution. As the Constitution already provided rules that entrenched important provisions which might be altered only following a popular referendum procedure, the Sri Lankan Court adopted a more cautious and modest approach in reviewing constitutional amendments, mainly through the lens of procedural scrutiny, as can be seen in *Re the Eighteenth Amendment to the Constitution*, and in *Re the Nineteenth Amendment to the Constitution*. In the latter case, the Sri Lanka Supreme Court was asked to consider whether the Thirteenth Amendment to the Constitution violated the basic structure of the Constitution.

In Re the Thirteenth Amendment to the Constitution and the Provincial Councils Bill
(1987) 2 Sri Lanka Law Reports 312 (Supreme Court, Sri Lanka)

Facts

In 1987, the Thirteenth Amendment to the Constitution Bill and the Provincial Councils Bill were passed. These laws made comprehensive changes to the original structure of the separation of powers in the Constitution. Each province was to establish a Provincial Council, with legislative and administrative powers invested in a Governor appointed by the President, who exercised his or her discretion according to the advice of the Board of the Council. They also sought to establish a High Court for each Province that should have original criminal jurisdiction and appellate jurisdiction from magistrates' courts and primary courts. The petitioners contended that the Thirteenth Amendment Bill was inconsistent with the Constitution, as it violated the Unitary State principle postulated by Article 2; sovereignty guaranteed by Articles 3 and 4; and Article 9 for giving the foremost place to Buddhism. They argued that under Article 83, a constitutional amendment making such constitutional changes required approval at a Bill Referendum. The petitioners further argued that even if the Bill received approval at a Bill Referendum, it was still unconstitutional for altering the basic structure of the Constitution.

P Colin-Thome, Atukorale & Tambiah JJ, and Sharvananda, CJ

It was submitted that the Bills seek to amend the basic structure of the Constitution. The basis of the submission was that the clauses 4 and 7 of the 13th Constitutional Amendment Bill seek to establish a Constitutional structure which is Federal or quasi-Federal and these Provisions take away the Unitarianism enshrined in Article 2. In our considered view, there is no foundation for the contention that the basic features of the Constitution have been altered or destroyed by the proposed amendments. The Constitution will survive without any loss of identity despite the amendment. The basic structure or framework of the Constitution will continue intact in its integrity. The unitary State will not be converted into a Federal or Quasi-federal State. We have already examined the question whether the amendment in any way affects entrenched Article 2 which stipulates a unitary State and after an analysis of the relevant provisions of the amending Bill, have come to the conclusion that the unitary nature of the State is in no way affected by the proposed amendments and that no new sovereign legislative body executive or judiciary is established by the amendment. The contra submission made by the petitioners is based on the misconception that devolution is a divisive force rather than an integrative force.

It was contended that the scope of amendment contemplated by Article 82 and 83 is limited and that there are certain basic principles or features of the Constitution which can in no event be altered even by compliance with Article 83. Reliance was placed for this proposition on the decisions of the Supreme Court of India in *Kesavananda v State of Kerala*, AIR 1973. SC 1461 and *Minerva Mills Ltd v Union of India* AIR 1980, SC 1789. Those decisions of the Supreme Court of India were based on Article 368 of the unamended Indian Constitution which reads as follows:

> An amendment of this Constitution may be initiated only by the introduction of a Bill for the purpose in either House of Parliament . . .

The said section 368 carried no definition of 'amendment' nor did it indicate its scope. It was in this context that the Supreme Court in the *Kesavananda* case, reached the conclusion by a narrow majority of seven to six that the power of amendment under Article 368 is subject to implied limitation and Parliament cannot amend those provisions of the Constitution which affect the basic structure or framework of the Constitution. The argument of the majority was on the following line:

> The word amendment postulates that the old Constitution survives without loss of its identity despite the change and continues even though it has been subjected to alterations. As a result of the amendment the old Constitution cannot be destroyed, and done away with it is retained though in the amended form. The words amendment of the Constitution with all their wide sweep and amplitude cannot have the effect of destroying and abrogating the basic structure-or frame work of the Constitution (per Khanna J) . . .

But both our Constitutions of 1972 and 1978 specifically provide for the amendment or repeal of any provision of the Constitution or for the repeal of the entire Constitution – vide Article 51 of the 1972 Constitution and Article 82 of the 1978 Constitution. In fact, Article 82(7) of the 1978 Constitution states 'in this chapter "Amendment" includes repeal, alteration and addition.' In view of this exhaustive explanation that amendment embraces repeal, in our Constitution we are of the view that it would not be proper to be guided by concepts of 'Amendment' found in the Indian judgments which had not to consider statutory definition of the word 'Amendment.' Fundamental principles or basic features of the Constitution have to be found in some provision or provisions of the Constitution and if the Constitution contemplates the repeal of any provision or provisions of the entire Constitution, there is no basis for the contention that some provisions which reflects fundamental principles or incorporate basic features are immune from amendment. Accordingly, we do not agree with the contention that some provisions of the Constitution are unamendable.

In Re the Nineteenth Amendment to the Constitution
(2002) 3 Sri Lanka Law Reports 85 (Supreme Court, Sri Lanka)

Facts

In September 2002, Sri Lanka's Parliament, which was dominated by the United National Party (UPN), passed the Nineteenth Amendment to the Constitution. Among other things, the Bill drastically reduced the discretionary power of the President. The petitioners challenged the constitutionality of clauses 4 and 5 of the legislation, arguing that such an amendment required approval at a Referendum under Article 83.

Held

The petitioners contend that these provisions require to be approved at a Referendum in terms of Article 83(a), as they are inconsistent with Article 3 read with Article 4 (b) of the Constitution . . . These Articles relate to the sovereignty of the People and the exercise of that sovereignty . . . Hence, it is necessary to examine the concept of the sovereignty of the People and the working thereof, as set out in Articles 3 and 4 from a slightly different perspective. Sovereignty, which ordinarily means power or more specifically power of the State as proclaimed in Article 1 is given another dimension in Article 3 from the point of the People, to include: (1) the powers of Government; (2) the fundamental rights; and (3) the franchise. Fundamental rights and the franchise are exercised and enjoyed directly by the people and the organs of government are required to recognize, respect, secure and advance these rights. The powers of government are separated as in most Constitutions, but unique to our Constitution is the elaboration in Articles 4(a), (b) and (c) which specifies that each organ of government shall exercise the power of the People attributed to that organ. To make this point clearer, it should be noted that subparagraphs (a), (b) and (c) not only state that the legislative power is exercised by Parliament; executive power is exercised by the President and judicial power by Parliament through Courts, but also specifically state in each sub paragraph that the legislative power 'of the People' shall be exercised by Parliament; the executive power 'of the People' shall be exercised by the President and the judicial power 'of the People' shall be exercised by Parliament through the Courts. This specific reference to the power of the People in each sub paragraph which relates to the three organs of government demonstrates that the power remains and continues to be reposed in the People who are sovereign, and its exercise by the particular organ of government being its custodian for the time being, is for the People. Therefore, the statement in Article 3 that sovereignty is in the People and is 'inalienable', being an essential element which pertains to the sovereignty of the People should necessarily be read into each of the sub paragraphs in Article 4. The relevant sub paragraphs would then read as follows: (a) the legislative power of the People is inalienable and shall be exercised by Parliament; (b) the executive power of the People is inalienable and shall be exercised by the President; and (c) The judicial power of the People is inalienable and shall be exercised by Parliament through Courts. The meaning of the word 'alienate', as a legal term, is to transfer anything from one who has it for the time being to another, or to relinquish or remove anything from where it already lies. Inalienability of sovereignty, in relation to each organ of government means that power vested by the Constitution in one organ of government shall not be transferred to another organ of government, or relinquished or removed from that organ of government to which it is attributed by the Constitution. Therefore, shorn of all flourishes of Constitutional Law and of political theory, on a plain interpretation of the relevant Articles of the Constitution, it could be stated that any power that is attributed by the Constitution to one organ of government cannot be transferred to another organ of government or relinquished or removed from that organ of government; and any such transfer, relinquishment or removal would be an 'alienation' of sovereignty which is inconsistent with Article 3 read together with Article 4 of the Constitution. It necessarily follows that the balance that has been struck between the three organs of government in relation to the power that is attributed to each such organ, has to be preserved if the Constitution itself is to be sustained.

This balance of power between the three organs of government, as in the case of other Constitutions based on a separation of power is sustained by certain checks whereby power is attributed to one organ of government in relation to another. The dissolution of Parliament and impeachment of the President are some of these powers which constitute the checks incorporated in our Constitution. Interestingly, these powers are found in chapters that contain provisions relating to the particular organ of government subject to the check. Mr HL de Silva, PC, submitted forcefully that they are 'weapons' placed in the hands of each organ of government. Such a description may be proper in the context of a general study of Constitutional Law, but would be totally inappropriate to our Constitutional setting, where sovereignty as pointed out above, continues to be reposed in the People and organs of government are only custodians for the time being, that exercise the power for the People. Sovereignty is thus a continuing reality reposed in the People. Therefore, executive power should not be identified with the President and personalised and should be identified at all times as the power of the People. Similarly, legislative, power should not be identified with the Prime Minister or any party or group in Parliament and thereby be given a partisan form and character. It should be seen at all times as the power of the People. Viewed from this perspective it would be a misnomer to describe such powers in the Constitution as 'weapons' in the hands of the particular organ of government. These checks have not been included in the Constitution to resolve conflicts that may arise between the custodians of power or, for one to tame and vanquish the other. Such use of the power which constitutes a check, would be plainly an abuse of power totally antithetic to the fine balance that has been struck by the Constitution. The power that constitutes a check, attributed to one organ of government in relation to another, has to be seen at all times and exercised, where necessary, in trust for the People. This is not a novel concept. The basic premise of Public Law is that power is held in trust . . .

. . . To sum up the analysis of the balance of power and the checks contained in the Constitution to sustain such balance, we would state that the power of dissolution of Parliament and the process of impeachment being some of the checks put in place, should be exercised, where necessary, in trust for the People only to preserve the sovereignty of the People, and to make it meaningful, effective and beneficial to the People. Any exercise of such power (constituting a check), that may stem from partisan objectives would be a violation of the rule of law and has to be kept within its limits in the manner stated by Bhagawati J There should be no bar to such a process to uphold the Constitution. Our conclusion on the matters considered above can be stated as follows: (1) The powers of government are included in the sovereignty of the People as proclaimed in Article 3 of the Constitution. (2) These powers of government continue to be reposed in the People and they are separated and attributed to the three organs of government; the Executive, the Legislature and the Judiciary, being the custodians who exercise such powers in trust for the People. (3) The powers attributed to the respective organs of government include powers that operate as checks in relation to other organs that have been put in place to maintain and sustain the balance of power that has been struck in the Constitution, which power should be exercised only in trust for the People. (4) The exercise of the sovereignty of the People can only be perceived in the context of the separation of powers as contained in Article 4 and other connected provisions of the Constitution, by the respective organs of government. (5) The transfer of a power which is attributed by the Constitution to one organ of government to another; or the relinquishment or removal of such power, would be an alienation of sovereignty inconsistent with Article 3 read with Article 4 of the Constitution . . .

Notes and Questions

1. Does the Sri Lankan Court really reject the idea of basic structure, or does it in fact apply this concept in a subtle and implicit manner? In the decision on the *Thirteenth Amendment Case*, the Court read the Constitution in a formal way and explicitly rejected the basic structure doctrine in its conclusion, while sparing no effort to discuss the basic structure in the Sri Lankan Constitution.

2. In the *Nineteenth Amendment* decision, the Court, though using no such terms, or any similar words, as 'basic structure' or 'limits to constitutional amendment', did elaborate on the nation's normative constitutional structure of the separation of powers. The Court started with the spirit of popular sovereignty and extended to the separation of powers. Do you think the Court changed its approach in reading the Constitution and understands the basic structure in a different way?

3. It has been observed that Sri Lanka constitutionalism is largely shaped by its fiercely confrontational partisan politics. As Gatmaytan-Magno noted:

    > Sri Lanka is an example of a country where amendments were used by the party in power to gain tactical advantage over other parties. In Sri Lanka, amendments deprived an opposition leader of civil liberties, expelled members of a political party (that subsequently lead to the loss of seats in parliament), empowered the President to determine the time of the presidential elections, and extended the life of parliament, depriving citizens of the choice of their local representatives. Other amendments ousted representatives of the Tamil-speaking regions from parliament and removed the safeguards for the extension of emergency powers. Courts have the power to require a referendum when the basic structure of the Constitution is amended but they have been reluctant to interfere with the decisions of the executive. The experience in Sri Lanka has led to disillusionment with the democratic process and with the ideology of constitutionalism.[71]

Given the increasing trend towards nationalism and democratic transition, it is not surprising to find that quite a few courts in Asia commonly develop limits to amending

---

[71] See Gatmaytan-Magno, above n 39, at 35–36.

constitutions. Though the substance of the implicit limits may differ from constitution to constitution, the common rationale these constitutional courts share in affirming the rule is to check the over-expansion of legislative power and to prevent it from undermining constitutional government.

Having been liberated from an authoritative regime, a democratising Taiwan undertook a series of constitutional revisions in the 1990s. In *JY Interpretation No 499*, the Constitutional Court of Taiwan was asked to adjudicate whether constitutional amendments had both procedural flaws and were against the principle of democracy contained in the Constitution. The Court declared the amendments unconstitutional and explicitly prescribed specific limits to constitutional amendments based on its interpretation of the general 'spirits' of the Constitution.

JY Interpretation No 499
24 Mar 2000 (Constitutional Court, Taiwan)

Facts

On 4 September 1999, the Third National Assembly passed Article 1 of the Amendment to the Constitution, which provided that from the Fourth National Assembly onwards, its members should be appointed from among the different political parties according to the ratio of votes received by them and independent candidates in the Legislative Yuan elections. This amendment proved controversial; the National Assembly is a very different body from the Legislative Yuan. The Court was asked to consider if the Amendment violated Article 25 of the Constitution, which states that the National Assembly shall exercise its powers on behalf of all nationals.

Held

The Constitution is the fundamental basis for and supreme law of the country. Its amendment greatly affects the stability of constitutional order and the well-being of all people as a whole and, therefore, must be made by the authorized [governmental] body in accordance with constitutional due process. Furthermore, because the process of amending the Constitution is the most direct action that reflects and realizes sovereignty, it must be conducted openly and transparently in order to satisfy the condition of rational communication and, hence, lay the proper foundation for a constitutional state . . . [T]he exercise of such power must be based upon the principles of openness and transparency and be in compliance with Article 174 of the Constitution as well as related rules of the National Assembly so as to satisfy the reasonable expectation and trust of the entire nation. As a result, Article 38, Paragraph 2, of the Regulations of the National Assembly Proceedings concerning anonymous balloting should be limited in its application in the readings on constitutional amendments. The act of amending the Constitution shall not take effect if the process is clearly and grossly flawed (Gravitaets-bzw. Evidenztheorie). 'Clearly' means [material] facts are so obvious that they can be determined without investigation; 'grossly' means, as far as parliamentary procedure is concerned, the flaw is so significant that due process is no longer present and the basic rule of the constitutional amendment is violated. In its Third Reading on September 4, 1999, in attempting to amend the Constitution, the National Assembly has violated the above-stated principle of openness and transparency. It also contradicted the then- still effective Article 38, Paragraph 2, of the Regulations of the National Assembly Proceedings.

Based upon the transcript, there were indeed [material] facts so obviously flawed that they could be determined without investigation. The general public was precluded from realizing how the National Assembly exercised its power to amend the Constitution, and the spirit of the Constitution, which dictates that delegates of the National Assembly be politically responsible for their respective electorate or political party, as incorporated in Article 133 of the Constitution or Judicial Yuan Interpretation No 331 could not be carried out. As a result, the act to amend the Constitution in question is clearly and grossly flawed and has violated the fundamental rule to render any constitutional amendment effective.

. . . Although the Amendment to the Constitution has equal status with the constitutional provisions, any amendment that alters the existing constitutional provisions concerning the fundamental nature of governing norms and order and, hence, the foundation of the Constitution's very existence destroys the integrity and fabric of the Constitution itself. As a result, such an amendment shall be deemed improper. Among the constitutional provisions, principles such as establishing a democratic republic under Article 1, sovereignty of and by the people under Article 2, protection of the fundamental rights of the people under Chapter Two as well as the check and balance of governmental powers are some of the most critical and fundamental tenets of the Constitution as a whole. The democratic constitutional process derived from these principles forms the foundation for the existence of the current Constitution and all [governmental] bodies installed hereunder must abide by this process.

Notes and Questions

1. *JY Interpretation No 499* – which declared the National Assembly's proposed constitutional amendments unconstitutional – was released right after the 2000 presidential and vice-presidential elections. The Government had only two options as the terms of the existing National Assembly delegates were due to expire on 19 May 2000. Either the Central Election Committee could immediately sponsor a new round of national elections (which was potentially volatile and impractical in terms of time and budget), or the National Assembly could call an extraordinary session to resolve the pending constitutional crisis. Due largely to public pressure (especially the general public's unfavourable attitude toward the National Assembly, with many questioning the value of its existence), the KMT and DPP, two major political parties, reconvened another extraordinary session of the National Assembly and amended the Constitution again. This was signed by the President and promulgated on 25 April 2000. Under this latest amendment, the original term for the Third National Assembly delegates was restored and allowed to expire. The National Assembly later became an ad hoc and 'reactive' institution, with its delegates being elected and called into session only if and when there was a bill to amend the Constitution or to change the territory. The *JY Interpretation 499* also paved the way for the final resolution of the notorious National Assembly problem. In 2005, the National Assembly approved a constitutional revision that formally abolished the National Assembly and assigned all its powers to the Legislative Yuan. Since then, the power to make law and revise the Constitution vests in the Legislative Yuan, in which all legislators are elected by people in Taiwan.

2. The basic features or basic structure doctrine has not found favour in many courts in Asia. In Malaysia and Singapore, cases heard in the 1970s and 1980s rejected the application of the basic structure doctrine.[72] However, later cases seem to endorse the concept. In the Malaysia case of *Sivarasa Rasiah v Badan Peguam Malaysia & Anor*,[73] the Federal Court rejected its earlier decision in *Loh Kooi Choon* which rejected the basic structure doctrine on grounds that it would involve the courts in policy questions and force them to enter into the political thicket. In *Sivarasa*, the Federal Court expressly referred to *Kesavananda* and stated that

    > it is clear from the way in which the Federal Constitution is constructed there are certain features that constitute its basic fabric. Unless sanctioned by the Constitution itself, any statute (including one amending the Constitution) that offends the basic structure may be struck down as unconstitutional. Whether a particular feature is part of the basic structure must be worked out on a case by case basis. Suffice to say that the rights guaranteed by Part II which are enforceable in the courts form part of the basic structure of the Federal Constitution.[74]

3. However, a number of courts have suggested that at the very least, a constitution cannot be called a constitution in the absence of the separation of powers between the three branches of government. An early case that reasoned along these lines was the Ceylonese case of *Liyanage v The Queen*.[75] There, the Judicial Committee of the Privy Council was asked to consider, inter alia, whether the absence of an express 'vesting' of 'judicial power' in the Ceylonese judiciary meant that the courts in Ceylon ceased to have such power. The Privy Council, after examining the structure and arrangement of the Constitution, concluded that it was clear that the framers of the Constitution had clearly intended that there be a separation of powers between the three branches – legislative, executive and judicial – and that judicial power lay where it had been for over a century: in the judicial branch.

4. In a recent Singapore High Court decision, *Mohammad Faizal bin Sabtu v Public Prosecutor*,[76] in the course of discussing the nature of 'judicial power' under Article 93 of the Singapore Constitution, Chief Justice Chan Sek Kong held that

    > under the Singapore Constitution, the sovereign power of Singapore is shared among the same trinity of constitutional organs, viz, the Legislature (comprising the President of Singapore and the Singapore parliament), the Executive (the Singapore government) and the Judiciary (the judges of the Supreme Court and the Subordinate Courts). The principle of separation of powers, whether conceived as a sharing or a division of sovereign power between these three organs of state, is therefore part of the basic structure of the Singapore Constitution.[77]

    Interestingly, the basic structure argument was never raised, yet the Court held that at least, a constitution has to separate the judiciary from the other branches of government.

---

[72] *Phang Chin Hock v PP* [1980] 1 MLJ 70 (Federal Court, Malaysia); *Loh Kooi Choon v Government of Malaysia* [1977] 2 MLJ 187 (Federal Court, Malaysia); and *Teo Soh Lung v Minister for Home Affairs* [1989] 1 SLR(R) 461 (High Court, Singapore).

[73] *Sivarasa Rasiah v Badan Peguam Malaysia & Anor* [2010] 2 MLJ 333 (Federal Court).

[74] Ibid at 342.

[75] *Liyanage v The Queen* [1967] AC 259.

[76] *Mohammad Faizal bin Sabtu v Public Prosecutor* [2012] 4 SLR 974.

[77] Ibid, para 11.

5. Assuming that courts accept the basic structure argument, how can the courts decide on what constitutes the basic features of the constitution? In *Kesavananda* all the majority judges agreed that there were certain basic features of the Indian Constitution, but did not agree on how many features there were and exactly what they were. Is the critique that courts who endorse the basic features doctrine engage in judicial legislation over-stated, given that this is essentially a conservative or protective doctrine?

C. International Law and Transnational Constitutionalism

International law is another source from which limits to constitutional change may take form, raising the issue of legal hierarchy and methods for receiving international law within the domestic context. While constitutions are the supreme law of the land, they are not immune from foreign influences, such as imposed constitutions or legal transplants borrowed from a colonial heritage. In addition, a state has the obligation under the international law to honour treaties to which it is party and generally binding customary international law, as well as peremptory norms and obligations *erga omnes*. The constitutional law of a state may thus be influenced by foreign precedents and models, as well as international law, and courts may seek to harmonise a constitution with transnational 'best practices', while negotiating local conditions. Foreign case law may of course serve as a model for emulation or an anti-model to rejection.[78]

Constitutionalism in Asian has been influenced by foreign cases and international law. The accelerated economic development and geo-political significance of many Asian states have attracted the attention of the international community, or at least, certain Western powers. As a result, many Asian states are responsive to the international and regional politics, and sensitive to external pressures. To some extent, constitutional change may be shaped by the normative pull of international law as well as the evolving state of international politics. However, as the case of *Kadir* shows, these two dimensions are not always compatible. In this case, the Indonesian Constitutional Court was asked to review the constitutionality of anti-terrorist legislation enacted after the notorious Bali bombings in 2002 and 2005. Following the 11 September 2001 terrorist attacks on American soil, the confrontation between Western states and politicised Islam escalated, such that terrorism associated with radical Islam became a central concern of the international community. Indonesia, a modernising Muslim-majority state, felt the need to adopt special counter-terrorist measures in response to the appeal of the mainstream international community, the urgency of which was exacerbated by the Bali bombings. It was argued that the anti-terrorist legislation was unconstitutional because it retroactively punished the Bali bombers, which was contrary to constitutional principles and minimal conditions for a criminal legal system prescribed by international law.

---

[78] See Li-ann Thio, 'Beyond the "Four Walls" in an Age of Transnational Judicial Conversations: Civil Liberties, Rights Theories and Constitutional Adjudication in Malaysia and Singapore' (2006) 19 (2) *Columbia Journal of Asian Law* 428.

Masykur Abdul Kadir Case
Constitutional Court Decision No 013/PUU-I/2003 (Constitutional Court, Indonesia)

Facts

On 1 October 2005, a series of terrorist suicide bombs were detonated in Bali, leaving 20 dead and a further 129 injured. This was the most recent attack in a spate of bombings, which included the 2002 Bali nightclub bombing, the 2003 Marriot Hotel bombing and the 2004 Australian Embassy bombing. Various members of Jemaah Islamiyah, a violent Islamist group, have been convicted in relation to the terrorist attacks, including three individuals who were sentenced to death. Seven days after the Bali attack in 2002, the Indonesian President issued a presidential decree empowering security forces to detain a suspect for seven days without charge, and subsequently for a further six months' detention without charge following a court appearance. In 2003, the Indonesian Government passed a law that applied the terrorism offences retrospectively to the Bali bombers.

Held

Considering that there be a group of people who believe that under a particular situation, the nonretroactive principle could be overridden (the nonretroactive principles of the World Organization Against Torture) by giving six (6) arguments as follows:

1. Argument of Gustav Radbruch which states that an act is liable for punishment even when the act is committed it has not been declared as a crime because the principle of superiority of justice may override the nonretroactive principle. However, Radbruch still believes that the nonretroactive principle is so important that overriding it may only be made in a most extreme situation, such as that which was once applied to the Nazi regime that had committed a genocide.
2. The argument saying that the knowledge of the perpetrator that his or her act is a punishable subject in the future, thought the act is legal when he or she commits it. The argument concludes that under any conditions the nonretroactive principle is not applicable to protect a person who is aware that his act is wrong.
3. The argument saying that the general principle of justice may override the existence of positive law. An act that may not be a crime when it is committed according to the positive law, may be applied with a retroactive law if the act is against the generally accepted justice.
4. The argument saying that the international law principles may override domestic law. Hence, though an act is according to domestic law not against the law, the nonretroactive principle may be overridden because the act is against the international positive law.
5. The argument saying that the nonretroactive may be overridden through a reinterpretation of the law that was effective before. By doing a reinterpretation of the law existing when the act was committed, an act that was before one that was not punishable may become a punishable act.
6. The argument saying that the act according to the prevailing law when it is committed is actually an obvious violation of the law prevailing at that time.

Considering that despite the views described above, it is apparent that the larger part of the legal scholars in the world – in observance of the development of the said viewpoints – still believe that somehow the nonretroactive principle cannot be overridden only for a cause as described in the above views. Accordingly, aside from the dissenting opinions among the judges of the Constitutional Court, the Court is of the opinion as follows:

1. That, essentially, law applies prospectively. It is not fair to punish a person for an act committed at the time when it was not a wrongful one. It is equally unfair if a person is charged under a heavier law to an act that when committed was punishable under a less severe law, whether it relates to procedural law or substance.
2. That the nonretroactive principle refers more to the philosophy of criminalization on retributive basis, while this principle is no longer the main reference of the criminalization system in our country that favors the preventive and educative principles.
3. That it has been a public knowledge that overriding the nonretroactive principle allows a particular regime to use the law as a tool for a revenge against its former political opponents. Such a revenge may not happen, and therefore, there should not be the slightest likelihood for such an opportunity.
4. That, currently, efforts are being made to ensure the rule of law including a fair trial. The minimum guarantee for a fair trial is: the principles of presumption of innocence, equal opportunities for the parties to the case, pronouncing a decision open to the public, the principle of ne bis *in idem*, the application of [a] less severe law for a pending process, and the prohibition of the application of retroactive principle. By referring to these minimum conditions, Law No 16 of 2003 moves in [the] opposite direction as a fair trial. . . .

Considering that it is true this principle was once overridden when prosecuting the war criminals in the Nuremberg Tribunal. However, as described above, this was done as an exception and an emotionally strong notion to punish the unfeeling Nazi, and after this trial has been completed, the international community has always been emphasizing that the nonretroactive principle shall not be overridden. This is reflected in the formulation on the human rights instruments. . . .

Considering that aside from whether or not the above definitions on terrorism are still confusing, the Court believes that all types of terrorism must be eradicated, even down to the roots of the problems and the initial causes thereof, as are the growing expectations among the international society. There must therefore be a law that assures the deterrence, suppression and eradication of terrorism. The law must provide, in addition to heavier penalt[ies], smooth arrangements for the process of probing, repression and apprehension.

Considering that Law Number 15 of 2003 on the Declaration of Government Regulation in lieu of Law Number 1 of 2002 on Suppression of Terrorism, as a Law, has fairly satisfied the expectations of the justiciables. However, Law Number 15 of 2003 must not be applied retroactively, because the elements and types of crime contained in terrorism according to this law are the types of crime that are subject to severe punishment.

Considering that the application of retroactive principle in criminal code is an exception that may only be permissible and applied to a case of gross violation on human rights, as a serious crime, that will protect the non-derogable rights. Meanwhile, the Roma Statute of 1998 categorizes gross violation of human rights include[ing] genocide, crime [against] humanity, war crime, and aggression crime; while Article 7 of Law No. 39 of 1999 on Human Rights categories of gross violation of human rights as only genocide and crime against humanity. Hence, a reference to the Rome Statute of 1998 as well as Law, Bali bombing does not still belong to an extraordinary crime that may be subjected to a retroactive principle of law, but an ordinary crime that is very cruel, but can still be prosecuted under the existing criminal code. Perpu No. 1 of 2002 and Perpu No. 2 of 2002 received many challenges, because, in formally legal view, the retroactive principle is actually inapplicable, because terrorism does not belong to the category of crime that will be subject to a retroactively applied law (Paper Position of Human Rights Foundation, No. 1, December 2002). . . .

Maruarar Siahaan, SH; I Dewa Gede Palguna, SH, MH; Prof HAS Natabaya, SH, LLM; and Dr Harjono, SH, MCL (dissenting)

In general, cases in which retrospective criminal laws have been applied have involved serious crimes against humanity, genocide, and war crimes. The application of retrospective laws has represented a demand for justice because if the human rights of the perpetrators were protected on the grounds that retrospective treatment was prohibited, this would be seen to strongly contradict human morality because it would, in fact, permit greater and grosser violations of human rights. Therefore, justice has been the rationale for overriding the principle of non-retroactivity with limitations in certain conditions. How must we view Article 28I of Indonesia's 1945 Constitution which states that the principle of non-retroactivity is a human right which cannot be set aside under any circumstances? Its literal wording implies that the principle of retroactivity is absolute. However, if viewed systematically, one human right is not absolute because in the exercise of their rights and freedoms people must respect the human rights of others and must be subject to limits as defined by Law.

Reading Article 28J(2) together with Article 28I(1), we can conclude that the principle of non-retroactivity is not absolute. Exceptions can, therefore, be recognised within the framework of 'satisfying just demands in accordance with moral considerations, religious norms, security and public order.' . . . We must consider whether a strict application of the principle of non-retrospectivity will give rise to injustice, and undermine religious values, security and public order because the Law did not intend to protect individuals in this manner. A balance must be struck between Legal certainty and Justice when attempting to ascertain the meaning of Article 28I(1) of the 1945 Constitution. This balance can be achieved using the following formula: a) Justice is not achieved through a high level of Legal certainty, but by balancing legal protection for the victims and perpetrators of crime; b) The more serious the crime committed, the greater the Justice that must be achieved over Legal certainty (Academic Research Paper on Human Rights, Supreme Court, 2003). Justice is a higher value than legal certainty. Thus, if there is a conflict between these two principles, the principle capable of bringing about real justice is prioritised. Therefore, enacting a limited Retrospective Law does not violate the 1945 Constitution, particularly in relation to crimes which are extraordinary in terms of the method used to perpetrate the crime and its consequences (victims). It was not the intention of those who made the 1945 Constitution to entrench the principle of Non-retroactivity absolutely without exception . . . From the above discussion it can be concluded that the essence of the principle of non-retroactivity is to protect against the criminalisation of an act that was not considered a crime when the act was perpetrated. Also prohibited are new laws which stipulate a harsher penalty or punishment than the penalty or punishment applicable at the time the act was committed. Retrospective legislation is justified provided that it does not violate the two prohibitions mentioned above . . .

. . . Based on the above considerations, there are insufficient grounds to declare that Law No 16 of 2003 has deviated both from normative limitations recognised in various international legal instruments and practical arguments in relation to setting aside the principle of non-retroactivity because: (a) The acts declared as crimes of terrorism by Interim Law No 1 of 2002 already constituted criminal acts or crimes under prior laws; (b) Interim Law No 1 of 2002 does not increase the penalties for the acts which under Interim Law No 1 of 2002 were declared to be crimes of terrorism.

. . . [T]he next question is, does the principle of non-retroactivity adopted in Interim Law No 1 of 2002 violate the 1945 Constitution, particularly Article 28I(1)? [The court set out Article 28I(1) of the Constitution.] . . . The inclusion of this Article in the 1945 Constitution, which is an adaptation of Article 15 of the International Covenant on Civil and Political

Rights (ICCPR), was coloured by long debate in both the Ad Hoc I Committee of the Peoples' Consultative Council – the committee which prepared the draft text of amendments to the 1945 Constitution – and hearings of Commission A during the Annual Session of the Peoples' Consultative Council in 2000 . . . The source of debate was the term 'non-derogable rights' used in Article 15 of the ICCPR, which was translated as 'cannot be diminished under any circumstances' . . .

The principles of non-retroactivity and legality were initially intended to protect members of the community from arbitrary rulers who, through law-making institutions, could create laws in accordance with their overtly repressive desires and use the law as a tool of oppression solely in their own interests. Terrorism is a crime which does not target distinct individuals; rather the community is the target. This differentiates terrorism from general crimes. Thus the Anti-Terrorist Law aims to directly protect the community from disturbances caused by acts that can create extraordinary fear or terror. The function of the State to protect members of the community is clear in this case; that is, it must exercise its mandate contained in the Preface to the 1945 Constitution: 'to protect all the people of Indonesia and their entire native land, improve public welfare, advance the intellectual life of the people and contribute to the establishment of a world order based on freedom, abiding peace and social justice' . . .

According to international law, human rights and civil and political rights are not absolute. A person's right may conflict with the right of another, and so one person's right must be sacrificed for the right of another. Individual rights can violate community values and the public interest. Both the Universal Declaration of the United Nations (UN) on Human Rights and the International Covenant on Civil and Political Rights recognise that a State can limit rights if it considers it necessary to protect certain public interests. Article 29(2) of the Universal Declaration of the UN states:

> In the exercise of his rights and freedoms, everyone shall be subject only to such limitations as are determined by law solely for the purpose of securing due recognition and respect for the rights and freedoms of others and of meeting the just requirements of morality, public order and the general welfare in democratic society.

Based on the above provisions of Article 29(2) of the Universal Declaration of the UN it can be concluded that limitations on human rights are permissible and can even satisfy the criteria of 'justice' in accordance with morality, public order and general welfare in a democratic society . . .

Indonesia recognises that Human Rights are universal. However, it is necessary to note that the international community, as declared in the Vienna Declaration of 1993, recognises and agrees that their implementation is the authority and responsibility of all state governments in observance of the diversity of value systems, history, culture, political systems, levels of social and economic growth and other factors of the nation in question . . . From the above two articles in the Universal Declaration and the International Covenant on Civil and Political Rights, it is apparent that the principle of *Nullum Delictum* only applies if the relevant crime was not a crime under national or international law. Consequently, if the crime in question is a crime under national and international law, the principle of *Nullum Delictum* cannot be employed. It is also appropriate to note that Article 15(2) of the International Covenant on Civil and Political Rights above states that nothing in this Article shall prejudice the trial and punishment of any person for any act or omission which, at the time it was committed, was criminal according to the general principles of law recognised by the community of nations. Based on this rule it can be concluded that if the act was a crime under the general principles of law recognised by the community of nations, the principle of *Nullum Delictum* can be overridden . . . In addition to the considerations in the above paragraph, the United Nations also issued two Conventions within the framework of suppressing international terrorism. These conventions include: (i) International Convention for the Suppression of Terrorist Bombings (1997); and (ii) International Convention for the Suppression of the Financing of Terrorism (1999). Further, previous to this the United Nations issued two Declarations: (i) Declaration on Measures to Eliminate International Terrorism (1994); and (ii) Declaration to Supplement the 1994 Declaration on Measures to Eliminate International Terrorism (1996). It is apparent that the international community had agreed to do away with all forms and manifestations of international terrorism and that those responsible for terrorist acts had to be brought before the courts.

Notes and Questions

1. The controversy surrounding Indonesia's constitutional prohibition against retrospective prosecution must be appreciated within the broader political context of the disputed Indonesian Bill of Rights and the Second Amendment to the Constitution. These were made to effect meaningful reform without constitutional indemnity like that enjoyed by the military under Soeharto's New Order regime. On 18 August 2000, the Indonesia's People's Consultative Assembly passed the Second Amendment to Indonesia's 1945 Constitution. In a 12-day sitting, the 700-member legislature, the *Majelis Permusyawaratan Rakyat* (MPR), significantly reformed the Constitution, particularly in the area of human rights. The Second Amendment was the culmination of nine months of preparation by the Ad Hoc Committee of the MPR's Working Committee, which included provincial consultation meetings and international study missions. Throughout the drafting process, experts engaged in intense negotiation with representatives of the MPR's political blocs, and the final draft tabled for debate was the product of political compromise – a feature common to all of Indonesia's recent constitutional amendments.

2. The Second Amendment included the addition of a Bill of Rights – Chapter XA of the Constitution. It is the first meaningful protection of human rights in Indonesia's 1945 Constitution, and it represents a radical shift in Indonesia's constitutional philosophy from an essentially authoritarian to a more liberal–democratic model. Chapter XA drew substantially from the Universal Declaration of Human Rights (UDHR) and it provides – on paper at least – a far more extensive list of constitutional rights than that offered by many developed states. The Second Amendment was made in the spirit of widespread reform, with the MPR focusing on using constitutional amendments to steer Indonesia's transition to democracy and to guarantee the protection of human rights. See R Clarke, 'Retrospectivity and the Constitutional Validity of the Bali Bombing and East Timor Trials' (2003) 5(2) *Australian Journal of Asian Law* 128.

3. The Government failed to respond to the holding of the Court in the *Masykur Abdul Kadir Case*, and the decision invited more controversy and even tainted the reputation of the Court. Though the Court declared the law never to have had binding force, the process under which the unconstitutionally convicted bombers could enforce the Constitutional Court's decision was unclear and untested. Some

legal commentators claimed that the Criminal Code allowed many of the accused persons to lodge a Supreme Court review against the sentences imposed upon them. Others claimed that the accused could simply lodge appeals against their convictions before the general courts. Fearing that the convictions would be lost or voided, Justice Minister Yusril Ihza Mahendra and Constitutional Court Chief Justice Professor Dr Jimly Asshiddiqie announced their own interpretation of the decision to the press. Expressing similar views, they claimed that the bombers would remain in jail because the Constitutional Court's decision could not operate retrospectively. In other words, while the decision was binding, it deals only with future investigations, prosecutions and convictions. It would not, therefore, have any impact upon convictions that have already been obtained. It took the Indonesian judiciary more than 30 years to obtain the power to review the constitutionality of statutes. If Constitutional Court decisions applied only prospectively, it would take a benevolent litigant aggrieved by an apparently unconstitutional law to challenge the legality of that law knowing that the decision will not actually benefit him or her in any way. See S Butt and D Hansell, 'Casenote: The *Masykur Abdul Kadir* Case: Indonesian Constitutional Court No 013/PUU-I/2003 ("Bali Bombing case")' (2004) 6(2) *Australian Journal of Asian Law* 176. Do you agree with this view? Was the reputation of the Indonesian Constitutional Court strengthened or weakened by this decision?

5

Judicial Review

I. INTRODUCTION

Alexander Hamilton considered judicial power to be 'the least dangerous to the political rights of the constitution'.[1] Compared to the executive who wields the sword or the legislature who commands the purse, the judiciary merely adjudicates cases or controversies and prescribes the rules by which duties and rights are accorded. This chapter focuses on the judicial review powers of the courts of Asia. In contrast to what Hamilton had envisioned, courts have, in modern constitutional states, been transformed into institutions so powerful that scholars have described this judicial dominance as a 'juristocracy'.[2]

This chapter is in seven further sections. Section II. addresses the nature and legal basis of judicial review, while section III. discusses institutional design in relation to judicial review. Section IV. examines the scope and subject of judicial review, and section V. considers judicial appointments and judicial independence. Section VI. addresses issues related to justiciability and *locus standi*, section VII. looks at judicial approaches to constitutional interpretation. Lastly, section VIII. concludes with a discussion of the various forms of judicial decisions and remedies.

II. NATURE OF JUDICIAL REVIEW

The origins of judicial review practice may possibly be traced to Athenian times,[3] but its practice flourished in more modern times with the establishment of the American republic and following the US Supreme Court's decision in *Marbury v Madison*.[4] By the twentieth century, states had adopted various approaches to judicial review, the main difference being that they were either 'centralised' or 'decentralised' forms and institutions of review.[5]

---

[1] A Hamilton, Federalist No 78, Benjamin Fletcher Wright (ed) (Cambridge: Belknap Press, 1961).
[2] R Hirschl, *Towards Juristocracy: The Origins and Consequences of New Constitutionalism* (Cambridge, Mass: Harvard University Press, 2004) 1; A Stone Sweet, Governing with Judges: Constitutional Politics in Europe (Oxford: Oxford University Press, 2000).
[3] See M Cappelletti, 'Judicial Review in Comparative Perspective' (1970) 58 *California Law Review* 1017, 1021–22. This article was published as chs 2 and 3 in M Cappelletti, *Judicial Review in the Contemporary World* (New York: Bobbs-Merrill, 1971) 25–68.
[4] *Marbury v Madison* (1803) 1 Cranch 137. See K Loewenstein, 'Reflections on the Value of Constitutions in Our Revolutionary Age' in AJ Zucher (ed), *Constitutions and Constitutional Trends Since World War II*, 2nd edn (New York: New York University Press, 1953) 191, 216–17.
[5] Cappelletti, 'Judicial Review in Comparative Perspective', above n 3, at 1033–50.

The 'decentralised' model 'had its origin in the United States, where judicial review remains a most characteristic and unique institution' and is 'found primarily in several of Britain's former colonies'.[6] Countries whose legal systems are derived from the common law model typically do not have separate constitutional tribunals or courts. The constitutional oversight of legislation and government action is undertaken by the superior courts – usually the High Court or Supreme Court. It is only in countries that draw their legal traditions from the Continental civil law tradition that have separate constitutional tribunals or courts.

The 'centralised' model, on the other hand, draws inspiration from the Austrian Constitution of 1920, which was based on proposals by Karl Renner and substantially drafted by Hans Kelsen.[7] For the first time, a special tribunal, the Constitutional Court (the *Bundes-Verfassungsgesetz* or *B-VG*), was to act as the sole and final arbiter of constitutional matters in a state. Although the Austrian Constitution was suspended from 1934 to 1945, it was re-enacted following the end of World War II, on 1 May 1945. The centralised system of judicial review was adopted by Italy (1948), Germany (1949) and then France (1958). It found favour primarily with civil law countries[8] for three principal reasons. First, the European states had a much stricter view about the separation of powers and institutions than the common law states, and were quick to recognise the inherently political nature of judicial review.[9] Secondly, in the absence of the rule of *stare decisis*, civil law judges are not bound by the decisions of superior courts, nor those of courts of corresponding jurisdiction. This could easily lead to a situation under which one court declares a statute unconstitutional, only for that judgment to be ignored by another judge, making for confusion and uncertainty.[10] Lastly, 'the traditional highest courts of most civil countries were found to lack the structure, procedures, and mentality required for effective constitutional adjudication'.[11]

A. Decentralised Systems of Review

In Asia, countries that continue to function under the common law system operate a decentralised system of judicial review. Typically, a Supreme Court or High Court is established under the constitution, vesting judicial power in the judicial branch of government. The combination of the constitutional supremacy clause and the vesting of judicial power in the judiciary accords these courts power to pronounce on the constitutionality of legislation. For example, Article 7(2) of the Bangladesh Constitution provides that the Constitution is 'the supreme law of the Republic and if any other law is inconsistent with this Constitution and other law shall, to the extent

---

[6] Ibid at 1034.

[7] Ibid at 1038. On the roles of Renner and Kelsen on the formation of the Austrian Constitution of 1920, see G Schmitz, 'The Constitutional Court of the Republic of Austria 1918–1920' (2003) 16(2) *Ratio Juris* 240.

[8] One notable exception was Cyprus, a former British colony. Its 1960 independence constitution provided for the establishment of a Supreme Constitutional Court. The Court comprised three judges: a Greek Cypriot, a Turkish Cypriot, and a contracted judge from a neutral country who served as president of the court.

[9] Cappelletti, 'Judicial Review in Comparative Perspective', above n 3, at 1040–41.

[10] Ibid at 1043–45.

[11] Ibid at 1046.

of the inconsistency, be void'. The declaration as to whether any law is 'inconsistent with' the Constitution must thus fall on the Supreme Court of Bangladesh. The Constitution of Singapore is rather more explicit. Article 4 declares the Constitution to be the 'supreme law' of the land, and any law that is inconsistent with the Constitution shall 'to the extent of the inconsistency, be void'. Article 93 further provides that the 'judicial power shall be vested in the Supreme Court and in such subordinate courts as may be provided by any written law for the time being in force'.

Countries that have adopted this mode of constitutional review are: Bangladesh; Bhutan (from 2008); Hong Kong (until 1997); India; Malaysia; Nepal; Pakistan; Sri Lanka and Singapore. Brunei has a variation of this model in that the Sultan may refer a constitutional provision for interpretation by an Interpretation Tribunal.[12] The 2008 Constitution of Myanmar provides for the establishment of a Constitutional Tribunal, whose task it is to

> interpret the provisions of the Constitution, to scrutinize whether or not laws enacted by the Pyidaungsu Hluttaw, the Region Hluttaws and the State Hluttaws and functions of executive authorities of Pyidaungsu, Regions, States and Self-Administered Areas are in conformity with the Constitution, to decide on disputes relating to the Constitution between Pyidaungsu and Regions, between Pyidaungsu and States, among Regions, among States, and between Regions or States and Self-Administered Areas and among Self-Administered Areas themselves, and to perform other duties prescribed in this Constitution.[13]

Given Myanmar's authoritarian system of government, there is little optimism that this Tribunal will be called upon seriously to pronounce on the constitutionality of laws in the country. For example, Article 22(f) of the Constitution proclaims the Defence Services to be 'mainly responsible for safeguarding the Constitution', thus making the military, rather than the courts, the guardians of the Constitution.

B. Centralised Systems of Review

Centralised systems of constitutional review have mainly been adopted by civil law countries. However, constitutional review bodies in these states are not necessarily top judicial bodies, especially in the communist states. In China and Hong Kong SAR, the body performing the constitutional review function is the Standing Committee of the National People's Congress (NPC), and not a constitutional tribunal or court. A similar situation exists in Vietnam and Laos, where the legislative arm – known as the National Assembly in both countries – is constitutionally mandated to perform the task of constitutional review. This is unsurprising, since communist doctrine treats law as an instrument to be wielded for the good of the people as expressed through the legislative branch.

In the civil law countries, the body performing constitutional review is typically a special constitutional court or tribunal. This body is set apart from the ordinary courts of law and typically has its own protocols and procedures. There are only six constitutional courts among the civil law countries covered in this volume. These are found in

---

[12] See Art 86, Constitution of Brunei Darussalam, 1984 rev edn.
[13] See Art 46, Constitution of the Republic of the Union of Myanmar 2008.

Cambodia, Indonesia, South Korea, Mongolia, Taiwan and Thailand. All of these are of fairly recent origin. The oldest of these courts is the Taiwanese Constitutional Court, which is not called by that name[14] but is part of the Judicial Yuan – one of the five branches of government under its 1946 Constitution[15] – and made up of a Council of Grand Justices. For much of its existence, the Taiwanese Constitutional Court was fairly inactive. Indeed, between 1947 and 1974, it declared a law unconstitutional on only one occasion, and this decision was promptly ignored by the political branches.[16] It was only after the political reforms of the 1990s that the Council became more active and daring.[17]

Like Taiwan, South Korea underwent great political changes and liberalisation in the 1980s, and the current Constitutional Court was established under the Constitution of the Sixth Republic in 1988. After World War II, South Korea's first constitution 'bifurcated constitutional review between a Supreme Court, with the power to adjudicate the constitutionality of administrative regulations, and a Constitutional Committee with the power to review legislation'.[18] This arrangement was changed under the Third Republic (1963–72) when the Constitution was amended to institute a decentralised system of constitutional review based on the American model.[19] The Constitutional Court of the Sixth Republic is modelled closely on the German Federal Constitutional Court.[20] Chapter VI of the Constitution establishes the Court with jurisdiction over the 'constitutionality of Acts upon the request of the courts'.[21]

Mongolia's Constitutional Court was established under Chapter 5 of its 1992 Constitution, with power to exercise 'supreme supervision over the implementation of the Constitution, making judgment on the violation of its provisions and resolving constitutional disputes. It shall be the guarantee for the strict observance of the Constitution.'[22]

Cambodia's 1993 Constitution was promulgated as a result of a United Nations initiative to convene a Constituent Assembly. Chapter X of the Constitution creates a Constitutional Council, a body that was quite clearly influenced by the French *Conseil Constitutionnel*, established in 1958 under Part VII of the French Constitution. The Council is duty-bound to 'safeguard respect for the Constitution, to interpret the Constitution, and the laws passed by the Assembly', as well as to 'examine and decide on contested cases involving the election of assembly members'.[23]

---

[14] Indeed, the Taiwanese Constitution makes no explicit provision for the creation of a constitutional court even if the members of the Council of Grand Justices have styled themselves the 'Justices of the Constitutional Court'. See, eg, the website of the Council at <http://www.judicial.gov.tw/constitutional-court/EN/p01_03.asp> (accessed 29 July 2013).

[15] The other branches are the Legislative Yuan, the Executive Yuan, the Control Yuan and the Examination Yuan. The National Assembly, which was designed to represent the people, exists outside this five-branch scheme.

[16] See T Ginsburg, *Judicial Review in New Democracies: Constitutional Courts in Asian Cases* (New York: Cambridge University Press, 2003) at 124.

[17] Ibid at 125.

[18] Ibid at 210.

[19] Ibid at 211.

[20] Ibid at 217.

[21] See Art 111(1), Constitution of South Korea.

[22] See Art 64, Constitution of Mongolia, 1992.

[23] See Art 117, Constitution of Cambodia, 1993.

The Constitutional Court of Thailand was established under its 1997 Constitution.[24] The Court of 15 judges[25] had final authority in the interpretation of the Constitution.[26] In 2006, following a bloodless coup, the Constitutional Court was dissolved, although a similar institution was established under the 2007 Constitution, but with nine instead of 15 judges.[27]

Indonesia's Constitutional Court (*Mahkamah Konstitusi*) was established in 1999 following wide-ranging political reforms in Indonesia. The Constitution of 1945 was amended and a new Article 24C was included to constitute the Court, empowering it to

> try a case at the first and final level and [the Court] shall have the final power of decision in reviewing laws against the Constitution, determining disputes over the authorities of state institutions whose powers are given by this Constitution, deciding over the dissolution of a political party, and deciding disputes over the results of general elections.[28]

Table 5.1 shows the form of review, the body designated for constitutional review and it date of establishment, in each of the countries studied.

C. Judicial Power and the Assertion of Judicial Review Powers

As already noted, most common law constitutions do not create constitutional tribunals or courts, and neither do they explicitly empower courts to conduct judicial review. Typically, constitutions may include a clause 'vesting' judicial power in the courts, or a supremacy clause declaring void all laws that are inconsistent with the constitution. But it is rare to find clauses explicitly giving common law courts judicial review powers. As a result, common law courts have from the earliest days asserted their power of judicial review. In England, Lord Coke CJ held, in *Dr Bonham's Case*,[29] that 'in many cases the Common Law will control Acts of Parliament and sometimes adjudge them to be utterly void: for when an Act of Parliament is against common right and reason, or repugnant, or impossible to be performed, the Common Law will control it and adjudge such Act to be void'.[30] In the absence of a written constitution, Lord Coke had to be content with relying on the common law as the basis for the assertion of the judicial review power. Almost two centuries later, the US Supreme Court asserted its power of judicial review in the celebrated case of *Marbury v Madison* when Chief Justice John Marshall expounded:

> It is emphatically the province and duty of the judicial department to say what the law is. Those who apply the rule to particular cases must of necessity expound and interpret that rule. If two laws conflict with each other, the courts must decide on the operation of each.[31]

---

[24] For an overview of the development of Thai constitutionalism, see P Nanakorn, 'The Remaking of the Constitution in Thailand' (2002) 6 *Singapore Journal of International & Comparative Law* 90.

[25] See Sec 255, Constitution of Thailand, 1997.

[26] See Sec 268, Constitution of Thailand, 1997, which provided that the 'decision of the Constitutional Court shall be deemed final and binding on the National Assembly, Council of Ministers, Courts and other State organs'.

[27] See Sec 204, Constitution of Thailand, 2007. Section 268 of the 1997 Constitution was re-enacted without change as Section 216 of the 2007 Constitution.

[28] Art 22 of the Constitution of Indonesia.

[29] *Dr Bonham's Case* (1610) 8 Co Rep 114 (Court of Common Pleas, England).

[30] Ibid at 118.

[31] *Marbury v Madison* (1803) 5 US (1 Cranch) 137, 177.

Table 5.1 Judicial Review in the States of Asia

Country	Form of Review	Court or Body Performing Review	Year Established
Bangladesh	Judicial Review	Supreme Court	1972
Bhutan	Judicial Review	High Court	2007
Brunei	No review, only interpretation	Interpretation Tribunal	1984
Burma	Constitutional Review	Constitutional Tribunal	2008
Cambodia	Constitutional Review	Constitutional Council	1993
China	Constitutional Review	Standing Committee of the National People's Congress	1949
Hong Kong SAR	Judicial Review and Constitutional Review	Court of Final Appeal Standing Committee of the National People's Congress	1997
India	Judicial Review	Supreme Court of India	1947
Indonesia	Constitutional Review	Constitutional Court (*Mahkamah Konstitusi*)	1947; 1997
Japan	Judicial Review	Supreme Court	1945
South Korea	Constitutional Review	Constitutional Court	1986
Laos	Constitutional Review	National Assembly Standing Committee	
Malaysia	Judicial Review	High Court	1957
Mongolia	Constitutional Review	Constitutional Tsets	1992
Nepal	Judicial Review	High Court	
Pakistan	Judicial Review	Supreme Court	1947
Philippines	Judicial Review	Supreme Court	
Singapore	Judicial Review	High Court	1969
Sri Lanka	Judicial Review	Supreme Court	
Taiwan	Constitutional Review	Council of Grand Justices of the Judicial Yuan	1947
Thailand	Constitutional Review	Constitutional Court	1997; 2008
Timor Leste	Judicial Review	Supreme Court	
Vietnam	No review, only supervision	National Assembly	

He further stated that 'the particular phraseology of the Constitution of the United States confirms and strengthens the principle, supposed to be essential to all written Constitutions, that a law repugnant to the Constitution is void, and that courts, as well as other departments, are bound by that instrument'.[32] The Court reasoned that

---

[32] Ibid at 179.

[t]he powers of the Legislature are defined and limited; and that those limits may not be mistaken or forgotten, the Constitution is written. It is a proposition too plain to be contested that the Constitution controls any legislative act repugnant to it, . . . The Constitution is . . . a superior, paramount law, unchangeable by ordinary means, . . . Certainly all those who have framed written Constitutions contemplate them as forming the fundamental and paramount law of the nation, and consequently the theory of every such government must be that an act of the Legislature repugnant to the Constitution is void.[33]

Courts in Asia have adopted Marshall's approach in asserting their power of judicial review. For example, the Supreme Court of Bangladesh, citing *Marbury v Madison* and the Indian Supreme Court decision of *Kesavananda v State of Kerala*[34] and other foreign authorities, firmly held in *Anwar Hossain Chowdhury v Bangladesh*[35] that judicial review on the constitutionality of parliamentary or executive acts is one of the basic structures in modern constitutionalism. It confirmed that it had the power to review not only parliamentary or executive acts but also constitutional amendment acts.[36] In Singapore, the Court of Appeal held, in the 1987 case of *Chng Suan Tze v Minister for Home Affairs*, that '[a]ll power has legal limits and the rule of law demands that the courts should be able to examine the exercise of discretionary power'.[37] The Singapore High Court, in the later case of *Chan Hiang Leng Colin v Public Prosecutor*, further held that it had 'the power and duty to ensure that the provisions of the Constitution are observed' and 'to declare invalid any exercise of power, legislative and executive, which exceeds the limits of the power conferred by the Constitution, or which contravenes any prohibition which the Constitution provides'.[38] In the Sri Lanka case of *Liyanage v The Queen*,[39] the Judicial Committee of the Privy Council held that even though the Constitution did not explicitly confer judicial power on the courts, this did not mean that the courts could not exercise such a power. Such vesting was to be implied by studying the structure of the Constitution and understanding how power was distributed between the various branches of government.

Not all courts in Asia are final arbiters of constitutionality in their own states. The communist states – China, North Korea, Vietnam and Laos – reserve the final power of constitutional adjudication and review for the legislative branch of government. In Vietnam, for example, Article 91 of the 1992 Constitution as amended in December 2001 entrusts the Standing Committee of the National Assembly with the power to interpret the Constitution, laws and ordinances. Under Article 67 of China's Constitution, the Standing Committee of the NPC is responsible for interpreting the Constitution and supervising its enforcement. In Hong Kong, as a special administrative region of China, Article 158(1) of the Basic Law also gives the power of interpretation of the Basic Law to the Standing Committee of the NPC. Only through the authorisation of the Standing Committee of the NPC in Article 158(2) are the courts

---

[33] Ibid at 178 and 179.

[34] *Kesavananda v State of Kerala* [1973] AIR SC 1461.

[35] *Anwar Hossain Chowdhury v Bangladesh* [1989] BLD (Supplement) 1.

[36] It should be noted that even before the independence of Bangladesh from Pakistan, despite the silence of the 1962 Pakistani Constitution, the judicial review power of legislation and executive acts was already established in the case law, following mostly the Indian examples. See R Hoque, *Judicial Activism in Bangladesh: A Golden Mean Approach* (Newcastle upon Tyne: Cambridge Scholars Publishing, 2011) at 101.

[37] *Chng Suan Tze v Minister for Home Affairs* [1988] AIR 2 SLR(R) 525, para 86.

[38] *Chan Hiang Leng Colin v Public Prosecutor* [1994] AIR 3 SLR (R) 209, para 50.

[39] *Liyanage v The Queen* [1967] AC 259.

in Hong Kong, in adjudicating cases, granted the power to interpret the provisions of the Basic Law within the limits of Hong Kong's autonomy. The following cases illustrate the role played by China's NPC as final arbiter of constitutionality in the case of Hong Kong. The final case in this section, *Qi Yuling v Chen Xiaoqi et al* (1999), sees a rather more activist judiciary in China, purporting to interpret the Constitution. Several observers have argued that this case represents a nascent form of judicial review in China.

Ng Ka Ling & Others v Director of Immigration
[1999] 1 HKLRD 315 (Court of Final Appeal, Hong Kong)

Facts

The applicants were Chinese nationals born on the Mainland, and each had a parent who was a Hong Kong permanent resident. They entered Hong Kong on 1 July 1997, upon the handover of Hong Kong to China, otherwise than through an immigration control point. After their arrival in Hong Kong, they reported to the immigration authority to assert their right of abode. However, they were arrested and their assertions rejected by the immigration authority.

Article 24(3) of the Hong Kong Basic Law ('the Basic Law') provides that permanent residents have the right of abode in the Hong Kong Special Administrative Region (the Region). Article 24(2) sets out categories of permanent residents, the third category of which includes persons of Chinese nationality born outside Hong Kong to permanent residents. Yet the Immigration Ordinance stated that permanent residence could be established only by affixing a certificate of entitlement to a valid travel document. A notice was later issued that applications should be made to the Mainland administration, and under the law on the Mainland, Chinese citizens required exit approval to travel to and from Hong Kong.

The applicants maintained that they belonged in the third category of permanent residents in Article 24(2) and enjoyed the right of abode as conferred by Article 24(3). They instituted judicial review proceedings to quash the decisions by the immigration authority. The judge in the High Court held against the applicants, and the Court of Appeal affirmed the judge's decision. One of the main issues in this appeal was whether the said Ordinance was unconstitutional pursuant to Article 24 of the Basic Law.

In addition, Article 158 of the Basic Law stipulates that if the courts in adjudicating cases need to interpret the provisions concerning affairs that are the responsibility of the Central Government or concerning the relationship between the Central Authorities and the Region, a reference shall be made to seek an interpretation from the Standing Committee of the NPC through the Court of Final Appeal before the final judgment. Article 22(4), in Chapter II of the Basic Law regarding the relationship between the Central Authorities and the Region, does state that for entry into the Region, people from other parts of China must apply for approval, and the quota shall be determined by the competent authorities of the Central Government. Hence, regarding the assertion of the right of abode by the applicants, whether any reference should be made by the Court of Final Appeal also became a point of debate.

Andrew Li CJ

This judgment is the unanimous judgment of the Court . . .

Questions involving the proper interpretation of the Basic Law are before us for the first time. These are questions of momentous importance for both the future of the people involved as well as the development of constitutional jurisprudence in the new order . . .

The Region is vested with independent judicial power, including that of final adjudication (art 19(1)). The courts of the Region at all levels shall be the judiciary of the Region exercising the judicial power of the Region (art 80).

In exercising their judicial power conferred by the Basic Law, the courts of the Region have a duty to enforce and interpret that law. They undoubtedly have the jurisdiction to examine whether legislation enacted by the legislature of the Region or acts of the executive authorities of the Region are consistent with the Basic Law, and if found to be inconsistent, to hold them to be invalid. The exercise of this jurisdiction is a matter of obligation, not of discretion so that if inconsistency is established, the courts are bound to hold that a law or executive act is invalid at least to the extent of the inconsistency. Although this has not been questioned, it is right that we should take this opportunity of stating it unequivocally. In exercising this jurisdiction, the courts perform their constitutional role under the Basic Law of acting as a constitutional check on the executive and legislative branches of government to ensure that they act in accordance with the Basic Law.

What has been controversial is the jurisdiction of the courts of the Region to examine whether any legislative acts of the National People's Congress or its Standing Committee (which we shall refer to simply as 'acts') are consistent with the Basic Law and to declare them to be invalid if found to be inconsistent. In our view, the courts of the Region do have this jurisdiction and indeed the duty to declare invalidity if inconsistency is found. It is right that we should take this opportunity of stating so unequivocally.

Under the Chinese Constitution (arts 57 and 58), the National People's Congress is the highest organ of state power and its permanent body is the Standing Committee and they exercise the legislative powers of the state. So their acts are acts of the sovereign. The [jurisdictions] of the Region's courts to examine their acts to ensure consistency with the Basic Law is derived from the sovereign in that the National People's Congress had enacted pursuant to art 31 of the Chinese Constitution the Basic Law for the Region. The Basic Law is a national law and is the constitution of the Region.

Like other constitutions, it distributes and delimits powers, as well as providing for fundamental rights and freedoms. As with other constitutions, laws which are inconsistent with the Basic Law are of no effect and are invalid. Under it, the courts of the Region have independent judicial power within the high degree of autonomy conferred on the Region. It is for the courts of the Region to determine questions of inconsistency and invalidity when they arise. It is therefore for the courts of the Region to determine whether an act of the National People's Congress or its Standing Committee is inconsistent with the Basic Law, subject of course to the provisions of the Basic Law itself.

This proposition gains added strength from the circumstances that the Basic Law was enacted to implement China's basic policies regarding Hong Kong to remain unchanged for 50 years as declared and elaborated in the Joint Declaration. Article 159(4) of the Basic Law provides that no amendment thereto shall contravene the established basic policies. The jurisdiction to enforce and interpret the Basic Law necessarily entails the jurisdiction stated above over acts of the National People's Congress and its Standing Committee to ensure their consistency with the Basic Law . . .

Article 158(1) [of the Basic Law] provides that the power of interpretation of the Basic Law shall be vested in the Standing Committee of the National People's Congress. Article 158(2) provides that the Standing Committee 'shall authorize' the courts of the Region 'to interpret on their own, in adjudicating cases, the provisions of this Law which are within the limits of the autonomy of the Region'. It is clear, as is accepted by both counsel, that this contains the constitutional authorization. The words 'on their own', in our view, emphasize the high degree of autonomy of the Region and the independence of its courts.

But the jurisdiction of the courts of the Region is not limited to interpreting such provisions. For art 158(3) provides that the courts of the Region 'may also interpret other provisions' of the Basic Law in adjudicating cases.

But there is a limitation on this jurisdiction as far as the Court of Final Appeal is concerned. If the courts of the Region:

> in adjudicating cases, need to interpret the provisions of this Law concerning affairs which are the responsibility of the Central People's Government, or concerning the relationship between the Central Authorities and the Region, and if such interpretation will affect the judgments on the cases, the courts of the Region shall, before making their final judgments which are not appealable, seek an interpretation of the relevant provisions from the Standing Committee of the National People's Congress through the Court of Final Appeal of the Region.

Since it is the Court of Final Appeal which can make final judgments which are not appealable, this provision limits the Court of Final Appeal's jurisdiction. Where the conditions there prescribed are satisfied, the Court of Final Appeal has a duty to seek an interpretation of the relevant provisions from the Standing Committee.

Article 158(3) goes on to provide that when the Standing Committee makes an interpretation of the provisions concerned, 'the courts of the Region, in applying those provisions, shall follow the interpretation of the Standing Committee. However, judgments previously rendered shall not be affected'.

Article 158(4) obliges the Standing Committee to consult its Committee for the Basic Law before giving its decision on interpretation. This Committee was established by a decision of the National People's Congress on 4 April 1990. Under that decision, the Committee is a working committee under the Standing Committee. It consists of twelve members, six respectively from the Mainland and Hong Kong, including persons from the legal profession appointed by the Standing Committee. The Hong Kong members shall be nominated jointly by the Chief Executive, President of the Legislative Council and the Chief Justice of the Region.

Under art 158, the power of the Hong Kong courts to interpret provisions of the Basic Law is 'in adjudicating cases'. It follows that the courts have no such power when not engaged in adjudicating cases. This reflects the well established principle in our system that the courts' role is adjudicative and not advisory. The power of interpretation of the Region's courts is as follows. Article 158 refers to:

(a) The provisions which are within the Region's autonomy; and
(b) Other provisions of the Basic Law. Within such other provisions are the two excluded categories: provisions which (i) concern affairs which are the responsibility of the Central People's Government; or (ii) concern the relationship between the Central Authorities and the Region. We shall refer to the provisions in (i) or (ii) as 'the excluded provisions'.

Under Article 158, the lower courts have the power to interpret (a) and (b) including the excluded provisions. The Court of Final Appeal has the power to interpret (a) and also the other provisions in (b) except the excluded provisions.

Thus, there is no limitation on the power of the lower courts to interpret all the provisions of the Basic Law. The only limitation is on the jurisdiction of the Court of Final Appeal. The language of art 158(2) emphasizes the power of all courts of the Region to interpret 'on their own' provisions which are within the limits of the Region's autonomy.

As far as the Court of Final Appeal is concerned, it has a duty to make a reference to the Standing Committee if two conditions are satisfied:

(1) First, the provisions of the Basic Law in question (a) concern affairs which are the responsibility of the Central People's Government; or (b) concern the relationship between the Central Authorities and the Region. That is, the excluded provisions. We shall refer to this as 'the classification condition'.
(2) Secondly, the Court of Final Appeal in adjudicating the case needs to interpret such provisions (that is the excluded provisions) and such interpretation will affect the judgment on the case. We shall refer to this as 'the necessity condition.'

In our view, it is for the Court of Final Appeal and for it alone to decide, in adjudicating a case, whether both conditions are satisfied. It is for the Court, not the National People's Congress, to decide whether the classification condition is satisfied, that is, whether the provision is an excluded provision. This is accepted by both counsel for the applicants and counsel for the Director.

If the classification is not satisfied, that would be an end of the matter. Even if the Court needs to interpret the provisions concerned and the interpretation will affect the judgment on the case, the necessity condition could not be satisfied since the provision in question would not be an excluded provision.

If the classification condition is satisfied, it is again for the Court of Final Appeal alone to decide whether the necessity condition is met in the case concerned.

If the Court of Final Appeal is satisfied of both conditions, it would be obliged to seek an interpretation of the relevant excluded provisions from the Standing Committee. It is significant that what has to be referred to the Standing Committee is not the question of interpretation involved generally, but the interpretation of the specific excluded provisions . . .

It is, in our view, of considerable significance that Article158 requires a reference to the Standing Committee of the interpretation of the relevant excluded provisions only. The article does not require a reference of the question of interpretation involved generally when a number of provisions (including an excluded provision) may be relevant to provide the solution of that question.

Applying that test, in adjudicating this case, as a matter of substance, the predominant provision which we are interpreting is art 24, which provides for the right of abode of a permanent resident, and the content of that right. That article is the very source of the right which is sought to be enforced by the applicant in these appeals. That being so, the Court, in our view, does not have to make a reference, although art 22(4) is *arguably* relevant to the interpretation of art 24 . . .

On this issue [regarding the constitutionality of the Ordinance] the key question is whether art 22(4) qualifies the right of abode in art 24(3) . . .

We have concluded that having defined the class of permanent residents, a generous approach should be adopted to the interpretation of the constitutional provisions guaranteeing their rights. . . .

Article 24(3) confers the right of abode in unqualified terms on permanent residents. If the argument that art 22(4) qualifies the right of abode in art 24(3) is correct, the right of abode of persons who are undoubtedly permanent residents but who are residing on the Mainland is a most precarious one . . .

It follows that the No 3 Ordinance is unconstitutional to the extent that it requires permanent residents of the Region residing on the Mainland to hold the one way permit before they can enjoy the constitutional right of abode.

Ng Ka Ling & Others v Director of Immigration (No 2)
[1999] 1 HKC 425 (Court of Final Appeal, Hong Kong)

Facts

After the Court of Final Appeal rendered the judgment in *Ng Ka Ling & Others v Director of Immigration* on 29 January 1999, a great deal of tension arose as regards the relationship between the Region and the Central Authorities. Both governments were worried about the estimated influx – from hundreds of thousands to even millions – of children from Mainland China to Hong Kong. Soon after the release of the judgment, the Hong Kong Government unprecedentedly requested the Court of Final Appeal for a clarification of its decision.

Li CJ

This is the unanimous judgment of the Court.

On 29 January 1999, the Court gave judgment in these appeals. On 24 February 1999, the Director of Immigration filed a notice of motion applying for clarification of that part of the judgment which relates to the National People's Congress and its Standing Committee. The ground stated in the motion is that the matter is of great constitutional, public and general importance.

This application invites the Court to take an exceptional course. After a judgment is given, it is for the public and the legal profession to consider that judgment. Where appropriate, the Court can be asked to consider it in a subsequent case. However, we are faced with an exceptional situation. Various different interpretations have been put on the part of the Court's judgment referred to in the motion and this has given rise to much controversy.

Having regard to these circumstances and the limitations on the proper exercise of judicial power, we are prepared to take the exceptional course under our inherent jurisdiction of stating the following.

The courts' judicial power is derived from the Basic Law. Article 158(1) vests the power of interpretation of the Basic Law in the Standing Committee. The courts' jurisdiction to interpret the Basic Law in adjudicating cases is derived by authorization from the Standing Committee under Articles 158(2) and 158(3). In our judgment on 29 January 1999, we said that the Court's jurisdiction to enforce and interpret the Basic Law is derived from and is subject to the provisions of the Basic Law which provisions include the foregoing.

The Court's judgment on 29 January 1999 did not question the authority of the Standing Committee to make an interpretation under Article 158 which would have to be followed by the courts of the Region. The Court accepts that it cannot question that authority. Nor did the Court's judgment question, and the Court accepts that it cannot question, the authority of the National People's Congress or the Standing Committee to do any act which is in accordance with the provisions of the Basic Law and the procedure therein.

The Interpretation by the Standing Committee of the National People's Congress of Articles 22(4) and 24(2)(3) of the Basic Law of the Hong Kong Special Administrative Region of the People's Republic of China
26 June 1999 (The Standing Committee of the Ninth National People's Congress, China)

Facts

The heated debate on *Ng Ka Ling & Others v Director of Immigration* continued even after the above clarification issued by the Court of Final Appeal. The Chief Executive, pursuant to his power vested by Articles 43 and 48(2) of the Basic Law that charged him with the responsibility for the implementation of the Basic Law and other laws in the Region, decided to seek an interpretation from the Standing Committee of the NPC. A report was sent to the State Council on the Mainland by the Chief Executive, and its assistance requested in seeking interpretation from the Standing Committee. Having studied the report, the State Council made a request to the Standing Committee for an interpretation.

Held

The Standing Committee of the Ninth National People's Congress examined at its Tenth Session the 'Motion Regarding the Request for an Interpretation of Articles 22(4) and 24(2)(3) of the Basic Law of the Hong Kong Special Administrative Region of the People's Republic of China' submitted by the State Council. The motion of the State Council was submitted upon the report furnished by the Chief Executive of [the Region] under the relevant provisions of Articles 43 and 48(2) of the Basic Law of the Hong Kong Special Administrative Region of the People's Republic of China. The issue raised in the Motion concerns the interpretation of the relevant provisions of the Basic Law of the Hong Kong Special Administrative Region of the People's Republic of China by the Court of Final Appeal of the Hong Kong Special Administrative Region in its judgment dated 29 January 1999. Those relevant provisions concern affairs which are the responsibility of the Central People's Government and concern the relationship between the Central Authorities and the Hong Kong Special Administrative Region. Before making its judgment, the Court of Final Appeal had not sought an interpretation of the Standing Committee of the National People's Congress in compliance with the requirement of Article 158(3) of the Basic Law of the Hong Kong Special Administrative Region of the People's Republic of China. Moreover, the interpretation of the Court of Final Appeal is not consistent with the legislative intent. Therefore, having consulted the Committee for the Basic Law of the Hong Kong Special Administrative Region under the Standing Committee of the National People's Congress, the Standing Committee of the National People's Congress has decided to make, under the provisions of Article 67(4) of the Constitution of the People's Republic of China and Article 158(1) of the Basic Law of the Hong Kong Special Administrative Region of the People's Republic of China, an interpretation of the provisions of Articles 22(4) and 24(2)(3) of the Basic Law of the Hong Kong Special Administrative Region of the People's Republic of China as follows:

1. The provisions of Article 22(4) of the Basic Law of the Hong Kong Special Administrative Region of the People's Republic of China regarding 'For entry into the Hong Kong Special Administrative Region, people from other parts of China must apply for approval' mean as follows: People from all provinces, autonomous regions, or municipalities directly under the Central Government, including those persons of Chinese nationality born outside Hong Kong of Hong Kong permanent residents, who wish to enter the Hong Kong Special Administrative Region for whatever reason, must apply to the relevant authorities of their residential districts for approval in accordance with the relevant national laws and administrative regulations, and must hold valid documents issued by the relevant authorities before they can enter the Hong Kong Special Administrative Region. It is unlawful for people from all provinces, autonomous regions, or municipalities directly under the Central Government, including persons of Chinese nationality born outside Hong Kong of Hong Kong permanent residents, to enter the Hong Kong Special Administrative Region without complying with the appropriate approval procedure prescribed by the relevant national laws and administrative regulations.

2. It is stipulated in the first three categories of Article 24(2) of the Basic Law of the Hong Kong Special Administrative Region of the People's Republic of China that the 'permanent residents of the Hong Kong Special Administrative Region shall be:

    (1) Chinese citizens born in Hong Kong before or after the establishment of the Hong Kong Special Administrative Region;
    (2) Chinese citizens who have ordinarily resided in Hong Kong for a continuous period of not less than seven years before or after the establishment of the Hong Kong Special Administrative Region;
    (3) Persons of Chinese nationality born outside Hong Kong of those residents listed in categories (1) and (2).'

The provisions of category (3) regarding the 'persons of Chinese nationality born outside Hong Kong of those residents listed in categories (1) and (2)' mean both parents of such persons, whether born before or after the establishment of the Hong Kong Special Administrative Region, or either of such parents must have fulfilled the condition prescribed by category (1) or (2) of Article 24(2) of the Basic Law of the Hong Kong Special Administrative Region of the People's Republic of China at the time of their birth. The legislative intent as stated by this Interpretation, together with the legislative intent of all other categories of Article 24(2) of the Basic Law of the Hong Kong Special Administrative Region of the People's Republic of China, have been reflected in the 'Opinions on the Implementation of Article 24(2) of the Basic Law of the Hong Kong Special Administrative Region of the People's Republic of China' adopted at the Fourth Plenary Meeting of the Preparatory Committee for the Hong Kong Special Administrative Region of the National People's Congress on 10 August 1996.

As from the promulgation of this Interpretation, the courts of the Hong Kong Special Administrative Region, when referring to the relevant provisions of the Basic Law of the Hong Kong Special Administrative Region of the People's Republic of China, shall adhere to this Interpretation. This Interpretation does not affect the right of abode in the Hong Kong Special Administrative Region which has been acquired under the judgment of the Court of Final Appeal on the relevant cases dated 29 January 1999 by the parties concerned in the relevant legal proceedings. Other than that, the question whether any other person fulfils the conditions prescribed by Article 24(2)(3) of the Basic Law of the Hong Kong Special Administrative Region of the People's Republic of China shall be determined by reference to this Interpretation.

Director of Immigration v Chong Fung Yuen
[2001] 2 HKLRD 533 (Court of Final Appeal, Hong Kong)

Facts

The applicant, Chong Fung Yuen, was a Chinese citizen born in Hong Kong on 29 September 1997. When he was born, his parents were not permanent residents of Hong Kong but were in Hong Kong lawfully with two-way permits from the Mainland. Chong Fung Yuen then claimed to be a permanent resident, and to enjoy the right of abode based on Article 24 of the Basic Law. However, his application was rejected by the immigration authority on the ground that neither of his parents was settled or had the right of abode in Hong Kong at the time of his birth or at any later time.

Article 24(3) of the Basic Law provides that permanent residents have the right of abode in the Hong Kong Special Administrative Region ('the Region'). Article 24(2)(1) states that Chinese citizens born in Hong Kong before or after the establishment of the Region are permanent residents. However, the Immigration Ordinance requires that for a Chinese citizen born in Hong Kong to be a permanent resident, one of his parents must have been settled or had the right of abode in Hong Kong at the time of his birth or at any later time.

The applicant, Chong Fung Yuen, sued against the immigration authority. The judge in the High Court held in his favour, ruling that the impugned provision of the Immigration Ordinance was inconsistent with Article 24(2)(1) of the Basic Law. The Court of Appeal affirmed that decision. Aside from the issue regarding constitutionality of the Ordinance, two other issues were also critical. First was whether the Interpretation made by the Standing Committee of the National People's Congress regarding Article 22(4) and Article 24(2)(3) of the Basic Law on 26 June 1999 should apply in this case. Second was whether the Court of Final Appeal should make a reference pursuant to Article 158(3) if relevant provisions in the present case were concerned with the affairs that are the responsibility of the Central Government or concerning the relationship between the Central Authority and the Region.

Andrew Li CJ

This is the unanimous judgment of the Court . . .

[W]here the Standing Committee has made an interpretation of the Basic Law pursuant to its power under Article 67(4) of the Chinese Constitution and art 158 of the Basic Law, the courts of Hong Kong are under a duty to follow it. The Court so held in *Lau Kong Yung* where the Court stated that the Standing Committee's power of interpretation of the Basic Law under art 158(1) originating from the Chinese Constitution 'is in general and unqualified terms'. In particular, that power of the Standing Committee extends to every provision in the Basic Law and is not limited to the excluded provisions referred to in art 158(3).

Equally, where the Standing Committee makes an interpretation of an excluded provision pursuant to a judicial reference from the Court under art 158(3), the courts in Hong Kong in applying the provisions concerned shall follow the Standing Committee's interpretation, although judgments previously rendered shall not be affected. This is expressly provided for in art 158(3).

The Standing Committee's power to interpret the Basic Law is derived from the Chinese Constitution and the Basic Law. In interpreting the Basic Law, the Standing Committee functions under a system which is different from the system in Hong Kong. As has been pointed out, under the Mainland system, legislative interpretation by the Standing Committee can clarify or supplement laws. Where the Standing Committee makes an interpretation of a provision of the Basic Law, whether under art 158(1) which relates to any provision, or under art 158(3) which relates to the excluded provisions, the courts in Hong Kong are bound to follow it. Thus, the authority of the Standing Committee to interpret the Basic Law is fully acknowledged and respected in the Region. This is the effect of the Basic Law implementing the 'one country, two systems' principle as was held by the Court in *Lau Kong Yung*. Both systems being within one country, the Standing Committee's interpretation made in conformity with art 158 under a different system is binding in and part of the system in the Region.

As has been pointed out, the Director accepts that the Standing Committee has not issued an interpretation of art 24(2)(1) which is binding on the courts in Hong Kong. He accepts that the statement in the Interpretation that 'together with the legislative intent of all other categories of art 242 . . . have been reflected' in the Opinions of the Preparatory

Committee on the implementation of art 24(2) of the Basic Law does not amount to a binding interpretation of art 24(2)(1). If there were such a binding interpretation, the courts in Hong Kong would be under a duty to follow it . . .

As was held in *Ng Ka Ling*, the Court is required to make a judicial reference under art 158(3) where both the classification and necessity conditions are satisfied. Here, as is common ground between the Director and the respondent, the necessity condition is satisfied. . . . The issue is whether the classification condition is satisfied . . .

Article 24(2)(1) prescribes the category of Chinese citizens born in Hong Kong before or after 1 July 1997 to be permanent residents. Its character is that of a provision defining one category of permanent residents who are entitled to the right of abode. In our view, having regard to its character, art 24(2)(1) does not concern affairs which are the responsibility of the Central People's Government or the relationship between the Central Authorities and the Region. It is a provision within the Region's autonomy and is not an excluded provision. Accordingly, a judicial reference to the Standing Committee is not required . . .

As discussed above, on the common law approach, the Court's task is to construe the language in art 24(2)(1) in the light of its context and purpose in order to ascertain *the legislative intent as expressed in the language*. As concluded earlier, the meaning of art 24(2) (1) is clear; there is no ambiguity. It means Chinese citizens born in Hong Kong before or after 1 July 1997. In conformity with the common law, the Court is unable, on the basis of the statement in question, to depart from what is considers to be the clear meaning of art 24(2)(1) in favour of a meaning which the language cannot bear.

Qi Yuling v Chen Xiaoqi et al
[1999] Lu Min Zhong No 258, 13 Aug 2001
(Higher People's Court of Shandong Province, China)

Facts

The applicant was accepted by a business school after taking an exam. However, because of a fraudulent act committed by the defendants, one of the defendants, Chen Xiaoqi, was able to enter the business school by using the name of the applicant. The applicant filed a suit against the defendants, claiming that they had violated her right to her name as well as her right to education protected by Article 46(1) of the Constitution of the People's Republic of China. She requested the court to award her compensatory damages. The defendant, Chen Xiaoqi, asserted that the applicant gave up the chance to go to school, and that since the right to education was not a civil right listed in the General Principles of Civil Law, the claim of the applicant was without any legal merit.

The judgment of the Intermediate Court confirmed that the right of name of the applicant was violated. However, the Intermediate Court affirmed that the applicant gave up the chance to go to school, and thus there was no violation of her right to education. The applicant appealed to the Higher Court of Shandong Province, asserting that she failed to go to school due to the fraudulent act committed by the defendants, and her right to education was indeed violated. The Higher Court found the fact in favour of the applicant, but had doubts on the application of law and thus made a request to the Supreme People's Court for interpretation.

According to Article 33 of the Organic Law of the People's Court, the Supreme People's Court may issue interpretations on questions concerning specific application of laws and decrees in judicial proceedings. In response to the request made by the Higher Court of

Shandong Province, the Supreme People's Court rendered the interpretation in 2001 ([2001] *Law Interpretation No 25*):

> Your inquiry in [1999] Lu Min Zhong No 258 'Concerning Qi Yuling v Chen Xiaoqi, Chen Kezheng, Jining City Business School in Shandong, the Eighth Middle School of Tengzhou, Shandong, and the Education Committee of Tengzhou, Shandong over a Dispute on Personal Name' was received. Given the facts in this case, we believe that, by means of infringing on Qi Yuling's right to select and use her own name, Chen Xiaoqi et al have violated Qi Yuling's fundamental constitutional right to education and have caused actual damages. Therefore, Chen Xiaoqi et al should bear corresponding civil liability.

Upon this interpretation, the Higher People's Court of Shandong Province made a decision on Qi Yuling's case.

Held

After passing her preliminary exam, appellant Qi Yuling filled out a form to express her willingness to accept student traineeship. She was assigned to take the entrance exam for both regular students and student trainees. This shows that she did have a desire to become a student trainee.

Appellee Chen Kezheng claimed that Qi Yuling was assigned to take the entrance exam for regular students and student trainees, because he provided the letter of recommendation and the training contract. However, there is no evidence to support his claim. Even if this was indeed the case, because of the illegal nature of Chen Kezheng's action, it still should be recognized that Qi Yuling filled out a form to express her desire to accept student traineeship of her own will. Chen Kezheng's claim that Qi Yuling gave up her right to becoming a trainee cannot be supported. Qi Yuling's test score exceeded the cut off score for student trainees. Appellee Jining Business School accepted her and sent her the admission letter. Because appellee Tengzhou Eighth Middle School failed to notify Qi Yuling personally of her score and the cut off score for acceptance as student trainees, and because it handed the admission letter to appellee Chen Xiaoqi, who picked it up in Qi Yuling's name, Chen Xiaoqi was able to steal the identity of Qi Yuling under a carefully crafted scheme orchestrated by Chen Kezheng. Also, because Jining Business School failed to carefully examine the paperwork of incoming students, Chen Xiaoqi was able to get accepted without showing a valid test registration ticket and other documentation. This failure allowed Chen Xiaoqi to attend school under a stolen identity and caused Qi Yuling to lose her opportunity to become a student trainee. After Chen Xiaoqi attended school under a stolen identity, appellee Tengzhou Education Committee helped Chen Kezheng forge a physical exam chart. Tengzhou Eighth Middle School assisted Chen Kezheng to forge a semester-by-semester performance review sheet. In violation of its file management procedure, Jining Business School allowed Chen Xiaoqi to gain access to her own file. This provided Chen Kezheng an opportunity to switch the records to enable Chen Xiaoqi not only to attend school under a false identity but also to work under a stolen identity. It enabled the violation of rights to continue. This violation was a result of deliberate acts committed by Chen Xiaoqi, Chen Kezheng, Tengzhou Eighth Middle School, and Tengzhou Education Committee and by the negligence of Jining Business School. These acts constituted a violation of Qi Yuling's right to her own name on the surface. In essence, it also violated the basic right to education granted to every citizen by the constitution of the People's Republic of China, including Qi Yuling. Therefore, each appellee should be held civilly liable for the consequences of their violation . . .

Aftermath of the Case

After the *Qi Yuling* case, there were a few cases in which claimants utilised constitutional provisions to claim for their rights violations. Few cases, however, were decided in favour of claimants on constitutional grounds. Most discussions were conducted within academic circles. In 2008, the Supreme People's Court issued an opinion stating that the judicial interpretation on the *Qi Yuling* case ceased to apply ([2008] *Law Interpretation No 15*). For further discussions on the subsequent development of the *Qi Yuling* case and its suspension, see Qianfan Zhang, 'A Constitution without Constitutionalism? The Path of Constitutional Development in China' (2010) 8(4) *I•CON* 960.

Notes and Questions

1.   What may we learn from the *Qi Yuling* case? To what extent can courts under a model of parliamentary supremacy still assert constitutional interpretative authority in adjudicating individual claims? In what ways may the interpretive power struggles presented in the series of cases with *Ng Ka Ling & Others* by the Hong Kong Court of Final Appeal and the interpretations by the Standing Committee of the NPC in China shed some light on such a question? Can the tension between the inherent power of judicial review derived from a written constitution and the interpretive power expressively assigned to the political institution be resolved or ameliorated? How?

2.   Are there alternative models to parliamentary supremacy or judicial supremacy? Based on recent developments in Canada, New Zealand or the United Kingdom with regard to the Human Rights Act, Stephen Gardbaum suggests a third model, in which the courts exercise the power to assess legislation for consistency with the Constitution or Bill of Rights while Parliament retains the final say on the validity of those statutes. Under this model, judicial declarations of constitutional inconsistency of statutes do not render the law void but merely put pressure on the legislature to amend the law (or even the constitution), thus maintaining sovereignty and supremacy in the legislature. One example of such a model is Section 33 of the Canadian Charter of Rights and Freedoms, which permits federal and provincial legislatures to declare – by an ordinary majority vote – that a statute shall continue to operate for a renewable period of five years even when it is found to be inconsistent with the rights and freedoms guaranteed by the Charter. In New Zealand, the Bill of Rights Act requires courts to interpret statutes consistently with the rights and freedoms contained in the Bill. However, it expressly rejects the notion that courts may invalidate or deny operative effect to any statute. In the United Kingdom, the Human Rights Act also obligates the courts to interpret laws consistently with the protected rights 'so far as it is possible to do so'. Where this is not possible, higher courts are empowered to issue a declaration of incompatibility, which does not affect the validity of the statute. See S Gardbaum, 'Reassessing the New Commonwealth Model of Constitutionalism' (2010) 8(2) *I•CON* 167.

3.   Another option is to create a constitutional court and entrust it – rather than all courts – with exclusive powers of constitutional interpretation and statutory

invalidation. According to Donald P Kommers, 'Kelsen's model [of constitutional review] distinguished itself from the British/Commonwealth and American models' in the presence of two paramount features, including '(a) the specialization of constitutional review, to be handled by distinct constitutional courts or special chambers of the highest appellate court; and (b) recognition of the political nature of constitutional review by, *inter alia*, making judicial appointments more overtly political'. Usually, justices of constitutional courts are appointed differently from those of ordinary courts with stronger parliamentary influence, and they may come from outside the judiciary, such as from ministers, parliamentarians or law professors. See DP Kommers, 'An Introduction to the Federal Constitutional Court' (2001) 2 *German Law Journal*, available at <http://www.germanlawjournal. com/ article.php?id=19> (accessed 2 March 2013).

4.   The majority of Asian constitutions embrace judicial review based on the supremacy of the constitution. Interestingly, a few jurisdictions choose to entrust the constitutional court with the power to invalidate legislation if constitutional inconsistency is found. The discussion of this choice and institutional design is included in section III. below. An interesting device exists in the 1992 Constitution of Mongolia to ameliorate the tension between judicial and parliamentary supremacy. Article 65 of the Constitution obliges the Constitutional Court to submit its conclusion on the constitutionality of laws to the Parliament. If the conclusion is not accepted by the Parliament, the Constitutional Court must re-examine it and render a final decision. If the Constitutional Court still finds the laws incompatible with the Constitution, they will be invalidated.

5.   In *Ng Ka Ling & Others*, the Court of Final Appeal in Hong Kong asserts two categories of judicial review power based on the Basic Law. The first category is the judicial power to examine whether legislative or executive acts are consistent with the Basic Law and to hold them invalid if inconsistent. The second – and more controversial – category of judicial review is the power of the Hong Kong courts to determine if an act of the NPC or its Standing Committee is inconsistent with the Basic Law. According to the Court of Final Appeal, the second category of powers is derived from the supremacy of the Basic Law in Hong Kong and the high degree of autonomy conferred on the Region, under which the courts in Hong Kong are to determine questions of inconsistency of any law with the Basic Law and invalidity of any law when they arise.

     This second proposition has generated a great deal of debate and political tension between China and Hong Kong. Article 67 of the PRC Constitution empowers the NPC Standing Committee to interpret the Constitution and supervise its enforcement. Even though the Basic Law is effectively Hong Kong's Constitution, it is technically a mere statutory product of the NPC. Article 158(1) of the Basic Law vests the power of interpreting the Basic Law in the NPC Standing Committee, and the Hong Kong courts' power of interpretation is a delegated power under Article 158(2). Doubts thus arise as to whether the courts in Hong Kong may review acts by the NPC or its Standing Committee, regarding their consistency with the Basic Law. For a comprehensive presentation of arguments from both sides, see Wenmin Chen, Hualing Fu and Yash P Ghai, *Hong Kong's Constitutional Debate: Conflicts over Interpretation* (Hong Kong: Hong Kong University Press, 2000).

6.   To date, the NPC Standing Committee has made four interpretations of the Basic
     Law. The first interpretation was issued in 1999 in response to the request made by
     Chief Executive Tung Chee Hwa following the decision of the Court of Final
     Appeal in *Ng Ka Ling & Others*. The second was in 2004, and related to methods
     for selecting the Chief Executive in 2007 and the Legislative Council in 2008. The
     third was in 2005 and concerned the term of office of Chief Executive Tung Chee
     Hwa's successor, since Tung resigned two years before the end of his term. None
     of these interpretations was made pursuant to Article 158(3) of the Basic Law,
     which obliges the Court of Final Appeal to make a reference to the NPC Standing
     Committee for an interpretation if such interpretation 'concern[s] affairs which
     are the responsibility of the Central Government, or concern[s] the relationship
     between the Central Authorities and the Region [HKSAR], and if such interpreta-
     tion will affect the judgments on the cases'.

     The fourth interpretation issued by the NPC Standing Committee on 26 August
     2011 was the only one made in response to a reference by the Court of Final
     Appeal under Article 158(3). In *Democratic Republic of Congo v FG Hemisphere
     Associates LLC*,[40] the Court of Final Appeal had to consider whether it should
     follow the Central Government's doctrine of absolute immunity for foreign sover-
     eigns, or whether it could adopt the common law doctrine of restrictive immunity.
     What was significant in this reference was that while requesting an interpretation
     from the NPC Standing Committee, the majority of the Court rendered a provi-
     sional judgment, expressing its views on the issue. According to Albert HY Chen,

     > the advantage of this approach is that it enables the [Court's] views on the interpretive
     > questions referred to the [NPC Standing Committee] to be made known to and considered
     > by the [NPC Standing Committee] as it proceeds to work out the answers to the questions.
     > . . . On the other hand, this approach is not without possible disadvantages and risks.
     > . . . The possible advantage of the [Court] . . . keeping silent on, and remaining 'neutral'
     > on, how the provision should be interpreted is that the Hong Kong court would not
     > assume any responsibility for the interpretation of the provisions.

     In the end, the NPC Standing Committee's interpretation was consistent with that
     expressed by the majority in the *Congo* case. See AHY Chen, 'The Congo Case'
     (2011) 41(2) *Hong Kong Law Journal* 371. For a collection of scholarly articles
     addressing issues on this reference, see (2011) 41 *Hong Kong Law Journal*, pt II,
     'Focus'.

7.   Lawyers understand judicial review as a necessary consequence of constitutional
     supremacy, but scholars of law and politics or law and society take a different
     view. For them, judges' constitutional authority to review popularly enacted laws
     is puzzling. Why would any self-interested politician accept this limit to the writ-
     ing of the constitution? Even in a parliamentary supremacy, parliament cannot
     bind its successors since its freedom to legislate cannot be limited or encumbered
     by anything previous parliaments have done. Why would any parliament restrain
     itself and its successors by institutionalising judicial review?

8.   Ginsburg argues that legislators' acceptance of limits on power is motivated by the
     buying of political insurance for the future. When constitutions are being drafted,

---

[40] *Democratic Republic of Congo v FG Hemisphere Associates LLC* [2011] 4 HKC 151.

political parties may view their post-constitutional options or positions differently. If they think their chances of winning elections are not high, they may prefer to establish minoritarian – rather than majoritarian – institutions to protect their prospective political interests and to place constraints on the majorities. These minoritarian devices as pre-commitment strategies also facilitate constitutional transactions. They help make possible constitutional bargains that might not otherwise occur. When political parties negotiate the constitution, they cannot accurately predict what their political position will be in post-constitutional politics, nor do they necessarily trust each other. Thus, it is in their self-interest to accede to these minoritarian devices, which can mitigate and check the party which wins the post-constitutional elections. See T Ginsburg, *Judicial Review in New Democracies: Constitutional Courts in Asian Cases* (New York: Cambridge University Press, 2003) at 25–26.

9. Hirschl offers another explanation. Based upon constitutional transitions in Canada, South Africa, New Zealand and Israel, he argues that the recent enhancement of judicial power is a result of 'hegemonic self-preservation'. To political actors, institutions such as judicial review put limits on their decision-making powers. Hegemonic elites support these institutions because the future opportunity cost is less than the limits imposed by the new institutional structure on rival political elements. See R Hirschl, *Towards Juristocracy: The Origins and Consequences of New Constitutionalism* (Cambridge, Mass: Harvard University Press, 2004) at 11.

10. Tate identifies eight conditions that facilitate the expansion of judicial power:

    (a) democracy;
    (b) separation of powers;
    (c) the politics of rights;
    (d) interest group use of the courts;
    (e) opposition use of the court;
    (f) ineffective majoritarian institutions;
    (g) perceptions of policy-making institutions; and
    (h) wilful delegation by majoritarian institutions.

    See C Neal Tate, 'Why the Expansion of Judicial Power' in C Neal Tate and T Vallinder (eds), *The Global Expansion of Judicial Power* (New York: New York University Press, 1995) 28–33. Among these conditions, separation of powers – both vertical and horizontal – and the politics of rights are most common in explaining the rise of judicial power. For further readings on judicialisation and constitutionalism, see M Shapiro and A Stone Sweet (eds), *On Law, Politics & Judicialization* (Oxford: Oxford University Press, 2002).

III. INSTITUTIONAL DESIGN OF JUDICIAL REVIEW

Two primary models of judicial review are adopted across Asia: the centralised model, with the creation of a constitutional court, and the decentralised model, with diffused exercise of judicial review at all levels of the court system. The former model has been adopted in Taiwan (in 1947), South Korea (1987), Mongolia (1992), Cambodia (1993), Thailand (1997), Indonesia (2001) and Myanmar (2008). The latter prevails in the jurisdictions that have experienced British colonial rule or American occupations: India, Pakistan, Bangladesh, Japan, Hong Kong, Malaysia, Philippines and Singapore. It is worth noting that Sri Lanka briefly adopted the constitutional court in its 1972 Constitution, but replaced it with a decentralised system in its 1978 Constitution.[41]

A. The Centralised Model: Constitutional Court

The first constitutional court in Asia was Taiwan's Constitutional Court, known as the Council of Grand Justices prior to 1993.[42] It was provided for in the 1947 Republic of China Constitution and formally established in 1948, four years earlier than the German Constitutional Court formed in 1952. Yet Taiwan's Constitutional Court did not become an effective judicial institution until the lifting of the Martial Law Decree in 1987.[43] Other Asian constitutional courts were all created in the context of democratisation and constitutional reforms in the late 1980s and early 1990s after the end of the Cold War.[44] South Korea established the Constitutional Court in its 1987 Constitution. The Constitutional Court (*Undsen Huuliin Tset*) of Mongolia was provided for in its 1992 Constitution. Cambodia's Constitutional Council was stipulated in the new Constitution of 1993 and began functioning in 1998. The Thai Constitutional Court was first established in the 1997 Constitution and was an influential institution for some time, as it was vested with the powers to resolve jurisdictional disputes among government authorities and to dissolve unconstitutional political parties, aside from constitutional interpretation. The 2007 Constitution – drafted after the 2006 coup – retained the Constitutional Court with minor alterations in the jurisdictions and the composition of justices. Indonesia began reforming its 1945 Constitution in 1999, and its 2001 constitutional revision created the Constitutional Court (*Mahkamah Konstitusi*) that began functioning in 2003. The most recent creation is the Constitutional Tribunal stipulated in the 2008 Constitution of Myanmar, which rendered its first interpretation in 2011.

i. Primary Jurisdictions

Constitutional courts are typically created to review the constitutionality of parliamentary or executive enactments, and to resolve competence disputes between central

---

[41] Jayampathy Wickramaratne, *Fundamental Rights in Sri Lanka*, 2nd edn (Pannipitiya: Stamford Lake, 2007) 66–67.

[42] The official English website of the Constitutional Court in Taiwan may be found at <http://www.judicial.gov.tw/constitutionalcourt/EN/p01_03.asp>.

[43] Wen-Chen Chang, 'The Role of Judicial Review in Consolidating Democracy: The Case of Taiwan' (2005) 2 *Asia Law Review* 73; Ginsburg, above n 16, ch 5, 'Confucian Constitutionalism? The Grand Justices of the Republic of China' at 106–57.

[44] For further readings of the constitutional courts in Asia, see B Dressel, *The Judicialization of Politics in Asia* (New York: Routledge, 2012); Ginsburg, above n 16; C Hill and J Menzel (eds), *Constitutionalism in Southeast Asia* (Singapore: Konrad-Adenauer-Stiftung Publisher, 2008); C Dürkop and Yap Hui Bin, *Present Status and Future Development of Constitutional Jurisdiction in Asia* (Singapore: Konrad-Adenauer-Stiftung Publisher, 2004).

and local governments or between government agencies.[45] Reviews by constitutional courts are often conducted *in abstracto* through petitions from the president, prime minister, parliament or other central or local government organs rather than through *cases or controversies* arising from courts. Table 5.2 illustrates four primary types of constitutional review by the constitutional courts in Asia. Aside from these primary jurisdictions, constitutional courts may also be provided with ancillary powers such as adjudication of impeachments, dissolution of political parties, referendum or electoral disputes. These will be discussed below.

Table 5.2 Primary Jurisdictions of Constitutional Courts in Asia

Constitutional Court	Primary Jurisdictions			
	Abstract Review	Concrete Review	Individual Complaint	Competence Dispute
Taiwan (1947)	O	O (1995)	O	O
South Korea (1987)		O	O	O
Mongolia (1992)	O		△*	O
Cambodia (1993)	O	O		O
Thailand (1997)	O	O	O (2007)	O
Indonesia (2001)	O		O	O
Myanmar (2008)	O	O		O

* Mongolian individual complaints differ from others in that citizens may petition on matters concerning unconstitutionality of a law but not on matters immediately concerning their own rights.

With respect to primary jurisdiction, all seven constitutional courts in Asia have jurisdiction over competence disputes. With the exception of the South Korean Constitutional Court, all courts have jurisdiction over abstract review of the constitutionality of statutes through petitions from central or local government agencies. Not all constitutional courts have jurisdiction of concrete review under which requests for constitutional review are brought by other courts, or jurisdiction of individual complaints, in which the request for constitutional review is brought by individuals.

a. Abstract Review

In *abstract review*, courts review the constitutionality of parliamentary enactments upon request from institutions such as the president, parliament (or parliamentary minority), prime minister, attorney-general, government agencies, local governments, ombudsman and national human rights commissions, among others. The exercise of abstract review usually takes place after laws have been passed (*ex post*), but may also occur prior to their promulgation (*ex ante*).

---

[45] For discussion of the jurisdictions of constitutional court based on the European model, see DP Kommers, *The Constitutional Jurisprudence of the Federal Republic of Germany*, 2nd edn (Durham, NC: Duke University Press, 1997) 10–15.

Abstract review is a common jurisdiction possessed by constitutional courts in Asia, except for the South Korean Constitutional Court. Article 111 of the South Korean Constitution confers on the Constitutional Court jurisdiction over:

(a) the constitutionality of a law upon the request of courts;
(b) impeachment;
(c) dissolution of a political party; and
(d) competence disputes between state agencies.

There is no abstract review.[46] Central or local government agencies may make requests to the Constitutional Court only if there is a dispute in competence granted by the Constitution or laws.[47]

In Taiwan, abstract review may be requested by any constitutional organ or government agency, such as the President, the executive, the legislature or one-third of the legislative members if they have doubts over the interpretation of constitutional provisions or the constitutionality of relevant laws or regulations.[48]

Article 66(2) of the Constitution in Mongolia provides the Constitutional Court with the jurisdiction to review the conformity of laws, decrees and other decisions by the Parliament and the President, as well as government decisions or international treaties signed by Mongolia. Requests for reviews may come from Parliament (the State Great Hural), the President, the minister or the prosecutor general under Article 66(1). Judicial deference to the legislature is constitutionally embedded, in that a decision of unconstitutionality must be sent to Parliament for acceptance. If it is not accepted, the Constitutional Court shall re-examine it and make a final decision, which shall become binding.[49]

Cambodia's Constitutional Council, which is partly influenced by the French practice of preliminary review, exercises abstract review both *ex ante* and *ex post*. Articles 140 and 141 of the Constitution state that the King, the Prime Minister, the President of the National Assembly, one-tenth of the members of the National Assembly, the President of the Senate and one-quarter of the members of the Senate may send drafts or laws by the National Assembly for constitutional review before, as well as after, promulgation. After promulgation of a law, citizens may also make a constitutional appeal against that law through their representative in the National Assembly or the Senate, or through the President of the National Assembly or Senate.

Both the 1997 and 2007 Thai Constitutions provide for abstract review. Like Cambodia, abstract review is provided both *ex ante* and *ex post*. The 2007 Constitution obliges the Constitutional Court to review the constitutionality of the drafts of the listed 'organic acts' prior to promulgation. These 'organic acts' include acts relating to the election of members of the House of Representatives and the Senate, the Election Commission, political parties, referenda, the procedure of the Constitutional Court, criminal procedures for holders of political positions, acts dealing with ombudsmen,

---

[46] Korean constitutional law scholars have suggested the addition of abstract review modelled on the French style of *ex ante* review or the German style of *ex post* abstract norm control into the Constitutional Court's jurisdictions. See eg Jongcheol Kim, 'The Structure and Basic Principles of Constitutional Adjudication in the Republic of Korea' in Kuk Cho (ed), *Litigation in Korea* (Northampton: Edward Elgar Press, 2010) at 115–34.

[47] See Art 61, Constitutional Court Act.

[48] See Art 5, Constitutional Interpretation Procedure Act.

[49] See Art 67, Constitution of Mongolia.

anti-corruption laws and state audit.[50] In the case of drafts of laws or rules of procedure for the House of Representatives or the Senate, if no fewer than one-tenth of the members of both the House of Representatives and the Senate are of opinion that such drafts contain provisions inconsistent with the Constitution, they may submit such opinions to the President of the House of Representatives or the President of the Senate, who in turn shall forward such opinions to the Constitutional Court.[51] In contrast with *ex ante* review by political institutions, the *ex post* abstract review of any promulgated laws can be requested only by the ombudsman or the National Human Rights Commission.[52]

Article 24C of the Constitution of Indonesia gives the Constitutional Court 'the final power of decision in reviewing laws against the Constitution'. Article 51 of the Law on Constitutional Court allows four categories of claimants to request for constitutional review of laws:

(a) individual citizens;
(b) public or private corporate bodies;
(c) customary law communities such as, but not limited to, indigenous tribes; and
(d) state agencies.[53]

Requests for constitutional review of statutes by state agencies are allowed if state agencies find their official functions infringed by the impugned statutes.

In Myanmar, the abstract review power of the Constitutional Tribunal is stipulated in Article 322 of the 2008 Constitution. This includes the power to interpret the provisions under the Constitution, review laws promulgated by the central, regional, local or autonomous legislatures to ensure they conform with the Constitution, and review whether the measures of the executive authorities in the central, regional, local or autonomous governments are in conformity with the Constitution. Aside from these general abstract review powers, the Constitution also grants the Constitutional Tribunal power to review matters initiated by the President relating to the Union territory and other functions and duties prescribed by the central legislature including both Houses (*Pyithu Hluttaw* and *Amyotha Hluttaw*).[54]

It interesting to note that Sri Lanka had a constitutional court between 1972 and 1978. This court only had the power to undertake abstract review of legislative drafts before enactment.[55]

b. Concrete Review

Concrete review refers to the power to review the constitutionality of statutes at the request of other collegial or lower courts. In Taiwan, neither the 1947 Constitution nor the Constitutional Interpretation Procedure Act confers jurisdiction of concrete review on the Constitutional Court. This jurisdiction was created by the Constitutional

---

[50] Arts 138 and 141, Constitution of the Kingdom of Thailand, 2007.
[51] Arts 154 and 155, Constitution of the Kingdom of Thailand, 2007.
[52] Arts 245 and 257, Constitution of the Kingdom of Thailand, 2007.
[53] For basic discussions of the powers and jurisdictions of the Indonesian Constitutional Court, see A Omara, 'Lessons from the Korean Constitutional Court: What Can Indonesia Learn from the Korean Constitutional Court Experience?' at <http://www.e-alin.org/file/attach/upload_2713727972977688331.pdf>.
[54] Arts 322(f) and 322(g), Constitution of the Republic of Myanmar, 2008.
[55] Jayampathy Wickramaratne, above n 41, at 67.

Court itself in *JY Interpretation No 371* in 1995, which referred to the similar jurisdiction enjoyed by European Constitutional Courts, like the German Constitutional Court. An excerpt from this *Interpretation* is included in section III.A.i.e. below.

The South Korean Constitutional Court's power to review the constitutionality of laws is triggered primarily by requests of lower courts.[56] Article 41(1) of the Constitutional Court Act stipulates that

> when the issue of whether or not statutes are constitutional is relevant to the judgment of the original case, the ordinary court (including the military court) shall request to the Constitutional Court, *ex officio* or by decision upon a motion by the party, adjudication on the constitutionality of statutes.

Thus, courts may suspend a proceeding to petition the Constitutional Court to review an impugned statute, upon the request of a party to litigation or *ex officio*. This jurisdiction is known as *Hun-Ka*. Such requests must be made through the Supreme Court. No appeal can be made against the decision of ordinary courts on requests of constitutional review.[57] However, after the ordinary courts reject a request, Article 68(2) of the Constitutional Court Act gives an independent right to the litigant to file a constitutional complaint directly with the Constitutional Court. This is known as the jurisdiction of *Hun-Ba*, one of two kinds for individual complaints. The *Hun-Ba* jurisdiction is distinctive in South Korea as no other Constitutional Court allows the litigant party to file a constitutional complaint immediately after the rejection of referral by ordinary courts. For example, in Taiwan, after the request of referral is rejected, the litigant cannot file any constitutional complaints until his or her case becomes final and after he or she has exhausted all available proceedings in the ordinary courts.

There is no concrete review in Mongolia and Indonesia. Constitutional review of statutes can be filed with both Constitutional Courts only through petitions from government organs or individuals. Noticeably however, in Mongolia, the Supreme Court may still make requests to the Constitutional Court – albeit not with any pending cases – for interpretations concerning the Constitution or laws, or the constitutionality of laws, decrees or other decisions.[58]

Article 141 of the Cambodian Constitution stipulates that the courts may request the Constitutional Council to review the constitutionality of statutes after their promulgation. If any litigant raises any issue concerning the unconstitutionality of statutes, decisions of state institutions such as Royal decrees, or administrative decisions in lower courts, the lower court must submit the issue to the Supreme Court. If the Supreme Court finds the complaint valid, it will forward the complaint to the Constitutional Council, and the lower court will suspend proceedings until the Constitutional Council makes a determination.[59]

Both the 1997 and 2007 Constitutions of Thailand adopt concrete review. Article 211 of the 2007 Constitution states that if in the application of any law a court is of the opinion the law is inconsistent with the Constitution, or if a party raises an objection on the constitutionality of any law, that court shall submit the matter to the

---

[56] Art 111, Constitution of the Republic of Korea.

[57] Art 41(4) and (5), Constitutional Court Act, South Korea.

[58] Art 66(1), Constitution of Mongolia. See also Tserenbaltav Sarantuya, 'The Constitution of Mongolia' in Dürkop and Yap Hui Bin (eds), above n 44, at 51–70, 60–61.

[59] The illustrative chart for the jurisdictions and the procedures of the Constitutional Council in Cambodia is available at <http:www.ccc.gov.kh/English/index.php> (accessed 1 March 2013).

Constitutional Court for consideration and decision. The Constitutional Court's decision will apply to the instant case as well as to other pending cases. However, it does not affect any prior final judgment.[60]

Like in the Thai system, the jurisdiction of concrete review of the Constitutional Tribunal of Myanmar is expressly provided for in the Constitution. Article 323 of the Constitution permits a court to stay a trial and submit its opinion to the Constitutional Tribunal if a dispute regarding the constitutionality of any law arises. The decision by the Constitutional Council also applies to all cases.

c. Individual Complaints

Individuals may file a complaint with the constitutional court to challenge the constitutionality of statutes. Subject to institutional design, individuals may be permitted to make such constitutional petitions, with or without exhausting available judicial remedies and on grounds that may or may not be related to their constitutional rights. In Taiwan and Thailand, individual complaints must be made only after exhaustion of available remedies. In Indonesia, there is no such strict limitation. South Korea provides the most extensive methods for individual complaints.

As a further illustration, in Taiwan, Article 5 of the Constitutional Interpretation Procedure Act permits individual citizens to make complaints against laws or regulations that infringe their constitutional rights after they exhaust all available judicial remedies. In South Korea, individual complaints may come from two sources. The first is linked to concrete review. As discussed earlier in section III.A.i.b. above, litigants may request ordinary courts to petition the Constitutional Court for a decision on the constitutionality of impugned laws relevant to their cases. If the request is rejected by the court, the litigant can file an independent constitutional complaint to the Constitutional Court, under the jurisdiction of *Hun-Ba*. The second source of individual complaints is provided for in Article 68(1) of the Constitutional Court Act, known as the jurisdiction of *Hun-Ma*. In making such *Hun-Ma* petitions, individuals must argue that their constitutional rights are violated by 'an exercise or non-exercise of governmental powers', but this excludes the judgments of ordinary courts.

The Mongolian Constitution is different. Article 66(1) of the Constitution empowers the Constitutional Court to exercise its powers on the basis of petitions and information received from citizens. As such, individual citizens may petition directly to the Constitutional Court on matters that may not immediately concern their own rights. They may, like other state organs, make constitutional petitions to challenge a law that is inconsistent with the Constitution.

Article 212 of the 2007 Thai Constitution allows individuals to file a motion to the Constitutional Court to determine the constitutionality of a law if his or her constitutional rights or liberties have been violated. This right of petition can be exercised only after the exhaustion of all other remedies, such as filing a complaint with the Ombudsman or the National Human Rights Commission.[61]

---

[60] Art 211(4), Constitution of the Kingdom of Thailand, 2007.
[61] Detailed procedures of all jurisdictions of the Constitutional Court of Thailand are available at <http://www.constitutionalcourt.or.th/english/>.

Constitutional review under Article 24C of the Indonesian Constitution permits petitions from both government agencies (for abstract review) and individual citizens. Article 51 of the Law on Constitutional Court prescribes that constitutional petitions of individuals may be allowed only when their constitutional rights are infringed by a law.

There is no individual complaint procedure available in Cambodia and Myanmar. Concrete review is recognised in both systems, however. Individual citizens may still have their complaints heard – albeit indirectly – in the ordinary courts through litigation and filing motions requesting presiding judges to seek a decision on the constitutionality of the impugned statute. Article 141 of the Cambodian Constitution provides that citizens may also make their complaints against a law through their elected representatives.

d. Competence Dispute

A classic function of modern constitutional courts is the adjudication of disputes over competences between central and local governments or between horizontal governmental branches, as exemplified in the practice of Austrian and German constitutional courts.[62] All seven Asian constitutional courts have this jurisdiction.

In Taiwan, if government organs or central/local governments doubt the constitutionality of certain powers or come into conflict with other organs or governments, they may petition the Constitutional Court for resolution. In South Korea, competence disputes between government organs or between central and local authorities are known as the jurisdiction of *Hun-Ra*, under Article 61 of the Constitutional Court Act.

In Mongolia and Cambodia, competence disputes may be brought through constitutional petitions made by the President, Parliament or Members of Parliament to the Constitutional Court. Under Article 214 of the Thai Constitution, where a dispute arises as to the powers and duties between two or more organs – such as the National Assembly, the Council of Ministers or a constitutional organisation other than the courts, the President of the National Assembly, the Prime Minister – such organs may submit the matter to the Constitutional Court.

Article 24C(1) of the Indonesian Constitution provides the Constitutional Court with the power to determine 'disputes over the authorities of state institutions whose powers are given by the Constitution'. In Myanmar, Article 322 of the Constitution provides that the Constitutional Council may decide constitutional disputes between 'the Union and a Region, between the Union and a State, between a Region and a State, among the Regions, among the States, between a Region or a State and a Self-Administered Area and among the Self-Administered Areas', as well as disputes arising out of the rights and duties of these various levels of governing entities.

e. Variations and Additions

While all seven constitutional courts in Asia have powers of abstract review, concrete review, individual complaint and competence dispute, variations exist. The South

---

[62] Kommers, above n 45, at 12–13.

Korean Constitutional Court may not conduct abstract reviews stemming from petitions of government organs or the legislative minority. Both the Indonesian and Mongolian constitutional tribunals do not have the jurisdiction of concrete review. There are no provisions allowing direct individual complaints to the constitutional tribunals in Cambodia and Myanmar. An interesting issue arises as to whether a constitutional court can add to or alter some of its jurisdictions or institutional variations through constitutional interpretation or review. Can a constitutional court justify this addition to its jurisdiction or powers by referring to the designs of other constitutional courts such as the German Constitutional Court or other collegial constitutional courts in Asia?

JY Interpretation No 371
20 Jan 1995 (Constitutional Court, Taiwan)

Facts

The 1947 Constitution is not explicit in specific details regarding the jurisdiction of the Constitutional Court. The Constitutional Interpretation Procedure Act of 1993 only provided the Supreme Court and the Supreme Administrative Court with power to initiate petitions before the Constitutional Court for review of laws or regulations. The petitions by both Supreme Courts were similar to those made by government organs, challenging impugned laws or regulations in the abstract rather than in conjunction with any pending cases or controversies. No concrete review was stipulated. However, an issue arose in the legislative debate on whether the judges of all levels should be given the power of judicial review in accordance with the Constitution. Consequently, the Legislative Yuan initiated the petition requesting the Constitutional Court for clarification.

Held

Based on the constitutional principle of separation of powers, modern countries with a written constitution and rule of law have set up a judicial review system. Those which do not have a special judicial tribunal for judicial review delegate this power to their ordinary courts through precedents, as the United States does, or through explicit constitutional provisions, as Japan does (Article 81 of the 1946 Constitution). In those countries which have special judicial tribunals for judicial review, the constitutionality of statutes is reviewed by the special judicial tribunals, such as the Constitutional Courts of Germany (Articles 93 and 100 of the 1949 Basic Law), Austria (Articles 140 and 141-1 of the 1929 Constitution), Italy (Articles 134 and 136 of the 1947 Constitution), and Spain (Articles 161 and 163 of the 1978 Constitution). Different countries with different situations could not be expected to have the same systems and applications. Nonetheless, their purposes are all to protect the constitution's highest authority in law, as well as to maintain a judge's independence in exercising his duties, in order that in trying a case, a judge shall obey nothing but the constitution and statutes without any interference. Because our legal system mainly adopted the statutes of continental countries, the development of our judicial review system has been very similar to those of the abovementioned continental countries since our Constitution went into effect.

   Article 171 of the Constitution provides: 'Statutes that contradict the Constitution shall be null and void. In case of doubts as to whether a given statute contradicts the Constitution, the matter shall be interpreted by the Judicial Yuan.' Article 173 of the Constitution provides: 'The Constitution shall be interpreted by the Judicial Yuan.' Article 78 of the Constitution provides: 'The Judicial Yuan shall interpret the Constitution and shall have the power to unify the interpretation of statutes and ordinances.' Article 79, Paragraph 2, of the Constitution and Article 4, Paragraph 2, of the Amendment to the Constitution clearly provide that the Grand Justices of the Judicial Yuan shall be responsible for the matters specified in Article 78 of the Constitution. Accordingly, the power to interpret a statute's constitutionality and to declare its nullity rests exclusively on the Grand Justices of the Judicial Yuan. Pursuant to Article 80 of the Constitution, judges of different levels shall try cases in accordance with law. In trying a case, a judge, therefore, shall base his decision on statutes that have been promulgated and effective in accordance with the legal procedure. A judge shall have no capacity to hold a statute unconstitutional, and shall not refuse to apply a statute for that reason. Nonetheless, since the Constitution is the state's highest authority, judges have an obligation to obey the Constitution over any other statutes. Therefore, in trying cases where judges of different levels have suspected, with reasonable assurance, that the statute applicable to the cases is unconstitutional, they shall be allowed to petition for interpretation of its constitutionality, regardless of the levels where the cases are pending. This may eliminate a judge's dilemma of obeying the Constitution and applying the controversial statute, as well as avoid the waste of judicial resources. In the abovementioned situation, judges of different levels may suspend the pending procedure on the ground that the constitutionality of the statute is a prerequisite issue. At the same time, they shall provide concrete reasons for objectively believing the unconstitutionality of the statute, and petition to the Justices of the Yuan to interpret its constitutionality. The provisions of Article 5, Paragraphs 2 and 3, of the Constitutional Interpretation Procedure Act which are inconsistent with the above interpretation shall no longer be applied. Petitions for interpretation of the constitutionality of statutes by judges of different levels shall be determined according to the interpretation of this case, and the form of the petition shall apply to Article 8, Paragraph 1, of the said Act.

Re: The application to the Constitutional Court for the interpretation of section 241 paragraph four and section 264 in conjunction with section 6 of the Constitution of the Kingdom of Thailand, BE 2540 (1997)
Ruling No 5/2541, 4 Aug 1998 (Constitutional Court, Thailand)

Facts

The applicant was accused of murder, but the Attorney-General issued a final non-prosecution order after investigation. Later, the applicant was prosecuted again due to the emergence of new material evidence. During the trial, the applicant's lawyer requested documentary evidence from the provincial court. Under section 241 of the Constitution, the suspect has the right to know a summary of evidence. The provincial court stated that the prosecutor need not deliver the requested documents. The applicant then requested the provincial court to initiate a petition to the Constitutional Court to determine the constitutionality of the refusal, but this was rejected. The applicant then initiated the petition before the Constitutional Court, although there was no provision in the Constitution or in the Act permitting individuals to bring an independent petition directly to the Constitutional Court after such rejection.

Held

The Constitutional Court considered the matter and held that section 264 paragraph one of the Constitution of the Kingdom of Thailand, BE 2540 (1997) provided that 'In the application of the provisions of any law to any case, if the Court by itself is of the opinion that, or a party to the case raises an objection that, the provisions of such law fall within the provisions of section 6 and there has not yet been a decision of the Constitutional Court on such provisions, the Court shall stay its trial and adjudication of the case and submit, in the course of official service, its opinion to the Constitutional Court for consideration and decision.' That provision meant that only the Court could submit, in the course of official service, the opinion to the Constitutional Court for consideration and decision. The applicant or the other party to the case was not entitled to directly submit the matter to the Constitutional Court. When it appeared that the applicant did not have the right to submit the matter to the Constitutional Court, the case therefore did not constitute a cause for the Constitutional Court to accept the application for consideration and ruling on whether such matter was contrary to or inconsistent with section 241 paragraph four in conjunction with section 6 of the Constitution of the Kingdom of Thailand, B.E. 2540 (1997) . . .

By reasons stated above, the Constitutional Court did not accept the application of the applicant for consideration.

Notes and Questions

1. The Constitutional Court of Taiwan in *JY Interpretation No 371* enlarged its own jurisdiction to conduct concrete review. In contrast, *The Constitutional Court Ruling No 5/2541* indicated the unwillingness of the Thai Constitutional Court to make additions or alterations to its existing jurisdiction. What sets the two courts apart on this issue? Which decision do you agree with, and why?

2. In *JY Interpretation No 371*, Taiwan's Constitutional Court made reference to the institutional designs of the European constitutional courts to justify its expansion of the concrete review jurisdiction. However, the Thai Constitutional Court chose to remain faithful to the constitutional text. In what ways do the methods of constitutional interpretation affect the decisions? Which interpretive method do you favour, and why? Note that the discussion of constitutional interpretation is also included in section VII.

ii. Ancillary Jurisdictions

Aside from their primary jurisdictions, constitutional courts may have certain ancillary jurisdictions such as adjudicating the impeachment of the president or other high-level government officials, the dissolution of political parties and resolving disputes relating to the holding of elections or a referendum.[63] Table 5.3 illustrates three kinds of ancillary jurisdictions exercised by Asian constitutional courts. Most constitutional courts have one or two types of ancillary jurisdictions. Only the Constitutional Court

---

[63] T Ginsburg. 'Ancillary Powers of Constitutional Courts' in T Ginsburg and RA Kagan (eds), *Institutions and Public Law: Comparative Perspectives* (New York: Peter Lang Publishing, 2004) 225; see also Kommers, above n 45, at 10–15.

Table 5.3 Ancillary Jurisdictions of Constitutional Courts in Asia

Constitutional Court	Ancillary Jurisdictions		
	Impeachment	Dissolution of political party	Election or referenda disputes
Taiwan (1947)	O	O	
South Korea (1987)	O	O	
Mongolia (1992)	O		O
Cambodia (1993)			O
Thailand (1997)		O	
Indonesia (2001)	O	O	O
Myanmar (2008)			

of Indonesia has all three powers. It is worth noting that the Myanmar Constitutional Council has not been given any of these ancillary powers.

a. Adjudication of Impeachment

Impeachment is traditionally a power possessed by Parliament, as a check against the other government branches. A typical comparative example is Article 1, Section 3(6) of the US Constitution, prescribing that 'the Senate shall have the sole power to try all Impeachments'. A trend developed after the World War II which shifted some power of impeachment from the legislature to the judiciary, especially the constitutional court. For example, the German Basic Law of 1949 vests the Federal Constitutional Court with the power to decide on the motion of presidential impeachment made by both Houses,[64] as well on cases of judicial impeachment.[65] In Asia, some constitutional courts have the jurisdiction of impeachment.

In Taiwan, the power to adjudicate impeachment was conferred on the Constitutional Court in the constitutional revision of 2005.[66] The Constitutional Court is provided with the power to decide the impeachment of the President and Vice-President only after the motion is passed by the legislature, excluding impeachment of other high-level government officials or judges. In contrast, the South Korean Constitutional Court has the power of impeachment over an array of high government officials including the President, the Prime Minister, members of the State Council, heads of executive ministries, justices of the Constitutional Court, judges, members of the National Election Commission, and the chairman and members of the Board of Audit and Inspection among others designated by the law. The motion for impeachment is decided by a parliamentary majority, except that a two-thirds vote is required for pres-

---

[64] Art 61, German Basic Law.
[65] Art 98, German Basic Law.
[66] Art 2 of the Additional Articles prescribes: 'Should a motion to impeach the President or the Vice-President initiated by the Legislative Yuan and presented to the grand justices of the Judicial Yuan for adjudication be upheld by the Constitutional Court, the impeached person shall forthwith be relieved of his duties.'

idential impeachment.[67] Article 66(1)(4) of the Mongolian Constitution provides the Constitutional Court with the power to examine 'the well-foundedness of the grounds for the removal of the President, Chairman of the State Great Hural and the Prime Minister, and for the recall of members of the State Great Hural'.

It is interesting that unlike other constitutional courts, the Indonesian Constitutional Court does not have a final say on the impeachment of the President and Vice-President. After a motion for the impeachment is passed by the House of Representatives (*Dewan Perwakilan Rakyat*, DPR), it must be sent to the Constitutional Court for a decision regarding the alleged constitutional violations by the President and Vice-President.[68] The Constitutional Court 'has the obligation to investigate, bring to trial, and reach the most just decision on the opinion of the DPR at the latetst 90 days after the request of the DPR was received'.[69] If the Constitutional Court decides that it has been proved that the President and Vice-President have committed such violations, the DPR shall hold a plenary session to submit the impeachment motion to the People's Consultative Assembly (*Majelis Permusyawaratan Rakyat*, MPR), which in turn shall hold a plenary session for final decision.

b. Dissolution of Political Parties

Another type of ancillary power exercised by constitutional courts is the dissolution of political parties. For example, under Article 21 of the German Basic Law the power to decide if political parties, 'by reason of their aims or the behaviour of their adherents, seek to undermine or abolish the free democratic order or to endanger the existence of the Federal Republic of Germany' rests with the Federal Constitutional Court. In Asia, four constitutional courts have such jurisdiction: Taiwan, South Korea, Thailand and Indonesia. The extent of their powers in supervising political parties varies from one to another. It is more extensive in the Thai and Indonesian constitutional courts, as compared to the courts in Taiwan and South Korea.

In a 1992 constitutional revision in Taiwan, the Constitutional Court was given the power to dissolve political parties whose 'goals or activities endanger the existence of the Republic of China or the nation's free and democratic constitutional order'.[70] Similarly, Article 4 of the 1987 South Korean Constitution prescribes that if the purpose or activities of a political party are contrary to the fundamental democratic order, the Government may bring an action to the Constitutional Court for dissolution.

There are extensive regulations on political parties in the Thai Constitution and laws, both of which accord great power to the Constitutional Court. Article 65 of the Thai Constitution requires that the internal organisation, management and regulations of a political party be consistent with fundamental principles of the democratic regime of government with the King as head of the state; it provides members of the House of Representatives who are members of a political party or members of the executive committee of a political party, with the right to refer to the Constitutional Court for decision the matter of the dissolution of unconstitutional political parties. In addition, the Constitutional Court may also:

---

[67] See Arts 65 and 111, Constitution of the Republic of Korea.
[68] Arts 7B and 24C, Constitution of the Republic of Indonesia.
[69] Art 7B, Constitution of the Republic of Indonesia.
[70] The Additional Article of the ROC Constitution, Art 5(5).

(a) determine whether a resolution or rule of a political party is inconsistent with the status and performance of functions of a member of the House of Representatives under the Constitution, or contrary to or inconsistent with the fundamental principles of a democratic form of government;[71]
(b) consider an appeal of a member of the House of Representatives whose membership of a political party has been terminated by resolution of the political party;[72] or
(c) determine whether a person or political party has unconstitutionally exercised political rights or liberties.[73]

Aside from the aforementioned constitutional provisions, the Organic Act on Political Parties accords further powers to the Constitutional Court in respect of political parties. The Constitutional Court may rule on:

(a) an order that denies the registration of a political party;
(b) an order that denies the registration of changes to a political party's policies or rules of a political party, changes of name or other matters;
(c) the membership of a political party member who holds office as a member of the House of Representatives;
(d) whether a political party leader, executive committee or executives should cease or remedy any act which constitutes a violation of political party policies or rules, or whether these leaders should retire from office;
(e) the termination of political party status; and
(f) the revocation of election rights of a political party leader or executive.[74]

Article 24C(1) of the Indonesia Constitution grants the Constitutional Court the power to decide whether a political party should be dissolved. Article 68 of the Law on the Constitutional Court stipulates further details regarding the requirement that the purpose and programmes of a political party be of a democratic nature, and regulates the motions made by the Government on the dissolution of an unconstitutional political party. The Cambodian Constitutional Council has no power to dissolve political parties. However, it does have the power to examine and decide on the complaint of a political party, where the Ministry of the Interior refuses to register it.

c. Resolution of Election or Referendum Dispute

Electoral disputes are common to judicial dockets in all democracies. Some courts may decline to decide these disputes under the political question doctrine. Others may, however, resolve these disputes on the basis of political equality or other constitutional principles. Certain constitutions rely on their constitutional courts for the exclusive resolution of electoral or similar disputes. For example, the French Constitutional Council can supervise the legality of elections for the President,[75] the legislature, and referenda (Articles 11 and 60). In Asia, only the Mongolian, Cambodian and

---

[71] Art 65, Constitution of the Kingdom of Thailand.
[72] Art 106.
[73] Arts 68 and 237.
[74] Detailed procedures of all jurisdictions of the Constitutional Court of Thailand are available at <http://www.constitutionalcourt.or.th/english/>.
[75] Arts 7 and 58, Constitution of France.

Indonesian constitutional courts have power to resolve election or referendum disputes.

Article 66(2)(2) of the Mongolian Constitution accords the Constitutional Court the power to review 'the constitutionality of decisions of the central election authorities on national referendums and the elections of the State Great Hural and its members as well as presidential elections'.

Under Article 136 of the Cambodian Constitution, the Constitutional Council may receive complaints and decide on disputes concerning the election of deputies and the election of members of the Senate. The Council may also decide on the elections of the members to the National Assembly and the Senate, and on complaints concerning the initial electoral rolls at the time of election registration as well as during the electoral campaign. In addition, during elections for members of the National Assembly and the Senate, a political party may file a direct complaint with the Constitutional Council within 72 hours after the release of the initial election result, or in appealing a decision of the National Election Committee which it contests.[76]

The Thai Constitutional Court is not empowered to resolve election or referendum disputes. Notably however, the Constitution gives the Constitutional Court power to rule on the membership or qualifications of a member of the National Assembly, a Minister and an Election Commissioner on grounds stipulated by the Constitution or laws.[77] Article 24C(1) of the Indonesian Constitution authorises the Constitutional Court to decide disputes regarding the result of general elections. Further details are provided in Article 74 of the Law on the Constitutional Court.

Notes and Questions

1. For discussion of the 'law-making' functions of constitutional courts, see A Stone Sweet and M Shapiro, *On Law, Politics, and Judicialization* (New York: Oxford University Press, 2002); AR Brewer-Carias (ed), *Constitutional Courts as Positive Legislators: A Comparative Study* (New York: Cambridge University Press, 2011).

2. The primary power of a constitutional court to invalidate unconstitutional statutes has been characterised as 'negative' law-making power in contrast with parliament's 'positive' law-making. The nature of ancillary powers, however, is more associated with dispute resolution rather than law-making, which may nevertheless presuppose high-profile political conflicts (see T Ginsburg, 'Ancillary Powers of Constitutional Courts' in T Ginsburg and RA Kagan (eds), *Institutions and Public Law: Comparative Approaches* (New York: Peter Lang Publishing, 2004) at 238). Judicial involvement in these political conflicts brings about the 'judicialisation of politics,' and possibly, the 'politicisation of the judiciary'. For example, in 2004, the South Korean Constitutional Court received the first motion of presidential impeachment and eventually decided not to impeach the President in *The Impeachment of the President (Roh Moo-hyun) Case*, 2004Hun-Na1, 14 May 2004 (Constitutional Court, South Korea). According to Chaihark Hahm:

   > Upon seeing the Court adjudicate the fall-out between the two political branches of the government, many citizens for the first time were alerted to the tremendous influence it

---

[76] Further details are available at <http:www.ccc.gov.kh/English/index.php>.
[77] Secs 91, 18 and 233, Constitution of Thailand, 2007.

could have on the political scene. Many were also led to ask about the democratic propriety of nine unelected justices deciding upon the fate of a popularly elected President . . . [T]he Korean decision cannot but be seen as an instance of judicialization of politics.

See, C Hahm, 'Beyond "Law vs politics" in constitutional adjudication: Lessons from South Korea' (2012) 10(1) *International Journal of Constitutional Law* 6, 22–23. Within two years, when the same President nominated a candidate to be the president of the Constitutional Court, the confirmation process was subject to a political struggle that lasted months between the ruling party and the opposition in the National Assembly. Eventually the nomination was withdrawn.

3.   Ancillary powers presuppose political conflicts, but constitutional interpretation or review of parliamentary enactments may also be politicised. In 2006, Taiwan's Constitutional Court was requested to interpret the scope of presidential immunity as the President and the first lady were charged with embezzlement. This almost led to his resignation, recall or impeachment. Wen-Chen Chang compares the interpretation by the Constitutional Court in Taiwan with the impeachment decision by the South Korean Constitutional Court, and argues that certain interpretive techniques may be employed by courts in adjudicating politically-charged cases. The techniques include the creation of 'win-win' situations, non-issuance of dissenting opinions, use of a textual approach to avoid accusations of infidelity to the constitution, and adoption of a strategy that empowers only the court but not any political institutions. See Wen-Chen Chang, 'Strategic Judicial Responses in Politically Charged Cases, East Asian Experiences' (2010) 8(4) *I·CON* 885.

B. The Decentralised Model

The decentralised model in Asia is mainly found in common law jurisdictions. In this model, courts at all levels may review the constitutionality of parliamentary or executive enactments in cases before them. This system has been characterised as a diffused one. The exercise of judicial review is understood as inherent and incidental to the general process of case adjudication. With or without express constitutional authorisation, courts exercise this power on the logic that the constitution is the supreme *law* of the land. In contrast, the centralised model requires express constitutional authorisation and the creation of a separate constitutional court dedicated to hearing constitutional questions.

Even in decentralised models, there may be times when judges are requested to issue advisory opinions on matters concerning laws or the constitution. Indeed, the power of English judges to deliver advisory opinions was well established in the seventeenth and eighteenth centuries.[78] However, the principle of separation of powers as applied in certain modern constitutional orders may impose limits on the issuance of advisory opinion by courts. Article III of the US Constitution, for example, prohibits federal

---

[78] DM O'Brien, *Constitutional Law and Politics: Struggles for Power and Government Accountability*, 4th edn (New York: WW Norton, 2000) at 103–04.

courts from exercising any advisory opinion. Some states in the US nevertheless still continue the practice of courts giving advisory opinions.[79]

Under Article 100 of the Singapore Constitution, the President, acting on the advice of Cabinet, may refer to an ad hoc constitutional tribunal consisting of no fewer than three judges of the Supreme Court, 'any question as to the effect of any provision of this Constitution which has arisen or appears to him likely to arise' in seeking its advisory opinion. Once a reference is made, the constitutional tribunal must consider the question referred and certify its opinion to the President no more than 60 days after the reference, with reasons and, if applicable, a minority opinion. The majority opinion shall be pronounced in open court. Article 100(4) further provides that no court has the jurisdiction to question the tribunal's opinion or validity, or any law or Bill which has been the subject of a constitutional reference before the tribunal. The first – and so far the only – reference rendered an opinion concerning the scope of the powers of the elected presidency. This is discussed below.

If the highest court in a decentralised system of judicial review may issue an advisory opinion or even some sort of abstract review of laws or regulations, it may exhibit mixed elements in both centralised and decentralised models. In Asia, perhaps only the Sri Lanka judicial system embodies such hybrid elements. The 1972 Constitution of Sri Lanka had briefly established the Constitutional Court, which was replaced by the Supreme Court with a decentralised system in the 1978 Constitution. Interestingly, however, some elements of abstract review were preserved. According to the 1978 Constitution, the Supreme Court of Sri Lanka – aside from its appellate and other jurisdictions typical in a decentralised system – is also solely and exclusively vested with four jurisdictions:

(a) constitutional review;
(b) legislative review;
(c) constitutional interpretation; and
(d) review of fundamental rights.

The Supreme Court of Sri Lanka is empowered to determine whether any bill of constitutional amendment requires a two-thirds parliamentary vote and a public referendum should such a bill seek to repeal and replace certain listed important constitutional provisions.[80] In addition, the Supreme Court is provided with the power to determine *in abstract* the constitutionality of any bill within one week of its placement before the Parliament, as invoked by the reference of the President or by the petition of any citizen addressed to the Chief Justice of the Supreme Court.[81] Once such a reference or petition is made, no parliamentary proceeding shall continue until the Supreme Court makes its decision, which shall ordinarily be delivered within three weeks. In the case of an urgent request, the decision must be made within 24 hours.[82] If the Supreme Court finds the bill is inconsistent with the Constitution, it shall require the bill to be passed by a supermajority or with a referendum.[83]

---

[79] *Flast v Cohen* 392 US 83, 96 (1968).
[80] Arts 83 and 120, Constitution of Sri Lanka.
[81] Art 121, Constitution of Sri Lanka.
[82] Art 122, Constitution of Sri Lanka.
[83] Art 123, Constitution of Sri Lanka.

The power to interpret the Constitution is also solely and exclusively vested in the Sri Lanka Supreme Court through references from any other court, tribunal or other institutions. The interpretation must be rendered within two months of the referral.[84] Lastly, the Supreme Court has exclusive jurisdiction to hear and determine any question involving the infringement of fundamental rights or language rights by executive or administrative action.[85] Any person alleging such violations may directly petition the Supreme Court. If other courts come across prima facie evidence of rights violations by executive or administrative actions, they shall refer those cases to the Supreme Court.

Besides these four exclusive forms of jurisdictions, the Sri Lanka Supreme Court is also vested with the power to issue advisory opinions on issues of public importance on the request of the President or Speaker of Parliament.[86] The Supreme Court further possesses some ancillary powers typical of constitutional courts, to resolve election or referendum disputes[87] and breaches of parliamentary privileges.[88]

The 1978 Constitution of Sri Lanka creates a hybrid model in relation to the jurisdiction of the Supreme Court. Without express constitutional authorisation, is it possible for courts to assume and develop similar hybrid powers within a decentralised system? In post-war Japan, the new Constitution adopted a decentralised system. Even so, many insisted that this did not prohibit the Supreme Court from exercising abstract review powers. In the case discussed below, the Japanese Supreme Court held that its power to review the constitutionality of laws or orders was within the limits of judicial power, and in this respect the Supreme Court was no different from the lower courts.

Case Concerning the National Police Reserve
6 Minshū 9 (Supreme Court, Japan)

Facts

After the Second World War, Japan explicitly renounced war as a sovereign right in Article 9 of its Constitution. However, pursuant to the need of defence during the Korean War, the Government created the National Police Reserve in 1950. The President of Japan Socialist Party (JSP) objected, arguing that this violated Article 9. He initiated a petition directly to the Supreme Court, claiming that the creation of the National Police Reserve, including all laws, ordinances and regulations concerning it, was null and void. He argued that the Supreme Court had the power to determine the constitutionality of all official acts in the abstract, because Article 81 of the Constitution prescribed the Supreme Court as 'the court of last resort with power to determine the constitutionality of any law, order, regulation or official act'. Although Japan's Supreme Court was modelled on the US Supreme Court, the President of the JSP contended that the Constitution did not limit its jurisdiction to cases or controversies.

---

[84] Art 125, Constitution of Sri Lanka.
[85] Art 126, Constitution of Sri Lanka.
[86] Art 129, Constitution of Sri Lanka.
[87] Art 130, Constitution of Sri Lanka.
[88] Art 131, Constitution of Sri Lanka.

Held

When the relevant institutions of other countries are examined, it is true that, in addition to countries where the power to review questions of constitutionality is vested in the judicial courts, there are other countries where this is not the case and where, instead, a special organ established for that purpose has been empowered to issue general and abstract declarations concerning the constitutionality of laws, orders, and the like and to render such laws, orders, and the like null and void, irrespective of the existence of concrete legal disputes. However, the authority that has been vested in our courts under the system now in force consists of the authority to exercise judicial power, and for judicial power to be invoked a concrete legal dispute must be brought before the courts. Our courts cannot exercise a power whereby, in the absence of such a concrete legal dispute, they render an abstract judgment anticipating the future and relating to a doubtful or controversial matter concerning the interpretation of the Constitution or other law, order, and the like.

In actuality, the Supreme Court possesses the power to review the constitutionality of laws, orders, and the like, but that authority may be exercised only within the limits of judicial power; in this respect, the Supreme Court is no different from the lower courts (cf Article 76, Paragraph 1 of the Constitution). The Plaintiff bases his claim on Article 81 of the Constitution; however, Article 81, which stipulates that the Supreme Court is the court of last resort for cases involving the Constitution, does not permit the inference that the Court has a power peculiar to itself to review constitutionality in the abstract, nor that it has exclusive jurisdiction (that is, jurisdiction as a court of first and last resort) over such cases.

The Plaintiff's argument regarding the special qualifications required of Supreme Court justices refers particularly to the intent of Article 41, Paragraph 1 of the Court Organization Law. However, these requirements pertain to the fact that the Supreme Court bears the grave responsibility of deciding important matters, such as questions of constitutionality, as the court of last resort.

Further, if the Supreme Court had authority to declare laws, orders, and the like invalid in the abstract as the Plaintiff contends, then, since anyone could bring a constitutionality case before the Court, the validity of laws, orders, and the like would be frequently contested, and the Court would risk appearing to be an organ superior to all other powers of the State, thereby contravening the fundamental principle of democratic government, namely, that the three powers [that is, judicial, legislative, and executive] are independent, that a balance should be maintained among them, and that they should be immune from each other's interference.

In short, under our present system, the decision of a court may be sought only when there exists a concrete legal dispute between specific parties. There is no basis whatsoever in the Constitution, laws, or statutes to support the view that the courts have authority to determine the constitutionality of laws, orders, and the like in the abstract and in the absence of a concrete case. It is clear from the Plaintiff's argument that his petition does not involve such a concrete legal dispute. Accordingly, this suit is not in conformity with law, and since neither the Supreme Court nor any lower court has jurisdiction in such a suit, it cannot be transferred to a lower court . . .

Constitutional Reference No 1 of 1995
[1995] SGCT 1 (Constitution of the Republic of Singapore Tribunal, Singapore)

Facts

In 1991, the Constitution of the Republic of Singapore (Amendment) Bill was passed to establish transform the office of Singapore's President into an elected one. A great number of provisions regarding the powers of the President were added. However, Article 5(2A), regarding the President's power to veto constitutional amendment bills, was kept in abeyance and was thus inoperative. Meanwhile, the Government sought to amend Article 22H(1) to restrict the President's power [to] non-constitutional bills. A question arose as to whether the President's assent was required, given that Article 5(2A) had not been brought into force.

Yong Pung How CJ

This Reference came about as a result of the Government suspending the operation of the newly enacted Art 5(2A) of the Constitution followed by the Government's desire to amend Art 22H(1) of the Constitution. Hence arose this question for determination by this tribunal:

> Whether because Art 5(2A) of the Constitution has not been brought into operation, the President has the power under Art 22H(1) of the Constitution to withhold his assent to any Bill seeking to amend any of the provisions referred to in Art 5(2A), and specifically to any Bill seeking to amend Art 22H to restrict the President's powers thereunder to any non-constitutional Bill which provides directly or indirectly for the circumvention or curtailment of the President's discretionary powers conferred upon him by the Constitution . . .

The 1990 Bill was passed on 3 January 1991 and contained, inter alia, the two new provisions, namely Arts 5(2A) and 22H(1), which give rise to this Reference. Article 5(2A) provided as follows:

> Unless the President, acting in his discretion, otherwise directs the Speaker in writing, a Bill seeking to amend this clause, Arts 17 to 22, 22A to 22O, 35, 65, 66, 69, 70, 93A, 94, 95, 105, 107, 110A, 110B, 151 or any provisions in Part IV or XI shall not be passed by Parliament unless it has been supported at a national referendum by not less than two-thirds of the total number of votes cast by the electors registered under the Parliamentary Elections Act.

Art 22H(1) provided that:

> The President may, acting in his discretion, in writing withhold his assent to any Bill passed by Parliament (other than a Bill to which Art 5(2A) applies) if the Bill provides, directly or indirectly, for the circumvention or curtailment of the discretionary powers conferred upon him by this Constitution.

When the 1990s Bill was passed, the Prime Minister accepted the Select Committee's recommendation to suspend the operation of Art 5(2A). At the Third Reading of the 1990 Bill, the Prime Minister, Mr GohChok Tong said:

> The Select Committee has quite rightly said that we should give ourselves a grace period for making amendments in the light of actual implementation. Such amendments ought

not be subject to the strict provisions of a referendum set out in new Art 5(2A). Hence, new Art 5(2A) should be brought into operation only after this period of adjustments and refinements. I agree with this comment. But the Select Committee was probably too optimistic in believing that a period of two years would be enough to iron out all of problems. I favour giving ourselves more time, to avoid having to go to referendum on procedural and technical provisions. I suggest we give ourselves at least four years for adjustments, modifications and refinements to be made.

The suspension of the operation of Art 5(2A) has given rise to a doubt as to the scope of Art 22H(1). The Government now wishes to make some adjustments to the system by seeking to amend, inter alia, Art 22H to restrict the President's powers thereunder to non-constitutional Bills which provide directly or indirectly for the circumvention or curtailment of the President's discretionary powers conferred upon him by the Constitution . . .

THE TRIBUNAL'S ANSWER

Statutory Interpretation

It is well established and not disputed by either parties that a purposive interpretation should be adopted in interpreting the Constitution to give effect to the intent and will of Parliament. The principle to be applied is that the words of the Act are to be read in their entire context and in their grammatical and ordinary sense, harmoniously with the scheme of the Act, the object of the Act and the intention of Parliament: EA Driedger, *Construction of Statute* (2nd Ed, 1983) p 87. The intention is to be found at the time the law was enacted or in some circumstances when it subsequently reaffirms the particular statutory provision . . .

In adopting the principles enunciated above, we are of the opinion that Parliament had intended Art 5(2A) to become part of the law, otherwise it would not have been enacted and the assent would not have been given to the Bill. This was further supported by the fact that the parenthesis to Art 22H(1) gave effect to that intention, bearing in mind that both Art 5(2A) and Art 22H(1) were enacted at the same time. We are disposed to agree with the AG [Attorney-General representing the Government] that the President's veto power under Art 22H(1) could not enlarge itself by reason only of Art 5(2A) not being in force as, at the time of enactment, Art 22H(1) did not confer such a wide veto power on the President. As such, we cannot accept the analogy to a '*testudo*' drawn by counsel for the Presidency, however novel and persuasive that argument may be . . .

Thus we are of the view that Art 22H(1) would not apply to any Bills which fall within the scope of Art 5(2A), and we note that the scope of Art 5A would essentially cover all constitutional Bills . . .

Notes and Questions

1. Notwithstanding the binary distinction between centralised and decentralised models, hybrids exist across jurisdictions. As discussed earlier, in a decentralised system, if the Supreme Court is vested with the power to issue advisory opinions, it may be seen as a kind of hybrid model. A variety of other hybrids may also exist within centralised systems. For example, in some jurisdictions, the constitutional court may be vested with the power to exercise review over the constitutionality of laws, but not of administrative regulations. Or the constitutional court may

exercise review over both laws and administrative regulations, but ordinary courts may also be permitted to review the constitutionality of administrative regulations. In these systems, the review of administrative regulations associated with ordinary courts is maintained within a decentralised system even though the review of unconstitutional statutes is centralised in the hands of the constitutional court. The judicial review systems of Taiwan, South Korea and Thailand reflect such a hybrid. A further hybrid model within centralised systems is found where ordinary courts may have the power to refuse to apply unconstitutional laws or regulations but only the constitutional court has the power to declare laws or regulations invalid. In Taiwan, for example, ordinary courts have the power to refuse to apply unconstitutional regulations, but only the Constitutional Court can invalidate them. Hybrid models may also emerge as a result of some external laws. For example, in many European countries, notwithstanding the centralised system of judicial review, ordinary courts may still engage in the review of laws or regulations on their consistency with the European Convention on Human Rights or some rights provisions of the European Union laws. For an examination of hybrid models in comparative perspective, see VC Jackson and M Tushnet, *Comparative Constitutional Law* (New York: Foundation Press, 2006) 466–67.

2.   In Latin American countries with Spanish colonial influences, the writ of *amparo* has been available as an extraordinary judicial proceeding for the protection of constitutional rights and freedoms from unconstitutional infringement by public or even private actors. The writ of *amparo* may co-exist with the writ of *habeas corpus*, which is directed at the protection of personal freedom and integrity, or *habeas data*, which focuses on the protection of personal data and information. Generally these writs may be issued by ordinary courts. However, in states like Costa Rica, El Salvador and Nicaragua, the writ of *amparo* can be issued only by the constitutional court or Supreme Court. A variety of hybrids may come from interesting combinations between the centralised/decentralised issuance of *amparo* and centralised/decentralised review of unconstitutional laws. For further discussions of *amparo* writs in Latin American countries, see G Gentili, 'A Comparative Perspective on Direct Access to Constitutional and Supreme Courts in Africa, Asia, Europe and Latin America: Assessing Advantages for the Italian Constitutional Court' (2011) 29 *Pennsylvania State International Law Review* 705, 710–16.

3.   In Asia, the writ of *amparo* is available in the Philippines as an extraordinary judicial proceeding for the protection of constitutional rights and freedoms from unconstitutional infringement by public or even private actors. This writ also covers extra-legal killings and enforced disappearances or threats. The writ of *amparo* may be petitioned for on any day and at any time before the Regional Trial Court when the impugned act occurs, or before the Court of Appeals, the Supreme Court or any justice of these courts. Any appeal against the writ of *amparo* is to be made to the Supreme Court. See Supreme Court of the Philippines, 'Annotation to the Writ of Amparo' at <http://sc.judiciary.gov.ph/admin%20matters/others/annotation.pdf>.

4.   The Supreme Court of Pakistan is vested with the power to act proactively in issuing *suomoto actions* in cases of public importance regarding the enforcement of

fundamental rights, especially where gross human rights violations are concerned. The existence of this sort of proactive power vested with the Supreme Court in a decentralised judicial review system is evidence of hybrids that may exist beyond the centralised and decentralised systems of judicial review. Article 184(3) of the Constitution of Pakistan empowers the Supreme Court, 'if it considers that a question of public importance with reference to the enforcement of any of the Fundamental Rights . . . is involved, [to] have the power to make an order of the nature mentioned in the said Article'.

IV. SUBJECT OF JUDICIAL REVIEW

The subject of judicial review usually includes parliamentary and executive enactments. Variations do, however, exist in centralised or decentralised systems. In centralised systems, some constitutional courts may have power to review treaty ratifications, presidential decrees or emergency orders, aside from laws and regulations. Others may be permitted to review only unconstitutional laws. Not all constitutional courts have the power to review judgments rendered by ordinary courts, a jurisdiction taken for granted by the highest court in decentralised systems. The subject of judicial review is thus a matter of institutional choices, but this may be inhibited, given the complex relationships between the executive, legislative and judicial powers, the balance of which may at times be delicate and difficult. This section discusses constitutional amendments, law and parliamentary resolutions, administrative rules and decisions, emergency decrees and judicial decisions as subjects of judicial review.

A. Constitutional Amendment

As discussed in chapter four, it is rare that under polities with written constitutions, constitutional revisions and amendments are the subject of judicial review. Constitutional amendments usually require a higher threshold in parliamentary voting or even a public referendum, thus representing the will of the people in deciding (and altering) the supreme law of the land. Subjecting constitutional amendments to judicial review is problematic, as a few elite judges may run against the most democratic expression of a supermajority on fundamental laws within a given political society. At the same time, however, fundamental laws forged by the democratic will may not always be consistent with the basic principles of modern constitutionalism. Abuses have occurred throughout history. For example, many popular presidents have pushed for constitutional amendments to the term limits just to stay in power. The Taiwan Constitution limits the President to two terms, but was once amended in 1960 to allow President Chiang Kai-shek a third term.[89] The Philippine Constitution limits a president to one six-year term. However, in 2009, President Arroyo's allies in Congress were considering constitutional amendments to move the country towards a parliamentary

---

[89] Jiunn-rong Yeh, 'Constitutional Reform and Democratization in Taiwan: 1945–2000' in P Chow (ed), *Taiwan's Modernization in Global Perspective* (Westport, Conn: Praeger Publishers, 2002) 47–77.

system so that she could serve as Prime Minister.[90] It thus becomes desirable, if not necessary, to adopt some degree of judicial supervision over constitutional revision or even constitution making.

The most well-known practice of judicial supervision over constitution making was by the Constitutional Court of South Africa. Article 71(2) of the 1993 Interim Constitution of South Africa empowered the Constitutional Court to certify that all the provisions of the new Constitution complied with the Thirty-Four Principles stipulated therein.[91] The most often-noted limitation to constitutional amendment is Article 79(3) of the German Basic Law, stipulating that Basic Law amendments affecting the division of the federation, participation of states in the legislative process or the principles laid down in the protection of fundamental rights, are not permitted. While not express, this provision recognises judicial oversight of inadmissible constitutional amendments. The German Constitutional Court has exercised the power to review constitutional amendments on grounds such as the principles of federal comity, liberal democratic order or militant democracy.[92]

In Asia, very few constitutions expressly authorise the judicial supervision of constitutional amendment. One example is Article 143 of the Constitution of Cambodia, which mandates that the King must consult with the Constitutional Council on all proposals to amend the Constitution.[93] Article 68 of the Constitution of Mongolia similarly allows the Constitutional Court to propose constitutional amendments to the State Great Hural, the Parliament. The most elaborate judicial function in constitutional revision is to be found in Article 120 of the Constitution of Sri Lanka, which empowers the Supreme Court to determine whether any constitutional amendment bill will have the effect of repealing or replacing important constitutional provisions listed in Article 83, which would require a two-thirds parliamentary vote and a public referendum. The constitutions of Cambodia and Sri Lanka adopt *ex ante* judicial review of constitutional amendments. It is particularly noteworthy that judicial review of constitutional amendments in Sri Lanka is provided not for the purpose of voiding unconstitutional amendments, but for ensuring whether further procedural checks, such as a supermajority vote or public referendum, are necessary. This device may better resolve the tension between democracy and constitutionalism.

Despite the absence of express constitutional authorisation, a few supreme and constitutional courts in Asia have assumed the power to review constitutional amendments. These include the courts in India, the Philippines, Bangladesh, Taiwan and Mongolia.

In India, the first unconstitutional constitutional amendment case was the 1967 case of *IC Golaknath v State of Punjab*,[94] in which the Supreme Court found the constitutional amendment infringing property rights unconstitutional. The Supreme Court

---

[90] Editorial, 'Fragile Philippine democracy', *The Washington Times*, 30 July 2009, at <http://www.washingtontimes.com/news/2009/jul/30/fragile-philippine-democracy/> (accessed 2 March 2013).

[91] The Constitutional Court of South Africa did reject some part of the new Constitution as inconsistent with the Thirty-Four Principles. For further discussions, see eg C Murray, 'A Constitutional Beginning: Making South Africa's Final Constitution' (2001) 23 *University of Arkansas at Little Rock Law Review* 809.

[92] Kommers, above n 45, at 48.

[93] Proposals for constitutional amendment may come from the King, the Prime Minister, the Chairman of the National Assembly at the suggestion of one-quarter of all of assembly members, according to Art 151 of the Constitution.

[94] *IC Golaknath v State of Punjab* [1967] AIR SCR (2) 762.

did not make a clear distinction between constitutional amendments and ordinary laws, and held that as parliamentary acts, both types of law should not contravene fundamental rights or run foul of Article 13 of the Constitution. In the seminal decision of *Kesavananda Bharati v State of Kerala*,[95] the Supreme Court held there were implied limits on the power to amend the Constitution. Departing from *Golaknath*, the majority held that Parliament had power to amend the Constitution, including the fundamental rights provisions, as long as the basic structure of the Constitution was not altered. In *Minerva Mills Ltd v Union of India*,[96] the Court struck down a constitutional amendment removing the power of judicial review on the ground that it violated the basic structure of the Constitution.

The Philippines Supreme Court, in *Javellana v Executive Secretary*,[97] tackled the question of whether the new 1973 Constitution had been made in accordance with the amendment procedure laid down in Article 15 of the 1935 Constitution. The Supreme Court unanimously declared it justiciable and not a political question, and defended the legitimacy of the new Constitution.

Influenced by India's basic structure doctrine, the Appellate Division of the Supreme Court of Bangladesh invalidated the eighth constitutional amendment in *Anwar Hossain Chowdhury v Bangladesh* on the ground that Parliament's amending power was subject to the inalterability of the Constitution's basic structure.[98] The impugned constitutional amendment diffused the jurisdiction of the High Court Division of the Supreme Court by adding several permanent benches outside the capital, Dhaka. In invalidating the amendment, the Appellate Division held that the High Court Division's plenary judicial power over the whole republic was part of the basic structure of the unitary state. It is interesting to note that the Constitution of Bangladesh specifically allows constitutional amendments to alter fundamental rights listed in the Constitution and saves them from being declared void.[99] Consequently, a distinct feature of the Bangladeshi basic structure doctrine is that it does not extend to insulate fundamental rights from amendment. In 2010, the High Court Division of the Supreme Court, in *Siddique Ahmed v Bangladesh*,[100] struck down the Seventh Amendment that ratified the martial law decree, and which prevented the decrees and orders issued between 1982 and 1986 from being subject to judicial review. The Court considered that the judicial power to review parliamentary acts was part of the basic features of the Constitution, in relation to which the independence of judiciary and the rule of law developed. Hence, it could not be altered by constitutional amendment.

Taiwan's Constitutional Court also reviewed and invalidated the entire constitutional revision of 1999 on both procedural and substantive grounds in *JY Interpretation No 499*.[101] The impugned constitutional amendment extended the term of the members of the National Assembly for more than a year, and in voting on the amendment,

---

[95] *Kesavananda Bharati v State of Kerala* [1973] AIR SC 1461.
[96] *Minerva Mills Ltd v Union of India* [1980] AIR SC 1789.
[97] *Javellana v Executive Secretary* GR No 36142, 31 Mar 1973.
[98] *Anwar Hossain Chowdhury v Bangladesh* [1989] 1989 BLD (Spl) 1.
[99] The relevant articles are Arts 26 and 142 of the Constitution. Art 26(2) of the Constitution provides that 'the State shall not make any law inconsistent with any provisions of this Part, and any law so made shall, to the extent of such inconsistency, be void'. Art 26(3) and Art 142(2), however, make clear that the aforesaid provision shall not apply to constitutional amendments made under Art 142.
[100] *Siddique Ahmed v Bangladesh* [2010] 39 CLC (HCD).
[101] *Interpretation No 499* [trans Andy Y Sun], 4 ROC Const Ct 1 (2007).

the National Assembly suddenly altered the voting rules. The Constitutional Court held that the sudden alteration of this voting rule amounted to 'clear and gross procedural flaws', rendering the constitutional amendment ineffective. More importantly, the Constitutional Court draws a line against which no constitutional amendment may transgress. In the view of the Court,

> any amendment alter[ing] the existing constitutional provisions concerning the fundamental nature of governing norms and order and, hence, the foundation of the Constitution's very existence destroys the integrity and fabric of the Constitution itself, [and hence] shall be deemed improper. Among the constitutional provisions, principles such as establishing a democratic republic under Article 1, sovereignty of and by the people under Article 2, protection of the fundamental rights of the people under Chapter Two as well as the check and balance of governmental powers are some of the most critical and fundamental tenets of the Constitution as a whole. The democratic constitutional process derived from these principles forms the foundation for the existence of the current Constitution and all [governmental] bodies installed hereunder must abide by this process.[102]

In 2000, the Constitutional Court of Mongolia reviewed and invalidated the constitutional amendment of 1999 on procedural grounds.[103] According to Article 68 of the Constitution of Mongolia, '[a]mendments may be initiated by organizations and officials enjoying the right to legislative initiative and/or proposed by the Constitutional Court to the State Great Hural' (Mongolia's legislature). However, the draft of the 1999 constitutional amendment was initiated by State Great Hural members and submitted for the State Great Hural's vote the next day. There was no public discussion or consultation with the Constitutional Court. Several citizens challenged the amendment in the Constitutional Court which found that the impugned constitutional amendment violated Article 68(1) of the Constitution and sent it back to the State Great Hural for reconsideration. After the State Great Hural refused to reconsider it, the Constitutional Court made a final conclusion invalidating the 1999 constitutional amendment.

B. Law or Parliamentary Resolution

In decentralised and centralised systems, the core function of judicial review is to enable courts to review laws made by parliament. Whether courts may review other acts of parliament, such as parliamentary resolutions, is a matter which often becomes a point of contention in decisions over institutional design or in constitutional adjudication. A few constitutions expressly authorise such review. For example, Article 66(2)(1) of the Mongolian Constitution authorises the Constitutional Court to review whether laws and other decisions made by the State Great Hural have been complied with. Article 155 of the Thai Constitution subjects draft rules of procedure for both Houses of Parliament for *ex ante* constitutional review. Others, such as Taiwan, however, make no such express authorisation. With or without express authorisation, the

---

[102] Ibid at 5–6.

[103] *Hearing on the matters of whether the amendments to the Constitution breach the Constitution*. The English translation of this decision, 29 Nov 2000, in *Decisions of the Constitutional Court of Mongolia* (2012), 94–100.

constitutional courts in Mongolia and Taiwan have both reviewed parliamentary resolutions and found them inconsistent with the Constitution.

Adjudication on the Matters Whether the Interpretation of the Constitution by the State Great Hural Breached or Not the Constitution
23 Mar 2001 (Constitutional Court, Mongolia)

Facts

Article 66(4) of the Constitution states that 'if the Constitutional Court decides that [the law is] incongruous with the Constitution, it shall be considered invalid'. The State Great Hural, however, passed a parliamentary resolution, interpreting this provision as meaning 'the law shall be valid until the issuance of the resolution by the Constitutional Court'. The petitioners argued that such parliamentary interpretation breached the Constitution, and applied for a decision of the Constitutional Court.

Held

The power to interpret the Constitution is not vested [in] the State Great Hural, according to article 25 prescribing the powers of the State Great Hural, and other provisions connected with the activities of the State Great Hural of the Constitution of Mongolia.

It finds grounds to comply with the complaint submitted ... concerning 'The interpretation of the Constitution by the State Great Hural is not vested to its powers, and is breaching the Constitution, as it is not in conformity with the Constitution' ...

JY Interpretation No 419
31 Dec 1996 (Constitutional Court, Taiwan)

Facts

In 1996, the Premier was elected as Vice-President but continued to serve in both positions concurrently. The Legislative Yuan considered this unconstitutional and issued a resolution demanding that the President nominate – as soon as possible – a new prime minister for parliamentary confirmation. Meanwhile, the legislature petitioned the Constitutional Court for an interpretation of whether it was unconstitutional for the Premier to hold both offices concurrently.

Held

These constitutionally mandated powers that belong to the Legislative Yuan and the various resolutions made by that Yuan through the legally mandated parliamentarian process in their very nature have binding effect on the entire population of the nation or related agencies. Yet any state agency must abide by the limits of the Constitution. For any particular power being taken out of the legislative, executive or judicial authority and transferred to another state agency to carry out in accordance with the separation-of-power principle, or mechanisms that the designers of the Constitution fundamentally do not adopt, each department has a constitutional obligation to strictly obey [those rules]. In the former situation, for instance, the investigative power that generally belongs to the legislature in other countries is under the authority of the Control Yuan under our Constitution; in the latter, for instance, our Constitution does not adopt the system where the parliament may cast a no confidence vote to the cabinet and the cabinet's countermeasure to dissolve the parliament. As to the appointment of the Premier, although the Legislative Yuan has the confirmation power, Article 55 of the Constitution clearly stipulates that such power must be exercised on the premises of the President's nomination and request the Legislative Yuan to carry out that power. Also in accordance with Article 57, Subparagraphs 2 and 3, of the Constitution, if the Legislative Yuan does not concur with an important policy of the Executive Yuan, it may, by resolution, request the Executive Yuan to alter that policy; if the Executive Yuan deems a resolution on a statutory, budgetary or treaty bill passed by the Legislative Yuan difficult to implement, it may, upon presidential approval, request the Legislative Yuan to reconsider; if two-thirds of the members of the Legislative Yuan present vote to sustain their original bill, the Premier must immediately accept that resolution or resign from office. This is the rule designed by the Constitution drafters to substitute for the no confidence vote and dissolution of parliament mechanism found in a country with a cabinet system, and the various constitutional amendments never sought to change it. If the Legislative Yuan were able to pass a resolution, with readings and [at least] over half of the vote cast in favor, to request the President to nominate a new Premier candidate so that it could exercise the power of confirmation, and the President did it accordingly, then it would be like creating the no confidence voting system that the Constitution drafters did not adopt. Furthermore, in accordance with the Constitution, the Executive Yuan is responsible to the Legislative Yuan. Except as otherwise stipulated by the Constitution, the Legislative Yuan does not have the authority to pass a resolution requesting the President to undertake or not to undertake a certain act. Therefore, the Legislative Yuan's resolution of June 11, 1996, requesting the President to renominate the candidate for the Premier of the Executive Yuan and to submit such renomination for the Legislative Yuan's confirmation as soon as possible exceeded the constitutional authority of the Legislative Yuan and shall be considered as advisory [opinion only] that carries no constitutional binding power over the President.

Notes and Questions

1. Aside from legislation or parliamentary resolutions, international treaties may also be subject to judicial review on procedural or substantive grounds. For example, Article 66(2)(1) of the Mongolian Constitution empowers the Constitutional Court to review the constitutional conformity of international treaties signed by Mongolia. Article 190(6) of the Thai Constitution grants the Constitutional Court power to resolve disputes over whether a treaty concluded by the executive requires the approval of the National Assembly, should such a treaty involve:

    (a) alteration of territory;
    (b) sovereign rights of Thailand;
    (c) implementation requiring legislation;
    (d) extensive impacts on national economic and social security; or
    (e) imposition of a significant obligation on national trade, investment or budget.

2. Even without an explicit mandate, the constitutional court may still assume this power through constitutional interpretation, as in South Korea[104] and Taiwan. In Taiwan, the Constitutional Court held that it had power to review treaties, as well as to balance the powers between the executive and the legislature in making and concluding international treaties or executive agreements. In *JY Interpretation No 329*, the Constitutional Court stated:

> According to the Constitution, the president has the power to conclude treaties. The premier and ministers shall refer those treaties that should be sent to the Legislation Yuan for deliberation to the Committee of the Executive Yuan. The Legislative Yuan has the power to review those treaties. All of these procedures are explicitly enshrined in Article 38, Article 58, Paragraph 2, and Article 63 of the Constitution, respectively. Treaties concluded according to the above procedures hold the same status as laws. Therefore, the term 'treaty' in the Constitution means an international agreement concluded between the ROC, including those institutions and groups authorized by governmental agencies, and other nations, including their authorized institutions and groups or international organizations, that employs the title of 'treaty,' 'convention' or 'agreement'; is involved directly in important national issues such as defense, diplomacy, finance, the economy or people's rights and duties, and has legal effect. Agreements that employ the title of 'treaty,' 'convention' or 'agreement,' and have ratification clauses should be sent to the Legislative Yuan for deliberation. Other international agreements, except those authorized by laws or pre-determined by the Legislation Yuan, should also be sent to the Legislative Yuan for deliberation. Those international agreements, which do not need to be sent to the Legislative Yuan for deliberation or cannot be regarded as treaties concluded by governmental agencies or their authorized institutions or groups, should be processed by responsible governmental agencies compliant with legislative or normal executive procedure. It is obvious that the 'Procedure Rules on Treaties and Agreements' enacted by the Ministry of Foreign Affairs should be amended in accordance with this interpretation.[105]

3. Compared to other courts in the region, the Thai Constitutional Court is vested with more extensive powers to review parliamentary acts and related political disputes. Aside from law, parliamentary resolutions and draft rules of parliamentary procedure, the Thai Constitutional Court is also vested with the powers to rule on:

    (a) whether a member of the House of Representatives, senator or committee member has committed an act in order to obtain a direct or indirect interest in budgetary appropriations (Article 168);
    (b) the membership or qualifications of a member of the National Assembly, a Minister and an Election Commissioner (Article 91);
    (c) whether the office of a Minister has been terminated (Article 182); and
    (d) whether an Election Commissioner lacks a qualification or is under a prohibition so as to be disqualified from office (Article 233).

4. It is interesting to note that the decision by the Mongolian Constitutional Court set out above concerned a parliamentary resolution that sought to limit the effect of constitutional decisions made by the Constitutional Court. Because of the

---

[104] Jongcheol Kim, 'The Structure and Basic Principles of Constitutional Adjudication in the Republic of South Korea' in Kuk Cho (ed), *Litigation in Korea* (Northampton: Edward Elgar, 2010) 115, 120.

[105] *JY Interpretation No 329* [trans FT Liao], 2 ROC Const Ct 438, 439–40 (2007).

tension generated by the judicial review of parliamentary acts, parliaments do enact laws or adopt resolutions which seek to constrain judicial powers. For example, in Indonesia, when the Parliament enacted the Constitutional Court Law (Law Number 24, 2003), it inserted an article that limited the scope of judicial review of laws to 'those which have been enacted after the introduction of the 2001 amendment to the 1945 Constitution of the Republic of Indonesia'. Thus, laws enacted prior to the establishment of the Constitutional Court would be beyond the scope of review. In *Case Number 066/PUU-II/2004*, the Constitutional Court of Indonesia insisted that

> Article 24C Paragraph (1) of the 1945 Constitution clearly states, 'The Constitutional Court shall have the authority to hear cases at the first and final level the decisions of which shall be final, in conducting judicial review on laws against the Constitution . . .', without containing the limitation concerning the enactment of the law reviewed; . . . It must be understood that the Constitutional Court is a state institution whose power and authority are determined by the constitution. The court is not an organ of laws, but rather it is an organ of the constitution. Therefore, the basis used by the Constitutional Court in carrying out its constitutional duties and authorities is the constitution. Even if other laws and regulations, in accordance with the principle of legality, must be followed by every person and institution as legal subjects of the national law, all laws and regulations concerned must be interpreted insofar as they are not contradictory to the 1945 Constitution.[106]

C. Administrative Rule

In addition to reviewing legislation or administrative rules, courts may also be called upon to conduct judicial supervision of emergency decrees. Judicial review of administrative acts is considered supervision on behalf of parliament (which represents the people's will). As such, the exercise of this power involves less tension between courts and political institutions.

In a decentralised system, all courts are vested with the power to review the legality and constitutionality of administrative rules and decisions. In a centralised system, ordinary courts may also review the legality and constitutionality of administrative rules and decisions. An issue may arise between the ordinary courts and the constitutional court over the allocation of judicial power in carrying out such review. Different jurisdictions adopt different institutional arrangements in this regard.

In some jurisdictions, ordinary courts may review administrative rules (but not laws), while the constitutional court reviews both laws and administrative rules. The effects of review by different courts may also be different. For instance, in Taiwan, although the ordinary courts can review and refuse to apply illegal (or unconstitutional) administrative rules, only the Constitutional Court can invalidate administrative rules. *JY Interpretation No 216* (below) illustrated how the Constitutional Court in Taiwan asserts its independent authority in interpreting laws as well as reviewing administrative rules.

---

[106] *Case Number 066/PUU-II/2004*, at <http://www.mahkamahkonstitusi.go.id/putusan/putusan_sidang_eng_Putusan%20066_PUU-II_2004%20(UU%20MKRI).pdf>.

A more sharply defined allocation may be adopted in other jurisdictions where ordinary courts review administrative rules (but not laws) and the constitutional court reviews laws (but not administrative rules). For example, under Article 24A of the Indonesian Constitution, the Supreme Court has the authority to review ordinances and regulations made under any law against such statute, while Article 24C empowers the Constitutional Court to review laws against the Constitution. The Thai Constitution has a similar arrangement. Its Constitutional Court refuses to adjudicate upon the constitutionality of administrative rules, in the absence of express constitutional authorisation. In South Korea, the Constitution also separates the judicial review of laws from that of administrative rules. The former is vested in the Constitutional Court and the latter in the Supreme Court. Article 107 states that the Supreme Court shall have the power to make a final review of the constitutionality or legality of administrative decrees, regulations or actions when their constitutionality or legality is at issue in a trial. In contrast, when the constitutionality of a law is at issue, courts must refer to the Constitutional Court. However, an interesting issue arises as to whether the Constitutional Court may still review and invalidate administrative regulations or decisions when circumstances so require.

Re: The Phra Nakhon Si Ayutthaya Provincial Court referred the objections of the defendants to the Constitutional Court for a ruling under section 264 of the Constitution of the Kingdom of Thailand, BE 2540 (1997)
Ruling No 14-15/2543, 4 Apr 2000 (Constitutional Court, Thailand)

Facts

The Prime Minister issued an order to suspend fresh-water shrimp farming to protect the environment. The provincial governor issued another order to implement the ministerial order. The applicant violated the governor's order and was prosecuted. He then challenged both the ministerial and provisional orders as violating the equal protection of the law and the rights guaranteed in the Constitution. However, under section 264 of the Constitution, the subject of judicial review is law. The Court had to consider if the Prime Minister's order was subject to judicial review by the Constitutional Court.

Held

The Constitutional Court held that the Order of the Prime Minister and the Order of PhraNakhon Si Ayutthaya Province were not issued by an organ which exercised legislative powers. Hence, they were not provisions of law within the definition in section 264 of the Constitution of the Kingdom of Thailand, BE 2540 (1997) and not within the jurisdiction of the Constitutional Court pursuant to Constitutional Court Ruling No 4/2542, dated 1st April BE 2542 (1999). It was therefore not necessary to rule on whether or not such orders were inconsistent with section 30, section 50 and section 60 of the Constitution of the Kingdom of Thailand, BE 2540 (1997) . . .

JY Interpretation No 216
19 Jun 1987 (Constitutional Court, Taiwan)

Facts

The petitioner challenged the legality of an interpretive rule issued by the Ministry of Judicial Administration (MOJA) regulating the conduct of public auctions of imported goods with customs duties on credit by the courts. An issue arose as to whether judges of ordinary courts were bound by such an interpretive rule.

Held

The provision that judges shall adjudicate independently according to law is specifically prescribed in Article 80 of the Constitution. Administrative rules adopted under the duty of pursuing the proper construction of laws by various government agencies may be applied by judges in the course of adjudication, who, not being bound thereby, may in a proper manner express their opinion in light of the law, as stated in *Interpretation No 137* of this Court. The provision that administrative ordinances issued by a judicial administration shall not intervene in adjudication is specifically prescribed in Article 90 of the Court Organic Act. Judicial administrations shall not put forth their own legal views and order judges to follow such views in the course of adjudication. If any legal views are presented, they are references for judges only and shall not bind judges in the course of adjudication. However, the rules, if and when cited by judges during the course of their adjudication, may be subject to a party's application for constitutional interpretation under Article 4, Paragraph 1, Subparagraph 2, of the Grand Justices Council Adjudication Act. We take the case accordingly.

Rules implementing the Certified Judicial Scriveners Act Case
89Hun-Ma178, 15 Oct 1990 (Constitutional Court, South Korea)

Facts

Article 4 of the Certified Judicial Scriveners Act delegates matters concerning certification and examination administration to the Supreme Court. Article 3(1) of Supreme Court Rule No 1108 stated that 'the Minister of Court Administration may administer the examination upon an approval from the Chief Justice of the Supreme Court when he recognizes [a] need for additional judicial scriveners'. However, only three examinations had been conducted since the founding of the Republic of Korea, because the need for scriveners was filled by retirees of the courts and the prosecutor's offices. The complainant was preparing to take the examination and argued that the rules discouraging regular examination took away his opportunity to take the examination and violated his right to equality. Under Article 107(2) of the Constitution, the Supreme Court has the final power of review over the constitutionality of rules and regulations. Furthermore, Article 68(1) of the Constitutional Court Act provides that '[a]ny person who claims that his basic right which is guaranteed by the Constitution has been violated by an exercise or non-exercise of governmental power may file a constitutional complaint, except [against] the judgments of the ordinary courts'. It does not exclude administrative rules from the Constitutional Court's jurisdiction. The question before the Court was whether it had power to review rules and regulations.

Held

The Court struck down Article 3(1) of the Rules implementing the Certified Judicial Scriveners Act for violating right of equality and occupational freedom after recognizing the rules of the Supreme Court as a proper subject of constitutional adjudication.

Article 107(2) of the Constitution grants the Supreme Court the final review power over the constitutionality of rules and regulations. However, it only means that, when a trial depends on the constitutionality of rules or regulations, there should be no need for the issue to be referred to the Constitutional Court but, unlike statutes, it should remain within the Supreme Court's jurisdiction and therefore subject to its final review. The provision does not apply to a constitutional complaint filed on grounds that basic rights have been violated by rules and regulations themselves. The 'governmental power' subject to constitutional adjudication, as in Article 68(1) of the Constitutional Court Act, refers to all powers including legislative, judicial and administrative. Statutes enacted by the legislature, regulations and rules promulgated by the executive, and rules made by the judiciary may directly violate basic rights without awaiting any enforcement action, in which case they are immediately subject to constitutional adjudication.

Article 4(1) of the Certified Judicial Scriveners Act grants the license not only to retirees with seven or more years of experience at the ordinary courts, the Constitutional Court or public prosecutor's offices, but also to those who have passed the examination. The intent behind such provision is to open the opportunity fairly to all people according to the constitutional principle of equality and allow anyone that passed the statutory exam to choose and practice in the occupation of a judicial scrivener. By doing so, it excludes the monopoly of the occupation by certain individuals or groups and aims at realizing the freedom to choose one's occupation as a means to nurture his or her individuality through free competition (Article 15 of the Constitution).

Article 4(1)(ii) grant of the license to the successful examinee is premised on the examination administered reasonably and surely. Accordingly, 'matters concerning exam administration,' delegated by Article 4(2) of the same Act to the Rules of the Supreme Court, mean the concrete methods and procedures of the examination and not whether or not it is given at all.

Article 3(1) of the Rules authorizes the Minister to not give the exam if he does not see the need for more judicial scriveners. The inferior law deprives the complainant and all others of the opportunity to become certified judicial scriveners, which was granted to them by its superior law, Article 4(1) of the Certified Judicial Scriveners Act. At the same time, it grants to the court and prosecutor's office retirees a monopoly on the work of judicial scriveners. In the end, it is the Supreme Court's departure from the delegated rule-making authority and a violation of the Article 15 occupational freedom and Article 11(1) right to equality belonging to the complainant and other people who wish to become a certified judicial scrivener.

May 18 Incident Non-institution of Prosecution Decision Case
95Hun-Ma221, etc, 15 Dec 1995 (Constitutional Court, South Korea)

Facts

In October 1979, President Park Chung Hee was assassinated. In December, General Chun Doo-Hwan staged a military coup, and protests and demonstrations broke out all over the place. On 18 May 1980, Chun ordered the military to suppress the demonstrations in

Kwangju. The city was under siege, and many people were killed. Later, when Chun became President, he labelled the Kwanju demonstrations a 'rebellion'. In 1993, Chun and several military leaders came under investigation, but in 1995 the prosecutors decided not to prosecute them and reasoned that a successful coup d'état was not punishable. The petitioners filed a constitutional complaint against the decision not to prosecute. Fearful that the Constitutional Court might hold that the action was time-barred, the petitioners made a last-minute withdrawal.

Held

Before the withdrawal, a super-majority of the justices had agreed that a successful coup is punishable during the deliberation. The new majority that declared the case closed acquiesced with the minority's publication of a part of the previously agreed-upon final decision, while leaving out the part about expiration of the statute.

Thus, the justices' prevailing view in the deliberation room saw the light of the day: a successful coup is punishable. The following is the summary of the opinion of the three Justices who were in the minority:

> The constitutional order protected by penalties against treason is one based on people's sovereignty and the basic order of free democracy, not the incumbent power or the order maintained by it. In addition, Article 84 of the Constitution, which stipulates 'the President shall not be prosecuted during the term except on crimes of treason internal or external,' stands as an unequivocal expression of a constitutional resolve that treason can be punished at all times regardless of its outcome. Therefore, even if a successful coup makes it practically impossible to punish the perpetrators during their incumbency, they can always be punished whenever the constitutional institutions recover their proper function and thereby regain de facto power to punish them. However, if treasonous activities were the means to create a democratic civil state and to restore the people's sovereignty previously suppressed and excluded under a feudal monarchy or despotism, they can be justified before or after the fact by the will of all the people. Therefore, a successful treason becomes not punishable under the exceptional circumstances that the people have ratified it through free expressions of their sovereign wills.

In this case, the treasonous acts of the two former Presidents were neither justified by the circumstances nor were ratified by free expressions of the people (denying legitimacy of the treasonous government does not mean denying the legal effects of all of its acts).

The prosecutor's non-institution of prosecution decision for reason of immunity of a successful coup engenders misunderstanding of the ideals of the Constitution and the criminal jurisprudence of treason.

Notes and Questions

1. Did the Constitutional Court of South Korea extend its power to review administrative rules in the case of *Rules Implementing the Certified Judicial Scriveners Act*? If so, how can such an extension be justified? Was there also a similar extension to the review of prosecutorial decisions in the case of *May 18 Incident Non-institution of Prosecution Decision*? What impacts would such extensions have on the relationship between the Constitutional Court and Supreme Court?

2. What would be a better model for the division of labour between the Constitutional Court and the Supreme Court regarding the power of reviewing legislation and

administrative regulations? Do you prefer the Taiwanese model, under which the Constitutional Court reviews and invalidates both legislation and administrative regulations, or the separatist model as exemplified by Indonesia, under which the Constitutional Court reviews and invalidates legislation while the Supreme Court deals only with administrative regulations? Why?

D. Emergency Decree

Most constitutions authorise the issuance of emergency decrees in extraordinary circumstances where national security is in peril or to avert a public calamity. This has implications on how power is allocated between the executive and the legislature, specifically, whether the executive may issue emergency degrees without parliamentary approval. However, scant attention is paid to the judicial reviewability of emergency decrees. This is because emergency decrees are constitutionally sanctioned and are thus regarded as non-justiciable. In Singapore, for example, Article 149 of the Constitution authorises the legislature – in the interests of national security – to enact anti-subversion measures that are broadly immune from judicial review, except on procedural grounds.

However, certain recent constitutions expressly authorise constitutional courts to review emergency decrees. Article 185 of the Thai Constitution, for example, permits the president of either House, upon a request by its members, to refer to the Constitutional Court a question concerning whether the emergency decree is issued in accordance with the Constitution regarding the conditions and procedures stipulated in Article 184. Even without such an express constitutional authorisation, can courts still review the constitutionality of emergency decrees? The following cases from Malaysia and Taiwan may shed some light on this issue.

Stephen Kalong Ningkan v Government of Malaysia
[1968] 2 MLJ 238 (Privy Council, on appeal from Malaysia)

Facts

In 1966, the Governor of Sarawak (a constituent State of the Federation of Malaysia) compelled the petitioner Chief Minister to vacate his office by an emergency decree. Ningkan challenged the constitutionality of the emergency decree, and in 1967 the Federal Court decided (per Barakbah LP) that only the head of the state had the power to determine if a state of emergency existed:

> In my view the question is whether a court of law could make it an issue for the purpose of a trial by calling in evidence to show whether or not His Majesty the Yang di-Pertuan Agong was acting in bad faith in having proclaimed the emergency. In an act of the nature of a Proclamation of Emergency, issued in accordance with the Constitution, in my opinion, it is incumbent on the court to assume that the Government is acting in the best interest of the State and to permit no evidence to be adduced otherwise. In short, the circumstances which bring about a Proclamation of Emergency are non justiciable.

Ningkan appealed to the Privy Council.

Lord McDermott

It is not for their Lordships to criticise or comment upon the wisdom or expediency of the steps taken by the Government of Malaysia in dealing with the constitutional situation which had occurred in Sarawak, or to enquire whether that situation could itself have been avoided by a different approach. But, taking the position as it was after Harley J had delivered judgment in September 1966, they can find, in the material presented, no ground for holding that the respondent Government was acting erroneously or in any way mala fide in taking the view that there was a constitutional crisis in Sarawak, that it involved or threatened a breakdown of stable government, and amounted to an emergency calling for immediate action. Nor can their Lordships find any reason for saying that the emergency thus considered to exist was not grave and did not threaten the security of Sarawak. These were essentially matters to be determined according to the judgment of the responsible Ministers in the light of their knowledge and experience. And although the Indonesian Confrontation had then ceased, it was open to the Federal Government, and indeed its duty, to consider the possible consequences of a period of unstable government in a State that, not so long before, had been facing the tensions of Confrontation and the subversive activities associated with it. That the appellant regarded the Federal Government's actions as aimed at himself is obvious and perhaps natural; but he has failed to satisfy the Board that the steps taken by the Government, including the Proclamation and the impugned Act were in *fraudem legis* or otherwise unauthorised by the relevant legislation.

Their lordships would add that, in their opinion, the continuing existence of earlier Emergency Proclamations or Acts (whether under article 149 or article 150 of the Federal Constitution) could not, in the circumstances, justify a different conclusion. The emergency, the subject of this appeal, was distinct in fact and kind from those that had preceded it, and the powers conferred by article 150 were in being and not spent when it arose.

For these reasons their Lordships find against the appellant on his first submission and would hold that the Emergency Proclamation of 14 September 1964, was intra vires and valid.

The issue of justiciability raised by the Government of Malaysia led to a difference of opinion in the Federal Court the LP of Malaysia and the CJ of Malaya holding that the validity of the Proclamation was not justiciable and Ong Hock Thye FJ holding that it was. Whether a Proclamation under statutory powers by the Supreme Head of the Federation can be challenged before the courts on some or any grounds is a constitutional question of far-reaching importance which, on the present state of the authorities, remains unsettled and debatable. Having regard to the conclusion already reached, however, their Lordships do not need to decide that question in this appeal. They do not, therefore, propose to do so, being of opinion that the question is one which would be better determined in proceedings which made that course necessary. . . .

JY Interpretation No 543
3 May 2002 (Constitutional Court, Taiwan)

Facts

On 21 September 1999, a severe earthquake hit Taiwan, causing significant loss of life and damage to property. The President issued an Emergency Decree. The Executive Yuan drafted 'Emergency Decree Execution Outline of September, 1999' and submitted it to the Parliament for notice. The Parliament thought that the Outline of the Emergency Decree might violate the Constitution and initiated this petition before the Constitutional Court.

Held

The issuance of emergency decrees under the Constitution is an endeavor to maintain the Nation's existence and restore its constitutional structure in the event of national emergency when the existing legal system is insufficient to eliminate danger or handle a major crisis. The criteria, procedures and review of emergency decrees are governed by the Constitution to prevent misconduct by government authorities and to safeguard therights of the people and the order of a democratic society. Article 2, Paragraph 3, of the Amendment to the Constitution provides that:

> The President may, in order to avert imminent danger affecting the national security or of the people or to cope with any major financial or economic crisis, issue emergency decrees and take all necessary measures through resolution of the Cabinet meeting, and is not subject to the restriction specified in Article 43 of the Constitution. However, such decrees shall, within ten days of issuance, be submitted to the Legislature for ratification. Where ratification is denied by the Legislature, the said emergency decrees shall cease to be valid.

Accordingly, emergency decrees are proclamations made by the President pursuant to resolution of the Cabinet, in order to avert imminent dangers to the State or the people or to deal with a major crisis, when the existing legal system and legislative process are unable to provide countermeasures. The effectiveness of such decree is restricted to a definite emergency period and location and has the effect of temporarily replacing or altering existing laws. Therefore, emergency decrees are an exception to the constitutional rules that the Legislature is to legislate on behalf of the people while the Executive Yuan is responsible for the execution of laws. As a principle, their content should be thorough and detailed so they can be executed forthwith without the need of supplementary regulations. In case of time constraint where provisions for detail and technicality are impracticable and supplementary regulations by the executive authorities are required to achieve objectives of emergency decrees, then the decrees must contain a provision expressing their objectives and be proclaimed only after ratification by the Legislature. To adhere to the constitutional structure, supplementary regulations (or by whatever term it is named) should be reviewed by the Legislature in accordance with the review procedures set out in the administrative orders. The issuance of emergency decrees, though not restricted by the principle of legal reservation stipulated in Article 23 of the Constitution, should observe the principle of proportionality. The requirement of ratification by the Legislature, within 10 days of issuance of emergency decrees, stipulated in the said Amendment to the Constitution is a representative review mechanism for the emergency measure. The Legislature, upon exercising its power of ratification, may only resolve as to the appropriateness of emergency decrees but not alter their contents. Where some parts of an emergency decree are considered to be inappropriate, partial ratification is available if the remainder of the decree has no impact on and is necessary to the entirety of the emergency measure.

Emergency decrees issued by the President pursuant to the said Amendment must be delivered to the Legislature for ratification under Article 15, Paragraphs 1 and 2, of the Legislative Yuan Functioning Act. During the recess of the Legislature, the legislators in recess shall meet within three days and ratify such decrees within seven days pursuant to Paragraph 3 of the said Article. Further, supplementary regulations contingent to an emergency decree issued by the Executive Yuan shall cease to be valid once the effective period of the decree elapses. Upon enactment of laws on the relevant emergency measures by the Legislature to replace the contents of emergency decrees, such decrees shall forthwith cease to be valid to the extent of the enactment.

The matters of whether executive authorities may issue supplementary regulations after issuance of emergency decrees and whether such orders should be presented for review by the legislative authorities were, prior to this Interpretation, pending under the existing laws. Thus, although the issuance of the said emergency decree on September 25, 1999, by the President, and the draft of the contingent Executive Outline by the Executive Yuan failed to comply with the procedures set out above, there was no breach of the Constitution.

Notes and Questions

1. In *Stephen Kalong Ningkan v Government of Malaysia*, did the Privy Council settle the issue? Did it provide some degree of judicial deference, or maintain the possibility for judicial inquiry into the emergency decree? Why?

2. On the *Ningkan* case, see Yash Ghai, 'The Politics of the Constitution: Another Look at the Ningkan Litigation' (1986) 7 *Singapore Law Review* 147; and V Sinnadurai, 'Proclamation of Emergency – Reviewable? Stephen Kalong Ningkan v Government of Malaysia' (1968) 10 *Malaya Law Review* 130.

3. What was the subject of review in *JY Interpretation No 543*? The emergency decree itself, or the supplementary regulation for the implementation of the emergency decree? Or both? Did the Constitutional Court of Taiwan review the emergency decree despite having no express constitutional authorisation? On what constitutional grounds did the Constitutional Court assert such a power? The Constitutional Court of Taiwan treated the emergency decree as law and the supplementary regulations as administrative rules, and required similar checks and balances as in ordinary times. Do you agree? How feasible is this constitutional requirement? Note that in the end of the *Interpretation*, the Court fell short of invalidating the emergency decree and the supplementary regulation despite unconstitutional flaws having been confirmed.

4. In the wake of the terrorist attacks of 11 September 2001, a scholarly debate on emergency constitutions ensued, particularly in the United States. Bruce Ackerman, in 'The Emergency Constitution' (2004) 113 *Yale Law Journal* 1029, advocated adopting a procedural, political check – rather than a substantive, judicial check – on the exercise of emergency powers. He proposed that a majority vote of the Congress be required to continue the state of emergency for the first two to three months, followed by a 60 per cent vote to extend the state of emergency two more months, and then by a 70 per cent vote for the next two months, and 80 per cent thereafter. In such a scheme, states of emergency are unlikely to last more than six to seven months as required by more than 80 per cent of a parliamentary vote, an extraordinary consensus. However, Tribe and Gudridge are concerned about the danger and ineffectiveness of procedural safeguards, preferring to rely on judicial supervision. See L Tribe and P Gudridge, 'The Anti-Emergency Constitutions' (2004) 113 *Yale Law Journal* 1801. Similarly, David Cole, in 'The Priority of Morality: The Emergency Constitution's Blind Spot'

(2004) 113 *Yale Law Journal* 1753, contends that the judiciary is a better institution to adjudicate legal and at times moral issues during extraordinary times. For a comparative view in Asia, see VV Ramraj and AK Thiruvengadam (eds), *Emergency Powers in Asia* (Cambridge: Cambridge University Press, 2010).

E. Judicial Decision

Judicial decisions are typically the subject of review by higher courts. However, in a centralised system of judicial review, constitutional courts are vested with the power to review laws or regulations *in abstract* and may not be granted the power to review judicial decisions rendered by ordinary courts. Taiwan, South Korea, Mongolia and Indonesia, among others, adopt this institutional design. Nonetheless, these constitutional courts may still find ways to review judicial decisions.

For example, in *JY Interpretation No 154*, the Constitutional Court treated selected judicial decisions (*Pan-li*) published by the Supreme Court and Administrative Court as having the same legal and binding force as regulations and, thus, subjected them to constitutional review. Similarly, while Article 68(1) of the South Korean Constitutional Court Act does not empower ordinary courts to conduct constitutional review, the Constitutional Court made an exception in invalidating a Supreme Court judgment that failed to observe the interpretation of the Constitutional Court. Only the Constitutional Court of Indonesia honoured its institutional constraints, as can be seen below.

JY Interpretation No 154
29 Sep 1978 (Constitutional Court, Taiwan)

Facts

The petitioner registered a land lease contract in a township administrative office. The officials mistakenly recorded the name of the lessor who had passed away years before. The officials refused to correct the record, and the petitioner took out an action at the administrative court but the case was dismissed. He then filed for a retrial on the ground that the judgment was 'clearly erroneous in the application of law', but this too was denied. The petitioner then filed again for a retrial on the ground that the court 'did not apply the appropriate law in the judgment'. The Administrative Court dismissed this request on the ground of a *Pan-li* (46) *Tsai Tze* No 41 of the Administrative Court, holding that a party in an administrative litigation may not petition for a retrial on the same facts. The petitioner then filed the case with the Constitutional Court and argued that the said *Pan-li* infringed his right to sue. The question before the Court was whether it had jurisdiction to review *Pan-li*.

Held

The applicable 'laws or regulations' concerning the finality of the judgment, in accordance with Article 4, Paragraph 1, Subparagraph, of the Grand Justices Council Adjudication Act, means the laws or regulations or their equivalents based on which the finality of the judgment is rendered. Furthermore, Article 25 of the Court Organic Act provides, '[if] a chamber of the Supreme Court should render legal opinions that differ from existing legal precedents, the President shall submit [the case] to the President of the Judicial Yuan who in turn shall call forth the Conference of the Alteration of Judicial Precedents to determine [the outcome of the opinion].' Article 24 of the Directives for the Operational Procedure of Administrative Court [also] provides, '[if] a chamber renders different legal opinions from existing legal precedents, the President shall submit [the case] to the President of the Judicial Yuan who in turn shall call forth the Conference of the Alteration of Judicial Precedents to determine [the outcome of the opinion]' (Currently Article 38, Paragraph 1). Suffice it to say that barring the modification or alteration process, the legal precedents of the Supreme Court and Administrative Court shall have binding effect and can be the bases for courts at all levels in rendering their respective judgments. Article 4, Paragraph 1, Section 2, of the Grand Justices Council Adjudication Act is applicable if and when the issue of constitutionality is present so that the rights of the people can be maintained . . .

Constitutional Review of Judgments Case
96Hun-Ma172, 24 Dec 1997 (Constitutional Court, South Korea)

Facts

A transfer profit tax was imposed on the complainant by the government agency, and he challenged the legality of this taxation. The suit was rejected by the High Court. When the case was pending before the Supreme Court, the Constitutional Court made a decision regarding the constitutionality of the impugned law on which the taxation was based. However, the Supreme Court failed to apply the interpretation of the Constitutional Court. In dismissing the complainant's case, the Supreme Court even held that it was not bound by Constitutional Court's decision. The complainant then filed an individual complaint against the Supreme Court's decision with the Constitutional Court.

Held

Although making the ordinary courts' judgments subject to review of the Constitutional Court would be more desirable to strengthen the protection of constitutional rights, the failure to do so in Article 68(1) does not amount to unconstitutionality since it does not clearly go beyond the legislative discretion. Nevertheless, to the extent that the provision is interpreted to exclude from constitutional challenge those judgments that enforce the laws struck down in whole or part by the Constitutional Court and thereby infringe upon people's basic rights, the provision in question should be unconstitutional.

Unconstitutionality decisions of the Constitutional Court could take such forms as unqualified unconstitutionality, limited constitutionality, limited unconstitutionality, and nonconformity to the Constitution, and the decisions in all these forms are binding. The Court's evaluation of a statute may vary according to how it interprets the text, meaning, and legislative intent of the statute. Then, the Court chooses the most favorable interpretation within the scope permitted by general rules of interpretation. After that, the Court may articulate the constitutional scope of the meaning of the statute and find it constitutional within that scope. Or the Court may articulate the possibilities of applying the statute beyond its constitutional scope and find it unconstitutional as applied outside that scope. The two forms are flip-sides of a coin and are the same for all practical purposes. They differ only in whether they actively or passively exclude the unconstitutional applications of an otherwise valid statute, and they are equally decisions of partial constitutionality.

The judgment of the Supreme Court enforces the statutory provision invalidated by the Constitutional Court in a decision of limited unconstitutionality, and it violates the binding force of the Constitutional Court's decisions. Therefore, the constitutional complaint against the Supreme Court's judgment must be allowed as an exception. Then, since the judgment infringes on the complainant's right to property, it should be cancelled according to Article 75(3) of the Constitutional Court Act.

Finally, since both the judgment and the original administrative action applied the law already struck down, the latter is clearly unconstitutional as well. Since it is desirable for the realization of the rule of law to eliminate the unconstitutional state of affairs in one stroke as well as provide swift and efficient redress to peoples' infringed rights, the administrative action is hereby annulled according to Article 75(3) of the Constitutional Court Act . . .

Decision Number 001/PUU-IV/2006
25 Jan 2006 (Constitutional Court, Indonesia)

Facts

The petitioners were a pair of mayoral and vice-mayoral candidates. In an election dispute, the High Court declared them winners of the election but this decision was invalidated by the Supreme Court. The petitioners challenged the Supreme Court's decision by filing a 'petition for judicial review of a law against the Constitution' to the Constitutional Court. They argued that the Supreme Court's decision should be subject to the jurisdiction of the Constitutional Court. According to Article 24C of the Constitution, the Constitutional Court has the final power to review the constitutionality of any law and to decide the results of general elections. The question before the Court was whether this gave the Constitutional Court power to review the constitutionality of a judicial decision.

Held

Whereas simply treating a Decision of the Supreme Court and jurisprudence as equal and also treating jurisprudence and law as equal is incorrect, because:

(a) both in formal and substantive sense, a law is not the same as jurisprudence. A Decision of the Supreme Court is a judicial decision (*een judicieele vonnis*), which belongs to the category of individual and concrete norms that are not binding in general (*erga omnes*), but which only bind parties (*inter-partes*). A Decision of the Supreme Court or jurisprudence is not a legislation which belongs to the category of general and abstract norms. Both types of legal norms cannot be treated as equal although both are sources of law in [a] formal sense.

(b) besides, not all Decisions of the Supreme Court are continuously followed by the next court decisions (*constant jurisprudentie*) and become permanent jurisprudence (*vaste jurisprudentie*). Even if they become permanent jurisprudence – quod non – they do not become the object of authorities of the Court to conduct review in the meaning of Article 24C Paragraph (1) of the 1945 Constitution;

(c) concerning review of law against the Constitution as intended by the 1945 Constitution, the Court is of the opinion that the review must be placed in the context of check and balances system because there is separation of power in the 1945 Constitution, and the Court is only granted the authority to conduct review of legislative product in the form of law, and it is not intended to review the product of judicial power in this matter the Supreme Court . . .

Soedarsono, SH & Maruarar Siahaan SH (dissenting)

Accordingly, we are of the opinion that the authorities of the Constitutional Court in Article 24C of the 1945 Constitution and Article 10 Paragraph (1) of Law 24 Year 2003 and Article 51 Paragraph (1) of Law 24/2003, are authorities that are open to possible development, insofar as they are still within the limits that are the main duties of the Constitutional Court, and therefore the petition of the petitioners – although formulated as a review of law by considering that the Decision of the Supreme Court a quo as a jurisprudence is equal to Law – in fact, which is filed by the Petitioners as an effort to meet the competence criteria of the Constitutional Court while the Decision of the Supreme Court argued by the Petitioners to be contradictory to basic rights recognized in the 1945 Constitution, actually constitutes a constitutional complaint, being admitted as one of the authorities of Constitutional Court in Germany and Korea and many Constitutional Courts of ex Communist countries under the Soviet Union. In our opinion with full confidence as a result of correct interpretation (comparative study interpretation), the choice of the drafters of amendments to the 1945 Constitution that form a Constitutional Court separately from the Supreme Court, having the authority to conduct judicial review, logically also contains a consequence that Decision of the Supreme Court as a judicative authority can be reviewed against the 1945 Constitution by the Constitutional Court, as an equal institution and in the context of horizontal functional supervision and not hierarchically vertical supervision. If it is not the intention of the drafters of amendments to the 1945 Constitution, it should have been selected the United States model and not Continental European model, which grants the authority to a judicial power organ separate from the Supreme Court; and if it is not the intent of the drafters of amendments to the 1945 Constitution, such consequence is inevitable. Thus, in our opinion, the petition of the a quo Petitioners shall be the authority of the Constitutional Court, in which the substance or principal case should be examined, considered and decided by the Constitutional Court, because the legal standing of the petitioners in such category of petition is entirely fulfilled in terms of constitutional rights of the Petitioners.

However, although we are of the opinion that the petition of the Petitioners is included as one of the authorities of the Constitutional Court, from the evidence obtained insofar as concerning the substance, the Supreme Court in its decision did not violate the basic rights of the Petitioners in the Regional Head Election dispute acknowledged and respected by the 1945 Constitution.

Notes and Questions

1. The Constitutional Courts of South Korea and Taiwan both made exceptions to review the constitutionality of judicial decisions, but the Constitutional Court of Indonesia did not. What do you think accounts for the adoption of these two different positions?

2. What is the impact on the relationship between the Taiwanese Constitutional Court and the Supreme Court, if the Constitutional Court enjoys the power to review judicial decisions? Note the earlier discussion of the institutional design of judicial review and hybrid models in section III.

V. JUDICIAL APPOINTMENT, ORGANISATION AND INDEPENDENCE

Judicial independence, the rule of law and the separation of powers stand at the core of modern constitutionalism. Judicial independence free from interference is an essential guarantee of the exercise of judicial powers as the third neutral arbiter between the legislature and the executive. This relates not only to the personal independence of judges in making decisions, but also to institutional independence of the courts from the pressures or influence of the political branches. This is secured by provisions to ensure judicial autonomy in budgets, judicial administration, and the process of judicial appointment and tenure. This section discusses these issues in turn, and draws comparisons between the centralised and decentralised systems of judicial review systems, with particular regard to the regime governing judicial appointment to constitutional courts and supreme courts.

A. Judicial Appointment

Designing mechanisms of judicial appointment is a challenging task that requires the striking of a balance between judicial independence and political accountability, especially since how judges are appointed bears directly on their impartiality, integrity and independence.[107] It may thus be argued that judicial appointments by political branches through some power-sharing mechanisms are more likely to be affected by political preferences than where appointments are made through less political mechanisms.[108] Furthermore, under political appointment systems, judges may be subject to a greater degree of accountability.[109]

   An even greater challenge is the appointment of judges to constitutional courts or the highest courts, which are usually vested with the final say on the interpretation of the constitution and laws. Given the institutional prominence of these courts, ensuring their independence and accountability is imperative. Let us now consider how judges are appointed to constitutional courts in Asia. While political involvement in judicial appointment ensures the political accountability or legitimacy of these constitutional courts, it may undermine their independence and even institutional authority.

i. Judicial Appointment to Constitutional Court

As Table 5.4 shows, all seven constitutional courts in Asia adopt power-sharing mechanisms in relation to judicial appointment. They may be further classified into two models: the co-operation model and the representation model.[110] The co-operation

---

[107] S Shetreet, *Judges on Trial* (New York: North-Holland Pub, 1976), 46.

[108] N Garopa and T Ginsburg, 'The Comparative Law and Economics of Judicial Councils' (2009) 27(1) *Berkeley Journal of International Law* 53, 57.

[109] Ibid.

[110] Jiunn-RongYeh, 'Politicization of Constitutional Courts in Asia: Institutional Features, Contexts and Legitimacy', paper presented at the *International Conference on New Perspectives in East Asian Studies*, Institute for the Advanced Studies in Humanities and Social Sciences, National Taiwan University, 1–2 June 2012, Taipei, 6–8.

Table 5.4 Methods of Appointments for Justices to Constitutional Courts

	Appointment of Justices		Appointment of Chief Justice	Term of Office
Taiwan (1947)	Nominated by President, with consent of the legislature		Nominated by President, with consent of the legislature	8 years/non-renewable
South Korea (1987)	3 by Chief Justice of the Supreme Court 3 by Parliament 3 by President		Appointed by President with Parliamentary consent	6 years/renewable
Mongolia (1992)	3 by Supreme Court 3 by Parliament 3 by President		Elected by all justices	6 year
Cambodia (1993)	3 by Supreme Council of the Magistracy 3 by National Assembly 3 by King		Elected by all justices	9 years/ non-renewable; one-third of members replaced every three years
Indonesia (2001)	3 by Supreme Court 3 by Parliament 3 by President		Elected by all justices	5 years/renewable for one consecutive term
Thailand (2007)	Appointed by King with the advice of the Senate	3 elected by Supreme Court Justices 2 elected by Supreme Administrative Court 2 (person qualified in law) 2 (person qualified in political science)	Appointed by King with the advice of the Senate	9 years/ non-renewable
Myanmar (2008)	3 by President 3 by Speaker of Lower House of Parliament 3 by Speaker of the Upper House of Parliament		Appointed by President with the approval of Lower House of Parliament	5 years/ on expiry of its term, the tribunal shall continue its functions till the President forms a new Tribunal.

model involves two government branches in effecting the appointment of all justices. Taiwan is such an example. Each constitutional court justice requires the nomination of the President and the consent of the Legislative Yuan.

The representation model emphasises the different interests of government branches in being fairly represented in the process of composing the bench of constitutional court justices. South Korea, Mongolia, Cambodia, Indonesia and Myanmar adopt this model, in which the executive, legislature and judiciary share the power to appoint constitutional justices. For example, in South Korea, there are nine constitutional court justices: three appointed by the Chief Justice of the Supreme Court, three by the Parliament and three by the President. Aside from the co-operation and representation models, Thailand has an interesting, complex and dynamic mechanism with elements of both models. Thai Constitutional Court justices are appointed by the King upon the advice of the Senate. However, the King's power of appointment is nominal, the appointment power in effect being shared by other government branches. Among the nine justices, five are selected by the judiciary (two elected by Supreme Court justices and two by Supreme Administrative Court justices) and the other four (two persons qualified in law and two in political sciences or other backgrounds) are selected by the Senate from a list submitted by the Selection Committee.

Other than Taiwan, which has 15 justices, all other Asian constitutional courts have nine justices each. The length of term ranges from five years, to six, eight or nine years, some of which are renewable and some are not. Staggered terms are adopted in Taiwan and Cambodia. In Cambodia, the Constitutional Council is composed of nine members whose term of office is limited to nine years, and one-third of the membership must be renewed every three years. In Taiwan, the 1997 constitutional revision stipulated the staggering of terms for constitutional court justices that would begin in 2003. Of the 15 justices appointed in 2003, eight served for only four years and seven for eight years, and as a result, half of justices would be renewed every four years.

As can be seen above, the method of appointing constitutional court justices usually involves a variety of power-sharing mechanisms and differs from the judicial appointment of ordinary court judges. In addition, constitutional court justices are not guaranteed life tenure but enjoy only a limited term, ranging from five to nine years. Due to these distinctive features, doubts may even arise as to the role of constitutional court justices and whether they are really independent, since they have no security of tenure or remuneration.

JY Interpretation No 601
22 Jul 2005 (Constitutional Court, Taiwan)

Facts

Dissatisfied with the decisions rendered by the Constitutional Court, the legislature decided to cut the budget for special premiums provided for all constitutional court justices for the fiscal year 2005. However, Article 81 of the Constitution guarantees that except in accordance with law, no judge shall be suspended or transferred or have his salary reduced. Concerned that the budget cut might violate the Constitution, some legislators submitted a petition to the Constitutional Court. One issue was whether the justices of the Constitutional Court were 'judges' within the meaning of the Constitution.

Held

II. The Justices [of the Constitutional Court] Are Judges in the Constitutional Context
With respect to Article 79-II of the Constitution and Article 5-IV of the Amendments to
the Constitution, which expressly provide that the Justices shall have the final authority to
interpret and construe the Constitution and laws and regulations, they merely stipulate a
division of labor among different courts under the judicial system, which makes no difference as to the fact that Justices and judges alike react passively to a case brought to their
attention pursuant to statutory procedure and independently and neutrally deliver a final,
authoritative opinion as to the Constitution or law in respect of the constitutional, legal or
factual issues in a particular case. Consequently, the Justices, like ordinary judges, are also
judges in the constitutional context who are mandated to exercise the judicial power.

Article 5-II of the Amendments to the Constitution unambiguously provides, inter alia,
that the Justices shall serve a term of eight years and may not be reappointed for a consecutive term. Article 5-III thereof further provides that, among the Justices nominated by
the President in the year 2003, eight of them shall serve for a term of four years. . . . It
should not be inferred that the Justices are not judges simply because they hold office for
a definite term. . . . As for the second half of Article 5-I of the Amendments to the
Constitution, which provides, 'Except those Justices who are transferred from the bench, a
Justice shall not enjoy lifetime tenure protection as provided in Article 81 of the
Constitution,' it is merely intended to exclude the status protection for those Justices who
are not transferred from the bench after they leave the office. Although it is not advisable
to omit a reasonable alternative provision, the aforesaid provision, however, has been set
forth on the premise that the Justices are also judges in the constitutional context. Otherwise,
the exclusionary provision would not be necessary. It is not plausible to deny the Justices
their judgeship for the aforesaid reason. Therefore, the first half of Article 5-IV of the
Organic Act of Judicial Yuan as amended and promulgated on May 23, 2001, provides,
'Any Justice who, upon expiration of his or her term, is not reappointed, shall be deemed
as a judge who has ceased taking cases, to whom the provisions of Article 40-III of the Act
Governing Judicial Personnel shall apply.' The said provision is formulated on the basis
that the Justices, in essence, exercise the same powers and authorities as judges of ordinary
courts do . . .

Decision Number 005/PUU-IV/2006
23 Aug 2006 (Constitutional Court, Indonesia)

Facts

The petitioners were 31 Supreme Court Justices who argued that their constitutional right
under Article 24(1) of the 1945 Constitution – the right to freedom as Supreme Court
Justices – was violated by certain provisions in the Law of the Republic of Indonesia
Number 22 Year 2004 concerning Judicial Commission and the Law of the Republic of
Indonesia Number 4 Year 2004 concerning Judicial Authority regarding supervision by the
Judicial Commission (KY). This petition involved three issues; (a) whether the definition
of 'judges' in Article 24B(1) of the 1956 Constitution concerning Judicial Commission
included Constitutional Justices; (b) whether such definition of judges covered Supreme
Court justices; and (c) whether the provisions of supervision in the Judicial Commission
Law (UUKY) and Judicial Authority Law (UUKK) contradicted the 1945 Constitution.

Held

Whereas if systematically reviewed and in accordance with the interpretation based on the 'original intent' of the formulation of the provisions of the 1945 Constitution, provisions concerning KY in Article 24B of the 1945 Constitution do not relate to provisions concerning MK [the Constitutional Court] set forth in Article 24C of the 1945 Constitution. Based on the [systematic placement] of the provisions of the Judicial Commission after the article setting forth about the Supreme Court, namely Article 24A, and before the article setting forth about the Constitutional Court, namely Article 24C, it is understood that the provisions on the Judicial Commission in Article 24B of the 1945 Constitution are not intended to include constitutional justices as set forth in Article 24C of the 1945 Constitution . . .

The exclusion of the attitude of constitutional justices in the definition of the attitude of judges according to Article 24B paragraph (1) of the 1945 Constitution is also contained in the provisions of UUMK [the Constitutional Court Law] and UUKK formulated prior to the formulation of UUKY. In UUMK, the function to supervise the attitude of Constitutional Justices is held by the Honorary Board set forth separately in Article 23 of UUMK. Likewise, Article 34 paragraph (3) of UUKK does not determine that Constitutional Justices become the objects of supervision by KY. In addition to that, different from ordinary judges, Constitutional Justices are basically not professional judges, but judges because of their position. Constitutional Justices are appointed for 5 (five) years and they shall return to their original profession after they no longer serve as Constitutional Justices . . .

Notes and Questions

1. The Constitutional Court of Taiwan in *JY Interpretation No 601* maintained that constitutional court justices, like ordinary court judges, were judges, while the Constitutional Court of Indonesia in *Decision Number 005/PUU-IV/2006* held otherwise. What sets these two courts apart on this issue? Different institutional design, or different conceptions of judges and judicial powers?

2. If constitutional court justices are not 'judges', what are they and on what ground can they exercise judicial powers?

ii. Judicial Appointment to Ordinary Courts and Supreme Courts

Unlike the process of appointing judges to Asian constitutional courts, which involves power-sharing mechanisms, the appointment of ordinary court judges is a far less politicised process. Typically, judges are appointed by the executive on the basis of qualifications or examinations. While this method prevents judicial appointment from becoming politicised, it may undermine judicial accountability and legitimacy. Hence, there has been a trend towards setting up an independent judicial council (or commission) – comprising members from the judiciary, the bar, the legal community, political branches or civil society – to participate in the judicial appointments process or other matters relating to the transfer, removal or performance evaluations of judges.[111] Some

[111] N Garopa and T Ginsburg, 'Guarding the Guardians: Judicial Councils and Judicial Independence' (2009) 57(1) *American Journal Comparative Law* 119.

constitutions establish judicial councils, like those of Hong Kong, Thailand, the Philippines and Pakistan. In other jurisdictions, they are created by statute, such as in Japan and Taiwan.

In Asia, there are four ways in which Supreme Court justices are appointed, each with a different level of power-sharing between the executive and the legislature. The first is the *executive model*, where justices are appointed by the president or cabinet. Japan and Bangladesh are typical examples. Under the Japanese Constitution, justices of the Supreme Court are appointed by the Cabinet, and the Chief Justice is appointed by the Emperor upon the designation of the Cabinet.[112] In Bangladesh, the Chief Justice and other Supreme Court Justices are appointed by the President.[113]

The second model is that of *executive appointment in consultation* with the Chief Justice of the Supreme Court. India, Singapore and China are examples. The Indian Constitution states that Supreme Court justices, except for the Chief Justice, shall be appointed by the President in consultation with the Chief Justice.[114] Similarly, the Singapore Constitution states that Supreme Court judges are appointed by the President on the advice of the Prime Minister and after consultation with the Chief Justice.[115] In China, judges of the Supreme People's Court are appointed by the Standing Committee of the NPC upon the recommendation of the president of the Supreme People's Court.[116]

The third model is executive appointment where *judicial councils or commissions* are consulted. Many jurisdictions in this region adopt this model. For example, in Hong Kong, judges are appointed by the Chief Executive on the recommendation of an independent commission.[117] In Pakistan, Supreme Court justices are appointed by the President with the recommendation of Judicial Commission.[118] In the Philippines, the members of the Supreme Court are appointed by the President from a list of at least three nominees prepared by the Judicial and Bar Council for every vacancy.[119]

The fourth model involves *power-sharing elements* in that justices of the Supreme Court are appointed by the executive with parliamentary consent. For example, according to the South Korea Constitution, Supreme Court justices are appointed by the President on the recommendation of the Chief Justice and with the consent of the National Assembly.[120] In Myanmar, Article 299(d) of the Constitution stipulates that the President, in co-ordination with the Chief Justice of the Union, shall submit the list of persons considered suitable to be appointed as Supreme Court Judges, to the *Pyidaungsu Hluttaw* (Parliament) for its approval.

Notes and Questions

1. What explains the different models adopted in different jurisdictions? Constitutional structure? Colonial influence? Legal culture? Do these models have any impact on judicial independence or judicial accountability?

---

[112] Arts 7 and 79, Constitution of Japan.
[113] Art 95, Constitution of Bangladesh.
[114] Art 124, Constitution of India.
[115] Art 95, Constitution of the Republic of Singapore.
[116] Art 67(11), Constitution of the People's Republic of Indonesia.
[117] Art 88, Hong Kong Basic Law.
[118] Arts 175A and 177, Constitution of Pakistan.
[119] Art VIII, Sec 9, Constitution of the Philippines.
[120] Art 104, Constitution of the Republic of Korea.

2. Judicial councils are institutions set up to protect the appointment, removal and discipline of judges from political interference, while securing some degree of judicial independence. Powers of judicial councils may vary but usually include three basic capacities: the appointment of judges, the evaluation of the performance of judges, and other housekeeping functions such as managing budgets, resources or other operations. The composition of judicial councils also varies but often includes three main groups: judges, members of other political branches and lawyers. Garopa and Ginsburg observe that if judges are in the majority on the judicial council and have strong powers, they can promote greater judicial independence. If non-judges comprise the majority on the judicial council and have powers limited to housekeeping functions, such council is likely to be politicised and weak. See N Garopa and T Ginsburg, 'Guarding the Guardians: Judicial Councils and Judicial Independence' (2009) 57(1) *American Journal Comparative Law* 119.

3. In Japan, the Judges Nominating Consultation Commission (JNCC) was created in 2003 to assist in the appointment of lower court judges. The JNCC comprises 11 members appointed by the Supreme Court. These members include two judges, one public prosecutor, two attorneys and six non-lawyers, and two of the members must be female. The JNCC mainly considers three kinds of appointment:

   (a) new graduates from the Judicial Training Institute applying to become assistant judges;
   (b) assistant judges seeking nomination to become judges, and judges seeking reappointments; and
   (c) attorneys applying for appointment as assistant judges or judges.

   The JNCC collects information about all applicants through its regional committees and related persons, and compiles a list of suitable candidates who are recommended to the Supreme Court. With the JNCC's participation, judicial appointment of lower court judges has become more transparent. Even so, challenges remain as to the composition of the JNCC, which is entirely in the hands of the Supreme Court. For further discussion, see Takayuki Ii, 'Japanese Way of Judicial Appointment and Its Impact on Judicial Review' (2010) 5(2) *National Taiwan University Law Review* 90.

iii. Qualification of Judge and Procedure of Judicial Appointment

Constitutions or statutes may stipulate qualifications for appointees to the Supreme Court or Constitutional Court. Nationality is a common requirement. For example, the Constitution of the Philippines provides that no person shall be appointed a member of the Supreme Court or any lower collegiate court unless he is a natural-born citizen of the Philippines.[121] The Constitution of Mongolia stipulates that a Mongolian national of 35 years of age with higher legal education and experience in judicial practice of not less than 10 years may be appointed as a judge of the Supreme Court.[122]

---

[121] Art VIII Sec (7)(1), Constitution of the Philippines.
[122] Art 51(3), Constitution of Mongolia.

It is interesting that in some jurisdictions, constitutional court justices are not necessarily appointed from among members of the legal profession. For example in Thailand, Section 204(1)(4) demands that two out of the nine justices are selected from 'qualified persons in the field of political science, public administration or other social science, who really [possess] knowledge and expertise in the administration of the State affairs'. In Taiwan, the qualifications of justices to the Constitutional Court are stipulated in the Organic Act of the Judicial Yuan. To be eligible for appointment as a Justice of the Constitutional Court, a candidate must:

(a) have served as a Justice of the Supreme Court for more than 10 years with a distinguished record; or
(b) have served as a Member of the Legislative Yuan for more than nine years with distinguished contributions; or
(c) have been a professor of a major field of law at a university for more than 10 years, who must have authored publications in a specialised field; or
(d) have served as a Justice of the International Court, or have had authoritative works published in the fields of public or comparative law; or
(e) be a person highly reputed in the field of legal research and who has had political experience.

In addition, the number of Justices qualifying under any single head of qualification listed above shall not exceed one-third of the total number of Justices. In practice, half of the Constitutional Court is usually composed of justices with the relevant academic background and half of career judges.[123]

In addition, some constitutions may prescribe appointment procedures or other limitations to regulate judicial appointments. For example, the Constitution of the Philippines stipulates that two months immediately before the next presidential elections and up to the end of his term, a President or Acting President shall not make appointments, except temporary appointments to executive positions when continued vacancies therein will prejudice public service or endanger public safety.[124] 'Midnight appointments' or other political manipulations may generate constitutional concerns calling for judicial resolution. In India, questions have also arisen as to whether the appointment of additional judges should follow the appointment procedure of ordinary judges, and whether a circular letter issued by the Law Minister to the Chief Justice regarding the appointment of judges was appropriate.

KiliosBayan Foundation, et al v Eduardo Ermita et al
GR No 177721, 3 Jul 2007 (Supreme Court, Philippines)

Facts

The petitioners filed a petition against the Executive Secretary and Gregory S Ong regarding the appointment in favour of Gregory S Ong as Associate Justice of the Supreme Court. They argued that Ong's appointment was patently unconstitutional, arbitrary and a grave abuse of discretion since Ong was not a natural-born Filipino citizen but, rather, a

---

[123] Wen-Chen Chang, 'The Role of Judicial Review in Consolidating Democracy: the Case of Taiwan' (2005) 2(2) *Asia Law Review* 73.
[124] Art VII Sec 15, Constitution of the Philippines.

Chinese citizen. Section 7(1) of Article VIII of the 1987 Constitution, on which the petitioners based their claim, provided that 'no person' shall be appointed Member of the Supreme Court or any lower collegiate court unless he is a natural-born citizen of the Philippines. Even if Ong's father was granted Filipino citizenship by naturalisation, the petitioners argued that this did not make him a natural-born Filipino citizen unless his birth certificate was changed by judicial order.

Azcuna J

[F]rom the records of this Court, respondent Ong is a naturalized Filipino citizen. The alleged subsequent recognition of his natural-born status by the Bureau of Immigration and the DOJ [Department of Justice] cannot amend the final decision of the trial court stating that respondent Ong and his mother were naturalized along with his father.

Furthermore, as petitioners correctly submit, no substantial change or correction in an entry in a civil register can be made without a judicial order, and, under the law, a change in citizenship status is a substantial change . . .

The series of events and long string of alleged changes in the nationalities of respondent Ong's ancestors, by various births, marriages and deaths, all entail factual assertions that need to be threshed out in proper judicial proceedings so as to correct the existing records on his birth and citizenship. The chain of evidence would have to show that DyGuiok Santos, respondent Ong's mother, was a Filipino citizen, contrary to what still appears in the records of this Court. Respondent Ong has the burden of proving in court his alleged ancestral tree as well as his citizenship under the time-line of three Constitutions. Until this is done, respondent Ong cannot accept an appointment to this Court as that would be a violation of the Constitution. For this reason, he can be prevented by injunction from doing so . . .

De Castro et al v Judicial and Bar Council et al Case
GR No 191002, 17 Mar 2010 (Supreme Court, Philippines)

Facts

Chief Justice Reynato S Puno of the Philippines Supreme Court was to retire by 17 May 2010. On the eve of her departure from presidential office, President Gloria Macapagal Arroyo appointed Justice Renato Corona as Chief Justice. However, Section 15, Article VII of the Constitution prohibits the President or Acting President from making appointments within two months immediately before the next presidential elections and up to the end of his term, except temporary appointments to executive positions when continued vacancies therein would prejudice public service or endanger public safety. The question before the Court was whether Corona's appointment as Chief Justice was unconstitutional.

Bersamin J

The first, Section 15, Article VII (Executive Department), provides:

> Section 15. Two months immediately before the next presidential elections and up to the end of his term, a President or Acting President shall not make appointments, except temporary appointments to executive positions when continued vacancies therein will prejudice public service or endanger public safety.

The other, Section 4(1), Article VIII (Judicial Department), states:

> Section 4. (1). The Supreme Court shall be composed of a Chief Justice and fourteen Associate Justices. It may sit en banc or in its discretion, in division of three, five, or seven Members. Any vacancy shall be filled within ninety days from the occurrence thereof
> . . .

Article VIII is dedicated to the Judicial Department and defines the duties and qualifications of Members of the Supreme Court, among others. Section 4(1) and Section 9 of this Article are the provisions specifically providing for the appointment of Supreme Court Justices. In particular, Section 9 states that the appointment of Supreme Court Justices can only be made by the President upon the submission of a list of at least three nominees by the JBC [Judicial and Bar Council]; Section 4(1) of the Article mandates the President to fill the vacancy within 90 days from the occurrence of the vacancy.

Had the framers intended to extend the prohibition contained in Section 15, Article VII to the appointment of Members of the Supreme Court, they could have explicitly done so. They could not have ignored the meticulous ordering of the provisions. They would have easily and surely written the prohibition made explicit in Section 15, Article VII as being equally applicable to the appointment of Members of the Supreme Court in Article VIII itself, most likely in Section 4(1), Article VIII. That such specification was not done only reveals that the prohibition against the President or Acting President making appointments within two months before the next presidential elections and up to the end of the President's or Acting President's term does not refer to the Members of the Supreme Court . . .

Moreover, the usage in Section 4(1), Article VIII of the word shall – an imperative, operating to impose a duty that may be enforced – should not be disregarded. Thereby, Section 4(1) imposes on the President the imperative duty to make an appointment of a Member of the Supreme Court within 90 days from the occurrence of the vacancy. The failure by the President to do so will be a clear disobedience to the Constitution.

The 90-day limitation fixed in Section 4(1), Article VIII for the President to fill the vacancy in the Supreme Court was undoubtedly a special provision to establish a definite mandate for the President as the appointing power, and cannot be defeated by mere judicial interpretation in Valenzuela to the effect that Section 15, Article VII prevailed because it was 'couched in stronger negative language.' Such interpretation even turned out to be conjectural, in light of the records of the Constitutional Commission's deliberations on Section 4(1), Article VIII . . .

Consequently, prohibiting the incumbent President from appointing a Chief Justice on the premise that Section 15, Article VII extends to appointments in the Judiciary cannot be sustained.

SP Gupta v President of India and Ors
[1982] AIR SC 149 (Supreme Court, India)

Facts

Article 217 of India Constitution stipulates that every Judge of a High Court shall be appointed by the President by warrant under his hand and seal after consultation with the Chief Justice of India and the Governor of the State. Article 224 states that the number of judges can be increased by reason of any temporary increase in the business of a High Court. In such cases, the President may appoint duly qualified persons to be additional Judges of the Court for such period not exceeding two years. In this case, the Law Minister issued a circular letter to the chief justices of each High Court and the Chief Minister of each State to obtain the consent [for] additional judges working in the High Court to be appointed as permanent judge.

The first four petitions challenged the constitutionality of the circular letter and the central Government's power in respect of the appointment or non-appointment of additional judges. The last four petitions attacked the constitutional validity of the orders of transfer of Chief Justice MM Ismail and Chief Justice KBN Singh. The issues were whether the appointment of the additional judges of the High Court complied with Articles 217 and 224, and whether the circular letter issued by the Law Minister was unconstitutional.

PN Bhagwati J

Appointment of Judges is a serious process where judicial expertise, legal learning, life's experience and high integrity are components, but above all are two indispensables – social philosophy in active unison with the socialistic Articles of the Constitution, and second, but equally important, built-in resistance to pushes and pressures by class interests, private prejudices, government threats and blandishments, party loyalties and contrary economic and political ideologies projecting into pronouncements . . .

The next question that arises for consideration is as to where is the power to appoint Judges of the High Courts and the Supreme Court located? Who has the final voice in the appointment of Judges of High Courts and the Supreme Court? The power of appointment of Judges of the Supreme Court is to be found in Clause (2) of Article 124 and this clause provides that every Judge of the Supreme Court shall be appointed by the President after consultation with such of the Judges of the Supreme Court and the High Courts in the States as the President may deem necessary for the purpose, provided that in the case of appointment of a Judge other than the Chief Justice, the Chief Justice of India shall always be consulted. . . .

The question immediately arises what constitutes 'consultation' within the meaning of Clause (2) of Article 124 and Clause (1) of Article 217, Fortunately, this question is no longer res integra and it stands concluded by the decision of this Court in Sankalch and Sheth's case. It is true that the question in Sankalch and Sheth's case related to the scope and meaning of 'consultation' in Clause (1) of Article 222, but it was common ground between the parties that 'consultation' for the purpose of Clause (2) of Article 124 and Clause (1) of Article 217 has the same meaning and content as 'consultation' in Clause (1) of Article 222. Chandrachud J, as he then was in his judgment in Sankalch and Sheth's case (supra) quoted with approval the following passage from the judgment given by Justice Subba Rao, when he was a Judge of the Madras High Court in *R Pushpam v State of Madras*, 'the word "consult" implies a conference of two or more persons or, an impact, of two or more minds in respect of a topic in order to enable them to evolve a correct or at-least a satisfactory solution' and added 'In order that the two minds may be able to confer and produce a mutual impact, It is essential that each must have for its consideration full and identical facts which can at once constitute both the source and foundation of the final decision' . . .

The power to appoint an additional Judge in a High Court is to be found in Clause (1) of Article 224 which reads as follows:

If by season of any temporary increase in the business of a High Court or by reason of arrears of work therein, it appears to the President that the number of the Judges of that Court should be for the time being increased, the President may appoint duly qualified persons to be additional Judges of the Court for such period not exceeding two years as he may specify . . .

The first question which arises for determination under Article 224 Clause (1) is as to when can an additional Judge be appointed by the President. This article confers power on the President to appoint an additional Judge, if by reason of any temporary increase in the business of a High Court or by reason of arrears of work therein, it appears to the President that the number of the judges of that Court should be for the time being increased and in that event, he can appoint an additional Judge for such period not exceeding two years as he may specify . . .

We are of the view that the provisions of Article 224 of the Constitution should be availed of and additional judges be appointed for the specific purpose of dealing with these arrears. The number of such additional judges required for each High Court for the purpose of dealing with the arrears will have to be fixed in consultation with the Chief Justice of India [and] the Chief Justice of the State High Court after taking into consideration the arrears in the particular Court, their nature and the average disposal of that Court . . .

It is clear on a plain reading of Article 217, Clause (1) that when an additional Judge is to be appointed, the procedure set out in that article is to be followed. Clause (1) of Article 217 provides that 'Every Judge' of a High Court shall be appointed after consultation with the Chief Justice of India, the Governor of the State and the Chief Justice of the High Court. The expression 'Every Judge' must on a plain natural construction include not only a permanent Judge but also an additional Judge . . . We must therefore, hold that no additional Judge can be appointed without complying with the requirement of Clause (1) of Article 217 . . .

But the question then arises what are the factors which can legitimately be taken into account by the Central Government in deciding whether or not to reappoint an additional Judge for a further term or to appoint him as a permanent Judge . . .

There are no limitations in the language of Clause (1) of Article 217 as to what factors shall be considered and what factors shall not be, but having regard to the object and purpose of that provision namely, appointment of a High Court Judge, it is obvious that fitness and suitability, physical, intellectual and moral, would be the governing considerations to be taken into account in deciding the question of appointment . . .

We must then turn to consider the question whether the circular letter issued by the Law Minister was unconstitutional and void. . . . The Law Minister is undoubtedly a member of the Cabinet and it is reasonable to assume that in issuing the circular letter he was acting on behalf of the Central Government but the circular letter does not appear to have been issued by the Law Minister in the exercise of any constitutional or legal power. The circular letter has no constitutional or legal sanction behind it and non-compliance with the request contained in it would not proprio vigore entail any adverse consequence to the additional Judge or to the person recommended for initial appointment, for not complying with such request . . . It is no more than a letter addressed to the Chief Minister of each State asking him to obtain the consent of the additional Judges as also of those recommended or to be recommended for initial appointment, for being appointed as Judges in a High Court outside the State . . .

The circular letter does not violate the provisions of Clause (1) of Article 217 or Clause (1) of Article 222 nor does it offend against any other constitutional or legal provision and the challenge against the validity of the circular letter must, therefore, fail . . .

We would therefore dismiss the first group of writ petitions in so far as they seek relief in respect of ON Vohra and SN Kumar. No relief can be granted in respect of ON Vohra because, though added as a party respondent, he has not appeared and claimed any relief against the decision of the Central Government to discontinue him as an additional Judge and has accepted such decision without protest or complaint. That is the reason why we have not examined the complaint of the petitioners in regard to discontinuance of ON Vohra as an additional Judge. So far as SN Kumar is concerned, we have rejected his claim for relief, because, in our opinion, and we have already given our reasons taking this view, the decision to discontinue him as an additional Judge was taken by the Central Government after full and effective consultation with the Chief Justice of Delhi and the Chief Justice of India and it was not based on any irrelevant considerations, We have taken the view that the circular letter issued by the Law Minister was not unconstitutional and void and hence the first group of writ petitions must also fail in so far as they challenge the constitutional validity of the circular letter. The other [reliefs] claimed in the first group of writ petitions [have] also been rejected by us and hence this group of writ petitions must wholly fail . . .

Notes and Questions

1. In *Kilosbayab v Ermita*, the Supreme Court of the Philippines dealt with whether the nominee for Associate Justice met the requirement of being a natural-born Filipino citizen. Why should judges be natural-born citizens? Why not naturalised citizens? Compare this with the composition of the Hong Kong Court of Final Appeals, which comprises the Chief Justice, three permanent judges and either one non-permanent Hong Kong judge or one foreign judge from another common law jurisdiction. See PY Lo, *The Hong Kong Basic Law* (Hong Kong: LexisNexis, 2011) at 472.

2. The case of *De Castro et al v Judicial and Bar Council et al* of the Philippines shows how the timing of a judicial appointment may be as important and politically controversial as the appointment itself. In Taiwan, the constitutional revision of 1997 altered the appointment mechanism for the justices of the Constitutional Court and stipulated that the new mechanism would become effective in 2003. However, the revision failed to provide any instructions on what mechanism to follow should any vacancy occur before 2003. Two cases were brought before the Constitutional Court. In *JY Interpretation No 470*, the Court held that

   the original legislative intent of the current Article 5 of the Constitution was that the newly appointed Justices shall succeed the current Justices following the expiration of the current term in October 2003. However, if vacancies do arise during this interim period, hindering the regular duties of the Judicial Yuan, the process of the nominations to fill the vacancies should follow Article 4 of the 1994 amended Constitution. The failure to provide specifically for such contingency in the current Constitution in Article 5 is a legislative omission and therefore, the nominations of the President, Vice President or Justices, Judicial Yuan, by the ROC President should be carried out pursuant to Article 4 of the Constitution as amended on August 1, 1994.[125]

   The Court in *JY Interpretation No 541* also decided that:

   As a result, if vacancies occur due to resignation or other reasons before the expiration of the 2003 legislative term, which adversely affect the normal operation of the Judicial Yuan, the President shall nominate, with the consent of the Legislative Yuan, the President of the Judicial Yuan, the Vice (Deputy) President of the Judicial Yuan and the Grand Justices.[126]

---

[125] *Interpretation No 470* [trans Baker and McKenzie], 3 ROC Const Ct 660, 664–65 (2007).
[126] *Interpretation No 541* [trans Li-Chih Lin], 4 ROC Const Ct 439, 448–49 (2007).

3.   In India, Article 224 of the Constitution permits the appointment of additional judges for a period not exceeding two years. Singapore has a similar short-term judicial appointment procedure for Judicial Commissioners. Article 94 of the Singapore Constitution provides for Judicial Commissioners (who have no security of tenure or remuneration) to be appointed for single cases only. This provision has never been invoked. While short-term judicial appointments are a convenient and pragmatic solution to a temporary increase in the judicial docket, the misuse or abuse of the system has the strong potential to undermine judicial independence, especially if the appointee desires and seeks a permanent position on the Bench. Arguably, such provisions are violations of the state's judicial power.

B. Judicial Transfer

Judicial transfer, if misused or abused, may gravely undermine judicial independence. As such, many constitutions have well-established restrictions on the transfer of judges. For example, in India, the Constitution stipulates that the President may transfer a judge from one High Court to any other High Court only after consultation with the Chief Justice.[127] The Constitution of Thailand prescribes that

> the transfer of a judge without his or her prior consent shall not be permitted except in the case of termly transfer as provided by law, promotion to a higher position, being under a disciplinary action or becoming a defendant in a criminal case, negative impacts on the administration of justice in the trial and adjudication, or a *force majeure* event or any other inevitable cause of necessity, as provided by law.[128]

Where judicial transfers are concerned, consultations with the head of the judiciary and/or the consent of transferred judges is usually required. However, in what ways can such consultations be made? Should any kind and any degree of consultation suffice? Or should there be some more 'effective' consultation?

Union Of India vs Sankal Chand Himatlal Sheth and Anr
[1977] AIR SC 2328 (Supreme Court, India)

Facts

On 27 May 1976, the President of India, after consultation with the Chief Justice, issued a notification to transfer Shri Justice Sankalch and Himatlal Sheth, Judges of High Court of Gujarat, to the High Court of Andhra Pradesh. Justice Sheth complied with this order, but before that he filed a writ petition in the Gujarat High Court challenging the constitutional validity of the order. One issue was whether the President had effectively consulted with the Chief Justice prior to issuing the transfer decision.

Chandrachud J

Thus, if the power of the President, who has to act on the advice of the Council of Ministers, to transfer a High Court Judge under article 222(1) is strictly limited to cases in

---

[127]   Art 222, Constitution of the Union of India.
[128]   Art 197(3), Constitution of the Kingdom of Thailand.

which the transfer becomes necessary in order to [serve the] public interest, in other words, if it be true that the President has no power to transfer a High Court Judge for reasons not hearing on public interest but arising out of whim, caprice or fancy of the executive or its desire to bend a Judge to its own way of thinking, there is no possibility of any interference with the independence of the judiciary if a Judge is transferred without his consent.

Once it is appreciated that a High Court Judge can be transferred on the ground of public interest only, the apprehension that the executive may use the power of transfer for its own ulterior ends and thereby interfere with the independence of the judiciary, loses its force . . .

A Judge of the High Court can be appointed by the President only after consultation with the Chief Justice of India, the Governor of the State and the Chief Justice of the High Court; and he can be transferred from one High Court to another only after consultation with the Chief Justice of India. This consideration takes us to the next question, as important as the one of consent which has been just disposed of, as to what is the true meaning and content of 'consultation provided for by article 222(1) of the Constitution . . .

It must, therefore, follow that while consulting the Chief Justice, the President must make [the relevant data available to him, on the, basis] of which he can offer to the President the benefit of his considered opinion. If the facts necessary to arrive at a proper conclusion are not made [available to the Chief Justice, he] must ask for them because, in casting on the President the obligation to consult the Chief Justice, the Constitution at the same time must be taken to have imposed a duty on the Chief Justice to express his opinion on nothing less than a full consideration of the matter on which he is entitled to be consulted. The fulfilment by the President, of his constitutional obligation to place full facts before the Chief Justice and the performance by the latter, of the duty to elicit facts which are necessary to arrive at a proper conclusion[,] are parts of the same process and are complementary to each other. The faithful observance of these may well earn a handsome dividend useful to the administration of justice . . .

After an effective consultation with the Chief Justice of India, it is open to the President to arrive at a proper decision of the question whether a Judge should be transferred to another High Court because, what the Constitution requires is consultation with the Chief Justice, not his concurrence with the proposed transfer. But it is necessary to reiterate what Bhagwati and Krishna Iyer JJ said in Shamsher Singh (supra) that in all conceivable cases, consultation with the Chief Justice of India should be accepted by the Government of India and that the Court will have an opportunity to examine if any other extraneous circumstances have entered into the verdict of the executive if it departs from the counsel given by the Chief Justice of India . . .

SP Gupta v President of India and Ors
[1982] AIR SC 149 (Supreme Court, India)

Facts

Article 222 of the Constitution provides that the President may transfer a Judge from one High Court to any other High Court after consultation with the Chief Justice of India; and when a Judge has been or is so transferred, he shall be entitled to receive, in addition to his salary, a compensatory allowance. This case was involved with constitutional validity of orders to transfer Chief Justice MM Ismail and Chief Justice KBN Singh in two separate High Courts.

PN Bhagwati J

The second group of writ petitions raises the question of constitutional validity of the orders transferring Chief Justice MM Ismail to the Kerala High Court and Chief Justice KBN Singh to the Madras High Court[.] However, so far as Chief Justice MM Ismail is concerned, the question has become academic because he has stated in the counter affidavit filed by him in reply to the writ petition of Miss Lily Thomas that he does not want anyone to litigate for or against him nor does he want anything about him to be argued or debated and he has subsequently resigned his office as Chief Justice of the Madras High Court. [T]he only question which therefore survives for consideration is whether the transfer of Chief Justice KBN Singh to the Madras High Court could be said to be constitutionally invalid. The determination of this question obviously depends upon the true scope and ambit of the power of transfer conferred under Clause (1) of Article 222. That Article reads as follows:

> Article 222(1). The President may, after consultation with the Chief Justice of India, transfer a Judge from one High Court to any other High Court . . .

Now it is obvious that when a Judge is transferred from one High Court to another by way of punishment, it can never be in [the] public interest for no public interest would countenance punishment of a Judge except by way of impeachment under proviso (b) to Clause (1) of Article 217 read with Clause (4) of Article 124. There is a clear antithesis between a transfer by way of punishment and a transfer. In [the] public interest and therefore, a transfer by way of punishment must be held to be outside the scope and ambit of Article 222 Clause (1) . . .

That takes me to a consideration [of] the question whether in the present case where there was full and effective consultation between the Central Government and the Chief Justice of India before the decision was taken to transfer Chief Justice KBN Singh to the Madras High Court and whether such transfer was effected in [the] public interest and not by way of punishment . . .

So far as the first question is concerned whether there was full and effective consultation between the Central Government and the Chief Justice of India, I have already pointed out, while discussing the scope and effect of Clause (1) of Article 217 as to what is the meaning and content of 'consultation'[.] It requires that the Central Government must make available to the Chief Justice of India relevant data in regard to the Judge proposed to be transferred and the Chief Justice of India must also elicit and ascertain all relevant material relating to the Judge either directly from him or from other reliable resources and place such material before the Central Govt. Each of the two constitutional authorities, the Central Govt. and the Chief Justice of India, must have for its consideration full and identical facts which can at once constitute both the source and foundation of the final decision. . . .

There is nothing to show that this particular difficulty of Chief Justice KBN Singh was brought to the notice of the Central Government by the Chief Justice of India before the decision was taken by the Prime Minister on 9th January, 1981, to transfer Chief Justice KBN Singh. The meeting between Chief Justice KBN Singh and the Chief Justice of India took place at 7.00 pm on 8th January, 1981 and on the next day, the Prime Minister made her endorsement on the file and there is absolutely nothing to show, nothing even in the counter-affidavit of the Chief Justice of India, that after his talk with Chief Justice KBN Singh, he telephoned either to the Law Minister or to the Prime Minister pointing out this particular difficulty of Chief Justice KBN Singh to the Central Government. There is nothing even in any nothings on the file showing that any such information was conveyed by the

Chief Justice of India to the Law Minister or to the Prime Minister in the evening of 8th Jan., 1981 or on 9th Jan., 1981. This omission to communicate the difficulty which would be experienced by Chief Justice KBN Singh as a result of transfer is sufficient to vitiate the process of consultation and it must be held that there was no full and effective consultation as required under Article 222 Clause (1) . . .

I would, therefore, allow the second group of writ petitions in so far as they challenge the constitutional validity of the order transferring Chief Justice KBN Singh and issue a writ declaring the order of transfer of Chief Justice KBN Singh as unconstitutional and void . . .

Notes and Questions

1. In *Union v SH Sheth*, the Supreme Court of India emphasised the need for an effective consultation between the Chief Justice and the President. After such an effective consultation with the Chief Justice, it is open to the President to arrive at a proper decision regarding judicial transfer. Why should such consultation be 'effective'? What is the rationale for this?

2. How may the court assess whether consultations between the Chief Justice and the Government and between the Chief Justice and the judges to be transferred are effective? In *SP Gupta v President of India*, Justice Bhagwati argued that an effective consultation

> requires that the Central Government make available to the Chief Justice of India relevant data in regard to the Judge proposed to be transferred and the Chief Justice of India must also elicit and ascertain all relevant material relating to the Judge either directly from him or from other reliable resources and place such material before the Central Government. Each of the two constitutional authorities, the Central Govt. and the Chief Justice of India, must have for its consideration full and identical facts which can at once constitute both the source and foundation of the final decision.

What do you think about the feasibility of such effective consultation? Can either one of the constitutional authorities, the President or the Chief Justice, refuse to provide information on privilege or other grounds?

C. Security of Remuneration and Judicial Budget

In order to ensure independence, judges must be provided with adequate compensation. Nearly all constitutions contain an explicit guarantee and impose restrictions on the reduction of judicial salary during a judge's term of office. For example, in Taiwan, the Constitution provides life tenure for a judge and, save in accordance with law, a judge's salary cannot be reduced.[129] South Korea also has a similar constitutional provision.[130] In the Philippines, the salary of all judges is fixed by law, and during their term of office their salary shall not be decreased.

---

[129] Art 81, Constitution of the Republic of China, 1947.
[130] Art 106, Constitution of the Republic of Korea.

Aside from security of remuneration for individual judges, a few constitutions also guarantee some degree of financial autonomy to the judiciary. For example, Article 5(6) of the Additional Articles of the Constitution in Taiwan prohibits the executive from eliminating or reducing the proposed budget submitted annually by the judiciary. The Constitution of the Philippines also provides the judiciary with some extent of fiscal autonomy. Article 8(3) states that appropriations for the judiciary may not be reduced by the legislature below the amount appropriated for the previous year and, after approval, shall be automatically and regularly released. However, if the government slashes the judicial budget for whatever reason, how can the courts deal with such a budget cut? Would it not be pointless to guarantee judges their salaries but make it impossible for them to function by depriving judicial administrative staff of their jobs?

JY Interpretation No 601
22 Jul 2005 (Constitutional Court, Taiwan)

Facts

Dissatisfied with some decisions of the Constitutional Court, the majority of members in the legislature decided to cut the budget for the specialty premiums of Justices of the Constitutional Court for the fiscal year 2005. Worried that such budget cuts would contradict the Constitution, some legislators submitted the issue to the Constitutional Court for determination.

Held

The Legislative Yuan, in Deleting the Budget for the Specialty Premiums for Judicial Personnel Payable to the Justices, Has Acted against the Constitutional Intent of Article 81 of the Constitution . . .

A literal reading of Article 81 of the Constitution, providing, inter alia, that no judge shall have his or her salary diminished except in accordance with law, would lead to the conclusion that a judge's salary may not be diminished except in accordance with a law referred to in Article 170 of the Constitution. No contrary construction is allowed to so interpret the said provision as to infer that a judge's salary may be diminished as long as such reduction is done pursuant to law. In particular, since the said provision is designed to ensure the security of the status of a judge for the purpose of judicial independence, it shall not be so construed as to run counter to the constitutional purpose by enabling a state organ to decrease a judge's existing remuneration through ex post facto law or by non-enactment of any law . . .

In order to honour the legal principle that the remuneration of a public functionary must be commensurate with his or her status and office, the remuneration of the Justices must either be included in a special law or in a special chapter of the law, or be expressly prescribed by law that the laws governing the remuneration for specially appointed public functionaries or judges shall apply mutatis mutandis thereto. Nonetheless, if the competent authority in charge of the preparation of budgets, at a time when the relevant legal framework remains to be built, having considered the status, position and function of the Justices in the hierarchy of public functionaries as a whole, prescribes by law and/or regulation the remuneration legally receivable by the Justices in accordance with the applicable provisions of the existing and valid laws governing the remunerations for public functionaries, it will not be contrary to the Constitution and/or the laws so long as such law and/or regulation serves the purpose of the laws governing the remunerations, as well as the constitutional intent . . .

While reviewing the Central Government's general budgets for the 2005 fiscal year, the Legislative Yuan altered the remuneration structure for the Justices which had existed for more than fifty years by deleting the budget for the specialty premiums for judicial personnel payable to the Justices. The Legislative Yuan has not done so according to any law, let alone any disciplinary law. If the Constitution should allow such act, it would be tantamount to encouraging the authority in charge of the preparation of budgets, through the review of annual budgetary bills, to influence the Justices in exercising their powers. If the Justices, who are empowered to conduct judicial review of the Constitution, do not have any adequate guarantee of their remuneration, but instead are at the beck and call of the authority in charge of the preparation of budgets year after year, the stability and soundness of the democratic and constitutional order will be in jeopardy, which is not consistent with the constitutional intent to render institutional protection to judges to ensure their independence in holding trials as the Justices should independently exercise their authorities under the Constitution and the law to preserve the constitutional structure of free democracy and protect fundamental human rights . . .

Bengzon v Drilon
GR No 103524, 15 Apr 1992 (Supreme Court, Philippines)

Gutierrez Jr J

The issue in this petition is the constitutionality of the veto by the President of certain provisions in the General Appropriations Act for the Fiscal Year 1992 relating to the payment of the adjusted pensions of retired Justices of the Supreme Court and the Court of Appeals.

The petitioners are retired Justices of the Supreme Court and Court of Appeals who are currently receiving monthly pensions under Republic Act No 910 as amended by Republic Act No 1797. They filed the instant petition on their own behalf and in representation of all other retired Justices of the Supreme Court and the Court of Appeals similarly situated . . .

It was the impression that Presidential Decree No 644 had reduced the pensions of Justices and Constitutional Commissioners which led Congress to restore the repealed provisions through House Bill No 16297 in 1990. . . .

The attempt to use the veto power to set aside a Resolution of this Court and to deprive retirees of benefits given them by Rep Act No 1797 trenches upon the constitutional grant of fiscal autonomy to the Judiciary.

Sec 3 Art VIII mandates that:

> Sec 3 The Judiciary shall enjoy fiscal autonomy. Appropriations for the Judiciary may not be reduced by the legislature below the amount appropriated for the previous year and, after approval, shall be automatically and regularly released.

We cannot overstress the importance of and the need for an independent judiciary . . .

As envisioned in the Constitution, the fiscal autonomy enjoyed by the Judiciary, the Civil Service Commission, the Commission on Audit, the Commission on Elections, and the Office of the Ombudsman contemplates a guarantee of full flexibility to allocate and utilize their resources with the wisdom and dispatch that their needs require . . .

The imposition of restrictions and constraints on the manner the independent constitutional offices allocate and utilize the funds appropriated for their operations is anathema to fiscal autonomy and violative not only of the express mandate of the Constitution but especially as regards the Supreme Court, of the independence and separation of powers upon which the entire fabric of our constitutional system is based . . .

The rationale behind the veto which implies that Justices and Constitutional officers are unduly favored is, again, a misimpression . . .

The provisions regarding retirement pensions of Justices arise from the package of protections given by the Constitution to guarantee and preserve the independence of the Judiciary.

The Constitution expressly vests the power of judicial review in this Court. Any institution given the power to declare, in proper cases, that acts of both the President and Congress are unconstitutional needs a high degree of independence in the exercise of its functions. Our jurisdiction may not be reduced by Congress. Neither may it be increased without our advice and concurrence. Justices may not be removed until they reach age 70 except through impeachment. All courts and court personnel are under the administrative supervision of the Supreme Court. . . . Our salaries may not be decreased during our continuance in office. We cannot be designated to any agency performing administrative or quasi-judicial functions. We are specifically given fiscal autonomy. The Judiciary is not only independent of, but also co-equal and coordinate with the Executive and Legislative Departments.

Any argument which seeks to remove special privileges given by law to former Justices of this Court on the ground that there should be no 'grant of distinct privileges' or 'preferential treatment' to retired Justices ignores these provisions of the Constitution and, in effect, asks that these Constitutional provisions on special protections for the Judiciary be repealed
. . .

For as long as these retired Justices are entitled under laws which continue to be effective, the government cannot deprive them of their vested right to the payment of their pensions
. . .

Notes and Questions

1. Both the Constitutional Court of Taiwan and the Supreme Court of the Philippines held that the reduction of the judicial budget regarding premiums for sitting justices or pensions for retired justices was unconstitutional on the ground of interference with judicial independence. Since the judiciary neither holds the sword nor commands the purse, in what ways can judges ensure compliance with and implementation of their decisions?

2. Because the judicial budget cut involved in *JY Interpretation No 601* was about the special premium for the sitting justices of the Constitutional Court, an issue arose as to whether all sitting justices needed to recuse themselves or were disqualified. If that were so, the case would inevitably be dismissed since there would be no judges to hear it. However, the Constitutional Court unequivocally rejected such a recusal argument:

   If the Justices opt to recuse themselves from hearing the case due to the indirect outcome of the constitutional interpretation out of reflective action, it is tantamount to a total failure of the judicial system to resolve any dispute between the judicial power and the executive or legislative power, or any case on the review of the constitutionality of a law or regulation involving every citizen (including, of course, the Justices). If such were the case, the purpose of the recusal system would be outright defeated and thus the system of constitutional interpretation expressly prescribed under the Constitution would inevitably be paralyzed, which would be no different from the Justices refusing to exercise their constitutional authority. As a result, the fundamental constitutional order of separation of powers as contemplated by a constitutional state would no longer exist.

D. Court Structure and Judicial Administration

Most constitutions do not prescribe courts' jurisdictions in detail. This is usually left to legislative enactments. However, some constitutions, such as that of Thailand, stipulate the whole structure and jurisdictions of all courts in relative detail. There is, however, a risk that in doing so, the legislature may encroach upon judicial powers or undermine judicial independence. Consequently, some checks and balances are necessary to restrict exercises of legislative powers seeking to alter the structures or jurisdictions of courts.

For example, in the Philippines, the Constitution gives the legislature powers to define, prescribe and apportion the jurisdiction of various courts, but not to deprive the Supreme Court of its jurisdiction over cases enumerated in the Constitution.[131] More importantly, the legislature may not impair the independence of judiciary in exercising its legislative powers, nor may it reorganise courts in ways that may undermine the security of judicial tenure. Even so, disputes may still arise. In the case of *Anwar Hossain Chowdhury v Bangladesh* (excerpted below), the Supreme Court of Bangladesh had to deal with the constitutionality of an alteration to the judicial structure by the Eighth Constitutional Amendment. There, the Court held that the unitary structure of courts was derived from a unitary state that was part of the basic structure in the Constitution, and hence unalterable.

Some constitutions grant the Supreme Court the power of judicial administration. For example, the Constitution of the Philippines exclusively vests in the Supreme Court administrative supervision over all courts and their personnel.[132] Similarly, Article 77 of the Japanese Constitution provides the Supreme Court with the power to decide on matters relating to attorneys, the internal discipline of the courts and the administration of judicial affairs. Others may not be as explicit, however. Matters concerning judicial administration may be undertaken by or shared with the Ministry of Justice or the executive, and concerns over interference with the judiciary may from time to time arise. The following cases from Taiwan, Bangladesh and Indonesia illustrate some of these disputes.

In *JY Interpretation No 530*, the Constitutional Court in Taiwan considered whether the Judicial Yuan could constitutionally exercise rule-making and supervisory powers over the lower courts. The Supreme Court of Bangladesh in *Secretary, Ministry of Finance v Md Masdar Hossain* was required to determine if members of the judicial service were part of the service of the republic and could thus be supervised and regulated by the civil service. Lastly, the Constitutional Court of Indonesia in *Decision*

---

[131] Art VIII, Sec 2, Constitution of the Philippines.
[132] Art VIII, Sec 6, Constitution of the Philippines.

Number 005/PUU-IV/2006 reviewed whether the provisions of supervision in the Judicial Commission Law (UUKY) and Judicial Authority Law (UUKK) violated judicial independence enshrined in Article 24B(1) of the Constitution.

Anwar Hossain Chowdhury v Bangladesh
1989 18 CLC (AD) (Supreme Court, Bangladesh)

Facts

Article 100 of the Constitution of Bangladesh originally read as follows:

> The permanent seat of the Supreme Court shall be in the capital, but sessions of the High Court Division may be held at such other place or places as the Chief justice may, with the approval of the President, from time to time appoint.

In 1988, the Parliament passed the Eighth Amendment to revise Article 100. The new Amendment stipulated in the following that:

(1)   Subject to this article, the permanent seat of the Supreme Court shall be in the capital;

(2)   The High Court Division and the Judges thereof shall sit at the permanent seat of the Supreme Court and at the seats of its permanent Benches;

(3)   The High Court Division shall have a permanent Bench each at Barisal, Chittagong, Comilla, Jessore, Rangpur and Sylhet, and each permanent Bench shall have such Benches as the Chief Justice may determine from time to time;

(4)   A permanent Bench shall consist of such number of Judges of the High Court Division as the Chief Justice may deem it necessary to nominate to that Bench from time to time and on such nomination the Judges shall be deemed to have been transferred to that Bench;

(5)   The President shall, in consultation with the Chief Justice, assign the area in relation to which each permanent Bench shall have jurisdictions, powers and functions conferred or that may be conferred on the High Court Division by this Constitution or any other Law; and the area not so assigned shall be the area in relation to which the High Court Division sitting at the permanent seat of the Supreme Court shall have such jurisdictions, powers and functions;

(6)   The Chief Justice shall make rules to provide for ail incidental, supplemental or consequential matters relating to the permanent Benches.

The petitioners questioned the constitutionality of the Eighth Amendment as Article 142 of the Constitution did not authorize the Parliament to alter or affect the basic structure of the Constitution or undermine judicial independence.

Badrul Haider Chowdhury J

In popular notion the High Court Division is the High Court as understood since the 19th Century. It overlooks the legal significance of the expression 'Division' – there are two Divisions of the Supreme Court eg Appellate Division and the High Court Division. Article 94 says 'comprising'. The dictionary meaning of the word is: 'to include, to comprehend; to consist of, to hold together'. That the High Court Division [is] an integral part of the Supreme Court as a Division, if overlooked, will cause all confusion . . .

Thus 'jurisdictions, 'powers' and 'functions' have been specifically conferred on two sets of courts the permanent Benches at the designated places and the court at the permanent seat. The newly created courts the permanent Benches, have achieved competitive status with the court in the permanent seat because both the sets of courts have been conferred jurisdictions, powers and functions of the High Court Division. Article 101 had not been amended but it has been dismantled structurally because the permanent Benches will exercise same jurisdictions, powers and functions of the High Court Division and in the residuary area at the permanent seat that court namely, the Dhaka Bench will also exercise the jurisdictions, powers and functions of the High Court Division. . . .

It has disrupted the provisions relating to the judiciary given in Article 94 because it has added some alien concept by way of introducing 'permanent Benches' conferring specifically 'jurisdictions, powers and functions' of the High Court Division, thereby creating seven courts in the name of permanent Benches. This has been done indirectly because it could not be done directly. It contravenes expressly Article 101 because it has set up rival courts to the High Court Division which has been given jurisdictions, powers and functions of the Constitution.

It has disrupted the Constitutional fabric of Article 102 by introducing territorial concept thereby creating innumerable difficulties and incongruities which has been cited by all the three learned counsels namely, Dr Kamal Hossain, Mr Syed Ishtiaq Ahmed and Mr Amir-ul-Islam . . .

Hence it appears (a) High Courts are courts of limited territorial jurisdiction; (b) [The] judges of these High Courts are transferable from one High Court to another; (c) Question of their possessing plenary judicial power of the Republic does not arise; (d) These High Courts may be created by sub-constitutional legislations. These characteristics distinguish the High Courts of India and Pakistan from the High Court Division which figures as [an] integral part of the Supreme Court in Article 94 . . .

No one has evaluated the performance of these outlying benches, their rate of disposal, reasons for decline in disposing cases, backlog of cases and the remedial measures that may be taken. It was only in the beginning of this year the Chief Justice had framed a [Committee] to look into these matters. But while proposing for setting up of Permanent Benches in the designated six places no endeavours were made to assess the position. Hence the criticism of Mr Asrarul Hossain that neither the President nor the Chief Justice did apply his mind cannot be brushed aside. Since the prerequisite in Article 100 (5) is consultation the absence of such consultation has demonstrated the arbitrariness in setting up of permanent benches which, on such, ground alone is unconstitutional . . .

JY Interpretation No 530
5 Oct 2001 (Constitutional Court, Taiwan)

Facts

The Judicial Yuan enacted rules and exercised supervisory powers over the lower courts. The Control Yuan, a functional equivalent of an ombudsman, challenged such practices on the ground that they might undermine judicial independence, and thus submitted this issue to the Constitutional Court.

Held

To realize the principle of judicial independence, the judiciary shall preserve judicial autonomy, entailing the independence of judges, judicial administration, and judicial rulemaking. Among them, judicial rulemaking implies that the highest judicial organ shall have its adjudicative members prescribe rules governing the details or technical matters involved in the procedures of litigation or non-litigation cases in order to ensure the litigation process as both fair and efficient and to guarantee the beneficiary the right to judicial access. Furthermore, the Constitution guarantees the right of instituting legal proceedings; thus, the State shall ensure that people have the right of instituting legal proceedings in accordance with legal proceedings and the right to fair and efficient trials. Consequently, the highest judicial organ shall have the supervisory power of judicial administration. Yet, both the preservation of judicial autonomy and the exercise of judicial supervisory powers shall aim at safeguarding judicial independence. As a result, while the highest judicial organ may prescribe rules governing judicial practice within the scope of judicial administration and supervision, it shall not violate the aforementioned principle of judicial independence. Rules concerning judicial administration and supervision prescribed by the highest judicial organ may lawfully provide concerned laws and rules, interpretative materials within its jurisdiction, or legal opinions governing judicial practice, in addition to judicial administrative matters, for lower courts and judicial staff in their legal enforcement and applications. Judicial rules, however, shall not be inconsistent with laws and these rules shall not add any further restrictions on the people's freedoms and substantive rights without the concrete and detailed delegation of law . . .

To guarantee both sufficiently and efficiently the people's beneficiary right to judicial access, the judicial administrative organ may, without encroachment on the principle of judicial independence, exercise its supervisory power over judges concerning their duties. Judges shall have the responsibility to handle cases before them lawfully, fairly, and promptly. If judges violate their duties or are negligent in the execution of their duties, they shall be notified, cautioned, or even punished according to relevant laws. Such cases may be exemplified as judges apply laws or rules that have been abrogated, or when judges leave the courtroom without due cause during hearings held by a tribunal en banc, thus resulting in the suspension of trials, or when judges prolong trial procedures or the completion of judgments has been delayed considerably. It is not only necessary but also consistent with the principle of judicial independence to exercise supervisory power when judges cannot provide reasonable explanations for the delays of the cases before them . . .

Article 77 of the Constitution prescribes that the Judicial Yuan shall be the highest judicial organ in charge of civil, criminal, administrative cases, and cases concerning disciplinary measures against public officials. Yet, according to the current Organic Act of Judicial Yuan, however, the Judicial Yuan shall have seventeen Justices in charge of constitutional interpretations and unified legal interpretations and the Justices shall form a Constitutional Court to adjudicate cases concerning the dissolution of unconstitutional parties. Thus, Article 4 of the Organic Act of Judicial Yuan promulgated on March 31, 1947, prescribed that the Judicial Yuan should have a civil, a criminal and an administrative tribunal, and a commission on the disciplinary punishment of public functionaries. Before going into effect, this Act was revised on December 25, 1947, and adhered to the previous court system of the tutelage period, to have the Supreme Court, the Administrative Court, and the Commission on the Disciplinary Sanction of Functionaries established under the Judicial Yuan. When the Organic Act of the Judicial Yuan was revised on June 29, 1980, it still prescribed that the Judicial Yuan should establish the Supreme Court, the Administrative Court, and the Commission on the Disciplinary Sanction of Functionaries. As a consequence, the Judicial Yuan, other than Justices vested with the power of judicial interpretations and the adjudication of cases concerning the dissolution of unconstitutional parties, has become merely the highest judicial administrative organ, resulting in the separation of the highest adjudicative organ from the highest judicial administration. In order to be consistent with the intent of the framers of the Constitution, the Organic Act of Judicial Yuan, the Court Organic Act, the Organic Act of the Administrative Court, and the Organic Act of the Commission on the Disciplinary Sanction of Functionaries must be reviewed and revised in accordance with the designated constitutional structure within two years from the date of this Interpretation.

Secretary, Ministry of Finance v Md Masdar Hossain
2000 29 CLC (AD) (Appellate Division, Supreme Court, Bangladesh)

Facts

The Services (Reorganisation and Conditions) Act, 1975 (Act No XXXII of 1975) conferred on the Government power to create new services or amalgamate or unify existing services. In exercise of these powers, the Government in 1988 issued the Bangladesh Civil Service (Reorganisation) Order to include the judicial service under the Bangladesh Civil Services (BCS). The petitioner challenged the constitutionality of this Order.

Mustafa Kamal CJ

Functionally and structurally [the] judicial service stands on a different level from the civil administrative executive services of the Republic. While the function of the civil administrative executive services is to assist the political executive in formulation of policy and in execution of the policy decisions of the Government of the day, the function of the judicial service is neither of them. It is an independent arm of the Republic which sits [in] judgment over parliamentary, executive and quasi-judicial actions, decisions and orders. To equal and to put on the same plane the judicial service with the civil administrative executive services is to treat two unequal[s] as equals. Article 116A of the Constitution was also lost sight of and it was conveniently forgotten that all persons employed in the judicial service and all magistrates are independent in the exercise of their judicial functions while the civil administrative executive services are not. The Government was also unmindful of the fundamental right enshrined in Article 35(3) of the Constitution which provides that 'Every person accused of a criminal offence shall have the right to a speedy and public trial by an independent and impartial court or tribunal established by law' . . . Judicial independence involves both individual and institutional relationships: the individual independence of a Judge as reflected in such matters as security of tenure and the institutional independence of the court as reflected in its institutional [or] administrative relationships to the executive and legislative branches of government . . .

The constitutional fallacy of treating the BCS (Judicial), as just one of the many cadres of civil administrative executive services of the Republic is that it has compromised, jeopardised and destroyed the institutional independence of the Judges of the subordinate courts . . .

The basic realisation that the members of the judicial service perform the judicial functions of the Republic while the civil administrative services perform a different kind of work altogether has never dawned on them from the very beginning. This amalgamation or mixing up or tying together of the judicial service with other civil administrative services has been a monumental constitutional blunder committed during the early years of liberation, the harmful legacy of which is the dogged and headstrong denial of the proper and rightful institutional status of the members of the judicial service and of magistrates exercising judicial functions at the implementational stage . . .

Thus while we reject the decision of the High Court Division that the members of the judicial service are not in the service of the Republic and do hold that they are in the service of the Republic. We hold at the same time that the High Court Division was correct in holding that the definition of the service of the Republic in Article 152(1) is broad and includes defence and judicial services, but that does not mean that the judicial service or the defence service is a part of the civil or administrative service. As we said, Part IX of the Constitution contains the heading The Services of Bangladesh, not just one service. Chapter I of Part IX, which begins with Article 133, is entitled Services of different categories and status are included in the service of the Republic. Members of the judicial service wield the judicial powers of the Republic. They cannot be placed on par with the civil administrative executive services in any manner. Their nomenclature of service must follow the language employed by the Constitution. Formation and composition of the judicial service and recruitment and appointment rules of the judicial service are to be made under Article 115 by the President. Service rules regarding posting, promotion, grant of leave, salary, remuneration and other privileges shall be made separately in each case from the civil administrative executive service Cadre rules under Article 133 or when applicable, under Article 136, and those separate rules shall, be consistent with Articles 116 and 116A . . .

Decision Number 005/PUU-IV/2006
23 Aug 2006 (Constitutional Court, Indonesia)

Facts

The petitioners are 31 Supreme Court Justices arguing that their constitutional right to freedom as Supreme Court Justices enshrined in Article 24(1) of the 1945 Constitution was violated by certain provisions in two laws: the Law of the Republic of Indonesia Number 22 Year 2004 concerning Judicial Commission; and Law of the Republic of Indonesia Number 4 Year 2004 concerning Judicial Authority regarding supervision by the Judicial Commission (KY). The Court had to consider whether the provisions of supervision in the Judicial Commission Law (UUKY) and the Judicial Authority Law (UUKK) contradicted the 1945 Constitution.

Held

As a state commission, the nature of the Judicial Commission's duties is related to the function of judicial authorities namely with respect to appointment of supreme court justices and other authorities in the context of maintaining and upholding the honor, dignity, and [conduct] of judges. Therefore, the existence of such state commissions is commonly referred to as the 'auxiliary state organs' or 'auxiliary agencies' which according to Soetjipno, a former member of PAH I of BP MPR in a Constitutional Court's session on May 10, 2006, the Judicial Commission constitutes a 'supporting element' in the system of judicial authorities (see the minutes of Court Hearing dated May 10, 2006). However, since the issues of justice appointment, honor, dignity and [conduct] of judges are deemed crucial, the provisions concerning the matters are expressly set forth in the 1945 Constitution. The position of the Judicial Commission is also stipulated in the 1945 Constitution as an independent state commission, the composition, position and membership of which are provided for in a separate law, therefore, this state commission is not under the influence of the Supreme Court or controlled by other power branches . . .

Considering whereas the Judicial Commission constitutes an organ the regulation of which is included in Chapter IX on Judicial Authorities, in which the Supreme Court is regulated in [Article] 24A, the Judicial Commission is regulated in 24A paragraph (3) and Article 24B, and the Constitutional Court is regulated in [Article] 24C. This regulation indicates that pursuant to the 1945 Constitution, the Judicial Commission is within the scope of judicial authorities, although it is not the actor of the judicial authorities. Article 24A paragraph (3) of the 1945 Constitution reads as [follows], 'Prospective supreme court justices shall be proposed by the Judicial Commission to the People's Legislative Assembly for approval and shall subsequently be stipulated as supreme court justices by the President'. The regulation indicates that the existence of the Judicial Commission in the state system is related to the Supreme Court. However, Article 24 paragraph (2) of the 1945 Constitution asserts that the Judicial Commission is not a judicial authorities executor, but as a supporting element or state auxiliary organ as asserted by the former member of PAH I BP MPR as described above that are not argued by other members of PAH I BP MPR. Therefore, in accordance with the spirit of the constitution above, the principles of checks and balances may not be applied in the internal relation pattern of judicial authorities, because the relation of checks and balances may not continue between the Supreme Court as a principal organ and the Judicial Commission as an auxiliary organ. The Judicial Commission is not the executor of the judicial authorities, but a supporting element in the context of supporting the judicial authorities which is independent, clean and dignified, although the Judicial Commission is independent in performing its duties . . .

(i) The formulation of Article 20 of the Law on the Judicial Commission is very clearly different from the formulation of Article 24B paragraph (1) of the 1945 Constitution. Article 20 of the Law on the Judicial Commission stipulates, '. . . in the context of upholding the honor, dignity of and maintaining judges' [conduct]'. Meanwhile Article 24B paragraph (1) of the 1945 Constitution stipulates, '. . . in the context of maintaining and upholding the honor, dignity and [conduct] of judges'. Hence, the scope of other authorities in the formulation of Article 20 on the Law on the Judicial Commission is different from the formulation of the Article 24B paragraph (1) of the 1945 Constitution which creates the implication of legal uncertainty (rechtsonzekerheid) in the application. Because, Article 24B paragraph (1) of the 1945 Constitution has been defined by Article 20 on the Law on the Judicial Commission merely as supervision on [conduct], while Article 24B paragraph (1) of the 1945 Constitution stipulates that the 'other authorities' of the Judicial Commission shall be 'in the context of maintaining and upholding' that can be interpreted as not only preventive and corrective measures, but also improving the understanding, consciousness, quality and professional commitment that lead to the expected level of honor, dignity and [conduct] of judges. It does not only result from supervision, but mainly from the development and education on professional ethics for judges, including education on judge ethics to the community. In such context, the partnership relation between the Judicial Commission and the Supreme Court is absolutely required without affecting their respective independence;

(ii) On the other hand, the elaboration of supervision concept in the Law on the Judicial Commission creates uncertainty because the object of 'other authorities' of the Judicial Commission pursuant to Article 24B paragraph (1) of the 1945 Constitution should be implementation of code of ethics and code of [conduct] of judges in the context of maintaining the honor, dignity and [conduct] of judges. Therefore, first there must be clarity on the norms regulating the definition and scope of judges' [conduct], especially those relating to the material norms including the certainty about who prepare the aforementioned code of ethics and code of conducts. The aforementioned matters are not at all provided for in the Law on the Judicial

> Commission. Matters that are provided for in detail in the Law on the Judicial Commission are only related to supervision. Such unclarity cause uncertainty because supervision is provided for in detail, while judges' conducts as the object to be supervised are not clear. Such unclarity causes inaccurate interpretation and even contradicts the 1945 Constitution, because it has created an interpretation that subsequently become the official stance of the Judicial Commission that assessment on judges' conducts shall be made through assessment on the decision . . .

Notes and Questions

1. If the power of judicial administration is not vested in the highest judicial organ but with (or partly with) the executive – typically the Ministry of Justice – it may undermine judicial independence. In Taiwan, prior to the 1980s, the lower courts were under the supervision of the Ministry of Judicial Administration (later renamed the Ministry of Justice), but not that of the Supreme Court or the Judicial Yuan. This practice was challenged by the Control Yuan as it gravely interfered with judicial independence, and the Control Yuan requested a constitutional interpretation from the Constitutional Court. In response, the Constitutional Court issued *JY Interpretation No 86* demanding that lower courts should be under the Judicial Yuan, the highest judicial organ designated by the Constitution.[133] Regrettably, the Government did not observe this *Interpretation* until the 1980s.

2. There are many institutional mechanisms to secure judicial independence. The mechanisms regarding appointment, transfer, tenure or security of remuneration are some examples. Another way to ensure judicial independence and maintain judicial authority is to adopt the offence of contempt of court. Civil contempt of court consists of disobedience to an order of the court made in civil proceedings. Criminal contempt of court includes scandalising the court, contempt in the face of the court, deliberative interference with particular judicial proceedings or unintended interference with prejudicial publications.[134] This topic is further discussed in chapter eight.

VI. JUSTICIABILITY AND *LOCUS STANDI*

The nature of the judicial function entails limiting the exercise of judicial power to cases or controversies, and is expressed through doctrines of justiciability and *locus standi* (standing to sue). These limits are set to prevent courts from becoming involved in abstract questions or dealing with issues that courts are unsuited to address. The following section discusses the doctrines of 'cases or controversies', political questions and *locus standi*.

---

[133] *Interpretation No 86* [trans FT Liao], 1 ROC Const Ct 155 (2007).
[134] O Hood Phillips, P Jackson and P Leopold, *Constitutional and Administrative Law*, 8th edn (London: Sweet & Maxwell, 2001) 431–48.

A. Cases or Controversies

Although courts in all jurisdictions exercise their powers over cases or controversies, few constitutions state this in as explicit a manner as Article 3 of the US Constitution. Yet many courts have adopted and applied this constraint in exercising their judicial powers. By deciding concrete legal disputes, courts must ensure that cases or controversies are actual, not academic or hypothetical, that they are ripe for adjudication and have not become moot.

The following cases illustrate how some courts in Asia define concrete legal disputes. In *Karpal Singh v Sultan of Selangor*, the petition was rejected on the grounds that there was no *lis* and the case was merely hypothetical. The Supreme Court of Singapore held in *Lim Mey Lee Susan v Singapore Medical Council* that 'the courts decide real controversies and do not entertain theoretical or hypothetical issues'. In *Joya v PCGG*, the Supreme Court of the Philippines dismissed the case as it had become moot.

Karpal Singh v Sultan of Selangor
[1988] 1 MLJ 64 (High Court, Malaysia)

Facts

The Sultan of Selangor – a constituent state of the Federation of Malaysia – allegedly made a public statement in the *New Straits Times* and *The Star* newspapers, stating that he would not pardon anyone who had been sentenced to the mandatory death penalty for drug trafficking in the State of Selangor. The plaintiff, Karpal Singh, who was a well-known lawyer and opposition politician, believed that this public statement violated Article 42 of the Federal Constitution, which required the Sultan's pardoning power to be exercised on the advice of a Pardons Board. Singh argued that the public statement effectively pre-empted any appeal to him for clemency, thereby resulting in the negation of a constitutional right. A preliminary issue that arose was whether Singh had a reasonable cause of action.

Abdul Hamid CJ

What seems obvious from the Originating Summons is that the declaration sought does not relate to specific facts or events, and if it does, these facts or events are hypothetical, that is to say, they have not yet occurred and may never occur. It is nothing but a mere conjecture or speculation on the part of the plaintiff when he implies that the events about which he is apprehensive, namely, the decision to dismiss the petition for clemency by convicted drug traffickers would be made arbitrarily without regard to the recommendation of the Pardons Board of the State of Selangor, is in breach of Article 42(8) of the Constitution and that a dispute as to breach of a right would arise. The pertinent question is whose right is it? Is it the right of the plaintiff? I hardly think so. It may well be the plaintiff is a Member of Parliament and his oath of office demands that he preserves, protects and defends the Constitution, but such oath is clearly spelt out in general terms and my view is that it can have no relevance to the particular circumstances of this case . . .

Lim Mey Lee Susan v Singapore Medical Council
[2011] 4 SLR 156 (High Court, Singapore)

Philip Pillai J

The Applicant seeks judicial review of the decision of the Singapore Medical Council ('SMC') to appoint a second disciplinary committee ('2nd DC') to hear and investigate a complaint following the recusal of the entire disciplinary committee ('1st DC') originally appointed to hear and investigate the same complaint.

The judicial remedies sought by the Applicant are that of a Quashing Order against the SMC's decision to appoint the 2nd DC to hear and investigate the complaint and a Prohibiting Order against the SMC taking any steps to bring disciplinary proceedings against the Applicant on the same subject matter covered in the charges set out in the Notice of Inquiry by the 1st DC dated 20 July 2009. Finally, the Applicant seeks a Declaration that the Medical Registration (Amendment) Regulations 2010 (S 528/2010) ('the S 528/2010 Amendment Regulations') are void . . .

This application is misconceived. The power to make regulations of general application is lawfully that of the SMC under s 70 of the MRA (Medical Registration Act). No authority was cited for the proposition that the courts would declare the mere enactment of regulations to be illegal generally. The courts will determine the legality of enactments only in a real controversy where the provision has been applied. It is quite clear that the courts decide real controversies and do not entertain theoretical or hypothetical issues. See Carleton Kemp Allen, *Law and Orders: An Inquiry into the Nature and Scope of Delegated Legislation and Executive Powers in English Law* (Stevens & Sons Limited, 2nd ed, 1956) at p 266–267. It is a principle of our jurisprudence – and, it is to be supposed, of most systems of law – that courts will not entertain purely hypothetical questions. They will not pronounce upon legal situations which may arise, but generally upon those which have arisen. If, however, there is an existing basis of right or obligation, it is sometimes of great advantage to an interested party to establish his position before it is put to the test of a joinder of issue. To take a simple illustration: nobody can come to the court to ascertain what his position will be if his rich uncle makes a promised disposition by will in his favour. This is, in legal terminology, a mere spes, and one which experience teaches is often frustrated . . .

Joya v PCGG
GR No 96541, 24 Aug 1993 (Supreme Court, Philippines)

Facts

All 35 petitioners sought to enjoin the Presidential Commission on Good Government (PCGG) from proceeding with an auction scheduled on 11 January 1991 by Christie's of New York of the Old Masters Paintings and the eighteenth- and nineteenth-century silver-ware seized from Malacañang and the Metropolitan Museum of Manila and placed in the custody of the Central Bank. The petitioners argued that this case should be resolved by the court as an exception to the rule on academic or moot cases.

Bellosillo J

[Regarding] the second requisite of actual controversy, petitioners argue that this case should be resolved by this Court as an exception to the rule on moot and academic cases; that although the sale of the paintings and silver has long been consummated and the possibility of retrieving the treasure trove is nil, yet the novelty and importance of the issues raised by the petition deserve this Court's attention . . .

For a court to exercise its power of adjudication, there must be an actual case of controversy – one which involves a conflict of legal rights, an assertion of opposite legal claims susceptible of judicial resolution; the case must not be moot or academic or based on extra-legal or other similar considerations not cognizable by a court of justice. A case becomes moot and academic when its purpose has become stale, such as the case before us . . .

We find however that there is no such justification in the petition at bar to warrant the relaxation of the rule . . .

Notes

1. Generally courts adjudicate concrete legal disputes as cases or controversies. However, as we have seen, the abstract review power of constitutional courts is an exception. In abstract review, constitutional courts are requested to review the constitutionality of parliamentary or executive enactments, sometimes even before the promulgation of laws or regulations. The Constitutional Court of Thailand and the Constitutional Council of Cambodia are two examples that have such *ex ante* reviewing power. The power to issue advisory opinions, such as that vested in *ad hoc* Constitutional Tribunals in Singapore or the Sri Lanka Supreme Court, is also an exception to the doctrine of cases or controversies in the decentralised judicial system.

2. Even if abstract review power permits adjudication of cases that may be premature, constitutional courts can still develop certain constraints to avoid hearing such cases. For example, in Taiwan, one-third of the legislators may petition the Constitutional Court to hear a question on the unconstitutionality of any law, but the Court has attached an additional requirement to such a petition, demanding that legislators first try to amend the law. In *JY Interpretation No 603*, the Constitutional Court held that

    > if more than one third of the incumbent members of the Legislative Yuan, in exercising their authority of enacting a law, believe that the law reviewed and passed by the majority of their fellow Legislators and promulgated by the president may be unconstitutional, or if more than one third of the incumbent members of the Legislative Yuan, in exercising their authority of amending a law, believe that the existing and valid law may be unconstitutional *but fail to so amend the law*, they may duly initiate a petition for constitutional interpretation in respect of the constitutionality of the law because this Court opines that it is in line with the intent of the aforesaid Article 5-I (iii) of the Constitutional Interpretation Procedure Act . . .[135] (emphasis added)

---

[135] See *JY Interpretation No 603* [trans Vincent C Kuan], 5 ROC Const Ct 531, 548–49 (2007).

B. Political Question

It is an established principle that it is political branches, and not courts, that must address non-justiciable political questions. This is because if judges were to resolve political questions, there would be no check on their resolutions as they are not accountable to any other branch or to the people. But 'political questions' are not the same as 'political cases', which should not easily be exempt from judicial review. To determine if a case is a non-justiciable political question, the US Supreme Court in *Baker v Carr* applied six indicators, that is:

> a textually demonstrable constitutional commitment of the issue to a coordinate political department; or a lack of judicially discoverable and manageable standards for resolving it; or the impossibility of deciding without an initial policy determination of a kind clearly for non-judicial discretion; or the impossibility of a court's undertaking independent resolution without expressing lack of the respect due coordinate branches of government; or an unusual need for unquestioning adherence to a political decision already made; or the potentiality of embarrassment from multifarious pronouncements by various departments on one question.[136]

A number of Asian courts have referred to the doctrine of political questions but have reached quite different results in its application. The political question doctrine has, for example, never stopped the Philippines Supreme Court from adjudicating highly-charged political cases, such as the validity of the new Constitution or the return of an exiled former president. In contrast, courts in Taiwan and Japan have invoked the doctrine to avoid such cases, as can be seen below.

Javellana v Executive Secretary
GR No L-36142, 31 Mar 1973 (Supreme Court, Philippines)

Facts

On 16 March 1967, Congress passed Resolution No 2, calling a Convention to propose amendments to the Constitution. The 1971 Constitutional Convention began on 1 June 1971, and while it was in session, President Ferdinand Marcos issued a martial law decree on 21 September 1972. On 29 November 1972, the Convention approved the new Constitution. The next day, the President issued Presidential Decree No 73, submitting the new Constitution for public referendum, scheduled for 15 January 1973. On 7 December 1972, one petitioner filed this case with the court on the grounds that Decree No 73 had no legal force or effect since the power to call the plebiscite was exclusively Congress's domain and there was no proper submission for the ratification of the new Constitution.

On 23 December, Marcos announced the postponement of the public referendum and issued another decree, No 86, which organised the Citizen Assembly for the ratification of the new Constitution on 1 January 1973. On the afternoon of 12 January 1973, the petitioners filed an urgent motion alleging that votes in the Citizen Assembly were cast by raising hands, hence violating the provisions of secrecy and of choice under Article XV of the 1935 Constitution. On 15 January 1973, while the cases were still pending at the court, the Secretary of Justice, acting upon Marcos's instruction, announced that the new Constitution was ratified by an overwhelming majority of all the votes cast by the members of all the

---

[136] *Baker v Carr* 369 US 186, 217 (1962).

Barangays (the Citizen Assembly). The question before the Court was whether the new Constitution was legal.

Concepcion CJ

Referring now more specifically to the issue on whether the new Constitution proposed by the 1971 Constitutional Convention has been ratified in accordance with the provisions of Article XV of the 1935 Constitution is a political question or not, I do not hesitate to state that the answer must be in the negative. Indeed, such is the position taken by this Court, in an endless line of decisions, too long to leave any room for possible doubt that said issue is inherently and essentially justiciable . . .

The reason why the issue under consideration and other issues of similar character are justiciable, not political, is plain and simple. One of the principal bases of the non-justiciability of so-called political questions is the principle of separation of powers – characteristic of the Presidential system of government – the functions of which are classified or divided, by reason of their nature, into three categories, namely: 1) those involving the making of laws, which are allocated to the legislative department; 2) those concerned mainly with the enforcement of such laws and of judicial decisions applying and/or interpreting the same, which belong to the executive department; and 3) those dealing with the settlement of disputes, controversies or conflicts involving rights, duties or prerogatives that are legally demandable and enforceable, which are apportioned to courts of justice . . .

We added that '. . . the term "political question" connotes, in legal parlance, what it means in ordinary parlance, namely, "a question of policy" in matters concerning the government of a State, as a body politic.'. . .

We have neither the authority nor the discretion to decline passing upon said issue, but are under the ineluctable obligation – made particularly more exacting and peremptory by our oath, as members of the highest Court of the land, to support and defend the Constitution – to settle it . . .

In cases of conflict, the judicial department is the only constitutional organ which can be called upon to determine the proper allocation of powers between the several departments of the government . . .

In the light of the foregoing, and considering that Art XV of our 1935 Constitution prescribes the method or procedure for its amendment, it is clear to my mind that the question whether or not the revised Constitution drafted by the 1971 Constitutional Convention has been ratified in accordance with said Art XV is a justiciable one and non-political in nature, and that it is not only subject to judicial inquiry, but, also, that it is the Court's bounden duty to decide such question . . .

Ferdinand E Marcos et al v Honorable Raul Manglapus et al
[1989] 177 SCRA 668 (Supreme Court, Philippines)

Cortes J

In February 1986, Ferdinand E Marcos was deposed from the presidency via the non-violent 'people power' revolution and forced into exile. In his stead, Corazon C Aquino was declared President of the Republic under a revolutionary government . . .

The accumulated foreign debt and the plunder of the nation attributed to Mr Marcos and his cronies left the economy devastated. The efforts at economic recovery, three years after Mrs Aquino assumed office, have yet to show concrete results in alleviating the poverty of the masses, while the recovery of the ill-gotten wealth of the Marcoses has remained elusive. Now, Mr Marcos, in his deathbed, has signified his wish to return to the Philippines to die. But Mrs Aquino, considering the dire consequences to the nation of his return at a time when the stability of government is threatened from various directions and the economy is just beginning to rise and move forward, has stood firmly on the decision to bar the return of Mr Marcos and his family . . .

One of issues is whether the decision of bar the return of Mr Marcos and his family is political question, which is non-justiciable . . .

There is nothing in the case before us that precludes our determination thereof on the political question doctrine . . . When political questions are involved, the Constitution limits the determination to whether or not there has been a grave abuse of discretion amounting to lack or excess of jurisdiction on the part of the official whose action is being questioned. If grave abuse is not established, the Court will not substitute its judgment for that of the official concerned and decide a matter which by its nature or by law is for the latter alone to decide . . .

It will not do to argue that if the return of the Marcoses to the Philippines will cause the escalation of violence against the State, that would be the time for the President to step in and exercise the commander-in-chief powers granted her by the Constitution to suppress or stamp out such violence. The State, acting through the Government, is not precluded from taking preemptive action against threats to its existence if, though still nascent they are perceived as apt to become serious and direct . . .

The President has determined that the destabilization caused by the return of the Marcoses would wipe away the gains achieved during the past few years and lead to total economic collapse. Given what is within our individual and common knowledge of the state of the economy, we cannot argue with that determination . . .

Action for Recognition of the Status as a Member of the House of Representatives and a Claim for Remuneration
14 Minshū 1206 (Supreme Court, Japan)

Facts

On 28 August 1952, the Japanese House of Representatives was dissolved by the Cabinet. One member of the House filed the suit, claiming that the dissolution was unconstitutional and that he was entitled to keep his seat as a legislative member.

Held

Dissolution of the House of Representatives deprives the members of their status as members of the House against their will and suspends the functioning of the House which is an essential part of the Parliament which is the supreme body of the nation, and by the subsequent general election, triggers the creation of a new House of Representatives and a cabinet, and therefore, its significance under the law of the nation is undeniable. Furthermore, dissolution takes place mostly when the cabinet intends to find out the general view of the people concerning the cabinet's important policies and subsequently, the continuation of the cabinet, and therefore, its political significance is extremely grave. Thus, the dissolution of the House of Representatives is a highly political act of the state involving the basis of ruling the nation and as explained above, it is evident that reviewing the legal validity of such an act is beyond the power of the court. The same applies when, as is in the present case, the dissolution of the House of Representatives is the preliminary issue in a litigation; in both instances, the matter is beyond judicial review . . .

JY Interpretation No 328
26 Nov 1993 (Constitutional Court, Taiwan)

Facts

In 1992, the Legislative Yuan reviewed the central government budget for the fiscal year of 1993. During the process, some members of the Legislative Yuan contended that Mainland China and Mongolia should not be considered as part of the constitutional territory of the Republic of China. In addition, the Mainland Affairs Council of the Executive Yuan should be merged with the Ministry of Foreign Affairs, and the Mongolian and Tibetan Affairs Commission should be dissolved and their budgets cut. Meanwhile, in reviewing the Act Governing Relations between People of the Taiwan Area and the Mainland Area, some legislatures had different views from that of the Executive Yuan on whether Mongolia was still part of the territory. To resolve these disputes, the Legislative Yuan brought the petition to the Constitutional Court, requesting the Court to decide whether Mainland China and Mongolia should be considered as part of the constitutional territory.

Held

How to delimit the national territory is a purely political question. It may also be called by some scholars an act of state. This question is not subject to judicial review according to the constitutional principle of separation of powers. Article 4 of the Constitution provides: 'The territory of the Republic of China according to its existing national boundaries shall not be altered except by resolution of the National Assembly.' Instead of enumerating the components of the ROC, a general provision was adopted and concurrently provided a special procedure for any change of national territory. It is understandable that this legislative policy was based upon political and historical reasons. Since the meaning of 'according to its existing national boundaries' is closely related to the delimitation of national territory, accordingly, it is a significant political question. Based on the above explanation, this application for interpretation is denied . . .

Notes and Questions

1. What explains the different attitudes toward the political question doctrine between the Supreme Court of the Philippines on the one hand and the Constitutional Court of Taiwan and the Supreme Court of Japan on the other? Political structure? Process of democratisation? Or legal culture?

2. The Philippines Supreme Court has held a consistent position on the political question doctrine. In the two Filipino cases excerpted above, the Court emphasised that if an issue was justiciable and non-political, it would be the Court's duty to decide it, and that should there be a 'grave abuse of discretion' committed by the executive officials, the judicial authority should not hide behind the political

question doctrine. In 1993, the Court, in *Oposa v Factoran* GR No 101083, 30 Jul 1993, considered whether the timber licence agreements made by the Secretary of the Department of Environment and Natural Resources (DENR) infringed the petitioners' right to a healthy environment and whether such an issue was a political question. The Court stressed that the political question doctrine was no longer an insurmountable obstacle to the exercise of judicial power or the impenetrable shield that once protected executive and legislative actions from judicial inquiry.

3.   Note that constitutional courts generally exercise jurisdiction through powers of constitutional review. They may also have ancillary powers to adjudicate questions of impeachment, dissolving unconstitutional political parties and election disputes. Should constitutional courts avoid addressing politically-charged issues by invoking the political question doctrine? Or do you consider that constitutional courts are created precisely to resolve such disputes? See the discussion regarding the ancillary powers of constitutional courts in the previous section III.A.ii. above.

C. *Locus Standi*

To establish *locus standi* (standing to sue), the litigant must demonstrate to the court that there is a sufficient connection between himself and the impugned law or action that resulted in harm to his interests. Every legal system develops such a doctrine to protect its judicial process from abuse and to filter out frivolous claims or vexatious litigants. In essence, litigant parties must demonstrate a direct and personal interest, or at least some real and substantial interest, in order to bring the case before the court.

An oft-cited formula was developed by the US Supreme Court in *Lujan v Defender of Wildlife*.[137] It comprises three elements. First, the plaintiff must have suffered an injury in fact, an invasion of a legally-protected interest which is concrete and particularised and actual or imminent, not conjectural or hypothetical. Secondly, there must be a causal connection between the injury and the conduct complained of, and the injury has to be fairly traceable to the challenged action. Thirdly, it must be likely that the injury will be redressed by a favourable decision. The elements of standing in *Lujan* are rudimentary and may thus be incorporated in varying degrees across jurisdictions. However, the degree of liberality of standing rules is premised on variations of separation of powers, detailed arrangements of judicial institutions or even judicial philosophy. As the following cases and discussions show, some Asian jurisdictions – for instance India and the Philippines – may formulate more liberalised rules of standing involving constitutional rights protection or public interests litigation.

i. *Individuals*

Usually an individual has *locus standi* if his constitutionally or legally protected rights or interests have been infringed. Those rights or interests are personal, but may involve the interests of third and unrelated parties. If a person challenges a government act, in

---

[137] *Lujan v Defender of Wildlife* 504 US 555, 560 (1992).

which a public right – as opposed to his own private right – has been interfered with, he must further demonstrate a substantial interest in order to initiate such litigation. For example, in the case of *Government of Malaysia v Lim Kit Siang* (excerpted below), the Supreme Court of Malaysia offered two situations in which an individual may challenge a government act without the Attorney-General's consent: first, where the litigant party's private right is also interfered with; and, secondly, where the litigant has not suffered an infringement of his private rights but has suffered special damage in relation to the infringement of the public right.

Due to the importance of constitutionally protected rights, a citizen has, prima facie, a sufficient interest to see that his or her constitutional rights are not violated. This is applicable in both decentralised and centralised judicial systems, as we shall see in the following cases from Singapore, Japan and Indonesia. Of special interest is *Tan Eng Hong v Attorney-General*, where the Singapore Court of Appeal held that the applicant still had *locus standi* to challenge the constitutionality of a criminal provision under which he was initially prosecuted and detained, even though the later substitution of the initial charge could have been unlawful.

Government of Malaysia v Lim Kit Siang
[1988] 2 MLJ 12 (Supreme Court, Malaysia)

Salleh Abas LP

The respondent who is the Leader of Opposition is seeking the aid of the court to interfere in the affairs of a proposed privatization contract for the construction of the North and South Highway due to be signed between United Engineers (M) Bhd (UEM) (appellant in Appeal No 456/1987) and the Government of Malaysia (appellant in Appeal No 434/1987) by asking for a declaration that the letter of intent issued by the Government to UEM in respect of the North and South Highway (NSH) contract is invalid, and based on the premise he also prays for a permanent injunction to restrain UEM from signing it with the Government . . .

A clear statement of it was stated by Buckley J in *Boyce v Paddington Borough Council* [1903] 1 Ch 109 as follows:

> A plaintiff can sue without joining the Attorney General in two cases: first, where the interference with the public right is such as that some private right of his is at the same time interfered with (eg where an obstruction is so placed in a highway that the owner of premises abutting upon the highway is specially affected by reason that the obstruction interferes with his private right to access from and to his premises to and from the highway); and, secondly, where no private right is interfered with, but the plaintiff, in respect of his public right, suffers special damage peculiar to himself from the interference with the public right. . . .

Locus standi is inseparable from, and indeed intertwined with, relator actions because if a private citizen, wishing to complain that a public authority has not legally performed its function or has failed to perform it altogether, has no locus standi, he must obtain the consent of the Attorney General in order to commence a relator action. Without locus standi, he cannot proceed on his own. In cases where the Attorney General has given his consent, there is, of course, no problem, because no locus standi needs to be shown since the Attorney General is constitutionally regarded as the guardian of public right . . .

Under this Order, a private citizen making an application for judicial review is required to show that he has 'a sufficient interest in the matter to which his application relates'. Thus English courts are required to interpret what 'sufficient interest' means . . .

Taking this approach, let us now examine the basis of the respondent's claim on locus standi.

First, he says he is the Leader of the Opposition, ie a politician. It is common knowledge that a politician works for voters' support. . . . The question is: is he motivated by public-spiritedness or an expectation of political gain and popularity? Would political grievances give him the locus standi? In my judgment, the court should be slow to respond to a politically motivated litigation unless the claimant can show that his private rights as a citizen are affected. . . . Thus as a politician, the respondent's remedy in this matter does not lie with the court, but with Parliament and the electorate.

Next, as a frequent road and highway user, I cannot see how he could be different from other road and highway users. There is nothing to show that he would be prevented from using roads and highways, already constructed or proposed to be constructed. If he objects to the tolls that are to be imposed for using the proposed NSH highway, he has, like any other users, an option either to use the highway or to use old or other roads. Thus, as a road and highway user, he also has no locus standi . . .

Chan Hiang Leng Colin v Minister for Information and Arts
[1996] 1 SLR 609 (Court of Appeal, Singapore)

Karthigesu JA

The appellants are ministers of a Christian religious denomination known as Jehovah's Witnesses. The International Bible Students Association (IBSA) and Watch Tower Bible and Tract Society (WTBTS) are organizations under the ambit of the denomination. By Order 179 of 1972 issued by the Minister for Home Affairs, the local chapter of the denomination, the Singapore Congregation of Jehovah's Witnesses (SCJW) was deregistered. At the same time, the Minister for Culture declared the publications of WTBTS prohibited publications by Order 123 of 1972. Neither of these two orders are being directly challenged. By Order 405/94 made under s 3 of the Undesirable Publications Act (Cap 338), the Minister for Information and the Arts (the Minister) prohibited the importation, sale or distribution of publications of IBSA. This order is the subject matter of the present proceedings.

The appellants sought leave to apply for an order of certiorari to remove into the High Court and quash Order 405/94. The appellants also sought a declaration that Order 405/94 is invalid. The learned judge below struck out the claim for the declaration on the ground that the High Court does not have the jurisdiction to grant a declaration in proceedings under O 53 of the Rules of the Supreme Court (RSC). The learned judge held that the appellants had sufficient locus standi to apply for judicial review. However, she refused to grant the appellants leave . . .

In the present case, what is complained of is an alleged violation of a citizen's constitutional right under art 15 of the Constitution to profess, practise and propagate his religion. Such rights are constitutionally enshrined. If a constitutional guarantee is to mean anything, it must mean that any citizen can complain to the courts if there is a violation of it . . .

There is thus no need for the appellants to show that they are office holders in IBSA or members thereof. Their right to challenge Order 405/94 arises not from membership of any society. Their right arises from every citizen's right to profess, practise and propagate his religious beliefs. If there was a breach of art 15, such a breach would affect the citizen *qua* citizen. If a citizen does not have sufficient interest to see that his constitutional rights are not violated, then it is hard to see who has.

It would indeed be strange if the only person who can complain of an alleged breach of art 15 in this case is IBSA, for IBSA is neither a citizen nor resident of Singapore. If Mr Reddy is right, then no citizen can complain of the alleged breach of art 15 in this case and the only person who can do so is a non-resident foreigner! This would be absurd, for art 15 of the Constitution only speaks of *citizens* having these rights . . .

Tan Eng Hong v Attorney-General
[2012] SGCA 45 (Court of Appeal, Singapore)

Facts

On 9 March 2010, Tan and the co-accused were arrested for engaging in oral sex in a cubicle in a public toilet of a shopping complex. In due course, Tan and the co-accused were separately charged under section 377A of the Penal Code which makes it an offence for any 'male person who, in public or private, commits, or abets the commission of, or procures or attempts to procure the commission by any male person of, any act of gross indecency with another male person'. A conviction under this section carried a punishment of imprisonment for a term which may extend to two years.

On 24 September 2010, Tan brought challenged the constitutionality of section 377A, arguing that it was inconsistent with his right to 'life' under Article 9 and the equal protection clause under Article 12 of the Constitution, as well as his right to freedom of speech and expression under Article 14 of the Constitution. On 15 October 2010, the Prosecution informed Tan that the section 377A charge against him had been substituted with a lesser charge under section 294(a) of the current Penal Code. On 7 December 2010, the Assistant Register (AR) struck out his application and Tan appealed. Tan subsequently pleaded guilty to the substituted charge and was convicted and sentenced to a fine of $3,000. The Court had to determine whether Tan had *locus standi* to challenge the constitutionality of section 377A.

VK Rajah JA

[T]he question of 'sufficient interest' must be judged in relation to the rights which are the subject matter of the application. Given the importance of constitutional rights, a citizen will prima facie have a 'sufficient interest to see that his constitutional rights are not violated' . . .

. . . [W]e find that violations of constitutional rights may occur not only at the point in time when an accused person is prosecuted under an allegedly unconstitutional law, but also when a person is *arrested and/or detained and/or charged under an allegedly unconstitutional law* . . .

Here, . . . a constitutional right may be violated by the very existence of an allegedly unconstitutional law in the statute books and/or by a threat of future prosecution under an allegedly unconstitutional law . . .

. . . [W]e state conclusively that we also reject the proposition that a subsisting prosecution under an allegedly unconstitutional law must be demonstrated in every case before a violation of constitutional rights can be shown. A law is either constitutional or it is not. The effects of a law can be felt without a prosecution, and to insist that an applicant needs to face a prosecution under the law in question before he can challenge its constitutionality could have the perverse effect of encouraging criminal behaviour to test constitutional issues. Even though a violation of constitutional rights may be most clearly shown where there is a subsisting prosecution under an allegedly unconstitutional law, we find that a violation may also be established in the absence of a subsisting prosecution. In certain cases, the very existence of an allegedly unconstitutional law in the statute books may suffice to show a violation of an applicant's constitutional rights . . .

To summarise, if an applicant is able to show that he is facing a real and credible threat of prosecution under an allegedly unconstitutional law, this may suffice to show that his constitutional rights have arguably been violated and that he should thus be granted standing to vindicate his rights . . .

It is common ground that Tan does not face a subsisting prosecution under s 377A. Even so, we have decided that a subsisting prosecution under an allegedly unconstitutional law is not a necessary requirement to show a violation of constitutional rights. The central issue here is whether it can be argued that Tan's constitutional rights were arguably violated on the facts of the case . . .

As we are of the view that s 377A is *arguably* unconstitutional for inconsistency with Art 12, it flows from this that Tan's right to personal liberty under Art 9(1) would have been violated by his arrest and detention under s 377A if the same were indeed unconstitutional . . .

Article 12(1) provides as follows: All persons are equal before the law and entitled to the equal protection of the law . . .

Applying this test, the Judge found . . . that s 377A engaged Tan's rights under Art 12(1). Although s 377A satisfied the first limb of the test as it was founded on an intelligible differentia (it applies to sexually-active male homosexuals), she found it arguable that s 377A failed the second limb as there was no obvious social objective that could be furthered by criminalising male but not female homosexual intercourse. We concur that there is an arguable case that s 377A engages Tan's rights under Art 12(1) . . .

The plain language of s 377A excludes both male–female acts and female–female acts. Tan professes to be a member of the targeted group, and the [Attorney-General] has not disputed this claim. Therefore, since we have found that s 377A arguably violates the Art 12(1) rights of its target group, as a member of that group, Tan's rights have arguably been violated by the mere existence of s 377A in the statute books. We also accept that there is a real and credible threat of prosecution under s 377A . . .

In conclusion . . . as we have found that s 377A is arguably inconsistent with Art 12, Tan's constitutional rights are at stake and Tan thus has *locus standi* to bring the Application. As noted above, in the present case, the issue of certainty of failure pivots solely on the issue of *locus standi*. As we have found that Tan has *locus standi*, Tan's case is not certain to fail . . .

Case to Seek Declaration of Illegality of Deprivation of the Right to Vote of Japanese Citizens Residing Abroad
59 Minshū 7 (Supreme Court, Japan)

Facts

The appellants were Japanese citizens residing abroad. They alleged that the Public Offices Election Law deprived them of their opportunity to exercise their right to vote simply because they resided abroad. This, they argued, violated Articles 14(1), 15(1) and (3), 43, and 44 of the Constitution, and Article 25 of the International Covenant on Civil and Political Rights. They had three claims, the third of which was for a declaration that they would be eligible to exercise the right to vote in the elections of the members of House of Representatives (HR) under the single-seat constituency system and the elections of the members of House of Councillors (HC) under the constituency system.

Held

The suit for the alternative claim for declaration can be understood as a suit brought under public law by a party to seek declaration on legal relations under public law. If Article 8 of the Supplementary Provisions of the Public Offices Election Law were not amended as required, the jokoku appellants indicated in the attached List of Parties 1 who are Japanese citizens residing abroad would be precluded from voting in an election of members under the single-seat constituency system in the next general election of HR members and in an election of members under the constituency system in the next regular election of HC members, or in other words, their right to exercise the right to vote would be violated. Therefore, the suit for the alternative claim for declaration can be deemed to be intended to obtain, in advance, declaration that the jokoku appellants will be eligible to exercise the right to vote in such elections on the grounds that Article 8 of the Supplementary Provisions of the Public Offices Election Law is unconstitutional and null, in order to prevent violation of the right to vote . . .

The right to vote is meaningless if it cannot be exercised, and it is impossible to restore the substance of its exercise once it is violated. In light of the importance of the right to vote, if a person files a suit to seek declaration that the person shall be eligible to exercise the right to vote in a specific election when there is a controversy over such eligibility, benefit of declaration can be found if such suit can be regarded as an effective and appropriate means. Therefore, the suit for the alternative claim in this case can be regarded as a suit to seek declaration on legal relations under public law and benefit of declaration can be found as mentioned above . . .

Next, we examine acceptability of the alternative claim. As mentioned above, the part of the provision of Article 8 of the Supplementary Provisions of the Public Offices Election Law that limits, for the time being, the applicability of the overseas voting system to elections of members of the Houses of the Diet under the proportional representation system is in violation of Article 15(1) and (3), Article 43(1), and the proviso of Article 44 of the Constitution and therefore invalid. Thus, the jokoku appellants indicated in the attached List of Parties 1 are eligible to vote in an election of members under the single-seat constituency system in the next general election of HR members and in an election of members under the constituency system in the next regular election of HC members on the grounds that they are listed on the overseas electoral register. Consequently, the alternative claim for declaration is well-grounded and it should be upheld without the need for further argument . . .

Decision Number 010/PUU-IV/2006
25 Jul 2006 (Constitutional Court, Indonesia)

Facts

The Indonesian Law Community (MHI) filed a petition to the Constitutional Court to review the constitutionality of the Law of the Republic of Indonesia Number 30 Year 2002 concerning the Commission for the Eradication of Criminal Acts of Corruption.

Held

Considering whereas, in a petition for judicial review of a Law against the 1945 Constitution, for a person or a party to be accepted as Petitioner having the legal standing before the Court, Article 51 Paragraph (1) of the Constitutional Court Law provides that,

'Petitioners shall be parties who deem that their constitutional rights are impaired by the coming into effect of a law, namely:

a.   individual Indonesian citizens; . . .
c.   public or private legal entities; . . .'

Meanwhile, Elucidation of Article 51 Paragraph (1) Sub-Paragraph a of the Constitutional Court Law reaffirms that 'individual' in Article 51 Paragraph (1) Sub-Paragraph a shall also include a group of people having a common interest; . . .
[P]ursuant to the provision of Article 51 Paragraph (1) of the Constitutional Court Law, the person or party concerned must:

(a) explain his qualification in the petition, whether as an individual Indonesian citizen, a customary law community unit, a legal entity, or a state institution;
(b) explain the impairment of constitutional rights and/or authorities, in the qualification as intended in item (a), due to the coming into effect of law petitioned for review; . . .

. . . [I]t has been decided by the Court that impairment of constitutional rights and/or authorities must meet the following criteria:

(1) The Petitioners must have constitutional rights and/or authorities granted by the 1945 Constitution;
(2) The Petitioners believe that such constitutional rights and/or authorities have been impaired by the coming into effect of a law petitioned for review;
(3) The impairment of such constitutional rights and/or authorities is specific and actual in nature, or at least potential in nature which, according to logical reasoning, will take place for sure;
(4) There is a causal relationship (causal verband) between such impairment and the law petitioned for review;
(5) If the petition is granted, it is expected that such impairment of constitutional rights and/or authorities argued will not or does not occur any longer . . .

Considering, after carefully evaluating the Petitioner's arguments in explaining the impairment of constitutional rights as described above, it has been evident to the Court that:

(1) The Petitioner could not explain the impairment of constitutional rights and/or authorities in its qualification as individual Indonesian citizen, in casu a group of

people having a common interest, due to the coming into effect of the provisions in the Corruption Eradication Commission Law petitioned for review;

. . .

(4) The Petitioner's unclear qualification and constitutional rights and/or authorities which are deemed by the Petitioner to have been impaired in such qualification have rendered this petitioned obscure (obscuur) due to confusion between the reasons for judicial review and legislative review which can be mutually supportive while both have differences. Hence, the a quo petition does not meet the criteria as intended in Article 51 Paragraph (1) of the Constitutional Court Law, neither does the petition meet the criteria as intended in Article 51 Paragraph (3) of the Constitutional Court Law . . .

ii. Public Interest Litigation and Taxpayer Suits

The doctrine of *locus standi* permits only individuals whose rights or legally protected interests are infringed, to bring cases before the court. However, this may not be sufficient to address state interference in public rights, or the infringement of rights of individuals who lack the means or resources to bring cases before the court. To address this problem, the Supreme Court of India extended *locus standi* to 'any member of the public'. In *SP Gupta v Union of India* (excerpted below) the Court stated:

[W]here a legal wrong or a legal injury is caused to . . . such person or determinate class of persons [as] is by reason of poverty, helplessness or disability or socially or economically disadvantaged position, unable to approach the Court for relief, any member of the public can maintain an application for an appropriate direction, order or writ.[138]

In this case, the Court allowed the practising lawyers – as concerned members of the public – to challenge the circular letter issued by the Law Minister on the appointment of additional High Court judges as well as the President's decision to transfer the Chief Justice of the High Court.

An equally all-encompassing criterion for *locus standi* is that of the taxpayer or ratepayer. In *Flast v Cohen*,[139] the US Supreme Court recognised a taxpayer to have standing to challenge allegedly unconstitutional federal taxing or spending programs so long as he or she had a sufficient interest. The Court stated that sufficiency of interest required the satisfaction of two criteria: first, the taxpayer must establish a logical link between his or her taxpayer status and government taxation or spending; and, secondly, the taxpayer must establish the nexus between that status and the precise nature of the alleged constitutional infringement. Perhaps the most generous taxpayer standing was offered by the Philippines Supreme Court in *Chavez v Presidential Commission on Good Government* (below). In that case, the Court granted *locus standi* so long as the issue was 'of transcendental importance [to] the public' or 'if the issues raised are of paramount public interest, and if they immeasurably affect the social, economic, and moral well-being of the people'.

---

[138] *SP Gupta v Union of India and Ors* [1982] AIR SC 149, para 17.
[139] *Flast v Cohen* 392 US 83 (1968).

SP Gupta v President of India and Ors
[1982] AIR SC 149 (Supreme Court, India)

Facts

Article 217 of the Constitution of India stipulates that every Judge of a High Court shall be appointed by the President by warrant under his hand and seal after consultation with the Chief Justice of India and the Governor of the State. Article 222 provides that the President may transfer a Judge from one High Court to any other High Court after consultation with the Chief Justice of India. Article 224 prescribes that the number of judges can be increased by reason of any temporary increase in the business of a High Court, and the President may appoint duly qualified persons to be additional Judges of the Court for such period not exceeding two years.

The Law Minister of the Government of India issued the circular letter to the Chief Justice of each High Court and the Chief Minister of each State to obtain the consent of additional judges working in one High Court to be appointed as permanent judges to another High Court. Lawyers practising in several High Courts challenged the constitutionality of the circular letter and the power of the central Government with respect to the appointment or non-appointment of additional judges. They also attacked the constitutional validity of orders of transfer of Chief Justice MM Ismail and Chief Justice KBN Singh. The first issue before the court was whether these petitioners had *locus standi*.

PN Bhagwati J

The traditional rule in regard to locus standi is that judicial redress is available only to a person who has suffered a legal injury by reason of violation of his legal right or legal protected interest by the impugned action of the State or a public authority or any other person or who is likely to suffer a legal injury by reason of threatened violation of his legal right or legally protected interest by any such action . . .

Even in our own country we have recognised this departure from the strict rule of locus standi in cases where there has been a violation of the constitutional or legal rights of persons who by reason of their socially or economically disadvantaged position are unable to approach the Court for judicial redress . . .

. . . [W]here a legal wrong or a legal injury is caused to a person or to a determinate class of persons by reason of violation of any constitutional or legal right or any burden is imposed in contravention of any constitutional or legal provision or without authority of law or any such legal wrong or legal injury or illegal burden is threatened and such person or determinate class of persons is by reason of poverty, helplessness or disability or socially or economically disadvantaged position, unable to approach the Court for relief, any member of the public can maintain an application for an appropriate direction, order or writ . . .

This broadening of the rule of locus standi has been largely responsible for the development of public law, because it is only the availability of judicial remedy for enforcement which invests law with meaning and purpose or else the law would remain merely a paper parchment, a teasing illusion and a promise of unreality . . .

There is also another reason why the rule of locus standi needs to be liberalised. Today we find that law is being increasingly used as a device of organised social action for the purpose of bringing about socio-economic change. The task of national reconstruction upon which we are engaged has brought about enormous increase in developmental activities and law is being utilised for the purpose of development, social and economic. It is creating more and more a new category of rights in favour of large sections of people and imposing a new category of duties on the State and the public officials with a view to reaching social justice to the common man. Individual rights and duties are giving place to meta-individual, collective, social rights and duties of classes or groups of persons. This is not to say that individual rights have ceased to have a vital place in our society but it is recognised that these rights are practically meaningless in today's setting unless accompanied by the social rights necessary to make them effective and really accessible to all. The new social and economic rights which are sought to be created in pursuance of the Directive Principles of State Policy essentially require active intervention of the State and other public authorities . . .

What is sufficient interest to give standing to a member of the public would have to be determined by the Court in each individual case. It is not possible for the Court to lay down any hard and fast rule or any strait-jacket formula for the purpose of defining or delimiting 'sufficient interest'[.] It has necessarily to be left to the discretion of the Court. The reason is that in a modern complex society which is seeking to bring about transformation of its social and economic structure and trying to reach social justice to the vulnerable sections of the people by creating new social, collective 'diffuse' rights and interests and imposing new public duties on the State and other public authorities, infinite number of situations are bound to arise which cannot be imprisoned in a rigid mould or a procrustean formula. The Judge who has the correct social perspective and who is on the same wavelength as the Constitution will be able to decide, without any difficulty and in consonance with the constitutional objectives, whether a member of the public moving the court in a particular case has sufficient interest to initiate the action . . .

We would, therefore, hold that any member of the public having sufficient interest can maintain an action for judicial redress for public injury arising from breach of public duty or from violation of some provision of the Constitution or the law and seek enforcement of such public duty and observance of such constitutional or legal provision. This is absolutely essential for maintaining the rule of law, furthering the cause of justice and accelerating the pace of realisation of the constitutional objective 'Law' . . .

In such cases, a member of the public having sufficient interest can certainly maintain an action challenging the legality of such act or omission, but if the person or specific class or group of persons who are primarily injured as a result of such act or omission, do not wish to claim any relief and accept such act or omission willingly and without protest, the member of the public who complains of a secondary public injury cannot maintain the action, for the effect of entertaining the action at the instance of such member of the public would be to foist a relief on the person or specific class or group of persons primarily injured, which they do not want.

If we apply these principles to determine the question of locus standi in the writ petition, . . . it will be obvious that the petitioners had clearly and indisputably locus standi to maintain their writ petition . . .

Chavez v Presidential Commission on Good Government
GR No 130716, 9 Dec 1998 (Supreme Court, Philippines)

Panganiban J

Petitioner Francisco I Chavez, as 'taxpayer, citizen and former government official who initiated the prosecution of the Marcoses and their cronies who committed unmitigated plunder of the public treasury and the systematic subjugation of the country's economy,' alleges that what impelled him to bring this action were several news reports bannered in a number of broadsheets sometime in September 1997. These news items referred to (1) the alleged discovery of billions of dollars of Marcos assets deposited in various coded accounts in Swiss banks; and (2) the reported execution of a compromise, between the government (through PCGG) and the Marcos heirs, on how to split or share these assets.

Petitioner, invoking his constitutional right to information and the correlative duty of the state to disclose publicly all its transactions involving the national interest, demands that respondents make public any and all negotiations and agreements pertaining to PCGG's task of recovering the Marcoses' ill-gotten wealth. He claims that any compromise on the alleged billions of ill-gotten wealth involves an issue of 'paramount public interest,' since it has a 'debilitating effect on the country's economy' that would be greatly prejudicial to the national interest of the Filipino people . . .

Petitioner, on the one hand, explains that as a taxpayer and citizen, he has the legal personality to file the instant petition. He submits that since ill-gotten wealth 'belongs to the Filipino people and [is], in truth [and] in fact, part of the public treasury,' any compromise in relation to it would constitute a diminution of the public funds, which can be enjoined by a taxpayer whose interest is for a full, if not substantial, recovery of such assets.

Besides, petitioner [emphasizes], the matter of recovering the ill-gotten wealth of the Marcoses is an issue 'of transcendental importance [to] the public.' He asserts that ordinary taxpayers have a right to initiate and prosecute actions questioning the validity of acts or orders of government agencies or instrumentalities, if the issues raised are 'of paramount public interest;' and if they 'immeasurably affect the social, economic, and moral well-being of the people.'

Moreover, the mere fact that he is a citizen satisfies the requirement of personal interest, when the proceeding involves the assertion of a public right, such as in this case. He invokes several decisions of this Court which have set aside the procedural matter of locus standi, when the subject of the case involved public interest . . .

Indeed, the arguments cited by petitioner constitute the controlling decisional rule as regards his legal standing to institute the instant petition. Access to public documents and records is a public right, and the real parties in interest are the people themselves . . .

Similarly, the instant petition is anchored on the right of the people to information and access to official records, documents and papers – a right guaranteed under Section 7, Article III of the 1987 Constitution. Petitioner, a former solicitor general, is a Filipino citizen. Because of the satisfaction of the two basic requisites laid down by decisional law to sustain petitioner's legal standing, ie (1) the enforcement of a public right (2) espoused by a Filipino citizen, we rule that the petition at bar should be allowed.

Notes and questions

1. The Supreme Court of India has liberalised *locus standi* to permit public interest litigation addressing concerns with public policies or issues of social justice on behalf of the general public or a determinate class of socially and economically disadvantaged people. For example, the Court, in *Ashok Kumar Pandey v State of West Bengal*,[140] states:

   A person acting bona fide and having sufficient interest in the proceeding of Public Interest Litigation will alone have a *locus standi* and can approach the court to wipe out

---

[140] *Ashok Kumar Pandey v State of West Bengal* [2004] 3 SCC 349.

violation of fundamental rights and genuine infraction of statutory provisions, but not for personal gain or private profit or political motive or any oblique consideration.

In *People's Union for Democratic Rights v Union of India*,[141] the Court determined that

> this Court has taken the view that, having regard to the peculiar socioeconomic conditions prevailing in the country where there is, considerable poverty, illiteracy and ignorance obstructing and impeding accessibility to the judicial process, it would result in closing the doors of justice to the poor and deprived sections of the community if the traditional rule of standing evolved by Anglo-Saxon jurisprudence that only a person wronged can sue for judicial redress were to be blindly adhered to and followed, and it is therefore necessary to evolve a new strategy by relaxing this traditional rule of standing in order that justice may became easily available to the lowly and the lost.

For further discussions on public interest litigation developed in India and challenges it has confronted, see S Deva, 'Public Interest Litigation in India: A Critical Review' (2009) 28(1) *Civil Justice Quarterly* 19.

2.   When public rights or interests are involved, courts may find it more appropriate to extend standing to social groups that represent whole citizens or a particular class of disadvantaged citizens, or who advocate on behalf of them. For example, in *Oposa v Factoran*,[142] the Supreme Court of the Philippines extended *locus standi* to environmental groups who brought a suit on behalf of generations yet unborn:

> The subject matter of the complaint is of common and general interest not just to several, but to all citizens of the Philippines. Consequently, since the parties are so numerous, it becomes impracticable, if not totally impossible, to bring all of them before the court. We likewise declare that the plaintiffs therein are numerous and representative enough to ensure the full protection of all concerned interests . . .. Their personality to sue in behalf of the succeeding generations can only be based on the concept of intergenerational responsibility insofar as the right to a balanced and healthful ecology is concerned.

Similarly, the Supreme Court of India also recognised the *locus standi* of women's organisations to sue on behalf of sexually harassed working women. In *Vishaka v State of Rajasthan*,[143] it opined:

> This writ petition has been filed for the enforcement of the fundamental rights of working women under Arts 14, 19 and 21 of the Constitution of India in view of the prevailing climate in which the violation of these rights is not uncommon. With the increasing awareness and emphasis on gender justice, there is increase in the effort to guard against such violations: and the resentment towards incidents of sexual harassment is also increasing. The present petition has been brought as a class action by certain social activists and NGOs with the aim of focusing attention towards this societal aberration, and assisting in finding suitable methods for realisation of the true concept of 'gender equality'; and to prevent sexual harassment of working women in all work places through judicial process, to fill the vacuum in existing legislation.

---

[141] *People's Union for Democratic Rights v Union of India* [1983] AIR SCR (1) 456, at 479.
[142] *Oposa v Factoran* GR No 101083, 30 Jul 1993.
[143] *Vishaka v State of Rajasthan* [1997] AIR SC 3011 [1].

3. The Supreme Court of Bangladesh recognised the *locus standi* of the Bangladesh Environmental Lawyers Association (BELA), which challenged a Flood Action Plan that had disregarded environmental impact assessments and caused environmental degradation and ecological imbalance, in *Dr Mohiuddin Farooque v Bangladesh*.[144] Under Article 102(1) of the Bangladesh Constitution, the Court may provide remedies on the application of any person aggrieved. In this case, the Court broadened the concept of 'any person aggrieved' by referring to the Principle of Rio Declaration on Environment and Development. The Court reasoned that

    > [a] group of environmental lawyers possessed of pertinent, bona fide and well-recognized attributes and purposes in the area of environment and having a provable, sincere, dedicated and established status is asking for a judicial review of certain activities under a flood action plan undertaken with foreign assistance on the ground, inter alia, of alleged environmental degradation and ecological imbalance and violation of several laws in certain areas of the district of Tangail. The question is: does it have sufficient interest in the matter for a standing under article 102?

    The Rio Declaration on Environment and Development containing 27 principles include, among [others], it may be noted for the present purpose:

    > Principle 10: Environmental issues are best handled with the participation of all concerned citizens, at the relevant level. At the national level, each individual shall have appropriate access to information concerning the environment that is held by public authorities, including information on hazardous materials and activities in their communities, and the opportunity to participate in decision-making processes. States shall facilitate and encourage public awareness and participation by making information widely available. Effective access to judicial and administrative proceeding, including redress and remedy, shall be provided.[145]

    Principle 10 above seems to be the theoretical foundation for all that have been vindicated in the writ petition and also provides a ground for standing. In this context of engaging concern for the conservation of environment, irrespective of the locality where it is threatened, I am of the view that a national organization like the appellant, which claims to have studied and made research on the disputed project, can and should be attributed a threshold standing as having sufficient interest in the matter, and thereby regarded as a person aggrieved to maintain the writ petition subject to the objection or objections as may be raised by the respondents if a Rule is issued ultimately.

4. As discussed earlier, in the centralised system of constitutional review, aside from individuals, many other institutional actors including the president, the premier, the legislature or legislative minority, may also initiate petitions before the constitutional courts. These petitions are often free from litigation fees. In what ways and to what extent does the centralised system of constitutional review facilitate public interest litigation? Wen-Chen Chang has characterised constitutional review in centralised judicial systems as an alternative form of public interest litigation that may effectuate broader social and policy changes, especially in times of democratic transitions. See Wen-Chen Chang, 'Public-Interest Litigation in Taiwan: Strategy for Law and Policy Reforms in Course of Democratization' in

---

[144] *Dr Mohiuddin Farooque v Bangladesh* [1996] 17 BLD (AD).
[145] Ibid.

Po Jen Yap and Holning Lau (eds), *Public Interest Litigation in Asia* (New York: Routledge, 2011) 136.

5. The global networking of non-governmental organisations may also facilitate public interest litigation, and become part of transnational lawyering and legal process. At the same time, however, transnational lawyering may also bring about concerns with democratic deficit and legitimacy, as such litigation often invokes outside actors and external norms. For further discussions, see H Hongju Koh, 'Transnational Legal Process' (1996) 75 *Nebraska Law Review* 181; and Jiunn-Rong Yeh and Wen-Chen Chang, 'The Emergence of Transnational Constitutionalism: Its Features, Challenges and Solutions' (2008) 27 *Pennsylvania State International Law Review* 89.

VII. APPROACHES TO CONSTITUTIONAL INTERPRETATION

Approaches to constitutional interpretation often give rise to polarising debates because battle lines tend to be drawn according to judges' views on political ideologies, constitutional tradition, judicial culture, or the perceived roles of courts and the relationship with political branches. At the same time, constitutional scholars generally agree that accepted approaches include interpretations based on text, the intent of the framers or the purposes that best explain constitutional provisions, precedents or, most controversially, free-standing subjective values.[146]

In some jurisdictions, laws may prescribe interpretive approaches for the courts. For example, in Taiwan, Article 13 of the Constitutional Interpretation Procedure Act privileges the interpretive method based on history:

> In case of rendering an interpretation, the Justices shall refer to materials concerning the enactment and amendments of the Constitution, and the legislative history of a statute or regulation.

Section 9A of Singapore's Interpretation Act also provides that the judiciary may consult materials that promote the purpose or object underlying the written law, where a literal interpretation is ambiguous. Notwithstanding any expressed legislative preferences, the choices of interpretive method ultimately lie with the courts, as it is their duty to interpret the written law and to declare the unwritten law. The following discussion includes interpretive approaches commonly used by Asian courts: text-based, history-based and purposive approaches, alongside the use of foreign and international laws.

A. Text-based Approach

Interpretation based upon the text is the most traditional and commonly-used approach, and is deployed as a starting point. When the text is plain and clear, a text-based

---

[146] RH Fallon Jr, 'A Constructivist Coherence Theory of Constitutional Interpretation' (1987) 100 *Harvard Law Review* 1189.

interpretive approach is appropriate. However, what may be accepted as a plain and clear text may itself not be clear. Although courts may make authoritative determinations over whether language is clear or not, different readings may still be invoked and lead to further debate or controversy. The following cases illustrate the primacy of the text-based approach in Asian courts. In *JY Interpretation No 392*, the Constitutional Court in Taiwan preferred a text-based approach over a historically-based one. In *SP Gupta v Union of India*, Justice Gupta of the Supreme Court of India asserted that only ambiguous language would require the court to adopt interpretive methods other than a textual one. In *Director of Immigration v Chong Fung Yuen*, the Court of Final Appeal in Hong Kong acknowledged the primary place of textual interpretation in common law systems, to ascertain the legislative intent as expressed in language.

JY Interpretation No 392
22 Dec 1995 (Constitutional Court, Taiwan)

Facts

Article 8 of the Constitution in Taiwan states:

> When a person is arrested or detained on suspicion of having committed a crime, the organ making the arrest or detention shall, within 24 hours, turn him over to a competent court for trial.

However, the Criminal Procedure Code allowed the prosecutors, rather than judges, to make detention decisions within 24 hours of arrest. This law was challenged as an obvious violation of Article 8. The Ministry of Justice defended the impugned practice by relying on the Provisional Constitution for the Period of Political Tutelage that had authorised 'tribunals' – including both courts and prosecutors – to make detention decisions, and urged the Constitutional Court to interpret Article 8 of the Constitution in light of the historical practice.

Held

Promulgated in 1931, Article 8 of the Provisional Constitution for the Period of Political Tutelage provides:

> When a person is arrested or detained on suspicion of having committed a crime, the executing or detention organ shall, within 24 hours, turn him over to a tribunal for trial. The said person, or any other person, may request the detainer to surrender the detainee for trial within 24 hours according to law.

The Double Five Constitutional Draft prepared in 1936, and the text of the current Constitution promulgated in 1947, did not used the term 'tribunal' as it appeared in the Basic Law. Instead, they used the term 'court.' This was due to the fact that, since the legal reformation movement which occurred in the latter part of the Ching Dynasty, in the Tribunal Organization Law for Da Li Yuan promulgated in the 30th year of the reign of the Emperor Kuan Shi (1906), and the Law for Court Organization promulgated in the 1st year of the reign of the Emperor Shuan Tong (1909), all government organs performing the functions of adjudication, except for the Da Li Yuan, were called 'tribunal' (eg higher tribunal, district tribunal). When the Republic was founded, the organization law was, in principle, adopted temporarily. As time passed and memories faded, the term 'tribunal' still lingered on. It cannot be said that later adoption of the term 'court' was a calculated move to deny the court or tribunal a restrictive connotation, and to assume an expansive definition for the court – that is, to include the prosecutor in it. Even for the connotation of 'court,' we should observe and judge from its functions. This has been discussed previously. The Constitution has used the term 'trial' explicitly. That should refer to a court of a restrictive definition, and no more. Moreover, the prosecutor's offices were made to be attached to courthouses. It can be inferred from this arrangement that the prosecutor's office, by its nature, is not a court. Otherwise, there would be no need to 'attach' it to another thing, not to mention these two organs each have different duties and functions. Thus, it cannot be said that the framers of the Constitution intended to have the prosecutor's office included in the 'court' as provided in the Article 8, Paragraph 2, second sentence, of the Constitution. Moreover, when we reviewed the constitutional history of the Republic, Article 5 of the 1913 ROC Constitutional Draft (the Tien Tan Constitutional Draft) used the term 'bench,' Article 6 of the 'Tsau Kun Constitution' promulgated in 1923 used the term 'court,' and Article 29 of the 'Tai Yuan Basic Law Draft' prepared in 1930 used the term 'court.' Although Article 8 of the Provisional Constitution for the Period of Political Tutelage promulgated in 1931 used the term 'tribunal,' Article 9 of the Draft of the Constitution (Double Five Constitutional Draft) prepared in 1936 and the Constitution promulgated in 1947 [the current Constitution] both used the term 'court.' It would appear that the various terms used at different times – 'bench,' 'court,' 'tribunal' and eventually 'court' – connoted the same organ of adjudication, ie, the court of a restrictive definition. There are various methods for constitutional interpretation. Comparing the objective theory with the subjective theory for this case, the former interpreted according to the normative intent reflected objectively in the words of constitutional articles, while the latter had to mirror the framer's subjective intent faithfully. Even so, the latter method still must abide by the letters of the Constitution chosen explicitly by the framers. Only when the literal meaning of the Constitution is ambiguous can the historical materials or the contextual information be supplemented. The search for the framers' original intent is not an easy task. It involves clarifying the relations between the drafter and the maker (the approver), and resolving the discrepancies among historical records from various sources. If there is no certain standard or criterion, the determination may become arbitrary and unscrupulous. Moreover, the fact that it existed in the time of the preparation of the Constitution was itself the normative object for the Constitution. How could the interpretation of the Constitution be built on this fact? The literal meaning of Article 8 of the Constitution is clear. The 'court' it refers to, if we take the language of the provision as a whole and give it an objective, literal interpretation, should mean a court composed of judges conducting trials and having authority to examine and to punish. The result from this line of interpretation will not only be in harmony with the spirit of the Constitution for the protection of physical freedom, but also in congruence with the system established by most modern constitutional democratic states for the protection of physical freedom. After all, the word 'court,' in general usage, commonly refers to an organ that exercises adjudicative power . . .

SP Gupta v Union of India
[1982] AIR SC 149 (Supreme Court, India)

Facts

Article 222 of the Constitution of India provides that 'the President may, after consultation with the Chief Justice of India, transfer a Judge from one High Court to any other High Court'. The petitioners argued that Article 222, as implied by Parliament's intention, connoted that the consent of the judges was required. As such, the transfer of any judges without their consent would be unconstitutional. While ruling the impugned transfer unconstitutional, Justice Gupta refuted the petitioners' reading of Article 222.

AC Gupta J

The question that now arises is if it can be said on a parity of reasoning that 'consent' also should be read as a part and parcel of the exercise of the power under Article 222. It is difficult to accede to this contention because if a Judge cannot be transferred without his consent then the power loses its significance and becomes an immunity to a Judge from transfer by withholding his consent. Thus, a power which is to be exercised by the President can be defeated or stalled by a simple act of the Judge in refusing to give his consent to the transfer. This could never have been the intention of the Founding Fathers of the Constitution. . . .

A perusal of Article 222 unmistakably shows that it is expressed in absolutely clear, explicit, intelligible, plain and unambiguous language which admits of no vagueness or ambiguity, Mr Seervai [the attorney of the petitioning judges], however, by an involved process of reasoning wants us to import the concept of 'consent' by reading the same into the Article by way of necessary intendment of the Parliament. It is not the function of the court to supply words to suit a particular course of action so as to be acceptable to a particular act of persons as a doctrine of implied consent. It is just like first raising a ghost and then trying to kill it. Before we enter into a detailed discussion of the Rules of interpretation of Statutes we might indicate that there is intrinsic evidence in the various constitutional provisions which clearly show that the word 'consent' has been dropped by the legislature deliberately or it is a case of deliberate omission rather than *casus omissus*.

. . . [T]he methodology of interpretation of statutes should be the same for constitutional provisions as it is for statutory provisions. It has further been held that external aids like Parliamentary debates, report of the Drafting or select committees, the Objects and Reasons of the Act are wholly inadmissible for the purpose of interpreting the provisions of a statute which would depend entirely on the language of the provisions concerned. Here also, some of the cases have held that, where the language of the provisions is shrouded in obscurity or is not fully intelligible so as to ascertain or find out the objects of the Act, external aids may be permissible.

. . . [T]he propositions that emerge from the decided cases of this Court and other foreign courts are as follows:

(1) Where the language of a statute is clear and unambiguous, there is no room for the application either of the doctrine of *casus omissus* or of pressing into service external aid, for in such a case the words used by the Constitution or the statute speak for themselves and it is not the function of the court to add words or expressions merely to suit what that courts think is the supposed intention of the legislature.

(2) Where however, the words or expressions used in the constitutional or statutory provisions are shrouded [in] mystery, clouded with ambiguity and are unclear and

unintelligible so that the dominant object and spirit of the legislature cannot be spelt out from the language, external aids in the nature of parliamentary debates, immediately preceding the passing of the statute, the report of the Select Committees or its Chairman, the Statement of Objects and Reasons of the statute, if any, or any statement made by the sponsor of the statute which is in close proximity to the actual introduction or insertion of the statutory provision so as to become, as it were, a result of the statement made, can be pressed into service in order to ascertain the [real] purport, intent and will of the legislature to make the constitutional provision workable. We might make it clear that such aids may neither be decisive nor conclusive but they would certainly assist the courts in interpreting the statute in order to determine the avowed object of the Act or the Constitution as the case may be.

(3)   Except in the aforesaid cases, a mere speech of any member made on the floor of the House during the course of a parliamentary or legislative debate would not be admissible at all because the views expressed by the speaker may be his individual views which may or may not be accepted by the majority of the members present in the House.

(4)   Legislative history of a constitutional provision though not directly germane for the purpose of construing a statute may, however, be used in exceptional cases to denote the beginning of the legislative process which results in the logical end and the finale of the statutory provision but in no case can the legislative history take the place of or be a substitute for an interpretation which is in direct contravention of the statutory provision concerned.

(5)   Where the scheme of a statute clearly shows that certain words or phrases were deliberately omitted by the legislature for a particular purpose or motive, it is not open to the Court to add those words either by conforming to the supposed intention of the legislature or because the insertion or the omission suite the ideology of the Judges deciding the case. Such a course of action would amount not to interpretation but to interpolation of the statutory or constitutional provisions, as the case may be, and is against, all the well established cannot of interpretation of statutes.

The main reason behind the principles enunciated above is that the legislature must be presumed to be aware of the expanding needs of the nation, the requirements of the people and above all, the dominant object which the legislation seeks to subserve.

Thus, where the language is plain and unambiguous the court is not entitled to go behind the language so as to add or supply omissions and thus play the role of a political reformer or of a wise counsel to the legislature . . .

Director of Immigration v Chong Fung Yuen
[2001] 2 HKLRD 533 (Court of Final Appeal, Hong Kong)

Facts

The applicant was a Chinese citizen born in Hong Kong on 29 September 1997. When he was born, his parents were not permanent residents of Hong Kong, but were in Hong Kong lawfully with two-way permits from the Mainland. On this basis, the applicant claimed to be a permanent resident of Hong Kong with a right of abode. This claim was based on Articles 24(2)(1) and Article 24(3), which gave the right of abode to 'Chinese citizens born in Hong Kong before or after the establishment of the Region'. However, the Immigration Ordinance further required that for a Chinese citizen born in Hong Kong, one of his parents must have been settled or had the right of abode in Hong Kong at the time of his birth or at any later time. A critical issue here was whether the plain reading of Article 24(3) barred the said ordinance from stipulating any additional requirements.

Andrew Li CJ

The courts' role under the common law in interpreting the Basic Law is to construe the language used in the text of the instrument in order to ascertain the legislative intent as expressed in the language. Their task is not to ascertain the intent of the lawmaker on its own. Their duty is to ascertain what was meant by the language used and to give effect to the legislative intent as expressed in the language. It is the text of the enactment which is the law and it is regarded as important both that the law should be certain and that it should be ascertainable by the citizen.

The courts do not look at the language of the article in question in isolation. The language is considered in the light of its context and purpose. . . . The exercise of interpretation requires the courts to identify the meaning borne by the language when considered in the light of its context and purpose. This is an objective exercise. Whilst the courts must avoid a literal, technical, narrow or rigid approach, they cannot give the language a meaning which the language cannot bear. As was observed in *Minister of Home Affairs v Fisher* [1980] AC 319 at 329E, a case on constitutional interpretation: 'Respect must be paid to the language which has been used and to the traditions and usages which have given meaning to that language'.

As the Court held in *Ng Ka Ling* . . . the courts should give a generous interpretation to the provisions in Chapter III that contain constitutional guarantees of freedoms that lie at the heart of Hong Kong's separate system. However, when interpreting the provisions that define the categories of permanent residents, the courts should simply consider the language in the light of any ascertainable purpose and the context.

To assist in the task of interpretation of the provision in question, the courts consider what is within the Basic Law, including provisions in the Basic Law other than the provision in question and the Preamble. These are internal aids to interpretation.

Extrinsic materials which throw light on the context or purpose of the Basic Law or its particular provisions may generally be used as an aid to the interpretation of the Basic Law. Extrinsic materials which can be considered include the Joint Declaration and the Explanations on the Basic Law (draft) given at the NPC on 28 March 1990 shortly before its adoption on 4 April 1990. The state of domestic legislation at that time and the time of the Joint Declaration will often also serve as an aid to the interpretation of the Basic Law. Because the context and purpose of the Basic Law were established at the time of its enactment in 1990, the extrinsic materials relevant to its interpretation are, generally speaking, pre-enactment materials, that is, materials brought into existence prior to or contemporaneous with the enactment of the Basic Law, although it only came into effect on 1 July 1997.

It is unnecessary for the purposes of this case to explore what assistance (if any) can be derived from extrinsic materials other than pre-enactment materials relating to context and purpose; in particular, whether post-enactment materials can be called in aid. For the purposes of this case, it is sufficient to state that on the common law approach which the courts are bound to apply in the absence of a binding interpretation by the Standing Committee, extrinsic materials, whatever their nature and whether pre or post-enactment, cannot affect interpretation where the courts conclude that the meaning of the language, when construed in the light of its context and purpose ascertained with the benefit of internal aids and appropriate extrinsic materials, is clear. The meaning of the language is clear if it is free from ambiguity, that is, it is not reasonably capable of sustaining competing alternative interpretations.

Once the courts conclude that the meaning of the language of the text when construed in the light of its context and purpose is clear, the courts are bound to give effect to the clear meaning of the language. The courts will not on the basis of any extrinsic materials depart from that clear meaning and give the language a meaning which the language cannot bear.

In a case where the courts have to consider the use of extrinsic materials other than pre-enactment materials relating to context and purpose, the courts should, in conformity with common law principles, approach the matter cautiously. The common law does not in general adopt the approach that all extrinsic materials can be considered leaving their weight to be assessed. A prudent approach is particularly called for where the courts are asked to consider post-enactment materials. This is because as discussed above, under a common law system which includes a separation of powers, the interpretation of laws once enacted is a matter for the courts.

Notes and Questions

1. What is the importance and function of the text-based approach? Why is it treated as the first and most basic interpretive method by most courts? Does it have anything to do with the legitimacy of courts or the counter-majoritarian nature of the judiciary?

2. The Hong Kong Court of Final Appeal in *Director of Immigration v Chong Fung Yuen* resorted to the plain text of Article 24(2)(3) of the Basic Law to resolve the claim to the right of abode, a sensitive political issue that has repercussions for the relationship between Hong Kong and China. As Wen-Chen Chang argues, a textual approach appeals to courts that have to deal with politically charged cases. She analyses the *Impeachment of the President (Roh Moo-hyun) Case* in South Korea and *JY Interpretation No 627* in Taiwan regarding presidential immunity from criminal investigations on the first lady's embezzlement of the state-secrets fund, and argues:

> Both courts understood the pivotal advantage in relying on nothing but the texts of their respective constitutions; this narrowed the site of what was being contested. The issues facing both courts were already very challenging, and there was certainly nothing to be gained in engaging in methodological disputes. Nevertheless, it is striking that both decisions relied on a single constitutional provision, article 52 in Taiwan, article 65 in South Korea. They declined – at least in any explicit terms – even to consult any other domestic interpretive sources; namely, other constitutional provisions, constitutional structures, government systems, constitutional histories, or the intents and purposes of the constitutional drafters. The attempt to narrow the field of contested normative authorities is certainly understandable, and that strengthened the Court's decisional authority.[147]

[147] See Wen-Chen Chang, 'Strategic Judicial Response in Politically Charged Cases: East Asian Experiences' (2010) 8 *I•CON* 885, 904.

B. The Historically-Based Approach

Interpretation based on history is another common approach in constitutional adjudication. Deployed when the text is not entirely clear, this approach looks to the intent of constitutional drafters or discussions held during constitutional conventions to help clarify what the text was originally understood to mean. The type of historical materials that courts may consult may include meeting records and even the essays or diaries of constitutional drafters. For example, the *Federalist Papers*, a collected volume of essays by James Madison, John Jay and Alexander Hamilton, three primary architects of the US Constitution, have served as an essential guide to the interpretation of the US Constitution and are cited by the US Supreme Court more often than any other historical document.[148] The following decision, rendered by the Constitutional Court in Taiwan, presents an exercise in history-based interpretation: how a court – faced with an issue not explicitly stipulated in the Constitution – may make inquiries about the discussion of and voting on the constitutional convention, as well as the teachings of Dr Sun Yat-sen, whose political theories greatly influenced the 1947 ROC Constitution.

JY Interpretation No 3
21 May 1952 (Constitutional Court, Taiwan)

Facts

Even though the ROC Constitution does not give the Control Yuan power to propose bills, it proposed the Control Yuan Organization Act to the Legislative Yuan. When this failed, the Control Yuan petitioned the Constitutional Court for an interpretation of the Constitution.

Held

The Constitution does not expressly provide whether the Control Yuan may propose bills of act to the Legislative Yuan concerning matters within its authority. Yet Article 87 of the Constitution stipulates that the Examination Yuan may propose bills of act to the Legislative Yuan for matters within its authority. Those who argue that the Control Yuan may not propose bills of act to the Legislative Yuan base their argument on the Latin [maxims] [in statutory construction] that *casus omissus pro omisso habendus est* ('a case omitted is to be held as intentionally omitted') and *expression unius est exclusio alterius* ('the expression of one thing is the exclusion of another'). In reality, however, [these maxims are not applicable] under all circumstances. For example, it is not applicable if there are apparent omissions or there is room for interpretation among related statutory provisions. Such omissions can be found in our Constitution as well. For example, for government bodies created by election, Article 34 and Article 64, Paragraph 2, expressly stipulate that the election of the delegates to the National Assembly and the members of the Legislative Yuan 'shall be regulated by [the enactment of] statute,' yet [somehow] only the election of members of the Control Yuan does not have a similar rule. Obviously, this omission cannot be considered to be because the election of members of the Control Yuan does not require

---

[148] For the legacy of the Federalist papers and its influence upon the interpretation of the US Constitution, see 'Symposium' (1993) 16 *Harvard Journal of Law & Public Policy* 579.

statutory regulation, or that the Constitution intentionally omits or purposefully precludes [the need for an election statute] as such.

Article 71 of the Constitution, as [derived from] Article 73 of the Constitution Draft, originally stated, '[a]t the meetings of the Legislative Yuan, the Premier of the Executive Yuan and the heads of all ministries and commissions may be present to express viewpoints.' Delegates of the Constitutional Conference later proposed to amend 'Premier of the Executive Yuan' to 'Head of other Branches concerned' for the reason that 'as far as the Examination Yuan, Judicial Yuan and Control Yuan are concerned, their Heads may naturally be present at the Legislative Yuan to present viewpoints on any statutory bill related to their discharged duties.' This amendment was accepted by the [Constitutional] Conference as in the current text, and is sufficient to demonstrate that Heads of other Branches concerned includes all Branch heads other than the Legislative Yuan. Also, Delegates of the Constitutional Conference proposed that [the language] in Article 87 of the Constitution, as [derived from] Article 92 of the Constitution Draft, '[w]hen the Examination Yuan proposes bills of act that are related to its duties of discharge, the Executive Secretary of the Examination Yuan shall be present at the Legislative Yuan to explain [the bill]' be deleted, the reason being 'the Examination Yuan, as with other Branches, may submit bills of act concerning its duties of discharge to the Legislative Yuan. If explanations need to be provided to the Legislative Yuan, the Head or his/her authorized representative responsible [for the bill] shall be present so that it is not necessary to provide that the Executive Secretary shall be present [at the Legislative Yuan] in the Constitution.' Having thoroughly examined the Records and all the propositions of the National Assembly (Constitutional Conference), there was not a single objection or difference of opinion concerning this issue, nor were there any other particular reasons why the Examination Yuan should independently be granted the power to propose [statutory] bills than the Judicial Yuan and Control Yuan. It is sufficient to demonstrate that it was without question that each Branch [of the Government] might propose [statutory] bills.

As stated in the Preamble, our Constitution was created from the teachings bequeathed by Dr Sun Yat-sen, who founded the Republic of China. The Five Branches were established in accordance with Article 53 (the Executive Yuan), Article 62 (the Legislative Yuan), Article 77 (the Judicial Yuan), Article 83 (the Examination Yuan), and Article 90 (the Control Yuan). Each Branch is the highest state agency independently discharging its duties, and is equal to the other Branches, within the scope of each respective power as originally bestowed by the Constitution. As far as the discharging duties are concerned, it is necessary for the Control Yuan and Judicial Yuan, as with the Examination Yuan, to respectively propose bills of act to the Legislative Yuan on matters within their authority. While the Examination Yuan may propose bills of act to the Legislative Yuan on matters within their authority, there is no reason for the Constitution to purposefully omit or intentionally preclude the granting of [the same] proposition [power] to the Judicial Yuan and Control Yuan. Whereas it is within the exclusive authority of the Legislative Yuan to resolve a [given] statutory bill, for other Branches, being more familiar with matters under their respective authorities and as providers of legislative opinions, it is not without reason or in violation of [any] law that they may indeed propose bills of act to the Legislative Yuan. In sum, since the Examination Yuan may propose bills of act to the Legislative Yuan for matters within its authority in accordance with Article 87 of the Constitution, based upon the system of the separation of the Five Powers and equal interdependence, [further] in reference to the legislative history of that Article and Article 71, it is in compliance with the spirit of the Constitution that the Control Yuan may propose bills of act to the Legislative Yuan concerning matters within its authority.

Notes and Questions

1. In Asia, many states have undergone democratisation and major constitutional reforms since their founding. Against this backdrop, how relevant is the history-based approach as regards constitutional interpretation? Can such changes be regarded as signifying a break from the constitutional past on account of their radicalism or revolutionary nature?

2. In *JY Interpretation No 3*, the five branches of government, a distinctive feature of the ROC Constitution and an important legacy from the political theories of Sun Yat-sen, were emphasised. Yet this Constitution has undergone a series of reforms in Taiwan since the 1990s, and the structure of the five branches and their respective functions have been greatly altered. In your view, to what extent would the political theories of Sun Yet-sen still be relevant to the interpretation of the ROC Constitution in Taiwan?

C. Purposive Approach

Aside from text or history, another thing courts can look at in the course of constitutional adjudication is the object or purpose of the constitutional provision in question. Discerning this may require looking back in history or to the future. The courts in Singapore and Hong Kong usually adopt a more historical approach to highlight legislative intention, to which the courts may defer. A purposive approach can also be forward-looking, in prioritising changing social conditions. A constitution is envisaged as a 'living' document whose meanings must evolve to meet the needs of a changing society. This has been adopted in activist jurisdictions like Canada, which sees the constitution through the metaphor of 'a living tree capable of growth and expansion within its natural limits'.[149] The constitution as a living document has also been recognised in the interpretation of the US Constitution.[150] One of the most renowned cases was *Brown v Board of Education*, where the Court adjusted the understanding of equal citizenship to the importance of modern education.[151] In Asia, the Supreme Court of India is renowned for its generous understanding of the living constitution. According to the Court, a constitution is 'a living and organic thing and must adapt itself to the changing situations and pattern in which it has to be interpreted'.[152] Nevertheless, detractors of the purposive approach are often concerned with the prospect of judicial legislation or a 'rule by judges', contrary to the rule of law and the separation of powers.

---

[149] *Edwards v Canada (Attorney General)* [1930] AC 124 (Privy Council on appeal from Supreme Court of Canada): 'The British North America Act planted in Canada a living tree capable of growth and expansion within its natural limits.'

[150] See eg DA Strauss, *The Living Constitution* (New York: Oxford University Press, 2010); and JM Balkin, 'The Roots of the Living Constitution' (2012) 92 *Boston University Law Review* 1129.

[151] *Brown v Board of Education* 347 US 483, 494 (1954).

[152] *Synthetics & Chemicals Ltd Etc v State of Uttar Pradesh* [1989] AIR SCR Supl (1) 623.

Constitutional Reference No 1 of 1995
[1995] SGCT 1 (Constitutional Tribunal, Singapore)

Facts

In 1991, the Constitution (Amendment) Bill was passed in Parliament to reduce the powers of the elected president. A question arose as to whether the President's assent to such an amendment was necessary under Article 22H given that Article 5(2A) – the key provision regulating constitutional amendments of this nature – had not yet been brought into force.

Yong Pung How CJ

It is well established and not disputed by either parties that a purposive interpretation should be adopted in interpreting the Constitution to give effect to the intent and will of Parliament. The principle to be applied is that the words of the Act are to be read in their entire context and in their grammatical and ordinary sense, harmoniously with the scheme of the Act, the object of the Act and the intention of Parliament: EA Driedger, *Construction of Statutes* (2nd Ed, 1983) p 87 . . .

This is also evident from s 9A of the Interpretation Act (Cap 1, 1985 Rev Ed) which states:

(1) . . . an interpretation that would promote the purpose or object underlying the written law (whether that purpose or object is expressly stated in the written law or not) shall be preferred to an interpretation that would not promote that purpose or object.

(2) Subject to subsection (4) . . . if any material not forming part of the written law is capable of assisting in the ascertainment of the meaning of the provision, consideration may be given to that material—

   (a) to confirm that the meaning of the provision is the ordinary meaning conveyed by the text of the provision taking into account its context in the written law and the purpose or object underlying the written law; or

   (b) to ascertain the meaning of the provision when—(i) the provision is ambiguous or obscure; or (ii) the ordinary meaning conveyed by the text of the provision taking into account its context in the written law and the purpose or object underlying the written law leads to a result that is manifestly absurd or unreasonable . . .

(4) In determining whether consideration should be given to any material in accordance with subsection (2), or in determining the weight to be given to any such material, regard shall be had, in addition to any other relevant matters, to—

   (a) the desirability of persons being able to rely on the ordinary meaning conveyed by the text of the provision taking into account its context in the written law and the purpose or object underlying the written law; . . .

This is clearly an instance where resort to contemporaneous speeches and documents is sanctioned: as an aid to the construction of legislation which is ambiguous or obscure or the literal meaning of which leads to an absurdity. Even in such cases references in court to Parliamentary material should only be permitted where such material clearly discloses the mischief aimed at or the legislative intention lying behind the ambiguous or obscure words. [Per Lord Browne-Wilkinson in *Pepper (Inspector of Taxes) v Hart* [1993] AC 593 at p 634]
. . .

> In the circumstances, it would be wrong to adopt a literal approach as suggested by counsel for the Presidency, even if Art 22H(1) was not ambiguous or inconsistent, if the literal approach did not give effect to the will and intent of Parliament . . .

Ng Ka Ling & Others v Director of Immigration
[1999] 1 HKLRD 315 (Court of Final Appeal, Hong Kong)

Facts

In this case, the issue of how to interpret Article 158 of the Basic Law arose, as to whether the Court of Final Appeal in Hong Kong could interpret Article 22(4) on its own or had to refer it to the Standing Committee of the NPC which had ultimate authority to interpret the Basic Law.

Andrew Li CJ

Approach to Interpretation of the Basic Law

We must begin by recognizing and appreciating the character of the document. The Basic Law is an entrenched constitutional instrument to implement the unique principle of 'one country, two systems'. As is usual for constitutional instruments, it uses ample and general language. It is a living instrument intended to meet changing needs and circumstances.

It is generally accepted that in the interpretation of a constitution such as the Basic Law a purposive approach is to be applied. The adoption of a purposive approach is necessary because a constitution states general principles and expresses purposes without condescending to particularity and definition of terms. Gaps and ambiguities are bound to arise and, in resolving them, the courts are bound to give effect to the principles and purposes declared in, and to be ascertained from, the constitution and relevant extrinsic materials. So, in ascertaining the true meaning of the instrument, the courts must consider the purpose of the instrument and its relevant provisions as well as the language of its text in the light of the context, context being of particular importance in the interpretation of a constitutional instrument.

As to purpose, the purpose of the Basic Law is to establish the Hong Kong Special Administrative Region being an inalienable part of the People's Republic of China under the principle of 'one country, two systems' with a high degree of autonomy in accordance with China's basic policies regarding Hong Kong as set out and elaborated in the Joint Declaration. The purpose of a particular provision may be ascertainable from its nature or other provisions of the Basic Law or relevant extrinsic materials including the Joint Declaration.

As to the language of its text, the courts must avoid a literal, technical, narrow or rigid approach. They must consider the context. The context of a particular provision is to be found in the Basic Law itself as well as relevant extrinsic materials including the Joint Declaration. Assistance can also be gained from any traditions and usages that may have given meaning to the language used.

Chapter III of the Basic Law begins by defining the class constituting Hong Kong residents including permanent and non-permanent residents and then provides for the rights and duties of the residents, including the right of abode in the case of permanent residents. What is set out in Chapter III, after the definition of the class, are the constitutional guarantees for the freedoms that lie at the heart of Hong Kong's separate system. The courts should give a generous interpretation to the provisions in Chapter III that contain these constitutional guarantees in order to give to Hong Kong residents the full measure of fundamental rights and freedoms so constitutionally guaranteed.

However, when interpreting the provisions that define the class of Hong Kong residents, including in particular the class of permanent residents (as opposed to the constitutional guarantees of their rights and freedoms), the courts should simply consider the language in the light of any ascertainable purpose and the context. The context would include other provisions of the Basic Law. Of particular relevance would be the provisions of the International Covenant on Civil and Political Rights ('the ICCPR') as applied to Hong Kong which remain in force by virtue of Article 39 and any relevant principles which can be distilled from the ICCPR.

What we have set out above cannot be and is not intended to be an exhaustive statement of the principles the courts should adopt in approaching the interpretation of the Basic Law. Constitutional interpretation, like other forms of interpretation, is essentially question specific. As and when questions of interpretation arise, the courts will address the challenges posed by the questions raised and develop principles as necessary to meet them. . . .

In deciding what test is to be applied in considering whether the classification condition is satisfied, a purposive interpretation has to be adopted. An important purpose of Article 158 is the Standing Committee's authorization to the Hong Kong courts including the Court of Final Appeal to interpret 'on their own' the provisions of the Basic Law which fall outside the excluded provisions, particularly provisions which are within the Region's autonomy. This is an essential part of the high degree of autonomy granted to the Region. . . .

. . . [Adopting the purposive approach, the Court holds that] Article 158 requires a reference to the Standing Committee of the interpretation of the relevant excluded provisions only. The Article does not require a reference of the question of interpretation involved generally when a number of provisions (including an excluded provision) may be relevant to provide the solution of that question.

Applying that test, in adjudicating this case, as a matter of substance, the predominant provision which we are interpreting is Article 24, which provides for the right of abode of a permanent resident, and the content of that right. That Article is the very source of the right which is sought to be enforced by the applicants in these appeals. That being so, the Court . . . does not have to make a reference, although Article 22(4) is arguably relevant to the interpretation of Article 24 . . .

Synthetics & Chemicals Ltd Etc v State of Uttar Pradesh
[1990] AIR 1927 (Supreme Court, India)

Facts

The petitioner, a corporation manufacturing ethyl alcohol, charged with impost by the State government, challenged the impugned State law as having no valid constitutional grounds. But the respondent State rebutted that the disputed legislation was authorised by the Constitution, which provided various entries and lists of vend fee and imposts levied by States.

Sabyasachi Mukharji J

The Constitution of India, it has to be borne in mind, like most other Constitutions, is an organic document. It should be interpreted in the light of the experience. It has to be flexible and dynamic so that it adapts itself to the changing conditions and accommodates itself in a pragmatic way to the goals of national development and the industrialisation of the country. This Court should, therefore, endeavour to interpret the entries and the powers in the Constitution in such a way that it helps to the attainment of [undisputed] national goals, as permitted by the Constitution. . . . [T]he relevant entries in the Seventh Schedule to the Constitution demarcate legislative fields and are closely linked and supplement one another. In this connection, reference may be made to entry 84 of list I which deals with the duties of excise on tobacco and other goods manufactured or produced in India except, inter alia, alcoholic liquors for human consumption. Similarly, entry 51, list II is the counterpart of entry 84 of list I so far as the State List is concerned. It authorises the State to impose duties of excise on alcoholic liquors for human consumption . . . produced or manufactured elsewhere in India. It is clear that all duties of excise save and except the items specifically excepted in entry 84 of list I are generally within the taxing power of the Central Legislature. The State Legislature has power, though limited it is, in imposing duties of excise. That power is circumscribed under entry 51 of list II of the Seventh Schedule to the Constitution. . . .

It has to be borne in mind that by common standards ethyl alcohol (which has 95%) is an industrial alcohol and is not fit for human consumption. The petitioner and the appellants were manufacturing ethyl alcohol (95%) (also known as rectified spirit) which is an industrial alcohol. ISI specification has divided ethyl alcohol (as known in the trade) into several kinds of alcohol. Beverage and industrial alcohols are clearly and differently treated. Rectified spirit for Industrial purposes is defined as 'spirit purified by distillation having a strength not less than 95% of volume by ethyl alcohol'. Dictionaries and technical books would show that rectified spirit (95%) is an industrial alcohol and is not potable as such. It appears, therefore, that industrial alcohol which is ethyl alcohol (95%) by itself is not only non-potable but is highly toxic. The range of spirit of potable alcohol is from country spirit to whisky and the Ethyl Alcohol content varies between 19 to about 43 per cent. These standards are according to the ISI specifications. In other words, ethyl alcohol (95%) is not alcoholic liquor for human consumption but can be used as raw material input after processing and substantial dilution in the production of Whisky, Gin, Country Liquor, etc. . . . It appears that in the light of the new experience and development, it is necessary to state that 'intoxicating liquor' must mean liquor which is consumable by human being[s] as it is.

Notes and Questions

1. The purposive approach has been commonly used in Hong Kong and Singapore. Especially in Hong Kong, the courts have repeatedly stressed that 'it is generally accepted that in the interpretation of a constitution such as the Basic Law a purposive approach is to be applied'. What explains such a great emphasis in these two jurisdictions? A relatively recent constitution? Common law tradition? Or political structure?

2. In *Ng Ka Ling & Others v Director of Immigration*, the purposive approach is understood to ascertain the true purpose of the Basic Law in light of the particu-

lar context in which the Basic Law was created, to establish Hong Kong as being an inalienable part of China. Based upon such an understanding and utilisation of the purposive approach, what difference has it from other approaches, such as the framers' intention or a history-based approach?

D. Use of Foreign and International Law

In recent years, scholars have engaged in a heated debate over the use of foreign or international law in the course of constitutional adjudication.[153] The debate has centered upon questions of methodology, correctness or the legitimacy of judicial reference to foreign or international laws. The tension over issues of legitimacy may be eased if the constitution expressly authorises reference to foreign or international law references. For example, Article 23 of the Constitution of Timor-Leste states that fundamental rights enshrined in the Constitution shall be interpreted in accordance with the Universal Declaration of Human Rights. Article 9 further states that the legal system of East Timor adopts the general or customary principles of international law, that 'rules provided for in international conventions, treaties and agreements shall apply' in its legal system, and all rules that are contrary to the provisions of international conventions, treaties and agreements applied in the internal legal system shall be invalid. Similarly, Article 31 of the Constitution of Cambodia makes an express recognition of respect for human rights under the United Nations Charter, the Universal Declaration of Human Rights, and the covenants and conventions relating to human rights, and women's and children's rights. Comparatively, an oft-cited example in the West is Article 39(1) of the Constitution of South Africa, demanding that courts consider international and foreign laws in interpreting constitutionally protected rights.[154]

Other implicit authorisations may include constitutional provisions that elevate the legal status of international laws in the domestic legal system, or suggest that courts apply generally recognised principles or norms in comparative or international laws in constitutional adjudication.[155] An arguably implicit authorisation may exist in provisions such as Article 6(1) of the Constitution of South Korea, which accords domestic legal status to treaties duly concluded and promulgated under the Constitution as well as the generally recognised rule of international law. A similar example is Article 141 of the ROC Constitution that requires the Government to respect treaties and the Charter of the United Nations.

Two contrasting attitudes, one embracing and the other resisting the use of foreign or international law in the course of constitutional adjudication, are both evident in the practice of Asian jurisdictions. As constitutional developments of this region have

---

[153] C Saunders, 'Judicial Engagement with Comparative Law' in T Ginsburg and R Dixon (eds), *Comparative Constitutional Law* (Northampton: Edward Elgar, 2011) 571; VC Jackson, 'Comparative Constitutional Law: Methodologies' in M Rosenfeld and A Sajó (eds), *Oxford Handbook of Comparative Constitutional Law* (Oxford: Oxford University Press, 2012) 54.

[154] Art 39(1) of the Constitution of South Africa: 'When interpreting the Bill of Rights, a court, tribunal or forum (a) must promote the values that underlie an open and democratic society based on human dignity, equality, and freedom; (b) must consider international law; and (c) may consider foreign law.

[155] See eg the Constitution of Hungary, Art 7(1); Constitution of Russia, Art 17; and Constitution of the Czech Republic, Art 19.

been heavily influenced by the West, frequent references to foreign or international laws are expected – and indeed taking place – in many jurisdictions.

At the same time, reticence towards foreign or international laws can be quite strong in some jurisdictions like Malaysia and Singapore, where the 'four walls approach' has been favoured. In *Government of the State of Kelantan v Government of the Federation of Malaya*, the Federal Court stated that 'the Constitution is primarily to be interpreted within its own four walls and not in the light of analogies drawn from other countries'.[156] However, the situation can change with time. In some recent Singapore cases, thorough consideration has been given to foreign cases and international law, even if they have been rejected on their merits as anti-models in developing an indigenised constitutional jurisprudence.

The following discussion is thus divided into three parts. The first illustrates the cases that affirm the use of foreign or international laws; the second includes cases where such reference is rejected; and the last draws on a distinctive function of invoking foreign or international laws in order to limit existing rights.[157]

i. Use of Foreign or International Law

Judicial reference to foreign or international laws usually acts to provide additional arguments for the protection of existing rights or, more importantly, to create new rights or nuanced understandings of existing rights. There is, nevertheless, a difference in how foreign and international sources are used. Foreign sources are merely persuasive, but not binding. When courts invoke foreign laws in the course of domestic decision making, they have been criticised on the bases of democratic legitimacy and rule of law.[158] In contrast, international law may apply directly to a domestic legal system through express or implicit constitutional authorisation, as can be seen in the Constitutions of East Timor, Cambodia, South Korea or Taiwan. Once international laws apply to the domestic legal system, further issues may arise as to where international law falls within the legal hierarchy: Does it rank higher than the constitution, as part of the constitution, lower than the constitution but higher than the statutes, or the same as statutes or common law? Much will depend on variations in the nature of international norms and the detailed arrangements of the domestic legal system.

As Thio notes,

> the utility of invoking international law to inform the crafting and structuring of public law arguments before municipal courts depends on how receptive a domestic legal order is to international law norms. At the international level, this rests on two key issues which determine the inter-relationship between international and domestic law. First, the status of an international legal norm: is the norm 'hard' or 'soft', does it have the status of being *jus cogens* (that is, having a peremptory or non-derogable character), or otherwise. Second, whether municipal courts recognise and accept international law rules automatically, or whether an intermediate act by a government body is required to give international law norms

---

[156] *Government of the State of Kelantan v Government of the Federation of Malaya* [1963] MLJ 355 (Federal Court, Malaysia).

[157] For various functions of referencing to foreign or international laws, see Wen-Chen Chang, 'The Convergence of Constitutions and International Human Rights: Taiwan and South Korea in Comparison' (2011) 36(3) *North Carolina Journal of International Law and Commercial Regulations* 593.

[158] The famous debate between Justices Scalia and Brennan is available at <http://www.freerepublic.com/focus/f-news/1352357/posts> (accessed 2 March 2013).

juridical effect within the domestic legal system. The question of what theory explains the binding quality of an international obligation, its status and effect within a domestic legal order, is a question of both international law and foreign relations law. How the content of a substantive international law norm or standard is deployed in public law arguments is a question of constitutional jurisprudence.[159]

The following cases illustrate how foreign or international laws are utilised to add new rights or provide persuasive arguments. In *JY Interpretation No 582*, a criminal defendant's right to cross-examine witnesses was affirmed not only from the constitutional text but also from foreign and international laws. In *Bangladesh Legal Aid and Services Trust (BLAST) v Bangladesh*, the Supreme Court relied on a case by the Privy Council as persuasive authority. In *Visakha v State of Rajasthan Case*, the Supreme Court of India invoked international treaty norms to fill the vacuum of domestic anti-sexual harassment law.

JY Interpretation No 582
23 Jul 2004 (Constitutional Court, Taiwan)

Facts

The petitioners were convicted primarily on the basis of a confession by their co-defendant. The defendants were petitioning against the admission of the confession without the ability to examine the witness. They challenged the related Supreme Court precedents that admitted such confessions as a violation of Article 16 of the Constitution that provides that 'The people shall have the right of presenting petitions, lodging complaints, or instituting legal proceedings.'

Held

Article 16 of the Constitution provides for the people's right to sue. As far as a criminal defendant is concerned, he should enjoy the right to adequately defend himself under a confrontational system, according to adversarial rules, so as to ensure a fair trial . . . The right of an accused to examine a witness is a corollary of such right. . . . Such right of a criminal defendant is universally provided – whether in a civil law country or a common law jurisdiction, and whether an adversarial system or an inquisitorial setting is adopted in administering a state's criminal justice. (*See, eg*, 6th Amendment to the United States Constitution, Article 37-II of the Japanese Constitution, Article 304 of the Code of Criminal Procedure of Japan, and Article 239 of the Code of Criminal Procedure of Germany) Article 6-III(iv) of the European Convention for the Protection of Human Rights and Fundamental Freedoms, effective on November 4, 1950, and Article 14-III(v) of the International Covenant on Civil and Political Rights, passed by the United Nations on December 16, 1966 and put into force on March 23, 1976, both provide, 'everyone charged with a crime shall be entitled to the following minimum guarantees: . . . to examine, or have examined, the witnesses against him and to obtain the attendance and examination of witnesses on his behalf under the same conditions as witnesses against him.'. . .

---

[159] Li-ann Thio, 'Reading Rights Rightly: The UDHR and its Creeping Influence on the Development of Singapore Public Law' (2008) *Singapore Journal of Legal Studies* 264.

Bangladesh Legal Aid and Services Trust (BLAST) v Bangladesh
[2010] 39 CLC (HCD) (Supreme Court, Bangladesh)

Facts

The petitioners were sentenced to death under section 6(2) of the *Nari-o-ShishuNirjatan (BishesBidhan) Ain* [Suppression of Cruelty to Women and Children Act] 2000, which prescribed a mandatory death penalty for such offences. They challenged the mandatory punishment, arguing that it was unconstitutional.

Muhammad Imman Ali J

When the legislature prescribes any punishment as a mandatory punishment the hands of the court are thereby tied. The court becomes a simple rubberstamp of the legislature. Upon finding the accused guilty, the Court can do no more than impose the mandatory punishment, which the legislature has prescribed for that offence. This certainly discriminates and prejudices the Court's ability to adjudicate properly taking into account all the facts and circumstances of the case. In the case of *Reyes* [*Reyes v The Queen*, [2002] 2 App Cas 235 (PC)] their Lordships considered the submission of counsel that 'a sentencing regime which imposes a mandatory sentence of death on all murderers, or all murderers within specified categories, is inhuman and degrading because it requires the sentence of death, with all the consequences such a sentence must have for the individual defendant, to be passed without any opportunity for the defendant to show why such sentence should be mitigated, without any consideration of the detailed facts of the particular case or the personal history and circumstances of the offender and in cases where such a sentence might be wholly disproportionate to the defendant's criminal culpability.' With respect, we would share the same view and observe that where the appellant is not a habitual criminal or a man of violence, then it would be the duty of the court to take into account his character and antecedents in order to come to a just and proper decision. But where the law itself prescribes a mandatory punishment then the court is precluded from taking into consideration any such mitigating or extenuating facts and circumstances. Their Lordships of the Privy Council observed, 'a law which denies a defendant the opportunity, after conviction, to seek to avoid imposition of the ultimate penalty, which he may not deserve, is incompatible with section 7 of the Constitution of the Belize because it fails to respect his basic humanity.'

In Bangladesh there is no provision or scope to argue in mitigation or to bring to the notice of the Court any extenuating facts and circumstances in any given criminal trial. There is no provision of sentence hearing. Such a provision existed in 1982 as section 255K of the Code of Criminal Procedure, but the provision was abolished in 1983. It is our view that it is imperative that such provision should exist, particularly in view of the fact that in our country the adversarial system denies the accused any opportunity to put forward any mitigating circumstances before the court. Even the most senior advocates will fight tooth and nail to maintain their client's innocence. . . .

To summarise, it may be stated that their Lordships of the Privy Council held: 'The Board is however satisfied that the provision requiring sentence of death to be passed on the appellant on his conviction of murder by shooting subjected him to inhuman or degrading punishment or other treatment incompatible with his right under section 7 of the constitution in that it required sentence of death to be passed and precluded any judicial consideration of the humanity of condemning him to death . . . To deny the offender the opportunity, before sentence is passed, to seek to persuade the court in all the circumstances to condemn him to death would be disproportionate and inappropriate is to treat him as no human being should be treated and thus to deny his basic humanity, the core of the right which section 7 exists to protect.'

In the light of the discussions, we are of the view that any mandatory provision of law takes away the discretion of the court and precludes the court from coming to a decision which is based on the assessment of all the facts and circumstances surrounding any given offence or the offender, and that is not permissible under the Constitution. The Court must always have the discretion to determine what punishment a transgressor deserves and to fix the appropriate sentence for the crime he is alleged to have committed. The court may not be degraded to the position of simply rubberstamping the only punishment which the legislature prescribed. There is such finality and irreversibility in the death penalty. If the discretion of the Court is taken away then the right of the citizen is denied.

We may also mention at this juncture that research has shown that in many cases it has been found many years after the death penalty was carried out that the accused was in fact not guilty of the crime alleged. Of course such finding is of little use to the accused, but it clearly exemplifies that mistakes can be made and the lives of innocent persons may be ended. This certainly was a factor taken into account in the abolition of the death penalty in UK and Europe. On the other hand, obviously the stark examples of injustice unearthed by use of scientific means have not led to the abolition of the death penalty in all the states of the USA. Whether the death penalty is to be abolished altogether cannot be decided lightly. It took the UK decades of research by various organisations and Law Commissions and also much public debate before the death penalty was finally abolished. After much debate and research by the Law Commission, India decided that abolition of the death penalty is not practicable. In the case of a developing country such as ours, it must be left to the public, parliament and researchers to debate extensively and decide after thorough and threadbare discussion whether the death penalty is to be retained.

Visakha v State of Rajasthan
[1997] AIR SC 3011 (Supreme Court, India)

Facts

After an incident of brutal gang rape of a social worker in a Rajasthan village, social activists and NGOs brought a class action petition in the Supreme Court of India for the enforcement of the fundamental right of working women under the Constitution. Because there was no legislation governing sexual harassment at the work place, the Court was asked to issue a writ of mandamus with accompanying guidelines to fill the vacuum.

Verma CJ

In the absence of domestic law occupying the field to formulate effective measures to check the evil of sexual harassment of working women at all work places, the contents of International Conventions and norms are significant for the purpose of interpretation of the guarantee of gender equality, right to work with human dignity in Articles 14, 15, 19(1) (g) and 21 of the Constitution and the safeguards against sexual harassment implicit therein. Any international convention not inconsistent with the fundamental rights and in harmony with its spirit must be read into those provisions to enlarge the meaning and content thereof, to promote the object of the Constitutional guarantee. This is implicit from Art 51(c) and the enabling power of the Parliament to enact laws for implementing the

International Conventions and norms by virtue of Art 253 read with Entry 14 of the Union List in Seventh Schedule of the Constitution. Article 73 also is relevant.

Thus, the power of this Court under Art 32 for enforcement of the fundamental rights and the executive power of the union have to meet the challenge to protect the working women from sexual harassment and to make their fundamental rights meaningful. Governance of the society by the rule of law mandates this requirement as [a] logical concomitant of the constitutional scheme. The exercise performed by the Court in this matter is with this common perception shared with the learned Solicitor General and other members of the Bar who rendered valuable assistance in the performance of this difficult task in public interest. . . .

The meaning and content of the fundamental rights guaranteed in the Constitution of India are of sufficient amplitude to encompass all the facets of gender equality including prevention of sexual harassment or abuse. Independence of judiciary forms a part of our constitutional scheme. The international conventions and norms are to be read into them in the absence of enacted domestic law occupying the field when there is no inconsistency between them. It is now an accepted rule of judicial construction [of] domestic law when there is no inconsistency between them and there is a void in the domestic law. The High Court of Australia in Minister for Immigration and *Ethnic Affairs v Teoh*, 128 ALR 353, has recognised the concept of legitimate expectation of its observance in the absence of a contrary legislative provision, even in the absence of a Bill of Rights in the Constitution of Australia. . . .

In view of the above, and the absence of enacted law to provide for the effective enforcement of the basic human right of gender equality and guarantee against sexual harassment and abuse, more particularly against sexual harassment at work places, we lay down the guidelines and norms specified hereinafter for due observance at all work places or other institutions, until legislation is enacted for the purpose. This is done in exercise of the power available under Art 32 of the Constitution for enforcement of the fundamental rights and it is further emphasised that this would be treated as the law declared by this Court under Art 141 of the Constitution.

ii. *Reticence Towards Foreign or International Law*

The objection to the use of foreign or international law may be founded on various grounds, ranging from political concerns to a deficit of democratic legitimacy, to institutional or cultural distinctions. The injunction to interpret a constitution 'within its four walls' and not in light of any foreign or international analogies reflects at least political and cultural concerns. In the following case, the High Court in Singapore declined to follow English cases on the changing legal circumstances, in that English laws had been greatly influenced by the European Court of Human Rights as a result of domestic incorporation. In *Attorney-General v Hertzberg Daniel and others*, the refusal to apply a test which had been generally recognised in common law countries was made in light of what the court held to be distinctive local conditions in Singapore.

Attorney-General v Chee Soon Juan
[2006] SGHC 54, 2 SLR 650 (High Court, Singapore)

Facts

The respondent was accused of contempt 'in the face of the court' at a hearing before an Assistant Registrar, in that he scandalised the Singapore judiciary through his statement to the High Court. Relying on recent UK case law, the respondent argued that the offence of contempt of court violated his right to free speech under the Constitution.

Lai Siu Chiu J

As a preliminary observation, case law from the Commonwealth cited by counsel for the Respondent and in particular recent jurisprudence from the UK had to be treated with considerable caution because of the differing legislation in those countries. To begin with, the position in UK has become statutorily regulated by the Contempt of Court Act 1981 (c 49) . . . Admittedly, the UK position on scandalising the court still falls to be regulated by the common law since the 1981 UK Act does not address the offence of scandalising the court. I should point out, however, that the UK's accession to the European Convention on Human Rights and Fundamental Freedoms . . . has indirectly incorporated the jurisprudence of the European Court of Human Rights . . . and pegs the UK position on the offence of scandalising the court to the standard imposed by the European Convention.

The case of *Attorney-General v Times Newspapers Ltd* [1974] AC 273 shows conflicts have arisen between the common law on contempt and the UK's obligation under the European Convention to protect the right of freedom of expression, with the former involving more extensive incursions on the freedom of expression than the European Court felt that the European Convention allowed . . . The enactment of the UK Human Rights Act 1998 (c 42) further entrenches the influence which the European Convention has since had on the development of UK common law.

Conditions unique to Singapore necessitate that we deal more firmly with attacks on the integrity and impartiality of our courts. To begin with, the geographical size of Singapore renders its courts more susceptible to unjustified attacks. In the words of the Privy Council in *Ahnee v Director of Public Prosecutions* [1999] 2 AC 294 at 305–306:

> In England [proceedings for scandalising the court] are rare and none has been successfully brought for more than 60 years. But it is permissible to take into account that on a small island such as Mauritius the administration of justice is more vulnerable than in the United Kingdom. The need for the offence of scandalizing the court on a small island is greater . . .

Attorney-General v Hertzberg Daniel
[2008] SGHC 218 (High Court, Singapore)

Facts

The Attorney-General (AG) applied for orders of committal for contempt of court against three respondents for their part in the publication and distribution of three publications, each of which contained passages that scandalised the Singapore judiciary. One respondent submitted that, in contempt of court cases, the 'real risk test' commonly accepted in other common law jurisdictions should supplant the test of 'inherent tendency' adopted in Singapore, as the former was of better clarity and offered greater protection of free speech.

Tay Yong Kwang J

The next question to ask then is whether Singapore should depart from the 'inherent tendency' test and adopt the 'real risk' test. Indeed, the 'real risk' test appears to be the test presently preferred by many common law countries. . . . The main reason for the adoption of the 'real risk' test in these jurisdictions is essentially the need to protect the right to freedom of speech and expression and the broader test based on 'inherent tendency' is considered to inhibit the right to freedom of speech and expression to an unjustifiable degree. . . . The 'inherent tendency' test is also criticised for its vagueness and is said to impose liability without the offence being defined in sufficiently precise terms. . . .

I agree with the AG that what are acceptable limits to the right to freedom of speech and expression imposed by the law of contempt vary from place to place and would depend on the local conditions . . . as well as the ideas held by the courts about the principles to be adhered to in the administration of justice. . . . As pointed out by Lai J in *Chee Soon Juan* . . . conditions unique to Singapore (ie, our small geographical size and the fact that in Singapore, judges decide both questions of fact and law) necessitate that we deal more firmly with attacks on the integrity and impartiality of our courts. Indeed, the ALRC [Australian Law Reform Commission] has also recognised the 'inherent tendency' test has two clear advantages . . . First, it does not call for detailed proof of what in many instances will be unprovable, namely, that public confidence in the administration of justice really was impaired by the relevant publication (cf the 'real risk' test which would require some evidence to show that there is more than a remote possibility of harm). Secondly, it enables the court to step in before the damage, ie, the impairment of public confidence in the administration of justice, actually occurs.

In the light of our local conditions and the advantages that the 'inherent tendency' test has, I agree that the 'inherent tendency' test should continue to govern liability for contempt of court committed by 'scandalising the court' in Singapore. If we need to ask in each case whether there is a real risk that public confidence in the administration of justice has been impaired by contemptuous remarks, it may lead to an absurd situation where a person at a dinner party who keeps shouting to all present that the Judiciary is completely biased will not be held in contempt of court simply because no one at the party bothers about his ranting or is affected by his remarks. It would be more logical in such a situation to hold that contempt of court has been committed and then go on to consider whether there is a real risk that public confidence in the administration of justice has been impaired in deciding whether or not to punish the contemnor and, if so, to what extent. In other words, the issue of the said real risk has no bearing on liability but is relevant only for mitigation or aggravation of the punishment (or even whether or not punishment should be imposed in a particular case at all).

iii. Balancing: Referencing for Restricting Rights

The reference to foreign or international laws does not necessarily guarantee greater protection for domestic rights. Sometimes courts may resort to foreign or international laws to justify rights restrictions, in service of other important values, including competing rights. For example, in the following case, the Constitutional Court of South Korea was faced with a conflict between protecting an individual's right of privacy and children's right to be free from sexual exploitation. Referring to the UN Convention on the Rights of the Child and the American laws, the Court gave greater weight to children's rights and justified the restriction on the right to privacy.

Disclosure of the Identity of Sex Offenders Convicted of Acquiring Sexual Favors from Minors in Exchange for Monetary Compensation
2002Hun-Ka14, 6 Jun 2003 (Constitutional Court, South Korea)

Facts

The petitioner was convicted for having sexual intercourse with a minor under the Juvenile Sex Protection Act. His personal information – including his name, age, birthdate, vocation, address, and a summary of his offence – was released by the Commission on Youth Protection under the Act. The petitioner sought to revoke this disclosure and challenged the constitutionality of Act's disclosure provisions.

Yun Young-chul, Ha Kyung-chull, Kim Hyo-jong & Kim Kyung-il JJ

(D) Appropriateness of the Means

Although there remains room for doubt as to whether the identity disclosure system is the most effective and appropriate means to achieve the above legislative purpose, common sense confirms that a disclosure to the public of the identity of the individual convicts concerned will have an impact on deterring or preventing the general adult population to not become a purchaser of sex from minors. Therefore, the identity disclosure system possesses the appropriateness of the means required by the principle of proportionality or the principle against excessive restriction.

Today the problem of sexual abuse of children including the purchase of sex is at the center of the concern all over the world and various countries adopt new legislative measures similar to the identity disclosure system. The United Nations Convention on the Rights of the Child of 1989 provides for an obligation of the member states to protect the child from all forms of sexual exploitation and sexual abuse (Article 34). Also, the participating countries in the 'First World Congress Against Commercial Sexual Exploitation of Children' held in Stockholm, Sweden in 1996 declared that they would develop within five (5) years measures to decrease the number of the children falling victims to commercial sexual exploitation.

In the United States, convicted sexual offenders are required to register regularly with the competent authorities of the name, address, vocation and the content of the judgment of guilt and also to submit their pictures and fingerprints, which are posted on the Internet (specifically in the State of Alaska). Also, in Taiwan, the Act to Prevent Purchase of Sex from Children and Minors (as revised on November 8, 2000) provides that the competent authority, upon final judgment in a criminal trial, should post and announce the name and the picture of the convicted criminals and the summary of the judgment, when a person eighteen (18) years of age or older is engaged in a sexual intercourse or obscene conduct with a child (under the age of 12) or a minor (under the age of 18), or criminal conduct involving sex with a child or a minor as provided by the Act, in exchange for monetary compensation (Article 34).

The above examples of legislation reflect the fact that the existing criminal punishment or preventive security measures are not sufficient to achieve the legislative purpose of protecting the sexual integrity of children and minors. This is grounded upon the special nature of the crime of purchasing sex from minors and also of the victims thereof.

Although there is criticism that the current identity disclosure system does not deter crime as it does not provide concrete information of the convicted criminals such as the face or the picture and it does not screen off minors who are the objects of the purchase, the appropriateness of the means can be confirmed because the purpose of this system itself is the prevention of the crime of purchasing sex from minors at a more general level that the system intends to protect the sexual integrity of minors thereby protecting the human rights of minors and helping them grow to be sound members of society by guiding and correcting the harm and the serious problem concerning the conduct of purchasing sex from minors, rather than a concrete and specific one to provide information to protect the potential victims and the community from the released sexual offenders such as in the so-called Megan's Law, and, also because the identity disclosure system has an impact upon the general public to suppress the impulse to commit sexual offenses against minors.

Notes and Questions

1. In 2011, the Singapore Court of Appeal re-evaluated the relationship between the inherent tendency test and the real risk test. In *Shadrake Alan v Attorney-General*, the Court also referred to foreign law, but held that the two tests were not conceptually contradictory and opted to adopt the *real risk* test. According to the Court:

   > The 'clear and present danger' test applies, in the main, in the United States' ('US') context . . . where the concept of freedom of speech is inextricably linked to the *unique* culture as well as constitutional position (*ie*, the First Amendment) in the US . . . [T]he 'clear and present danger' test appears to apply in no other Commonwealth jurisdiction. . . . The US First Amendment is clearly quite different from the corresponding articles in the respective constitutions of Commonwealth jurisdictions (of which Art 14 of the Singapore Constitution is a representative illustration). . . . This is not to state that freedom of speech is absent – or even lacking, for that matter – in Commonwealth countries. There is, instead, far more attention accorded to the issue of *balance* between the right to freedom of speech on the one hand and its abuse on the other (*inter alia*, by conduct amounting to contempt of court).[160]

   How would you compare *Attorney-General v Hertzberg Daniel* with *Shadrake Alan v Attorney-General*, particularly regarding the reference and utilisation of foreign law? Do you think that the courts in Singapore now consider foreign law not only on form but also on its merits?

2. Many former British colonies in Asia inherited the English common law system, including India, Pakistan, Bangladesh, Sri Lanka, Malaysia, Singapore, Brunei and Hong Kong. As British colonies were not vested with judicial sovereignty, appeals to the Privy Council were mandatory.[161] Some jurisdictions (eg Singapore and Malaysia) retained appeals to the Privy Council even after achieving independence, while others (eg India) abolished the Privy Council as their final court of appeal and created a final court of appeal of their own immediately after inde-

---

[160] *Shadrake Alan v Attorney-General* [2011] SGCA 26 para 41.

[161] In the case of Brunei, appeals are made to the Sultan of Brunei, who then refers the case to the Judicial Committee for advice but not directly to the Council.

pendence. Irrespective of whether appeals to the Privy Council were retained, these courts still have a penchant for referring to Privy Council decisions, even today. The above case, *Bangladesh Legal Aid and Services Trust (BLAST) v Bangladesh*, is an example where the court invoked a decision by the Privy Council as persuasive authority.

3. British influence over former colonies extends beyond frequent reference to Privy Council decisions, and even to the domestic incorporation of international laws. The United Kingdom had made the international treaties it signed applicable to its colonies. When acceding to the International Covenant on Civil and Political Rights (ICCPR), the UK made it applicable to Hong Kong by enacting the Hong Kong Bill of Rights Ordinance[162] and giving this Bill supremacy over domestic laws of Hong Kong.[163] After Hong Kong was returned to China, the Basic Law of Hong Kong maintained the applicability of the ICCPR along with other international covenants. As a result, even after 1997, Hong Kong courts continue to refer to international laws, particularly the ICCPR. For instance, in *HKSAR v Ng Kung Siu*,[164] the disputed issue was whether the statute prohibiting the desecration of both national and regional flags in public fell within the public order exception under Article 19(3) ICCPR. The Court of Final Appeal held that Article 19 ICCPR was incorporated into the Basic Law by Article 39, which provided that the provisions of the ICCPR and other international human rights conventions should remain in force and be implemented through the laws. In addition, the Bill of Rights Ordinance provided for the incorporation of the provisions of the ICCPR into the laws of Hong Kong. For further discussions on the domestic incorporation of international laws in Hong Kong, see A Hung-Yee Chen, 'International Human Rights Law and Domestic Constitutional Law: Internationalization of Constitutional Law in Hong Kong' (2009) 4(3) *National Taiwan University Law Review* 237.

Besides creating or restricting rights, references to foreign or international laws may perform alternative functions such as:

(a) providing the benchmark for further legislative change; or
(b) promoting judicial or legislative engagement with domestic and international laws.

Both these functions are evident in the decisions of constitutional courts in Taiwan and South Korea.[165] For example, In *JY Interpretation No 549*, the Constitutional Court in Taiwan requested that

> an overall examination and arrangement, regarding the survivor allowance, insurance benefits and other relevant matters, should be done in accordance with the principles of this Interpretation, international labor conventions and the pension plan of the social security system.[166]

[162] Hong Kong Bill of Rights Ordinance (hereinafter 'Bill of Rights'), (1991) Cap 383, s 8.
[163] *R v Chan* [1994] 3 HKC 145, 153; cited by the Court of Appeal itself in *Lee v Attorney-General* [1996] 1 HKC 124, 127.
[164] *HKSAR v Ng Kung Siu* [1999] 2 HKCFAR 442.
[165] Wen-Chen Chang, above n 157.
[166] *Interpretation No 549* [trans Chin-Chin Cheng], 4 ROC Const Ct 524 (2007).

In *JY Interpretation No 578*, the Court advised the Government to conduct a comprehensive examination of the current scheme regarding labour retirement payments and stressed that 'the provisions of international labour conventions and the overall development of the nation shall also be taken into account'.[167] Similarly, in *Constitutional Complaint against Article 8(1) of the Support for Discharged Soldiers Act*,[168] the South Korean Constitutional Court referred to the Convention on the Elimination of all Forms of Discrimination against Women (CEDAW) to review the veterans' extra point system in the public officer exam, and suggested that the Government revise the system accordingly. The Court stated that CEDAW and other international treaties ban discrimination against women and treat the protection of rights for women and the disabled as fundamental. The veterans' extra point system, despite its benign attempt to support economically disadvantaged veterans, came at the expense of vulnerable groups, such as women and the disabled. Thus, the Court held that the extra point system, as a means of aiding veteran soldiers, fell short of reasonableness and had to be revised accordingly.

The other alternative purpose in referring to foreign or international laws is that it promotes dialogue between majority and minority opinions regarding the understanding of domestic and international norms. A good example of this is the South Korean case of *Ban on Civil Servants' Labor Movement*,[169] where international human rights laws shaped judicial dialogue. The majority had a very different understanding of the legal effect of international human rights law and its application to the domestic legal system from the dissenting opinion. The majority insisted that international human rights covenants allowed the 'restriction of basic labor rights by statutes as long as the restriction does not infringe upon the essence of the right and takes place in accordance with . . . democratic procedure'. The majority also noticed that relevant 'declarations, conventions and recommendations under international law concerning basic labor rights have not been ratified' by South Korea and thus could not provide a standard to review the constitutionality of domestic laws. In sharp contrast, the dissenting judges held that

> the Universal Declaration of Human Rights, international human rights covenants, the treaties related to the International Labor Organization concerning civil servants' basic labor rights, and recommendations of international bodies . . . can become important guidelines in interpreting the meaning, content, and scope of application of highly abstract provisions of the Constitution . . .

even though they had not been ratified by South Korea. The justices held that domestic constitutional provisions must be understood in light of these persuasive or guiding international legal authorities, and the Court found that in so doing, the challenged provisions violated the Constitution.

Rather than merely disputing with one another on the definition or scope of constitutional rights, justices may rely on their understanding of international norms to reinterpret domestic constitutional rights. This opens up an entirely different channel for judicial debate. Admittedly, these dialogues may be quite tense if majority and

---

[167] *Interpretation No 578* [trans CY Huang], 5 ROC Const Ct 91 (2007).
[168] *Constitutional Complaint Against Article 8(1) of the Support for Discharged Soldiers Act Case*, 98Hun-Ma363, 23 Dec 1999.
[169] *Ban on Civil Servants' Labor Movement*, 2003Hun-Ba50 and 2004Hun-Ba96, 27 Oct 2005.

minority opinions hold contrasting views on the understanding of international and domestic laws. But they may create a new possibility for the justices holding different positions in relation to domestic constitutional law questions, to find a new common ground through the intermediation of international law.

VIII. FORMS OF JUDICIAL DECISIONS AND REMEDIES

Asia has both centralised and decentralised systems of judicial review. As discussed above, the constitutional court is typically vested with the abstract review power over legislative enactments in the centralised systems. Such review may be requested – prior to or after enactment – by the president, parliament, government agencies, courts or individuals, with or without the cases being litigated before the courts. In the decentralised judicial review system, all courts may review the constitutionality of legislative or executive enactments involved in cases or controversies, and rule on the constitutionality of those enactments as they are or as they apply to the cases or controversies.

Beyond rulings that legislative or executive enactments are either constitutional or unconstitutional, many supreme and constitutional courts have presented an interesting array of decisional forms, ranging from findings of limited constitutionality (or unconstitutionality), prospective rulings, the imposition of judicial deadlines, making a declaration of unconstitutionality without invalidating the law, or mere judicial warnings.[170] These forms of decisions help courts mediate tensions with political branches and provide some degree of flexibility in filling the legal vacuum resulting from the invalidation of impugned laws or regulations.

The following section surveys the application of these forms by supreme and constitutional courts across Asia. Aside from ruling on the constitutionality of legislative or executive enactments, courts may provide various forms of remedies for individuals whose constitutionally protected rights are infringed. This is particularly so in the decentralised system of judicial review, in which courts adjudicate over concrete cases and controversies. For example, in the Philippines, influenced by both Spanish and American legal systems, courts may issue writs of *habeas corpus*, directed at the protection of personal freedom and integrity, writs of *habeas data*,[171] focused on the protection of personal data and information, as well as writs of *amparo*, available as an extraordinary judicial proceeding for the protection of constitutional rights and freedoms from unconstitutional infringement by public or even private actors.[172] The Supreme Court of India is granted the power to issue various writs, including *habeas corpus, mandamus, prohibition, quo warranto* and *certiorari*.[173] In addition, the Supreme

---

[170] These various forms of constitutional rulings are also seen in German and other European constitutional courts. See, eg, Kommers, above n 45, 52–55.

[171] See Supreme Court of the Philippines, 'Rule on the Writ of Habeas Data' at <http://sc.judiciary.gov.ph/rulesofcourt/2008/jan/A.M.No.08-1-16-SC.pdf>.

[172] See Supreme Court of the Philippines, 'Annotation to the Writ of Amparo' at <http://sc.judiciary.gov.ph/admin%20matters/others/annotation.pdf>.

[173] Art 32 of the Constitution of India provides: 'The Supreme Court shall have power to issue directions or orders or writs, including writs in the nature of habeas corpus, mandamus, prohibition, quo warranto and certiorari, whichever may be appropriate, for the enforcement of any of the rights conferred by this Part.'

Court of Pakistan is vested with the power to act proactively in issuing *suo moto* actions for cases of public importance regarding the enforcement of fundamental rights, especially those involving gross human rights violations.[174] These various writs empower courts to remedy gross violations of constitutionally protected rights, besides enjoining or invalidating government acts that may threaten or result in such violations.

A. Limited Constitutionality or Limited Unconstitutionality

To respect legislative powers, courts may adopt the presumption of constitutionality in reviewing laws. By invoking this presumption, courts assume the constitutionality of the impugned law, which means that as long as it is possible to interpret the law harmoniously and consistently with the constitution, the courts will do so rather than strike down the law. Even if courts cannot save the impugned law in its entirety, they may decide that the impugned law has limited constitutionality or limited unconstitutionality.

In South Korea, Article 113 of the Constitution stipulates that at least six out of nine justices must concur in the decision regarding the constitutionality of a law. Similarly, in Taiwan, a two-thirds majority (out of 15 justices) is required in the decision concerning constitutionality of a law, whereas a simple majority is sufficient with respect to the constitutionality of administrative rules. The supermajority requirement may account for judicial decisions finding limited constitutionality or limited unconstitutionality. If no consensus is reached by a two-thirds majority in either saving or striking down the law in its entirety, compromises may be made in rendering a decision with limited constitutionality or limited unconstitutionality. Of the following two cases decided by the Constitutional Court of South Korea, the first illustrates various forms of constitutional decisions and the second shows the impact a supermajority requirement may have on the finding of constitutionality.

Constitutional Review of Judgments Case
96Hun-Ma172 et al, 24 Dec 1997 (Constitutional Court, South Korea)

Facts

This case was also excerpted in section IV.E. above, involving the question of whether the Supreme Court should follow the decision of the Constitutional Court that found a statute to have limited constitutionality. In the reasoning, the Constitutional Court prescribes various forms of decisions it may apply to an impugned statute, including limited constitutionality.

Held

Unconstitutionality decisions of the Constitutional Court could take such forms as unqualified unconstitutionality, limited constitutionality, limited unconstitutionality, and

---

[174] Art 184(3) of the Constitution of Pakistan provides: '[T]he Supreme Court shall, if it considers that a question of public importance with reference to the enforcement of any of the Fundamental Rights . . . is involved, have the power to make an order of the nature mentioned in the said Article.'

nonconformity to the Constitution, and the decision[s] in all these forms are binding. The Court's evaluation of a statute may vary according to how it interprets the text, meaning, and legislative intent of the statute. Then, the Court chooses the most favorable interpretation within the scope permitted by general rules of interpretation. After that, the Court may articulate the constitutional scope of the meaning of the statute and find it constitutional within that scope. Or the Court may articulate the possibilities of applying the statute beyond its constitutional scope and find it unconstitutional as applied outside that scope. The two forms are flip-sides of a coin and are the same for all practical purposes. They differ only in whether they actively or passively exclude the unconstitutional applications of an otherwise valid statute, and they are equally decisions of partial constitutionality.

Joint and Several Liability of Executive Officers and Oligopolistic Stockholders Case
2000Hun-Ka5, 29 Aug 2002 (Constitutional Court, South Korea)

Facts

Under the disputed Mutual Savings and Finance Company Act, executive officers and oligopolistic stockholders were jointly and severally liable for debts of mutual savings banks. The petitioners, who were directors or stockholders of mutual savings banks that had gone bankrupt due to improper management, petitioned the Court arguing that the relevant provision infringed their right of equality and property rights under the Constitution.

Opinion of Limited Unconstitutionality by Five Justices

Executive officers are held jointly and severally liable for the debts of the mutual savings banks under the instant statutory provision on the premise that they took active parts in unsound or evasive lending, or that they either cooperated [in] or overlooked unreasonable demands of the oligopolistic stockholders. Oligopolistic stockholders, on the other hand, are held jointly and severally liable for the debts of mutual savings banks on the premise that they, using their influence as oligopolistic stockholders, directed or demanded officers to make decisions, thus taking part in improper management of the banks. If the legislative objective of the instant statutory provision is to prevent the bankruptcy of mutual savings banks from improper management or privatization of the savings, thus [to] protect the bank customers, individuals subject to the regulation by the provision should be limited to 'persons who took part in improper management of the banks.'

There might be some executive officers who may be registered as directors of the company in the register but who had not taken any part in management of the savings banks or who were excluded from the decision making process in making decisions. These officers should not be held liable for improper management of the banks. It would be excessive to hold these officers jointly and severally liable during their tenure as well as for three years after their retirement. It would effectively prevent corporate governance by professional managers who may be equipped with the expertise and efficiency but do not have special ties with the oligopolistic stockholders. This would not promote separation of management and ownership, but instead, would promote unification of management and ownership against the legislative objectives of the above statute.

In [the] case of oligopolistic stockholders, too, only those 'individual stockholders who directly caused an undesirable result either through exercise of shareholders' rights or through use of his influence on the bank management by ordering or demanding officers to take certain actions' should be burdened with joint and several liabilities for the company debts. It would only be justified to burden oligopolistic stockholders with almost unlimited liability equal to that borne by members in a partnership or partners with unlimited liability in limited partnership company when there is no separation of management and ownership or when such stockholders wielded influence on management. Not all oligopolistic stockholders take part in management of the savings bank. Some may be formally oligopolistic stockholders because they are relatives of other stockholders, but they may not take any part in the management of the banks. It would be against the legislative spirit of the instant statutory provision as well as that of the entire Mutual Savings and Finance Act to hold such oligopolistic stockholders liable for improper management of the banks.

Considering its legislative purpose, the scope of application of the instant statutory provision should be limited to only those 'executive officers responsible for mismanagement of the bank' and 'oligopolistic stockholders who wielded their influence on the management.' Since every executive officer and oligopolistic stockholders, without exception, are jointly and severally liable for the debts of the savings bank under the instant provision, the provision violates the freedom of association, property rights, and the principle of equality.

It is not unconstitutional to hold executive officers and oligopolistic stockholders jointly and severally liable for the debts of the banks. However, it is unconstitutional to hold those officers and oligopolistic stockholders who had no part in improper management of the banks liable for the debts of the banks. The unconstitutionality of the statute could be removed by limiting the scope of executive officers and oligopolistic stockholders to be jointly and severally liable. If the Court were to declare the statutory provision simply unconstitutional, all of the executive officers and oligopolistic stockholders of the savings banks will only bear responsibilities stipulated under the Commercial Act, and this would not protect the interests of bank customers, creditors of the banks. Therefore, the Court should interpret the law maintaining its effect if at all possible. Considering the legislative objective of the instant statutory provision, the scope of executive officers to be held jointly and severally liable for bank debts should be limited to those officers directly responsible for mismanagement of the bank, and the scope of oligopolistic stockholders to bear the financial responsibilities should be limited to those stockholders who wielded their influence on the management, thereby causing the financial crisis. It would be against the Constitution to hold jointly and severally liable for the company debts, those officers who are not responsible for improper management or those oligopolistic stockholders who did not cause improper management of the bank using their influence.

Opinion of Nonconformity by One Justice

To interpret the instant statutory provision in a limited manner as done by the majority of Justices would exceed the limits of interpretation of law, and it would be tantamount to legislation by the Constitutional Court, ignoring the opinion of the legislators objectively expressed in the written statute. In such case, it would be constitutionally more desirable if the Constitutional Court were to render a decision of nonconformity to the Constitution and let the legislators enact a new law reflecting the opinion of this Court within a short period of time.

Notes and Questions

1. Consider the case of *Joint and Several Liability of Executive Officers and Oligopolistic Stockholders* above. What difference is there between the finding of limited unconstitutionality by five justices and the finding of constitutional non-conformity by one justice? To what extent are these variations of findings due to the requirement for a strict quorum for a declaration of unconstitutionality, requiring six out of nine justices to agree on the invalidation of unconstitutional statutes?

2. The main concern about a decision of limited unconstitutionality is the potential abuse of judicial interpretation that may lead to a distortion of legislation or leg-islative intent. In *JY Interpretation No 585* of the Constitutional Court of Taiwan, a dissenting opinion conveyed a similar worry. The issue was the constitutionality of the Act of Special Commission on the Investigation of the Truth in Respect of the 319 Shooting, which created an independent Commission to investigate the failed presidential assassination one day before the 2004 election. The majority opinion narrowly construed the Commission's power as exercising an inherent parliamentary power of investigation, and thus held that it had limited constitu-tionality. The dissenting opinion, however, argued that such a narrow reading of the impugned statute distorted not only the legislative intent in creating a commis-sion to exercise and share the judicial power in carrying out an investigation, but also the intent of constitutional framers, who gave no such investigative power to the legislature.

B. Prospective Ruling, Temporal Validity and Judicial Deadlines

When a law is found to be contrary to the constitution, it must be invalidated. Yet whether such invalidation should be retroactively applied becomes an issue of con-cern. In *Linkletter v Walker*, the US Supreme Court held that 'the Constitution neither prohibits nor requires retrospective effect' and that courts 'must then weigh the merits and demerits in each case by looking to the prior history of the rule in question, its purpose and effect, and whether retrospective operation will further or retard its operation'.[175] Indeed, giving only prospective effect to the unconstitutional pronounce-ment of impugned laws may ease tensions between courts and the legislature and maintain legal stability.

In centralised systems of judicial review which give greater emphasis to the stability of laws, constitutional courts usually give prospective effect to decisions of unconsti-tutional invalidation. If circumstances so require, constitutional courts may even give additional time for impugned laws to remain in force before the legislature can revise or enact new laws. This practice was established by the Austrian Constitutional Court, the world's first. Article 140 of the Constitution of Austria stipulates that '[t]he judg-ment by the Constitutional Court which rescinds a law as unconstitutional enters into force on the day of publication if the Court does not set a deadline for the rescission',

---

[175] *Linkletter v Walker* 381 US 618, 629 (1965).

and that 'the deadline may not exceed one year'. For unconstitutional ordinances, the deadline may not exceed six months.[176] Before the expiry of the deadline, the impugned laws or ordinances 'shall continue to apply to the circumstances effected before the rescission, the case in point excepted, unless the Court in its rescissory judgment decides otherwise'. The German Constitutional Court also developed similar practices. Article 78 of the German Constitutional Court Act gives prospective effect to decisions in which laws are found unconstitutional and hence invalidated. However, retroactive exceptions are granted to criminal convictions and extraordinary civil cases in which claims of unjustified benefit may be made.[177] The German Constitutional Court may also allow statutes declared unconstitutional but not yet voided to remain in force for some time. In so doing, the Court may stipulate conditions by which the impugned laws remain effective, and lower courts may not proceed with pending cases arising under such laws unless following the Constitutional Court's instructions or until the revision of the laws.[178]

The following cases from India, Malaysia and Singapore demonstrate a general approach towards giving prospective effect to decisions finding impugned laws or orders unconstitutional. The American practice and *Linkletter v Walker*[179] were referred to in the Indian and Malaysian decisions. More noteworthy is the Hong Kong decision of *Koo Sze Yiu v Chief Executive*, in which the Final Court of Appeal not only gave prospective effect to the decision, but also accorded temporal validity to the impugned law that had been declared unconstitutional. Extending some time for the laws or regulations declared unconstitutional to remain effective is a strategy often used by constitutional courts in Taiwan and South Korea, two jurisdictions heavily influenced by the practice of the German Constitutional Court. As illustrated in *The Right to Vote of Nationals Residing Abroad Case*, the Constitutional Court of South Korea declared the impugned law unconstitutional but kept it temporarily valid before the deadline of invalidation.

IC Golaknath v State of Punjab
[1967] AIR SC 1643 (Supreme Court, India)

Facts

The question before the Supreme Court was whether or not to overrule the earlier case of *Sankari Prasad* which had become the basis of subsequent constitutional amendments. A retrospective overruling would have jettisoned the Indian Government's agrarian reform programme.

Subbarao CJ

[In] America the doctrine of prospective overruling is now accepted in all branches of law, including constitutional law. But the carving of the limits of retrospectivity of the new rule is left to courts to be done, having regard to the requirements of justice.

---

[176] Art 139, Constitution of Austria.
[177] Art 79, Constitution of the Federal Republic of Germany.
[178] Kommers, above n 45, at 54.
[179] *Linkletter v Walker* 381 US 618 (1965).

. . . We consider that [the House of Lords also] accepts, though not expressly but by necessary implication the doctrine of 'prospective overruling.'

Let us now consider some of the objections to this doctrine. The objections are: (1) the doctrine involved legislation by courts; (2) it would not encourage parties to prefer appeals as they would not get any benefit therefrom; (3) the declaration for the future would only be obiter; (4) it is not a desirable change; and (5) the doctrine of retroactivity serves as a brake on court which otherwise might be tempted to be so facile in overruling. But in our view, these objections are not insurmountable. If a court can overrule its earlier decision – there cannot be any dispute now that the court can do so – there cannot be any valid reason why it should not restrict its ruling to the future and not to the past. Even if the party filing an appeal may not be benefited by it, in similar appeals which he may file after the change in the law he will have the benefit. The decision cannot be obiter for what the court in effect does is to declare the law but on the basis of another doctrine restricts its scope. Stability in law does not mean that injustice shall be perpetuated.

. . . It is a modem doctrine suitable for a fast moving society. It does not do away with the doctrine of stare decisis, but confines it to past transactions. It is true that in one sense the court only declares the law, either customary or statutory or personal law. While in strict theory it may be said that the doctrine involves making of law, what the court really does is to declare the law but refuses to give retroactivity to it. It is really a pragmatic solution reconciling the two conflicting doctrines, namely, that a court finds law and that it does make law. It finds law but restricts its operation to the future. It enables the court to bring about a smooth transition by correcting its errors without disturbing the impact of those errors on the past transactions. It is left to the discretion of the court to prescribe the limits of the retroactivity and thereby it enables it to [m]ould the relief to meet the ends of justice.

In India there is no statutory prohibition against the court refusing to give retroactivity to the law declared by it. Indeed, the doctrine of res judicata precludes any scope for retroactivity in respect of a subject-matter that has been finally decided between the parties. Further, Indian Courts by interpretation reject retroactivity to statutory provisions though couched in general terms on the ground that they affect vested rights. The present case only attempts a further extension of the said rule against retroactivity.

. . . Our Constitution does not expressly o[r] by necessary implication speak against the doctrine of prospective overruling. . . . The law declared by the Supreme Court is the law of the land. If so, we do not see any acceptable reason why it, in declaring the law in supersession of the law declared by it earlier, could not restrict the operation of the law as declared to [the] future and save the transactions, whether statutory or otherwise[,] that were effected on the basis of the earlier law. To deny this power to the Supreme Court on the basis of some outmoded theory that the Court only finds law but does not make it is to make ineffective the powerful instrument of justice placed in the hands of the highest judiciary of this country.

As this Court for the first time has been called upon to apply the doctrine evolved in a different country under different circumstances, we would like to move warily in the beginning. We would lay down the following propositions : (1) The doctrine of prospective overruling, can be invoked only in matters arising under our Constitution; (2) it can be applied only by the highest court of the country, ie, the Supreme Court as it has the constitutional jurisdiction to declare [law] binding on all the courts in India; (3) the scope of the retroactive operation of the law declared by the Supreme Court superseding its earlier decisions is left to its discretion to be moulded in accordance with the justice of the cause or matter before it. . . .

Public Prosecutor v Dato' Tap Peng
[1987] 2 MLJ 311 (Supreme Court, Malaysia)

Facts

This case concerned the constitutionality of section 418A of the Criminal Procedure Code which gave the Public Prosecutor power to request any trial before a Sessions Court to be transferred to the High Court for trial. It was argued that section 418A was unconstitutional as it was in breach of the judicial power under Article 121(1) of the Federal Constitution. One issue that arose was whether the Court should give retrospective or prospective effect if it declared the law unconstitutional.

Eusoffe Abdoolcader SCJ

I would accordingly declare that s 418A is in violation of the provisions of Article 121(1) and therefore unconstitutional and void under the provisions of Article 4(1). The Deputy submits that any such pronouncement will create chaos as the section in question has been resorted to and trials held in the High Court as a result. The section has indeed been implemented and convictions and acquittals secured as a result over a span of some eleven years in view of the decision in the Hong Kong Bank case, and it will therefore be necessary in these circumstances to apply the doctrine of prospective overruling in this case.

The general principle of retroactivity of a judicial declaration of invalidity of a law was overturned by the Supreme Court of the United States of America in *Linkletter v Walker* . . . when it devised the doctrine of prospective overruling in the constitutional sphere in 1965 as a practical solution for alleviating the inconveniences which would result from its decision declaring a law to be unconstitutional, after overruling its previous decision upholding its constitutionality. This doctrine was applied by the Supreme Court of India in *IC Golak Nath v State of Punjab* . . . The doctrine – to the effect that when a statute is held to be unconstitutional, after overruling a long-standing current of decisions to the contrary, the Court will not give retrospective effect to the declaration of unconstitutionality so as to set aside proceedings of convictions or acquittals which had taken place under that statute prior to the date of the judgment which declared it to be unconstitutional, and convictions or acquittals secured as a result of the application of the impugned statute previously will accordingly not be disturbed – can be applied by the Supreme Court as the highest court of the country in a matter arising under the Constitution to give such retroactive effect to its decision as it thinks fit to be moulded in accordance with the justice of the cause or matter before it – to be adhibited however with circumspection and as an exceptional measure in the light of the circumstances under consideration.

In England this doctrine has been recognised . . . predicated on conditions of legal certainty which required the court, as an exceptional measure, to declare the law for the future only.

At the conclusion of argument on 19 March 1987, the Court accordingly by a majority . . . declared s 418A to be unconstitutional and void as being an infringement of the provisions of Article 121(1) and applied the doctrine of prospective overruling so as not to give retrospective effect to the declaration made with the result that all proceedings of convictions or acquittals which had taken place under that section prior to the date of the our judgment in this matter would remain undisturbed and not be affected, and the appeal was dismissed on this basis . . .

Abdul Nasir bin Amer Hamsah v Public Prosecutor
[1997] SGCA 38 (Court of Appeal, Singapore)

Facts

The appellant was a detainee in the lock-up of the Criminal Investigation Department. In his attempt to escape, he confined two police corporals and held them for ransom (car and weapons). When arrested, he was charged with an offence under the Kidnapping Act, convicted, and sentenced to imprisonment for life and 12 strokes of the cane. In the course of its judgment, the Court adopted a new interpretation on the meaning of 'life imprisonment' which went against all previous interpretations. The question before the Court was whether this new interpretation should take effect prospectively.

Karthigesu & LP Thean JJA, Yong Pung How CJ

We . . . embarked on the more difficult question of whether the judicial pronouncement above should have a retroactive or prospective effect which, unfortunately, neither counsel had touched on. And, if there should be prospective effect, then when should the reference point for this pronouncement be? Should it apply to all offenders convicted or sentenced after the pronouncement, irrespective of when the offence was committed? Or should it apply only to offences committed after its pronouncement?

There were three obvious considerations. First, there has never been a local judicial pronouncement on what life imprisonment means. Second, the Penal Code does not prescribe a meaning for life imprisonment. Third, the existing practice has been to equate life imprisonment with 20 years' imprisonment. Hence, of considerable importance to us was whether a first-time judicial pronouncement on the meaning of life imprisonment should be given retroactive or prospective effect, especially in the light of such a practice.

One approach was to maintain that the declaration and determination of life imprisonment would not actually pronounce any new law, but merely maintain and expound an old one. In a sense, this court would be merely making clear what has always been the law. To this extent, it could be said that a first-time judicial pronouncement should be retroactive since it merely affirms the position at law, as opposed to creating a new liability or punishment . . .

In other words, all prisoners presently serving life sentences should remain incarcerated until the end of their natural lives, even if they had been assured by lawyers and the Prisons Department that life imprisonment in practice means 20 years. Accused persons who decided to plead guilty on the basis that life imprisonment means 20 years would equally be caught by the pronouncement. However, in our view, such a result would be contrary to justice and fairness to the accused. To simply turn around and dismiss the original understanding of life imprisonment as erroneous, and adopt a retroactive approach for our pronouncement, would surely defeat the legitimate expectations of such accused persons.

In the circumstances, we had to consider how best to safeguard such legitimate expectations and whether a prospective approach for a first-time judicial pronouncement could be justified and adopted . . .

In the instant case, although we had concluded that life imprisonment should mean imprisonment for the remaining natural life of the prisoner, we could not ignore that, in practice, it has been consistently given a technical meaning of 20 years' imprisonment, excluding remission . . . Lawyers, the Prison Department, police officers and other law enforcement officers have come to know and understand the practice to be so. Advice might have been dispensed on the basis of such a practice. This seemed to be a clear example of a legitimate expectation engendered by a practice of many years. Therefore, the courts ought to protect individuals who arranged their affairs according to this expectation, bearing in mind that we were here concerned with the fundamental matter of a person's liberty for the rest of his life.

Consequently, a prospective approach must be adopted . . .

We were certainly not suggesting that the practice of 20 years' imprisonment had represented the state of the law on life imprisonment at any time. But, on an analogous reasoning with prospective judicial overruling, if the first-time interpretation of a particular punishment as prescribed by law would result in an expanded meaning, contrary to what could be reasonably and legitimately expected all along, then such a judicial pronouncement must also be given prospective effect to prevent prejudice and injustice to the accused.

This left only the question as to the reference point for this new pronouncement to affect offenders. Should it be determined by the date of conviction, date of sentence or date of commission of the offence? It seemed to us that an outcome based on the dates of conviction or sentence would depend on the efficiency of the criminal justice system. It could also depend on the administrative efficiency of the prosecuting agencies . . .

Consequently, for fairness and for consistency with the position taken in Manogaran, this pronouncement which we now make shall affect only offences committed after the date of delivery of this judgment . . .

Koo Sze Yiu v Chief Executive of the HKSAR
[2006] 3 HKLRD 455 (Court of Final Appeal, Hong Kong)

Facts

Covert surveillance under section 33 of the Telecommunication Ordinance was found incompatible with the Basic Law and was to be suspended by the Interception of Communications Ordinance (the IOCO) in 1997. However, because the date at which the IOCO would enter into force had not been designated, the proposed scheme never came into operation. Nonetheless, the Chief Executive published an executive order refining the covert surveillance procedures. The petitioners challenged the constitutionality of this order, section 33 of the Telecommunications Ordinance and the failure to bring the IOCO into operation. In invalidating the order, an issue arose as to whether any temporary validity of the impugned order should be provided despite its being declared unconstitutional, since there would be a legal vacuum.

Bokhary PJ

Declaring a law or executive action unconstitutional does not normally leave any void in the legal order let alone a void that dissolves society or imperils the rule of law. The effect of such a striking-down may be purely to rid the legal order of an unconstitutional encrustation. That would be normal. So would striking down an unconstitutional way of doing something that would be worthwhile if done constitutionally. In such a situation corrective legislation would be a likely sequel. Mere inconvenience in the meantime would not, however, justify temporary validity or suspension. But what if the circumstances are exceptional and the problem goes well beyond mere inconvenience? . . .

In some circumstances the doctrine of necessity is involved as a source of jurisdiction, and confers on the court powers that are exceptional to the point of being anomalous. But in other circumstances necessity comes into the picture only in the sense of providing justification, in any given case, for exercising jurisdiction that the court has without recourse to the doctrine of necessity. . . .

The rule of law involves meeting the needs of law and order. It involves providing a legal system able to function effectively. In order to meet those needs and preserve that ability, it must be recognized that exceptional circumstances may call for exceptional judicial measures. Temporary validity or suspension are examples of what courts have seen as such measures. . . .

A point to be noted in regard to the difference between temporary validity and suspension is as follows. Where temporary validity is accorded, the result would appear to be twofold. First, the executive is permitted, during such temporary validity period, to function pursuant to what has been declared unconstitutional. Secondly, the executive is shielded from legal liability for so functioning. Looking at the decided cases involving scenarios such as a virtual legal vacuum or a virtually blank statute book, it may be that the courts there thought that, absent such a shield, there would be, even after corrective legislation, chaos between persons and the state and also between persons and persons. . . .

The scenario in the present case is nothing like a virtual legal vacuum or a virtually blank statute book. It is by no means as serious as that. I see nothing to justify temporary validity in the present case.

This leaves the question of suspension, which would not involve the shield to which I have been referring. The judicial power to suspend the operation of a declaration is a concomitant of the power to make the declaration in the first place. It is within the inherent jurisdiction. There is no need to resort to the doctrine of necessity for the power. Necessity comes into the picture only in its ordinary sense: not to create the power but only for its relevance to the question of whether the power should be exercised in any given case. . . .

The decided case show that once temporary validity or suspension was considered justified, it became a question of whether to set a fixed period or require expedition by a form of words.

At least in general, I think that a fixed period should be set, subject to the possibility of further extension for good cause shown. A fixed period makes for greater certainty, and keeps the situation under better control.

The Right to Vote of Nationals Residing Abroad Case
2004Hun-Ma644 et al, 28 Jun 2007 (Constitutional Court, South Korea)

Facts

According to the Public Official Election Act and the National Referendum Act, voters and candidates had to be registered as residents. Absentee voting was allowed only for those who resided in Korea. The petitioners were Korean nationals who were unable to vote or register for absentee voting because they did not live in Korea. They argued that the provision infringed their right to vote, the principle of popular election and the equal protection clause.

Held

The Articles in question in this case infringe the basic rights of Korean nationals residing abroad, who cannot register as residents, by preventing them from exercising their right to vote in presidential and national assembly elections as well as their right to vote in national referendum simply because they are not registered as residents, even though they are still citizens of the Republic of Korea. They also deny the Korean nationals living abroad the right to vote or be elected in local elections simply because they are not registered as residents, despite the fact that they are residents who are nationals. However, as explained below, it does not seem appropriate to render a decision stating that the Articles in question are simply unconstitutional.

When laws violate the Constitution, it is procedure to declare them unconstitutional in order to ensure the validity of the Constitution. However, when removing unconstitutional Articles of law from the system through a decision of unconstitutionality may cause confusion and leave a legal void, a declaration of non-conformity can be made with an order to continue enforcing the articles in question temporarily. If it is determined that the unconstitutional state of temporarily enforcing the unconstitutional articles of law is constitutionally more desirable than the constitutional state of no legal regulation arising from the declaration of unconstitutionality, the Constitutional Court may decide maintain the unconstitutional regulations for a certain period of time and enforce them temporarily until the legislative branch amends the articles to conform with the Constitution in order to prevent an unbearable legal void and the ensuing confusion. . . .

If the articles in question are declared unconstitutional and are immediately rendered ineffective, it is clear that a state of confusion [will ensue] in which it will be impossible to properly hold the upcoming 17th presidential elections and 18th national assembly elections. Also, though it is a Constitutional requirement that all Korean nationals residing abroad be granted the right to vote as a matter of [principle], there still remain many issues that must be solved in terms of ensuring fair elections and technicalities involved therein. For example, if we were to allow Korean nationals residing abroad including overseas sojourners the right to vote in state elections and the right to vote in national referendum, we would require time to conduct a sufficient review of and prepare for matters such as installing voting booths and an agency to manage the elections, establish a process for checking the ID of Korean Nationals residing abroad, the method of voting, method of campaigning, and other specific methods on conducting fair elections. In the case of giving the nationals residing abroad but currently living within the country the right to vote in local elections, we must review issues such as whether to impose residential requirements, and if so how long the term of residing should be. These such issues should ultimately be decided by the legislative branch through extensive discussion and social consensus.

Therefore the Articles in question are hereby declared not to be in conformity with the Constitution, but they are to be temporarily enforced until the legislature amends them. The legislative branch must make the proper amendments at the latest by December 31, 2008, and if no such amendments are made by then, the Articles in question will become null and void starting on January 1, 2009.

Notes and Questions

1. What constitutional concerns would you have in applying prospective ruling or judicial deadlines? Legal certainty, rule of law, separation of powers, protection of rights or all of them? How can the courts be assured of progress in legal revision when imposing deadlines?

2. By giving temporary validity to laws that are declared unconstitutional, the courts allow the legislature time to revise the laws before the date on which they becomes invalid. A similar strategy has been employed by Taiwan's Constitutional Court in a variety of cases, ranging from the rights of criminal defendants, to equal protec-

tions or even to politically sensitive cases such as the re-election of national representatives. In this form of decision, the Court often imposes a deadline, ranging from one to three years, by which time the impugned law remains temporarily valid but beyond which time it becomes invalidated. For example, in *JY Interpretation No 251*, 19 Jan 1990, the Court stated:

> The existing procedure regarding the detention and forced labor indicated in the former interpretation and the punishments addressed in this interpretation will be null and void after July 1, 1991. All relevant laws also have to be revised by that date.

3. In a high-profile political case regarding the re-election of national representatives who had not stood for any re-election after 1948 but continued to serve in office, the Constitutional Court in *JY Interpretation No 261*, 21 Jun 1990, stated:

> To cope with the present situations, those first-term national representatives who have not been re-elected on a periodical basis shall cease the exercise of their powers no later than December 31, 1991. Among them, those who have been de facto incapable of exercising or constantly failed to exercise their powers shall be immediately dismissed, after thorough investigation, from their offices. The Central Government is further mandated to hold, in due course, a nationwide second-term election of the national representatives, in accordance with the spirit of the Constitution, the essence of this Interpretation and the relevant regulations, so that the constitutional system will function properly.

4. When the court finds an organic act unconstitutional, there is usually a need to provide temporary validity for the impugned act so that the legislature will have sufficient time to revise the law and to reorganise the agency implementing it. For example, in *JY Interpretation No 613*,[180] the Constitutional Court found the method of appointment of members to the National Communication Commission (NCC), an independent regulatory commission, unconstitutional, but decided to give the Commission temporary validity for two-and-a-half years. The Court states:

> As such, the purpose of establishing the NCC as an independent agency is defeated, and the constitutional intent of safeguarding the freedom of communications is not complied with. Therefore, the foregoing provisions shall become void no later than December 31, 2008. Prior to the voidance of the aforesaid provisions due to their unconstitutionality as declared by this Court, the legality of any and all acts performed by the NCC will remain unaffected, as will the transfer of personnel and affairs.

5. If impugned laws are involved with controversial social policies, there may be an even stronger need to give them temporary validity so that policy makers and the general public have sufficient time to deliberate new policies. For example, the Constitutional Court in *JY Interpretation No 666*, 6 November 2009, struck down the law that penalised only prostitutes but not those also engaged in sexual transactions, on the ground that it violated the principle of equality. Understanding that it might take some time for the legislature to decide on the policy, the Constitutional Court provided for a two-year period during which the legislature could debate and take a decision on the policy issue. It stated:

---

[180] *JY Interpretation No 613*, 5 ROC Const Ct 682, 687 (2007).

In order to carry out the legislative purpose of maintaining citizens' health as well as *ordre public* and morality, the government agency may implement different kinds of management or counselling measures for those [engaging in sexual transactions for financial gain] in accordance with the law such as physical examinations or safe sex awareness; may also provide job training, career counselling or other educational methods to enhance their work capacity and economic condition so that it is no longer necessary [for them] to use sexual transactions as the means for livelihood; or [adopt] other effective management measures. Other than providing the most possible protection and assistance to the socio-economically disadvantaged people, in order to prevent sexual transaction activities from [negatively] impacting on third party's interests, or to avoid sexual transaction activities infringing on other important public interests, the State may, when necessary to restrict sexual transactions, enact statutes or authorize the promulgation of regulations to provide reasonable and precise rules to control or penalize. Given that this requires substantial time for careful planning, the disputed provision shall cease to be effective no later than two years from the issuance of this Interpretation.[181]

C. Unconstitutional Declaration without Invalidation and Judicial Warnings

The German Constitutional Court has, over the years, developed various strategies 'to soften the political impacts of its decisions'.[182] Among these strategies is the practice of declaring a law unconstitutional without invalidating it, and the other is the issuance of judicial warnings (or admonitory decisions) to tender advice to Parliament for consideration of legal revisions. In applying the former strategy, the defective law continues in force until it is replaced by a new law. In applying the latter strategy, the law is constitutional but the legislature is advised to proceed with revisions. Unlike the case of temporary validity, the legislature is not under immediate pressure to revise the law and retains its discretion in deciding when and how to proceed with legal revisions. However, in cases where the law is declared unconstitutional, legislative inaction – and the longer it lasts – may gravely undermine the legitimacy of the impugned law and the institutional authority of both the court and the legislature.

The following two cases from the Constitutional Court in Taiwan illustrate the use of alternative constitutional decisions. *JY Interpretation No 86* was an unconstitutional declaration without invalidation. However, regrettably, the impugned law remained effective for nearly two decades before being revised. *JY Interpretation No 211* was a judicial warning. Absent any legislative revision for about a decade, the Constitutional Court eventually declared the law unconstitutional when the impugned law was challenged again.

---

[181] See *JY Interpretation No 666*, 6 ROC Const Ct 594, 598–99 (2007).
[182] Kommers, above n 45, at 53.

JY Interpretation No 86
15 Aug 1960 (Constitutional Court, Taiwan)

Facts

Under the Court Organization Act, the District and High Courts were placed under the supervision of the Ministry of Judicial Administration (later renamed the 'Ministry of Justice') instead of the Supreme Court or the Judicial Yuan. Article 77 of the Constitution stipulates that the Judicial Yuan is the highest judicial organ in charge ofcivil and criminal litigation, as well as other judicial matters. Consequently, the Control Yuan – which is functionally equivalent to an ombudsman – petitioned the Constitutional Court, arguing that the Court Organization Act was unconstitutional.

Held

Article 77 of the Constitution stipulates that the Judicial Yuan is the highest judicial organ of the State and holds the judicial power over trials of civil and criminal litigation, the trials of which shall include trials of civil and criminal litigation at courts of all levels. In view of this fact, Article 82 of the Constitution, which stipulates that the structure of the Judicial Yuan and courts of all levels shall be organized by law and is incorporated into the chapter of the Judiciary intending to establish the consistency of the judicial system, contributes as cross-evidence. Based on this reason, all levels of courts and subsidiary courts below the High Court shall be subordinate to the Judicial Yuan. All relevant acts and regulations shall respectively be amended to comply with the concept of Article 77 of the Constitution.

Aftermath of the case

Notwithstanding this interpretation, no revisions were undertaken until in the early 1980s, when the Government was faced with both internal and external demands for political and judicial reforms. The Court Organization Act was finally revised on 29 June 1980 to make the structure of lower courts consistent with the Constitution.

JY Interpretation No 211
5 Dec 1986 (Constitutional Court, Taiwan)

Facts

The petitioner was fined for importing goods without authorisation. He filed a complaint which was dismissed as he had not paid the deposit for lodging complaints under the Customs Smuggling Control Act. He then initiated a petition before the Constitutional Court, arguing that the deposit requirement for lodging complaints violated the principle of equality and his right to sue.

Held

Article 7 of the Constitution, [which] provides that 'All citizens of the Republic of China, irrespective of sex, religion, race, class or party affiliation shall be equal before the law,' is to protect the substantial equality of the legal position of the people. It does not restrict the competent authority, with due authorization by the law, from rendering reasonably different treatments by reference to the differences de facto of any particular case and the purposes of legislation. Article 49 of the Customs Smuggling Control Act provides that 'For any protest cases, and in case no goods were seized or the goods seized were not sufficient to pay for the fine or the short-paid duty, the Customs may order the person to pay in deposit, within 14 days, half of the original fine or insufficient amount or furnish an adequate security equal to the same amount. In case no payment was made or no security was furnished within the prescribed time limit, that protest will not be accepted.' The wording that follows the word 'may' is meant to authorize the Customs, after examination, and subject to the particular facts, to render appropriate punishment. This is to prevent the person subjected to administrative punishment, by submitting a protest, from delaying or evading the execution of duty payment and punishment. It is not that Customs shall whatsoever order the person subjected to administrative punishment to pay a deposit or furnish the security needed. Though this provision limits the opportunity for relief of the person subjected to administrative punishment, it aims to prevent the person subjected to administrative punishment, who have no goods seized or whose goods seized were not sufficient to pay for the fine or the short-paid duty, from submitting a protest deliberately under the circumstance that the original administrative punishment was not obviously contrary to law or did not constitute undue punishment. It aims to fulfill the Customs policy of preventing smuggling, which is necessary to promote the public interest and is not contrary to Articles 7 and 16 of the Constitution. As to the person subjected to administrative punishment submitting administrative appeal or litigation against the administrative punishment on paying a deposit or furnishing the security, the administrative authority accepting the administrative appeal or the administrative court shall, subject to the above-mentioned, examine and determine whether that administrative punishment was illegal or improper. Under this circumstance, in case it is found that the Customs' original administrative punishment on supplementary levying or punishment was illegal or undue, the higher administrative authority may put it to proper disposition, subject to its power of supervision over the relevant administrative authority. In addition, it is to be noted here that some of the wording in the section on administrative litigation procedure stipulated in the Customs Smuggling Control Act is imprecise and may cause deviation in the administrative execution; thus, such wording should be examined and amended in order to concur with the preservation of administrative execution and the adequate exercise of the rights of administrative appeal and litigation of the people.

Aftermath of the case

Despite the warnings in this Interpretation that Article 49 of the Customs Smuggling Control Act concerning administrative litigation procedure was 'imprecise and . . . should be examined and amended', no legislative action was undertaken. Years later, a new petition was initiated before the Constitutional Court, arguing that the provision in the Customs Smuggling Control Act violated the principle of equality and the right to sue. On 30 October 1997, the Constitutional Court made *JY Interpretation No 439*, eventually invalidating those impugned provisions.

Notes and Questions

1. Do you think a unconstitutional declaration without invalidation or judicial warning are appropriate forms of judicial decision-making? Do they indicate too great a judicial deference to the political institutions? Or do they reflect judicial comity and modesty, especially in light of the counter-majoritarian nature of the judiciary?

2. Did *JY Interpretation No 86* and *JY Interpretation No 211* have any immediate effect? Despite the unconstitutional declaration and warnings, the laws remained unchanged for quite a while. What do you think actually brought about the subsequent legal change? The impact of the declaration or warning? Or the progress in democratisation and rule of law since the late 1980s in Taiwan?

D. Judicial Law-Making

As Kemel Bokhary, Permanent Judge of the Court of Final Appeal of Hong Kong SAR noted, 'exceptional circumstances may call for exceptional judicial measures'.[183] In extraordinary situations, the creation of a legal vacuum and the grave dangers it may bring to the public may foster temporary judicial law-making that offers a wide range of measures. In the following case, absent any legislation dealing with sexual harassment, the Supreme Court of India decided to write the law itself, and make the law applicable until such time as Parliament enacted the necessary legislation. Unlike judicial warnings or unconstitutional declarations that seek to 'soften the political impacts' of constitutional rulings, judicial law-making inevitably creates tensions between courts and the legislature, underscoring the counter-majoritarian difficulty associated with judicial law-making.

> **Vishaka and others v State of Rajasthan and others**
> **[1997] AIR SC 3011 (Supreme Court, India)**
>
> **Facts**
>
> This case was instigated after the gang rape of a social worker in Rajasthan. One request by the petitioner was that the Supreme Court provide as detailed a set of rules as possible regulating sexual harassment, since there was no appropriate legislation.
>
> **Verma CJ**
>
> In the absence of domestic law occupying the field, to formulate effective measures to check the evil of sexual harassment of working women at all work places, the power of this Court under Art 32 for enforcement of the fundamental rights and the executive power of the union have to meet the challenge to protect the working women from sexual harassment and to make their fundamental rights meaningful. Governance of the society by the rule of law mandates this requirement as [a] logical concomitant of the constitutional scheme.

---

[183] *Koo Sze Yiu v Chief Executive of the HKSAR* [2006] 3 HKLRD 455, para 28.

The progress made at each hearing culminated in the formulation of guidelines to which the Union of India gave its consent through the learned Solicitor General, indicating that these should be the guidelines and norms declared by this Court to govern the behaviour of the employers and all others at the work places to curb this social evil.

Gender equality includes protection from sexual harassment and right to work with dignity, which is a universally recognised basic human right. The common minimum requirement of this right has received global acceptance. The International Conventions and norms are, therefore, of great significance in the formulation of the guidelines to achieve this purpose. . . .

Independence of judiciary forms a part of our constitutional scheme. The international conventions and norms are to be read into them in the absence of enacted domestic law occupying the field when there is no inconsistency between them. It is now an accepted rule of judicial construction domestic law when there is no inconsistency between them and there is a void in the domestic law . . .

In view of the above, and the absence of enacted law to provide for the effective enforcement of the basic human right of gender equality and guarantee against sexual harassment and abuse, more particularly against sexual harassment at work places, we lay down the guidelines and norms specified hereinafter for due observance at all work places or other institutions, until a legislation is enacted for the purpose. This is done in exercise of the power available under Art 32 of the Constitution for enforcement of the fundamental rights and it is further emphasised that this would be treated as the law declared by this Court under Art 141 of the Constitution. . . .

Accordingly, we direct that the above guidelines and norms would be strictly observed in all work places for the preservation and enforcement of the right to gender equality of the working women. These directions would be binding and enforceable in law until suitable legislation is enacted to occupy the field.

Notes and Questions

1. In *Vishakav State of Rajasthan*, the Supreme Court of India assumed the initiative to prescribe rules on sexual harassment, which were to be in force until Parliament legislated on the subject. While temporary law-making by the judiciary is rare, temporary injunctions against the enforcement of legislation are even rarer. In the context of constitutional courts exercising the power of abstract judicial review, judicial orders to enjoin the enforcement of a law the constitutionality of which is in serious doubt are also quite rare since they may generate political tensions. In Taiwan, the Constitutional Court in *JY Interpretation No 599* laid down the rules according to which the Court may issue an injunctive order:

    The preventive system used to ensure the effectiveness of the interpretations given or judgments rendered by the judiciary is one of the core functions of the judicial power, irrespective of whether it involves constitutional interpretations or trials, or concerns civil, criminal or administrative litigations. The Grand Justices, in exercising the power of constitutional interpretation, may grant the declaration of a preliminary injunction in the event that the continuance of doubt or dispute as to the constitutional provisions at issue, the application of the law or regulation in dispute, or the enforcement of the judgment for the case at issue may cause irreparable or virtually irreparable harm to any fundamental right of the people, fundamental constitutional principle or any other major public interest, that the granting of a preliminary injunction on the motion of a petitioner prior to the delivery of an interpretation for the case at issue may be imminently necessary to prevent any harm, that no other means is available to prevent such harm, and that, after weighing the advantages for granting a preliminary injunction and the disadvantages for not granting the same, the granting of the injunction obviously has more advantages than disadvantages.[184]

In this case, the Constitutional Court was concerned about Article 8 of the Household Registration Act, which required every national to be fingerprinted before he or she applied for an identity card. In March 2005, the Ministry of the Interior was planning to implement such fingerprinting scheme. Having balanced with all the factors, the Constitutional Court decided to issue a preliminary injunction in June. In September, the Constitutional Court issued *JY Interpretation No 603* invalidating Article 8 of the Household Registration Act.

2. What constitutional concerns might you have with judicial law-making even temporarily? Democratic legitimacy, separation of powers, rule of law or all of them? To what extent would temporary judicial law-making be an effective trigger for further political action?

---

[184] *Interpretation No 599* [trans VC Kuan], 5 ROC Const Ct 442, 445–46 (2007).

6

Democracy and
the Right to Political Participation

I. INTRODUCTION

Notwithstanding the contested meanings of democracy, we live in an era when it has become an international marker of legitimacy and in which democratisation has had a global impact. At minimum, there is broad consensus that democracy entails a government elected by individuals with equal suffrage. As opposed to dictatorships or oligarchies ruled by one or a few elite persons, democracy in principle guarantees that every citizen has an equal right to vote to form the government, both as an expression of the consent of the governed as well as embodying the principle of democratic accountability. Hence, the periodic holding of free, fair and transparent elections is a central feature of democracy which affirms as a core value the equal right to political participation, which includes but transcends voting, to encompass taking part in public affairs.

To ensure the accountability of the governors, there must be a set of binding rules to which they must be subject. Such rules are usefully enforced by an independent judiciary. So understood, democracy and constitutionalism may become synonymous, in that both ensure that those who govern must be governed by themselves as well as the rules they make.[1] In terms of institutional design, democracy implies a system of majority decision making; where these decisions relate to fundamental matters affecting individuals and the polity, a substantive political ideology or normative theory is implicated as the reference point for shaping and guiding these decisional choices. Encompassed within the parameters of democratic discourse are complex ideas related to a diversity of democratic models, such as liberal democracy, communitarian democracy, capitalist democracy, socialist democracy or deliberative democracy.[2]

The focus of this chapter is on forms of electoral democracy, within which context the right of individuals to engage in political participation assumes centre-stage. We first examine the concepts and types of democracy, and democratisation trends in Asia after World War II. This is followed by a discussion about the forms and institutions of political representation, and the exercise and enjoyment of the right to political

---

[1] N Dorsen et al, *Comparative Constitutionalism: Cases and Materials*, 2nd ed (St Paul, Minn: West, 2010) at 1414.

[2] See generally MJ Sandel, *Democracy's Discontent* (Cambridge, Mass: Belknap Press, 1996); A Gutmann and D Thompson, *Democracy and Disagreement* (Cambridge, Mass: Belknap Press, 1996); Li-ann Thio, 'Constitutionalism in Illiberal Polities' in M Rosenfeld and A Sajó (eds), *The Oxford Handbook of Comparative Constitutional Law* (Oxford: Oxford University Press, 2012) 133, 134; Li-ann Thio, 'The Right to Political Participation in Singapore: Tailor-Making a Westminster-Modelled Constitution to fit the Imperatives of "Asian" Democracy' (2002) 6 *Singapore Journal of International & Comparative Law* 181.

participation through methods such as electoral schemes, state referenda and the initiative provided by the facility of citizen petitions.

II. DEMOCRACY AND DEMOCRATISATION IN ASIA

Asian states are amongst the many that have transformed into democratic polities in the last three decades. While India and Japan became democracies after World War II, states like South Korea, Taiwan, the Philippines, Mongolia, Thailand and Indonesia underwent this process in more recent decades. This section introduces various conceptions of democracy and discusses the recent waves of democratisation in Asia.

A. Concepts and Types of Democracy

Democracy as a principle is enshrined in the majority of Asian constitutions. Many constitutions declare or commit their states to be a democratic state, a democracy, a liberal democracy or a socialist democracy. For example, the constitutions of South Korea, Taiwan, and the Philippines expressly commit the state to be a democratic republic. The Interim Constitution of Nepal ensures that the state is responsible for adopting a political system which fully abides by the concept of multi-party competitive democratic system.[3] The Constitution of Cambodia commits the state to the principle of liberal democracy and pluralism.[4] In addition, several constitutions refer to socialist democracy. The constitutions of both Sri Lanka and Vietnam, for example, define the state as a democratic socialist republic. The Constitution of People's Republic of China ensures that the state is a socialist state under the people's democratic dictatorship.

Democracy entails the rule of the people, as opposed to a monarchy or an oligarchy. Where democracy is direct, the people make political decisions directly. Where democracy is representative, the equal right to vote for one's choice of representatives and stand for elections is a primary feature.[5] Elected representatives make political decisions on behalf of the people to whom they are accountable. Political scientists consider that holding a free and open election based upon universal suffrage indicates the beginning of a transition to democracy or democratisation.[6] While direct democracy has its appeal in broad-based democratic legitimacy, it is nevertheless inefficient and costly. Most modern states adopt a form of representative democracy, supplemented by a limited form of direct democracy operating at the local levels.

Aside from procedural understandings of democracy in terms of direct and indirect democracy, other concepts or types of democracy may illustrate substantive under-

---

[3] Art 33(c), Interim Constitution of Nepal.

[4] Art 1, Interim Constitution of Cambodia.

[5] T Paine, 'Dissertation on the First Principles of Government' in *The Political Writings of Thomas Paine* (Boston, Mass: JP Mendum Investigator Office, 1859) at 335.

[6] JJ Linz and A Stepan, *Problems of Democratic Transition and Consolidation* (Baltimore, Md: Johns Hopkins University Press, 1996) at 8–9, 14.

standings of democracy according to normative values or political ideologies that provide guidance for political decisions made by the people's representatives. These may be liberal, illiberal or communitarian forms of democracy. In general, liberal democracy is premised on normative individualism that prioritises individual autonomy through constitutional rights, as well as on the purported neutrality of the state that does not espouse a shared conception of the good, individuals being free to pursue their own aspirations.[7] In contrast, illiberal or communitarian democracy prioritises community interests and actively promotes a particular version of public life. In an illiberal democracy, the state is expressly non-neutral, privileging a substantive vision of the good, informed by ethnicity, religion or communal morality.[8] Political institutions elected to uphold the collective version of public good – such as the parliament or president – enjoy considerable respect in the constitutions of illiberal or communitarian democracy. Some non-liberal democracies highlight a particular religion in public life as a source of national identity. Sri Lanka or Thailand stand as examples. Others may choose particular community values as the basis of public life, thus restricting the choices of individuals vis-à-vis the collective. Malaysia and Singapore may be considered communitarian democracies which recognise diverse religious and racial groups in their unifying national ideologies.[9]

Notwithstanding these competing substantive conceptions, the discourse on democracy in an age of widespread democratic transitions is centred on electoral democracy, which in turn focuses on periodic elections and equal voting rights of citizens.

B. Waves of Democratisation

The democratisation process in Asia began at the end of World War II with Japan.[10] Notwithstanding the external influence from the victorious Allies, the adoption of the 1946 Constitution was the first step in the transformation of Japan from military oligarchy to liberal democracy.[11] From this time on, other nascent democracies emerged in Asia, such as India and Pakistan, but not all were consolidated and some failed.[12] For example, South Korea and Taiwan both had military dictatorships by the end of the 1950s; martial law was imposed in the Philippines in 1972; and in 1975, a state of emergency was declared in India.

---

[7] Thio, above n 2, at 133 and 134.

[8] Ibid at 136.

[9] Ibid at 144.

[10] SP Huntington, *The Third Wave: Democratization in the Late 20th Century* (Norman, Okla: University of Oklahoma Press 1993) at 18.

[11] The Supreme Commander for the Allied Powers under the leadership of General MacArthur, suggested a draft to the Japanese Government in February 1946, which became the basis for the subsequent discussion of the new Constitution. In April, the Japanese Government submitted its own draft to the newly elected Parliament, which later passed the new Constitution. For detailed discussions on the making of the new Constitution, see Wen-Chen Chang, 'East Asian Foundations for Constitutionalism: Three Models' (2008) 3(2) *National Taiwan University Law Review* 111, 117; Jiunn-Rong Yeh and Wen-Chen Chang, 'The Emergence of East Asian Constitutionalism: Features in Comparison' (2011) 56 *American Journal of Comparative Law* 805, 807.

[12] Huntington, above n 10, at 20.

The 1980s saw another wave of democratisation in Asia.[13] In 1987, South Korea undertook a far-reaching constitutional revision. By 1992, Kim Young Sam, a key figure from the former opposition, was elected President and became the first civilian leader. Since then, government powers have been diffused among various political parties. Similarly in Taiwan, democratisation followed a gradual but steady path from one-party rule to a liberal democracy in the 1980s and 1990s, with seven rounds of constitutional revisions. In 2000, the Nationalist Party (*Kuomintang* or KMT) lost the power it had held since World War II to the long-time opposition, the Democratic Progressive Party (DPP). Eight years later, the KMT regained political power when it won both the presidential and parliamentary elections. Both South Korea and Taiwan have passed the 'two-turnover test' political scientists use to characterise the beginning of democratic consolidation.[14] In 1986, the Philippines transformed into a democracy and, since then, general elections have become the regularised and normal way of transferring governing powers.[15] Indonesia took strides towards democracy in 1998, after the fall of Indonesia's authoritarian 'New Order' with the resignation of President Suharto. Vice President BJ Habibie succeeded to the presidency and started political reforms, including large-scale constitutional revisions.[16]

However, the process of democratisation in Asian jurisdictions does not always proceed smoothly. Notwithstanding a gradually open political environment, the elected rulers or political parties may not respect democratic rules and the rights of political opposition. Worse still, some governments may manipulate state resources or the media to influence the outcome of elections in their favour. Regressive developments took place after an initial wave of democratisation. For example, in Cambodia, the Paris Peace Accord of 1991 made possible the first free parliamentary elections in 1993, but a coup occurred four years later. In Nepal, the election of 1991 brought about democratic rule, but this was sustained for only a short period before civil conflict broke out between the Government and the Maoists. In Thailand, the new Constitution of 1997 improved the institutional framework for democratic governance but was suspended in 2006 after a coup, which yielded another Constitution in 2007.[17]

Notes and Questions

1. Can the reversal of democratic gains in some Asian jurisdictions in the late 1990s be explained as the expression of various conceptions of democracy, such as illiberal or communitarian democracy, rather than as regression into authoritarianism?

2. Li-ann Thio observes that 'many Asian states with communitarian traditions are gradually liberalising, while remaining committed to protecting a particular culture or religion' and 'all societies have a mix of liberal and illiberal practices'. See

---

[13] A Croissant, 'From Transition to Defective Democracy: Mapping Asian Democratization' (2004) 11(5) *Democratization* 156, 157; Jiunn-Rong Yeh and Wen-Chen Chang, above n 11, at 813.
[14] Jiunn-Rong Yeh and Wen-Chen Chang, above n 11, at 813.
[15] Doh Chull Shin, 'The Third Wave in East Asia: Comparative and Dynamic Perspective' (2008) 4(2) *Taiwan Journal of Democracy* 91, 99–101.
[16] Ibid at 157.
[17] Ibid at 157–62.

Li-ann Thio, 'Constitutionalism in Illiberal Polities' in M Rosenfeld and A Sajó (eds), *The Oxford Handbook of Comparative Constitutional Law* (Oxford: Oxford University Press, 2012) at 133, 137 and 144.

C. Forms of Political Representation

Modern states generally practice a system of representative democracy, in which everyone is guaranteed an equal right to choose representatives who are delegated with the task of public decision making through a voting system predicated on universal suffrage. Within the frame of liberal democracy, representatives are chosen to act on behalf of atomic individuals rather than racial, ethnic or religious groups or any special communities.

However, communitarian or other forms of non-liberal democracy – given their primary focus on racial harmony, national unity or community values – may choose alternative forms of political representation. For example, a system may have a quota system to ensure parity of representation of the sexes to correct under-representation,[18] or it may administer some kind of group-based representation, where group interests are represented through functional constituencies, proportional representation, or special ethnic or religious legislative quotas. According to Iris Young, heterogeneous public and group representation are crucial to a democracy that promotes social justice, and 'a democratic republic should provide mechanisms for the effective recognition and representation of the distinct voices and perspectives of those of its constituent groups that are oppressed or disadvantaged'.[19]

Both liberal and alternative forms of political representation are adopted throughout Asia. The proportional representation (PR) system is implemented in many jurisdictions, including Japan, South Korea, Taiwan, Thailand and the Philippines. As part of its colonial legacy, the system of functional constituency remains in Hong Kong. To cater to the needs of disadvantaged groups such as women, the 1947 ROC Constitution implemented a special quota for women in electoral politics, being the first Asian constitution to do so.[20] The Constitution of India reserves parliamentary seats for Scheduled Castes and Tribes under Article 330. The following section discusses these various forms of political representation in Asian jurisdictions and analyses what constitutional challenges they may face.

i. Electoral Representation: Apportionment and Voting Disparity

The equal right of individuals to vote is crucial to political representation in a liberal democracy. Equality of voting may not be fully guaranteed if the weight, value or

---

[18] B Rodríguez-Ruiz and R Rubio-Marín, 'The Gender of Representation: On Democracy, Equality and Parity' (2008) 6 *International Journal of Constitutional Law* 287.

[19] IM Young, *Justice and the Politics of Difference* (Princeton, NJ: Princeton University Press, 1990) at 184.

[20] R Rubio-Marin and Wen-Chen Chang, 'Sites of Constitutional Struggle for Women's Equality' in M Tushnet, T Fleiner and C Saunders (eds), *Routledge Handbook of Constitutional Law* (New York: Routledge, 2012) 301, 308.

effect of votes is not equal. As Chief Justice Warren of the US Supreme Court stated in *Reynolds v Sims*,

> if a State should provide that the votes of citizens in one part of the State should be given two times, or five times, or 10 times the weight of votes of citizens in another part of the State, it could hardly be contended that the right to vote of those residing in the disfavoured areas had not been effectively diluted.[21]

However, many political and technical factors – such as the total number of parliamentary seats, the density of population in various districts or the administrative unity of districts – may affect the value or effect of a vote. Chief Justice Warren admitted

> it is a practical impossibility to arrange legislative districts so that each one has an identical number of residents, or citizens, or voters. Mathematical exactness or precision is hardly a workable constitutional requirement.[22]

If mathematical precision is unattainable, what other constitutional standards may guide electoral representation based upon the principle of 'one person, one vote'? Most constitutions confer on parliament the power to enact electoral rules. The Constitution of Japan, for instance, leaves all important details – such as the choice of the electoral system, the method of voting, the number of legislators, the boundaries of districts and the apportionment of seats among the districts – to Parliament.[23] A few other constitutions, however, may entrust to a neutral and independent constitutional commission the power to prescribe electoral rules, such as the Commission on Elections (COMELEC) created by Article IX(C) of the Constitution of the Philippines. Whether electoral rules are formulated by parliament or an independent commission, should the courts treat these deferentially? What disparity in the value of votes should be deemed unconstitutional under the principle of equality of voting rights? When should legislative apportionment or districting be found unconstitutional, or to constitute unlawful gerrymandering[24] in which the excessive manipulation of district boundaries may be to give effect to an intention to dilute the voting strength of certain groups or voters? The following cases illustrate how voter rights may be affected by actions to divide an electoral district, or failure to do so, as well as where the principle of proportionality has been breached.

Case to Seek Invalidation of Election
65 Minshū 2 (Supreme Court, Japan)

Facts

Under the Act for Establishment of the Demarcation Council, one seat would be reserved for each prefecture. Based on the results of the population census conducted in October 2000, the Demarcation Council revised the apportionment of seats by adding one seat each to five prefectures while taking one seat each from five others, and drafted a plan for

---

[21] *Reynolds v Sims* 377 US 533, 562 (1964).
[22] Ibid at 577.
[23] Arts 43 and 47, Constitution of Japan.
[24] DH Lowenstein, RL Hasen and DP Tokaji (eds), *Election Law – Cases and Materials* (Durham, NC: Carolina Academic Press, 2008) at 243.

revision of constituencies within each prefecture. This culminated in the enactment of the Act for Partial Revision of the Public Offices Election Act.

However, this Partial Revision resulted in serious voting disparities, and the appellants challenged the apportionment, arguing that any apportionment should be proportionate to population and that the Diet (Parliament) did not have a broad discretion in apportionment. While the Supreme Court urged the Diet to take legislative measures to 'meet the requirement of equality in the value of votes, such as abolishing, as quickly as possible, the rule of reserving one seat per prefecture', it nevertheless sustained the impugned demarcation and dismissed the appeal.

Held

It is understood that the Constitution requires equality in the substance of the right to vote, or in other words, equality in the value of votes. However, equality in the value of votes is not the absolute criterion for determining the design of an election system, but it must be realized in harmony with other policy purposes and grounds that the Diet is duly authorized to consider. Insofar as specific matters determined by the Diet are justified as a reasonable exercise of its discretion, it cannot be helped even when such determination might lead to asking for a concession to a certain extent on the part of equality in the value of votes.

The Constitution requires that, in the case of adopting a system for holding an election of members of the House of Representatives by dividing the whole area of the country into a number of constituencies, securing equality in the number of voters or population per member to the greatest possible extent should be the most important and essential criterion for determining the apportionment of seats and the demarcation of constituencies as features of the design of an election system. The Constitution also allows the Diet to take other factors into consideration as long as it is reasonable to do so.

In the process of determining specific features of an election system, prefectures have been regarded as the basis for the apportionment of seats and the demarcation of constituencies as they have been considered to serve as important units in social life and also for their political and social functions. Under the election system for members of the House of Representatives, prefectures have been the primary basis for the apportionment of seats. Municipalities or other administrative districts created by subdividing prefectures have been supposed to be specific constituencies, while taking into account various factors including the size, population density, composition of residents, transportation conditions, and geographical situations of the respective areas. Amid the changes in population, the Diet is required to, while taking these various factors into account, ensure that the will of the people will be reflected properly so as to carry out national politics, and at the same time, reconcile this with the requirement of securing equality in the value of votes. Consequently, determination as to the constitutionality of an election system is to be made by examining whether or not, even when all of these circumstances are comprehensively taken into account, the election system is justifiable as a reasonable exercise of the discretion vested in the Diet . . .

The criteria for demarcation of single-seat constituencies under the Election System are specified in Article 3 of the Act for Establishment of the Demarcation Council (these criteria and the relevant provisions shall hereinafter be referred to as the 'Criteria for Demarcation' and the 'Provisions on Criteria for Demarcation' respectively). Paragraph (1) of said Article provides that the drafting of a revision plan shall be performed in accordance with the principle of ensuring that the maximum disparity between constituencies in terms of population will be below two. This can be a reasonable criterion established with due consideration given to equality in the value of votes.

On the other hand, as mentioned above, paragraph (2) of said Article adopts the rule of reserving one seat per prefecture, and as described in 2(3) above, it was explained that the purpose of this rule was to apportion more seats to relatively less populated prefectures, so that the will of the people living in less populated prefectures will also be fully reflected in national politics. However, members to be elected under this election system are, irrespective of in which regions their constituencies are located, required to take part in national politics as representatives of all the people. Consideration to relatively less populated regions is a matter that these members should take into account when making laws and performing other duties from a nationwide perspective in the course of carrying out such political activities. It can hardly be justified as being reasonable to cause, only for the purpose of coping with problems arising from regional circumstances, inequality in the value of votes between voters in particular regions (prefectures) and those in other regions (prefectures). What is more, at the time of the Election, the maximum disparity between prefectures in terms of the value of votes already reached around the level of 1:2 after the first stage of apportionment of seats to each prefecture under the rule of reserving one seat per prefecture. Thus, it is obvious that the rule of reserving one seat per prefecture became the major factor causing the disparity between constituencies in terms of the value of votes as described in 2(5) above. The significance of the rule of reserving one seat per prefecture seems to have been somewhat explained at the time of legislation, ie consideration to the sudden decrease in the number of seats to be apportioned to less populated regions. More specifically, in light of the history of the election system in Japan as described above, and in particular, the situation where it was extremely difficult to reduce the number of seats in response to population changes, if, upon the introduction of a new election system, seats for Diet members were apportioned to each prefecture exclusively in proportion to population, the number of seats to be apportioned to less populated prefectures would be reduced suddenly and considerably, and therefore it was necessary to secure stability and continuity in national politics, and said rule was adopted under the circumstances where, without consideration to such necessity of securing stability and continuity, among others, the reform of the election system in itself was difficult to achieve.

Assuming so, the rule of reserving one seat per prefecture is reasonable only for a limited period of time, and once a new election system has been established and put into stable operation, it is no longer reasonable. The aforementioned judgment of the Grand Bench of the Supreme Court of June 13, 2007, indicated a determination on the general election that was held on September 11, 2005, when ten years had not yet passed since the first general election held in 1996 following the introduction of the Election System, and when the population census for 2005 had not yet been conducted. In said judgment, the court determined that at the time of said date, it seems to have been reasonable to some extent to maintain the rule of reserving one seat per prefecture, and therefore it cannot be deemed to have become contrary to the constitutional requirement of equality in the value of votes. We can affirm this judgment from the viewpoints shown above. The same applies to similar determinations indicated in the aforementioned judgments of the Grand Bench of the Supreme Court of November 10, 1999, relating to the general elections held in 1996 and 2000, respectively, as well as in 2001 (Gyo-Tsu) No 223, the judgment of the Third Petty Bench of the Supreme Court of December 18, 2001, Minshu Vol 55, No 7, at 1647. On the other hand, when the Election was held, more than ten years had passed since the first general election held in 1996 following the introduction of the Election System. During this period, through the procedure prescribed in the Act for Establishment of the Demarcation Council, revision of constituencies took place in 2002 based on the results of the population census conducted in 2000, and then in light of the results of the population census conducted in 2005, review was considered but it was decided not to make a revision of constituencies, and accordingly, a general election was held twice based on the aforementioned revised constituencies. In view of these circumstances, we can evaluate that the Election System was established and put into stable operation, and we should say that the rule of reserving one seat per prefecture was no longer reasonable as described above. In addition, as mentioned in 2(5), the maximum disparity between constituencies in terms of the value of votes that existed at that time based on the Demarcation of Constituencies reached 1:2.304, and the number of constituencies with the ratio being 1:2 or larger has increased. The rule of reserving one seat per prefecture has been the major factor causing such a disparity between constituencies in terms of the value of votes, or to put it another way, unreasonableness of said rule has come to the surface in the form of the disparity in the value of votes. Then, we should say that the part of the Criteria for Demarcation which pertains to the rule of reserving one seat per prefecture, at the time of the Election at the latest, was no longer reasonable as it had been at the time of legislation but incompatible with equality in the value of votes, and by that time, said part itself had become contrary to the constitutional requirement of equality in the value of votes. Because the Demarcation of Constituencies was established based on the Criteria for Demarcation, including the rule of reserving one seat per prefecture, which were in the aforementioned state at the time of the Election, it had also become contrary to the constitutional requirement of equality in the value of votes by that time.

However, the aforementioned judgment of the Grand Bench of the Supreme Court of June 13, 2007, found that neither the Criteria for Demarcation, including the rule of reserving one seat per prefecture, nor the Demarcation of Constituencies, by the time of the general election held in 2005, had become contrary to the constitutional requirement of equality in the value of votes as described above. Considering this, we cannot conclude that no correction had been made within a reasonable period of time as required by the Constitution only because, by the time when the Election was held, the rule of reserving one seat per prefecture, which is included in the Criteria for Demarcation, had not been abolished, nor had the Provisions on Demarcation, premised on this rule, been corrected.

. . . According to the reasoning shown above, the part of the Criteria for Demarcation under the Provisions on Criteria for Demarcation, which pertains to the rule of reserving one seat per prefecture, by the time of the Election, had become contrary to the constitutional requirement of equality in the value of votes, and the Demarcation of Constituencies under the Provisions on Demarcation as revised according to said criteria, by that time, had also become contrary to the constitutional requirement of equality in the value of votes; yet, it cannot be said that no correction had been made to either of them within a reasonable period of time as required by the Constitution, and in conclusion, the Provisions on Criteria for Demarcation and the Provisions on Demarcation cannot be found to be in violation of Article 14, paragraph (1) or other provisions of the Constitution.

An election system that can properly reflect the will of the people is the foundation of democracy. In the rapidly changing society, it is not an easy task to realize such an election system, while meeting the constitutional requirement of equality in the value of votes, and in order to perform that task properly, the legislature is vested with a broad discretion. However, the rule of reserving one seat per prefecture is regarded as being reasonable only for a limited period of time, in the situation where it was adopted upon the first drastic post-war reform of the election system for members of the House of Representatives. Viewed away from such situation, said rule should inevitably be judged to be incompatible with the constitutional requirement of equality in the value of votes. The House of Representatives, in light of its power, the term of office of its members, the existence of the rule of its dissolution, and other features, is required to always reflect the will of the people properly, and it is subject to a more severe requirement in respect of equality in the value of votes in elections of its members. Consequently, within a reasonable period of time as required for correction depending on the nature of the respective problems, legislative measures must be taken to meet the requirement of equality in the value of votes, such as abolishing, as quickly as possible, the rule of reserving one seat per prefecture, which is included in the Criteria for Demarcation, and revising the Provisions on Demarcation in line with the purport of Article 3, paragraph (1) of the Act for Establishment of the Demarcation Council.

National Assembly Election Redistricting Plan Case
2000Hun-Ma92, 25 Oct 2001 (Constitutional Court, South Korea)

Facts

There were two complaints in the case. The first was brought by residents in an electoral district with a population of 331,458, arguing that the weight of their vote was seriously diluted compared to that of another district with a population of only 90,656. The second complaint concerned the merger of electoral districts that were geographically 20 km apart. The petitioners argued that there was no solidarity between the two districts and that it was very difficult to convey their political opinions to the residents of the other district. As such, the redistricting plan infringed their right to pursue happiness, the right to equality and the right to vote.

Held

[A] wide scope of legislative discretion is recognized in creating the National Assembly Election Redistricting Plan. The legislature can take into consideration not only the population disparity, but also administrative districts, geography of particular area, traffic, living sphere, sense of historical or traditional solidarity, or any other policy or technical factors when realigning the electoral districts . . .

The total number of National Assembly seats, or the size of the legislature, is also a factor to be considered in rezoning the electoral districts . . .

But, a wide scope of legislative discretion in constituency rezoning does not mean that the redistricting of electoral districts is free from constitutional control. In other words, the constitutional principle of equal election limits legislative discretion in such matters. First, the equality in the value of each vote is the most important and basic factor in constituency rezoning. Accordingly, unreasonable redrawing of electoral districts, violating the constitutional mandate of equal weight of votes, is arbitrary, and hence, is unconstitutional. In this light, there is an inherent limit to legislative discretion in readjusting the electoral constituencies . . .

Second, gerrymandering is not within the constitutional limits of legislative discretion, and is unconstitutional. Gerrymandering refers to an intentional discrimination of electors in a particular region through arbitrary division of electoral districts. It would be gerrymandering if electors in a particular electoral district lose opportunities to participate in political affairs, because of an arbitrary division of electoral districts, or if a district is redrawn to prevent the election of a candidate supported by electors from a particular region . . .

In suggesting the permissible limit on population disparity, the Court could employ either the population of the smallest electoral district or the average population of electoral districts as a basis of comparison . . .

Next, the Court needs to decide whether to use different standards in reviewing the constitutionality of population disparities in urban electoral districts and rural electoral districts . . . However, because it is not easy to distinguish an urban electoral district from a rural electoral district, such classification would be either improper or unnecessary. Therefore, the Court will not distinguish between an urban electoral district from a rural electoral district when reviewing the instant case. However, the existing difference between population in urban and rural areas resulting from the concentration of population to urban areas should be taken into consideration when formulating the permissible maximum deviation of population in an electoral district . . .

Population disparity in electoral constituencies is not a problem limited only to Korea, and over the years, the standards used to review the constitutionality of population disparities have become more exacting in countries around the world . . .

Population remains the most important factor in redistricting constituencies, but secondary factors other than population have to be taken into consideration as well. To set limits on legislative discretion in constituency rezoning, or more specifically, to suggest constitutionally permissible limits on population disparity in electoral districts, is a problem of easing the strict application of the principle of equality in the value of each vote by considering factors other than population . . .

Under such circumstance, it would not be difficult to predict that there would arise many problems if the Court adopted the $33^1/_3\%$ criterion. It has only been 5 years since the Court first deliberated on the problem of population disparity in electoral districts, and a too idealistic of an approach disregarding practical limits would be imprudent. Therefore, the Court will review the instant case using the 50% criterion . . .

When revising the Election Redistricting Plan for the 16th National Assembly Election, the legislature decided to set the minimum population of an electoral district at 90,000. Under such a guideline, Kangwha-Kun did not have enough population to form an independent electoral district, and it still would not meet the minimum population requirement if Kangwha-Kun was combined with Ongjin-Kun to form an electoral district. Thus, the legislature decided to separate a part of Incheon Seo-Ku, which is closer to Kangwha-Kun than Incheon Kyeyang-Ku, and combine it with Kangwha-Kun to form an independent electoral district. The reason the legislature chose to separate Kumdan-Dong was because Kumdan-Dong, being located in the north part of Incheon Seo-Ku, was relatively close to Kangwha-Kun, and because it would be easier to meet the minimum population requirement to add Kumdan-Dong, the most populated of all administrative districts in Seo-Ku, to Kangwha-Kun. Such constituency rezoning by the legislature is not against the Court's decision in the 96Hun-Ma54 case. Also, since population of Kumdan-Dong is about 43% of total population of Incheon Seo-Ku and Kangwha-Kun B Electoral District, it would be difficult to say Kumdan-Dong was incorporated into Kangwha-Kun. When all factors are considered, it cannot be concluded that the legislators arbitrarily realigned the electoral districts with an intention to discriminate against the people of Kumdan-Dong. Thus, the Incheon Seo-Ku and Kangwha-Kun B Electoral District part of the instant Election Redistricting Plan does not violate the complainants' right to vote or right to equality, and hence, is constitutional.

Robert v Tobias Jr v Hon City Mayor Benjamin S Abalos
GR No L-114783, 8 Dec 1994 (Supreme Court, Philippines)

Facts

The petitioners, invoking their rights as taxpayers and residents of Mandaluyong, assailed the constitutionality of Republic Act No 7675, which divided the municipalities of

Mandaluyong and San Juan into separate congressional districts. They argued that the division of the two municipalities into separate congressional districts would result in an increase in the composition of the House of Representatives, which would violate Article VI, Section 5(1) of the Constitution which vested legislative power in Congress, except to the extent reserved to the people by the provision on initiative and referendum. The petitioners also argued that the law resulted in gerrymandering by dividing the two districts.

Bidin J

The said Act enjoys the presumption of having passed through the regular congressional processes including due consideration by the members of Congress of the minimum requirements for the establishment of separate legislative districts. At any rate, it is not required that all laws emanating from the legislature must contain all relevant data considered by Congress in the enactment of said laws.

As to the contention that the assailed law violates the present limit on the number of representatives as set forth in the Constitution, a reading of the applicable provision, Article VI, Section 5(1), as aforequoted, shows that the present limit of 250 members is not absolute. The Constitution clearly provides that the House of Representatives shall be composed of not more than 250 members, 'unless otherwise provided by law.' The inescapable import of the latter clause is that the present composition of Congress may be increased, if Congress itself so mandates through a legislative enactment. Therefore, the increase in congressional representation mandated by RA No 7675 is not unconstitutional

. . .

Similarly, petitioners' additional argument that the subject law has resulted in 'gerrymandering', which is the practice of creating legislative districts to favor a particular candidate or party, is not worth of credence. As correctly observed by the Solicitor General, it should be noted that Rep Ronaldo Zamora, the author of the assailed law, is the incumbent representative of the former San Juan/Mandaluyong district, having consistently won in both localities. By dividing San Juan/Mandaluyong, Rep Zamora's constituency has in fact be[en] diminished, which development could hardly be considered as favorable to him.

Bagabuyo v COMELEC
GR No 176970, 8 Dec 2008 (Supreme Court, Philippines)

Facts

According to the Republic Act No 9371, the legislative district of Cagayan de Oro was divided into two. COMELEC (Commission on Elections) issued a resolution to implement the Act. The petitioner argued that both the Act and the resolution were unconstitutional without a plebiscite, which was indispensable for the division of a local government unit, and thus prayed for an order directing the ceasing of the Act and the resolution, and re-establishing a single legislative district of Cagayan de Oro.

Brion J

The Legislature undertakes the apportionment and reapportionment of legislative districts, and likewise acts on local government units by setting the standards for their creation, division, merger, abolition and alteration of boundaries and by actually creating, dividing, merging, abolishing local government units and altering their boundaries through legislation. Other than this, not much commonality exists between the two provisions since they are inherently different although they interface and relate with one another . . .

As above stated, the aim of legislative apportionment is 'to equalize population and voting power among districts.' Hence, emphasis is given to the number of people represented; the uniform and progressive ratio to be observed among the representative districts; and accessibility and commonality of interests in terms of each district being, as far as practicable, continuous, compact and adjacent territory . . .

In contrast with the equal representation objective of Article VI, Section 5, Article X, Section 10 expressly speaks of how local government units may be 'created, divided, merged, abolished, or its boundary substantially altered.' Its concern is the commencement, the termination, and the modification of local government units' corporate existence and territorial coverage; and it speaks of two specific standards that must be observed in implementing this concern, namely, the criteria established in the local government code and the approval by a majority of the votes cast in a plebiscite in the political units directly affected . . .

A pronounced distinction between Article VI, Section 5 and, Article X, Section 10 is on the requirement of a plebiscite. The Constitution and the Local Government Code expressly require a plebiscite to carry out any creation, division, merger, abolition or alteration of boundary of a local government unit. In contrast, no plebiscite requirement exists under the apportionment or reapportionment provision.

J & K National Panthers Party v The Union of India & Ors
[2010] INSC 937 (Supreme Court, India)

Facts

Jammu and Kashmir National Panthers Party, a political party in the State of Jammu and Kashmir, filed this suit seeking to impugn the judgment of the Jammu and Kashmir High Court dated 2 June 2009. The Supreme Court was called upon to decide whether the Government, in postponing the delimitation of territorial constituencies until the relevant census figures were published after 2026, was acting constitutionally. The appellant argued that the postponement of the delimitation of constituencies caused an imbalance in the composition of various constituencies, and if the demographical changes could not be reflected in the composition of constituencies, the nature of democracy would be eroded.

Ganguly J

This position has been again reiterated in para 126 in Poudyal's case in the following words: 'An examination of the constitutional scheme would indicate that the concept of "one person one vote" is in its very nature considerably tolerant of imbalances and departures from a very strict application and enforcement. The provision in the Constitution indicating proportionality of representation is necessarily a broad, general and logical principle but not intended to be expressed with arithmetical precision . . . The principle of mathematical proportionality of representation is not a declared basic requirement in each and every part of the territory of India. Accommodations and adjustments, having regard to the political maturity, awareness and degree of political development in different parts of India, might supply the justification for even non-elected Assemblies wholly or in part, in certain parts of the country. The differing degrees of political development and maturity of various parts of the country, may not justify standards based on mathematical accuracy.'

. . . In the matter of delimitation of constituencies, it often happens that the population of one constituency differs from that of the other constituency and as a result although both the constituencies elect one member, the value of the vote of the elector in the constituency having lesser population is more than the value of the vote of the elector of the constituency having a larger population . . .

[W]e are of the opinion that a right [to cast a vote] is a valuable right but to demand any uniform value of one's voting right through the process of delimitation, disregarding the statutory and constitutional dispensation based on historical reasons is not a justiciable right . . .

It is, therefore, clear that there is an express constitutional bar to any challenge being made to the delimitation law which is made under Constitutional provisions. Therefore, the substantial challenge of the appellant in this proceeding is not to be entertained by any Court, including this Court.

Notes and Questions

1. The Supreme Court of Japan, in the *Case to Seek Invalidation of Election* on 23 March 2011, was critical of 'the disparity between constituencies in terms of the value of votes with the ratio being 1:2 or larger', thus urging the Diet to undertake reform as soon as possible. On 17 October 2012, the Court ruled again that the vote disparity of 1:5 in the 2010 House of Councillors Election represented a significantly unequal state that questioned the legitimacy of the election while falling short of nullification (see 'Top court says vote disparity unconstitutional', available at <http://www.houseofjapan.com/local/top-court-says-vote-disparity-unconstitutional>). These recent decisions are not the first time the Court has expressed concerns with vote–value disparity. As early as 1976, the Court had ruled that a disparity of 1:5 so gravely violated 'the constitutional [requirement] for equality in the right to vote' as to justify the nullification of the impugned election.[25] In 1996, the Court again found the disparity ratio of 1:6 as unconstitutional and advised legislative reform.[26] Similarly, in South Korea, in the *National Assembly Election Redistricting Plan Case* of 2001, the Constitutional Court decided to use the 50 per cent criterion (1:2) to review the vote–value disparity instead of the 33.3 per cent criterion (1:3) it had used in a decision rendered in 1995.[27]

2. What ratio of vote disparity would you consider reasonable from the standpoint of liberal democracy? Given the unattainability of mathematical precision, is it possible to develop a formula across jurisdictions? In what manner might the conception of atomic individuals in liberal democracy provide an answer to the question?

---

[25] See *Kurokawa v Chiba Prefecture Election Commission*, 30 Minshū 223, 30 Apr 1976.
[26] See *Case on Election Invalidity*, 1994 (Gyo-Tsu) No 59, 11 Sep 1996.
[27] See *Excessive Electoral District Population Disparity* Case, 95Hun-Ma224, 27 Dec 1995.

3. The disparity of vote value is usually a complex function of technical and political factors. In Japan, the disparity is largely due to the rule of reserving one seat per prefecture. In Korea, the Constitutional Court, in the *National Assembly Election Redistricting Plan Case*, stated that aside from the population, the legislature can take into consideration other reasonable factors such as 'administrative districts, geography of particular area, traffic, living sphere, sense of historical or traditional solidarity, or any other policy or technical factors when realigning the electoral districts'. In *Bagabuyo v COMELEC*, the Supreme Court of the Philippines accepted that accessibility and commonality of interests in each district may be taken into account. The Supreme Court of India, in *J & K National Panthers Party v The Union of India & Ors*, stressed that the concept of 'one person one vote' is tolerant of imbalances, and that accommodations and adjustments, having regard to the political maturity, awareness and degree of political development in different parts of India, may be justifications.

4. Do you think that taking considerations other than population into account is consistent with the premise of liberal democracy in terms of electoral design? Why should administrative unity, a sense of historical or traditional solidarity, or even political maturity be considered? Given the prioritisation of individual preferences within liberal democracies as compared to illiberal/communitarian democracies, in what ways may complex electoral designs reflect a mix of liberal and communitarian elements?

5. Given the complex nature of electoral apportionment or reapportionment, should courts afford some degree of latitude to legislative decisions? Notably, in the seminal US reapportionment case of *Baker v Carr*,[28] the Supreme Court, in supporting a strong judicial role in preserving political equality, rejected the applicability of the political questions doctrine in electoral decisions on the constitutional ground of 'one person one vote'.

6. The Supreme Courts of both India and the Philippines accord a great deal of deference to legislative apportionment. While the Supreme Court of Japan condemned the disparity of vote value in several decisions, it rarely invalidated any election as a result of such disparity. In Taiwan, a constitutional amendment was passed in 2005, reducing the number of legislative members from 225 to 113, while preserving one seat per county and city. As a result, extreme vote–value disparities occurred in the election of January 2008. However, when minority legislative members challenged the constitutionality of the impugned constitutional amendment, the Constitutional Court dismissed the case on the ground that the legislature should have sought to revise the provisions first. What explains the judicial deference to legislative apportionment or reapportionment? Is it due to varying conceptions of democracy, or to the complex nature of the right to vote as both an individual right and a collective right? For discussion of the nature of the right to vote, see VD Amar and A Brownstein, 'The Hybrid Nature of Political Rights' (1998) 50 *Stanford Law Review* 915.

---

[28] *Baker v Carr* 369 US 186 (1962).

D. Functional or Sectoral Representation

Hong Kong's functional representatives in its Legislative Council are a legacy of the elite appointment process under British colonial rule. This functional constituency was created in 1985 as part of political negotiations between the British and Chinese Governments during the transition before the handover.[29] The Basic Law of Hong Kong stipulates the method for constituting the Legislative Council and its procedure for voting in Annex II. The current fifth Legislative Council has 70 members, with 35 members elected by geographical constituencies through direct elections and 35 members by functional constituencies.[30] Under the new arrangements for the election of the Legislative Council, there are five super functional constituency seats representing all 18 districts and voted in by all resident voters of Hong Kong.[31] In addition, three members are from labour and nine other groups such as law, accounting, medical, tourism, business, finance, information technologies and engineering.[32]

Similar functional representation can be found in Singapore's Parliament. The Constitution of Singapore provides that the Members of the Parliament include elected members, non-constituency members and nominated members.[33] Elected members can represent either Single Member Constituencies or Group Representation Constituencies (GRCs). In GRCs, political parties compete in teams of between four and six candidates, at least one of whom must be a member from an ethnic minority. This requirement ensures that the contests in GRCs are multi-racial, and that minority races have their own representative in the Parliament. In addition, the Constitution also provides that up to nine non-constituency members may be appointed from among the best-performing defeated opposition candidates.[34] In 1990, the Constitution was amended to allow for the appointment of up to nine Nominated Members of the Parliament (NMPs) to ensure wide representation of community views.[35] These are 'persons who have rendered distinguished public service, or who have brought honour to the Republic, or who have distinguished themselves in the field of arts and letters, culture, the sciences, business, industry, the professions, social or community service or the labour movement'. They are appointed by the President for a term of two-and-a-half years on the recommendation of a Special Select Committee, chaired by the Speaker, who must ensure that those appointed 'reflect as wide a range of independent and non-partisan views as possible'.[36] Singapore's NMPs represent groups like busi-

---

[29] LF Goodstadt, 'Business Friendly and Politically Convenient – the Historical Role of Functional Constituencies' in C Loh (ed), *Functional Constituencies: A Unique Feature of the Hong Kong Legislative Council* (Hong Kong: Hong Kong University Press, 2006) 41.

[30] On 28 August 2010, the standing Committee of the Eleventh National People's Congress in China at its Sixteenth Session approved that the amendment to Annex II to Basic Law of the Hong Kong Special Administrative Region of People's of China Concerning the Method for the Formation of the Legislative Council of Hong Kong Special Administrative Region. See PY Lo, *The Hong Kong Basic Law* (Hong Kong: LexisNexis, 2011) 878, 890.

[31] Art 3.3 of ch 3 of Guidelines on Election-related Activities in respect of the Legislative Council Election, available at <http://www.eac.gov.hk/pdf/legco/2012lc_guide/en/chapter_3.pdf>.

[32] Ibid.

[33] Art 39(1), Constitution of the Republic of Singapore.

[34] Art 39(1b), Constitution of the Republic of Singapore.

[35] Art 39(1b), Constitution of the Republic of Singapore.

[36] Sec 3(2), Fourth Schedule, Constitution of the Republic of Singapore.

ness and industry; the professions; media, arts and sports; social service organisations; the labour movement; tertiary institutions; and the civil sector.

In functional constituencies, some classes of voters are more privileged than others in their political representation. For example, in Hong Kong, those who belong to the functional constituencies of law, medicine and business, among others, are given one more vote than those who do not. In Singapore, the appointment of non-constituency members and nominated members distorts equal political representation of the general public. The varying degrees of distortion give rise to doubts about the constitutionality of these functional arrangements. The following case from the Court of Final Appeal in Hong Kong illustrates this debate.

Chan Yu Nam & Anor v the Secretary for Justice
[2010] 1 HKC 4937 (Court of First Instance, Hong Kong)

Facts

The applicants, a taxi driver and a renovation worker, were not entitled to cast a vote at any elections for the functional constituency. They argued that Article 26 of the Basic Law and Article 21(b) of the Hong Kong Bill of Rights gave permanent residents equal rights to vote, and because corporations were not natural persons and would never be permanent residents of Hong Kong, they should not have the right to vote. It was therefore unconstitutional for corporations to be allowed to vote in elections for the functional constituencies of the Legislative Council.

Held

According to the evidence, the functional constituencies have evolved over the years 'as a means of enabling, for example, important sectors in Hong Kong's industrial and commercial activities and also its leading professionals to be appropriately represented in the [Legislative Council]'. Functional constituencies had [their] origin in the replacement of the system of appointment of unofficial members of the Legislative Council . . .

Functional constituencies came into being as a more systematic way of representing the various functional constituencies' interests in the Legislative Council. In turn, those interests represented, at least in terms of political theory, people's common interests in the society. Elections for functional constituencies were developed as a formal representative system to replace the previous informal system of selecting members from a wide range of functional constituencies under the appointment system.

That being the case, corporate voting is not surprising at all. In many of the functional constituencies or the economic or social interests that they represent, the key players and stakeholders are corporate bodies. It is simply natural, therefore, for corporate bodies, alongside with, or as opposed to, individuals, to be given the right to vote in the relevant elections. That has been the case from day one . . .

Viewed in that historical context, up to the time when the Basic Law was promulgated, Hong Kong had never had any elections for seats in the Legislative Council which only involved voting by permanent residents of Hong Kong (or by individuals who could satisfy a minimum residence or some other form of connection requirement). Up to that point of time, corporate voting had always been an intrinsic part of Legislative Council elections . . .

Article 26 gives the right to vote 'in accordance with law'. 'Law' in this context must include the Basic Law . . .

It must be remembered that the companies are made constituents of a functional constituency because of their interests and contributions in the constituency. The system of elections for functional constituencies seeks to give these companies a say in returning members to the Legislative Council. The say is intended to be given to the companies . . .

[T]he legislative intent of the National People's Congress, when enacting the Basic Law (including article 39), must have been to allow corporate voting to continue in elections for functional constituencies after the establishment of the Hong Kong Special Administrative Region, just as it had always been the case up to 1990 . . .

According to the evidence, election of members through functional constituencies is to enable important social, economic, occupational and other sectors in Hong Kong to be represented in the Legislative Council, and for their sectoral interests to be properly taken into account when bills or motions in the Legislative Council are debated. Its purpose, according to the evidence, is to help to maintain stability and prosperity and facilitate the development of the capitalist economy in Hong Kong. To serve this purpose, members in functional constituencies are returned through voting by the key players and stakeholders in the respective sectors. These key players and stakeholders are identified having regard to the significance of the persons or bodies in the sector. Understandably, in some sectors, the key players and stakeholders often take the form of well-established corporations. It is quite plain that the purpose of enabling the particular interests of these sectors to be represented will be defeated if all individuals who are in any way connected to these sectors are given a right to vote . . .

The mere fact that an individual has the ability to form a company therefore does not automatically give that individual the right to vote in a functional constituency through that company. In functional constituencies whose electorate consists of representative bodies, a body must assume certain degree of importance in the sector in order to qualify. For functional constituencies whose electorate is defined by reference to umbrella organisations, there is no evidence that umbrella organisations would accept any company to be a member . . .

The two applications for judicial review are dismissed.

Notes and Questions

1. The Court of Final Appeal in Hong Kong considered that functional constituencies present 'a more systematic way of representing the various interests in the Legislative Council'. How would you evaluate this assertion along the lines of liberal/illiberal/communitarian conceptions of democracy?

2. Notwithstanding the decision in *Chan Yu Nam v the Secretary for Justice*, many proposals to reform the Legislative Council have been made. One proposal is to abolish corporate voting and to give partners or the managing staff of corporations the right to vote. See SNM Young and A Law, 'Privileged to Vote: Inequalities and Anomalies of the FC System' in C Loh (ed), *Functional Constituencies: A Unique Feature of the Hong Kong Legislative Council* (Hong Kong: Hong Kong University Press, 2006) at 93–94. Another proposal is to reorganise functional constituencies to include more mixed ranges of constituencies. Under this scheme, each constituency would have two legislators, except for the labour constituency which would have three seats. See C Loh, 'Functional Constituencies: The Way Forward' in C Loh (ed), *Functional Constituencies: A Unique Feature of the Hong Kong Legislative Council* (Hong Kong: Hong Kong University Press, 2006) 333–35.

3. The GRC in Singapore was introduced in 1988 to ensure that minorities are permanently represented in Parliament. Under this scheme, at least one member of a team of between four and six members, must belong to a stipulated minority group. However, critics of the scheme saw this as a method to entrench the dominance of the ruling People's Action Party (PAP), given the difficulties of opposition parties in assembling such teams, and especially in securing minority candidates. Most seats in Singapore's 90-seat Parliament are drawn from GRC wards. Prior to the 2011 General Election, Prime Minister Lee Hsien Loong proposed raising the number of Single Member Constituencies (SMCs) from nine to 12, and requiring a minimum of eight seats from SMCs. This was effected before the elections. Between 1988 (when the scheme was introduced) till 2006, the PAP won all GRC wards. However, it lost its monopoly on GRCs in the 2011 General Elections when it lost the five-member Aljunied GRC to the Worker's Party. What may have once have been a method of entrenching political power (many GRCs going uncontested in previous elections) in the past has now demonstrated its theoretical neutrality. The trend appears to be towards the full contestation of all GRC wards by opposition parties, as Singapore's polity seeks ever more alternative voices in Parliament. For discussion of these changes and the impact on the election, see KYL Tan, 'Legal and Constitutional Issues' in KYL Tan and T Lee (ed), *Voting in Change: Politics of Singapore's 2011 General Election* (Singapore: Ethos Books, 2011) 50, 53–54. For an in-depth analysis of the GRC scheme and how it was used to implement non-constitutional objectives relating to PAP renewal, limited town council devolution and community governance, see Thio Li-ann, 'The Right to Political Participation in Singapore: Tailor-Making a Westminster-Modelled Constitution to fit the Imperatives of "Asian" Democracy' (2002) 6 *Singapore Journal of International & Comparative Law* 181.

E. Proportional Representation and Anti-hopping Laws

Proportional representation (PR) is an electoral scheme that seeks to ensure representation of minority interests. In a PR system, voters usually choose from political parties rather than individual candidates. Representatives to the legislature are then selected by the political parties in proportion to the number of votes won at the election. Concerns that the PR system may contravene the idea of political equality or the principle of direct election and the role of political parties are discussed below.

i. Proportional Representation

In recent decades, PR has gained popularity in Asian jurisdictions. In Japan, it was first adopted in the House of Councillors' election in the early 1980s, and then by the House of Representatives in the mid-1990s.[37] Many new democracies – such as South Korea, Taiwan and the Philippines – also adopted proportional systems of representation.

---

[37] Jiunn-rong Yeh and Wen-Chen Chang, 'The Emergence of East Asian Constitutionalism: Features in Comparison' (2010) 59 *American Journal of Comparative Law* 805, 820–21.

The PR system usually runs alongside an electoral system based on the size of the population or geographical districts. For example, in Taiwan, the Constitution sets aside 34 seats (out of 113) to be elected from the lists of political parties in proportion to the number of votes won by political parties obtaining at least five per cent of the total vote.[38] In the Philippines, the Constitution stipulates that the House of Representatives shall be composed of no more than 250 members, 20 per cent of whom are elected from the party-list representatives.[39] In Japan, the party-list representatives occupy half the parliamentary seats. Similarly, the Thai Constitution of 2007 stipulates that the election of 80 out of 480 members of the House of Representatives on a PR basis shall be conducted by reference to party-lists prepared by political parties, and for this purpose, a voter in any constituency shall have the right to cast only one vote for a political party that has prepared a list of candidates for that constituency.[40]

Variations of PR may also exist in terms of an open or closed list of candidates submitted by political parties, providing voters with one vote or two votes, and the option of limiting the number of political parties that may contest through PR. In a closed-list PR system, such as that in Taiwan, voters can vote only for political parties that decide the list of candidates. In an open-list system, such as that in Japan, voters can still cast votes for candidates who appear on the list prepared by the political parties, and voter preferences will affect the order by which the listed candidates are selected. In mixed systems of district elections and PR, some jurisdictions like Japan and Taiwan provide voters with two votes: one vote for candidates in district elections and the other vote for the PR elections. However, other voters in district elections in countries like South Korea have only one vote, and the PR among political parties is allocated according to the number of votes those parties win in district elections. Nearly all jurisdictions set limits on the number of political parties that may have seats distributed to them through PR: mostly by the percentage of votes – such as two per cent or five per cent – political parties win in the election. Worthy of note is the Philippines, where, unlike other PR systems, the seats set aside for PR in the Parliament (20 per cent) are to be distributed only among political parties of the 'marginalised and underrepresented'.

Given these variations, the abiding principle in all systems of PR is that political parties rather than individual voters exert the most influence over the selection of party-list representatives to sit in the legislative body. Is this consistent with the concept of democracy, or is this an undue intervention with individual voting rights, particularly where voters may not identify with or support existing political parties? In what ways and to what extent does the power of political parties to select the list of candidates whence legislators will be chosen make politics more inclusive? The next two cases highlight how controversies arose in the operation of PR systems in Japan and South Korea. The two Filipino cases that follow concern the meaning of 'marginalised and underrepresented' for the purposes of PR; and whether a political party made up of lesbians, gays, bisexuals and transgendered individuals could be barred on grounds of 'immorality'.

---

[38] Art 4(1)(2), Additional Articles to the Constitution of the Republic of China (Taiwan).
[39] Art VI, sec 5. Constitution of the Philippines.
[40] Arts 93 & 95, Constitution of the Kingdom of Thailand, 2007.

Case Seeking Nullification of an Election
58 Minshū 1 (Supreme Court, Japan)

Facts

In this appeal, it was argued that the provisions regarding the method of electing PR members of the House of Councillors (HC) in the Public Offices Election Law violated the Constitution, and that the election of the HC on 29 July 2001 was null and void.

Held

[I]t is clearly within the Diet's discretion, in light of the fact that political parties play such an important role in the national administration, to adopt a list-based proportional representation system that is designed to reflect the people's political intentions in the administration of the nation via political parties, as an election system to be used for HC elections. As a list-based proportional representation system does not allow voting without choosing a political party, it is inappropriate to go so far as to regard the Open-List Proportional Representation System as infringing the right to vote and violating Article 15 of the Constitution on the ground that, under this system, voters are not allowed to realize their intention to cast a vote for a particular person on the House of Councillors List without also casting a vote for the political party or group which has submitted the list and to which the person belongs. In addition, under a list-based proportional representation system, persons on the List are regarded as candidates who belong to particular political parties or groups. Therefore, it is not unreasonable that the Amended Public Offices Election Law stipulates that votes cast for a particular person on the List shall be counted as votes won by the political party or group which has submitted the List and to which the person belongs, and this cannot be regarded as going beyond the bounds of the Diet's discretion.

One may argue that it is problematic that, under the Open-List Proportional Representation System, even when a member elected under the proportional representation system resigns office or breaks away from the political party or group to which the member belongs, the number of votes won by the member will not be deducted from the number of votes won by the party or group, and therefore the number of successful candidates assigned to the party or group will not be reduced. In such cases, however, if the number of votes won by the member is deducted from the number of votes won by the political party or group to which the member belongs, thereby determining anew the number of successful candidates, it would require overly complicated procedures. Furthermore, if the resignation of a member elected under the proportional representation system or breaking away from the party to which the member belongs causes invalidation of successful election results of other candidates who belong to the same party or group, it might be criticized as diverging from voters' intentions. As mentioned above, it is reasonable to regard votes cast for a particular person on the List as having been cast for the political party or group which has submitted the List and to which the person belongs. For this reason, even if a successful candidate resigns as a member elected under the proportional representation system or breaks away from the party to which the candidate belongs, it is not immediately unreasonable that the effect of votes cast for such candidate remains, and therefore, the Open-List Proportional Representation System cannot be regarded as going beyond the bounds of the Diet's discretion because of this . . .

This election system is to determine successful candidates based on the voting results, or voters' collective opinions, and in this respect, it is by no means different from an election system in which voters cast votes directly for individual candidates. In the case where two or more persons on the same political party's or group's List have won the same number of votes, the ranking for being chosen as successful candidates between them shall be determined by lot by the Chief Electoral Officer. However, even in such case, the determination of successful candidates does not depend on the intention of persons other than voters. For this reason, an election under the Open-List Proportional Representation System cannot be regarded as not falling under the category of direct election and therefore it cannot be deemed to be in violation of Article 43(1) . . .

However, as mentioned in 2(2) above, the Open-List Proportional Representation System has been introduced in order to solve problems found in the fixed-list proportional representation system which was applied before the Amendment, in response to criticisms that profiles of individual candidates were not sufficiently focused on in election campaigns and voters' voting decision, the fixed-list system particularly strengthened the power of political parties in the House of Councillors Election Law, and the process of determining the ranking of the persons on the list was difficult to understand, as well as to allow voters to cast votes for particular persons on the List while maintaining a party-oriented election system. This legislative purpose cannot be regarded as unjust and the Open-List Proportional Representation System cannot be regarded as unreasonable in light of the legislative purpose, and therefore the introduction of this system cannot be regarded as going beyond the bounds of the Diet's discretion.

One-Person One-Vote Case
2000Hun-Ma91, 19 Jul 2001 (Constitutional Court, South Korea)

Facts

The complainants alleged that Articles 146(2) and 189(1) of the Public Election Act were unconstitutional. Article 146(2) provided that one person should be entitled to one vote in the electoral district and did not allow a separate vote for the party nominees of proportional representatives. However, a vote for an independent candidate in the electoral district only counted for the member of district election, and had no value in the allocation of seats for proportional representatives. Article 189(1) stipulated that the allocation of seats for proportional representatives would be proportional to the sum of votes obtained by all candidates of a particular political party in the district elections, assuming that the voter's choice would be in accordance with his or her support for a particular political party. The complainants argued that these provisions violated their constitutional right to equality, to vote and to be elected into public office, as well as the principle of direct election.

Held

Article 146(2) and Article 189(1) are closely related. Combined, the statutory provisions allow only one vote for the election of a district lawmaker and do not allow a separate vote for a political party of one's choice. With such statutory provisions in place, the current election system assumes that the voter's choice of a candidate in the electoral district is the same as his or her support for a particular political party. The question is whether such provisions are in accordance with the principle of democracy, the principle of direct election, and the principle of equality in public elections.

The proportional representation system refers to an election system where parliamentary seats are allocated to political parties in proportion to voters' support for a particular party or its nominees . . .

When implemented properly, the proportional representation system can be used to produce representatives of various social groups, positively promote party politics, and prevent political monopoly by fostering competition among the political parties . . .

. . . [W]hen the proportional representation system requiring submission of a slate of party nominees is implemented, the election should also accurately reflect people's support for a particular political party, and allocation of seats for proportional representatives to a specific party should correspond to people's support and preference for that party.

However, the present system of allocation of seats for proportional representatives in the National Assembly under Article 189(1) of the Public Election Act combined with the one-person one-vote system actively distorts the public support for a particular party.

When an elector supports either a candidate in one's electoral district or a political party, but not both, half of the message in the elector's ballot is not conveyed whether the elector votes for one's favorite candidate or for the political party of one's choice. The present election system even distorts the honest political opinion of electors. When an elector casts a ballot for one's favorite candidate, this is counted toward the party that nominated the candidate in allocating the seats of the proportional representatives in the National Assembly even if the elector does not support the party which nominated the candidate, and this would contribute to allocation of seats for proportional representatives to be directly against the elector's choice. On the other hand, when an elector casts a ballot for a party of one's choice, the vote would contribute to the election of a candidate that the elector may not support, and this does not accurately reflect the elector's choice for the candidate.

Moreover, the distribution of parliamentary seats under the current election system cannot accurately reflect the people's support for a newly formed political party, and the existing major parties may be assigned more proportional representative seats than actual support they receive from the people. Generally, a nominee of a newly formed party is in a relative disadvantage compared to a nominee of an existing major party, in terms of candidate recognition, party organization, and resources . . .

The current election system, which assumes that the voter's choice of a candidate in the electoral district is the same as his or her support for a particular political party and does not allow a separate vote for the slate of party nominees for the seats of the proportional representatives, is contrary to the principle of direct election . . .

Under the present election system adopting the allocation of seats for proportional representatives in the National Assembly, when an elector votes for a party nominee in the electoral district, his or her vote contributes to the election of a lawmaker from the electoral district, and to the allocation of seats for proportional representatives. On the other hand, when an elector votes for an independent in the electoral district, his or her vote only contributes to the election of a lawmaker from the electoral district, and the vote has no value in the allocation of seats for proportional representatives.

Hence, there arises inequality in the value of a vote. One has to endure such inequality if it is a result of his or her choice – under an election system where separate votes are allowed for individual candidates and the party, an elector may choose to vote for an independent, and not cast a ballot expressing one's support for a political party. On the other hand, when a person votes for an independent because the party of one's choice has not nominated a candidate, the elector is forced to suffer against his or her will inequality in the value of one's vote . . .

In this light, the present election system discriminates against voters who support independent candidates from voters who support party nominees, without a reasonable basis, and it violates the principle of equality in election.

Article 189(1) of the Public Election Act states that the seats of the proportional representatives in the National Assembly will be allocated to the Party which has obtained five or more seats in the general election for the National Assembly or upward of 5/100 of the total valid votes, and that one seat of the proportional representative is to be allocated to each political party which has obtained more than 3/100 and fewer than 5/100 of the total valid votes in the general election. Such statutory provision setting forth a limit for allocation of seats for proportional representatives is called the 'blockade clause.' . . .

Whether the blockade clause is necessary or legally justified is a matter to be decided with due consideration to the present state of political affairs in a particular country . . .

A political system limiting parliamentary participation of a political party which obtained a number of votes less than the minimum required votes must be based on the premise that the election outcome accurately reflects people's support for particular political parties. The present election system, allocating seats for proportional representatives, while only allowing one vote per voter, is unable to accurately reflect people's support for a particular party, and in some cases, it even actively distorts the amount of support that each party receives . . . Because the present election system employs an unreasonable yardstick to assess people's support for a particular political party, the blockade clause is in violation of the principle of equal election, no matter what the minimum required number of votes is.

Ang Bagong Bayani-OFW Labor Party v Commission on Elections
GR No 147589, 26 Jun 2001 (Supreme Court, Philippines)

Facts

The Petitioner filed two petitions to challenge Omnibus Resolution No 3785 issued by the Commission on Elections (COMELEC) on 26 Mar 2001. The two petitions were also approved by 154 organisations and parties who participated in the 2001 party-list elections. They argued that the party-list system was designed to benefit the 'marginalized and underrepresented' and not mainstream political parties, and requested the Court to disqualify the private respondents.

Panganiban J

The foregoing provision mandates a state policy of promoting proportional representation by means of the Filipino-style party-list system, which will 'enable' the election to the House of Representatives of Filipino citizens,

1. who belong to marginalized and underrepresented sectors, organizations and parties; and
2. who lack well-defined constituencies; but
3. who could contribute to the formulation and enactment of appropriate legislation that will benefit the nation as a whole . . .

'Proportional representation' here does not refer to the number of people in a particular district, because the party-list election is national in scope. Neither does it allude to numerical strength in a distressed or oppressed group. Rather, it refers to the representation of the 'marginalized and underrepresented' as exemplified by the enumeration in Section 5 of the law; namely, 'labor, peasant, fisherfolk, urban poor, indigenous cultural communities, elderly, handicapped, women, youth, veterans, overseas workers, and professionals.'

However, it is not enough for the candidate to claim representation of the marginalized and underrepresented, because representation is easy to claim and to feign. The party-list organization or party must factually and truly represent the marginalized and underrepresented constituencies mentioned in Section 5. Concurrently, the persons nominated by the party-list candidate-organization must be 'Filipino citizens belonging to marginalized and underrepresented sectors, organizations and parties.' ...

In the end, the role of the COMELEC is to see to it that only those Filipinos who are 'marginalized and underrepresented' become members of Congress under the party-list system, Filipino-style ...

While the enumeration of marginalized and underrepresented sectors is not exclusive, it demonstrates the clear intent of the law that not all sectors can be represented under the party-list system. It is a fundamental principle of statutory construction that words employed in a statute are interpreted in connection with, and their meaning is ascertained by reference to, the words and the phrases with which they are associated or related. Thus, the meaning of a term in a statute may be limited, qualified or specialized by those in immediate association ...

This Court, therefore, cannot allow the party-list system to be sullied and prostituted by those who are neither marginalized nor underrepresented. It cannot let that flicker of hope be snuffed out. The clear state policy must permeate every discussion of the qualification of political parties and other organizations under the party-list system ...

From its assailed Omnibus Resolution, it is manifest that the COMELEC failed to appreciate fully the clear policy of the law and the Constitution. On the contrary, it seems to have ignored the facet of the party-list system discussed above ...

The linchpin of this case is the clear and plain policy of the law: 'to enable Filipino citizens belonging to marginalized and underrepresented sectors, organizations and parties, and who lack well-defined political constituencies but who could contribute to the formulation and enactment of appropriate legislation that will benefit the nation as a whole, to become members of the House of Representatives.' ...

Clearly, therefore, the Court cannot accept the submissions of the COMELEC and the other respondents that the party-list system is, without any qualification, open to all. Such position does not only weaken the electoral chances of the marginalized and underrepresented; it also prejudices them. It would gut the substance of the party-list system. Instead of generating hope, it would create a mirage. Instead of enabling the marginalized, it would further weaken them and aggravate their marginalization.

Ang Ladlad LGBT Party v Commission on Elections
GR No 190582, 8 Apr 2010 (Supreme Court, Philippines)

Facts

The Commission on Elections (COMELEC) disqualified the Ang Ladlad LGBT Party – which is made up of lesbians, gays, bisexuals or transgendered individuals – from running in the 2007 general election on the ground that it did not have nationwide membership. On 11 November 2009, the COMELEC again refused Ang Ladlad LGBT's petition for permission to run in the 2010 elections, on grounds of 'immorality'. The petitioner argued that the Party represented a marginalised and under-represented sector because of their sexual orientation and gender identity, and that they were victims of exclusion, discrimination and violence due to negative societal attitudes. After the COMELEC denied its motion for reconsideration, Ang Ladlad LGBT filed this suit, arguing that the COMELEC violated the Constitution on various grounds.

Del Castillo J

The COMELEC denied Ang Ladlad's application for registration on the ground that the LGBT sector is neither enumerated in the Constitution and RA 7941, nor is it associated with or related to any of the sectors in the enumeration . . .

Nonetheless, we find that there has been no misrepresentation. A cursory perusal of Ang Ladlad's initial petition shows that it never claimed to exist in each province of the Philippines. Rather, petitioner alleged that the LGBT community in the Philippines was estimated to constitute at least 670,000 persons; that it had 16,100 affiliates and members around the country, and 4,044 members in its electronic discussion group. Ang Ladlad also represented itself to be 'a national LGBT umbrella organization with affiliates around the Philippines composed of the following LGBT networks . . .

. . . [W]e find that Ang Ladlad has sufficiently demonstrated its compliance with the legal requirements for accreditation. Indeed, aside from COMELEC's moral objection and the belated allegation of non-existence, nowhere in the records has the respondent ever found/ruled that Ang Ladlad is not qualified to register as a party-list organization under any of the requisites under RA 7941 or the guidelines in Ang Bagong Bayani. The difference, COMELEC claims, lies in Ang Ladlad's morality, or lack thereof . . .

We are not blind to the fact that, through the years, homosexual conduct, and perhaps homosexuals themselves, have borne the brunt of societal disapproval. It is not difficult to imagine the reasons behind this censure – religious beliefs, convictions about the preservation of marriage, family, and procreation, even dislike or distrust of homosexuals themselves and their perceived lifestyle. Nonetheless, we recall that the Philippines has not seen fit to criminalize homosexual conduct. Evidently, therefore, these 'generally accepted public morals' have not been convincingly transplanted into the realm of law . . .

As such, we hold that moral disapproval, without more, is not a sufficient governmental interest to justify exclusion of homosexuals from participation in the party-list system. The denial of Ang Ladlad's registration on purely moral grounds amounts more to a statement of dislike and disapproval of homosexuals, rather than a tool to further any substantial public interest . . .

The COMELEC's differentiation, and its unsubstantiated claim that Ang Ladlad cannot contribute to the formulation of legislation that would benefit the nation, furthers no legitimate state interest other than disapproval of or dislike for a disfavored group.

From the standpoint of the political process, the lesbian, gay, bisexual, and transgender have the same interest in participating in the party-list system on the same basis as other political parties similarly situated. State intrusion in this case is equally burdensome. Hence, laws of general application should apply with equal force to LGBTs, and they deserve to participate in the party-list system on the same basis as other marginalized and underrepresented sectors . . .

We do not doubt that a number of our citizens may believe that homosexual conduct is distasteful, offensive, or even defiant. They are entitled to hold and express that view. On the other hand, LGBTs and their supporters, in all likelihood, believe with equal fervor that relationships between individuals of the same sex are morally equivalent to heterosexual relationships. They, too, are entitled to hold and express that view . . .

As a final note, we cannot help but observe that the social issues presented by this case are emotionally charged, societal attitudes are in flux, even the psychiatric and religious communities are divided in opinion. This Court's role is not to impose its own view of acceptable behavior. Rather, it is to apply the Constitution and laws as best as it can, uninfluenced by public opinion, and confident in the knowledge that our democracy is resilient enough to withstand vigorous debate.

Notes and Questions

1. Notwithstanding challenges to the PR system on the basis of the equal right to vote, courts have been reluctant to adjudge such systems invalid. Is this because the choice of an electoral system is usually stipulated in the constitution, or is it because by its nature, such a choice is better made by political institutions?

2. The Indonesian Constitutional Court was deferential towards the legislative choice of adopting a PR system. In the case of *Judicial Review on Regulation No 12 year 2003 concerning General Election of House of Representatives*, the Constitutional Court held that:

   > The Legislators are free to determine the substance of a law, except for matters expressly laid down by the Constitution, . . . includ[ing] the principles of a direct, public, free, secret, honest and fair election, periodization (every five years), objective of election (electing DPR and DPRD members), election participants (political parties), and election organizer (KPU). The election system, whether majority pluralistic (district), semi proportional or proportional, with their variations; electoral districts, whether based on administrative territory/region or not; and other technical matters shall be delegated to the Legislators. In the Law on the General Election of DPR, DPD and DPRD Members, the Legislators have chosen the proportional system with an open candidate list for the election of DPR and DPRD members.[41]

   Similarly in Japan, the electoral system for the House of Representatives was reformed from a medium-sized district-based system to a mix of a small single district system and PR in 1993. When faced with a challenge on the constitutionality of the new system, the Supreme Court in *Claim for the Invalidity of an Election* held it constitutional, applying the reasonableness test and holding that the reform would be deemed unconstitutional only if it could never be regarded as reasonable.[42]

3. Proportional representation systems usually establish a threshold on the percentage of votes a political party must obtain to be allocated seats in parliament. In Taiwan the threshold is five per cent, while in the Philippines it is two per cent. What do you think is a reasonable percentage? Should courts make such an assessment, and if so, what criteria might they use? The Supreme Court of the Philippines, in *Veteran Federation Party v Commission on Elections*, held:

   > The two percent threshold is consistent not only with the intent of the framers of the Constitution and the law, but with the very essence of 'representation.' Under a republican or representative state, all government authority emanates from the people, but is exercised by representatives chosen by them. But to have meaningful representation,

---

[41] *Judicial Review on Regulation No 12 year 2003 concerning General Election of House of Representatives*, 002/PUU-II/2004.

[42] *Claim for the Invalidity of an Election*, 1999 (Gyo-Tsu) No 8, 10 Nov 1999.

the elected persons must have the mandate of a sufficient number of people. Otherwise, in a legislature that features the party-list system, the result might be the proliferation of small groups which are incapable of contributing significant legislation, and which might even pose a threat to the stability of Congress. Thus, even legislative districts are apportioned according to 'the number of their respective inhabitants, and on the basis of a uniform and progressive ratio' to ensure meaningful local representation.[43]

ii. Anti-hopping Laws

Political parties play an important role in determining the success of a scheme of electoral representation, especially in PR. Party-list candidates are submitted by political parties, such that, apart from voting, voters exercise little influence, especially in relation to a closed-list system. An issue that has arisen is whether a party-list representative who loses his/her party membership should be able to continue to serve as a representative in the parliament? In Asian jurisdictions that have adopted PR, few constitutions address this issue directly, preferring to leave it to the courts. Article 106 of the Thai Constitution states that the membership of the House of Representatives terminates when a member resigns from his political party or where his political party is dissolved by a Constitutional Court order. Likewise, Singapore's Constitution provides that a member of Parliament loses his seat if 'he ceases to be a member of, or is expelled or resigns from, the political party for which he stood in the election'.[44] In Taiwan, no such provision exists, and the Constitutional Court was called upon to decide if a party-list representative who lost his party membership would lose his seat as well. The Constitutional Court of South Korea was faced with a similar case in 1994. Both these cases are excerpted below.

JY Interpretation No 331
30 Dec 1993 (Constitutional Court, Taiwan)

Facts

In May 1992, the Control Yuan, a functional equivalent to the ombudsman, requested the Constitutional Court to decide whether Article 69(2) of the Public Officials Election and Recall Act, governing the recall procedure, applied to representatives elected based upon the party-list.

Held

Articles 1, 2 and 4 of the Amendment to the Constitution introduced the system of party-list proportional representation for the election of congressmen who represent overseas Chinese and the National Sector. The legislative intent of such Articles is to ensure that a certain portion of congressmen, while they are exercising the power conferred, do not yield to the will of regional voters in particular precincts, so that they may learn the genuine will of the people as a whole and preserve national interests; in addition, said Articles also are meant to prompt political parties to nominate the most talented, virtuous and reputable members to be said congressmen within the quota proportionate to total ballots won in a

---

[43] *Veteran Federation Party v Commission on Elections*, GR No 136781, 6 Oct 2000.
[44] Art 46(2)(b), Constitution of the Republic of Singapore.

particular election and allocated to each party, so that such congressmen may serve their country. Nonetheless, if any of said congressmen should lose his membership in the political party from which he is elected, it is certain that he will also be deprived of his eligibility for the position in the Congress, since the legal foundation of his election is forfeited. Only then can the constitutional intent of introducing such a system be met.

National Seat Succession Case
92Hun-Ma153, 28 Apr 1994 (Constitutional Court, South Korea)

Facts

A representative from national (proportional) seats left his party, and the party requested the National Election Commission to transfer his seat to a successor within the political party. The Commission refused, citing lack of legal grounds to unseat the representative. The political party initiated a constitutional complaint before the Constitutional Court, questioning the constitutionality of the Commission's decision.

Held

Whether or not a member from national seats defecting from his party leaves his seat vacant depends on the legal relationship between the assemblypersons who are people's representatives and the people who elect them. Article 7(1) of the Constitution states public officials shall be servants of the entire people and shall be responsible to the people. Article 45 also states no member of the National Assembly shall be held responsible outside the National Assembly for the opinions officially expressed, or the votes cast, in the Assembly.

Article 46(2) states members of the National Assembly shall give the first priority to national interests and shall perform their duties in accordance with their conscience. All these provisions, taken together, put assemblypersons on their own discretion pursuant to the principle of free mandate and, therefore, their membership is not affected by their defection from a party that nominated them to their seats.

Kim Yang-Kyun (dissenting)

According to the constitutional principle of free mandate, members from regional seats do not, even by operation of law, lose their seats upon defecting from their parties. Members from national seats, on the other hand, should lose their seats in consideration of the practical implications of the principle of people's sovereignty, right to vote, right to hold public offices, the constitutional protection of political parties, and the system of electing national seats in proportion to the number of each party's regional seats. If there is no legal mechanism bringing about that effect, the National Assembly is violating its legislative duty under the Constitution and should discharge its duty of protection through appropriate laws.

Notes and Questions

1. Compare the decisions of the Taiwanese and South Korean courts, paying special attention to the dissenting opinion of Justice Kim Yang-Kyun. Does a party-list representative obtain his mandate from the people or his party? In what way does

the mandate of a party-list representative depart from that of a representative standing in district-based elections? What might explain the difference with respect to the Taiwanese and South Korean judicial decisions?

2.   Anti-hopping laws may also be made in the attempt to strengthen political party discipline and cohesion in the legislature. For instance, in Singapore, the anti-hopping law is used to restrict the capacity of political party members to change political parties once elected, so that political party leaders can ensure that their members toe the party line in voting on key constitutional and legislative votes over the course of a parliamentary term. However, a similar legislative measure was held unconstitutional by the Supreme Court of Malaysia in *Nordin bin Salleh v The Kelantan State Assembly*, on the ground of the right to free association. According to the Court:

> In this case the Kelantan Constitution – a state law – by art XXXIA, seeks to impose a restriction on the fundamental right of a member of the legislature to form associations, which of course includes the right to dissociate, and it operates by way of disqualification, once the member exercises that right.
>
> It is, in our view, inconceivable that a member of the legislature can be penalized by any ordinary legislation for exercising a fundamental right which the Constitution expressly confers upon him subject to such restrictions as only Parliament may impose and that too on specified grounds, and on no other grounds.[45]

3.   The absence of anti-hopping laws makes it easy for members of parliament to 'cross the floor' without worrying about losing their seats. This is a legacy of the British tradition, where 'crossing the floor' is a fairly common practice. Winston Churchill famously crossed the floor from the Conservative Party to join the Liberals in 1904, and crossed the floor again in 1924 to rejoin his old party. When a government's majority in Parliament is wafer thin, the crossing of the floor could mean the collapse of the government and a change of Prime Ministers. This happened dramatically in Singapore in 1961, when a radical faction of the ruling People's Action Party (PAP), comprising 13 Assemblymen, broke away to form a new opposition party, the Barisan Sosialis. Overnight, the PAP's majority fell from 43 out of 51 to 30 out of 51. The Government teetered on the brink of collapse when more MPs defected to the Barisan camp and two PAP MPs died. At one point the PAP held only 25 seats in the House but remained the Government. It was after the PAP won a resounding victory in the 1963 general election following the preventive detention of many leaders of the Barisan Sosialis that the Constitution was amended, so that any Member crossing the floor would cease to be a Member of the House.

4.   In more recent times, a constitutional crisis was precipitated in the Malaysian State of Perak with a series of floor-crossings. Perak had, since 2008, been ruled by the Pakatan Rakyat party (Pakatan), which had 32 members in the Legislative Assembly, just five more seats than its main rival, the Barisan Nasional (BN). In February 2009, three members of Pakatan declared that they intended to resign from their party and sit as independents, and that in confidence motions, they would support BN. This effectively reduced the Pakatan's membership to 29, and

---

[45] *Nordin bin Salleh v The Kelantan State Assembly* [1992] 1 MLJ 697, para 4.

although it did not increase BN's membership, it did increase the number of votes it could count on in confidence motions – 30. Having now the command of 30 votes, the head of Perak BN, Najib Abdul Razak (who was also Malaysia's Prime Minister), sought an audience with Perak's Sultan Azlan Shah to inform him that BN now had the support of the majority of the Assembly and that he should appoint a Chief Minister from within the ranks of BN instead of Pakatan. In the meantime, the incumbent Chief Minister, Nizar Jamaluddin – anxious to renew his mandate with the voting public – requested the Sultan to dissolve the Assembly so that fresh elections could be held. The Sultan refused, instead proceeding to declare the post of Chief Minister vacant – effectively firing Nizar – and appointing Zambry Abdul Kadir of the BN as Chief Minister. This action was controversial, not least because Sultan Azlan Shah had, when he was Lord President (Malaysia's highest judicial officer), admonished rulers to dissolve the legislature if requested to do so by the Chief Minister or Prime Minister. A series of cases were filed, challenging the constitutionality of the Sultan's action, but the Federal Court ultimately upheld the Sultan's action. See generally, A Quay (ed), *Perak: A State of Crisis – Rants, Reviews and Reflections on the Overthrow of Democracy and the Rule of Law in Malaysia* (Petaling Jaya: Loyar Burok Publications, 2011).

F. Quotas

Reserving quotas by allocating parliamentary seats for certain minority groups based on race or gender is the most direct way of ensuring diverse political representation. A number of Asian constitutions contain such quotas. For example, quotas for female representatives are secured in Pakistan, Bangladesh and Taiwan, while quotas for particular tribes have long been implemented in India.

The 1947 ROC Constitution implemented in Taiwan was among the first Asian constitutions to stipulate quotas for women in electoral politics. Article 134 of the Constitution states that in various kinds of elections, the number of women to be elected shall be fixed, with these measures to be prescribed by law. The 2005 constitutional revision altered the electoral system for Parliament, but not the provisions relating to PR. The number of elected female members on each party's list must not be less than one-half of the total number. Article 51 of the Pakistan Constitution states that 60 of the 342 seats in the Parliament (17.5 per cent) are reserved for women. In Bangladesh, the Constitution reserves 50 seats exclusively for women members within the context of the PR scheme.[46]

In India, Article 330 of the Constitution prescribes that seats shall be reserved in the House of the People for:

(a) the Scheduled Castes;
(b) the Scheduled Tribes, except those in the autonomous districts of Assam; and
(c) the Scheduled Tribes in the autonomous districts of Assam.

---

[46] Art 65, Constitution of Bangladesh.

The number of seats reserved in any State or Union territory for the Scheduled Castes or the Scheduled Tribes shall bear the same proportion to the total number of seats allotted to that State or Union territory in the House of the People.

Does the preservation of quotas for certain minority groups violate the principle of 'one person, one vote'? In what ways does the system of quotas better reflect political inclusiveness or the idea of communitarian democracy, or aid in overcoming gender stereotypes? Are quotas likely to become a ceiling for women or minority representation in the parliament, and is this a risk worth taking? How should courts handle such issues, taking into consideration the socio-political context? These issues were canvassed in the following two cases.

Dr Ahmed Hossain v Bangladesh
21 CLC (AD) 109 (Supreme Court, Bangladesh)

Facts

The Petitioner challenged the Constitution (Tenth Amendment) Act of 1990, which provided that 30 seats should be reserved exclusively for women members elected according to law. He argued that after the period for reservation of 30 seats expired on 16 December 1987, no extension could be made. In addition, he also contended that the impugned Act violated Article 121 (single electoral roll for each constituency) and Article 122(1) (elections to Parliament based on adult franchise) of the Constitution.

MH Rahman J

Clause (3) of Article 65 was never deleted. It remained in the Constitution. The substitution of the earlier clause (3) by the new one cannot be challenged as ultra vires . . .

The Constitution on the date of its commencement provided for two different Ends of elections. Three hundred members of the Parliament are to be elected in accordance with law from single territorial constituency by direct election. Members for seats reserved exclusively for women are to be elected by the members of the Parliament, according to law . . .

We find no conflict between the impugned amendment and Articles 121 and 122(1) of the Constitution . . .

A system of indirect election cannot be called undemocratic. It is provided in the Constitution itself. The amendment is not also violative of Article 28. Clause (4) in Article 28 provides that nothing in that Article shall prevent the State, which expression includes Parliament, from making special provision in favour of women. We find no merit in this petition and, accordingly, it is dismissed.

Union of India v Rakesh Kumar and Ors
[2010] AIR SC 3244 (Supreme Court, India)

Facts

Article 244 of the Constitution of India explicitly states that the provisions of the Fifth Schedule shall apply in respect of the administration and control of the Scheduled Areas in any State other than the States of Assam, Meghalaya, Tripura and Mizoram. The provisions of the Sixth Schedule guide the administration of tribal areas in those States to protect the interest of Scheduled Tribes. Under the provisions of Constitution, the Government of India enacted several special laws to guarantee the autonomy of the Scheduled Tribes.

Several petitions challenged the constitutionality of the second proviso to Section 4(g) of Panchayats Extension to the Scheduled Areas Act of 1996 (PESA) and Section 21(B), Section 40(B) and Section 55(B) of Jharkhand Panchayati Raj Act of 2001 (JPRA) because they preserved all chairperson positions of Panchayats in the Scheduled Tribes. Another issue was whether it was constitutionally permissible to provide reservations in favour of Scheduled Castes (SC), Scheduled Tribes (ST) and Other Backward Classes (OBC) that together amount to 80 per cent of the seats in the Panchayati Raj Institutions.

KG Balakrishnan J

We must make it abundantly clear that this pattern of reservation has been designed only for Scheduled Areas which merit such exceptional treatment. In the present case, it should be noted that the Scheduled Areas under consideration are restricted only to certain Districts in the State of Jharkhand. In some Districts where STs are not predominantly in occupation, only certain blocks have been notified as Scheduled Areas by themselves. On account of migration of non-tribal people in some areas, there may be a relatively lesser proportion of tribal population but historically these areas were occupied almost exclusively by Tribal people . . .

We hold that in Panchayats located in Scheduled Areas, the exclusive representation of Scheduled Tribes in the Chairperson positions of the same bodies is constitutionally permissible. This is so because Article 243-M(4)(b) expressly empowers Parliament to provide for 'exceptions and modifications' in the application of Part IX to Scheduled Areas. The provisos to Section 4(g) of the PESA contemplate certain exceptions to the norm of 'proportionate representation' and the same exceptional treatment was incorporated in the impugned provisions of the JPRA . . .

It may be noted that under Article 243-D there is a clear mandate for the State Legislature to reserve seats for SCs and STs in every panchayat and the number of seats so reserved shall bear, as nearly as may be, the same proportion to the total number of seats to be filled by direct election in that Panchayat as the population of the SCs or of the STs in that Panchayat area bears to the total population of the area under consideration . . .

When examining the validity of affirmative action measures, the enquiry should be governed by the standard of proportionality rather than the standard of 'strict scrutiny'. Of course, these affirmative action measures should be periodically reviewed and various measures are modified or adapted from time to time in keeping with the changing social and economic conditions. Reservation of seats in Panchayats is one such affirmative action measure enabled by Part IX of the Constitution . . .

We believe that the case of Panchayats in Scheduled Areas is a fit case that warrants exceptional treatment with regard to reservations. The rationale behind imposing an upper ceiling of 50% in reservations for higher education and public employment cannot be readily extended to the domain of political representation at the Panchayat-level in Scheduled Areas . . . Especially in the context of Scheduled Areas, there is a compelling need to safeguard the interests of tribal communities with immediate effect by giving them an effective voice in local self-government . . .

By reserving at least half of the seats in panchayats located in Scheduled Areas in favour of STs, the legislature has adopted a standard of compensatory discrimination which goes beyond the ordinary standards of 'adequate representation' and 'proportionate representation'. The standard of 'adequate representation' comes into play when it is found that a particular community is under-represented in a certain domain and a specific threshold is provided in order to ensure that the beneficiary group comes to be adequately represented with the passage of time . . .

There is of course a rational basis for departing from the norms of 'adequate representation' as well as 'proportionate representation' in the present case. This was necessary because it was found that even in the areas where Scheduled Tribes are in a relative majority, they are under-represented in the government machinery and hence vulnerable to exploitation. Even in areas where persons belonging to Scheduled Tribes held public positions, it is a distinct possibility that the non-tribal population will come to dominate the affairs. The relatively weaker position of the Scheduled Tribes is also manifested through problems such as land-grabbing by non-tribals, displacement on account of private as well as governmental developmental activities and the destruction of environmental resources. In order to tackle such social realities, the legislature thought it fit to depart from the norm of 'proportional representation'. In this sense, it is not our job to second-guess such policy-choices . . .

. . . [T]he legislative intent behind the impugned provisions of the JPRA is primarily that of safeguarding the interests of persons belonging to the Scheduled Tribes category. In light of the preceding discussion, it is our considered view that total reservations exceeding 50% of the seats in Panchayats located in Scheduled Areas are permissible on account of the exceptional treatment mandated under Article 243-M(4)(b).

Notes and Questions

1. In *Dr Ahmed Hossain v Bangladesh*, Judge Rahman states that 'a system of indirect election cannot be called undemocratic'. What conception of democracy does he have in mind?

2. Women or gender quotas have generally been regarded as an effective means to secure sex/gender equality and – more generally – parity democracy, in which women are coequal partners of democracy. It is intriguing that gender quotas entered the constitutional scheme earlier in Asia than in the West. A few constitutions enacted after World War II already stipulated quotas to enhance the political representation of women. However, in the West, gender quotas were mostly developed in the mid-1990s, through legislation and constitutional litigation, influenced in part by CEDAW and related international movements.

3. For further comparative discussions on gender quotas in Asia and beyond, see R Rubio-Marin and Wen-Chen Chang, 'Sites of Constitutional Struggle for Women's Equality' in M Tushnet, T Fleiner and C Saunders (eds), *Routledge Handbook of Constitutional Law* (New York: Routledge, 2012) 301–12; and SM Rai, 'Reserved Seats in South Asia: A Regional Perspective' in J Ballington and A Karam, *Women in Parliament: Beyond Numbers* (Stockholm: International Institute for Democracy and Electoral Assistance, 2005) at 174–76.

4. In India, political quotas reserved for Scheduled Castes or Tribes were implemented to enhance their political representation. This was an attempt to combat the legacy of colonial stratification and subordination. It also reflected a constitutional commitment to substantive equality as explicitly recognised by Articles 15(4) and 16(4) of the Constitution. For further discussions related to the concept

of equality, see chapter 7 of this book. For discussions on the history and culture of Scheduled Castes or Tribes, see M Galanter, *Law and Society in Modern India* (New York: Oxford University Press, 1989) at 185–207.

III. INSTITUTIONS FOR POLITICAL REPRESENTATION

A crucial element for the functioning of open and free elections is competition among political parties, the medium through which citizens form their political opinions and participate in electoral politics. This section discusses these institutions, which are crucial for democracy: first, in relation to the formation and dissolution of political parties; secondly, elections; and, lastly, on election commissions as impartial guardians with respect to the conduct of elections.

A. Political Parties and Militant Democracy

Political parties are the vital link between the state and civil society, mediating government and private interests within society.[47] Throughout history, political parties have played crucial functions in the development of modern states and constitutions. In the first half of the twentieth century, political parties – nationalist, fascist or communist – all tried to monopolise state power with attempts at reconstructing state and society in particular ways. In Asia, a number of 'nationalist' political parties in countries like Japan, China and India, became very popular and were perceived as the main vehicle for constructing national unity and driving colonial rulers out of the homeland.[48]

As many states in Asia become liberal democracies, political parties must also be of a liberal democratic nature. Karl Loewenstein in 1937 advised all democracies 'to become militant' by developing legal techniques against the threats of fascism, such as enacting anti-extremist legislation that 'applies the ban indiscriminately to all political groupings which fall under the general category of a subversive party, an unlawful association, or an organization inimical to the state'.[49] Many modern constitutions now have safeguards built in to ensure that a polity is safeguarded from political parties espousing illiberal or non-democratic visions for that polity. This raises the question of 'militant democracy' and its legality, that is, whether a constitutional democracy may act in an anti-democratic manner to combat threats to its own existence. For example, Article 21(2) of the German Basic Law stipulates that 'parties which, by reason of their aims or the behavior of their adherents, seek to impair or abolish the free democratic basic order or to endanger the existence of the state are unconstitutional'. The power of adjudicating that a political party is unconstitutional is usually vested with the Constitutional Court (see chapter five).

---

[47] A Heywood, *Politics* (New York: Palgrave, 2002) at 247.
[48] R Hague and & M Harrop, *Political Science: A Comparative Introduction* (New York: Palgrave Macmillan, 2010) at 203.
[49] K Loewenstein, 'Militant Democracy and Fundamental Rights, I' (1937) 31(3) *The American Political Science Review* 417, 430; K Loewenstein, 'Militant Democracy and Fundamental Rights, II' (1937) 31(4) *The American Political Science Review* 638, 647.

A few Asian jurisdictions, for example South Korea, Taiwan, Thailand and Indonesia, include provisions regarding political parties in their respective constitutions. For instance, Article 8 of the Constitution of South Korea provides that 'the establishment of political parties is free, and the plural party system is guaranteed'. However, political parties must be democratic in their objectives, organisation and activities, and have the necessary organisational arrangements for the people to participate in the formation of the political will. As long as political parties maintain a democratic nature, they enjoy the protection of the State.

i. Formation of Political Parties

Forming political parties is an exercise of the rights both to political participation and to free association. The formation of political parties requires prior approval in most jurisdictions, and the statutory requirements usually embody elements of 'militant democracy', demanding that political parties observe liberal democratic values and be of a liberal democratic nature in their purpose, organisation and activities. A requirement of note is that a few jurisdictions require national or federal political parties to have members or branches across various regions. As the following cases illustrate, courts usually hold these requirements to a standard of reasonableness.

Registration Requirement of Political Parties
2004Hun-Ma246, 30 Mar 2006 (Constitutional Court, South Korea)

Facts

Article 25 of the Political Parties Act provides that all political parties, for registration, should have at least five city or provincial branches, and Article 27 of the same Act stipulates that each city or provincial branch shall have at least 1,000 party members. The Socialist Party, as a small party having difficulty meeting all these requirements, filed a constitutional complaint arguing that the said provisions violated the freedom of party formation guaranteed by Article 8 of the Constitution.

Held

Article 25 of the Instant Provisions aims to exclude 'regional parties' and Article 27 aims to exclude 'minor parties.' Exclusion of minor parties is a legitimate legislative purpose because proper functioning of representative democracy under our Constitution requires a stable majority within the legislature. Also, exclusion of regional parties representing the political wills of only certain regions cannot be said to be an illegitimate purpose under the Constitution when party politics depending excessively on regional affiliation has become problematic in our political reality. Therefore, the Instant Provisions have a requisite legitimate purpose.

The Instant Provisions require for party registration two constants, namely, 5 or more city or provincial branches and each city or provincial branch having more than 1,000 party members, for the purpose of excluding regional parties and minor parties. These regulations prevent the parties from being organized only from certain areas, and require city and provincial organizations in at least five cities or provinces, in each of which at least a certain number of members are active. Therefore, these regulations are appropriate means to suppress election-related entities and minor regional political organizations from indiscriminately participating in party politics. The Instant Provisions also concretize the requirement in Article 8 Section 2 of the Constitution concerning 'the organization necessary for participating in people's political will-formation' in the form of the minimum 5 city or provincial branches and the minimum 1,000 members for each of the branches. The legislator's decision that at least 5 city or provincial branches are required for fulfilling faithfully the functions and position of a national party is not irrational. Also, the requirement of at least 1,000 members for each city or provincial branch is not excessive even for minor or newly formed parties such as Petitioners in light of the size of the populations of the cities and provinces of our country.

The Instant Provisions do restrict people's freedom of party formation with the requirements of 5 or more city or provincial branches and 1,000 or more party members for each of the branches. However, these restrictions are reasonable restrictions materializing the constitutional concept of a political party through which people shall participate in political will-formation 'for a substantial time' in substantial areas.' These restrictions are constitutionally justified.

Dr Mohd Nasir bin Hashim v Menteri Dalam Negeri
[2006] 6 MLJ 213 (Court of Appeal, Malaysia)

Facts

The appellant and 12 other people formed the Parti Sosialis Malaysia (PSM) on 15 February 1998. They organised a committee of seven and made an application to the Registrar of Societies (ROS) to register themselves as a political society at the national level. The ROS rejected their application because they did not meet the conditions set by section 7 of the Societies Act 1966, but they could still register as a party in the State of Selangor. The appellant was dissatisfied with the result and complained to the respondent, the Minister for Home Affairs. However, the complaint was dismissed. The appellant thus appealed to the Court of Appeal.

Gopal Sri Ram JCA

The real question that appears to have been missed by learned counsel for the appellant is this. Is the departmental policy formulated by the ROS for himself when considering applications to register political societies at the national level an unreasonable administrative act? In my judgment this is the true question because the first limb of art 8(1) of the Constitution demands fairness of any form of State action . . .

It is axiomatic that a statutory power or discretion is exercised unfairly if it is exercised unreasonably and without due consideration.

To answer the question posed a moment ago, it is my judgment that the departmental policy requiring a political party's committee to comprise of representatives from at least 7 States of the Federation where registration is sought at the national level is not an unreasonable exercise of the statutory power conferred upon the ROS by s 7(1) of the Act. Since Malaysia has 13 States the ROS probably had in mind that a political party seeking registration at the national level must seek to represent 50% plus one State in the Federation. There is nothing unreasonable about this. Some policy is necessary to guide the discretion conferred by s 7. Otherwise it may become an unprincipled discretion . . .

The general rule is that anyone who has to exercise a statutory discretion must not 'shut [his] ears to the application' (to quote from Bankes LJ). I do not think that there is any great difference between a policy and a rule. There may be cases where an officer or authority ought to listen to a substantial argument reasonably presented urging a change of policy. What the authority must not do is to refuse to listen at all. But a Ministry or large authority may have had to deal already with a multitude of similar applications and then they will almost certainly have evolved a policy so precise that it could well be called a rule. There can be no objection to that provided the authority is always willing to listen to anyone with something new to say – of course I do not mean to say that there need be an oral hearing. In the present case the Minister's officers have carefully considered all that the appellants have had to say and I have no doubt that they will continue to do so.' . . .

. . . Here the ROS formulated a policy which, as I have already said, is not unreasonable in an objective sense. It may well have been different if the ROS and the Minister had required a person from every State in the Federation to be in PSM's committee. But that is not what happened. Like British Oxygen and Sagnata, here too, the ROS and the Minister provided the appellant an opportunity to make representations as to why the policy should not be applied to PSM. The evidence shows that the appellant and other pro-tem committee members met with officials of the ROS and that written representations were also made. So this is not the kind of case which Lord Reid had in mind in British Oxygen or which the Master of the Rolls had in Sagnata. There was no shutting of the ears in this case. The ROS acted fairly and reasonably at all times.

Political Party Registrar's application for an order to dissolve Patiroop Party
Ruling 2/2542, 4 Mar 1999 (Constitutional Court, Thailand)

Facts

Section 29 of the Organic Act on Political Parties stipulated that the political party, for registration, had to prepare to have no fewer than 5,000 members, comprising those from each Region, and at least one branch in each Region. Section 65 of the same Act provided that a political party – if failing to comply with section 29 – had to be dissolved. Although the Patiroop Party and its members met with section 29, it had not established any branch in the region. As a result, the political party registrar filed an application to the Constitutional Court to dissolve the Patiroop Party.

Held

[T]he political party registrar submitted the application to the Constitutional Court for an order to dissolve Patiroop Party, because such Party failed to comply with section 29 of the Organic Act on Political Parties, BE 2541 (1998) which provided that 'Within one hundred and eighty days from the date the registrar has acknowledged the establishment of a political party, such political party shall prepare to have not less than five thousand members, which shall comprise those from each Region according to the list of Regions and Changwats notified by the registrar and shall have at least one branch of the political party in each Region.' Section 92 of the Organic Act on Political Parties, BE 2541 (1998) provided that 'A political party registered under the Act on Political Parties, BE 2524 (1981) shall be a political party under this Organic Act. In the case where such political party has not complied with section 29, it shall completely comply with it within one hundred and eighty days from the date this Organic Act comes into force.' Section 94 paragraph one provided that 'In the case where a political party under section 92 failed to completely comply with section 29, such political party shall be dissolved under section 65 and the Registrar shall comply with section 65 paragraph two.' The facts as stated in the application made by the political party registrar and the response statement made by Patiroop Party revealed that a cause under section 65 paragraph one subparagraph (5) of the Organic Act on Political Parties, BE 2541 (1998) occurred to Patiroop Party pursuant to the application of the political party registrar, by which the Constitutional Court could order the dissolution of that Party.

ii. Dissolution of Political Parties

The constitutional courts of South Korea, Taiwan, Thailand and Indonesia may dissolve political parties if their objectives, organisation or activities are found to be in violation of the constitution and inconsistent with democratic values. In Thailand, political parties may also be dissolved on legal grounds as prescribed by the Organic Act on Political Parties. Thus far, there has been no case on the dissolution of political parties in South Korea or Taiwan, in sharp contrast with the decisions of the Thai Constitutional Court. In other jurisdictions where there is no constitutional court, an elections commission may also exercise the power to recognise or withhold recognition from political parties wishing to contest elections. Such decisions are reviewable by courts.

Re: Request of the Attorney-General for dissolution orders against Pattana Chart Thai Party, Paen Din Thai Party and Thai Rak Thai Party
Ruling No 3-5/2550, 30 May 2007 (Constitutional Court, Thailand)

Facts

In order to avoid only one candidate contesting in the election of House of Representatives held on 2 April 2006, the Thai Rak Thai Party provided financial support to the candidates of the Pattana Chart Thai Party and the Paen Din Thai Party. In addition, the Thai Rak Thai Party was accused that it conspired with the Pattana Chart Thai Party and officials of the Election Commission to change the party membership and help the members of the Pattana Chart Thai Party who lacked certain qualifications to become eligible candidates. Also the leaders of the Pattana Chart Thai Party and the Paen Din Thai Party allegedly filed erroneous party information for the election. All of the impugned acts of the Thai Rak Thai Party violated section 66(1) and (3) of the Organic Act on Political Parties. The acts of the Pattana Chart Thai Party and the Paen Din Thai Party violated section 66(2) and (3) of the same Act. The Attorney-General thus filed an application to the Constitutional Court to dissolve all three political parties.

Held

The acts of Thai Rak Thai Party were committed to acquire national governing powers through means which were not provided in the Constitution and posed a threat to the security of the state or inconsistent with law or public order or good morals of the people. There was a lack of regard for the essential principles of the democratic form of government, lack of due respect for the laws of the nation and lack of capability to remain as a political party that could create legitimate politics or the further implementation thereof in the democratic form of government. Therefore, there were causes for the dissolution of Thai Rak Thai Party.

As for Pattana Chart Thai Party and Paen Din Thai Party, these were parties founded for the interests of the founders or party executives showing no characters of a legitimate political party. Therefore, there were causes for the dissolution of Pattana Chart Thai Party and Paen Din Thai Party.

The Announcement of the Council for Democratic Reform No 27 was applicable to the causes for party dissolution under section 66 subsections (1), (2) and (3) of the Organic Act on Political Parties BE 2541 (1998) because the provisions of section 66 subsections (1), (2) and (3) were inherently clear as prohibitory provisions. Any political party violating any such prohibition could be dissolved. Such provisions were equivalent to a prohibition against a political party committing any such act.

The Announcement of the Council for Democratic Reform No 27, dated 30 September BE 2549 (2006), which revoked election rights, did not impose criminal penalties. The provisions merely constituted legal measures consequential of laws which authorized the dissolution of a political party that had violated a prohibition under the Organic Act on Political Parties BE 2541 (1998). These measures were implemented in order to deprive party executives who had caused detriment to society and the democratic form of government of the opportunity to recommit acts which would cause further detriment to society within a period of time. Even though election rights were fundamental rights of citizens in a democratic society, the enactment of laws stipulating the persons entitled to vote as appropriate to society conditions, or in order to maintain the continued existence of the democratic form of government, were justifiable . . .

. . . The Constitutional Tribunal therefore issued an order to dissolve Thai Rak Thai Party, Pattana Chart Thai Party and Paen Din Thai Party, and revoked the election rights of 111 executives of Thai Rak Thai Party, 19 executives of Pattana Chart Thai Party and 3 executives of Paen Din Thai Party for a period of 5 years as from the date of political party dissolution order.

Re: The Attorney-General requested for a Constitutional Court order to dissolve Neutral Democratic (Matchima Thippathai) Party
Ruling No 18/2551, 2 Dec 2008 (Constitutional Court, Thailand)

Facts

This case involved an order to dissolve the respondent party, as one party executive and the deputy leader of the party, also a candidate in the election of members of the House of Representatives for Prachinburi Province, had allegedly committed acts to acquire national governing powers through means in violation of section 237 of the Constitution and section 94(1) and (2) of the Organic Act on Political Parties, resulting in fraudulent and unfair elections.

Held

Section 237 paragraph two of the Constitution of the Kingdom of Thailand BE 2550 (2007) was a mandatory provision that if there was a commission of an offence by an election candidate, and if there was reasonable cause to believe that the political party leader or any political party executive connived at or neglected or was aware of the commission of an offence by the election candidate and failed to enforce preventive or remedial actions to enable the election to proceed in an honest and fair manner, such political party would be deemed as having committed an act to acquire national governing powers through means which were not in accordance with the Constitution. Even though according to the explanation of the respondent and statement of the respondent party leader affirmed that the political party, party leader and party executives were not the committers, the law still deemed such persons as committers. Such facts were therefore unobjectionable. Even the Constitutional Court was not entitled to rule otherwise since the offence of fraud by buying votes in an election was a special offence in which the committer could employ deceitful means that were difficult to detect. The law imposed a duty on party executives to select persons who would be involved in party activities and to control, supervise and monitor those persons to avoid any wrongdoing. In this regard, there were provisions for the political party and party executives to also be accountable for the acts of party executives who had committed the offence. This was analogous to the general liability of juristic persons that a representative of a juristic person or a person authorized to act on behalf of the juristic person committed an act within the objectives of such juristic person and caused damages to another person, the juristic person should also be liable for the acts of the representative or person authorized to act on behalf of such juristic person and would not be able to deny such responsibility. Therefore, there was cause under the law in this case for the court to decide on whether or not the respondent party should be dissolved.

As the respondent was a political party, which was a very important organ in the democratic form of government, it should therefore be a model of rightfulness, legitimacy and honesty. The obtaining of members of the House of Representatives of the respondent should be achieved in good faith principally from the popularity of the election candidates and the respondent party, not from benefits or bribes to entice the electorate to cast votes in their favour. All party executives should also collaborate in performing the functions of controlling and supervising election candidates fielded by the party, as well as the party executives themselves, to prevent the commission of any act that would violate the law. However, Mr Sunthorn Wilawan, deputy leader and executive of the respondent party, employed unlawful means to get himself elected, increasing the number of members of [the] House of Representatives gained by the respondent. Thus, the respondent was deemed as having benefitted from the act, being a serious matter . . .

. . . [T]he Constitutional Court found that if an offender under paragraph one was a party executive himself, it was inherently apparent that such party executive had an intention and committed the offence even more so than just a mere connivance. It was therefore not necessary for the party leader or other party executives to connive, neglect or be aware and fail to prevent or remedy the acts to enable honest and fair elections, since the party executive who committed the offence under paragraph one also had the status of a party executive at the time of the commission of the offence. This case was therefore more serious than the case of an offence committed by another person who was not a party leader or executive, in accordance with the legal principle that when the law prohibited an evil, other things which were more even would also be prohibited. This was consistent with the conscience of honest people generally and consistent with the logic that 'it is more so'. The argument raised by the respondent was therefore not accepted.

As Mr Sunthorn Wilawan, deputy leader and party executive of the respondent party, had an important role in the party, he was under a duty to control and monitor party members under his administration to ensure honest and fair elections. However, by committing an offence himself, which was a serious offence and a threat to the development of the country's democratic form of government. This case, therefore, showed cause for the dissolution of the respondent party so that a precedent for exemplary political behaviour be set and in order to have a preventive effect on the same offence in the future.

Janata Dal (Samajwadi) v The Election Commission of India
[1996] AIR 577 (Supreme Court, India)

NP Singh J

The appellant was recognised as a national political party on 16-4-1991. The general elections to the Lok Sabha and to the Legislative Assemblies of the States of Assam, Haryana, Kerala, Tamil Nadu, Uttar Pradesh, West Bengal and the Union Territory of Pondicherry were held in the months of April–June, 1991. A statement showing the number of votes polled by the appellant at the aforesaid general elections held in the months of April–June, 1991 showing the performance of the appellant at the poll was prepared by the Election Commission and thereafter a show cause notice dated 4.12.1991 was issued to the appellant by the Election Commission as to why the recognition of the appellant as a national party should not be withdrawn under the provisions of the Symbols Order . . .

[In view of paragraph] 6(2) a political party shall be treated as a recognised political party in a State, if and only if either the condition specified in clause (A) or the condition specified in Clause (B) is fulfilled by the party. Clause (A) requires such party to have been engaged in political activity for a continuous period of five years and [have] at the general election in that State to the House of the People, or, as the case may be, to the Legislative Assembly, for the time being in existence and functioning returned at least one member to the House of the People for every twenty-five members of that House or any fraction of that number elected from that State or at least one member to the Legislative Assembly of that State for every thirty members of that Assembly or any fraction of that number. The alternative condition as specified in clause (B) is regarding the total number of valid votes specified in the said Clause (B) polled at the General Election in the State to the House of the People or to the Legislative Assembly for time being in existence and functioning. The conditions for being recognised as a 'national party' or 'state party' have been specified in paragraph 7(1), saying that if a political party is treated as a recognised political party in accordance with paragraph 6 aforesaid in four or more States, it shall be known as, and enjoy the status of a 'National party' throughout the whole of India; on the other hand if a political party is treated as a recognised political party in accordance with paragraph 6 aforesaid in less than four States, it shall be known as, and shall have and enjoy the status of, a 'State party' in the State or States in which it is a recognised political party. There is no dispute that when the appellant was recognised as a national party on 16.4.1991 it fulfilled the conditions prescribed in paragraphs 6(2) and 7(1) of the Symbols Order. It is also an admitted position that when the show cause notice was given by the Election Commission to the appellant as to why it should not be derecognised as a national party on the basis of the election results of the Legislative Assemblies in the States mentioned above in the months of April–June, 1991, the appellant did not fulfil the conditions prescribed in paragraphs 6(2) and 7(1) for being recognised as a national party. As such the question which is to be answered is as to whether once a political party is recognised as a national party having fulfilled conditions prescribed for the same in the Symbols Order can it be derecognised as a national party under the provisions of the same Symbols Order?

It is true that there is no specific provision under the Symbols Order vesting power in the Election Commission after having recognised a political party as a national party to declare that such political party has ceased to be a national party, not being entitled to the exclusive use of the symbol allotted to it. But at the same time, it cannot be conceived that a political party having been recognised as a national party or State party as the case may be on having fulfilled the conditions prescribed in paragraph 6(2) shall continue as such in perpetuity although it has forfeited the right to be recognised as a national party or a State party . . .

The General Elections in all the States at one time in India [have] now become a matter of history. For one reason or other the elections are being held in group of States under different situations prevailing from time to time. Apart from that as the condition prescribed in paragraph 7(1) for recognising a political party as a national party is that it should be treated as a recognised political party is accordance with paragraph 6, in four or more States; then for purpose of withdrawing such recognition also it has to be examined as to whether after elections the said political party can be treated as a recognised political party in accordance with paragraph 6 in four or more states. If for purpose of recognising a political party as a national party the performance of such party in four or more States has to be examined in accordance with paragraphs 6 and 7 then it cannot be urged that for withdrawing such recognition it must await till elections are held in all the States within Union of India. If this stand is accepted then even for recognising a political party as a national party, such recognition should await till elections are held in all the States in India. Can recognition of a political party as a national party be not given, no sooner it fulfils the conditions specified in paragraph 6(2), in four or more States in view of paragraph 7(1) of the Symbols Order? If for purpose of recognition of a political party as a national party the conditions of paragraph 6(2) have to be fulfilled only in four or more States, then on the same principle even for withdrawing the said recognition the question has to be examined in the light of paragraph 6(2) on the basis of the results in four or more States. Once the Election Commission is satisfied that a political party recognized as a national party, has ceased to fulfil the conditions prescribed in paragraph 6(2) of the Symbols Order not even in four States as a result of any election, it can derecognise such a political party as a national party . . .

The Election Commission on the materials produced before it rightly came to the conclusion that the appellant had ceased to be a national party or a State party . . . We find no reason to take a different view. Accordingly, the appeal fails and it is dismissed.

Notes and Questions

1. Why do constitutions entrust constitutional courts with the power to adjudicate on the legality of political parties? Are constitutional courts a reliable safeguard for 'militant democracy'? Can election commissions or supreme courts provide the same functions as effectively? (See chapter five for further discussion.)

2. Comparatively, the Thai Constitutional Court has the greatest number of cases involving the dissolution of political parties. Table 6.1 lists the names of political parties dissolved by the Constitutional Court and the grounds for their respective dissolutions. What explains this high rate of dissolution? Could this be attributed to the state of transitional politics, an immature democracy, or any other particular cultural or political factors?

Table 6.1 List of Dissolved Political Parties in Thailand

Name of Political Party	Reason for Dissolution
Maharadthipat Party	Maharadthipat Party failed to have the number of its members and establish its branch as specified in section 29 of the Organic Act on Political Parties, BE 2541 (1998).
Chivit Party	After the expiration of the period of 180 days as prescribed by law, Chivit Mai Party failed to prepare to have the number of its members and to establish its political branch as prescribed by section 29 of the Organic Act on Political Parties, BE 2541 (1998).
Chatniyom Party	After the expiration of the period of 180 days as prescribed by law, it appeared that Chatniyom Party failed to prepare to have the number of its members and to establish its political branch as prescribed by section 29 of the Organic Act on Political Parties, BE 2541 (1998).
Chat Samakkee Party	Chat Samakkee Party had not submitted a response statement within a prescribed time limit, without stating any reason, to the Constitutional Court; this could therefore constitute a cause for the dissolution of a political party under section 65(1)(5) of the Organic Act on Political Parties, BE 2541 (1998).
Thai Kaona Party	That Thai Kaona Party had a misunderstanding over the computation of a specified period of time was untenable, since the Organic Act on Political Parties, BE 2541 (1998) specified such period of time unambiguously.
Dharmarat Party	After the period of 180 days had elapsed, the establishment of four political branches of Dharmarat Party had not been complied with its by laws.
Ruk Chat Party	After the time period of 180 days had elapsed, Ruk Chat Party had not complied with section 29 of the Organic Act on Political Parties, BE 2541 (1998).
Chat Kasertrakorn Thai Party	Chat Kasertrakorn Thai Party failed to comply with section 29 of the Organic Act on Political Parties, BE 2541 (1998).
Chat Prachachon Party	Chat Prachachon Party had not prepared to have no fewer than 5,000 members, which had to comprise those from each Region pursuant to the list of Regions and Changwats notified by the Registrar, and failed to have at least one branch of the political party in each Region by the date of 14 August BE 2544 (2001).
Num Thai Party	Num Thai Party failed to prepare to have no fewer than 5,000 members, which had to comprise those from each Region according to the list of Regions and Changwats notified by the Registrar, and failed to have at least one political branch in each Region within the date of 8 September BE 2545 (2002).
Prachachon Thai Party	Prachachon Thai Party failed to have no fewer than 5,000 members as provided by section 29 of the Organic Act on Political Parties, BE 2541 (1998).

3. While the government may place regulations on political parties, it must avoid excessive interference with their internal matters. The Supreme Court of the Philippines, in *LDP v COMELEC LDP v Comelec*,[50] held that it was within the Commission of Election's power to ensure the truth of a person's identity and that he was in fact a party member who held party ideals. According to the Court:

> It is . . . in the interest of every political party not to allow persons it had not chosen to hold themselves out as representatives of the party. Corollary to the right of a political party 'to identify the people who constitute the association and to select a standard bearer who best represents the party's ideologies and preference' is the right to exclude persons in its association and to not lend its name and prestige to those which it deems undeserving to represent its ideals. A certificate of candidacy makes known to the COMELEC that the person therein mentioned has been nominated by a duly authorized political group empowered to act and that it reflects accurately the sentiment of the nominating body. A candidate's political party affiliation is also printed followed by his or her name in the certified list of candidates. A candidate misrepresenting himself or herself to be a party's candidate, therefore, not only misappropriates the party's name and prestige but foists a deception upon the electorate, who may unwittingly cast its ballot for him or her on the mistaken belief that he or she stands for the party's principles. To prevent this occurrence, the COMELEC has the power and the duty to step in and enforce the law not only to protect the party but, more importantly, the electorate, in line with the Commission's broad constitutional mandate to ensure orderly elections.

B. Elections

Elections are democratic processes through which citizens select their governors and hold them to account. Election campaigns are also sites of communications between voters and political parties, and between government and society.[51] Usually the government decides when to hold elections and how to administer them, but increasingly, independent election commissions are assuming this role (see section III.C. below). Courts may adjudicate election-related disputes with an eye to issues of time. The following cases illustrate disputes that may arise concerning when to hold elections to fill a vacancy and the scope of judicial review with respect to the administration of elections.

> ### *Day and Time of, and Method of Determining the Elect at the Re-election and the Vacancy Election for Members of the National Assembly*
> **2003Hun-Ma259, 27 Nov 2003 (Constitutional Court, South Korea)**
>
> #### Facts
>
> The Act on the Election of Public Officials and the Prevention of Election Malpractices provides that the re-election and vacancy election for members of the National Assembly shall take place from 6:00 am to 6:00 pm on a Thursday. Regardless of voter turnout, a candidate who obtains a simple majority of the votes will win the election. The complainant

---

[50] *Laban ng Demokratikong Pilipino v COMELEC*, GR No 161265, 24 Feb 2004.
[51] Hague and & Harrop, above n 48, at 179.

candidates filed this constitutional complaint, arguing that the aforementioned provisions violated the principle of people's sovereignty, and the rights to equality and equal vote.

Held

The Act on the Election of Public Officials and the Prevention of Election Malpractices provides identically for the general election for members of the National Assembly and the re-election and vacancy election for members of the National Assembly in terms of the day of the week of the election and the time period available for voting. Therefore, it does not discriminate between voters and candidates at the general election and voters and candidates at the re-election and vacancy election, in these regards.

The government designates the election date for the general election as an official holiday. However, as indicated above, this is pursuant to the Regulation on Public Office's Official Holidays. Therefore, implementing the re-election and the vacancy election without designating the date therefor as an official holiday is not a question for the Act on the Election of Public Officials and the Prevention of Election Malpractices itself in this regard

. . .

It would be desirable, in light of the principle of representative democracy, to secure representativeness of the elected by promoting convenience of voting on the part of the voters and increasing the voting rate. However, matters concerning whether or not to designate the date of the re-election and vacancy election for members of the National Assembly as an official holiday and whether or not to extend time for voting until after the normal business hours fall within the meaning of such other 'matters concerning the election' duly delegated by the Constitution to the purview of the legislators' law making power.

The current provision of the Act on the Election of Public Officials and the Prevention of Election Malpractices that designates a Thursday as the election date and designates the time for voting identically for both the general election and the re-election and vacancy election for members of the National Assembly does not fall outside the scope of such legislative discretion of the legislators.

The Constitution requires that the method of election be that of general, equal, direct, secret, and free vote. The representativeness of the election is sufficiently secured and realized under the current method that provides all voters with an opportunity to participate in voting without discrimination thereagainst, assesses the votes of the voters participating in the election at equal value, and determines the candidate who has obtained a majority of valid votes to be elected.

There can be found no clear constitutional provision or constitutional principle that requests an additional requirement of the minimum voting rate system in order to further secure the representativeness of the election.

If the minimum voting rate system were to be introduced, as argued by the complainants, in case the actual voting rate would turn out to be lower than the required minimum voting rate, voting should be repeated until the voting rate would reach the minimum voting rate, which might cause complication and waste of time and cost. If such methods as civil penalties or fine were to be adopted in order to prevent such situation thereby compelling the voters to vote, this would unjustly abridge the freedom to form opinions of the voters and, as the result, might infringe upon the right to vote, thereby violating the principle of free election.

To conclude, the provisions of the Act on the Election of Public Officials and the Prevention of Election Malpractices concerning the date and the time of the re-election and the vacancy election for members of the National Assembly are within the scope of the legislators' law making power and, as such, do not abridge the right to equality or equal vote or the right to participate in politics of the complainants who are the voters. The provision of the Act on the Election of Public Officials and the Prevention of Election Malpractices determining the election by a simple majority of the valid votes is not in violation of the essence of representativeness of the election or the principle of people's sovereignty.

NP Ponnuswami v Returning Officer
[1952] AIR SC 64 (Supreme Court, India)

Facts

Article 329 of the Constitution provides that:

329. Notwithstanding anything in this Constitution –

(a) the validity of any law relating to the delimitation of constituencies or the allotment of seats to such constituencies, made or purporting to be made under Article 327 or Article 328, shall not be called in question in any court;

(b) no election to either House of Parliament or to the House or either House of the Legislature of a State shall be called in question except by an election petition presented to such authority and in such manner as may be provided for, by, or under any law made by the appropriate Legislature.

The appellant filed nomination papers for election to the Madras Legislative Assembly from the Namakkal Constituency in the district of Salem. The Returning Officer rejected the appellant's nomination paper. The appellant the applied for a writ of certiorari to quash the order of the Returning Officer's rejection, and for mandamus to direct the Returning Officer to include his name in the list of valid nominations to be published. The High Court dismissed the application on the ground that it had no jurisdiction to interfere with the order of the Returning Officer by reason of Article 329(b) of the Constitution. The case was then appealed to the Supreme Court.

Held

Now, the main controversy in this appeal centres around the meaning of the words 'no election shall be called in question except by an election petition' in article 329(b), and the point to be decided is whether questioning the action of the Returning Officer in rejecting a nomination paper can be said to be comprehended within the words, 'no election shall be called in question.' The appellant's case is that questioning something which has happened before a candidate is declared elected is not the same thing as questioning an election, and the arguments advanced on his behalf in support of this construction were these:

(1) That the word 'election' as used in article 329(b) means what it normally and etymologically means, namely, the result of polling or the final selection of a candidate;

(2) That the fact that an election petition can be filed only after polling is over or after a candidate is declared elected, and what is normally called in question by such petition is the final result, bears out the contention that the word 'election 'can have no other meaning in article (b) than the result of polling or the final selection of a candidate;

(3)   That the words 'arising out of or in connection with' which are used in article 324(1) and the words 'with respect to all matters relating to, or in connection with' which are used in articles 327 and 328, show that the framers of the Constitution knew that it was necessary to use different language when referring respectively to matters which happen prior to and after the result of polling, and if they had intended to include the rejection of a nomination paper within the ambit of the prohibition contained in article 329(b) they would have used similar language in that article and

(4)   That the action of the Returning Officer in rejecting a nomination paper can be questioned before the High Court under article 226 of the Constitution for the following reason: – Scrutiny of nomination papers and their rejection are provided for in section 36 of the Representation of the People Act, 1951. Parliament has made this provision in exercise of the powers conferred on it by article 327 of the Constitution which is 'subject to the provisions of the Constitution'. Therefore, the action of the Returning Officer is subject to the extraordinary jurisdiction of the High Court under article 226.

These arguments appear at first sight to be quite impressive, but in my opinion there are weightier and basically more important arguments in support of the view taken by the High Court. As we have seen, the most important question for determination is the meaning to be given to the word 'election' in article 329(b). That word has by long usage in connection with the process of selection of proper representatives in democratic institutions, acquired both a wide and a narrow meaning. In the narrow sense, it is used to mean the final selection of a candidate which may embrace the result of the poll when there is polling or a particular candidate being returned unopposed when there is no poll. In the wide sense, the word is used to connote the entire process culminating in a candidate being declared elected . . .

The question now arises whether the law of elections in this country contemplates that there should be two attacks on matters connected with election proceedings, one while they are going on by invoking the extraordinary jurisdiction of the High Court under article 226 of the Constitution (the ordinary jurisdiction of the courts having been expressly excluded), and another after they have been completed by means of an election petition. In my opinion, to affirm such a position would be contrary to the scheme of Part XV of the Constitution and the Representation of the People Act, which, as I shall point out later, seems to be that any matter which has the effect of vitiating an election should be brought up only at the appropriate stage in an appropriate manner before a special tribunal and should not be brought up at an intermediate stage before any court. It seems to me that under the election law, the only significance which the rejection of a nomination paper has consists in the fact that it can be used as a ground to call the election in question. Article 329(b) was apparently enacted to prescribe the manner in which and the stage at which this ground, and other grounds which may be raised under the law to call the election in question could be urged. I think it follows by necessary implication from the language of this provision that those grounds cannot be urged in any other manner, at any other stage and before any other court. If the grounds on which an election can be called in question could be raised at an earlier stage and errors, if any, are rectified, there will be no meaning in enacting a provision like article 329(b) and in setting up a special tribunal. Any other meaning ascribed to the words used in the article would lead to anomalies, which the Constitution could not have contemplated, one of them being that conflicting views may be expressed by the High Court at the pre-polling stage and by the election tribunal, which is to be an independent body, at the stage when the matter is brought up before it . . .

In discharging the statutory duty imposed on him, the Returning Officer does not call in question any election. Scrutiny of nomination papers is only a stage, though an important stage, in the election process. It is one of the essential duties to be performed before the election can be completed, and anything done towards the completion of the election proceeding can by no stretch of reasoning be described as questioning the election. The fallacy of the argument lies in treating a single step taken in furtherance of an election as equivalent to election. The decision of this appeal however turns not on the construction of the single word 'election', but on the construction of the compendious expression – 'no election shall be called in question' in its context and setting, with due regard to the scheme of Part XV of the Constitution and the Representation of the People Act, 1951. Evidently, the argument has no bearing on this method of approach to the question posed in this appeal, which appears to me to be the only correct method.

C. Election Commissions

The impartial and fair administration of elections is an essential component of democratic governance. Many countries in Asia have election commissions to administer and supervise elections. Such commissions are established either by the constitution or by statute. The Indian Election Commission is one of the most powerful commissions in this region. Article 324(1) of the Indian Constitution provides that the superintendence, direction and control of the preparation of the electoral rolls for, and the conduct of, all elections to Parliament and to the Legislature of every State, and of elections to the offices of President and Vice-President held under the Constitution, shall be vested in a Commission. It further provides that the Election Commission shall consist of the Chief Election Commissioner and such other election commissioners as the President may appoint. The independence of the Election Commission is guaranteed by a special provision stipulating that the Chief Election Commissioner shall not be removed from office except in the same manner and on the same grounds as a Supreme Court judge.[52]

i. Independence of the Election Commission

The independence of an election commission is important to the fair administration of elections. Usually commissioners are appointed for a limited term based upon their expertise, and like judges, they are independent from the executive and parliament.

In Thailand, for example, the Constitution stipulates that the Election Commission shall consist of a chairperson and four other commissioners with a non-renewable term of seven years.[53] The chairperson and commissioners are appointed by the King with the advice of the Senate on the basis of apparent political impartiality and integrity.[54] To qualify for appointment, a candidate for commissioner should be at least 40 years of age, have graduated with at least a Bachelor's degree or its equivalent, and not be serving as a judge of the Constitutional Court, an Ombudsman, or a member of other independent constitutional commissions.[55]

---

[52] Art 324(5), Constitution of the Union of India.
[53] Arts 229 and 232, Constitution of the Kingdom of Thailand, 2007.
[54] Art 229, Constitution of the Kingdom of Thailand, 2007.
[55] Art 230, Constitution of the Kingdom of Thailand, 2007.

Notwithstanding institutional designs to ensure independence, the election commission is as vulnerable as the judiciary. The following cases illustrate the kind of interference an election commission may face in the appointment process or with respect to administrative supervision.

Macalintal v COMELEC
GR No 157013, 10 Jul 2003 (Supreme Court, Philippines)

Facts

The petitioner filed the instant petition as a taxpayer and as a lawyer. Among the questions raised was the issue of the independence of the Commission on Elections (COMELEC). The petitioner challenged that constitutionality of the Joint Congressional Oversight Committee which Congress created under Section 25 of Republic Act (RA) No 9189. The petitioner argued that this Committee's power to review, revise, amend and approve the Implementing Rules and Regulations promulgated by COMELEC, violated the independence of the COMELEC under Article IX-A, Section 1 of the Constitution.

Austria-Martinez J

Petitioner avers that Sections 19 and 25 of RA No 9189 violate Article IX-A (Common Provisions) of the Constitution, to wit:

Section 1

The Constitutional Commissions, which shall be independent, are the Civil Service Commission, the Commission on Elections, and the Commission on Audit. (Emphasis supplied)

He submits that the creation of the Joint Congressional Oversight Committee with the power to review, revise, amend and approve the Implementing Rules and Regulations promulgated by the COMELEC, RA No 9189 intrudes into the independence of the COMELEC which, as a constitutional body, is not under the control of either the executive or legislative departments of government; that only the COMELEC itself can promulgate rules and regulations which may be changed or revised only by the majority of its members; and that should the rules promulgated by the COMELEC violate any law, it is the Court that has the power to review the same via the petition of any interested party, including the legislators . . .

The ambit of legislative power under Article VI of the Constitution is circumscribed by other constitutional provisions. One such provision is Section 1 of Article IX-A of the 1987 Constitution ordaining that constitutional commissions such as the COMELEC shall be 'independent.'

Interpreting Section 1, Article X of the 1935 Constitution providing that there shall be an *independent* COMELEC, the Court has held that '[w]hatever may be the nature of the functions of the Commission on Elections, the fact is that the framers of the Constitution wanted it to be independent from the other departments of the Government.' . . .

The Court has no general powers of supervision over COMELEC which is an independent body 'except those specifically granted by the Constitution,' that is, to review its decisions, orders and rulings. In the same vein, it is not correct to hold that because of its recognized extensive legislative power to enact election laws, Congress may intrude into the independence of the COMELEC by exercising supervisory powers over its rule-making authority.

By virtue of Section 19 of RA No 9189, Congress has empowered the COMELEC to 'issue the necessary rules and regulations to effectively implement the provisions of this Act within sixty days from the effectivity of this Act.' This provision of law follows the usual procedure in drafting rules and regulations to implement a law – the legislature grants an administrative agency the authority to craft the rules and regulations implementing the law it has enacted, in recognition of the administrative expertise of that agency in its particular field of operation. Once a law is enacted and approved, the legislative function is deemed accomplished and complete. The legislative function may spring back to Congress relative to the same law only if that body deems it proper to review, amend and revise the law, but certainly not to approve, review, revise and amend the IRR of the COMELEC . . .

The second sentence of the first paragraph of Section 19 stating that '[t]he Implementing Rules and Regulations shall be submitted to the Joint Congressional Oversight Committee created by virtue of this Act for prior approval,' and the second sentence of the second paragraph of Section 25 stating that '[i]t shall review, revise, amend and approve the Implementing Rules and Regulations promulgated by the Commission,' whereby Congress, in both provisions, arrogates unto itself a function not specifically vested by the Constitution, should be stricken out of the subject statute for constitutional infirmity. Both provisions brazenly violate the mandate on the independence of the COMELEC.

Sixto S Brillantes Jr v Yorac
GR No 93867, 18 Dec 1990 (Supreme Court, Philippines)

Facts

The petitioner challenged the designation by the President of the Philippines of the Associate Commissioner of the Commission of Elections (COMELEC) as Acting Chairman in place of former Chairman. He argued that this designation was contrary to the Constitution in violating COMELEC's independence.

Cruz J

The petitioner contends that the choice of the Acting Chairman of the Commission on Elections is an internal matter that should be resolved by the members themselves and that the intrusion of the President of the Philippines violates their independence. He cites the practice in this Court, where the senior Associate Justice serves as Acting Chief Justice in the absence of the Chief Justice. No designation from the President of the Philippines is necessary.

In his Comment, the Solicitor General argues that no such designation is necessary in the case of the Supreme Court because the temporary succession cited is provided for in Section 12 of the Judiciary Act of 1948. A similar rule is found in Section 5 of BP 129 for the Court of Appeals. There is no such arrangement, however, in the case of the Commission on Elections. The designation made by the President of the Philippines should therefore be sustained for reasons of 'administrative expediency,' to prevent disruption of the functions of the COMELEC.

Expediency is a dubious justification. It may also be an overstatement to suggest that the operations of the Commission on Elections would have been disturbed or stalemated if the President of the Philippines had not stepped in and designated an Acting Chairman. There did not seem to be any such problem. In any event, even assuming that difficulty, we do not agree that 'only the President (could) act to fill the hiatus,' as the Solicitor General maintains.

Article IX-A, Section 1, of the Constitution expressly describes all the Constitutional Commissions as 'independent.' Although essentially executive in nature, they are not under the control of the President of the Philippines in the discharge of their respective functions. Each of these Commissions conducts its own proceedings under the applicable laws and its own rules and in the exercise of its own discretion. Its decisions, orders and rulings are subject only to review on Certiorari by this Court as provided by the Constitution in Article IX-A, Section 7.

The choice of a temporary chairman in the absence of the regular chairman comes under that discretion. That discretion cannot be exercised for it, even with its consent, by the President of the Philippines.

A designation as Acting Chairman is by its very terms essentially temporary and therefore revocable at will. No cause need be established to justify its revocation. Assuming its validity, the designation of the respondent as Acting Chairman of the Commission on Elections may be withdrawn by the President of the Philippines at any time and for whatever reason she sees fit. It is doubtful if the respondent, having accepted such designation, will not be estopped from challenging its withdrawal.

It is true, as the Solicitor General points out, that the respondent cannot be removed at will from her permanent position as Associate Commissioner. It is no less true, however, that she can be replaced as Acting Chairman, with or without cause, and thus deprived of the powers and perquisites of that temporary position.

The lack of a statutory rule covering the situation at bar is no justification for the President of the Philippines to fill the void by extending the temporary designation in favor of the respondent. This is still a government of laws and not of men. The problem allegedly sought to be corrected, if it existed at all, did not call for presidential action. The situation could have been handled by the members of the Commission on Elections themselves without the participation of the President, however well-meaning.

In the choice of the Acting Chairman, the members of the Commission on Elections would most likely have been guided by the seniority rule as they themselves would have appreciated it. In any event, that choice and the basis thereof were for them and not the President to make.

The Court has not the slightest doubt that the President of the Philippines was moved only by the best of motives when she issued the challenged designation. But while conceding her goodwill, we cannot sustain her act because it conflicts with the Constitution.

ii. Functions of an Election Commission

Generally an election commission is entrusted with all relevant powers to administer elections. The Thai Constitution vests extensive powers in the Thai election commission, which includes the power to monitor the registration of voters to ensure that all eligible voters are registered, to lay down rules relating to election campaigns and any activities of political parties or candidates in an election and to voters to ensure their honesty and fairness, to regulate donations to political parties, the expenditure of political parties and candidates in an election, to conduct fact-finding investigations and inquiries into election problems, and to order a new election or a new vote at a referendum to be held in any or all polling stations in an honest and fair manner.[56]

---

[56] Art 236, Constitution of the Kingdom of Thailand, 2007.

Election commissions often possess quasi-legislative and quasi-judicial powers aside from executive powers in the administration of elections. For example, the Commission on Elections of the Philippines may exercise exclusive original jurisdiction over all contests relating to the elections; returns; qualifications of all elective regional, provincial and city officials; and appellate jurisdiction over all contests involving elective municipal officials decided by trial courts of general jurisdiction, or involving elective barangay officials decided by trial courts of limited jurisdiction.[57]

If disputes concerning the administration of elections arise, should courts review the decisions of election commission, and in so doing, adopt a deferential approach? These disputes arose in the following three cases.

Mohinder Singh Gill & Anr v Chief Election Commissioner
[1978] AIR SC 851 (Supreme Court, India)

Krishna Iyer J

The historic elections to Parliament, recently held across the country, included a constituency in Punjab called 13-Ferozepore Parliamentary Constituency. It consisted of nine assembly segments and the polling took place on March 16, 1977. The appellant and the third respondent were the principal contestants.

The appellant's version is that he had all but won on the total count by a margin of nearly 2000 votes when the panicked opposite party havoced and halted the consummation by muscle tactics. The postal ballot papers were destroyed . . .

Disturbed by the disruption of the declaratory part of the election, the appellant, along with a former Minister of the State, met the Chief Election Commissioner . . . with the request that he should direct the returning officer to declare the result of the election. Later in the day, the Commission issued an order which has been characterised by the appellant as a law-less and precedentless cancellation, of the whole poll, acting by hasty hunch and without rational appraisal of facts . . . [T]he Election Commission made the impugned order, the bulk of the electoral results in the country bad beamed in. The gravamen of the grievance of the appellant is that while he had, in all probability, won the poll, he has been deprived of this valuable and hard-won victory by the arbitrary action of the Commission going contrary to fair play and in negation of the basic canons of natural justice . . . [T]he Commission did not stop with the cancellation but followed it up a few days later with a direction to hold a fresh poll for the whole constituency.

Can the Election Commission, clothed with the comprehensive functions under Article 324 of the Constitution, cancel the whole poll of a constituency after it has been held, but before the formal declaration of the result has been made, and direct a fresh poll without reference to the guidelines under ss 58 and 64(a) of the Act, or other legal prescription or legislative backing . . .

Election, [w]ide or narrow be its connotation, means choice from a possible plurality monolithic politics not being our genius or reality, and if that concept is crippled by the Commissioner's act, he holds no election at all. A poll is part – a vital part – of the election but with the end of the poll the whole election IS not over. Ballots have to be assembled, scrutinised, counted recount claims considered and result declared. The declaration determines the election. The conduct of the election thus ripens into the elector's choice only when processed, screened and sanctified, every escalatory step up to the formalised finish being unified in purpose, forward in movement, fair and free in its temper . . .

---

[57] Art IXC Sec 2(2), Constitution of the Philippines.

Nobody will deny that the Election Commission in our democratic scheme is a central figure and a high functionary . . .

This question of the soundness of the cancellation of the entire poll is within the court's power under s 98 of the Act. All are agreed on this. In that eventuality, what are the follow-up steps? Everything necessary to resurrect reconstruct and lead on to a consummation of the original process. Maybe, to give effective relief by way of completion of the broken election the Commissioner may have to be directed to hold [a] fresh poll and report back together with the ballots. A recount of all or some may perhaps be required. Other steps suggested by other developments may be desired. If anything integrally linked up with and necessitated by the obligation to grant full relief has to be undertaken or ordered to be done by the election machinery, all that is within the orbit of the Election Court's power . . .

Having regard to statutory setting and comprehensive jurisdiction of the Election Court, we are satisfied that it is within its powers to, direct a re-poll of particular polling stations to be conducted by the specialised agency under the Election Commission and report the results and ballots to the Court. Even a re-poll of postal ballots, since those names are known, can be ordered taking care to preserve the secrecy of the vote. The Court may, if necessary, after setting aside the election of R. 3 (if there are good grounds therefore keep the case pending, issue directions for getting available votes, order recount and or partial re-poll, keep the election petition pending and pass final orders holding the appellant elected if – only if – valid grounds are established . . .

In sum, a pragmatic modus vivendi between the Commission's paramount constitutional responsibility vis-à-vis elections and the rule of law vibrant with fair acting by every authority and remedy for every right breached, is reached. We conclude stating that the bar of Art 329(b) is as wide as the door of s 100 read with s 98. The writ petition is dismissible but every relief (given factual proof) now prayed for in the pending election petition is within reach. On this view of the law *ubi jus ibi remeditum* is vindicated, election injustice is avoided, and the constituency is allowed to speak effectively. In the light of and conditioned by the law we have laid down, we dismiss the appeal.

ABS-CBN Broadcasting Corporation v Commission on Elections
GR No 133486, 28 Jan 2000 (Supreme Court, Philippines)

Panganiban J

Before us is a Petition for *Certiorari* under Rule 65 of the Rules of Court assailing Commission on Elections (Comelec) *en banc* Resolution No 98-1419 dated April 21, 1998 . . .

The Resolution was issued by the Comelec allegedly upon 'information from [a] reliable source that ABS-CBN (Lopez Group) has prepared a project, with PR groups, to conduct radio-TV coverage of the elections . . . and to make [an] exit survey of the . . . vote during the elections for national officials particularly for President and Vice President, results of which shall be [broadcast] immediately.' The electoral body believed that such project might conflict with the official Comelec count, as well as the unofficial quick count of the National Movement for Free Elections (Namfrel). It also noted that it had not authorized or deputized Petitioner ABS-CBN to undertake the exit survey.

On May 9, 1998, this Court issued the Temporary Restraining Order prayed for by petitioner. We directed the Comelec to cease and desist, until further orders, from implementing the assailed Resolution or the restraining order issued pursuant thereto, if any. In fact, the exit polls were actually conducted and reported by media without any difficulty or problem . . .

The holding of exit polls and the dissemination of their results through mass media constitute an essential part of the freedoms of speech and of the press. Hence, the Comelec cannot ban them totally in the guise of promoting clean, honest, orderly and credible elections. Quite the contrary, exit polls – properly conducted and publicized – can be vital tools in eliminating the evils of election-fixing and fraud. Narrowly tailored countermeasures may be prescribed by the Comelec so as to minimize or suppress the incidental problems in the conduct of exit polls, without transgressing in any manner the fundamental rights of our people . . .

An exit poll is a species of electoral survey conducted by qualified individuals or groups of individuals for the purpose of determining the probable result of an election by confidentially asking randomly selected voters whom they have voted for, immediately after they have officially cast their ballots. The results of the survey are announced to the public, usually through the mass media, to give an advance overview of how, in the opinion of the polling individuals or organizations, the electorate voted. In our electoral history, exit polls had not been resorted to until the recent May 11, 1998 elections . . .

Admittedly, no law prohibits the holding and the reporting of exit polls. The question can thus be more narrowly defined: May the Comelec, in the exercise of its powers, totally ban exit polls? . . .

In the case at bar, the Comelec justifies its assailed Resolution as having been issued pursuant to its constitutional mandate to ensure a free, orderly, honest, credible and peaceful election . . .

Such arguments are purely speculative and clearly untenable. First, by the very nature of a survey, the interviewees or participants are selected at random, so that the results will as much as possible be representative or reflective of the general sentiment or view of the community or group polled. Second, the survey result is not meant to replace or be at par with the official Comelec count. It consists merely of the opinion of the polling group as to who the electorate in general has probably voted for, based on the limited data gathered from polled individuals. Finally, not at stake here are the credibility and the integrity of the elections, which are exercises that are separate and independent from the exit polls. The holding and the reporting of the results of exit polls cannot undermine those of the elections, since the former is only part of the latter. If at all, the outcome of one can only be indicative of the other.

The Comelec's concern with the possible non-communicative effect of exit polls – disorder and confusion in the voting centers – does not justify a total ban on them. Undoubtedly, the assailed Comelec Resolution is too broad, since its application is without qualification as to whether the polling is disruptive or not. Concededly, the Omnibus Election Code prohibits disruptive behavior around the voting centers. There is no showing, however, that exit polls or the means to interview voters cause chaos in voting centers. Neither has any evidence been presented proving that the presence of exit poll reporters near an election precinct tends to create disorder or confuse the voters.

Moreover, the prohibition incidentally prevents the collection of exit poll data and their use for any purpose. The valuable information and ideas that could be derived from them, based on the voters' answer to the survey questions will forever remain unknown and unexplored. Unless the ban is restrained, candidates, researchers, social scientists and the electorate in general would be deprived of studies on the impact of current events and of election-day and other factors on voters' choices . . .

The absolute ban imposed by the Comelec cannot, therefore, be justified. It does not leave open any alternative channel of communication to gather the type of information obtained through exit polling. On the other hand, there are other valid and reasonable ways and means to achieve the Comelec end of avoiding or minimizing disorder and confusion that may be brought about by exit surveys . . .

With the foregoing premises, we conclude that the interest of the state in reducing disruption is outweighed by the drastic abridgment of the constitutionally guaranteed rights of the media and the electorate. Quite the contrary, instead of disrupting elections, exit polls – properly conducted and publicized – can be vital tools for the holding of honest, orderly, peaceful and credible elections; and for the elimination of election-fixing, fraud and other electoral ills . . .

In exit polls, the contents of the official ballot are not actually exposed. Furthermore, the revelation of whom an elector has voted for is not compulsory, but voluntary. Voters may also choose not to reveal their identities. Indeed, narrowly tailored countermeasures may be prescribed by the Comelec, so as to minimize or suppress incidental problems in the conduct of exit polls, without transgressing the fundamental rights of our people.

Jatiya Party v Election Commission for Bangladesh and Ors
2001 BLD (AD) 10, 30 Nov 2000 (Supreme Court, Bangladesh)

Facts

This case concerned a dispute over the allocation of party symbols for electoral candidates. A key issue was whether the Acting Chief Election Commissioner could exercise the powers vested in the entire Election Commission.

Latifur Rahman CJ

[T]he Election Commission which shall consist of a Chief Election Commissioner along with other Election Commissioners as may be appointed by the President and the Commission shall be subject to the provisions of any law made in that behalf by the President. Sub-article (9) of Article 118 speaks that when the Election Commission consists of more than one person, the Chief Election Commissioner shall act as the Chairman thereof. This is about the establishment of Election Commission under the Constitution. . . .

In the present case the order was passed by the Acting Chief Election Commissioner alone and not b[y] the Election Commission. The moot question is whether a member who was acting as Chief Election Commissioner can perform all or any of its powers and functions under the Representation of the People Order, 1972, briefly, the Order, without there being any authorization the Commission itself. It has been referred earlier that the Election Commission is constituted under Article 118(1) of the Constitution and it consists of a Chief Election Commissioner and such other Election Commissioners as may be appointed by the President and they, in fact, constitute the Election Commission for Bangladesh. In that sense, Election Commission is a composite body, an individual member can only act under section 4 of the Order when he is authorized by the Commission itself. In this particular case as a matter of fact there is no delegation/authorization by the Commission itself. What we find is that the Chief Election Commissioner being unwell he went on leave for treatment abroad and he verbally nominated a [member] to act as Acting Chief Election Commissioner. As a matter of fact, this may at best be said to be a direction of the Chief Election Commissioner to perform functions of the office in his absence as Acting Chief Election Commissioner, but for exercising and performing any powers or functions under this Order he must get authorization from the Commission itself, otherwise his action under the Order will be corum non judice and without jurisdiction. As a matter of fact the [function] that the Acting Chief Election Commissioner was doing in this particular case, was a function vested in him under this Order . . .

In the present case the controversy was with regard to allocation of symbol which the Returning Officer was authorized to do under Article 20(1) of the Order and that order was challenged before the Election Commission and the Election Commission of Bangladesh has got the power of review under Article 91(b) of the Order. Thus the Election Commission has got the authority to decide the matter. Without entering into the question as to whether the authority exercised by the Acting Chief Election Commissioner is a quasi judicial order or an order in its administrative capacity, it can be safely said that there was no delegation by the Election Commission itself to perform such function under the Order . . .

Thus on a careful consideration of law and subject we are of the view that the Acting Chief Election Commissioner had acted corum non judice in exercising its power in this particular case the learned Judges of the High Court Division are necessarily wrote a long judgment without touching on the vital issue raised in the present case before it.

Since we are holding that the order of Acting Chief Election Commissioner is *corum non judice* it is needless for us to go into the question as to whether the action of the Acting Chief Election Commissioner was quasi-judicial one or one in his administrative capacity.

For the foregoing reasons, the judgment of High Court Division is set aside and the appeal is allowed without any order as to cost.

Notes and Questions

1. What explains such a high degree of judicial deference to the decisions of election commissions? Notably, the process for appointing election commission members, especially where a commission is constitutionally established, is similar to that adopted for judicial appointments. Do you think judicial deference is a result of the similarity between the position of courts and that of election commissions, or is it because the nature of election disputes makes these issues better resolved by non-judicial institutions?

2. As the election commission is usually vested with quasi-judicial powers in the adjudication of election disputes, certain jurisdictional conflicts may arise between an election commission and the courts. In *Perfecto V Galido v Commission on Elections*, the Supreme Court of the Philippines held that courts may review the decisions rendered by the COMELEC, while giving it a high degree of deference. The Court held:

   > The Commission on Elections (COMELEC) has exclusive original jurisdiction over all contests relating to the elections, returns, and qualifications of all elective regional, provincial, and city officials and has appellate jurisdiction over all contests involving elective municipal officials decided by trial courts of general jurisdiction or involving elective barangay officials decided by trial courts of limited jurisdiction. (Article IX(C), Section 2(2), paragraph 1 of the 1987 Constitution).
   >
   > In the present case, after a review of the trial court's decision, the respondent COMELEC found that fifteen (15) ballots in the same precinct containing the letter 'C' after the name Galido are clearly marked ballots. May this COMELEC decision be brought to this court by a petition for certiorari by the aggrieved party (the herein petitioner)?

We resolve this issue in favor of the petitioner. The fact that decisions, final orders or rulings of the Commission on Elections in contests involving elective municipal and barangay offices are final, executory and not appealable, does not preclude a recourse to this Court by way of a special civil action of certiorari. The proceedings in the Constitutional Commission on this matter are enlightening.

We do not, however, believe that the respondent COMELEC committed grave abuse of discretion amounting to lack or excess of jurisdiction in rendering the questioned decision. It is settled that the function of a writ of certiorari is to keep an inferior court or tribunal within the bounds of its jurisdiction or to prevent it from committing a grave abuse of discretion amounting to lack or excess of jurisdiction.[58]

3.   In addition to election commissions, an independent tribunal may also be created to deal with the election disputes . A good example is the Electoral Tribunal in the Philippines. The Constitution of the Philippines provides that the Senate and the House of Representatives shall each have an Electoral Tribunal which shall be the sole judge of all contests relating to the election, returns and qualifications of their respective Members. It further stipulates that each Electoral Tribunal shall be composed of nine Members, three of whom shall be Justices of the Supreme Court, to be designated by the Chief Justice, and the remaining six of whom shall be Members of the Senate or the House of Representatives chosen on the basis of proportional representation from the political parties and the parties or organisations registered under the party-list system represented therein. The senior Justice in the Electoral Tribunal shall be its Chairman (Article VI Section 17). With regard to jurisdictional conflicts which might occur between the Commission of Election and the Electoral Tribunal, the Supreme Court of the Philippines, in *Arnold V Guerrero v Commission on Elections*, held:

> Under Article VI, Section 17 of the Constitution, the House of Representatives Electoral Tribunal (HRET) has the sole and exclusive jurisdiction over all contests relative to the election, returns, and qualifications of members of the House of Representatives. Thus, once a winning candidate has been proclaimed, taken his oath, and assumed office as a member of the House of Representatives, COMELEC's jurisdiction over election contests relating to his election, returns, and qualifications ends, and the HRET's own jurisdiction begins. Thus, the COMELEC's decision to discontinue exercising jurisdiction over the case is justifiable, in deference to the HRET's own jurisdiction and functions.
>
> . . . [A]s we already held, in an electoral contest where the validity of the proclamation of a winning candidate who has taken his oath of office and assumed his post as Congressman is raised, that issue is best addressed to the HRET. The reason for this ruling is self-evident, for it avoids [duplication] of proceedings and a clash of jurisdiction between constitutional bodies, with due regard to the people's mandate.[59]

IV. RIGHT TO POLITICAL PARTICIPATION

The right to political participation is essential to democratic governance and enjoys constitutional protection as well as certain treaty-based human rights guarantees. For

---

[58] *Perfecto V Galido v Commission on Elections* GR No 95346, 18 Jan 1991.
[59] *Arnold V Guerrero v Commission on Elections* GR No 137004, 26 Jul 2000.

instance, Article 25 of the International Covenant on Civil and Political Rights (ICCPR) states that

> every citizen shall have the right and the opportunity . . . to take part in the conduct of public affairs, directly or through freely chosen representatives; . . . to vote and to be elected at genuine periodic elections which shall be by universal and equal suffrage and shall be held by secret ballot, guaranteeing the free expression of the will of the electors; . . . to have access, on general terms of equality, to public service in his country.

In a nutshell, the right to political participation encompasses the right to vote, the right to stand for election, and the rights to hold public office and to participate in public affairs.

A. Qualification of Voters

Central to the guarantee of a right to political participation is the component of equality. Ideally, every person, regardless of his or her status, should enjoy the *equal right* to vote, to stand for elections, to hold public office through elections, appointments or examinations, and to participate in public affairs. In reality, however, the exercise of these rights is subject to eligibility and other qualifications.

In most democracies, the right to vote is limited to nationals or citizens. With globalisation and more frequent travel across national borders, the issue of whether to extend the right to vote to citizens residing abroad, or even to permanent residents or foreigners residing locally, has increasingly become a heated one. In Hong Kong, a similar issue may arise in terms of who are eligible 'indigenous villagers' enjoying the right to vote for village representatives. Whether prisoners should be allowed to vote is another issue discussed below.

Kim v Osaka Electoral Commission
49 Minshū 639 (Supreme Court, Japan)

Facts

The appellant was a Korean citizen and permanent resident of Japan. He was denied registration at the registration of voters in the local Kita Ward election in Osaka. He sued the local election officials for infringing his right of equal political participation enshrined in the Constitution.

Held

Guarantee of fundamental rights by the provisions of Chapter Three of the Constitution also extends to foreign nationals on sojourn in Japan except for those rights that, by their nature, are intended for Japanese nationals only. Whether or not the right to elect and dismiss public officials as guaranteed by Article 15, para 1 extends to foreign nationals on sojourn in Japan should be considered in the following. These provisions of the Constitution are understood to have declared that the ultimate power of electing and dismissing public officials lies with the people based upon the principle of people's sovereignty. Judging from the preface and Article 1 of the Constitution which declares that sovereignty lies with

'Japanese nationals', it is obvious that 'people' in 'people's sovereignty means' Japanese nationals, ie those with Japanese citizenship. Therefore, it is reasonable to conclude that Article 15, para 1 which guarantees the right to elect and dismiss public officials, by its nature, addresses Japanese nationals only and that the guarantee of this provision does not extend to foreign nationals on sojourn in Japan. Furthermore, Chapter Eight of the Constitution which covers local self-government, in Article 93, para 2, provides that the chief executive of the local self-government, members of the local assembly, and other officials provided by law should be elected by the inhabitants of the said local self-government. In the light of the above-mentioned principle of people's sovereignty and Article 15, para 1 of the Constitution which is based upon this principle, and taking into account that local self-governments are an integral part of the ruling system of Japan, it is reasonable to understand 'inhabitants' as provided in Article 93, para 2 of the Constitution to mean Japanese nationals who have residence in the territory of the said local self-government. This provision cannot be construed to have guaranteed the right to vote for foreign nationals on sojourn in Japan in the election for the chief executive of the local self-government, members of the local assembly, and others. . . .

Thus, Article 93, para 2 of the Constitution cannot be construed as guaranteeing the right to vote in the election for local self-governments. However, in the light of the significance of the local self-government in a democratic society, provisions on local self-government accommodated in Chapter Eight of the Constitution are designed, to institutionally guarantee a political system in which public administration closely related to the day-to-day life of the inhabitants is handled by the local self-government of the territory based upon the will of the inhabitants. Therefore, as regards foreign nationals on sojourn in Japan, it is reasonable to understand that the Constitution does not prohibit taking measures to grant voting rights to those permanent residents and others who have come to have an especially close relationship with the local self-government in the area of residence in elections for the chief executive of the local self-government, members of the local assembly, and other officials by law. However, whether or not such measures should be taken is exclusively a matter of the legislative policy of the state, and even if such measures are not taken, it is not a matter of unconstitutionality.

Case to Seek Declaration of Illegality of Deprivation of the Right to Vote of Japanese Citizens Residing Abroad
59 Minshū 7 (Supreme Court, Japan)

Facts

The appellants were Japanese citizens residing abroad. They were eligible to vote in the elections of the House of Representatives (HR) and the House of Councilors (HC), but only under the proportional representation system and not the district-based constituency system. They alleged that the Public Offices Election Law deprived them of the opportunity to exercise the right to vote and was thus unconstitutional.

Held

Citizens' right to choose members of the National Diet as their representatives through elections, which is a fundamental right that guarantees citizens the opportunity to take part in national administration, serves as the core of parliamentary democracy, and a democratic nation should give this right equally to all citizens who have reached a certain age.

The Constitution of Japan, in its preamble and Article 1, proclaims that sovereign power resides with the people, and provides that the people shall act through their duly elected representatives in the National Diet. Article 43(1) provides that both Houses of the Diet shall consist of elected members, representative of all the people. Article 15(1) further provides that the people have the inalienable right to choose their public officials and to dismiss them. Thus, the Constitution guarantees the people, as the sovereign, the right to take part in national administration by voting in elections of members of the Houses of the Diet. Article 15(3) of the Constitution also guarantees universal adult suffrage with regard to the election of public officials, and the proviso of Article 44 prohibits discrimination as to the qualification of electors of members of both Houses because of race, creed, sex, social status, family origin, education, property or income. In light of the provisions mentioned above, it is reasonable to construe that the Constitution, under the principle of popular sovereignty, guarantees the people the right to take part in national administration by voting in elections of members of the Houses of the Diet as their inalienable right, and in order to achieve this goal, guarantees the people equal opportunity to vote.

In light of the purport of the Constitution mentioned above, it is unallowable in principle to restrict the people's right to vote or their exercise of the right to vote, aside from imposing certain restrictions on the right to vote of those who have acted against fair elections, and it should be considered that in order to restrict the people's right to vote or their exercise of the right to vote, there must be grounds that make such restriction unavoidable. Such unavoidable grounds cannot be found unless it is deemed to be practically impossible or extremely difficult to allow the exercise of the right to vote while maintaining fairness in elections without such restrictions. Therefore, it must be said that it is in violation of Article 15(1) and (3), Article 43(1), and the proviso of Article 44 to restrict the people from exercising the right to vote without such unavoidable grounds. This also applies where the people are unable to exercise the right to vote due to the State's failure to take necessary measures to enable them to exercise the right to vote.

Japanese citizens residing abroad, unlike those residing in Japan, are generally unable to exercise the right to vote due to lack of eligibility to be listed on the electoral register.

However, they still have the constitutional right to vote, and the State is responsible for taking necessary measures to practically enable them to exercise the right to vote while giving consideration to maintenance of fairness in elections. The State may argue unavoidable grounds to take no such measures only when it is deemed to be practically impossible or extremely difficult to take such measures while maintaining fairness in elections.

. . . [C]onsidering the repeated use of the overseas voting system and remarkable progress in communication technology on a global scale . . . it is no longer extremely difficult to provide Japanese citizens residing abroad with correct information on individual candidates. Furthermore, the Law for Partial Amendment of the Public Offices Election Law (Law No 118 of 2000) was promulgated . . . with the aim of adopting an open list for elections of HC members under the proportional representation system. After this amendment, voters are, in principle, required to write the names of persons on the HC Candidates List as prescribed in Article 86-3(1) of the Public Offices Election Law when voting in elections of HC members under the proportional representation system. Furthermore, Japanese citizens residing abroad exercised the right to vote under this system in elections held in 2001 and 2004. Taking these facts into account, it cannot be said that there will be unavoidable grounds to preclude Japanese citizens residing abroad from voting in elections of HR members under the single-seat constituency system and elections of HC members under the constituency system, at least at the time of the first general election of HR members or regular election of HC members to be held after this judgment is handed down. Therefore, it must be said that the part of the provision of Article 8 of the Supplementary

Provisions of the Public Offices Election Law that limits, for the time being, the applicability of the overseas voting system to elections of members of the Houses of the Diet under the proportional representation system is in violation of Article 15(1) and (3), Article 43(1), and the proviso of Article 44 of the Constitution.

Secretary for Justice v Chan Wah
[2000] 3 HKCFAR 459 (Court of Final Appeal, Hong Kong)

Facts

The applicant Chan was a non-indigenous villager living in the village of Po Toi O in the New Territories. Although he had lived in the village his entire life and married an indigenous female villager, he was not deemed eligible to elect his village representatives on the ground that he was not an indigenous villager. He then sought judicial review, arguing that the registration rejection infringed his right to participate in public life right under the Bill of Rights.

Andrew Li CJ

As a matter of fact, there must have been a point of time when all villagers were indigenous. By definition, this was the case in 1898. For a good part of the 20th century, it may well be that with the relatively slow pace of economic and social change, mobility was relatively limited so that the villagers continued to be entirely or predominantly indigenous. In that situation, there would have been a close, if not virtually a complete, identity between the village and the indigenous villagers who make up its population. Apart from the certification and facilitation functions which are only relevant to indigenous villagers as they relate to their traditional rights and interests, the village representative represented the village, for example, in liaising with Government. And that meant representing the indigenous villagers since they made up predominantly the population of the village.

But with rapid change coming to the New Territories in the last few decades of the 20th century, economic and social forces have resulted in mobility. . . . [In the village concerned], the non-indigenous villagers make up a substantial portion of their population. . . . With such shifts in the make-up of the population . . . the village representative in discharging his functions beyond certification and facilitation, would as a matter of fact no longer be representing only the indigenous villagers but the village as a whole consisting of both indigenous and non-indigenous villagers. This would be so for example, in his functions in liaising with the Government.

As to the Kuk [Rural Council], its statutory functions are not limited to representing the interests of indigenous inhabitants. Whatever may have been the position in the past, the present composition of its Full Council is that there is now a significant portion (about 25%) who are non-indigenous inhabitants. . . . The amendment to the Kuk Ordinance in 1988 was evidently to facilitate the participation of non-indigenous inhabitants.

Leaving aside the position as a matter of fact, and turning to the proper construction of the phrase, 'a person . . . to represent a village', should it be construed to mean to represent only the indigenous villagers? Even assuming that in 1959 when the Kuk Ordinance was enacted, the population in the villages consisted only of indigenous villagers, there is no justification for suggesting that the meaning of the statute was intended to be frozen at the time of its enactment. The Kuk Ordinance providing for the Kuk's incorporation and its functions looks to the future. As is usual with statutes, the Court should construe it in accordance with the need to treat it as continuing to operate as current law. . . . So construing it, the phrase 'to represent a village' carries its ordinary meaning of representing the whole village. It cannot be read to mean only a part of the village. Accordingly, both indigenous villagers and non-indigenous villagers which make up its population would be represented.

Public affairs would cover all aspects of public administration including at the village level. Apart from the certification and facilitation functions which relate to the traditional rights and interests of indigenous villagers, the village representative represents the village as a whole in liaising with the authorities on matters affecting the village and the welfare of the villagers. Such matters concern public administration at the village level. Further, the village representative has a role to play beyond the village level. . . . [T]his role, played directly or indirectly through chairmen and vice-chairmen of Rural Committees elected by village representatives from among themselves, extends to various bodies in the public arena; the Rural Committee, the District Council, the Kuk and ultimately the Kuk as a functional constituency in the Legislative Council. Having regard to the functions of the village representative and the person's role beyond the village level, the village representative should be regarded as engaged in the conduct of public affairs within article 21(a) of the Bill of Rights. This is reflected by the requirement that to become a village representative, the person elected has to be approved by a public official, the Secretary.

Having concluded that the village representative should be regarded as engaged in the conduct of public affairs, the next question which arises is whether the restrictions excluding Mr Chan from voting . . . are unreasonable restrictions.

The question whether restrictions are reasonable or unreasonable has to be considered objectively. One must have regard to the nature of the public affairs the conduct of which is involved and the nature of the restrictions on the right and the opportunity to participate and any reason for such restrictions. What may be considered reasonable or unreasonable restrictions in one era may be different from those in quite a different era.

Mr Chan . . . [has] lived in [the village all his life] and can plainly be properly regarded as [a villager]. But [he has been] excluded from voting . . . on the ground that [he is] not indigenous, that is, [he is not descendant] by patrilineal descent of ancestors who in 1898 were residents of villages in the New Territories. But bearing in mind that the village representative by statute is to and in fact does represent the village as a whole (comprising both the indigenous and the non-indigenous villagers) and further has a role to play beyond the village level, the restriction on the ground of not being indigenous cannot be considered a reasonable restriction.

Accordingly, the electoral arrangements in restricting Mr Chan from voting . . . [are] unreasonable and inconsistent with Article 21(a) of the Bill of Rights.

Restriction on Prisoner's Right to Vote Case
2007Hun-Ma1462, 29 Oct 2009 (Constitutional Court, South Korea)

Facts

The former portion of Article 18, Section 1, Item 2 of the Public Official Election Act (the 'Instant Provision') stipulated that 'a person who is sentenced to imprisonment without prison labor or a heavier punishment, but whose sentence execution has not been terminated shall be disfranchised.' The complainant, who had been sentenced to one-and-half years in prison, tried to cast a vote in the 2007 presidential election while in prison, but failed. He filed this constitutional complaint, alleging that the Instant Provision infringed his basic rights including the right to vote.

Held

The deprivation of the right to vote by the Instant Provision functions as retribution for crime as an extension of criminal sanction against criminals, which can be regarded as an important purpose for the legislators to impose criminal sanctions or restrictions against grave crimes.

Further, the deprivation of the right to vote imposed on a prisoner by the Instant Provision, on top of the capital punishment or deprivation of liberty to which the prisoner is sentenced, can contribute to heighten the responsibility of general citizens including the prisoner himself/herself as a citizen and reinforce the their respect toward the rule of law.

Such legislative purposes of the Instant Provision are legitimate, and the restriction on prisoners' voting right is one of the effective and proper measures to achieve the legislative purposes. Therefore, the Instant Provision cannot be said to meet legitimate legislative purposes and appropriateness of means . . .

Election is a system that forms state institutions by competition and majority vote. Majority opinion expressed by election also has binding force on minority, and the legitimacy of such binding force comes from the fact that the same chance to participate in election is also equally given to individuals who fall under the minority group, in other words, the principle of universal suffrage is observed. Therefore, the principle of universal suffrage both shows the limitation of the principle of majority rule and provides legitimacy to the rule of majority rule. This is why Article 41 and Article 67 of our Constitution specifically elucidate the principle of universal suffrage for the election of the National Assembly members and the Presidential Election. Therefore, the principle of universal suffrage and the right to vote based on it should be restricted to the minimum extent if necessary.

Meanwhile, the core of punishments, . . . is 'deprivation of life' or 'incarceration in correctional facility,' and the decision as to which part of other freedoms and rights prisoners may enjoy as citizens would be restricted is not made directly. . . . So, a prisoner, in principle, still has right to enjoy their basic rights other than those restricted by the particular punishment sentenced to him/her. As restriction on the right to vote does not naturally derive from the essence of capital punishment or imprisonment sentenced to prisoners, prisoner's right to vote should be restricted to minimum necessary extend based on the principle of universal suffrage.

The Instant Provision, however, fully and uniformly restrict the right to vote of those who are sentenced to imprisonment without prison labor or a heavier punishment, but whose sentence execution has not been terminated. . . . [T]he scope of application of the Instant Provision is very broad, spanning from and neither does consider the type of crimes such as whether it is a criminal negligence or intentional offence nor the type of legal interests infringed by the crimes such as whether it is state interest, social interest or personal interest.

Further, the Instant Provision's wide-ranging restriction on the right to vote, even applying to the one who is sentenced to a short term imprisonment for a crime of little gravity nothing to do with any anti-state offence that denies the constitutional order such as the democracy, seems discrepant from the election system of a liberal democratic country that aims at creating and maintaining order within the community by allowing various people with diverse ideological backgrounds and personal history to freely participate in elections based on pluralistic worldview.

Therefore, the Instant Provision violates the rule of least restrictive means in restricting basic rights.

The right to vote, as a means through which the right holders can realize their political opinions, is a right every citizen holds. Further, maximum guarantee of the right to vote pursuant to the principle of universal suffrage is the core element for realizing 'the representative democracy on the basis of the popular sovereignty,' which is the basic tenant of our Constitution and has the public value of guaranteeing democratic legitimacy of state power achieved by election to the maximum level. Therefore, arbitrary restriction on the voting right infringes on not only private interests of the right holders but also the above mentioned public interest.

As the restriction on prisoner's right to vote by the Instant Provision, however, is too broad . . . and . . . not directly related to the specific characteristics of a crime, the public interests expected to be achieved by the restriction including 'sanction against criminals who commit grave crimes or reinforcement of citizens' respect to the rule of law' is less valuable than 'prisoner's private interests or the public value of democratic election system' expected to be infringed by the Instant Provision.

Therefore, the Instant Provision fails to strike balance between the conflicting legal interests regarding the restriction on the basic rights.

As reviewed above, the constitutional complaint should be upheld and the Instant Provision should be declared unconstitutional.

Notes and Questions

1. Compare *Kim v Osaka Electoral Commission* and the *Case to Seek Declaration of Illegality of Deprivation of the Right to Vote of Japanese Citizens Residing Abroad*, both decisions of the Supreme Court of Japan. In the former case, the Court deferred to the legislative decision not to extend voting rights to non-nationals, while in the latter case the Court held it unconstitutional not to extend the full right to vote to nationals residing abroad. What explains the difference between these two decisions? Is it due to the gradual liberalising of judicial attitudes towards the equal right to vote, or due to a preference towards nationals with respect to voting?

2. In both *Secretary for Justice v Chan Wah* by the Final Court of Appeal and the *Restriction on Prisoner's Right to Vote Case* (South Korean Constitutional Court), the principle of proportionality was applied and the restrictions held unconstitutional. To what extent is the principle of proportionality a helpful test in guaranteeing the equal right to vote? How stringent is the test of adopting the least restrictive means?

3. Although the exercise of the right to vote is usually limited to nationals or citizens, there has been an increasing trend in European countries to extend such right to foreigners at local levels. Article 6(1) of the Convention on the Participation of Foreigners in Public Life at Local Level, a Council of Europe treaty, provides:

    > Each Party undertakes . . . to grant to every foreign resident the right to vote and to stand for election in local authority elections, provided that he fulfils the same legal requirements as apply to nationals and furthermore has been a lawful and habitual resident in the State concerned for the 5 years preceding the elections.

In addition, 15 EU countries have granted suffrage to foreigners, including but not limited to EU citizens, in local level elections. See J Shaw, *The Transformation of Citizenship in the European Union: Electoral Rights and the Restructuring of the Political Space* (Cambridge: Cambridge University Press, 2007) at 76. Some countries explicitly extend the right to vote to foreigners in the constitution. For instance, the Constitution of the Netherlands provides that 'the right to elect members of a municipal council and the right to be a member of a municipal council may be granted by Act of Parliament to residents who are not Dutch nationals provided they fulfil at least the requirements applicable to residents who are Dutch nationals'. Most other countries extend such rights by statutes. For example, in Denmark, section 1 of the Consolidated Act on Danish Municipal and Regional Elections stipulates that 'anyone shall have the franchise in municipal and regional elections who, on election day, has turned 18 years of age and who is domiciled in the municipality or the region, respectively, and who, in addition . . . has been domiciled continuously in the Kingdom of Denmark during the last 3 years prior to election day'.

4.   In contrast with the liberal attitude exhibited by the Supreme Court of Japan in the *Case to Seek Declaration of Illegality of Deprivation of the Right to Vote of Japanese Citizens Residing Abroad*, the Constitutional Court of South Korea upheld similar residential requirements in two cases. In the *Overseas Citizens Voting Rights Ban Case*,[60] when reviewing the law that conditioned the exercise of the right to vote, tax obligations and mandatory military service, the Court held that 'it is needed to impose residential requirements on voting rights in order to protect the essential content of the voting right, the fairness in voting, and other public interests'. In a later case (97Hun-Ma99, 25 Mar 1999), the Court upheld Article 38(1) of the Act, reasoning that overseas absentee ballots would be costly and difficult to administer fairly, and the absent voting system was only an administrative amenity subject to legislative discretion. As a result, the lack of voting opportunity for overseas nationals was not in violation of the Constitution. In the *Restriction on Prisoner's Right to Vote Case*, the Constitutional Court of South Korea held unconstitutional an overly-broad restriction on prisoners' voting rights. In relation to prisoners' voting rights, the Human Rights Committee stated, in General Comment 25:

> If conviction for an offence is a basis for suspending the right to vote, the period of such suspension should be proportionate to the offence and the sentence. Persons who are deprived of liberty but who have not been convicted should not be excluded from exercising the right to vote.

See UN Human Rights Committee, 'General Comment 25, The right to participate in public affairs, voting rights and the right of equal access to public service (article 25)' UN Doc CCPR/C/21/Rev.3/Add.7 (1996), para 14.

5.   A similar sense of proportionality in respecting prisoner voting rights is evident in various decisions by the European Court of Human Rights. In *Scoppola v Italy (No 3)*,[61] the Court upheld the Italian disenfranchisement system under Article 3 of Protocol 1 to the European Convention on Human Rights as the system was

---

[60] *Overseas Citizens Voting Rights Ban Case*, 97Hun-Ma253, 28 Jan 1999.
[61] *Scoppola v Italy (No 3)*, App No 126/05 (ECtHR, 22 May 2012), para 106.

not applied to 'all individuals sentenced to a term of imprisonment but only to those sentenced to a prison term of three years or more. Italian law also adjusts the duration of the measure to the sentence imposed and thus . . . to the gravity of the offence'. Article 3 of Protocol 1 to the European Convention on Human Rights provides that 'The High Contracting Parties undertake to hold free elections at reasonable intervals by secret ballot, under conditions which will ensure the free expression of the opinion of the people in the choice of the legislature'. Based upon the observation, the Court ruled (at para 110) that '[t]he margin of appreciation afforded to the respondent Government [of Italy] in this sphere has therefore not been overstepped'.

B. Qualifications of Candidates

Individuals under almost every Asian constitutional order enjoy the equal right to stand for elections or to hold public office, subject to certain restrictions. These relate typically to nationality, citizenship, educational background, criminal record or membership of political parties, among others. The following cases illustrate some of these restrictions and the constitutional concerns raised.

Mercado v Manzano
307 SCRA 630 (1999) (Supreme Court, Philippines)

Facts

The petitioner Mercado and respondent Manzano were candidates for the post of Vice Mayor of the City of Makati in the 11 May 1998 elections. The petitioner filed a petition before Election Day, alleging that the respondent was an American citizen and should thus be disqualified as a candidate. The respondent argued that although he was born in the United States, he did not lose his Filipino citizenship because he was born of a Filipino father and a Filipino mother.

Mendoza J

The disqualification of private respondent Manzano is being sought under §40 of the Local Government Code of 1991 . . . which declares as 'disqualified from running for any elective local position: . . . (d) Those with dual citizenship.' This provision is incorporated in the Charter of the City of Makati.

To begin with, dual citizenship is different from dual allegiance. The former arises when, as a result of the concurrent application of the different laws of two or more states, a person is simultaneously considered a national by the said states. For instance, such a situation may arise when a person whose parents are citizens of a state which adheres to the principle of *jus sanguinis* is born in a state which follows the doctrine of *jus soli*. Such a person, *ipso facto* and without any voluntary act on his part, is concurrently considered a citizen of both states. . . .

Dual allegiance, on the other hand, refers to the situation in which a person simultaneously owes, by some positive act, loyalty to two or more states. While dual citizenship is involuntary, dual allegiance is the result of an individual's volition.

Clearly, in including §5 in Article IV on citizenship, the concern of the Constitutional Commission was not with dual citizens per se but with naturalized citizens who maintain their allegiance to their countries of origin even after their naturalization. Hence, the phrase 'dual citizenship' in RA No 7160, §40(d) and in RA No 7854, §20 must be understood as referring to 'dual allegiance.' Consequently, persons with mere dual citizenship do not fall under this disqualification. Unlike those with dual allegiance, who must, therefore, be subject to strict process with respect to the termination of their status, for candidates with dual citizenship, it should suffice if, upon the filing of their certificates of candidacy, they elect Philippine citizenship to terminate their status as persons with dual citizenship considering that their condition is the unavoidable consequence of conflicting laws of different states. As Joaquin G Bernas, one of the most perceptive members of the Constitutional Commission, pointed out: '[D]ual citizenship is just a reality imposed on us because we have no control of the laws on citizenship of other countries. We recognize a child of a Filipino mother. But whether or not she is considered a citizen of another country is something completely beyond our control.' . . .

By electing Philippine citizenship, such candidates at the same time forswear allegiance to the other country of which they are also citizens and thereby terminate their status as dual citizens. It may be that, from the point of view of the foreign state and of its laws, such an individual has not effectively renounced his foreign citizenship.

The record shows that private respondent was born in San Francisco, California on September 4, 1955, of Filipino parents. Since the Philippines adheres to the principle of *jus sanguinis*, while the United States follows the doctrine of *jus soli*, the parties agree that, at birth at least, he was a national both of the Philippines and of the United States.

Until the filing of his certificate of candidacy on March 21, 1998, he had dual citizenship. The acts attributed to him can be considered simply as the assertion of his American nationality before the termination of his American citizenship. . . .

To recapitulate, by declaring in his certificate of candidacy that he is a Filipino citizen; that he is not a permanent resident or immigrant of another country; that he will defend and support the Constitution of the Philippines and bear true faith and allegiance thereto and that he does so without mental reservation, private respondent has, as far as the laws of this country are concerned, effectively repudiated his American citizenship and anything which he may have said before as a dual citizen.

On the other hand, private respondent's oath of allegiance to the Philippines, when considered with the fact that he has spent his youth and adulthood, received his education, practiced his profession as an artist, and taken part in past elections in this country, leaves no doubt of his election of Philippine citizenship.

His declarations will be taken upon the faith that he will fulfill his undertaking made under oath. Should he betray that trust, there are enough sanctions for declaring the loss of his Philippine citizenship through expatriation in appropriate proceedings.

JY Interpretation No 290
24 Jan 1992 (Constitutional Court, Taiwan)

Facts

The applicant was an influential Taiwanese writer and social activist. She was refused registration to run for the National Assembly election due to her educational background; she had attended only elementary school due to her rheumatoid arthritis. The applicant challenged the Public Service Election and Recall Law on the grounds that the requirements of educational backgrounds and working experience of candidates for all levels of elected representatives infringed the fundamental right to equality and the right to hold public office.

Held

Article 130 of the Constitution provides: '. . . any citizen who has attained the age of 23 years shall have the right to be elected in accordance with law.' Accordingly, the law provides some latitude by stipulating some conditions to regulate the exercise of the right to be elected within reasonable discretion. Article 32, Section 1, of the . . . Public Service Election and Recall Law . . ., revised and publicized on February 3, 1989, with regard to the restrictions on educational background and working experience of candidates for all levels of elected representatives, though not typical in comparison with other countries, shall not be deemed contrary to the Constitution for the purpose of promoting the efficacy and quality of all levels of representative organs in light of the current state of this country. However, as the pursuit of education grows even more popular and voters' ability to make informed choices becomes better, whether such restrictions should be maintained should be considered in light of the examples of other democracies. Should they be deemed necessary, their underlying reasoning should be supported by evidence. The circumstances of those who have difficulty completing compulsory education should also be considered (eg, those with physical or other disabilities who have difficulties completing a normal education) and appropriate rules should be stipulated accordingly by reasonable discretion of the legislature.

Tse Hung Hing v Medical Council of Hong Kong
[2010] 1 HKLRD 111 (Court of First Instance, Hong Kong)

Facts

Section 4(2)(b) of the Medical Practitioners Regulations ('the Regulations') provided that a registered medical practitioner would be disqualified from nomination in an election or from holding office as a member of the Medical Council of Hong Kong ('the Council') if he had been convicted in Hong Kong or elsewhere of any offence punishable with imprisonment. The applicant questioned the constitutionality of the blanket ban on the right to stand for election and to hold office in the Medical Council upon conviction for an offence punishable with imprisonment.

Hon Chu J

At the heart of this application is the constitutionality of section 4(2)(b) of the Regulations. . . . [T]he section is a restriction that interferes with the right to take part in the conduct of public affairs directly or through freely chosen representatives. The right is guaranteed under Article 25 of the International Covenant on Civil and Political Rights, as applied to Hong Kong by Article 21 of the Hong Kong Bill of Rights ('HKBOR'), and enshrined in Article 39 of the Basic Law. The Council is a public body and its members are engaged in the conduct of public affairs within the meaning of Article 21(a) of the HKBOR.

I accept the submission that the restriction under section 4(2)(b) is unreasonable having regard to the factors identified in *Secretary for Justice & Ors v Chan Wah & Ors* [2000]

3 HKCFAR 459, namely, (i) the nature of the public affairs in question; (ii) the nature of the restriction; and (iii) the reason for the restriction under the section. Members of the Council primarily function as the regulator of the medical profession. *Prima facie*, the reason for the disqualification in section 4(2)(b) is to ensure that Council members are trustworthy persons of high moral probity. In setting out to achieve this objective, the section imposes a blanket ban on the right to stand for election and to hold office upon conviction of an offence punishable with imprisonment, giving no regard to the nature, gravity and culpability of the offence involved. Thus analysed, the blanket restriction cannot pass the reasonableness requirement. The point is exemplified by the facts of the present case. The conviction involved is a motoring offence of careless driving and a fine of $1000 was imposed. It is common ground that this is a minor conviction. It also has no apparent relevance to the applicant's suitability to be a Council member. Nonetheless, on an application of the section, the applicant became automatically disqualified from being nominated for election and from holding office as a member of the Council.

Judicial Review on Regulation No 23 year 2003 Regarding General Election of President and Vice President
007/PUU-II/2004, 23 Jul 2004 (Constitutional Court, Indonesia)

Facts

The petitioner was an independent presidential candidate. He could not participate in the presidential election because there was no provision to register candidates without any political party affiliation. The petitioner then filed a judicial review petition, alleging that Article 51 Paragraph (1) of the Law of the Republic of Indonesia Number 24 Year 2003 was unconstitutional since it only allowed party nominees to be presidential candidates.

Held

[T]he 1945 Constitution appears to distinguish between the constitutional right of a citizen and that of a political party. The right to become President is the constitutional right of a citizen, but it does not mean that every citizen may automatically become President; rather, they must comply with the requirements and procedures set by the Constitution and the law as the implementation of the provisions of the Constitution.

    ... [P]ursuant to ... Article 6A Paragraph (2) of the 1945 Constitution, the party that has the constitutional right to nominate Presidential and Vice Presidential candidates shall be a political party ... This provision is not intended to eliminate the right of citizens to become President. Meanwhile, the provision of Article 25 of Law Number 23 Year 2003 which states that 'Presidential Candidate and Vice Presidential Candidate are nominated by a political party or a coalition of political parties participating in the General Election' is a mere reiteration and confirmation of the provision of Article 6A Paragraph (2) of the 1945 Constitution so that consequently, it is not contradictory to the 1945 Constitution.

    ... Therefore, although the Petitioner has the constitutional right to become a Presidential Candidate pursuant to the Constitution, if he is not nominated by a political party or coalition of political parties participating in the general election, the Petitioner *in casu* shall not have the constitutional right as referred to in Article 6A Paragraph (2) of the Constitution. Hence, the Petitioner cannot argue that he has suffered impairment due to the coming into effect of Article 25 of Law Number 23 Year 2003.

Notes and Questions

1. Just as there is a growing trend to extend voting rights to foreigners across Europe, foreigners have also been given the right to stand for elections. Article 6(1) of the Council of Europe's Convention on the Participation of Foreigners in Public Life at Local Level stipulates that each state party shall grant to every foreign resident the right to stand for election 'in local authority elections, provided that he fulfils the same legal requirements as apply to nationals and furthermore has been a lawful and habitual resident in the State concerned for the 5 years preceding the elections'. A few EU countries also grant aliens the right to stand for local level elections. The Local Government Act of Sweden entitles a non-citizen who has been a registered resident of Sweden for three consecutive years before election day, the right to stand for election to a municipal or county assembly.

2. Since those serving in public office are usually subject to higher responsibilities, the qualifications for standing for election to or holding public office are usually found permissible, as can be seen in *JY Interpretation No 290* of the Constitutional Court in Taiwan.

3. In Pakistan, section 99(cc) of the Representation of the People Act of 1976 requires members of an assembly to possess 'a bachelor's degree in any discipline or any degree recognized as equivalent thereto by the University Grants Commission'. Notwithstanding this strict requirement, corrupt practices have allowed this requirement to be circumvented. In *Mian Najibuddin Oawaisi v Aamir Yar* [2011] PLD 1, the Supreme Court of Pakistan held that both the Election Commission and the Chief Commissioner were competent to lodge complaints about suspect candidates who lacked the requisite educational qualifications.

4. The European Court of Human Rights has held that states enjoy broad latitude in determining what criteria they demand of election candidates; though they must 'ensure both the independence of elected representatives and the freedom of electors, these criteria vary in accordance with the historical and political factors specific to each State'.[62] In addition, 'any electoral legislation must be assessed in the light of the political evolution of the country concerned, so that features that would be unacceptable in the context of one system may be justified in the context of another'. Nevertheless, these qualifications are not without any limits. As the Human Right Committee recommended, 'persons who are otherwise eligible to stand for election should not be excluded by unreasonable or discriminatory requirements such as education, residence or descent, or by reason of political affiliation'. See UN Human Rights Committee, 'General Comment 25, The right to participate in public affairs, voting rights and the right of equal access to public service (article 25)' UN Doc CCPR/C/21/Rev.3/Add.7 (1996), para 15.

5. In South Korea, independent candidates at the time of registration were required to deposit 20 million Korean won with the local Election Commission, twice the amount required of party nominees. The Constitutional Court of South Korea found that the relevant Act failed to conform to the Constitution. It held:

---

[62] See *Podkolzina v Latvia* ECHR 2002-II 443, para 33.

The role of political parties is indispensable to democratic polity. The Constitution does extend special protection to parties. However, the deposit requirement for independent candidates amounting to twice the amount required of party nominees gives the independent candidates substantial competitive disadvantages and suppress[es] their candidacy. . . . The average amount of savings of the economically active in this country is 6.93 million won. The deposit requirement of ten or twenty million is prohibitive to people of ordinary income or in their twenties' or thirties', and therefore permits only the wealthy to the candidacy. Therefore, it is excessive.[63]

6. In Taiwan, the full-amount deposit requirement for independent candidates was also stipulated in the Public Officials Election and Recall Act. Intriguingly, unlike the South Korean Constitutional Court, the Constitutional Court of Taiwan held such a requirement necessary to foster 'a healthy development of party politics'. The Court reasoned:

Paragraph II of the Public Officials Election and Recall Act provides, 'The guarantee deposit for a party-recommended area or aboriginal candidate will be reduced by half provided, however, that the same shall be paid in full if the political party withdraws its recommendation.' The said provision is tantamount to requiring a candidate who is not recommended by a political party to pay a higher amount of guarantee deposit than a party recommended candidate.

If and when the amount of the guarantee deposit published by the competent authority is too high, a person intent on running for the public office concerned may simply bring together a handful [or small group] of people and form a political party by means of placing the same on record pursuant to law, and then lessen his or her financial burden in the name of a party-recommended candidate. As a result, smaller parties will be mushrooming, which may not be conducive to a healthy development of party politics. Hence, the aforesaid provision of the Public Officials Election and Recall Act has imposed unnecessary restrictions on the people's suffrage and qualifies as unreasonable discrimination.

Similarly, in Taiwan, the Presidential and Vice Presidential Election and Recall Act required that independent candidates garner at least 1.5 percent of the total number of electors in the most recent national election within forty-five days when the Central Election Commission proclaimed the candidates for the joint-endorsement campaigns. The Constitutional Court again upheld the Act, reasoning that: 'the adoption of the joint-endorsement system, which signifies a reasonable degree of political support for the candidate opting for the system, serves not only to equitably balance against the requirement for a candidate recommended by a political party,' but also 'to prevent the people from needlessly participating in presidential and vice presidential elections, thus wasting social resources.[64]

7. Reflecting Confucian culture that emphasises education and the merit of civil servants, some East Asian jurisdictions explicitly grant their citizens the right to take civil service examinations in the constitution. See HG Frederickson, 'Confucius and the Moral Basis of Bureaucracy' (2002) 33 *Administration & Society* 610, 618. For instance, in Taiwan, Article 18 of the Constitution specifically provides that 'the people shall have the right of taking public examinations

---

[63] See *National Assembly Candidacy Deposit Case*, 88Hun-Ka6, 8 Sep 1989.
[64] See *JY Interpretation No 340*, 2 ROC Const Ct 489, 491 (2007); and *JY Interpretation No 468*, 3 ROC Const Ct 640, 646–47 (2007).

and of holding public offices'. Article 25 of the Constitution of South Korea stipulates that 'all citizens shall have the right to hold public office under the conditions as prescribed by Act', which is further supplemented by the Decree on Civil Service Entrance Examination.

8. Although the Constitution of Japan does not explicitly provide for the right to take examinations, a similar issue arose in the Supreme Court of Japan.[65] A Japanese permanent resident holding Korean citizenship applied to sit the examination for Management Selection to Hachioji Public Health Center in Tokyo in 1994. However, her application was refused as she was not of Japanese nationality, even though no such a requirement was stipulated in the Outline of Management Selection by the Personnel Commission of the Tokyo Metropolitan Government. The appellant sought non-pecuniary compensation for deprivation of her right to take such examinations. The Court held:

> As promotion to managerial posts generally involves advancement to superior job grades, reasonable grounds would be required when appointing foreign residents as employees under the condition that they cannot be promoted to managerial posts.
>
> With respect to local government employees who are engaged in performing duties that involve exercise of public authority, such as directly creating rights and obligations of inhabitants or defining the scope thereof, or decision-making or participation in the decision-making process relating to important policies of an ordinary local public body, ... it is appropriate to consider as follows. The performance of duties of local government employees with public authority is directly or indirectly related to the lives of inhabitants to a significant extent, because it defines the rights and obligations of inhabitants or their legal status or has in effect a significant influence on these matters. Therefore, considering that the Japanese people shall, as the sovereign of the nation under the principle of sovereignty of the people, have final responsibility for governance by the national government and ordinary local public bodies (see Article 1 and Article 15, Para 1 of the Constitution), it is contemplated that, in principle, Japanese nationals shall take office as local government employees with public authority, and it is not contemplated under the Japanese legal framework that foreign nationals who belong to a nation other than Japan and have rights and obligations as the people of the nation, may take office as local government employees with public authority in Japan.[66]

V. REFERENDUM, INITIATIVE AND PETITION

The majority of constitutions include certain mechanisms in which direct democracy is used to supplement representative decision making. This section discusses referendum practices in Asian jurisdictions, as well as the initiative and petition system, which draws mainly from the Chinese Letter and Visit (*Xinfang*) system.

---

[65] See *Case to Seek Declaration of Eligibility to Become a Candidate for an Examination for Selecting Management Level Employees*, 59 Minshū 1.

[66] Ibid para 4(2).

A. Referendum

The referendum is an important mechanism through which citizens realise their right to political participation. The Human Rights Committee stated that citizens participate directly in the conduct of public affairs 'when they choose or change their constitution or decide public issues through a referendum or other electoral process'.[67] In the Committee's view, the right to vote in a referendum is no different from the right to vote in an election, and 'persons entitled to vote must be free to vote for any candidate for election and for or against any proposal submitted to referendum or plebiscite'.[68]

The referendum is widely available in many Asian jurisdictions. Table 6.2 shows the variations of referendum mechanisms provided for in 12 Asian constitutions, which may be supplemented by a statutory regime. As can be seen, the majority of the Asian

Table 6.2 Referendum Mechanisms in Asian Constitutions

Level of Exercise		Issues Involved		Power to Propose a Referendum (at national level)	
National	Sub-national	Constitutional Changes	Only Issues Other than Constitutional Changes	President	Parliament
Bangladesh Japan Mongolia Pakistan Philippines Singapore South Korea Sri Lanka Taiwan Thailand Timor-Leste Vietnam	Japan South Korea Philippines Thailand Taiwan	Bangladesh Japan Mongolia Philippines** Singapore South Korea Sri Lanka Taiwan Timor-Leste	Pakistan* Thailand Vietnam***	Bangladesh South Korea Sri Lanka	Japan Mongolia Pakistan Singapore Taiwan Vietnam Thailand Timor-Leste

*   Any matter of national importance (Art 48).

**   Philippines: 'Amendments to this Constitution may likewise be directly proposed by the people through initiative upon a petition of at least twelve per centum of the total number of registered voters, of which every legislative district must be represented by at least three per centum of the registered voters therein.' (Art XVII, Sec 2)

Any issue that may affect national or public interests, or in the case where a referendum is required by the law (Sec 165).

*** 'Citizens have the right to take part in managing the State and society, in debating on general issues of the whole country or of the locality, and make petitions or recommendation to the state offices and vote at any referendum held by the State' (Art 53)

---

[67] UN Human Rights Committee, 'General Comment 25, The right to participate in public affairs, voting rights and the right of equal access to public service (article 25)' UN Doc CCPR/C/21/Rev.3/Add.7 (1996), para 6.

[68] Ibid, para 19.

jurisdictions provide for referenda at the national level, including Bangladesh, Japan, Mongolia, Pakistan, the Philippines, Singapore, South Korea, Sri Lanka, Taiwan, Thailand and Timor-Leste. The right to referenda at the sub-national level is granted in Japan, South Korea, the Philippines, Thailand and Taiwan.

Matters that are subject to the referendum process are mainly those involving constitutional revision, matters of national importance or which relate to local autonomy. The majority of the 12 jurisdictions permit or even demand the exercise of referenda for constitutional revision. However, in Pakistan, Thailand and Vietnam, a referendum can be held for other issues too. The President in Bangladesh, South Korea and Sri Lanka has the power to propose a referendum, while the other nine countries leave that power to the legislature.

Impeachment of the President Case
2004Hun-Na1, 14 May 2004 (Constitutional Court, South Korea)

Facts

The respondent President of Korea stated that he intended to implement a national confidence referendum for himself. A constitutional complaint was filed on the basis that his statement was unconstitutional, since Article 72 of the Constitution mandated a national referendum only for 'important policies relating to diplomacy, national defense, unification and other matters relating to the national destiny'. It was further argued that such a referendum infringed upon the citizens' basic rights, including the right to vote. The Constitutional Court dismissed the complaint on the ground that the President's statement was merely an expression of political proposition, rather than an 'exercise of governmental power'. Months later, the National Assembly sought to impeach the President for suggesting a confidence vote in the form of a national referendum.

Held

Since the National Assembly's impeachment resolution specifically mentions the President's 'unconstitutional suggestion to have a confidence referendum' with respect to its third stated ground for impeachment of 'unfaithful performance of official duties and reckless administration of state affairs' and the National Assembly further specified on this issue in its brief submitted subsequent to the initiation of the impeachment adjudication, we examine this issue as a subject matter of this impeachment adjudication.

The President, during 'his speech' at the National Assembly on October 13, 2003 . . . suggest[ed] a confidence vote to be instituted in December of 2003. Debates concerning the constitutional permissibility of a confidence vote were thereby caused. Finally, such debates upon the constitutionality of a confidence referendum reached the Constitutional Court through a constitutional petition, but the Constitutional Court, in its majority opinion of five Justices in 2003Hun-Ma694 . . ., dismissed such constitutional petition on the ground that the 'act of the President that is the subject matter of the case was not an act accompanying legal effect but an expression of a mere political plan, therefore did not constitute an exercise of governmental power.'

Article 72 of the Constitution vests in the President the authority to institute national referendum by providing that the 'President may submit important policies relating to diplomacy, national defense, unification and other matters relating to the national destiny to a national referendum if he or she deems it necessary.' Article 72 of the Constitution connotes a danger that the President might use national referendum as a political weapon and politically abuse such device by employing it to further legitimize his or her policy and to strengthen his or her political position beyond as a mere means to confirm the will of the public toward a specific policy, as the President monopolizes the discretionary authority to institute national referendum including the authority to decide whether to institute a national referendum, its timing, and the specific agendas to be voted on and the questions to be asked at the referendum, under Article 72 of the Constitution. Thus, Article 72 of the Constitution vesting within the President the authority to institute a national referendum should be strictly and narrowly interpreted in order to prevent the political abuse of national referendum by the President.

From this standpoint, the 'important policy matters' that can be subjected to a national referendum under Article 72 of the Constitution do not include the 'trust of the public' in the President.

An election is for the 'decision on persons,' that is, an election is to determine the representatives of the public as a premise to make representative democracy possible. By contrast, the national referendum is a means to realize direct democracy, and its object or subject matter is the 'decision on issues,' that is, specific state policies or legislative bills. Therefore, by the own nature of the national referendum, the 'confidence the public has in its representative' cannot be a subject matter for a national referendum and the decision of and the confidence in the representative under our Constitution may be performed and manifested solely through elections. The President's attempt to reconfirm the public's trust in him that was obtained through the past election in the form of a referendum constitutes an unconstitutional use of the institution of a national referendum provided in Article 72 of the Constitution in a way not permitted by the Constitution.

The Constitution does not permit the President to ask the public's trust in him by way of national referendum. The constitution further prohibits as an unconstitutional act the act of the President subjecting a specific policy to a referendum and linking the matter of confidence thereto. Of course, when the President institutes a referendum for a specific policy and fails to obtain the consent of the public concerning the implementation of such policy, the President may possibly resign by regarding such outcome as [the] public's distrust in him or her. However, should the President submit a policy matter to a referendum and declare at the same time that 'I shall regard the outcome of the referendum as a confidence vote,' this act will unduly influence the decision-making of the public and employ the referendum as a means to indirectly ask confidence in the President, therefore will exceed the constitutional authority vested in the President. The Constitution does not vest in the President the authority to ask the confidence in him or her by the public through a national referendum, directly or indirectly.

Furthermore, the Constitution does not permit a national confidence referendum in any other form than the national referendum that is expressly provided in the Constitution. This is also true even when a confidence referendum is demanded by the people as the sovereign or implemented under the name of the people. The people directly exercise the state power by way of the election and the national referendum, and the national referendum requires an express basis therefor within the Constitution as a means by which the people exercise the state power. Therefore, national referendum cannot be grounded on such general constitutional principles as people's sovereignty or democracy, and, instead, can only be permitted when there is a ground expressly provided in the Constitution.

In conclusion, the President's suggestion to hold a national referendum on whether he should remain in office is an unconstitutional exercise of the President's authority to institute a national referendum delegated by Article 72 of the Constitution, and thus it is in violation of the constitutional obligation not to abuse the mechanism of the national referendum as a political tool to fortify his own political position. Although the President merely suggested an unconstitutional national referendum for confidence vote and did not yet actually institute such referendum, the suggestion toward the public of a confidence vote by way of national referendum, which is not permitted under the Constitution, is itself in violation of Article 72 of the Constitution and not in conformity with the President's obligation to realize and protect the Constitution.

Dharmadasa Gomes v Commissioner of Elections
[2000] 3 SLR 207 (Court of Appeal, Sri Lanka)

Facts

Article 86 of the Constitution in Sri Lanka gave the President power to submit any matter of national importance to the people for decision by referendum. Article 85(2) further stipulated that the President

> . . . may in his discretion submit to the People by Referendum any Bill (not being a Bill for the repeal or amendment of any provision of the Constitution, or for the addition of any provision to the Constitution, or for the repeal and replacement of the Constitution, or which is inconsistent with any provision of the Constitution), which has been rejected by Parliament.

The petitioner sought a writ of prohibition to prevent the Commissioner of Elections from holding a referendum directed by a proclamation by the President on the ground that the President had no power to issue such a proclamation and the Commissioner of Elections had discretion not to execute the illegal directions, for [the reason] that the matters submitted to the people by referendum are limited to bills concerning the Constitution.

Jan de Silva J

The main contention of the petitioner was that the President has no power to issue a Proclamation and the Commissioner of Elections has a discretion not to carry out the directions given by the President as such directions are illegal. We are not in agreement with this proposition. We hold that the Commissioner of Elections has no judicial power to consider the validity of the acts of the Hon President in calling for Referendum or Elections.

We are also mindful of the fact that Section 24 of the Interpretation Ordinance has placed limitations on Court with regard to the issuing of injunctions on State Officers.

Section 24(1) of the Interpretation Ordinance precludes any Court from granting injunctions against the State, a Minister or Deputy Minister upon any ground whatsoever. Furthermore, by Section 24(2), a Court is even precluded from granting an injunction against a public officer if the effect of so doing would amount to directly or indirectly [restraining] the State.

It is observed that if the relief prayed for in this application is granted, it would amount to an injunction against the State, as the President under whose direction the Commissioner of Elections is to hold the Referendum, is the Head of State.

The Commissioner of Elections being a public officer is covered by Section 24 of the Interpretation Ordinance. Therefore this Court cannot grant any of the reliefs prayed for by the petitioner. In the circumstances this application is dismissed however without costs.

Notes and Questions

1. What explains the different attitudes of the Constitutional Court of South Korea and the Court of Appeal in Sri Lanka, given that the former was willing to review the constitutionality of the referendum proposed by the President while the latter was not? Is the difference due mainly to the degree of democratic maturity or the state of party politics?

2. Consider the institutional design of commissions or agencies that are responsible for the administration of referenda. In *JY Interpretation No 645*, the Constitutional Court in Taiwan declared the institutional design of the referendum review committee unconstitutional given the involvement of party politics in the selection of committee members. The Court reasoned:

   > In order to safeguard the rights of initiative and referendum of the people and to ensure smooth and proper implementation of referendum, the legislative body shall establish comprehensive procedural and substantive regulations with respect to referendum. It shall in particular enact statutes to prescribe clearly and precisely the substantive elements required for the presentation of a bill of referendum and the procedure of holding the vote, and also establish a fair and impartial organization to take charge of the review of such bills so as to win the confidence of the people and to encourage the people to take part in referendum. To make such laws, however, the legislators must, in addition to making appropriate regulations on the principle of sovereignty by the people, adhere to the principle of separation of powers by refraining from making laws that go beyond the border of check and balance of powers to the extent of depriving completely the Executive Yuan of its power to make decisions on personnel management.[69]

B. Initiative

The initiative refers to a form of direct democracy by which a petition signed by a certain number of voters may trigger a plebiscite on a constitutional amendment, or a proposed statute or ordinance at the national or local level. A few Asian constitutions provide citizens with the right to initiate and propose constitutional amendments. For example, Article XVII, Section 2 of the Constitution of the Philippines stipulates:

> Amendments to this Constitution may likewise be directly proposed by the people through initiative upon a petition of at least twelve per centum of the total number of registered voters, of which every legislative district must be represented by at least three per centum of the registered voters therein.

In addition, citizens are empowered to initiate legislation at the national or local levels. The Philippines and Taiwan Constitutions both provide for the right of initiative at both national and local level.[70] In contrast, Japan and South Korea permit initiative measures for the legislation of local ordinances under the Local Autonomy Act.[71] Under that system,

---

[69] See *JY Interpretation No 645*, 6 ROC Const Ct 332, 339–40 (2012).
[70] Art VI Sec 32 of the 1987 Philippine Constitution; Arts 17 and 123 of the Constitution of the Republic of China.
[71] Local Autonomy Law, Art 74 (Japan); Local Autonomy Act (2009), Art 15 (South Korea).

the residents of certain number or more, over nineteen years of age, and residing in the pertinent local self-government unit may request the chief executive officer of that self-government unit to prepare a bill and submit it to the corresponding local legislature for the enactment, revision or repeal of an ordinance.[72]

Nevertheless, the local legislature still holds the ultimate authority to pass or reject the bill as law.[73] The following case shows how the Philippines Supreme Court extended the subjects of initiative to guarantee the original power of the people to legislate.

Enrique T Garcia v Commission on Elections
237 SCRA 279 (1994) (Supreme Court, Philippines)

Facts

The Sangguniang Bayan ng Morong (Council Municipality of Morong) agreed to include the municipality of Morong as part of the Subic Special Economic Zone via its Pambayang Kapasyahan (public resolution) Blg 10, Serye 1993. The people of Morong filed a petition with the Council Municipality to annul this decision, but to no avail. They then began soliciting the required number of signatures to repeal the resolution through their initiative power. The petition for local initiative was denied by the Commission on Elections (COMELEC) because its subject was 'merely a resolution (pambayang kapasyahan) and not an ordinance'. The petitioners then filed a suit in the Supreme Court, asked for certiorari to set aside the resolution of the Commission and a writ of mandamus to command the COMELEC to schedule the continuation of the signing of the petition, and set a date for the initiative.

Puno J

The 1987 Constitution is borne of the conviction that people power can be trusted to check excesses of government. One of the means by which people power can be exercised is thru initiatives where local ordinances and resolutions can be enacted or repealed. An effort to trivialize the effectiveness of people's initiatives ought to be rejected.

The case at bench is of transcendental significance because it involves an issue of first impression – delineating the extent of the all important original power of the people to legislate. Father Bernas explains that 'in republican systems, there are generally two kinds of legislative power, original and derivative. Original legislative power is possessed by the sovereign people. Derivative legislative power is that which has been delegated by the sovereign people to legislative bodies and is subordinate to the original power of the people.'

For the first time in 1987, the system of people's initiative was thus installed in our fundamental law. To be sure, it was a late awakening. . . . In any event, the framers of our 1987 Constitution realized the value of initiative and referendum as an ultimate weapon of the people to negate government malfeasance and misfeasance and they put in place an overarching system. Thus, thru an initiative, the people were given the power to amend the Constitution itself. Sec. 2 of Art. XVII provides: 'Amendments to this Constitution may likewise be directly proposed by the people through initiative upon a petition of at least twelve per centum of the total number of registered voters, of which every legislative

---

[72] Woo-young Rhee, 'Recently Introduced Measures of Direct and Participatory Democracy and their Constitutional Ramifications in the Republic of Korea' (2009) 4(2) *National Taiwan University Law Review* 41, 48.

[73] Ibid.

district must be represented by at least three per centum of the registered voters therein.' Likewise, thru an initiative, the people were also endowed with the power to enact or reject any act or law by congress or local legislative body.

In light of this legal backdrop, the essential issue to be resolved in the case at bench is whether Pambayang Kapasyahan Blg. 10, serye 1993 of the Sangguniang Bayan of Morong, Bataan is the proper subject of an initiative. Respondents take the negative stance as they contend that under the Local Government Code of 1991 only an ordinance can be the subject of initiative. They rely on section 120, Chapter 2, Title XI, Book I of the Local Government Code of 1991 which provides: 'Local Initiative Defined. – Local initiative is the legal process whereby the registered voters of a local government unit may directly propose, enact, or amend any ordinance.'

We reject respondents' narrow and literal reading of the above provision for it will collide with the Constitution and will subvert the intent of the lawmakers in enacting the provisions of the Local Government Code of 1991 on initiative and referendum.

The Constitution clearly includes not only ordinances but resolutions as appropriate subjects of a local initiative. Section 32 of Article VI provides in luminous language: 'The Congress shall, as early as possible, provide for a system of initiative and referendum, and the exceptions therefrom, whereby the people can directly propose and enact laws or approve or reject any act or law or part thereof passed by the Congress, or local legislative body . . .' An act includes a resolution. Black defines an act as 'an expression of will or purpose . . . it may denote something done . . . as a legislature, including not merely physical acts, but also decrees, edicts, laws, judgments, resolves, awards, and determinations . . .' It is basic that a law should be construed in harmony with and not in violation of the constitution. In line with this postulate, we held in *In Re Guarina* that 'if there is doubt or uncertainty as to the meaning of the legislative, if the words or provisions are obscure, or if the enactment is fairly susceptible of two or more constructions, that interpretation will be adopted which will avoid the effect of unconstitutionality, even though it may be necessary, for this purpose, to disregard the more usual or apparent import of the language used.'

The constitutional command to include acts (ie, resolutions) as appropriate subjects of initiative was implemented by Congress when it enacted Republic Act No 6735 entitled 'An Act Providing for a System of Initiative and Referendum and Appropriating Funds Therefor.' Thus, its section 3(a) expressly includes resolutions as subjects of initiatives on local legislations. . . .

We note that respondents do not give any reason why resolutions should not be the subject of a local initiative. In truth, the reason lies in the well-known distinction between a resolution and an ordinance – ie, that a resolution is used whenever the legislature wishes to express an opinion which is to have only a temporary effect while an ordinance is intended to permanently direct and control matters applying to persons or things in general. Thus, resolutions are not normally subject to referendum for it may destroy the efficiency necessary to the successful administration of the business affairs of a city.

In the case at bench, however, it cannot be argued that the subject matter of the resolution of the municipality of Morong merely temporarily affects the people of Morong for it directs a permanent rule of conduct or government. The inclusion of Morong as part of the Subic Special Economic Zone has far reaching implications in the governance of its people. . . .

Considering the lasting changes that will be wrought in the social, political, and economic existence of the people of Morong by the inclusion of their municipality in the Subic Special Economic Zone, it is but logical to hear their voice on the matter via an initiative. It is not material that the decision of the municipality of Morong for the inclusion came in the form of a resolution for what matters is its enduring effect on the welfare of the people of Morong.

Finally, it cannot be [gainsaid] that petitioners were denied due process. . . . This procedural lapse is fatal for at stake is not an ordinary right but the sanctity of the sovereignty of the people, their original power to legislate through the process of initiative. Ours is the duty to listen and the obligation to obey the voice of the people. It could well be the only force that could foil the mushrooming abuses in government . . .

C. Petition

The right to petition has deep cultural roots in Asia. In ancient China, people used to beat the drum outside government offices to voice their appeals.[74] A few Asian constitutions include the right of the people to voice their grievances, in addition to their right to sue in court. In Taiwan, such a right is explicitly guaranteed under Article 17. Article 53 of the Constitution of Vietnam also stipulates that citizens have the right to take part in managing the state and society, and to make petitions or recommendations to the state offices.

Article 75 of the Local Autonomy Law of Japan provides local residents with the right to petition the executive for audit,[75] for dissolution of a local assembly,[76] to remove any member of the elected assembly[77] and for recall of 'the chief executive's assistants, chief accountant or treasurer, or any member of the election administration commission, any audit commissioner, or any member of the public safety commission'.[78] Article 124 provides for issuing petitions to the local assembly.

This ancient cultural heritage also sheds light on the contemporary practice of citizen petitions in China. China established the 'Letter and Visit' system ('*Xinfang*' system), based on Article 41 of the Constitution, as a way to overcome bureaucratic inefficiencies and to keep governments in close contact with the people, to protect the rights and interests of the people.[79] The number of letters and visits have steadily risen in recent years, to such an extent that the system has been paralysed. Some reforms have been carried out, such as the promulgation of the new 'Regulations on Petitions by Letters and Calls', but the inefficiency of the petition system has bred concerns: only 0.2 per cent of petitions were settled directly through the letter and visit procedure.[80] The relationship between the letter and visit system and the courts also remains ambiguous.[81] There has been a heated debate over whether to abolish the system. Some suggest that the NPC can serve as a supervisory body over the system,[82] while others

---

[74] Li Jianguo, 'Protect the Right to Petition', *Beijing Review*, 10 November 2005.
[75] Art 75, the Local Autonomy Law of Japan, 1947.
[76] Art 76, the Local Autonomy Law of Japan, 1947.
[77] Art 80, the Local Autonomy Law of Japan, 1947.
[78] Art 86, the Local Autonomy Law of Japan, 1947.
[79] Regulations on Petitions by Letters and Calls, Art 1.
[80] Zou Keyuan, 'The Right to Petition in China: New Developments and Prospects Petition: An Essential Element to Build a Harmonious Society?' (2006) 285 *EAI Background Brief* 3.
[81] Ibid.
[82] Yu Jianrong, 'Xinfang System Reform and Constitutional Construction' (2005) 89 *Twenty-First Century* 73 (in Chinese).

urge that it be transformed into an impartial ombudsman system.[83] Notwithstanding the debate, the system seems likely to continue, as it has placed certain checks on the exercise of government powers and provided channels for citizens to address their grievances without recourse to formal dispute resolution venues such as courts. The less adversarial nature of the Chinese system of letters and visits and general citizen petitions, might reflect the cultural preference in some Asian societies for harmonious relationships between the ruler and the ruled, as the ruling elite must remain vigilant to the needs of the ruled.

[83] Zou Keyuan, above n 80.

7

The Right to Equality and Equal Protection

I. EQUALITY AND THE LAW

Throughout history, human beings have cried out for the right to be treated with greater fairness and equality. It is, as Pennock argues, the 'greatest motivating force in politics'.[1] As the British philosopher John Lucas put it:

> Equality is the great political issue of our time. Liberty is forgotten: Fraternity never did engage our passions: the maintenance of Law and Order is at a discount: Natural Rights and Natural Justice are outmoded shibboleths. But Equality – there men have something to die for, kill for, agitate about, be miserable about. The demand for Equality obsesses all our political thought. We are not sure what it is . . . but we are sure that whatever it is, we want it: and while we are prepared to look on frustration, injustice or violence with tolerance, as part of the natural order of things, we will work ourselves up into paroxysms of righteous indignation at the bare mention of Inequality.[2]

Over time, the concept of 'equality' found its way into the world's leading constitutional documents. Thomas Jefferson's opening words of the American Declaration of Independence, proclaiming it a self-evident truth that 'all men are created equal', must surely be one of the most memorable and powerful lines ever penned. That in turn laid the foundation for the Fourteenth Amendment of the American Constitution, and almost two centuries later, echoes of Jefferson can be found in Article 1 of the Universal Declaration of Human Rights which states that 'All human beings are born free and equal in dignity and rights'.[3] Today, equality clauses and provisions are found in all constitutions around the world.

Equality rhetoric often fails to distinguish between *factual equality*, which is empirically determined, and *legal equality*, which is a legally-recognised status. This flows from a normative premise that human beings are of intrinsic worth. The idea of 'equality' resonates and conflicts with religious and philosophical teachings,[4] in so far

---

[1] See his entry on 'Equality and Inequality' in J Krieger (ed), *The Oxford Companion to Politics of the World* (New York: Oxford University Press, 1993) at 271.

[2] JR Lucas, 'Against Equality' (1965) XL *Philosophy* 296–207, at 296.

[3] A notable contribution of Mrs Hansa Mehta (1897–1995), the Indian delegate to the Universal Declaration of Human Rights Drafting Commission, was the insistence on amending Art 1 of the Declaration to remove the gendered wording, that 'all men are created equal'. The reference to 'men', argued Mehta, might give the impression that the Declaration was meant to protect only men and not women. See S Waltz, 'Universalizing Human Rights: The Role of Small States in the Construction of the Universal Declaration of Human Rights' (2001) 23 *Human Rights Quarterly* 44, 62–63.

[4] See, eg, SA Lakoff, 'Christianity and Equality' in JR Pennock and JW Chapman (eds), *Equality: NOMOS IX* (New York, Atherton Press, 1967) 115 at 132 ('As an ultimate ideal . . . equality was very much

as these assert equality of men and women. It also conflicts with religious or philo-sophical tenets espousing a hierarchical ordering of social relationships. The idea of equality as a political concept has been elucidated by European Enlightenment politi-cal theorists such as Hobbes, Rousseau and Locke,[5] for whom the political equality of man was the basis of democracy. It continues to receive sustained treatment by notable contemporary philosophers like John Rawls[6] and Ronald Dworkin.[7] Rawls's book, *A Theory of Justice*, gave rise to the 'first wave' of liberal egalitarianism concerned primarily with 'what should be equalized' in the realm of economic inequality.[8] The 'second wave' of equality discourses focused on 'those claims carried out by minority groups regarding cultural, racial and gender inequalities', with concerns about 'mar-ginalization, domination and cultural imperialism'.[9]

The egalitarian tenor of the 1948 Universal Declaration of Human Rights is pro-claimed in Article 1, which declares, in the face of racism and sexism: 'All human beings are born free and equal in dignity and rights. They are endowed with reason and conscience and should act towards one another in a spirit of brotherhood.' Its anti-colonial spirit is contained in its universality, in applying globally to all states, without jurisdictional exemption, as reflected in Article 2. Lastly, Article 7 states: 'All are equal before the law and are entitled without any discrimination to equal protec-tion of the law.' Similar clauses are found in most constitutions in Asia.

The appearance of equality provisions in Asian constitutions came rather later than in the United States. Asia's first modern constitution, the Meiji Constitution of 1889, had no equality clause.[10] However, the 1912 Provisional Constitution of the Republic

---

an element of Christian teaching from the outset'). See also in the same volume, E Rackman, 'Judaism and Equality' at 154, and AH Somjee, 'Individuality and Equality in Hinduism' at 177.

[5] To John Locke, the notion of original equality was a fundamental principle of government, and given the equality of men, political authority could be justified only by consent. There is 'nothing more evident than that creatures of the same species and rank, promiscuously born to all the same advantages of nature, and the use of the same faculties, should also be equal amongst one another without subordination or sub-jection' (J Locke, *Second Treatise on Civil Government*, 1689 (Mineola, New York: Dover Publications, 2002), ch 2).

[6] J Rawls, *A Theory of Justice* (Cambridge, Mass: Belknap Press, 2005) at 507ff. See also MC Segers, 'Equality in Contemporary Political Thought: An Examination and an Assessment' (1979) 10(4) *Administration & Society* 409.

[7] See R Dworkin, 'What is Equality? Part 1: Equality of Welfare' (1981) 10(3) *Philosophy & Public Affairs* 185; and R Dworkin, 'What is Equality Part 2: Equality of Resources' (1981) 10(4) *Philosophy & Public Affairs* 283.

[8] M Helvia and J Colon-Rios, 'Contemporary Theories of Equality: A Critical Review' (2005) 74 *Revista Juridica UPR* 133 at 134.

[9] This shifted the discourse from the moral equality of human beings to controversial assertions of the moral equivalence of forms of human behaviour: see CF Stychin, 'Essential Rights and Contested Identities: Sexual Orientation and Equality Rights Jurisprudence in Canada' in C Gearty and A Tomkins (eds), *Understanding Human Rights* (London and New York: Pinter, 1996) at 218; and LJ Moran, 'The Homosexualisation of Human Rights' in Gearty and Tomkins (eds), ibid, at 313. A panel of experts put forth their views in the non-binding Yogyakarta Principles (*Principles on the Application of International Human Rights Law in Relation to Sexual Orientation and Gender Identity*) which have been criticised as devaluing the concept of family: Principle 24 seeks to recognise a diversity of family forms; Principles 20 and 21 could also have the effect of restricting free speech: see PA Tozzi, 'Six Problems with the "Yogyakarta Principles"' *Catholic Family and Human Rights Institute: International Organizations Research Group Briefing Paper No 1* (2007), text available at <http://www.c-fam.org/docLib/20080610_Yogyakarta_Principles.pdf>. The Principles are available at <http://www.yogyakartaprinciples.org/principles_en.pdf>. The issue of whether sexual orientation is genetic and an immutable trait, or a question of sexual preference and environment, remains heavily controversial and politicised.

[10] See generally, H Tomatsu, 'Equal Protection of the Law' (1990) 53(2) *Law & Contemporary Problems* 109.

of China, drafted just three decades later, did. Clearly inspired by the American model, Article 5 of the latter reads: 'Citizens of the Chinese Republic are all equal, and there shall be no racial, class or religious distinctions.'[11] By this time, the idea that equality of treatment could be attained through the law had taken firm root.

The absence of an equality clause in the Meiji Constitution did not stop the Japanese delegation to the Paris Peace Conference of 1919 from proposing that a racial equality clause be worked into Article 21 of the Covenant of the League of Nations.[12] At the end of World War I, a major peace conference was convened in Paris at which the Allied victors negotiated the peace terms with the defeated Central Powers. Delegates from more than 32 countries were present, including Japan, which was included on account of its being Britain's ally during the War. Japan had three main demands at this Conference, the first two of which were territorial in nature and the third, the demand for a racial equality clause to be inserted into the Covenant of the League of Nations as follows:

> The equality of nations being a basic principle of the League of Nations, the High Contracting Parties agree to accord as soon as possible to all alien nationals of states, members of the League, equal and just treatment in every respect making no distinction, either in law or in fact, on account of their race or nationality.[13]

The proposal was not initially intended to be universalist in nature. Japan, the only non-white power at the Conference, was anxious to place itself on an equal footing with the major powers and proposed this amendment in an effort to ensure that it would be treated as an equal in the conduct of international affairs. As Shimazu puts it:

> It is evident that the original intention of the racial equality proposal was defensive in nature . . . There can be no doubt that the government's racial equality demand . . . was a highly particularistic and nationalistic expression of Japan's desire to prevent itself and its nationals as a state from suffering the humiliation of racial prejudice in the League of Nations. It underlined the anticipatory fear that the new international order would continue to be disadvantageous to Japan, as was the existing one. It suggests strongly, therefore, that one of the motivations for the proposal was pre-emptory, to secure Japan's great power status in the League of Nations at its inception.[14]

This early effort by an Asian state to constitutionalise equality at an international level failed. Met with strong objections from Australia – whose Prime Minister Billy Hughes defended his state's 'White Australia' policy which restricted non-white immigration to Australia – and with Great Britain refusing to upset its Dominion, only 11 of the 17 delegates voted for Japan's amendment. Anxious not to alienate his British allies, President Woodrow Wilson, who chaired the session, declared that as a major objection had arisen, a unanimous decision on this matter was necessary. Japan's proposed racial equality clause never made it into the Covenant.[15]

---

[11] Art 5, Provisional Constitution of the Republic of China, as reproduced in (1912) 6(3) *American Journal of International Law* 149.

[12] See generally, N Shimazu, *Japan, Race and Equality: The Racial Equality Proposal of 1919* (London: Routledge, 1998).

[13] Ibid at 20.

[14] Ibid at 113.

[15] See M MacMillan, *Paris 1919: Six Months that Changed the World* (New York: Random House, 2003) at 306–21.

For all its rhetorical power, 'equality' remains a problematic concept. Philosopher Thomas Nagel once described 'equality' as 'the most controversial of the great social ideals'.[16] In purely abstract terms, equality means 'that people who are similarly situated in morally relevant respects should be treated similarly', but the problem lies in determining 'what kinds of similarity count as relevant, and what constitutes similar treatment'.[17] A further difficulty with the concept of equality is that it is necessarily relative and does not in itself mean very much.

The following two extracts succinctly highlight the philosophical and legal difficulties of the concept.

RJ Pennock, 'Equality and Inequality' in J Krieger (ed), *The Oxford Companion to Politics of the World* (New York: Oxford University Press, 1993) at 271

The emphasis here is on *inequality*, rather than *equality* simply because equality, literally, is not to be found outside of the world of mathematics. It means identity. When people cry out for equality, they are actually demanding equality with respect to some particular thing or things. They may not express their demands in terms of 'equality'. They merely demand *more*, or they may seek legislative or administrative action that they believe will give them more, of something they desire, whether it be an economic or psychic good. But most of the time, they have their eyes on how others in their reference group, or in other categories not far removed in status or monetary income, are faring. It is relative rather than absolute equality that they are seeking.

M Schwarzchild, 'Constitutional Law and Equality' in D Patterson (ed), *A Companion to Philosophy of Law and Legal Theory* (Oxford: Blackwell Publishers, 1999) at 156–58

No two people (or things) are exactly alike. In that sense, none is equal to another. Yet all share points in common. At a minimum, all people are people (as, for that matter, all things are things). To that extent, at least, they are equal. Whatever the ways people might be equal or unequal, they can be *treated* equally or unequally in a wide variety of different ways. They might receive equal respect, or equal rights at law, or equal opportunities to distinguish themselves, or equal property and other resources, or equal welfare and happiness. Equality might be reckoned by individuals, or it may be by groups. There might be absolute equality: the same for everyone, regardless of what is thought to be deserved or otherwise proper. Or equality might be proportional: the same for everyone according to what is deserved or otherwise proper.

These different kinds of equality, it is fairly obvious, can often be mutually exclusive. Equal opportunity to distinguish oneself amounts to an equal opportunity to become unequal. Equal rights for people whose skills or whose luck is unequal may ensure unequal possession of property and other human resources. To ensure equality of possessions, conversely, may require unequal rights, by way of equalizing or 'handicapping' people with unequal abilities. Equal possessions are apt to mean unequal welfare and happiness for people with different needs, tastes, and personality types; equal welfare may require unequal resources. Individual equality, at least of some kinds such as equality of opportunity, is apt

---

[16] See his entry on 'Equality' in T Honderich (ed), *The Oxford Companion to Philosophy* (New York: Oxford University Press, 1995) at 248.

[17] Ibid.

to mean group inequality, since groups – almost however defined – will have differing distributions of skills, luck, and ambition. Absolute equality and proportional equality are sharply different: honors and possessions or prison sentences for all, say, as against honor or possessions or prison sentences according to a scale of who deserves them.

Equality, in truth, might mean almost anything. The crucial questions are 'Who is to be equal to whom? With respect to what?' Yet as an ideal, equality exerts great moral force, especially in modern places and times. What are the sources of equality's power as an ideal? And toward what sorts of equality ought people and their laws strive?

. . . [T]he secular Enlightenment was the most important source for modern ideals of equality. For Hobbes, Locke, and Rousseau, men are equal in a state of nature. Hume – echoing Diderot and Adam Smith – wrote that all mankind are 'much the same in all times and places.' The American Declaration of Independence, perhaps the greatest political document of the Enlightenment, proclaimed it a self-evident truth that all men are created equal. And the French Revolutionaries, calling for *égalité*, claimed the mantle of the Enlightenment, as did the nineteenth and twentieth-century socialist movements.

If equality was a salient Enlightenment idea, what sort of equality, among the myriad conflicting possibilities, was meant? As an intellectual and social movement, the Enlightenment arose to repudiate what it saw as the backwardness, superstition, and intolerance of medieval Christianity, and the frozen, hierarchical society of medieval Christendom. The Enlightenment rejected the idea that a person's worth, identity, and destiny should be overwhelmingly bound up in birth and kinship. In Sir Henry Maine's later expression, the Enlightenment was a great step away from the 'society of status.'

Instead, the Enlightenment thinkers put a high value on the individual, endowed as a person with natural rights. The supreme natural right is the right to pursue happiness, each person in his own way, according to his own faculties. Natural rights attach to every person, regardless of birth. As such, they are equal rights.

But for the Enlightenment, including the American founders, this meant equal rights before the law. It did not mean equal outcomes in life. On the contrary, life's happiest outcome is to achieve enlightened reason, and the Enlightenment accepted that people's capacities for this are unequal. Moreover, trying to ensure equal human happiness would have to be a collectively imposed definition of happiness in order to administer an equal distribution of it.

As for any idea of equal wealth or resources, the American founders followed Locke in emphasizing the right to property as a fundamental human right, with the recognition that property rights inevitably mean differences in wealth. For these Enlightenment thinkers, property rights were important in at least two ways: first, they encourage industriousness and hence promote prosperity; and second, they afford each person a practical opportunity to pursue personal goals, a personal idea of happiness, independent of any collective orthodoxy about what constitutes a good life. (The paradigm orthodoxy, of course, was that of the church, against which the Enlightenment defined itself in the first place) The characteristic social ideal of the Englightenment was the *carrière ouverte aux talents*: equal opportunity to pursue various (and hence unequal) careers, for unequal rewards, without legal disabilities found on irrelevant accidents of birth.

Notes and Questions

1. The philosophical difficulties in determining the content of the constitutional right to equality have led Peter Westen to label equality an 'empty idea'. See P Westen, 'The Empty Idea of Equality' (1982) 95 *Harvard Law Review* 537, and

rejoinders: K Greenawalt, 'How Empty is the Idea of Equality?' (1983) 83 *Columbia Law Review* 1167; E Chemerinsky, 'In Defense of Equality: A Reply to Professor Westen' (1983) 81 *Michigan Law Review* 575; and A D'Amato. 'Is Equality a Totally Empty Idea?' (1983) 81 *Michigan Law Review* 600.

2. If equality is a concept empty of content, an empty vessel into which any political theory or public philosophy may be poured, do you agree with Westen that we can do without equality altogether? What is the strategic utility of deploying an equality-based argument? Does it obscure anything?

3. Every constitution in Asia – with the exception of Brunei, which has no bill of rights – contains an equality clause. Naturally, the wording of these clauses varies considerably. Quite a number of constitutions were inspired by the wording of Article 14 of the Indian Constitution: 'The State shall not deny to any person equality before the law or the equal protection of the laws within the territory of India.' In particular, the phrases 'equality before the law' and 'equal protection of the law' are embedded in these constitutions, which include those of: Bangladesh (Article 27); Bhutan (Article 15); Malaysia (Article 8); Myanmar (Article 347); Nepal (Article 13, Interim Constitution); Pakistan (Article 25); Singapore (Article 12); Sri Lanka (Article 12); and Thailand (Section 30).

4. Some other constitutions merely contain the 'equal before the law' or 'equality before the law' phrase: China (Article 33); Hong Kong SAR (Article 25, Basic Law); Japan (Article 14); Laos (Article 35); Macau (Article 25); Mongolia (Article 14); South Korea (Article 11); Taiwan (Article 7); Timor-Leste (Article 16); and Vietnam (Article 52). Equality before the law is not universally applicable in all states. Other phraseology used include 'equal treatment before the law' (Indonesia, Article 28D) and 'equal protection of the law' (Philippines, Article III(1)).

5. In a number of states, the right to equality before the law is guaranteed only to *citizens*: Bangladesh (Article 27); China (Article 33); North Korea (Article 65); Laos (Article 35); Macau (Article 25 – residents only); Mongolia (Article 14); Pakistan (Article 25); South Korea (Article 11); Taiwan (Article 7); Timor-Leste (Article 16); and Vietnam (Article 52).

6. For a discussion of the concept of equality in Confucian thought, see Chenyang Li, 'Equality and Inequality in Confucianism' (2012) 11 *Dao* 295.

II. EQUALITY BEFORE THE LAW

A. Introduction

A commitment to equality is an aspect of the rule of law in its assertion that no one should be above the law and that the law should be 'blind' in treating all parties equally. This contrasts with privileged treatment, which featured in aristocratic, feudal or caste-based societies. In Malaysian case of *PP v Tengku Mahmood Iskandar & Anor* [1973] 1 MLJ 128, a member of the Johor royal family was convicted of causing hurt, and the court took into account the 'position of the accused' in the sentencing process.

This was challenged on appeal, and the High Court held this to be in conflict with Article 8 (equality clause) of the Malaysian Constitution:

> [T]his implies that there is only one kind of law in the country to which all citizens are amenable. With us, every citizen, irrespective of his official or social status, is under the same responsibility for every act done without legal justification. This equality of all in the eyes of the law minimizes tyranny.

The judgment in *Tengku Mohamood Iskandar* thus follows in the long line of cases interpreting the second leg of Victorian jurist Albert Venn Dicey's concept of the Rule of Law, that is,

> equality before the law, or the equal subjection of all classes to the ordinary law of the land administered by the ordinary law courts; the 'rule of law' in this sense excludes the idea of any exemption of officials or others from the duty of obedience to the law which governs other citizens or from the jurisdiction of the ordinary tribunals.[18]

The first Asian constitution to include the phrase 'equal before the law' was the Constitution of the Republic of China 1923, Article 5 of which read:

> 5. Citizens of the Republic of China shall be equal before the law, without distinction of race, class, or religion.

This provision later morphed into Article 7 of the 1946 Constitution, which provided:

> 7. All citizens of the Republic of China, irrespective of sex, religion, ethnic origin, class, or party affiliation, shall be equal before the law.

The first time it was adopted as a universal concept – as applicable to all persons, rather than to just citizens – was in 1947, when it appeared in Article 14 of the Constitution of Japan. Interestingly, the wording of Article 14 did not mirror that of the Fourteenth Amendment of the American Constitution but instead adopted a phraseology that gave 'more concrete expression' to the 'concept of equality':[19]

> 14. All of the people are equal under the law and there shall be no discrimination in political, economic or social relations because of race, creed, sex, social status or family origin.

The reason for this can be attributed to the fact that the woman entrusted with drafting the civil rights section of the Constitution, 22-year-old Beate Sirota (b 1923), felt more greatly inspired by Article 109 of the Weimar Constitution of 1919[20] than by the Fourteenth Amendment of the American Constitution which she felt contained insufficient protection for the rights of women.[21]

---

[18] AV Dicey, *An Introduction to the Study of the Law of the Constitution*, 10th edn (with an introduction by ECS Wade) (London: MacMillan, 1959) at 202.

[19] H Tomatsu, 'Equal Protection of the Law' (1990) 53(2) *Law & Contemporary Problems* 109, 109.

[20] Art 109 of the Weimer Constitution 1919 provides: 'All Germans are equal before the law. In principle, men and women have the same rights and obligations. Legal privileges or disadvantages based on birth or social standing are to be abolished. Noble titles form part of the name only; noble titles may not be granted any more. Titles may only be granted, if they indicate an office or occupation; academic degrees are not affected by this regulation. The state may no more bestow orders and medals. No German may accept titles or orders from a foreign government.'

[21] See JM Gleich-Anthony, *Democratizing Women: American Women and the US Occupation of Japan 1945–1951*, unpublished PhD dissertation (College of Arts & Sciences, Ohio University, 2007) at 48–58; see also B Sirota Gordon, *The Only Woman in the Room: A Memoir* (Tokyo: Kodansha International, 2001) at 103–38.

The British influence on constitution-drafting was more in evidence in their former colonies. In Burma, the task of drafting the constitution fell on the Constituent Assembly – elected in 1947 – under the leadership of U Chan Htoon (1906–88), who was the Assembly's constitutional adviser.[22] In preparation for his task, U Chan Htoon was 'sent to New Delhi to make an intensive study of the constitutions of different countries, to watch how the Indian constituent assembly was getting on' and 'to make friends with Indian colleagues in the freedom movement'.[23] In New Delhi, he befriended Sir Benegal Narsing Rau (better known as BN Rau), who not only helped U Chan Htoo to polish up his draft but also played a vital role as constitutional adviser to the Indian Constituent Assembly from 1946 to 1949. Rau himself recalls:

> The Constitutional Adviser of Burma came to Delhi in April, 1947, for discussion and collection of materials; a first draft of the new Constitution was then prepared and he took it back with him to Rangoon in May. There it underwent certain modifications and its provisions as so modified were accepted in substance by the Constituent Assembly of Burma. A Drafting Committee was then appointed to give it final shape. The Committee sat for about a fortnight in August and September and completed its work in time for the final draft to be brought before the Constituent Assembly about the middle of September. The Constituent Assembly passed it on September 24, 1947, with a provision that it would come into operation on such date as the Provisional President might announce by proclamation.[24]

While the Burmese Constitution was promulgated before that of India, its drafting was heavily influenced by the deliberations and recommendations of the Indian Constituent Assembly. In respect of the rights provisions, Rau said:

> The fundamental rights in the Burma Constitution follow closely, both in form and content, those recommended by the Advisory Committee of the Indian Constituent Assembly; rights of equality, rights of freedom, rights relating to religion, cultural and educational rights, economic rights, and rights to constitutional remedies.[25]

Thus, it can be said that the inclusion of the 'equal before law' clause in Article 13 of the 1947 Constitution[26] was largely influenced by the Indian proposals.

The equality provisions in the Indian Constitution originated from a draft submitted by Dr KM Munshi on 17 March 1947, which among other things provided that 'All persons irrespective of religion, race, colour caste, language, or sex are equal before the law and are entitled to the same rights, and are subject to the same duties.'[27] This was considered in the Sub-Committee on Fundamental Rights and amended as follows:

---

[22] On the framing of Burma's Constitution, see Maung Maung, *Burma's Constitution* (The Hague: Martinus Nijhoff, 1961).

[23] Maung Maung, 'Mr Justice Chan Htoon' in RH Taylor (comp), *Dr Maung Maung: Gentleman, Scholar, Patriot* (Singapore: Institute of Southeast Asian Studies, 2008) 110 at 115.

[24] BN Rau, 'The Constitution of the Union of Burma' (1948) 23 *Washington Law Review & State Bar Journal* 288, 288.

[25] Ibid at 291.

[26] The clause read: 'All citizens irrespective of birth, religion, sex or race are equal before the law; that is to say, there shall not be any arbitrary discrimination between one citizen or class of citizens and another.'

[27] See KM Munshi's 'Note and Draft Articles on Fundamental Rights', 17 March 1947, as reproduced in B Shiva Rao et al, *The Framing of India's Constitution; Select Documents*, vol 2 (New Delhi: Indian Institute of Public Administration, 1967) at 74.

All persons within the Union shall be equal before the law. No person shall be denied the equal protection of laws within the territories of the Union. There shall be no discrimination against any person on grounds of religion, race, caste, language or sex.

In his explanatory note on this particular article, constitutional adviser BN Rau stated that the first part of the main clause – 'equality before the law' – was based on Article 109 of the Weimar Constitution of 1919, while the second part – 'equal protection of the law' – was based on the Fourteenth Amendment of the US Constitution.[28] The final version as enacted reads:

The State shall not deny to any person equality before the law or the equal protection of the laws within the territory of India.

B. Meaning of 'Equality Before the Law'

The effect of the two segments of Article 14 of the Indian Constitution was explicated by the Indian Supreme Court in 1959 in *Basheshar Nath v The Commissioner of Income Tax, Delhi & Rajasthan & Anor*,[29] where Das CJ held:

The underlying object of this Article is undoubtedly to secure to all persons, citizen or non-citizens, the equality of status and of opportunity referred to in the glorious preamble of our Constitution. It combines the English doctrine of the rule of law and the equal protection clause of the 14th Amendment to the American Federal Constitution which enjoins that no State shall deny to any person within its jurisdiction the equal protection of the laws. There can, therefore, be no doubt or dispute that this Article is founded on a sound public policy recognised and valued in all civilised States. Coming then to the language of the Article it must be noted, first and foremost that this Article is, in form, an admonition addressed to the State and does not directly purport to confer any right on any person as some of the other Articles, eg, Article 19, do.[30]

The following year, the Supreme Court further elaborated in *State of Uttar Pradesh v Deoman*:[31]

The doctrine of equality may be briefly stated as follows: All persons are equal before the law is fundamental of every civilised constitution. Equality before law is a negative concept; equal protection of laws is a positive one. The former declares that every one is equal before law, that no one can claim special privileges and that all classes are equally subjected to the ordinary law of the land; the latter postulates an equal protection of all alike in the same situation and under like circumstances. No discrimination can be made either in the privileges conferred or in the liabilities imposed. But these propositions conceived in the interests of the public, if logically stretched too far, may not achieve the high purpose behind them. In a society of unequal basic structure, it is well nigh impossible to make laws suitable in their application to all the persons alike. So, a reasonable classification is not only permitted but is necessary if society should progress. But such a classification cannot be arbitrary but must be based upon differences pertinent to the subject in respect of and the purpose for which it is made.

---

[28] See B Shiva Rao, *The Framing of India's Constitution*, 2nd edn (Subhash C Kashyup, ed) (New Delhi: Universal Law Publishing Co Pte Ltd, 2004) at 179.

[29] *Basheshar Nath v The Commissioner of Income Tax, Delhi & Rajasthan & Anor* 1959 SCR Supp (1) 528.

[30] Ibid at 550–52.

[31] *State of Uttar Pradesh v Deoman* 1960 AIR 1125 SC.

Notes

1. In his *The Law of the Constitution* (London: University of London Press, 1968), Sir Ivor Jennings noted that the concept of 'Equality before the law means that among equals the law should be equal and should be equally administered, that like should be treated alike.' This clearly introduces the element of classification which would, according to the Indian Supreme Court, be more suited for application under the 'equal protection of the law' clause. See generally JK Mittal, 'Right to Equality and the Indian Supreme Court' (1965) 14(3) *American Journal of Comparative Law* 422; and SR Chowdhury, 'Equality Before the Law in India' [1961] *CLJ* 223.

2. The reading of the Indian Supreme Court in respect of Article 14 has been adopted by the courts in Bangladesh, Pakistan, Malaysia and Singapore.

3. In Japan, Article 14 provides that 'All of the people are equal under the law'. This provision came under consideration in the tragic patricide case, *Aizawa v Japan*.[32] The appellant, Chiyo Aizawa, had been raped and sexually abused by her father since she was 14 years old. She even bore him five children, two of whom died in infancy. At the age of 29, she fell in love and married a co-worker. Her jealous father threatened to kill her three children if she left him, and locked her up. After weeks of psychological abuse, Chiyo strangled her father. Under Article 200 of the Japanese Criminal Code, the penalty for the murder of one's 'own ascendant' or one's 'spouse's lineal ascendant' was death or life imprisonment with forced labour. The appellant argued that Article 200 of the Criminal Code violated Article 14 of the Constitution in that it prescribed a heavier punishment for the crime of killing an ascendant than under other types of murder under Article 199 of the Criminal Code. By a majority, the Court – sitting as a full bench of 11 – held Article 200 to be unconstitutional. The majority held that Article 200 was not in itself unconstitutional, since murder of ascendants was a serious breach of social morality, but did violate Article 14 in the extremity and seriousness of the punishment prescribed. For an English translation of the case, see LW Beer and H Itoh, *The Constitutional Case Law of Japan, 1970 through 1990* (Seattle and London: University of Washington Press, 1996) at 143–70.

4. South Korea's Criminal Act also provided for enhanced punishment for the murder of a person's lineal ascendant or his or her spouse's lineal ascendant. The constitutionality of this provision was challenged in *Manslaughter of a Lineal Ascendant of the Offender or His Spouse Resulting from Bodily Injury Case*.[33] In contrast to the Japanese Supreme Court, the South Korean Constitutional Court held that the legislation did not violate the equality provisions of Article 11(1) of the Constitution for the following reasons:

    > Respect and love are the pillars of relationship between relatives formed by marriage or blood. A lineal ascendant rears his descendant to become a successful member of the society, and takes upon [himself] legal and moral responsibilities for the descendant's

---

[32] *Aizawa v Japan* 27 Keishu 265 (Sup Ct, GB, 4 Apr 1973).

[33] *Manslaughter of a Lineal Ascendant of the Offender or His Spouse Resulting from Bodily Injury Case* 14-1 KCCR 159, 2000Hun-Ba53, 28 Mar 2002.

action. A descendent, on the other hand, shares the responsibilities of the lineal ascendant as a family member, pays respect and strives to requite for the ascendant's sacrifice. Such is the natural and overarching morality dominant in the historically and socially confirmed family relationships. Such morality should be protected by the Criminal Act because it forms a basic order that maintains and develops each family and the society. A crime of causing death of a lineal ascendant of the offender or his spouse resulting from bodily injury, then, is contrary to the universal social order, and morality, and there are ample reasons for more social censure of the immorality of this crime than that of a crime of causing death resulting from bodily injury of an ordinary person.[34]

However, the Constitutional Court was not prepared to uphold section 53(1) of the Military Criminal Act which provided for enhanced punishment for the murder of a military superior, on grounds that the punishment was disproportionate to the crime.[35] Capital punishment is not unconstitutional *per se* in South Korea.[36] On Korean perceptions of equality, see I Lee, 'Korean Perception(s) of Equality and Equality' (2008) 31 *Boston College International & Comparative Law Review* 53.

5. There are special exceptions to the application of the 'equality before the law' clause. While kings and princes cannot claim immunity from the law or preferential treatment, diplomats and statesmen can, by dint of the law governing state and diplomatic immunities enacted in the various states on the basis of comity between states and the international law governing their relations. The Vienna Convention on Diplomatic Relations (1961), of which there are almost 190 states parties, provides for the immunity of diplomats, their homes and their missions. Article 29 provides that 'the person of the diplomatic agent shall be inviolable' and that he 'shall not be liable to any form of arrest or detention'. Article 30 further provides that the diplomat's private residence 'shall enjoy the same inviolability and protection as the premises of the mission'.

6. Such grants of immunity are, quite naturally, susceptible to abuse by diplomats. One of the most blatant abuses of diplomatic immunity involved two Asian states. In 1979, the Burmese ambassador to Sri Lanka killed his wife after an argument over her boy-band lover. He then proceeded to build a funeral pyre in his backyard and cremated her body, all this in broad daylight and in full view of his neighbours and the Sri Lankan police, who could do nothing on account of his status. He was later recalled and nothing more was heard of him.[37]

---

[34] Ibid, para 1 of Summary of Decision.

[35] See *Request for Constitutional Review of Article 53 Section 1 of the Military Criminal Act* 19-2 KCCR 535, 2006Hun-Ka13, 29 Nov 2007.

[36] See *Capital Punishment Case* 161 KCCG 452, 2008Hun-Ka23, 25 Feb 2010.

[37] See 'Dominique Strauss-Kahn: Diplomatic Immunity's Greatest Hits', *Guardian*, News Blog, 28 March 2012, available at <http://www.guardian.co.uk/world/blog/ 2012/mar/28/dominique-strauss-kahn-diplomatic-immunity-scandal> (accessed 1 December 2012).

III. EQUAL PROTECTION OF THE LAW

A. Introduction

The phrase 'equal protection of the law' has found its way into no fewer than 12 constitutions in Asia.[38] This is an almost exact reproduction of the equal protection clause of the Fourteenth Amendment of the US Constitution. Passed in 1868 as part of the Reconstruction Amendments, Section 1 reads:

> All persons born or naturalized in the United States, and subject to the jurisdiction thereof, are citizens of the United States and of the State wherein they reside. No State shall make or enforce any law which shall abridge the privileges or immunities of citizens of the United States; nor shall any State deprive any person of life, liberty, or property, without due process of law; nor deny to any person within its jurisdiction the *equal protection of the laws*. (emphasis added)

Most of this section of the Fourteenth Amendment had been introduced by John A Bingham (1815–1900), the Republican Congressman from Ohio whom Supreme Court Justice Hugo Black once called the 'Madison of the first section of the Fourteenth Amendment'.[39] It is unclear what the Joint Committee for Reconstruction had in mind when adopting Bingham's draft and presenting it to Congress,[40] and over the next century and a half, its meaning has been left to extensive interpretation by the US Supreme Court.[41]

The first time this phrase appeared in an Asian constitution was when it was incorporated into the Indian Constitution as enacted by its Constituent Assembly in 1949. Despite the fact that the phrase 'equal protection of the law' is drawn from the Fourteenth Amendment to the Constitution of the United States, no judiciary in an Asian state with a similar clause in its constitution has followed the approach of the US Supreme Court in interpreting it.

Although enacted in 1868, much of the current jurisprudence of the US Supreme Court relating to the equal protection clause was developed after the 1938 decision of *United States v Carolene Products Co*,[42] in which we find the famous 'Footnote 4' of Justice Harlan Stone. The third paragraph of this footnote, which suggested that

---

[38] The 'equal protection of the law' clause and its variations can be found in the constitutions of: Bangladesh (Art 27); Bhutan (Art 15); India (Art 14); Indonesia (Art 28D); Malaysia (Art 8); Myanmar (Art 347); Nepal Interim Constitution (Art 13); Pakistan (Art 25); the Philippines (Art III(1)); Singapore (Art 12); Sri Lanka (Art 12); and Thailand (Secs 5 and 30).

[39] *Adamson v California* 332 US 46, 74 (1947).

[40] See WE Nelson, *The Fourteenth Amendment: From Political Principle to Judicial Doctrine* (Cambridge, Mass: Harvard University Press, 1988) at 55–57; and DA Faber and JE Muench, 'The Ideological Origins of the Fourteenth Amendment' (1994) 1 *Constitutional Comment* 235, 270–72.

[41] On the jurisprudence of the US Supreme Court concerning the Fourteenth Amendment, see: S Morrison, 'Does the Fourteenth Amendment Incorporate a Bill of Rights?' (1949–1950) 2 *Stanford Law Review* 140; R Berger, *Government by Judiciary: The Transformation of the Fourteenth Amendment* (Cambridge, Mass: Harvard University Press, 1977); JA Baer, *Equality Under the Constitution: Reclaiming the Fourteenth Amendment* (Ithaca, NY: Cornell University Press, 1983); A Reed Amar, 'The Bill of Rights and the Fourteenth Amendment' (1992) 101(6) *Yale Law Journal* 1193; R West, *Progressive Constitutionalism: Reconstructing the Fourteenth Amendment* (Durham, NC: Duke University Press, 1994); and MJ Perry, *We the People: The Fourteenth Amendment and the Supreme Court* (New York: Oxford University Press, 1999).

[42] *United States v Carolene Products Co* 304 US 144 (1938).

legislation which prejudiced 'discrete and insular minorities' may 'call for a correspondingly more searching judicial inquiry', formed the basis for the current three-tiered test of strict scrutiny (for suspect categories); intermediate scrutiny (for quasi-suspect categories); and minimal or rational basis scrutiny (for all other discriminatory legislation).

Suspect classifications – those pertaining to immutable characteristics such as race, gender or descent – are constitutional only if a 'compelling state interest' in such classification can be demonstrated. Intermediate scrutiny applies to classifications like gender and illegitimacy, which are upheld only if a substantial relationship exists between the means and ends of the legislation and the classification. Rational basis classification review requires the state to show only that the classification is rationally related to serving a legitimate state interest.

B. Prohibited Categories of Discrimination

Following from our discussion above, it should be noted that Section 1 of the Fourteenth Amendment of the US Constitution does not prohibit discrimination on any particular or specific ground; most constitutions in Asia, on the other hand, contain explicit clauses prohibiting discrimination on certain specific grounds, although such prohibitions relate primarily to citizens rather than to all persons. For example, Article 29(2) of the Bangladesh Constitution provides that: 'No citizen shall, on grounds only of religion, race, caste, sex or place of birth, be ineligible for, or discriminated against in respect of, any employment or office in the service of the Republic.' There are of course, exceptions to this general trend. Article 14(2) of the Mongolia Constitution provides that 'No person shall be discriminated against on the basis of ethnic origin, language, race, age, sex, social origin and status, property, occupation and position, religion, opinion and education.' Prohibited grounds of discrimination vary from constitution to constitution, although most constitutions forbid discrimination on the basis only of 'religion', 'race' and 'gender'.[43] Other forbidden grounds of discrimination to be found in Asian constitutions include: caste;[44] place of birth;[45] descent or status;[46] language;[47] political affiliation or belief;[48] wealth or property;[49] education;[50] and physical or health condition.[51]

---

[43] Gender discrimination is not absolutely forbidden in North Korea, Hong Kong, the Philippines and Singapore.

[44] Bangladesh, India, Nepal, Sri Lanka, South Korea.

[45] Bangladesh, Cambodia, India, Malaysia, Myanmar, Singapore and Sri Lanka.

[46] Bhutan, Cambodia, Japan, Malaysia, Mongolia, Myanmar, Nepal, Singapore, South Korea, Thailand and Timor-Leste.

[47] Bhutan, Cambodia, Macau, Mongolia, Nepal, Sri Lanka and Timor-Leste.

[48] Bhutan, Cambodia, Macau, Mongolia, Nepal, Sri Lanka and Timor-Leste.

[49] Cambodia and Mongolia.

[50] Macau, Mongolia and Timor-Leste.

[51] Thailand and Timor-Leste.

C. Positive Discrimination

Some constitutions contain provisions that single out certain groups for special or privileged treatment. This has been done to redress past injustices and to protect certain minorities, such as indigenous peoples. One of the most well-known examples of this is Article 153 of the Malaysian Constitution, which provides:

> 153.(1) It shall be the responsibility of the Yang di-Pertuan Agong[52] to safeguard the special position of the Malays and natives of any of the States of Sabah and Sarawak and the legitimate interests of other communities in accordance with the provisions of this Article.
> (2) Notwithstanding anything in this Constitution, but subject to the provisions of Article 40 and of this Article, the Yang di-Pertuan Agong shall exercise his functions under this Constitution and federal law in such manner as may be necessary to safeguard the special position of the Malays and natives of any of the States of Sabah and Sarawak and to ensure the reservation for Malays and natives of any of the States of Sabah and Sarawak of such proportion as he may deem reasonable of positions in the public service (other than the public service of a State) and of scholarships, exhibitions and other similar educational or training privileges or special facilities given or accorded by the Federal Government and, when any permit or license for the operation of any trade or business is required by federal law, then, subject to the provisions of that law and this Article, of such permits and licenses.

Article 13(3) of the Interim Constitution of Nepal specifically provides for 'special provisions' for certain groups:

> (3)   The State shall not discriminate among citizens on grounds of religion, race, caste, tribe, gender, origin, language or ideological conviction or any of these.
>
> Provided that nothing shall be deemed to prevent the making of special provisions by law for the protection, empowerment or advancement of women, Dalits, indigenous ethnic tribes [Adivasi Janajati], Madhesi or farmers, labourers or those who belong to a class which is economically, socially or culturally backward, or children, the aged, disabled or those who are physically or mentally incapacitated.

i. Constitutional Protection of Indigenous Peoples

Several Asian constitutions specifically single out indigenous peoples for protection: India, Malaysia, Nepal, the Philippines and Singapore. In the case of Nepal, the Philippines and Singapore, the constitutional protection is cast in general terms with no specific responsibility being demanded of the state. As noted above, Article 13(3) of the Interim Constitution of Nepal facilitates the making of special provisions 'for the protection, empowerment or advancement of', among other groups, the Adivasi Janajati or indigenous ethnic tribes. The Government may also form such commissions as are necessary to safeguard and promote the rights and interests of these tribes.[53] In the same vein, Article XIV, Section 17 of the Philippines Constitution provides:

---

[52] The Yang di-Pertuan Agong is the Malaysian King. The kingship is rotational, the king being elected from among the members of the Council of Rulers every five years.
[53] Art 154.

17. The State shall recognize, respect, and protect the rights of indigenous cultural communities to preserve and develop their cultures, traditions, and institutions. It shall consider these rights in the formulation of national plans and policies.

Article XVI, Section 12 further empowers Congress to 'create a consultative body to advise the President on policies affecting indigenous cultural communities, the majority of the members of which shall come from such communities'.

Article 152 of the Singapore Constitution is slightly more detailed in that it:

(a) clearly identifies who the indigenous peoples are; and
(b) spells out the broad areas of state protection.

152. – (1) It shall be the responsibility of the Government constantly to care for the interests of the racial and religious minorities in Singapore.

(2) The Government shall exercise its functions in such manner as to recognise the special position of the Malays, who are the indigenous people of Singapore, and accordingly it shall be the responsibility of the Government to protect, safeguard, support, foster and promote their political, educational, religious, economic, social and cultural interests and the Malay language.

In some constitutions, the protection of indigenous peoples does not stop at guaranteeing equal rights but extends to forms of *positive discrimination* or affirmative action for these peoples. Such positive discrimination may manifest itself in special quotas in educational institutions or government service for indigenous or historically disadvantaged peoples. Some of the most detailed provision for such forms of guarantees can be found in the Indian Constitution and in the Malaysian Constitution.

The most detailed provisions are found in the Indian Constitution, which has a Scheduled list of Tribes who have been singled out for special treatment. Among other things, members of Scheduled Tribes enjoy reservation of seats in the legislatures of the Union[54] as well as in the States,[55] and special claims on appointments to public office.[56] Article 338A establishes the National Commission for Scheduled Tribes which is charged with:

(a) investigating and monitoring all matters relating to the safeguards provided for the Scheduled Tribes under the Constitution, or under any other law for the time being in force or under any order of the Government, and evaluating the working of such safeguards;
(b) inquiring into specific complaints with respect to the deprivation of rights and safeguards of the Scheduled Tribes;
(c) participating in and advising on the planning process of socioeconomic development of the Scheduled Tribes, and evaluating the progress of their development under the Union and any State;
(d) presenting to the President, annually and at such other times as the Commission may deem fit, reports upon the working of those safeguards;
(e) making such reports, recommendation as to the measures that should be taken by the Union or any State for the effective implementation of those safeguards and

[54] Art 330.
[55] Art 332. This reservation of seats will expire after 70 years from the date of the commencement of the Constitution – 2021 – see Art 334.
[56] Art 335.

other measures for the protection, welfare and socio-economic development of
the Scheduled Tribes; and

(f) discharging such other functions in relation to the protection, welfare, and development and advancement of the Scheduled Tribes as the President may, subject to
the provisions of any law made by Parliament, by rule specify.[57]

The Malaysian Constitution is also very specific. While Article 8(1) guarantees that
all persons are equal before the law and entitled to the equal protection of the law, the
state may take steps to ensure the 'protection, well-being or advancement of the aboriginal peoples of the Malay Peninsula (including the reservation of land) or the reservation to aborigines of a reasonable proportion of suitable positions in the public
service'.[58] An 'aborigine' is defined rather tautologically as 'an aborigine of the Malay
Peninsula'.[59] Other than aborigines, other persons considered indigenous are the
'natives' of the States of Sabah and Sarawak, and the majority Malays. The special
steps to be taken with regard to all these peoples are set out in full in Art 153(1) and
(2).[60] Land may also be specifically reserved for Malays[61] and natives of Sabah and
Sarawak.[62]

Most challenges on indigenous rights have been with respect to the expropriation or
alienation of traditional or native lands. The following two cases were decided on first
principles and the common law rather than any specific constitutional provisions to
protect the indigenous peoples of either Malaysia or Japan.

Adong bin Kuwau & Ors v Kerajaan Negeri Johor & Anor
[1997] 1 MLJ 418 (Court of Appeal, Malaysia)

Facts

The 52 plaintiffs ('the plaintiffs') were heads of families representing a group of aboriginal
people living around the Sungai Linggiu catchment area ('the Linggiu valley'), while the
defendants were the Johor government and the Director of Lands and Mines, Johor. The
relief sought was in the form of two declarations: (i) that all the lands acquired by the
defendants for the purpose of constructing the Sungai Linggiu Dam near Kota Tinggi,
Johor were an aboriginal area or reserve; and (ii) that the defendants were jointly or severally liable to pay the plaintiffs all the compensation received by them from the Government
of Singapore (who had contracted with the Johor State Corporation to build a dam and
supply water to Singapore and the State of Johor) or a sum deemed just by the Court.

Mokhtar Sidin JCA

[T]his is the first case in this country where the aboriginal people have sued the government
for their traditional rights under law.
 ... It is established from the various articles [submitted by the plaintiffs' counsel] that the
aboriginal people inhabiting the Linggiu valley are of the Jakun tribe and have been in

---

[57] See Art 338A(5).
[58] Art 8(5)(c).
[59] Art 160(2).
[60] See the text accompanying n 52 above
[61] Art 89.
[62] Art 161A(5).

inhabitation of that land from time immemorial. Prior to 1954, there was no specific authority established to take care of the affairs of the aborigines. In 1954, the British Colonial Government established the Department of the Aboriginal Peoples' Affairs. That department took over the control of administering the socio-economic welfare of the aborigines of the Federation of Malaya. In 1961, after Malaysia had gained her independence, the Federal Government, in order to eliminate the influence of communist terrorists amongst the aborigines, relocated most of the aborigines including the plaintiffs from the deep jungles to the jungle fringes where the authorities could keep an eye on them . . . some of them were recruited by the government to fight against communist terrorists.

However, the legal recognition of the aboriginal peoples' rights in Malaysia was first enacted in 1939 under the State of Perak Enactment No 3 of 1939. It was enacted to protected the aboriginal tribes of Perak whereby a 'protector' was appointed by the Ruler in the State Council to take charge of the aboriginal peoples' affairs (this post was redesignated as 'the commissioner' in 1967). Currently, the Federal Government has a special department to take care of the affairs of the aborigines and to improve their living conditions. This clearly shows the government's interest in the affairs of the aborigines. The Aboriginal Peoples Ordinance was revised in 1974 (the 'Act'). The Act provides for a commissioner to be appointed for the protection, well-being and advancement of the aborigines of West Malaysia.

. . . [I]t is clear to me that the plaintiffs and their families, and also their ancestors, were the aboriginal people who lived in the Linggiu valley, or, at the very least, in the surrounding areas. It is also established that the plaintiffs depend on the produce of the jungle in the Linggiu valley and its surrounding areas for their livelihood. The jungle produce are the fauna, flora, fruits and the animals which include land animals and water animals like fish, crab, etc. The defendants have not denied the plaintiffs' claim that the Linggiu valley was the source of their livelihood until the jungle was cleared for the purpose of building a dam.

. . . [I]t was found that the JHEOA (Department of the Aboriginal Peoples' Affairs) had recommended to the State Authority that the plaintiffs' families ought to be compensated as a result of the acquisition of the land . . . [I]n a letter dated 16 April 1990 addressed to Ketua Pengarah Alam Sekitar, Kementerian Sains, Tknologi dan Alam Sekitar, the JHEOA admitted that the land involved are the plaintiffs' ancestral land for which they should be compensated under ss 11 and 12 of the Act. The letter went on to recommend a compensation of a sum of RM 560,535 to the plaintiffs. This letter . . . is an admission of the defendants' liabilities to pay compensation to the plaintiffs.

[The question of] . . . aboriginal peoples' land rights . . . has gained much recognition after the Second World War, with the establishment of the United Nations of which the UN Charter guarantees certain fundamental rights. Native rights have been greatly expounded on by the courts in Canada, New Zealand and Australia restating the colonial laws imposed on native rights over their land. It is worth noting that these native peoples' traditional land rights are now firmly entrenched in countries that had and/or are still practising the Torrens land law – namely Canada, New Zealand and Australia – where special statutes have been enacted or tribunals set up in order for natives to claim a right over their traditional lands. In Malaysia, as we do not have special statutes or tribunals, the courts is the only forum whereby the natives can make their claim, and this case being the first of such a claim by a group of aboriginal people in Malaysia, I will now set out the plaintiffs' right under the different headings of common law, statutory land and under the Federal Constitution.

Plaintiffs' right under common law

The study of native land rights shows that common law recognizes native land rights, even in countries practising the Torrens land system where the authorities issue title pursuant to statutory powers.

[The learned judge undertook a study of judgments on native title from jurisdictions like the United States of America, and Privy Council decisions from Southern Rhodesia, Southern Nigeria, New Zealand and India as well as from Canada. He approved the statement by the US Supreme Court that 'it is a settled principle that their rights to occupancy is considered as sacred as the fee simple of the whites'.][63]

. . . Much closer to us, the High Court of Australia consisting of seven judges including the Chief Justice, in the case of *Mabo & Ors v State of Queensland & Anor* (1986) 64 ALR 1 sealed the statement of law pronounced in the *Calder* case [*Calder v Attorney-General of British Columbia* (1973) 34 DLR (3d) 145, British Columbia] by according rights to the aboriginal peoples of the Torrens Island of Queensland and overturning two centuries of court ruling that Australia was founded terra nullius, that is, Australia was an uninhabited island discovered by the British, or in other words, legally not recognizing the existence and/or occupation of Australia by Australian aboriginal people. The *Mabo case (No 2)* decision was succinctly condensed by the Federal Court of Australia in the case of *Pareroultja & Or v Tickner & Ors* (1993) 117 ALR 206 at p 213 where the court held:

> As mentioned earlier, *Mabo (No 2)* is authority for the proposition that the common law of Australia recognizes a form of native title which, except where it has been extinguished, reflects the entitlement of the indigenous inhabitants in accordance with their laws or customs to their traditional land which is preserved as native title. Native title has its origins in and is given its content by the traditional laws acknowledged by, and the traditional customs observed by, the indigenous inhabitants of the territory. The nature of native title must be ascertained by reference to the traditional laws and customs of the indigenous inhabitants of the land. Native title does not have the customary incidents of common law title to land, but it is recognized by the common law. It may not be alienated under the common law. If a group of aboriginal people substantially maintains its traditional connection with the land by acknowledging the laws and observing the customs of the group, the traditional native title of the group to the land continues to exist. Once the traditional acknowledgment of the laws and observance of the customs of the group ceases, the foundation of native title to the land expires and the title of the Crown becomes a full beneficial title.

The possession of land under native title may be protected by representative action brought on behalf of the people concerned . . .

. . . [This] decision is authority for the proposition that native rights over their land existed and is recognized by the common law of Australia. Consequentially, the Australian Parliament enacted 'The Native Title Act' just before Christmas 1990 which came into effect on 1 January 1994, creating the mechanism for Australian natives to claim their traditional and ancestral lands.

The question now is whether the plaintiffs have any right over their traditional and ancestral lands. For this purpose, it is better for me to trace the plaintiffs' historical claim on the said land.

It is not disputed that traditionally, Peninsula Malaysia was occupied by two groups of people; namely, the Malays who lived along the coast and the rivers and the aboriginal people who lived in the interiors or locally known as the 'Ulus', each group occupying their

---

[63] *Mitchel v United States* 34 US 711 (1835), per Baldwin J at 746.

own areas or spheres and living in harmony. Within the Malay Peninsula were found the Malay Sultanates and, within the Malay Sultanates, some areas were occupied by aboriginal peoples without any dispute as to their occupation of the lands. Land disputes in this part of the world began with the coming of the Europeans. The British introduced their system of government and administration which included the demarcation of lands.

The British introduced the Torrens land system, which introduced alienation and title for the first time. This system brought within it all the people except the aborigines who continued to live in the jungle and roamed freely and sheltered wherever they wanted. These people continue to live from the produce of the jungle and the jungles are still their hunting grounds. Before the introduction of the Torrens land system, these lands were unclaimed land in the present sense but were 'kawasan saka' to the aboriginal people. On the introduction of the Torrens land system, all the kawasan saka became state land but the aboriginal people were given the freedom to roam about these lands and harvest the fruits of the jungle. Some of these lands have been gazetted as forest reserves. The plaintiffs however, continue to live and/or depend on these lands, and all of them still consider the jungle as their domain to hunt and extract the produce of the jungle just like their forefathers had done.

My view is that . . . the aboriginal peoples' rights over the land include the right to move freely about their land, and without any form of disturbance or interference and also to live from the produce of the land itself, but not to the land itself in the modern sense that the aborigines can convey, lease out, rent out the land or any produce therein since they have been in continuous and unbroken occupation and/or enjoyment of the rights of the land from time immemorial . . . in Malaysia, the aborigines common law rights include, inter alia, the right to live on their land as their forefathers had lived and this would mean that even future generations of the aboriginal people would be entitled to this right of their forefathers.

Statutory rights

Recognizing these rights of the aboriginal people, the government enacted the Aboriginal Peoples Act 1939 which is 'an enactment for the protection of the aboriginal tribes of Perak.' In the same year, this enactment was extended to the states of Selangor, Negeri Sembilan and Pahang which were then known as the Federated Malay States.

. . . Under s 11, the State Authority must pay compensation when acquiring by alienation or leasing any land upon which are fruit and rubber trees claimed by the aboriginal peoples.

These people live from the hunting of animals in the jungle and the collection of jungle produce. These are the only source of their livelihood and income. Can these rights be taken away by the government without compensation? . . . [A]dequate compensation must be made for these trees (on reserved land) but not for the land. In the present case, I am of the view that adequate compensation for loss of livelihood and hunting ground ought to be made when the land where the plaintiffs normally went to look for food and produce was acquired by the government. The compensation is not for the land but for what is above the land over which the plaintiffs have a right.

[The learned judge noted that common law rights and statute rights were complementary and that the latter did not extinguish the former.]

Constitutional rights of the aboriginal peoples

When Malaysia gained its independence on 31 August 1957, the Federal Constitution became the supreme law of the country. See art 4 of the Federal Constitution. All laws passed after independence day, which are inconsistent with the Federal Constitution, are void to the extent of the inconsistency.

... Under the Federal Constitution, the aboriginal people of Malaysia enjoyed a special position. This is found in art 8(5)(c):

> (5) This Article does not invalidate or prohibit:
>
>> (c) any provision for the protection, well-being or advancement of the aboriginal peoples of the Malay Peninsula (including the reservation of land) or the reservation to aborigines of a reasonable proportion of suitable positions in the public service.

... The plaintiffs' counsel submitted that rights accorded to the aboriginal people by common law and statutory law are proprietary rights within the ambit of art 13(1) of the Federal Constitution and that when these rights are taken away by the defendants, the plaintiffs should be compensated pursuant to art 13(2) ...

The word 'property' appearing in art 13(1) is a legal word and should be accorded its legal meaning. There is a similar provision to our art 13 in the Indian Constitution arts 19(1)(f) and 31. There are numerous Indian constitutional cases which have defined the word 'property' and I rely on the case of *Rabindra Kumar v Forest Officer* AIR 1955 Manipur 49 at pp 53–54 which eloquently sets out the meaning of the word 'property' as used in a constitutional context:

The words 'property' has been explained in Corpus Juris, Vol 73 p 136 as follows:

> In legal usage, 'property' is perhaps the comprehensive word which can be employed and it may signify either the subject matter in which interest exists or it may signify valuable rights and interests protected by law or it may signify both. It is generally recognized that property includes certain rights such as the right of acquisition, possession, use, enjoyment and disposition.
>
> In legal usage, the word property is a generic term. According to the authorities on this question it is a term of broad and extensive application and it is also a term of large import with the very broadest and most extensive signification. It is a very comprehensive word having broad and comprehensive and exceedingly complex meanings ...
>
> The word property includes both real and personal property ...
>
> In the strict legal sense, the word property signifies valuable rights or interests protected by law and this is the primary appropriate and broader signification of the term. In modern legal system, property includes practically all valuable rights, the term being indicative and descriptive of every possible interest which a person can have in any and every thing that is the subject of ownership by man and including every valuable interest, it can be enjoyed as property and recognized as such equitable interests as well as legal interests and extending to every species of valuable rights or interests in either real or personal property or in easements ...
>
> The term comprises also all rights which are incidental to the use, enjoyment and disposition of intangible things ...
>
> ... the word 'property' means not only the thing but also the rights in the physical and corporeal thing which are created and sanctioned by law.

The Federal Court in the case of *Selangor Pilot Association (1946) v Government of Malaysia & Anor* [1975] 2 MLJ 66 at p 69, per Suffian LP said:

> The language of our art 13 is not identical with, but it certainly approximates to, the language of the Indian art 31 before the 1959 amendment which added the new cl (2A). The absence of a similar clause from our art 13 persuades me to adopt the construction placed on the Indian article by the Indian Supreme Court on the unamended art 31.

I would therefore agree with the wide interpretation given to proprietary rights under art 13 and hold that the plaintiffs' rights both under common law and statutory law are proprietary rights protected by art 13 of the Federal Constitution.

At the time the defendants entered into an agreement with the Government of the Republic of Singapore and built a dam in the Linggiu Valley, the plaintiffs' right of free access into Linggui valley and to harvest the fruits of the jungle were unchallenged and recognized in law. It is the building of the dam that brought the plaintiffs' freedom of movement within the Linggiu valley, which is guaranteed by the Federal Constitution art 9(2), to an end and subsequently extinguished the plaintiffs' rights to collect the forest produce which are recognized at common law and statutory law.

The plaintiffs' statement that the forest was a source of their livelihood was not rebutted by the defendants and neither was there evidence there was a break in the continuous occupation and traditional connection in the land for their livelihoods.

It has been long recognized under our law that when a person is deprived of any proprietary right under an executive exercise pursuant to powers given by statute, the person must be compensated.

. . . Since the defendants have failed to establish the right to deprive the plaintiff of their rights, I will hold that this deprivation without compensation was unlawful. I therefore hold that the plaintiffs are entitled to compensation in accordance with art 13(2).

The Federal Constitution art 13 supersedes both statutory law and common law and mandates that all acquisition of proprietary rights shall be compensated and that any law made for the compulsory acquisition or use of property without compensation shall be rendered void in accordance with art 4 of the Federal Constitution. I assume that the alienation of the Linggiu valley lands in four titles was done under the National Land Code 1965 [which] . . . does not provide for compensation of land acquired. However, the National Land Code 1965 must be read as being subservient to art 13 of the Federal Constitution and where there is no provision for compensation under statutory law, art 13(2) should be read into that statute.

. . . I would state that the plaintiffs had suffered deprivation of the following types of interest in the land:

1   deprivation of heritage land;
2   deprivation of freedom of inhabitation or movement under art 9(2);
3   deprivation of produce of the forest;
4   deprivation of future living for himself and his immediate family; and
5   deprivation of future living for his descendants.

. . . In awarding the compensation, I have in my mind that the sum would not only reflect a just figure, but also be a sum which would enable the plaintiffs to put into good use and regenerate [RM 26.5m ordered as compensation] . . . In parting, it is my sincere hope that the plaintiffs would make good use of the compensation awarded so that they and their families would be able to survive for generations to come.

Kayano et al v Hokkaido Expropriation Committee (The Nibutani Dam Decision)
(Sapporo District Court, Civil Division No 3), 27 Mar 1997
(1999) 38 *International Legal Materials* 397 (trans MA Levin)

Facts

The plaintiffs were the owners or heirs of the owners of land in the Nibutani River valley in the eastern part of Hokkaido island which was subject to expropriation by the Japanese Government for the building of the Nibutani Dam Project. The plaintiffs opposed the project and claimed for the restoration of land rights lost by the Ainu people in the course of modernisation, and sought compensation accordingly.

Held

i. Considerations Pertaining to Comparative Balancing

The conditions prescribed by Land Expropriation Law Article 20(3) contemplate a comparative balance of the public benefits to be gained by the completion of a planned project with the project's detriment to public and private interests, and that the former benefits be found to be greater than the latter harms. As indicated above, we recognize the discretionary authority of the administrative entity to make this judgment.

However, there may be cases where, in making this judgment, the administrative entity unjustly and carelessly makes light of various factors and values which deserve the utmost regard from the start, with the result that where the greatest consideration is obviously due, it lacks instead. And there may be cases where less significant matters, which from the start were being considered, were overvalued. If it can be found that these kinds of improprieties influenced the judgment, then error in the manner and process of the discretionary judgment requires that the decision be recognized as illegal.

In the instant case, the former element, *ie* the public benefits to be gained by the completion of the planned project, are flood control, maintaining correct functioning of the river flow, supplying water service for various uses, and electrical power generation, and clearly, there is little difference here from most other projects of this type carried out before. But on the other hand, in this case, the latter element, *ie* the project's detriment to public and private interests, involves the culture of the Ainu people who are a minority, and this has not been discussed previously.[64] Moreover, because the points which follow *infra* are also present, this is a question that demands careful review.

ii The Legal Quality of Interests Held by Minorities in their Culture

Defendants argue that, even *assuming arguendo* that a minority's rights to enjoy its culture should be respected, when considering whether those rights are pertinent the [to] Land Expropriation Law's stipulations, there is no basis to interpret those rights as deserving a position higher than any other circumstances that should be considered under the statute. To address this, we choose to include herein a study of the legal quality of interests held by minorities in their culture.

---

[64] This means the issue raises a matter of first instance before the Japanese courts.

(a) Nexis to the ICCPR

The United Nations General Assembly adopted the ICCPR in 1969 [*sic*], and after undergoing ratification by our country's parliament in 1979, it was promulgated as Treaty No 7
of the same year.[65] This treaty recognizes the inherent dignity of the individual and inviolable right to equality for all members of humankind as the foundation for freedom, justice,
and peace worldwide. Following a preface text which confirms the inherent dignity of the
individual as the source for these rights, there are fifty-three separate provisions, and
Articles 2 (1), 26, and 27 therein address the instant right of the Ainu people to enjoy their
culture. These articles provide:

> Article 2(1): Each State Party to the present Covenant undertakes to respect and to
> ensure to all individuals within its territory and subject to its jurisdiction the rights
> recognized in the present Covenant, without distinction of any kind, such as race, colour,
> sex, language, religion, political or other opinion, national or social origin, property,
> birth or other status.

> Article 26: All persons are equal before the law and are entitled without any discrimination
> to the equal protection of the law. In this respect, the law shall prohibit any discrimination
> and guarantee to all persons equal and effective protection against discrimination on any
> ground such as race, colour, sex, language, religion, political or other opinion, national
> or social origin, property, birth or other status.

> Article 27: In those States in which ethnic, religious or linguistic minorities exist, persons
> belonging to such minorities shall not be denied the right, in community with the other
> members of their group, to enjoy their own culture, to profess and practise their own
> religion, or to use their own language.

In 1991, the Government of Japan, participating party herein, presented its third report to
the UN Human Rights Committee based upon ICCPR Art 40. The report states that
because the Ainu people have their own religion and language, and because the uniqueness
of their culture is being preserved, etc, they may be fairly described as a minority as defined
by ICCPR Art 27. In this action, ([based upon] the undisputed facts indicated *supra* and
facts obvious to the court), the Government accepts that the Ainu people are a minority
within the scope of ICCPR Art 27.

It is proper to understand that the ICCPR, as set out above, guarantees to individuals
belonging to a minority the right to enjoy that minority's distinct culture. Together with
this, there is an obligation [*sekimu*] imposed upon all contracting nations to exercise due
care with regard to this guarantee when deciding upon, or executing, national policies
which have the risk of adversely affecting a minority's culture, etc. Thus, the Ainu people,
as a minority which has preserved the uniqueness of its culture, are guaranteed the right to
enjoy their culture by ICCPR Art 27, and accordingly, it must be said that, as set out in the
provisions of Art 98 (2) of the Constitution,[66] our nation has a duty [*gimu*] to faithfully
observe this guarantee.[67]

---

[65]   *Shiminteki oyobi seijiteki kenri ni kan suru kokusai kiyaku* [International Covenant on Civil and Political
Rights], Treaty No 7 of 1979.

[66]   The treaties concluded by Japan and established laws of nations shall be faithfully observed. Kempó,
art 98 para 2.

[67]   *Sekimu* (translated here as 'obligation') and *gimu* (translated here as 'duty') differ in nuance. *Sekimu* is
narrower and indicates 'a responsibility plus duty', ie there must be a responsibility (*sekinin*) which creates
the duty. '*Gimu*' (ie duty) is broader and implies legal and ethical or moral imperatives together. See *Ruigo
Reikai Jiten* [*Illustrated Dictionary Of Usage*] under *tsutome* (Microsoft/Shogakukan Bookshelf CD-ROM
Version 2.0 1998) (1994).

Indeed, the rights arising under ICCPR Art 27, are not unlimited. It is true that as the defendants correctly argue, those rights are subject to the limits for the public welfare included in Articles 12 and 13 of the Constitution.[68] But in light of the aims of ICCPR Art 27, any limits on the guarantee of rights must be kept to the narrowest degree necessary.

(b) Nexis to Article 13 of the Constitution

Article 13 of the Constitution provides:

> All of the people shall be respected as individuals. Their right to life, liberty, and the pursuit of happiness shall, to the extent that it does not interfere with the public welfare, be the supreme consideration in legislation and in other governmental affairs.

In light of its wording and historical origin, this provision demands the highest regard for the individual in his or her relationship with the state. It manifests the principals we call individualism and democracy as the recognition of the particular worth of all citizens, who collectively constitute the state, in the state's exercise of governance.

Diversity exists in an unmistakable fashion as the respective differences in the particulars faced by each individual, *eg* gender, ability, age, wealth, etc. Premised upon this diversity and these differences, Article 13 demands meaningful, not superficial, respect for individuals and the differences arising between them. And when, in any given social setting, stronger persons take care of those weaker with humility and grace, a diverse society though which the entire community can prosper is established and preserved. There are no other means to pursue the likes of happiness.

If we look at these points in terms of the relationship between a dominant majority and a minority who do not belong to the majority, it often happens that the majority people, being a majority, consequently tend to ignore or forget the interests of the minority. When the minority's interests relate to the minority's unique culture and are difficult to appreciate in the generally accepted values of the majority, those tendencies are likely to become all the more stronger.

The minority's distinct ethnic culture is an essential commodity to sustain its ethnicity without being assimilated into the majority. And thus, it must be said that for the individuals who belong to an ethnic group, the right to enjoy their distinct ethnic culture is a right that is needed for their self-survival as a person. We believe the guarantee of that right fulfills the basic tenets of democracy by meaningfully respecting the individual while striving for the majority's comprehension of and respect for the circumstances faced by the socially weak.

Furthermore, this conclusion is in accord with the movement of the United Nations and the rest of the society of nations, which has sought through the creation and reception of the above-mentioned ICCPR, and subsequently all the more, to ensure the essential equality of minorities and to enable co-existence with a majority within a single national entity.

Accordingly, we agree that Constitution Art 13 guarantees to the plaintiffs the right to enjoy the distinct ethnic culture of the Ainu people, which is the minority to which the plaintiffs belong.

Of course, in speaking of this right, we understand it to be subject to the public welfare limitation included expressly within the provisions of Constitution Art 13, but in consider-

---

[68] 'Article 12: The freedoms and rights guaranteed to the people by this Constitution shall be maintained by the constant endeavor of the people, who shall refrain from any abuse of these freedoms and rights *and shall always be responsible for utilizing them for the public welfare.*' Kempó, Art 12 (emphasis added). Re Art 13, see text accompanying note 62. For authoritative guidance on Japan's public welfare limits in the Japanese Constitution, see Nobuyoshi Ashibe, Kempó [Constitutional Law] §6(1) (new edn 1997).

ation of the character of the human right involved, that limitation must be kept to the narrowest degree necessary.

iii The Indigenous Character of the Ainu People

ICCPR Article 27 only addresses 'minorities' and therefore, an ethnic group's indigenous character is not a condition for considering the guarantee of a right to enjoy a distinct ethnic culture. [But let us suppose two kinds of minority groups.] If one minority group lived in an area prior to being ruled over by a majority group and preserved its distinct ethnic culture even after being ruled over by the majority group, while another came to live in an area ruled over by a majority after consenting to the majority rule, it must be recognized that it is only natural that the distinct ethnic culture of the former group requires greater consideration.

This notion [that indigenous peoples' circumstances warrant greater consideration] clearly follows with a growing international movement towards seeing indigenous peoples' culture, lifestyle, traditional ceremonies, customary practices, etc, as deserving respect regardless of whether or not such recognition goes so far as there being so-called indigenous rights, meaning indigenous peoples' right of self-determination with regard to land, resources, political control, etc.

1. Before we try to investigate the indigenous character of the Ainu people, we must first ascertain what is an indigenous people. In the first place, it should be noted that there is no uniform understanding of the notion of an 'indigenous people' and some even question whether the notion is appropriate for being defined at all. (Briefly put, [the argument would be that] even admitting that indigenous peoples exist, the differences in those groups' historical background, their current circumstances, etc, vary based upon the country with which they are now associated. That being the case, it is only natural that the groups cannot be understood collectively by a single term.) In the instant case, among other matters, it is necessary to study the importance of the interest that has been violated, *ie* Ainu culture, and the extent of the guarantee of the right to enjoy that culture. Because we must inevitably make reference to the indigenousness of the Ainu people to carry out such a study, we set out a definition of indigenous people to the degree necessary.

Comprehensively viewing the evidence (omitted herein), we regard an indigenous people as a social group who live and have lived in a region which historically existed outside of a state's rule and was brought within that state's rule as a minority group with a culture and identity which differed from the majority of the parent ruling state, and who have retained a unique culture and identity that originate and continue from the past, such that even while subject to the rule of the above-mentioned majority, that group has not since lost the unique culture and identity which derives and continues from the past.

2. Next, we consider whether the Ainu people are an indigenous people within the meaning explained above. However, the Ainu people have had no written language and thus, to establish proof of their indigenousness as described above, there is no contemporaneous historical written record drafted by Ainu hands. Nothing in any of the evidence in this case clarifies when the Ainu people became established as a social grouping and began inhabiting Hokkaido and Northern Honshu. Therefore, we find it necessary to judge the indigenous character of the Ainu people against the interpretation set out above using documents written primarily by non-Ainu Japanese persons (following the plaintiffs' usage, hereinafter '*wa-jin*') about the Ainu people during the middle feudal and early modern periods as evidentiary sources.[69]

---

[69] In Japanese historical usage, the 'middle feudal period' refers to the Kamakura (1180–1333) and Muramachi (1336–1573) eras.

We recognize from the overall evidence (omitted herein):

At least by the late Kamakura period, intercourse between Hokkaido's[70] Ainu people and *wa-jin* arose from trade in the form of barter transactions involving unique products of Hokkaido including varieties of fish and wild animals in exchange for *wa-jin* products, between Ainu people living in Hokkaido and *wa-jin* merchant traders.

In the middle of the fifteenth century, powerful small and mid-sized *wa-jin* family clans relocated to the southern portion of Hokkaido mainly around [present-day] Hakodate. There was repeated fighting both among those family clans and between the clans and Ainu people (*eg,* the battle of 1456 led by [the Ainu leader] Koshamain.)

Around the mid-sixteenth century, the Kakizaki family, which later founded the Matsumae domain, proclaimed a edict to maintain orderly trade between themselves and the Matsumae-area Ainu called the 'Ordinance concerning Trade Exchanges with Barbarians'. The nature of trade between Ainu and *wa-jin* around that time was that Ainu people would come to the Matsumae region from the various places in Hokkaido in which they lived to carry out barter exchange with *wa-jin* merchants from Honshu who had gathered together there.

In 1604, the Matsumae domain entered the Edo Shogunate's regime as a fief, and that domain passed on trade sites (places where trading was carried out) as land tenures to its retainers. From that time forward, trade with the Ainu people was directed to those sites and the domain ensured its fiscal foundation by levying taxes on trading profits.

Around that time as well, free travel by *wa-jin* in Hokkaido was not recognized but it was permitted for the Ainu.

In 1669, [the Ainu leader] Shakushain led battles between *wa-jin* and Ainu people.

At least by the second half of the eighteenth century, *wa-jin* traders monopolistically managed fishing grounds in areas around the Matsumae domain, and trade with the Ainu was carried out at designated contract locations that were set up. At those contract locations, the Ainu people began to be used as the labor force for fisheries production.

By the end of the eighteenth century, these contract locations had been extended as far as the Eastern portion of Hokkaido, and were the source of exploitation of Ainu people by *wa-jin*.Incidents of fighting between Ainu people and *wa-jin* arose (*eg* the 1789 Kunashiri Menashi fighting).

Around the end of the Tokugawa Shogunate rule, in the Saru River area, a *wa-jin* named Bunemon Yamada contracted for the Saru Site (the fishing areas from present-day Tomakomai City to Shizunai Township), and that Yamada escorted the Ainu people who were the principal workforce to the Akkeshi contract site and other places as transient labor, exploiting them in this way.[71]

Depending on the location, entire households were caused to be re-located from place to place.

In 1858, Takeshiro Matsuura,[72] while carrying out an investigation of Hokkaido (Ezochi), visited to the Nibutani area, and recorded the population, ages, and living conditions of the Ainu people living there.

[70] The Court's use of the place name 'Hokkaido' conforms to modern usage, however that name did not come into existence until 1868. Prior to that time, the island had been known to *wa-jin* as *Ezochi* and to the Ainu as *Ainu Moshiri*; see R Siddle, *Race, Resistance and the Ainu of Japan* (London: Routledge, 1996) at 53.

[71] It is roughly 225 kilometers (140 miles) from the Saru area to Akkeshi. At the time, the journey would have been by foot through rugged mountainous areas.

[72] Matsuura (1818–88) was a famed Japanese explorer who made six trips through the Ainu lands. 'Much of the information that exists on labour practices, the mistreatment of Ainu women, and the plight of those left behind in the villages in the early nineteenth century comes from his writings.' (Siddle, above n 70, at 212, fn 99)

The Matsumae domain completely segregated *wa-jin* and Ainu people, and by virtue of such policies stopping contact through trade, etc., Ainu people could maintain their culture and traditions as an ethnic group apart from the *wa-jin*.

From the latter half of the eighteenth century to the middle of the ninteenth century, the Edo Shogunate feared the advance of Russian hegemony into the land of Hokkaido. Thus, in order to transform Ainu people into *wa-jin,* they repeatedly put forward the so-called assimilationist policies under which the Ainu people were made to use the Japanese language, to eat rice, and the like. In the end, these policies failed owing to strong resistance by the Ainu people.

Putting the above-recognized facts together with the overall purport of the arguments submitted, we further find as follows: Prior to the imposition of rule in the Edo period by the Matsumae domain under the Shogunate's feudal system, there were numerous places where Ainu people resided in Nibutani and throughout Hokkaido. The Matsumae domain's subsequent rule over Hokkaido did not extend completely and the Ainu people's unique societal lifestyle continued. Even while enduring tremendous political and economic influence from the Shogunate feudal system, Ainu people lived throughout Hokkaido preserving the enjoyment of their unique culture. As we find below in section iv, it was later that their unique culture, lifestyle, etc deteriorated as a direct consequence of various policies adopted towards the Ainu people.

According to evidence (omitted herein), the Ainu people presently are living amidst the general society in our country with little difference, linguistically or culturally, from other citizens and the number of people speaking their unique language is extremely limited. However, based upon a sense of ethnic belonging and ethnic pride arising both individually and through the action of organized groups seeking renewal and enhancement of the ethnic rights of the Ainu people, efforts are being made for the preservation and continuation of the Ainu language and traditional culture. These efforts include the collection, preservation, and opening of museums for Ainu artifacts, the popularization of the Ainu language, the compilation of Ainu dictionaries, the transcription of Ainu oral legends, lectures relating to Ainu culture, etc. Moreover, these efforts are bearing fruit.

3. Comprehensively viewing the above recognized facts, we can see that for the most part the Ainu people have inhabited Hokkaido from before the extension of our country's rule. They formed their own culture and had an identity. And even after their governance was assumed by our country, even after suffering enormous social and economic devastation wrought by policies adopted by the majority, they remain a social group that has not lost this unique culture and identity. Accordingly, the definition provided above of an 'indigenous people' should certainly apply.

iv Various Public Policies Relating to the Ainu People

After governance was assumed by our country over the indigenous Ainu people, they became a minority and consequently suffered enormous social and economic devastation wrought by the rule of the our country's majority members. As a result, they lost their ethnic culture, lifestyle, traditional customs, and the like. That being the case, this historical background must be taken into consideration in the comparative balancing we conduct presently.

We recognize the following facts according to evidence (omitted herein).

• The Meiji Government deemed the colonization of Ezochi [Hokkaido] to be an important policy upon which the nation's fate would rest. To tackle this task, the government sent the Colonization Commission (Kaitaku-shi) to Hokkaido.

- In September 1872, land rights were established which designated into bounded lots the entire Hokkaido territorial area including land that had been used by Ainu people for removing trees, hunting, and fishing. Lots were given to Ainu people but the fact that they were not accustomed to agriculture made self-sufficiency difficult to achieve.
- In 1873, the felling of trees and the removal of bark without permission was prohibited. Moreover, the use of uray nets (*ie*, catching fish by placing stakes across a river to bar the fish from traveling up except for at a single open space where nets are set), one of the traditional Ainu fishing methods, was prohibited for salmon fishing at the Toyohira, Hassamu, Kotani, and Shinoro Rivers.[73]
- In 1876, criminal punishment was imposed to prohibit traditional customary styles of Ainu earrings, tattoos, and the like. Furthermore, the Ainu traditional hunting method using poisoned arrows was prohibited.
- In 1878, fishing for salmon and trout was banned entirely for all rivers around Sapporo.
- In 1880, criminal punishment was imposed to prohibit the traditional customary manner of Ainu burning the home of a deceased and relocating elsewhere. Moreover, education was provided in spoken and written Japanese language.
- Thereafter, poaching salmon in the rivers of the Chitose area was prohibited. And after the traditional Ainu fishing method by tesu nets was prohibited, salmon and trout fishing even for personal household consumption was prohibited in 1897.
- In this way, the prohibitions against taking fish and the like became stronger while *wa-jin* robbed the Ainu people's land for development. As such things became common, the Ainu lifestyle became impoverished. To address this, the Hokkaido Former Aboriginals Protection Act was passed in 1899.[74] This law sought to encourage through allocations of land a stable means of support based upon agriculture. However, the law's five chobu[75] as the maximum amount of land to be granted to an Ainu person was woefully inadequate and moreover, nearly twenty percent of the allocated land was unfit for cultivation. Therefore, the Ainu people's standard of living remained extremely poor and the goal of lifestyle stabilization went unfulfilled.

Putting the above-recognized facts together with the overall purport of the arguments submitted, we further find as follows: Because their livelihood had been sustained principally by fishing, the above-described prohibitions on fisheries, etc plunged the Ainu people into destitution. Even the Hokkaido Former Aboriginals Protection Act which was enacted for the purpose of lifestyle stabilization was entirely inadequate to create self-sufficiency for the Ainu people. Furthermore, while prohibitions against traditional Ainu customs, Japanese language education, and similar policies may have been intended to secure a lifestyle environment on the same level as *wa-jin,* they were so-called assimilationist policies which were based on values that unilaterally set *wa-jin* culture as pre-eminent and forced *wa-jin* culture on the Ainu people. To say that those policies failed to consider the Ainu people's unique dietary customs, manners and customs, language, etc. is unavoidable. And the deterioration of the Ainu people's unique manners and customs, language, etc was a direct consequence thereof.

---

[73] These were the principal rivers flowing through the newly urbanised colonial capital of Sapporo.

[74] Hokkaidó Kyúdojin Hogo Hó [Hokkaido Former Aboriginals Protection Act], Law No 27 of 1899. The title of this statute is sometimes translated with 'Natives' or 'Aborigines' in the place of of 'Aboriginals'. See eg Siddle, above n 70, at 70. 'Aborginals' is selected here to evoke the obsolescence and political incorrectness of the Japanese term *Kyúdójin.*

[75] One chobu is approximately one hectare.

v Contemplation and Reflection

(a) The public benefits from the accomplishment of the instant Project Plan as recognized above show its public nature to be high. To wit,

1 controlling flood waters, to protect persons and property from flooding and to eliminate residents' anxiety with regards to flooding;
2 maintaining correct functioning of the river flow, to obtain a stable flow of water through the river course preventing the occurrence of water shortages and eliminating residents' anxiety with regards to water shortages and furthermore, to prevent obstructions at the mouth of the river, which both forestall internal water flooding in the vicinity of the mouth of the river and make it easier for the upstream migrations of rainbow trout, smelt, and other fish;
3 supplying irrigation water service, to provide a foundation for regional agricultural production offering greater security for farm management;
4 supplying municipal water service, to distribute municipal water in keeping with the various municipal water plans for Biratori and Monbetsu Townships;
5 supplying industrial use water, to make possible Hokkaido's predicted 1995 industrial use water needs for the East Tomakomai Industrial Park, allowing the region's industrial production and economic activity to contribute of course to the economic and social development of all of Hokkaido; and,
6 supplying water to an electric power generating station constructed with the Nibutani Dam, to make possible up to 3,000 kilowatts of electrical power to the Saru River area, which moreover, will address increasing needs for electrical power in that area.

On the other hand, as recognized above, among the losing interests and accompanying costs that may arise out of the execution of the project are:

The vicinity of the Instant Confiscated Properties is said to be a holy place to Ainu people, and furthermore, an extremely high proportion of the residents in the vicinity are Ainu people. That proportion stands out as high even in comparison with other places in Hokkaido where many Ainu people live.

In the Nibutani area, traditional Ainu spiritual and technological culture is preserved. And it is not just that many who hand down the folklore to future times have been from there, but many scholars from Japan and abroad have visited there, and it is known as the birthplace of Ainu cultural scholarship.

The fundamental characteristics of Ainu culture are focused around hunting, gathering, and fishing, spending their lives together with nature. Because this culture was born from worshiping the bounty of nature together with their gods, [the culture's notion of] nature bonds together an area's culture with the land cherished by that culture in a connection so extraordinarily close that it can never be severed.

Historically, the Ainu culture in the Nibutani area also was forcibly changed after experiencing contact with wa-jin and suffered as a result. Nevertheless, the essence and/or spirit of Ainu culture's close connection with nature has continued even to the present.

Specifically, the Chippusanke ceremony, today, has become a place for interaction between Ainu and wa-jin. It has taken on an importance not only in helping *wa-jin* better understand Ainu culture, but even for Ainu people to achieve for themselves a renewed sense of ethnic belonging. Thus, in light of its original significance as well as its present day effects, it is easy to understand that the event's staging grounds are extremely important for handing down Ainu culture.

The Yuoy Chashi and Poromoy Chashi located in the vicinity of the Instant Confiscated Properties are important remains for understanding the history of the Ainu people.

The *chinomishir* located in three places in the vicinity of the Instant Confiscated Properties are holy places for Nibutani area Ainu people.

(b) Incidentally, as explained above, attempts to comparatively balance the above two positions are informed by the fact that the latter interests [*ie* the losing interests and accompanying costs] involve human rights which are guaranteed by ICCPR Article 27 and Article 13 of the Constitution and any restrictions on those rights should be recognized only to the narrowest possible degree. Together with that recognition is the fact that the Minister of Construction, who represents an administrative entity of the nation, when determining or executing policies which risk an adverse effect upon an indigenous minority's culture etc, is bound by an obligation to give generous consideration for the above-mentioned interests associated with an indigenous minority group's culture, etc., to ensure that that improper infringement of these rights not occur.

Because the Ainu people have no written language, the *Chippusanke* and similar ceremonies and the *Chashi* relicts which have been preserved through their [social and physical] forms are precious irreplaceable resources in the quest for understanding Ainu ethnic culture. Without a doubt, their importance exists on a level that is incomparable with what would be for ethnic groups who have written languages. Furthermore, because the *chinomishir* are places which fulfill a religious meaning as sites of spiritual refuge for the Ainu people whose principals are found in the worship of nature, it deserves to be said that people from other ethnic groups need to humbly show due respect for these places without arguing about trifling points.

Continuing from there, it is manifest that the Ainu people in the vicinity of the Instant Confiscated Properties hold many environmental, ethnic, cultural, historical, and religious values which are important to them. But the worth of these various elements also appertains to the broad reach of citizens who are not members of the Ainu people. This is because, in our country which is a physically isolated island nation, it is inevitable that opportunities to contact the cultures of many ethnic groups are comparatively limited. This in turn causes a tendency to succumb to simplistic values. Facing those circumstances, we believe that the opportunity to contact a culture associated with the indigenous locale of an indigenous minority people in Japan greatly contributes to fostering more diverse values and a better understanding of ethnic diversity overall.

Moreover, in support of the above values, it is not enough that Ainu language, food culture, lifestyle customs, traditional ceremonies, principals of nature worship, etc, all of which continue to be taken from and lost by the Ainu people as a consequence of the continuing influence of the so-called assimilationist policies, be told to future generations, but rather the real life practices themselves should also be maintained and preserved to be passed on the future.

Yet if the Project Plan is accomplished, the environment in the Nibutani area, which is known as an Ainu holy place, a place where Ainu culture is rooted, and the birthplace of Ainu ethnic scholarship, will undergo great change. Without a doubt, it will become markedly more difficult to keep for future generations the many ethnic, cultural, historical, and religious values of the Ainu people, who are an indigenous minority people closely associated with the area with a spiritual culture founded upon togetherness with nature.

Of course, it is conceivable that these various values may be compromised for the public interest. But in cases where such concessions are to be sought, there must also be the greatest degree of consideration that includes a sense of remorse concerning matters such as that described above of the historical background of the coerced deterioration of the Ainu people's unique ethnic culture caused by assimilationist policies.

Absent such remorseful consideration, what results is the thoughtless theft of nature, including land in an indigenous region that is deeply connected to a distinct ethnic culture. That nature is stolen from the Ainu people who have their own ethnic group pride and sense of belonging. And such results take place in the context of governance by the society's majority members without remorse for a historical background of numerous afflictions carried out by the majority causing the deterioration of Ainu ethnicity. The Ainu lived as an indigenous people, managing their lives around hunting, gathering, and fishing, deeply placing in the highest regard the nature that they were so closely connected to. Their traditional hunting and fishing methods were stolen. Fishing for salmon, which was the very basis for their food and clothing, was prohibited. Many lifestyle customs and manners were prohibited. Such occurrences robbed the Ainu of unique ethnic customs and dietary practices. On top of all this, land benefits pursuant to the Hokkaido Former Aboriginals Protection Act were issued forcing the Ainu to go over to an agricultural lifestyle qualitatively different from their ethnic way of living. And this enumeration could continue.

It should also be noted that the Instant Confiscated Properties were properties originally issued pursuant to the Hokkaido Former Aboriginals Protection Act. Thus, less than one hundred years after issuing land to Ainu people to force them into an agricultural lifestyle to which they were unaccustomed and representing a significant factor in the deterioration of their ethnicity, that land is now to be taken away. Of course, there is absolutely no bar on using land originally issued pursuant to the Hokkaido Former Aboriginals Protection Act for the public interest, but here too, the greatest degree of consideration seems warranted. If such consideration is lacking, it reflects the majority's careless and selfish policymaking, and our judgment finding illegality cannot be avoided.

(c) Now we consider the question of whether or not sufficient consideration can be found in the instant case.

At least by the time of the [April 25, 1986] application for the Project Authorization, the enterprise authority/participating party realized that a majority of the residents in the planned enterprise area were members of the Ainu people, and that Ainu culture was being preserved and handed down there. Yet, prior to that application for the Project Authorization, there was not sufficient research or study of the degree of impact that the proposed project would have on Ainu culture.

It is clear that, from the very beginning, there was meager understanding generally of Ainu culture as a culture of a minority group residing within Japan, and the details of that culture were similarly unknown. Accordingly, in such a case, the equivalent of a preliminary environmental assessment should have been carried out, *ie* a carefully conducted comparative balancing of investigative results found after unhurried study of the project's impact on Ainu culture.

Specifically, a decision of whether or not to permit construction of the Nibutani dam in the Nibutani area should have been based on results from an investigation as above. And even assuming that construction would be permitted, then a determination of the location of the construction site should not have been based merely on ground form, structure, and economic factors, as was done in the present case. A comparative balancing should have been carried out including the nexus with the concrete burdens imposed on Ainu culture, asking, for example, what construction locations might have been available to keep clear of the *Chashi* and *Chipusanke* locations, etc. The Project Plan should have been determined and the application for a Project Authorization should have been submitted pursuant to this process.

[Ultimately,] the authorizing entity, *ie* Minister of Construction, in making the Project Authorization, needed to sufficiently investigate whether this sort of careful comparative balancing etc. was indeed carried out. This was a legal obligation[76] imposed upon the Minister of Construction.

However, the consideration with regard to Ainu culture taken by the participating party by the time of the application for the Project Authorization was nothing more than taking steps pursuant to the Cultural Assets Protection Law for buried assets protection of the *Chashi* and contemplating an alternative location for the *Chipusanke.* And even in the buried assets protection, the participating party's way of thinking was exactly the same as would be seen for buried assets protection of *wa-jin* cultural artifacts; there was not a scintilla of particular consideration for the Ainu *per se.* Moreover, in carrying out the buried assets protection measures, the participating party carried out the procedures by submitting its request to the involved government agencies taking the construction of the Nibutani dam at the planned location as a foregone conclusion. And the fact that the Construction Implementation Plan, the Fundamental Plan, and the Project Plan all completely lacked mention of Ainu culture causes us to presume that at the time that the Project Plan was decided upon, Ainu culture had not been separately considered whatsoever.

Putting all of these contemplations together, we find no particular awareness of Ainu culture on the side of the enterprise authority/participating party in preparing the Project Plan. Subsequent requests from the Ainu plaintiffs' and local community councils, etc, sought consideration for Ainu culture and regional support. But because the enterprise authority/participating party was seeking smooth execution of voluntary land acquisitions, it took a posture to ignore what could have been properly addressed. Consequently, things proceeded through to the Confiscatory Administrative Rulings without obtaining the plaintiffs' understanding.

Moreover, the defendants have argued that Ainu culture was considered when, in 1981 and afterwards, the Hokkaido Development Bureau, which is a local administrative operating entity for the nation/participating party, promoted area environment maintenance and carried out comprehensive research and investigation by establishing investigation committees with participation of persons learning and experience, local council members, and others. However, as explained above, not only were the results from those investigations hardly clear, but both investigative committees' principal goal was regional improvement which was understood to relate to social welfare measures only. Here again, particular consideration for and assessment of Ainu culture was lacking.

Defendants have argued that their ignorance of the locations of *chinomishir* was unavoidable, not only because they were unknown to the general public, but because Plaintiff Kayano did not identify those locations until the time of his request for an examination of the Confiscatory Administrative Rulings. However, as explained above, had the participating party allowed sufficient time and properly investigated the impact of the Nibutani Dam construction on Ainu culture in advance, the possibility can not be denied that their lack of awareness might have been avoided. For these reasons, a finding of impropriety is inescapable.

(d) Taking all that has been written above together, we find that the Minister of Construction, who was the authorizing agency and the agent for the enterprise authority in the instant matter, neglected the investigative and research procedures that were necessary to judge the priority of the competing interests accompanying the accomplishment of the Project Plan. He unreasonably made little of and ignored various factors and values that should have been given the highest regard. Furthermore, despite being unable to make a proper judgment, he recognized only the smallest possible impact on Ainu culture and left any damages thereupon unremedied.

[76] *Sekimu* – see above n 67.

After all of this, the Minister of Construction determined to give precedence to the public benefits of the project over losing interests and associated values, and consequently issued the Project Authorization. Nothing more can be said except that such action exceeded the administrative discretion given to the authorizing agency pursuant to Land Expropriation Law Article 20 (3) and was illegal.

Therefore, we conclude that the instant Project Authorization was in violation of Land Expropriation Law Article 20 (3) and that such illegality succeeded to the Confiscatory Administrative Rulings.

Notes

1. The rights of the Ainu came up for consideration again in the case of *Ogawa v Hokkaido*, also known as the *Ainu Communal Property (Trust Assets) Litigation*. See G Stevens, 'Ogawa v Hokkaido (Governor), the Ainu Communal Property (Trust Assets) Litigation' (2005) 4 *Indigenous Law Journal* 219; and MA Levin and T Tsunemoto, 'A Comment on the Ainu Trust Assets Litigation in Japan' (2003) 39 *Tulsa Law Review* 399.

2. The leading Indian case on indigenous rights is *Samatha v State of Andhra Pradesh & Ors*.[77] In this case, the Supreme Court had to consider whether a concession to a reserved forest area had been issued illegally by the State Government of Andhra Pradesh. In a very lengthy decision, the Court held that as the lands concerned were lands reserved for the benefit of Scheduled Tribes, the grant of a mining lease in favour of a non-tribal was bad in law.

3. Native land rights in Malaysia were again litigated in *Kerajaan Negeri Selangor & Ors v Sagong bin Tasi & Ors*,[78] where the Court of Appeal once again affirmed the existence of native title to the Temuans, an Orang Asli tribe on Peninsula Malaysia. On the status of aboriginals under Article 153 of the Malaysian Constitution, see R Bulan, 'Native Status under the Law' in Wu Min Aun (ed), *Public Law in Contemporary Malaysia* (Kuala Lumpur: Longman, 1999) 249. See also R Knox Dentan, *Malaysia and the 'Original People': A Case Study of the Impact of Development on Indigenous Peoples* (London: Allyn & Bacon Inc, 1996); C Wuiling, '*Sagong Tasi* and Orang Asli Land Rights in Malaysia: Victory, Milestone or False Start?' (2004)(2) *Law, Social Justice & Global Development Journal*, available at <http://www2.warwick.ac.uk/fac/soc/law/elj/lgd/2004_2/cheah/>; and S Osman, 'Globalisation and Democratisation: The Response of the Indigenous Peoples of Sarawak' (2000) 21(6) *Third World Quarterly* 977.

4. It is interesting that in Malaysia, positive discrimination is constitutionally mandated for the *bumiputeras* (literally 'sons of the soil'), defined by the Constitution as 'Malays and natives of any of the States of Sabah and Sarawak', who together form the majority of the population. Article 153 has been invoked in relation to cases concerning the extinguishment of native customary rights under the Sarawak

---

[77] *Samatha v State of Andhra Pradesh & Ors* [1997] AIR SC 3297.
[78] *Kerajaan Negeri Selangor & Ors v Sagong bin Tasi & Ors* [2005] 6 MLJ 289.

Land Code as a subsidiary argument.[79] Article 153 forms the basis for the New Economic Policy which was launched in 1971 to reduce the socio-economic disparity between the Chinese and the *bumiputeras*.

5.   In *TSC Education Sdn Bhd v Kolej Yayasan Pelajaran Mara & Anor*, the Malaysian High Court, upholding the constitutionality of an Act creating an educational institution to provide education and training to *bumiputeras*, made some observations about Article 153:

> I am constrained to hold that the whole purpose of the said Act and the said Order being enacted was exclusively for the advancement of Bumiputera students. It would certainly be absurd if foreign students from the People's Republic of China – the China students, were allowed entry but, on the other hand, the entry of local students who are non-Bumiputeras are disallowed. To adopt the argument of the learned counsel for the plaintiff would defeat the purpose of enacting the said Act and the said Order. The plaintiff seemed to suggest and advocate that local non-Bumiputera students should also be allowed entry because this would also 'promote and stimulate the economic and social development of Malaysia.' But the long line of authorities as alluded to earlier would certainly put an end to that kind of suggestion. The exclusive rights of the Bumiputeras are enshrined in the Federal Constitution ('the Constitution'). Article 153 of the Constitution provides for reservation of special benefits for the Malays and natives of any of the States of Sabah and Sarawak . . . [80]

6.   On the implementation of the New Economic Policy in Malaysia and its impact, see AJ Harding, *The Constitution of Malaysia: A Contextual Analysis* (Oxford: Hart Publishing, 2012) at 78–83.

7.   Article 152 of the Singapore Constitution[81] provides that it shall be 'the responsibility of the Government constantly to care for the interests of the racial and religious minorities in Singapore', and further the Government

> shall exercise its function in such manner as to recognize the special position of the Malays, who are the indigenous people of Singapore, and accordingly it shall be the responsibility of the Government to protect, safeguard, support, foster and promote their political, educational, religious, economic, social and cultural interests and the Malay language.

---

[79]   *Jalang anak Paran & Anor v Government of the State of Sarawak & Anor* [2007] 1 MLJ 412; *Bato Bagi & Ors v Government of the State of Sarawak* [2008] 5 MLJ 547.

[80]   *TSC Education Sdn Bhd v Kolej Yayasan Pelajaran Mara & Anor* [2002] 5 MLJ 577, 595–96.

[81]   The genesis of this article is derived from the Preamble of the 1958 Order-in-Council for Singapore which reads: 'That it shall be the responsibility of the Government of Singapore constantly to care for the interests of racial and religious minorities in Singapore. It should also be the deliberate and conscious policy of the Government of Singapore at all times to recognise the special position of the Malays, who are the indigenous people of the Island and are most in need of assistance, and within the framework of the general good of Singapore, to support, foster and promote their political, economic, social and cultural interests, and the Malay language.' The declaration of Malays as being 'most in need of assistance' and the need to balance the 'general good of Singapore' against recognising their special position and protecting their interests was left out of Art 89 of the Constitution of the State of Singapore when Singapore became part of the Federation of Malaysia in 1963. Art 89 is identical to the current Art 152 of the Constitution: see KYL Tan, 'The Legal and Institutional Framework and Issues of Multiculturalism in Singapore' in Lai Ah Eng (ed), *Beyond Rituals and Riots: Ethnic Pluralism and Social Cohesion in Singapore* (Singapore: Eastern Universities Press, 2004) at 98.

D. Privilege and Equality

Sometimes, the juxtaposition of guarantees to the right of equality and provisions designed to privilege certain groups gives rise to conflict. This happened in Taiwan, when the Justices of the Constitutional Court had to consider the validity of Article 37(1) of the Physically and Mentally Disabled Citizens Protection Act – which among other things provided that 'those who are not vision-impaired . . . shall not engage in the massage business' – in the light of the Constitution's equality provision (Article 7).

Judicial Yuan Interpretation No 64982
31 Oct 2008 (Constitutional Court, Taiwan)

Facts

This case concerned the constitutionality of Article 37(1) of the Physically and Mentally Disabled Citizens Protection Act as amended in 2001, which prohibited persons who were *not* visually-impaired from obtaining licences to practise as massagers. The Court held that this law violated Article 7 of the Constitution and that it would be invalid no later than three years after the issue of this Interpretation.

Held

Vision impairment is a physical condition beyond any human control. The disputed statutory provision, which based its discriminatory treatment on such a category over who can engage in massage business, has a profound impact on the majority of population who are not vision-impaired. While the legislators have taken into consideration the limited occupation and career options available to the vision-impaired in light of many obstacles they need to overcome, such as their growth, movement, learning and education, as well as the vulnerability of their social status, together with the reality that vision-impaired individuals have traditionally been dependent upon massage business for their livelihood, such legislation, in order to achieve an important public interest and comply with the right of equal protection, should nevertheless adopt a measure not to be excessively restrictive to the rights of those who are not vision-impaired, and to ensure that the protective measure for the vision-impaired have a substantial nexus with the objectives it intends to accomplish. The Constitution provisions concerning fundamental rights have emphatically focused on the protection of socially disadvantaged. Article 155 of the Constitution states, '. . . [t]o the aged and the infirm who are unable to earn a living, and to victims of unusual calamities, the State shall provide appropriate assistance and relief.' Article 10, Paragraph 7 of the Additional Articles of the Constitution states, '[t]he State shall guarantee availability of insurance, medical care, obstacle-free environments, education and training, as well as support and assistance in everyday life for physically and mentally handicapped persons, and shall also assist them to attain independence and to develop [their] potentials. . . .' These provisions have clearly demonstrated the principle for assisting the disadvantaged. As a result, there is a significant public interest in protecting the vision-impaired right to work, and the objectives for preferential or discriminatory treatment are justified under the relevant provisions of the Constitution.

[82] Official translation and edits by Professor Andy Y Sun.

When the Handicapped Welfare Act was enacted and promulgated in 1980, there were few career options available for vision-impaired individuals. The prohibition against non-vision impaired to engage in massage business was beneficial for the vision-impaired willing to engage in such business, and the reality was that a high percentage of vision-impaired have chosen massage business as their livelihood. However, the nature of massage and the skill required for those intend to engage in the massage business is not limited to vision-impaired only. With the expansion of market for massage career and service consumption, the disputed provision has become excessively restrictive to non-vision impaired individuals, which include other physically or mentally disabled but [who] are not vision-impaired who do not otherwise enjoy the preference on occupation reservation. With the knowledge and capability of [many] vision-impaired enhanced gradually, and the selectable occupation categories increased by the day, the statutory provision in question tends to make the governing authority overlook the fact that the talents of vision-impaired are not limited to massage business alone. Consequently, after nearly thirty years of the statute's promulgation and in light of the multiple availabilities of various occupations, the social-economic condition of vision-impaired has yet to see any significant improvement. Since there is hardly a substantial nexus between the objectives and the means, [the provision] contradicts the meaning and purpose of Article 7 of the Constitution on the right of equal protection.

The right of citizens' employment must be protected under Article 15 of the Constitution, the Judicial Interpretations No 404, 510, 584, 612, 634 and 637 further illustrate the freedom to engage in employment and to choose occupation. The Constitution has set forth different permission standards, based upon difference of contents, on restrictions over freedom of employment. The legislators, in pursuance of general public interest, may impose proper restrictions on the methods, time and location that an occupation may be carried out. Yet on the freedom to choose an occupation, if [the restrictions] concern the subjective condition needed, which means professional capability or license to perform the specific occupation, and such capability or [license] status can be gained through training and fostering, such as knowledge, degree or physical capability, no restrictions may be permitted without justification of important public interest. The objective condition needed for people to choose an occupation means those restrictions on the pursuance of an occupation that cannot be achieved by individual efforts, such as monopoly of certain sectors. Such restrictions may be justified only with showing of especially critical public interest. Without regard to under which condition the restrictions were imposed, the means adopted must not violate the principle of proportionality.

The disputed provision that prohibits non-vision impaired to engage in massage business amounts to restrictions on the objective conditions concerning the freedom to choose occupation. Since that provision was designed to protect the employment opportunity for vision-impaired, taking into consideration of the purpose of the last paragraph of Article 155 of the Constitution and Article 10, Paragraph 7 of the Additional Articles of the Constitution, it concerns an especially critical public interest, and the objective [of the statutory provision] is proper. Yet in light of the social development, expansion of the need for massage occupation, provided that the hand skills required for massage business are quite broad, including, among other things, 'effleuraging, kneading, chiropractics, pounding, stroking, hand arcuation, movement and other special hand skill.'[83] The prohibition in the disputed provision against the non vision-impaired does not have a clearly defined scope, and has resulted in inconsistent enforcement standards; thereby greatly increase the

---

[83] See Art 4 of the Regulations Governing the Qualifications and Management of Vision-Impaired Engaged in Massage Occupation, repealed on 5 March 2008; and Art 4, Sec 1 of the current Regulations Governing the Qualifications and Management of Vision Functionally-Impaired Engaged in Massage and Physical Therapy Massage Occupation.

possibility of violations by non vision-impaired engaged in similar work or business. This can be seen by many cases pending before different levels of the Administrative Courts. Given that anyone interested in massage business should have been eligible to engage in the occupation after receiving corresponding training and qualification review, by only permitting the vision-impaired to be able to conduct such business has resulted in non-vision impaired transfer to other occupation or lose their jobs, and a multi-facet competitive environment for consumers to choose not being able to form. This is not in parity with the interest to protect the right of employment for the vision-impaired. Consequently, the restriction of the disputed provision is not in conformity with principle of proportionality under Article 23 of the Constitution, and contravenes the protection over the right of employment stipulated in Article 15 of the Constitution.

It is an especially important public interest to protect the right of employment for the vision-impaired, and the governing authority shall adopt multiple, concrete measures to provide training and guidance for occupations deemed suitable for the vision-impaired [and] retain appropriate employment opportunities. In addition, [the governing authority] should provide adequate management on massage occupation and related matters, take into consideration the interests of both vision-impaired and non-vision impaired, the consumers and the suppliers, as well as the balance between the protection of [the] disadvantaged and market mechanism[s], so that the employment opportunities for the vision-impaired and other physically or mentally disabled [individuals] can be enhanced, the objectives of the Constitution to assist the disadvantaged in independent development can be fulfilled, and the principle and spirit of substantive equality enhanced. Since all of these measures require delicate planning and execution, the disputed provision shall be invalid no later than three years since the issuance of this Interpretation.

A similar provision exists in the Constitution of South Korea. In 2008, the South Korean Constitutional Court was called upon to consider the operation of Article 34, Section 5 of the Constitution, which required the state to protect citizens who were 'incapable of earning livelihood due to a physical disability, disease, old age or other reason'.

Visually Impaired Massagers Case
20-2(A) KCCR 1089, 2006Hun-Ma1098·1116·1117 (consolidated),
30 Oct 2008 (Constitutional Court, South Korea)

Facts

Under Article 61(1) of the Medical Service Act, only blind persons are permitted to obtain licences to be masseurs or masseuses ('massagers'). The complainants argued that by barring non-visually impaired persons from obtaining massager licences, the Act had infringed their rights of occupational choice. The provision was upheld by a majority of 6:3.

Justices Kim Hee-ok, Kim Jong-dae, Min Hyeong-ki, Lee Dong-heub, Mok Young-joon, Song Doo-hwan

(1) Fundamental Rights at Issue and Constitutional Review Method

(A) Article 34 Section 1 of the Constitution provides that, 'The State shall have the duty to endeavor to promote social security and welfare', and therefore stipulates the State's duty to ensure people's right to livelihood. Also, Article 34 Section 5 of the Constitution stipulates that, 'Citizens who are incapable of earning a livelihood due to a physical disability, disease, old age or other reasons shall be protected by the State', and thus proclaims the State's duty to protect the physically disabled and other people lacking self sufficiency.

As such, legislators have the obligation to formulate welfare policies actively corresponding to the constitutional commitment to the livelihood rights of the physically disabled, the underprivileged in society, but there is a likelihood that legislation in this regard may clash with other people's fundamental rights. In the case of the Instant Provision that stipulates exclusive massage licensing for those with visual impairment, the State duty specified in Article 34 Section 5 of the Constitution may conflict with fundamental rights such as people's freedom of occupation, which should be fully considered in constitutional review of the Instant Provision. In this case, the least restrictive legislation under Article 37 Section 2 of the Constitution will continue to apply, but, in the process of reviewing conformity with the least restrictive means and balance of interests, it would be necessary to determine the appropriate sentence also based on comprehensive consideration of the extent as to how far people's fundamental rights are restricted, fundamental rights of visually impaired persons and their welfare policies, exclusive massage licensing for the visually impaired and its alternatives.

(B) Meanwhile, in case the fundamental rights including the freedom of occupation are restricted as a result of the preferential treatment for the visually impaired as in the Instant Provision, excessive restriction of one's occupational freedom and equality rights violation both are at issue. In this context, it would be appropriate to review the violation of occupational freedom and equality rights together as a package instead of separately examining the two elements, since the two issues, the restriction of occupational freedom and unequal treatment suffered by the group applicable or non applicable by the discriminatory policy set by legislators, are very closely related. In particular, the legislative purpose of the Instant Provision is to favor the visually impaired over the unimpaired that results in the restriction of others' freedom of occupation, so it appears to be more adequate to review the justification of both the restriction on the freedom of occupation and the discriminatory treatment.

(2) Constitutionality of the Instant Provision

(A) As viewed earlier, Article 34 Section 5 of the Constitution proclaims the State's duty to protect the citizens who are incapable of earning a livelihood, and this corresponds to the spirit of Article 8 Section 1 of the Welfare of Disabled Persons Act that prohibits discrimination of the disabled and 'Declaration on the Rights of Disabled Persons' that promotes social security and employment. Such duty of the State needs to be materialized by legislation of legislators. In other words, legislators should devise welfare policies required for job training, job arrangements, employment, etc in order for the disabled to receive adequate training and have suitable jobs that fit their aptitudes and abilities according to their age, ability and the type and level of disability. The severely disabled barely self sufficient, in particular, will need a more active policy.

The primary purpose of the welfare policies for the disabled lies with guaranteeing their livelihood rights, but the purpose must not limit such a goal. The policies should also be focused on providing overall environment with the disabled as the minority in which they are treated as true members of the society and enabling them to have their dignity and value respected and lead a humane livelihood pursuant to Article 10 and 34 of the Constitution. However, active welfare policies for the disabled sometimes take the form of favoring the disabled against other citizens, which may result in the restriction of non-disabled persons' fundamental rights. In that case, legislators should be able to find harmony and balance between the two interests of protecting the disabled and guaranteeing people's fundamental rights, and the legislators will have to exercise their legislative discretion within such limitations.

(B) The Instant Provision, as aforementioned, aims to provide the visually impaired with livelihood based on the stated constitutional commitment to protecting the physically disabled and the principles of welfare policy for the disabled, and the legislative purpose of the Instant Provision lies ultimately in making their lives rewarding and realizing their right to live a humane livelihood. In this sense, the Instant Provision fully meets the requirement for legitimacy of purpose.

Furthermore, provided that the massage business barely requires spatial movement and mobility and is friendly to the visually impaired with developed sense of touch, the Instant Provision, which gives massage licenses exclusively to the visually impaired and thereby supporting their livelihood and offer opportunities for employment, serves as a suitable means to serve the stated legislative purpose.

(C) At the same time, there are several alternatives to serving the legislative purpose other than granting exclusive license to the visually impaired: first, to offer direct financial assistance; second, to favor the visually impaired over others in choosing and performing one's occupation; third, to provide a program promoting employment and vocational rehabilitation. In practice, the Welfare of Disabled Persons Act, taking into account the level of disability and financial conditions, articulates systems such as disability allowances (Article 49), supply of medical expenses (Article 36), instant provision of educational expenses for children (Article 38), supply of self-reliance training expenses (Article 43), loan of fund, etc (Article 41). In order to provide for income sources and vocational rehabilitation there are also other alternatives such as support for business (Article 42), which gives priority to the disabled in installing stores selling daily necessities or vending machines in the public facilities or in selling tobacco and postage stamps, and an incentive system that encourages state agencies to preferentially purchase goods produced (Article 44). Yet, it cannot be denied that the welfare of the disabled in reality in fact is far from these provisions, particularly the visually impaired. For instance, those eligible for financial support such as disability allowances and supply of medical expenses are very limited and the amount of money is extremely small, which therefore is not substantially helpful to the visually impaired. Not many disabled persons benefit from the business support, such as giving priority in tobacco retail business or installation of vending machines, either, and the said benefits are particularly rarely enjoyed by visually impaired persons due to their physical characteristics. Also, even compulsory employment of massagers in certain work places of certain sizes or incentives such as tax benefits in business activities of the visually impaired may not be very effective when assuming that the visually impaired will be competing against the non-visually impaired.

If we consider such realistic aspects of the welfare policy for the visually impaired, in order to ensure welfare and the right to humane livelihood of visually impaired persons in our society, it would be inevitable to allow the visually impaired monopoly over the massage practice as a legislative decision. Indeed, because denying non-visually impaired persons the opportunity to obtain massager licenses in the first place results in an extremely serious restriction of fundamental rights, it is undoubted that the discrimination is inevitable in serving the legislative purpose and should be adopted only as the last resort. Still, it is not easy for the visually impaired to choose jobs even if support for employment in other areas is provided because not even their right to mobility is guaranteed in our society. The occupation of massager is one of the very few jobs that for the visually impaired can opt for, and barely no other occupation would be available in reality. In particular, according to many statistics confirmed so far, it is not difficult to find that quite a few number of persons with severe visual impairment have obtained massager licenses and rely on massage practice for their livelihoods. Given this reality alone, the massage practice is almost the only profession that the visually impaired can choose and engage in.

As verified through cases of many other countries such as the United States and United Kingdom equipped with developed welfare policies for the visually impaired, if more financial support is provided to the visually impaired and if they are in an environment to engage in job activities other than massaging, there would be no need to go so far as to grant the visually impaired monopoly over the massage practice. Still, as Korea is not yet ready for such an environment, the aforementioned means alone cannot be an effective alternative to serve the legislative purpose, and the welfare policy must be implemented in a way that fits our current socioeconomic conditions. This conclusion is well exhibited in Taiwan, which grants the monopoly right for the massage practice to the visually impaired as a form of employment reservation, and Japan, where a certain percentage of massager positions is allotted to those with visual impairment.

It is true that people's freedom of occupation is restricted as a result of the Instant Provision that grants monopoly of the visually impaired over the massage practice, but this policy is an inevitable choice to ensure their livelihood rights since the massage practice is almost the only occupation they can normally engage in. In contrast, the scope of profession that non-visually impaired persons can choose is extensive and they have many options other than the massage practice. In particular, physical therapists are almost similar to massagers, and it is possible that one can engage in the practice by taking a series of training courses and tests and obtaining licenses, which means it is not true that other routes to choosing massagers and other similar occupations is totally blocked.

Having considered the above, it cannot be contested that the Instant Provision stipulating exclusive licensing for the visually impaired contradicts the principle of the least restrictive means.

(D) Visually impaired persons have been under visible and invisible forms of discrimination in [their] overall daily lives, and it is undeniable that they have been severely discriminated against in sectors such as education and employment. There were no welfare policies for their income compensation or vocational rehabilitation that can ensure a humane livelihood. In that sense, exclusive massage licensing for the visually impaired is the minimum preferential treatment to guarantee their livelihood and a humane life in this reality and has been adopted as a means to compensate for the discrimination and realize substantial equality.

In this regard, some may point out that social welfare should be achieved by financial compensation by the government and that restriction on other people's fundamental rights is inappropriate. However, providing the visually impaired with financial support would evidently forgo the basic idea of Article 10 and Article 34 Section 5 of the Constitution that stipulates the protection of the physically disabled as members of the community. What visually impaired persons want is not mere financial assistance but to engage in a proper and rightful profession. Whether it be from the point of social integration or protection of fundamental rights, the State should offer special protection for the disabled, which is not a special favor of benefit but a constitutional right. A humane livelihood allows the visually impaired, as others, to meet the conditions to earn their livelihood by engaging in the profession through which they can manifest their personality as fitting their abilities, so actively engaging in a profession, instead of simply receiving financial support from the government, would elevate their occupational awareness and prevent sense of alienation. Moreover, as the majority of visual impairment is acquired, not congenital, those with no visible impairment can develop one anytime. In this context, giving priority to the disabled, in particular the visually impaired, is hardly an unjust discrimination against the non-visually impaired.

(E) In short, the legislators legislated this Instant Provision as part of welfare policies for the visually impaired in accordance with Article 10 and Article 34 Section 5 of the Constitution. In the course of the legislation, overall circumstances as reviewed earlier have been fully considered and deserve to be respected: working as massagers is almost the only occupational choice for the visually impaired; there are not enough alternatives to the massage practice to ensure livelihood of the visually impaired if the practice is also open to people without visual impairment; and visually impaired persons are a minority who have long been discriminated against in sectors such as education and employment, so realizing substantial equality requires preferential treatment. The Instant Provision has appropriately weighted diverse circumstances surrounding visually and non-visually impaired persons pursuant to the constitutional commitment to ensuring their right to livelihood. When comparing the public interest to be achieved by the Instant Provision, such as the livelihood rights of the visually impaired, and the consequently sacrificed private interest, such as the freedom of occupation of the others, it cannot be concluded immediately that there is an imbalance between the two interests.

Therefore, the Instant Provision hardly discriminates the non-visually impaired against the visually impaired in violation of the principle of proportionality, and it is also difficult to view that the Instant Provision violates the Constitution by excessively infringing on the freedom of occupation.

(F) The Instant Provision is a means taken by legislators to provide the visually impaired with livelihood and a humane life and thus does not violate the Constitution, but a more serious consideration is required on disadvantages that the non-visually impaired have to suffer from the Instant Provision. It is undeniable that, so far since adopting the exclusive massage licensing for the visually impaired, the disadvantage for non-visually impaired persons of not being able to choose the massage practice as profession and the resulting conflict of attrition has remained in place. In this regard, in light of the fact that the problem of not being able to choose massager as occupation is a social issue no less important than protecting the socioeconomically underprivileged, the legislature and other government authorities should not neglect resolving the issues in carrying out welfare policies for the visually impaired. As aforementioned, the Instant Provision is an inevitable policy measure that we have adopted because other efficient alternatives to ensure livelihood and job activities of the visually impaired are yet not functioning properly. Therefore, if socioeconomic conditions improve and welfare policies for the visually impaired further develop, it would be difficult to maintain the current policy measure of securing their livelihood rights at the expense of others' fundamental rights.

In this respect, the legislature and other government authorities need to actively come up with welfare policies for the visually impaired in order to promptly resolve the issue of fundamental law restriction, but it is currently difficult to find other efficient policy measures to ensure livelihood of the visually impaired other than exclusive massage licensing. Based on serious recognition of such issues, the legislature and other government authorities, for this reason, should commit themselves to more serious and active review on measures to enable harmonious coexistence of the two conflicting fundamental rights – the livelihood rights of the visually impaired and the occupational freedom of the visually unimpaired-particularly on measures that can allow persons with visual impairment to enjoy a humane livelihood based on job activities.

(3) Sub-Conclusion

Therefore, it is not likely that the Instant Provision infringes on the complainants' freedom of occupation and equality rights under the Constitution. . . .

Justices Lee Kang-kook (Presiding), Lee Kong-hyun & Cho Dae-hyen (Dissenting)

We believe that the Instant Provision infringes on the freedom of occupation by contradicting the rule against excessive restriction and thereby violates the Constitution. For this reason, we state the following dissenting opinion.

A. Restriction of Occupational Freedom by Objective Reasons

Occupation is not only an activity of earning necessary income but also an essential element in maintaining market economy order, as well as a means to develop one's individual personality by freely manifesting one's personality. The Korean Constitution guarantees the freedom of occupation (Article 15, Constitution).

Therefore, restriction on occupational freedom should by all means be consistent with law and regulations and is only achievable by appropriate means and methods to achieve legitimate and major common goals of society, such as securing national safety, public order or welfare (1 KCCR 329, 336, 89Hun-Ka102, November 20, 1989).

In particular, the Constitutional Court previously held that the restriction of occupational freedom based on objective requirement for permission regardless of one's abilities or qualifications can be justified provided that it is necessary to 'prevent clear and evident risk for the purpose of serving public interests of high importance', so the rule against excessive restriction, namely the principle of strict proportionality, under Article 37 Section 2 of the Constitution serves as a criterion for review (14-1 KCCR 410, 427, 2001Hun-Ma614, April 25, 2002).

The exclusive massage licensing pursuant to the Instant Provision directly violates the occupational freedom of the non-visually impaired. Because such restriction is based on relevant objective requirements irrespective of one's abilities and qualifications, it should be consistent with the rule against excessive restriction under Article 37 Section 2 of the Constitution (18-1(B) KCCR 112, 123-124, 2003Hun-Ma715, May 25, 2006).

B. Review on the Instant Provision

Although the massage practice itself, by its essence, is not unsuitable for the non-visually impaired, the Instant Provision restricts the freedom of occupation based on an objective reason or condition – visual disability. It is only when the purpose of restriction goes beyond simple public welfare to prevent clear and evident risk for the sake of public interest, which is far more important than the occupational freedom, that legitimacy of purpose is achieved. It is fully understood that guaranteeing the visually impaired their livelihood and offering them the opportunity to engage in job activities is a major public interest purpose, but it is difficult to see that there is a clear and evident risk that can justify the restriction on the occupational freedom given the following: as of late March, 2007, the number of visually impaired persons registered as massagers is a mere 6,000 to 7,000 out of the 209,968 registered as those with visual impairment, and removal of exclusive licensing will not make it impossible for the visually impaired to work as licensed massagers but will just place them under competition against the non-visually impaired.

At the same time, it is to be reviewed whether the Instant Provision is a suitable means to provide the visually impaired with livelihood and the opportunity for job activities. As of late March, 2007, of the total visually impaired persons registered, 170,685 persons with level 3 to 6 visual impairment (level 3–11,365, level 4–10,605, level 5–17,532, level 6–131,183) excluding 39,283 with level 1 and 2 severe visual impairment are working in relatively diverse job sectors[;] approximately 17 percent of those with severe visual disabilities, or 6,000 to 7,000 persons, are registered as massagers; and only over 500,000 persons with light visual impairment are registered as massagers. This considered, it is doubted whether the Instant Provision is effective in guaranteeing them livelihood, and simply allowing monopoly of the massage practice hardly leads to the opportunity to choose one's occupation as a means to self actualization and development of individual personality. Therefore, it is difficult to say that the Instant Provision fully contributes to the said legislative purpose in reality.

Furthermore, it is not that there is no other means to provide the visually impaired with livelihood and job opportunities aside from the monopoly over the massage practice pursuant to the Instant Provision. There can be many other forms of support for the visually impaired related to their massage business: to expand the scope of health and welfare related facilities where massagers can work for to health service centers, welfare facilities for the elderly, welfare facilities for the disabled, etc as well as massage parlors; to reduce the number of test subjects of massager certificate examinations for the visually impaired; implement a compulsory employment quota for visually impaired massagers in massage parlors of certain sizes; to provide the visually impaired with financial assistance in starting massage businesses and tax benefits; to give monopoly to the visually impaired over massage businesses over or under certain sizes, such as out call massage services without business places; to classify the visually impaired into those with severe and light visual impairment and offer appropriate vocational training courses related to job opportunities other than the massage practice; and to enforce improvement in the test system, such as introduction of voice tests and advantage in test time, so that fair verification of abilities can be administered. Given these alternatives, it would be difficult to view that monopoly over the massage practice prescribed by the Instant Provision is an inevitable means to serve the legislative purpose and would violate the least restrictive means. Also, legislators who are trying to settle for the Instant Provision without review thereon or development of alternatives despite the many alternatives mentioned before have neglected the State's duty to promote social security and welfare (Article 34 Section 2, Constitution) based on the constitutional Instant Provision that the State shall protect those incapable of earning livelihood as prescribed by law (Article 34 Section 5, Constitution).

Besides, the Instant Provision denies the non-visually impaired the opportunity to obtain massager licenses in the first place, and it can be found that balancing of interests is barely realized by just considering the aspect of ensuring livelihood of the visually impaired, particularly some of those with severe impairment. If non-visually impaired persons are also entitled to massager licenses, this will inevitably bring competition with those with severe visual impairment. Although this may lead to an actual disadvantage that abilities of visually impaired persons are unjustly assessed due to prejudices, it is not likely that such will lead to denial of the livelihood rights of those with severe visual impairment. Also, prejudice and discrimination against the disabled is a different challenge that our society and others in this world need to overcome. Even now, it is easily found that so many disabled persons without visual impairment unlawfully engage in the massage practice, and the general public who are laymen to law receive massage service provided by unlicensed non-visually impaired persons in order to relieve physical fatigue and psychological stress from work or workouts, thereby joining in unlawful acts regardless of their true intentions. In that sense, there is a possibility that opening the massager profession to the non-visually impaired and strictly controlling and banning unlawful massage practices result in opportunities for the visually impaired by increasing demand for massage services and normalizing the market. In conclusion, it is fully acknowledged that the public interest to be served by the Instant Provision such as guarantee of livelihood of the visually impaired is important, but it is difficult to decide that the significance of public interest outweighs that of the private interest since denying the non-visually impaired the freedom of occupation infringes on even the essence of fundamental rights.

Therefore, the Instant Provision violates the Constitution by contradicting the rule against excessive restriction and thus the essence of freedom of occupation (18-1(B) KCCR 112, 123–126, 2003Hun-Ma715, May 25, 2006).

Notes and Questions

1. Compare the results and reasoning in the blind massagers cases from Taiwan and South Korea. What do you think are the key reasons for the different approaches adopted and the outcomes? What attitude did the respective courts adopt in respect of blind persons and their ability to eke out a living? Why are they – or are they not proper subjects of protection?

2. For a comparative study between the Taiwanese and South Korean cases on blind massagers, see Chun-Yuan Lin, 'Livelihood v Equality: A Comparison of Visually Impaired Massage Law in Taiwan and Korea' (2010) 5(1) *National Taiwan University Law Review* 229.

3. In 2003, prior to its decision in the *Visually Impaired Massagers Case* (2008), the South Korean Constitutional Court upheld the Promotion, etc of Employment of Disabled Persons Act which required employers who constantly employ 300 employees or more, to employ disabled persons totalling at least two per cent of the employer's workforce. This was decided in *Mandatory Employment of Disabled Persons,*[84] where the Court held:

> The Preamble of the Constitution declares that an equal opportunity is guaranteed for all citizens and seeks to realize a welfare state by presenting the direction of the guarantee of the social basic rights. Article 32 of the Constitution provides that all citizens are entitled to the right to work, and that the state shall make effort to promote employment and to guarantee appropriate wages by social and economic means. Article 34 of the Constitution declares that every citizen is entitled to a life worthy of human beings; at the same time, it obligates the state to promote social security and social welfare to specifically realize such humane living conditions, and emphasizes that especially those citizens lacking capability of living due to such factors as disability, ailment, or aging shall be protected by the state pursuant to the relevant statutes. Also, Article 119(2) of the Constitution provides that the state may regulate and coordinate in order for the democratization of economy through harmonization among various subjects and actors within the economy.
>
> Disabled persons often face extreme hardship in reality in obtaining a vocation appropriate to their ability, due to their physical or mental condition, which requires a measure at the social and national level in order to guarantee the right to work of disabled persons. From this perspective, despite the guarantee of the freedom of economic activities of business entities and the declaration of the freedom of contract among private individuals under the Constitution, it is an inevitable measure to restrict such freedom to a certain degree in order to recognise human dignity and value, and to guarantee humane living conditions for disabled persons who are in a socially and economically weaker position. As the creation of jobs relies on general private business entities as well as the state, it is inevitable to obligate private businesses with respect to

---

[84] *Mandatory Employment of Disabled Persons* 15-2(A) KCCR 58, 2001Hun-Ba96, 24 Jul 2003.

the guarantee of employment for disabled persons to an appropriate extent. Therefore, the mandatory employment of disabled persons provision at issue in this case does not excessively restrict the freedom of contract and other economic liberties of the employers.

The state and local governments are the public actors responsible for carrying out education, publicity campaigns and employment promotion drives for disabled persons to increase understanding of the employers and the general public with respect to the employment of disabled persons, carrying out support and subsidyies for the employers, the disabled employees and other parties concerned, and vocational rehabilitation measures reflecting the unique characteristics concerning disabled individuals, and effectively carrying out measures necessary to promote employment and job security for disabled persons. Also, the Act relaxes the employment requirement when applied to private industry, where the Act acknowledges a considerable portion thereof consists of the vocation for which it is difficult to employ disabled persons. Therefore, although the Act provides that the state and the local governments shall make efforts to recruit and retain two-hundredths of the public officials employed therein among disabled persons unlike private business entities with the exceptional exclusion of certain public offices as set forth in the presidential decree, it is a differential treatment based on a reasonable ground and is thus not against the principle of equality.

E. Rational Classification and the Reasonable Nexus Test

i. The Indian Test and Its Progeny

Equality under the law does not require all persons to be treated alike. People differ in their abilities, personalities and culture, and it makes no sense to treat a child in the same manner as an adult in matters of voting or criminal culpability. As was noted previously, all that equality requires is that a rational basis exists for classifying persons into a particular class, and to demonstrate that such a classification bears a reasonable nexus to a legitimate state interest and object. Put another way, all the law requires is that like persons in like circumstances should be treated alike. Under the doctrine of classification, one may in certain instances discriminate *between* classes, but no one *within* a particular class should be singled out for discriminatory treatment.

The following cases illustrate the workings of this doctrine of classification.

The State of West Bengal vs Anwar Ali Sarkar
[1952] AIR 75; [1952] SCR 284 (Supreme Court of India)

Facts

In this case, the Supreme Court of India was asked to consider the constitutionality of the West Bengal Special Courts Act (No X of 1950) which had been enacted to 'provide for the speedier trial of certain offences'. Section 3 of the Act empowered the West Bengal Government to constitute such Special Courts by way of a notification in the *Gazette*. In addition, section 5 of the Act provided that: 'A Special Court shall try such offences or classes of offences or cases or classes of cases, as the State Government may by general or special order in writing, direct.' The respondent, who had been convicted by the Special

Court, argued that section 5 of the Act was unconstitutional as it violated Article 14 of the Constitution which guaranteed citizens equal protection of the law.

Patanjali Sastri CJ (dissenting)

The question next arises as to whether the provision, thus understood, violates the prohibition under article 14 of the Constitution. The first part of the article, which appears to have been adopted from the Irish Constitution, is a declaration of equality of the civil rights of all persons within the territories of India and thus enshrines what American Judges regard as the 'basic principle of republicanism' [cf *Ward v Flood*[85]].The second part which is a corollary of the first and is based on the last clause of the first section of the Fourteenth Amendment of the American Constitution, enjoins that equal protection shall be secured to all such persons in the enjoyment of their rights and liberties without discrimination or favouritism, or as an American Judge put it 'it is a pledge of the protection of equal laws' [*Yick Wo v Hopkins*[86]], that is, laws that operate alike on all persons under like circumstances. . . .

And as the prohibition under the article is directed against the State, which is defined in article 12 as including not only the legislatures but also the Governments in the country, article 14 secures all persons within the territories of India against arbitrary laws as well as arbitrary application of laws. This is further made clear by defining 'law' in article 13 (which renders void any law which takes away or abridges the rights conferred by Part III) as including, among other things, any 'order' or 'notification', so that even executive orders or notifications must not infringe article 14. This trilogy of articles thus ensures non-discrimination in State action both in the legislative and the administrative spheres in the democratic republic of India. This, however, cannot mean that all laws must be general in character and universal in application. As pointed out in *Chiranjit Lal's* case[87] and in numerous American decisions dealing with the equal protection clause of the 14th Amendment, the State in the exercise of its governmental power must of necessity make laws operating differently on different groups or classes of persons within its territory to attain particular ends in giving effect to its policies, and it must possess for that purpose large powers of distinguishing and classifying persons or things to be subjected to such laws. But classification necessarily implies discrimination between persons classified and those who are not members of that class. 'It is the essence of a classification' said Mr Justice Brewer in *Atchison, Topeka & Santa Fe R Co v Matthews*,[88] 'that upon the class are cast duties and burdens different from those resting upon the general public. Indeed the very idea of classification is that of inequality, so that it goes without saying that the mere fact of inequality in no manner determines this matter of constitutionality'. Commenting on this observation in his dissenting opinion in *Connoly v Union Sewer Pipe Co*[89] *(which later prevailed in Tigner v Texas)*[90] Mr Justice McKenna posed a problem and proceeded to answer it:

> It seems like a contradiction to say that a law having equality of operation may yet give equality of protection. Viewed rightly, however, the contradiction disappears . . . Government is not a simple thing. It encounters and must deal with the problems which come from persons in an infinite variety of relations. Classification is the recognition of those relations, and, in making it, a legislature must be allowed a wide latitude of

---

[85] *Ward v Flood* 17 Am Rep 405 (1874).
[86] *Yick Wo v Hopkins* 118 US 356, 369 (1888).
[87] *Chiranjit Lal Chowdhury v The Union of India and Others* [1950] SCR 869.
[88] *Atchison, Topeka & Santa Fe R Co v Matthews* 174 US 96 (1899), at 106.
[89] *Connolly v Union Sewer Pipe Co* 184 US 540 (1902), at 566, 567, 568.
[90] *Tigner v Texas* 310 US 141, at 296.

discretion and judgment . . . Classification based on those relations need not be constituted by an exact or scientific exclusion or inclusion of persons or things. Therefore it has been repeatedly declared that classification is justified if it is not palpably arbitrary.

Thus, the general language of article 14, as of its American counterpart, has been greatly qualified by the recognition of the State's regulative power to make laws operating differently on different classes of persons in the governance of its subjects, with the result that the principle of equality of civil rights and of equal protection of the laws is only given effect to as a safeguard against arbitrary State action. It follows that in adjudging a given law as discriminatory and unconstitutional two aspects have to be considered. First, it has to be seen whether it observes equality between all the persons on whom it is to operate. An affirmative finding on the point may not, however, be decisive of the issue. If the impugned legislation is a special law applicable only to a certain class of persons, the court must further enquire whether the classification is founded on a reasonable basis having regard to the object to be attained, or is arbitrary. Thus, the reasonableness of classification comes into question only in those cases where special legislation affecting a class of persons is challenged as discriminatory. But there are other types of legislation such as, for instance, the Land Acquisition Act, which do not rest on classification, and no question of reasonable classification could fairly arise in respect of such enactments. Nor, obviously, could it arise when executive orders or notifications directed against individual citizens are assailed as discriminatory.

It is interesting to find that the trend of recent decisions in America has been to lean strongly toward sustaining State action both in the legislative and in the administrative spheres against attacks based on hostile discrimination. Classifications condemned as discriminatory have been subsequently upheld as being within the powers of the legislature. In *Tigner v Texas*,[91] the majority view in *Connolly's* case[92] holding that an Illinois anti-trust law, which made certain forbidden acts criminal if done by merchants and manufacturers but declared them to be civil wrongs if done by farmers and stockmen, was 'manifestly a denial of the equal protection of the laws' was considered to be no-longer 'controlling'. While in *Gulf, Colorado & Santa Fe R Co v Ellis*[93] a Texas statute imposing an attorney's fee in addition to costs upon railway corporations which unsuccessfully defended actions for damages for stock killed or injured by their train was struck down as discriminatory because such corporations could not recover any such fee if their defence was successful, a similar provision in a Kansas statute in respect of an action against railroad companies for damages by fire caused by operating the rail-road was upheld as not discriminatory in *Atchison, Topeka & Santa Fe R Co v Matthews*,[94] the earlier case being distinguished on some ground which Harlon J in his dissenting opinion confessed he was not 'astute enough to perceive'. And the latest decision in *Kotch v Pilot Comm'rs*[95] marks, perhaps, the farthest swing of the pendulum. A Louisiana pilotage law authorised the appointment of State pilots only upon certification by a State Board of river pilot commissioners who were themselves State Pilots. Among the prescribed qualifications was apprenticeship under a State pilot for a certain period. By admitting only their relatives and friends to apprenticeship, the members of the board made it impossible, with occasional exceptions, for others to be appointed as State pilots. Upholding the constitutionality of the law as well as the manner in which it was administered, the Court said:

[91] *Tigner v Texas* 310 US 141.
[92] *Connolly v Union Sewer Pipe Co* 184 US 540 (1902).
[93] *Gulf, Colorado & Santa Fe Railway Co v Ellis* 165 US 150 (1891).
[94] *Atchison, Topeka & Santa Fe R Co v Matthews* 184 US 540 (1891).
[95] *Kotch v Pilot Comm'rs* 330 US 552 (1947).

The constitutional command for a State to afford equal protection of the laws sets a goal not attainable by the invention and application of a precise formula. This Court has never attempted that impossible task. A law which affects the activities of some groups differently from the way in which it affects the activities of other groups is not necessarily banned by the 14th Amendment. Otherwise, effective regulation in the public interest could not be provided, however essential that regulation might be.

These decisions seem, to my mind, to reveal a change of approach marked by an increasing respect for the State's regulatory power in dealing with equal protection claims and underline the futility of wordy formulation of so called 'tests' in solving problems presented by concrete cases. Great reliance was placed on behalf of the respondent upon the decision in *Truax v Corrigan*[96] and *Yick Wo v Hopkins*.[97] In the former case it was held by a majority of 5:4 that a law which denied the remedy of injunction in a dispute between employer and his ex-employees was a denial of the equal protection of laws, as such a remedy was allowed in all other cases. But it is to be noted that the minority, which included Holmes and Brandeis JJ, expressed the opinion that it was within the power of the State to make such differentiation and the law was perfectly constitutional. The legislation was obviously applicable to a class of persons and the decision was an instance where the classification was held to be arbitrary and is not of much assistance to the respondent. In the other case a San Francisco Ordinance, which prohibited the carrying on of a laundry business within the limits of the City without having first obtained the consent of the Board of Supervisors unless it was located in a building constructed of brick or stone, was held discriminatory and unconstitutional. The undisputed facts disclosed in the record were that out of 320 laundries in San Francisco about 310 were constructed of wood, and about 240 of the 320 were owned and conducted by subjects of China. The petitioner, a Chinaman, and about 200 of his countrymen applied to the Board of Supervisors to continue their clothes washing business in wooden buildings which they had been occupying for many years, but in all cases licence was refused, whereas not a single one of the petitions presented by 80 persons who were not subjects of China had been refused. Dealing with these facts the court observed:

> Though the law itself be fair on its face and impartial in appearance, yet if it is applied and administered by public authority with an evil eye and an unequal hand so as to practically make unjust and illegal discrimination between persons in similar circumstances, material to their rights, the denial of equal justice is still within the prohibition of the Constitution.

It is to be noted that the law was 'administered', ie, not merely applied in a few stray cases, but regularly and systematically applied, making a hostile discrimination against a particular class of persons on grounds of race and colour. Such systematic discriminatory administration in practice of the ordinance though impartial on its face, was, evidently, taken to give rise to the inference that it was designed to be so administered. That is how the decision has been explained in later cases. For instance, in *Atchison Topeka & Santa Fe R. Co v Matthews*[98] it was said

> In that case (*Yick Wo's* case)[99] a municipal ordinance of San Francisco designed to prevent the Chinese from carrying on the laundry business was adjudged void. This Court looked beyond the mere letter of the ordinance to the condition of things as they

---

[96] *Truax v Corrigan* 257 US 312.
[97] *Yick Wo v Hopkins* 118 US 356 (1886).
[98] *Atchison Topeka & Santa Fe Railway Co v Matthews* 174 US 96 (1899), 105.
[99] *Yick Wo v Hopkins* 118 US 356 (1886).

existed in San Francisco and saw under the guise of regulation an arbitrary classification was intended and accomplished.

That is to say, the ordinance was what the Privy Council called a 'colourable legislative expedient' which, under the 'guise or pretence' of doing what is constitutionally permissible, 'in substance and purpose seeks to effect discrimination': *Morgan Proprietary Ltd v Deputy Commissioner of Taxation for New South Wales*.[100] Thus explained, the *Yick Wo* case is no authority for the view that the vesting in a public authority of a discretion which is liable to abuse by arbitrary exercise contrary to its intendment is a sufficient ground for condemning a statute as discriminatory and unconstitutional.

On the other hand, there is ample authority in the American decisions for the view that the necessarily large powers vested in a legislature must include the power of entrusting to an administrative body a plenary but not arbitrary discretion to be exercised so as to carry out the purpose of an enactment. In *Engel v O' Malley*[101] a New York statute prohibiting individuals or partnerships to engage in the business of receiving deposits of money without a licence from the controller 'who may approve or disapprove the application for a licence in his discretion' was sustained as constitutional. In answer to the argument that the controller might refuse a licence on his arbitrary whim, Holmes J said:

> We should suppose that in each case the controller was expected to act for cause. But the nature and extent of the remedy, if any, for a breach of duty on his part, we think it unnecessary to consider; for the power of the state to make the pursuit of a calling dependent upon obtaining a licence is well established where safety seems to require it.

In *New York ex rel Lieberman v Van De Carr*[102] a provision in the Sanitary Code of the City of New York vested discretion in Local Health Boards to grant or withhold licences for carrying on milk business in the City. Upholding the constitutionality of the provision, Day J observed after referring to certain prior decisions:

> These cases leave in no doubt the proposition that the conferring of discretionary power upon administrative boards to grant or withhold permission to carry on a trade or business which is the proper subject of regulation within the police power of the state is not violative of rights secured by the 14th Amendment. There is no presumption that the power will be arbitrarily exercised, and when it is shown to be thus exercised against the individual, under sanction of state authority, this court has not hesitated to interfere for his protection, when the case has come before it in such manner as to authorise the interference of a Federal Court.

And Holmes J added that, although it did not appear from the statute that the action of the Board of Health was intended to be subject to judicial revision as to its reasonableness, he agreed that it was not hit at by the 14th Amendment.

In the light of the foregoing discussion, it seems to me difficult to hold that section 5(1) in whole or in part is discriminatory. It does not, either in terms or by necessary implication, discriminate as between persons or classes of persons; nor does it purport to deny to any one equality before the law or the equal protection of the laws. Indeed, it does not by its own force make the special procedure provided in the Act applicable to the trial of any

---

[100] *Morgan Proprietary Ltd v Deputy Commissioner of Taxation for New South Wales* [1940] AC 838, at 858.
[101] *Engel v O' Malley* 219 US 128 (1911).
[102] *New York ex rel Lieberman v Van De Carr* 199 US 552 (1905).

offence or classes of offences or classes of cases; for, it is the State Government's notification under the section that attracts the application of the procedure. Nor is that procedure,
as I have endeavoured to show, calculated to impair the chances of a fair trial of the cases
to which it may be made applicable, and no discriminatory intent or design is discernible on
its face, unless every departure from the normal procedure is to be regarded as involving a
hostile discrimination. . . .

Fazl Ali J

I have come to the conclusion that these appeals should be dismissed, and since that is also
the conclusion which has been arrived at by several of my colleagues and they have written
very full and elaborate judgments in support of it, I shall only supplement what they have
said by stating briefly how I view some of the crucial points arising in the case.

There is no doubt that the West Bengal Special Courts Ordinance, 1949, which was later
replaced by the impugned Act (West Bengal Special Courts Act X of 1950, to be hereinafter referred to as 'the Act'), was a valid Ordinance when it was promulgated on the 17th
August, 1949. The Act, which came into effect on the 15th March, 1950, is a verbatim
reproduction of the earlier Ordinance, and what we have to decide is whether it is invalid
because it offends against article 14 of the Constitution. In dealing with this question, the
following facts have to be borne in mind:

(1) The framers of the Act have merely copied the provisions of the Ordinance of 1949
     which was promulgated when there was no provision similar to article 14 of the present
     Constitution.
(2) The provision of the American Constitution which corresponds to article 14 has, ever
     since that Constitution has been in force, greatly exercised the minds of the American
     Judges, who, notwithstanding their efforts to restrict its application within reasonable
     limits, have had to declare a number of laws and executive acts to be unconstitutional.
     One is also amazed at the volume of case-law which has grown round this provision,
     which shows the extent to which its wide language can be stretched and the large
     variety of situations in which it has been invoked.
(3) Article 14 is as widely worded as, if not more widely worded than, its counterpart in
     the American Constitution, and is bound to lead to some inconvenient results and
     seriously affect some pre-Constitution laws.
(4) The meaning and scope of article 14 have been elaborately explained in two earlier
     decisions of this Court, viz, *Chiranjit Lal Chowdhury v The Union of India and
     Others*[103] and *The State of Bombay and Another v FN Balsara*,[104] and the
     principles laid down in those decisions have to be kept in view in deciding the present
     case. One of these principles is that article 14 is designed to protect all persons placed
     in similar circumstances against legislative discrimination, and if the legislature takes
     care to reasonably classify persons for legislative purposes and if it deals equally with
     all persons belonging to a well-defined class, it is not open to the charge of denial of
     equal protection on the ground that the law does not apply to other persons.
(5) There is nothing sacred or sacrosanct about the test of reasonable classification, but it
     has undoubtedly proved to be a useful basis for meeting attacks on laws and official
     acts on the ground of infringement of the equality principle.
(6) It follows from the two foregoing paragraphs that one of the ways in which the
     impugned Act can be saved is to show that it is based on a reasonable classification of

---

[103] *Chiranjit Lal Chowdhury v The Union of India and Others* [1950] SCR 869.
[104] *The State of Bombay and Another v FN Balsara* [1951] SCR 682.

the persons to whom or the offences in respect of which the procedure laid down in it is to apply, and hence it is necessary to ascertain whether it is actually based on such a classification. . . .

Mahajan J

I had the advantage of reading the judgment prepared by my brother Mukherjea and I am in respectful agreement with his opinion. . . .

Mukherjea J

These two appeals are directed against the judgment of a Special Bench of the Calcutta High Court dated the 28th of August, 1951, and they arise out of two petitions presented, respectively, by the respondent in the two appeals under article 226 of the Constitution praying for writs of certiorari to quash two criminal proceedings, one of which has ended in the trial court, resulting in conviction of the accused, while the other is still pending hearing. The questions requiring consideration in both the appeals are the same and the whole controversy centres round the point as to whether the provision of section 5(1) of the West Bengal Special Courts Act, 1950, as well as certain notifications issued under it are *ultra vires* the Constitution by reason of their being in conflict with article 14 of the Constitution. . . .

. . . In order to appreciate the points that have been canvassed before us, it would be convenient first of all to refer to the provision of article 14 of the Constitution with a view to determine the nature and scope of the guarantee that is implied in it. The article lays down that 'the State shall not deny to any person equality before the law or the equal protection of the laws within the territory of India.' It is, in substance, modelled upon the equal protection clause, occurring in the Fourteenth Amendment of the American Constitution with a further addition of the rule of 'equality before the law', which is an established maxim of the English Constitution. A number of American decisions have been cited before us on behalf of both parties in course of the arguments; and while a too rigid adherence to the views expressed by the Judges of the Supreme Court of America while dealing with the equal protection clause in their own Constitution may not be necessary or desirable for the purpose of determining the true meaning and scope of article 14 of the Indian Constitution, it cannot be denied that the general principles enunciated in many of these cases do afford considerable help and guidance in the matter.

It can be taken to be well settled that the principle underlying the guarantee in article 14 is not that the same rules of law should be applicable to all persons within the Indian territory or that the same remedies should be made available to them irrespective of differences of circumstances.[105] It only means that all persons similarly circumstanced shall be treated alike both in privileges conferred and liabilities imposed.[106] Equal laws would have to be applied to all in the same situation, and there should be no discrimination between one person and another if as regards the subject matter of the legislation their position is substantially the same. This brings in the question of classification. As there is no infringement of the equal protection rule, if the law deals alike with all of a certain class, the legislature has the undoubted right of classifying persons and placing those whose conditions are 'substantially similar under the same rule of law, while applying different rules to persons differently situated. It is said that the entire problem under the equal protection clause

---

[105] *Chiranjit Lal Chowdhuri v The Union of India* [1950] SCR 869.
[106] *Old Dearborn Distributing Co v Seagram Distillers Corporation* 299 US 183 (1936).

is one of classification or of drawing lines.[107] In making the classification the legislature cannot certainly be expected to provide 'abstract symmetry.' It can make and set apart the classes according to the needs and exigencies of the society and as suggested by experience. It can recognise even 'degrees of evil',[108] but the classification should never be arbitrary, artificial or evasive. It must rest always upon real and substantial distinction bearing a reasonable and just relation to the thing in respect to which the classification is made; and classification made without any reasonable basis should be regarded as invalid.[109] These propositions have not been controverted before us and it is not disputed also on behalf of the respondents that the presumption is always in favour of the constitutionality of an enactment and the burden is upon him who attacks it, to show that there has been transgression of constitutional principles. . . .

. . . A point was made by the Attorney-General in course of his arguments that the equality rule is not violated simply because a statute confers unregulated discretion on officers or on administrative agencies. In such cases it may be possible to attack the legislation on the ground of improper delegation of authority or the acts of the officers may be challenged on the ground of wrongful or mala fide exercise of powers; but no question of infringement of article 14 of the Constitution could possibly arise. We were referred to a number of authorities on this point but I do not think that the authorities really support the proposition of law in the way it is formulated. In the well known case of *Yick Wo v Hopkins*,[110] the question was, whether the provision of a certain ordinance of the City and County of San Francisco was invalid by reason of its being in conflict with the equal protection clause. The order in question laid down that it would be unlawful for any person to engage in laundry business within the corporate limits 'without having first obtained the consent of the Board of Supervisors except the same to be located in a building constructed either of brick or stone.' The question was answered in the affirmative. It was pointed out by Matthews J, who delivered the opinion of the court, that the ordinance in question did not merely prescribe a rule and condition for the regulation of the laundry business. It allowed without restriction the use for such purposes of building of brick or stone, but as to wooden buildings constituting nearly all those in previous use, it divided the owners or occupiers into two classes, not having respect to their personal character and qualifications of the business, nor the situation and nature and adaptation of the buildings themselves, but merely by an arbitrary line, on one side of which were those who were permitted to pursue their industry by the mere will and consent of the supervisors and on the other those from whom that consent was withheld at their will and pleasure. This sort of committing to the unrestrained will of a public officer the power to deprive a citizen of his right to carry on lawful business was' held to constitute an invasion of the Fourteenth Amendment. The learned Judge pointed out in course of his judgment that there are cases where discretion is lodged by law in public officers or bodies to grant or withhold licences to keep taverns or places for sale of spirituous liquor and the like. But all these cases stood on a different footing altogether. The same view was reiterated in *Crowley v Christensen*[111] which related to an ordinance regulating the issue of licences to sell liquors. It appears to be an accepted doctrine of American courts that the purpose of the equal protection clause is to secure every person within the States against arbitrary discrimination, whether occasioned by the express terms of the statute or by their improper application through duly constituted agents. This

---

[107] N Dowling, *Cases on Constitutional Law*, 4th edn, at 1139.
[108] *Skinner v Oklahoma* 316 US 535 (1942), at 540.
[109] *Southern Railway Co v Greene* 216 US 400 (1910), at 412.
[110] *Yick Wo v Hopkins* 118 US 356 (1886).
[111] *Crowley v Christensen* 137 US 86 (1890).

was clearly laid down in *Sunday Lake Iron Cornparty v Wakefield*.[112] In this case the complaint was against a taxing officer, who was alleged to have assessed the plaintiff's properties at their full value, while all other persons in the county were assessed at not more than one third of the worth of their properties. It was held that the equal protection clause could be availed of against the taxing officer; but if he was found to have acted bona fide and the discrimination was the result of a mere error of judgment on his part, the action would fail. The position, therefore, is that when the statute is not itself discriminatory and the charge of violation of equal protection is only against the official, who is entrusted with the duty of carrying it into operation, the equal protection clause could be availed of in such cases; but the officer would have a good defence if he could prove bona fides. But when the statute itself makes a discrimination without any proper or reasonable basis, the statute would be invalidated for being in conflict with the equal protection clause, and the question as to how it is actually worked out may not necessarily be a material fact for consideration. As I have said already, in the present case the discrimination arises on the terms of the Act itself. The fact that it gives unrestrained power to the State Government to select in any way it likes the particular cases or offences which should go to a Special Tribunal and withdraw in such cases the protection which the accused normally enjoy under the criminal law of the country, is on the face of it discriminatory. It may be noted in this connection that in the present case the High Court has' held the provision of section 5(1) of the West Bengal Special Courts Act to be *ultra vires* the Constitution only so far as it allows the State Government to direct any case to be tried by the Special Court. In the opinion of the learned Chief Justice, if the State Government had directed certain offences or classes of offences committed within the territory of West Bengal to be tried by the Special Court, the law or order could not have been impeached as discriminatory. It is to be noted that the Act itself does not mention in what classes of cases or offences such direction could be given; nor does it purport to lay down the criterion or the basis upon which the classification is to be made. It is not strictly correct to say that if certain specified offences throughout the State were directed to be tried by the Special Court, there could not be any infringement of the equality rule. It may be that in making the selection the authorities would exclude from the list of offences other offences of a cognate character in respect to which no difference in treatment is justifiable. In such circumstances also the law or order would be offending against the equality provision in the Constitution. This is illustrated by the case of *Skinner v Oklahoma*.[113] There a statute of Oklahoma provided for the sterilization of certain habitual criminals, who were convicted two or more times in any State, of felonies involving moral turpitude. The statute applied to persons guilty of larceny, which was regarded as a felony but not to embezzlement. It was held that the statute violated the equal protection clause. It is said that in cases where the law does not lay down a standard or form in accordance with which the classification is to be made, it would be the duty of the officers entrusted with the execution of the law, to make the classification in the way consonant with the principles of the Constitution.[114] If that be the position, then an action might lie for annulling the acts of the officers if they are found not to be in conformity with the equality clause. Moreover, in the present case the notification by the State Government could come within the definition of law as given in article 13(3) of the Constitution and can be impeached apart from the Act if it violates article 14 of the Constitution. I do not consider it necessary to pursue this matter any further, as in my opinion even on the limited ground upon which the High Court bases its decision, these appeals are bound to fail.

---

[112] *Sunday Lake Iron Cornparty v Wakefield* 247 US 350.
[113] *Skinner v Oklahoma* 316 US 555 (1942).
[114] HE Willis, *Constitutional Law of the United States* (Bloomington, Indiana: The Principia Press, 1936) at 587.

Das J

Article 14 of our Constitution, it is well known, corresponds to the last portion of section 1 of the Fourteenth Amendment to the American Constitution except that our article 14 has also adopted the English doctrine of rule of law by the addition of the words 'equality before the law.' It has not, however, been urged before us that the addition of these extra words has made any substantial difference in its practical application. The meaning, scope and effect of article 14 of our Constitution have been discussed and laid down by this Court in the case of *Chiranjit Lal Chowdhury v The Union of India and Others*[115] . . . Those principles were again considered and summarised by this Court in *The State of Bombay v FN Balsara*.[116] It is now well established that while article 14 is designed to prevent a person or class of persons from being singled out from others similarly situated for the purpose of being specially subjected to discriminating and hostile legislation, it does not insist on an 'abstract symmetry' in the sense that every piece of legislation must have universal application. All persons are not, by nature, attainment or circumstances, equal and the varying needs of different classes of persons often require separate treatment and, therefore, the protecting clause has been construed as a guarantee against discrimination amongst equals only and not as taking away from the State the power to classify persons for the purpose of legislation. This classification may be on different bases. It may be geographical or according to objects or occupations or the like. Mere classification, however, is not enough to get over the inhibition of the Article. The classification must not be arbitrary but must be rational, that is to say, it must not only be based on some qualities or characteristics which are to be found in all the persons grouped together and not in others who are left out but those qualities or characteristics must have a reasonable relation to the object of the legislation. In order to pass the test, two conditions must be fulfilled, namely, (1) that the classification must be founded on an intelligible differentia which distinguishes those that are grouped together from others and (2) that that differentia must have a rational relation to the object sought to be achieved by the Act. The differentia which is the basis of the classification and the object of the Act are distinct things and what is necessary is that there must be a nexus between them. In short, while the Article forbids class legislation in the sense of making improper discrimination by conferring privileges or imposing liabilities upon persons arbitrarily selected out of a large number of other persons similarly situated in relation to the privileges sought to be conferred or the liability proposed to be imposed, it does not forbid classification for the purpose of legislation, provided such classification is not arbitrary in the sense I have just explained. The doctrine, as expounded by this Court in the two cases I have mentioned, leaves a considerable latitude to the Court in the matter of the application of article 14 and consequently has the merit of flexibility.

The learned Attorney-General, appearing in support of these appeals, however, contends that while a reasonable classification of the kind mentioned above may be a test of the validity of a particular piece of legislation, it may not be the only test which will cover all cases and that there may be other tests also. In answer to the query of the Court he formulates an alternative test in the following words: If there is in fact inequality of treatment and such inequality is not made with a special intention of prejudicing any particular person or persons but is made in the general interest of administration, there is no infringement of article 14. It is at once obvious that, according to the test thus formulated, the validity of State action, legislative or executive, is made entirely dependent on the state of mind of the authority. This test will permit even flagrantly discriminatory State action on the specious plea of good faith and of the subjective view of the executive authority as to

---

[115] *Chiranjit Lal Chowdhury v The Union of India and Others* [1950] SCR 869.
[116] *The State of Bombay v FN Balsara* [1951] SCR 682.

the existence of a supposed general interest of administration. This test, if accepted, will amount to adding at the end of article 14 the words 'except in good faith and in the general interest of administration.' This is clearly not permissible for the Court to do. Further, it is obvious that the addition of these words will, in the language of Brewer J, in *Gulf, Colorado and Santa Fe Railway Co v WH Ellis*,[117] make the protecting clause a mere rope of sand, in no manner restraining State action. I am not, therefore, prepared to accept the proposition propounded by the learned Attorney-General, unsupported as it is by any judicial decision, as a sound test for determining the validity of State action.

Chandrasekhara Aiyar J

The short question that arises for consideration in these cases is whether the whole, or any portion of the West Bengal Special Courts Act, X of 1950, is invalid as being opposed to equality before the law and the equal protection of the laws guaranteed under article 14 of the Constitution of India. . . .

> It is well settled that equality before the law or the equal protection of laws does not mean identity or abstract symmetry of treatment. Distinctions have to be made for different classes and groups of persons and a rational or reasonable classification is permitted, as otherwise it would be almost impossible to carry on the work of Government of any State or country. To use the felicitous language of Mr Justice Holmes in *Bain Peanut Co v Pinson*[118] 'We must remember that the machinery of government could not work if it were not allowed a little play in its joints.' The law on the subject has been well stated in a passage from *Willis on Constitutional Law* (1936 Edition, at page 579) and an extract from the pronouncement of this Court in what is known as the *Prohibition Case*, *The State of Bombay and Another v FN Balsara*,[119] where my learned brother Fazl Ali J has distilled in the form of seven principles most of the useful observations of this Court in the Sholapur Mills case, *Chiranjit Lal Chowdhury v The Union of India and Others*.[120] Willis says:

> The guaranty of the equal protection of the laws means the protection of equal laws. It forbids class legislation, but does not forbid classification which rests upon reasonable grounds of distinction. It does not prohibit legislation, which is limited either in the objects to which it is directed or by the territory within which it is to operate. It merely requires that all persons subject to such legislation shall be treated alike under like circumstances and conditions both in the privileges conferred and in the liabilities imposed. The inhibition of the amendment was designed to prevent any person or class of persons from being singled out as a special subject for discriminating and hostile legislation. It does not take from the states the power to classify either in the adoption of police laws, or tax laws, or eminent domain laws, but permits to them the exercise of a wide scope of discretion, and nullifies what they do only when it is without any reasonable basis. Mathematical nicety and perfect equality are not required. Similarity, not identity of treatment, is enough. If any state of facts can reasonably be conceived to sustain a classification, the existence of that state of facts must be assumed. One who assails a classification must carry the burden of showing that it does not rest upon any reasonable basis.

> The seven principles formulated by Fazl Ali J are as follows: –

---

[117] *Gulf, Colorado and Santa Fe Railway Co v WH Ellis* 165 US 150 (1891).
[118] *Bain Peanut Co v Pinson* 282 US 499 (1931) at 501.
[119] *The State of Bombay v FN Balsara* [1951] SCR 682.
[120] *Chiranjit Lal Chowdhury v The Union of India and Others* [1950] SCR 869.

1.   The presumption is always in favour of the constitutionality of an enactment, since it must be assumed that the legislature understands and correctly appreciates the needs of its own people, that its laws are directed to problems made manifest by experience and its discriminations are based on adequate grounds.
2.   The presumption may be rebutted in certain cases by showing that on the face of the statute, there is no classification at all and no difference peculiar to any individual or class and not applicable to any other individual or class, and yet the law hits only a particular individual or class.
3.   The principle of equality does not mean that every law must have universal application for all persons who are not by nature, attainment or circumstances in the same position, and the varying needs of different classes of persons often require separate treatment.
4.   The principle does not take away from the State the power of classifying persons for legitimate purposes.
5.   Every classification is in some degree likely to produce some inequality, and mere production of inequality is not enough.
6.   If a law deals equally with members of a well-defined class, it is not obnoxious and it is not open to the charge of denial of equal protection on the ground that it has no application to other persons.
7.   While reasonable classification is permissible, such classification must be based upon some real and substantial distinction bearing a reasonable and just relation to the object sought to be attained, and the classification cannot be made arbitrarily and without any substantial basis.

After these citations, it is really unnecessary to refer to or discuss in detail most of the American decisions cited at the Bar. Their number is legion and it is possible to alight on decisions in support of propositions, apparently even conflicting, if we divorce them from the context of the particular facts and circumstances and ignore the setting or the background in which they were delivered. With great respect, I fail to see why we should allow ourselves to be unduly weighted-down or over-encumbered in this manner. To say this is not to shut out illumining light from any quarter; it is merely to utter a note of caution that we need not stray far into distant fields and try to clutch at something which may not after all be very helpful. What we have to find out is whether the statute now in question before us offends to any extent the equal protection of the laws guaranteed by our written Constitution. Whether the classification, if any, is reasonable or arbitrary, or is substantial or unreal, has to be adjudicated upon by the courts and the decision must turn more on one's commonsense than on over-refined legal distinctions or subtleties. The Attorney-General argued that if the principle of classification has to be applied as a necessary test, there is a classification in the impugned Act as it says that it is intended to provide for the speedier trial of certain offences; and in the opinion of the legislature certain offences may require more expeditious trial than other offences and this was a good enough classification. But as speedy administration of justice, especially in the field of the law of crimes, is a necessary characteristic of every civilised Government, there is not much point in stating that there is a class of offences that require such speedy trial. Of course, there may be certain offences whose trial requires priority over the rest and quick progress, owing to their frequent occurrence, grave danger to public peace or tranquillity, and any other special features that may be prevalent at a particular time in a specified area. And when it is intended to provide that they should be tried more speedily than other offences, requiring in certain respects a departure from the procedure prescribed for the general class of offences, it is but reasonable to expect the legislature to indicate the basis for any such classification. If the Act does not state what exactly are the offences which in its opinion need a speedier trial and why it is so considered, a mere statement in general words of the object sought to be achieved, as we find in this case, is of no avail because the classification, if any, is illusive or evasive. The policy or idea behind the classification should at least be adumbrated, if not stated, so that the court which has to decide on the constitutionality might be seized of something on which it could base its view about the propriety of the enactment from the standpoint of discrimination or equal protection. Any arbitrary division or ridge will render the equal protection clause moribund or lifeless.

Bose J

We are concerned here with article 14 of the Constitution and in particular with the words 'equality before the law' and 'equal protection of the law.' Now I yield to none in my insistence that plain unambiguous words in a statute, or in the Constitution, must having regard to the context, be interpreted according to their ordinary meaning and be given full effect. But that predicates a position where the words are plain and unambiguous. I am clear that that is not the case here.

Take first the words 'equality before the law'. It is to be observed that equality in the abstract is not guaranteed but only equality before the law. That at once leads to the question, what is the law, and whether 'the law' does not draw distinctions between man and man and make for inequalities in the sense of differentiation? One has only to look to the differing personal laws which are applied daily to see that it does; to trusts and foundations from which only one particular race or community may benefit, to places of worship from which all but members of particular faith are excluded, to cemeteries and towers of silence which none but the faithful may use, to the laws of property, marriage and divorce. All that is part and parcel of the law of the land and equality before it in any literal sense is impossible unless these laws are swept away, but that is not what the Constitution says, for these very laws are preserved and along with equality before the law is also guaranteed the right to the practice of one's faith.

Then, again, what does 'equality' mean? All men are not alike. Some are rich and some are poor. Some by the mere accident of birth inherit riches, others are born to poverty. There are differences in social standing and economic status. High sounding phrases cannot alter such fundamental facts. It is therefore impossible to apply rules of abstract equality to conditions which predicate in equality from the start; and yet the words have meaning though in my judgment their true content is not to be gathered by simply taking the words in one hand and a dictionary in the other, for the provisions of the Constitution are not mathematical formula which have their essence in mere form. They constitute a framework of government written for men of fundamentally differing opinions and written as much for the future as the present. They are not just pages from a text book but form the means of ordering the life of a progressive people. There is consequently grave danger in endeavouring to confine them in watertight compartments made up of readymade generalisations like classification. I have no doubt those tests serve as a rough and ready guide in some cases but they are not the only tests, nor are they the true tests on a final analysis.

What, after all, is classification? It is merely a systematic arrangement of things into groups or classes, usually in accordance with some definite scheme. But the scheme can be anything and the laws which are laid down to govern the grouping must necessarily be arbitrarily selected; also granted the right to select, the classification can be as broad-based as one pleases, or it can be broken down and down until finally just one solitary unit is divided off from the rest. Even those who propound this theory are driven to making qualifications. Thus, it is not enough merely to classify but the classification must not be 'discriminatory', it must not amount to 'hostile action', there must be 'reasonable grounds for distinction', it must be 'rational' and there must be no 'substantial discrimination'. But what then becomes of the classification? and who are to be the judges of the reasonableness and the substantiality or otherwise of the discrimination? And, much more important, whose standards of reasonableness are to be applied? – the judges'? – the government's? – or that of the mythical ordinary reasonable man of law which is no single man but a composite of many men whose reasonableness can be measured and gauged even though he can neither be seen nor heard nor felt? With the utmost respect I cannot see how these vague generalisations serve to clarify the position. To my mind they do not carry us one whit beyond the original words and are no more satisfactory than saying that all men are equal before the law and that all shall be equally treated and be given equal protection. The problem is not solved by substituting one generalisation for another.

To say that the law shall not be discriminatory carries us nowhere for unless the law is discriminatory the question cannot arise. The whole problem is to pick out from among the laws which make for differentiation the ones which do not offend article 14 and separate them from those which do. It is true the word can also be used in the sense of showing favouritism, but in so far as it means that, it suffers from the same defect as the 'hostile action' test. We are then compelled to import into the question the element of motive and delve into the minds of those who make the differentiation or pass the discriminatory law and thus at once substitute a subjective test for an objective analysis. I would always be slow to impute want of good faith in these cases. I have no doubt that the motive, except in rare cases, is beyond reproach and were it not for the fact that the Constitution demands equality of treatment these laws would, in my opinion, be valid. But that apart. What material have we for delving into the mind of a legislature? It is useless to say that a man shall be judged by his acts, for acts of this kind can spring from good motives as well as bad, and in the absence of other material the presumption must be overwhelmingly in favour of the former.

I can conceive of cases where there is the utmost good faith and where the classification is scientific and rational and yet which would offend this law. Let us take an imaginary case in which a State legislature considers that all accused persons whose skull measurements are below a certain standard, or who cannot pass a given series of intelligence tests, shall be tried summarily whatever the offence on the ground that the less complicated the trial the fairer it is to their sub-standard of intelligence. Here is classification. It is scientific and systematic. The intention and motive are good. There is no question of favouritism, and yet I can hardly believe that such a law would be allowed to stand. But what would be the true basis of the decision? Surely simply this that the judges would not consider that fair and proper. However much the real ground of decision may be hidden behind a screen of words like 'reasonable', 'substantial', 'rational' and 'arbitrary' the fact would remain that judges are substituting their own judgment of what is right and proper and reasonable and just for that of the legislature; and up to a point that, I think, is inevitable when a judge is called upon to crystallise a vague generality like article 14 into a concrete concept. Even in England, where Parliament is supreme, that is inevitable, for, as Dicey tells us in his *Law of the Constitution*, 'Parliament is the supreme legislator, but from the moment Parliament has uttered its will as lawgiver, that will becomes subject to the interpretation put upon it by the judges of the land, and the judges, who are influenced by the feelings of magistrates no less than by the general spirit of the common law, are disposed to construe statutory exceptions to common law principles in a mode which would not commend itself either to a body of officials, or to the Houses of Parliament, if the Houses were called upon to interpret their own enactments.'

This, however, does not mean that judges are to determine what is for the good of the people and substitute their individual and personal opinions for that of the government of the day, or that they may usurp the functions of the legislature. That is not their province and though there must always be a a narrow margin within which judges, who are human, will always be influenced by subjective factors, their training and their tradition makes the main body of their decisions speak with the same voice and reach impersonal results what-ever their personal predilections or their individual backgrounds. It is the function of the legislature alone, headed by the government of the day, to determine what is, and what is not, good and proper for the people of the land; and they must be given the widest latitude to exercise their functions within the ambit of their powers, else all progress is barred. But, because of the Constitution, there are limits beyond which they cannot go and even though it fails to the lot of judges to determine where those limits lie, the basis of their decision cannot be whether the Court thinks the law is for the benefit of the people or not. Cases of this type must be decided solely on the basis whether the Constitution forbids it. I realise that this is a function which is incapable of exact definition but I do not view that with dismay. The common law of England grew up in that way. It was gradually added to as each concrete case arose and a decision was given ad hoc on the facts of that particular case. It is true the judges who thus contributed to its growth were not importing personal predilec-tions into the result and merely stated what was the law applicable to that particular ease. But though they did not purport to make the law and merely applied what according to them, had always been the law handed down by custom and tradition, they nevertheless had to draw for their material on a nebulous mass of undefined rules which, though they existed in fact and left a vague awareness in man's minds, nevertheless were neither clearly definable, nor even necessarily identifiable, until crystallised into concrete existence by a judicial decision; nor indeed is it necessary to travel as far afield. Much of the existing Hindu law has grown up in that way from instance to instance, the threads being gathered now from the rishis, now from custom, now from tradition. In the same way, the laws of liberty, of freedom and of protection under the Constitution will also slowly assume recog-nisable shape as decision is added to decision. They cannot, in my judgment, be enunciated in static form by hidebound rules and arbitrarily applied standards or tests.

I find it impossible to read these portions of the Constitution without regard to the back-ground out of which they arose. I cannot blot out their history and omit from consider-ation the brooding spirit of the times. They are not just dull, lifeless words static and hide-bound as in some mummified manuscript, but, living flames intended to give life to a great nation and order its being, tongues of dynamic fire, potent to mould the future as well as guide t, he present. The Constitution must, in my judgment, be left elastic enough to meet from time to time the altering conditions of a changing world with its shifting empha-sis and differing needs. I feel therefore that in each case judges must look straight into the heart of things and regard the facts of each case concretely much as a jury would do; and yet, not quite as a jury, for we are considering here a matter of law and not just one of fact: Do these 'laws' which have been called in question offend a still greater law before which even they must bow?

Doing that, what is the history of these provisions ? They arose out of the fight for free-dom in this land and are but the endeavour to compress into a few pregnant phrases some of the main attributes of a sovereign democratic republic as seen through Indian eyes. There was present to the collective mind of the Constituent Assembly, reflecting the mood of the peoples of India, the memory of grim trials by hastily constituted tribunals with novel forms of procedure set forth in Ordinances promulgated in haste because of what was then felt to be the urgent necessities of the moment. Without casting the slightest reflection on the Judges and the Courts so constituted, the fact remains that when these tribunals were declared invalid and the same persons were retried in the ordinary Courts, many were acquitted, many who had been sentenced to death were absolved. That was not the fault of the judges but of the imperfect tools with which they were compelled to work. The whole proceedings were repugnant to the peoples of this land and, to my mind, article 14 is but a reflex of this mood. What I am concerned to see is not whether there is absolute equality in any academical sense of the term but whether the collective conscience of a sovereign democratic republic can regard the impugned law, contrasted with the ordinary law of the land, as the sort of substantially equal treatment which men of resolute minds and unbiased views can regard as right and proper in a democracy of the kind we have proclaimed ourselves to be. Such views must take into consideration the practical necessities of government, the right to alter the laws and many other facts, but in the forefront must remain the freedom of the individual from unjust and unequal treatment, unequal in the broad sense in which a democracy would view it. In my opinion, 'law' as used in article 14 does not mean the 'legal precepts which are actually recognised and applied in the tribunals of a given time and place' but 'the more general body of doctrine and tradition from which those precepts are chiefly drawn, and by which we criticise, them.'[121] I grant that this means that the same things will be viewed differently at different times. What is considered right and proper in a given set of circumstances will be considered improper in another age and vice versa. But that will not be because the law has changed but because the times have altered and it is no longer necessary for government to wield the powers which were essential in an earlier and more troubled world. That is what I mean by flexibility of interpretation.

This is no new or startling doctrine. It is just what happened in the cases of blasphemy and sedition in England. Lord Sumner has explained this in *Bowman's* case[122] and the Federal Court in *Niharendu Dutt Majumdar's* case[123] and so did Puranik J and I in the Nagpur High Court in *Bhagwati Charan Shukla's* case.[124]

Coming now to the concrete cases with which we have to deal here. I am far from suggesting that the departures made from the procedure prescribed by the Criminal Procedure Code are bad or undesirable in themselves. Some may be good in the sense that they will better promote the ends of justice and would thus form welcome additions to the law of the land. But I am not here to consider that. That is no part of a Judge's province. What I have to determine is whether the differentiation made offends what I may call the social conscience of a sovereign democratic republic. That is not a question which can be answered in the abstract. but, viewed in the background of our history. I am of opinion that it does. It is not that these laws are necessarily bad in themselves. It is the differentiation which matters; the singling out of cases or groups of cases, or even of offences or classes of offences, of a kind fraught with the most serious consequences to the individuals concerned, for special, and what some would regard as peculiar, treatment. It may be that justice would be fully done by following the new procedure. It may even be that it would be more truly done. But it would not be satisfactorily done, satisfactory that is to say, not from the point of view of the governments who prosecute, but satisfactory in the view of the ordinary reasonable man, the man in the street. It is not enough that justice should be done. Justice must also be seen to be done and a sense of satisfaction and confidence in it engendered. That cannot be when Ramchandra is tried by one procedure and Sakharam, similarly placed, facing equally serious charges, also answering for his life and liberty, 'by another which differs radically from the first. The law of the Constitution is not only for those who govern or for the theorist, but also for the bulk of the people, for the common man for whose benefit and

---

[121] R Pound, 'Judge Holmes's Contributions to the Science of Law' (1921) 34 *Harvard Law Review* 449 at 452.
[122] *Bowman v Secular Society* [1917] AC 406, 454, 466 and 467.
[123] [1942] FCR 32, 42.
[124] ILR 1946 Nag 865, 878 and 879.

pride and safeguard the Constitution has also been written. Unless and until these fundamental provisions are altered by the constituent processes of Parliament they must be interpreted in a sense which the common man, not versed in the niceties of grammar and dialectical logic, can understand and appreciate so that he may have faith and confidence and unshaken trust in that which has been enacted for his benefit and protection.

Tested in the light of these considerations, I am of opinion that the whole of the West Bengal Special Courts Act of 1950 offends the provisions of article 14 and is therefore bad.

Notes

1.   The test advanced by the Indian Supreme Court in *The State of West Bengal v Anwar Ali Sarkar* and *Chiranjit Lal Chowdhury v The Union of India and Others* has been followed and adopted in several other jurisdictions. In Pakistan, the leading case on equal protection is *IA Sherwani v Government of Pakistan*,[125] where the Supreme Court held:

   (i)   that equal protection of law does not envisage that every citizen is to be treated alike in all circumstances, but it contemplates that persons similarly situated or similarly placed are to be treated alike;

   (ii)   that reasonable classification is permissible but it must be founded on reasonable distinction or reasonable basis;

   (iii)   that different laws can validity be enacted for different sexes, persons in different age groups, persons having different financial standings and persons accused of heinous crimes;

   (iv)   that no standard of universal application to test responsibilities of a classification can be laid down as what may be reasonable classification in a particular set of circumstances, may be unreasonable in the other set of circumstances;

   (v)   that a law applying to one person or one class of persons may be Constitutionally valid if there is sufficient basis or reason for it, but a classification which is arbitrary and is not founded on any rational basis is no classification as to warrant its exclusion from the mischief of Article 25 [Equality of Citizens];

   (vi)   that equal protection of law means that all persons equally placed be treated alike both in privileges conferred and liabilities imposed;

   (vii)   that in order to make a classification reasonable, it should be based:–

      (a)   on an intelligible differentia which distinguishes persons or things that are grouped together from those who have been left out; and

      (b)   that the differentia must have rational nexus to the object sought to be achieved by such classification.

2.   In Bangladesh, the test was similarly adopted in *SA Sabur v Returning Officer*, *Retired Government Employees Association v Bangladesh*, *Jibendra Kishore v East Pakistan* and *Akramuzzaman v Bangladesh*.[126] The position is similar in Sri Lanka

---

[125]   *IA Sherwani v Government of Pakistan* [1991] SCMR 1041, at 1086.
[126]   *SA Sabur v Returning Officer* 41 DLR (AD) 30; *Retired Government Employees Association v Bangladesh* 46 DLR 426; *Jibendra Kishore v East Pakistan* 9 DLR (SC) 21; and *Akramuzzaman v Bangladesh* 52 DLR 209.

(see Jayampathy Wickramaratne, *Fundamental Rights in Sri Lanka*, 2nd edn (Colombo: Stamford Lake, 2007) at 285–90).

3.   The Indian approach to interpreting 'equal protection of the law' was likewise adopted by the Malaysian Federal Court in the cases of *Datuk Haji bin Harun Idris v Public Prosecutor* and *Malaysian Bar & Anor v Government of Malaysia;*[127] and by the Singapore Court of Appeal in *Public Prosecutor v Taw Cheng Kong.*[128]

4.   One of the main difficulties in applying the reasonable nexus test is in determining the ambit of the impugned statute's object. Different judges can, on the basis of the same material, arrive at diametrically opposed views on the legislature's object. In the *Taw Cheng Kong* case, the High Court in Singapore, in considering the object of section 37 of the Prevention of Corruption Act, held, after an examination of the Act's history and legislative debates:

> Two elements stand out. The first is that the Act was targeted primarily at the civil service. Secondly, the Act was aimed at corruption which infringed on the efficient running of the Singapore civil service or corrupt practices amongst fiduciaries in Singapore. The objective was not to eradicate corruption globally, irrespective of national boundaries. If, therefore, the Act was given an extraterritorial dimension in 1966, the natural inference is that the objective of a corruption-free Singapore was being frustrated by acts of corruption taking place outside the territorial boundaries of Singapore. In my view, the objective of s 37 is therefore to address acts of corruption taking place outside Singapore but affecting events within it.[129]

When the case went on appeal to the Court of Appeal, the same material was consulted but the Court held that the language of section 37 was wide enough to capture 'all corrupt acts by Singapore citizens outside Singapore, irrespective of whether such corrupt acts have consequences within the borders of Singapore or not', and that as it was against international comity for the Singapore legislature to make laws for non-Singapore citizens, 'it was rational to draw the line at citizenship and leave out non-citizens so as to observe international comity and the sovereignty of other nations'.[130]

5.   A problem associated with using the rational nexus test for determining the constitutionality of discriminatory legislation is that classification can be either under-inclusive or over-inclusive. The difficulty is described in a pioneering article by Joseph Tussman and Jacobus ten Broek, 'The Equal Protection of the Laws' (1949) 37 *California Law Review* 341:

> The purpose of a law may be either the elimination of a public 'mischief' or the achievement of some positive public good. To simplify the discussion we shall refer to the purpose of a law in terms of the elimination of mischief, since the same argument holds, in either case. We shall speak of the defining character or characteristics of the legislative classification as the trait. We can thus speak of the relation of the classification to the purpose of the law as the relation of the Trait to the Mischief.

---

[127] *Datuk Haji bin Harun Idris v Public Prosecutor* [1977] 2 MLJ 155 and *Malaysian Bar & Anor v Government of Malaysia* [1987] 2 MLJ 165.
[128] *Public Prosecutor v Taw Cheng Kong* [1998] 2 SLR 410.
[129] *Taw Cheng Kong v Public Prosecutor* [1998] 1 SLR 943 (High Court, Singapore).
[130] *Public Prosecutor v Taw Cheng Kong* [1998] 2 SLR 410 (Court of Appeal, Singapore).

Under this classification, the fairness of any law must depend on how closely the Trait matches the Mischief, both of which are not always easy to match. Classification may include some people in a group which may not have the Trait, or conversely, some people having the Trait are left out of the classification.

6. The foundational article on the doctrine of reasonable classification is SM Huang-Thio, 'Equal Protection and Rational Classification' [1963] *Public Law* 412.

7. Another problem associated with discriminatory legislation and the rational classification test is that the legislature may be able to define its objectives so narrowly that the courts will find it difficult to find fault with the classification. If the objectives are themselves discriminatory, eg based on race or religion, or descent, then the test of classification is impotent and cannot be used to strike down the discriminatory legislation.

ii. *The American Test*

Among the Asian states, only the Philippines has adopted the approach of the United States Supreme Court in the interpretation of its equality clause. Article III Section 1 of its Bill of Rights reads: 'No person shall be deprived or life, liberty, or property without the due process of the law, nor shall any person be denied the equal protection of the law.' This is taken, almost word for word, from the latter portion of Section 1 of the Fourteenth Amendment of the American Constitution. The South Korean Constitutional Court has also adopted, in the instance of *Act on the Immigration and Legal Status of Overseas Koreans Case*, a strict scrutiny approach redolent of the American approach.

Quinto v Commission on Elections
GR No 189698, 22 Feb 2010 (Supreme Court, Philippines)

Facts

In the run-up to the 2010 national elections, the Commission on Elections issued Resolution 8678, section 4 of which reads:

4. Effects of Filing of Certificates of Candidacy

    (a) Any person holding a public appointive office or position, including active members of the Armed Forces of the Philippines, and other officers and employees in government-owned or controlled corporations, shall be considered ipso facto resigned from his office upon the filing of his certificate of candidacy.

    (b) Any person holding an elective office or position shall not be considered resigned upon the filing of his certificate of candidacy for the same or any other elective office or position.

The petitioners intended to contest the upcoming elections and filed a petition for *certiorari* and *prohibition* to nullify section 4(b) of the Resolution on grounds that it violated the equal protection clause of the Constitution of the Philippines in giving an undue advantage to incumbent elected officials. The Supreme Court had to consider:

(a) if the remedies petitioned for were the proper remedies;
(b) if the petitioners had standing to bring the case to court; and
(c) whether the application of the 'resign-to-run' rule to appointed officials but not to elected ones violated the equal protection clause of the Constitution.

Although the outcome of this decision was highly controversial, unpopular as the Arroyo Government was at the time, the test for equal protection is authoritatively stated.

Puno CJ

IV. Section 4(a) of Resolution 8678, Section 13 of RA 9369, and Section 66 of the Omnibus Election Code Do Not Violate the Equal Protection Clause

We now hold that Section 4(a) of Resolution 8678, Section 66 of the Omnibus Election Code, and the second proviso in the third paragraph of Section 13 of RA 9369 are not violative of the equal protection clause of the Constitution.

i. Fariñas, et al v Executive Secretary, et al is Controlling

In truth, this Court has already ruled squarely on whether these deemed-resigned provisions challenged in the case at bar violate the equal protection clause of the Constitution in *Fariñas et al v Executive Secretary et al.*[131]

In *Fariñas*, the constitutionality of Section 14 of the Fair Election Act, in relation to Sections 66 and 67 of the Omnibus Election Code, was assailed on the ground, among others, that it unduly discriminates against appointive officials. As Section 14 repealed Section 67 (*ie*, the deemed-resigned provision in respect of elected officials) of the Omnibus Election Code, elected officials are no longer considered *ipso facto* resigned from their respective offices upon their filing of certificates of candidacy. In contrast, since Section 66 was not repealed, the limitation on appointive officials continues to be operative – they are deemed resigned when they file their certificates of candidacy.

The petitioners in *Fariñas* thus brought an equal protection challenge against Section 14, with the end in view of having the deemed-resigned provisions 'apply equally' to both elected and appointive officials. We held, however, that the legal dichotomy created by the Legislature is a reasonable classification, as there are material and significant distinctions between the two classes of officials. Consequently, the contention that Section 14 of the Fair Election Act, in relation to Sections 66 and 67 of the Omnibus Election Code, infringed on the equal protection clause of the Constitution, failed muster. We ruled:

The petitioners' contention, that the repeal of Section 67 of the Omnibus Election Code pertaining to elective officials gives undue benefit to such officials as against the appointive ones and violates the equal protection clause of the constitution, is tenuous.

The equal protection of the law clause in the Constitution is not absolute, but is subject to reasonable classification. If the groupings are characterized by substantial distinctions that make real differences, one class may be treated and regulated differently from the other. The Court has explained the nature of the equal protection guarantee in this manner:

The equal protection of the law clause is against undue favor and individual or class privilege, as well as hostile discrimination or the oppression of inequality. It is not intended to prohibit legislation which is limited either in the object to which it is directed or by territory within which it is to operate. It does not demand absolute equality among

---

[131] *Fariñas et al v Executive Secretary et al* GR No 147387, 10 Dec 2003, 417 SCRA 503.

residents; it merely requires that all persons shall be treated alike, under like circumstances and conditions both as to privileges conferred and liabilities enforced. The equal protection clause is not infringed by legislation which applies only to those persons falling within a specified class, if it applies alike to all persons within such class, and reasonable grounds exist for making a distinction between those who fall within such class and those who do not.

Substantial distinctions clearly exist between elective officials and appointive officials. The former occupy their office by virtue of the mandate of the electorate. They are elected to an office for a definite term and may be removed therefrom only upon stringent conditions. On the other hand, appointive officials hold their office by virtue of their designation thereto by an appointing authority. Some appointive officials hold their office in a permanent capacity and are entitled to security of tenure while others serve at the pleasure of the appointing authority.

Another substantial distinction between the two sets of officials is that under Section 55, Chapter 8, Title I, Subsection A. Civil Service Commission, Book V of the Administrative Code of 1987 (Executive Order No 292), appointive officials, as officers and employees in the civil service, are strictly prohibited from engaging in any partisan political activity or take [*sic*] part in any election except to vote. Under the same provision, elective officials, or officers or employees holding political offices, are obviously expressly allowed to take part in political and electoral activities.

By repealing Section 67 but retaining Section 66 of the Omnibus Election Code, the legislators deemed it proper to treat these two classes of officials differently with respect to the effect on their tenure in the office of the filing of the certificates of candidacy for any position other than those occupied by them. Again, it is not within the power of the Court to pass upon or look into the wisdom of this classification.

Since the classification justifying Section 14 of Rep Act No 9006, *ie*, elected officials vis-à-vis appointive officials, is anchored upon material and significant distinctions and all the persons belonging under the same classification are similarly treated, the equal protection clause of the Constitution is, thus, not infringed.[132]

The case at bar is a crass attempt to resurrect a dead issue. The miracle is that our assailed Decision gave it new life. We ought to be guided by the doctrine of *stare decisis et non quieta movere*. This doctrine, which is really 'adherence to precedents,' mandates that once a case has been decided one way, then another case involving exactly the same point at issue should be decided in the same manner.[133] This doctrine is one of policy grounded on the necessity for securing certainty and stability of judicial decisions. As the renowned jurist Benjamin Cardozo stated in his treatise *The Nature of the Judicial Process*:

> It will not do to decide the same question one way between one set of litigants and the opposite way between another. 'If a group of cases involves the same point, the parties expect the same decision. It would be a gross injustice to decide alternate cases on opposite principles. If a case was decided against me yesterday when I was a defendant, I shall look for the same judgment today if I am plaintiff. *To decide differently would raise a feeling of resentment and wrong in my breast; it would be an infringement, material and moral, of my rights.' Adherence to precedent must then be the rule rather than the exception if litigants are to have faith in the even-handed administration of justice in the courts.*[134]

---

[132] Ibid at 525–28.

[133] *Tan Chong v Secretary of Labor*, 79 Phil 249 (1941).

[134] BN Cardozo, *The Nature of the Judicial Process* (New Haven, Conn, and London: Yale University Press, 1921) at 33–34.

Our *Fariñas* ruling on the equal protection implications of the deemed-resigned provisions cannot be minimalized as mere *obiter dictum*. It is trite to state that an adjudication on any point within the issues presented by the case cannot be considered as *obiter dictum*.[135] This rule applies to all pertinent questions that are presented and resolved in the regular course of the consideration of the case and lead up to the final conclusion, and to any statement as to the matter on which the decision is predicated.[136] For that reason, a point expressly decided does not lose its value as a precedent because the disposition of the case is, or might have been, made on some other ground; or even though, by reason of other points in the case, the result reached might have been the same if the court had held, on the particular point, otherwise than it did.[137] As we held in *Villanueva, Jr v Court of Appeals, et al*:[138]

> ... *A decision which the case could have turned on is not regarded as obiter dictum merely because, owing to the disposal of the contention, it was necessary to consider another question*, nor can an additional reason in a decision, brought forward after the case has been disposed of on one ground, be regarded as dicta. So, also, where a case presents two (2) or more points, any one of which is sufficient to determine the ultimate issue, but the court actually decides all such points, *the case as an authoritative precedent as to every point decided, and none of such points can be regarded as having the status of a dictum, and one point should not be denied* authority merely because another point was more dwelt on and more fully argued and considered, nor does a decision on one proposition make statements of the court regarding other propositions dicta.[139] (italics supplied)

ii. Classification Germane to the Purposes of the Law

The *Fariñas* ruling on the equal protection challenge stands on solid ground even if reexamined.

To start with, the equal protection clause does not require the universal application of the laws to all persons or things without distinction.[140] What it simply requires is equality among equals as determined according to a valid classification.[141] The test developed by jurisprudence here and yonder is that of reasonableness,[142] which has four requisites:

(1)   The classification rests on substantial distinctions;
(2)   It is germane to the purposes of the law;
(3)   It is not limited to existing conditions only; and
(4)   It applies equally to all members of the same class.[143]

Our assailed Decision readily acknowledged that these deemed-resigned provisions satisfy the first, third and fourth requisites of reasonableness. It, however, proffers the dubious conclusion that the differential treatment of appointive officials vis-à-vis elected officials is not germane to the purpose of the law, because 'whether one holds an appointive office or an elective one, the evils sought to be prevented by the measure remain,' *viz.*:

---

[135] *Villanueva, Jr v Court of Appeals, et al*, GR No 142947, 19 Mar 2002, 379 SCRA 463, 469 citing 21 *Corpus Juris Secundum* §190.

[136] Ibid at 469–70.

[137] Ibid at 470.

[138] Above n 134.

[139] Ibid at 470.

[140] *The Philippine Judges Association et al v Prado et al*, GR No 105371, 11 Nov 1993, 227 SCRA 703, 712.

[141] Ibid.

[142] *The National Police Commission v De Guzman et al*, GR No 106724, 9 Feb 1994, 229 SCRA 801, 809.

[143] *People v Cayat*, 68 Phil 12, 18 (1939).

... For example, the Executive Secretary, or any Member of the Cabinet for that matter, could wield the same influence as the Vice-President who at the same time is appointed to a Cabinet post (in the recent past, elected Vice-Presidents were appointed to take charge of national housing, social welfare development, interior and local government, and foreign affairs). With the fact that they both head executive offices, there is no valid justification to treat them differently when both file their [Certificates of Candidacy] for the elections. Under the present state of our law, the Vice-President, in the example, running this time, let us say, for President, retains his position during the entire election period and can still use the resources of his office to support his campaign.[144]

Sad to state, this conclusion conveniently ignores the long-standing rule that to remedy an injustice, the Legislature need not address every manifestation of the evil at once; it may proceed 'one step at a time.'[145] In addressing a societal concern, it must invariably draw lines and make choices, thereby creating some inequity as to those included or excluded.[146] Nevertheless, as long as 'the bounds of reasonable choice' are not exceeded, the courts must defer to the legislative judgment.[147] We may not strike down a law merely because the legislative aim would have been more fully achieved by expanding the class.[148] Stated differently, the fact that a legislative classification, by itself, is under-inclusive will not render it unconstitutionally arbitrary or invidious.[149] There is no constitutional requirement that regulation must reach each and every class to which it might be applied;[150] that the Legislature must be held rigidly to the choice of regulating all or none.

Thus, any person who poses an equal protection challenge must convincingly show that the law creates a classification that is 'palpably arbitrary or capricious.'[151] He must refute *all* possible rational bases for the differing treatment, whether or not the Legislature cited those bases as reasons for the enactment,[152] such that the constitutionality of the law must be sustained even if the reasonableness of the classification is 'fairly debatable.'[153] In the case at bar, the petitioners failed – and in fact did not even attempt – to discharge this heavy burden. Our assailed Decision was likewise silent as a sphinx on this point even while we submitted the following thesis:

> ... [I]t is not sufficient grounds for invalidation that we may find that the statute's distinction is unfair, under-inclusive, unwise, or not the best solution from a public-policy standpoint; rather, we must find that there is no reasonably rational reason for the differing treatment.[154]
>
> In the instant case, is there a rational justification for excluding elected officials from the operation of the deemed resigned provisions? I submit that there is.

[144] *Quinto v Tolento*, GR No 189698, at 23.

[145] *Greenberg v Kimmelman*, 99 NJ 552, 577, 494 A 2d 294 (1985).

[146] *New Jersey State League of Municipalities, et al v State of New Jersey*, 257 NJ Super 509, 608 A 2d 965 (1992).

[147] *Taxpayers Ass'n of Weymouth Tp v Weymouth Tp*, 80 NJ 6, 40, 364 A 2d 1016 (1976).

[148] *Robbiani v Burke*, 77 NJ 383, 392–93, 390 A 2d 1149 (1978).

[149] *De Guzman, et al v Commission on Elections*, GR No 129118, 19 Jul 2000, 336 SCRA 188, 197; *City of St Louis v Liberman*, 547 SW 2d 452 (1977); *First Bank & Trust Co v Board of Governors of Federal Reserve System*, 605 F Supp 555 (1984); *Richardson v Secretary of Labor*, 689 F 2d 632 (1982); *Holbrook v Lexmark International Group, Inc*, 65 SW 3d 908 (2002).

[150] *State v Ewing*, 518 SW 2d 643 (1975); *Werner v Southern California Associated Newspapers*, 35 Cal 2d 121, 216 P 2d 825 (1950).

[151] *Chamber of Commerce of the USA v New Jersey*, 89 NJ 131, 159, 445 A 2d 353 (1982).

[152] *Werner v Southern California Associated Newspapers*, 35 Cal 2d 121, 216 P 2d 825 (1950).

[153] *Newark Superior Officers Ass'n v City of Newark*, 98 NJ 212, 227, 486 A 2d 305 (1985); *New Jersey State League of Municipalities, et al v State of New Jersey*, 257 NJ Super 509, 608 A 2d 965 (1992).

[154] *New Jersey State League of Municipalities, et al v State of New Jersey* 257 NJ Super 509, 608 A 2d 965 (1992).

An election is the embodiment of the popular will, perhaps the purest expression of the sovereign power of the people.[155] It involves the choice or selection of candidates to public office by popular vote.[156] Considering that elected officials are put in office by their constituents *for a definite term*, it may justifiably be said that they were excluded from the ambit of the deemed resigned provisions in utmost respect for the mandate of the sovereign will. In other words, complete deference is accorded to the will of the electorate that they be served by such officials until the end of the term for which they were elected. In contrast, there is no such expectation insofar as appointed officials are concerned.

The dichotomized treatment of appointive and elective officials is therefore germane to the purposes of the law. For the law was made not merely to preserve the integrity, efficiency, and discipline of the public service; the Legislature, whose wisdom is outside the rubric of judicial scrutiny, also thought it wise to balance this with the competing, yet equally compelling, interest of deferring to the sovereign will.[157] (emphasis in the original)

In fine, the assailed Decision would have us 'equalize the playing field' by invalidating provisions of law that seek to restrain the evils from running riot. Under the pretext of equal protection, it would favor a situation in which the evils are unconfined and vagrant, existing at the behest of both appointive and elected officials, over another in which a significant portion thereof is contained. The absurdity of that position is self-evident, to say the least.

The concern, voiced by our esteemed colleague, Mr Justice Nachura, in his dissent, that elected officials (vis-à-vis appointive officials) have greater political clout over the electorate, is indeed a matter worth exploring – but *not* by this Court. Suffice it to say that the remedy lies with the Legislature. It is the Legislature that is given the authority, under our constitutional system, to balance competing interests and thereafter make policy choices responsive to the exigencies of the times. It is certainly within the Legislature's power to make the deemed-resigned provisions applicable to elected officials, should it later decide that the evils sought to be prevented are of such frequency and magnitude as to tilt the balance in favor of expanding the class. This Court cannot and should not arrogate unto itself the power to ascertain and impose on the people the best state of affairs from a public policy standpoint.

Act on the Immigration and Legal Status of Overseas Koreans Case
13-2 KCCR 714, 99Hun-Ma494, 29 Nov 2001
(Constitutional Court, South Korea)

Facts

The complainants were ethnic Koreans with Chinese nationality and descendants of a person who emigrated prior to the establishment of the Korean Government in 1948. They argued that the Act on the Immigration and Legal Status of Overseas Koreans – which provided a wide range of benefits to ethnic Koreans who emigrated after the establishment of the Republic of Korea, but not for those who emigrated prior to its establishment – was unconstitutional and in violation of the right of equality under Article 11 of the Constitution.

---

[155] *Taule v Santos, et al*, GR No 90336, 12 Aug 1991, 200 SCRA 512, 519.
[156] Ibid.
[157] Dissenting Opinion of Chief Justice Reynato S Puno, at 60–61.

Held

. . .

(1) Meaning of the Principle of Equality

Article 11(1) of the Constitution states that 'all citizens shall be equal before the law, and there shall be no discrimination in political, economic, social or cultural life on account of gender, religion, or social status.' The principle of equality prescribed by Article 11(1) is the supreme principle in the field of protection of basic rights. It provides a standard which the state must abide by in interpreting or executing laws, and it is a mandate by the State not to discriminate without a reasonable basis. Everyone is entitled to the right to claim equal treatment, and the right to equality is the most basic of all basic rights (1 KCCR 1, 2, 88Hun-Ka7, 25 Jan 1989). The constitutional principle of equality, however, does not require absolute equality negating any form of differential treatment whatsoever. Rather, it means relative equality forbidding discrimination in legislating and executing laws without reasonable basis. Therefore, differentiation or inequality with reasonable basis is not against the principle of equality. Whether a discrimination is grounded on a reasonable basis or not depends on whether such discrimination is a necessary and adequate means to achieve a legitimate legislative purpose, while upholding the constitutional principle for respect for human dignity (6-1 KCCR, 72, 75, 92Hun-Ba43, 24 Feb 1994; 10-2 KCCR 461, 476, 98Hun-Ka7 and etc, 30 Sep 1998).

(2) Standard and Effect of Discrimination

(A) The Act classifies a group of Koreans with foreign nationalities (Article 2[2] of the Overseas Koreans Act) into two categories: one group consists of persons or lineal descendents of persons who emigrated after the establishment of the Korean Government and who lost Korean nationality (Article 3[1] of the Enforcement Decree of the Act); the other consists of persons or lineal descendants of persons who emigrated after the establishment of the Korean Government and who were explicitly recognized as Korean nationals before obtaining the nationality of a foreign country (Article 3[2] of the Enforcement Decree of the Act). As a consequence, the Overseas Koreans Act deny the privileges under the Act to ethnic Koreans with foreign nationalities who are 'persons or lineal descendants of persons who emigrated before the establishment of the Korean Government and who were not explicitly recognized as Korean nationals before obtaining the nationality of a foreign country'. This is because of the following reasons: According to Article 2(1) of the Enforcement Regulation of the Act on the Immigration and Legal Status of Overseas Koreans, 'a person who was explicitly recognized as a Korean national' is an individual who registered oneself at one of the Korean diplomatic establishments or at other authorized agencies or organizations in the country of his or her residence, pursuant to the provisions of the Registration of Korean Nationals Residing Abroad Act (enacted on November 24, 1949 as Act No70; wholly amended on December 28, 1999 by Act No 6057); Because Korea and China agreed to establish diplomatic relations with each other on August 24, 1992 and because the Korean embassy in China opened on August 28, 1992 (The Beijing Office of the Korea Trade-Investment Promotion Agency, or KOTRA, opened on January 30, 1991), it was physically impossible for ethnic Koreans in China to fulfill the registration requirement; The situation is not much different for Koreans living in the former Soviet Union ('Investigation Report' on the Bill on the Immigration and Legal Status of Overseas Koreans by the Legislation and Judiciary Committee of the National Assembly, p 8, August 1999).

(B) The statutory provisions on review are definition clauses on ethnic Koreans with foreign nationalities, and an individual classified as an ethnic Korean with a foreign nationality under the Act receives a wide variety of benefits and privileges as seen above. In principle, ethnic Koreans with foreign nationalities are 'foreigners', and, therefore, they cannot become public officials of the Republic of Korea (Article 35 of the State Public Officials Act; Article 33 of the Local Public Officials Act; Article 9 of the Diplomatic Public Officials Act). They also cannot enjoy the freedom of residence and the right to move at will (Article 14 of the Constitution; Article 7 and 17 of the Immigration Control Act), freedom of occupation (Article 15 of the Constitution; Article 5 of the Fisheries Act; Article 6 of the Pilotage Act), right to property (Article 23 of the Constitution; Article 3 of the Foreigner's Land Acquisition Act; Article 25 of the Patent Act; Article 6 of the Aviation Act), right to vote and right to hold public office (Article 24 and 25 of the Constitution; Article 15 and 16 of the Act on the Election of Public Officials and the Prevention of Election Malpractices), right to claim compensation (Article 29(2) of the Constitution; Article 7 of the State Compensation Act), right to receive aid for injury from criminal acts (Article 30 of the Constitution; Article 10 of the Crime Victims Aid Act), right to vote on Referendum (Article 72 and 130(2) of the Constitution; Article 7 of the National Referendum Act) and other social rights, or can only enjoy them in a limited fashion (12-2 KCCR 167, 183, 97Hun-Ka12, August 31, 2000). The Overseas Koreans Act lifts some of these restrictions for a limited group of ethnic Koreans with foreign nationalities, and the standard employed to distinguish qualified beneficiaries under the Act discriminates against the complainants and other ethnic Koreans who emigrated before the establishment of the Republic of Korea in their exercise of basic or legal rights.

(3) Violation of the Right to Equality

(A) The principle of equality prohibits the legislature from treating essentially equal things arbitrarily unequally, or treating unequal things arbitrarily equally. The legislature violates the principle of equality when it enacts laws discriminating facts that are essentially equal without reasonable justification for the discrimination. When things being compared are identical not in every aspect, but only in certain aspects, whether to see them as identical in legal terms or not depends on the standard employed to determine such identity. In general, such standard draws upon the intent and meaning of the statute in question (8-2 KCCR 680, 701, 96Hun-Ka18, 26 Dec 1996). As we have seen previously, the provisions on review distinguish ethnic Koreans who emigrated after the establishment of the Republic of Korea, mostly Korean-Americans in the US or ethnic Koreans in European countries, from those who emigrated before the establishment of the Republic of Korea, mainly ethnic Koreans in China and the former Soviet Union. The Overseas Koreans Act provides various privileges to those belonging to the first group while denying those in the latter group the same privileges. However, ethnic Koreans belonging to these two categories are identical in that they are ethnic Koreans with foreign nationalities. The only difference between them is the time of their emigration. This difference is not so essential as to affect equal treatment of individuals belonging to the two groups. In other words, whether ethnic Koreans emigrated before or after the establishment of the Republic of Korea cannot be a decisive factor warranting discrimination between the two groups.

(B) Legislation discriminating a group of people from others naturally has a specific legislative objective. In order for such discrimination with regard to basic rights to be a reasonable one, the objective should be legitimate and in accordance with the Constitution. In addition, the standard for such discrimination should be substantially related to the legislative purpose, and resulting discrimination should not be excessive (8-2 KCCR 46, 56, 93Hun-Ba57, 29 Aug 1996).

The Overseas Koreans Act provides a wide scope of benefits and privileges to an ethnic Korean who emigrated to a foreign country after the establishment of the Korean Government, and virtually grants him or her a status as that of a dual citizenship. However, the statutory provisions on review deny such privileges to an ethnic Korean who emigrated before the establishment of the Korean Government, thereby treating him or her merely as another foreigner. As such, the Overseas Koreans Act grants basically all the requests of those who emigrated to a foreign country after the establishment of the Korean Government (mostly Korean-Americans, especially first generation Korean-Americans with US citizenship), while ethnic Koreans who emigrated before the establishment of the Korean Government (mainly ethnic Koreans in China and the former Soviet Union) were not included in the scope of application of the Act, thereby being denied opportunities they desperately seek – opportunities to enter and exit Korea and opportunities for employment in Korea. Supplementary measures to meet the needs of the ethnic Koreans in the latter group proposed by the Ministry of Justice are not giving sufficient help to ethnic Koreans with foreign nationalities. The fact that the Act was legislated based on the requests of ethnic Koreans who emigrated after the establishment of the Korean Government cannot be a decisive factor justifying such great discrimination. Needs of ethnic Koreans who emigrated before the establishment of the Korean Government are equal to, if not greater than, those of ethnic Koreans who emigrated after the establishment of the Korean Government. While the State cites socio-economic and security reasons for this discriminatory legislation, such argument cannot be said to have gone through a thorough review in the light of the fact that lawmakers originally planned to include ethnic Koreans who emigrated before the establishment of the Korean Government but excluded them in the latter process of legislation. It does not seem that the State conducted a thorough research and analysis of possible results of legislation which includes ethnic Koreans who emigrated before the establishment of the Korean Government within the scope of the Act.

The State argues that ethnic Koreans who emigrated before the establishment of the Korean Government are excluded and denied the privileges under the Act as a consequence of the adoption of the 'Past Nationality Principle' when defining ethnic Koreans with foreign nationalities in the Act, according to international customs. The State emphasizes that legislation adopting 'Jus Sanguinis', or the principle that a person's citizenship is determined by the citizenship of the parents, would be against the general principle of public international law and contrary to international customs; that it could bring about diplomatic friction with other countries; and that the notion is too vague so that the application of the Act may be extended without limit. The State cited Ireland, Greece and Poland as countries adopting the 'Past Nationality Principle' and allowing special treatment in entry and departure of expatriates who obtained the nationality of another country ('Investigation Report' on the Bill on the Immigration and Legal Status of Overseas Koreans by the Legislation and Judiciary Committee of the National Assembly, p. 8, August 1999). However, the extent of past nationality recognized in these countries is drastically different from that in the instant case. Although there may be an apprehension of diplomatic friction, the instant provisions defining ethnic Koreans with foreign nationalities cannot be seen as a necessary and adequate legislation resulting from a through review of policy alternatives. Instead of enacting a singular special act to address the existing difficulties that ethnic Koreans with foreign nationalities face in Korea, the State should first have reviewed if it would be possible to achieve the same objective by individually relieving restrictions, considering all circumstances. If legislation adopting 'Jus Sanguinis' has problems, instead of approaching the matter by guaranteeing a certain legal status to ethnic

Koreans with foreign nationalities, it would be better if the State started by improving the status of foreigners in Korea in general while focusing on supporting the activities aiming to instill a sense of national identity and strengthen cultural solidarity in the countries of their residence in the case of overseas Koreans.

(C) As we have seen previously (Section 4(A)(3)), ethnic Koreans who emigrated before the establishment of the Korean Government are excluded and denied the privileges under the Act not because the State adopted the 'Past Nationality Principle' from the beginning. The State adopted the 'Past Nationality Principle', a somewhat neutral term, in the Overseas Korean Act in defining ethnic Koreans with foreign nationalities, while through the Enforcement Decree, requiring those ethnic Koreans who emigrated before the establishment of the Korean Government, mostly ethnic Koreans living in China or the former Soviet Union who were forced to leave their motherland to join the independence movement, or to avoid military conscription or forced labor by the Japanese imperialist force, to prove that they were explicitly recognized as Korean nationals before obtaining foreign citizenship, thereby making it virtually impossible for these ethnic Koreans to receive benefits bestowed under the Act. Legislation of an act discriminating ethnic Koreans who were involuntarily displaced due to historical turmoil sweeping over the Korean peninsula cannot be justified from a humanitarian perspective, let alone from a national perspective, in the sense that no country on earth has legislated an act to discriminate against such compatriots, when it seems only appropriate to assist them. The public interest to be achieved by this legislation is too minor compared to the injury inflicted on individuals being discriminated by the Act.

Article 2 of the Overseas Korea Foundation Act (enacted on March 27, 1997, by Act No 5313) which was legislated before the Overseas Koreans Act defines overseas Koreans as persons with the nationality of the Republic of Korea who have stayed overseas for a long time or who have obtained the permanent resident status in a foreign country (Article 2[1]) or persons with Korean lineage who reside and make a living in a foreign country regardless of their nationality (Article 2[2]). The first definition corresponds to 'Korean nationals residing abroad' under the Overseas Koreans Act, and the second corresponds to 'Koreans with foreign nationalities'. The two Acts may differ in their respective legislative purposes, but it would lead to confusion in the application of the Acts if different definitions are to be used for the same term ('overseas Koreans') in the two Acts.

(4) Sub-conclusion

In sum, discrimination based on the statutory provisions in the instant case that deny the complainants and other ethnic Koreans who emigrated before the establishment of the Republic of Korea the privileges under the Act is arbitrary and is without legitimate reasons.

Since the standard used for such discrimination is not substantially related to achieving the legislative purpose and the extent of discrimination cannot possibly be seen as reasonable, these provisions are against the principle of equality stated in Article 11 of the Constitution, and thereby violate the complainants' right to equality.

Notes

1. The Constitutional Court of Taiwan has held that the phrase 'equal before the law' in Article 7 of its Constitution 'does not mean absolute and mechanical equality in formality, but is for the protection of substantive equal status under

the law, which requires matters identical in nature to be treated and handled identically without being subjected to differential treatment arbitrarily or for no proper justification'.[158] In *Judicial Interpretation No 618* (3 Nov 2006), the Constitutional Court had occasion to consider the constitutionality of Article 21-I of the Act Governing Relations between People of the Taiwan Area and Mainland Area. Under that Act, no person from 'the Mainland Area who has been permitted to enter into the Taiwan area may serve as a public functionary unless he or she has had a household registration in the Taiwan Area for at least ten years'. The Court held:

> The said provision is an extraordinary one with reasonable and justifiable objectives in that a public functionary, once appointed and employed by the State, shall be entrusted with official duties by the State under public law and shall owe a duty of loyalty to the State, that the public functionary shall not only obey the laws and orders but also take every action and adopt every policy possible that he or she considers is in the best interests of the State by keeping in mind the overall interests of the State since the exercise of his or her official duties will involve the public authorities of the State; and, further, that the security of the Taiwan Area, the welfare of the people of Taiwan, as well as the constitutional structure of a free democracy, must be ensured and preserved in light of the status quo of two separate and antagonistic entities which are on opposite sides of the strait and significant differences in essence between the two sides in respect of the political, economic and social systems.
>
> Given the fact that a person who came from the Mainland Area but has had a household registration in the Taiwan Area for less than ten years may not be as familiar with the constitutional structure of a free democracy as the Taiwanese people, it is not unreasonable to give discriminatory treatment to such a person and not to the Taiwanese people of the Taiwan Area with respect to the qualifications to serve as a governmental employee, which is not in conflict with the principle of equality as embodied in Article 7 of the Constitution, nor contrary to the intent of Article 10 of the Amendments to the Constitution.
>
> In addition, the said provision, which requires a person who originally came from the Mainland Area to have had a household registration for at least ten years before he or she may be eligible to hold a public office, is based on the concerns that those who originally came from the Mainland Area have a different view as to the constitutional structure of a free democracy and may need some time to adapt to and settle into the society of Taiwan. Moreover, it also may take a while for the Taiwanese people to place their trust in a person who came from the Mainland Area if and when he or she serves as a public functionary. If the review is conducted on a case-by-case basis, it would be difficult to examine an individual's subjective intentions and character, as well as his or her level of identification with the preservation of the constitutional structure of a free democracy. Besides, it would also needlessly increase the administrative costs to a prohibitive level with hardly any hope of accuracy or fairness.
>
> Therefore, the ten-year period as specified by the provision at issue is nonetheless a necessary and reasonable means. In respect of such matters as the types of public functionaries and public offices that may affect the security of the Taiwan Area, the welfare of the people of Taiwan, as well as the constitutional structure of a free democracy, the constitutional interpreters should give due respect to the decisions made by the legislative body in that regard. Despite the failure of the law at issue to make any differential treatment and thus impose different restrictions, no noticeable or significant

---

[158] See *Judicial Yuan Interpretation No 666*, 6 Nov 2009.

oversights have been made. Hence, there is no violation of the principle of proportionality under Article 23[159] of the Constitution.

2.   In Thailand, 'equality before the law' and 'equal protection under the law' are guaranteed in Section 30 of the Constitution. In *Constitutional Court Ruling No 15/2549* (22 Aug 2006), the Constitutional Court had to consider whether the Supreme Court's application of section 156 of the Thai Civil Procedure Code – which allowed impoverished persons to file a motion to appeal as a pauper – was consistent with section 30 of the Constitution. In the court of first instance, an order had been made against the applicants, Chumpol Kantawiworn and others, to repay their loan to the bank. The applicants filed an appeal to the Court of Appeals along with a motion under section 156 of the Code to appeal as paupers. The court of first instance held that as the applicants were not completely impoverished and could likely afford a proportion of the court fees. Leave was granted to proceed in the Court of Appeals and they were exempted from providing a deposit for court fees and lawyers' fees payable to the plaintiff bank in the submission of the appeal. They were, however, still required to provide a deposit for court fees to the Couert of Appeals. The applicants appealed this decision, but it was upheld by the Court of Appeals, and the applicants argued before the Constitutional Court that their rights under Section 30 of the Constitution had been violated. The Constitutional Court held that section 156 of the Code applied generally and was not directed at any particular party or person, and in any case applied equally to the parties: 'All parties were treated equally and enjoyed equal protection under the law without any regard to the status of the parties.' In an earlier case – *Constitutional Court Ruling No 61/2548* (15 Nov 2005) – a similar approach to interpreting equality was adopted by the Constitutional Court, this time with respect to the application of section 229 of the Civil Procedure Code.

3.   The present American approach towards reviewing discriminatory statutes is three-tier. First, the least probing standard is 'mere rationality' review, where the classification need only bear a rational relationship to a legal statutory objective. This test applies mostly to cases involving socio-economic issues. Secondly, the 'strict scrutiny' test, which applies to statutes based on 'suspect classifications' like race or where 'fundamental rights' like the right to vote are affected.[160] Such classifications will be upheld only if necessary to promote a compelling government interest. Lastly, 'intermediate scrutiny', whereby the courts will require that the classification be substantially related to an important government purpose. This has been applied mostly to cases involving discrimination on the basis of gender or alienage.[161] See JHaWilkinson III, 'The Supreme Court, the Equal Protection Clause and the Three Faces of Constitutional Equality' (1975) 63 *Virginia Law Review* 94; MJ Perry, 'Modern Equal Protection: A Conceptualization and Appraisal' (1979) 79 *Columbia Law Review* 1023.

---

[159] 'Article 23: All the freedoms and rights enumerated in the preceding Articles shall not be restricted by law except by such as may be necessary to prevent infringement upon the freedoms of other persons, to avert an imminent crisis, to maintain social order or to advance public welfare.'

[160] *Brown v Board of Education* 347 US 483 (1954).

[161] See *Craig v Boren* 429 US 190 (1976); *Michael M v Sonoma County Superior Court* 450 US 464 (1980); *US v Virginia* 518 US 515 (1996).

4. How does one determine whether the classification bears a rational nexus to the object of the act? Is there is a limit on the legislature's power to formulate discriminatory policies and to pass relevant legislation to effectuate them? Does the function of the court in rational classification analysis blur the distinction between legality (the judicial province) and desirability (the legislature's province) of legislative classification? Should it? Is there a doctrine of a suspect category, eg race or religion?

iii. Beyond Classification: Proportionality

The Constitutional Courts in Taiwan and Korea have, in a number of important decisions, introduced 'proportionality' as a salient ground in determining if impugned legislation violates the equality clause in their respective constitutions. Historically, the concept of proportionality in constitutional adjudication was developed in Germany,[162] and even though both Taiwan and South Korea drew inspiration from German constitutional law, the word 'proportionality' does not feature in either constitution. As such, the proportionality principle is read into the constitution by implication. In the case of Taiwan, Article 23 of the Constitution provides that all freedoms and rights 'shall not be restricted by law except by *such as may be necessary* to prevent infringement upon the freedoms of other persons, to avert an imminent crisis, to maintain social order or to advance public welfare' (emphasis added). The highlighted phrase has been interpreted to keep curbs on fundamental freedoms to the minimum.[163] In a similar vein, Article 37(2) of the South Korean Constitution provides that the 'freedoms and rights of citizens may be restricted by Act *only when necessary* for national security, the maintenance of law and order or for public welfare' (emphasis added). This allowed the South Korean Constitutional Court to develop the doctrine of excessive restriction under Article 37(2), under which the test of 'excess' is based on the proportionality principle. In the *Nationality Act Case* 12-2 KCCR 167, 7Hun-Ka12, 31 Aug 2000, the full bench of the Korean Constitutional Court held:

> The principle of equality in Article 11(1) of the Constitution is a fundamental mandate of the order of rule of law. It prohibits all state agencies from treating adversely a person or a certain group without just cause in applying laws. Therefore, all people bear the same obligations and enjoy the same rights under the laws, and no state actor can apply or cannot apply law to certain people disadvantageously or advantageously. The normative meaning of Article 11(1) does not stop at 'equality in application of law.' It also re- quires the legislature to justify its standard of value used in distributing the rights and responsibilities through legislation. Hence 'equality in law-making.' Therefore, the principle of equality rejects any criterion of discrimination aimed at extending different legal effects to people if the criterion cannot be objectively justified. How much the legislature is bound by the Article 11(1) principle of equality is determined by the regulated subject matter and the characteristics of the criterion of discrimination.
>
> In equality review, whether a strict or relaxed standard shall be used depends on the scope of the legislative-formative power given to the legislature. However, those cases where the

---

[162] See B Schlink, 'Proportionality in Constitutional Law: Why Everywhere But Here?' (2012) 22 *Duke Journal of Comparative and International Law* 291, at 294–97.

[163] One of the earliest cases to apply the proportionality principle was *Judicial Interpretation No 476*, 29 Jan 1999.

Constitution specially demands equality shall be scrutinized under a strict standard. If the Constitution itself designates certain standards not to be used as reasons for discrimination or certain domains in which discrimination shall not take place, it is justified to strictly scrutinize the discrimination based on that standard of . . . that domain. Also, if differential treatment causes a great burden on the related basic rights, the legislative-formative power shall be curtailed and strictly scrutinized.

Pledge to Abide by the Law Case
14-1 KCCR 351, 98Hun-Ma425, etc, (consolidated), 25 Apr 2002
(Constitutional Court, South Korea)

Facts

Article 14 of the Ordinance for Parole Review provided that inmates who had been imprisoned for violation of the National Security Act or the Assembly and Demonstration Act must submit a pledge to abide by the national laws of Korea in order for their paroles to be considered. The 31 complainants had been detained for violating the National Security Act and sentenced to varying periods of imprisonment. They had all been excluded from parole release for refusing to submit the pledge to abide by the law as required by the Ordinance.

Held

(A) Standard of Review

Whether a strict or relaxed standard is to be used for equality review of a particular case depends on the scope of the legislative-formative power given to the legislature. Those cases where the Constitution specifically demands equality shall be scrutinized under a strict standard. If the Constitution itself designates certain standards not to be used as basis for discrimination or certain domains in which discrimination shall not take place, strict scrutiny should be employed to determine whether there is discrimination. Next, if differential treatment causes a great burden on the related basic rights, the legislative-formative power shall be curtailed, and strict scrutiny should be used for the constitutional review of the case(11-2 KCCR 770, 787, 98Hun-Ma363, December 23, 1999).

The instant provision deals with the review procedure for parole review, and the criminal administrative authority is allowed a large degree of discretion in the matter. Moreover, the Constitution does not explicitly proscribe discrimination in this field. As seen above, the instant provision concerning the pledge to abide by the law does not infringe on the freedom of conscience or other basic rights of the complainants, and thus, there is no burden on the related basic rights caused by differential treatment. Therefore, constitutional review of the instant provision does not require use of a strict standard, and it suffices to use a relaxed standard to determine reasonableness of the provision.

(B) Legislative Purpose of Requiring Submission of the Pledge to Abide by the Law

Since its inception, the Republic of Korea has confronted North Korea, and under such special conditions of the nation, many persons have been imprisoned for violation of the public security laws. Many inmates incarcerated for violation of the public security laws have either remained hostile or disapproved the constitutional regime of the Republic of Korea. Considering such tendency of these inmates, the instant statutory provision requires them to pledge allegiance to the existing constitutional order to the maximum degree permissible under the Constitution in order to preserve the existing constitutional system of the Republic of Korea. It replaced the ideological conversion program requiring inmates imprisoned for violation of the public security laws such as the National Security Act to renounce their belief in communist ideologies. The present requirement of submission of the pledge aims to silence criticism on the past ideological conversion program that it violated the freedom of conscience. It also aims to satiate the constitutional requirement only by reconfirming the duty to abide by the law that is duly required of all citizens while relieving the psychological burden of inmates subject to parole review.

(C) Proportionality in Differential Treatment

The instant provision does not require all inmates to submit the pledge to abide by the law regardless of their convicted crimes, but only demand[s] the pledge from those inmates imprisoned for perpetration of the National Security Act and the Assembly and Demonstration Act for parole consideration.

North Korea still endeavors to bring about a communist revolution to the entire peninsula, and to protect itself against such external threats. The government of South Korea has no choice but to defend against North Korea's attempts at a radical revolution of South Korea. Illegal activities by individuals aiming to disturb the basic order of free democracy or overthrow the government, either in alliance with the North Korean government, or through independent decision of its own, have largely been dealt with either the National Security Act or the Assembly and Demonstration Act because of the nature of such activities. It is under such circumstance that the parole review board examines, in addition to things ordinarily taken into consideration to determine eligibility for parole, whether inmates imprisoned for violation of the National Security Act or the Assembly and Demonstration Act are willing to observe the national laws once released on parole. Thus, differential treatment of such inmates is not without a reasonable basis, and is appropriate as a means to achieve the policy objectives.

The purpose of differential treatment of inmates convicted for violation of the National Security Act or the Assembly and Demonstration Act is clear and important while the means to achieve the legislative objective is a mere reconfirmation of the general duty required of all citizens that does not entail any infringement on the basic rights of citizens. Thus, it is obvious that the principle of proportionality is observed in differential treatment of different groups, and therefore, the instant provision does not violate the constitutional principle of equality.

4. Conclusion

The complaints filed by complainants Cho O-rok and Cho O-won are rejected, and the complaints filed by other complainants are dismissed.

This decision is pursuant to the consensus of all justices except Justice Kwon Seong who wrote a concurring opinion and Justices Kim Hyo-jong and Choo Sun-hoe who wrote a dissenting opinion.

Justices Kim Hyo-jong and Choo Sun-hoe (dissenting)

. . .

(4) Let us next see whether requiring submission of the pledge violates the principle of proportionality.

Even if one argues that requiring submission of the pledge is not a matter of inner freedom but only a restriction on the freedom to realize conscience, the instant provision violates the principle of proportionality.

The instant provision of the Ordinance may have a valid legislative purpose in that the pledge is used to judge the likelihood of recidivism of an inmate. However, appropriateness of the means chosen to achieve the legislative purpose is questionable. While there may be some individuals who adamantly object to the legal order of the Republic of Korea among violators of the public security laws, failure to submit the pledge is passive refusal. Recidivism can be said to be a form of active refusal of the existing legal order, and the likelihood of recidivism is affected by numerous contingencies such as political or social conditions of the society when an inmate is released, and individual living environments. It is not clear whether an inmate released on parole after submitting the pledge is not likely to commit another crime or whether likelihood of recidivism would be higher if inmates were to be released without submitting the pledge.

If requiring submission of the pledge aims to assist judgment whether the released inmate is likely to be a recidivist, other means used for parole review of ordinary inmates could be employed to achieve such a legislative purpose. A potential candidate for parole could first be screened by using the incarceration record during the imprisonment term. The members of Parole Review Board could question the inmate about the status of mind and future plans during the interview for parole review, and could indirectly make assessment about the inmate's ideology and about whether he accepts the constitutional order of the Republic of Korea. Likelihood of recidivism could thus be examined thoroughly.

The instant provision excessively restricts freedom of conscience because it forces an inmate to make a written confession about things related to fundamental beliefs or conscience.

An individual asked to submit the pledge in order to be reviewed for parole release suffers a serious mental conflict: he can either express his intent to change his fundamental belief to be released, or he can choose to retain his inner belief by remaining silent. Thus, the injury inflicted on individuals' conscience by requiring the pledge to abide by the law is far greater than the public interest of acquisition of information for parole review, and the instant provision fails the balance of interest test.

D. Conclusion

In conclusion, we think that the instant provision is unconstitutional because it infringes upon the inner freedom of conscience, encroaches upon the basic rights of citizens not based on acts legislated by the National Assembly, and violates the principle of proportionality even when one deems it as restriction of freedom to realize one's conscience.

IV. DISCRIMINATION AND THE PROTECTION OF MINORITIES

A. Introduction

Ordinarily, the word 'minority' is used to refer to the smaller of two groups of individuals or things, whether they be distinguished by race, religion, language, descent or gender. The marks of distinction are infinite: age, education, place of birth, sexual orientation, social status, financial condition, vocational experience, professional training, ownership of property, . . . etc. With such a wide range of possibilities, how do we decide on what a 'minority' in law should be. Put another way, with what sorts of minorities should a constitution concern itself with? Democracies function on the basis of majoritarianism, but majorities can sometimes be insensitive and tyrannical, and those who are not part of the majority – the 'minorities' – suffer. Thus, all modern constitutional democracies attempt to protect their minoritiesmajorities from the worst excesses of the majority.

The idea of 'minorities' as a legal subject may be traced to the Paris Peace of 1919, when American President Woodrow Wilson proposed the establishment of the League of Nations. Paragraph VI of his supplementary agreement to the Draft Covenant of the League read:

> The League of Nations shall require all new states to bind themselves as a condition precedent to their recognition as independent or autonomous states, to accord to all racial or national minorities within their jurisdiction exactly the same treatment and security, both in law and in fact, that is accorded the racial or national majority of their people.[164]

In the debate over this provision, the Japanese delegation proposed a racial equality clause (discussed earlier in section I above) which was not only defeated but also ensured that paragraph VI never made it into the Covenant. It was not till the end of World War II that new efforts were made to place 'minority rights' on a legal footing. The Universal Declaration of Human Rights 1948 does not mention minorities but does, in Article 7, provide that:

> All are equal before the law and are entitled without any discrimination to equal protection of the law. All are entitled to equal protection against any discrimination in violation of this Declaration and against any incitement to such discrimination.

Article 23(2) further provides that all persons 'without any discrimination, [have] the right to equal pay for equal work'.

In his capacity as Special Rapporteur to the United Nations Sub-Commission on Prevention of Discrimination and Protection of Minorities, the Italian jurist, Franceso Capotorti, defined a 'minority' as

> [a] group numerically inferior to the rest of the population of a State, in a non-dominant position, whose members – being nationals of the State – possess ethnic, religious or linguistic characteristics differing from those of the rest of the population and show, if only implicitly, a sense of solidarity, directed towards preserving their culture, traditions, religion or language.[165]

In 1992, the United Nations Declaration on the Rights of Persons Belonging to National or Ethnic, Religious and Linguistic Minorities was adopted at the UN General Assembly. Article 1 of this Declaration enjoined states to 'protect the existence and the national or ethnic, cultural, religious and linguistic identity of minorities within their territories'. The four bases of minority protection – nationality, ethnicity, religion, language – are also to be found in most Asian constitutions as prohibited grounds for discrimination (see section III. B above).

While discrimination has historically been against minorities, there are some groups that may not be numerically inferior but have traditionally be discriminated against. Women and children, for example, have often been discriminated against, even though

---

[164] See W McKean, *Equality and Discrimination Under International Law* (Oxford: Clarendon Press, 1983) at 14.

[165] E/CN4/Sub2/384/Rev 1, para 568.

they make up a substantial and sometimes major part of the population. In South Africa, the Blacks were a majority but the minority Whites were in a dominant position, with power to mete out discriminatory treatment to the majority.

Beyond the Carpotorti definition, other groups, such as persons with disabilities, or those belonging to certain political groups or identities, claim the right to equal treatment on the basis of the general 'equal protection' clauses. In this section we take a look at some of the battles for equality taking place in the legal and political spheres throughout Asia. The choice of material is necessarily selective, given the vastness of the subject.

B. Gender Discrimination

i. Women

Women – who are hardly minorities in most states – have historically been discriminated against, in Asia and elsewhere. Although the Preamble to the Charter of the United Nations (1945) affirmed the faith of the peoples of the United Nations 'in the dignity and worth of the human person, in the equal rights of men and women', it was not till 1979 that a separate, comprehensive convention was adopted to manifest this aspiration. The Convention for the Elimination of All Forms of Discrimination Against Women (CEDAW) was adopted by the UN General Assembly in 1979 by a vote of 130:0, with 10 abstentions. As at the end of 2012, the Convention had 187 parties, making it one of the most universally-adopted human rights treaties in the world. Practically every state is a party to the Convention.

Article 4 of CEDAW mandates the adoption of temporary affirmative measures to ameliorate the subordinate position of women in society, and Article 5 requires states to adopt measures to counter gender stereotypes. Article 2 also imposes an obligation on states to adopt appropriate measures to eliminate discrimination against women through legal and informal means, including amending constitutions and laws to embody the principle of equality of men and women, to ensure the effective protection of women against discrimination through competent national tribunals, to ensure public authorities do not engage in any act and practice of discrimination as well as to 'take all appropriate measures to eliminate discrimination against women by any person, organization or enterprise'.

Parties to CEDAW are obliged to submit to the Secretary-General of the United Nations,a report on the legislative, judicial, administrative or other measures they adopted to implement the Convention within one year of its entry in force, and then at least every four years thereafter or whenever the Committee on the Elimination of Discrimination against Women so requests. Full texts of the initial and subsequent reports by states parties are readily available on the website of the Convention.[166]

---

[166] http://www.un.org/womenwatch/daw/cedaw/

Notes

1. Most constitutions in Asia contain explicit sexual equality clauses,[167] while the remainder rely on the general equality provisions[168] for the protection of women against discrimination. The Philippines Constitution relies on the general equal protection clause in Article III Section 1, but also provides in Article II Section 14 that the state 'shall ensure the fundamental equality before the law of women and men'. Timor-Leste's Constitution goes even further, by stating that 'Women and men shall have the same rights and duties in all areas of family, political, economic, social and cultural life.'[169] In keeping with its CEDAW obligations, Article 17 of Bhutan's Constitution enjoins the state to 'take appropriate measures to eliminate all forms of discrimination and exploitation against women including trafficking, prostitution, abuse, violence, harassment and intimidation at work in both public and private spheres'. Upon signing CEDAW, Malaysia amended Article 8(2) of its Constitution to insert 'gender' as a prohibited ground of discrimination, such that it now reads:

   > (2) Except as expressly authorized by this Constitution, there shall be no discrimination against citizens on the ground only of religion, race, descent, place of birth or *gender* in any law or in the appointment to any office or employment under a public authority or in the administration of any law relating to the acquisition, holding or disposition of property or the establishing or carrying on of any trade, business, profession, vocation or employment. (emphasis added)

2. There is a wealth of information available online in relation to reports to the CEDAW Committee, the discussion of issues with that Committee and its concluding observations (see <http://www.un.org/womenwatch/daw/cedaw/cedaw. htm>). Another useful site is the UN Office of the High Commissioner for Human Rights (see <http://www.ohchr.org/EN/countries/AsiaRegion/Pages/AsiaRegion Index. aspx>).

3. Despite the fact that most Asian states are parties to CEDAW, the fact remains that governments have an uphill task battling traditional biases against women in many of these states. Even in the most advanced and prosperous Asian societies, like Japan, Korea and Singapore, women continue to face challenges such as glass ceilings in the workplace.[170] The situation becomes even more critical in societies where women are treated as mere objects. In one of the most heinous incidents recorded, a group of six men gang-raped a 23-year-old student as she was returning home with her fiancé after a movie. This happened not on some country road

---

[167] Bangladesh (Arts 28(2) and 28(3)); Cambodia (Art 31); China (Art 48); India (Art 15); Japan (Art 14); Laos (Art 35); Macau (Art 25); Malaysia (Art 8(2)); Mongolia (Art 14(2)); Myanmar (Art 348); Nepal (Art 13(2) Interim Constitution); North Korea (Art 77); Pakistan (Art 25(2)); South Korea (Art 11(1)); Sri Lanka (Art 12(2)); Taiwan (Art 7); Thailand (Sec 5); and Vietnam (Art 63).

[168] Hongkong (Art 25); Indonesia (Art 27); and Singapore (Art 12).

[169] Art 17, Constitution of the Democratic Republic of Timor-Leste.

[170] See Tamako Nakanishi, 'Equality or Protection? Protective Legislation for Women in Japan' (1983) 122(5) *International Labour Review* 609; E Cho, 'Caught in Confucius' Shadow: The Struggle for Women's Legal Equality in South Korea' (1998) 12(2) *Columbia Journal of Asian Law* 125; and L Wolff, 'Eastern Twists on Western Concepts: Equality Jurisprudence and Sexual Harassment in Japan' (1996) 5(3) *Pacific Rim Law & Policy Journal* 509.

but in the Indian capital of New Delhi at 9.30 pm, on 16 December 2012. After gang-raping the student, the perpetrators then beat her up and threw her off the bus, leaving her for dead. The victim was rescued, underwent several emergency operations, and eventually died at a Singapore hospital to which she had been flown for specialist attention. The incident sent shockwaves throughout India and sparked off a series of street protests that led the Indian Government to give repeated assurances of better measures to protect women.

4.   See generally R Cook (ed), *Human Rights of Women: National and International Perspectives* (Philadelphia: University of Pennsylvania Press, 1995); AS Fraser, 'Becoming Human: The Origins and Development of Women's Human Rights' (1994) 21(4) *Human Rights Quarterly* 853; S Linton, 'ASEAN states, their reservations to human rights treaties and the proposed ASEAN Commission on Women and Children' (2008) 30 *Human Rights Quarterly* 436; C Evans and A Whiting (eds), *Mixed Blessings: Law, Religions, and Women's Rights in the Asia-Pacific Region* (Leiden: Brill, 2006); I Jaising, *Elusive Equality: Constitutional Guarantees and Legal Regimes in South Asia, Malaysia and China* (New Delhi: Women Unlimited, 2011); K Carmit Yefet, 'What's the Constitution Got to Do With It? Regulating Marriage in Pakistan' (2009) 16 *Duke Journal of Gender, Law & Policy* 347.

5.   In the Malaysian context, see JLC Neo, ' "Anti-God, Anti-Islam and Anti-Quran": Expanding the Range of Participants and Parameters in Discourse over Women's Rights and Islam in Malaysia' (2003) 21 *UCLA Pacific Basin Law Journal* 54; Z Anwar and JS Rumminger, 'Justice and Equality in Muslim Family Laws: Challenges, Possibilities, and Strategies for Reform' (2007) 64 *Washington & Lee Law Review* 1529; A Aziz Bari, 'The Right to Equality under the Constitution: The Implication of the Federal Court decision in Beatrice Fernandez' [2005] *The Laws Review* 373.

ii. Gender Selection and Abortion

Discrimination against women reaches its zenith in states where female infanticide is practised. This has happened in states like India[171] and China,[172] where males were traditionally prized and females despised. The British were so appalled by this practice in India that immediate steps were taken to put an end to it. Starting from 1805, Lieutenant-Colonel Alexander Walker, Resident at Baroda (present-day Vadodara) in the state of Gujarat, put in place several measures to suppress female infanticide.[173] Later the British Government established the Infanticide Committee to study the

---

[171] See R Venkatachalam and V Srinivasan, *Female Infanticide* (New Delhi: Har-Anand Publications, 1993); R Dube Bhatnagar, R Dube and R Dube, *Female Infanticide in India: A Feminist Cultural History* (Albany, NY: State University of New York Press, 2005); R Patel, 'May You Be the Mother of a Hundred Sons: The Practice of Sex Selective Abortion in India' (1996) 3(1) *Carolina Papers in International Health and Development*; N Ahmad, 'Female Feticide in India' (2010) 26 *Issues in Law & Medicine* 13; T Patel, *Sex-Selective Abortion in India: Gender, Society and New Reproductive Technologies* (New Delhi: Sage, 2007); and R Muthulakshmi, *Female Infanticide: Its Causes and Solutions* (New Delhi: Discovery Publishing House, 1997).

[172] For a historical view, see BJ Lee, 'Female Infanticide in China' (1981) 8(3) *Historical Reflections* 163.

[173] See Measures Adopted for the Suppression of Female Infanticide in the Province of Kattywar, etc by the late Colonel Alexander Walker (Bombay: Government of India, 1856).

problem, and this led to the passage of the Female Infanticide Prevention Act 1870.[174] A recent news report stated that between 2005 and 2011, almost 79,000 girls in the Indian State of Andhra Pradesh were victims of infanticide or foeticide.[175]

In earlier times, female infants were simply strangled or drowned, but in recent years, parents have used advanced medical diagnosis techniques to determine the sex of the foetus and have the foetus aborted if she if found to be female. This practice, known as 'sex-selective abortion',[176] led the Indian legislature to enact the Pre-Conception and Pre-Natal Diagnostic Techniques (Prohibition of Sex Selection) Act in 1994.[177] Among other things, this Act prohibits the use of pre-natal diagnostics to determine the sex of the foetus. Persons conducting such pre-natal diagnostics are also prohibited from disclosing the sex of the foetus to anyone.

Centre for Enquiry into Health & Allied Themes (CEHAT) & Ors v Union of India & Ors
(2003) 8 SCC 398, [2003] AIR SC 3309 (Supreme Court, India)

MB Shah J

It is an admitted fact that in the Indian society, discrimination against the girl child still prevails, maybe because of prevailing uncontrolled dowry system despite the Dowry Prohibition Act, as there is no change in the mindset or also because of insufficient education and/or tradition of women being confined to household activities. Sex selection/sex determination further adds to this adversity. It is also known that a number of persons condemn discrimination against women in all its forms, and agree to pursue, by appropriate means, a policy of eliminating discrimination against women, still however, we are not in a position to change the mental set-up which favours a male child against a female. Advanced technology is increasingly used for removal of foetus (may or may not be seen as commission of murder) but it certainly affects the sex ratio. The misuse of modern science and technology by preventing the birth of a girl child by sex determination before birth and thereafter abortion is evident from the 2001 Census figures which reveal greater decline in sex ratio in the 0–6 age group in States like Haryana, Punjab, Maharashtra and Gujarat, which are economically better off.

Despite this, it is unfortunate that law which aims at preventing such practice is not implemented and, therefore, non-governmental organisations are required to approach this Court for implementation of the Prenatal Diagnostic Techniques (Regulation and Prevention of Misuse) Act, 1994 renamed after amendment as 'the Preconception and Prenatal Diagnostic Techniques (Prohibition of Sex Selection) Act' (hereinafter referred to as 'the PNDT Act') which is the normal function of the executive.

In this petition, it was inter alia prayed that as the prenatal diagnostic techniques contravene the provisions of the PNDT Act, the Central Government and the State Governments

---

[174] Act VIII of 1870. On the Act, see M Kasturi, 'Law and Crime in India: British Policy and the Female Infanticide Act of 1870' (1994) 1 *Indian Journal of Gender Studies* 169.

[175] B Baseerat, 'Over 78K girls killed in Andrhra Pradesh in 6 years', *Times of India*, 29 December 2012, at <http://articles.timesofindia.indiatimes.com/2012-12-29/hyderabad/ 36050585_1_female-foeticide-ultrasound-centres-female-infanticide> (accessed 30 December 2012).

[176] See F Arnold, S Kishor and TK Roy, 'Sex-Selective Abortion in India' (2002) 28(4) *Population & Development Review* 759.

[177] For discussion of this controversial legislation, see K Lemoine and J Tanagho, 'Gender Discrimination Fuels Sex Selective Abortion: The Impact of the Indian Supreme Court on the Implementation and Enforcement of the PNDT Act' (2007–2008) 15(2) *University of Miami International & Comparative Law Review* 203.

be directed to implement the provisions of the PNDT Act (a) by appointing appropriate authorities at State and district levels and the Advisory Committees; (b) the Central Government be directed to ensure that the Central Supervisory Board meets every 6 months as provided under the PNDT Act; and (c) for banning of all advertisements of prenatal sex selection including all other sex-determination techniques which can be abused to selectively produce only boys either before or during pregnancy.

After filing of this petition, notices were issued and thereafter various orders from time to time were passed to see that the Act is effectively implemented.

The Court ordered

It is unfortunate that for one reason or the other, the practice of female infanticide still prevails despite the fact that gentle touch of a daughter and her voice has soothing effect on the parents. One of the reasons may be the marriage problems faced by the parents coupled with the dowry demand by the so-called educated and/or rich persons who are well placed in the society. The traditional system of female infanticide whereby female baby was done away with after birth by poisoning or letting her choke on husk continues in a different form by taking advantage of advance medical techniques. Unfortunately, developed medical science is misused to get rid of a girl child before birth. Knowing full well that it is immoral and unethical as well as it may amount to an offence, foetus of a girl child is aborted by qualified and unqualified doctors or compounders. This has affected overall sex ratio in various Slates where female infanticide is prevailing without any hindrance.

For controlling the situation, the Parliament in its wisdom enacted the Pre-natal Diagnostic Techniques (Regulation and Prevention of Misuse) Act, 1994 (hereinafter referred to as 'the PNDT Act'). The Preamble, inter alia, provides that the object of the Act is to prevent the misuse of such techniques for the purpose of pre-natal sex determination leading to female foeticide and for matter connected therewith or incidental thereto. The Act came into force from 1st January, 1996. It is apparent that to a large extent, the PNDT Act is not implemented by the Central Government or by the State Governments. Hence, the petitioners are required to approach this Court under Article 32[178] of the Constitution of India. One of the petitioners is the Central for Enquiry into Health and Allied Themes (CEHAT) which is a research centre of Anusandhan Trust based in Pune and Mumbai. Second petitioner is Mahila Sarvangeen Utkarsh Mandal (MASUM) based in Pune and Maharashtra and third petitioner is Dr Sabu M, Georges who is having experience and technical knowledge in the field.

After filing of this petition, this Court issued notices to the concerned parties on 9 May 2000. It took nearly one year for the various States to file their affidavits in reply/written submissions, Prima facie it appears that despite the PNDT Act being enacted by the Parliament five years back, neither the State Governments nor the Central Government has taken appropriate actions for its implementation. Hence, after considering the respective submissions made at the time of hearing of this matter, as suggested by the learned Attorney General for India, Mr Soli J Sorabjee following directions are issued on the basis of various provisions for the proper implementation of the PNDT Act:

[The Court then went on to issue very detailed and specific directions to the Central Government, the Central Supervisory Board, State Governments and Union Territories (UT) Administrations and other relevant authorities.]

---

[178] The relevant provisions of Art 32 read: '(1) The right to move the Supreme Court by appropriate proceedings for the enforcement of the rights conferred by this Part is guaranteed. (2) The Supreme Court shall have power to issue directions or orders or writs, including writs in the nature of habeas corpus, mandamus, prohibition, quo warranto and certiorari, whichever may be appropriate, for the enforcement of any of the rights conferred by this Part.'

Notes

1. In the *Ban on Fetus Sex Identification Case*,[179] the Korean Constitutional Court held that the provisions of the Medical Service Act, which forbade the disclosure of the sex of a foetus, were incompatible with the Constitution on the ground that they violated the physician's freedom of occupation, as well as the parents' right to know the sex of their child without interference.

2. The issue of sex-selective abortion is just as serious in China. See Jing-Bao Nie, 'Non-medical Sex-Selective Abortion in China: Ethical and Public Policy Issues in the Context of 40 Million Missing Females' (2011) 98 *British Medical Bulletin* 7; and Jiang-Bao Nie, 'Limits of State Intervention in Sex-Selective Abortion: The Case of China' (2010) 12(2) *Health & Sexuality* 205.

3. A related problem confronting women in India is that of dowry murder. In India, it is customary for the bride's family to provide a dowry at the time of a marriage. Depending on the social standing of the bride and groom, this dowry can be quite sizeable. Dowry deaths occur when young brides are murdered or driven to suicide by constant harassment, torture and ill-treatment by their husbands and in-laws after extracting a large dowry. Even though the demand for a dowry – regardless of its amount – was made illegal with the passage of the Dowry Prohibition Act in 1961, this practice continues. According to India's National Crime Records Bureau, there were an average of 8,200 dowry death convictions between 2007 and 2010. See V Talwar Oldenburg, *Dowry Murder: The Imperial Origins of a Cultural Crime* (New York: Oxford University Press, 2002); A Newman, 'For Richer, For Poorer, Til Death Do Us Part: India's Response to Dowry Deaths' (1992) 15 *ILSA Journal of International Law* 109; L Remers Pardee, 'The Dilemma of Dowry Deaths: Domestic Disgrace or International Human Rights Catastrophe?' (1996) 13 *Arizona Journal of International & Comparative Law* 491; JG Greenberg, 'Criminalizing Dowry Deaths: The Indian Experience' (2002–2003) 11 *American University Journal of Gender, Social Policy & Law* 801; J van Willigen and VC Channa, 'Law, Custom and Crimes Against Women: The Problem of Dowry Deaths in India' (1991) 50(4) *Human Organization* 369; and W Teays, 'The Burning Bride: The Dowry Problem in India' (1991) 7(2) *Journal of Feminist Studies in Religion* 29.

iii. Homosexuals and the Third Sex

In many Asian states, lesbians, gays, bisexuals and transgenders (LGBT) have been marginalised and discriminated against. No Asian state recognises same-sex marriages, nor the right of LGBTs to form family nuclei and adopt children. A pressing *legal* issue has been the criminalising of sodomy in several Asian states. Sodomy is a crime in Pakistan, Malaysia, Singapore and, until recently, India. In Nepal, the Supreme Court has recognised the status of the 'third sex' and ordered the Government to form a committee to undertake a study of discrimination against LGBTs.

---

[179] *Ban on Fetus Sex Identification Case* 20-2(a) KCCR 236, 2004Hun-Ma1010, 2005Hun-Ba90, 31 Jul 2008.

Naz Foundation v Government of Delhi & Ors
WP(C) No 7455/2001, 2 Jul 2009 (High Court, Delhi)

Ajit Prakah Shah CJ

1. This writ petition has been preferred by Naz Foundation, a Non Governmental Organisation (NGO) as a Public Interest Litigation to challenge the constitutional validity of Section 377 of the Indian Penal Code, 1860 (IPC), which criminally penalises what is described as 'unnatural offences', to the extent the said provision criminalises consensual sexual acts between adults in private. The challenge is founded on the plea that Section 377 IPC, on account of it covering sexual acts between consenting adults in private infringes the fundamental rights guaranteed under Articles 14, 15, 19 & 21 of the Constitution of India. Limiting their plea, the petitioners submit that Section 377 IPC should apply only to non-consensual penile non-vaginal sex and penile non-vaginal sex involving minors. . . .

Section 377 IPC Targets Homosexuals as a Class

94. Section 377 IPC is facially neutral and it apparently targets not identities but acts, but in its operation it does end up unfairly targeting a particular community. The fact is that these sexual acts which are criminalised are associated more closely with one class of persons, namely, the homosexuals as a class. Section 377 IPC has the effect of viewing all gay men as criminals. When everything associated with homosexuality is treated as bent, queer, repugnant, the whole gay and lesbian community is marked with deviance and perversity. They are subject to extensive prejudice because [of] what they are or what they are perceived to be, not because of what they do. The result is that a significant group of the population is, because of its sexual nonconformity, persecuted, marginalised and turned in on itself.[180]

95. As Justice O'Connor succinctly stated in her concurring opinion in *Lawrence v Texas* [539 US 558 (2003)]:

> While it is true that the law applies only to conduct, the conduct targeted by this law is conduct that is closely correlated with being homosexual. Under such circumstances, Texas's sodomy law is targeted at more than conduct. It is instead directed towards gay persons as a class. [Page 583]

96. In *Romer v Evans*, 517 US 620 (1996), the challenge was to an amendment to Colorado's Constitution which named as a solitary class persons who were homosexuals, lesbians, or bisexual either by 'orientation, conduct, practices or relationships' and deprived them of protection under the state anti-discrimination laws. The US Supreme Court concluded that the provision was 'born of animosity towards the class of persons affected' and further that it had no rational relation to a legitimate governmental purpose. Justice Kennedy speaking for the majority observed:

> It is not within our constitutional tradition to enact laws of this sort. Central both to the idea of the rule of law and to our own Constitution's guarantee of equal protection is the principle that government and each of its parts remain open on impartial terms to all who seek its assistance. 'Equal protection of the laws is not achieved through indiscriminate imposition of inequalities'. *Sweatt v Painter*, 339 US 629, 635 (1950) (quoting *Shelley v Kraemer*, 334 US 1, 22 (1948)). Respect for this principle explains why laws

---

[180] Sachs J in *The National Coalition for Gay and Lesbian Equality v The Minister of Justice*, Case CCT 11/98 (South Africa) para 108.

singling out a certain class of citizens for disfavoured legal status or general hardships are rare. A law declaring that in general it shall be more difficult for one group of citizens than for all others to seek aid from the government is itself a denial of equal protection of the laws in the most literal sense. 'The guaranty of equal protection of the laws is a pledge of the protection of equal laws . . .' [Page 633]

A second and related point is that laws of the kind now before us raise the inevitable inference that the disadvantage imposed is born of animosity towards the class of persons affected. "[I]f the constitutional conception of 'equal protection of the laws' means anything, it must at the very least mean that a bare . . . desire to harm a politically unpopular group cannot constitute a legitimate governmental interest . . ." [Page 634].

97. The Supreme Court of Canada in *Vriend v Alberta*, (1998) 1 SCR 493, held:

Perhaps most important is the psychological harm which may ensue from this state of affairs. Fear of discrimination will logically lead to concealment of true identity and this must be harmful to personal confidence and self-esteem. Compounding that effect is the implicit message conveyed by the exclusion, that gays and lesbians, unlike other individuals, are not worthy of protection. This is clearly an example of a distinction which demeans the individual and strengthens and perpetrates [*sic*] the view that gays and lesbians are less worthy of protection as individuals in Canada's society. The potential harm to the dignity and perceived worth of gay and lesbian individuals constitutes a particularly cruel form of discrimination. [para 102]

These observations were made in the context of discrimination on grounds of sexual orientation in the employment field and would apply with even greater force to the criminalisation of consensual sex in private between adult males.

98. The inevitable conclusion is that the discrimination caused to MSM and gay community is unfair and unreasonable and, therefore, in breach of Article 14 of the Constitution of India.

Infringement of Article 15: Whether 'Sexual Orientation' is a Ground Analogous To 'Sex'

99. Article 15 is an instance and particular application of the right of equality which is generally stated in Article 14. Article 14 is genus while Article 15 along with Article 16 are species although all of them occupy same field and the doctrine of 'equality' embodied in these Articles has many facets. Article 15 prohibits discrimination on several enumerated grounds, which include 'sex'. The argument of the petitioner is that 'sex' in Article 15(1) must be read expansively to include a prohibition of discrimination on the ground of sexual orientation as the prohibited ground of sex discrimination cannot be read as applying to gender *simpliciter*. The purpose underlying the fundamental right against sex discrimination is to prevent behaviour that treats people differently for reason of not being in conformity with generalization concerning 'normal' or 'natural' gender roles. Discrimination on the basis of sexual orientation is itself grounded in stereotypical judgments and generalization about the conduct of either sex. This is stated to be the legal position in International Law and comparative jurisprudence. Reliance was placed on judgments of Human Rights Committee and also on the judgments of Canadian and South African courts.

100. International Covenant on Civil and Political Rights (ICCPR) recognises the right to equality and states that, 'the law shall prohibit any discrimination on any ground such as race, colour, sex, language, religion, political or other opinion, national or social region, property, birth or other status'. In *Toonen v Australia* (Communication No. 488/1992, U.N. Doc CCPR/C/50/D/488/1992 (1994)), the Human Rights Committee, while holding that

certain provisions of the Tasmanian Criminal Code which criminalise various forms of sexual conduct between men violated the ICCPR, observed that the reference to 'sex' in Article 2, paragraphs 1 and 26 (of the ICCPR) is to be taken as including 'sexual orientation'.

101. Despite the fact that Section 15(1) of the Canadian Charter does not expressly include sexual orientation as a prohibited ground of discrimination, the Canadian Supreme Court has held that sexual orientation is a ground analogous to those listed in Section 15(1):

> In Egan, it was held, on the basis of 'historical, social, political and economic disadvantage suffered by homosexuals' and the emerging consensus among legislatures (at para 176), as well as previous judicial decisions (at para 177), that sexual orientation is a ground analogous to those listed in s 15(1). [Vriend v Alberta per Cory J para 90].

102. Similarly, in *Corbiere v Canada* [1999] 2 SCR 203, the Canadian Supreme Court identified the thread running through these analogous grounds – 'what these grounds have in common is the fact that they often serve as the basis for stereotypical decisions made not on the basis of merit but on the basis of a personal characteristic that is immutable or changeable only at unacceptable cost to personal identity.' [para 13].

103. The South African Constitutional Court recognised in *Prinsloo v Van Der Linde* 1997 (3) SA 1012 (CC) that discrimination on unspecified grounds is usually 'based on attributes and characteristics' attaching to people, thereby impairing their 'fundamental dignity as human beings'. In *Harksen v Lane* 1998 (1) SA 300 (CC), the Court further developed the idea to say that there will be discrimination on an unspecified ground if it is based on attributes or characteristics which have the potential to impair the fundamental dignity of persons as human beings, or to affect them adversely in a comparably serious manner. Elaborating on what it means by potential impairment of dignity, the Court resisted the temptation of laying down any such 'test' for discerning 'unspecified' grounds, but has this to say by way of guidelines, 'In some cases they relate to immutable biological attributes or characteristics, in some to the associational life of humans, in some to the intellectual, expressive and religious dimensions of humanity and in some cases to a combination of one or more of these features'. It needs to be noted that on account of the prevalent wider knowledge of the discrimination on account of sexual orientation, the South African constitution, when it was drafted, specifically included that as a ground.

104. We hold that sexual orientation is a ground analogous to sex and that discrimination on the basis of sexual orientation is not permitted by Article 15. Further, Article 15(2) incorporates the notion of horizontal application of rights. In other words, it even prohibits discrimination of one citizen by another in matters of access to public spaces. In our view, discrimination on the ground of sexual orientation is impermissible even on the horizontal application of the right enshrined under Article 15.

Sunil Babu Pant & Ors v Government of Nepal
Writ No 917 of 2007 (Supreme Court, Nepal)
English translation in (2008) 2(1) NJA Law Journal 262

Facts

The applicant filed the case on behalf of LGBTs for an order of mandamus, to require that gender identity be based on the subjective feelings of individuals and to recognise their right to cohabit in accordance with their sexual orientation.

Balram & Pawan Kumar Ohja JJ

[O]ur traditional society has recognized only two types of sexes ie male and female. A dominant role has been provided to these two sexes 'male' and 'female' in the society. There exist practices of treating the people of third sex differently. The Court should take this matter into the judicial notice. Due to the lack of awareness, education and knowledge the tradition and practices of treating the third gender, other than the male or female, differently continues not only in our society but also in other countries. Therefore, the claim that the people of third gender may not file the petition on their own behalf cannot be held otherwise.

Part III of the Constitution confers various fundamental rights to the Nepali citizens. The Directive Principles and Policies of the State stipulated [in] Part IV of the Constitution have kept the State at the centre for the upliftment and development of the citizens. All human beings including the child, the aged, women, men, disabled, incapacitated, third genders etc are Nepali citizens. All the territory of this country including all citizens collectively constitutes the nation. The third genders among the population are also part of the Nepalese population as a whole. The third gender are still considered as disadvantaged class of citizens because of the social perception towards them and social behavior as well as lack of education, knowledge and economic backwardness within the society of third gender. . . .

The second question raised above, relates to the basis of identification of homosexual or third gender people and whether it happens because of the mental perversion of an individual or such characteristics appears naturally. It seems to us that there is a practice of using the term 'sex' to depict the difference between the individuals on the basis of genitals whereas the term 'gender' is used for the role assigned by the society on the basis of sex. There are people having the identity of 'third gender' in minority in the society other than the 'male' and 'female', which are categorized as the mainstream on the basis of gender identity.

It is found that the medical science and psychology have categorized three types of people of different sexual attraction on the basis of sexual orientation. According to this practice, sexual relation or sexual attraction between the people of same sex is called homosexual relation. On the contrary, sexual relation or sexual attraction between the people of opposite sex is called heterosexual relation and the sexual relation or the sexual attraction between the people either of same sex or of opposite sex equally is called bisexual relation. Similar to what men and women are considered as the mainstream of the society on the basis of gender identity, from the point of view of the sexual orientation, the heterosexual people, because of their number, are considered as the mainstream of that group. On the other hand, the number of homosexual and bi-sexual people is not large in the society. Among the homosexuals also two types female homosexual (lesbian) and male homosexual (gay) are found. Similarly, persons who are born with the physical characteristics of one sex but psychologically feel and behave like members of opposite sex are called transsexual.

The other category of sexual minority are intersexuals who are born naturally with the both genetic sex organs of male and female. The number of such people is very few. Their gender is determined on the basis of their sexual orientation when they become adult. Thus, in totality, the five categories are found within the group of sexual minority, namely lesbian, gay, bisexual, transgender, intersexual which are known as LGBTI in an abbreviated form. The main contention of the writ petitioners is that this group has not been recognized yet on the basis of sexual orientation and gender identity. . . .

Another claim of the petitioners pertains to the protection of the fundamental right of the lesbians, gays and bisexual people by the state though appropriate legal provisions which, by granting them legal and social recognition from the state and society on the basis of their sexual orientation, ensures a life of freedom as other heterosexual people have. In reality, this claim is specific in regard to the issue of same sex marriage or co-habitation of such couple. Looking at the issue of same sex marriage, we hold that it is an inherent right of an adult to have marital relation with another adult with her/his free consent and according to her/his will. The same sex marriage should be viewed from the view point of interest and rights of the concerned people as well as that of the society, family and all others. It seems appropriate to reach a conclusion after studying the legal provisions and practices of other countries regarding gay and lesbian marriage. It has already been recognized in some countries whereas in some others it yet to be recognized. Therefore, it is essential to carry out a thorough study and analysis of international instruments relating to the human rights, the values recently developed in the world in this regard, the experience of the countries where same sex marriage has been recognized, and its impact on the society as well. The Government of Nepal has hereby been directed to form a committee as mentioned below in order to undertake the study on . . . all issues in this regard . . .

Notes

1. For a commentary on the *Pant* case, see M Bochenk and K Knight, 'Establishing a Third Gender Category in Nepal: Process and Prognosis' (2012) 26 *Emory International Law Review* 11.

2. As this book goes to print, the Court of Appeal of Singapore will determine whether section 377A of the Penal Code violates the equal protection provision under Article 12 of the Constitution. Section 377A reads:

    Any male person who, in public or private, commits, or abets the commission of, or procures or attempts to procure the commission by any male person of, any act of gross indecency with another male person, shall be punished with imprisonment for a term which may extend to 2 years.

C. Discrimination Against Indigenous Peoples

i. Indigenous Peoples and the Right to Self-Determination

In many states, indigenous peoples – most of whom are in the minority – have been the subjects of discrimination. In 1982, the United Nations' Economic and Social Council (ECOSOC) established a Working Group on Indigenous Populations to study the problem of discrimination against indigenous peoples. In 1985, the Working Group began work on a Draft Declaration on the Rights of Indigenous Peoples. This was completed in 1993 and submitted to the Sub-Commission on the Prevention of Discrimination and Protection of Minorities which approved it the following year. In the meantime, the International Labour Organisation adopted, in 1989, Convention No 169, the Indigenous and Tribal Peoples Convention. However, the Convention received limited endorsement; the only Asian state to ratify this Convention was Nepal, which did so on 2007.

The Draft Declaration was referred to the Commission on Human Rights which established another Working Group to study it. Between 1993 and its adoption in 2006, almost a dozen meetings were held to discuss and fine-tune the provisions. A number of states were concerned over issues such as the right of indigenous peoples to self-determination and control over traditional lands and natural resources. On 29 June 2006, the Human Rights Council (successor body of the Commission on Human Rights) approved the Draft Declaration, which was then put before the General Assembly for adoption on 13 September 2007 during its 61st regular session. The votes in favour of the Declaration were 144:4 with 11 abstentions. Every Asian state voted in favour of the Declaration, with the exception of Bangladesh and Bhutan, who abstained.

Unlike the ILO Indigenous and Tribal Peoples Convention, this Declaration is not legally binding and imposes no legal obligation on those who have endorsed it. That said, the Declaration proclaims the right of indigenous peoples to self-determination[181] and a nationality.[182] In addition, indigenous peoples have the right to: practise and revitalise their cultural traditions and customs;[183] manifest, practise and teach their spiritual and religious traditions, customs and ceremonies;[184] revitalise, use, develop and transmit to future generations their histories, languages, oral traditions, philosophies, writing systems and literatures;[185] designate and retain their own names for communities, places and persons;[186] establish and control their educational systems and institutions providing education in their own languages;[187] preserve dignity and diversity of their cultures, traditions, histories and aspirations;[188] establish their own media in their own languages and have access to all forms of non-indigenous media without discrimination;[189] participate in decision making in matters affecting their rights;[190] be consulted prior to the implementation of legislative or administrative measures affecting them;[191] maintain and develop their political, economic and social systems or institutions;[192] determine and develop priorities and strategies for exercising their right to development;[193] their traditional medicines and maintain their health practices (including the conservation of their vital medicinal plants, animals and minerals);[194] maintain and strengthen their distinctive spiritual relationship with their traditionally owned or otherwise occupied and used lands, territories, waters and coastal seas;[195] lands, territories and resources which they have traditionally owned, occupied or otherwise used or acquired;[196] conservation and protection of the environment and the productive capacity of their lands or territories and resources;[197] maintain, control, protect and develop their cultural heritage, traditional knowledge and traditional cultural expressions, as well as manifestations of their sciences, technologies and

[181] Art 3.
[182] Art 6.
[183] Art 11.
[184] Art 12.
[185] Art 13.
[186] Art 13.
[187] Art 14.
[188] Art 15.
[189] Art 16.
[190] Art 18.
[191] Art 19.
[192] Art 20.
[193] Art 23.
[194] Art 24.
[195] Art 25.
[196] Art 26.
[197] Art 29.

cultures, including human and genetic resources, seeds, medicines, knowledge of the properties of fauna and flora, oral traditions, literatures, designs, sports and traditional games and visual and performance arts;[198] maintain, control, protect and develop their intellectual property over such cultural heritage, traditional knowledge and traditional cultural expressions;[199] determine and develop priorities and strategies for the development or use of their lands or territories and other resources;[200] determine their own identity or membership according to their customs and traditions;[201] promote, develop and maintain their institutional structures and their distinctive customs, spirituality, traditions, procedures, practices and juridical systems or customs in accordance with international human rights standards;[202] determine the responsibilities of individuals to their communities;[203] recognition, observance and enforcement of treaties, agreements or other constructive arrangements concluded with states or their successors;[204] access to financial and technical assistance from states for the enjoyment of rights embodied in the Declaration;[205] and access to and prompt decision through just and fair procedures for the resolution of conflicts and disputes with states or other parties.[206]

The Declaration mandates the organs and specialised agencies of the United Nations to 'contribute to the full realization of the provisions' of the Declaration 'through mobilization, inter alia, of financial cooperation and technical assistance'.[207] Article 42 of the Declaration further states that the United Nations, 'its bodies, including the Permanent Forum on Indigenous Issues, and specialized agencies, including at the country level, and States shall promote respect for and full application of the provisions' of the Declaration.

The Declaration is, as we can see, extremely comprehensive and wide-reaching, but it is next to impossible to enforce precisely for that reason. Problems of definition are the first to be overcome. Exactly who constitutes a distinct 'people'? Assuming clear definitions can be formulated, what does the right to 'self-determination' entail? Does every people have a right to have its own state? Surely, that would completely destabilise the state system as we understand it. A small island like Taiwan has over a dozen aboriginal tribes,[208] and there are at least 10 distinct groups in the Andaman Islands alone. The main task then is to accommodate and protect these indigenous peoples within existing polities. After all, very few constitutions have secession clauses.

Notes

1. The literature on minority rights, indigenous peoples and self-determination is copious. An excellent starting point would be A Cassese, *Self-Determination of*

---

[198] Art 31.
[199] Art 31.
[200] Art 32.
[201] Art 33.
[202] Art 34.
[203] Art 35.
[204] Art 37.
[205] Art 39.
[206] Art 40.
[207] Art 41.
[208] Among these are: Amis, Atayal, Bunun, Kavalan, Paiwan, Puyuma, Rukai, Saisiyat, Sakizaya, Seediq, Tao, Thao, Tsou and Truku.

Peoples: A Legal Appraisal (Cambridge: Cambridge University Press, 1995). Other useful general works are: H Hannum, 'The Right to Self-Determination in the Twenty-First Century' (1998) 55 *Washington & Lee Law Review* 773; C Tomuschat, 'Self-Determination in a Post-Colonial World' in C Tomuschat (ed), *Modern Law of Self-Determination* (Leiden: Martinus Nijhoff, 1993) 1–20; J Anaya, *Indigenous Peoples in International Law*, 2nd edn (Oxford: Oxford University Press, 2004); and Li-ann Thio, *Managing Babel: The International Legal Protection of Minorities in the Twentieth Century* (Leiden: Martinus Nijhoff, 2005). On Asia, see C Nicholas and R Singh (eds), *Indigenous Peoples of Asia: Many Peoples, One Struggle* (Bangkok: Asia Indigenous Peoples Pact, 1996); Li-ann Thio, 'International Law and Secession in the Asia and Pacific Regions' in MG Kohen (ed), *Secession: International Law Perspectives* (Cambridge: Cambridge University Press, 2006) 297; B Kingsbury, 'The Applicability of the International Legal Concept of Indigenous Peoples in Asia' in J Bauer and DA Bell (eds), *The East Asian Challenge for Human Rights* (Cambridge: Cambridge University Press, 1999) 336; and J Castellino and E Dominguez Redondo, *Minority Rights in Asia: A Comparative Legal Analysis* (Oxford: Oxford University Press, 2006).

2. Useful country-specific writings include: VP Nanda, 'Self-Determination in International Law: The Tragic Tale of Two Cities – Islamabad (West Pakistan) and Dacca (East Pakistan)' (1972) 66 *American Journal of International Law* 321; P Harris, 'Is Tibet Entitled to Self Determination?', *Occasional Paper No 18* (Centre for Comparative and Public Law, Faculty of Law, University of Hong Kong, 2008); Zhu Guobin and Yu Lingyun, 'Regional Minority Autonomy in the PRC: A Preliminary Appraisal from a Historical Perspective' (2000) 7 *International Journal on Minority & Group Rights* 39; Baogang He, 'Minority Rights with Chinese Characteristics' in W Kymlicka and Haogang He (eds), *Multiculturalism in Asia* (Oxford: Oxford University Press, 2005) 56; MD Moneyhon, 'China's Great Western Development Project in Xinjiang: Economic Palliative or Political Trojan Horse?' (2003) 31(3) *Denver Journal of International Law & Policy* 491; C Mackerras, 'Ethnicity in China: the Case of Xinjiang' (2004) 8(1) *Harvard Asia Quarterly* 6; and M Kumar Sinha, 'Minority Rights: A Case Study of India' (2005) 12(4) *International Journal on Minority & Group Rights* 355.

D. Discrimination Against Aliens or Foreigners

Arudou v Earth Cure
Judgment of 11 Nov 2002 (Sapporo District Court, Japan)
(2008) 9(2) Asian-Pacific Law & Policy Journal 297
(trans T Webster)

Facts

David Aldwinckle sought to enter the Yunohana bathhouse in Otaru, Japan. He wanted to test the firmness of the 'No Foreigners' policy posted on its door. He assembled a multinational, multiracial cast outside the bathhouse, bought tickets, and attempted to enter. With him were his Japanese wife and their two daughters; his German friend, Olaf Karthaus, his Japanese wife and their two daughters; and a Japanese husband and his Chinese wife.

The bathhouse did not strictly apply its 'No Foreigners' policy. It allowed the Chinese woman to enter, but not the white men. When pressed, the bathhouse manager admitted he would have accepted the more 'Asian-looking' of Aldwinckle's two daughters, but not the more phenotypically Caucasian one.

In October 2000, Aldwinckle returned to Yunohana, under the name Arudou Debito, as a naturalized citizen of Japan. But Yunohana's policy had not changed and he was refused entrance. Arudou then did what foreigners are increasingly doing in Japan: he sued Yunohana bathhouse for racial discrimination.

Held

. . .

B. Based on the facts premised and acknowledged above, we examine the first dispute: Whether Earth Cure has a legal obligation.

1. Plaintiffs allege that Earth Cure's refusals are illegal violations of Article 14(1) of the Constitution Article 26 of the International Covenant on Civil and Political Rights (ICCPR), and Articles 5(f) and 6 of the Convention on the Elimination of Racial Discrimination (CERD). But Article 14(1) of the Constitution only applies to relations between the state and the individual; it should not apply to relations between private persons such as Plaintiffs and Earth Cure. As a practical matter, applying this provision to private relations would unjustly infringe on the private sphere inherent in the principle of private autonomy. Likewise, even if the ICCPR and CERD had legal force as domestic law, their provisions would regulate relations between the state and the individual; it would prescribe international obligations on the state, but would not directly regulate interpersonal relationships. The Public Bath Law sets out proper standards for maintaining public hygiene at public baths. Though it licenses bathhouses, it does not empower courts to determine the legality of conduct such as this, which is not related to public hygiene. Thus, Plaintiffs' claim cannot be accepted.

2. As noted, Article 14(1) of the Constitution, the ICCPR, and CERD do not apply directly to relations between private persons. But if private conduct specifically violates, or risks violating, another person's basic rights or equality, these provisions can be used to evaluate social norms. Articles 1 and 90 of the Civil Code, among others, generally regulate private autonomy, and protect an individual's interests against illegal infringements of basic rights and equality. Thus, Article 14(1) of the Constitution, the ICCPR, and CERD can serve as one standard in interpreting the above provisions of private law.

With regard to the refusals, it seems that the signs banning foreigners posted at the entrance of Yunohana evince discrimination based on nationality. But there are situations, such as in the second refusal, when one cannot differentiate national origin from physical appearance; Arudou was refused even after taking Japanese nationality. The substantive issue is not discrimination based on nationality, but whether one appears to be foreign. This is discrimination based on race, skin color, descent, ethnic origin or racial origin. In light of the meaning of Article 14(1) of the Constitution, Article 26 of the ICCPR, and CERD, these amount to private acts of racial discrimination that ought to be eliminated.

We acknowledge that Earth Cure, with respect to Yunohana, enjoys a right to a profession based on the protection of property rights. However, pursuant to the Public Bath Law,

Yunohana is a public bath operating under the license of the governor of Hokkaido. Because it contributes to maintaining and advancing public hygiene, Yunohana has a public nature. Patrons, upon paying the appropriate fee, can enjoy a bath unlike the ones in their own homes, and thereby maintain cleanliness. As far as public baths are concerned, patrons should be able to use them without regard to nationality or race. However, though called a 'public' bath, one who causes trouble to other patrons may be ejected or denied use. Thus, Earth Cure may – with the assistance of [the city of] Otaru and the Otaru police – eject people who do not follow bathing etiquette after receiving instructions. Earth Cure can also refuse persons who are drunk or possess alcohol. There are undeniably situations where the implementation of such methods will not be easy. But as a *public* bath, Earth Cure should implement the above methods to the extent it is able. In situations where it might not be easy, Earth Cure cannot just categorically refuse foreigners. That would clearly be irrational. Furthermore, there was absolutely no risk that these Plaintiffs were causing trouble for other patrons.

Thus, categorically refusing all foreigners constitutes irrational discrimination, exceeds social norms, and amounts to an illegal act.

Defendant Earth Cure claims that the refusals do not exceed social norms. Because Plaintiffs visited Yunohana to appeal to the mass media and protest Earth Cure's policies, the violation they suffered does not substantively compare to the economic freedom enjoyed by Earth Cure. By contrast, Plaintiffs claim that even if they intended to publicize their protest of Earth Cure, such facts do not alter their basic desire to take a bath. Since Plaintiffs suffered irrational discrimination, their intent does not change the illegality of the refusals.

Notes

1. Earth Cure was ordered to pay the plaintiff 1 million yen in damages, plus five per cent interest beginning 16 February 2001, and one-half of its own attorney's fees and one-quarter of the plaintiff's attorney's fees. The plaintiff was ordered to pay all remaining fees, including those incurred by the city of Otaru.

2. In 1999, the Shizuoka District Court had awarded 1.5 million yen in damages to the plaintiff Brazilian reporter who had been subject to 'no foreigner' treatment by Goro Itsuyama, owner of a shop which she had entered. Thinking that she was 'French', Itsuyama was initially friendly to the plaintiff, but turned hostile and evicted her from his store when he found out that she was from Brazil. As the Court did not consider Article 14 of the Japanese Constitution relevant, since it was concerned with citizens, it is difficult to discern from the long and convoluted judgment the exact grounds upon which the award was made except that Itsuyama's behaviour hurt the 'plaintiff's feelings'.[209]

3. States and governments have long regarded it their sovereign right to exclude persons who are not citizens from their territory. A recent case which attracted worldwide attention – on account of the number of foreign domestic workers abroad – was *Vallejos v Commissioner of Registration & Anor*.[210] The applicant, a national

---

[209] See *Bortz v Suzuki*, Judgment of October 12, 1999, Hamamatsu Branch, Shizuoka District Court (2007) 16(3) *Pacific Rim Law & Policy Journal* 631.

[210] *Vallejos v Commissioner of Registration & Anor* [2012] 2 HKC 185 (Court of Appeal, Hong Kong SAR).

of the Philippines, had been employed in Hong Kong as a foreign domestic helper since 1986. In 2008, she applied for a permanent identity card on grounds that she had resided in Hong Kong for over 22 years and that she had satisfied the requirements of Article 24(2) of the Basic Law of Hong Kong SAR to become a permanent resident. Her application was rejected by the Commissioner of Registration on the ground that under section 2(4)(a)(vi) of the Immigration Ordinance (Cap 115), a person will be not considered to have been ordinarily resident in Hong Kong for the purpose of the Ordinance 'while employed as a domestic helper who is from outside Hong Kong'. She appealed to the Registration of Persons Tribunal but her appeal was dismissed. She then applied for judicial review against the decision of the respondents, arguing that section 2(4)(a)(vi) of the Immigration Ordinance was inconsistent with Article 24(2)(4) of the Basic Law. The High Court ruled in her favour and the Commissioner appealed to the Court of Appeal, which held that this was 'not a case about discrimination and that

> it must be up to the sovereign authority to decide the extent to which the status of permanent resident should be conceded to foreign nationals. It is a fundamental principle in international law that a sovereign state has the power to admit, exclude and expel aliens: *Januzi v Secretary of State for the Home Department* [2006] 2 AC 426, 439G. As Bokhary PJ said in *Fateh Muhammad* (at p 285I–J), different treatment of citizens and non-citizens in regard to the right of abode is a common if not invariable feature of the laws of countries throughout the world, including those with constitutions which prohibit discrimination. That difference of treatment flows inevitably from the fact of the political boundaries which are drawn across the globe. The question of who can and who cannot qualify for permanent resident status is governed by the same principles. There simply cannot be any complaint that art 24(2)(4) confers the permanent resident status on some people but not others.[211]

The Hong Kong Court of Final Appeal reversed the decision of the High Court on 26 March 2013, ruling that foreign domestic workers had no right to apply for permanent residency. See A Chiu and P Moy, 'Foreign helpers' plea for permanent residency fails', *South China Morning Post*, 26 March 2013.

---

[211] Ibid, at para 132.

8

Free Speech and *Res Publica*

I. INTRODUCTION

The protection of free speech is essential to modern constitutional democracies. There are various rationales for guaranteeing freedom of expression. One object is to facilitate democratic governance as a facet of popular sovereignty, by enabling every citizen to freely express his or her opinions, to participate in public debate, and to influence law and public policy.[1] The protection of free speech also facilitates our common search for truth, which requires free enquiry and dissent. According to John Stuart Mill, 'the peculiar evil of silencing the expression of an opinion' amounts to 'robbing the human race'.[2] In the words of Justice Oliver Wendell Holmes Jr, 'the best test of truth is the power of the thought to get itself accepted in the competition of the market'.[3] Other rationales include the development of individual personality,[4] cultivating a tolerant community and sustaining a reason-based public culture.[5]

Freedom of speech is strongly linked to freedom of assembly and freedom of association. Indeed, the very idea of republican government recognised in nearly all modern constitutions entails a right for its citizens to meet peacefully and express opinions on public affairs.[6] Similarly, freedom of association 'encourages those with a sense of citizenry to actively participate in political affairs through the formation of civic associations'[7] that advance democratic governance. Freedom of expression, assembly and association are classic civil and political rights which are not only protected in most domestic constitutions, but also enshrined in most international human rights conventions, such as Articles 19 to 22 of the International Covenant on Civil and Political Rights (ICCPR).

Nearly all Asian constitutions have free speech guarantees, although few adopt the American absolutist formulation of free speech protection in the First Amendment that states: 'Congress shall make no law abridging the freedom of speech.' Article III Section 4 of the Philippines Constitution provides '[n]o law shall be passed abridging the freedom of speech . . . or of the press'. Most Asian constitutions regard free speech as a fundamental right, which may be subject to reasonable restrictions, such as in

---

[1] A Meiklejohn, *Free Speech and Its Relation to Self-Government* (New York: Harper Brothers Publishers, 1948) at 15–16, 24–27.

[2] JS Mill, *On Liberty* (New York: The Modern Library, 2002) at 17–19.

[3] *Abrams v United States* 250 US 616 (1919), 630 (Holmes J, dissenting).

[4] DAJ Richards, 'Free Speech and Obscenity Law: Toward A Moral Theory of the First Amendment' (1974) 123 *University of Pennsylvania Law Review* 62.

[5] LC Bollinger, *The Tolerant Society: Freedom of Speech and Extremist Speech in America* (New York: Oxford University Press, 1986); TI Emerson, *The System of Freedom of Speech* (New York: Random House, 1970); CR Sunstein, 'Free Speech Now' (1992) 59 *University of Chicago Law Review* 255.

[6] *United States v Cruikshank* 92 US 542 (1876), 552.

[7] *JY Interpretation No 644* [trans Andy Y Sun], 6 ROC Const Ct 319, 322–23 (2012).

Article 19(2) of the Indian Constitution. In general, there are two main models under which freedom of expression is guaranteed. The first model prescribes the protection of free speech, subject to a general limitation clause. In this model, courts may apply tests based on proportionality, reasonableness or the principle of excessiveness in adjudicating the constitutionality of free speech restrictions. This model is adopted in Japan, Hong Kong, Taiwan and the Philippines, among others. For example, Article 21 of the Constitution of Japan stipulates that 'freedom of assembly and association as well as speech, press and all other forms of expression are guaranteed'. A general limitation clause is provided in Article 12 that is applicable to all fundamental rights and freedoms. There is no other specific limitation or restriction made on freedom of expression.

The second model departs from the first by the inclusion of specific limitations or restrictions made to freedom of expression. Constitutions under the second model tend to highlight other comparable basic rights or interests to freedom of expression and prescribe specific limitations to the exercise of free speech. Under this model, the right of reputation or honour may be explicitly recognised as a limit to defamatory speech; the equality of racial or ethnic groups or community values are highlighted as justifications to curb hate speech; the proper functioning of the judiciary sets the limits to speech which is critical of the courts and may fall foul of contempt of court laws. Jurisdictions adopting this approach include Bangladesh, India, Malaysia, Nepal, Pakistan, Singapore, South Korea and Sri Lanka.

An illustrative example is the Constitution of South Korea. Although Article 21(1) guarantees freedom of speech enjoyed by all citizens, Article 21(4) explicitly states that 'neither speech nor the press shall violate the honour or rights of other persons nor undermine public morals or social ethics' and that 'should speech or the press violate the honour or rights of other persons, claims may be made for the damage resulting therefrom'. This specific limitation in Article 21(4) is made in addition to the general limitation clause in Article 37(2) which is applicable to all fundamental rights and freedoms.[8]

Another typical illustration is Article 14 of the Constitution in Singapore which is drawn from Article 10 of the Malaysian Constitution. This provision expressly subjects free speech guarantee to laws which the Parliament deems 'necessary or expedient' to serve eight specified grounds of derogation, that is, 'the interest of the security of Singapore or any part thereof, friendly relations with other countries, public order or morality and restrictions designed to protect the privileges of Parliament or to provide against contempt of court, defamation or incitement to any offence'.

These two models of free speech guarantee reflect the dynamics of liberal/illiberal/communitarian democracies discussed in chapter six. Generally, liberal democracy prioritises individual autonomy and assumes the neutrality of the state. In contrast, illiberal or communitarian democracies prioritise community interests and actively promote a particular version of public life. Accordingly, while the constitution of a liberal democracy may adopt a laissez-faire approach to freedom of expression, the constitution of a communitarian democracy may bar speech that attacks the national

---

[8] Art 37(2) of the Constitution of South Korea states that the freedoms and rights of citizens may be restricted by Act only when necessary for national security, the maintenance of law and order, or for public welfare. Even when such restriction is imposed, no essential aspect of the freedom or right shall be violated.

identity of the state or group identity.[9] A socialist constitution may require speech to be 'patriotic' and not contradict state ideology, and a non-liberal theocratic democracy may have substantive limits to religious speech, as exemplified in blasphemy laws as discussed in chapter nine.

In recent years, many Asian jurisdictions have undergone a process of increasing democratisation, resulting in a more open political environment for the realisation and enjoyment of freedom of expression and cognate liberties. However, Asian states are diverse, with liberal, illiberal, communitarian or theocratic democracies. For example, in an illiberal, theocratic democracy such as Sri Lanka or Thailand, a particular religion may be highlighted and associated with certain state institutions as a source of national identity. Lèse majesté or other speech that defames protected identities and respected institutions may continue to be restricted. In a communitarian democracy like Malaysia or Singapore, the justification for restraining freedom of expression may be drawn from culture in the form of the 'Asian values' discourse dating back to the 1990s, which argued that Asian societies favoured duties over rights and economic and social security over civil and political freedoms.[10] It is intriguing to see the dynamics created by these various forms of democracy on the different models of free speech in the region.

This chapter discusses the freedoms of expression, assembly and association. The focal point of enquiry is on understanding the scope of these guaranteed freedoms in various Asian constitutional jurisdictions, and to interrogate the underlying political and cultural contexts which shape the extent of protection accorded to these freedoms.

II. FREE SPEECH

Freedom of expression is not an absolute right and may be restricted by constitutionally permissible purposes and means. This section addresses key selected issues regarding prior restraint, press and media, sedition and hate speech, lèse majesté, contempt of court and symbolic speech, defamation, obscene speech and, lastly, judicially enforced apologies.

A. Prior Restraints on Speech

Prior restraints as a method of regulating speech have roots that pre-date the creation of modern constitutions, at a time when printing presses were generally licensed by the government and no books were published without prior government censorship and approval. However, as early as 1695, in England, the rights of the press or of individuals to be free from licensing and government censorship assumed the status of a

---

[9] M Rosenfeld and A Sajó, 'Spreading Liberal Constitutionalism: An Inquiry into the Fate of Free Speech Rights in New Democracies' in S Choudhry et al (eds), *The Migration of Constitutional Ideas* (New York: Cambridge University Press, 2005) 146.

[10] WT De Barry, *Asian Values and Human Rights: A Confucian Communitarian Perspective* (Cambridge, Mass: Harvard University Press, 1998).

common law right.[11] According to Blackstone, 'the liberty of the press is indeed essential to the nature of a free state' and 'consists in laying no previous restraints upon publications'.[12] Perhaps due to this common law tradition, the United States developed – through its federal Constitution and case law – a strong resistance to any form of prior restraint. In contrast, European countries continue 'to allow, under certain circumstances, the suppression of writings whether by way of a court injunction or by a decision of the executive'.[13]

Against this comparative backdrop, it is worth noting that a few Asian constitutions enacted after World War II explicitly ban government censorship. For instance, Article 21 of Japan's Constitution stipulates that 'freedom of speech, press and all other forms of expression are guaranteed' and that 'no censorship shall be maintained'. Similarly, Article 21 of the Constitution of South Korea explicitly states that 'licensing or censorship of speech and the press, and licensing of assembly and association shall not be recognized'. In some jurisdictions, while the ban of prior censorship may not be explicitly stipulated in the constitution, it can be effected by statutes. For example, the guarantee of freedom of publication has become one of the strongest liberties in Taiwan, where in 1999 the legislature repealed the Publication Act that required prior approval for all publications and has since provided no further regulation.

In jurisdictions without express constitutional or statutory bans, courts may be requested to adjudicate on constitutionality of prior restraints. The following cases illustrate different judicial attitudes towards prior restraints with respect to the printed press or other publications. Special attention is paid to the difference between prior restraints prescribed by the courts in the form of injunction and those imposed by the government in the form of censorship.

Brij Bhushan v Delhi
[1950] SCR 605 (Supreme Court, India)

Facts

The applicants were the publisher of *Organizer*, an English weekly published in Delhi, and its editor. Under section 7(1)(c) of the East Punjab Public Safety Act, 1949, the Delhi Province had power to prohibit publication if it believed such publication violated public order or public law. The applicants received an order from the Chief Commissioner of Delhi stating:

> Whereas the Chief Commissioner, Delhi, is satisfied that *Organizer*, an English weekly of Delhi, has been publishing highly objectionable matter constituting a threat to public law and order and that action as is hereinafter mentioned is necessary for the purpose of preventing or combating activities prejudicial to the public safety or the maintenance of public order.

The applicants sought writs of certiorari and examination against the order.

---

[11] GR Stone, LM Seidman, CR Sunstein and MV Tushnet, *Constitutional Law*, 3rd edn (New York: Aspen Publishers, 1996) at 1183.
[12] W Blackstone, *Commentaries on the Laws of England*, vol 4 (Oxford: Clarendon Press, 1769) at 151–52.
[13] R Errera, 'The Freedom of the Press: The United States, France and Other European Countries' in L Henkin and AJ Rosenthal (eds), *Constitutionalism and Rights: The Influence of the United States Constitution Abroad* (New York: Columbia University Press, 1990).

Patanjali Sastri J

The petitioners claim that this provision infringes the fundamental right to the freedom of speech and expression conferred upon them by article 19(1)(a) of the Constitution inasmuch as it authorises the imposition of a restriction on the publication of the journal which is not justified under clause (2) of that article. There can be little doubt that the imposition of pre-censorship on a journal is a restriction on the liberty of the press which is an essential part of the right to freedom of speech and expression declared by article 19(1)(a). As pointed out by Blackstone in his *Commentaries* . . . 'the liberty of the press consists in laying no previous restraint upon publications, and not in freedom from censure for criminal matter when published. Every freeman has an undoubted right to lay what sentiments he pleases before the public; to forbid this, is to destroy the freedom of the press'. The only question therefore is whether section 7(1)(c) which authorises the imposition of such a restriction falls within the reservation of clause (2) of article 19. As this question turns on considerations which are essentially the same as those on which our decision in Petition No XVI of 1950 was based, our judgment in that case concludes the present case also. Accordingly, for the reasons indicated in that judgment, we allow this petition and hereby quash the impugned order of the Chief Commissioner, Delhi, dated the 2nd March, 1950.

Persatuan Aliran Kesadran Negara v Minister of Home Affairs
[1987] 1 MLJ 442 (High Court, Malaysia)

Facts

The applicant was the publisher of a monthly English magazine, *The Aliran Monthly*. His publishing permit had been renewed annually since 1984. However, in November 1986, his application for publishing a fortnightly magazine in Bahasa Malaysia called 'Seruan Aliran' was rejected. While the Minister had full discretionary powers according to section 12(2) of the Printing Presses and Publications Act 1984, the applicant argued that the rejection violated the Constitution, and sought orders of certiorari and mandamus against the Minister.

Harun J

Aliran's application in wanting two separate publications is clearly to reach a wider reading public. That is in the interest of Aliran and I fail to see how it could be in the interest of Aliran by not allowing two publications. If the 'interest' is financial, then that is the concern of Aliran and should not be a consideration for refusing the permit. I also fail to see how the interest of the public at large is being protected by denying it access to a Bahasa Malaysia magazine particularly where the contents of the proposed magazine are already available to the English reading public.

The Minister says he exercised his discretion under s 12(2) of the 1984 Act. That subsection reads: 'The Minister shall have the absolute discretion to refuse an application for a licence or permit or the renewal thereof.'

It is common ground that although the discretion is absolute it is not unfettered. It follows that the exercise of the discretion is subject to judicial review. In the instant case, Aliran has complied with all the requirements for a permit. There is no evidence that the granting of the permit asked for is against the public interest.

In my view the granting of a permit to print and publish a magazine under the 1984 Act should be made as a matter of course provided of course, if all the requirements for such a permit have been complied with. The 1984 Act is a regulating Act and generally intended to police publications available to the public by requiring a permit to print and publish so that the authorities know who the printers and publishers are and the desirability of such publications being exposed to the general public. At the granting of permit stage the consideration for the exercise of the Minister's discretion is limited to protecting the public interest or national interest in respect of public order, morality and security as is shown in ss 4 and 7 of the 1984 Act. But these considerations must be obvious from the application itself or from other information made available to the Minister. In the present case the Minister relied entirely on the information supplied by the applicant. Except in obvious cases, the discretion to refuse to grant a permit cannot be exercised in anticipation that the applicant is likely to publish material which may offend against any law. Should such undesirable material be published, then the Minister has the power to revoke the permit under s 6(2) of the 1984 Act. The printer and publisher is open to prosecution under the Official Secrets Act, the Sedition Act, the Penal Code and to suits for defamation. Both the government and the public are well protected by these laws.

On the facts of this case, I found that the Minister had no good reasons in refusing the application for a permit and accordingly granted the orders prayed for with costs.

Order accordingly.

Judgment upon Case of Injunctions against Publication In Relation To the Freedom of Expression
40 Minshū 872 (Supreme Court, Japan)

Facts

The appellant published a magazine entitled *Hoppo (North) Journal*. In February 1979, one of the defendants, who was a candidate for the post of Governor of Hokkaido, claimed that an article in *Hoppo* would damage his reputation, and sought a provisional injunction against the magazine at the Sapporo District Court. The court issued an order prohibiting the appellant from printing and publishing. However, the court did not hold oral hearings nor make any inquiries of the appellant. The appellant argued that the provisional order of the prior ban on the magazine article violated his freedom of speech and violated Article 21(2) of the Constitution. Both courts of the first and second instance dismissed the claim and affirmed the legality of the injunction. The case was brought to the Supreme Court.

Held

'[C]ensorship' as provided in the former part of paragraph 2, Article 21 of the Constitution should be interpreted to indicate what has a special quality of prohibition of publication of matters being deemed objectionable by the administrative authorities as the main organ, based on a comprehensive and general examination of the contents of specific matters of expression prior to publication, such as the substance of thought conducted for the purpose of prohibiting publication in whole or in part. Now, prior restraint of printing, bookbinding, selling, distribution, etc of a magazine or any other publication containing certain articles by an injunction, not necessarily based on the result of oral proceedings or examination of the respondent, allowing prima facie evidence as the means of proof, can be ordered through such informal proceeding though conducted in a form of trial. This regulates the relative rights in dispute as a so-called 'provisional disposition settling the state of legal affairs'. So it cannot be said to not have the same character as Cases on Noncontentious Matters. However, it should be said that prior restraint by an injunction does not constitute censorship, because it is ordered after a court of judicature ascertains the existence of the right alleged to be preserved such as claim for injunction and the necessity of preservative measures based on the petition by the concerned party with regard to the individual private dispute. This is unlike cases where prior restraint is conducted by administrative authorities with the objective of prior restraint itself after a comprehensive and general examination of the substance of the matters of expression. Accordingly, the decision of the court below which held that the issuance of the injunction by the Sapporo District Court based on the petition by the Appellee Igarashi (hereinafter referred to as 'the injunction in this case') against the publication of the April 1979 issue of 'Hoppo Journal', a monthly magazine published by the Appellant, which printed an article entitled 'An Authoritarian's Temptation' (hereinafter referred to as 'the article in this case') does not amount to censorship, is justifiable and the Appellant's argument cannot be accepted. . . .

Next, whether the injunction conducted by a court against distribution, etc of a publication constitutes so-called prior restraint, and thus violating the provision of paragraph 1, Article 21 of the Constitution will be examined.

. . . Prior restraint in acts of expression, hindering the matters of expression, such as publication of newspapers, magazines and other publications and broadcasts, etc from reaching free society, shutting the door on communication of its contents to readers or viewers, or delaying the communication and thus destroying its significance has the effect of reducing the opportunities for public criticism. Moreover, due to characteristics of prior control being such that it cannot be but presupposed, it easily becomes more far-reaching than after-the-fact sanctions, and in addition to the possibility of its abuse, it is considered to have a more deterrent effect, in reality, than after-the-fact sanctions. Therefore, it should be said that in light of the purport of Article 21 of the Constitution which guarantees the freedom of expression and prohibits censorship, prior restraint on acts of expression is allowed only under strict and definite requirements.

Injunction against distribution and other processes of publication corresponds to the above-mentioned prior restraint. Particularly when the objective is relative to the evaluation or criticism of public servants or candidates for public office, from that in itself it may be generally said to relate to matters of public interest. It must be said an injunction against the relevant act of expression should not be granted as a general rule in light of the aforesaid purport of the paragraph 2, Article 21 of the Constitution . . ., and considering that under the Constitution such expressions having social values superior to a private right of reputation should be specially protected. However, even in such a case as above, it must be said that an injunction should be exceptionally allowed only when it is obvious that the contents of expression are not true or its objectives are not solely in the public interest, and, moreover, when the victim may suffer serious and irreparable damage. Because when the foregoing substantial requirements are satisfied, and additionally it is obvious that the value of the relevant act of expression is inferior to the reputation of the victim, and the need for an injunction is affirmed as an effective, appropriate and necessary remedy. We hold this construction is not contrary to the above- mentioned purport of the Constitution. . . .

JY Interpretation No 105
7 Oct 1964 (Constitutional Court, Taiwan)

Facts

In this case, the Control Yuan, a functional equivalent to ombudsmen, argued that the Publication Act, that required all publications to obtain prior approval of the Government, was unconstitutional, and petitioned the Constitutional Court.

Held

Administrative acts of interlocutory injunction against publication and deregistration under the Publication Act, Articles 40 and 41, fall within the scope of 'necessary' restriction stipulated in Article 23 of the Constitution, [stipulating that freedoms and rights shall not be restricted by law except by such as may be necessary to prevent infringement upon the freedoms of other persons, to avert an imminent crisis, to maintain social order or to advance public welfare]. Regarding the restriction on freedom of publication, this Yuan holds the same opinion as that contained in the Application to this Interpretation. The Constitution places no limitation on the means of penalization for illegal publication. Hence, the means of administrative penalty is adopted to achieve efficient restriction and can hardly be regarded as infringing upon the Constitution. Prescribed conditions for administrative acts under the aforesaid Articles are restrictive. Administrative agencies must act according to the itemized process prescribed therein. Persons so affected may still make an administrative appeal and administrative litigation to the Administrative Court seeking remedy and protection.

South Korea Periodicals Registration Case
90Hun-Ka23, 26 Jun 1992 (Constitutional Court, South Korea)

Facts

Under Article 7(1) of the Registration, etc of Periodicals Act (RPA) (amended by Law No 4441), the publisher of periodicals is required to register his rotary press machines with the Ministry of Public Information. Article 6(iii) of the same Act allows registration only when the application is accompanied by proof of ownership of at least one rotary printing press and ancillary facilities. Those found violating these provisions could be sentenced up to one year in prison, or ordered to pay a fine of up to five million won under Article 22(iii) of the Act. The complainants published periodicals twice a month from 10 March to 25 June 1989 without registering with the Government, and were prosecuted at the Seoul District Criminal Court. They argued that Article 7(1) of the RPA violated Article 21(2) of the Constitution.

Held

Freedom of speech and press in the Constitution protects the methods and the contents of essential and inherent manifestation of that freedom, but does not protect the objects needed to materialize such expression or the business activities of the entrepreneur controlling the media. Therefore, legally requiring periodical publishers to maintain and safeguard a certain level of facilities for sound growth of the press must clearly be distinguished from interfering with the essential contents of freedom of speech and press. Registration is not required for formulating and presenting views, nor for gathering and disseminating information – the substantive freedom of press – but is required of the business entity and the facilities that are the means of reporting and periodicals publication. They can be required to be registered without infringing the essential content of freedom of speech and press. . . .

However, requiring proof of ownership of the printing facilities as a precondition of registration is too stringent to be constitutional. The printing facilities can be procured by rent or lease. Reading the ownership requirement out of Article 7(1)(ix) is not only an arbitrary construction of the elements of a crime violating the Article 12 principle of *nulla poena sine lege*; but also an exaggerated construction of 'matters necessary for proper functioning of the press' in Article 21(3), which violates the Article 37(2) rule against excessive restriction.

Notes and Questions

1. What are the differences between prior restraints imposed by the courts and those imposed by the government? While the courts in both India and Malaysia struck down the administrative censorship, the Supreme Court of Japan sustained the legality of a judicially ordered injunction against the publication of a magazine. In the Court's view, such a 'prior restraint by an injunction does not constitute censorship', because it is ordered after a court ascertains the relevant facts and adjudicates the conflict of rights. Following a similar line of reasoning, the Taiwan Constitutional Court in *JY Interpretation No 105* justified the government censorship on the condition that judicial remedies were available to challenge these decisions. Do you agree with such a view? Why?

2. In the *South Korea Periodicals Registration Case*, the Constitutional Court found the requirement of providing the proof of ownership of printing facilities too stringent. Why? Is the law requiring publishers to register information with the Government, particularly regarding the ownership of rotary press machines and other ancillary facilities, a form of censorship or prior restraints? If not, what would be the nature of such restrictions?

3. Government censorship may be allowed with respect to certain special types of speech, for example statements or advertisements relating to drugs or food, which implicate public health. In the *Case Prohibition of Censorship and Article 18(1) (5) of the Functional Health Foods Act*,[14] the South Korean Constitutional Court decided that it was constitutional for the law to require the censorship of labels or advertisements of health foods:

   If false or exaggerated advertisements of functional health foods are not prevented, it would cause various damages to the health of people; and even if false or exaggerated advertisements are punished later, the physical or health harms of consumers cannot be recovered, implying its imperfect efficacy. On the other hand, advertisements of functional health foods, which are purely commercial, are rarely related to political expression on ideas or knowledge; and the censorship on such advertisements would not

[14] *Case Prohibition of Censorship and Article 18(1)(5) of the Functional Health Foods Act* 2006Hun-Ba75, Jul 29 2010.

affect the originality and creativity of artistic activities or freedom of speech, which has possibility to limit the freedom of expression to that which satisfies the whim of the person in authority.

In *JY Interpretation No 414*,[15] Taiwan's Constitutional Court also ruled that '[b]ecause the commercial speech of drug advertisements is closely related to the health of nationals, it thus should be strictly regulated by law to protect the public interest'. Both courts recognise that public health interests may outweigh freedom of speech in the context of food and drug regulation.

4.   Prior restraint of speech may be acceptable during a period of state of emergency. In *Siriwardena v Liyanage*,[16] however, the Supreme Court of Sri Lanka justified such restrictions, stating :

> The restrictions on the freedoms enshrined in the Constitution will necessarily be greater during a period of emergency than in periods of peace, and tranquility. What is obnoxious during a crisis or a State of Emergency may not be so in normal times. The necessity for quick action for the preservation of public order, which means the prevention of disorder, and for the maintenance of peace and tranquility has to be recognised.

Similarly, Article 4(2) of the ICCPR excludes freedom of expression (Article 19) from the list of rights from which no derogation may be made, even in times of public emergency. As the guarantee of constitutional rights may be considerably undermined during emergencies, having judicial checks and balances over the power of emergency becomes even more important. For discussions related to this issue, see chapters three and five.

5.   Some degree of censorship may apply to video or audio expressions. In South Korea, the Constitutional Court found the withholding of a rating for video products unconstitutional, as it amounted to censorship. According to the Constitutional Court,

> video products, of which ratings are withheld, are prevented from distribution . . . Penalties can be imposed to those who provided such products for distribution or viewing, and rating of video products can be withheld for an indefinite period of time as there is no limit on the frequency of withholding a rating. Therefore, . . . withholding of a rating of video products amounts to a system conducting review prior to distribution and prohibiting publication of unauthorized contents, namely censorship, which contradicts the Constitution.[17]

6.   In contrast, the Supreme Court of India upheld the classification and pre-censorship system of movies on the ground of public interest and the need to protect children and adolescents. In *KA Abbas v The Union of India*, the Supreme Court held:

> That censorship is prevalent all the world over in some form or other and pre-censorship also plays a part where motion pictures are involved, shows the desirability of censorship in this field . . . Further it has been almost universally recognised that the treatment of motion pictures must be different from that of other forms of art and expression. . . . The

[15] *JY Interpretation No 414* (2007) 3 ROC Const Ct 155, 156.
[16] *Siriwardena v Liyanage* SC Application 120/82, 17 Dec 1982.
[17] See *Withholding of Video Product Classification Case*, 2004Hun-Ka18, 30 Oct 2008.

art of the cameraman, with trick photography, vista vision and three dimensional representation thrown in, has made the cinema picture more true to life than even the theatre or indeed any other form of representative art. The motion picture is able to stir up emotions more deeply than any other product of art. Its effect particularly on children and adolescents is very great since their immaturity makes them more willingly suspend their disbelief than mature men and women. They also remember the action in the picture and try to emulate or imitate what they have seen. . . . With this preliminary discussion we say that censorship in India (and pre-censorship is not different in quality) has full justification in the field of the exhibition of cinema films. We need not generalize about other forms of speech and expression here for each such fundamental right has a different content and importance.[18]

7. Given its contemporary prevalence, the Internet has become another important space for expression. With the increasing number of speakers over the Internet, governments have to grapple with how to regulate cyberspace. The censorship of cyber-speech has become a topic of concern. In South Korea, Article 53 of the Telecommunications Business Act prohibits communications that 'harm the public peace and order or social morals and good customs' over the Internet. A student published a critical comment on a political figure on the Internet, and this message was deleted by the system manager pursuant to an order issued by the Minister of Information and Communication. In the constitutional review of this case, the Constitutional Court ruled that the impugned law was too broad and imposed an unnecessary restraint on Internet speech. The Constitutional Court stated:

> Necessity of such regulatory measures as deletion of messages cannot be denied considering the rapid speed of online information dissemination. However, while restriction of circulation of expression to protect juveniles could be allowed, generally, regulation or suppression of online expression based on its contents should not be allowed unless it contains materials clearly illegal or obviously detrimental to the public good . . . This would inevitably have a chilling effect on the users of telecommunication services . . . The Internet has become the largest and most powerful [medium], and regulation of expression on the Internet with emphasis on maintenance of order would be detrimental to the promotion of freedom of expression. Technological advance [regarding] the media continue to widen the scope of freedom of expression and bring about changes in the quality of such expression. In this light, new regulatory measures within Constitutional limits should be developed to keep up with the continuously changing environment in this field.[19]

8. In Singapore, the Government has recognised that the Internet may be used to benefit or to harm, and as a result, the laws relating to real space, such as the libel law, are transferrable to virtual space. For instance, a Singaporean student at the University of Illinois closed down his blog which criticised A*STAR, a statutory body, after receiving the threat of a defamation suit. For further discussion on this and related issues, see Thio Li-ann, 'The Virtual and the Real: Article 14, Political Speech and the Calibrated Management of Deliberative Democracy in Singapore' (2008) *Singapore Journal of Legal Studies* 37.

---

[18] *KA Abbas v The Union of India* [1971] AIR 481, [1971] SCR (2) 446.
[19] See *Ban on Improper Communication on the Internet Case*, 99Hun-Ma480, 27 Jun 2002.

B. Press, Media and Right to Reply

Thomas Carlyle observed in 1840 that the printing press was far more important than the Three Estates in Parliament, and decided to call it 'the Fourth Estate', under which 'whoever can speak, speaking now to the whole nation, becomes a power, a branch of government, with inalienable weight in law-making, in all acts of authority'.[20] Through their news and reports, the press and other media function as a watchdog over government conduct, facilitating open discussion in a democratic society.

However, there are concerns that this power may be abused or misused, especially when press companies do not merely report on news but also seek to advance a preferred political agenda. For example, Law Minister Shanmugam of Singapore once commented on the role of media and the democratic process:

> Journalists, like the rest of us, are human, and subject to the same influences and vices. They can be biased, unfair and prejudiced, as much as any of us can be. Media companies are often profit-driven, like other commercial entities. It is not uncommon for journalistic values to be sacrificed in pursuit of profit. Media companies and journalists, like other entities and people, can be bought, suborned and corrupted – particularly in developing countries. Competition and the need for the advertising dollar can compromise ethics. . . . The media can have tremendous influence in the political process. It can set the agenda for discussion, it can shape public opinion about Government and government policies, and it can make or break politicians. As the Fourth Estate, it is an active participant in the political process. Yet it is the only institution in the political process that is often not subject to any checks or balances . . .[21]

Given the institutional importance of the press and the need to prevent the abuse and misuse of its powers, many Asian constitutions contain express provisions relating to the press. The guarantee of a free press is included in the constitutions of Japan,[22] South Korea,[23] Bangladesh[24] and Laos.[25] The Constitution of the Philippines not only guarantees freedom of the press, but also requires the state to develop policies that respect the press.[26]

Article 45 of the 2007 Thai Constitution has perhaps the most elaborate press freedom clause. This bans any pre-publication censorship of news or articles except during wartime, and prohibits the closure of a newspaper or other mass-media business except by legal process. To secure press neutrality, the Thai Constitution forbids state subsidy or financial support for private mass media, and protects mass media personnel from government intervention to facilitate the free presentation of news and opinions, subject to the requirements of professional ethics or law.[27] Any government

---

[20] T Carlyle, Sartor Resartus, and on Heros, Hero-Worship, and the Heroic in History (London: JM Dent & Sons LTD, 1908) at 392.

[21] Speech by Minister for Home Affairs and Minister for Law, K Shanmugam at the inaugural forum, 'A Free Press for a Global Society', at Columbia University, 4 November 2010, archived at <http://www.mlaw.gov.sg/news/speeches/speech-by-minister-for-home-affairs-and-minister-for-law-k-shanmugam-at-the-inaugural-forum-a.html> (accessed 21 February 2013).

[22] Art 21, Constitution of Japan.

[23] Art 21, Constitution of the Republic of Korea.

[24] Art 39, Constitution of Bangladesh.

[25] Art 44, Constitution of Laos.

[26] Art 3, Secs 4 and 10, Constitution of the Philippines.

[27] Sec 46, Constitution of the Kingdom of Thailand, 2007.

agency or official attempting to interfere with the press freedoms would be deemed to be guilty of the 'intentionally undue exercise of powers and duties' which would be 'of no effect'.[28] In addition, the Thai Constitution demands the establishment of an independent regulatory agency with power over allocation of frequencies, and supervision over the operation of radio or television broadcasting businesses.[29] Government measures are also required to prevent mergers, cross right holding or market dominance amongst mass media businesses, or by any other person.[30] Individuals holding a political position are barred from holding shares in a radio or television broadcasting or telecommunications business.[31]

However, there are a few Asian constitutions, such as those of India, Indonesia, Malaysia, Singapore and Taiwan, that do not include such an explicit guarantee. Nevertheless, this may be implied or found within general freedom of expression clauses, such as in India. The Indian Supreme Court has held that freedom of speech and expression includes freedom of the press and circulation.[32] Similarly, the Constitutional Court of Taiwan held that as 'radio and television broadcasts are important media through which people state their ideas and commentary, thereby allowing public opinion to be expressed, the freedom of speech through radio and television must be protected'.[33] Other courts have taken a more circumspect view, in distinguishing their press models from those associated with western liberal democracies. For example, the Singapore Court of Appeal has expressed the view, obiter, that 'there is no room in our political context for the media to engage in investigative journalism which carries it with a political agenda'.[34]

This section discusses constitutional issues relating to freedom of the press, including entry regulations of media and access to media, particularly the right to reply.

i. Entry Regulation of Media

The right of every individual to speak, write and publish must be distinguished from the right to broadcast, since access to broadcast facilities is not unlimited. While government censorship or licensing of the printed press, periodicals or publications may be barred, other considerations apply with respect to radio or cable broadcasting. As explained by Justice White in *Red Lion Broadcasting Co v FCC*:[35]

> If 100 persons want broadcast licenses but there are only 10 frequencies to allocate, all of them may have the same 'right' to a license; but if there is to be any effective communication by radio, only a few can be licensed and the rest must be barred from the airwaves. It would be strange if the First Amendment, aimed at protecting and furthering communications, prevented the Government from making radio communication possible by requiring licenses to broadcast and by limiting the number of licenses so as not to overcrowd the spectrum.[36]

---

[28] Ibid.
[29] Sec 47, Constitution of the Kingdom of Thailand, 2007.
[30] Ibid.
[31] Sec 48, Constitution of the Kingdom of Thailand, 2007.
[32] *Bennett Coleman v Union of India* [1973] AIR 1973 SC 107.
[33] *JY Interpretation No 364* [trans Professor Tsung-Fu Chen], 2 ROC Const Ct 612, 613 (2007).
[34] *Review Publishing Co Ltd v Lee Hsien Loong* [2010] 1 SLR 52 at 177.
[35] *Red Lion Broadcasting Co v FCC* 395 US 367 (1969).
[36] Ibid at 388–89.

In the following two decisions, both the Constitutional Court of Taiwan and the Supreme Court of India address the question of the right to broadcasting in the face of limited resources.

JY Interpretation No 678
29 Jul 2010 (Constitutional Court, Taiwan)

Facts

In May, 2002, the petitioner began utilising the 95.9Hz radio frequency and established a radio station without authorisation in Taichung County in violation of Articles 48(1), 58(2), and 60 of the Telecommunications Act. While such illegal broadcasting did not interfere with other lawful uses of radio waves, the radio station was raided by the police in March 2003. The case was reviewed by Taichung District Court and the appellate panel of the same court, which ordered the detention of the petitioner for 50 days and confiscated all the equipment involved. The petitioner argued that the law violated his constitutional right to freedom of speech under Article 11 of the Constitution and property rights under Article 15 of the Constitution.

Held

Radio frequencies are public resources that belong to all nationals. In order to prevent usage interference and to ensure efficient and harmonious usage so as to maintain the order of wave usage, public resources and to enhance important public interest, the government must naturally manage with appropriate caution. [Taking] the above into consideration, the legislative body stipulates in Article 48, Paragraph 1 of the Telecommunications Act that the people's use of radio frequency shall be subject to prior approval. The purpose of such legislation is appropriate. While this regulation restricts the freedom of communications concerning the usage of radio frequency, in light of protecting the licensed users' rights and interests, preventing interruptive interferences and maintaining the orderly usage of radio wave and the safety of radio communications (see Article 18 of the Radio Regulations of International Telecommunication Union and Article 109 of the United Nations Convention on the Law of the Sea), and in balance, the restrictive measures under this provision [are] necessary and helpful in achieving the above-stated purposes, and do not contradict the principle of proportionality or the protection of free speech under Article 11 of the Constitution.

To fulfill the pre-approval system under the front portion of Article 48, Paragraph 1 of the Telecommunications Act, Article 58, Paragraph 2 of the same Act provides that anyone who arbitrarily use[s] or alter[s] radio frequency without authorization shall be penalized with detention, and/or a fine of not more than NT$200,000. The legislators consider the act of unauthorized and arbitrary use of radio frequencies a violation of the license system and the measure of administrative penalty is not sufficient to achieve the legislative purpose of maintaining the order of radio frequency usage as well as thoroughly and effectively banning the illegal usage activities (see the Legislative Yuan Gazette, vol 88, no 37, p 248), thus stipulate criminal penalty as the measure of control, which does not contradict the principle of proportionality under Article 23 of the Constitution. As to Article 60 of the Telecommunications Act, which stipulates that the telecommunication equipment used in violation of Article 58, Paragraph 2, regardless of ownership, shall be confiscated, is intended to prevent repeated unlawful use with the same equipment at different locations after the [initial] ban and is meant to prevent recidivism. Furthermore, radio transmitters or other devices used by radio stations to transmit radio frequencies are controlled goods that cannot be possessed or used at will (see Article 49, Paragraph 1 and Article 67, Paragraphs 3 and 4 of the same Act). Therefore, the confiscation regulation under Article 60 for violation of Article 58, Paragraph 2 contradicts neither the principle of proportionality under Article 23 of the Constitution nor the protection of people's property rights under Article 15 of the Constitution . . .

Secretary, Ministry of I & B v Cricket Association of Bengal
[1995] AIR 1995 SC 1236 (Supreme Court, India)

Facts

In March 1993, the Cricket Association of Bengal (CAB) began negotiating with the Director-General of Doordarshan (DD) about an offer which required DD to create a broadcaster signal. In addition, the offer granted DD exclusive right to live telecast cricket matches in the tournament. Meanwhile, CAB planned to sell the worldwide TV rights to the cricket matches to another party. Though CAB invited DD to join the plan and share the rights fee, DD responded that it would not join CAB's right-selling plan and would like to stick to the original offer made by CAB which allowed DD to have exclusive TV rights in India. CAB eventually signed an agreement with the World Production Establishment (WPE) to allow Trans World International (TWI) to telecast all the matches. CAB only kept radio rights for India. When DD found out the agreement between CAB and WPE, DD refused to telecast the matches by refusing TWI the TV right to telecast the event.

TWI had no choice but to seek recourse from Videsh Sanchar Nigam Limited (VSNL), the government agency controlling frequency of telecasting, for permission to uplink signals created by TWI, TWI's agency cameras or its earth station to a foreign satellite. However, the problem was still unresolved, since TWI needed to get signals from DD for up-linking through VSNL. To resolve the dispute, CAB attempted to negotiate new terms with DD, but failed. In the end, CAB filed a lawsuit in the Calcutta High Court requesting DD to provide telecasting and broadcasting of all the cricket matches by supporting TWI. On appeal, the High Court passed an interim order to allow DD to be the host broadcaster, and asked the Ministry of Telecommunication to consider granting a licence to TWI within three days. The matches were then broadcast. But the Ministry of Broadcasting (MIB), Government of India and DD filed two Special Leave Petitions to the Supreme Court. Unsatisfied with the order which gave DD the exclusive right to telecast matches in India, CAB filed a writ petition independently.

Sawant J

We may now summarise the law on the freedom of speech and expression under Article 19[1](a) as restricted by Article 19[2]. The freedom of speech and expression includes [the] right to acquire information and to disseminate it. Freedom of speech and expression is necessary, for self-expression which is an important means of free conscience and self-fulfillment. It enables people to contribute to debates of social and moral issues. It is the best way to find a truest model of anything, since it is only through it, that the widest possible range of ideas can circulate. It is the only vehicle of political discourse so essential to democracy. Equally important is the role it plays in facilitating artistic and scholarly endeavours of all sorts. The right to communicate, therefore, includes right to communicate through any media that is available whether print or electronic or audio-visual such as advertisement, movie, article, speech etc. That is why freedom of speech and expression includes freedom of the press. The freedom of the press in terms includes right to circulate and also to determine the volume of such circulation. This freedom includes the freedom to communicate or circulate one's opinion without interference to as large a population in the country as well as abroad as impossible to reach.

This fundamental right can be limited only by reasonable restrictions under a law made for purpose mentioned in Article 19[2] of the Constitution.

The burden is on the authority to justify the restrictions. Public order is not the same thing as public safety and hence no restrictions can be placed on the right to freedom of speech and expression on the ground that public safety is endangered. Unlike in the American Constitution, limitations on fundamental rights are specifically spelt out under Article 19(2) of our Constitution. Hence no restrictions can be placed on the right to freedom of speech and expression on grounds other than those specified under Article 19(2).

What distinguishes the electronic media like [the] television from the print media or other media is that it has both audio and visual appeal and has a more pervasive presence. It has a greater impact on the minds of the viewers and is also more readily accessible to all including children at home. Unlike the print media, however, there is a built-in limitation on the use of electronic media because the airwaves are a public property and hence are owned or controlled by the Government or a central national authority or they are not available on account of the scarcity, costs and competition.

The next question to be answered in this connection is whether there can be a monopoly in broadcasting/telecasting. Broadcasting is a means of communication and, therefore, a medium of speech and expression. Hence in a democratic polity, neither any private individual, institution or Organisation nor any Government or Government Organisation can claim exclusive right over It. Our Constitution also forbids monopoly either in the print or electronic media. The monopoly permitted by our Constitution is only in respect of carrying on a trade, business, industry or service under Article 19(6) to subserve the interests of the general public. However, the monopoly in broadcasting and telecasting is often claimed by the Government to utilise the public resources in the form of the limited frequencies available for the benefit of the society at large. It is Justified by the Government to prevent the concentration of the frequencies in the hands of the rich few who can information to suit their interests and thus in fact to control and manipulate public opinion in effect smothering the right to freedom of speech and expression and freedom of information of others. The claim to monopoly made on this ground may, however, lose all its raison d'être if either any section of the society is unreasonably denied an access to broadcasting or the Governmental agency claims exclusive right to prepare and relay programmes. The ground is further not available when those claiming an access either do not make a demand on the limited frequencies controlled by the Government or claim the frequency which is not utilised and is available for transmission. The Government sometimes claims monopoly also on the ground that having regard to all pervasive presence and impact of the electronic media, it may be utilised for purposes not permitted by law and the damage done by private broadcasters may be irreparable. There is much to be said in favour of this view and it is for this reason that the regulatory provisions including those for granting licences to private broadcasting where it is permitted, are enacted. On the other hand, if the Government is vested with an unbridled discretion to grant or refuse to grant the license or access to the media, the reason for creating monopoly will lose its validity. For then it is the government which will be enabled to effectively suppress the freedom of speech and expression instead of protecting it and utilising the licensing power strictly for the purposes for which it is conferred. It is for this reason that in most of the democratic countries an independent autonomous broadcasting authority is created to control all aspects of the operation of the electronic media. Such authority is representative of all sections of the society and is free from control of the political and administrative executive of the State. . . .

The law on the subject discussed earlier makes it clear that the fundamental right to freedom of speech and expression includes the right to communicate effectively and to as large a population not only in this country but also abroad, as is feasible. There are no geographical barriers on communication. Hence every citizen has a right to use the best means available for the purpose. At present, electronic media, viz, TV and radio, is the most effective means of communication. The restrictions which the electronic media suffers in addition to those suffered by the print media, are that (i) the airwaves are a public property and they have to be used for [the] benefit of the society at large; (ii) the frequencies are limited (iii) media is subject to pre-censorship. The other limitation, viz, the reasonable restrictions imposed by law made for the purposes mentioned in Article 19(2) is common to all the media. In the present case, it was not and cannot be the case of the NM that the telecasting of the cricket matches was not for the benefit of the society at large or not in the public interest and, therefore, not a proper use of the public property. It was not the case of the MIB that it was in violation of the provisions of Article 19[2]. There was nothing to be pre-censored on the grounds mentioned in Article 19[2]. As regards the limitation of resources, since the DD was prepared to telecast the cricket matches, but only on its terms it could not plead that there was no frequency available for telecasting. The DD could also not have ignored the rights of the viewers which the High Court was at pains to emphasise while passing its orders and to which we have also made a reference. The CAB/BCCI being the organisers of the event had a right to sell the telecasting rights of [their]event to any agency. Assuming that the DD had no frequency to spare for telecasting the matches, the CAB could certainly enter into a contract with any agency including a foreign agency to telecast the said matches through that agency's frequency for the viewers in this country [who could have access to those frequencies] as well as for the viewers abroad. The orders passed by the High Court in effect gave a right to DD to be the host broadcaster for tele-casting in this country and for the TWI, for telecasting for the viewers outside this country as well as those viewers in this country who have an access to the TWI frequency. The order was eminently in the interests of the viewers whatever its merits on the other aspects of the matter.

The orders passed by the High Court have to be viewed against the backdrop of the events and the position of law discussed above. The circumstances in which the High Court passed the orders and the factual and legal considerations which weighed with it in passing them speak for themselves. However, since the cricket matches have already been telecast, the question of the legality or otherwise of the orders has become academic and it is not necessary to pronounce our formal verdict on the same. Hence we refrain from doing so.

We, therefore, hold as follows:

(i)   The airwaves or frequencies are a public property. Their use has to be controlled and regulated by a public authority in the interests of the public and to prevent the invasion of their rights. Since the electronic media involves the use of the airwaves, this factor creates an in-built restriction on its use as in the case of any other public property.

(ii) The right to impart and receive informaiton is a species of the right of free [speech, which is] the best means of imparting and receiving informaiton and as such to have an access to telcating for the prupose. However, this right to have an access to telecasting has limitations on account of the use of the public property, viz, the airwaves, involved in the exercise of the right and can be controlled and regulated by the public authority. This limitation imposed by the nature of the public property involved in the use of the electronic media is in addition to the restrictions imposed on the right to freedom of speech and expression under Article 19(2) of the Constitution.

(iii) The Central Government shall take immediate steps to establish an independent autonomous public authority representative of all sections and interests in the society to control and regulate the use of the airwaves. [iv] Since the matches have been telecast pursuant to the impugned order of the High Court, it is not necessary to decide the correctness of the said order.

Notes and Questions

1. What is the legal nature of radio frequencies or airwaves? On what constitutional grounds do the courts in Taiwan and India justify the prior approval of broadcast and the allocation of frequencies by the government? To what extent might technological innovations change the argument?

2. In *Secretary, Ministry of I & B v Cricket Association of Bengal*, the Supreme Court of India stated that the use of frequencies must be controlled and regulated by the public authority, and yet held that the government refusal to grant frequencies to a private entity was unconstitutional. Do you think this is a contradiction? Why, or why not?

3. Both courts in the above decisions advised the government to create an independent autonomous public authority in order to distribute frequencies and issue licences. A similar proposal was also made by András Sajó in the context of new democracies in Eastern Europe. According to Sajó, the government should take steps to establish an independent autonomous public authority representative of all sections and interests in the society, to control and regulate the use of the airwaves. Such an independent autonomous agency is to enforce government neutrality and must be independent and beyond partisan politics. See A Sajó, 'Neutral Institutions: Implications for Government Trustworthiness in East European Democracies' in J Kornai and S Rose-Ackerman (eds), *Building a Trustworthy State in Post-Socialist Transition* (New York: Palgrave Macmillan, 2004) at 29.

4. How do we ensure the independence of such an independent autonomous public authority vested with regulatory powers of distributing broadcast and telecast frequencies? By creating an independent regulatory commission? In this regard, a critical issue would be how to compose such a commission, and how to appoint its members to ensure political impartiality.

5. In Taiwan, the controversy surrounding the appointment of the first independent regulatory commission, the National Communication Commission (NCC), provides some insight to these issues. The appointment regime of the Organic Act of the NCC allowed the main political parties in the legislature to recommend candidates for membership, based on the percentage of the number of seats of the respective parties in the legislature. In *JY Interpretation No 613*,[37] the Constitutional Court ruled this method of appointment unconstitutional, as it transferred the power of appointment from the executive to the various political parties in the

---

[37] *JY Interpretation No 613* (2007) 5 ROC Const Ct 682, 683–90.

legislature, thus overstepping the limits of participation and running counter to the separation of powers. More importantly, the Constitutional Court stressed that the purpose of the Organic Act of the NCC was to reduce the political clout of the executive and legislature on the NCC's exercise of powers, and to promote further public confidence in its fair enforcement of the law. However, the partisan method of appointment

> accomplished exactly the opposite by inviting active intervention from political parties and granting them a special status to recommend and, in essence, nominate, members of the NCC based on the percentages of the numbers of their seats, thus affecting the impartiality and reliability of the NCC in the eyes of the people who believe that it shall function above politics.

The NCC Organic Act was changed after this constitutional ruling. It now stipulates that commissioners, who shall possess professional knowledge or practical experience in telecommunications, information, broadcast, law or finance, among other matters, are to be appointed by the executive with the approval of the legislature. The Act explicitly limits the number of commissioners with affiliations to the same political party, which is not to exceed one-half of the total number of commissioners.

6. In *JY Interpretation No 678*, the Constitutional Court in Taiwan upheld the imposition of a criminal penalty on the unauthorised use of frequencies, which was rather severe compared to the use of civil penalties in other jurisdictions. As previously discussed, the strong regulatory power of government in allocating and regulating frequencies is justified on the basis of the scarcity of airwaves. However, technological advancements, and in particular the availability of Internet and social media, have greatly challenged such a premise. Unlike traditional media, today's networks and social media are more decentralised and accessible to individuals. Individuals may send information to millions of readers and become at times more influential than even some traditional media corporations. These new developments in technological innovation have led some to believe that it is no longer necessary for the government to exercise regulatory powers in allocating communication channels. See J Berman and DJ Weitzner, 'Abundance and User Control: Renewing the Democratic Heart of the First Amendment in the Age of Interactive Media' (1995) 104 *Yale Law Journal* 1624; and O Fiss, 'In Search of a New Paradigm' (1995) 104 *Yale Law Journal* 1613, 1614–15. Others maintain the need for the continued exercise of government regulatory powers. The abundance of communication channels does not necessarily guarantee the realisation of equal rights to speech in these various forums, and new forms of discrimination and disadvantages may continue to emerge. See TG Krattenmaker and LA Powe Jr, 'Converging First Amendment Principles for Converging Communications Media' (1995) 104 *Yale Law Journal* 1719, 1725–26.

ii. Access to Media and Right to Reply

Freedom of speech ensures that everyone has the freedom to speak through any medium of his or her choice. This right extends to the ownership of newspapers or periodicals in which the owners can express their opinions. In actuality, however, only a few individuals can own and operate the printed press due to economic and market factors. The scarcity of frequencies means that in practice, only a few powerful corporations own broadcast and telecast facilities. As a result, free speech guarantees inevitably entail 'the right of access to the media'. Some constitutions may entrench a constitutional right of reply generally or in particular contexts.[38] For example, when stipulating the responsibilities of the Commission on Elections, Article IXC, Section 4 of the Philippines Constitution emphasises that relevant supervision or regulations must aim to ensure equal opportunity, time and space, and the right to reply in connection with the holding of elections. Even without an express constitutional guarantee, courts may still derive the right to reply from freedom of expression, equality and other constitutional grounds. The Constitutional Court of Taiwan stated in *JY Interpretation No 364* that the right of access to the media includes a person's right to express his or her objections through the media – such as the right to reply – as well as the right to demand that media owners make available telecast or broadcast time schedules.[39]

However, granting individuals the right of access to the media limits the freedom of the press and other media. It was due to this concern that the US Supreme Court, in *Miami Herald Publishing Co v Tornillo*,[40] unanimously held invalid a statute that gave candidates running for political offices the right to reply if their personal characters or official records were assailed by newspapers. In the view of the Court, a newspaper is more than a passive receptacle or conduit for news, comment and advertising, and the right of free speech guarantees a newspaper editorial freedom, including the right to choose what material to publish.[41] Yet this may itself undermine an important free speech rationale, which is to promote truth or accuracy. To assume there exists a 'free marketplace of ideas' is fallacious, as it assumes that entry barriers governing the right of access to the press and media are low or inexpensive.

The solution to bad speech is not 'more free speech', in the sense that it is not easy simply to go out and create a co-equal newspaper with the same reach and impact as one which refuses to publish a right to reply. Hence, the challenge facing all courts is to strike a proper balance between the right of access to the press and media and the freedom of the press. The following cases illustrate the divergent ways in which Asian courts strike such a balance.

JY Interpretation No 364
23 Sep 1994 (Constitutional Court, Taiwan)

Facts

In reviewing the amendments to the Radio and Television Act, a few legislators had doubts about the meaning and scope of Article 11 of the Constitution that guarantees freedom of speech, and decided to initiate a petition to the Constitutional Court for clarification.

---

[38] Art 5 V of the Constitution of Brazil ensures a right to reply (*direito de resposta*) generally.
[39] *JY Interpretation No 364* [trans Professor Tsung-Fu Chen] 2 ROC Const Ct 612, 614–15 (2007).
[40] *Miami Herald Publishing Co v Tornillo* 518 US 241 (1974).
[41] Ibid at 258.

Held

Freedom of speech is the very foundation of a constitutional democracy. Radio and television broadcasts are important media through which people may state their ideas and commentary, thereby allowing public opinion to be expressed. This results in the reinforcement of democracy, the advancement of knowledge, and the promotion of cultural, moral and economic development. As such, the freedom of speech through radio and television is protected under Article 11 of the Constitution. However, because the messages disseminated via radio waves are boundless, radio and television engender a great and deep impact on society. The enjoyment of this freedom of information dissemination carries with it, under the principle of self-regulation, certain social obligations so as to avoid the abuse of these rights. The state is entitled to enact laws to restrict the freedom of the media should they demonstrate immorality, disturb the public peace, endanger the state, or infringe upon the rights of others.

Radio wave frequencies are a limited public resource. In order to avoid monopolies, the state must enact laws that govern their distribution. Under such laws, the responsible authority is empowered to work out a fair and reasonable system concerning the lifting of the ban on radio wave frequencies. This system will serve to ensure the balanced development of radio and television and increase the availability of media for the average person.

In theory, the 'right of access to the media' indicates the right to demand the mass media station owner publicly to provide a printed broadcast time schedule. This will serve to promote the truthfulness and fairness of media reports and commentary by enabling the public their rightful opportunity to express their opinions. That is to say, when an individual's right is infringed upon due to wrongful media reports or commentary, he or she is entitled to offer a response or request the media to revise their reports or commentary. An example of the means by which radio and television media are able to improve the quality of democratic politics is by way of holding impartial political debates during election campaigns.

Nonetheless, granting public access to the media in effect places limitations on media station owners in terms of editing and selection of information. It may serve to deprive media station owners of their right to free editing should they be required to accept unconditionally any individual's demands to express his or her objections through broadcast media. As a result of losing their freedom to edit, media station owners will be subject to excessive compromise and hesitate to report the full truth. Accordingly, the function of the media to report in a true and fair manner will be undermined. Therefore, both the public right to media access and the media's freedom of editing must be simultaneously considered. The law must set conditions on the public's access to the media in order to implement the equal integrity of the public right of access and the media's freedom of editing.

In conclusion, the freedom of expression through radio or television media is included under the freedom of speech of Article 11 of the Constitution. To protect this freedom, the state must distribute the use of radio wave frequencies in a fair and reasonable manner. The laws must be enacted with a balanced regard for the public's equal right to media access and the media's right to edit freely.

Request for a Corrective Report Case
89Hun-Ma165, 16 Sep 1991 (Constitutional Court, South Korea)

Facts

Article 16(3) of the Registration, etc of Periodicals Act entitles a person whose right to personality has been infringed by stories in periodicals, to request a corrective report. Pursuant to Article 19(3) of the same Act, the court is authorised to dispose of the issue through preliminary orders. The complainant published a story on the Pasteur Dairy Corporation in 23 July 1988, and was later sued by the corporation. When the complainant was ordered to print a corrective statement he sought constitutional review of the statute, alleging that it infringed the freedom of press and the press's right to trial.

Held

Although the relevant provisions mention 'correction', they in reality mean a right to request that the reporting agency publish rebuttal by those affected by the report, [namely], right to reply. Reply does not aim to contest the truth of the report or compel correction of a false report. A right to reply gives the injured person an opportunity to present [a] reply to the factual reports by the press, thereby protecting his right to personality. It also enhances the objectivity of the report and thus the systemic security of the press by allowing the defamed victim to participate in generating a balanced public opinion. Obviously, such a right is derived from the general right to personality, right to privacy, freedom of privacy guaranteed by the Constitution.

Right to a corrective report restricts the editing and the layout of the periodicals and may impose indirect limitations on reporting, and therefore should adhere to the rule against excessive restriction so that all rights complementing freedom of press are given the maximum effects. The right to reply has a legitimate end and applies only to reply [to] factual assertions (Article 16(1)). It allows a periodical to refuse to carry the reply under certain circumstances, narrowing the permissible scope of exercise of the right (Article 16(3)). The Act requires the request to be made within certain time limits in order to protect the press from long periods of uncertainty. Finally, reply is done not by the press but under the name of the injured party, and therefore does not directly denigrate the reputation and the credibility of the media agency. In short, the challenged law achieves a well-struck balance between the two conflicting interests.

Article 19(3) submission of the matter to preliminary order processes also does not violate the complainant's right to trial because it is needed for swift remedies to injuries.

The statutes above mentioned do not violate the essential content of freedom of the press or their right to trial.

Against this majority opinion, Justices Han Byong-chae and Lee Shi-yoon dissented, arguing that right to a corrective report does not operate like right to reply, and disposing of it through summary procedures such as preliminary orders, instead of full trials, discriminates against the publishers of periodicals unreasonably, violating the equality before law and procedural basic rights.

Japan Communist Party v Sankei Newspaper Inc
875 Hanrei Jihō 30, 1977 (Supreme Court, Japan)

Facts

In 15 November 1973, the ruling Liberal Democratic Party (LDP) planned to publish large-scale, seven-column opinion advertisements, and contacted seven newspaper companies. This action drew the attention of the Japanese Communist Party (JCP) as the advertisements directly attacked the JCP. In response, the JCP requested the seven newspapers to review the advertisements and not publish them. Four newspapers, including *Asahi*, *Mainichi*, *Yomiuri* and *Tokyo* complied, but *Sankei Shimbun* eventually published the advertisement.

On 11 December, the JCP requested *Sankei Shimbun* to make redress for publishing the untrue advertisement. *Sankei Shimbun* responded that if the JCP held a press conference, they would report it based on their editorial policy. On 15 December, the JCP provided a draft of rebuttal without any indication of whether it should be published in the form of an article or advertisement, but insisted that it be published free of charge. *Sankei Shimbun* replied that the newspaper would not publish the rebuttal for free, but if the JCP could show that its opponent the LDP would pay for such publication, the newspaper would charge LDP for the publication. After rounds of negotiations, no consensus or compromise was reached, and JCP decided to sue *Sankei Shimbun* in the courts.

Held

Since plaintiff first set forth freedom of speech (Article 21 of the Constitution) as the foundation reason for their claim in this case, let us consider this point.

a) The guarantee of freedom of speech under Article 21 of the Constitution naturally guarantees the freedom of speech of the party who is the object of that speech. And freedom of speech as a concept can be said to include the freedom to argue to the contrary. As argued by plaintiff, this freedom of counterargument has as its content the right to engage in effective rebuttal sufficient to the particular nature of the methods and contents of an attack. In other words, as long as it is not contrary to the public welfare, the plaintiff is not prevented from any speech or rebuttal. However, many problems must be considered to go from such an affirmation of plaintiff's right of rebuttal to recognition of a claim to publish the particular rebuttal of the defendant demanded in this case.

b) Plaintiff lists eight conditions regarding the advertisement at issue and contends that in the present case where these concrete facts exist, plaintiff can directly demand that the defendant publish a rebuttal based on Article 21 of the Constitution:

1) The means is an advertisement in a general interest newspaper which has a firm readership of 2,000,000.
2) It mentions the plaintiff by name.
3) It attacks important basic policies of the plaintiff, using expressions which intentionally distort.
4) From the standpoint of the common sense of the community, it is of a form which demands an answer of the plaintiff in the same newspaper.
5) If plaintiff does not rebut these attacks, it will create conditions which give the impression that the contents of those attacks are the truth.
6) As a consequence, political trust in plaintiff will be damaged and plaintiff's political activities will be obstructed.

7) Knowing that plaintiff was not in a position to make a counterargument by other method, they published and distributed the advertisement at issue with the above special characteristics.

8) Since the defendant is engaged in the newspaper industry, it should on its own initiative carry in the Sankei newspaper the rebuttal text as requested by plaintiff. It can thus restore the loss of political trust in the plaintiff and remove the obstruction of their political activities.

c) . . . We must try to consider [these matters] as criticism of political parties. Political parties in a democratic society aim for political power by competing for the support of the people with debate as a major weapon based on the freedoms of speech and expression. As a result, that the disputes among political parties should become relentless and acrimonious is naturally unavoidable, and one appealing for support for himself with speech must be resigned on the other hand to [being the object of] harsh attack and criticism.

That political parties are in this situation is a publicly known fact among the people, and the people undeniably keep this premise in mind when they look at disputes among political parties. That is, the disputes and attacks of conflicting political parties are not taken at face value by the people, and their effect is diminished just because they issue from opposing parties . . .

Just because the LDP, not a party in this suit, attacked plaintiff in the advertisement at issue, it is not appropriate to quickly say that it hindered the political activities of plaintiff. It is very doubtful whether the political trust of the people in the plaintiff was damaged by the ad in this case.

d) The most important point of dispute in this case is of course plaintiff's civil claim on the defendant to publish the rebuttal. Here . . . plaintiff contends that they can directly demand of the defendant publication of the rebuttal in this case based on Article 21 of the Constitution, but . . . [setting aside problems raised above], this court cannot understand why such conditions suddenly give rise to a civil right in plaintiff to demand publication of a rebuttal. It goes without saying that based on the freedom of speech, plaintiff has a right to rebut by any means, including an 'advertisement' rebuttal in the Sankei newspaper, the same paper used by the LDP for its attacks. The great importance of the freedoms of speech and expression under Article 21 guarantees is as plaintiff has argued.

However, there must naturally be a foundation for guaranteeing as a means of counterargument the charging of another with responsibilities and burdens. Plaintiff argues that the right to demand publication of a rebuttal based on Article 21 of the Constitution arises even without defamation. But it is a great principle of modern law that in a case where an illegal act does not arise, provided for as an illegality of defamation, in a case where no illegality of the defendant exists, no responsibility is imposed on the defendant. If we speak of the present case, on the matter of illegality, except for cases where a defendant must bear responsibility, there should be no reason for the defendant to be required to contribute advertising space, which is a commercial item. Since, in spite of this, plaintiff argues that they demand publication of the rebuttal in this case as a civil claim against the defendant, plaintiff must show sufficient reason. However, as shown above, plaintiff's argument is only a contention that the above-mentioned eight factual requisites [suffice] as a direct foundation. Otherwise, the factual inability of plaintiff to [present a] rebuttal is only an argument from Inconvenience. But since the details of the above eight requisites as the foundation for a claim for publication of a rebuttal go beyond the understanding of the present court, . . . let us consider other foundations indirectly indicated in plaintiff's detailed explanation.

Life Insurance Corporation v Manubhai
[1993] AIR 171, [1992] SCR (3) 595 (Supreme Court, India)

Facts

This was a consolidation of two separate lawsuits, with Professor Manubhai D Shah as the common plaintiff in both. The defendant in the first case was the Life Insurance Corporation (LIC), while the defendant in the second case was a public service broadcaster, Doordarshan.

In the first case, Manubhai, acting as an executive trustee of the Consumer Education & Research Centre, published a study paper stating that the LIC treated insurance holders unequally, with extremely high premiums and denials of coverage to many individuals. The LIC published a response in *The Hindu*, challenging Manubhai's arguments. Manubhai then wrote another article which he published in *The Hindu*. Then, as a final rebuttal, the LIC published a paper in its own company magazine *Yogakshema*. Believing that the readers of *Yogakshema* should have the chance to read his rebuttal, Manubhai then requested the LIC to republish his earlier article in *Yogakshema*, but LIC rejected his request.

In the second case, Manubhai produced a documentary, *Beyond Genocide*, which won the Golden Lotus award for being the best non-feature film of 1987. At the presentation of the award, the Central Minister for Information stated that the short film would be telecasted on Doordarshan, a publicly-funded broadcasting media. However, when Manubhai requested Doordarshan to telecast the film, Doordarshan refused.

Ahmadi J

[The LIC case]

The words 'freedom of speech and expression' must be broadly construed to include the freedom to circulate one's views by word of mouth or in writing or through audio-visual instrumentalities. Therefore, [it] includes the right [to] propagat[e] one's views through the print media or through any other communication channel eg the radio and the television. . . .

The right extends to the citizen being permitted to use the media to answer the criticism levelled against the view propagated by him. . . .

No serious exception can be taken to the approach which [has been]commended to the High Court. The LIC is a State within the meaning of Article 12 of the Constitution [which provides 'the State includes the Government and Parliament of India and the Government and the Legislature of each of the States and all local or other authorities within the territory of India or under the control of the Government of India']. It is created under an Act, namely, the Life Insurance Corporation Act, 1956, which requires that it should function in the best interest of the community. The community is, therefore, entitled to know whether or not this requirement of the Statute is being satisfied in the functioning of the LIC.

By refusing to print and publish the rejoinder, the LIC had violated the respondent's fundamental right. The rejoinder . . . is not in any manner prejudicial to the members of the community nor is it based on imagin[a]ry or concocted material. It does not contain any material which can be branded as offensive, in the sense that it would fall within anyone of the restrictive clauses of Article 19(2) [which states 'Nothing in [freedom of speech and expression] shall affect the operation of any existing law, or prevent the State from making any law, in so far as such law imposes reasonable restrictions on the exercise of the right conferred by the said sub clause in the interests of the sovereignty and integrity of India, the security of the State, friendly relations with foreign States, public order, decency or morality or in relation to contempt of court, defamation or incitement to an offence.'].

That being so on the fairness doctrine the LIC was under an obligation to publish the rejoinder since it had published its counter to the study paper.

The LIC's refusal to publish the rejoinder in its magazine financed from public funds is an attitude which can be described as both unfair and unreasonable; unfair because fairness demanded that both view points were placed before the readers, however, limited be their number, to enable them to draw their own conclusions[;] and unreasonable because there was no logic or proper justification for refusing publication. . . .

[The Doordarshan case]

The freedom conferred on a citizen by Article 19(1)(a) [which states 'All citizens shall have the right (a) to freedom of speech and expression;'] includes the freedom to communicate one's ideas or thoughts through a newspaper, a magazine or a movie. . . .

Once it is recognised that a film-maker has a fundamental right under Article 19(1)(a) to exhibit his film, the party which claims that it was entitled to refuse enforcement of this right by virtue of law made under Article 19(2), the onus lies on that party to show that the film did not conform to the requirements of that law, in the present case the guidelines relied upon.

The respondent had a right to convey his perception of the gas disaster in Bhopal through the documentary film prepared by him. The film not only won the Golden Lotus award but was also granted the 'U' Certificate by the censor. . . .

In the circumstances it cannot be said that the film was not consistent with the accepted norms. Doordarshan being a State controlled agency funded by public funds could not have denied access to the screen to the respondent except on valid grounds.

Notes and Questions

1. In the above decisions, the Constitutional Courts of both South Korea and Taiwan held it constitutional to demand the right to reply against the media. However, the Supreme Court of Japan, in *Japan Communist Party v Sankei Newspaper, Inc,* refused to grant a political party the right to reply in a newspaper against an advertisement published by its opponent. What gives rise to these departing views?

2. In *Life Insurance Corporation v Manubhai,* the Supreme Court of India held that the public broadcaster service must open access to opposing views. Does it mean that only government or public authorities can be ordered to grant a right to reply? Does the government also enjoy the right to reply against private media? In Singapore, the Government has stressed the right to reply. Law Minister K Shanmugam outlined the Government's stand:

   > [O]ur approach on press reporting is simple: The press can criticize us, our policies. We do not seek to proscribe that. But we demand the right of response, to be published in the journal that published the original article. We do not accept that they can decide whether to publish our responses. That irks the press no end.

   See, 'Singapore government demands right of reply to press criticism', BBC Monitoring International Reports, 28 October 2009, available at <http://www.accessmylibrary.com/article-1G1-210705890/singapore-government-demands-right-of-reply>.

3. In the case excerpted above, the Supreme Court of Japan decided that *Sankei Shimbun* need not give the JCP free space to reply since the JCP could simply pay for publication of a rebuttal advertisement. This position reflects the 'marketplace of ideas' ideal espoused by the US Supreme Court in *Miami Herald Publishing Co v Tornillo*.[42] As mentioned in section II. B, such a premise often fails to address the unequal access of individuals to the media due to factors like economic wherewithal, and is likely to entrench structural inequalities regarding freedom of expression and even participation in public affairs.

4. A few international human rights conventions also recognise the right to reply as part of an independent right to free speech. Most renowned is Article 14 of the American Convention on Human Rights (ACHR) which formally recognises the right of reply and correction, stating that 'anyone injured by inaccurate or offensive statements or ideas disseminated to the public in general by a legally regulated medium of communication has the right to reply or to make a correction using the same communications outlet, under such conditions as the law may establish', and that the correction or reply shall not in any case remit other legal liabilities that may have been incurred. The Inter-American Court of Human Rights further held that the right to reply and make a correction is an enforceable right under the American Convention, and hence state parties were obliged to take legislative or other measures for implementation.[43] What do you think about Article 14 of the ACHR? Is it supportive or undermining of the free speech rationale in search of accuracy and truth?

5. While the European Convention on Human Rights does not explicitly mention the right of reply, the European Court of Human Rights has nevertheless recognised this as integral to free expression, holding that Member States have 'a positive obligation to help an individual exercise free speech rights in media'.[44] In the Indian case excerpted above, the Supreme Court stressed that publicly-owned insurance and broadcasting companies must guarantee to citizens the right of reply. Such a distinction between public and private media owners is worthy of note, and to some extent resonates with what the European Court of Human Rights has also emphasised – the positive duty of states to ensure the rights of individuals to speech through media. For further discussions of the right to reply in international and comparative perspectives, see Kyu Ho Youm, 'The Right of Reply and Freedom of the Press: An International and Comparative Perspective' (2008) 76 *George Washington Law Review* 1017; A Czepek, M Hellwig and E Nowak, *Press Freedom and Pluralism in Europe: Concepts and Conditions* (Bristol: Intellect, 2009); DA Cifrino, 'Press Freedom in Latin America and the Emerging International Right to Communicate' (1989) 9 *Boston College Third World Law Journal* 117.

6. The free press and media are important institutions whose autonomy must be ensured. See P Stewart, 'Or of the Press' (1975) 26 *Hastings Law Journal* 631, 633–34. However, this carries with it special responsibilities. After all, by broadcasting

---

[42] *Miami Herald Publishing Co v Tornillo* 418 US 241 (1974).

[43] See *Enforceability of the Right to Reply or Correction (Arts 14(1), 1(1) and 2 American Convention on Human Rights)*, Advisory Opinion OC-7/85, Inter-Am Ct HR (ser A) No 7, para 35 (29 Aug 1986).

[44] See *Melnychuk v Ukraine* App No 28743/03 (ECtHR, 5 July 2005) 6–7.

and telecasting images and sounds, the media transmit ideas that quickly occupy minds of citizens and generate impacts greater than any other methods of communication. The Singapore Government has raised various questions about the qualities and responsibilities of the media:

(a) Does [the press] always pursue the truth and seek to enlighten the readers?

(b) Do parts of the media act as campaign arms of politicians, peddle half-truths and present very biased perspectives?

(c) Do viewers really get to the truth, or do they rely on their preferred media, which may often seek to confirm their existing prejudices?

(d) Is it financially more lucrative for the media to serve up 'red meat' to a secure base of viewers, rather than seek the middle ground?

(e) To what extent does money affect the traditional theory of a marketplace of ideas?

(f) If a particular group can buy more campaign ads, will that group have a clear advantage? How does it help democracy and informed choice if, pursuant to the principles of free speech, large groups can play a big financial role in elections – would that not advantage vested interests?

See K Shanmugam, 'A Free Press For A Global Society', speech at Columbia University Low Memorial Library Rotunda, 4 November 2010, available at <http://www.singaporeunited.sg/cep/index.php/cluster/Our-News/The-Role-of-the-Media-Singapore-s-Perspective-by-Mr-K-Shanmugam-Minister-for-Home-Affairs-Law/%28cluster%29/MHA>.

7. In Singapore, the statutory regime of the Newspaper Printings and Presses Act (NPPA) provides tailor-made, calibrated controls over foreign media. Under section 24(1) of the Act, the Minister is empowered to declare any foreign newspaper published outside Singapore to be 'engaging in the domestic politics of Singapore'. If the foreign press are deemed to contravene this, penalties such as circulation reduction may apply. The Court of Appeal adopted a wide and generous interpretation of the phrase 'engaging in domestic politics' on account of the fact that 'since 1974 the government has amended the NPPA to prohibit any newspaper published in Singapore being managed or controlled by non-citizens so that it could not be used to promote political and other causes or ideas which are not, in the opinion of the government of the day, in the interest of Singapore'.[45]

8. Similarly, in *National Press Club v Commission on Elections*,[46] the Supreme Court of the Philippines was mindful of the extraordinary influence the media might exert, when upholding legislation that made it unlawful for the press or any other media to sell or to give free of charge print space or air time for candidates during the campaign period, except as designated by the Election Commission. According to the Court,

> the nature and characteristics of modern mass media, especially electronic media, cannot be totally disregarded. Realistically, the only limitation upon the free speech of candidates imposed is on the right of candidates to bombard the helpless electorate with paid

---

[45] See *Dow Jones Publishing Company (Asia) Inc v Attorney General* [1989] 2 MLJ 385.

[46] *National Press Club v Commission on Elections*, GR No 102653, 5 Mar 1992.

advertisements commonly repeated in the mass media ad nauseam. Frequently, such repetitive political commercials when fed into the electronic media themselves constitute invasions of the privacy of the general electorate. It might be supposed that it is easy enough for a person at home simply to flick off his radio o[r] television set. But it is rarely that simple. For the candidates with deep pockets may purchase radio or television time in many, if not all, the major stations or channels. Or they may directly or indirectly own or control the stations or channels themselves. The contemporary reality in the Philippines is that, in a very real sense, listeners and viewers constitute a 'captive audience.'

The paid political advertisement[s] introjected into the electronic media and repeated with mind-deadening frequency, are commonly intended and crafted, not so much to inform and educate as to condition and manipulate, not so much to provoke rational and objective appraisal of candidates' qualifications or programs as to appeal to the non-intellective faculties of the captive and passive audience. The right of the general listening and viewing public to be free from such intrusions and their subliminal effects is at least as important as the right of candidates to advertise themselves through modern electronic media and the right of media enterprises to maximize their revenues from the marketing of 'packaged' candidates.[47]

9.   As discussed section II B, in order to prevent power abuse or misuse of the media, the Thai Constitution requires government measures to prevent mergers, cross right holding or market dominance amongst mass media businesses or by any other person (Article 47). In Singapore, the NPPA was enacted (see 7. above), replacing the 1920 Printing Press Ordinance. It contained provisions designed to ensure that foreigners would not own local newspapers. Section 10 of NPPA created two categories of shares for newspaper companies publishing in Singapore which were required to go public: ordinary shares and management shares. In addition, all directors in newspaper companies were required to be Singapore citizens. In 1977, an amendment was passed, and no person could own more than three per cent of ordinary shares. Furthermore, section 13 of the NPPA provides that a Minister may approve an application to be or continue to be a 12 per cent controller or substantial shareholder, if 'satisfied' that the person is a 'fit and proper person', that the newspaper company, having regard to the applicant's 'likely influence', will continue to conduct business prudently and where it serves the national interest. These measures are designed to prevent the newspapers from being controlled by one person or a small group of persons. What do you think about these measures? Do they function against the ideal of 'free market of ideas' or, on the contrary, have they been prescribed to cure malfunctions of the market?

C. Sedition and Hate Speech

If the expression of particular ideas or information has the potential to cause harm to the government, society in general, or particular racial or religious groups, the state may have legitimate interests in restricting such expression. The protection of harmonious relationships between various social groups or the integrity of state institutions

---

[47] Ibid.

is a typical and recognised restriction on free speech. For example, Article 15 of the Sri Lanka Constitution prescribes that free speech should be subject to laws enacted in the interests of racial and religious harmony and which prohibit incitement to an offence.[48] In Nepal, Article 12(3)(1) of the Constitution emphatically states that freedom of expression may not undermine the sovereignty and integrity of the state, jeopardise harmonious relations among diverse groups of people or incite offences.[49] Thus, expressions that are seditious or instigate disharmony or discrimination against a group may be excluded from constitutional protection in many Asian jurisdictions.

At the same time, however, a line must be drawn between impermissible speech that causes real social and political harms, and permissible expressions of critical views or unpleasant remarks. How serious must social and political harm be before restriction of speech is justified? How impending must the harm be before action is taken? Should the speaker's intentions be taken into consideration? Can the legislature and courts fashion a clear, coherent standard that reasonably distinguishes between permissible and impermissible expressions?

In the context of sedition, a state undoubtedly has the legitimacy to outlaw acts against its own existence, including words that threaten or cause insurrection against the constitutional order, imperilling state survivability through incitements to disorder and violence. Yet seditious acts and seditious words are significantly different. Words that incite imminent violence and threaten the existence of state and government must be distinguished from words that are merely critical of the state and government. For example, the US Supreme Court developed 'a clear and present danger test' to determine if words used in such circumstances would bring about the substantive evils that Congress had a right to prevent under the 1919 Espionage Act.[50] The tests later elaborated by the courts provided that the Government could prohibit unlawful words directed to inciting or producing imminent lawless action.[51] Similar standards have also been developed in other jurisdictions.[52]

In Asia, most states have criminal provisions punishing sedition, including seditious words that incite seditious acts. The processes of democratisation in certain states have brought about the liberalisation of such laws or the narrow construction of the elements of the offence. For example, in Taiwan, the old Article 100 of the Criminal Code – which punished any person intending to destroy the state or overthrow the Government – had long been used to criminalise political dissidents who published or disseminated words critical of the state and Government. In 1992, after many serious

---

[48] Art 15(2) of the Constitution of Sri Lanka states: 'The exercise and operation of the fundamental right declared and recognized by Article 14(1)(a) shall be subject to such restrictions as may be prescribed by law in the interests of racial and religious harmony or in relation to parliamentary privilege, contempt of court, defamation or incitement to an offence.'

[49] Art 12(3)(1) of the Constitution of Nepal stipulates that 'nothing in sub-clause (a) shall be deemed to prevent the making of laws to impose reasonable restrictions on any act which may undermine the sovereignty and integrity of Nepal, or which may jeopardize the harmonious relations subsisting among the peoples of various castes, tribes, religion or communities, or on any act of defamation, contempt of court or incitement to an offence; or on any act which may be contrary to decent public behaviour or morality'.

[50] *Schenck v United States* 249 US 47 (1919).

[51] *Brandenburg v Ohio* 395 US 444 (1969), 447–48.

[52] N Dorsen, M Rosenfeld, A Sajó and S Baer, *Comparative Constitutionalism: Cases and Materials* (St Paul, Minn: West, 2010) 863–64. Eg, in *Ceylan v Turkey* App No 23556/94 (ECtHR, 8 Jul 1999), the European Court of Human Rights found a criminal provision punishing speeches inciting lawless actions to be in violation of the free speech guarantee.

protests, this law was altered to criminalise only the actions of persons who by violence or threats committed an overt act with intent to destroy the state and Government.

It is important to note, however, that in some Southeast Asian jurisdictions the law of sedition has extended beyond protecting the state's or government's existence to encompass a capacious reading of 'public order' to include the maintenance of racial and religious harmony, to preserve the social fabric. Under section 3 of the Singapore Sedition Act, a 'seditious tendency' includes words which 'promote feelings of ill-will and hostility between different races or classes of the population of Singapore', which may be punished under section 4(1) with a fine and imprisonment not exceeding five years. A similar provision is to be found in the Malaysian Sedition Act.[53] This broad interpretation of 'sedition' has been criticised.[54]

In other jurisdictions, seditious utterances which damage racial and religious harmony may be treated not as seditious speech but speech designed to incite hatred towards religious or racial groups, or 'hate speech'. 'Hate speech' legislation is designed to address speech which 'wounds' or 'offends' defined groups of people, which may vary across jurisdictions. This poses a substantive restriction to free speech, which is qualified by reference to public order considerations. For example, Sections 298 and 298A of the Penal Code in Singapore punish offensive expressions wounding religious or racial feelings.[55] Such provisions are not unique to Asia. To some extent, such a restrictive attitude towards hate speech is sanctioned by international human rights conventions. Article 20(2) of the ICCPR allows Member States to prohibit by law 'any advocacy of national, racial or religious hatred that constitutes incitement to discrimination, hostility or violence'. Laws on hate speech have a chilling effect and where applied over-zealously, curtail diversity of viewpoint.[56] The debate over the constitutionality of hate speech

---

[53] Art 4(1) of the Sedition Act 1948 of Malaysia provides: '(1) Any person who – (a) does or attempts to do, or makes any preparation to do, or conspires with any person to do, any act which has or which would, if done, have a seditious tendency; (b) utters any seditious words; (c) prints, publishes, sells, offers for sale, distributes or reproduces any seditious publication; or (d) imports any seditious publication, shall be guilty of an offence and shall, on conviction, be liable for a first offence to a fine not exceeding five thousand ringgit or to imprisonment for a term not exceeding three years or to both, and, for a subsequent offence, to imprisonment for a term not exceeding five years; and any seditious publication found in the possession of the person or used in evidence at his trial shall be forfeited and may be destroyed or otherwise disposed of as the court directs.'

[54] See Thio Li-ann, *A Treatise on Singapore Constitutional Law* (Singapore: Academy Publishing, 2012) at 774–91; and Tan Yock Lin, 'Sedition and its New Clothes in Singapore' [2011] *Singapore Journal of Legal Studies* 212.

[55] Sec 298 provides: 'Whoever, with deliberate intention of wounding the religious or racial feelings of any person, utters any word or makes any sound in the hearing of that person, or makes any gesture in the sight of that person, or places any object in the sight of that person, or causes any matter however represented to be seen or heard by that person, shall be punished with imprisonment for a term which may extend to 3 years, or with fine, or with both.' Sec 298A further stipulates: 'Whoever – (a) by words, either spoken or written, or by signs or by visible representations or otherwise, knowingly promotes or attempts to promote, on grounds of religion or race, disharmony or feelings of enmity, hatred or ill-will between different religious or racial groups; or (b) commits any act which he knows is prejudicial to the maintenance of harmony between different religious or racial groups and which disturbs or is likely to disturb the public tranquility, shall be punished with imprisonment for a term which may extend to 3 years, or with fine, or with both.' Recently, an assistant director at National Trade Union Congress in Singapore was released from her job because she posted a slanderous rant about Malay wedding on her Facebook page. These words immediately spread and criticisms flared up. Legal counsel pointed out that she is likely to be investigated under Sections 298 or 298A. See L Lim, 'Amy Cheong "could face charges" for online rant', *Straits Times*, 11 October 2012, available at <http://www.straitstimes.com/breaking-news/singapore/story/amy-cheong-could-face-charges-online-rant-20121011> (accessed 11 October 2012).

[56] See J Waldron, *The Harm in Hate Speech* (Cambridge, Mass: Harvard University Press, 2012).

restrictions is discussed in the following readings from Korea, Malaysia, Singapore and India.

Praising and Encouraging under National Security Act Case
89Hun-Ka113, 2 Apr 1990 (Constitutional Court, South Korea)

Facts

Article 7(1) of the National Security Act of South Korea provided that

> any person who praises, encourages, sympathizes with, or benefits through other means operation, an anti-state organization, its members, or any person under its direction shall be punished by imprisonment for up to seven years.

Article 7(5) of the Act further stipulated that

> any person who, for the purpose of performing the acts mentioned in (1), (2), (3) or (4) of this section, produces, imports, duplicates, possesses, transports, distributes, sells or acquires a document, a drawing or any other expressive article shall be punished by a penalty prescribed in each subsection respectively.

The petitioners were supporters of an anti-state organization and were prosecuted and tried at the Choongmoo Branch of the Masan Local Court for possessing and distributing materials containing anti-government expressions. During the trial, they filed a motion for the constitutional review of the statute and the presiding judge granted the motion.

Held

The expressions such as 'member', 'activities', 'sympathizes with', or 'benefits' used in the challenged provisions are too vague and do not permit a reasonable standard for ordinary people with good sense to visualize the covered types of conduct. They are also overbroad to determine the contents and boundaries of their definitions. Interpreted literally, they will merely intimidate and suppress freedom of expression without upholding any public interest in national security. Furthermore, they permit the law enforcement agencies to arbitrarily enforce the law, infringing freedom of speech, freedom of press, and freedom of science and arts, and ultimately violating the principle of rule of law and the principle of statutory punishment. In addition, the broadness of those expressions can potentially permit a punishment of a pursuit of reunification policy pursuant to the basic order of free democracy or a promotion of the national brotherhood. This result is not consistent with the preamble to the Constitution calling for unity of the Korean race through justice, humanity, and national brotherhood pursuant to the mandate of peaceful unification, and the Article 4 [of the South Korea Constitution] directing us toward peaceful reunification [which reads: 'The Republic of Korea shall seek unification and shall formulate and carry out a policy of peaceful unification based on the principles of freedom and democracy.'].

This multiplicity, however, does not justify total invalidation of the entire provision. Pursuant to a general constitutional principle, the terms in a legal provision permitting multiple definitions or multiple interpretations within the bounds of their literal meanings should be interpreted to make the provision consistent with the Constitution and to avoid unconstitutional interpretation of these terms, giving life to its constitutional and positive aspects . . .

Public Prosecutor v Oh Keng Seng
[1977] 2 MLJ 206 (Federal Court, Malaysia)

Facts

The respondent was charged with uttering seditious words in a speech, but was acquitted without being called for his defence. The Public Prosecutor appealed.

Wan Suleiman FJ

At the trial the prosecution contended that many passages in the speech were seditious, but here before us they maintained that only two passages were seditious, namely the passage dealing with the incidents of 13 May 1969, and the passage dealing with the Army.

The first passage reads as follows:

> Our condition made the ALLIANCE to be in great fear. Therefore they brought about the 13 May incidents. In the 13 MAY incidents, we all know who created it. We, the DAP challenged the Government, asking it to set up a Commission of Inquiry to investigate into 13 MAY who caused it. Many people died in 13 May who was responsible for it? This was brought about by some racialists. Some who feared to lose his position, he who feared of not becoming the Mentri Besar, he who feared of not becoming State Assemblyman, he who feared of not becoming Member of Parliament. Therefore he brought about a 13 May incidents. I shall give an example. Just like in a football tournament or a basketball tournament, why do they fight suddenly in the process of play? Who created it? Was it created by the winning side? No, it was certainly created by the losers. So, the same conditions apply in politics. 13 May was created by those losers. Why was the government afraid? Why did it not want a Commission of Inquiry to investigate into the truth? Why did the MCA have no courage to stand out and explain to the people? Therefore, the MCA and the UMNO, they are indulging in racialism, in dirty politics. They want to intimidate, using bloodshed to intimidate the people.

The learned judge holds that this was not seditious. He said at page 112 of the appeal record, 'The accused referred to the 13 May incidents and said that the government had failed to set up a Commission of Inquiry to investigate the causes of the incidents. The DAP had asked for an inquiry and he criticised the MCA for not doing so. The accused said further that the incidents were brought about by racialists who were afraid of losing their positions in the government. This statement by the accused and his reference to 13 May might be somewhat sensitive but it does not come within the definition of seditious tendency under the Sedition Act.'

The second passage reads as follows:

> Army, in the army, 100% are their people. This is unfair. We want to speak, to speak it out. MALAYSIA wants to be multi-racial. We, the DAP, proposes that MALAYSIA wants a multi-racial army, not of one race. MCA professes to represent the Chinese, do they dare to talk? What about the condition in the army? Very dangerous, isn't it? The power of the army is 'not in your hands, it is really dangerous. Dares the MCA speak? Dares not speak. I dare to speak. Arrest, so be it! Still want to arrest, then let him arrest! But if this problem is not brought forth, it is really dangerous. UMNO says, 'Economy is in the hands of the Chinese.' Therefore, if there is political strength, UMNO says, 'With political power and without economic strength, very dangerous.' It says, 'One day, the Malays will be chased out by other people.' It utilises such saying to attract the

Malays to support them. So they now have political strength, have economic strength. In fact, the economic strength is not in the hands of the Chinese. Of 100 Chinese, only one is rich, 99 others are poor Chinese. It said that the economy is in the hands of the Chinese. This is telling lie. To divert the people's line of vision, to divert the Malays' line of vision, so that they can always remain in that post. However, the MCA dares not deny, the MCA dares not say that the political strength is not in the hands of the Chinese. If the MCA is holding a mass rally over here tomorrow, I will ask it to explain on these problems. Why can't they speak? Why don't they dare to speak? These are very important problems. Economy, political, military. MAO Tse-Tung also says, 'Power, political power grows out of gun barrels.' Without the army, what strength you can talk about. With money, without strength, it is useless. Hence this is very important.

The learned judge held that this was not seditious either. He said at pages 112 and 113:

> . . . the accused referred to the army. He said that the army consists of their people which in the context of the speech refers clearly to one race. The accused says that Malaysia being a multi-racial country its army should not consist of one race but should be multi-racial. I must say that this particular passage taken into isolation might well come near to having a seditious tendency for it might be inferred that the government is partial to only one race in recruiting people into the armed forces. However, this passage has to be read together with the whole speech and in my view it cannot be said that taking the speech as a whole the accused had charged the government with such gross partiality as to have a tendency to raise discontent or disaffection amongst the subjects of the country. I agreed with Mr Yeap Ghim Guan that when the accused said that the army was 100% their people he was speaking figuratively. So too when he quoted Mao Tse-Tung the accused was trying to impress his audience that he was well acquainted with the works of the Chinese leader.

Now the question before us is whether or not the passages in question were seditious. Sedition is dealt with in the Sedition Act 1948 (Revised – 1969) Act 15. By s 2 a speech is seditious if it has a seditious tendency. Seditious tendency is defined by s 3(1) which contains paragraphs (a) to (f) [which read: A 'seditious tendency' is a tendency – (a) to bring into hatred or contempt or to excite disaffection against any Ruler or against any Government; (b) to excite the subjects of any Ruler or the inhabitants of any territory governed by any Government to attempt to procure in the territory of the Ruler or governed by the Government, the alteration, otherwise than by lawful means, of any matter as by law established; (c) to bring into hatred or contempt or to excite disaffection against the administration of justice in Malaysia or in any State; (d) to raise discontent or disaffection amongst the subjects of the Yang di-Pertuan Agong or of the Ruler of any State or amongst the inhabitants of Malaysia or of any State; (e) to promote feelings of ill will and hostility between different races or classes of the population of Malaysia; or (f) to question any matter, right, status, position, privilege, sovereignty or prerogative established or protected by the provisions of Part III of the Federal Constitution or Article 152, 153 or 181 of the Federal Constitution.] We are only in partial agreement with what the learned trial judge considered to be the proper approach to the question as to whether those parts of the speech now alleged by Mr Mahalingam to be seditious are indeed so. We agree that particular words or sentences taken out of context 'may sound obnoxious or innocuous and that this might convey an altogether wrong impression'. However to say that to determine whether particular passages are seditious the speech in which such words are uttered should be read as a whole is, with respect going too far if by that is meant that in a long speech two passages (or for that matter four) cannot be seditious if numerous other topics discussed are not seditious.

At most one could say that the speech as a whole would assist in giving the court a proper perspective of, and so assist it to decide whether the passages giving offence were mere episodes of over exuberance in a speech coming fairly under the exceptions envisaged in s 3(2) [which defined act, speech, words, publication or other thing shall be deemed to have seditious tendency by several reasons] or something more than that. Again whilst we would with respect agree that the prosecution is not obliged to prove that anything said in the speech was true or false, evidence to show that the allegations made were false whether will-fully or inadvertently so, would increase the likelihood that such utterances would have a seditious tendency. For instance to suggest falsely that the army is composed 100% of one ethnic group, because of Government policy to favour such ethnic group to ensure its polit-ical hegemony can be expected to bring into hatred or contempt or to excite disaffection against the government – s 3(1)(a) or to promote ill-will etc between two ethnic groups – the Malays and the Chinese – s 3(1)(c). That is where the uncontradicted evidence of Col Yaacob . . . on the racial make-up of the army, and on recruiting policy is highly relevant. We agree that to determine whether the speaker had exceeded the bounds of free speech here, the contemporary situation has to be taken into account. If there is a state of unrest, of strained relations between the different ethnic groups in this country, a tendency to bring about one of the undesirable results set out in s 3(1)(a) to (c) would be more likely than if the situation is such that peace and harmony have ruled for decades. But whether the set-ting of the utterances complained of is a local by-election or a general election is with respect not a relevant matter. Here there was a crowd of a few hundred, but I should think that words having a tendency to bring about hatred or contempt etc. of any Ruler or against any Government, or to promote feelings of ill-will and hostility among the various ethnic groups etc can be uttered before a handful of persons and yet be seditious under our law. Before us Inche Mahalingam abandoned that part of his appeal on two of the passages alleged to be seditious at the trial – those dealing with education and land alienation. Be that as it may, it should be noted that the same 4 matters were raised in the speech which lead to *Fan Few Teng* 1 MLJ 176; [1975] 2 MLJ 235 FC prosecution and conviction. Indeed, it seems to us that respondent had in his speech dealt with these very matters at greater length and with greater vehemence. The only factor which can be said to be in respondent's favour was that it was made on behalf of a Malay candidate. However the race of the can-didate espoused seems to us to have been completely forgotten in a speech meant for a Chinese audience the tenor of which was to belabour the perennial racial issues – Chinese versus Malay – and to make extravagant allegations of gross partiality of a Government towards the latter ethnic group to the detriment of the former, with such vituperation and in such exaggerated terms as to make the promotion of feelings of ill-will and hostility between the two ethnic groups (and between the Malays and other minority groups) an unavoidable tendency. The constant repetition of these issues invested them with distinctive communal connotations synonymous with doing away with the special privileges of the Malays permitted by the Constitution.

From his speech it is clear that the respondent knew that the police were present and that his speech was being taped. Whilst some may be expected to be cautious in their utterances under such circumstances, it seems to us that the respondent was stirred by such knowledge into acts of oral bravado. Whatever his intention might have been respondent has in our view gone beyond the limit of freedom of speech, that both passages are not legitimate criticism of the sort permissible under s 3(2) of the Act, but utterances clearly having a seditious tendency of the sort envisaged in both s 3(1)(a) and 3(1)(c). We would therefore allow the appeal, set aside the order of acquittal and in its place direct that the respondent be called upon to make his defence.

Appeal allowed.

Public Prosecutor v Koh Song Huat Benjamin
[2005] SGDC 272 (District Court, Singapore)

Facts

Benjamin Koh Song Huat was convicted of two charges under section 4(1)(a) of the Sedition Act. Among other things, it was alleged that by posting anti-Malay and anti-Muslim remarks on his web log, Koh was promoting feelings of ill-will and hostility between different races and classes of population in Singapore. Another accused, Lim Yew Nicholas, was convicted of the same charge due to his posting of anti-Muslim remarks on a general discussion forum.

Senior District Judge Richard Magnus

While an offence under section 4(1)(a) [of the] Sedition Act is rare, it is necessary for this Court to make it clear that such an offence will be met, upon conviction, with a sentence of general deterrence. 'Seditious tendency' is defined in section 3 of the Sedition Act. For our present purposes, section 3(1)(e) is relevant:

Seditious Tendency

3. – (1) A seditious tendency is a tendency –

> (a) to bring into hatred or contempt or to excite disaffection against the Government;
>
> (b) to excite the citizens of Singapore or the residents in Singapore to attempt to procure in Singapore, the alteration, otherwise than by lawful means, of any matter as by law established;
>
> (c) to bring into hatred or contempt or to excite disaffection against the administration of justice in Singapore;
>
> (d) to raise discontent or disaffection amongst the citizens of Singapore or the residents in Singapore;
>
> (e) to promote feelings of ill-will and hostility between different races or classes of the population of Singapore.

The doing of an act which has a seditious tendency to promote feelings of ill-will and hostility between different races or classes of the population in Singapore, which is the section 4(1)(a) offence, is serious. Racial and religious hostility feeds on itself. This sentencing approach of general deterrence is because of three main reasons: the section 4(1)(a) offence is *mala per se*; the especial sensitivity of racial and religious issues in our multi-cultural society, particularly given our history of the Maria Hertogh incident in the 1950s and the July and September 1964 race riots; and the current domestic and international security climate. The Court will therefore be generally inclined towards a custodial sentence for such an offence.

Young Singaporeans, like the accused persons before this Court, may have short memories that race and religion are sensitive issues. They must realize that callous and reckless remarks on racial or religious subjects have the potential to cause social disorder, in whatever medium or forum they are expressed. In this case, it is the medium of the Internet and with it, its ubiquitous reach . . . But one cannot hide behind the anonymity of cyberspace, as each the accused has done, to pen diatribes against another race or religion.

. . . The right of one person's freedom of expression must always be balanced by the right of another's freedom from offence, and tampered by wider public interest considerations. It is only appropriate social behaviour, independent of any legal duty, of every Singapore citizen and resident to respect the other races in view of our multi-racial society. . . . A fortiori, the Sedition Act statutorily delineates this redline on the ground in the subject at hand. Otherwise, the resultant harm is not only to one racial group but to the very fabric of our society.

The two accused persons have crossed the red line by wantonly breaching these ground rules. . . .

The Court however notes that the remarks by Benjamin Koh posted on his blog were particularly vile, to use the words of the Learned DPPs [Directors of Public Prosecution]. Paragraph 10 of the Learned DPPs' submission on sentence says:

> The accused's remarks on his blog at www.upsaid.com were highly inflammatory and insulting. He parodied the halal logo and placed it next to a pig's head, spewed vulgarities at the Muslim Malay community, derided and mocked their customs and beliefs and profaned their religion. He even compared their religion to Satanism.

His remarks provoked a widespread and virulent response. They sparked off more than 200 comments, some of which involved the slinging of racial slurs at Chinese and Malays. This is an aggravating factor. In the case of Nicholas Lim, the Learned DPPs say that his comments are less serious than those by Benjamin Koh. This is borne out by a comparison of the offending materials.

The Court considers the relative offensiveness of the materials against the established sentencing principle that the moral culpability of the offender is always an important factor. As HLA Hart states in Hart HLA, *Law, Liberty, and Morality* (London: Oxford University Press, 1963) at page 37:

> . . . when the question of the quantum for such conduct is raised, we should [defer] to principles which make relative moral wickedness of different offenders a partial determinant of the severity of punishment.

The quantum of sentence on each of the accused persons, therefore, varies according to their level of blameworthiness . . .

These sentences turn on the peculiar facts of the cases before the Court. The Court will not hesitate to impose appropriate salutary and stiffer sentences in future cases.

Virendra v The State of Punjab
[1957] AIR 896 (Supreme Court, India)

Facts

The *Daily Pratap* was a daily newspaper printed in Urdu and published simultaneously in Jullundur and New Delhi. *Vir Arjun* was a Hindi daily newspaper that was published in the same places as the *Daily Pratap*. On 30 May 1957, a movement called 'Save Hindi Agitation' was started by Hindi Raksha Samiti. The sponsor of the 'Save Hindi Agitation' claimed that it had the support of almost all segments of Hindus in the State. The petitioners, who were the editors, printers and publishers of *Pratap* and *Vir Arjun*, supported the agitation. On 13 July 1957, a notification under section 2(1)(a) of the Punjab Special Powers Act was issued against Virendra (one of the petitioners), who was the editor, printer and publisher of the *Daily Pratap*. Virendra was prohibited from printing and publishing any material relating to the 'Save Hindi Agitation' for two months. On 14 July 1957, two other notifications under section 3 of the Act were issued against K Narendra (the other petitioner). The petitioners argued that sections 2 and 3 of the Act respectively infringed the constitutional freedom of speech.

Sudhi Ranjan Das CJ

In these two petitions under Art 32 of the Constitution of India the petitioners call in question the validity of the Punjab Special Powers (Press) Act, 1956 (being Act No 38 of 1956), hereinafter referred to as 'the impugned Act,' and pray for an appropriate writ or order directing the respondents to withdraw the Notifications issued by them on the two petitioners as the editors, printers and publishers of two newspapers, *Pratap* and *Vir Arjun* . . .

. . . The provisions of the impugned Act, in so far as they are material, may now be referred to. Section 2(1)(a) runs as follows:

> 2(1) The State Government or any authority so authorised in this behalf if satisfied that such action is necessary for the purpose of preventing or combating any activity prejudicial to the maintenance of communal harmony affecting or likely to affect public order, may, by order in writing addressed to a printer publisher or editor – (a) prohibit the printing or publication in any document or any class of documents of any matter relating to a particular subject or class of subjects for a specified period or in a particular issue or issues of a newspaper or periodical; Provided that no such order shall remain in force for more than two months from the making thereof; Provided further that the person against whom the order has been made may within ten days of the passing of this order make a representation to the State Government which may on consideration thereof modify, confirm or rescind the order;

Section 2(1)(b) authorises the State Government or any authority so authorised in this behalf to require that any matter covering not more than two columns be published in any particular issue or issues of a newspaper or periodical on payment of adequate remuneration and to specify the period (not exceeding one week) during which and the manner in which such publication shall take place. Clause (c) of s 2(1) authorises the State Government or the delegated authority to impose pre-censorship. Sub-section (2) of s 2 enables the State Government or the authority issuing the order in the event of any disobedience of an order made under s 2 to order the seizure of all copies of any publication and of the printing press or other instrument or apparatus used in the publication. Section 3(1) runs as follows: 'The State Government or any authority authorised by it in this behalf, if satisfied that such action is necessary for the purpose of preventing or combating any activity prejudical to the maintenance of communal harmony affecting or likely to affect public order, may, by notification, prohibit the bringing into Punjab of any newspaper, periodical, leaflet or other publication.' Sub-section (2) of s 3 gives power to the State Government or the authority issuing the order, in the event of any disobedience of an order made under s 3, to order the seizure of all copies of any newspaper, periodical, leaflet or other publication concerned. Section 4 provides punishment for the contravention of any of the provisions of the Act [either by imprisonment] which may extend to one year or with [a] fine up to one thousand rupees or with both. . . .

. . . There is and can be no dispute that the right to freedom of speech and expression carries with it the right to propagate and circulate one's views and opinions subject to reasonable restrictions. The point to be kept in view is that the several rights of freedom guaranteed to the citizens by Art 19(1) of the Indian Constitution [which protects certain rights regarding freedom of speech] are exercisable by them throughout and in all parts of the territory of India. The Notifications under s 2(1)(a) prohibiting the printing and publishing of any article, report, news item, letter or any other material of any character whatsoever relating to or connected with 'Save Hindi Agitation' or those under s 3(1) imposing a ban against the entry and the circulation of the said papers published from New Delhi in the State of Punjab do not obviously take away the entire right, for the petitioners are yet at liberty to print and publish all other matters and are free to circulate the papers in all other parts of the territory of India. The restrictions, so far as they extend, are certainly complete but whether they amount to a total prohibition of the exercise of the fundamental rights must be judged by reference to the ambit of the rights and, so judged, there can be no question that the entire rights under Arts 19(1)(a) and 19(1)(g) have not been completely taken away, but restrictions have been imposed upon the exercise of those rights with reference to the publication of only articles etc relating to a particular topic and with reference to the circulation of the papers only in a particular territory and, therefore, it is not right to say that these sections have imposed a total prohibition upon the exercise of those fundamental rights. . . .

. . . The powerful influence of the newspapers, for good or evil, on the minds of the readers, the wide sweep of their reach, the modern facilities for their swift circulation to territories, distant and near, must all enter into the judicial verdict and the reasonableness of the restrictions imposed upon the Press has to be tested against this background. It is certainly a serious encroachment on the valuable and cherished right to freedom of speech and expression if a newspaper is prevented from publishing its own views or the views of its correspondent relating to or concerning what may be the burning topic of the day. Our social interest ordinarily demands the free propagation and interchange of views but circumstances may arise when the social interest in public order may require a reasonable subordination of the social interest in free speech and expression to the needs of our social interest in public order. Our Constitution recognises this necessity and has attempted to strike a balance between the two social interests. It permits the imposition of reasonable restrictions on the freedom of speech and expression in the interest of public order and on the freedom of carrying on trade or business in the interest of the general public. Therefore, the crucial question must always be: Are the restrictions imposed on the exercise of the rights under Arts 19(1)(a) and 19(1)(g) reasonable in view of all the surrounding circumstances? In other words are the restrictions reasonably necessary in the interest of public order under Art 19(2) or in the interest of the general public under Art 19(6)? It is conceded that a serious tension had arisen between the Hindus and the Akalis over the question of the partition of the State on linguistic and communal [bases]. The people were divided into two warring groups, one supporting the agitation and the other opposing it. The agitation and the counter agitation were being carried on in the Press and from the platforms. Quite conceivably this agitation might at any time assume a nasty communal turn and flare up into a communal frenzy and factious fight disturbing the public order of the State which is on the border of a foreign State and where consequently the public order and tranquility were and are essential in the interest of the safety of the State. It was for preserving the safety of the State and for maintaining the public order that the Legislature enacted this impugned Statute. Legislature had to ask itself the question, who will be the appropriate authority to determine at any given point of time as to whether the prevailing circumstances require some restriction to be placed on the right to freedom of speech and expression and the right to carry on any occupation, trade or business and to what extent? The answer was obvious, namely, that as the State Government was charged with the preservation of law and order in the State, as it alone was in possession of all material facts it would be the [best] authority to investigate the circumstances and assess the urgency of the situation that might arise and to make up its mind whether any and, if so, what anticipatory action must be taken for the prevention of the threatened or anticipated breach of the peace. The court is wholly unsuited to gauge the seriousness of the situation, for it cannot be in possession of materials which are available only to the executive Government. Therefore, the determination of the time when and the extent to which restrictions should be imposed on the Press must of necessity be left to the judgment and discretion of the State Government and that is exactly what the Legislature did by passing the statute. . . .

The observations hereinbefore made as to the safeguards set forth in the provisions of s 2(1)(a) and (b) cannot, however, apply to the provisions of s 3. Although the exercise of the powers under s 3(1) is subject to the same condition as to the satisfaction of the State Government or its delegate as is mentioned in s 2(1)(a), there is, however, no time limit for the operation of an order made under this section nor is there any provision made for any representation being made to the State Government. The absence of these safeguards in s 3 clearly makes its provisions unreasonable and the learned Solicitor-General obviously felt some difficulty in supporting the validity of this section. It is surprising how in the same statute the two sections came to be worded differently.

For reasons stated above petition No 95 of 1957 (*Virendra v The State of Punjab*) which impugns the Notifications issued under s 2(1)(a) must be dismissed and petition No 96 of 1957 (*K. Narendra v The State of Punjab*) which challenges s 3 must be allowed. In the circumstances of these cases we make no order as to the costs of these applications.

Petition No 95 of 1957 dismissed.
Petition No 96 of 1957 allowed.

Notes and Questions

1. In the *Praising and Encouraging under National Security Act Case*, how did the South Korea Constitutional Court construe the National Security Act to exclude the possibility of punishing words that are merely critical of the state and Government? Did this method of interpretation distort the legislative intent?

2. How did the courts in Malaysia and Singapore interpret 'words which promote feelings of ill-will and hostility between different races' as having 'seditious tendencies'? Does it matter in what contexts these words are uttered? Compare the diverse contexts of race and ethnicity in Malaysia, Singapore and India. Note that in *Virendra v The State of Punjab*, the Supreme Court of India held that it was impermissible for the statutory regime not to have time limit in the restraining order on the impugned publication. Should there be any time consideration in the maintenance of racial harmony? Why?

3. The Canadian Supreme Court tackled the constitutionality of hate speech laws in *R v Keegstra*.[57] A high school teacher was charged with unlawfully advocating hatred against a specific group by making anti-Semitic statements in the classroom. He described Jews as 'treacherous', 'subversive', 'sadistic', 'money-loving', 'power hungry' and 'child killers.' He was convicted under section 319(2) of the Criminal Code, which provided that

   > everyone who, by communicating statements, other than in private conversation, willfully promotes hatred against any identifiable group is guilty of (*a*) an indictable offence and is liable to imprisonment for a term not exceeding two years; or (*b*) an offence punishable on summary conviction.

   The Court upheld this provision by applying the principle of proportionality:

---

[57] *R v Keegstra* [1990] 3 SCR 697.

[I]t would be impossible to deny that Parliament's objective in enacting s 319(2) is of the utmost importance. Parliament has recognized the substantial harm that can flow from hate propaganda, and in trying to prevent the pain suffered by target group members and to reduce racial, ethnic and religious tension in Canada has decided to suppress the willful promotion of hatred against identifiable groups . . .

The criminal nature of the impugned provision, involving the associated risks of prejudice through prosecution, conviction and the imposition of up to two years imprisonment, indicates that the means embodied in hate propaganda legislation should be carefully tailored so as to minimize impairment of the freedom of expression. It therefore must be shown that s 319(2) is a measured and appropriate response to the phenomenon of hate propaganda, and that it does not overly circumscribe the s 2(*b*) guarantee [of free speech] . . .

. . . [I]n light of the great importance of Parliament's objective and the discounted value of the expression at issue I find that the terms of s 319(2) create a narrowly confined offence which suffers from neither overbreadth nor vagueness. This interpretation stems largely from . . . the provision possesses a stringent *mens rea* requirement, necessitating either an intent to promote hatred or knowledge of the substantial certainty of such, and is also strongly supported by the conclusion that the meaning of the word 'hatred' is restricted to the most severe and deeply felt form of opprobrium. Additionally, however, the conclusion that s 319(2) represents a minimal impairment of the freedom of expression gains credence through the exclusion of private conversation from its scope . . .[58]

4. In *R v Keegstra*, the Canadian Supreme Court referred to various international human rights conventions as justifications for restricting hate speech. In addition to Article 20(2) of the ICCPR, Article 4 of International Convention on the Elimination of All Forms of Racial Discrimination (CERD) was discussed. Article 4 of the CERD provides:

> States Parties condemn all propaganda and all organizations which are based on ideas or theories of superiority of one race or group of persons of one colour or ethnic origin, or which attempt to justify or promote racial hatred and discrimination in any form, and undertake to adopt immediate and positive measures designed to eradicate all incitement to, or acts of, such discrimination and, to this end, with due regard to the principles embodied in the Universal Declaration of Human Rights and the rights expressly set forth in article 5 of this Convention, inter alia: a) Shall declare [as] an offence punishable by law all dissemination of ideas based on racial superiority or hatred, incitement to racial discrimination, as well as all acts of violence or incitement to such acts against any race or group of persons of another colour or ethnic origin, and also the provision of any assistance to racist activities, including the financing thereof.

5. Aside from Canada, other jurisdictions may also restrict hate speech on similar or more narrow grounds. For example, the US Supreme Court in *Chaplinsky v New Hampshire*[59] described certain 'fighting words' as examples of low-value speech, the prevention and punishment of which would never raise any constitutional problem. According to the Court, 'such utterances are no essential part of any exposition of idea, and are of such slight social value as a step to truth that any benefit that may be derived from them is clearly outweighed by the social interest in order and morality'.

---

[58] Ibid, 758, 771, 785–86.
[59] *Chaplinsky v New Hampshire* 315 US 568 (1942), 571–72.

6.   A similar judgment was delivered by the German Federal Constitutional Court in the *Holocaust Denial Case*.[60] The Court was confronted with the dilemma of whether to prohibit a controversial speaker, who asserted that the mass extermination of Jews never took place, from participating in a meeting. The Bavarian State government permitted the meeting while restricting any promotion of the 'Auschwitz Hoax' theory. The host of the meeting, a regional association called National Democratic Party of Germany, claimed that its right to free speech was unconstitutionally restrained. The Federal Constitutional Court ruled that such prohibition was not in contradiction to the essence of free speech, stating that

> matters do not change if one considers that Germany's attitude to its national socialist past and the political consequences thereof, which were the subject of the meeting, is a question concerning the public in an important way. It is true that in this case there is a presumption in favor of free speech, but this does not apply if the utterance constitutes a formal insult or vilification, nor does it apply if the offensive utterance rests on demonstrably untrue representations of fact.
>
> Overstretching the requirements of truth as regards the factual core of the utterance in a manner incompatible with Art 5(1) of the Basic Law is not then the result of this balancing.[61]

7.   Three types of hate-speech legislation, reflective of the existing Singapore legislation aimed at protection of minorities, public order and preservation of the state, have been identified. First, hate-speech legislation that focuses on intentional racist speech. Secondly, public order-orientated legislation seeking to prohibit inter-religious or inter-racial speech that harms public tranquillity. Lastly, the law of sedition, which outlaws seditious words that jeopardise state security by causing racial or religious disharmony. Arguably, the prohibition of racially or religiously discriminatory words has a distinct legislative goal from that of sedition law, such that 'sedition' should be reserved for matters relating to the subversion of the constitutional order. See JLC Neo, 'Seditious in Singapore! Free speech and the Offence of Promoting Ill-will and Hostility Between Different Racial Groups' (2011) *Singapore Journal of Legal Studies* 366 at 366–70.

8.   Blasphemy law relates to the suppression of speech which challenges religious orthodoxy and which may incidentally spark religious disharmony. This places a substantive limit on free speech and inhibits the free marketplace of ideas, as it is predicated on the belief that truth has been revealed or discovered and is not to be questioned. Chapter nine deals more extensively with this topic.

D. Lèse Majesté, Contempt of Court and Symbolic Speech

The government has a legitimate interest in defending the integrity and authority of state institutions. Hence, speech that seriously threatens or undermines institutional authority may be restricted. However, these restrictions may chill speech critical of the

---

[60]   *Holocaust Denial Case* [1994] 90 BVerfGE 241 (Federal Constitutional Court, Germany).
[61]   *Holocaust Denial Case* [1994] 90 BVerfGE 241, para 51 (Federal Constitutional Court, Germany) (in German). For English translation, see DP Kommers, *The Constitutional Jurisprudence of the Federal Republic of Germany*, 2nd edn (Durham: Duke UP, 1997) 382.

government which is necessary to the effective functioning of democracy and securing the accountability of government bodies. It falls to the courts to draw a line between permissible and impermissible speech that criticises government institutions and which may be offensive and threatens their integrity. This section discusses the offences of lèse majesté and contempt of court by scandalising the judiciary, two types of speech which critically address royalty and the courts, and the implications of restricting such speech.

Aside from defending the integrity of state institutions, the government may have legitimate interests in protecting national symbols, such as national flags, statues or portraits of national figures. It is a criminal offence in many states physically to abuse or deface national symbols. However, whether criminal punishment should extend to symbolic speech or expressive conduct undertaken to express critical views of the state and government is a much-debated constitutional issue. In *Texas v Johnson*,[62] a flag-burning case, the US Supreme Court ruled that the symbolic, communicative element in such conduct should be constitutionally protected. In contrast, the German Constitutional Court upheld a law which makes it a crime to revile or damage the German flag, which captures expressive conduct that physically abused national symbols, justified on the basis of appealing to citizens' sense of 'civic responsibility'.[63] A Hong Kong Court of Final Appeal flag-burning case is discussed below.

i. Lèse Majesté

Lèse majesté, literally meaning 'injured majesty', is a crime against the dignity of a reigning sovereign or against the state. As recently as in the 2000s, it has applied in some European states, the Middle East, Asia and elsewhere.[64] In Asia, quite a number of states – Bhutan, Brunei, Cambodia, Japan, Malaysia and Thailand – maintain a monarchical system. For example, Section 112 of the Thai Penal Code provides: 'Whoever, defames, insults or threatens the King, the Queen, the Heir-apparent or the Regent, shall be punished with imprisonment of three to fifteen years.' These laws have attracted criticism for being anachronistic and harsh.[65] However the prosecution of lèse majesté has increased in recent years: 36 cases in 2010, compared to 18 in 2005 and just one in 2000.[66]

In a non-monarchical system, lèse majesté may apply to offences in relation to the head of state. For example, in Indonesia, the criminal law punishes intentional defamation of the President or Vice-President. The Constitutional Court of Indonesia, however, found such a criminal provision contrary to the Constitution, as it 'may be used to obstruct the democratic processes' and 'decrease the freedom to express ideas and opinions'.

---

[62] *Texas v Johnson* 491 US 397 (1989).
[63] *Flag Desecration Case* (1990) 81 BVerfGE 278.
[64] See   <http://www.bangkokpost.com/opinion/opinion/334000/somyot-case-stirs-fiery-emotional-talk-on-lese-majeste-enforcement>. In Europe, lèse majesté is not aggressively enforced and sentence is limited to five years.
[65] 'An inconvenient death', *The Economist*, 12 May 2012.
[66] See <http://sg.news.yahoo.com/thailands-lese-majeste-laws-under-scrutiny-105212675.html>.

Dr Eggi Sudjana, SH, MSi, Pandapotan Lubis
013-022/PUU-IV/2006 [2006] IDCC 26, 6 Dec 2006
(Constitutional Court, Indonesia)

Facts

The case involved two petitioners. One of the petitioners, Dr Eggi Sudjana, visited the office of the Commission for Corruption Eradication (KPK) on Tuesday, 3 January 2006, expecting to meet the Chairperson of the KPK to clarify matters concerning rumours about luxurious gifts to the President's family. He was later prosecuted and tried by the Central Jakarta District Court for intentional defamation of the President. The petitioner then filed a petition for judicial review of Articles 134 and 136 *bis* of the Criminal Code, which criminalised intentional defamation of the President or Vice-President and broadly defined the crime of defamation, respectively. He argued that these laws violated Article 28F of the 1945 Constitution, which reads:

> Every person shall have the right to communicate and obtain information for the development of his personal life and his social environment, and shall have the right to seek, acquire, possess, keep, process and convey information by using all available channels.

On 16 May 2006, the other petitioner, Pandapotan Lubis, and other activists were arrested and charged for displaying flags, banners and posters at the Hotel Indonesia traffic circle in Jakarta, criticising the President and Vice-President and asking them to step down. He filed a petition for judicial review of Articles 134, 136 *bis* and 137 of the Criminal Code. Article 137 of the Criminal Code read as follows:

> [A]ny person who distributes, openly exhibits or puts up a writing or depiction which contains a defamation against the President or Vice President, with the intent to make the defaming contents widely known or increase the publicity thereof, shall be subject to a maximum imprisonment of one year and four months, or a maximum fine of four thousand five hundred Rupiah; In the event that the guilty person commits the crime in his profession and that, during the commission of the crime two years have not yet elapsed since that earlier conviction for a similar crime has become irrevocable, he can then be deprived from practicing that profession.

Pandapotan Lubis argued that these statutes violated his constitutional right to equality under Article 27 and his right to free speech under Article 28 of the 1945 Constitution.

Held

Considering, whereas at the time the Petitioners' petition for the substantiation of Article 134, Article 136 *bis*, and Article 137 of the Indonesian Criminal Code was submitted, the third amendment to the 1945 Constitution had been drawn up (and binding). Article 1 Paragraph (2) of the 1945 Constitution reads: 'Sovereignty is held by the people and implemented pursuant to the Constitution.' Sovereignty is held by the people and the President and/or Vice President are directly elected by the people. Therefore, they are responsible to the people. The dignity of the President and/or Vice President is entitled to be respected in protocol terms, but the two leaders elected by the people may not be granted the privileges resulting in their status and treatment as human [beings]whose dignity is substantively different from other citizens. . . . Therefore, the aforementioned matter is constitutionally contradictory to Article 27 Paragraph (1) or the 1945 Constitution;

Considering, whereas Article 134, Article 136 *bis*, and Article 137 of the Indonesian Criminal Code may result in legal uncertainty (*rechtsonzekerheid*) because they are extremely prone to the interpretation whether or not a protest, statement, or opinion constitutes a [criticism] or defamation against the President and/or Vice President. The aforementioned matter is constitutionally contradictory to Article 28D Paragraph (1) of the 1945 Constitution and may one day obstruct communications and efforts to obtain information, as guaranteed Article 28F of the 1945 Constitution;

... Considering, whereas in addition to that, the existence of Article 134, Article 136 *bis*, and Article 137 of the Indonesian Criminal Code will also hamper and/or obstruct the possibilities to clarify whether or not the President and/or Vice President has committed the violation(s) as intended in Article 7A of the 1945 Constitution that reads: 'The President and/or Vice President may be terminated during their terms of office by the People's Consultative Assembly based on the recommendation by the People's Legislative Assembly if they have been proven of committing legal violations . . .', because the efforts to make such clarifications may be interpreted as defamations against the President and Vice Presidents;

Considering, whereas based on the aforementioned matters, the Court is of the opinion that Indonesia as a democratic rule of law state in the form of a republic, the sovereignty of which is held by its people, and that highly respects human rights as stated in the 1945 Constitution, it is not relevant to have articles such as Article 134, Article 136 *bis*, and Article 137 in its Criminal Code that negate the principle of equality before the law and decrease the freedom to express ideas and opinions, the freedom to obtain information, and the principle of legal certainty. Therefore, the Draft Indonesian Criminal Code constituting an effort to reform the Indonesian Criminal Code colonially inherited must not contain any Article the provisions of which are identical or similar to Article 134, Article 136 *bis*, and Article 137 of the Indonesian Criminal Code. Moreover, the six-year maximum imprisonment sanction for violations against Article 134 may be used to obstruct the democracy processes, especially accesses to public positions requiring that persons applying for such positions must have not been sentenced for committing criminal acts threatened with imprisonment for five years or more;

Considering, whereas based on all the reasons in the considerations stated above, the Court is of the opinion that the arguments of the Petitioners are reasonable and the petition must be granted; . . .

- Declaring that the entire petition of the Petitioners is granted;
- Declaring that Article 134, Article 136 *bis*, and Article 137 of the Indonesian Criminal Code are contradictory to the 1945 Constitution of the Republic of Indonesia;
- Declaring that Article 134, Article 136 *bis*, and Article 137 of the Indonesian Criminal Code have no binding legal force;
- Ordering the proper announcement of these Decisions in the Official Gazette.

Notes and Questions

1. The Constitutional Court of Indonesia struck down the law of lèse majesté on the ground that Indonesia was now 'a democratic rule of law state in the form of a republic, the sovereignty of which is held by its people'. Is the law of lèse majesté a major impediment to free speech? Does it still have any relevance today? What about states that still retain monarchs?

2.   The offence of lèse majesté has been recognised in Japan. In May 1946, a mass meeting was held, and during the demonstration a communist worker at a machine factory carried a placard mocking the Tenno (Emperor of Japan), which read:

> Imperial Edict (Hirohito says)
> The *kokutai* has been maintained.
> I stuff
> myself.
> You people,
> starve to death.
> Imperial sign and seal (in katakana)
> The Japan Communist Party Tanaka Precision Machine Cell

The worker was indicted for lèse majesté. On 9 October, however, General MacArthur issued a decision suspending all prosecutions on lèse majesté in light of the new Constitution just adopted by the Diet. In MacArthur's view, as the new Constitution promoted an open and democratic society in which everyone was to be accorded freedom of expression and equal protection, the Emperor as a symbol of state should not be granted special protection, let alone use lèse majesté to punish citizens for expressing views critical of the Emperor. MacArthur's decision suspending lèse majesté was ignored, and on 2 November 1946, one day before the promulgation of the new Constitution, the worker was convicted of the offence and sentenced to eight months' imprisonment by the district court in Tokyo. Both sides appealed.

Together with the promulgation of the new Constitution, an order of amnesty was issued, including those indicted for lèse majesté. However, on 28 June 1947, the appellate court in Tokyo sustained the conviction, contending that as the head of state, the Emperor continued to enjoy a special status in the New Constitution. The case went up to the Supreme Court, which on 26 May 1948 dismissed the appeal, stating that the amnesty should have already vacated the prosecution. See N Kawagishi, 'The Birth of Judicial Review in Japan' (2007) 5(2) *I•CON* 308, 326–31.

3.   While the use of lèse majesté is decreasing and its recognition is diminishing in many jurisdictions, recent developments in Thailand indicate a trend to the contrary. On 10 October 2012, the Thai Constitutional Court upheld a law criminalising defamation of the royal family. In addition, there was another lèse majesté case involving a foreigner who translated part of a banned biography of the royal family and put it on the Internet. He was arrested, but was later released after receiving a pardon. The incident raised serious concerns in the United Nations. The UN Special Rapporteur on freedom of expression, Frank La Rue, pointed out:

> The threat of a long prison sentence and vagueness of what kinds of expression constitute defamation, insult, or threat to the monarchy, encourage self-censorship and stifle important debates on matters of public interest, thus putting in jeopardy the right to freedom of opinion and expression . . . This is exacerbated by the fact that the charges can be brought by private individuals and trials are often closed to the public.

See D Singer, 'UN Expert Condemns Thailand Royal Insult Law', *Jurist*, 11 October 2011, available at <http://jurist.org/paperchase/2011/10/un-expert-

condemns-thailand-royal-insult-law.php>. La Rue stated that under the ICCPR, to which Thailand has been a party since 1996, Member States were allowed to impose only very clear and limited exceptions to free speech, such as to protect the reputation of individuals and to safeguard national security. According to him, 'the Thai penal code and the Computer Crimes Act do not meet these criteria' and 'the laws are vague and overly broad, and the harsh criminal sanctions are neither necessary nor proportionate to protect the monarchy or national security'. See F Jordan, 'UN Expert Urges Reform of Thai Royal Insult Laws', *NBC NEWS*, 10 October 2011, available at <http://www.msnbc.msn.com/id/44849939/ns/world_news-asia_pacific/t/un-expert-urges-reform-thai-royal-insult-laws/#.UIjqXG_MiNU>.

ii. Contempt of Court

The offence of contempt of court is designed to ensure judicial independence through maintaining public confidence in the integrity and independence of the courts. Civil contempt of court consists of disobedience to a court order made in civil proceedings. Criminal contempt of court includes scandalising the court, contempt in the face of the court, deliberate interference with particular judicial proceedings or unintended interference with prejudicial publications.[67] Many common law jurisdictions in Asia maintain the offence of contempt by scandalising the court, even while this has come under criticism for being obsolete or otherwise ill-suited to a democratic society.[68]

However, while not all civil law jurisdictions include such an offence as contempt of court in their respective criminal codes, the majority of common law jurisdictions in Asia do, and even expressly include it as a permissible ground for limiting free speech. For example, the Constitution of Singapore recognises contempt of court as one of the grounds restricting the right to freedom of speech and expression.[69] The Constitution of Malaysia permits the legislature to enact legislation dealing with contempt of court.[70] The Constitutions of Bangladesh,[71] India,[72] Nepal,[73] Pakistan[74] and Sri Lanka[75] all include similar provisions. Interestingly, while the Philippines Constitution does not expressly provide for contempt of court as a restriction on free speech, it expressly confers upon the Commission on Human Rights the power to cite for contempt.[76]

In adjudicating cases concerning contempt of court, the question of what test should be used to distinguish words scandalising the court from expressions critical of

---

[67] See O Hood Phillips, P Jackson and P Leopold, *Constitutional and Administrative Law*, 8th edn (London: Sweet & Maxwell, 2001) at 431–48.

[68] O Litaba, 'Does the "Offence" of Contempt by Scandalising the Court have a Valid Place in the Law of Modern Day Australia?' (2003) 8(1) *Deakin Law Review* 113. See also the Australian Law Reform Commission Report 35, *Contempt* http://www.alrc.gov.au/report-35.

[69] Art 14, Constitution of the Republic of Singapore.

[70] Art 10, Constitution of the Federation of Malaysia.

[71] Art 39, Constitution of Bangladesh.

[72] Art 19, Constitution of the Union of India.

[73] Art 12, Interim Constitution of Nepal.

[74] Art 19, Constitution of Pakistan.

[75] Art 15, Constitution of Sri Lanka.

[76] Art XVIII, Sec 18, Constitution of the Philippines.

the judiciary in the performance of its functions, is critical to avoid unduly repressive laws that may diminish freedom of expression in a democratic society. Many common law countries adopt the 'real risk' test, in which statements are held to be contemptuous only if they pose a real risk of undermining public confidence in the administration of justice. The Hong Kong courts, for example, have adopted the 'real risk' test. Until the 2011 Court of Appeal decision in *Shadrake Alan v Attorney-General*, the applicable test in Singapore was the vague and lax 'inherent tendency' test. In *Shadrake*, the High Court rejected the 'inherent tendency' test that had been applied uniformly to all relevant cases and held that the proper test should be that of 'real risk'. This was affirmed by the Court of Appeal.[77] Despite adopting a test more protective of the right to free speech, the impugned speakers were still convicted for contempt of court on the facts.

In contrast to cases in Hong Kong and Singapore, cases from Malaysia and Sri Lanka indicate deliberate judicial efforts to narrow the findings for contemptuous speech. In the view of the Supreme Court of Malaysia, 'mere abuse of a judge, however defamatory, is not a contempt of court'. To constitute criminal contempt of court, the abusive words 'must relate to the performance of a judicial duty by the judge'. The Supreme Court of Sri Lanka considered all the mitigating factors and found contemptuous statements to be punishable only where there was a deliberate intention to undermine public confidence in the administration of justice.

Shadrake Alan v Attorney-General
[2011] SGCA 26 (Court of Appeal, Singapore)

Andrew Phang Boon Leong JA

This is an appeal against the decisions of the trial judge ('the Judge') in *AG v Shadrake Alan* [2011] 2 SLR 445 ('*Shadrake 1*') and *AG v Shadrake Alan* [2011] 2 SLR 506 ('*Shadrake 2*'). In *Shadrake 1*, the Judge found Mr Alan Shadrake ('the Appellant') in contempt of court for 11 of the 14 impugned statements [noting that in *Shadrake 1* the Judge had already apply the test of 'real risk' with regard to the matter]. In *Shadrake 2*, the Judge sentenced the Appellant to six weeks' imprisonment and a fine of $20,000 (in default of which, two weeks' imprisonment, to run consecutively to the first term of imprisonment).

This case arose from an application by the Attorney-General ('the Respondent') to commit the Appellant, the author of *Once a Jolly Hangman: Singapore Justice in the Dock* (Strategic Information and Research Development Centre, 2010) ('the book'), for contempt of court in relation to certain passages contained in the book.

... [T]he 'real risk' test is an adequate formulation in and of itself and requires no further theoretical elaboration. It is, at bottom, a test that means precisely what it says: is there a real risk that the impugned statement has undermined – or might undermine – public confidence in the administration of justice (here, in Singapore)? In applying this test, the court must avoid either extreme on the legal spectrum, viz, of either finding that contempt has been established where there is only a remote or fanciful possibility that public confidence in the administration of justice is (or might be) undermined or finding that contempt has been established only in the most serious situations (which is, as we shall see in the next section of this judgment, embodied within the 'clear and present danger' test). In under-

---

[77] See *Attorney-General v Shadrake Alan* [2010] SGHC 327; and *Shadrake Alan v Attorney-General* [2011] SGCA 26.

taking such an analysis, the court must not substitute its own subjective view for the view of the average reasonable person as it is clear that the inquiry must necessarily be an objective one. Much would depend, in the final analysis, on the precise facts and context in which the impugned statement is made. . . .

It is important, in our view, to emphasise that if a particular statement poses a 'real risk', this would be sufficient to render that statement contemptuous. . . .

In summary, the 'clear and present danger' test does not represent the law in Singapore and Mr Ravi's attempt to introduce it under the guise of the 'real risk' test fails. . . .

The 'inherent tendency' test was first articulated by the Singapore High Court in *AG v Wain Barry* [1991] 1 SLR(R) 85 ('*Wain*') (the related judgment with regard to sentence is reported at *AG v Wain* Barry J [1991] 1 SLR(R) 108), where TS Sinnathuray J observed as follows (at [54]):

> . . . it is not a requirement of our law . . . that in contempt proceedings it must be proved that the publication constitutes a real risk of prejudicing the administration of justice. In my judgment, it is sufficient to prove that the words complained of have the inherent tendency to interfere with the administration of justice.

With respect, there does not appear to be any clear authority for the 'inherent tendency' test and, indeed, the learned judge in *Wain* did not cite any such authority. However, as the Judge correctly observed, this particular test was 'subsequently referred to in decisions of the [Singapore] High Court and seems to have developed a life of its own' . . .

The Relationship Between the 'Inherent Tendency' Test and the 'Real Risk' Test

The test laid down in *Wain* is somewhat ambiguous in so far as it does not clearly set out the precise relationship between 'real risk' and 'inherent tendency'.

It may be possible, on one reading at least, to interpret *Wain* as conceptualising 'inherent tendency' in contradistinction to 'real risk'; indeed, this is what several courts have done in subsequent cases.

However, a holistic reading of *Wain* suggests that the learned judge did not intend to divorce the test from its actual or potential impact on public confidence in the administration of justice. It is, in fact, axiomatic that the law in general and the law relating to scandalising contempt in particular do not – and cannot – operate in a hermetically sealed environment. That this is the case is clearly illustrated by the actual application of the law to the facts by the learned judge himself (and a similar interpretation could arguably be taken of *Lovitt*). This must surely be the case as, in our view, it would be contrary to both logic as well as commonsense for the 'inherent tendency' test – or any test for that matter– to be stated only at a purely abstract or theoretical level. Indeed, even a theoretical formulation must have in view the vital sphere of application, having regard of course to the particular facts and context of the case in which that formulation is applied. In our view, in none of the decisions cited above (at [52]) is there any indication whatsoever that the court concerned had ignored the particular facts and context of the case at hand in arriving at its decision. Looked at in this light, the apparent distinction between the 'inherent tendency' test on the one hand and the 'real risk' test on the other is, in our view, a 'legal red herring'.

As stated earlier, however, we note that subsequent courts have appeared to define the 'inherent tendency' test in contradistinction to the 'real risk' test. Although those cases would have been decided the same way even if the 'real risk' test was applied, this provides us reason enough to eschew the use of the term 'inherent tendency'. As the Judge noted (at [50] of *Shadrake 1* ([1] supra)), emphasizing the test to be that of 'real risk' would avoid controversy and misunderstanding by conveying precisely the legal test to layperson and lawyer alike. We therefore unequivocally state that the 'real risk' test is the applicable test vis-à-vis liability for scandalising contempt in Singapore.

Attorney-General v Tan Liang Joo John & Ors
[2009] SGHC 41 (High Court, Singapore)

Judith Prakash J

These were applications by the Attorney-General ('the Applicant') seeking orders of committal against Tan Liang Joo John ('the First Respondent'), Isrizal bin Mohamed Isa ('the Second Respondent') and Muhammad Shafi'ie Syahmi bin Sariman ('the Third Respondent') (collectively 'the Respondents') for contempt of court . . .

The ground upon which the applications against the Respondents were made was that they had scandalised the Singapore judiciary in the following manner:

(a) in respect of all the Respondents, by publicly wearing a white T-shirt, imprinted with a palm-sized picture of a kangaroo dressed in a judge's gown . . ., within and in the vicinity of the Supreme Court on 26 May 2008, when a hearing (the 'assessment of damages hearing') was being held before Justice Belinda Ang in . . . the Supreme Court for the assessment of damages payable by . . . the Singapore Democratic Party to Minister Mentor Lee Kuan Yew and Prime Minister Lee Hsien Loong in defamation actions instituted by the Minister Mentor and the Prime Minister . . .;

(b) additionally, in respect of the First Respondent only:

    (i) by publicly wearing the contemning T-shirt within and in the vicinity of the Supreme Court on 27 May 2008, during the continuation of the assessment of damages hearing; and

    (ii) by pointing to the picture of the kangaroo on the contemning T-shirt and saying, 'This is a kangaroo court', to Minister Mentor Lee Kuan Yew when the latter walked past him outside Court . . .; and

(c) by posting, or acquiescing in the posting of, an article entitled 'Police question activists over kangaroo T-shirts' which appeared on the Singapore Democratic Party ('SDP') website on 27 July 2008 ('the SDP article'), which article was accompanied by a photograph of the Respondents wearing the contemning T-shirts and standing outside the main entrance of the Supreme Court building ('the photograph of the Respondents')
. . .

The jurisdiction of the Singapore court to punish for contempt is given statutory effect by s 7(1) of the Supreme Court of Judicature Act (Cap 322, 2007 Rev Ed), which provides that: 'The High Court and the Court of Appeal shall have power to punish for contempt of court.' It is settled law in Singapore that it is a contempt of court to scandalise a court or judge . . .

. . . [T]here are limits to the right of fair criticism. The criticism must be made in good faith and must also be respectful. In determining whether *mala fides* has been proved, the court can take into account a wide range of factors.

One relevant factor is the extent to which the allegedly fair criticism is supported by argument and evidence. There must be some reason or basis for the criticism or else it would amount to an unsupported attack on the court. . . .

. . . The criticism must generally be expressed in a temperate and dispassionate manner, since an intention to vilify the courts is easily inferred where outrageous and abusive language is used . . .

. . . [C]ourts have also taken into consideration such factors as the party's attitude in court . . . and the number of instances of contemning conduct . . . The list of relevant factors is not closed. The court is entitled to take into account all the circumstances of the case which in its view go towards showing bad faith.

There is another, more contentious, limit on the right of criticism. It appears from the English authorities above that the act or words in question must not impute improper motives to nor impugn the integrity, propriety and impartiality of judges or the courts . . .

The need to maintain public confidence in the administration of justice must, however, be balanced against the public interest in rooting out bias and impropriety where it in fact occurs. We ought not to be so complacent as to assume that judges and courts are infallible or impervious to human sentiment . . .

The fear of baseless imputations of bias or impropriety is unfounded as the court is able to take into account factors such as the existence of evidence for such allegations under the requirement of *bona fides*. To my mind, therefore, the second limit on the right to criticise is unnecessary and potentially overly restrictive of legitimate criticism.

Applying the law to the facts of the cases before me, I shall deal first with the Second Respondent's submission that the contemning T-shirt could be interpreted in various ways. Given the entire context in which the T-shirt had been worn (*viz*, in and around the Supreme Court, at the same time as the assessment of damages hearing . . .), I concluded that a reasonable viewer would apprehend that it was a reference to the expression 'kangaroo court' and intended to cast aspersions on the way in which the assessment of damages hearing was being conducted in particular and the Singapore justice system in general. This was especially since the Second Respondent could not give any satisfactory explanation why he put on the T-shirt depicting (as he claimed) a dressed wallaby . . .

The First Respondent did not deny that he had worn the contemning T-shirt within and in the vicinity of the Supreme Court on 26 May 2008 (as well as in its vicinity on 27 May 2008) and that he had distributed similar T-shirts inside the Supreme Court on 26 May 2008. He also admitted that he had some editorial say in the SDP website, and did not deny being in some way involved in the posting of the SDP article and the photograph of the Respondents on the SDP website. Instead, he claimed that these acts were done in the spirit of fair criticism. I did not agree with him. No reasons accompanied the assertion (by the image on the T-shirt) that the court was a kangaroo court. Far from expressing his criticism in a temperate manner, the First Respondent had chosen to make a statement by wearing the T-shirt and, even worse, inciting others to wear it within the court's premises. This amounted to a deliberate and provocative attack on the court, falling far outside the realm of fair and reasoned criticism.

The Second Respondent also did not deny wearing the T-shirt within and in the vicinity of the Supreme Court on 26 May 2008. Instead, he asserted that he had had no intention to scandalise the Singapore judiciary. However, as I have set out above, intention is irrelevant in establishing liability for the contempt. Furthermore, the Second Respondent's assertion that he had had no intention to scandalise the Singapore judiciary was doubtful in the light of his subsequent refusal to apologise for his acts on the basis that it would go against his conscience. . . .

A powerful and evocative image has as much inherent power as a written article to shake public confidence in our justice system. Images can convey messages and meaning by implication and association. . . . The Respondents had posed for the photograph of the Respondents at a location where it was obvious that they would be seen by and photographed by the press (not to mention that the First Respondent had distributed the contemning T-shirts within the Supreme Court and was also involved in the posting of the SDP article on the SDP website). It was clear to me that this case was about much more than merely wearing a T-shirt. The conduct of the Respondents communicated to an average member of the public the Respondents' conviction that the Singapore courts are 'kangaroo courts' . . .

For all these reasons, I found that the First Respondent was in contempt of court by wearing the contemning T-shirt within and in the vicinity of the Supreme Court on 26 May 2008 (as well as in its vicinity on 27 May 2008), distributing similar T-shirts in the Supreme Court on 26 May 2008, and being involved in or acquiescing in the posting of the SDP article and the photograph of the Respondents on the SDP website. I also found that the Second and Third Respondents were in contempt of court by wearing the T-shirt within and in the vicinity of the Supreme Court on 26 May 2008.

Wong Yeung Ng v Secretary for Justice
[1999] 2 HKC 24; [1999] 2 HKLRD 293 (Court of Final Appeal, Hong Kong)

Facts

Wong Yeung Ng was the editor of the *Oriental Daily News*. In 1996, the Obscene Articles Tribunal ruled the *Oriental Daily News* indecent as it published several photographs containing naked women. That same year, the Oriental Daily Group sued the *Apple Daily* newspaper for copyright infringement of the photograph of a famous singer. The suit failed. One judge in the Court of Appeal, Justice Godfrey JA, publicly criticised the Oriental Daily Group for their intrusion into the singer's privacy. The tension between the Oriental Daily Group and the judiciary department escalated. Between 11 December 1997 and 13 January 1998, Wong Yeung Ng began publishing articles, allegedly containing passages of crude and vicious abuse of the judiciary and including threats to the judiciary. From 13 to 15 January 1998, the *Oriental Daily News* carried out a daily campaign to 'educate' Justice Godfrey JA. On 23 June 1998, Wong was convicted of two indictments of contempt of court by the High Court: (1) for efforts to 'threaten, harass and/or intimidate Godfrey JA thereby wrongfully interfering with the administration of justice'; and (2) for publishing 'articles calculated to undermine public confidence in the administration of justice'. Wong appealed.

Justice Litton PJ

Charge 2 came first in time. It related to a campaign of vilification and intimidation aimed at members of the Obscene Articles Tribunal and the judiciary, conducted by the applicant in the pages of the *Oriental Daily News* over a period of time, which the High Court in sentencing the applicant described as 'without parallel in modern times': The features of the campaign which made it so unique included 'the venom of the language used, the outrageousness of the motives ascribed to the targets and the impact the campaign had on confidence in the ability of the judges to dispense justice conscientiously and impartially'. Counsel for the applicant accepts that the articles were published maliciously, in bad faith, and were 'scurrilous, abusive, shocking and reprehensible'. Counsel also accepts that there was a *real risk* of the articles diminishing the authority of the court and impairing public confidence in the administration of justice. In other words the articles were 'calculated to undermine public confidence in the administration of justice in Hong Kong', in terms of charge 2. It is said, nevertheless, that arguably Article 16(2) of the Hong Kong Bill of Rights [which read '(2) Everyone shall have the right to freedom of expression; this right shall include freedom to seek, receive and impart information and ideas of all kinds, regardless of frontiers, either orally, in writing or in print, in the form of art, or through any other media of his choice.'] and Article 27 of the Basic Law [which read 'Hong Kong residents shall have freedom of speech, of the press and of publication; freedom of association, of assembly, of procession and of demonstration; and the right and freedom to form and join trade unions, and to strike.'], guaranteeing to the applicant freedom of expression, [render] the conviction for contempt unlawful.

As to charge 1, this relates to a campaign to threaten, harass and intimidate Godfrey JA, by having him pursued night and day by employees of the Oriental Daily News, following an appeal in the Court of Appeal in which Godfrey JA had given the leading judgment adverse to the Oriental Press Group. The avowed purpose of the campaign was to 'educate' the judge, but the real purpose, as the High Court found, was to take revenge for the Court of Appeal's judgment and to punish the judge for his part in it. This was, as the High Court said in sentencing the applicant, unprecedented in the common law world.

The constitutional right of free speech as contained in the Basic Law, adopting the norms set out in the International Covenant on Civil and Political Rights, is not an absolute right. Every civilized community is entitled to protect itself from malicious conduct aimed at undermining the due administration of justice. It is an important aspect of the preservation of the rule of law. Where the contemnor goes way beyond reasoned criticism of the judicial system and acts in bad faith, as the applicant has done in this case, the guarantee of free speech cannot protect him from punishment. . . .

The courts below have given detailed and cogent reasons for reaching their conclusion on what, as counsel accepts, is an extreme case: The likes of which, hopefully, will never be seen again. There is no prospect of the Court of Final Appeal differing from their conclusion. Despite the Court of Appeal's certification, we refuse to give leave to appeal against conviction.

As to the sentence, this was carefully weighed by both courts below. Having regard to the gravity of the contempts, the applicant's own role as editor and his admitted bad faith, the sentence of 4 months' imprisonment appears extremely lenient. The notion that a substantial and grave injustice has been done is absurd. We decline to give leave to appeal against that sentence.

Attorney-General, Malaysia v Manjeet Singh Dhillion
[1991] 1 MLJ 167 (Supreme Court, Malaysia)

Harun Hashim SCJ (dissenting)

This is an application by the Attorney General to commit the respondent [the Malaysian Bar and its representatives] to prison for alleged contempt of court. It arises out of an affidavit affirmed by the respondent on 25 April 1989 and filed in this court in support of an application for leave for an order of committal to prison of the Lord President of the Supreme Court (Tun Dato Abdul Hamid bin Omar) for alleged contempt of this court.

The grounds on which this application is sought is the alleged conduct of the respondent in making various accusations and allegations in the aforesaid affidavit as set out hereunder against the Lord President who was at the material time the acting Lord President and the Chief Justice of the High Court of Malaya:

(a) . . . [T]he respondent herein alleged that the 'respondent [ie the Lord President] on 2 July 1988 did commit contempt of the Supreme Court by attempting to prevent, frustrate and interfere with the sitting of the Supreme Court' in connection with the application by YAA Tun Mohamed Salleh Abas referred to therein.

(b) . . . [T]he respondent accused the Lord President of 'abusing his official position as Acting Lord President by taking the actions . . . to prevent, frustrate and to interfere with a sitting of the Supreme Court to hear a matter in which the respondent [ie the Lord President] himself was a party thereto'. The respondent herein further alleged that 'As such, the aforesaid action . . . constitutesof' the Lord President 'constitute contempt of court of the grossest imaginable. Contempt apart, the aforesaid conduct of the respondent [ie the Lord President] also constitutes misbehaviour within the meaning of art 125 of the Constitution [which read: 'If the Prime Minister, or the Lord President after consulting the Prime Minister, represents to the Yang di-Pertuan Agong that a judge of the Supreme Court oath to be removed on the ground of misbehaviour or of inability, from infirmity of body or mind or of any cause, properly to discharge the functions of his office, the Yang di-Pertaun Agong shall appoint a tribunal in accordance with Clause (4) and refer the representation to it; and may on the recommendation of the tribunal remove the judge from office.'], deserving his removal from office.'

(c) . . . [T]he respondent accused that the Lord President, 'by using his position [as] the Acting Lord President interfered in the course and the administration of justice in the proceedings brought by Tun Salleh Abas.

(d) . . . [T]he respondent alleged that the conduct of the Lord President as described therein 'is an affront to the dignity and impartiality of the courts.'

(e) . . . [T]he respondent alleged that the acts of the Lord President as described therein 'amount to an exercise of powers for improper motives and an interference with the course of justice.' The Attorney General contends that the conduct of the respondent in making the accusations and allegations as set out above amounts to scandalizing the Lord President in his judicial capacity and warrants the committal of the respondent to prison for contempt of court.

. . . In the instant case, the first fact to consider is that the criticism of the respondent is not directed at any judgment of this court whether present or pending or the judiciary as a whole or this court in particular but criticism of a judge as a judge in his capacity at the material time as the acting Lord President and the Chief Justice of the High Court of Malaya . . .

There can be no doubt that these statements are *ex facie* defamatory of the Lord President. The question is whether this defamatory attack is purely a libel for the Lord President to proceed against the respondent if he so chooses or has crossed the line to scandalizing the Lord President in his judicial capacity. Bearing in mind that the power to commit for contempt which consists of scandalizing a judge as a judge should be treated with much discretion and always with reference to the administration of justice, it is necessary to determine, on the facts of each particular case, whether the line has been crossed. In so determining, it is also necessary to apply the common law according to the circumstances prevailing in this country (s 3 of the Civil Law Act 1956) [which read: In so determining, it is also necessary to apply the common law according to the circumstances prevailing in this country (s 3 of the Civil Law Act 1956) [which read: (1) Save so far as other provision has been made or may hereafter be made by any written law in force in Malaysia, the Court shall – (a) in West Malaysia or any part thereof, apply the common law of England and the rules of equity as administered in England on the 7th day of April, 1956] and not what it would be in the United States, the United Kingdom or other common law countries . . .

The defamatory statements made by the respondent in his affidavit relate entirely to the single act of the Lord President in giving his instructions to the Chief Registrar to prevent a sitting of the Supreme Court on 2 July 1988. It was held by this court that that sitting was an unlawful sitting. There was therefore no court in existence for the Lord President to be guilty of contempt. The respondent therefore has made a false allegation. The statement itself is undoubtedly defamatory if only on account of its falsity but a defamatory statement against a judge by itself is not a contempt of court . . .

It is contended that the statements made by the respondent amount to scandalizing the Lord President in his judicial capacity. To uphold this contention it must be shown that the Lord President was exercising some judicial power. It is not enough if the statements are made against the person of the Lord President only . . . The instruction given to the Chief Registrar was not in exercise of judicial powers. At best it was advice not to sit. In any event they were not carried out. Indeed the Lord President did nothing on 2 July 1988 which was related to the administration of justice which could be the subject-matter of contempt proceedings against the respondent . . .

As the Lord President was not doing anything in his judicial capacity it was defamatory of the respondent to allege the Lord President of abusing his official powers, imputing improper motives, misbehaviour and interfering with the course of justice.

The statements made by the respondent are wholly unjustified. They are blatantly defamatory and must have caused acute embarrassment to the Lord President, more particularly in this case as the statements were preceded in a blaze of publicity as evident from the press statements issued, the several meetings of the Bar Council and the Malaysian Bar. In short, the Lord President has been publicly ridiculed. . . . The only material complained of is the affidavit affirmed by the respondent and filed in this court in the course of court proceedings. The extent of publication of such an affidavit is very limited . . .

I am of the firm opinion on the authorities I have referred to, that the respondent has not crossed the line from libel to scandalizing the Lord President in his judicial capacity. Mere abuse of a judge, however defamatory, is not a contempt of court. The abuse must relate to the performance of a judicial duty by the judge for it to be a criminal contempt of court. The offence alleged against the respondent has not been proved.

For the reasons stated, I would dismiss this application.

Mohamed Yusoff SCJ

I have had the advantage of reading Harun Hashim SCJ's final judgment last Saturday morning. I do not agree with the conclusion and would state my views as follows.

At the outset I would say that I do not agree with the contention of the respondent's counsel that the common law contempt of court as has hitherto been applied in this court by virtue of s 3 of the Civil Law Act 1956 is inconsistent with art 10(1) of the Federal Constitution.

The Supreme Court has this far consistently applied the common law principle of contempt of court as seen in the judgments in some of these cases . . . I see no reason now to depart from these principles. Further, the common law, as has been expounded, applied and decided by our courts after 7 April 1956, by virtue of the Civil Law Act 1956, has become part of our law.

. . . Turning to the present case, the respondent is cited for contempt for scandalizing a judge as a judge, indeed the highest judge in the country, by criticizing the conduct of the Acting Lord President (as he then was), in his affidavit of 25 April 1989.

. . . On the law applicable to this case, I agree with the Attorney General that, as mentioned earlier, the principle of common law of contempt as stated in *R v Gray* still applies

696 Free Speech and Res Publica

in our country. Parliament has not imposed any restriction by law relating to contempt of court under art 10(2) of the Constitution. As such the common law provision under s 3 of the Civil Law Act 1956 is preserved.

I also agree that this is the present law applicable in Australia for scandalizing the court as seen in *Gallagher v Durack* (1983) 45 ALR 53, and also in New Zealand, *SG v Radio Avon Ltd* [1978] 1 NZLR 225, though as pointed out by the respondent's counsel that this is not the same in Canada after 1982 with the specific legislation in Canadian Charter of Fights and Freedoms Act and in Pakistan and India with their constitutional provisions on the common law contempt of court. But in this regard the Attorney General submitted that in the present case the test in *Arthur Lee's* case should apply that the respondent's remark was not made within the limit of reasonable courtesy and good faith. . . .

. . . On these authorities I agree with the respondent's counsel's proposition that the specie[s] of contempt of court cited against the respondent in the present case is of the kind known as scandalizing the court itself.

The proof that is required to establish this type of contempt in scandalizing the court is stringent. In *Lim Kit Siang's* case this court has held that for proceedings for contempt constituting an attack on the judiciary [the strictest burden of proof is required]. The proof that was envisaged in that case was as suggested by the applicant there. This was as laid down in *Surendra v Nabakrishma* AIR 1958 Orissa 168, ie 'Any act done, or writing published calculated to bring a court or the judge of a court into contempt, or to lower his authority, is a contempt of court.'

Or as another quorum of this court in *Malaysian Bar v Tan Sri Dato Abdul Hamid bin Omar* at p 283, deciding on the respondent's expunged application for leave puts it 'what amounts to contempt are acts done calculated to obstruct or interfere with the lawful process of the court'.

The criticism made by the respondent in this case does not relate to any particular case in court but specifically directed at the Lord President's conduct in the exercise of his function. The words used in the criticism were: 'abusing his official position as Ag LP'; 'his acts amount to exercise of powers for improper motives' and 'the conduct of the LP constitutes misbehaviour, deserving his removal from office.'

. . . In my assessment of the case resting on the authorities cited, it is correct to say that the first contempt was committed in respect of criticism against the judge in his judicial capacity, in whose court the case was pending, and that the alternative contempt, calculated to interfere in the course of justice, described in *R v Gray*, was established against the respondent in respect of his criticism scandalizing the court and all the judges generally in their duties.

. . . It is pertinent to note that the respondent's motion before the court was only to cite contempt against the Lord President but not to seek a remedy for the removal of the Lord President from office. The statement 'that the conduct of the Lord President deserved his removal from office' is in effect a declaration of the respondent's wilfulness in intent and purpose. It is not relevant to the present issue at hand.

To find contempt the court requires strict proof and before a contemner can be found in contempt, the act complained of must not only be wilful and calculated but must also be made with the intention of bringing the judge into contempt or casting suspicion on the administration of justice. Our own authorities have established that even where proceedings are not actually pending there can be contempt of court if there is a reflection upon the administration of justice in the country – see *PP v The Straits Times Press Ltd* [1949] MLJ 81. It has been shown that the respondent's violent criticism of the Lord President would have that effect on the future administration of the law in the courts.

Our authorities have also established that when applying the law of contempt the court will not lose sight of local conditions and for that reason it would be necessary to take a stricter view here of matters pertaining to dignity of the court – see *The Straits Times Press* case and *PP v SRN Palaniappan & Ors* [1949] MLJ 246. Confining myself to the facts mentioned herein, I find that the criticism made by the respondent if repeated would [i]ndisputably undermine the authority of the Lord President and lower the dignity of the court in the eyes of the public.

Sentence: The respondent is found in contempt of court in his representative capacity as secretary of the Malaysian Bar in affirming an affidavit criticizing the Lord President. The contemptuous words used in the respondent's affidavit are repetitions of similar criticism of the Lord President made by the Malaysian Bar at its meeting and similar statements made elsewhere.

The respondent's responsibility is, in our opinion vicarious. Although this is not itself a defence in contempt proceedings against him, nevertheless it is a mitigating factor to be considered in his favour.

For these reasons we do not consider a custodial sentence appropriate. A fine of $5,000 in default [of] three months' imprisonment would be sufficient in the circumstances. Each party to pay its own costs.

Gunn Chit Tuan SCJ allowed the application on grounds similar to those given by Mohamed Yusoff SCJ.

Hewamanne v Manik de Silva & Another
[1983] 1 Sri LRI (Supreme Court, Sri Lanka)

Facts

In this case, an editor, the owner, printer and publisher respectively of the *Daily News* were charged with contempt of court for publishing the following headlines in the *Daily News* of 7 March 1983:

Select Committee probe of Mr KCE de Alwis' representations. FDB's pleadings prepared in Judge's chambers?

The respondents stated that the headlines originated from the political conflict between Justice KCE de Alwis, a member of the Special Presidential Commission, and Felix Dias Bandaranaike, former Prime Minister and, at that time, a Member of the Parliament.

Wanasundera J

The Supreme Court is the 'highest and final superior court of record in the Republic' and has been established by the Constitution. It is vested with a power to punish for contempt and this power is found in Article 105 (3). The law of contempt, which is a concept known to English law, was well known in this country from early British times. This English law of contempt, modified to some extent in its application here, was in operation immediately prior to the coming into operation of this 1978 Democratic Socialist Republican Constitution. It had been continued in operation by the earlier Republican Constitution of 1972, which also kept alive the then existing law of contempt of court. . . .

The short answer, therefore, to Mr Choksy's first submission is that the law of contempt of court which had hitherto existed would operate untrammeled by the fundamental right of freedom of speech and expression contained in Article 14 [which read '(1) Every citizen is entitled to – (a) the freedom of speech and expression including publication; . . .'].

. . . [T]here is a consensus that in the hierarchy of values and principles that sustain a democratic society, preponderance must be given to the proper functioning of the administration of justice, as this is central to the very conception of the administration of justice[.] Therefore the reasoning in the passages cited is no less valid in the present situation as in the circumstances referred to in those cases. This cannot in any way imply that judges are above the law. Apart from the authorised channels available for making complaints, the law at all times allow[s] fair and temperate comments on decisions and the administration of justice. I am therefore unable to assent to the proposition that judges and the judiciary should be exposed for wide open discussion by the mass media and the general public. The latter view, I believe, would in the long term be actually counterproductive and destructive of the public welfare. . . .

The texts are very clear that the privilege will not extend, however fair and accurate, to the matters which are blasphemous, seditious, immoral, etc. These are essentially public matters and the publication of such matters, far from being for the public interest, would be against the public welfare. I think the distinction made by Mr Nadesan [counsel for the petitioner] is a valid one and the reasoning in the libel cases which deal with harm to an individual cannot hold good when we are confronted with the case of a larger public interest as in a matter of Contempt. The principles set out in the cases cited by the respondents therefore do not in themselves solve or throw any real light on the present problem.

While I hold that the respondents are guilty of a contempt of court, I am [p]repared to accept their statement that they did not have a deliberate intention of interfering with the administration of justice, though their publication has that effect. In meting punishment we have to consider the totality of the circumstances relating to this matter. The fact that a parliamentary motion impliedly reflecting on the conduct of a Judge had previously been published without attracting thereto the laws of contempt of court and the uncertainty of the [l]egal position in view of the recent constitutional changes, which may have misled even the legal advisers, are mitigating factors which [we] will take into consideration. It is therefore possible for a merciful view to be taken of the conduct of the respondents. But, having regard to the proposed order of the majority, it is unnecessary to pursue the question of punishment any further.

This court, by its majority decision, therefore, confirms the Rule issued on the respondents but, in view of the mitigatory circumstances, imposes no punishment. They are accordingly discharged.

Notes and Questions

1. Read carefully and compare the articulation of the 'real risk' test by the Singapore court in the case of *Shadrake Alan v Attorney-General*, and that in the Hong Kong decision in *Wong Yeung NG v Secretary for Justice*. Is the 'real risk' test articulated the same way in these cases? If not, what are the differences?

2. In *Attorney-General v Tan Liang Joo John & Ors*, the High Court of Singapore stressed that the criticism 'must be made in good faith and must also be respectful' – in other words, *bona fide* – and 'must generally be expressed in a temperate and dispassionate manner, since an intention to vilify the courts is easily inferred where outrageous and abusive language is used'. Why? What would be the impact of *mala fide* contemptuous speech on judicial functions?

3. Why do you think the Singapore courts decided to adopt the 'real risk' test in place of the 'inherent tendency' test? Which test do you think is preferable, and why? How

does each test achieve a balance between the right to free speech and the interests in ensuring judicial independence and proper functioning of the judiciary?

4. In reading the above decisions, do you discern any 'local conditions' that must be taken into account in the Asian or particularly Singapore context? In *Attorney-General v Wain*,[78] Sinnathuray J adopted the test of 'inherent tendency' in seeking to balance the right to free speech and the public interests in maintaining proper functioning of the judiciary. He stressed that 'the conditions local to Singapore are many and varied. I am not going to touch on the socio-political and economic conditions of our island nation which is markedly different from many other countries'. The factors identified were the fact that Singapore is a 'small island' and that because judges were triers of both fact and law, they require more protection from critical speech which would undermine public confidence in the administration of justice. See Thio Li-ann and D Chong Gek Sian SC, 'The Chan Court and Constitutional Adjudication: A Sea Change into Something Rich and Strange?' in Chao Hick Tin et al (eds), *The Law in His Hand: A Tribute to Chief Justice Chan Sek Keong* (Singapore: Academy Publishing, 2012) 92–93.

5. The *Wain* line of reasoning was subsequently affirmed and elaborated upon at the greater length in the High Court decision in *Attorney-General v Hertzberg Daniel & Ors*.[79] In *Hertzberg*, the court argued in favour of the 'inherent tendency' test because it did not 'call for detailed proof of what in many instances will be unprovable, namely, that public confidence in the administration of justice really was impaired by the relevant publication', and because it enabled 'the court to step in before the damage, ie the impairment of public confidence in the administration of justice, actually occurs'. This line of authorities found no favour with the Court of Appeal in *Shadrake Alan v Attorney-General*, reproduced above.

6. In finding contemptuous speech, what other public interests should be balanced with the protection of free speech? Dignity of the court? Should the age of the court be taken into consideration? In *Attorney-General v Arthur Lee Meng Kuang*,[80] for example, the Supreme Court of Malaysia indicated while the English common law principle of contempt of court applied to Malaysia, local conditions require a modification of the English approach in so far as it is necessary to take a 'stricter view . . . of the matters pertaining to the dignity of the court'. Moreover, the vulnerability of the Supreme Court due to its relative youth should also be one important consideration. According to the Court:

> The Supreme Court was given birth only on 1 January 1985, and its sensitivity need not be the same as courts of similar jurisdictions in England or other countries. Having regard to local conditions, criticisms which are considered within the limit of reasonable courtesy elsewhere are not necessarily so here. For the present, except possibly – and we say this with great reservation – for the limited purpose of proving it in actual court proceedings, any allegation of injustice or bias however couched in respectful words and even if expressed in temperate language, cannot be tolerated particularly when such allegations are made for the purpose of influencing or exerting influence upon the court in the exercise of its judicial function.[81]

---

[78] *Attorney-General v Wain* [1991] 1 SLR(R) 85.
[79] *Attorney-General v Hertzberg Daniel & Ors* [2009] 1 SLR(R) 1103.
[80] *Attorney-General v Arthur Lee Meng Kuang* [1987] 1 MLJ 207.
[81] Ibid.

What do you make of this argument? Is it persuasive? Does it follow that in relatively new constitutional states, the law of contempt should be more stringent? Is this a matter of judicial confidence, or sociological judgment?

iii. Symbolic Speech

Expressive conduct may be considered symbolic speech, which attracts constitutional protection. Yet expressive conduct can be distinguished from other conduct. For example, when expressing discontent with the state and government, some protesters may vandalise national flags, statues, or portraits of national figures or other objects that symbolise state authority. Many states have laws criminalising the physical abuse of national symbols. The extent of constitutional protection also varies, so while the US extends such protection, many European countries do not.[82] In the following case, the Hong Kong Court of Final Appeal upheld the criminal provision that punishes expressive conduct such as the desecration of national and regional flags, as a necessary restriction to freedom of expression.

HKSAR v Ng Kung Siu
[1999] 8 BHRC 244 (Court of Final Appeal, Hong Kong)

Facts

The respondents participated in a peaceful demonstration which defaced national and regional flags. After the demonstration, they were arrested and charged with publicly desecrating both the national and regional flags in violation of section 7 of the National Flag and National Emblem Ordinance and section 7 of the Regional Flag and Regional Emblem Ordinance. The Eastern Magistrates' Court ruled that the restriction on the defendants' right to freedom of expression was necessary for the protection of public order. The Court of Appeal allowed their appeal and quashed the conviction. The prosecution appealed.

Andrew Li CJ

Freedom of expression is a fundamental freedom in a democratic society. It lies at the heart of civil society and of Hong Kong's system and way of life. The courts must give a generous interpretation to its constitutional guarantee. This freedom includes the freedom to express ideas which the majority may find disagreeable or offensive and the freedom to criticise governmental institutions and the conduct of public officials.

. . . It is common ground that the statutory provisions criminalising desecration of the national and regional flags restrict the freedom of expression. Before considering whether the restriction is justified, it is important to examine first the extent of the restriction. This is because when one comes to consider the issue of justification, one must have in mind what it is that has to be justified, in particular, whether it is a wide or limited restriction that has to be justified. The wider the restriction, the more difficult it would be to justify. The appellant submits that the freedom of expression is implicated only in a minor way as only one mode of expression is prohibited. The respondent argues that the restriction is wide. The argument is that it prohibits not merely one mode of expression but by rendering unlawful one form of political protest also the substance of what may be expressed.

---

[82] Dorsen et al, above n 52, at 866.

As has been observed, flag desecration is symbolic expression or non-verbal expression. A person desecrating a national flag as a means of expression would usually be expressing a message of protest. But the message he seeks to convey may not be clear. The message may be one of hatred or opposition directed to the nation. Or it may be one of protest against the ruling government. Or the person concerned may be protesting against a current policy of the government. Or some other message may be intended. One has to consider the surrounding circumstances of the flag desecration in question to ascertain the message which is sought to be communicated. In the present case, the respondents were protesting against the system of government on the mainland. This appears from the fact that the Chinese character 'shame' had been written on the flags taken together with the chanting of 'build up a democratic China' during the procession and what the second respondent was reported to have stated to the press at the time.

The prohibition of desecration of the national and regional flags by the statutory provisions in question is not a wide restriction of the freedom of expression. It is a limited one. It bans one mode of expressing whatever the message the person concerned may wish to express, that is the mode of desecrating the flags. It does not interfere with the person's freedom to express the same message by other modes. Further, it may well be that scrawling words of praise on the flags (as opposed to words of protest which is usually the message sought to be conveyed) would constitute offences within s 7 of both ordinances, namely, that of desecrating the flag by scrawling on the same. If this be right, then it would mean that the prohibition not only bans expression by this mode of a message of protest, but also other messages including a message of praise. But a law seeking to protect the dignity of the flag in question as a symbol, in order to be effective, must protect it against desecration generally.

Freedom of expression is not an absolute. The preamble to the ICCPR recognises that the individual has duties to other individuals and to the community to which he belongs. Article 19(3) itself recognises that the exercise of the right to freedom of expression carries with it special duties and responsibilities and it may therefore be subject to certain restrictions. But these restrictions shall only be such as are provided by law and are necessary: (a) For respect of the rights or reputation of others; (b) For the protection of national security or of public order (ordre public), or of public health or morals.'

The requirement that the restriction be provided by law is satisfied by the two statutory provisions which are in question in this case. In considering the extent of a restriction, it is well settled that any restriction on the right to freedom of expression must be narrowly interpreted. . . . It is common ground that the burden rests on the government to justify any restriction.

Here, the government principally relies on the restriction as necessary for the protection of public order (*ordre public*). Two questions arise. First, are the legitimate societal and community interests in the protection of the flags in question, which I have held to exist, within the concept of public order (*ordre public*)? Secondly, if the answer is in the affirmative, is the restriction to the right to freedom of expression necessary for their protection?

. . . The following points can be drawn from the materials referred to above. First, the concept is an imprecise and elusive one. Its boundaries cannot be precisely defined. Secondly, the concept includes what is necessary for the protection of the general welfare or for the interests of the collectivity as a whole. Examples include: prescription for peace and good order; safety; public health; aesthetic and moral considerations and economic order (consumer protection, etc). Thirdly, the concept must remain a function of time, place and circumstances.

As to the time, place and circumstances with which we are concerned, Hong Kong has a new constitutional order. On 1 July 1997, the People's Republic of China resumed the exercise of sovereignty over Hong Kong being an inalienable part of the People's Republic of China and established the HKSAR under the principle of 'one country, two systems'. The resumption of the exercise of sovereignty is recited in the preamble of the Basic Law, as 'fulfilling the long-cherished common aspiration of the Chinese people for the recovery of Hong Kong'. In these circumstances, the legitimate societal interests in protecting the national flag and the legitimate community interests in the protection of the regional flag are interests which are within the concept of public order (*ordre public*). As I have pointed out, the national flag is the unique symbol of the one country, the People's Republic of China, and the regional flag is the unique symbol of the HKSAR as an inalienable part of the People's Republic of China under the principle of 'one country, two systems'. These legitimate interests form part of the general welfare and the interests of the collectivity as a whole.

. . . In applying the test of necessity, the court must consider whether the restriction on the guaranteed right to freedom of expression is proportionate to the aims sought to be achieved thereby . . . As concluded above, by criminalising desecration of the national and regional flags, the statutory provisions in question constitute a limited restriction on the right to freedom of expression. The aims sought to be achieved are the protection of the national flag as a unique symbol of the nation and the regional flag as a unique symbol of the HKSAR in accordance with what are unquestionably legitimate societal and community interests in their protection. Having regard to what is only a limited restriction on the right to the freedom of expression, the test of necessity is satisfied. The limited restriction is proportionate to the aims sought to be achieved and does not go beyond what is proportionate.

Hong Kong is at the early stage of the new order following resumption of the exercise of sovereignty by the People's Republic of China. The implementation of the principle of 'one country, two systems' is a matter of fundamental importance, as is the reinforcement of national unity and territorial integrity. Protection of the national flag and the regional flag from desecration, having regard to their unique symbolism, will play an important part in the attainment of these goals. In these circumstances, there are strong grounds for concluding that the criminalisation of flag desecration is a justifiable restriction on the guaranteed right to the freedom of expression.

Further, whilst the court is concerned with the circumstances in the HKSAR as an inalienable part of the People's Republic of China, the court notes that a number of democratic nations which have ratified the ICCPR have enacted legislation which protects the national flag by criminalising desecration or similar acts punishable by imprisonment. These instances of flag protection indicate that criminalisation of flag desecration is capable of being regarded as necessary for the protection of public order (*ordre public*) in other democratic societies.

Accordingly, s 7 of the National Flag Ordinance and s 7 of the Regional Flag Ordinance are necessary for the protection of public order (*ordre public*). They are justified restrictions on the right to the freedom of expression and are constitutional.

Notes and Questions

1. In *HKSAR v Ng Kung Siu*, the issue in dispute was whether the statutes prohibiting the public desecration of national and regional flags would fall within the scope of 'public order', with the Court finding the restriction reasonable based upon the principle of proportionality. To what degree should the symbols of state

be protected against the freedom of expression? Is the principle of proportionality a helpful doctrine in deciding the issue? Why, or why not?

2. The standards applied to restricting symbolic speech may vary as between jurisdictions. Comparatively, the US Supreme Court in *United States v O'Brien*[83] heightened the level of scrutiny, demanding the existence of substantial interests to justify a similar restriction. According to the Court:

    > We cannot accept the view that an apparently limitless variety of conduct can be labeled 'speech' whenever the person engaging in the conduct intends thereby to express an idea. However, even on the assumption that the alleged communicative element in O'Brien's conduct is sufficient to bring into play the First Amendment, it does not necessarily follow that the destruction of a registration certificate is constitutionally protected activity. This Court has held that when 'speech' and 'nonspeech' elements are combined in the same course of conduct, a sufficiently important governmental interest in regulating the nonspeech element can justify incidental limitations on First Amendment freedoms. To characterize the quality of the governmental interest which must appear, the Court has employed a variety of descriptive terms: compelling; substantial; subordinating; paramount; cogent; strong. Whatever imprecision inheres in these terms, we think it clear that a government regulation is sufficiently justified if it is within the constitutional power of the Government; if it furthers an important or substantial governmental interest; if the governmental interest is unrelated to the suppression of free expression; and if the incidental restriction on alleged First Amendment freedoms is no greater than is essential to the furtherance of that interest.

    What is your view of the US position? How does it compare with *HKSAR v Ng Kung Siu*? What gives rise to the difference in judicial protection of such symbolic speech?

3. *HKSAR v Ng Kung Siu* is regarded by many Hong Kong constitutional scholars as a landmark decision because the Court of Final Appeal asserted its judicial power in continuously applying the ICCPR to Hong Kong in a very delicate political context. Professor Albert Chen regards this case as 'probably the most theoretically significant constitutional case on civil liberties and human rights in the legal history of Hong Kong'. See A Chen, '"The Rule of Law under 'One Country, Two Systems'": The Case of Hong Kong 1997–2010,' (2011) 6(1) *National Taiwan University Law Review* 279. The demonstration in which flag defacement occurred was against the handover of Hong Kong to China in July 1997, an event which provoked serious tensions between the regional and national governments. Although the Court of Final Appeal upheld the flag desecration law, it nevertheless recognised the operative force of the Bill of Rights and the ICCPR in Hong Kong, along with the judicial power to review the constitutionality of Hong Kong legislation on human rights grounds, a stand that the Central Chinese Government was strongly against.

---

[83] *United States v O'Brien* 391 US 367, 376–77 (1968).

E. Political Defamation

One recognised ground for restricting free speech is the protection of an individual's reputation from slander or libel. Reputation is a fundamental right or interest, and may be understood from three perspectives as a form of honour, property or aspect of human dignity.[84] 'Reputation' refers to a person's honour, which is typically ascribed to his or her social status in the community. The law of defamation seeks to protect personal reputation from false and scurrilous attacks, and restores and vindicates the person maligned through damages. Reputation is sometimes seen as a proprietary right that is founded on individual exertion in the marketplace; it may thus also fluctuate according to market conditions. For example, a baker's reputation is based on the quality of his bread. Lastly, reputation can be linked to a person's dignity and is rooted in any decent system of ordered liberty.[85]

Many Asian constitutions expressly stipulate that reputation is a legitimate ground on which freedom of expression may be restricted. For example, Article 21(4) of the South Korean Constitution provides that neither speech nor the press shall violate the honour of other persons; and in the event of violations, claims may be made for damages. Similar provisions are also included in the constitutions of Bangladesh,[86] India,[87] Malaysia,[88] Nepal,[89] Pakistan,[90] Singapore[91] and Sri Lanka,[92] by which the legislature may by law restrict acts of defamation. Noticeably, the protection of women's reputation is especially recognised under Article 46 of the Constitution of Cambodia.[93]

The law of defamation is designed to protect reputation and deter and redress malicious allegations. A delicate balance needs to be struck between free speech and reputational protection, to prevent aimless or malicious attacks on the reputation of individuals, while maintaining an open environment where critical speech, particularly that concerning public affairs or public figures, may be expressed. In this section, we consider the nature of political libel or defamation targeted at public figures.

Comparatively, the leading American case is *New York Times v Sullivan*, in which the Supreme Court formulated a test under which a libel is actionable only if it is actuated by malice or made with reckless disregard to the facts.[94] Subsequently, in *Gertz v Welch*, the Court decided that the standard in *New York Times v Sullivan* applied only to public officials or public figures because private individuals have fewer effective opportunities for rebuttal, and are thus more vulnerable to injury from defamation.[95] Thus, in the United States, one's liability for defamation depends on whether those defamed are public figures or private individuals. Public figures receive less protection

---

[84] RC Post, 'The Social Foundations of Defamation Law: Reputation and the Constitution' (1986) 74(3) *California Law Review* 691.

[85] As expressed by Justice Stewart of the US Supreme Court in *Rosenblatt v Baer* 383 US 75, 92 (1966).

[86] Art 39, Constitution of Bangladesh.

[87] Art 19, Constitution of the Union of India.

[88] Art 10, Constitution of the Federation of Malaysia.

[89] Art 12, Interim Constitution of Nepal.

[90] Art 19, Constitution of Pakistan.

[91] Art 14, Constitution of the Republic of Singapore.

[92] Art 15, Constitution of Sri Lanka.

[93] Art 46 of the Cambodia Constitution provides: 'The commerce of human beings, exploitation by prostitution and obscenity which affect the reputation of women shall be prohibited.'

[94] *New York Times v Sullivan* 376 US 254 (1964).

[95] *Gertz v Welch* 418 US 323, 324 (1974).

as they are subject to greater criticism in a democratic polity because of the need to ensure political accountability and free, open and robust debate on politicians and their policies.

In Asia, the *New York Times v Sullivan* line of reasoning has influenced similar cases on defamation of public officials in some jurisdictions such as Japan, South Korea and Taiwan,[96] and been rejected in other common law jurisdictions as it unduly protects speech at the expense of other important interests.[97] For example, in Singapore, the court in *JB Jeyaretnam v Lee Kuan Yew* expressly rejected the position adopted by the US Supreme Court cases and held that under Singaporean law, politicians or public office holders should enjoy the same protective regime as private individuals.[98] This position was subsequently affirmed in *Goh Chok Tong v Jeyaretnam JB*, in which the Court of Appeal reasoned:

> The Prime Minister is entitled to his reputation no less than the ordinary citizen and it is not required for the Prime Minister to prove malice on the part of the defendant to succeed in this claim. Whilst there is an undeniable public interest in protecting freedom of speech as a means of exposing wrongdoing or abuse of office by public officials, there is an equal public interest in allowing those officials to execute their duties unfettered by false aspersions.[99]

The following discussion is in two parts. The first deals with the defence of truth and the related defence of actual malice or reckless disregard. This is a primary topic of discussion in some Asian jurisdictions, such as Japan, South Korea and Taiwan, which have been influenced – in varying degrees – by American free speech jurisprudence. The second part addresses the defence of fair comment and qualified privilege, a topic that preoccupies courts in common law jurisdictions.

i. Defence of Truth

The defence of truth or justification is possibly one of the strongest defences to an allegation of defamation. In recent years, there has been a trend towards modifying this rule to give greater protection to free speech, following the line of reasoning in *New York Times v Sullivan*. The courts in Japan, South Korea and Taiwan all agree that even if a statement is not true, so long as the speaker has a reasonable ground to believe it is true, the speaker bears no responsibility. This rule was first articulated by the Tokyo High Court in a civil case, and subsequently extended to criminal defamation, which influenced developments in South Korea and Taiwan.

---

[96] See N Kitajima, 'The Protection of Reputation in Japan: A Systematic Analysis of Defamation Cases' (2012) 37 *Law and Social Inquiry* 89, 89–90; Kyu Ho Youm, 'Freedom of Expression and the Law: Rights and Responsibility in South Korea' (2002) 38 *Stanford Journal of International Law* 136; and Kyong Whan Ahn, 'The Influence of American Constitutionalism on South Korea' (1997) 22 *Southern Illinois University Law Journal* 72.

[97] A Stone, 'Freedom of Speech and Defamation: Developments in the Common Law World' (2000) 26(2) *Monash University Law Review* 362.

[98] *JB Jeyaretnam v Lee Kuan Yew* [1992] 2 SLR 310.

[99] *Goh Chok Tong v Jeyaretnam JB* [1998] 1 SLR 547, 561.

Case to Seek Damages and Compensation for Non-Pecuniary Damages Caused
by Libel and Damage to Credit
20 Minshū 5 (Tokyo High Court, Japan)

Facts

The appellant was a candidate in the general election for the House of Representatives in February 1955. The respondent published an article in the paper alleging that the appellant had misrepresented his educational and personal background and was in fact under police investigation for a breach of the Public Offices Election Law. While the report proved to be false, the appellant's suit in the lower court for defamatory damage was denied. He appealed to the Supreme Court.

Held

Concerning libel which is a tortious act under the Civil Code, in cases where the libel act involved facts which concern the public interest and was effected solely for the purpose of the public interest, if the facts stated were proved to be true, the act lacks unlawfulness and shall not constitute a tort. Even if it was not proved that the stated facts were true, if there was a reasonable ground for this person to believe that the facts were true, the act lacks intent or negligence, and therefore, in the end, it does not constitute a tort. This is sufficiently evident from the purpose of Article 230-2 of the Penal Code.

In the present case, according to the judgment of the original instance court (including the judgment of the first instance court cited by the original instance court; the same hereinafter), the jokoku appellant was a candidate for the general election for the House of Representatives which took place in February 1955. The jokoku appellee, as indicated in the judgment of the original instance court, published in the paper which he manages a report that the jokoku appellant had misrepresented his educational and personal history, had been investigated by the police for a breach of the Public Offices Election Law and had a prior conviction. The content of the report, except for the part on misrepresentation, was true, and also regarding the part on misrepresentation, the jokoku appellee at least had a reasonable ground to believe that it was true. The finding of the facts and the ruling are sufficiently justifiable in the light of the evidence indicated in the judgment of the original instance court.

Furthermore, according to the above facts, it is evident that these facts involve the public interest, since the jokoku appellant was a candidate for a member of the House of Representatives, and it is clearly understandable from the text of the judgment of the original instance court that the act of the jokoku appellee was solely for the purpose of pursuing the public interest. Therefore, it is evident from what has been explained in the preceding paragraph that the publication of the report by the jokoku appellee in the paper lacks unlawfulness, or lacks intent or negligence and does not constitute libel as a tort.

There are parts in the judgment of the original instance court which are explained differently from the above, but it has denied that the act constitutes tortious libel, and thus, in conclusion, the ruling of the original instance is justifiable.

Judgment Concerning the Case where a Newspaper Company, when Printing an Article Distributed from a News Agency in the Newspaper that it Publishes, is Deemed to have Reasonable Grounds for Believing the Fact Alleged in Said Article to be True
2009 (Ju) No 2057, 28 Apr 2011 (Supreme Court, Japan)

Facts

The appellant was a physician who worked at a university and an institute in 2001. The respondents were members (and subscribers) of the News Agency Z, an incorporated association with which local newspapers nationwide were affiliated as its members (subscribers). News Agency Z engaged in gathering domestic and overseas news and distributing articles to the subscribers. On 5 July 2002, the respondents printed an article alleging that the appellant made a mistake in handling a heart-lung machine and caused the death of a patient during an the operation performed at the University on 2 March 2001. This article was distributed from the News Agency Z, and the respondents printed it in their respective newspapers without further investigation. The appellant sued for damages, but failed in the lower court. He appealed to the Supreme Court.

Held

In the case of defamation as civil tort, where the defaming act relates to matters of public interest and was conducted solely for the benefit of the public, if the alleged facts are not proven to be true but the person who is accused of having performed the act has reasonable grounds for believing those facts to be true, such person has no intent or negligence in performing said act and there is no tort on his/her part (See 1962 (O) No 815, judgment of the First Petty Bench of the Supreme Court of June 23, 1966, Minshu Vol 20, No 5, at 1118.)

The news reporting system, wherein newspaper companies use news agencies so as to provide readers with a variety of domestic and overseas news, has an important social significance in enriching the content of news reports provided by newspaper companies, and thus serving for the people's right to know, and this system is well recognized in society as a type of modern news reporting system. Under this news reporting system that uses news agencies, newspaper companies are generally not supposed to carry out [a] search for supporting evidence regarding the content of articles distributed from news agencies, and it is in reality difficult for newspaper companies to carry out such search.

. . . Assuming so, where a newspaper company has printed an article distributed from a news agency in the newspaper that it publishes, if, at least, the news agency and the newspaper company can be recognized as forming one news reporting unit throughout the process from news gathering to production, distribution, and printing of articles, it is appropriate to deem the newspaper company to have used the news agency as its news gathering division and had the news agency gather news on its behalf, and in that case, it is reasonable to identify the news gathering by the news agency as the news gathering by the newspaper company. If the news agency has reasonable grounds for believing the facts alleged in the distributed article to be true, the newspaper company should also be deemed to have reasonable grounds for believing the facts alleged in the article that it has printed in the newspaper that it publishes to be true, unless there are special circumstances such as that the newspaper company printed the distributed article in the newspaper carelessly, even though there existed a fact that should have given rise to the newspaper company's suspicion with regard to the trueness of the facts alleged in the distributed article.

Case of Defamation
1966(A) No 2472, 25 Jun 1969 (Supreme Court, Japan)

Facts

The defendant published an article headlined 'Wicked Acts of Tokuichiro Sakaguchi, the Blood-sucker' in the *Yukan Wakayam Jiji* of 18 February 1963. Sakaguchi was proprietor of the *Wakayama Tokudane Shimbun* (newspaper) and the article alleged that he, or a subordinate under his instructions, bribed officials in the Public Works Department of Wakayama City Office and that he had threatened a government official by saying: 'A tender feeling always finds a ready response, they say. Well, my boy, you are suspected of corruption, too. Shall we settle the matter over a glass in a proper place?' Sakaguchi sued the defendant, alleging that the publication was defamatory. The trial court found for Sakaguchi, and on appeal the trial court's judgment was upheld. The defendant took the case up to the Supreme Court.

Held

The court of first instance applied in its judgment Paragraph 1 of Article 230 of the Penal Code [which read '(1) A person who defames another by alleging facts in public shall, regardless of whether such facts are true or false, be punished by imprisonment with or without work for not more than 3 years or a fine of not more than 500,000 yen.'] to the above-mentioned facts and pronounced the accused guilty.

The attorneys in the court below contended, 'Mens rea of defamation is negative in the light of the fact that he believed in the existence of the facts he published on such information and grounds as to enable him to prove it. And the accused is not guilty.' The court below rejected the contention in its judgment, saying, 'It is the purport of the Decision of the Supreme Court (Decision of the 1st Petty Bench, May 7, 1969, Supreme Court Criminal Report Vol 13, No 5, p 641) that the accused is not entitled to be exempted from criminal liability for defamation, notwithstanding his mistaken belief in the existence of the facts so long as it is not proved', and held that the accused could not be exempted from criminal liability for defamation, even if there had been good reason for his mistaken belief in the existence of the facts.

It should be observed, however, that Article 230-2 of the Penal Code has been enacted to reconcile the personal security to honour of an individual and the freedom of speech provided for in Article 21 of the Constitution. Giving thought to the reconciliation and balance of these two interests, it should be construed that, even if there is no proof of the existence of the facts under Paragraph 1 of Article 230-2 of the Penal Code, no crime of defamation was committed because of the absence of mens rea, when the publisher believed mistakenly in the existence of the facts and there was good reason for his mistaken belief on the basis of reliable information and grounds. We are of the opinion that the Decision of the Petty Bench of this Court (Decision of the 1st Petty Bench, May 7, 1959, Case Number (A) No 2698 of 1958, Supreme Court Criminal Report Vol 13 No 5, p 641) diverging from this construction and holding that the accused is not entitled to be exempted from criminal liability for defamation notwithstanding such mistaken belief so long as the existence of the facts is not proved, should be overruled. It follows that the aforementioned holding in the judgment of the court below is incorrect in the construction and application of law.

JY Interpretation 509
7 Jul 2000 (Constitutional Court, Taiwan)

Facts

The petitioners were the chief editor and journalist of *Business Weekly*. In November 1996, they published two articles alleging that the Minister of Transportation and Communication spent public funds on his personal mansion, and described the Minister as 'stingy,' 'acrimonious' and 'ruthless'. The Minister sued them for defamation under Article 310(2) of the Criminal Code and won. The petitioners challenged the constitutionality of the criminal provision.

Held

Article 11 of the Constitution guarantees the right to enjoy the freedom of speech. Such freedom is essential for the diversity of a democratic society. For the freedom of speech not only allows each individual to achieve self-fulfillment, utter his/her opinion freely, pursue the truth, and realize his/her right to know, but also to help the society form a consensus, and encourage civil participation in all manners of rational political and social activities. Thanks to its functions, the government must endeavor to grant a maximum amount of protection to the freedom of speech. However, in light of protecting other individual rights such as personal reputation and privacy and public interests as well, the government may impose reasonable restrictions upon the communication media. The restrictive mechanisms adopted could be civil remedies and/or punitive measures. To make a choice, all of the following factors must be considered: constituents' habit of abiding by the law, constituents' respectfulness for the rights of their peers, effectiveness and availability of the prevailing civil remedies, the media professionals' willingness to comply with their ethics standards in performing their duties, and the effectiveness of sanctions imposed by self-regulatory organizations. Considering our citizenry and all of the above factors, the failure to decriminalize defamation hardly constitutes a violation of the freedom of speech protected under the Constitution. If the law allowed anyone to avoid penalty for defamation by offering monetary compensation, it would be tantamount to issuing them a license to defame, a choice obviously not in line with the constitutional protection of the people's fundamental rights.

. . .

Article 310, the first sentence of Paragraph 3, of the Criminal Code provides that 'to the extent that a statement is defamatory, an accused must be found not guilty if the accused is able to show that the statement is true.' This provision prescribes the elements of a defense; that is, a perpetrator who originated or circulated a defamatory statement may be found not guilty of criminal defamation, if the statement is true. Nevertheless, it does not imply that the accused must carry the burden of proof that the defamatory statement is in fact a truthful statement. In the case where the accused has no way of showing the truthfulness of the statement, the court must find the accused not guilty when the evidence proffered for the court's review shows that the accused has reasonable grounds to believe that the statement was true at the moment of dissemination. Furthermore, this provision does not exempt a public or private prosecutor from his/her statutory burden to prove that the accused has intended to damage another person's reputation, a burden mandated by the criminal procedures, nor does the provision exempt the court from its duty of discovering the truth.

Letter of Condolence for Kim Il-sung Case
97Hun-Ma265, 24 Jun 1999 (Constitutional Court, South Korea)

Facts

The complainant was a member of the Kang-won Province Assembly. To promote a South–North exchange program initiated by Kang-won Province, he sent a letter addressed to Kim Jung-il requesting co-operation for the programme. The letter contained the following words:

Dear the Commander-in-Chief of People's Army for the Democratic People's Republic of Korea; Have you been well? You must have passed many days in grief since Premier Kim Il-sung passed away. I would like to express sympathy and encouragement for you.

The letter further explained that the complainant once received a letter from Kim Jung-il and expressed his anti-dictatorship struggle against the past military regime. The letter and its delivery route were investigated by the Board of Reunification and law enforcement agencies. On 9 April 1995, *Kwang-won Daily News* reported the investigation under a headline 'Three Provincial Assemblymen in Contact with North under Probe' and a sub-title 'Police and Prosecutor on a Letter of Condolence for Kim Il-sung to Kim Jung-il'. The newspaper continued using the expression 'a condolence letter for Kim Il-sung' 17 more times until 6 September. The complainant sued the publisher and reporters of the newspaper for defamation in publishing a false report with a derogatory purpose. The prosecutors dismissed the charges and the complainant brought the case to the Constitutional Court.

Held

The Court unanimously rejected the complaint. The Court laid out a general standard for balancing the competing interests of protecting freedom of expression and one's reputation concerning a newspaper report on a public person's public activities as follows:

The standard for constitutional scrutiny of a defamatory newspaper report should vary, depending on the public or private nature of the defamed person and the subject matter reported. Objective facts of sufficient public and social value to people contribute to the opinion-making and public discourses that form the basis of democracy, and should not be suppressed for fear of criminal prosecution. Expeditious reporting is the life of a newspaper. The newspaper should be free from all threat of criminal prosecution for those reports that were delivered under the justified belief of truth but turned out to be false, or that were false on minor points. A newspaper report competes with time. The attendant errors in its reports are unavoidable in guaranteeing unlimited, free publication of thoughts and opinions. These expressions are necessary for free discussion and truth-finding and should be protected alike. Only the falsities published knowingly or unconfirmed despite the lack of any basis for truth are outside the protection.

Therefore, we hold that criminal defamation provisions must be interpreted narrowly when they are applied against defamatory reports on a public person's public activities.

Firstly, even absent a proof of truth of the report, when the charged acted with mistaken but justified belief in its truth, the crime is not established. Secondly, the Article 310 Criminal Act exemption for those reports 'solely concerned with the interest of the public' should be broadened in its application. Thirdly, the element of 'derogatory purpose' in Article 309 of Criminal Act should be interpreted narrowly. A judge must find a derogatory purpose only on stringent proof.

In this case, we do not find major falsities in the report. Even where trivial falsities can be found, we also find the charged justified in believing them to be true.

Notes and Questions

1. Study the above decisions by the courts in Japan, South Korea and Taiwan. Is the standard by which an untrue statement may be excused the same? What gives rise to similarity in doctrine? Similar extent of political liberalisation? Legal system? Regional affinity? Or cross-jurisdiction judicial dialogues?

2. To protect reputational rights, many countries have both civil and criminal defamation laws. In Western jurisdictions like Germany, Canada and several US States, criminal defamation laws are maintained. In Asia, the majority of states also have criminal defamation laws, including Japan, South Korea, China, Taiwan, India, Burma, Bangladesh, Pakistan, Indonesia, the Philippines, Singapore, Malaysia and Thailand. Typically, the criminal defamation law sets a higher bar for successful prosecution. Intention to harm or knowledge that harm will be suffered are the usual thresholds for criminal prosecutions, which must also be proved beyond reasonable doubt. The enforcement of criminal defamation laws may have an unduly chilling effect, which deters free speech and thwarts open discussion in a democracy. To enhance free speech protection, the Human Rights Committee has recommended the liberalisation or decriminalisation of defamation laws. General Comment No 34 asserts:

    > Defamation laws must be crafted with care to ensure that they . . . do not serve, in practice, to stifle freedom of expression. All such laws, in particular penal defamation laws, should include such defences as the defence of truth and they should not be applied with regard to those forms of expression that are not, of their nature, subject to verification. At least with regard to comments about public figures, consideration should be given to avoiding penalizing or otherwise rendering unlawful untrue statements that have been published in error but without malice. In any event, a public interest in the subject matter of the criticism should be recognized as a defence. Care should be taken by States parties to avoid excessively punitive measures and penalties. Where relevant, States parties should place reasonable limits on the requirement for a defendant to reimburse the expenses of the successful party. States parties should consider the decriminalization of defamation and, in any case, the application of the criminal law should only be countenanced in the most serious of cases and imprisonment is never an appropriate penalty. It is impermissible for a State party to indict a person for criminal defamation but then not to proceed to trial expeditiously – such a practice has a chilling effect that may unduly restrict the exercise of freedom of expression of the person concerned and others.[100]

3. Criminal defamation laws accompanied by severe punishment raise constitutional concerns. The Philippines Supreme Court issued a restraining order on the implementation of the Cybercrime Prevention Act as one of its provisions regarded libel as a type of cybercrime that was punishable with up to 12 years' imprisonment.[101] Under the new Act, a person found guilty of making defamatory comments online, including on social networks, may be fined or jailed. Government

---

[100] Human Rights Committee, General Comment No 34: *Freedoms of Opinion and Expression* (para 47), 102nd Session, 2011.

[101] C Diola and CM Arcibal, 'SC Issues TRO on New Cyber Law', *The Philippines Star*, 9 October 2012, at <http://www.philstar.com/nation/article.aspx?publicationsubcategoryid=63&articleid=857646>.

officials have the power to search and seize data from the online accounts of individuals. This new law was heavily criticised as it offered the Government tremendous power which it might use to target political opponents. In January 2013, the Supreme Court heard 15 consolidated petitions challenging this Act,[102] and on 6 February 2013, the Philippines Supreme Court extended indefinitely the temporary restraining order it had made earlier.

ii. Fair Comment and Qualified Privilege

Fair comment as a defence against defamation is typically raised in common law jurisdictions like Hong Kong and Singapore. The issues centre on whether a comment is made in the public interest, how to distinguish comment from statement of facts, whether the statement is made by an honest person without malice, and the question of who suffers if clarification of facts and comment is unattainable. Qualified privilege as a defence to political defamation confers an immunity from suit; this rests on the showing of a special relationship or special facts, such that there is a public interest strong enough to give rise to a legal, social or moral duty on the part of the speaker or publisher to communicate.

The Hong Kong Court of Final Appeal held in the case of *Eastern Express Publisher Ltd v Mo Man Ching* that

> in a society which greatly values the freedom of speech and safeguards it by a constitutional guarantee, it is right that the courts when considering and developing the common law should not adopt a narrow approach to the defence of fair comment.[103]

This generous approach to the right of fair comment on the matters of public interest has been maintained with full vigour.[104] In *Albert Cheng v Tse Wai Chun Paul*, the Court of Final Appeal discussed in detail elements of fair comment and considered whether the purpose or motive for which a defendant states an honestly held opinion may deprive him or her of the protection of the defence. It concluded that although motives may evince the absence of a genuine belief, this is not conclusive and such speech warranted protection.

Certain jurisdictions may recognise a qualified privilege with respect to subject matter like political communication,[105] or specific to actors like the media. Singapore law does not recognise a general category of qualified privilege at common law for media defendants. In *Review Publishing Co Ltd v Lee Hsien Loong*,[106] the Singapore Court of Appeal considered whether developments in relation to defences to defamation were part of the law of qualified privilege in Singapore, or whether they should be adopted as part of the Singapore common law. In particular, it considered the *Reynolds* privilege ('responsible journalism' media privilege) developed by the House of Lords in *Reynolds v Times Newspapers Ltd*[107] and developments in other Commonwealth juris-

---

[102] 'SC tackles cybercrime law cases today', *The Philippines Star*, 5 February 2013, at<http://www.philstar.com/headlines/2013/02/05/904997/sc-tackles-cybercrime-law-cases-today>.

[103] *Eastern Express Publisher Ltd v Mo Man Ching* [1999] 2 HKCFAR 264, 278.

[104] As expressed by Chief Justice Andrew Li in *Albert Cheng v Tse Wai Chun Paul* [2000] 4 HKC 1, 1.

[105] Eg *Lange v ABC* (1997) 145 LR 96.

[106] *Review Publishing Co Ltd v Lee Hsien Loong* [2009] SGCA 46.

[107] *Reynolds v Times Newspapers Ltd* [2001] 2 AC 127.

dictions, and noted that in balancing free expression against reputational interests, the House of Lords shifted the balance in favour of free speech. The Court further noted that the categories of qualified privilege were not closed, as these were affected by public policy considerations, and rejected any special privilege for media defendants, and noted that the development of qualified privilege would depend on the 'political, social and cultural values' of the day.

Albert Cheng & Anor v Tse Wai Chun Paul
[2000] 4 HKC 1 (Court of Final Appeal, Hong Kong)

Facts

In September 1991, two Hong Kongers, Au Wing Cheung (a tour guide) and Wong Chuen Ming, were arrested for drug trafficking in the Philippines. They were convicted and sentenced to life imprisonment. Their arrests aroused much interest in Hong Kong and different groups organized campaigns seeking their release. The plaintiff Tse was legal adviser to one of these groups, the Tourist Industry Rescue Group. Meanwhile, the first defendant, Cheng, organized another group to agitate for Au's and Wong's release. In July 1996, Au and Wong were released and returned to Hong Kong, accompanied by Tse and Cheng and others. On 1 August 1996, Cheng and one Lam Yuk Wah were co-hosts of a call-in radio talk show called 'Teacup in a Storm'. Part of the program consisted of a dialogue between Cheng and Lam. Unhappy with remarks made in the course of this dialogue, Tse sued Cheng, Lam and the Hong Kong Commercial Broadcasting Co Ltd. Their defence was that their statements were not defamatory; that they were true or substantially true; and that they consisted of expressions of opinion that were fair comment on a matter of public interest. Tse alleged that the defendants made the statements maliciously.

Andrew Li CJ

This is an appeal in a defamation action. It raises an important point on the defence of fair comment. The title of this defence is misleading. Comment, or honest comment, would be a more satisfactory name. In this judgment I adhere, reluctantly, to the traditional terminology.

Fair comment: the objective limits

In order to identify the point in issue I must first set out some non-controversial matters about the ingredients of this defence. These are well established. They are fivefold. First, the comment must be on a matter of public interest. Public interest is not to be confined within narrow limits today.

Second, the comment must be recognisable as comment, as distinct from an imputation of fact. If the imputation is one of fact, a ground of defence must be sought elsewhere, for example, justification or privilege. Much learning has grown up around the distinction between fact and comment. For present purposes it is sufficient to note that a statement may be one or the other, depending on the context. Ferguson J gave a simple example in the New South Wales case of *Myerson v Smith's Weekly* (1923) 24 SR (NSW) 20, 26:

> To say that a man's conduct was dishonourable is not comment, it is a statement of fact. To say that he did certain specific things and that his conduct was dishonourable is a statement of fact coupled with a comment.

Third, the comment must be based on facts which are true or protected by privilege: see, for instance, *London Artists Ltd v Littler* [1969] 2 QB 375, 395. If the facts on which the comment purports to be founded are not proved to be true or published on a privilege occasion, the defence of fair comment is not available.

Next, the comment must explicitly or implicitly indicate, at least in general terms, what are the facts on which the comment is being made. The reader or hearer should be in a position to judge for himself how far the comment was well founded.

Finally, the comment must be one which could have been made by an honest person, however prejudiced he might be, and however exaggerated or obstinate his views . . . It must be germane to the subject matter criticised. Dislike of an artist's style would not justify an attack upon his morals or manners. But a critic need not be mealy-mouthed in denouncing what he disagrees with. He is entitled to dip his pen in gall for the purposes of legitimate criticism: see Jordan CJ in *Gardiner v Fairfax* (1942) 42 SR (NSW) 171, 174.

These are the outer limits of the defence. The burden of establishing that a comment falls within these limits, and hence within the scope of the defence, lies upon the defendant who wishes to rely upon the defence.

Malice

That is not the end of the matter. Even when a defendant has brought his case within these limits, he will not necessarily succeed. The plaintiff may still defeat ('rebut') the defence by proving that when he made his comment the defendant was, in the time-hallowed expression, 'actuated by malice'.

It is here that the storm clouds begin to appear. In ordinary usage malice carries connotations of spite and ill-will. This is not always so in legal usage. In legal usage malice sometimes bears its popular meaning, sometimes not. It is an imprecise term. Historically, even within the bounds of the law of defamation, malice has borne more than one meaning. Historically, defamation lay in publishing the words complained of 'falsely and maliciously'. In this context malice meant merely that publication had been a wrongful act, done intentionally and without lawful excuse: see Bayley J in *Bromage v Prosser* (1825) 4 B&C 247, 255. This was sometimes called malice in law, as distinct from malice in fact. But even malice 'in fact', otherwise known as express malice or actual malice, may cover states of mind which are not malicious in the ordinary sense of the word. This is so in the context of the defence of qualified privilege. It is no wonder that Lord Bramwell described malice as 'that unfortunate word': see *Abrath v North Eastern Railway Co* (1886) 11 App Cas 247, 253.

The question raised by this appeal concerns the meaning of malice in the context of the defence of fair comment. On this, two matters are clear. First, unlike the outer limits (as I have called them) of the defence of fair comment, which are objective, malice is subjective. It looks to the defendant's state of mind. Second, malice covers the case of the defendant who does not genuinely hold the view he expressed. In other words, when making the defamatory comment the defendant acted dishonestly. He put forward as his view something which, in truth, was not his view. It was a pretence. The law does not protect such statements. Within the objective limits mentioned above, the law protects the freedom to express opinions, not vituperative make-believe. . . .

Motive

. . . Proof of malice is the means whereby a plaintiff can defeat a defence of fair comment where a defendant is abusing the defence. Abuse consists of using the defence for a purpose other than that for which it exists. The purpose for which the defence of fair comment exists is to facilitate freedom of expression by commenting on matters of public interest. This accords with the constitutional guarantee of freedom of expression. And it is in the public interest that everyone should be free to express his own, honestly held views on such matters, subject always to the safeguards provided by the objective limits mentioned above. These safeguards ensure that defamatory comments can be seen for what they are, namely, comments as distinct from statements of fact. They also ensure that those reading the comments have the material enabling them to make up their own minds on whether they agree or disagree. . . .

The purpose and importance of the defence of fair comment are inconsistent with its scope being restricted to comments made for particular reasons or particular purposes, some being regarded as proper, others not. Especially in the social and political fields, those who make public comments usually have some objective of their own in mind, even if it is only to publicise and advance themselves. They often have what may be described as an 'ulterior' object. Frequently their object is apparent, but not always so. They may hope to achieve some result, such as promoting one cause or defeating another, elevating one person or denigrating another. In making their comments they do not act dispassionately, they do not intend merely to convey information. They have other motives.

The presence of these motives, and this is of crucial importance for present purposes, is not a reason for excluding the defence of fair comment. The existence of motives such as these when expressing an opinion does not mean that the defence of fair comment is being misused. It would make no sense, for instance, if a motive relating to the very feature which causes the matter to be one of public interest were regarded as defeating the defence.

On the contrary, this defence is intended to protect and promote comments such as these. Liberty to make such comments, genuinely held, on matters of public interest lies at the heart of the defence of fair comment. That is the very object for which the defence exists. Commentators, of all shades of opinion, are entitled to 'have their own agenda'. Politicians, social reformers, busybodies, those with political or other ambitions and those with none, all can grind their axes. The defence of fair comment envisages that everyone is at liberty to conduct social and political campaigns by expressing his own views, subject always, and I repeat the refrain, to the objective safeguards which mark the limits of the defence.

Nor is it for the courts to choose between 'public' and 'private' purposes, or between purposes they regard as morally or socially or politically desirable and those they regard as undesirable. That would be a highly dangerous course. That way lies censorship. That would defeat the purpose for which the law accords the defence of freedom to make comments on matters of public interest. The objective safeguards, coupled with the need to have a genuine belief in what is said, are adequate to keep the ambit of permissible comment within reasonable bounds.

Spiteful comments

One particular motive calls for special mention: spite or ill-will. This raises a difficult point. I confess that my first, instinctive reaction was that the defence of fair comment should not be capable of being used to protect a comment made with the intent of injuring another out of spite, even if the person who made the comment genuinely believed in the truth of what he said. Personal spite, after all, is four square within the popular meaning of malice. Elsewhere the law proscribes conduct of this character; for instance, in the field of nuisance, as exemplified by the well known case of the householder who made noises on musical instruments with the intention of annoying his neighbour (*Christie v Davey* [1893] 1 Ch 316).

On reflection I do not think the law should attempt to ring-fence comments made with the sole or dominant motive of causing injury out of spite or, which may come to much the same, causing injury simply for the sake of doing so. In the first place it seems to me that the postulate on which this problem is based is a little unreal. The postulate poses a problem which is more academic than practical. The postulate is that the comment in question falls within the objective limits of the defence. Thus, the comment is one which is based on fact; it is made in circumstances where those to whom the comment is addressed can form their own view on whether or not the comment was sound; and the comment is one which can be held by an honest person. This postulate supposes, further, that the maker of the comment genuinely believes in the truth of his comment. It must be questionable whether comments, made out of spite and causing injury, are at all likely to satisfy each and every of these requirements. There must be a query over whether, in practice, there is a problem here which calls for attention.

Moreover, in so far as this situation is ever likely to arise, it is by no means clear that the underlying public interest does require that the person impugned should have a remedy. Take the case of a politician or a journalist who genuinely believes that a minister is untrustworthy and not fit to hold ministerial office. Facts exist from which an honest person could form that view. The politician or journalist states his view, with the intention of injuring the minister. His reason for doing so was a private grudge, derived from a past insult, actual or supposed. I am far from persuaded that the law should give the minister a remedy. The spiteful publication of a defamatory statement of fact attracts no remedy if the statement is proved to be true. Why should the position be different for the spiteful publication of a defamatory, genuinely held comment based on true fact?

There is a further consideration. The law of defamation is, in all conscience, sufficiently complex, even tortuous, without introducing further subtle distinctions which will be hard to explain to a jury. The concept of intent to injure is easy enough. But, as already noted, intent to injure is not inconsistent with the purpose for which the defence of fair comment exists. So, if spite and cognate states of mind are to be outlawed for the purposes of this defence, the directions to the jury would have to be elaborate and sophisticated.

Review Publishing Co Ltd & Anor v Lee Hsien Loong & Anor
[2009] SGCA 46 (Court of Appeal, Singapore)

Facts

The Review Publishing Co Ltd ('RP') was publisher of the *Far Eastern Economic Review* ('FEER'). It published an article following an interview with Chee Soon Juan, Secretary-General of the Singapore Democratic Party. In this article entitled 'Singapore's Martyr', Chee said this about former Prime Minister Lee Kuan Yew:

> Why is he still so afraid? I honestly think that through the years he has accumulated enough skeletons in his closet that he knows that when he is gone, his son and the generations after him will have a price to pay. If we had parliamentary debates where the opposition could pry and ask questions, I think he is actually afraid of something like that.

Lee Hsien Loong (son of Lee Kuan Yew) and his father commenced this action for defamation, arguing that anyone reading it would assume that they were corrupt and suppressed the opposition unfairly, and were thus unfit for office. One defence raised by RP was 'fair comment'.

Chan Sek Keong CJ

Ground (f): The Defence of Fair Comment

There are four elements which the defendants must establish in order to succeed on the plea of fair comment:

(i) the words complained of are comments, though they may consist of or include inference[s] of facts;
(ii) the comment is on a matter of public interest;
(iii) the comment is based on facts; and
(iv) the comment is one which a fair-minded person can honestly make on the facts proved.

. . . As mentioned earlier, whether a statement is a comment or a statement of fact is '[a question] of fact, dependent upon the nature of the imputation conveyed, and the context and circumstances in which it is published' (see *Evans on Defamation* ([26] supra) at p 103). The Judge gave extensive reasons as to why he considered the Relevant Statements, when read in the context of the Article as a whole and taking into account the circumstances of the present case, to be statements of fact rather than comments (see the Judgment at [152]–[153]). We agree with those reasons. To avoid unnecessary repetition of these reasons here, it suffices for us to say that the context of the Article as well as the tone and language employed therein would leave the ordinary reasonable person with no doubt that the Appellants were putting across factual statements rather than comments. . . .

At this juncture, we would like to add an observation on the defence of fair comment. The Appellants are no strangers to court actions for defamation in so far as publications in FEER have previously been the subject of defamation suits in Singapore. As a matter of prudence, all reputable publishers, especially those whose publications have an international readership, have lawyers to advise them on the law of defamation in the various jurisdictions in which they publish. We assume that RP [respondent] must also have followed this salutary practice. Given the applicable legal principles on the defence of fair comment (as articulated by case law) and the difficulty of distinguishing comments from statements of fact, it is incumbent upon the media to make it clear in its editorials or opinion pieces which statements are comments and which statements are simply factual statements or imputations of fact.

Ultimately, if a publisher is sued for defamation, the burden would be on it to establish the defence of fair comment. It should be borne in mind that, if the publisher fails to distinguish clearly between statements of facts and comments, the statements in question would not be protected by the plea of fair comment and would be considered by the court to be statements of facts (see *Evans on Defamation* at p 103). The rationale for this approach was explained by Fletcher Moulton LJ in the English CA case of *Hunt v The Star Newspaper Company, Limited* [1908] 2 KB 309 ('Hunt') at 319–320, as follows:

> The law as to fair comment, so far as is material to the present case, stands as follows: In the first place, comment in order to be justifiable as fair comment must appear as comment and must not be so mixed up with the facts that the reader cannot distinguish between what is report and what is comment . . . The justice of this rule is obvious. If the facts are stated separately and the comment appears as an inference drawn from those facts, any injustice that it might do will be to some extent negatived by the reader seeing the grounds upon which the unfavourable inference is based. But if fact and comment be intermingled so that it is not reasonably clear what portion purports to be inference, he will naturally suppose that the injurious statements are based on adequate grounds known to the writer though not necessarily set out by him. In the one case the

insufficiency of the facts to support the inference will lead fair-minded men to reject the inference. In the other case it merely points to the existence of extrinsic facts which the writer considers to warrant the language he uses. . . . Any matter, therefore, which does not indicate with a reasonable clearness that it purports to be comment, and not [a] statement of fact, cannot be protected by the plea of fair comment.

. . . The media has a responsibility to its readers and, in particular, to the potential plaintiff whose reputation may be seriously damaged by careless words which the ordinary reasonable person may view as statements of fact rather than comments. In this regard, the media can easily avoid the pitfall of its comments being mistaken by the ordinary reasonable person as statements of fact by making it clear that the statements concerned are comments and not statements of facts, and by identifying the facts on which the comments are based so as to ensure that there is no confusion on the reader's part as to which portions of the statements are comments and which portions are statements of facts. Of course, such measures (in cases where they are taken) would not conclusively denote whether the statements in question are comments or statements of fact. These measures would, however, serve as a strong indicator to the court of how the statements concerned are likely to be understood (ie, whether as comments or as statements of fact) by the ordinary reasonable person. As pertinently noted in Geoffrey Robertson & Andrew Nicol, *Robertson & Nicol on Media Law* (Sweet & Maxwell, 4th Ed, 2002) at p 120:

> The fair comment defence relates only to comment – to statements of opinion and not to statements of fact. This is the most important, and most difficult, distinction in the entire law of libel. . . . Writers can help to characterise their criticisms as comment with phrases like 'it seems to me', 'in my judgment', 'in other words', etc, although such devices will not always be conclusive. . . . Where a defamatory remark is made baldy, without reference to any fact from which the remark could be inferred, it is not likely to be defensible as comment, especially if it imputes dishonesty or dishonourable conduct.

In short, a person who wishes to write anything about another person that is prima facie defamatory of the latter has the means to state clearly whether what is being written is meant to be a comment or a statement of fact. If the writer fails to do so, there is no reason why he (and, likewise, the publisher of the statement) should be given the benefit of the defence of fair comment.

With regard to the defence of fair comment in the instant case, we are unable to say that the Judge was wrong in finding (at [152] of the Judgment) that, even if the Relevant Statements were comments, they were not comments based on facts (see the third element of this defence as laid down in Chen Cheng ([139] supra) at [33]). (Indeed, it appears to us that the Relevant Statements also do not satisfy the fourth element of the defence of fair comment in so far as they are not comments which a fair-minded person could honestly make on the facts proved. . . .

Ground (h): The Defence of Qualified Privilege

The last ground of appeal advanced by the Appellants is that they are entitled to rely on the Reynolds privilege and/or its offshoot, the neutral reportage defence. We should point out that the application of this privilege, after it was laid down in *Reynolds* (HL) ([20] supra), was subsequently clarified (likewise by the House of Lords) in *Jameel (Mohammed) v Wall Street Journal Europe Sprl* [2007] 1 AC 359 ('Jameel'). In using the expression 'the Reynolds privilege' in this judgment, we are referring to the Reynolds privilege as so clarified . . .

(1) The Key Question

The crucial question vis-à-vis Singapore citizens (which we shall hereafter refer to as 'the key question') is whether or not, in the context of publication of matters of public interest, the Reynolds rationale ought to apply so that (to paraphrase Lord Steyn's words in *Reynolds* (HL) at 208) constitutional free speech becomes the rule and restrictions on this right become the exception. This question has not hitherto been decided by this court.

. . . We would suggest that the following considerations are particularly pertinent to how the key question may be answered by our courts, namely:

(a) The balance in Singapore between constitutional free speech and protection of reputation has remained unchanged since it was struck on 16 September 1963 when freedom of speech became a constitutional right here.

(b) Our common law of defamation has all along been held, implicitly, in numerous decisions of this court to strike the appropriate balance between constitutional free speech and protection of reputation.

(c) Unlike the legislative policy in England (as expressed in s 12 of the HRA), Singapore does not have any law recognising journalistic material as being of special importance in the context of publishing matters of public interest. Instead, as stated at [251] above, Parliament has enacted laws to restrict the constitutional free speech conferred by Art 14(1)(a) of the Singapore Constitution (and its predecessor provisions), and there is no room in our political context for the media to engage in investigative journalism which carries with it a political agenda.

(d) Our local political culture places a heavy emphasis on honesty and integrity in public discourse on matters of public interest, especially those matters which concern the governance of this country.

We shall now elaborate on these considerations.

(A) The Existing Balance Between Constitutional Free Speech and Protection of Reputation is Appropriate

. . . [C]onstitutional free speech under Art 14(1)(a) of the Singapore Constitution (and its predecessor provisions) has existed in Singapore since 16 September 1963 (see [237] above). The balance between constitutional free speech and protection of reputation was struck on that date and, in the intervening years, our courts have consistently held that our common law of defamation is not incompatible with constitutional free speech even though it is a restriction on the latter (see, inter alia, *JBJ v LKY* (1990) ([238] supra) and *JBJ v LKY* (1992) ([19] supra); see also Lee Hsien Loong (HC) ([32] supra), which was decided after Reynolds (HL)). This suggests that our courts regard the balance struck on 16 September 1963 between constitutional free speech and protection of reputation as still being appropriate in the prevailing circumstances in Singapore today. . . .

(B) The Media's Role in Our Society

. . . In contrast, we do not have a law directing the courts to have special regard, where journalistic materials are concerned, to the extent to which it is or would be in the public interest for the materials in question to be published (cf s 12(4)(a)(ii) of the HRA). Furthermore, as counsel for the Respondents pointed out to us, in our political context, the notion that '[t]he press discharges vital functions as . . . a watchdog' (per Lord Nicholls in *Reynolds* (HL) at 205) is not accepted. The media has no special role beyond reporting the news and giving its views on matters of public interest fairly and accurately.

... In short, the media's role in Singapore has hitherto been and continues to be limited to what Lord Nicholls referred to in *Reynolds* (HL) as 'the traditional activities of reporting and commenting' (id at 200). Our political context therefore militates against applying the Reynolds rationale to extend the scope of the traditional qualified privilege defence where the publication of matters of public interest is concerned. The media can, however, as Mr Goh acknowledged, report on 'things [that] are wrong' (for instance, where there is corruption in the Government). When 'things are wrong' in relation to matters that affect the way in which the State is governed, citizens obviously have a right to know about what has gone wrong. It also goes without saying that Mr Goh's statement that the media can report on 'things [that] are wrong' does not mean that the media is free to publish defamatory statements.

(C) Our Local Emphasis on Honesty and Integrity in Public Discourse

... In contrast, it is questionable whether the marketplace of ideas rationale is applicable to false statements. Such statements are (by definition) inaccurate and society does not derive any value from their publication as 'there is no interest in being misinformed'
   ... In Singapore, there is no place in our political culture for making false defamatory statements which damage the reputation of a person (especially a holder of public office) for the purposes of scoring political points. Our political culture places a heavy emphasis on honesty and integrity in public discourse on matters of public interest, especially those matters which concern the governance of the country.
   ... Reverting to the issues which this court needs to decide in the present appeals, we agree with and affirm the Judge's ruling on the natural and ordinary meaning of the Disputed Words in relation to the Respondents. We also uphold the Judge's decision to allow LHL [Lee Hsien Long] to amend his SOC [statement of claim] and to reject the Appellants' pleaded defences.

Notes and Questions

1. Chief Justice Andrew Li of the Hong Kong Court of Final Appeal has emphasised a generous approach to the right of fair comment on matters of public interest. Do you think that the elements of fair comment articulated and applied in *Albert Cheng & Anor v Tse Wai Chun* were construed generously in favour of free speech? Why, or why not?

2. Compare the case of *Albert Cheng v Tse Wai Chun* with *Review Publishing Co v Lee Hsien Loong*. Is there any difference in their articulation of the fair comment defence? What gives rise to such difference?

3. What is the role of media in relation to the law of political defamation? Contrast the Singapore case of *Review Publishing Co v Lee Hsien Loong* with those from Japan and South Korea excerpted above.

4. In the *Judgment Concerning the Case where a Newspaper Company, when Printing an Article Distributed from a News Agency in the Newspaper that it Publishes, is Deemed to have Reasonable Grounds for Believing the Fact Alleged in Said Article to be True*, the Supreme Court of Japan emphasised that the news reporting system 'has an important social significance in enriching the content of news reports provided by newspaper companies, and thus serving for the people's right to

know', thus privileging the media which enjoys greater protection of free speech. Similarly, in the *Letter of Condolence for Kim Il-sung Case*, the Constitutional Court of South Korea also stressed that 'expeditious reporting is the life of a newspaper', and thus 'the newspaper should be free from all threat of criminal prosecution for those reports that were delivered under the justified belief of truth but turned out to be false, or that were false on minor points'.

5. In contrast, in *Review Publishing Co v Lee Hsien Loong*, the Singapore Court of Appeal, when discussing the role of the media and responsible journalism, stated that

    > [t]he media has a responsibility to its readers and, in particular, to the potential plaintiff whose reputation may be seriously damaged by careless words which the ordinary reasonable person may view as statements of fact rather than comments.

    Law Minister K Shanmugam also expressed the Government's concern that the media might engage in investigative journalism which carried with it a political agenda.[108]

6. What is your view of the role of media in public debate and democratic govern-ance? What gives rise to the different approaches in different countries? Is it a question of different conceptualisation of democracy, or the ideal of public debate in which the media assume the role? What about different social realities in the media market?

7. In Singapore, while politicians and public figures have the same protection as pri-vate individuals, when it comes to the assessment of the quantum of damages this egalitarianism disappears, the courts holding that a 'prominent public figure' deserves higher damages. In *Goh Chok Tong v Chee Soon Juan (No 2)*, the award of damages was high, SGD$300,000, 'because it constituted a severe indictment against a senior member of the government for the disposal of a large sum of the nation's fund'.[109] In *Lee Hsien Loong v Singapore Democratic Party*, it was noted that the libel against the plaintiffs, including Minister Mentor Lee Kuan Yew (LKY) and Prime Minister Lee Hsien Loong (LHY), was 'the gravest imaginable', attacking the core of their 'integrity, honour, courage, loyalty and achievements', and having taken into account 'the position, standing and the reputation of the plaintiffs', large awards of damages, $330,000 (LHY) and $280,000 (LKY) were made.[110]

8. In contrast, as Noriko Kitajima points out, in Japan, 'politicians and officials are less likely to win in defamation cases than are [business] executives and criminals, and they received lower damages than athletes and entertainers'.[111] What do you think about such a difference? Does it relate to different political cultures, to the image of politicians, to visions of democratic governance?

---

[108] *Review Publishing Co Ltd v Lee Hsien Loong* [2009] SGCA 46.
[109] *Goh Chok Tong v Chee Soon Juan (No 2)* [2005] 1 SLR 573, 581.
[110] *Lee Hsien Loong v Singapore Democratic Party* [2009] 1 SLR 642 [148], [154].
[111] Kitajima, above n 96, 119.

F. Obscenity and Pornography

The law may differentiate between valuable and less valuable speech, and calibrate the degree of protection afforded on this basis. What is considered to be high-value or low-value speech depends on the background political philosophy, culture and context. What may be considered art in one country may be considered worthless pornography which degrades women in another. Categories of low-value speech typically relate to laws regulating obscenity and pornography. While this sort of speech may be unprotected in many jurisdictions, in a postmodern and plural world it is not surprising that definitions of what constitute 'pornography' or 'obscenity' continue to be subject to debate. If they are construed too broadly, this may unduly chill expression, just as the failure to protect public goods like public morality and the moral ecology can have deleterious effects and cause personal and social harm.[112]

What possible justifications are there to curtail 'speech' that is 'obscene' or 'pornographic'? Ronald Dworkin discussed four possible justifications in an article entitled 'Liberty and Pornography'.[113] One possible justification is that such speech causes great harm to women, as some forms of pornography significantly increase the danger of women being sexually violated. Yet empirical difficulty in proving the causal link between pornography and sexual violence does exist. Another justification is that pornography causes subordination of women, and has contributed to an unequal economic and social structure in which women are trapped. A third justification is that a negative liberty – which is the liberty not to be obstructed by others – for expressing obscene speech conflicts with the positive liberty – the power to control or participate in public decisions – for women to be recognised as coequal partners in the political sphere. The fourth ground of justification is that regarding the conflict between two negative liberties: the negative liberty to express obscene speech may curtail – in fact, silence – women's negative liberty to express themselves freely. Public morals provide an additional ground for restricting pornographic speech. According to Robert George, 'the central harm of pornography is moral harm – harm to character and thus to the human goods and institutions'.[114]

Aside from finding justifications to restrict obscene speech, formulating the definitions of obscenity or pornography is another challenge. It is worth referring to an old English definition originating from *Regina v Hicklin*, which is frequently applied in Indian cases, where the court held:

> [W]hether the tendency of the matter charged as obscenity is to deprave and corrupt those whose minds are open to such immoral influences, and into whose hands a publication of this sort may fall . . ., it would . . . suggest . . . thoughts of a most impure and libidinous character.[115]

---

[112] Eg see RP George, 'The Concept of Public Morality' (2000) 45 *American Journal of Jurisprudence* 17, 17–18: 'The central harm of pornography is not . . . that it shocks and offends people, any more than the central harm of carcinogenic smoke is that it smells bad. Rather, the central harm of pornography is moral harm – harm to character and thus to the human goods and institutions, such as the good and institution of marriage, which are preserved and advanced by a disposition to act uprightly, and damaged and defiled by a contrary disposition, in respect to them.'

[113] R Dworkin, 'Liberty and Pornography', *The New York Times Review of Books*, 15 August 1991, vol 38 no 14, at 12.

[114] George, above n 112.

[115] *Regina v Hicklin* (1868) LR 3 QB 360.

In *Miller v State of California*, the US Supreme Court offered a relatively modern guideline to determine if something was obscenity: first, whether the average person, applying contemporary community standards, would find that the work, taken as a whole, appeals to the prurient interest; secondly, whether the work depicts or describes, in a patently offensive way, sexual conduct specifically defined by law; and, lastly, whether the work, taken as a whole, lacks serious literary, artistic, political or scientific value.[116]

The standard in *Miller* has been applied in Taiwan and Japan, where obscenity is defined as 'by objective standards stimulating or satisfying a prurient interest, generating among common people a feeling of shame or distaste, thereby offending their sense of sexual morality, and undermining societal cultural ethics'.[117] However, as societal values evolve and coarsen, recent cases show a liberalising trend, where the courts have narrowly construed obscenity to allow more freedom for sexual expression. For instance, the Constitutional Court of Taiwan in *JY Interpretation No 617* (excerpted below) restricted only materials that 'include violence, sexual abuse or bestiality but are lacking in artistic, medical or educational value'. A 2008 Japanese case, (also excerpted below), also demonstrates similar liberalisation toward sexually explicit speeches. It is interesting to note that in Japan and India, the judicial formulation of 'obscenity' revolved around DH Lawrence's *Lady Chatterley's Lover* in the 1950s and 1960s. Relying on a similar definition of obscenity, both courts decided to uphold the prosecution of the publishers as the book contained sexual descriptions 'harmful to the normal feeling of shame'.

Judgment Upon Case of Translation and Publication of Lady Chatterley's Lover and Article 175 of the Penal Code
1953(A) No 1713, 13 Mar 1957 (Supreme Court, Japan)

Facts

A translation of the English novel, *Lady Chatterley's Lover*, was considered as obscene within the meaning of Article 175 of the Penal Code in Japan, and the publisher of the book was prosecuted. The trial court declared the defendant not guilty for lack of evidence. The appellate court reversed the trial court's decision and found the defendant guilty. The defendant appealed to the Supreme Court.

Held

As has already been stated, the book as a whole is a work of art and ideological in nature, and it has been valued considerably among English literary circles. This special artistic literary quality has been manifested not only throughout the book but can also be perceived even in the description of the sex acts at twelve places as indicated by the prosecutors. However, it must be clearly noted that art and obscenity are concepts which belong to two separate, distinct dimensions; and it cannot be said that they cannot exist side by side. If it is to be asserted that an obscene writing cannot be called true art, or that true art can never be obscene, it would merely be a matter of theoretical discussions. Such a mental manipulation

---

[116] *Miller v State of California* 413 US 15, 24–25 (1973).
[117] *JY Interpretation No 407* (2007) 3 ROC Const Ct 104, 106. *Judgment upon case of translation and publication of Lady Chatterley's Lover and Article 175 of the Penal Code*, 1953(A)No 1713, 13 Mar 1957.

is like engaging in an argument as to whether a bad law should be recognized as law. Just as the content of a positive law can be evil, it is possible to find an obscene element in a work of art which we generally accept as valid art, because pornographic writings usually lack artistic quality. This writing which is truly a valid piece of art is not a pornographic writing, as already established by the decisions since the trial in the first instance. However, the obscene nature of the work cannot be denied solely for the reason that the work in question is artistic literature. This is so because even the finest piece of artistic product can be evaluated as being obscene from the ethical and legal point of view. Such a conclusion is not impossible because art, law and morality can exist in entirely different dimensions. We cannot give our support to the principle of 'art-for-art's sake' which places emphasis only upon the artistic quality of production and denies criticism from the moral and legal points of view. No matter how supreme the quality of art, it does not necessarily wipe out the stigma of obscenity. Art, even art, does not have the special privilege of presenting obscene matters to the public. Be he an artist or a literary man, he may not violate the duty imposed upon the general public, the duty of respecting the feeling of shame and humility and the law predicated upon morality.

The same thing said with respect to art can be said in connection with various scientific and educational texts dealing with the subject of sex. An artistic production, however, differs from a scientific text book which treats a given subject objectively and dispassionately, in that it strongly appeals to the sense and emotion; and, consequently, instead of nullifying the obscene quality in the work, it may even serve to intensify the degree of stimulation and excitement.

Existence or non-existence of obscenity in a writing must be judged from a purely objective point of view, that is, by analyzing the piece of work in question itself; and in its determination, one should not be influenced by any assertion of subjective intention of the author. The attorney for the defense defines obscene literature as a 'malicious writing on the subject of sex, designed and calculated to stir avid curiosity only in the mind of a minor person who is incapable of exercising mature, independent judgment; deny the true function of the sexual instinct in a human body as that which is necessary for the procreation of the species or cause him to forget the same; turn the flesh into a tool of profligation and dissipation; and bring about irreparable injury to the mind and body of the minor,' and criticizes the decision of the previous court, asserting that the book in question was written with sincere intent. If we were to accept this definition, no matter how obscene a writing might be, as long as it was intended for esthetic or educational purpose, it would be excluded from the category of obscene literature; and so-called obscene literature would be limited only to an out-and-out pornographic writing. Sincerity of writing does not necessarily nullify the obscene quality of the writing. Consequently, the assertion of the appellants on this issue cannot be accepted. . . .

In the appellants' brief, their Attorney, Shoichi Tamaki, contended that the guarantee of freedom of expression contained in Article 21 of the Constitution is almost without limitation, and even if it is to be admitted that it can be limited in the name of 'public welfare,' the basis for the determination of restriction must clearly be established before the fact; that under the new Constitution which nullified the system of censorship, the question of whether or not any given writing is contrary to the 'public welfare' clause of the Constitution must be left to the discretion of the individual persons concerned; that in the present case, the court of previous instance failed to accept the exercise of discretion by the individual persons concerned in connection with the translation in question and imposed punishment against the defendants; that therein lies the error in adjudicating the case in the instant case; and that in short, it violated Article 21 of the Constitution. However, it must be remembered that the basis for making the determination against the translation in this case lies in the social concept, the conscience of the general public. Therefore, it cannot be said that the criteria was not clear before the fact. Furthermore, whether or not a writing runs counter to the welfare of the public must be decided from the objective point of view and must not be left to the discretion of individual persons concerned. For these reasons, the contention of the defense counsel cannot be accepted.

Ranjit D Udeshi v Maharashtra
[1965] 1 SCR 65 (Supreme Court, India)

Facts

The appellant, a bookseller, was convicted for selling a copy of the unexpurgated edition of *Lady Chatterley's Lover* which was alleged to be obscene. He was prosecuted under section 292 of the Penal Code that prohibited the selling of books deemed obscene. The trial court found the appellant guilty, and the Bombay High Court upheld that decision. The appellant appealed to the Supreme Court.

Held

Mr Garg who argued the case with ability, raised these two issues. He bases his argument on three legal grounds which briefly are:

(i)   that s 292 of the Indian Penal Code is void as being an impermissible and vague restriction on the freedom of speech and expression guaranteed by Art 19(1)(a) and is not saved by cl (2) of the same article;

(ii) that even if s 292, Indian Penal Code, be valid, the book is not obscene if the section is properly construed and the book as a whole is considered; and

(iii) that the possession or sale to be punishable under the section must be with the intention to corrupt the public in general and the purchasers in particular.

In short, according to these precedents, to be obscene the literature in question must be such that it is harmful to the normal feeling of shame, it excites and stimulates sexual desire, and runs counter to good moral concepts regarding sex.

On the subject of obscenity his general submission is that a work of art is not necessarily obscene if it treats with sex, even with nudity, and he submits that a work of art or a book of literary merit should not be destroyed if the interest of society requires that it be preserved. He submits that it should be viewed as a whole, and its artistic or literary merits should be weighed against the so-called obscenity, the context in which the obscenity occurs and the purpose it seeks to serve. If on a fair consideration' of these opposite aspects, [he] submits, the interest of society prevails, then the work of art or the book must be preserved, for then the obscenity is overborne. In no case, he submits, can [a]stray passage or passages serve to stamp an adverse verdict on the book. He submits that the standard should not be that of an immature teenager or a person who is abnormal but of one who is normal, that is to say[,] with a [*mens sana in corpore sano*]. He also contends that the test adopted in the High Court and the Court below from *Queen v Hicklin* [(1868) LR 3 QB 360] is out of date and needs to be modified and [h]e commends for our acceptance the views expressed recently by the courts in England and the United States. . . .

. . . Section 292, Indian Penal Code, manifestly embodies such a restriction because the law against obscenity, of course, correctly understood and applied, seeks no more than to promote public decency and morality. The word obscenity is really not vague because it is a word which is well-understood even if persons differ in their attitude to what is obscene and what is not. Lawrence thought James Joyce's *Ulysses* to be an obscene book deserving suppression but it was legalised and he considered *Jane Eyre* to be pornographic but very few people will agree with him. The former he thought so because it dealt with excretory functions and the latter because it dealt with sex repression. . . . Condemnation of obscenity depends as much upon the mores of the people as upon the individual. It is always a question of degree or as the lawyers are accustomed to say, of where the line is to be drawn. It is, however, clear that obscenity by itself has extremely 'poor value in the propagation of ideas, opinions and informations of public interest or profit.' When there is propagation of ideas, opinions and informations of public interest or profit, the approach to the problem may become different because then the interest of society may tilt the scales in favour of free speech and expression. It is thus that books on medical science with intimate illustrations and photographs, though in a sense immodest, are not considered to be obscene but the same illustrations and photographs collected in book form without the medical text would certainly be considered to be obscene. Section 292, Indian Penal Code deals with obscenity in this sense and cannot thus be said to be invalid in view of the second clause of Art 19. The next question is when can an object be said to be obscene?

. . . We shall now consider what is meant by the word 'obscene' in s 292, Indian Penal Code. The Indian Penal Code borrowed the word from the English Statute. As the word 'obscene' has been interpreted by English Courts something may be said of that interpretation first. The Common law offence of obscenity was established in England three hundred years ago when Sir Charles Sedley exposed his person to the public gaze on the balcony of a tavern. Obscenity in books, however, was punishable only before the spiritual courts because it was so held down to 1708 in which year *Queen v Read* (II Mod 205 OB) was decided. In 1727 in the case against one Curl it was ruled for the first time that it was a Common Law offence (2 Stra 789 KB). In 1857 Lord Campbell enacted the first legislative measure against obscene books etc and his successor in the office of Chief Justice interpreted his statute (20 & 21 Viet C 83) in *Hicklin's* case. The section of the English Act is long (they were so in those days), but it used the word 'obscene' and provided for search, seizure and destruction of obscene books etc and made their sale, possession for sale, distribution etc a misdemeanour. The section may thus be regarded as substantially *in pari materia* with s 292, Indian Penal Code, in spite of some differences in language. In *Hicklin's* case the Queen's Bench was called upon to consider a pamphlet, the nature of which can be gathered from the title and the colophon which read: 'The Confession Unmasked, showing the depravity of Romish priesthood, the iniquity of the confessional, and the questions put to females in confession'. It was bilingual with Latin and English texts on opposite pages and the latter half of the pamphlet according to the report was 'grossly obscene[,] as relating to impure and filthy acts, words or ideas'. Cockburn CJ laid down the test of obscenity in these words

> I think the test of obscenity is this, whether the tendency of the matter charged as obscenity is to deprave and corrupt those whose minds are open to such immoral influences, and into whose hands a publication of this sort may fall . . . it is quite certain that it would suggest to the minds of the young of either sex, or even to persons of more advanced years, thoughts of a most impure and libidinous character.

This test has been uniformly applied in India.

JY Interpretation No 407
5 Jul 1996 (Constitutional Court, Taiwan)

Facts

The appellant translated and published two books, entitled *Making Love* and *Sensual Massage*, on 1 June 1992. The Department of Information in the City Government of Taipei ordered the two books not to be sold or disseminated and be detained under Article 32(3) of the Publication Act, as the two books contained pictures with nude human body parts deemed obscene. The appellant filed a complaint to the Department of Information and then to the administrative court. All his actions failed. He then petitioned the Constitutional Court, arguing that Article 32(3) of the Publication Act violated his constitutional right of free speech.

Held

What laws may prescribe are often abstract norms. For the purpose of implementing the rule of certain laws, an agency may issue interpretive rulings, so as to provide a necessary basis for future action by the same agency or its subordinate agencies. The standard for judging whether a publication constitutes a crime of obscenity by instigating obscene conduct may vary because of differences in customs and ethics in various nations, but one thing in common among different nations is the governmental regulation of obscene publications. Obscene publications are those publications that, by objective standards, can stimulate or satisfy a prurient interest, generate among common people a feeling of shame or distaste, thereby offending their sense of sexual morality, and undermining societal cultural ethics. To distinguish obscene publications from legitimate art, medical or educational publications, one must examine the features and aims of the publications at issue as a whole, and adapt them to the contemporary common values of society.

JY Interpretation No 617
26 Oct 2006 (Constitutional Court, Taiwan)

Facts

The two appellants offered for sale in their bookstore, publications that allegedly contained sexual descriptions. These allegedly obscene publications were seized by the police, and the appellants were convicted for violation of Article 235 of the Criminal Code. Article 235 states that 'a person who distributes, broadcasts, sells, publicly displays, or by other means to show an obscene writing, picture, audio record, video record, or any other object to another person shall be sentenced to imprisonment for not more than two years, short-term imprisonment, in lieu thereof, or in addition thereto, a fine of thirty thousand yuan may be imposed' and that 'the writing, picture, audio or video object shall be confiscated whether it belongs to the offender or not'. The appellants challenged the constitutionality of Article 235.

Held

Any depiction or publication of, or relating to, sex is considered sexually explicit language or material. Obscene language or an obscene publication is something that, by objective standards, can stimulate or satisfy a prurient interest, generate among average people a feeling of shame or distaste, thereby offending their sense of sexual morality and undermining social decency. To distinguish obscene language or an obscene publication from legitimate artistic, medical or educational language or publications, one must examine the features and aims of the respective language or publications at issue as a whole, and render a judgment according to the contemporary common values of the society. . . .

Furthermore, in order to protect a minority cultural group's sense of sexual morality and its cognition of social decency regarding the circulation of sexually explicit speech or material, criminal punishment should be imposed only to the extent necessary to maintain the common sexual values and mores of the majority of the society. As such, the distribution, broadcast, sale, public display of obscene material or objects or otherwise enabling others to read, view or hear same as provided under Paragraph I of the aforesaid article should be so interpreted as to refer to such act where any obscene material or object whose content includes violence, sexual abuse or bestiality but is lacking in artistic, medical or educational value is disseminated, or where no adequate protective and isolating measure (eg, no covering, warning, or limiting to places designated by law or order) is adopted before disseminating to the general public any other obscene material or object that is so sexually stimulating or gratifying from an objective standpoint that the average person will either find it not publicly presentable or find it so intolerable as to be repulsive. Likewise, the manufacture or possession of obscene material with the intent to distribute, broadcast or sell as provided in Paragraph II of said article merely refers to such act where any obscene material or object whose content includes violence, sexual abuse or bestiality but is lacking in artistic, medical or educational value is manufactured or possessed with the intent to disseminate same, or where, with the intent not to adopt adequate protective and isolating measures before disseminating to the general public any other obscene material or object that is so sexually stimulating or gratifying by objective standards that the average person will either find it not publicly presentable or find it so intolerable as to be repulsive, such material or object is manufactured or possessed.

Case to Seek Revocation of the Disposition of Notification to the Effect that the Goods to be Imported Fall Within the Category of Prohibited Goods
2003 (Gyo-Tsu) No 157, 19 Feb 2008 (Supreme Court, Japan)

Facts

The appellant brought back a collection of photographs from his travels. The Director-General of the Narita Branch Customs of Tokyo Customs deemed the collection to be obscene prohibited goods under Article 21(1)(4) of the Customs Tariff Act, which stipulates that books, pictures, sculptures and any other articles prejudicial to public security or good morals should not be imported. The appellant sought a reversal of the decision, arguing the said provision conflicted with his freedom of speech.

Held

Among the aforementioned holdings of the court of prior instance, although we can affirm the conclusion that dismissed the claim for damages under the Act on State Liability for Compensation, we cannot affirm the rest of the holdings, on the following grounds.

According to the facts mentioned above, all of the Photographs directly and concretely show male genitals arranged at the center of the planes thereof in an eye-catching manner, and in light of such mode of depiction, the relative importance of the depicted objects on the entire plane of individual Photographs, and the composition of the plane, we should say that all of the Photographs should inevitably be construed to emphasize the genitals themselves and emphasize the depiction of them. However, according to the facts mentioned above, Mapplethorpe released photographs taken under themes that were related to the root of the existence of human beings, such as the human body, sex, and the naked body, and established a high reputation among art critics as a leading authority of modern photographic art. The Photograph Collection can be deemed to be significant in that it was edited and composed from an artistic viewpoint, ie compiling, in one book, major works of such a photographic artist and reviewing the entirety of his photographic art, expecting that it would be bought and enjoyed by people who were very interested in photographic art or modern art, and the Photographs can also be deemed to be regarded as his major works from such viewpoint and therefore chosen for the Photograph Collection. Also according to the facts mentioned above, the Photograph Collection covers a variety of works such as photographs of portraits, flowers, still lifes, male and female nudes, and among its total pages (384 pages), the Photographs (including two photographs that are reduced-size versions of other photographs) appear only on 19 pages. Considering this, we should say that the relative importance of the Photographs in the Photograph Collection as a whole is significantly small. Furthermore, the Photographs are black-and-white (monochrome) photographs and they do not directly depict scenes of sexual intercourse. If we see the Photograph Collection in light of these factors—the existence of the artistic quality and other aspects of the Photograph Collection that diminish sexual stimulation, the relative importance of the Photographs in the Photograph Collection as a whole, and the mode of expression applied, we should inevitably say that it is difficult to find the Photograph Collection to be appealing primarily to the sexual interest of people who see it.

Notes and Questions

1. Is the standard by which obscene expression is judged similar in the above cases from the different jurisdictions? If so, how? To what extent does the standard that applied in Japan and Taiwan reflect the guideline provided in the US case of *Miller v State of California*?

2. Both the courts in India and Japan decided to uphold the prosecution of respective publishers of DH Lawrence's *Lady Chatterley's Lover*. In the words of the Supreme Court of India, this book contained sexual descriptions 'harmful to the normal feeling of shame'. How is public morality understood here? Does it evolve through time?

3. Compare the two Japanese cases: the *Judgment Upon Case of Translation and Publication of Lady Chatterley's Lover and Article 175 of the Penal Code* in 1957 and the *Case to Seek Revocation of the Disposition of Notification to the Effect that the Goods to be Imported Fall Within the Category of Prohibited Goods* in 2008. Did the standard by which obscene materials are judged change? Why, or why not? If it did not, how did the 2008 decision give greater protection to obscene speech?

4.   One additional justification to regulate obscene materials is for the protection of children. Sexual exposure without proper guidance may have harmful effects on the personal development of children. In Germany, a balance was struck between the protection of children and limited access to obscene materials, restricting this to adult consumption instead of adopting a total ban.[118]

5.   South Korea adopted a similar non-substantive limit in restricting the circulation of obscene materials rather than imposing a blanket ban. In *Registration Revocation of Obscenity Publishers Case*,[119] the Socho District Office in Seoul revoked the registration of a publisher who published and distributed the 'Semi-Girl' photo binder, allegedly violating Article 5-2(V) of the Registration of Publishing Companies and Printers Office Act. This authorises the revocation of licences if publishers are found to have published obscene or indecent materials harmful to children. The publisher appealed to the Constitutional Court, which struck down the provision in part as a total ban was considered excessive as a means to protect juveniles:

> In the meantime, 'indecency' is a sexual or violent and cruel expression, a swearing, or other expressions of vulgar and base content, not reaching the level of obscenity and remaining within the domain protected by the Constitution. The concept of 'indecency' justifying revocation of registration is so broad and abstract that a judge's supplementary interpretation cannot sharpen its meaning, and therefore does not inform a publisher's decision in adjusting the contents of the material, violating the rule of clarity and the rule against over breadth. Corrupt sexual expressions or overly violent and cruel expressions do need be regulated away from the minds of juveniles, but such regulation should be limited to only juveniles and only such narrowly defined means as blocking the chain of supply to them. Totally banning indecent materials and revoking registration of the publisher is excessive as a means for juvenile protection, and debases adults' right to know to the level of a juvenile's, violating the rule against excessive restriction.[120]

6.   The Constitutional Court of Taiwan also made a comparable decision in *JY Interpretation No 623*,[121] where it upheld the constitutionality of Article 29 of the Child and Juvenile Sexual Transaction Prevention Act which prohibits the spreading, broadcasting or publishing of information of unlawful sexual transactions. The Court construed the provision narrowly and applied it only to children under the age of 18:

> To protect children and juveniles from being sexually exploited due to engaging in any unlawful sexual activity is a universally recognized fundamental right which should be treated as a significant interest to be legally protected by the State. By imposing criminal punishment, the aforesaid provision is designed to outright eliminate sexual exploitation of children and juveniles by means of eliminating the information that induces people to engage in unlawful sexual transaction[s]. As such, it is an effective means to achieve the legislative purpose of deterring and eliminating the cases where children or juveniles become objects of sexual transaction[s]. Furthermore, in light of the significant state interest in protecting a child or juvenile from engaging in any unlawful sexual activity as

---

[118] See *Mutzenbacher Case* [1990] BVerfGE 83, 130 1 BvR 402/87 Mutzenbacher–decision (Federal Constitutional Court, Germany).

[119] See *Registration Revocation of Obscenity Publishers Case* 95Hun-Ka16, 30 Apr 1998.

[120] Ibid.

[121] *JY Interpretation No 623* (2012) 6 ROC Const Ct 1, 11.

contrasted with the restraints imposed by law on the rights and interests of those who provide information regarding unlawful sexual transaction[s], the aforesaid provision does not go beyond the necessary and reasonable scope by imposing criminal punishment to achieve the legislative purpose of deterring and eliminating the cases where children or juveniles become objects of sexual transaction[s] in that the law limits its application to the information whose content includes child or juvenile sexual transaction[s] or inducement of same to engage in sexual transaction[s], or the distribution to children or juveniles who are eighteen years of age or younger or the general majority of uncertain age any information that may induce the average person to engage in unlawful sexual transaction[s].[122]

7. In almost all jurisdictions, obscenity is defined as expression that appeals to what the community considers base or prurient interests. However, whose view can be said to represent the community? Elected government officials, judges, juries? Who is most competent and best suited to define obscenity at any given point in time? What criteria are to be applied, and is there even a need for a comprehensive definition? As Justice Potter Stewart noted of 'hard-core pornography' in *Jacobellis v Ohio*,[123] this was hard to define but 'I know it when I see it'. In *Miller v State of California*,[124] the US Supreme Court suggested that jurors may act as fact-finders in seeking to capture the meaning of obscenity in the view of the general public:

> Under a National Constitution, fundamental First Amendment limitations on the powers of the States do not vary from community to community, but this does not mean that there are, or should or can be, fixed, uniform national standards of precisely what appeals to the 'prurient interest' or is 'patently offensive.' These are essentially questions of fact, and our Nation is simply too big and too diverse for this Court to reasonably expect that such standards could be articulated for all 50 States in a single formulation, even assuming the prerequisite consensus exists. When triers of fact are asked to decide whether 'the average person, applying contemporary community standards' would consider certain materials 'prurient,' it would be unrealistic to require that the answer be based on some abstract formulation. The adversary system, with lay jurors as the usual ultimate factfinders in criminal prosecutions, has historically permitted triers of fact to draw on the standards of their community, guided always by limiting instructions on the law. To require a State to structure obscenity proceedings around evidence of a national 'community standard' would be an exercise in futility.

8. In *Case to Seek Revocation of the Disposition of Notification to the Effect that the Goods to be Imported Fall Within the Category of Prohibited Goods*, the Japanese Supreme Court in 2008 liberalised the regulation of obscene or pornographic materials. Although the decision has been praised as remarkable in providing greater freedom of speech, some remain critical, feeling that it fell short of touching upon the sensitive issue of state ideology and cultural identity. For example, Yuri Obata contends that the reason the Supreme Court chose to protect the photography was because

> [t]he book did not contain any clear and detailed photos of female genitals, or of heterosexual intercourse, and the nineteen disputed black and white photographs were either close-ups of male genitals or images of homosexual acts by foreign males. These

---

[122] Ibid, 11–12.
[123] *Jacobellis v Ohio* 378 US 184 (1964).
[124] *Miller v State of California* 413 US 15, 23–30 (1970).

facts possibly indicate that the explicit homoerotic images represented in Mapplethorpe's photographs may be viewed by the Court as foreign and fantasized images, and therefore outside of the Court's concern since they have a less offending impact on the state ideology of cultural identity.[125]

9. Sexual expressions have been under strict control in India. As Ratna Kapur explains, the national identity and culture of India can be constructed and understood as an attempt to protect the chastity and purity of Indian women:

> Women's sexual purity, confined to and safeguarded within the home and representing in turn the purity of Indian culture, was a constituting feature in the emergence of the Indian nation. Paradoxically, just as the emerging Indian nationalist bore the mark of Western conceptions of nationalism, so too did the reconstituted space of Indian sexuality bear more than a slight resemblance to Victorian sexuality. The idea of sex and sexuality as a dangerous corrupting force, to be carefully contained at all costs within family and marriage, was as Victorian as it was Indian.

Thus, the justification for restrictions of prurient expressions is not so-called 'Indian culture' but the need to construct a national identity. See R Kapur, 'Postcolonial Erotic Disruptions: Legal Narratives of Culture, Sex, and Nation in India' (2001) 10 *Columbia Journal of Gender and Law* 337, 338–39.

10. Feminist jurisprudence has advocated strong restrictions on pornographic materials as these are degrading to women and perpetuate harmful sexual stereotypes. The Supreme Court of Canada captures, in a nutshell, the argument of certain Western feminists:

> There has been a growing recognition in recent cases that material that may be said to exploit sex in a 'degrading or dehumanizing' manner will necessarily fail the community standards test, even in the absence of cruelty or violence. This is because such material is perceived as harmful to society, particularly women.[126]

Similar debates on this complex issue took place before the Indonesian Parliament in 2005. The RUU-APP, a controversial anti-pornography bill, sought to incorporate 'pornoaksi' into the law, defined as 'an action in public that exploits sex, obscenity and/or erotica'. While most Indonesians supported the regulation of production and distribution of pornography materials, the incorporation of 'pornoaksi' generated a great deal of controversy due to its broad definition. Many Indonesian women's groups considered the bill to be discriminatory against women as it implied that women were the prime cause of national moral decay and their subordination to men. However, other women's groups jointed with Islamic groups to support the bill, on grounds that it would prevent women from being degraded and protect Islamic national culture. A series of demonstrations for and against the bill took place in Jakarta in 2006. Debates and protests notwithstanding, the anti-pornography bill was passed on 30 October 2008. In 2010, the Constitutional Court upheld the constitutionality of the anti-pornography law on the ground that the law was to safeguard morality, ethics and national

---

[125] See Yuri Obata, 'Public Welfare, Artistic Values, and the State Ideology: The Analysis of the 2008 Japanese Supreme Court Obscenity Decision on Robert Mapplethorpe' (2010) 19 *Pacific Rim Law and Policy Journal* 542.
[126] *R v Butler* [1992] 1 SCR 452.

identity. The Court also noted that the law should be construed narrowly to exclude materials whose content caused no sexual excitement, and was appropriate according to the morality of the time and place where it was presented. See P Allen, 'Women, Gendered Activism and Indonesia's Anti-Pornography Bill' (2009) 19(1) *Intersections: Gender and Sexuality in Asia and the Pacific*, para 42, paras 70–73.

11. What are your views on this debate? Note that Article 28(2) of the Indonesian Constitution states that in exercising his or her rights and freedoms, every person shall have the duty to respect of the rights and freedoms of others and of satisfying just demands based upon considerations of morality, religious values, security and public order in a democratic society. How does this provision justify the restriction on the expression of obscene or pornographic speech?

12. The South Korea Constitutional Court addressed the question of obscenity and the scope of free speech in a series of cases. The leading cases include the *Nude Maja case*, the *Revolting Slaves case*, the *Married Life case*, the *Happy Sara case*, the *Santa Fe case*, and the *Lie to Me case*. Having studied these cases, Jaewan Moon concludes that in defining obscenity, the Constitutional Court has relied on the standard of 'prurient interest', similar to that in Japan and Taiwan. However, Moon is critical of this standard, as it may not be able to distinguish materials with artistic or educational values from those with have a solely sexual appeal, neither does it takes into consideration the varying impact of printed words or images. She notes that no dissenting opinions were published in these obscenity related cases. See J Moon, 'Obscenity Law in a Paternalistic Country: The Korean Experience' (2003) 2 *Washington University Global Study Law Review* 362.

G. Judicially Enforced Apologies

Can a court order a forced apology to restore a damaged reputation or to compensate for intangible losses? A common objection is that a forced apology may violate the right of speech that includes the right not to speak. A forced apology may also intrude upon freedom of thought and conscience. Notwithstanding these objections, judicially enforced apologies are not uncommon in many Asian jurisdictions.

Except in South Korea, court-ordered apologies – where available – have been held constitutional in the majority of Asian jurisdictions. The Constitutional Court of South Korea, in the *Notice of Apology case* (below), stressed the paramount importance of protecting individual conscience and freedom of silence, and held that reputation could be restored by other, less restrictive means such as publishing a judgment in the newspaper. In Hong Kong, the Court of Final Appeal held constitutional a court-ordered apology, but warned that this should be ordered only in 'exceptional' cases in which the degree of gravity of the illegal conduct and the nature of the loss and damage must all be taken into consideration. In Taiwan and Japan, judicially enforced apologies were held constitutional as a proper disposition to restore one's reputation.

Notice of Apology Case
89Hun-Ma160, 1 Apr 1991 (Constitutional Court, South Korea)

Facts

Kim Song-hi, a former Miss Korea, brought a civil suit against the complainants, *Dong-a Ilbo*, its president and the Chief of Editorial of Women, Dong-a. She sought compensation and an apology for a defamatory story about her published by them in June 1988. The complainants requested the civil court to petition the Constitutional Court to review the constitutionality of court-ordered apologies under Article 764 of the Civil Code. The civil court denied such a request, but the complainants filed their own petition to the Constitutional Court.

Held

Conscience' protected by Article 19 of the Constitution includes a world view, a life view, an ideology, a belief and also, even if not rising to the level of the mentioned above, those value or ethical judgments in inner thoughts affecting one's formation of personality. Freedom of 'conscience protects freedom of inner thought from the state's intervention [into] people's ethical judgment of the right or wrong and the good or bad, and also protects people being forced by the state into making ethical judgments public, hence freedom of silence.

An order of public apology compels an individual admitting no wrong on his part to confess and apologize for his conduct. It distorts his conscience and forces a dual personality upon him by ordering him to express what is not his conscience as his conscience. Therefore, it violates the prohibition against compelling one to commit an act against one's conscience, which is derived from freedom of silence. Therefore, the Court cannot help but find limitation on freedom of conscience (in case of a corporation, forcing its representative to express his fabricated conscience). Furthermore, the right to personality, allowing free development of personality either for a human being or a corporation, is impaired in the process. State-coerced distortion of external personality is necessarily followed by fragmentation in personality.

State-coerced apology is an improper attempt to achieve, through civil liability, the policy goal of satisfying the sentiments of retribution that can only be achieved through a criminal punishment. It is inconsistent with the intent and the purpose of the system set up by Civil Act Article 764, and violates the rule against excessive restriction of Article 37 (2) of the Constitution. That is, the Article 764's goal of restoration of reputation can be achieved by such means as using the defendant's fund to publish civil or criminal judgment against him in newspapers and magazines in general or an advertisement withdrawing the defaming story. Therefore a public apology, which involves imposing coerced expression of one's conscience and other disgraces on the defendant, is an excessive and unnecessary restriction of rights.

Ma Bik Yung v Ko Chuen
[2001] 4 HKC 119 (Court of Final Appeal, Hong Kong)

Facts

The appellant was a paraplegic who was insulted by the respondent when he boarded the latter's taxi. The appellant considered such an insult discriminatory and a harassment under the Disability Discrimination Ordinance, and sued the respondent in the district court. The district court ordered the respondent to pay damages and make an apology to the appellant. The respondent appealed to the Court of Appeal to quash the order of apology and reduce the compensation, and succeeded. The appellant appealed.

Andrew Li CJ

The question of principle is therefore raised whether the court has the power to order an unwilling defendant to give an apology. In this context, an unwilling defendant is one who does not feel sorry. As he has no sense of regret, any apology by him would be insincere and an empty gesture. It is in this sense that the phrase 'unwilling defendant' is used in this judgment. The question is whether the court has the power to order an unwilling defendant to make an apology which would in the circumstances be an insincere one. In the worst scenario, an unwilling defendant may even go to the extreme of defying the order which would then have to be enforced by contempt proceedings.

. . . To apologise is simply to say sorry. An apology is a regretful acknowledgement of a wrong done. It can be made privately or publicly. The making of an apology will usually redress, at least to some extent, the loss or damage, particularly injury to feelings, suffered by the plaintiff as a result of the defendant's unlawful conduct under the Ordinance. Where a defendant voluntarily makes an apology at early stage, for example, soon after the incident, during the conciliation process or before legal proceedings, it will usually mitigate the plaintiff's loss or damage. And the earlier it is made, the stronger will be its mitigating effect. . . .

The cases that may arise will involve circumstances of infinite variety. The questions whether (1) the freedom of thought or conscience would be infringed or (2) the freedom to manifest one's belief or the freedom of expression would be infringed and if so, whether the prescribed restrictions are applicable, must depend on the circumstances of each case. . . .

The circumstances to be considered in each case will include the defendant's circumstances and the defendant's reasons for his unwillingness to apologise. Where the prescribed restrictions are relevant, the matters to be considered may include the nature and aim of the legislation, the interests of the community, the gravity of the unlawful conduct and the plaintiff's circumstances, including the extent of the loss and damage suffered. It is only upon an examination of all the circumstances in a particular case that one can answer the question whether the guaranteed rights and freedoms are infringed (including the question of whether the prescribed restrictions are applicable). . . .

. . . Whether an apology made by an unwilling defendant, albeit insincere, has the effect of redressing the plaintiff's loss and damage to some extent would depend on the circumstances of each case. In some cases, it may have such an effect.

Before an order for an apology could be made against an unwilling defendant, s 72(4)(b) requires the court to be satisfied that an apology is a reasonable act for the defendant to perform in the circumstances of the case in question. The requirement of 'reasonable' in the provision may not necessarily lead to the conclusion that an order for an apology can never be made against an unwilling defendant. With an unwilling defendant, it may well be that an apology, which will be an insincere one, would usually not be a reasonable act for him to perform. In this context, it must be borne in mind that there are many other remedies at the court's disposal which could be considered. But there may be rare cases where the court could be satisfied that an apology, albeit insincere, would be a reasonable act for the defendant to perform. Further, in these rare cases, enforcement could not be said to be futile or disproportionate and contrary to the interests of the administration of justice. The circumstances in these rare cases, including the degree of gravity of the defendant's unlawful conduct as well as the nature and extent of the plaintiff's loss and damage, would have to be exceptional. Under s 72(4)(b) the court does have the power to order an unwilling defendant to make an apology. It is in these rare cases that the court could consider exercising this power against an unwilling defendant.

Although the court has the power to make such an order against an unwilling defendant, the court, even in the rare cases where the circumstances are exceptional, has to proceed with great circumspection. The court would have to consider carefully the parties' representations, including any submissions in relation to the guaranteed rights and freedoms. The court should take a global approach and consider the wide range of available remedies. Even where the court concludes that an order would not infringe the defendant's rights and freedoms, such an order should not be lightly made against an unwilling defendant. Other available and appropriate remedies would at least include a substantial increase in the amount of damages. An order under s 72(4)(b) directing the defendant to publish a summary of the court's judgment could also be considered. This would only require the defendant to publish facts and information, that is, a summary of what is contained in the judgment, and is different in kind from an order for an apology. . . .

As has been stated, both in the Court of Appeal and in this Court, the matter has proceeded on the basis that the defendant would be unwilling to apologise, that is, he was not contrite and repentant and had never indicated that he was and an apology would therefore be an empty gesture. The defendant's harassment of the plaintiff on account of her disability which occasioned the plaintiff considerable distress must be condemned by this Court. By outlawing such conduct, the community has made clear that such conduct is not to be tolerated in our society. However, the circumstances of this case do not come within the rare cases with exceptional circumstances where the Court should consider ordering an apology against the unwilling defendant.

. . . As stated above, on a fair reading of the judgment, the judge's finding on harassment should be taken to have been based on the defendant's conduct throughout the incident. This may not have been fully appreciated by the Court of Appeal, although it recognised that the two aspects were closely interrelated. Halving the judge's award so that $10,000 was awarded for harassment alone led to an award which is clearly on the low side, especially as the order for an apology was quashed.

JY Interpretation No 656
3 Apr 2009 (Constitutional Court, Taiwan)

Facts

The petitioner was a publishing company which, in 2000, published an article allegedly implying that Vice-President Annette Lu was plotting against President Chen Shui-bian. Lu sued the publisher, requesting restoration of her reputation. The district court ordered the petitioner to publish an open apology along with the full text of the court judgment in major newspapers for one day. Arguing the forced apology unconstitutional, the petitioner requested an Interpretation from the Constitutional Court.

Held

The right to reputation, necessary in the realization of human dignity, aims to maintain and protect the individual sovereignty and moral integrity. It is guaranteed under Article 22 of the Constitution (see *JY Interpretation Nos 399, 486, 587* and *603*). Article 195, Paragraph 1 of the Civil Code stipulates: 'For any unlawful offense against the body, health, reputation, freedom, credibility, privacy, chastity of an individual, or aggravated unlawful infringement on other moral legal interests, the injured individual may petition for proper monetary compensation. Those whose reputation is injured may further petition for proper disposition to restore that reputation.' Based on the latter part of this provision (hereinafter 'the disputed provision'), an individual whose reputation is injured may petition the court, in addition to monetary compensation, to render proper disposition to restore his/her reputation, tak[ing] into consideration the substantive circumstances of each case[.] With regard to the means for restoring the reputation, numerous civil trial practices have used the publication of apologies [i]n the newspaper as the proper disposition to restore reputation, and incorporate [this method] into judicial precedents.

In accordance with the meaning and purpose of *JY Interpretation No 577*, people's freedom of speech under Article 11 of the Constitution protects not only the active freedom of expression, but also the passive freedom to withhold expression. Given that the disputed provision entails a court-imposed public apology on the newspaper, it necessarily touches upon the freedom to withhold expression under Article 11 of the Constitution. While the State may impose limitations on the freedom to withhold expression in accordance with law, given that there may be a wide variety of causes to withhold, the inner beliefs and values that concern morality, ethics, justice, conscience, and faith are essential to the spiritual activities and self-determination of individuals, and are indispensable for to maintain and protect the individual sovereignty and moral integrity ([S]ee *JY Interpretation No 603*). Hence, in the case where it is necessary to limit the offender's freedom to withhold expression so that the reputation of the injured party may be restored, [the court] should carefully weigh the severity of the unlawful infringement on the moral interest against the contents of the imposed expression before rendering a proper decision so as to comply with the Principle of Proportionality under Article 23 of the Constitution.

The purpose of the disputed provision is to maintain the reputation and to protect the moral rights of the injured party. In light of the fact that individual cases concerning the injury of reputation vary and monetary damages may not necessarily be sufficient to compensate or restore [the injured] reputation, it is a justifiable objective to authorize the court to render proper disposition. That the court orders the offender to make a public apology as what it deems to be a proper disposition does not exceed the scope of necessity, if the court should find such measures as having the offender [bear] all expenses for the publication of a clarification statement, a note on the injured party's judicial vindication, or the contents of the court judgment, in whole or in part, are still not sufficient to warrant the restoration of the injured party's reputation; provided that the court has weighed in the severity of damage to the reputation, the identity of both parties, and the offender's economic status. However, if an order for public apology induces self-humiliation to the point that human dignity is disparaged, it then has exceeded the scope of necessity to restore the reputation and excessively limit[s] the people's freedom to withhold expression. In accordance with the interpretation above, the disputed provision does not contradict the meaning and purpose of the Constitution to preserve human dignity and respect the free development of morality.

Notes and Questions

1. What explains the different judicial attitudes toward judicially enforced apologies in South Korea, Taiwan and Hong Kong? Why is it deemed unconstitutional in South Korea but constitutional in Taiwan, and imposed only as an exception in Hong Kong?

2. In Japan, the landmark decision on the constitutionality of compulsory apology is *Oguri v Kageyama*,[127] involving a libel suit between two candidates for the 1952 House of Representatives election. In this case, the defendant stated in a public speech that the plaintiff received a bribe in connection with a government contract. The lower court found in favour of the plaintiff and ordered the defendant to publish an apology in local newspapers and radio broadcasts, a decision affirmed by the Supreme Court. The majority of the Supreme Court held that the freedom of expression did not include an implicit freedom of silence. They quoted the provision of the Civil Code under which the trial court ordered the apology, noting that court-ordered apologies had been granted in past cases. Freedom of conscience was more thoroughly discussed in three concurring opinions, one of which compared right of conscience to the freedom of religion or faith and contended it was not applicable to this case. In their dissenting judgments, two judges prohibited court-ordered apologies, on the understanding that freedom of conscience included the right of inner thoughts and opinions held by individuals.

3. A number of scholars attempt to explain this decision on social and cultural grounds. For example, Inazo Nitobe argues that harmony, hierarchy, collectivism and shaming are not only the emotions and feelings shared among members of society, but are also the benchmark upon which the social respect an individual deserves is based. See I Nitobe, *Bushido: The Soul of Japan* (Rutland, Ver: Charles E Tuttle Company, 1969). Hiroshi Wagatsuma and Arthur Rosett argue that the deeply rooted cultural regard for group harmony and social hierarchy has shaped the use of apology in Japan. See H Wagatsuma and A Rosett, 'The Implications of Apology: Law and Culture in Japan and the United States' (1986) 20 *Law and Society Review* 461. According to them, in a Japanese relationship, when one's actions have resulted in another's injury, efforts are made toward accommodation and compromise, and an apology is necessary to restore the 'positive relationship' between the parties and acknowledge 'the authority of the hierarchical structure upon which social harmony is based' (at 472–73).

4. Although a forced apology is usually ordered in civil suits against private parties, it may also be used in litigation against the government. As Brent T White argues, citizens in lawsuits against the government should be entitled to court-ordered apologies as an equitable remedy. See BT White, 'Say You're Sorry: Court-Ordered

---

[127] *Oguri v Kageyama* 10 Minshū 785 (1956).

Apologies as a Civil Rights Remedy' (2006) 91 *Cornell Law Review* 1261. White suggests that traditional forms of compensation are unable to provide proper relief to civil rights victims because they do not address emotional distress and injuries. Judicially enforced apologies can serve to heal mental wounds, reinforce legal norms and re-establish social equilibria. He argues that for public apologies made by the government, sincerity is not required since public officials act on behalf of their institutions and offices rather than on their own will.

III. RIGHT TO ASSEMBLY AND THE POLITICAL PROCESS

The right to assembly originates from traditional petitions made by individuals to demonstrate grievances to the government and fellow citizens. The importance of this right persists, even in this world of virtual meetings made possible by the Internet which tends to be available only to certain classes in each society. For the poor and underprivileged, public assemblies or even street protests are the only way to express opinions openly.[128] The right to assembly is thus essential to the practice and realisation of democratic governance and popular sovereignty. Many new democracies in Asia in the last two decades have experienced massive demonstrations and street protests, which have generated tensions and precipitated crises that have at times led to profound political change and constitutional transformation.[129]

A classic civil and political right, the right to assembly is also enshrined in major international human rights conventions.[130] For instance, Article 21 of the ICCPR guarantees the right of peaceful assembly, upon which no restrictions may be placed except 'those imposed in conformity with the law and which are necessary in a democratic society in the interests of national security or public safety, public order (*ordre public*), the protection of public health or morals or the protection of the rights and freedoms of others'. This has become an important standard by which international and national judiciaries review legal restrictions regulating holding of assemblies and parades.[131] While the government may restrict the right to assembly on those legitimate grounds, it is also obliged to provide sufficient public facilities for the realisation of this right and to take 'reasonable and appropriate measures to enable lawful assemblies to take place peacefully'.[132]

The following section discusses restrictions on the right of assembly in various Asian jurisdictions. As public assemblies and parades usually involve the use of public

---

[128] A similar concern with the access to the media by the underprivileged was conveyed in a constitutional interpretation by the Constitutional Court of Taiwan involving the right of assembly. See *JY Interpretation No 445* [trans Vincent C Kuan], 3 ROC Const Ct 423, 461–62 (2007).

[129] For the development of new democracies and the process of democratisation in Asia, see ch 6 of this volume.

[130] Eg, Art 21 of the ICCPR, Art 11 of the ECHR, Art 15 of the AmCHR, and Art 11 of the AfCHR. The Asian Human Rights Charter recognises the right to democracy that guarantees 'a tolerant and pluralistic system, in which people are free to express their views and to seek to persuade others', which shall imply the protection of the right to assembly.

[131] M Nowak, *UN Covenant on Civil and Political Rights: CCPR Commentary* (Rhein: Engal, 2005) at 380–83.

[132] *Leung Kwok Hung v HKSAR* [2005] 8 HKCFAR 229, para 22. The same obligation is also affirmed in *JY Interpretation No 445*, above n 124, by the Constitutional Court in Taiwan. See also Nowak, above n 131, at 375–76.

facilities (like public parks, open spaces or roads), many jurisdictions require prior notification or approval for the holding of outdoor assemblies and parades. Such a prior restraint on free speech has been challenged in many courts, as we shall see. We also consider other substantial and procedural restrictions to the right of assembly and their constitutional concerns

A. Prior Notification or Approval

The requirement of prior notification for holding outdoor assemblies and parades has been found legitimate in most jurisdictions both in the West[133] and in Asia. As the Court of Final Appeal in Hong Kong admitted,

> [i]t was not seriously argued that the mere statutory requirement for notification is unconstitutional. Plainly, such an argument would be untenable. Apart from anything else, notification is required to enable the Police to fulfill the positive duty resting on Government to take reasonable and appropriate measures to enable lawful demonstrations to take place peacefully. The statutory requirement for notification is constitutional. A legal requirement for notification is in fact widespread in jurisdictions around the world.[134]

A similar line of reasoning has been taken by various courts in this region. In Taiwan, for example, the Constitutional Court in *JY Interpretation No 445* applied the principle of proportionality when considering punitive, reporting and approval systems, stating:

> In deciding whether the relevant provisions regarding prior administrative control are in line with the principle of proportionality set forth in Article 23 of the Constitution, the provisions of law relevant and necessary to a specific case must be examined one by one. It ought not to be reasoned that the system will be unconstitutional unless either the punitive system or reporting system is adopted, or that the system will be in violation of the freedom of assembly as a fundamental human right if the system of approval is used. . . . In conducting a prior review of an application for an assembly or a parade, if the focus is on such formal requirements as time, place and methods, which are clearly prescribed by law, but not on the purposes or contents of the assembly or parade, there should be no infringement upon the freedom of expression. In order to maintain important public interests such as traffic safety or social peace, the competent authority may also take necessary precautions in advance and respond properly.[135]

In the view of the Taiwan Constitutional Court, the system of obtaining prior approval for staging outdoor assemblies is constitutional so long it involves only administrative review of the time, place or method of the activity, and not its purpose or content, and satisfies the principle of proportionality. In South Korea, the Constitutional Court also upheld the constitutionality of the prior reporting system in holding outdoor assemblies and parades, on the ground that such a system did not violate the principle of excessive restraint. The Court reasoned:

> [A]dvance report for outdoor assembly cannot be construed as advance permit which is prohibited under the Constitution, Article 21(2). Advance report for outdoor assembly is

---

[133] Dorsen et al, above n 52 at 1012.
[134] *Leung Kwok Hung* [2005] 8 HKCFAR 229, 261.
[135] *JY Interpretation No 445* (2007) 3 ROC Const Ct 423, 465.

enacted in order to ensure peaceful and effective assembly and to protect public safety with legitimate legislative purpose. Further, it intends to increase the communication and cooperation between the organizer of an assembly and relevant administrative agency through advance report and therefore is deemed to be a proper measure to implement these goals. A requirement for information and schedule of an assembly is not excessive to make the report impossible and therefore not against the principle of the least restrictive means. Further, report provision satisfies the balancing test between the restricted private interest from inconvenience incurred by the organizer of an assembly and the protected public interest.[136]

Notes and Questions

1. Prior notification or approval of outdoor assemblies and parades has been held constitutional in all of the above decisions in Hong Kong, Taiwan and South Korea. Do you agree? How do the courts justify such a restriction on the right of assembly and parade? Is it perhaps also relevant for realisation of the right? How?

2. The Supreme Court of Malaysia affirmed the licensing system for regulating outdoor assembles on the ground that this fell within the powers of Parliament. In a case involving the conviction of an individual who acted beyond the conditions of the licence, the Court stated that

   > Parliament has deemed it fit to give full powers to OCPDs [Officers-in-Command Police District] under sub-s (2) of s 27 to define conditions upon which an assembly is permitted which, inter alia, must include the power to restrict the number of speakers and the topic of their speeches, if they are deemed necessary in the interest of security or to prevent a disturbance of the peace.[137]

3. The organisers of assemblies and parades who do not comply with the reporting, notification or approval requirements of the system, may be fined or even face imprisonment. For such minor illegalities, imprisonment, even for a short time, may raise a constitutional concern of excessive sanction. In Taiwan, the Assembly and Parade Act authorises the Government to suspend and disperse any unapproved outdoor assembly or parade. Non-compliance with these orders may attract a further fine or term of imprisonment for up to two years. In reviewing whether this severe sanction was constitutional, the Constitutional Court in *JY Interpretation No 445* examined various statutory grounds by which such unlawful activities could be punished, and advised the lower courts to weigh various factors when imposing the sentence. According to the Court,

   > [t]he requisite elements for breach of [the] peace and order as provided in Article 64-I of the Social Order Maintenance Act are to 'assemble a crowd haphazardly at a park, station, seaport, airport or any other public place with the intent to cause trouble, which is likely to interfere with the public order, and to not disperse after an order to disperse is given by the public functionary in charge.' And, as to the offense of a flagrant assembly of a crowd without regard to an order to disperse provided by Article 149 of the Criminal Code, the criminal penalty will be inflicted upon a person who 'flagrantly assembles a crowd with the intent to engage in violence or coercion, and does not disperse it after

---

[136] *Advance Report Duty for Outdoor Assembly Case*, 2007Hun-Ba22, 28 May 2009.
[137] See *Lau Dak Kee v Public Prosecutor* [1976] 2 MLJ 229.

three or more orders to disperse are given by the public functionary in charge.' The aforesaid provisions and Article 29 of the Assembly and Parade Act vary in their levels of severity as far as both subjective and objective elements are concerned, and thus there is no violation of the principle of necessity as provided in Article 23 of the Constitution. Additionally, . . . [a] criminal court, in weighing the offense and imposing a penalty, should make a precise determination as to whether the requisite elements of the criminal act are met. Needless to say, attention should also be paid to the existence of intent, especially, as a requisite element for the punishment of the act at issue.[138]

Do you think such criminal punishment against unauthorised outdoor assembly and parade too excessive? Why, or why not?

B. Restrictions on Right to Assembly

The holding of assemblies may be restricted by other procedural and substantive limits beyond the requirements of prior notification and approval. These limits must not undermine the right to assembly as a fundamental civil and political right which facilitates democratic governance. Article 21 of the ICCPR provides helpful guidance, requiring that the restrictions must be prescribed by law, and that the rights or interests such restrictions seek to protect must be necessary in a democratic society.

The 'prescribed by law' requirement has been interpreted by both the Hong Kong Court of Final Appeal and the Taiwan Constitutional Court as including not only compliance with legal procedure, but also that the law itself should have legal clarity and certainty. According to the Court of Final Appeal in Hong Kong, if a statute conferred discretion on a public official to restrict the right to assembly, 'such a discretion must give an adequate indication of the scope of the discretion with a degree of precision appropriate to the subject matter'.[139] For the Taiwan Constitutional Court, 'in conducting a prior review of an application for an assembly or a parade, if . . . requirements . . . are clearly prescribed by law . . . there should be no infringement upon the freedom of expression'.[140]

Many jurisdictions have applied the principle of proportionality in deciding whether restrictions to the right of assembly are 'necessary in a democratic society'. However, its application and the balance struck between the right to free assembly and public interests may vary from jurisdiction to jurisdiction. The following cases from Hong Kong, Japan and Singapore illuminate these differences. In addition, the distinction between 'content-based' or 'content-neutral' restrictions developed in the United States[141] also finds a comparable line of reasoning in a few jurisdictions, as is illustrated by the Taiwanese case of *JY Interpretation No 445* and the Indian case of *Himat Lal K Shah v Commissioner of Police*.

---

[138] *JY Interpretation No 445* (2007) 3 ROC Const Ct 423, 483–85.
[139] *Leung Kwok Hung* [2005] 8 HKCFAR 229, para 76.
[140] *JY Interpretation No 445* (2007) 3 ROC Const Ct 423, 465.
[141] The dichotomy of 'content-based' and 'content-neutral' regulations over speeches has been established in the US First Amendment cases laws since the 1930s in *Schneider v States* 308 US 147 (1939), along with other cases. See GR Stone et al, *Constitutional Law*, 5th edn (New York: Aspen Publishers, 2005) 1291–92.

Leung Kwok Hung v HKSAR

[2005] 8 HKCFAR 229 (Court of Final Appeal, Hong Kong)

Facts

The petitioners held an unauthorised assembly contrary to section 17A(3)(b)(i) of the Public Order Ordinance. Despite police advice, the petitioners refused to comply with the notification procedure. Section 13A of the Ordinance provided that before an assembly could take place, the Commissioner of Police must be notified in writing of its purpose, time, route and estimated numbers. The Commissioner then had a discretion to object to the procession under section 14(1) if he reasonably considered that it was 'necessary in the interests of national security or public safety, public order or the protection of the rights and freedom of others'. The petitioners challenged the Ordinance on the ground that it violated their right to assembly.

Andrew Li CJ

As has been emphasized at the outset of this judgment, the freedom of peaceful assembly is a fundamental constitutional right. It is well established in our jurisprudence that the courts must give such a fundamental right a generous interpretation so as to give individuals its full measure . . . Plainly, the burden is on the Government to justify any restriction. This approach to constitutional review involving fundamental rights, which has been adopted by the Court, is consistent with that followed in many jurisdictions. Needless to say, in a society governed by the rule of law, the courts must be vigilant in the protection of fundamental rights and must rigorously examine any restriction that may be placed on them. . . .

   . . . Turning to the constitutional requirement of necessity, any restriction on the right of peaceful assembly must be necessary in a democratic society in the interests of national security or public safety, public order (*ordre public*), the protection of public health or morals or the protection of the rights and freedoms of others. . . .

   In considering whether the Commissioner's discretion in relation to 'public order (*ordre public*)' satisfies the constitutional requirement of 'prescribed by law', it is essential to distinguish between the use of the concept at the constitutional level on the one hand and its use at the statutory level on the other.

The Constitutional Level

The concept of 'public order (*ordre public*)' operates at the constitutional level in Hong Kong. This is because art 39(2) of the Basic Law requires any restriction of rights and freedoms to comply with the ICCPR as applied to Hong Kong, and the concept is specified in a number of ICCPR articles as a legitimate purpose for the restriction of rights, including the right of peaceful assembly.

   There is no doubt that the concept of 'public order (*ordre public*)' includes public order in the law and order sense, that is, the maintenance of public order and prevention of public disorder. But it is well recognised that it is not so limited and is much wider. . . .

   A constitutional norm is usually and advisedly expressed in relatively abstract terms. There is no question of challenging a constitutional norm and the concept 'public order (*ordre public*)' as a constitutional norm must be accepted. . . .

   As has been discussed in relation to the constitutional requirement of necessity, the proportionality test has to be applied, that is: (a) whether the Commissioner's statutory discretion to restrict the right of peaceful assembly for the purpose of public order is rationally connected with the wider constitutional legitimate purpose of 'public order (*ordre public*)';

and (b) whether such a statutory discretion is no more than is necessary to accomplish that constitutional purpose.

The first limb of the proportionality test is obviously satisfied. The constitutional purpose of public order within 'public order (*ordre public*)' is incorporated into the statute and the statutory discretion is of course rationally connected with the legitimate purpose laid down at the constitutional level.

In considering the second limb, the following matters must be taken into account:

(1)   The right of peaceful assembly involves a positive duty on the part of Government to take reasonable and appropriate measures to enable lawful assemblies to take place peacefully.

(2)   The statutory scheme is limited to the regulation of public processions consisting of more than 30 persons on a public highway or thoroughfare or in a public park.

(3)   Upon being notified of a public procession, the Commissioner would have to consider various facets of public order such as traffic conditions and crowd control. Depending on the case in question, factors that may be relevant include the date and time of the proposed procession, the topography of the route, the possible presence of rival groups and the reaction of members of the public. The Commissioner has to approach the matter in a flexible manner but his discretion to object or to impose conditions is constrained: In considering its exercise, the Commissioner must apply the proportionality test: Whether the potential restriction (i) is rationally connected with the purpose of public order; and (ii) is no more than is necessary to accomplish that purpose.

(4)   If the Commissioner objects to the proposed public procession, he must do so within the statutory time limits. And where he imposes conditions, he must do so within a reasonable time.

(5)   If the Commissioner objects or imposes conditions, he is under a duty to give reasons which must be adequate.

(6)   His decision is subject to appeal to the Appeal Board. And his decision, assuming it is upheld by the Appeal Board, is subject to judicial review.

Taking into account all these matters, the Commissioner's discretion to restrict the right in relation to public order should be held to be no more than is necessary to accomplish the constitutional legitimate purpose of 'public order (*ordre public*)'. It is limited to public processions consisting of more than 30 persons on a public highway or thoroughfare or in a public park. The discretion is of assistance in enabling Government to fulfil its positive duty. It is a limited discretion, constrained by the proportionality test. Adequate reasons have to be given for any objection or imposition of conditions. There is a right of appeal and a right of recourse to judicial review.

Accordingly, the Commissioner's statutory discretion to restrict the right of peaceful assembly for the purpose of public order must be held to satisfy the proportionality test and therefore the constitutional necessity requirement.

Japan v Teramae
(1975) 29 Keishu 489 (Supreme Court, Japan)

Facts

The appellant, a labour union official and leader of the local anti-war group, participated in a demonstration held by the prefectural anti-war youth committee. The assembly demanded that '[m]ilitary bases in Matsumo and Wada islands should be removed and laws against rioting should be abolished'. In the assembly, several members of the group, including the appellant, walked in a 'zig-zag' fashion on the road and violated the permit condition 'not to take action which may cause disturbance of traffic order'. They were duly charged. The court of first instance decided that the appellant had violated Articles 77(3) and 119(1)(13) of the Road Traffic Law but was not guilty as regards Articles 3(3) and 5. The Takamatsu High Court upheld the original judgment, but the public prosecutor appealed to the Supreme Court.

Held

Next, it must be examined whether the wording of the stipulation 'to maintain traffic order' is definite as a factor composing the elements of an offence.

Taking a literal reading of the above stipulation, the stipulation orders only to maintain road traffic order in an abstract manner, but it [does not] concretely mention the content of duty, for example, what kind of act must be done or must be avoided. For a large number of public safety regulations, the following method is adopted: That is, to adopt a permission system for a parade and in rendering such permission, to specify the duty to be observed in conditions with respect to the matters concerning the maintenance of traffic orders. Even in the case of the Ordinance, which stipulates duties to be observed, it is to be regarded as extremely inappropriate as legislative proceedings, because it does not make any consideration on specifying the content of duties as much as possible by enumerating typical acts which may infringe traffic order, although it is quite possible to clarify the content of the duties. However, for the following reason, a case where the element of on offence in a penal provision is regarded to contravene Article 31 of the Constitution and therefore, it is invalid due to its ambiguity and indefiniteness. That is, such a provision does not show the criterion that enables the discrimination of prohibited acts from other acts for an ordinary person who has a usual sense of judgment, therefore it does not carry out the function of notifying the public to what acts are covered by a penalty by the provision in advance. Additionally, how to implement the stipulation depends on the subjective judgment of the state or local public entities that are going to apply it, therefore, it tends to become arbitrary, which may cause a serious and harmful effect. Laws in general have a limitation in their expression and due to their characteristics, they are abstractive to some extent. Penal provisions are no exception, therefore, the criterion that enables one to distinguish between prohibited acts and an accepted act is not always an absolute one, but it may require a rational decision for some cases. Therefore, in deciding that a penal provision contravenes Article 31 of the Constitution because of ambiguity should depend on whether a person with ordinary judgment can understand the criterion, by which he can decide whether the provision is applicable to an act in a specific case.

First of all, a parade on a road involves a group of many people occupying some part of the road continuously, and using the roads by means of walking and other forms, therefore, it cannot deny the possibility of infringing on traffic order to a certain extent, which can be maintained when such an act is not performed. Considering that a parade has some elements to be guaranteed by the Constitution as a form of expression, the Ordinance adopts the notification system, by means of which it accepts a disturbance of traffic order on roads to be occurred inevitably by such a parade. Therefore, it is fairly evident that infringement of traffic order that is prohibited by Article 3, sub-para 3 of the Ordinance does not mean infringement inevitably accompanied by said parade. However, a parade as an act of expressing thought is carried out, as previously mentioned, by a large number of participants in order to make an appeal to the general public with respect to their common claim, demand, and thought by means of a unified act such as a parade, and its substantial significance and value exist solely in showing it in a form of a unified act. Against such an act, even though it is demanded to be carried out in good order and quietly, and not to disturb local public peace and order more than necessary, it can only be regarded that the substantial significance and value of a parade as an act of expressing said thought would be lost and freedom of expression guaranteed by the Constitution would be restricted unreasonably. As one of the items to be observed in order to maintain public peace by a person intending to carry out a parade, Article 3 sub-para 3 of the Ordinance mentions the matter, 'to maintain traffic order.' It can be interpreted that it is stipulated because it orders to prevent an act of particular disturbance of traffic order which exceeds the degree of traffic disturbance accompanied by an ordinary parade on roads in good order and smoothly. When a person with ordinary judgment decides in a specific case, whether his intended act would violate the prohibited matter by said stipulation or not, it would not be very difficult to generally determine this by taking the following matters into consideration; that is, whether their intended act would solely cause a usual disturbance of traffic accompanied by a parade carried out in good order and smoothly, or a particular disturbance of traffic order. For example, the following acts which can be seen often in a parade on a road in various places, such as walking in a weaving fashion, parading in a circle, a sit-down and a French demonstration that is carried out by occupying the road entirely, can easily be determined as being regarded as acts of disturbing traffic order in particular, which exceed the degree of traffic disturbance accompanied by a parade that is carried out in good order and smoothly.

As previously mentioned, said acts that would cause particular traffic disturbance are not essential elements of an act of expressing one's thoughts, therefore, when they were prohibited, it would not restrict the legitimate execution of the constitutional rights of the people. Usually, it is not very difficult to decide whether an act is regarded as an act of disturbing traffic order in particular, therefore, there are no cases where Article 3, sub-para 3 of the Ordinance may disturb the legitimate execution of the constitutional right of the people, or it may allow an arbitrary operation by the organizations of state and local public entities. . . .

From all of the above, it is true that the wording of Article 3, sub-para 3 of the Ordinance is abstract, however, it is possible to determine some criterion concerning the observance of road traffic order in a case of a parade, and it cannot be concluded that it lacks the clarity as an element of an offence and contravenes Article 31 of the Constitution. In conclusion, in the judgment of the original instance and that of the first instance maintained by the original instance, which decided otherwise, it is to be concluded Article 21 of the Constitution was mistakenly interpreted and applied, therefore, the given line of argument can be accepted.

Chee Siok Chin & Ors v Minister for Home Affairs & Anor
[2006] 1 SLR(R) 582 (High Court, Singapore)

Facts

The three applicants and another person held a peaceful protest outside the Central Provident Fund ('CPF') Building. The police arrived and ordered the protestors to disperse on the basis that they were being a public nuisance under the Miscellaneous Offences Act (Cap 184) (MOA). The applicants argued that they were exercising their rights to freedom of speech and expression, and freedom of peaceful assembly under Article 14(1) of the Constitution. The applicants were arrested, and they sought declarations that the Minister for Home Affairs and the Commissioner of Police (the respondents) acted in an unlawful and/or 'unconstitutional manner' in ordering them to disperse and in seizing their belongings. The applicants further argued that under Article 14 of the Constitution, four or fewer persons were free to assemble in any public place to stage 'peaceful protests' which the police had no right to disrupt. The freedom to assemble in this manner was thus wholly unfettered as long as there was no breach of public peace.

VK Rajah J

Constitutionality of the MOA

As the applicants tirelessly assert that their constitutional rights in relation to free speech and assembly have been infringed, it is not only appropriate but necessary when assessing the striking out application, that the subtext of this argument be immediately, fairly and squarely addressed. This arises in the context of the police having characterised their conduct as a 'public nuisance' offending the MOA. Can the provisions of the MOA restrict or curtail Art 14 rights as declared in the Constitution?

The right to freedom of speech and expression and the right to assemble peaceably without arms are rooted in Art 14 of the Constitution. These fundamental rights are however not absolute and are circumscribed by limits clearly articulated in Art 14(2) of the Constitution. The article stipulates:

Freedom of speech, assembly and association
14. – (1) Subject to clauses (2) and (3) –

    (a) every citizen of Singapore has the right to freedom of speech and expression;
    (b) all citizens of Singapore have the right to assemble peaceably and without arms; and
    (c) all citizens of Singapore have the right to form associations.

(2) Parliament may by law impose –

    (a) on the rights conferred by clause (1)(a), such restrictions as it considers necessary or expedient in the interest of the security of Singapore or any part thereof, friendly relations with other countries, public order or morality and restrictions designed to protect the privileges of Parliament or to provide against contempt of court, defamation or incitement to any offence;
    (b) on the right conferred by clause (1)(b), such restrictions as it considers necessary or expedient in the interest of the security of Singapore or any part thereof or public order; and
    (c) on the right conferred by clause (1)(c), such restrictions as it considers necessary or expedient in the interest of the security of Singapore or any part thereof, public order or morality.

(3) Restrictions on the right to form associations conferred by clause (1)(c) may also be imposed by any law relating to labour or education.

In short, Parliament may by law impose restrictions on the rights of freedom of speech and expression and assembly if it considers such restrictions *necessary or expedient* in the interest of (a) the security of Singapore, or (b) *public order*.

. . . It bears emphasis that the phrase 'necessary or expedient' confers on Parliament an extremely wide discretionary power and remit that permits a multifarious and multifaceted

approach towards achieving any of the purposes specified in Art 14(2) of the Constitution.
. . .

It is also crucial to note that the legislative power to circumscribe the rights conferred by Art 14 of the Constitution is, *inter alia*, delineated by what is 'in the interest of public order' and not confined to 'the maintenance of public order'. This is a much wider legislative remit that allows Parliament to take a prophylactic approach in the maintenance of public order. This necessarily will include laws that are not purely designed or crafted for the immediate or direct maintenance of public order . . .

There is nothing irregular, arbitrary, or unusual about Parliament's right to limit the right of assembly or freedom of speech. . . .

The right of assembly can never be absolute and may be subordinated to public convenience and good order for the protection of the general welfare whenever it is 'necessary or expedient'. From time to time, for the common welfare and good, individual interests have to be subordinated to the wider community's interests. There is also nothing inherently wrong or unreasonable in requiring permission from the relevant authorities to be sought prior to the holding of a public meeting or assembly. This can be viewed as a facilitative arrangement.

The nub of the matter is that Arts 14(1)(*a*) and 14(1)(*b*) of the Constitution do not confer absolute or immutable rights. The rights conferred by these Articles can be restricted in the wider interests of, *inter alia*, the public order so that they do not impinge on or affect the rights of others. The framework of the Constitution deems it crucial and necessary to authorise the imposition of restrictions in the wider and larger interests of the community and country.

Returning to the MOA, it is evident from its short title that the Act was enacted for the purpose of ensuring good order in, *inter alia*, public places. The long title of the MOA now states: 'An Act relating to offences against *public order*, nuisance and property' [emphasis added]. The relevant Parliamentary debates as well as the content and purport of the MOA place beyond any doubt that the MOA has as an objective the upholding of public order.

Parliament has therefore considered and has intended through the MOA to impose restrictions on the freedom of speech and/or assembly that are 'necessary or expedient' to ensure public order in certain situations. Accordingly, in my view, there can be no challenge as such to the constitutionality of the MOA.

. . . In Singapore, Parliament has through legislation placed a premium on public order, accountability and personal responsibility. As Lord Reid observed with his customary incisive acuity in *Cozens v Brutus* [1973] AC 854 at 862, free speech should not 'go beyond any one of three limits. It must not be threatening. It must not be abusive. It must not be insulting.' Free speech is neither impaired nor impeded by ruling out such conduct. Nor is the right of assembly curtailed by expecting or exacting from citizens responsibility for their conduct. While it is axiomatic that in every democratic society those who hold office must remain open to criticism, such criticism must be founded on some factual or other legitimate basis. The object of contesting and changing government policy has to be effected by lawful and not unlawful means. Wild and scurrilous allegations should be neither permitted nor tolerated under the pretext and in the guise of freedom of speech. Disseminating false or inaccurate information or claims can harm and threaten public order.

JY Interpretation No 445
23 Jan 1998 (Constitutional Court, Taiwan)

Facts

The petitioners applied to the police for a permit to hold a demonstration, the purpose of which was to protest against the illegal disposal of waste by the city government. The police denied the application and the petitioners decided to deliver a petition to the city government instead. When they went to the City Hall, they were deemed an unlawful demonstration and ordered to disperse by the police. The petitioners refused and were arrested. The district court convicted them of violations under the Assembly and Parade Act, and the appeal court affirmed the decision. The petitioners brought the case to the Constitutional Court, challenging the Act as unconstitutional.

Held

[T]he protection of the freedom of assembly should not only extend to the extrinsic freedom in form, but also to the intrinsic freedom in essence, thus enabling the participants in an assembly or a parade to proceed without fear. Therefore, in restricting the rights of assembly and parade by law, the principle of necessity as provided in Article 23 of the Constitution, as well as the principle of clarity and definiteness of law, must be complied with. Thus, the competent authority, in deciding if said right of the people should be restricted, will have a clearly defined legal basis to act upon, whereas the people, on the same basis, may also express their opinions under due process of law so as to preserve their constitutional right.

An assembly or a parade may be held either indoors or outdoors. An outdoor assembly or parade inevitably will affect public peace and safety, traffic order, quality of residence, or environmental sanitation. In order to prevent infringement upon other people's freedom, to maintain social order or public interests, the State may certainly make laws to impose necessary restrictions. Having considered the value of the freedom of expression and that of other legally recognized and protected interests of the society affected by said freedom, in formulating relevant regulations, the extent of restrictions should then be determined, using proper methods and selecting the least intrusive means . . .

Article 11 of the Assembly and Parade Act provides that an application for an outdoor assembly or parade shall be approved unless any of the situations described in said Article exists. Hence, excepting any of the various situations described in said article, the competent authority is not allowed to deny any application for an assembly or a parade. As such, it is a system of guided approval. The constitutionality of the various situations enumerated in Article 11 of the Assembly and Parade Act will be explained as follows:

Subparagraph I: 'Any violation of Articles 4, 6 or 10.' Article 4 thereof provides, 'There shall be no advocacy of communism or secession of territory during an assembly or a parade.' . . . By making violation of Article 4 of the Assembly and Parade Act a requirement for denial of an assembly or a parade, the competent authority is empowered to conduct a substantive review of the contents of the speech prior to the assembly or parade. In that regard, if an applicant does not specify in the application the purposes of an assembly or a parade in accordance with Article 9-I (ii) of the Assembly and Parade Act, then the competent authority will not be able to review such purposes. If such advocacy is later found during a previously approved outdoor assembly or parade, the permission may certainly be withdrawn in accordance with Article 15-I of said Act to achieve the objective of prohibiting the assembly or parade based on the facts and circumstances and as dictated by the urgency and necessity of maintaining social order, public interests or the safety of the assembly or parade. If, at the beginning of the application for an assembly or parade, the mere existence of such advocacy does not pose any clear and present danger to social order or public interests, but the application is nonetheless denied or an approval thereof is withdrawn, it is tantamount to prohibiting the assembly or parade merely for its advocacy of communism or secession of territory. As such, it not only interferes with the participants' freedom to express their political opinions, but also goes beyond the necessity as set forth in Article 23 of the Constitution. . . .

Subparagraph II: 'There are facts showing the likelihood that national security, social order or public welfare will be jeopardized.' An assembly or a parade is a group activity engaged in by numerous persons to achieve a particular common goal, which, in a democratic society, is a means through which the people express their opinions in respect of the administrative measures of the government so as to form the public will. In order to ensure social order and safety, the constitutionally protected assemblies and parades must be conducted in a peaceful manner. Furthermore, the law shall not impose any restrictions thereupon unless an assembly or a parade is in violation of the law, provided that such law shall still be clear and definite in formulating its restrictive conditions. The phrase 'national security, social order or public welfare will be jeopardized' as contained in said subparagraph is a generalized provision lacking specificity and definiteness, which empowers the competent police agency to pass judgment on the existence or non-existence of said facts within a short period. As such, it is likely to infringe upon the aforesaid legally recognized and protected interest. Since an outdoor assembly or parade inevitably will affect the freedom of other people, social order or public interests, it is more likely than not that the people's freedom of assembly will be interfered with and thus such provision is not in line with the legislative intent of Article 11 of the Assembly and Parade Act . . .

Subparagraph III: 'There is likelihood that public safety or freedom will be jeopardized, or there will be serious damage to property.' The provision of said subparagraph is inconsistent with the constitutional intent partly due to the reasons described in the preceding paragraph. Additionally, in respect of the 'likelihood that public safety or freedom will be jeopardized, or there will be serious damage to property,' is it appropriate to deny other participants the right to hold an assembly or a parade if merely a couple of participants have acted to that effect? Besides, even though there is the abovementioned 'likelihood', it has not gone so far as to give rise to criminal liability. In case any behavior breaches peace or order, resort to the penal provisions of the Social Order Maintenance Act should suffice. If an assembly or a parade is prohibited simply due to such situation, the principle of proportionality will be violated. Since the criteria for determining 'likelihood' is neither specific nor clear, a substantive review thereof conducted by the competent authority prior to the assembly or parade will be in violation of the constitutional intent to protect such right. . . .

Subparagraph V: 'An application is submitted by a group that is not established according to the law, or permission for its establishment has been withdrawn, or it has been ordered to dissolve.' The provision of said subparagraph limits an applicant for an assembly or a parade to a natural or juristic person, or any other group duly established pursuant to law . . . A complete background check may be conducted on the representative of a group duly established according to the law, and an objective basis also exists, on which the identity of the responsible person will be determined. As such, it falls within the scope of legislative discretion and, therefore, is not in violation of the constitutional intent.

Subparagraph IV: 'The same time, place, and route have been applied for by another and been approved.' . . . According to Article 26 of the Assembly and Parade Act, if the competent authority denies an application in accordance with said provision, it shall still do so in an equitable manner within the necessary scope of achieving the objectives after taking into consideration the balance and preservation of the people's right to assemble and parade and other legally recognized and protected interests. Thus, the provision of said subparagraph is consistent with the constitutional intent. . . .

Subparagraph VI: 'The application does not conform to the provisions of Article 9.' Article 9-I of the Assembly and Parade Act provides that the person in charge of an out-door assembly or parade shall fill out an application form, which shall be submitted to the competent authority for approval six days prior to the assembly or parade . . . Article 14 of the Constitution guarantees the people's freedom of assembly, which does not prohibit an incidental assembly or parade. In view of the requirements listed in Article 9-I of the Assembly and Parade Act, any and all applications for assemblies or parades not filed within the statutorily prescribed period due to the suddenness of the events will be denied for violation of the provisions of said Article 9. Restraining the people's constitutionally guaranteed fundamental right to assemble and parade in accordance with said provisions is not consistent with the Constitution and thus requires prompt and speedy review and revision.

Himat Lal K Shah v Commissioner of Police
[1973] SCR (2) 266 (Supreme Court, India)

Facts

The appellant applied to hold a public meeting on a public street, but permission was denied. He brought the case to the High Court, arguing that Article s 33(1)(o) of the Bombay Police Act 1951 was ultra vires as the subsection did not authorise the requirement of prior permission for public meetings. As such, his fundamental right under the Constitution was infringed. The High Court dismissed his case, and he appealed to the Supreme Court.

SM Sikri CJ

It seems to us that it follows from the above discussion that in India a citizen had, before the Constitution, a right to hold meetings on public streets subject to the control of the appropriate authority regarding the time and place of the meeting and subject to consider-ations of public order. Therefore, we are unable to hold that the impugned rules are ultra vires s 33(1) of the Bombay Police Act insofar as they require prior permission for holding meetings.

. . . It is not surprising that the Constitution-makers conferred a fundamental right on all citizens 'to assemble peaceably and without arms'. While prior to the coming into force of the Constitution the right to assemble could have been abridged or taken away by law, now that cannot be done except by imposing reasonable restrictions within Art 19(3). But it is urged that the right to assemble does not mean that that right can be exercised at any and every place. This Court held in *Railway Board v Narinjan Singh* that there is no funda-mental right for any one to hold meetings in government premises. It was observed '[t]he fact that the citizens of this country have freedom of speech, freedom to assemble peace-ably and freedom to form associations or unions does not mean that they can exercise those freedoms in whatever place they please.' This is true but nevertheless the State cannot by law abridge or take away the right of assembly by prohibiting assembly on every public street or public place. The State can only make regulations in aid of the right of assembly of each citizen and can only impose reasonable restrictions in the interest of public order. . . .

If the right to hold public meetings flows from Art 19(1)(b) and Art 19(1)(d) it is obvious that the State cannot impose unreasonable restrictions. It must be, kept in mind that Art 19(1)(b), read with Art 13, protects citizens against State action. It has nothing to do with the right to assemble on private streets or property without the consent of the owners or occupiers of the private property. This leads us to consider whether s 33(1)(o) of the Act and the rules violate Art 19(1)(b). . . .

. . . It is clearly unconstitutional to enable a public official to determine which expressions of view will be permitted and which will not or to engage in invidious discrimination among persons or groups either by use of a statute providing a system of broad discretionary licensing power or, as in this case, the equivalent of such a system by selective enforcement of an extremely broad prohibitory statute. It is, of course, undisputed that appropriate, limited discretion, under properly drawn statutes or ordinances, concerning the time, place, duration, of manner of use of the streets for public assemblies may be vested in administrative officials, provided that such limited discretion is exercised with 'uniformity of method of treatment upon the facts of each application, free from improper or inappropriate considerations and from unfair discrimination' . . . and with a systematic, consistent and just order of treatment, with reference to the convenience of public use of the highways. . . .

. . . We may make it clear that there is nothing wrong in requiring previous permission to be obtained before holding a public meeting on a public street, for the right which flows from Art 19(1)(b) is not a right to hold a meeting at any place and time. It is a right which can be regulated in the interest of all so that all can enjoy the right. In our view rule 7 confers arbitrary powers on the officer authorised by the Commissioner of Police and must be struck down. The other Rules cannot survive because they merely lay down the procedure for obtaining permission but it is not necessary to strike them down for without Rule 7 they cannot operate. Rule 14 and Rule 15 deal both with processions and public meetings. Nothing we have said affects the validity of these two rules as, far as processions are concerned.

In view of this conclusion it is not necessary to decide the other points raised by the learned counsel for the appellants.

. . . In the result we set aside the judgment of the High Court, allow the appeal and declare that r 7 of the Rules framed by Commissioner of Police, Ahmedabad, is void as it infringes Art 19(1)(b) of the Constitution. We need hardly say that it will be open to the Commissioner of Police, Ahmedabad, to frame a proper rule or rules.

Notes and Questions

1. Is the principle of proportionality an effective legal technique to balance the right to free assembly and other public interests? Compare the balance arrived at by the Hong Kong Court of Final Appeal in *Leung Kwok Hung v HKSAR* with that of the Supreme Court of Japan and of the High Court in Singapore. Why did the Hong Kong Court find the restriction unconstitutional, while the other two courts found similar restrictions not unreasonable?

2. What kind of 'public interest' can be weighed against the right to free assembly? Should the power to define such public interest be stated in the constitution or delegated to legislature? In the Japanese case above, the Supreme Court recognised that the maintenance of traffic order could be a legitimate purpose for

restricting the right to outdoor assembly or parades. The High Court in Singapore stated that it was within the power of Parliament to define and ensure public order in imposing restrictions on freedom of assembly. In contrast, the Hong Kong Court of Final Appeal distinguished two kinds of 'public order' – constitutional and statutory – permitting only constitutional 'public order' to be a valid justification for restricting the right to assembly. Which approach is preferable? Why?

3. The distinction between 'content-based' or 'content-neutral' restrictions is accepted and relied upon in the cases above from India and Taiwan as the justification for restricting the right of assembly. In *Himat Lal K Shah v Commissioner of Police*, the Supreme Court of India asserts unequivocally that '[i]t is clearly unconstitutional to enable a public official to determine which expressions of view will be permitted and which will not', but restrictions concerning the time, place, duration and manner of use of the street for public assemblies may be permitted. In *JY Interpretation No 445*, the Constitutional Court in Taiwan ruled that in approving or disapproving applications for outdoor assemblies or parades, the competent authority should not be empowered to review the speech itself. As a result, the Constitutional Court struck down a provision in the Assembly and Parade Act stipulating that '[t]here shall be no advocacy of communism or secession of territory during an assembly or a parade'. In other words, content-based restrictions are not permitted in restricting freedom of assembly, while content-neutral ones are permitted. Do you agree with this approach? Are content-neutral regulations necessarily less restrictive? Are restrictions based on time, place and manner entirely unconnected to the purpose of outdoor assemblies and parades? Might restrictions on time, place and manner in conducting assemblies diminish to some extent the intensity of expression which the activity seeks to accomplish? Read the following cases in point 4 below from South Korea regarding time and place restrictions before you reflect on these questions.

4. The distinction between 'content-based' and 'content-neutral' restrictions also applies in South Korea, barring public demonstrations from taking place in proximity to certain government institutions, including foreign embassies. In the case on *Prohibition of Assembly in the Vicinity of Diplomatic Institutions*,[142] however, the Constitutional Court of South Korea held such a general ban without any exceptions was excessively restrictive. In this case, a nationwide civil organisation intended to hold an outdoor assembly in a location close to a few foreign embassies, which however were not the target of the demonstration. But the government authority still denied the application. In the constitutional ruling, the Constitutional Court held:

> [A]lthough the legislators may prohibit, in principle, all assemblies on certain locations on the premise of the presumption that an 'assembly in the vicinity of a diplomatic institution has a general tendency of inflicting serious conflicts between legally protected interests,' there should be at the same time those provisions setting forth exceptions to such general prohibition in order to mitigate the possibility of excessive limitation upon the basic right that may result out of such general and abstract provision of law. The provision at issue in this case nonetheless imposes a prohibition without permitting

---

[142] *Prohibition of Assembly in the Vicinity of Diplomatic Institutions* 2000Hun-Ba67, 30 Oct 2003.

exceptions for those situations where there exists no specific danger premised under the provision at issue in this case. It is an excessive limitation beyond the scope of measures necessary to achieve the legislative purpose. . . .

. . . [T]he provision at issue in this case . . . excessively restricts the freedom of assembly in violation of the principle of proportionality.[143]

Nevertheless, the restriction on public assembly held in close proximity to court-houses was deemed constitutional to secure the 'proper functioning of courts'. According to the South Korea Constitutional Court:

The legislative purpose of the Instant Provision is protection of the proper functioning and peace of courts to the extent that peace of courts contributes to the proper functioning of the courts. The function of a court can be properly maintained only when the fairness and independence of judicial functions is secured. The fairness and independence of judicial functions is a constitutional mandate. The core legislative purpose of the Instant Provision, protection of the proper functioning of courts, is strongly mandated by the Constitution, and is, therefore, found legitimate. Also, protection of such functioning of courts is special in that it is required by the Constitution, and therefore, an absolute ban, without exception, on all assemblies and demonstrations adjacent courts is an indispensable means to prevent materialization of abstract risks, and therefore satisfies the rule of minimum restriction.[144]

Why did the South Korea Constitutional Court find the location restriction regarding diplomatic institutions unconstitutional, while that regarding court-houses was found to be constitutional? What is the underlying rationale? Do you agree?

5. Time-based restrictions on outdoor assemblies and parades are quite common. However, the South Korea Constitutional Court, in the *Night-time Outdoor Assembly Ban Case*, held the restriction on night-time assemblies unconstitutional. The Court stated:

The Assembly and Demonstration Act (hereinafter, 'ADA'), Article 10 prescribes that the head of a competent police department, as an administrative authority, may ban an outdoor assembly scheduled either before sunrise or after sunset (hereinafter, 'night time') as a general rule with an exception that the authority may decide not to ban it based on the review of the contents of an assembly in advance. Evidently, Article 10 prescribes a permit system for night time outdoor assembly and we cannot read it otherwise. Therefore, it is against the Article 21 Section 2 of the Constitution and the entire Article 23 Item 1 of 'ADA' based on it is against the Constitution as well.[145]

6. In some jurisdictions, there may be special restrictions on the right to assembly of civil servants due to their special status. However, the Supreme Court of India, in *Kameshwar Prasad & Ors v The State of Bihar & Anor*,[146] held unconstitutional the Bihar Government Servants' Conduct Rules of 1956, which prohibited govern-ment servants from demonstrating and participating in any form of strike in rela-

---

[143] Ibid.

[144] See, *Ban on Outdoor Assembly and Demonstration Adjacent to Courthouses Case*, 2004Hun-Ka17, 24 Nov 2005.

[145] See, Summary of the Decision, *Night time Outdoor Assembly Ban Case*, 2008Hun-Ka25, 24 Sep 2009.

[146] *Kameshwar Prasad & Ors v The State of Bihar & Anor* [1962] AIR 1166.

tion to 'any matter pertaining to [their] conditions of service', as overly restrictive to the right to free assembly of government servants who could enjoy this right within reasonable limitations:

> We have rejected the broad contention that persons in the service of government form a class apart to whom the rights guaranteed by Part III do not, in general, apply. By accepting the contention that the freedoms guaranteed by Part III and in particular those in Art. 19(1)(a) [freedom of speech and expressions] apply to the servants of government we should not be taken to imply that in relation to this class of citizen, the responsibility arising from official position would not by itself impose some limitations on the exercise of their rights as citizens.[147]

7. In 2000, Singapore introduced a Speakers' Corner in Hong Lim Park. This venue is exempt from the licensing requirements of the Public Entertainments and Meetings Act (PEMA), but it is subject to an administrative regime imposing conditions for speaking there. Interestingly, control of the space is in the hands of the National Parks Board. Certain content-neutral rules require speakers to register with the nearby police station 30 days before speaking. Speakers must be Singapore citizens and the use of amplification devices is limited to 'handheld, self-powered amplification equipment'. Use of these devices is also restricted to between 9.00 am and 10.30 pm, and no sale of food or drinks is permitted without a relevant permit. Speakers are required to speak in four official languages only, including Malay, Mandarin Chinese, Tamil and English. Content-specific regulations require speakers to abstain from any matter 'which relates, directly or indirectly, to any religious belief or to religion generally' or 'which may cause feelings of enmity, hatred, ill-will or hostility between the different racial or religious groups in Singapore'. Demonstrations are also allowed at the Speakers' Corner, provided the organiser is a Singapore citizen and its participants are either Singapore citizens or permanent residents. Again the content of the protest is restricted in the same manner as speeches at the Corner. Might these conditions be seen as a restriction on or as a guarantee of freedom of expression?

IV. FREEDOM OF ASSOCIATION AND CIVIL SOCIETY

The freedom of association empowers individuals to form groups freely to pursue their common goals, express their collective wills, and participate in the private and the public sphere. This right is both individual and collective.[148] It guarantees individuals the freedom to associate or not to associate with others. As a collective right, it ensures the freedom of association to promote and advance disparate activities, whether they be social, economic, professional, religious or political in nature. This facilitates an open market and a vibrant civil society, integral to a modern democratic state.

The freedom of association is recognised in many human rights instruments. Article 22 of the ICCPR addresses the economic dimension of this right by protecting the right of every person to form and join trade unions. Asian constitutions like those of

---

[147] Ibid, 384.
[148] *JY Interpretation No 644* (2012) 6 ROC Const Ct 319, 322–23; see also Nowak, above n 130, at 497.

Malaysia (Article 10) and Singapore (Article 14) guarantee freedom of association while permitting parliament to impose such legal restrictions as it deems necessary or in the interest of the security of the state or public order.

The following section first discusses individual rights of association and the freedom of societies or associations in relation to their organisation, management and the running of their activities. For organisational purposes, the rights to form political parties and religious groups are discussed in chapter six ('Democracy and the Right to Political Participation') and chapter nine ('Religion and State').

A. The Right of Individuals to Associate/Disassociate

Freedom of association guarantees individuals the right to join or not to join any associations. At the beginning of the twentieth century, the development of forced unionism as a collective response of labour to the manipulation of industrial capitalists generated a heated debate as to whether it curtailed the freedom of association of individual labourers. The debate was put to an end with the adoption of the two Covenants – the ICCPR and International Covenant on Economic, Social and Culture Rights (ICESCR) – that explicitly grant individuals the right to join (and not to join) trade unions for the protection of their interests.[149] The following cases demonstrate how the courts in Sri Lanka and Japan have adopted the same normative stand as these two Covenants, to which both are states parties. Neither employers nor labour unions can force individual labourers to join or not to join any particular labour union.

Certain classes of individuals may be restricted in the exercise of their right to free association due to their special status or function. Article 22(2) ICCPR, for example, provides that members of the armed forces and police may be subject to greater restrictions on their rights of association than ordinary individuals. The following cases from South Korea, Malaysia and Taiwan deal with the constitutional issue of whether the right of free association held by teachers and technicians working in public schools, as well as private attorneys, can be restricted due to their status.

Ariyapala Gunaratne v The People's Bank
[1985] 1 Sri LR 338 (Supreme Court, Sri Lanka)

Wanasundera J

The facts in this case are not in dispute. The Emergency Regulations were in operation in this country from the beginning of 1971 due to the insurrection and insurgency that threatened our country at that time. Under those Emergency Regulations, service in the People's Bank (in which the appellant was employed as a Grade III officer in the Bank Service) had been declared an 'essential service' and this had the effect of prohibiting strikes. Notwithstanding those regulations, on 1st September 1972 the Ceylon Bank Employees' Union, a registered trade union of which the appellant was a member, called out its membership on strike.

---

[149] Art 22(1) ICCPR; Art 8(a) ICESCR.

On the next day, 2nd September 1972, the respondent Bank notified the strikers that they would be regarded as having vacated their posts unless they returned to work by the 6th September, which was the deadline fixed by the Bank The strikers paid no heed to this notice. Sometime later, on 17th December, the Bank Employees' Union called off the strike and directed its members to resume work from the 18th December 1972.

When the appellant reported for work on the 18th, he was informed by the Bank authorities that he could only come in as a new entrant, for which he should make an application. The appellant had been in employment with the Bank since 1961 and had been promoted to Grade III in 1964. On the appellant making such an application, he was issued a letter of appointment . . . [subject] to the following conditions:

> . . . [T]he Bank will not permit the employees in Grade III and above to be a member of any Trade Union the membership of which is open to employees of Grade V and below.
>
> If you are a member of such a Trade Union you should resign that membership before you get the proposed promotion and you should give an undertaking that you will not hold membership in any such Trade Union in the future as long as you hold a post in Grade III or above.

The appellant after considerable delay, perhaps after much soul-searching and after a reminder was sent to him, replied . . . that he was not prepared to resign his membership in the union of which he was a member. He was thereby staking his future on his convictions. All the material events relating to this matter took place during the existence of the 1972 Republican Constitution and it is those provisions that govern this case . . .

In the lower Court the learned District Judge held with the appellant and granted judgment in his favour[;] in appeal the Court of Appeal has reversed this judgment and dismissed the appellant's action without costs. . . .

. . . The right of all employees (except a few prescribed categories) to voluntarily form unions is part of the law of this land. It exists both in the Constitution and in statute form. No employer can take away this statutory right by imposing a term to the contrary in a contract of employment. But of course where the State considers a restriction of this right is necessary for good cause, it is enabled to do so by section 18(2) of the 1972 Constitution. Such a restriction can be imposed only by law and only for grounds set out in section 18(2) and no other.

This right of association is of great value and has varied scope. It embraces associations which are political, social, economic and includes even such entities as clubs and societies. But trade unions enjoy pride of place. They play a significant role as an integral part of the democratic structure of government, and are a part of the contemporary political and social landscapes. When Article 18(1)(f) of our Constitution speaks of the freedom of association, it means primarily the freedom of forming trade unions. Restraints or limitations on it would be permitted only in the most exceptional circumstances and that could only be done by law in the interests of national security or in the interests of law and order etc. There may be some employers even today who are against unionisation of labour. They may in all sincerity think that their factories or work places would be run much better and more effectively without union interference. If the law were to permit it, they would be ever ready, in the name of order and discipline to prohibit unionisation of the workers by imposing such a condition in the letter of appointment. If the courts were to adopt the view of the Court of Appeal, we would be erasing Article 18(1)(f) of the Constitution and writing off trade unions and the trade union movement in this country which had, after a long and protracted struggle fraught with great hardship and suffering, succeeded in gaining this right and seeing it enshrined in the Constitution.

Judgment Concerning Whether the Agreement Concluded Between an Employee and Employer, which Obliges the Employee Not to Exercise the Right to Withdraw From a Particular Labour Union, is Contrary to Public Policy
2004 (Ju) No 1787, 2 Feb 2007 (Supreme Court, Japan)

Facts

On 1 April 1989, the appellant began his employment with Appellee Y2, a company manufacturing electric appliances, and worked at the First Manufacturing Department of Factory A. Appellee Y1 was a labour union consisting of employees working at Factory A. Since the appellant was a worker of Factory A, on 1 July 1989, he joined the union. The collective agreement concluded between the company and the union included a union shop clause and a check-off clause, which entitled the company to check off (withhold) union dues payable to the union from its members' wages. The appellant became dissatisfied with the management over extra wages as well as the union's handling of his complaints. He then joined Regional Federation C of B National Union of General Workers ('Regional Federation C') around the end of September 1995 and submitted a letter of withdrawal to Appellee Y1 on 3 October 1995. However, Appellee Y1 (union) did not accept the appellant's letter of withdrawal and tried to dissuade him from withdrawing. On 3 October 1995, the appellant and Regional Federation C informed the company that appellant had joined Regional Federation C and made an offer for collective bargaining. The company rejected the offer, arguing that the union suspended acceptance of the appellant's letter of withdrawal.

Believing that the union's rejection constituted unfair labour practice, the appellant and Regional Federation C filed a petition for relief (the 'Petition for Relief') with the District Labour Relations Commission of the local government (the 'Kanagawa Labour Commission'). On 24 November, they reported to the Kawasaki Minami Labour Standards Office, alleging a violation of the Labour Standards Act, including non-payment of extra wages at Factory A. Subsequent settlements were made between the company, the appellant and Regional Federation C later on. According to these settlements, the appellant and Regional Federation C should withdraw their petition to the government and Appellee Y2 would pay Regional Federation C and the appellant 2.5 million yen. Nevertheless, even after the settlements, the appellant was dissatisfied with his transfer within Factory A. Therefore, on 12 September 2000, he asked for withdrawal from Appellee Y1 again. His request was denied.

Held

[T]he determination of the court of second instance mentioned above cannot be affirmed, on the following grounds.

(1)   In general, it is construed that members of a labour union have freedom of withdrawal, or more specifically, they are free to quit as union members on their own will (see 1973 (O) No 498, judgment of the Third Petty Bench of the Supreme Court of November 28, 1975, Minshu Vol 29, No 10, at 1634; 1987 (O) No 515, judgment of the First Petty Bench of the Supreme Court of December 21, 1989, Saibanshu Minji, No 158, at 659). Given the facts mentioned above, the Ancillary Agreement can be construed to restrict the appellant's freedom of withdrawal and promise to Appellee Y2 [employer] that the appellant will never exercise his right to withdraw from Appellee Y1 [union].

(2)   Since the Ancillary Agreement was concluded between the appellant and Appellee Y2 [employer], it shall, in principle, become effective between the appellant and Appellee Y2 [employer], the other party to the agreement, and therefore, even if the appellant exercises the right to withdraw from Appellee Y1 [union] in breach of the Ancillary

Agreement, the appellant's withdrawal would only raise issues regarding his responsibility for default in the relationship with Appellee Y2 [employer]. According to the facts mentioned above, we cannot find any special reasons to consider that the appellant's withdrawal would raise such issues in the relationship with Appellee Y1 [union], which is not a party to the agreement.

(3) Furthermore, a labour union is legally vested [with] the power to exercise control over its members, and the members under its control cannot avoid the obligations, for example, to participate in the activities decided by the union and pay union dues. Such treatment can be permitted only where the members have the freedom of withdrawal from the union. The part of the Ancillary Agreement that obliges the applicant never to exercise the right to withdraw from Appellee Y1 [union], thereby preventing the appellant's withdrawal from becoming effective at all, deprives the appellant of freedom of withdrawal, which is an important right, and compels him to be eternally subject to the control of the union. Such part of the agreement should be deemed to be contrary to public policy and therefore void.

(4) For these reasons, in any case, we cannot say that the Withdrawal is ineffective because it is in breach of the Ancillary Agreement.

. . . The determination of the court of second instance that is contrary to this reasoning contains a violation of laws and regulations that apparently affects the judgment. The appellant's argument is well-grounded in that it alleges such violation, and the judgment of prior instance should inevitably be quashed with respect to the part for which the appellant lost the case, without needing to make judgment on other points.

Since the appellant no longer has membership in Appellee Y1 [union] as a result of the Withdrawal, his claim to seek against Appellee Y1 [union] a declaration of this fact is well-grounded. Also, according to the facts mentioned above and other facts determined by the court of second instance as well as the facts for which there is no dispute between the parties, other claims made by the appellant against Appellee Y1 [union] are well-grounded, including the claim to seek refund of 28,590 yen of unjust enrichment arising from the monthly union dues for April to September 2003, which is a claim newly added in the second instance, and to seek payment of delay damages thereon.

Prohibition of Political Party Membership of Primary and Middle School Teachers
2001Hun-Ma710, 25 Mar 2004 (Constitutional Court, South Korea)

Facts

The complainants were middle-school teachers who wanted to take part in election campaign activities by joining a political party. However, they were barred from the election campaign activities because of a statutory prohibition against general public officials joining political parties. They filed suits for constitutional review, claiming that their freedom of political expression, freedom of political party membership and party activities, freedom to conduct election campaigns and the right to equality had been infringed.

Held

First, Section 1 of Article 7 of the Constitution provides that 'All public officials shall be servants of the entire people and shall be responsible to the people,' thereby clearly indicating that the public officials are in the position to serve the interest of the entire citizenry and not in the position to serve the interest of particular sections of the citizens or a particular political sector or political party. Section 2 of Article 7 of the Constitution provides for the 'political neutrality of the public officials' so that the consistency and continuance of the administration will not be deprived by the change of the political powers and the administration will not be depend[ent] upon the political beliefs of the public officials, by expressly providing that 'The status and political impartiality of public officials shall be guaranteed as prescribed by Act.'

Second, Section 4 of Article 31 of the Constitution declares that 'political impartiality of education shall be guaranteed under the conditions as prescribed by Act,' thereby institutionally guaranteeing the political neutrality requested for the public officials upon the educational civil servants serving in the area of education. The political neutrality of education means not only that the education should be free from unjust interferences from state authority or political power, but also that education should not intervene in the realm of politics in deviation from its original or primary function. The ground for the Constitution's request [for] the 'political neutrality of education' is that it is desirable to keep a certain distance between education and politics, as education is in its essence in pursuit of ideals and not prone to power, while politics seeks reality and power.

Third, it is true that the political fundamental right of the complainants is restricted by the prohibition of the freedom of political party membership and election campaign activities of the teachers of primary school and middle-school in the entirety including off-duty hours. However, the impact of the political activities of the teacher upon the students at primary school and middle-school who are fully sensitive, imitative and receptive is massive; the activities of the teacher over both on-duty and off-duty hours constitute part of the potential education process significantly affecting the formation of the personality and the basic life-style habits of the students; and the political activities of the teacher might infringe upon the right to learn in class from the perspective of the students who are the beneficiaries of the education. Considering in totality that priority should be given at the current point to the public interest that may be achieved by further guaranteeing the fundamental right of education of the citizens, the restriction of the freedom of political party membership and election campaign activities of the primary school and middle-school educational civil servants is constitutionally justifiable.

JY Interpretation No 373
24 Feb 1995 (Constitutional Court, Taiwan)

Facts

The petitioner was a technician in the Mandarin Experimental Elementary School in Taipei. In 1989, he prepared to organise a labour union and applied to the city government to form a labour union comprising technicians and journeymen in educational enterprises. The city government rejected his request, citing Article 4 of the Labour Union Law, which provides that 'persons employed in administrative or educational agencies of government at any level, and persons employed in munitions industries should not organize a labour union'. The petitioner challenged the constitutionality of the said provision.

Held

Article 14 of the Constitution stipulates that citizens shall have the freedom of association. Additionally, Paragraph 1 of Article 153 of the Constitution reiterates the duty of the State to enact laws and implement policies that protect workers so as to better their livelihood and improve productive skills. Workers employed in all lines of work organize labour unions in order to improve labour conditions, and to raise their social and economic status. This basic labour right is generally recognized by countries with modern legal systems, and its safeguarding was the intent of Article 153 of the Constitution. Labour union laws promulgated by the State shall allow workers to enjoy the right to collective bargaining and dispute resolution, as long as social order and public welfare are secured. Article 4 of the Labour Union Law stipulates that: 'Persons employed in administrative or educational agencies of government at any level, and persons employed in munitions industries shall not organize a labour union,' and among those groups, technicians and journeymen working for educational agencies are not permitted to organize labour unions. Although the nature of their work is linked to the citizenry's right to education, by prohibiting the formation of labour unions, it deprives the aforementioned workers of their basic rights, exceeds the imposed threshold of Article 23 of the Constitution and infringes upon these workers' constitutionally guaranteed right of association.

Sivarasa Rasiah v Badan Peguam Malaysia & Anor
[2010] 2 MLJ 333 (Federal Court, Malaysia)

Gopal Sri Ram FCJ

The appellant is an advocate and solicitor. He is also an office bearer of a political party and a Member of Parliament. He wishes to stand for and, if elected, serve on the Bar Council which is the governing body of the Malaysian Bar. Section 46A(1) of the Legal Profession Act 1976 ('the Act') prohibits him from doing so. It says, among other things not relevant here:

> A person shall be disqualified for being a member of the Bar Council or a Bar Committee or of any committee of the Bar Council or a Bar Committee:
> (b) if he is a member of either House of Parliament, or of a State Legislative Assembly, or of any local authority . . .

The appellant challenged the constitutionality of Section 46A(1). His challenge failed before the High Court and the Court of Appeal . . .

. . . The first question to ask is whether a statutory body like the Malaysian Bar is an 'association' within art 10(1)(c). A careful examination of the authorities provides a negative response. . . .

The Malaysian Bar was created by statute and has, from its inception, been governed by statute, namely the Act and the subsidiary legislation made thereunder. As such, no complaint can be made on the ground that the appellant's right of freedom of association has been violated. In short, art 10(1)(c) does not apply to the Malaysian Bar. Accordingly no question can arise on the issue of the right to serve on the Bar Council.

Even if Daman Singh and the cases that have applied it were wrongly decided, and the Malaysian Bar is an association and even if the appellant has a fundamental right to serve on the Bar Council, the disqualifications that s 46A imposes are reasonable restrictions within art 10(2)(c). That provision says that 'Parliament may by law impose . . . (c) on the right conferred by paragraph (c) of Clause (1), such restrictions as it deems necessary or expedient in the interest of the security of the Federation or any part thereof, public order or morality.' As earlier pointed out, the clause must be read as 'such reasonable restrictions'. The restrictions are reasonable because they are justifiable on the ground of morality. . . .

Part of public morality is the proper conduct and regulation of professional bodies. Matters of discipline of the legal profession and its regulation do form part of public morality. This is because it is in the public interest that advocates and solicitors who serve on the governing body behave professionally, act honestly and independent of any political influence. An independent Bar Council may act morally in the proper and constitutional sense of that term. The absence of political influence secures an independent Bar Council. Hence, as stated earlier, the restriction is entirely reasonable and justifiable on grounds of public morality. It follows that the challenge based on art 10(1)(c) fails.

Notes and Questions

1. What are pros and cons of forced unionism? What normative values are involved in guaranteeing an individual labourer's right to join or not to join a union? What difference does it make if we approach this issue from the perspective of socialist or communist state philosophy?

2. What are the nature and function of public schools? Why should teachers of public schools be further restricted in their freedom of association? Note that the Constitutional Court of South Korea justified the statute banning school teachers from joining any political party on the need to maintain the 'political impartiality of education' under Article 31(4) of the Constitution. Taiwan's Constitutional Court justified a similar ban on individuals working in public schools from forming or joining any labour unions, but exempted technicians who work in public schools.

3. In *Sivarasa Rasiah v Badan Peguam Malaysia & Anor*, the Supreme Court of Malaysia held constitutional a statutory ban on Bar Council members holding parliamentary office, to ensure the independence and impartiality of the Bar Council. Is such a restriction on the right of free association, as well as the right to political participation held by private lawyers, necessary?

4. Another class of individuals whose right to free association is usually restricted is judicial officers, including judges and prosecutors. For example, in Taiwan, Article 15 of the Judges Act stipulates: 'A judge shall not participate in any political party, political organization, or their activities during the term of service, and shall withdraw therefrom if already joined before being appointed.' To ensure political neutrality, judges may not join political parties or organisations. Whether such a general ban is overly restrictive has been contested since the right of judges to political participation are restricted. See discussion in chapter six.

B. Rights and Freedoms of Associations

Societies formed by individuals in the exercise of their rights of association enjoy certain freedoms with respect to their formation, purpose, organisation, maintenance and activities. However, these societies may be regulated by law, and the degree of regulation will depend on their nature and functions. For example, in Singapore and Taiwan, the law regarding the formation of associations distinguishes political associations from other types of associations. In Singapore, the Societies Act has a two-tier automatic and non-automatic registration scheme. Voluntary welfare organisations, for example, enjoy automatic registration. Listed groups require prior ministerial approval and include any society lobbying to promote or discuss issues relating to 'religion, ethnic group, clan, nationality, or a class of persons defined by reference to their gender or sexual orientation', the use and status of any language, governance of Singapore society and societies seeking to promote 'any civil or political right (including human rights, environmental rights, animal rights)' and 'martial arts'. This red-flags issues that are deemed politically contentious or destabilising.[150] In relation to political associations, the Registrar may, under section 4(2)(e) of the Societies Act, refuse to register a society if 'its rules do not provide for its membership to be confined to citizens of Singapore or it has such affiliation or connection with any organisation outside Singapore as is considered by the Registrar to be contrary to the national interest'. The law in Taiwan is just the opposite, in so far as the formation of political parties requires no prior government approval, while the formation of other civic, social or occupational associations does.[151]

The following cases from Taiwan illustrate the scope of the constitutional guarantee of the freedom or autonomy of associations with respect to their purposes and functions.

JY Interpretation No 644
20 Jun 2008 (Constitutional Court, Taiwan)

Facts

The Petitioner Chen applied to the city government of Taipei for the formation of the 'Goa-Seng-Lang Association for Taiwan Independence.' His application was rejected pursuant to Article 2 of the Civic Organizations Act which stipulates that 'the organization and activities of a civic association shall not advocate Communism or the partition of national territory'. He filed a complaint against the city government but lost in the administrative court. He then sought a constitutional review of the disputed article.

Held

Any restrictions by law on freedom of expression must meet the principle of proportionality. The use of so-called 'advocating Communism or partition of national territory,' each constituting a kind of political advocacy (or speech), as grounds for disapproving the establishment of a civic association amounts to bestowing on the governing authority (or

---

[150] Thio, above n 54, at 861.
[151] The Civic Organizations Act, Arts 8, 44 and 46.

agency) the power to review the content of the speech itself, which directly restricts the people's fundamental right of free speech. Article 5, Paragraph 5 of the Amendment of the Constitution of the Republic of China provides, '[a] political party shall be deemed unconstitutional in the event its goals or activities endanger the existence or the democratic constitutional order of the Republic of China.' Since there is no prerequisite that the organization of a political party should seek prior approval, a political party may be disbanded only by the judgment of the Constitutional Court after it has been established and its goals or activities have been deemed to endanger the existence or the democratic constitutional order of the Republic of China. Conversely, disapproval based on Article 2 of the Civic Organizations Act gives the governing authority (or agency) the power to conduct substantive review of the content of such speech before an organization is established. As such, if it should discover that an association advocates the above-mentioned activities, and the facts [collected] at the time are sufficient, the governing authority may then revoke (which has been amended to 'repeal' as of December 11, 2002) the approval in accordance with the latter portion of the first paragraph of Article 53, as amended and promulgated on January 27, 1989, to achieve the purpose of disbandment. If disapproval is rendered from the outset of a petition to form a civic organization, it is not different from the prohibition of establishment of a civic association merely on the ground that it advocates Communism or partition of national territory. This has clearly exceeded the scope of necessity under Article 23 of the Constitution, and is not in conformity with the purpose of constitutional protection of people's freedom to associate and freedom of speech. Therefore, Article 2 and the front portion of the first paragraph of Article 53 of the Civic Organizations Act, as indicated above, shall be deemed invalid within the scope of this Interpretation as of the date this Interpretation is issued.

JY Interpretation No 479
1 Apr 1999 (Constitutional Court, Taiwan)

Facts

The petitioner was an association named 'China Society of Comparative Law'. In 1995, members of the association renamed the association 'Taiwan Law Society' and applied to the Ministry of the Interior for approval of the name change. The application was rejected because Section 4 of the Regulations for Registration of Social Entities required that any social organization be named according to the administrative district where it was located. Since the petitioner was a national association, it must be named with 'China' or 'Republic of China' instead of 'Taiwan'. The petitioner filed a suit in the administrative court but failed, and thus petitioned to the Constitutional Court for a review of the law.

Held

Article 14 of the Constitution that guarantees freedom of association as one of the people's fundamental rights is to empower people by way of freely forming associations to formulate their common wills, pursue their common beliefs, and ultimately realize their common goals. Freedom of association not only includes the people's right to freely determine the purposes and forms of their associations, but also the right to join or not join any associations and related activities. It also guarantees any associations that individuals form and join, along with their creation, maintenance, naming, and promotion of their related activities from any unlawful infringement. With such a protection, associations may freely, in accordance with common consensus reached by a majority principle, decide their own business affairs related to associations including naming and openly express ideas consistent with the purpose of associations. By choosing their own names, associations express their existence as associations and show their own distinctiveness from that of others. Using their own names, associations will be able to, internally, strengthen the identity of their members, and externally, further their business relations as well as promote their activities under said names. Should associations have been deprived of the freedom to choose their own names, the nature of free association, being able to freely determine their own business affairs, would not have been incarnated, and that recruitment and maintenance of their members as well as external expressions of their own wills would have been disadvantaged. Hence, associations' right to choose their own names, at the time of their creation, or the right to change their names afterwards, shall be protected under the right of freedom of association that Article 14 of the Constitution guarantees. The infringement of the associations' right to choose their own names shall not be permitted unless under the circumstances specified by Article 23 of the Constitution and by laws or specifically delegated rules.

Article 3 of the Civil Organizations Act assigns agencies to regulate civil associations at the national, provincial, and county levels. Article 5 of the same Act prescribes that organizational areas of civil associations shall be limited to the abovementioned administrative areas. Although Article 12 of the Act requires that names and organizational areas of associations be specified in their own charters, it does not intend to limit associations' internal or external activities to such administrative areas specified in their own charters. According to the original intent of the Article, the purpose of specifying organizational areas of associations is to assign agencies to regulate the civil associations as well as to determine which courts have jurisdiction with regard to registering matters on their legal person. Names and organizational areas of associations manifest differently such that between them there are no necessary relations. While administrative agencies, based on their mandate of executing laws, may make necessary rules to supplement laws, the administrative rules shall not go beyond the mandate of delegating laws and shall be limited to details and technicalities concerning the execution of related laws. This fundamental principle has been previously upheld in Interpretations Nos 367, 390, 443 and 454. Hence, Section 4 of the Regulations for Registration of Social Entities, made by the Ministry of the Interior, requiring that civil associations be named in accordance with their administrative areas, infringes upon the peoples' freedom of association guaranteed by Article 14 of the Constitution and shall be declared null and void.

Damyanti Naranga v The Union of India & Ors
[1971] AIR 966, [1971] SCR (3) 840 (Supreme Court, India)

Facts

The Hindi Sahitya Sammelan was a registered society founded to develop and promote Hindi culture. Later, Parliament enacted the Hindi Sahitya Sammelan Act, declaring the Hindi Sahitya Sammelan of national importance. Section 4(1) of the Act stipulated that the Sammelan was to consist of the first members of the Society. All other applications for membership must be decided by relevant rules and procedures. The petitioner challenged the Act, arguing that it violated the right of individuals to form association guaranteed by Article 19 of the Constitution.

Vishishtha Bhargava J

It was argued that the right guaranteed by Article 19(1)(c) is only to form an association and, consequently, any regulation of the affairs of the Association, after it has been formed, will not amount to a breach of that right. It is true that it has been held by this Court that, after an Association has been formed and the right under Art 19(1)(c) has been exercised by the members forming it, they have no right to claim that its activities must also be permitted to be carried on in the manner they desire. Those cases are, however, inapplicable to the present case. The Act does not merely regulate the administration of the affairs of the Society, what it does is to alter the composition of the Society itself as we have indicated above. The result of this change in composition is that the members, who voluntarily formed the Association, are now compelled to act in that Association with other members who have been imposed as members by the Act and in whose admission to membership they had no say. Such alteration in the composition of the Association itself clearly interferes with the right to continue to function as members of the Association which was voluntarily formed by the original founders. The right to form an association, in our opinion, necessarily, implies that the persons forming the Association have also the right to continue to be associated with only those whom they voluntarily admit in the [association]. Any law, by which members are introduced in the voluntary Association without any option being given to the members to keep them out, or any law which takes away the membership of those who have voluntarily [j]oined it, will be a law violating the right to form an association. If we were to accept the submission that the right guaranteed by Art 19(1)(c) is confined to the initial stage of forming an Association and does not protect the right to continue the Association with the membership, either chosen by the founders or regulated by rules made by the Association itself, the right would be meaningless because, as soon as an Association is formed, a law may be passed interfering with its composition, so that the Association formed may not be able to function at all. The right can be effective only if it is held to include within it the right to continue the Association with its composition as voluntarily agreed upon by the persons forming the Association.

Dr Mohd Nasir Hashim v Menteri Dalam Negeri
[2006] 6 MLJ 213 (Court of Appeal, Malaysia)

Gopal Sri Ram JCA

On 15 February 1998 the appellant and twelve others met to form the Parti Sosialis Malaysia ('PSM'). They formed a committee of seven. An application was then made to the Registrar of Societies (ROS) to register themselves as a political society. The ROS declined to grant registration at national level. But [the ROS] was prepared to grant registration in the State of Selangor. Dissatisfied with the result the appellant appealed to the respondent, the Minister for Home Affairs. The appeal was dismissed. . . . Judicial review was sought and refused. The appellant now appeals to us.

. . . As I have already said, the legislative response of Parliament under art 10(2)(c)[152] is

---

[152] This refers to Art 10 of the Malaysian Constitution. Art 10(1)(c) guarantees to all citizens the right to form associations. Art 10(2)(c) empowers Parliament by law to impose such restrictions on the right con-

the Act itself and for present purposes it is s 7(1).[153] The only issue is whether this is a reasonable legislative restriction. In my judgment, there is nothing in s 7 that amounts to an unreasonable restriction on the freedom of association conferred by art 10(1)(c). All it does is to regulate the registration of associations to conform with the criteria set out in art 10(2)(c). Accordingly I would hold that s 7(1) is a valid law.

The real question that appears to have been missed by learned counsel for the appellant is this. Is the departmental policy formulated by the ROS for himself when considering applications to register political societies at the national level an unreasonable administrative act? In my judgment this is the true question because the first limb of art 8(1) of the Constitution demands fairness of any form of State action. Thus, in *Palm Oil & Research & Development Board Malaysia v Premium Vegetable Oils Sdn Bhd* [2004] 2 CLJ 265 it was held by the Federal Court as follows:

Article 8(1) has two limbs. The first limb guarantees equality before the law. In other words, it requires fairness in all forms of State action. As Thommen J said of the equipollent art 14 of the Indian Constitution in *Shri Sitaram Sugar Co Ltd v Union of India & Ors* [1990] 3 SCC 223 at p 251:

Any arbitrary action, whether in the nature of a legislative or administrative or quasi-judicial exercise of power, is liable to attract the prohibition of art 14 of the Constitution. As stated in *EP Royappa v State of Tamil Nadu* [1974] 4 SCC 3: 'equality and arbitrariness are sworn enemies; one belongs to the rule of law in a republic while the other, to the whim and caprice of an absolute monarch'. Unguided and unrestricted power is affected by the vice of discrimination: *Maneka Gandhi v Union of India*. The principle of equality enshrined in art 14 must guide every State action, whether it be legislative, executive, or quasi-judicial: *Ramana Dayaram Shetty v International Airport Authority of India* [1979] 3 SCC 489 at 511–512, *Ajay Hasia v Khalid Mujib Sehravardi* [1981] 1 SCC 722 and *DS Nakara v Union of India* [1983] 1 SCC 305.

In *Savrimuthu v Public Prosecutor* [1987] 1 CLJ 368; [1987] CLJ (Rep) 322, Salleh Abas LP said:

. . . any statutory power must be exercised reasonably and with due consideration.

It is axiomatic that a statutory power or discretion is exercised unfairly if it is exercised unreasonably and without due consideration.

To answer the question posed a moment ago, it is my judgment that the departmental policy requiring a political party's committee to comprise of representatives from at least 7 States of the Federation where registration is sought at the national level is not an unreasonable exercise of the statutory power conferred upon the ROS by s 7(1) of the Act. Since Malaysia has 13 States the ROS probably had in mind that a political party seeking registration at the national level must seek to represent 50% plus one State in the Federation. There is nothing unreasonable about this. Some policy is necessary to guide the discretion conferred by s 7. Otherwise it may become an unprincipled discretion . . .

Here the ROS formulated a policy which, as I have already said, is not unreasonable in an objective sense. It may well have been different if the ROS and the Minister had required a person from every State in the Federation to be in PSM's committee. But that is not what happened. Like British Oxygen and Sagnata, here too, the ROS and the Minister provided

---

ferred by Art 10(1)(c) 'as it deems necessary or expedient in the interest of the security of the Federation or any part thereof, public order or morality'.

[153] This means s 7(1) of the Societies Act 1966, stipulating that 'upon receipt of an application under s 6, the Registrar shall, subject to the provisions of this section and to such conditions as the Registrar may deem fit to impose, register the local society making the application'.

the appellant an opportunity to make representations as to why the policy should not be applied to PSM. The evidence shows that the appellant and other pro-tem committee members met with officials of the ROS and that written representations were also made. So this is not the kind of case which Lord Reid had in mind in British Oxygen or which the Master of the Rolls had in Sagnata. There was no shutting of the ears in this case. The ROS acted fairly and reasonably at all times.

Secretary of Aircraft Engineers of BD & Anor v Registrar of Trade Union & Ors 1993, 22 CLC (AD) (Supreme Court, Bangladesh)

Facts

Under section 8 of the Industrial Relations Ordinance 1969, the Registrar of Trade Unions registered the five petitioners and two unions as trade unions of the Biman. Under section 22 of the same Ordinance, the five appellants were authorised as the Collective Bargaining Agents of the Biman. Later, the Industrial Relations Act made amendments to the Ordinance and the Registrar served on the seven registered trade unions of Biman an order stating that under the Amendment, an enquiry was made which found that the seven trade unions were not constituted in accordance with the new provisions to the Ordinance. The trade unions were asked to submit documents to obtain proper registration certificates. A notification was then made in the *Bangladesh Gazette* naming the seven trade unions that were at risk of having their registration cancelled. The petitioners submitted objections and challenged the Registrar's notification. The High Court held that section 5 of the Amendment Act did not violate Article 38 of the Constitution protecting the freedom of association, and did not decide on the validity of the two provisions added to the Ordinance. The petitioners then sought constitutional review of the amendments to the Ordinance.

Mustafa Kamal J

The Ordinance, 1969 was amended by the Industrial Relations (Amendment) Act, 1990, shortly, the Amendment Act, 1990. By section 2 thereof two provisions were added to sub-section (2) of section 7 of the Ordinance, 1969 so that the entire sub-section (2) of section 7 now reads as follows:

> A trade union of workers shall not be entitled to registration under this Ordinance unless it has a minimum membership of thirty percent of the total number of workers employed in the establishment or group of establishment in which it is formed:
>   Provided that more than one establishment under the same employer, which are allied to and connected with one 'another for the purpose of carrying on the same industry irrespective of their place of situation, shall be deemed to be one establishment for the purpose of this sub-section:
>   Provided further that where any doubt or dispute arises as to whether any two of more establishments are under the same employer or whether they are allied to or connected with one another for the purpose of carrying on the industry, the decision of the Registrar shall be final'.

. . . The basic right involved in these appeals is not so much a right of registration, but a right to a particular form of organisational set up of trade unions. If the appellant trade unions had organised themselves along the lines indicated in the amended legislation and ha[d] wanted to survive as a trade union simpliciter, without being registered, then perhaps the validity of section 11A of the Ordinance, 1969 could be considered. But that is not their case. Nor is section 11A under challenge in these appeals.

What has been sought to be achieved by the amended legislation is that it aims to put an end to the concept of 'as many trade unions as establishments' and introduce a scheme of 'one employer, one establishment'. The erstwhile registered trade unions can claim a fundamental right to their continuance only if they can establish that they have a fundamental right to the continuation of the old concept of organisational set-up. The changed concept is applicable to all employers and all then allied and connected establishments, without any distinction whatsoever[.] Neither is this concept [a] totally new one nor a radical departure from the past. This changed concept has its origin in section 28B of the Trade Unions Act, 1926. This Act contained no provision for determination of collective bargaining agent as in the Ordinance, 1969. After registration, there was a further need of recognition by the employer. And the employer was to follow the concept of 'same or allied industries, one trade union'. Section 28B of the Trade Unions Act, 1926 was as follows:

> 28B(1) An employer shall recognise a Trade Union if it fulfils the following conditions, namely:
> (b) that all its ordinary members are workmen employed in the same industry or in industries allied to or connected with one another;

Note clause (b) above. It is only when a trade union was recognised by an employer that it acquired the right to negotiate with the employer in respect of trade union matters, a right given to collective bargaining agents under section 22(12) of the Ordinance, 1969. The point to notice is that to meet the requirement of recognition of an employer under the Trade Unions Act, 1926, members of a trade union had to be employed in the same industry or in industries allied to or connected with one another and also had to have not less than ten percent of the total number of workmen employed in such industry or industries and also had to exceed the number of members of every other trade union in such industry or industries. What was sought to be achieved at the employees level (after registration) under the Trade Unions Act, 1926 is now sought to be achieved at the Registrar's level under the newly amended Ordinance, 1969, because recognition by the employer is no longer necessary and a collective bargaining agent is determined either by operation of law (section 22(1)) or by the Registrar in secret ballot (section 22(2) to 22(10)). The amended legislation has thus nothing to do with restrictions on the right of association or union or restrictions on its continuance. It is a re-organisational statute and no one has a fundamental right to a particular form of trade union. The appellant-union in CA No 15 of 1993, Aircraft Workshop Technical Workers Union, was no doubt an 'establishment' within the meaning of section 2 (iv) of the Ordinance, 1969, because its members were drawn up from an aircraft workshop of the Biman, but its apprehended loss of registration is similarly due to an organisational re-structuring and not due either to any restrictions on its members' right to association or union or to any restrictions on its continuance. The re-structuring is not arbitrary or fanciful or even innovative. It is applicable to all industries with one employer. It was there previously, only resuscitated anew. . . .

. . . In the result all the appeals are dismissed without costs. However, this Judgment will not affect the existing Agreements, if any, between any of the appellants and the Biman.

Notes and Questions

1. Does the distinction between content-based and content-neutral regulations also apply to freedom of association? In *JY Interpretation No 644*, the Constitutional Court invalidated a ban on civil organisations 'advocating Communism or partition of national territory' as amounting to 'bestowing on the governing authority ... the power to review the content of the speech itself'.

2. *JY Interpretation No 479* of Taiwan's Constitutional Court affirmed the freedom of associations to decide their own affairs, including the name of the association. What other rights and freedoms may associations enjoy?

3. In *Damyanti Naranga v The Union of India*, the Supreme Court of India held that an association, once lawfully formed, enjoyed the right to continue its own purposes and functions notwithstanding subsequent legal change. However, the courts in Bangladesh and Malaysia held that associations may be subject to reasonable regulations with respect to their organisation and administration. What might be considered reasonable restrictions on the organisation and administration of civic associations? What is the appropriate standard in reviewing these restrictions? Why?

4. In Taiwan, the formation of civic, social or occupational associations requires prior government approval, while that of political parties does not. However, if any political party engages 'in illegal activities that endanger the existence of the state or the nation's free and democratic constitutional order', it may be dissolved by the Constitutional Court pursuant to Article 5 of the Additional Article of the Constitution in Taiwan. The dissolution of illegal political parties is also possible in other Asian jurisdictions, such as Indonesia, South Korea and Thailand: see chapters five and six.

9

Religion and State

I. WHAT IS RELIGION?

The definition of 'religion' or what constitutes a 'religious practice' is an important threshold question, as it determines what claims enjoy the cover of a religious freedom guarantee. Are the criteria subjective (insider perspective) or objective (outsider perspective)? Are courts or legislative bodies equipped to determine whether a belief system contains the 'necessary spiritual content' to qualify as a religion, or would this be undue intrusion into theology?

A. Defining Religion: A Broad or Restrictive Approach?

There are a multiplicity of approaches to this complex and pressing question.[1] Where legal definitions of 'religion' are under-inclusive, they deny protection to (disfavoured) religious groups. For example, the Singapore Court of Appeal in *Nappalli Peter Williams v Institute of Technical Education*[2] adopted a narrow reading of 'religion' which excluded humanistic ideologies such as state patriotism from the ambit of the definition. Religion 'is not about a system of belief in one's own country but about a citizen's faith in a personal God, sometimes described as a belief in a supernatural being'. It noted that the state 'commands no supernatural existence in a citizen's personal belief system', rejecting an argument by Jehovah's Witnesses that compelling a teacher to participate in a flag and anthem ceremony in public school forced him to participate in idolatry and violated his religious freedom.

Various Asian courts have recognised the reality that a theistic definition of religion would not serve the variety of non-theistic religions extant in Asia. For example, the Supreme Court of India in *The Commissioner, Hindu Religious Endowments, Madras v Sri Lakshmindra Thirtha Swamiar of Sri Shirur Mutt*[3] rejected the definition of 'religion' in the American case of *Davie v Benson*[4] as 'one's views of his relation to his Creator and to the obligations they impose of reverence for His Being and character and of obedience to His will'. It stated:

---

[1] On the problem of defining religion, see TJ Gunn, 'The Complexity of Religion and the Definition of "Religion" in International Law' (2003) 16 *Harvard Human Rights Journal* 189 at 193–94.

[2] *Nappalli Peter Williams v Institute of Technical Education* [1999] 2 SLR 569 at [26].

[3] *The Commissioner, Hindu Religious Endowments, Madras v Sri Lakshmindra Thirtha Swamiar of Sri Shirur Mutt* [1954] AIR 282.

[4] *Davie v Benson* 133 US 333, 342 (1890).

[W]e have great doubt whether a definition of 'religion' as given above could have been in the minds of our Constitution-makers when they framed the Constitution. Religion is certainly a matter of faith with individuals or communities and it is not necessarily theistic. There are well known religions in India like Buddhism and Jainism which do not believe in God or in any Intelligent First Cause. A religion undoubtedly has its basis in a system of beliefs or doctrines which are regarded by those who profess that religion as conducive to their spiritual well being, but it would not be correct to say that religion is nothing else, but a doctrine or belief. A religion may not only lay down a code of ethical rules for its followers to accept, it might prescribe rituals and observances, ceremonies and modes of worship which are regarded as integral parts of religion, and these forms and observances might extend even to matters of food and dress.

Another case in point is the Hong Kong decision in *Chu Woan Chyi v Director of Immigration*,[5] which rejected a narrow or rigid approach to defining 'religious belief' and 'religious activities' under the Basic Law. While religion 'needs to be something more than a set of shared ethical beliefs' in the Asian context, the court held it did not 'demand a belief in the existence of God or any first cause', noting that 'clearly recognised religions' that are not based on a belief in the existence of God included Buddhism and Taoism.

However, an over-inclusive formulation may include belief systems which are broadly not considered to be religious, such as ecology, secular humanism[6] or anything which constitutes 'a sincere and meaningful belief occupying in the life of its possessor a place parallel'[7] to a belief in God(s). With this caution in mind, the disparity of perspectives in assessing whether a belief or practice is considered 'religious' is apparent. Take transcendental meditation (TM), for example. Indian courts have held that TM is not a religion but a science with beneficial calming effects: *Hiralal Mallick v State of Bihar.*[8] It noted that ancient vedic insights were validated by scientific studies, bequeathing mankind 'new meditational, yogic and other therapeutics, at once secular, empirically tested and trans-religious'. This included studies of TM in America, Canadia and Germany that yielded improved creativity and better behaviour. In contrast, Malaysian Islamic authorities issued a fatwa against yoga since they did not consider it a sport but an integral part of Hinduism and feared that its Hindu roots would corrupt Muslims.[9] The 'modernist' approach by the secular Indian court considered the 'scientific' benefits of TM and highlighted its observance beyond the context of Hindu worship, while the theological view by a Malaysian religious body fixed on the religious roots and spiritual impact of the practice.

Courts have had to decide whether a group was a religious group and entitled to the benefit of laws prohibiting discrimination on grounds of religion, or laws protecting religious group autonomy from state interference. Factors relevant to this enquiry range from subjective self-identification to more 'objective' factors like the doctrines and ceremonies of a belief system and its leadership structures. The Hong Kong Court of First Instance in *Chu Woan Chyi v Director of Immigration* had to consider if the

---

[5] *Chu Woan Chyi v Director of Immigration* [2007] HKCFI 267.
[6] See Justice Black's Opinion in *Torcaso v Watkins* 367 US 488 (1961), at fn 11: '[A]mong religions in this country which do not teach what would generally be considered a belief in the existence of God are Buddhism, Taoism, Ethical Culture, Secular Humanism and others.'
[7] *United States v Seeger* 380 US 163 (1965).
[8] *Hiralal Mallick v State of Bihar* [1978] 1 SCR 301.
[9] 'Malaysia clerics issue yoga fatwa', *BBC News*, 22 November 2008.

Falun Gong movement should be recognised as a religion, despite being declared an illegal 'evil cult'[10] on the Mainland in 1999. Hartmann J noted that

> practitioners of Falun Gong, while they describe it as a spiritual movement, do not classify it as a 'religion'. The Falun Gong movement is founded in large measure on Buddhist teachings but incorporates elements of Daoism. There is no requirement to believe in an identified deity. But Falun Gong practitioners do accept the supernatural . . . By means of meditation and exercises they seek to place themselves in harmony with this transcendent reality. Falun Gong practitioners see their movement as entirely benevolent. They adhere to a moral code, they say, which ensures a life of spiritual purpose.

He adopted guidelines set out by the Australian High Court in *Church of the New Faith v Commissioner of Pay-Roll*:[11]

> One of the more important indicia of 'a religion' . . . involves belief in the supernatural . . . that really extends beyond that which is capable of perception by the senses. If that be absent, it is unlikely that one has 'a religion'. Another is that the ideas relate to man's nature and place in the universe and his relation to things supernatural. A third is that the ideas are accepted by adherents as requiring or encouraging them to observe particular standards or codes of conduct or to participate in specific practices having supernatural significance. A fourth is that, however loosely knit and varying in beliefs and practices adherents may be, they constitute an identifiable group or identifiable groups.

These factors are both subjective, in terms of self-belief and perception, and objective, such as group distinctiveness. Courts in different jurisdictions ascribe different weight to these factors in the adjudicatory process. Most of these criteria relate to the 'supernatural' dimension of a belief system. Hartmann J noted that Falun Gong adherents were an identifiable group who believed in the supernatural and a moral code integral to their spiritual aspiration. The Hong Kong approach did not consider as decisive Falun Gong's belief that it was not a religion. The test was applied by examining its belief structure, and the conclusion was that it was entitled to be recognised as a religious movement with religious beliefs, warranting religious freedom protections.

In contrast, the Singapore High Court in *Ng Chye Huay v PP*[12] applied an exclusively subjective test in determining if certain Falun Gong practitioners convicted of unlawful assembly could claim Article 15 religious freedom protection. The court gave conclusive weight to the declaration of Falun Gong members that theirs was not a religion but just a specific form of *qigong* (meditation exercises). Self-identification was determinative. In contrast, other quasi-judicial bodies have adopted other definitional tests incorporating objective criteria.[13]

A practical 'mixed' test is discernible in the approach that identifies, non-exhaustively, the 'elements' of a religion, like that applied by the Indian Supreme

---

[10] See ASY Cheung, 'In Search of a Theory of Cult and Freedom of Religion in China: The Case of Falun Gong' (2004) 13 *Pacific Rim Law & Policy Journal* 1.

[11] *Church of the New Faith v Commissioner of Pay-Roll* (1982) 154 CLR 120, per Wilson and Deane JJ at 174.

[12] *Ng Chye Huay v PP* [2006] 1 SLR(R) 157 [34].

[13] In *Ontario Human Rights Commission v Daiming Juang* 2006 Human Rights Tribunal of Ontario 1, Falun Gong was found to satisfy both the subjective elements of being a 'deeply and sincerely held personal belief' about spirituality and the objective criteria of being 'a professed system and confession of faith' not requiring the belief in God(s).

Court in *SP Mittal v Union of India*.[14] The Court had to determine if the teachings of
Sri Aurobindo (Aurobindoism) constituted a religion. The process by which the Court
concluded that Aurobindoism was not a religion is illuminating. First, it considered
how secular authorities, such as various Encyclopaedias of Philosophy, viewed it as a
religion and identified Aurobindo as an 'Indian metaphysician' who synthesised older
Indian religious ideas with Christian theism. Secondly, the Court noted that there was
a religious following, evidenced by some 300 Aurobindonian centres worldwide.
Thirdly, it examined the rituals, which included identified places of pilgrimage and
chanting mantras. Fourthly, it examined the writings of Sri Aurobindo or his associates which indicated that the Aurobindo Ashram was not a religious association, as its
members included people of all religions, including anti-theists, who subscribed to
Aurobindo's teachings about the discovery of the divine self and certain psychological
practices of meditation and Integral Yoga. The Memorandum of Association did not
mention religion, and it was on the basis of its being a scientific research association
that the Society collected funds from the Indian Government and non-governmental
agencies. The majority judgment concluded that the Aurobindo society was not a religious denomination, and that Aurobindo's teachings represented only his philosophy
and not a religion. The insiders' perspective that theirs was not a religion was accorded
great weight.

Courts have had to delimit the boundaries of 'religion' by distinguishing this from
'custom' or 'superstition'. In jurisdictions like Indonesia, which recognises six official
religions (Islam, Buddhism, Hinduism, Protestantism, Catholicism and Confucianism),
the state distinguishes between religion (*agama*) and mystical belief (*aliran kepercayaan*). This has implications for the legitimacy of a belief system and whether practitioners of the latter are able to access funding for religious groups.[15]

In *Kakunaga v Sekiguchi* (*Tsu City Shinto Ground-breaking Ceremony Case*),[16] the
Japanese court had to consider if Shintoism was a religion such that state involvement
in a Shinto ceremony would violate the separation of state and religion. Specifically, a
municipal public authority organised and paid for a ground-breaking ceremony presided over by a Shinto priest. If this were a 'religious activity', it would be prohibited
under Article 20(3) of the 1946 Constitution of Japan, which relates to the separation
of religion and state.

One must recognise the complex nature of Shintoism, given its long history with
Japanese identity. Shintoism held a revered place in the Meiji Constitution before
World War II, and was intimately linked with Japanese nationalism. The belief was
that the Emperor was the direct divine descendant in an unbroken line from the first
Emperor, and was both the ruler and the high priest of Shinto. The Shinto Directive
issued by the General Headquarters of the Allied Occupation ordered religious reform
by separating religion from the state to prevent the misuse of religion for political
ends.[17] In his dissenting opinion, Judge Fujibayashi Ekizo considered whether Shinto

---

[14] *SP Mittal v Union of India* [1983] AIR 1, (1983) SCR(1) 729, 741–45, 772–88.
[15] See M Crouch, 'Law and Religion in Indonesia: The Constitutional Court and the Blasphemy Law'
(2012) 7(1) *Asian Journal of Comparative Law* 1.
[16] *Kakunaga v Sekiguchi* (*Tsu City Shinto Ground-breaking Ceremony Case*) 31 Minshū533 (Supreme
Court of Japan, 13 July 1977); trans ref in LW Beer and H Itoh (eds), *The Constitutional Law of Japan
1970–1990* (Seattle, Wash: University of Washington Press 1996) at 478–91.
[17] Y Ashizu, 'The Shinto Directive and the Constitution' at <http://nirc.nanzan-u.ac.jp/nfile/3118>.

was a folk custom or religion, and noted that after the Meiji Restoration (1868) – when Japan modernised and imported many institutions from the West – it retained Shintoism as a spiritual foundation, but held that while it was not a religion it had the status of a national religion. It became a matter of cultural practice, regardless of personal belief, for students to be brought to Shinto shrines for worship, and for government ministers to worship at Ise Shrine, for example. He stated that such requirements were accepted as customary because:

> Shrine Shinto was a simple religion. It had no organized theology; its view of the divine was elemental, and it had very few supernatural or miraculous components . . .
>
> Historically, there had been few conflicts between Japanese Buddhism and Shrine Shinto . . . The doctrine that the Japanese gods were incarnations of Buddhas and bodhisattvas provided a theoretical basis for the harmony, unity, and coexistence of the deities of the two religions. Some Buddhist temples had shrines dedicated to a Shinto guardian deity within their grounds, and most Japanese were, at the same time, both Buddhists and parishioners of their local Shinto shrine. In other words, they were content to believe in Buddhism as individuals and worship at shrines as a people, without finding this duality strange in any way . . . In any case, a thousand years leading a dual life combining Buddhism and Shrine Shinto meant the Japanese people had little difficulty accepting the State's policy toward Shrine Shinto after the Meiji Restoration.[18]

The religious consciousness of the Japanese people developed within a tradition of Shrine Shinto and Buddhism, and was therefore not sufficiently sensitive to the question of religious freedom. As the two religions are polytheistic or pantheistic, not monotheistic like Christianity with its personal God, they did not encourage a sense of the individual person or stimulate the development of concepts of basic human rights. Thus, they did little to raise awareness of the importance of religious freedom. This historical circumstance is probably a major reason why the issue of shrine worship was not viewed as a serious infringement of the freedom of religion.

The majority in the *Tsu City Shinto Ground-breaking Ceremony Case* considered prayers offered at ground-breaking ceremonies a customary practice or secular in nature, since the average citizen would regard them as a mere formality. Judge Ekizo recognised that certain customs had certainly lost all religious significance in Japan, such as Christmas trees as a family treat for children, but disagreed that the ground-breaking ceremony was a mere formality. This is because it appealed to the worker's desire for human safety 'beyond human powers', such that it was irrelevant whether the Mayor believed in it or not. Further, it was no mere folk practice, as four Shinto priests in their professional capacity conducted the ceremony, Judge Ekizo noting that Shinto rituals were 'gestures of giving thanks to the gods', constituting 'religious acts of the highest order'. In his view, to define religion too restrictively would be to open the door to 'close ties between religion and State'. Once again, we see divided perspectives, one arising from the external or social perception of an activity and another more internal perspective ascribing the religious quality of an act to how a Shinto practitioner would regard it.

---

[18] *Tsu City Shinto Ground-breaking Ceremony Case*, above n 16, para 2(b) available at <http://www.courts.go.jp/english/judgments/text/1977.7.13-1971.-Gyo-Tsu-.No.69.html>.

The Philippines Supreme Court held that the indigenisation of a formerly religious ritual could transform it into a custom, in *Garces v Estenzo.*[19] Here, favouring social perceptions, it held that the purchase by private donations of a wooden image of a saint in conjunction with the celebration of a barrio fiesta, involving the celebration of mass, did not establish any religion or favour the Catholic Church. This is because the fiesta was consider 'a socio-religious affair' and 'ingrained tradition in rural communities'.

B. Religion or Custom?

Another closely related question is whether a particular form of conduct is 'religious' so as to attract the protection of religious freedom. In *Hjh Halimatussaadiah bte Hj Kamaruddin v Public Services Commission, Malaysia,*[20] the issue was whether wearing a 'purdah' (an item of clothing covering the face except for eye slits) was an Islamic practice or merely a cultural expression. A female Muslim government employee had been dismissed for wearing purdah which contravened a government circular relating to work conditions. She challenged this as violating her Article 11(1) rights to practise her Islamic faith. Before the Malaysian High Court, she argued from the Quran and certain *hadiths* (religious teaching) that she believed she had to cover her entire face, except her eyes, to avoid '*fitnah*'.[21] Eusoff Chin J noted that the highest Islamic authority in the form of the Mufti (Sunni Islamic scholar) agreed that the Quran required a woman to cover her body, except for 'the face, palms and fingers, and feet'. However, the Mufti had issued a *fatwa* (religious ruling) that

> [w]here a woman's face is painted with cosmetics to make her exceptionally beautiful and attractive so that it evokes a sexual desire on all men who behold her beautiful face, which would invite 'fitnah' [and] may cause a breach of the peace or lead to public disorder, then the woman is obliged to cover her face and should only expose her face to members of her family. She is allowed to use make-up to beautify her face for her husband. Whether the woman's face is exceptionally beautiful is not for the woman herself to judge.

The Court took as conclusive the Mufti's opinion that Malaysian Muslim women were not required to cover their faces and accepted his evidence that old Arab women, in a practice pre-dating Islam, wore purdah as customary dress. The Court considered that the Quran neither prohibited nor prevented a Muslim woman from wearing purdah. The Islamic Division of the Prime Minister's Department also issued its opinion that the relevant circular was not contrary to Islamic teachings. The High Court found the circular legal, giving weight to official religious expert opinion and the opinion of political authorities, over that of the personal interpretation of what a faith requires. For good measure, the High Court noted that for purposes of maintaining the sanctity of state secrets, a man could wear a purdah and pose as a female officer, which could undermine government interests! The circular thus did not undermine public order, morality or health.

---

[19]   *Garces v Estenzo* GR No 53487, 25 May 1981.
[20]   *Hjh Halimatussaadiah bte Hj Kamaruddin v Public Services Commission, Malaysia* [1992] 1 MLJ 513 (Kuala Lumpur High Court, Malaysia).
[21]   An Arabic term connoting chaos or upheaval.

The Supreme Court[22] affirmed this ruling, noting from Islamic teachings that the Prophet's instructions ordering women to wear outer garments (whether 'hijab' or 'jilbab') was to protect their dignity, not to restrict their liberty, 'but to protect them from harm and molestation under the conditions then existing in Medina'. It concluded that Islam did not make it obligatory to display a woman's face, except in a haram, leaving it to the choices of Muslims of various nations to practise their own customs of hijab. It said of the appellant's interpretation of Surah 24:

> [W]e find that there is a misconception on her part with regard to her interpretation of Surah 24 that she must not expose her body including her face. Otherwise, there would be 'fitnah' against her. The message in verses 27–34 of Surah 24 seems to be that 'privacy should be respected and the utmost decorum should be observed in dress and manners.' (The Holy Quran – Text, Translation and Commentary, Abdullah Yusuf Ali)[23]

This raises the issue of whether the determination of the scope of religious obligation should be left to the believer, a civil court or religious authority. The question whether a judge may utilise his religious knowledge to help decide a case, or whether he should confine himself to expert evidence, arose in acute form in the Malaysian case of *Meor Atiqulrahman v Fatimah Binti Sihi.*[24]

Here, the Court adopted the Indian test of essential practice (discussed in section I.C. below) in concluding that wearing *serban* (male turban) was not an essential practice of Islam, upholding as constitutional a school uniform policy banning the *serban*. Abdul Hamid Mohamad FCJ proposed a three-step test in balancing religious freedoms against public goods like public order and morality, set out in Article 11(1), (5). This included:

(a) looking to see whether religion was involved;
(b) examining whether a practice was part of that religion, and how important it was to the practise of the religion; and
(c) considering all relevant circumstances.

In deciding whether it was integral, the Court considered its importance, such that if it was compulsory, greater weight ought to be accorded to it. Mohamad FCJ noted that the classification made by Islamic jurists on the '*hukum*'[25] regarding a particular practice was helpful, such that prohibiting '*wajib*' (mandatory) as opposed to '*sunat*' (commendable) practices would be viewed more seriously. He affirmed the judicial role in deciding whether a religious practice was involved, and its importance, with the assistance of expert witnesses or the views of state and federal religious bodies. On whether wearing turbans was a religious practice, he noted:

> Islam is not about turban and beard. The pagan Arabs . . . wore turbans and kept beards. It was quite natural for the Prophet (PBUH), born into the community and grew up in it, to do the same. As it was not repugnant to the teaching of Islam, he continued to do so . . . [L]earned counsel tried to equate the wearing of turban with the 'Hajj': the 'Hajj' too was performed in pre-Islamic days and continued to be performed after the coming of Islam. That, with respect, is misconceived. The 'Hajj' performed by the pagan Arabs was completely

---

[22] *Hjh Halimatussaadiah bte Hj Kamaruddin v Public Services Commission, Malaysia* [1994] 3 MLJ 61
[23] Ibid, 71 at [23].
[24] *Meor Atiqulrahman v Fatimah Binti Sihi* [2006] 4 MLJ 605, 610–11 (Federal Court, Putrajaya).
[25] Ruling on religious law.

different from the 'Hajj' taught by the Prophet (PBUH). Furthermore, there are clear provisions in the Al-Quran that make the performance of the 'Hajj' mandatory and one of the pillars of Islam. Turbans were (and are) not only worn by Arabs. Other peoples, living in the desert or semi-desert areas, eg the Afghans and Persians wore/wear them too ... Nowadays, the turbans, distinguished by their designs and the way they are tied or worn, symbolize the nationality of the persons wearing them, eg whether they are Saudis, Sudanese, Afghans, Omanis, etc. The turban has become part of the national dress of those countries.[26]

In underscoring that wearing *serban* was more a cultural than religious practice, Mohamad FCJ made a few sociological statements. He noted the turban was rarely won in Malaysia during the 1960s, save as a sign of piety by Muslims who had made the Hajj (pilgrimage) to Mecca. This became popularised in the 1970s with the appearance of certain *dakwah* (missionary groups) associated with a more fundamentalist brand of Islam. Mohamad FCJ observed, however, that in contemporary Malaysia, 'very few of our Muftis and hardly any Shari'ah Court judge wears the turban'. He noted that the syariah placed different obligations on Muslim boys and men, such that mandatory practices like the five daily prayers applied only to Muslims of the age of majority (15 years). In assessing whether Muslim boys of the appellant's age wore turbans, Mohamad FCJ said, as a matter of personal observation:

> The best place to see whether it is the practice of boys, I am speaking about Arab and Arabic-speaking boys (not Malay boys living in a FELDA settlement) ... is to go to Masjid Al-Haram, the birthplace of the Prophet (PBUH), where the 'House of Allah' ('Baitullah' or the 'Kaabah') stands. Go there after the 'Asar' prayer. One can see scores of boys of the age of the appellants sitting cross-legged learning to read and reciting the Al-Quran. None of them wears turban ...[27]

He noted there was no fatwa in Malaysia on turban wearing by the religious authorities, and that the Quran itself did not mention the turban; the various hadiths cited, which were not to be read in isolation, mentioned only how the Prophet used to wear the turban, not whether it was required:

> I accept that the Prophet (PBUH) wore turban. But he also rode a camel, built his house and mosque with clay walls and roof of leaves of date palms and brushed his teeth with the twig of a plant. Does that make the riding a camel a more pious deed than travelling in an aeroplane? Is it preferable to build houses and mosques using the same materials used by the Prophet (PBUH) and the same architecture adopted by him during his time? In Malaysia, Muslim houses and mosques would leak when it rains! There would be no Blue Mosque or Taj Maha ... that the Muslims can be proud of! Again, is it more Islamic to brush one's teeth with a twig than using a modern tooth brush with tooth paste and water to wash in the privacy of one's bathroom? It is not everything that the Prophet (PBUH) did or the way he did it that is legally (according to Shariah) or religiously binding on Muslims or even preferable and should be followed.[28]

He noted the distinction between non-legal and legal Sunnah (the Prophet's acts and tacit enactments), as established in *Principles of Islamic Jurisprudence* by Mohammad Hashim Kamali (1991):

---

[26]   *Meor Atiqulrahman v Fatimah Binti Sihi*, above n 24 612–13 at [24]–[25].
[27]   Ibid, 612 at [30].
[28]   Ibid, 613 at [35]

Non-legal Sunnah (*Sunnah ghayr tashri'iyyah*) mainly consists of the natural activities of the Prophet (*al-af 'al al'jibilliyyah*) such as the manner in which he ate, slept, dressed, and such other activities as do not seek to constitute a part of the Shari'ah. Activities of this nature are not of primary importance to the Prophetic mission and therefore do not constitute legal norms. According to the majority of ulema, the Prophet's preferences in these areas, such as his favourite colours, or the fact that he slept on his right side in the first place, etc, only indicate the permissibility (ibahah) of the acts in question . . .

On a similar note, Sunnah which partakes in specialized or technical knowledge, such as medicine, commerce and agriculture, is once again held to be peripheral to the main function of the Prophetic mission and is therefore not a part of the Shari'ah. As for acts and sayings of the Prophet that related to particular circumstances such as the strategy of war, including such devices that misled the enemy forces, timing of attack, siege or withdrawal, these too are considered to be situational and not a part of the Shari'ah . . .

Certain activities of the Prophet may fall in between the two categories of legal and non-legal Sunnah as they combine the attributes of both. Thus it may be difficult to determine whether an act was strictly personal or was intended to set an example for others to follow. It is also known that at times the Prophet acted in a certain way which was in accord with the then prevailing custom of the community. For instance, the Prophet kept his beard at a certain length and trimmed his moustache. The majority of ulema have viewed this not as a mere observance of the familiar usage at the time but as an example for the believers to follow. Others have held the opposite view by saying that it was a part of the social practice of the Arabs which was designed to prevent resemblance to the Jews and some non-Arabs who used to shave the beard and grow the moustache. Such practices were . . . optional. Similarly, it is known that the Prophet used to go to the 'id prayers (salat al-'id) by one route and return from the mosque by a different route, and that the Prophet at times performed the hajj pilgrimage while riding a camel. The Shafi'i jurists are inclined to prefer the commendable (mandub) in such acts to mere permissibility whereas the Hanafis consider them as merely permissible, or mubah.[29]

The Court downgraded the appellant's view that wearing turban was 'sunat', noting that he cited the views of traditional jurists living at a time when wearing turban was 'customary or fashionable', and underscoring that great jurists revised their rulings after observing the customs of a people, such as Imam Shafie who lived in Egypt. The Court concluded that even if wearing the turban was 'sunat', it was not as important as other 'sunat' practices like 'sunat prayers', buttressing the judicial conclusion that the practice in question 'is of little significance' from the perspective of Islam, such that the restrictions on it were constitutional.

C. The Test of Essential Practice

The Indian Supreme Court, in its influential decision in *The Commissioner, Hindu Religious Endowments, Madras v Sri Lakshmindra Thirtha Swamiar of Sri Shirur Mutt*,[30] held that an essential part of a religion warranted protection, with the implication that non-essential practices are subject to state regulation. 'Essentiality' was to be 'primarily ascertained with reference to the doctrines of that religion itself'. As such, if a Hindu sect required certain food offerings to an idol at particular times, the fact

---

[29] Ibid, 614 at [36].
[30] *The Commissioner, Hindu Religious Endowments, Madras v Sri Lakshmindra Thirtha Swamiar of Sri Shirur Mutt* [1954] AIR 282.

that monetary expenditure was involved did not make that activity 'secular' despite the economic aspect of the activity. The Supreme Court has noted that 'purely secular practices' not essential to a religion may 'be clothed with a religious form'; in addition, religious practices 'may have sprung from merely superstitious beliefs and may in that sense be extraneous and unessential accretions to religion itself'.[31] This appears to open the door to greater judicial rationalisation of religion, both in terms of the essential/non-essential test and dividing superstition from authentic religion. This engagement by a secular court in theological questions is distinct from the view of Latham CJ in *Adelaide Company of Jehovah's Witnesses Incorporated v Commonwealth*[32] that 'What is religion to one is superstition to another.'

An example of theological engagement is found in *Saraswathi Ammal v Rajagopal Ammal.*[33] The Court, referring to Hindu scriptures, held as invalid under Hindu Law a woman's perpetual endowment of properties to ensure the conduct of worship at her deceased husband's *samadhi* (burial place), which she believed would produce spiritual benefit rather than general public benefit. The Court considered that the test to determine whether an act was conducive to spiritual benefit and was for a 'religious purpose' was to be decided on the basis of Hindu writings, ie had a Shastraic basis as far as Hindus were concerned. Where permanently tying up property for religious rather than public benefit was concerned, the Court required evidence that a purpose must 'have obtained wide recognition and constitute the religious practice of a substantial and large class of persons' rather than being merely the belief of one or more individuals. Some degree of consensus of the importance of a religious purpose within the religious community itself was thus important in enabling a secular court to decide upon the validity of the perpetual dedication of property without public benefit. In other words, the view of the mainstream religious community matters.

The High Court (Punjab) also cautioned against courts requiring what it might consider to be a 'progressive' reading of a religious faith in *Gurleen Kaur v State of Punjab.*[34] It upheld the decision of a Sikh minority institute to treat a Sikh girl as an inappropriate candidate for a reserved Sikh quota in its medical college, because she had trimmed her eyebrows contrary to the requirement to keep hair unshorn and was not considered an observant Sikh. In concluding that this tenet was essential to the Sikh religion, the Court referred to Sikh teachings, history, old and new Rehatnamas, daily Sikh 'Ardas' or prayers to God seeking the blessing of retaining bodily hair unshorn to his last breath, various Gurdwara Acts and Guru Granth Sahib to determine the meaning of 'Sikh' for the purposes of the Gurdwara Act of 1925. To Sikhs, hair is a gift of God, and to trim or shave it constitutes a form of apostasy. So too, Sikh tenets on preserving hair were a reaction to the Hindu observance of tonsure; thus, wearing hair unshorn was a primary distinguishing feature between a Sikh and a Hindu. The Court concluded that maintaining hair unshorn was a 'fundamental tenet' of the Sikh faith and not trivial. It noted that the courts should abstain from deciding whether a religious tenet was progressive or regressive:[35]

---

[31] *Durgah Committee Ajmer v Syed Hussain Ali* [1962] SCR (1) 383.

[32] *Adelaide Company of Jehovah's Witnesses Incorporated v Commonwealth* [1943] ALR 193.

[33] *Saraswathi Ammal v Rajagopal Ammal* [1954] SCR 277, 286–88.

[34] *Gurleen Kaur v State of Punjab* CWP No 14859 of 2008, [2009] INPBHC 21163 (30 May 2009).

[35] This is distinct from the constitutional mandate under Art 25(2)(b) that courts should reform aspects of Hinduism.

Religion must be perceived as it is, and not as another would like it to be. The followers of a faith do not allow their beliefs to be questioned. Once a Court arrives at the conclusion that a particular aspect of a religion, is fundamental and integral, as per the followers of the faith, it must be given effect to, irrespective of the views expressed . . . based either on science or logic. It is not for the Court to determine whether it is forward-looking or retrograde.[36]

Indian courts have found that a practice was not 'essential' to a religion by reference to history as opposed to their views of whether a practice was progressive. The Supreme Court in *Commissioner of Police v Acharya Jagdishwarananda Advadhuta*[37] held that the performance of Tandava dance in public (involving banned items like human skulls, daggers and tridents) was not an essential practice of the Ananda Margie order, upholding the police decision to declare as an unlawful assembly a religious procession where the Tandava dance was performed. While this order was established in 1955, Tandava dance as a religious rite was introduced later in 1966, casting doubt as to whether it was an essential rite. Additionally, nothing in the religious writings indicated that such a dance, even if it was 4,000 years old, had to be performed publicly. Judge Lakshmann in his dissenting judgment stated that if adherents to a religion accepted the dance as spiritually uplifting, the court should not judge their professed view but accept it as part of their religion.

The state's view that a particular practice was optional rather than an obligatory practice was judicially preferred by the Supreme Court in *Mohd Hanif Quareshi v State of Bihar*,[38] where a group of Muslims who were butchers and tanners challenged various laws banning the slaughter of certain animals, including a total ban on cow slaughter, without making an exception for bona fide religious purposes. They alleged that this violated religious freedom under Article 25. The Court referred to a non-judicially enforceable directive principle of state policy in Article 48, where the State, among other objectives, was to organise agriculture and animal husbandry, including taking steps to prohibit the slaughter of cows, calves and other milch and draught cattle. Notably, in Hinduism, the cow is sacred, revered as a source of good and a symbol of life, and may never be killed.[39] Das CJ noted that only scanty materials had been presented to substantiate the claim that cow sacrifice on Bakr Id Day was enjoined by Islam. No religious expert opinion on this point was offered, and only general Quranic verses were cited to the effect that the faithful are enjoined to pray and make sacrifices to their God.

The Court noted from a translation of the Hedaya Book XLIII, that Muslims were duty-bound to offer a sacrifice on this day in the form either of one goat per person, or a cow or camel for seven persons. From this, it inferred and concluded that cow sacrifice was not an obligatory religious practice, as 'the very fact of an option seems to run counter to the notion of an obligatory duty'. Empirically, many Muslims did not sacrifice cows on Bakr Id Day; the mandatory nature of the alleged duty was also watered down by dint of Indian history, where Moghul Emperors like Babar had seen 'the wisdom' of prohibiting cow slaughter by way of religious sacrifice and directed his

[36] *Gurleen Kaur v State of Punjab* CWP No 14859 of 2008 [149].
[37] *Commissioner of Police v Acharya Jagdishwarananda Advadhuta* [2004] INSC 155 (11 March 2004).
[38] *Mohd Hanif Quareshi v State of Bihar* [1958] AR 731.
[39] For a comparison between laws prohibiting cow and pig slaughter in India and Israel respectively, see D Barak Erez, 'Symbolic Constitutionalism: On Sacred Cows and Abominable Pigs' (2010) 6(3) *Law, Culture and the Humanities* 420.

son to do likewise. In so ruling, the secular Court partially appeased Hindus through its own interpretation of the Quran in rejecting the claims that cow slaughter was 'an essential practice of Islam', which is a matter of concern to religious minorities.

By way of comparison, the German Federal Constitutional Court[40] recognised the religious right of a Turkish Muslim to perform Islamic ritual slaughter under the Basic Law, prohibiting the application of a pre-slaughter stunning law. The US First Amendment's free exercise clause was held to protect both ritual slaughter and animal sacrifices practised by the Santeria religion, which could not be restricted by laws that ostensibly protected public health or animal welfare.[41] Such exemptions from general laws are a method of accommodating religious minorities.

II. CONTENT OF RELIGIOUS FREEDOM

Religious freedom is one of the most widespread constitutional rights.[42] This typically relates to rights belonging to the *forum internum* (conscience-based rights to hold or not hold a religious belief) and the *forum externum* (external manifestation of religious beliefs through publication, communal worship, teaching, preaching and evangelism). While religious free conscience is a vital element constituting the religious identity and worldview of believers, freedom of thought 'is also a precious asset for atheists, agnostics, skeptics and the unconcerned'.[43]

Within secular liberal constitutions, where individual autonomy is prioritised and the state is agnostic, religious freedom is predicated on voluntarist conceptions of religious identity. Profession of religion is safeguarded as an absolute freedom, while religious action is qualified by reference to public good. However, states with confessional constitutions may actively promote and protect a particular religious worldview as a substantive good or facet of indigenous national identity. Today, constitutional debates over freedom of profession of religion are evident in cases relating to blasphemy, apostasy and anti-propagation legislation, which ostensibly protect state-defined vulnerable groups. This is contrary to the liberal state, which does not advocate, enforce or punish belief but adopts a laissez-faire approach to protect individual choice through exposure to the broadest range of religious (and non-religious) worldviews. This allows religions to co-exist peacefully and each religion to 'flourish according to the zeal of its adherent and the appeal of its dogma'.[44] This ideal fades away when states adopt protectionist approaches towards an official religion, thereby intruding into personal choice and maintaining religious majorities that may translate into votes at the ballot box.

---

[40] 1 BvR 1783/99 (15 Jan 2002). See generally R Miller, 'The Constitutional Court's "Traditional Slaughter" Decision: The Muslims' Freedom of Faith and Germany's Freedom of Conscience', 3 German Law Journal (2002) at <http://www.germanlawjournal.com/article.php?id=128>.

[41] *Church of Lukumi Babalu Aye v City of Hialeah* 508 US 520 (1993). See T Shaddow, 'Religious Ritual Exemptions: Sacrificing Animal Rights for Ideology' (1991) 24 *Loyola of Los Angeles Law Review* 1367.

[42] As of 2006, it was entrenched in 97% of constitutions. See DS Law and M Versteeg, 'The Evolution and Ideology of Global Constitutionalism' (2011) 99 *California Law Review* 1163, 1167 and 1200.

[43] *Leyla Sahin v Turkey*, App no 44774/98 (ECtHR, 10 November 2005), para 39.

[44] Per Douglas J in *Zorach v Clauson* 343 US 306 (1952).

A. Right to Profess

The robustness of religious freedom turns on how its content is interpreted and evaluated against competing rights and goods. Religious freedom is based on free conscience, as reflected in Article 18 of the Universal Declaration of Human Rights, which states that everyone has 'the right to freedom of thought, conscience and religion', including 'freedom to change his religion or belief'. However, Saudi Arabia numbered among the detractors who objected to the right to change one's religion, on the basis it was contrary to its Islamic tradition.[45] The right to profess a belief implicates various issues, including a right to convert and not to be converted, a right to try to convert someone else non-coercively and negotiating parental rights over their children's faith.

The Malaysian cases that follow reject a voluntarist conception of religious identity, specifically where Malay Malaysians want to leave the Islamic faith.

Daud bin Mamat v Majlis Agama Islam [2001] 2 MLJ 390 (High Court, Malaysia)

Facts

The plaintiffs, four Malays from the state of Kelantan, issued affidavits that they had left the Muslim faith. They were charged and sentenced to imprisonment for heresy under section 69 of the Kelantan Enactment on the Administration of Muslim Law (1994) [*Enakmen Majlis Agama Islam dan Adat Istiadat Melayu Kelantan*, 1994] which fell within the Ninth Schedule, List II (State List). They argued they should be exempt from the Kelantan Syariah Court whose jurisdiction extends only to Muslims. The Syariah Appeal Court varied the order by requiring the plaintiffs in lieu of imprisonment to make monthly visits to the Syariah Judge to express their regrets or 'taubat'. The affidavit attracted a further charge and successful conviction under section 102 for apostasy. The civil Kelantan High Court had to determine whether the plaintiffs had, under Article 11(1) of the Federal Constitution, the right to profess their religion of choice such that Muslim-specific laws no longer applied to them.

Suriyadi Halim Omar J

[The judge noted that section 102(1) required a fact-finding exercise to ascertain whether a person was a Muslim.] Mohamed Dzaiddin FCJ in *Soon Singh Bikar Singh* [1999] 2 CLJ 5 commented:

> The Kelantan Enactment No 4 of 1994, s 102 also provides that no person who has confessed that he is a Muslim by religion may declare that he is no longer a Muslim until a court has given its approval to that effect. Before the court gives its approval, the person shall be presumed to be a Muslim and any matter which is connected with the religion of Islam shall be applied to him.
>
> These provisions and the spirit behind them . . . are in line with the teachings and tenets of Islam, as the Koran is quite explicit in that if one is forced to pronounce something that amounts to apostasy, while his heart remains a Muslim, he will not be

---

[45] A Saeed and H Saeed, *Freedom of Religion, Apostasy and Islam* (Burlington, VT: Ashgate, 2004) at 10–13.

charged with it in those circumstances (Quran, ch 16:106) . . . as the plaintiffs are yet to be found guilty of the second charges of apostasy . . . I have to conclude that they still are Muslims.

The down to earth legal requirement of imposing a duty upon the Syariah Court to ascertain, and not by any other person or institution, whether a person had indeed apostatized is not only sound but practical. The jurists in the Syariah Court, apart from being conversant with religious matters, will also be in a more elevated position to make a sound judgment of the status of any would-be apostate, bearing in mind their constant interaction with the Muslim populace, if they are legally qualified that will be a plus factor. Pertaining to this matter Mohamad Yusof CJ in *Dalip Kaur* [1991] 3 CLJ 2768 had occasion to remark:

> . . . such a serious issue would, to my mind need consideration by eminent jurists who are properly qualified in the field of the Islamic Jurisprudence . . . it is imperative that the determination of the question in issue requires substantial consideration of the Islamic law by relevant jurists qualified to do so. The only forum qualified to do so is the syariah court.

[Concluding that he lacked jurisdiction to hear the case because of Article 121(1A) of the Federal Constitution [46] and that the plaintiffs were 'legally Muslims' and subject to syariah court jurisdiction, but going on to pronounce on Article 11(1)] . . . the plaintiffs have unwittingly alluded to Article 11(1) of the Federal Constitution as the main ground of their grouses. This provision reads that every person has the right to profess and practise his religion and, subject to cl (4), to propagate it. This brief but meaningful article in crystal clear terms guarantees the right and freedom of every citizen, of whatever race or religion to profess and practise his or her beliefs unhindered. [The next issue is] whether any individual or institution in this country had infringed the constitutionally guaranteed religious rights of the plaintiffs in any way. After perusing the affidavits, I could not escape the conclusion that the issue of the plaintiffs having been prevented from practising their religion of choice, really did not exist here. In fact the complaints actually revolved around the issue of their right to apostate. It was undisputed that the plaintiffs had voluntarily declared themselves as having left the Islamic faith. How could their constitutional rights to profess and practise their supposed religion of choice have been compromised or infringed, when their actions indicated otherwise? The act of exiting from a religion is certainly not a religion, or could be equated with the right 'to profess and practise' their religion. To seriously accept that exiting from a religion may be equated to the latter two interpretations, would stretch the scope of Article 11(1) of the federal Constitution to ridiculous heights, and rebel against the canon of construction . . . I reject the contention of the plaintiffs that their rights pursuant to Article 11(1) of the federal Constitution had been infringed.

Needless to say if Article 11(1) of the federal Constitution were to read, inter alia, that 'everyone has the right to renounce or profess and practise his religion, and subject to cl (4), to propagate it', my conclusion would certainly be steered towards a different course . . . as the impugned article does not contain that additional hypothetical ingredient, the plaintiffs' action to resort to that article is surely misdirected and misconceived . . . (originating summons dismissed)

---

[46] Article 121(1A) provides that the two Federal High Courts referred to in Article 121(1) 'shall have no jurisdiction in respect of any matter within the jurisdiction of the Syariah courts'. In *Latifah Mat Zin v Rosmawati bte Sharibun* [2007] 5 MLJ 101 at 53, the Court held that Art 121(1A) was not designed to oust the jurisdiction of civil courts which could consider the constitutionality of any law, and that a syariah court had that jurisdiction expressly provided by statute, not implied.

Notes and Question

1. What is the relevance of the Judge citing a Quranic passage that one remains a Muslim if one is coerced into declaring the contrary, given that the plaintiffs voluntarily issued an affidavit that they had left the Muslim faith? Is there any role for personal decision here?

2. Is it 'ridiculous' to read into Article 11(1) the right to exit a religion? How does the Malaysian court apprehend religious identity, and does this secure religious freedom?

B. Religious Conversion as a Public Order Issue

Apostasy offences curtail freedom of religious profession and conversion. Malaysian courts have characterised the issue of a Muslim wanting to convert not as a personal choice but as a public order concern, within a Muslim-majority country. Malaysian syariah law applies only to Muslims, but who decides whether a person is a Muslim? The individual, or a state/officially recognised religious body? This issue was central to the *Lina Joy* case, when a Malay woman wanted to convert out of Islam to Catholicism. Significant pronouncements were made about the content of religious freedom (which varies with context and interpretation), religious identity and public order considerations.

Lina Joy v Majlis Agama Islam Wilayah & Anor
[2004] 2 MLJ 119 (High Court, Malaysia)

Facts

The National Registration Department (NRD) rejected Azlina bte Jailani's application to change her name to Lina Joy on her identity card and to remove 'Islam' as her religion. She issued an affidavit stating she had become a Christian. She did not apply to a syariah court for a declaration of apostasy but sought various declarations from the High Court that section 2 of the Administration of Islamic Law (Federal Territories) Act and any laws imposing restrictions on conversions out of Islam were inconsistent with the guarantee of religious freedom under Article 11(1) of the Federal Constitution. She argued that various state enactments which applied only to Muslims, no longer applied to her. The defendants argued she was still a Muslim and the issue of religious conversions fell within the syariah court's exclusive jurisdiction by dint of Article 121(1A) of the Constitution which provided the High Court 'shall have no jurisdiction in respect of any matter within the jurisdiction of the Syariah courts'.

Faiza Tamby Chik J

[The plaintiff contends] . . . that she has a freedom to profess a religion of her choice under Article 11(1) of the FC [Federal Constitution], which supersedes any other Federal or State laws and that her freedom to profess is a matter of personal choice and not to be dictated by any party . . . [T]he plaintiff is so obsessed with the first part of Article 11(1) of the FC [which she said] gives her the right to profess and practise the religion of her choice. I think Article 11 of the FC actually speaks of freedom of religion and not freedom of choice, which are distinct. Looking at the wording of the first part of Article 11(1) . . . there is no restriction on the right of any person to profess and practise his religion . . . Hence, if a Muslim wishes to renounce/leave his original religion for another . . . the first part of Article 11(1) is subject to the second part of Article 11(1) and also to Article 11(4) and Article 11(5) of the FC, because the issue of change of a person's religion is directly connected to the rights and obligations of that person as a Muslim. Clauses (1), (4) and (5) of Article 11 of the FC provide as follows:

> Article 11
> (1) Every person has the right to profess and practise his religion and, subject to cl (4), to propagate it.
> (4) State law and in respect of the Federal Territories of Kuala Lumpur and Labuan, Federal law may control or restrict the propagation of any religious doctrine or belief among persons professing the religion of Islam.
> (5) This Article does not authorise any act contrary to any general law relating to public order, public health or morality.

. . . It is clear that cll (4) and (5) above preserve and protect the harmony and preserve the affairs and interests of Muslims and non-Muslims in this country whereby the rights of the various races and religions are also protected. When a Muslim wishes to renounce/leave the religion of Islam, his other rights and obligations as a Muslim will also be jeopardized and this is an affair of Muslims falling under the first defendant's jurisdiction as provided by Article 11(3)(a) of the FC read with s 7(1) of the 1993 Act. Article 11(3)(a) clearly states that every religious group has the right to manage its own religious affairs whereas the 1993 Act was created to provide for the Federal Territories a law concerning the enforcement and administration of Islamic Law, the constitution and organization of the Syariah Court, and related matters as stated in the preamble of the 1993 Act . . . the plaintiff can[not] hide behind [Article 11(1)] without first settling the issue of renunciation of her religion (Islam) with the religious authority which has the right to manage its own religious affairs under Article 11(3)(a) . . . If the plaintiff is allowed to do so, this will create chaos and confusion with the administrative authority which manages the affairs of Islam and the Muslim community and consequently the non-Muslim community as a whole . . . this threatens public order and . . . cannot have been the intention of the legislature when drafting the FC and the 1993 Act.

. . . [S]ince the Plaintiff is still a Muslim and she wanted to convert out of Islam, the issue then is whether her rights to affirm or declare her faith in Christianity is subject to the relevant syariah laws on apostasy, declared by *Soon Singh v Pertubuhan Kebajikan Malaysia (PERKIM) Kedah* [1994] 1 MLJ 690 to be within the jurisdiction of the Syariah Courts. In short, whether the plaintiff's rights to convert out of Islam under Article 11(1) is subject to the syariah laws.

. . . I am of the view by looking at the constitution as a whole, it is the general tenor of the constitution that Islam is given a special position and status, with Article 3 declaring Islam to be the religion of the Federation. Tun Mohamed Suffian in his book, *An Introduction to the Legal System of Malaysia* second edition at p 10, said that this provision constitute one of the basic features of the Malayan Constitution. Article 3(1) reads:

> Islam is the religion of the Federation, but other religions may be practised in peace and harmony in any part of the Federation.

In *Teoh Eng Huat v Kadhi, Pasir Mas & Anor* [1990] 2 MLJ 300, Abdul Hamid LP adopted the opinion of Lord Denning on constitutional interpretation '. . . to ascertain for ourselves what purpose the founding fathers of our constitution had in mind when our constitutional laws were drafted . . .'. The starting point would be the Reid Commission which makes a finding after negotiations, discussions and consensus between the British Government, the Malay Rulers and the Alliance party representing various racial and religious groups. Paragraph 169 of the Reid Report is on religion, where the report is based on the unanimous recommendation of the Alliance party stated (at pp 301–302):

> The religion of Malaysia shall be Islam. The observance of this principle shall not impose any disability on non-Muslim nationals professing and practising their own religion and shall not imply that the state is not a secular state.

From the Reid Report is the Federation of Malaya Constitutional Proposal 1957 (The White Paper). The recommendation on religion in the White Paper is in para 57 which states:

> There has been included in the proposed Federation Constitution a declaration that Islam is the religion of the Federation. This will in no way affect the present position of the Federation as a Secular state . . .

It is pertinent to note that Tun Mohamed Suffian in his book *An Introduction to the Constitution of Malaysia* (2nd Ed) at p 45 said:

> Islam had long been established in the country before the conquest of Malacca by the Portuguese in 1511. It was left undisturbed by the British in the century or so they controlled the country. It is not therefore surprising when the constitution by Article 3(1) provides that Islam is the religion of the Federation [while guaranteeing . . .] the freedom of everybody to practice in peace and harmony his own religion.

Therefore from the inception of the FC, the religion of Islam has been given the special status of being the main and dominant religion of the Federation. Dr Mohammad Imam in his article *Freedom of Religion Under Federal Constitution of Malaysia: A Reappraisal* [1994] 2 CLJ lvii has adopted the purposive interpretation to Article 3(1) to the extent that Article 3(1) '. . . cast upon the "Federation" a positive obligation to protect, defend and promote the religion of Islam . . .'

. . . [T]he plaintiff has made a fundamental error in constitutional interpretation when she asserts that Article 3(4) reaffirms the primacy and precedence of Article 11(1). There is nothing in the FC to even suggest that Article 11(1) takes precedence over Article 3(1). The term 'derogates' in Article 3(4) simply means that Article 3 'does not reduce' other provisions in the constitution . . . Article 3(4) does not have the effect of reinforcing the status of the Federation as a secular state as suggested by the plaintiff. In *Freedom of Religion in Malaysia* by Lee Choon Min, the writer is of the opinion that Malaysia is not purely a secular state like India or Singapore but is a hybrid between the secular state and the theocratic state. The constitution of this hybrid model accord official or preferential status to Islam but does not create a theocratic state like Saudi Arabia or Iran. Contrary to the plaintiff's assertion, the subject and purpose of Article 3(1) is not merely 'to fix' the official religion of a nation. The case of *Che Omar bin Che Soh v Public Prosecutor* [1988] 2 MLJ 55 did not decide on Article 3(1), that is, the meaning of Islam as the Religion of the Federation (see Sheridan, 'The Religion of the Federation' [1988] 2 MLJ xiii). Article 3(1) has a far wider and meaningful purpose than a mere fixation of the official religion. One of the natural consequences from the fact that Islam is the religion of the Federation is the limitation imposed on the propagation among persons professing the religion of Islam in Article 11(4). Other consequences which emanate from the pronouncement of Islam in Article 3(1) is the establishment of Islamic institution for the furtherance of the religion of

Islam with funds to be expended for the advancement of the Islamic religion . . . The plaintiff's interpretation of Article 11(1) is by reading it in a limited and isolated manner, without due regard to the other provisions in the FC. This restrictive interpretation advocated by the plaintiff would result in absurdities not intended by the framers of the FC, namely, how would one reconcile the restrictive interpretation of Article 11(1) with the relevant provisions on the Islamic religion in the FC itself, such as Articles 3(1), 12(2), 74 and 121(1A) . . . Applying the principle of harmonious construction is to read Article 11(1) together with Articles 3(1), 12(2), 74, 121(1A) and 160 so as to give effect to the intention of the framers of our constitution. When read together Article 11(1) must necessarily be qualified by provisions on Islamic law on apostasy enacted pursuant to Article 74 List II in respect of the plaintiff's intention to convert out of the Islamic religion. Her purported renunciation of Islam can only be determined by the Syariah Courts and not the Civil Courts pursuant to Article 121(1A).

There is also a clear nexus between Articles 3(1) and 11(1) as both articles dealt with the issue of religion. Article 11(4) is the consequence of the declaration that Islam is the religion of the Federation. The declaration in Article 3(1) has the consequence of qualifying a Muslim's absolute right to murtad in Article 11(1) by requiring that compliance to the relevant syariah laws on apostasy is a condition precedent. Another fundamental error in the plaintiff's case is her assertion that the principle of freedom of conscience is housed in Article 11(1). Here, the plaintiff sought to equate Article 11(1) to Article 25 of the Indian Constitution, which reads:

> 25   Freedom of conscience and free profession, practice and propagation.
> (1)   Subject to public order morality and health and to the other provisions of this Part all persons are equally entitled to freedom of conscience and the right to freely profess, practise and propagate religion.

The most obvious distinction between Article 11(1) and Article 25 of the Indian Constitution is the conspicuous absence of the words 'freedom of conscience' and 'free profession . . .' in Article 11(1). 'The freedom of conscience is the absolute inner freedom of the citizen to mould his own relation with God in whatever manner he pleases . . .' The plaintiff's conclusion that her right to murtad is not circumscribed in any manner except in her own choice would be correct if read in the context of freedom of conscience in Article 25 of the Indian Constitution. But in the absence of such 'freedom of conscience' in Article 11(1), the plaintiff cannot assert that Article 11(1) gives her the absolute and unqualified right to convert out of the Islamic religion. The same is to be determined by the Syariah Courts. The plaintiff's extensive reference to the Indian Constitution in her submission is clearly misplaced. The Forty Second Amendment of 1976 has declared India to be a secular state. There is no such pronouncement in the FC . . . the position of Islam in Article 3(1) is that Islam is the main and dominant religion in the Federation [which] the Federation has a duty to protect, defend and promote . . . This proposition is reinforced by the Fourth Schedule where it states that in his oath of office, the Yang di-Pertuan Agong among other things solemnly and truly declares that he shall at all time protect the religion of Islam and to uphold the rule of law and order of the country. As such, the country could impose syariah laws on Muslim which are not inconsistent with the Constitution . . . since the Applicant is still a Muslim, the finality of her decision to convert out of Islam is within the competency of a Syariah Court (see *Md Hakim Lee* [1998] 1 MLJ 681 (HC)).

[Referring to Article 3(1) . . .] The very fact that people professing religion other than Islam are constitutionally guaranteed the right to practise their faith in peace and harmony, must necessarily mean that Muslims are also similarly guaranteed the right to practise Islam in a like manner . . .

[Notes that Article 74(2), read with the Second List of the Ninth Schedule, empowers state legislatures to enact laws on Islamic personal and family law and to establish syariah courts which may exercise jurisdiction only over Muslims; Thamby J noted in *Md Hakim Lee*, that the absence of legislative provisions providing that syariah courts had jurisdiction over religious conversions out of Islam 'would not make the jurisdiction exercisable by a the civil court '. He discussed inconsistent cases, rejecting the view that the syariah court, as a creature of statute, only had that jurisdiction which was conferred by express statutory terms; he favoured the view that the jurisdiction listed in List II of the Ninth Schedule 'is part of the Syariah Court's inherent jurisdiction.']

Apart from Article 3, other provisions in the constitution enforce the special position of Islam as the main and dominant religion of the Federation. The propagation of any religious doctrine or belief among persons professing the religion of Islam may be controlled or restricted by law (Art 11(4)). The purpose of this restriction is to provide the States with the power to pass a law to protect the religion of Islam from being exposed to the influences of the tenets, precepts and practices of other religions or even of certain schools of thoughts and opinion within the Islamic religion itself (see *Mamat bin Daud v Government of Malaysia* [1988] 1 MLJ 199). [Notes other constitutional provisions which authorise the Federation or State to support Islamic institutions, distribute state legislative powers, the royal patronage given Islam by the various Sultans and Article 121(1A), citing cases supporting the view that this clause gives exclusive jurisdiction to Syariah courts in administrating Islamic personal and family laws, to prevent conflicting jurisdictions between the civil and syariah courts.] . . .

. . . Article 11(1) must be construed harmoniously with the other relevant provisions on Islam, namely Articles 3(1), 74(2), 121(1A), 12(2) and 160 (where a Malay is defined as a person who professes the religion of Islam). When construed harmoniously, the inevitable conclusion is that the freedom to convert out of Islam in respect of a Muslim is subject to qualifications, namely the Syariah laws on those matters. Only such construction would support the 'smooth workings of the system', namely the implementation of the Syariah law on the Muslims as provided by the constitution. To grant Muslims the rights to convert out of Islam without final determination by the Syariah Courts would '. . . lead to uncertainty and confusion . . .' and would contradict the enabling syariah laws on apostasy '. . . since the question of whether a person was a Muslim or had renounced the faith of Islam transgressed into the realism of the Syariah law which needs serious consideration and proper interpretation of such law . . .' (per Mohamed Yusoff J in *Dalip Kaur* [1992] 1 MLJ 1 (SC).

. . . [T]he issue of apostasy is an issue coming under the category of religious affairs as provided under Article 11(3)(a) of the FC and . . . under 'related matters' as provided by the 1993 Act and therefore it . . . ought to be determined by eminent jurists who are properly qualified in the field of Islamic jurisprudence and definitely not by the civil court . . .

. . . Article 11(1) read with cll (3), (4) and (5) of the FC is created for the harmony and well-being of the multi-racial and multi-religious communities of this country . . . When a person wishes to renounce/leave his original religion, he/she has first to resolve the issue of renunciation of religion with the body/authority which protects and preserves the well-being of people professing that religion based on the laws or provisions relating to that religion. This is in accordance with Article 11(3) of the FC . . . [T]here are numerous matters related to the status of the plaintiff as a Muslim which must be resolved first and these matters can only be considered by eminent jurists who are properly qualified in the field of Islamic jurisprudence that is the Syariah Court . . . I think the plaintiff cannot seek relief from the Civil Court especially when she has yet to exhaust her remedy(s) under the jurisdiction of the Syariah Court. It is difficult to imagine how the administration of justice can be served if the plaintiff is allowed to abuse the process of the court by hopping from one jurisdiction to another over the same subject matter. I think that . . . there is no conflict or inconsistency between the first part of Article 11(1) of the FC and the provisions in the 1993 Act . . . as alleged by the plaintiff.

The first part of Article 11(1) is actually a general provision and to protect the affairs and preserve the interests of each religion and its followers as is provided under Article 11(3) of the FC. In the case of the Islamic religion for the purpose of Article 11(3)(a), the 1993 Act was created to smoothen [*sic*] the administration of Islam amongst the Muslim community so that the harmony and well-being of the Muslim community in particular (including the plaintiff) and the Malaysian community in general will be protected and preserved. The . . . provisions in the 1993 Act are not unconstitutional and are not violative of . . . Article 11 . . . The restrictions imposed by the provisions cannot but be said to be in the interest of public order and within the ambit of permissible legislative interference with that fundamental right. The provisions strike the correct balance between individual fundamental rights and the interest of public order . . . in interpreting an enactment, the court should have regard not merely to the literal meaning of the words used, but also take into consideration the antecedent history of the legislation, its purpose and the mischief it seeks to redress . . .

The fundamental teaching of Islam pertaining to the freedom of religion is expressed clearly in the Holy Quran . . .

'Let there be no compulsion in religion' (Surah Al-Baqarah 2:256).

This is endorsed in a number of other places in the Quran. (quotes Surah Al-Kafirun: 109: 1-6; Surah Al'Ankabut: 29:46; Surah Al Baqarah: 2:62; Surah Al Nisa': 4:137; Surah Al Kahf: 18:29; Surah Yunus: 10:99; Surah Al Tawbah: 9:6) . . .

The Holy Quran therefore declares the freedom of the individual to profess the religion of his or her choice without compulsion. According to Islam, if a man whose religion is Islam makes a declaration by deed poll that he renounces the religion of Islam, he removes himself from the religion of Islam and is a murtad. However, in order to decide whether he is a murtad or not . . . there must be a decision of the Syariah Court that he is a murtad [otherwise] . . . the person remains a Muslim (see *Dalip Kaur*). The religion of Islam depends on faith. Islam itself means submission to the will of Allah; and the willing submission of oneself to the will of Allah must be attained through conviction and reasons. And so when a Plaintiff who is a Muslim wishes to repudiate his submission to the will of Allah it is only imperative that the determination of such a serious issue is carried out by Syariah Court judges who are properly qualified in the field of Islamic jurisprudence. In this connection, we must not overlook that Article 11(1) also applies to Muslims in that they are not to be compelled or be put under undue influence so as to become apostates. Conversion out of Islam is not just a personal or private matter: it is capable of serious consequences such as on matters relating to marriage and inheritance. . . .

In *Soon Singh* [1994] 1 MLJ 690, the High Court held that it is clear from the fatwa that a Muslim who renounced the Islamic faith by a deed poll or who went through a baptism ceremony to reconvert to Sikhism continue to remain in Islam until a declaration has been made in a Syariah Court that he is a 'murtad'. Therefore, in accordance with the fatwa, the plaintiff is still a Muslim. He should go to the Syariah Court for the declaration. Whether or not his conversion is invalid is also a matter for the Syariah Court to determine in accordance with hukum syarak and the civil courts have no jurisdiction [holding that if the Syariah court had jurisdiction to determine cases of conversion into Islam, it should by implication have jurisdiction to deal with conversions out of Islam even where not expressly conferred] . . .

Therefore, it can be concluded that the validity of a person's renunciation of Islam can only be determined by the Syariah Courts based on hukum syarak. To conclude, Article 11(1) gives a person the freedom to profess a religion of his choice, but on the issue of conversion out of Islam, a Muslim is bound by the syariah law on the matter.

Section 2 of the 1993 Act provides a Muslim to mean:

(1) person who profess the religion of Islam;
(2) a person either or both of whose parents were, at the time of the persons birth, Muslim;
(3) a person whose upbringing was conducted on the basis that he was a Muslim;
(4) a person who has converted to Islam in accordance with the requirements of s 85;
(5) a person who is commonly reputed to be a Muslim; or
(6) a person who is shown to have stated, in circumstances in which he was bound by law to state the truth, that he was a Muslim, whether the statement be verbal or written.

The plaintiff was born a Muslim, she was brought up as a Muslim or her upbringing was conducted on the basis that she was a Muslim, she lived as a Muslim with her family and is commonly reputed to be a Muslim. All this is strong evidence of her being a person who professes the religion of Islam. Therefore, the plaintiff is a Muslim at all material times, within the meaning of 'Muslim' in the 1993 Act. Hence, her well-being as a Muslim is the duty and care of the first defendant in accordance with Article 11(3) of the FC and s 7(1) of the 1993 Act which were enacted in accordance with Islamic Law.

Article 11(3)(a) of the FC provides:

Every religious group has the right: (a) . . . to manage its own religious affairs . . .

Section 7(1) of the 1993 Act states:

It shall be the duty of the Majlis to promote, stimulate, facilitate and undertake the economic and social development and well-being of the Muslim community in the Federal Territories consistent with Islamic law,

. . . I am of the opinion that there is no inconsistency between Article 11(1) and s 2 of the 1993 Act. Article 11(1) is on the freedom of religion whereas s 2 of the 1993 Act is on the definition of a Muslim. There is nothing in s 2 that can be said to expressly forbid, restrict or curtail religious freedom under Article 11(1) . . . I am of the view that s 2 of the 1993 Act is enacted pursuant to Article 74(2) of the FC. The enabling Article 74(2) confers wide jurisdiction to the Federal Government to enact syariah laws to the same extent as provided in item 1 in the State list (see para 6(e) list 1, Ninth Schedule). Section 2 of the 1993 Act is directly designed for the purpose of implementing syariah laws on the Muslim and it is not in any way designed to curtail the freedom of religion under Article 11(1) . . . The purpose of s 2 of the 1993 Act is merely to define a Muslim since the FC did not provide any definition. This is important because syariah laws are applicable only to Muslim . . . Without a definition section (s 2 of the 1993 Act), only then could the 1993 Act be said to be ultra vires Article 11(1) since it imposes syariah law on everyone regardless of religion. Therefore, s 2 of the 1993 Act complements Article 11(1) by limiting the application of the syariah law to Muslims only.

From the definition in s 2 of the 1993 Act, the plaintiff is still a Muslim until there is a declaration to the contrary by the Syariah Court . . . As a Muslim she is therefore subject to the relevant syariah laws including the 1993 Act and the 1997 Act . . .

The new cl (1A) of Article 121 of the FC effective from 10 June 1988 has taken way the jurisdiction of the Civil Courts in respect of matters within the jurisdiction of the Syariah Courts . . .' (per Hashim Yeop Sani CJ (Malaya) at p 7 in *Dalip Kaur*). I am of the view that in the instant application, the root of the plaintiff's complaint and the practical effect of the declaratory orders is to enable her to convert out of Islam, an issue within the exclusive jurisdiction of the Syariah Courts . . .

This case raises an issue of constitutional importance. It concerns the religious position of a person born a Malay as defined in art 160 of the FC . . .

It is noted that as from 10 June 1988 by virtue of cl 1A of Article 121 of the FC, the civil courts have no jurisdiction in respect of matters within the jurisdiction of the Syariah Courts. It must also be noted that the civil courts are for general application; their jurisdiction is general, it is applicable to both Muslims and non-Muslims throughout the country, whereas the Syariah Courts are established by the various State Enactments and are of limited application in the sense that the jurisdiction covers Muslims only if they commit any Syariah offences in those States . . . I am not going to decide this case based on my Syariah qualification because I am more comfortable to leave it to the Syariah Court to make a decision on the matter of faith or belief of a Muslim person. Instead I am going to decide this case as a civil matter in accordance with the FC.

The FC has clarified the religious position of a Malay Article 160 of the FC is the interpretation article. The definition of a 'Malay' in cl (2) is inclusionary in nature. It is an anthropological classification rather than based on race. This means that if a Javanese was before Merdeka Day born in Malaysia or Singapore or born of parents one of whom was born in Malaysia or in Singapore and the said Javanese professes the religion of Islam, habitually speaks the Malay language and conforms to Malay custom, he/she is a Malay by definition under Article 160(2) of the FC . . . It defines a 'Malay' as a person who professes the religion of Islam . . . habitually speaks the Malay language, conforms to Malay custom and (a) was before Merdeka Day born in the Federation or in Singapore . . . or born of parents one of whom was born in the Federation or in Singapore, or is on that day domiciled in the Federation or in Singapore; or (b) is the issue of such a person. Therefore a person as long as he/she is a Malay and by definition under Article 160 cl (2) is a Malay, the said person cannot renounce his/her religion at all. A Malay under Article 160(2) remains in the Islamic faith until his or her dying days. The said Malay cannot renounce his or her religion through a deed poll . . . Even if one is a non-Malay and embrace Islam and becomes a Muslim convert (mualaf) and later decides to leave the Islamic faith he or she is still required to report and see the relevant State Islamic authority who will decide on her renunciation of Islam (see *Hun Mun Meng* [1992] 2 MLJ 676).

. . . I therefore conclude that the plaintiff is a Malay. By Article 160 of the FC, the plaintiff is a Malay and therefore as long as she is a Malay by that definition she cannot renounce her Islamic religion at all. As a Malay, the plaintiff remains in the Islamic faith until her dying days . . . My decision is based purely on the interpretation on Article 160 of a Malay under the FC.

Notes and Questions

1. Does or should religious freedom include a right to enter or exit a religious community?

2. For a general critique, see Thio Li-ann, 'Apostasy and Religious Freedom: Constitutional Issues Arising from the *Lina Joy* Litigation' [2006] 2 *MLJ* I; and M Azam Adil, 'Restrictions in Freedom of Religion in Malaysia: A Conceptual Analysis with Special Reference to the Law of Apostasy' (2007) 4 *Muslim World*

Journal of Human Rights 2. While apostasy is a criminal offence in many Malaysian states, section 90A of the *Administration of Muslim Law (Negri Sembilan) Enactment* 1991 (NS En 1/1991) stipulates a procedure for converting out of Islam:

> A Muslim shall not renounce or be deemed to have renounced Islam as his religion, unless and until he has obtained a declaration to that effect from the Mahkamah Tinggi Syariah
>
> The applicant shall state the grounds upon which he wishes to renounce Islam and the application shall be supported by affidavit stating all the facts that support the grounds of the application
>
> The judge may defer the hearing for 30 days and refer the applicant to the Mufti for counseling with a view to advise the applicant to reconsider his wishes to renounce Islam
>
> The judge may, upon the facts presented before him, declare that the applicant has renounced Islam or may refuse the declaration
>
> The order that he has renounced Islam shall be registered and until such order is registered, he shall be treated as a Muslim.

3. Does constitutional history support the view 'Islam' in Article 3(1) is meant to be ceremonial, or that it takes precedence over the Article 3(4) constitutional supremacy clause such that Islam becomes a grundnorm of sorts? See J Fernando, 'The Position of Islam in the Constitution of Malaysia' (2006) 37(2) *Journal of Southeast Asian Studies* 249. Is there a concern that Malay religious conversions out of Islam would diminish Malay political power?

4. The Supreme Court in *Che Omar bin Che Soh v PP*[47] rejected the argument that the mandatory death penalty for a firearms offence was void as contravening Islam. Salleh Abas LP discussed Article 3, distinguishing between Islam as rituals and ceremonies and Islam as a comprehensive system of life covering all fields of human activities, including its jurisprudence and moral standards. Malay states were truly Islamic before the British colonial era, when state sultans were both religious vice-regents and political leaders, applying Muslim law to Muslim subjects. The effect of colonialism was described thus:

> When the British came, however, through a series of treaties with the sultans beginning with the Treaty of Pangkor and through the so-called British advisers, the religion of Islam became separated into two separate aspects, viz, the public aspect and the private aspect. The development of the public aspect of Islam had left the religion as a mere adjunct to the ruler's power and sovereignty. The ruler ceased to be regarded as god's vicegerent on earth but regarded as a sovereign within his territory. The concept of sovereignty ascribed to humans is alien to Islamic religion because in Islam, sovereignty belongs to god alone. By ascribing sovereignty to the ruler, ie to a human, the divine source of legal validity is severed and thus the British turned the system into a secular institution. Thus all laws including administration of Islamic laws had to receive this validity through a secular fiat . . . during the British colonial period, through their system of indirect rule and establishment of secular institutions, Islamic law was rendered isolated in a narrow confinement of the law of marriage, divorce, and inheritance only. (See MB Hooker, *Islamic Law in South-east Asia*, 1984). In our view it is in this sense of dichotomy that the framers of the Constitution understood the meaning of the word 'Islam' in the context of Art 3 . . .

---

[47] *Che Omar bin Che Soh v PP* [1988] 2 MLJ 55.

It is the contention of Mr Ramdas Tikamdas that because Islam is the religion of the Federation, the law passed by parliament must be imbued with Islamic and religious principles . . . this submission [is] contrary to the constitutional and legal history of the federation and also the Civil Law Act which provides for the reception of English common law in this country.

. . . [W]e have to set aside our personal feelings because the law in this country is still what it is today, secular, where morality not accepted by the law is not enjoying the status of law. Perhaps that argument should be addressed at other forums or at seminars and perhaps, to politicians and parliament. Until the law and the system is changed, we have no choice but to proceed as we are doing today.[48]

5. With reference to Thamby J's opinion in *Lina Joy*, is the Federal Constitution or his conception of Islam supreme, such that Article 3 determines the content of the Article 11 religious freedom guarantee? Is it appropriate for civil court judges to refer to religious texts, as he did?

6. Did the judicial references to Islam in the Malay archipelago from the fifteenth century seek to construct a certain vision of an Islamic past, ignoring prior practices of animism and Hinduism? How does this myth/vision buttress Thamby J's attempt to interpret constitutional provisions through the lens of Article 3?

7. How would you assess the application of public order considerations to what is conventionally considered part of the *forum internum* (right to profess)? The Court of Appeal in *Lina Joy* noted:

The Muslim community regards it as a grave matter not only for the person concerned, in terms of the afterlife, but also for Muslims generally, as they regard it to be their responsibility to save another Muslim from the damnation of apostasy. The incidence of apostasy is therefore a highly sensitive matter among Muslims. Apart from the spiritual aspect, Muslims in this country, where Islam is the official religion, are subject to special laws that no other community is subject to.[49]

If it is destabilising to evangelise Muslims within multi-religious societies, is it equally inflammatory for Muslims to proselytise non-Muslims or minority Islamic sects like the Shi'a?

8. Is the implementation of Administration of Muslim Law enactments an exercise or curtailment of religious liberty? How are clashes between group and individual interests prioritised?

9. Why did Thamby J proclaim, on his reading of Articles 3, 11 and 162, that the plaintiff was a Muslim, if he considered that the syariah court should decide this question?

10. Did Thamby J effectively carve out an exception for Muslims wanting to convert out of Islam (there being no issue if a non-Muslim wanted to change faiths), or was the privileged position of Islam used via Article 3 to read Article 11 in a certain way? If Islam, as Thamby J indicated, provides there is 'no compulsion in Islam', why did this not influence his reading of Article 11?

---

[48] Ibid 55, 56 at [5], [9]–[11].
[49] *Lina Joy* [2005] 6 MLJ 193, 208.

11. Is there a different regime governing conversions out of a faith for *murtads* (Malay Muslims), *muallafs* (non-Muslim converts to Islam) and all other Malaysians? What are the implications for equality under the law (Article 8)?

12. Assess Thamby J's bare reference to India as being an inappropriate comparator as it was a secular state, whereas Malaysia was a 'hybrid' one, 'a secular state with Islamic characteristics and bias'? See Wu Min Aun, 'Islamic Law' in *The Malaysian Legal System* (Kuala Lumpur: Longman, 2000) at 154. From constitutional history and precedent alone, Malaysia was designed to be a 'secular' state. Does Thamby J's view of the religion–state model reflect political statements asserting that Malaysia is an Islamic state? Consider what then Deputy Prime Minister Najib said:

> Islam is the official religion and we are an Islamic state . . . [but] it does not mean that we don't respect the non-Muslims. The Muslims and the non-Muslims have their own rights (in this country) . . . We have never been secular because being secular by Western definition means separation of the Islamic principles in the way we govern a country . . . We have never been affiliated to that position. We have always been driven by our adherence to the fundamentals of Islam.[50]

Lina Joy v Majlis Agama Islam Wilayah
[2007] 4 MLJ 585 (Federal Court, Malaysia)

Editors' Note: Only Richard Malanjum FCJ's dissenting judgment was reported in English; the following is an unofficial majority judgment translation from Bahasa, available at <http://www.becketfund.org/files/1f27b.pdf>.

Ahmad Fairuz Chief Justice (delivering majority judgment)

[T]here is no conclusive certainty that the appellant no longer professes Islam. Therefore the statement that she can no longer be under the authority of the Syariah Court . . . should not be stressed . . . The Freedom of Religion under Article 11 of the Federal Constitution requires the Appellant to comply with the practices or law of the Islamic religion in particular with regards to converting out of the religion . . . one cannot at one's whims and fancies renounce or embrace a religion . . . [concludes that apostasy is within the exclusive jurisdiction of syariah courts by dint of Article 121(1A)] . . .

. . . If a person professes and practices Islam, it would definitely mean that he must comply with the Islamic law which has prescribed the way to embrace Islam and converting out of Islam . . . To profess and practice Islam should definitely mean practicing not only the theological aspect of the religion but also the laws of the said religion.

. . . Section 102 of the Kelantan Enactment 1994 prevents a Muslim from declaring that he is not Muslim unless he obtains a Court's certificate. This, says the appellant, contravenes Article 11 and therefore is null and void. Based on this submission by the Appellant, Abdul Hamid Mohamad, HMR in the case of *Kamariah* says:

> If that was the meaning of the provision then not only are laws that fix a way for a person to embrace Islam and renounce Islam void, but also the laws that make it an offence if a Muslim commits adultery, close proximity, not pay zakat etc . . . Article 11 grants a

---

[50] 'Malaysia not secular state, says Najib', Bernama.com, 17 July 2007 at <http://www.bernama.com/bernama/v3/news_lite.php?id=273699.>.

right to a person to practice his religion, therefore, it is left to him [to decide which religious instructions] he wishes to practice and which he doesn't . . . any law that requires a person to perform something or renounce something that contravenes with the freedom granted by Article 11 is therefore void in its entirety.

I am of the opinion that with regards to Islam (I do not decide with regards to other religion), Article 11 cannot be construed or defined in such a wide meaning to the extent it annuls all laws that require a Muslim to perform an Islamic obligation or that restrict them from performing a matter that is prohibited by Islam or which prescribe the method of conducting a matter in relation to Islam. This is because the position of Islam in the Federal Constitution differs from the position of other religions [citing Article 3(1)] . . . [rejecting the argument which, if accepted, meant that all other Islamic laws such as those relating to marriage and divorce would potentially be null and void as contradicting Article 11] . . .

Based on the above authorities, it is evident that:–

(a) The issue of religious conversion is directly connected with the rights and obligations of the Appellant as a Muslim before the conversion;
(b) Article 11(1) should not be argued as a provision that provides unrestricted right of freedom;
(c) The right to profess and practice a religion should always be subject to the principles and practices prescribed by the said religion. (dismissing the appeal)

Richard Malanjum CJ (Sabah & Sarawak) (Dissenting)

Article 3(1) of the Constitution placed Islam [in] a special position in this country. However, Article 3(4) clearly provides that nothing in the Article derogates from any other provision of the Constitution thereby implying that Article 3(1) was never intended to override any right, privilege or power explicitly conferred by the Constitution (see *Che Omar bin Che Soh v PP*) . . . [T]his is . . . consonant with Article 4 of the Constitution which places beyond doubt that the Constitution is the supreme law of this country . . .

. . . [L]egislative powers are derived from the Constitution itself. Hence, one is not wrong to say that the Legislative Lists are subordinate to the fundamental liberties provisions enshrined in the Constitution . . .

Just as any legislation or any part thereof will be struck down if it fails to conform with any of the provisions of the Constitution, so too with administrative, departmental and executive discretions, policies and decisions . . . [Discusses the availability of judicial review on grounds of illegality, irrationality and procedural impropriety to check executive discretion; in reviewing the National Registration Regulations (1990), the learned judge found that only requiring Muslims to provide details of their religion in change of name applications contravened the equal protection of the law under Article 8, which was unjustified as it did not relate to personal law. He found the appellant was entitled to have an identity card where the word 'Islam' did not appear, considering it unreasonable for the NRD [National Registration Department] to ask for a certificate of apostasy from the syariah court, which the Regulations did not require, particularly since the appellant had provided a statutory declaration that she was a Christian, rendering a syariah court certificate an irrelevant document in processing the appellant's application.]

In the majority judgment it was said that the policy adopted by NRD was reasonable and that it was justified for NRD to request for a certificate of apostasy since *renunciation of Islam is a question of Islamic law* and that it *is not within the jurisdiction of the NRD and that the NRD is not equipped or qualified to decide* . . . [T]he majority judgment erred in considering an issue which should not have been there in the first place, namely affirming the insistence by NRD for a certificate of apostasy when the appellant had in fact met all the requirements stipulated in [the regulations] . . .

Further, the conclusion in the majority judgment that the impugned policy adopted by NRD was reasonable within the test of *Wednesbury* [1966] 2 QB 275 has unfortunately missed one cardinal principle. The implementation of the policy has a bearing on the appellant's fundamental constitutional right to freedom of religion under art 11 of the Constitution. Being a constitutional issue it must be given priority, independent of any determination of the *Wednesbury* reasonableness. A perceived reasonable policy could well infringe a constitutional right. Hence, before it can be said that a policy is reasonable within the test of *Wednesbury* its constitutionality must be first considered . . .

[Rejecting the view that apostasy is a matter within exclusive syariah court jurisdiction] . . . In my view apostasy involves complex questions of constitutional importance especially when some States in Malaysia have enacted legislations to criminalize it, which in turn raises the question involving federal–state division of legislative powers . . . Since constitutional issues are involved especially on the question of fundamental rights as enshrined in the Constitution it is of critical importance that the civil superior courts should not decline jurisdiction by merely citing Article 121(1A). In my view the said article only protects the Syariah Court in matters within their jurisdiction which does not include the interpretation of the provisions of the Constitution. Hence when jurisdictional issues arise civil courts are not required to abdicate their constitutional function. Legislations criminalizing apostasy or limiting the scope of the provisions of the fundamental liberties as enshrined in the Constitution are constitutional issues in nature which only the civil courts have jurisdiction to determine . . .

. . . [T]he insistence by NRD for a certificate of apostasy from the Federal Territory Syariah Court or any Islamic Authority was not only illegal but unreasonable. This is because under the applicable law, the Syariah Court in the Federal Territory has no statutory power to adjudicate on the issue of apostasy. It is trite law that jurisdiction must come from the law and cannot be assumed. Thus the insistence was unreasonable for it required the performance of an act that was almost impossible to perform . . .

Another aspect of the unreasonableness of the policy of NRD is in its consequence if followed. In some States in Malaysia apostasy is a criminal offence. Hence, to expect the appellant to apply for a certificate of apostasy when to do so would likely expose her to a range of offences under the Islamic law is in my view unreasonable for its means the appellant is made to self-incriminate . . .

[On the issue of jurisdiction] . . . The doctrine of implied powers must be limited to those matters that are incidental to a power already conferred or matters that are necessary for the performance of a legal grant. And in the matters of fundamental rights there must be as far as possible be express authorization for curtailment or violation of fundamental freedoms. No court or authority should be easily allowed to have implied powers to curtail rights constitutionally granted . . . to rely on implied power as a source of jurisdiction would set an unhealthy trend. For instance under List 1, Item 15 Schedule 9 of the Constitution, Parliament is authorized to pass laws relating to 'social security'. To date no law has been passed governing minimum wages in this country. If the implied jurisdiction doctrine is adopted there is nothing to prevent the Industrial Court from assuming jurisdiction relying on Item 15 and thus adjudicating on matters pertaining to minimum wages. If that were to occur, then all that is required will be a list of what Parliament or the State Assembly can enact and that will entitle the courts to have jurisdiction on such matters irrespective of whether there is any specific legislation enacted. I am therefore inclined not to follow the reasoning in *Soon Singh* . . .

Note and Questions

1. While the majority decision effectively deconstitutionalised the issues by framing them as whether the policy was reasonable, the dissenting judgment brought a rights-based approach to bear on administrative law. Which serves constitutional supremacy?

2. There are cases where non-Malay converts to Islam (*muallaf*) were allowed to leave the Islamic faith. For example, Nyonya Tahir was allowed to be buried according to Buddhist rites after the Syariah High Court decided she was not a Muslim.[51] In 2006, a living woman was allowed by the Syariah High Court to convert from Islam to her original religion of Buddhism, as her Iranian husband and Penang religious authorities gave her improper religious advice.[52]

3. Where one spouse converts to Islam and converts minor children as well against the other spouse's wishes, may this be unilaterally effected? Article 12(4) of the Malaysian Constitution provides that 'the religion of a person under the age of eighteen years shall be decided by his parent or guardian'. The Federal Court held that the reference to 'parent' in Article 12(4) referred to one parent, so the conversion by a formerly Hindu husband of his elder son to Islam under the Selangor Enactment was not unconstitutional.[53] The wife, who remained Hindu, could not rely on the equal protection of parental rights provided for under the Guardianship of Infants Act 1961, since it did not apply to Muslims.[54]

C. Propagation and Conversion

Propagation or evangelism is a form of religious free speech closely allied to freedom of conscience and conversion. It exposes the individual seeker to a diversity of beliefs so that he or she can make an informed choice. This logic stems from the liberal ideal, facilitates religious missionary mandates and is constitutionally recognised in many Asian jurisdictions, and subject to state regulation, falling with the *forum externum.*

The endgame of religious propagation is not merely to inform but to win religious converts, through persuasion on questions of religious truth. The state does not participate in this discourse but facilitates it, as is the view within secular democracies without official religions, like Singapore. The Court of Appeal in *Nappalli v ITE* noted that 'the protection of freedom of religion under our Constitution is premised on removing restrictions to one's choice of religious belief. This has been described as accommodative secularism'.[55] Article 15(1) of the Singapore Constitution provides

---

[51] 'Syariah Court Decides Nyonya Tahir Not A Muslim', Bernama.com (Malaysia), 23 January 2006. at < http://bernama.com.my/bernama/v3/news_lite.php?id=177118>.

[52] 'Malaysian court allows Muslim convert to go back to Buddhism', *New York Times*, 8 May 2008. But see 'The Moorthy Maniam Case: Compassion and Justice Missing' (2005) 25(11) *Aliran Monthly* at <http://aliran.com/archives/monthly/2005b/11b.html>.

[53] *Subashini Rajasingam v Saravanan Thangathoray* [2008] 2 MLJ 147.

[54] See *Shamala Sathiyaseelan v Dr Jeyaganesh Mogarajah* [2004] 2 CLJ 416 (High Court, Kuala Lumpur).

[55] *Nappalli v ITE* [1999] 2 SLR(R) 529 [28].

that '[e]very person has the right to profess and practise his religion and to propagate it', while clause (4) provides that acts 'contrary to any general law relating to public order, public health or morality' are not authorised. However, this privatist model is not accepted across all Asian jurisdictions, especially where the Constitution recognises an official religion or accords that religion preferential state support. Religious propagation may be viewed not as a good rooted in free conscience but as an evil to be eradicated, or as an activity having social costs to be managed, because it threatens the state, a majority religion or social harmony. Further diversities in practice are evident where the state becomes involved in propagating a religion; the Malaysian Government practises a form of state-sanctioned inducement in propagating Islam to indigenous communities like the Orang Asli, promising material benefits.[56]

Religious freedom is further threatened where state officials undertake campaigns to force citizens to recant their beliefs. Members of Christian communities in Laos were reportedly forced to renounce their faith,[57] to preserve social unity and harmony. In extreme cases, village authorities evicted Christians from their homes, or asked them to sign a letter indicating that they would burn the Bible or face detention for refusal. Their children were also harassed and denied access to public schools. Article 43 of the Lao Constitution provides that Lao citizens have the right and freedom to believe or not to believe in religions. Under Article 9, the

> State respects and protects all lawful activities of Buddhists and of followers of other religions, and mobilizes and encourages Buddhist monks and novices as well as the priests of other religions to participate in activities that are beneficial to the country and people.

It prohibits 'all acts creating division between religions and classes of people'. Government officials have referenced Article 9 to justify limits on religious practice, especially proselytising, fearing the expansion of Protestantism among minority ethnic groups.[58]

This brings to the fore questions of what constitutes legitimate and illegitimate proselytising, issues of expressive liberty, personal and cultural identity, and the need to theorise what the 'public order' constitutes, beyond an absence of strife. Are questions of constitutional, cultural or group identity implicated?

i. Constitutionalising the Right to Propagate Religion

The inclusion of the right to propagate one's faith in Article 25 of the Indian Constitution was a contentious matter, as these Constituent Assembly debates extracts demonstrate.

---

[56] Ding Jo-Ann, 'JHOEA involved in Orang Asli conversion', *The Nut Graph*, 4 May 2010, archived at <http://www.thenutgraph.com/jheoa-involved-in-orang-asli-conversion/>; C Nicholas, *The Orang Asli and the Contest for Resources: Indigenous Politics, Development and Identity in Peninsula Malaysia* (INEIA Document No 95, 2000) at 98–102.

[57] *Report*, Special Rapporteur on Freedom of Religion or Belief, Mission: Lao People's Democratic Republic, Addendum, A/HRC/13/40/Add.4 27 Jan 2010 at [40]–[41].

[58] Available at <http://www.state.gov/documents/organization/171656.pdf>.

Constituent Assembly of India Debates
6 December 1948, Vol VII (Article 25, Constitution of India)
available at <http://www.indiankanoon.org/doc/1933556/>

Shri Lokanath Misra (Orissa)

[M]aking propagation of religion a fundamental right is . . . dangerous. Justice demands that the ancient faith and culture of the land should be given a fair deal, if not restored to its legitimate place after a thousand years of suppression. We have no quarrel with Christ or Mohammad . . . Vedic culture excludes nothing . . . [the cry of religion is dangerous and divisive] . . . In the present context [the word 'propagation' in Article 19] can only mean paving the way for the complete annihilation of Hindu culture . . . Islam has declared its hostility to Hindu thought. Christianity has worked out the policy of peaceful penetration by the back-door on the outskirts of our social life. This is because Hinduism did not accept barricades for its protection. Hinduism is just an integrated vision and a philosophy of life and cosmos, expressed in organised society to live that philosophy in peace and amity. But Hindu generosity has been misused and politics has over run Hindu culture. Today religion in India serves no higher purpose than collecting ignorance, poverty and ambition under a banner that flies for fanaticism . . . let us say nothing about rights relating to religion . . . It is a device to swallow the majority in the long run.

Shri TT Krishnamachari (Madras)

[Supporting the inclusion of a right to propagate, noting this was open to all religions including the Hindus, Arya Samaj Muslims, Jains and Buddhists] . . . as a person who has studied for about fourteen years in Christian institutions . . . no attempt had been made to convert me from my own faith and to practise Christianity. I am very well aware of the influences that Christianity has brought to bear upon our own ideals and our own outlook, and I am not prepared to say here that they should be prevented from propagating their religion. I would ask the House to look at the facts so far as the history of this type of conversion is concerned. It depends upon the way in which certain religionists and certain communities treat their less fortunate brethren. The fact that many people in this country have embraced Christianity is due partly to the status that it gave to them . . . An untouch-able who became a Christian became an equal in every matter along with the high-caste Hindu, and if we remove the need to obtain that particular advantage . . . the incentive for anybody to become a Christian will not probably exist . . .

Shri K Santhanam (Tamil Nadu)

[Noting that Article 19 was to be read with the free speech guarantee and that it dealt less with religious freedom and more with religious toleration subject to public order, morality and health] . . . propagation is merely freedom of expression . . . the word 'convert' is not there. Mass conversion was a part of the activities of the Christian Missionaries in this country and great objection has been taken by the people to that. Those who drafted this Constitution have taken care to see that no unlimited right of conversion has been given . . . the State has every right to regulate attempts at mass conversion through undue influence . . .

Shri KM Munshi (Bombay)

[Noting that Christian missionaries lost their influence with District Collectors through which converts were acquired when the Congress Ministry came into power in Bombay,

1937] . . . since then whatever conversions take place . . . are only the result of persuasion and not because of material advantages offered to them . . . [W]e are now creating under this Constitution . . . a secular State. There is no particular advantage to a member of one community over another; nor is there any political advantage by increasing one's fold. In those circumstances, the word 'propagate' cannot possibly have dangerous implications . . . I was a party from the very beginning to the compromise with the minorities . . . and I know it was on this word that the Indian Christian community laid the greatest emphasis, not because they wanted to convert people aggressively, but because the word 'propagate' was a fundamental part of their tenet. Even if the word were not there, [it would be open under the free speech guarantee for] any religious community to persuade other people to join their faith . . .

Shri L Krishnaswami Bharathi (Madras)

[T]he word 'propagate' is intended only for the Christian community . . . So far as my experience goes, the Christian community have not transgressed their limits of legitimate propagation of religious view . . . It is for other communities to emulate them and propagate their own religions as well . . . It is not to be understood that when one propagates his religion he should cry down other religions . . . [A secular state] does not side with one religion or another. It tolerates all religions . . . To say that some religious people should not do propaganda or propagate their views is to show intolerance on our part . . .

Notes and Questions

1. What is the scope and content of the right to propagate? Is its linkage with the free conscience clause (Article 25(1), India Constitution) significant? On the debates surrounding the inclusion of religious propagation, see S Kim, *In Search of Identity: Debates on Religious Conversion in India* (India: Oxford University Press, 2005) 37–58.

2. Not all constitutions protect religious propagation: Article 13 of the Greek Constitution prohibits proselytism, while Article 3 recognises 'the Eastern Orthodox Church of Christ' as the prevailing religion. The term 'proselytism' has pejorative connotations, framing the discourse in terms of 'illegitimate proselytism' and 'legitimate evangelism'. See L Uzzell, 'Don't call it Proselytism' (2004) 146 *First Things* 14. Is the inclusion of 'propagation' as a constitutional right dangerous?

3. What are the theoretical justifications for constitutionalising religious propagation? What are the competing rights and goods? Does religious propagation as religious speech and as a religious duty have distinctive rationales for protection and warrant special treatment? See J Garvey, 'The Real Reason for Religious Freedom' (1997) 71 *First Things* 13. Consider the following:

   If critics were somehow able to convince even the most fervent zealots that evangelization is wrong, what would be the long-term social repercussions? In many cases the former evangelizer would no longer see humanity as his brothers and sisters who need to be turned to the truth, but as a separate community to be shunned. If a zealot honestly believes he is part of the chosen, and that it is impractical or impossible to convert others through persuasion, what is to prevent him from making his spiritual tribalization a physical one? . . . If we rule out a marketplace of ideas where all faiths and persuasions can share their opinions, the alternative might be a sectarian balkanization far more dangerous than the rhetorical rough-and-tumble of genuine religious freedom.

The critics insist that they do not wish an end to learning about other faiths, but rather an end to attempts to change someone else's faith. Indeed, they often encourage people to learn as much as they can about other religions. The former proselytizer, convinced that it is wrong to evangelize, will rightly ask – 'Why?' If one already knows the truth, and cannot or will not share it with others, why study other faiths? If they are all damned and there is nothing anyone can do about it, why bother?

In order to both prevent evangelization and preserve an environment where all faiths are respected and studied, one must not only convince evangelists that their missionary work is dangerous, but that they do not really hold the Truth at all. This is the deep irony: critics of conversion have a conversionist agenda of their own, [to] convert believers . . . to adopt a relativist persuasion. Eliminating evangelism would not usher in the utopia of interreligious tolerance and peace that critics imagine. Religion has been a motivator of violence but it is only one among many . . . The solution for religious violence lies not in the cessation of evangelism, but its encouragement in the context of a level playing field. The more faiths that sincerely seek to save humanity, through authentic living and persuasion, the better.[59]

4.   How does one balance a speaker's right to religious propagation with another's individual's right to be free from religious persuasion or not to have his religious feelings hurt? How might the prospect of eroded group identity caused by individual members converting to universal faiths be addressed, where group membership is kinship-based rather than volitional? For ancestral worshippers, to convert out of a faith is to neglect family and community. See *Bermuda Trust (Singapore) Ltd v Richard Wee*,[60] where a trust for the observance of Sinchew rites failed as the testator's children had converted to Christianity.

ii.   The Right to Propagate Religion

Assertions of the right to religious propagation have caused disquiet in Asian states whose constitutions accord a particular religion a privileged status, as this may bring about a diminution in the 'flock'.

a. Bhutan and its Attitude Towards the Propagation of Religion: A Virtual Theocracy?

Bhutan was a Buddhist theocracy until the early twentieth century; it remains primarily Buddhist in composition (75 per cent) and is the world's only Vajray na Buddhist country, a form of Tantric Buddhism closely associated with Tibetan Buddhism. Article 3(1) of the 2008 Constitution proclaims Buddhism as Bhutan's spiritual heritage, with the King as protector of all religions (Article 3(2)). Article 7(4) guarantees religious liberty and prohibits compelling a person 'to belong to another faith by means of coercion or inducement'. Article 7(15) prohibits discrimination on religious

---

[59] D Fink, 'Critics of Conversion', Institute for Global Engagement, 22 September 2003, at <http://www.globalengage.org/issues/articles/freedom/652-critics-of-conversion.html >.
[60] *Bermuda Trust (Singapore) Ltd v Richard Wee* (2000) 2 SLR 126.

grounds. Bhutanese citizens are required to foster tolerance under Article 8(3). Officially, religion is separate from politics (Article 3(3)), although the Constitution reflects a strong Buddhist identity. For example, the Preamble references the 'Triple Gem' (Buddha, Dharma and Sangha), Article 3 provides for the establishment of the Chief Abbot of the Central Monastic Body (*Je Khenpo*) and Monastic Affairs Commission (*Dratshang Lhentsang*).

The Government is hostile towards certain proselytising religions like Christianity (Bhutan has about 12,000 Christians), despite the role Jesuits played in establishing high schools.[61] Christianity is viewed suspiciously as a divisive 'foreign' religion, threatening Bhutanese values. The Government banned the public preaching of Christianity in 1979 on these principles:

(a) The Christians are not allowed to preach their religion in public.
(b) Only academic studies are to be taught in schools and no Christian religion and practice are to be taught.
(c) The Christians are allowed to practise their religion in their homes.
(d) Any person found preaching Christianity in public shall be expelled from the country.[62]

This ban was reiterated in 1982 and extended to Islam and any alien religion.[63] The National Assembly debated Christianity in 2000; the Speaker noted that the main problem with the proselytisation of Christianity was that it 'condemned' Bhutan's two religions, Buddhism and Hinduism, induced the poor through material benefit, undermined cultural traditions,[64] caused family discord, and would undermine peace and unity in a small country.[65]

In October 2010, a court in south Bhutan jailed a man for three years for showing a Christian film.[66] There is an official suspicion that most Bhutanese Christian converts were very poor and were monetarily induced to convert. Home Minister Dorji said there was freedom to convert voluntarily, but the growth of Christianity would threaten Bhutan's unique Buddhist-rooted culture: '[I]f we lose our culture, we will lose everything.'[67] Parliamentarians have debated the issue, opining that having a third religion in a small society would threaten social stability.[68]

There is no registered Christian religious organisation, nor official recognition of Christians. An objective of the 2007 Religious Organisations Act is to 'facilitate the establishment of ROs [religious organisations] in order to benefit the religious

[61] Footprints Recruiting, Education in Bhutan, at <http://www.footprintsrecruiting.com/teaching-in-bhutan/1020-education-in-bhutan>; D Malone, 'Our Man in Bhutan: How a Canadian Jesuit founded a secular education system in a remote mountain nation', online *Literary Review of Canada*, 1 March 2008.

[62] 'Preaching of Christianity Prohibited', Bhutan, National Assembly – 51st Session at 9 (18 November 1979), available at <http://www.nab.gov.bt/downloads/4151st%20Session.pdf>.

[63] Bhutan, National Assembly – 56th Session at 16 (25 June 1982), available at <http://www.nab.gov.bt/downloads/3656th%20Session.pdf>.

[64] Specifically, *Thadamtsi* (honour and sacred commitment) and *Leyjumdrey* (the idea of karma). See Tashi Wangyal, 'Ensuring Social Sustainability: Can Bhutan's Education System Ensure Intergenerational Transmission of Values?' (2001) 3(1) *Journal of Bhutan Studies* 106.

[65] Bhutan, National Assembly – 78th Session at 142–149 (25 June 2000), available at <http://www.nab.gov.bt/downloads/378th%20session.pdf>.

[66] 'Christian in Bhutan Imprisoned for Showing Film on Christ', *Compass Direct News*, 18 October 2010.

[67] 'Official recognition eludes Christian groups in Bhutan', *Compass Direct News*, 3 February 2010.

[68] Ugyen Penjore, 'Proselytisation: a threat to a small society', *Kuensel Online*, 21 July 2001, at <http://www.kuenselonline.com/proselytisation-a-threat-to-a-small-society/#.UiwZ9p2wq74>.

institutions and protect the spiritual heritage of Bhutan'. Of the 16 religious organisations registered with Chhoedey Lhentshog, only one is Hindu. A government official stated this Act was designed to protect and preserve Bhutan's spiritual heritage: 'We need to see if such preconditions can be met if we register a Christian organization.'[69] The Act stipulates that registered organisations will not 'compel any person to belong to another faith, by providing reward or inducement'.

These concerns motivated the adoption of anti-proselytism legislation. When discussed in 2003, the Minister referenced conflicts between the Irish Catholics and Protestants, Sunni and Shi'ite Muslims, noting:

> Bhutan, a small country with small population, has mainly Buddhists or Hindus, generally known for their deep religious sentiments and close family ties. The Kingdom cannot afford to have too many divisive entities, which would divide and even lead to conflicts and crisis within families, communities and eventually at the national level.[70]

He asserted that improved socio-economic development would deter proselytism.[71] The National Assembly amended the Penal Code in 2011.[72] Section 463(B) grades as a misdemeanour the section 463(A) offence of 'compelling others to belong to another faith if the defendant uses coercion or other forms of inducement to cause the conversion of a person from one religion or faith to another'. Christians saw this law as a way to curb the growth of Christianity[73] and were concerned that its vagueness captured charitable acts. Prime Minister Jigmi Yoser Thinley described this clause as 'essentially . . . to deter conversion'; while there was no difficulty having a few Christians and followers of other faiths in Bhutan, as 'we promote diversity of cultures', there was no reason why Christians should seek to gain converts. He described attempts to convert others 'without understanding the values, the principles, and the essence of the other religion' as 'the worst form of discrimination'. Christians denied using monetary inducements or having an attitude of spiritual superiority in seeking converts.[74]

The National Assembly treated complaints about the spread of 'different sects of Hinduism' more tolerantly, during the 65th session in 1986. The *Dratshang Lhenthog* Secretary noted that 'the Hindus and Buddhists worship almost the same gods and goddesses', causing no problems thus far, but warned that it would act if proselytisers disturbed the peace or cheated people of property.[75]

The official Bhutanese conception of tolerance is rooted in the belief in the moral equality of all religions rather than the concept of an absolute truth, and the imperative of protecting Bhutanese culture (Article 8). Officials have viewed religious conversions negatively, as the antithesis of intolerance:

> [C]onversion is the worst form of intolerance. . . . The first premise [of seeking conversion] is that you believe that your religion is the right religion, and the religion of the convertee is

[69] 'Official Recognition eludes Christian Groups in Bhutan', *Compass Direct News*, 1 February 2011.

[70] 'Chathrim to govern religious practice', Bhutan, National Assembly – 81st Session at 68–71(28 June 2003), available at <http://www.nab.gov.bt/downloads/681%20resolution.pdf>.

[71] Ibid.

[72] Penal Code (Amendment) Act of Bhutan 2011, Attorney-General Office, at <http://oag.gov.bt/wp-content/uploads/2010/05/Penal-Code-Amendment-Act-of-Bhutan-2011.pdf>.

[73] 'Buddhist Bhutan Proposes "Anti-Conversion" Law', *Compass Direct News*, 21 July 2010.

[74] 'Christians in Bhutan Seek to Dispel Regime's Mistrust', *Compass Direct News*, 12 September 2011.

[75] Bhutan, National Assembly – 65th Session at 12 (13 July 1987), available at <http://www.nab.gov.bt/downloads/2565th%20Session.pdf>.

wrong . . . that your religion is superior and that you have this responsibility to promote your way of life, your way of thinking, your way of worship . . . it divides families and societies.[76]

Notes and Questions

1. How does the Bhutanese conception of tolerance compare with the Lockean view that social stability would be strengthened where the liberties of all religious groups are safeguarded?

2. Is the Bhutanese Government unduly paternalist when it comes to religious liberty? Are you persuaded by the argument that the element of rational choice is absent from most conversions as many Bhutanese are poor and uneducated? See P Kumar, 'Religious freedom and religious conversion in Bhutan', *Bhutan Observer: The Independent Voice*, 4 November 2009, at <http://www.bhutan observer.bt/religious-freedom-and-religious-conversion-in-bhutan/>. Does this undermine the assumptions underlying liberal conceptions of religious liberty? Do only the rich and educated make rational choices?

3. Religious conversion to any religion other than Buddhism (and Hinduism) is viewed as a threat to Buddhism and social order. Despite the constitutional separation of religion and politics, does this signify a theocratic order inimical to religious freedom?

4. The UN Special Rapporteur on Freedom of Religion or Belief has stated that Article 18 ICCPR recognised missionary activity as a legitimate expression of religious belief, provided the parties involved were adults able to reason on their own, where no hierarchical or dependent relationship existed. See *Report*, Special Rapporteur on Freedom of Religion or Belief, Mission to the Lao People's Democratic Republic, Addendum, A/HRC/13/40/Add.4 27 Jan 2010, [43].

5. The European Court of Human Rights in *Kokkinakis v Greece*,[77] distinguished between true evangelism and improper proselytism. See KN Kyriazopoulos, 'Proselytization in Greece: Criminal Offence vs Religious Persuasion and Equality' (2004–2005) 20(1) *Journal of Law and Religion* 149.

6. T Stahnke, 'The Right to Engage in Religious Persuasion' in T Lindholm, W Cole Durham Jr and Bahia Tahzib-Lie (eds), *Facilitating Freedom of Religion or Belief: A Deskbook* (The Hague: Martinus Nijhoff, 2004) 641, identifies four important factors aiding the line-drawing process: (i) characteristics of the source; (ii) the target; (iii) where proselytism takes place; (iv) the nature of the proselytising act and its propensity to generate coercive pressure.

iii. Anti-Propagation Legislation

Within secular states with a multi-religious society, religious conversion arouses strong passions, particularly in South Asia which has a complex history of religious interactions between Hindus, Sikhs, Buddhists, Muslims and Christians, among others,

---

[76] 'Religious Conversion Worst Form of "Intolerance," Bhutan PM Says', *Compass Direct News*, 14 April 2011.

[77] *Kokkinakis v Greece* App No 14307/88 (ECtHR, 25 May 2013) [48].

complicated by colonial influences and conflation of ethnic-religious identity. A paternalistic legalistic approach to regulate conversions is evident in the adoption of anti-conversion or anti-propagation laws in countries like India, Sri Lanka and Nepal, where the speaker is cast as predator, and the hearer, the vulnerable victim.

a. Constitutionally Mandated Constraints on Conversion and Propagation

Nepal

The 1990 Constitution of the Kingdom of Nepal established the world's only 'sovereign, monarchical Hindu Kingdom' under Article 39(1). Article 19 expressly forbade religious conversions: 'every person may profess his own religion as handed down from ancient times and may practice it having regard to tradition. Provided that no person shall be entitled to convert another person from one religion to another.' The 2007 Interim Constitution declares that Nepal is an 'independent, indivisible, sovereign, secular, inclusive and fully democratic State' (Art 4(1)), departing from the Hindu monarchy. Article 23 substantially reiterates the qualified religious freedom clause:

> (1) Every person shall have the right to profess, practise and preserve his or her own religion as handed down to him or her from ancient times paying due regard to social and cultural traditions. Provided that no person shall be entitled to convert another person from one religion to another, and no person shall act or behave in a manner which may infringe upon the religion of others.

Proselytising remains illegal in Nepal, punishable by fines or imprisonment or the expulsion of foreigners . . . Non-governmental organisations (NGOs), or individuals, are permitted to file reports on proselytising people or groups, which the authorities investigate.[78] This hostility towards religious conversions flows from the perception that external religions or cultures threaten internal cultural norms; this close association of religion and ethnicity heightens the insecurity amongst groups that declining numbers will erode communal identity, breeding inter-group suspicion which hampers interfaith discourse necessary to religious tolerance.

Malaysia

Johor Legislative Assembly, Control and Restriction of the Propagation of Non-Islamic Religions Enactment 1991 (State of Johor) No 13 of 1991

The Control and Restriction of the Propogation of Non-Islamic Religious Enactment 1991 (State of Johor) No 13 of 1991 was enacted by the Johor Legislative Assembly in 1991, pursuant to Article 11(4) of the Constitution which authorises state legislatures to enact laws restricting propagation of other faiths to Muslims.

  Section 2 defines 'Muslim' as 'a person professing the religion of Islam,' to be determined by the 'criterion of general reputation' without reference to the faith or conduct of the person in question (section 3). Section 4 makes it an offence, punishable by a maximum 10,000 ringgit fine, four years imprisonment or both, where the perpetrator 'persuades, influences, coerces or incites' or 'holds or organizes any activity' designed

---

[78] Australian Government Refugee Review Tribunal, *Country Advice Nepal*, at <http//:www.mrt-rrt.gov.au/ArticleDocuments/97/npl37529.pdf.aspx>.

to make a Muslim become 'a follower or member' of a non-Islamic religion or be inclined towards this or 'to forsake or disfavour' Islam. The offence is not dependent on the speech having any effect on the person in question, and it is a defence if the accused reasonably believed that the other person was not a Muslim.

'Non Islamic religion' is statutorily defined as

. . . Christianity, Hinduism, Buddhism, Sikhism, Judaism, or any variation, version, form, or offshoot of any of the said religions, and includes any creed, ideology, philosophy, or any body of practices or observances, which has as one of its characteristics the worship of some spiritual or supernatural being or power, whether real or supposed, or which purports to have as its aim or one of its aims the attainment of spiritual enlightenment, spiritual protection or spiritual existence, being a creed, ideology, philosophy, or body of practices or observances which is not recognised by the religion of Islam as belonging to it

Other offences include causing a Muslim under 18 to receive instruction in a non-Islamic religion or to participate in religious ceremony (section 5), arranging a meeting with a Muslim to subject him to 'any speech on or display of any matter concerning a non-Islamic religion' (section 6), or sending unsolicited religious publications from within or without the state (section 7), or delivering non Islamic publications to a Muslim, unless specifically requested in a manner unprompted by the accused (section 8). It is an offence if a person in writing or speech addressed to a gathering of persons which he knew or reasonably knew would be published or broadcasted 'uses any of the words of Islamic origin' or their derivatives to express any aspect of a belief or activity pertaining to any non-Islamic religion (section 9). The Ruler in Council may appoint any public officer to be an authorized officer with powers of arrest (sections 10–11), investigation (section 12) and to prosecute such offences in any court (section 15).

Questions

1. What role is there for human agency with respect to religious affiliation within the context of these anti-propagation clauses?

2. Do anti-propagation laws and the predator paradigm run the risk of stifling the individual's search for religious truth within an open system? Do they rest on the inconsistent assumption that individuals cannot autonomously change religions but can autonomously retain religion?

iv. Legislative Schemes

a. Anti-Conversion Legislation: India

There is a long history of anti-conversion legislation in India, dating back to the 1930s when Hindu princely states enacted it to preserve Hindu religious identity against the efforts of British Christian missionaries. Today, Hindu nationalism is the primary driving force behind such legislation, advanced by the Bharatiya Janata Party (BJP). The first post-colonial laws were the Orissa Freedom of Religion Act of 1967[79] and

---

[79] Now rr 4, 5(1) of the Orissa Freedom of Religion Rules (1989), available at <http://indianchristians.in/news/images/resources/pdf/orissa_freedom_of_religion_rules-text_only.pdf>.

Madhya Pradesh Dharma Swatantraya Adhiniyam of 1968, which remain in force.[80] These were adopted ostensibly to prevent or regulate 'unethical conversions' through 'allurement', 'fraud', 'inducement' or 'force', which are terms vague enough to include charitable gifts or prayers of blessing. This manifests a paternalistic ethos.

While coercive conversion violates free conscience and should be banned, the underlying motive behind these laws may be to entrench the political interests of dominant religious groups, in the name of preserving social harmony. This is evident in the large-scale conversion in India of Dalits (untouchables), who are at the lowest rung of the Hindu caste system, to other faiths like Buddhism, Islam or Christianity.[81] Notably, the Father of the Constitution, BR Ambedkar, led 500,000 Dalits out of Hinduism into Buddhism in a 1956 mass conversion ceremony.[82]

Constitutional challenges against the validity of these anti-propagation laws have been made. The Orissa High Court, in *Yulitha Hyde v State of Orissa*,[83] held the Orissa Freedom of Religion Act 2 of 1968 was ultra vires the powers of the state legislature, finding that the right to convert another into one's religion was part of Article 25(1) of the Indian Constitution. Counsel cited biblical passages and Vatican writings to establish the duty to propagate faith, which the Court accepted as a 'a part of religious duty for every Christian'. Thus, the Article 25(1) guarantee 'must be taken to extend to propagate religion and as a necessary corollary of this proposition, conversion into one's own religion has to be included in the right so far as a Christian citizen is concerned'. While finding the statutory definition of 'force' and 'fraud' acceptable, 'inducement' was too wide a term, such that even invoking the blessings of the Lord or saying 'by His grace your soul shall be elevated' might be captured by the legislation.

The Madhya Pradesh High Court, in *Rev Stainislaus v State of Madhya Pradesh*,[84] upheld the relevant Act as a public order Act, finding that it guaranteed equality of religious freedom to all, including those susceptible to force, fraud or allurement.

Both the above decisions were appealed and came before the Supreme Court in the following case.

Rev Stainislaus v State Of Madhya Pradesh
[1977] AIR 908, [1977] SCR (2) 611

Facts

The Supreme Court, in upholding anti-propagation laws, pronounced on the meaning of 'propagation' in Article 25 of the Constitution which provides that 'all persons are equally entitled to freedom of conscience and the right freely to profess, practise and propagate religion'.

---

[80] See JA Huff, 'Religious Freedom in India and Analysis of the Constitutionality of Anti-Conversion Laws' (2009) 10 *Rutgers Journal of Law & Religion* 1.

[81] L Jenkins, 'Legal Limits on Religious Conversion in India' (2008) 71 *Law & Contemporary Problems* 109; S Kim, 'Freedom of Religion: Legislation in India' (2002) 9 *Mission and Theology* 227.

[82] B Rogers, 'Untouchable – The Human Face of India's Caste System', 8 May 2007, *Catholicity*, at <http://www.catholicity.com/commentary/brogers/00060.html>.

[83] *Yulitha Hyde v State of Orissa* [1973] AIR Ori 116.

[84] *Rev Stainislaus v State of Madhya Pradesh* [1975] AIR MP 163.

Ray CJ

Counsel for the appellant has argued that the right to 'propagate' one's religion means the right to convert a person to one's own religion. On that basis, counsel has argued further that the right to convert a person to one's own religion is a fundamental right guaranteed by Article 25(1) . . .

. . . The expression 'propagate' has been defined in the *Shorter Oxford Dictionary* to mean 'to spread from person to person, or from place to place, to disseminate, diffuse (a statement, belief, practice, etc)' . . . [I]t is in this sense that the word 'propagate' has been used in Article 25(1), for what the Article grants is not the right to convert another person to one's own religion, but to transmit or spread one's religion by an exposition of its tenets. It has to be remembered that Article 25(1) guarantees 'freedom of conscience' to every citizen, and not merely to the followers of one particular religion, and that, in turn, postulates that there is no fundamental right to convert another person to one's own religion because if a person purposely undertakes the conversion of another person to his religion, as distinguished from his effort to transmit or spread the tenets of his religion, that would impinge on the 'freedom of conscience' guaranteed to all the citizens of the country alike.

The meaning of guarantee under Article 25 of the Constitution came up for consideration in this Court in *Ratilal Panachand Gandhi v State of Bombay* [1954] SCR 1055 and it was held as follows:

> Thus, subject to the restrictions which this Article imposes, every person has a fundamental right under our Constitution not merely to entertain such religious belief as may be approved of by his judgment or conscience but to exhibit his belief and ideas in such overt acts as are enjoined or sanctioned by his religion and further to propagate his religious views for the edification of others.

This Court has given the correct meaning of the Article, and we find no justification for the view that it grants a fundamental right to convert persons to one's own religion. It has to be appreciated that the freedom of religion enshrined in the Article is not guaranteed in respect of one religion only, but covers all religions alike, and it can be properly enjoyed by a person if he exercises his right in a manner commensurate with the like freedom of persons following the other religions. What is freedom for one, is freedom for the other, in equal measure, and there can therefore be no such thing as a fundamental right to convert any person to one's own religion . . .

Notes and Question

1. This judgment holds there is no right to carry propagation to its logical conclusion of conversion, rendering it an empty right. Leading Indian Jurist HM Seervai criticised this case as causing 'the greatest public mischief'; it warranted overruling to dispel the myth that conversion was unconstitutional. He regretted that the Court considered neither Article 25's legislative history nor the central issue – whether conversion was part of the Christian religion – which the Orissa High Court had affirmed in *Yulitha Hyde v State of Orissa*.[85] Seervai argued that A's propagation of his religion to B did not violate B's free conscience but gave 'an opportunity to B to exercise his free choice of a religion', and that conversion by persuasion was a legitimate aspect of religious freedom:

---

[85] *Yulitha Hyde v State of Orissa* [1973] AIR Ori 116.

The right to propagate religion gives a meaning to freedom of choice, for choice involves not only knowledge but an act of will. A person cannot choose if he does not know what choices are open to him. To propagate religion is not to impart knowledge and to spread it more widely, but to produce intellectual and moral conviction leading to action, namely, the adoption of that religion. *Successful* propagation of religion would result in conversion.

See HM Seervai, *Constitutional Law of India*, 4th edn (New Delhi: Universal, 1996) at 1286–90.

2. If the Supreme Court had read into propagation the right to try to convert by persuasion rather than coercion, could the anti-propagation legislation be upheld as a permissible restriction to serve public order and the community's conscience against reprehensible conversions?

Evangelical Fellowship of India v State of Himachal Pradesh
CWP No 438 of 2011A (High Court, Himachal Pradesh)

Facts

The petitioners challenged the constitutionality of the Himachal Pradesh Freedom of Religion Act, 2006 (HP Act) for violating Articles 14, 19(2), 21 and 25 of the Constitution. The Court considered *Stanislaus v State of MP* 1977 SC 908 and *Satya Ranjan Majhi v State of Orissa* (2003) 7 SCC 439, which upheld the relevant Acts.

Deepak Gupta J

[T]he Madhya Pradesh Act provides for the prohibition of conversion from one religion to another by use of force or allurement, or by fraudulent means . . . Section 3 of the Orissa Act prohibits forcible conversion by the use of force or by inducement or by any fraudulent means, and Section 4 penalises such forcible conversion. The Acts . . . clearly provide for the maintenance of public order . . .
   . . . [T]his Court in *Ramesh Thapper v State of Madras* (1950) SCR 594 [held] that 'public order' is an expression of wide connotation and signifies state of tranquility which prevails among the members of a political society as a result of internal regulations enforced by the Government . . . Reference may also be made to . . . *Ramjilal Modi v State of UP* (1957) SCR 860 where this Court held that the . . . freedom of religion guaranteed by Articles 25 and 26 of the Constitution is expressly made subject to public order, morality and health . . . Reference may . . . be made to . . . *Arun Ghosh v State of West Bengal*, AIR 1970 SC 1228 where it has been held that if a thing disturbs the current of the life of the community, and does not merely affect an individual, it would amount to disturbance of the public order . . . The impugned Acts . . . fall within the purview of Entry 1 of List II of the Seventh Schedule as they are meant to avoid disturbances to the public order by prohibiting conversion from one religion to another in a manner reprehensible to the conscience of the community.
   Dr Subramanian Swamy has drawn our attention to the *Collected Works of Mahatma Gandhi,* wherein certain questions were posed by Mahatma Gandhi and answered by himself:

WOULD YOU PREVENT MISSIONARIES COMING TO INDIA IN ORDER TO BAPTIZE?
   . . . If I had power and could legislate, I should certainly stop all proselytizing. It is the cause of much avoidable conflict between classes and unnecessary heartburning among

missionaries. But I should welcome people of any nationality if they came to serve here for the sake of service. In Hindu households the advent of a missionary has meant the disruption of the family coming in the wake of change of dress, manners, language, food and drink.

IS IT NOT THE OLD CONCEPTION YOU ARE REFERRING TO? NO SUCH THING IS NOW ASSOCIATED WITH PROSELYTIZATION?

The outward condition has perhaps changed but the inward mostly remains. Vilification of Hindu religion, though subdued, is there . . . Only the other day a missionary descended on a famine area with money in his pocket, distributed it among the famine stricken, converted them to his fold, took charge of their temple and demolished it. This is outrageous. The temple could not belong to the converted Hindus, and it could not belong to the Christian missionary. But this friend goes and gets it demolished at the hands of the very men who only a little while ago believed that God was there.

He has also drawn our attention to the issue raised in the Constituent Assembly that conversion from one religion to another brought about by coercion or undue influence shall not be recognized by law . . . Dr Subramanian Swami contends that conversions are against Hindu philosophy and . . . should not be permitted . . . The question whether conversions should be permitted or not is not for the Court to decide . . . Conversions in our country are permissible if . . . by the free will of the convertee . . .

. . . A comparative analysis of the HP Act, the Madhya Pradesh Act and the Orissa Act shows that the definitions of the words 'conversion', 'force', 'fraud' and 'minor' are identical . . . In the Madhya Pradesh Act, the word 'allurement' has been used to describe offer of any temptation in the form of any gift or gratification either in cash or kind or grant of any material benefit, either monetary or otherwise. In the HP and Orissa Acts, instead of the word 'allurement' the word 'inducement' has been defined, but the definition is identical.

. . . It has been urged . . . that the definition of the words 'force', 'fraud' and 'inducement' are very vague and liable to be misused. Merely because a definition is liable to be misused does not mean that the Act should be struck down. As and when the provisions of the Act are misused, the affected party can approach the Court for redressal . . . It has . . . been urged . . . that Article 13(2) prohibits the Legislature from enacting any law which infringes the rights guaranteed under Part III of the Constitution [including Article 25] . . . It has . . . been urged before us that there are two proselytizing religions, *ie* Islam and Christianity, [and] to spread the word of God is an inherent part of these religions . . . the State cannot put any restriction on this religious practice of proselytization. We cannot accept this argument because the Apex Court in no uncertain terms has held that though the right to propagate may be a fundamental right . . . there is no fundamental right to convert.

We are proud of our multicultural heritage where people belonging to all religions, thoughts and beliefs have amalgamated into our society. Indian culture is such that we have accepted into our fold believers and nonbelievers. Indian Society has not discriminated against any religion or thought. At the same time, we cannot permit religions, which advance proselytization and encourage conversions, to carry out these conversions by 'force', 'fraud' or 'inducement'.

Christianity entered and flourished in India right from the time when St Thomas came to India in 52 AD. Jews found asylum in India both in Kochi in Kerala and in the North Eastern parts of the country. Zoroastrians entered India at Navsari to escape persecution in Persia. Today, though the number of Jews may have dwindled, Christians and Parsis have flourished and attained high offices in the country. Islam is now the second largest religion of the country. Though, by peaceful propagation, each religion may expand the number of its followers, there have to be limitations on the manner in which conversions are carried out and no civilized society can permit conversions to be carried out by 'force', 'fraud' or 'inducement'. The word of God cannot be spread either through the sword or by the use of money power.

The right to propagate one's religion may entitle a person to extol the virtues of the religion which he propounds. He, however, has no right to denigrate any other religion, thought or belief. One may promise heaven to the followers of one's religion, but one cannot say that damnation will follow if that path is not followed. The essence of secularism is tolerance and acceptance of all religions. The right to propagate can never include the right to denigrate any other thought, religion or belief . . .

. . . The right of freedom of opinion, the right of freedom of conscience by themselves include the extremely important right to disagree. Every society has its own rules and over a period of time when people only stick to the age-old rules and conventions, society degenerates. New thinkers are born when they disagree with well-accepted norms of society . . . If a person does not ask questions and does not raise issues questioning age-old systems, no new systems would develop and the horizons of the mind will not be expanded. Whether it be Budha, Mahavira, Jesus Christ, Prophet Mohammad, Guru Nanak Dev, Martin Luther, Kabir, Raja Ram Mohan Roy or Swami Dayanand Saraswati, new thoughts and religious practices would not have been established, if they had quietly submitted to the views of their forefathers and had not questioned the existing religious practices, beliefs and rituals.

In a secular country, every belief does not have to be religious. Even atheists enjoy equal rights under our Constitution. Whether one is a believer, an agnostic or an atheist, one enjoys complete freedom of belief and conscience . . . There can be no impediments on the aforesaid rights except those permitted by the Constitution. This right of freedom of conscience and belief also includes the very important right to change one's own belief. Every person has a right to question the beliefs of others in a civilized manner without deriding or casting aspersions on the beliefs of the others . . . However, this change must be an act of his own conscience . . . If a person changes his religion or belief of his own volition then the State has no role to play. On the other hand, if persons are made to change their religion due to 'force', 'fraud' or 'inducement', this would wreck the very basic framework of our society and lead India to total annihilation. No law can be permitted to be interpreted in such a manner that the very being of our secular country is put at stake . . .

Coming to the provisions of the Act and the Rules, which are not found in the Madhya Pradesh and Orissa Acts, we may refer to Section 4 of the HP Act, which reads as follows:

4(1) A person intending to convert from one religion to another shall give prior notice of at least thirty days to the District Magistrate of the district concerned of his intention to do so and the District Magistrate shall get the matter enquired into all by such agency as he may deem fit:

Provided that no notice shall be required if a person reverts back to his original religion.

(2) Any person who fails to give prior notice, as required under subsection (1), shall be punishable with fine which may extend to one thousand rupees.

Section 8 of the Act empowers the State to frame rules . . . we are concerned with Rules 3, 4, 5 and 6:

3. Notice before conversion

(1) Any person domiciled in the State, intending to convert his religion, shall give a notice to the District Magistrate of the District in which he is permanently resident, prior to such conversion, in Form A.

(2) The District Magistrate shall cause all notices received under subrule (1) of rule 3 to be entered in a Register of Notices and Complaints of conversion in Form B, and may within fifteen days from the receipt of said notice, get the matter enquired into by such agency as he may deem fit and record his findings as regards the particulars of notice given:

Provided that the person giving notice and any other person likely to be prejudicially affected shall be given adequate opportunity to associate himself with any such enquiry.

4. Inquiries in other cases

Where on the basis of any complaint or any information laid before him, the District Magistrate is of the opinion, for reasons to be recorded,

(a) that force or inducement have been used or is likely to be used in any conversion within the local limits of his jurisdiction; or
(b) that a conversion has taken place without notice in contravention of the provisions of this Act,

he may cause an inquiry to be made in the matter and proceed in the manner as provided in Rule 3.

Every such complaint so received shall be entered in the Register of Notices and Complaints of conversion in Form B.

5. Registration and investigation of case

If after enquiry under rule 3 or rule 4 . . . the District Magistrate records a finding that a conversion has taken place or is likely to take place through the use of force or inducement or without the requisite notice, he shall enter the particulars of the case in the Register of Forced Conversion in Form C and refer the case along with all material adduced during the course of the enquiry to the Police Station in which the person is resident or where the conversion is intended or done for registration of a case and its investigation.

6. Sanction for prosecution

If after investigating the matter, it appears that an offence under section 4(2) or under section 5 has been committed, the Investigation Officer shall place all relevant material before the authority empowered under Section 7 to grant prosecution sanction and such sanction shall be granted or refused within a period of 7 days, giving reasons in writing.

An important issue . . . raised . . . is with regard to the right to privacy of a person wanting to change his beliefs. [Discusses section 4 of the HP Act and Rules 3, 5, 6.]

. . . In this case, the main issue with which we are concerned is whether the fundamental rights of the person, who is converting (the convertee), are being adversely affected by Section 4 and Rules 3 and 5?

. . . Neither the Madhya Pradesh Act nor the Rules made thereunder provide that the convertee should give notice before conversion. In the Madhya Pradesh Act, it is the person who is converting any other person from one religious faith to another, such as a religious priest, who is required to give notice of such conversion to the District Magistrate. Every conversion may not entail the performance of a ceremony. True it is, that in some religions, before initiation into the religion, some ceremony has to be performed, but this is not applicable to all religions.

Under the Orissa Act, there is . . . no provision for giving advance notice by the convertee. However, Rule 4 of the Orissa Freedom of Religion Rules (1999) [provides that] . . . any person intending to convert his religion is directed to give a declaration before a Magistrate 1st Class prior to such conversion that he intends to convert his religion of his own free will. There is no time period prescribed. The non-filing of such declaration is not an offence. Under Rule 8 of the Orissa Rules, only contravention of Rules 5 and 6 is an offence, but contravention of Rule 4 is not an offence.

. . . [T]he HP Act has gone much further than the Madhya Pradesh or Orissa Acts as far as the convertee is concerned . . . our Constitution ensures that no person living in India can be denied equality under the law or the . . . freedoms . . . guaranteed under Part III . . . These rights, which are commonly known as fundamental rights, are, in fact, human rights. These rights inhere in every human being and in every civilized society, we must respect such rights. The right to privacy is one of such rights and has been the subject matter of interpretation in a number of cases. [Discusses the right to privacy, an unenumerated right, as elaborated in *Govind v State of Madhya Pradesh* [1975] AIR SC 1378, and finds restrictions to it subject to the 'compelling state interest test'. Gupta J also noted that an over-extensive definition of privacy raised 'serious questions about the propriety of judicial reliance' on an unenumerated right and discussed other cases like *Ram Jethmalani v UOI* (2011) 8 SCC 1.

. . . A person not only has a right of conscience, the right of belief, the right to change his belief, but also has the right to keep his beliefs secret. No doubt, the right to privacy is, like any other right, subject to public order, morality and the larger interest of the State. When rights of individuals clash with the larger public good, then the individual's right must give way to what is in the larger public interest. However, this does not mean that the majority interest is the larger public interest. Larger public interest would mean the integrity, unity and sovereignty of the country, the maintenance of public law and order. Merely because the majority view is different does not mean that the minority view must be silenced.

. . . [T]he State must have material before it to show what are the very compelling reasons which will justify its action of invading the right to privacy of an individual . . . A man's mind is the impregnable fortress in which he thinks and there can be no invasion of his right of thought unless the person is expressing or propagating his thoughts in such a manner that it will cause public disorder or affect the unity or sovereignty of the country.

Why should any human being be asked to disclose what is his religion? Why should a human being be asked to inform the authorities that he is changing his belief? What right does the State have to direct the convertee to give notice in advance to the District Magistrate about changing his rebellious thought?

A person's belief or religion is something very personal to him. The State has no right to ask a person to disclose what is his personal belief. The only justification given is that public order requires that notice be given. We are of the considered view that in case of a person changing his religion and notice being issued to the so-called prejudicially affected parties, chances of the convertee being subjected to physical and psychological torture cannot be ruled out. The remedy proposed by the State may prove to be more harmful than the problem.

In case such a notice is issued, then the unwarranted disclosure of the voluntary change of belief by an adult may lead to communal clashes and may even endanger the life or limb of the convertee. We are not, in any manner, condoning or espousing conversions especially by 'force', 'fraud' or 'inducement' [which must be] dealt with strictly in accordance with law . . . At the same time, the right to privacy and the right to change the belief of a citizen cannot be taken away under the specious plea that public order may be affected. We are unable to comprehend how the issuance of a notice by a convertee will prevent conversions by 'fraud', 'force' or 'inducement'. In fact, this may open a Pandora's box and once notice is issued, this may lead to conflicts between rival religious outfits and groups. No material has been placed on record by the State to show that there has been any adverse effect on public order by any conversion in the State whether prior to or after the enactment of the Himachal Pradesh Act. In fact, till date only one case has been registered under this Act.

. . . [C]onversions may not require any ceremony in some religions and how will the Government determine when the thought process of a person has changed. A person who belongs to A religion and willingly wants to convert to B religion will not change his religion overnight, except in case of forced [or induced] conversions . . . Change of religion, when it is of its own volition, will normally be a long drawn out process . . . there is no way that one can measure or fix the date on which he has ceased to belong to religion A and converted to religion B. This has to be an ongoing process and therefore, there can be no notice of thirty days as required under the Himachal Pradesh Act.

. . . [T]he proviso to Section 4 is also discriminatory and violative of Article 14 of the Constitution of India.[86] 'Original religion' has not been defined in the Himachal Act . . . The general consensus of opinion used was that the original religion would be the religion of the convertee by birth, ie the religion he was born into.

We fail to understand the rationale why if a person is to revert back to his original religion, no notice is required. It was urged before us that since he was born in his religion and knows his religion well, therefore, it was thought that while reverting back to his original religion, no notice be issued. This argument does not satisfy the parameters of Article 14 . . . Supposing a person born in religion A converts to religion B at the age of 20 and wants to convert back to religion A at the age of 50, he has spent many more years, that too mature years, being a follower of religion B. Why should he not be required to give notice? Another question which is troubling us is if a person born in religion A, converts to religion B, then converts to religion C and then to religion D. If he converts back to religion B or C, he is required to give notice, but if he converts back to religion A, then no notice is required. This also, according to us, is totally irrational and violative of Article 14 . . .

We also fail to understand why a person, who fails to give such notice, should be required to pay a fine, which may extend up to (rupees) 1,000 . . . We are also of the view that conversion by 'force', 'fraud' or 'inducement' should be dealt with strictly and should be discouraged. But, by and large, it is the poor and the downtrodden, who are converted by 'force', 'fraud' or 'inducement'. By enacting Section 4 and making the non-issuance of the notice a criminal offence, the State has, in fact, made these poor and downtrodden people criminals, whereas the main thrust of the Act should have been to deal strictly with the persons who convert people by 'force', 'fraud' or 'inducement'.

We also found many flaws in the Rules. Rule 3 requires that any person domiciled in the State intending to convert must give notice to the District Magistrate of the District of which he is a permanent resident. Supposing a person is a permanent resident of District Shimla, who is staying in Delhi. He decides to convert at Delhi . . . The State of Himachal Pradesh has no jurisdiction over the Union Territory of Delhi. In Delhi, there is no law corresponding to the HP Freedom of Religion Act. If such conversion is not illegal in Delhi, why should such person be required to give notice in Himachal Pradesh? How can such a person be virtually treated to be a criminal when the act of conversion is legal at Delhi? There are other flaws also in the Rules inasmuch as they are totally vague and do not specify the agency, through which the District Magistrate should carry out the enquiry. But, since we are of the view that Section 4 itself is ultra vires the Constitution of India, the corresponding rules must fall . . .

. . . [W]e allow the petitions to a limited extent and strike down Section 4 of the HP Freedom of Religion Act, 2006 and Rule 3 of the HP Freedom of Religion Rules, 2007 [for violating Article 14] . . . Rule 5 only insofar as it relates to actions relating to Section 4 is

---

[86] Art 14 of the Constitution of India (1949) provides: 'The State shall not deny to any person equality before the law or the equal protection of the laws within the territory of India.'

also held to be ultra vires. However, all other provisions of the Act and the Rules are held to be legal and valid.

Notes and Questions

1. What are the strongest arguments for and against regulating conversion? Which best protects free conscience, human dignity and privacy? Conversion has been statutorily defined to exclude 'reconversion': section 2(b) of the Arunachal Act defines conversion as renouncing an indigenous faith ('religion of our forefathers') and adopting another. See S Suleman, 'Freedom of Religion and Anti-Conversion Laws' (2010) 1(1) *Indian Law Institute Law Review* 106, 119. Does this raise equal protection issues? Is induced conversion as offensive as induced reconversion?

2. Is the Gandhian notion that all religions are of equal validity or veracity as dogmatic as the absolute truth-claims made by certain faiths?

3. There have been few complaints and convictions under Indian anti-propagation laws. Is the object of prohibiting forcible conversion suspect? Bibu argues that although anti-conversion laws have been in force in Orissa, Madhya Pradesh and Chhattisgarh for over 40 years, no one has been found guilty of forced conversion: G Bibu, 'The Anti Conversion Laws examined in Light of the Indian Constitution' at <http://www.sakshitimes.org/index.php?option=com_content&task=view&id =316&Itemid=40>, p 51. Are these laws a method for harassing religious minorities and entrenching the status quo, as they apply 'only to cases of conversion by the Hindus to a non-Hindu religion, and not vice versa'.

4. May anti-propagation laws promote more violence and injustice against religious minorities, through their misuse by Hindu Nationalists to prevent conversions out of Hinduism, by making allegations against Christians even where no force was involved? For example, two priests and a nun were penalised for converting Hindus without registering them with the local police, despite the ex-Hindus sending letters to the police vouching for the authenticity of their conversions. See A Anant, 'Anti Conversion Laws', *The Hindu*, 17 December 2002. We should note that Hindus constitute a 82 per cent majority, while Christians account for 2.3 per cent of the population.

b. Anti-Propagation Legislation: Sri Lanka

Buddhism is deeply rooted in Sri Lankan history, where Sri Lankan Buddhists were the first to write down the Buddha's teachings (first century CE) and create a Buddhist historical record (second to fourth centuries CE). The King was duty-bound to defend the *Sangha* (monastic community); and where the *Sangha* felt the King had exceeded his boundaries, it could rouse the peasantry to revolt. There is a history of hostility between Buddhism and Christian missionaries, and Buddhism later developed a strong anti-colonial bias.[87] The relevant constitutional provisions are:

[87] Y Liston, 'The Transformation of Buddhism during British Colonialism' (1999–2000) 14 *Journal of Law & Religion* 189. Earlier initiatives to insert the words 'Hinduism, Islam, Christianity' into Article 9,

– Article 9: 'The Republic of Sri Lanka shall give to Buddhism the foremost place and accordingly it shall be the duty of the State to protect and foster the Buddha *Sasana*, while assuring to all religions the rights granted by Articles 10 and 14(1)(e).'

– Article 10: 'Every person is entitled to freedom of thought, conscience and religion, including the freedom to have or to adopt a religion or belief of his choice.'

– Article 14(1): 'Every citizen is entitled to (e) the freedom, either by himself or in association with others, and either in public or in private, to manifest his religion or belief in worship, observance, practice or teaching'.

– Article 15(1): Article 14(1) may be subject to restrictions, 'in the interests of racial and religious harmony'.

A series of decisions known as the 'incorporation' cases implicate the right to propagate a religion. Religious groups do not need to register with the government but require incorporation by an Act of Parliament to conduct financial transactions as a business under the Companies Act or under the Societies or Trust Ordinance. Threatened by the increasing number of Christian evangelical groups since the 1970s, some have been accused of engaging in 'unethical conversions' and have found it difficult to register new churches or re-register under the Companies Act. In the 2000s, the Supreme Court heard challenges against attempts to incorporate Christian organisations via Private Members Bills, broadly on the basis that their economic, commercial or humanitarian activities, such as providing social-welfare services or job training, would give rise to the potential for economically induced conversions.[88]

Teaching Sisters of the Holy Cross in Menzingen v Sri Lanka
SC Special Determination No 19/2003 (Supreme Court, Sri Lanka)

Facts

A petitioner challenged the constitutionality of a Private Member's Bill under Article 121(1) of the Sri Lanka Constitution. The impugned Provincial of the Teaching Sisters of the Holy Cross of the Third Order of Saint Francis in Menzingen of Sri Lanka (Incorporation) Bill sought to propagate the Catholic religion in a manner that took advantage of certain vulnerable persons. The Bill sought to incorporate a Catholic Order whose objects included spreading the knowledge of Catholicism (clause 3) and obtaining legal recognition to run schools and nursing homes as Christian institutions. This would involve providing crèches, nursing homes, orphanages and mobile clinics to care for infants, the aged, orphans, the destitute and the sick. The petitioner argued that the Bill, contrary to Article 10, sought to allure persons of other religions by providing material benefits, to take advantage of their youth, inexperience or physical/mental disability, and that the Bill provided facilities to the organisation to convert non-Catholic children.

'while assuring to all religions the rights granted by Articles 10 and 14(1)(e)', were rejected given the place the Buddhism had in Ceylon's history and tradition: J Cooray, *A Commentary on the Constitution and the Law of Public Administration of Sri Lanka* (Colombo, Sri Lanka: Sumathi Publishers, 1995) at 618–23.

[88] See A Owens, 'Using Legislation to Protect Against Unethical Conversions in Sri Lanka' (2006–2007) 22(2) *Journal of Law & Religion* 323.

Shirani A Bandaranayake, HS Yapa & Nihal Jayasinghe JJ

Article 10 could be regarded as an absolute right . . . [Discusses the Indian Supreme Court decision of *Rev Stainislaus v State of Madhya Pradesh* [1977] AIR SC. 908] The Indian Constitution spells out the word 'propagate' in Article 25(1). Article 10 and 14(1)(e) of our Constitution do not refer to the word 'propagate' and therefore, it could be said that the provisions in our Constitution are more restrictive than that of Article 25(1) . . . Ray CJ, referring to the word 'propagate' in Article 25(1) was of the view that [propagation only extends to transmission of information and not the right to convert another person which would impugn free conscience] . . . In such circumstances, as pointed out in SC Determination No 2 of 2001, the reasoning of Ray CJ, would apply more forcefully with regard to Articles 10 and 14(1)(e) of our Constitution. [Referred to Article 18, UDHR and Article 18(2), ICCPR.]

The decision of the European Court in *Larissis v Greece*[89] is a case in point with regard to the circumstances given in clause 3 of the Bill which seeks to 'spread knowledge of catholic religion.' An examination of clause 3(c), (d) and (e) indicate strong relationships –that of teacher–student, nurse/doctor/patient, curator/refugee and that of guardian/minor. In the *Larissis* case, three officers of the Greek Air Force, who were followers of the Pentecostal Church, were convicted for proselytising three airmen of a lesser rank . . . the European Court was of the view that,

> The Commission found that the interference could be justified as ensuring that the three airmens' religious beliefs were respected, in view in particular of the special character of the relationship between a superior and a subordinate in the armed forces, which rendered the subordinate more susceptible to influence in a variety of matters including religious beliefs . . .

In a situation where toddlers, children, invalids, [the] aged and refugees are concerned, they would be in a similar or a worse position as that of an airman under a superior officer in an air force, and the reasoning of the European Court to the susceptibility of subordinate officers to superiors should apply with greater force. Where there are special relationships that exist, preaching would create a situation where there could be infringement of freedom of thought of the person, who is under authority as there could be compulsion to that effect. Executing pressure on people by offering material or social advantage in order to convert into their religion was discussed in the European Court decision in *Kokkinakis v Greece*.[90] This decision deals with a situation similar to the instances referred to in the Preamble and clause 3 of the Bill.

In that case a Jehovah's Witness was convicted for proselytism, when an attempt was made to convert a wife of a Cantor in the Orthodox Church by visiting her house to teach their religion. Considering the activities of offering material or social advantage, the Court was of the view that,

> First of all, distinction has to be made between bearing Christian witness and improper proselytism. The former corresponds to true evangelism, which a report drawn up in 1956, under the auspices of the World Council of Churches describes as an essential mission and a responsibility of every Christian and every church. The latter represents a corruption or deformation of it. It may . . . take the form of activities offering material or social advantages with a view to gaining new members for a Church or exerting improper pressure on people in distress or in need; it may even entail the use of violence

---

[89] *Larissis v Greece* App nos 140/1996/759/958–960 (ECtHR, 24 February 1998).
[90] *Kokkinakis v Greece* App nos 3/1992/348/421 (ECtHR, 25 May 1993).

or brainwashing; more generally, it is not compatible with respect for the freedom of thought, conscience and religion of others.

The provisions in the Bill, viz, the Preamble, clause 3 and also clause 5, which deal with the powers of the organization that includes inter alia to be able to receive and hold property both movables and immovables and or to dispose of such property, create a situation which combines the observance and practice of a religion or belief with activities which would provide material and other benefits to the inexperienced, defenceless and vulnerable people to propagate a religion. The kind of activities projected in the Bill would necessarily result in imposing unnecessary and improper pressures on people, who are distressed and in need, with their free exercise of thought, conscience and religion with the freedom to have or to adopt a religion or belief of his choice as provided in Article 10 of the Constitution. What Article 10 postulates is to adopt a religion or belief of his or her choice and the execution of improper inducement would not be compatible with such a provision.

. . . [W]e hold that the provisions in clauses 3 and 4 of the Bill are inconsistent with Article 10 of the Constitution. The petitioner submitted that the objects enumerated in clause 3 also violates Article 9 . . . [A]lthough it is permissible under our Constitution for a person to manifest his or her religion, spreading another religion would not be permissible as the Constitution would not guarantee a fundamental right to propagate religion . . . [W]hen there is no fundamental right to propagate, if efforts are taken to convert another person to one's own religion, such conduct could hinder the very existence of the Buddha Sasana. What is guaranteed under the Constitution is the manifestation, observance and practice of one's own religion, and the propagation and spreading of Christianity as postulated in terms of clause 3 would not be permissible as it would impair the very existence of Buddhism or the Buddha Sasana . . .

Notes and Questions

1. Buddhists make up the majority religious group in Sri Lanka (70 per cent), compared with Christians (7 per cent) who have long suffered acts of violence. After the Supreme Court declared organisations like the Teaching Sisters unlawful, a wave of violence against Christians and church burnings followed: US State Department, *International Religious Freedom Reports (Sri Lanka)*, 2004 and 2005.

2. Is it satisfactory merely to assert that propagating other faiths might 'impair the very existence of Buddhism'? Is it mandated by Article 9, or is a Supreme Court in a multi-religious polity obliged to protect the rights of majorities and minorities? Could the Court have construed Article 9 more harmoniously in tandem with Articles 10 and 14(1)(e)? Are the illiberal restrictions on religious practice of concern, or is upholding exclusivist majoritarianism justified?

3. The Sri Lanka Court, in citing decisions of the European Court of Human Rights, did not apply the sequential legal tests in determining whether a fundamental right had been infringed (ie prescribed by law, necessary in a democratic society to achieve a legitimate aim, etc), in contrast to free speech cases like *Sunila Abeysekera v Ariya Rubesinghe*.[91] In *Larissis v Greece*, the Strasbourg Court noted (at [50] and

---

[91] *Sunila Abeysekera v Ariya Rubesinghe* (2000) 1 SLR 314.

[59]) that military hierarchy 'may colour every aspect of the relations between military personnel, making it difficult for a subordinate to rebuff the approaches of an individual of superior rank or to withdraw from a conversation initiated by him', and found it 'of decisive significance *that the civilians whom the applicants attempted to convert were not subject to pressures and constraints of the same kind as the airmen*' (emphasis added). The Supreme Court in *Menzingen* analogised military relations with those of teacher/student, doctor/patient, curator/refugee, which is to miss the point of *Larissis.* See A Welikala, 'The Menzingen Determination and the Supreme Court: A Liberal Critique', at <http://www.lankaliberty.com/legal/index.html>.

4. The Human Rights Committee received a communication that Sri Lanka had violated Articles 18, 19, 26 and 27 of the ICCPR relating to religious freedom, free expression, equality under the law and religious minority rights: *Sister Immaculate Joseph and 80 Teaching Sisters of the Holy Cross of the Third Order of Saint Francis in Menzingen of Sri Lanka v Sri Lanka*, No 1249/2004, UN Doc CCPR/C/85/D/ 1249/2004 (2005) [7.3]. The Committee found that Article 18 of the ICCPR had been violated as the state party cited only the Supreme Court decision to justify the infringement of the rights of others, which held the Order's activities sought improperly to propagate religion through providing material benefits to vulnerable people. From the perspective of the Committee, this was insufficient to show that restrictions were necessary for a permissible purpose:

> The decision failed to provide any evidentiary or factual foundation for this assessment, or reconcile this assessment with the analogous benefits and services provided by other religious bodies that had been incorporated. Similarly, the decision provided no justification for the conclusion that the Bill, including through the spreading [of] knowledge of a religion, would 'impair the very existence of Buddhism or the *Buddha Sasana*'. The Committee notes moreover that the international case law cited by the decision does not support its conclusions. In one case, criminal proceedings brought against a private party for proselytisation was found in breach of religious freedoms. In the other case, criminal proceedings were found permissible against military officers, as representatives of the State, who had proselytised certain subordinates, but not for proselytising private persons outside the military forces.[92]

5. Can a more generous construction of Article 14(1)(e) offer an alternative to the view that the constitutional drafters excluded the right to propagate under Article 10?

6. In the Indian case of *Christian Sahanaye Doratuwa Prayer Centre (Incorporation)*, SC Determination No 2/2001, a Private Member's Bill was held inconsistent with Article 10, as clause 3 listed objects including encouraging the active observance of Christianity, and assisting persons to obtain jobs and drug rehabilitation, while clause 4 empowered the Corporation to borrow and raise money and run bank accounts. The Supreme Court, noting the 'particular sensitivity' attendant on issues of religious conversion and conscience, stated:

---

[92] *Sister Immaculate Joseph and 80 Teaching Sisters of the Holy Cross of the Third Order of Saint Francis in Menzingen of Sri Lanka v Sri Lanka*, No 1249/2004, UN Doc CCPR/C/85/D/1249/2004 (2005) [7.3].

The free exercise of these rights is of high emotive significance in a pluralistic society. Any legislative measure which places one religious group at an advantage which directly or indirectly would permit the conversion by allurement or other subtle means of a person of a particular religion to another would indeed result in social disturbances . . .

In discussing Article 10, it stated:

The Constitution guarantees to every person that the basic choice he makes with regard to his religion or belief would be taken with complete freedom without being exposed to any undue influence, allurement or fraud.

Affirming *Stanilaus v State of Madya Pradesh*[93] in so far as the right to propagate does not entail a right to convert, the Court noted that

the freedom guaranteed to every citizen by Article 14(1)(c) of the Constitution to practice a religion and engage in worship and observance, by himself or in association with others, should be taken as distinct from the freedom guaranteed by Article 14(1)(g) to engage in a lawful occupation, trade, business or enterprise. A prayer centre that seeks special legislative recognition by way of incorporation cannot avail itself of these two freedoms together. If it is sought to be done in that manner, there is a likelihood of the fundamental right guaranteed by Article 10 being infringed.

Is this decision unduly intolerant? Does it infringe on the charitable mission of certain faiths such as Christianity, which are integral to the faith? Within the Sri Lankan context where the Constitution privileges the majority's religion, did the Supreme Court sufficiently protect the interests of religious minorities within a plural society? What was its attitude towards vulnerable groups in relation to predatory actions to convert by allurement/fraud?

c. Subsequent Attempts at Enacting Anti-Propagation Laws in Sri Lanka

In *Supreme Court Determinations Nos 02 to 22/2004 on 'Prohibition of Forcible Conversion of Religion' Legislation*,[94] the Supreme Court held unconstitutional a Private Member's Bill while making certain recommendations to bring it into conformity with the Constitution. Clause 3(a) and (b), which required the convert, facilitator and the witness to such ceremony to notify the Divisional Secretary of the conversion, contravened Article 10.

In 2009, the Jathika Hela Urumaya (JHU National Heritage Party)[95] re-introduced the Prohibition of Forcible Conversion of Religion Bill LDO/INC/7/2004.[96] Section 2(1) states:

No person shall convert or attempt to convert, either directly or otherwise, any person from one religion to another by the use of force or by allurement or by any fraudulent means.

Section 6 provides:

---

[93] *Stanilaus v State of Madya Pradesh* [1977] AIR SC 908.

[94] *Supreme Court Determinations Nos 02 to 22/2004 on 'Prohibition of Forcible Conversion of Religion' Legislation*, at <http://www.lankaliberty.com/legal/SCdetermination.pdf>.

[95] J Whitehall, 'Sri Lanka: Sectarian, anti-Christian bill re-appears', *News Weekly*, 21 March 2009, at <http://newsweekly.com.au/article.php?id=3934>.

[96] Text at <http://www.srilankanchristians.com/media/pdf/anti-conversion-legislation.pdf>.

(a) 'allurement' means offer of any temptation for the purpose of converting a person professing one religion to another religion, in the form of –

   (1) any gift or gratification whether in cash or kind;

   (2) grant of any material benefit, whether monetary or otherwise;

   (3) grant of employment of grant of promotion in employment;

'convert' means to make one person to renounce one religion and adopt another religion;

'force' shall include a show of force including a threat [of] harm or injury of any kind or threat of religious disgrace or condemnation of any religion or religious faith for the purpose of converting a person from one religion to another;

'fraudulent' meals any wilful misinterpretation or any other fraudulent contrivance used for the purpose of converting persons from one religion to another religion . . .

A breach incurs up to five years' imprisonment or a fine of 150,000 rupees, unless the act was committed against a minor, a woman or a person stipulated in the Schedule, such as students, prison inmates or the mentally disabled, which carries a penalty of seven years' imprisonment or a fine of 500,000 rupees (section 3). Section 4 provides that offences shall be instituted 'upon a complaint made to the Police, following the procedure laid down in section 136 of the Code of Criminal Procedure Act, No.15 of 1979. The prior written sanction of the Attorney-General should be obtained for the institution of proceedings under this Act'.

Notes and Questions

1. Is the 2009 anti-conversion Bill likely to promote unity or conflict between persons of different religious groups, considering the criminal sanctions under it? What impact would it have on fundamental rights? Is it a remedy proportionate to the harm it seeks to redress, to 'save the Buddhists, Hindus and Christians . . . from American evangelical Christian missions': see 'Sri Lanka Buddhist party wants to bring Anti Conversion Bill back', *Colombo Page*, 11 November 2011, at <http://www.colombopage.com/archive_11B/Nov11_1320982985KA.php>.

2. The Government drafted its own anti-propagation bill with a broader reach (available at <http://www.lankaliberty.com/legislation/index.html>). See T Hresko, 'Rights Rhetoric as an Instrument of Religious Oppression in Sri Lanka' (2006) 29 *Boston College International & Comparative Law Review* 123.

3. What impact would the Bill have on free speech or charitable activities, like providing shelter and medical attention, given the vague nature of its terms and the broad discretion conferred on state officials to determine what legitimate proselytism is?

4. What tests could state officials use to determine what motivates conversion? Does imposing more onerous penalties for proselytising 'vulnerable' women and children treat them like contemporary state wards?

5. In 2004, the Jathika Hela Urumaya (JHU – National Heritage Party) issued a draft Constitutional Amendment Bill to make Buddhism the state religion. The proposed *Nineteenth Amendment to the Constitution (Constitutional Amendment Bill)* was published in the *Gazette* on 1 November 2004 and presented before Parliament by the Venerable Ellawala Medhananda Thero, MP, on 18 November

2004. This proposed *Nineteenth Amendment* was challenged before the Supreme Court in December 2004, and the Court held Clauses 9(1) to 9(5) inconsistent with Articles 3, 10, 12(1), 12(2) and 14(1)(e) of the Constitution and concluded that since the Bill sought to repeal Article 9 of the Constitution in terms of Article 83(a), it must be passed by a Parliamentary special majority and approved by the people at a Referendum in order to become law. See 'Sri Lanka Court deems Buddhism bill unconstitutional', *Dhamma Times*, 7 January 2005, at <http://www.dhammathai.org/e/news/m01/bnews07_2.php>.

6. What impact would this currently stalled Bill have on the religious freedoms of the non-Buddhist minorities? Would this product of militant Buddhist nationalism effectively end religious freedom? See generally M Deegalle, 'Politics of the Jathika Hela Urumaya Monks: Buddhism and Ethnicity in Contemporary Sri Lanka' (2004) 5(2) *Contemporary Buddhism* 83.

d. Restrictions on Religious Propagation: Intrinsic and Instrumental Motivations

Restrictions on the freedom of religious propagation may flow from intrinsic motivations independent of substantive restrictions. For example, Article 3 of the Malaysian Constitution identifies 'Islam' as the Federation's religion, but as Shia Islam is considered deviationist in a Sunni-majority country, the propagation of Shia Muslim teaching is an offence.[97] The Indonesian Ministry of Religion issued Decree 70/1978 on the Guidelines for the Propagation of Religion, providing that there should be no targeting of someone who already has a religion and no use of deceptive means.

In Singapore, there are no substantive or person-based restrictions on religious propagation, although ministerial statements have urged religionists not to evangelise Muslims but to focus on other citizens instead, given geopolitical sensitivities, Singapore being located between two Muslim-majority states: Malaysia and Indonesia. Propagation, a constitutional right, is viewed as a public order threat

> when followers become over-zealous and self-righteous in their missionary activities, and carry them out in an aggressive and insensitive manner, disregarding the feelings of other religions. Unlike previously, devotees of the different faiths today appear to be less tolerant over perceived slights to their religion, and are more ready to retaliate.[98]

Religious citizens involved in proselytising activities have been charged under the Sedition Act (Cap 290), where a capacious definition of 'sedition' includes as an offence having seditious tendencies, the promotion of 'feelings of ill-will and hostility between different races or classes of the population of Singapore' (section 3(1)). In Singapore, 'race' is closely correlated with 'religion' with respect to the overwhelmingly Muslim indigenous Malay population. A Protestant Christian couple was convicted under the Sedition Act for distributing tracts to people with Muslim sounding names in *Ong Kian Cheong v PP*.[99] The District Court observed:

---

[97] J Liow, *Piety and Politics: Islamism in Contemporary Malaysia* (Oxford: Oxford University Press, 2009) at 163.

[98] Speech by Deputy Prime Minister Wong Kan Seng, 'ISD Intelligence Service Promotion Ceremony', 14 March 2010, [19], at <http://www.mha.gov.sg/news_details.aspx?nid=MTcwNQ%3d%3d-?,Q9CJuc52SKk%3d>.

[99] *Ong Kian Cheong v PP* [2009] SGDC 163.

81. The observations the court made with regard to race in *PP v Koh Song Huat Benjamin* [2005] SGDC 272 apply equally to making insensitive and denigrating remarks about religion or religious beliefs. In our multi-racial and multi-religious society, distributing tracts with callous, denigratory, offensive and insensitive statements on religion with aspersions on race do have a tendency to cause social unrest thereby jeopardizing racial and religious harmony.

82. As citizens of Singapore, both the accused cannot claim to be ignorant of the sensitivity of race and religion in our multi-racial and multi-religious society. Common sense dictates that religious fervor to spread the faith, in our society, must be constrained by sensitivity, tolerance and mutual respect for another's faith and religious beliefs. Both the accused by distributing the seditious and objectionable tracts to Muslims and to the general public clearly reflected their intolerance, insensitivity and ignorance of delicate issues concerning race and religion in our multi-racial and multi religious society. They both acted on their own accord without ensuring that the tracts were suitable for distribution to the general public.

This raises the question of whether the exercise of the constitutional right of propagation may be considered seditious.[100] A rights-based orientation to religious free speech would yield a different approach, as seen in the Philippines case of *Iglesia ni Cristo v Court of Appeals*,[101] where the petitioner, a religious group, challenged a government board's decision to prohibit the airing of a religious programme which was highly critical of Catholicism (the Philippines' dominant religion). Religious freedom was a fundamental right and infringements would be subject to heightened scrutiny to ascertain whether a substantive and imminent evil existed to justify the restriction:

> Under our constitutional scheme, it is not the task of the State to favor any religion by protecting it against an attack by another religion. Religious dogmas and beliefs are often at war and to preserve peace among their followers, especially the fanatics, the establishment clause of freedom of religion prohibits the State from leaning towards any religion . . . Neutrality alone is its fixed and immovable stance . . . [the] respondent board cannot squelch the speech of petitioner Iglesia ni Cristo simply because it attacks other religions, even if said religion happens to be the most numerous church in our country . . . the remedy against bad theology is better theology. The bedrock of freedom of religion is freedom of thought and it is best served by encouraging the marketplace of duelling ideas.[102]

Question

1. Is this an adequate response, in the face of volatile inter-religious conflict?

e. Legal Regulation, Relational Constitutionalism, and Religious Propagation and Harmony

Where the state's primary object is to maintain inter-religious harmony, it may deploy a variety of approaches to deal with religious disputes with public order implications. First, it can apply punitive legislative sanctions as a deterrent. For example, section 298 of Singapore's Penal Code criminalises acts that the perpetrator knows to be 'prej-

---

[100] See generally Thio Li-ann, 'Contentious Liberty: Regulating Religious Propagation in a Religiously Diverse Secular Democracy' (2010) *Singapore Journal of Legal Studies* 484.

[101] *Iglesia ni Cristo v Court of Appeals*, GR No 119673, July 26, 1996, at < http://www.lawphil.net/judjuris/juri1996/jul1996/gr_119673_1996.html>.

[102] Ibid.

udicial to the maintenance of harmony between different religious or racial groups' and disturb public tranquillity. The wrongdoer is punished for violating fundamental social values and undermining public order by provoking inter-group disharmony. Secondly, the state may adopt pre-emptive measures, as in the case of Singapore's Maintenance of Religious Harmony Act (Cap 167A) which authorises ministerial restraining orders to be issued against a religious leader, such as a priest or *imam*, who has committed or is attempting to commit action which causes 'feelings of enmity, hatred, ill-will or hostility between different religious groups'.[103] This pre-empts religious disharmony by restraining the potential perpetrator.

Where the Singapore Government seeks to manage inter-religious group tensions arising from the actions of religionists or irreligious conflict entrepreneurs, a form of relational constitutionalism is evident:

> This operates against the background legal framework and seeks to promote the relational well-being of individuals and groups and to preserve sustainable relationships in a polity where disparate religious groups and their members are able to co-exist, maintain their distinct identities, while being unified by a national identity and a shared commitment to the common good. While public order speaks to the absence of disorder or disruption to public life, the goal of maintaining 'racial and religious harmony' speaks to the quality of relationships and a vision of community. As social trust is essential, the methods of relational constitutionalism may downplay strict insistence on rights; this favours informal regulation to promote reconciliation where social ties are strained, by appealing to hortatory norms in non-binding instruments adopted with some degree of formality, such as the 2003 Declaration on Religious Harmony, drafted by a committee of religious representatives chaired by a junior government minister. This contains broad guidelines designed to influence the expectations and behaviour of constitutional actors, through the reciprocal internalization of social norms as a form of self or co-regulation.[104]

Where an inter-religious dispute arises, and a complaint is made and investigated by the authorities, the Government has stood in the background and through quiet diplomacy urged the relevant religious parties and grass-roots leaders to discuss the issue with common sense and reconciliatory intent. It has then reiterated 'soft constitutional norms' contained in non-binding instruments such as White Papers or Declarations as 'best practices', extolling the virtues of 'inter-religious communication', 'religious tolerance', and 'racial and religious harmony' as aspirations better given to persuasion than coercion.

The Singapore Government has stressed the liberty to propagate one's religion while underscoring a prudential rule of non-denigration in the responsible exercise of a constitutional liberty, to reinforce community expectations. The Government has warned that no one should be allowed to exploit any issue to stir emotions and tensions between ethnic and religious communities, and has voiced approval of the reconciliatory efforts of alienated religious leaders. For example, the Prime Minister attended a Taoist function where Taoist and Church leaders sought to overcome frictions and offenc,es and to develop friendly relations by singing Hokkien ballads. This reflects a concern not merely with peace but with solidarity, which requires social trust, a

---

[103] Maintenance of Religious Harmony Act (Cap 167A), s 8(1)(a).
[104] Li-ann Thio, 'Relational Constitutionalism and the Management of Religious Disputes: The Singapore "Secularism with a Soul" Model' (2012) *Oxford Journal of Law & Religion* 1, 3.

function of relational well-being and appreciation of the mutuality of responsibilities necessary for peaceful co-existence.[105]

Relational well-being is also promoted through creating bodies with dialogical and interactive functions, such as Singapore's Presidential Council of Religious Harmony which advises the President on associated matters, two-thirds of which is composed of religious leaders, and the creation of inter-racial and religious confidence circles in 2002, to promote dialogue between religious leaders.

In 2005, the Indonesian Ministry of Religious Affairs and the Ministry of Interior issued an Ordinance establishing the Inter-Religious Harmony Forum (*Forum Kerukunan Umat Beragama*). This is composed of local religious leaders tasked with conducting dialogue with religious leaders and believers, accommodating the aspirations of religious community organisations, formulating policy recommendations in conjunction with government officials to ensure inter-religious harmony and educating the community on relevant laws relating to religious harmony. It provides a formal channel where religious leaders and the Government can discuss inter-religious issues, and a formal mechanism where religious leaders can gather to address sectarian issues before they escalate into conflict.

In February 2010, the Special Committee to Promote Inter-religious Understanding and Harmony was created under the Malaysian Prime Minister's Office,[106] to promote dialogue among religious groups and to diffuse inter-religious tensions, such as the announcement of a seminar by Johor authorities on the 'threat of Christianisation' to Muslims, which sparked outrage.[107]

In August 2012, a Pakistan Minister announced his Government's intention to creation an inter-faith council for religious harmony, comprising religious scholars to discuss the promotion of sectarian harmony.[108] The volatility of religious conflict necessitates a multi-pronged approach to the problem which transcends legal solutions; it introduces into the vocabulary of constitutional discourse something beyond rights; the focus is on other aspects of human relations such as duty, prudence, forbearance, sensitivity, common sense and forgiveness, with the overall goal of preserving a relationship through rapprochement, rather than terminating a relationship through sustained antagonism or intimidation. Social trust cannot be mandated by law, but legally established dialogue forums or exhortatory norms which generate community expectations of compliance can help nurture this commodity.

III. RIGHT TO PRACTICE

The right to religious practice, which includes teaching, worship and observance individually or in community with fellow believers, is part of the *forum externum* and subject to state regulation. The scope of permissible limitations will be shaped by the

---

[105] Ibid at 19–22.

[106] 'New Acts to Provide a Balance for Individual Rights, Civil Liberties and Public Order Safeguards', 1Malaysia.com, at <http://1malaysia.com.my/zh/news_archive/new-acts-to-provide-a-balance-for-individual-rights-civil-liberties-and-public-order-safeguards/>.

[107] S Teoh, 'Inter-faith chief says will act on provocative "Christian threat" seminar', *Malaysian Insider*, 28 March 2012.

[108] 'Govt to create inter-faith council for religious harmony', *Express Tribune* (Pakistan), 24 August 2012.

public philosophy shaping state attitudes towards religion. Zones of conflict emerge in the tussle between traditional religious practices and individual rights, or the practices of religious minorities and majoritarian law.

A. Religious Dress Codes in Public Schools/Institutions

There has been a great deal of constitutional and human rights litigation over clashes between religious dress and state policies mandating school uniforms to create a religion-free zone where all citizens are guaranteed equality, in Western polities and beyond.[109] The German, Swiss and Turkish constitutional courts[110] have accepted the state's characterisation of the *hijab* (Islamic veil) as a fundamentalist threat to secularism, democracy, public order, tolerance and gender equality,[111] the 'proselytising effect' of which, as a powerful religious symbol, might affect the religious freedom of others, particularly when worn by teachers in their capacity as state representatives.[112] The House of Lords in the United Kingdom held that a public school could ban the *jilbab* (loose head-to-toe Muslim dress), even though this restricted religious practice, to ensure other girls were not pressured into wearing more extreme forms of Islamic dress.[113] In other jurisdictions, proportionality reviews and invocations of multiculturalism as part of religious freedom have invalidated policies barring Sikhs from wearing *kirpans* (ceremonial daggers) in schools,[114] and the ripping away of religious traditions by a school ban on *hijab* has been considered unreasonable.[115]

In Singapore, a ban on the *tudung* (female scarf) in primary schools was justified by the Government as a legitimate restriction on religious freedom on two primary grounds. First, the uniforms policy was to facilitate integration among the different racial groups and to promote national unity through ensuring public schools were 'common spaces' where similarities were emphasised. This could conceivably be related to particularistic 'public order' concerns. Secondly, the fear was that exempting the *tudung* from the uniforms policy would spark similar demands for exemptions, such as Muslims demanding that girls be segregated from boys in secular schools. Notably, there is no blanket ban on religious symbols, as Christians may wear non-ostentatious crosses and Sikhs their turbans. The Government justified this differentiated treatment

---

[109] See Li-ann Thio, 'Judges and Religious Questions: Adjudicating Claims to Wear Religious Dress in Public Schools' (2007) 2 *Journal of Religion and Human Rights* 119.

[110] *Teacher Headscarf decision*, Judgment of 24 September 2003, BVerfGE 108, 282; Case No 2 BvR 1436/02 (Bundesverfgassungsgericht [BVerfG] Constitutional Court, 24 Sept 2003); *Sahin v Turkey* App no 44774/98 (ECtHR, 10 November 2005). For example, the Grand Chamber in *Sahin* adopted the Turkish Constitutional Court's view (Judgments of 7 March 1989, 9 April 1991) that the headscarf had been 'regularly appropriated by religious fundamentalist movements for political ends', threatening women's rights: *Sahin v Turkey*, App No 44774/98 (ECtHR, Grand Chamber, 29 June 2004) para 11.

[111] See J Marshall, 'Freedom of Religion and Gender Equality: Sahin v Turkey' (2006) 69(3) *MLR* 452.

[112] See the Swiss Federal Court decision of 12 November 1997, cited in *Dahlab v Switzerland* App no 42393/98 (ECtHR, 15 February 2001), translation at <http//:www.strasbourgconference.org/ caselaw/ DahlabvSwissDecision.pdf> at 15; *US v Board of Education of School District & Commonwealth Philadelphia* 911 F 2d 882, 889 (1990) (noting a child's 'possible conclusion of endorsement' of religion over non-religion).

[113] *R (on the application of Begum) v Head Teacher and Governors of Denbigh High School* [2005] 2 All ER 487 (HL).

[114] *Multani v Commission Scolaire Marguerite-Bourgeoys* (2006) SCC 6 (Supreme Court, Canada).

[115] *Sumayyah Mohammed v Moraine* [1996] 3 LRC 475, 486 (High Court, Trinidad & Tobago).

on pragmatic grounds, noting that Sikhs could not carry *kirpans* in schools and that the wearing of turbans was a practice dating back to British colonial times.[116]

Clearly, the issues engaged in clashes between religious dress and symbols and general laws are complex, often involving a tension between 'the feminist freedom of state education over the patriarchal dominance of their families' and the 'liberal principle of respect for individual autonomy and cultural diversity'.[117] There have been cases in Asian jurisdictions which transcend these tensions: one involving the state enforcement of a religious dress code from Bangladesh, and the other, a ban on a form of male Islamic headwear associated with more fundamentalist expressions of Islam within Malaysia. These are explored in more detail below.

i. State Enforcement

Salahuddin Dolon v Government of Bangladesh
Writ Petition No 4495 of 2009 (High Court, Bangladesh)

Facts

Article 2A of the Bangladesh Constitution provides that the state religion is Islam, 'but other religions may be practiced in peace and harmony in the Republic'. Article 102 empowers the High Court division, on application of an aggrieved person, to give directions or orders to any person or authority 'as may be appropriate' to enforce Part III fundamental rights. An Upazila District Primary Education Officer directed that all female teachers were to wear *burqa* at a meeting; 50 female teachers protested. The Officer then derogatorily called the primary school Headmistress a 'prostitute' and uncultured, whereupon she fell senseless and was hospitalised. The Deputy Director of Primary Education later apologised. Advocate Sara Hossain for the co-petitioner argued that the impugned action of attempting to impose dress codes on women constituted sexual harassment and gender discrimination, violating their constitutional rights of personal liberty, freedom of expression, movement and religion. The following extract relates to religious freedom issues.

Syed Mahmud Hossain, J

How an educated man of the status of a Thana Education officer could utter the word . . . (uncultured prostitute) to a Headmistress of a Government Primary School is not comprehensible. It is the personal choice of a woman to wear veil or to cover her head. Any such attempt to control a woman's movement and expression – and further in this case threatening the teacher concerned for her failure to do so – is clearly a violation of her right to personal liberty.

In Bangladesh there has been no uniform practice of veiling or head covering among women. However, in recent years, there have seen such attempts to forcibly impose dress codes not only by private persons and extremist political organizations, claiming to act on the basis of religion, but also by persons in authority, including those in public office.

---

[116] Thio Li-ann, 'Recent Constitutional Developments: Of Shadows and Whips, Race, Rifts and Rights, Terror and Tudungs, Women and Wrongs' (2002) *Singapore Journal of Legal Studies* 328, 355–66.
[117] Per Baronness Hale, *R (on the application of Begum) v Headteacher and Governors of Denbigh High School* [2006] 2 All ER 487 [96].

In the absence of any legal sanction, attempts to coerce or impose a dress code on women clearly amount to a form of sexual harassment. To the extent the derogatory term used against the teacher was sexually coloured and it also targeted her as a woman by requiring her to cover her head, a requirement which was not made to any other male teacher in the school, such action amounts to sexual harassment and to a form of gender discrimination.

As Article 29 occurring in chapter III of [the] Constitution states . . . there shall be equality of opportunity for all citizens in respect of employment or office in the service of the Republic and that no citizen shall, on the grounds only of religion, race, caste, sex or place of birth, be ineligible for, employment or office in the service of the Republic and that no citizen shall, on the grounds only of religion, race, caste, sex or place of birth, be ineligible for, or discriminated against, in respect of any employment or office in the service *of* the Republic . . . [Article 28(2)] . . . specifically provides that women should have equal rights with men in all spheres of the State and of public life . . . Article 39 of the Constitution guarantees freedom of thought, conscience and expression. Freedom of expression ranges from the articulation of words and images to actions and lifestyle choices, including choices around one's manner of dress and behaviour. Subjecting a woman to harassment [for failing] to cover her head, is a discriminatory act [violating the constitutional equality clause] and inconsistent with international standards.

Arbitrary and intrusive gender-based codes for acceptable demeanour and dress also violate the rights to privacy and to free expression protected under international law, as well as the right of women to protection from violence.

[The court referred to relevant international instruments, including the ICCPR, UDHR and ICESCR, regarding rights of privacy, expression, life, liberty and security, the prohibition against torture or cruel and inhuman punishment, non-discrimination, and just and favourable work conditions. The court took note of General Recommendation 19 (1992) of the CEDAW Committee. Conventions are not judicially enforceable unless incorporated by domestic legislation, although the court will look to ratified conventions to facilitate the interpretation of Part III fundamental liberties.]

. . . [H]arassment of women and girls is endemic in public spaces, schools, institutes of higher education and workplaces, both public and private sectors . . . [T]his Court in *Bangladesh National Women Lawyers Association (BNWLA) v Government of Bangladesh* . . . (2009) 29 BLD (HCD) 415 issued guidelines for the prevention of sexual harassment directing the Government to enact legislation to address this issue immediately, pending which the guidelines would have the force of law . . . [Under these guidelines] . . . sexual harassment includes:

4(i)(c) Sexually coloured verbal representation;
4(i)(f) Sexually coloured remark or gesture.

. . . Rule 27A [of the Government Servants (Discipline and Appeals) Rules] states:

(Conduct towards female colleagues):
No Government servant shall use any language or behave with his female colleagues in any manner which is improper and goes against the official decorum and dignity of female colleagues.

This Rule 27 is to be read with the definition of sexual harassment given in Guideline 4 [as] formulated by this Court in *Bangladesh Jatiya Mahila Ainjibi Samity v Government of Bangladesh*, (2009) 29 BLD (HCD) 415 in the case of Government servants [which should also be followed in public and private educational institutions pending legislation] . . .

Since respondent no 3 has tendered [an] unqualified apology and since the victim accepted that apology, we have decided not to impose any prescribed punishment on respondent no 3 but [he] should be immediately withdrawn/transferred so the victim could not be subjected to any further harassment . . . by this respondent.

. . . [T]he Rule is disposed of with the following direction:

(1) The Ministry of Education (MOE) . . . is directed to ensure that the women working in different educational institutions . . . both in public and private sectors are not subjected to similar harassment by their superior and others.

(2) The MOE shall ensure that the women working in educational institutions both in public and private sectors are not subjected to wearing [a] veil or covering their head against their will . . .

(3) The MOE is also directed to implement guidelines formulated in *Bangladesh Jatiya Mahila Ainjibi Samity v Government of Bangladesh* for all educational institutions under [its control], both in private and public sectors, and to report through the Registrar of the Supreme Court about action taken on those guidelines.

Note and Questions

1. Is wearing *burqa* an expression or suppression of religious liberty? Who decides? See A Sengupta, 'Burqa freedom in Bangladesh', *Telegraph* (India), 5 October 2010.

ii. State Restraint (Singapore and Malaysia)

Meor Atiqulrahman bin Ishak v Fatimah bte Sihi
[2006] 4 MLJ 605 (Federal Court, Malaysia)

Facts

Four schoolboys were prohibited from wearing the *serban* (Muslim turban) to public school as this violated uniforms policy under the Ministry of Education's School Regulations.

Abdul Hamid Mohamad FCJ (delivering judgment of the court)

[L]earned counsel for the appellants argued that the regulation prohibiting students from wearing turban violates the provisions of art 11(1) of the Federal Constitution . . .:

11(1) Every person has the right to profess and practise his religion and, subject to clause (4), to propagate it.

. . . He submitted that the right to practise one's religion includes every religious practice 'which have some basis or become part of that religion whether they are mandatory or otherwise.' That right can only be restricted if, by exercising such rights, it affects public order, public health and public morality enshrined in art 11(5) of the Federal Constitution. Learned counsel further submitted that the right to wear turban, even though not mandatory, is part of 'Islamic prophetic teaching'.

The Court of Appeal . . . applied the test of whether 'the right to wear a "serban" is an integral part of the religion of Islam' [noting there was insufficient evidence placed before it that wearing serban was mandated by Islam] . . .

. . . The Court of Appeal was criticised for relying on Indian authorities, especially because of the differences between the provisions of the Indian Constitution and the

Federal Constitution, in particular, the preamble to the Indian Constitution declares India to be a secular state and no religion of the state is provided. It is also said, who is to decide whether a particular practice is an integral part of a religion or not?

. . . [W]e are only concerned with the words 'practise his religion'. There is no doubt that the 'integral part of the religion' approach has its merits. Otherwise, in a country with many religions being practised, to allow a regulation or law to be declared unconstitutional just because someone claims that it prohibits his 'religious practice' no matter how trivial it is and even though in a very limited way, would lead to chaos. However, in my view, that test has its demerits too, because it would lead to the following results: so long as a practice is an integral part of a religion, any restriction or limitation, even regulatory, would be unconstitutional. On the other hand, if the practice is not an integral part of a religion, it can even be prohibited completely. The circumstances under which the law or regulation is made may be such that it is justifiable to restrict or regulate it during a period and at the place when and where it is to operate. A constitution is expected to be in force so long as the country exists but circumstances may change dramatically from time to time, even from place to place. On the other hand, a practice may not be an integral part of the teaching of a religion, in the Islamic sense, it may be a 'sunat' eg performing the 'sunat' prayers. Using this test, it can be prohibited absolutely and forever. I do not think that is right.

. . . [W]hether a practice is or is not an integral part of a religion is not the only factor that should be considered. Other factors are equally important in considering whether a particular law or regulation is constitutional or not under art 11(1) . . . I would therefore prefer the following approach. First, there must be a religion. Secondly, there must be a practice. Thirdly, the practice is a practice of that religion. All these having been proved, the court should then consider the importance of the practice in relation to the religion [noting that greater weight should be accorded if it was a compulsory or mandatory practice] . . .

The next step is to look at the extent or seriousness of the prohibition. A total prohibition certainly should be viewed more seriously than a partial or temporary prohibition. For example, a regulation that prohibits an adult Muslim male from leaving his job to perform the Friday prayer is more serious than a regulation that requires adult male Muslims employees to take turns to perform their 'Asar' prayer, all within the 'Asar' period. Then, we will have to look at the circumstances under which the prohibition is made. An air traffic controller will have to be at his post even during Friday prayers, where replacement by a non-Muslim or a female employee is not possible. A surgeon who starts an emergency operation just before the 'Maghrib' prayer may have to miss his prayer. (Even the Shariah provides exceptions and relaxation of its application under certain circumstances.)

. . . [A]ll these factors should be considered in determining whether the 'limitation' or 'prohibition' of a practice of a religion is constitutional or unconstitutional under art 11(1) [concludes that wearing turban was of little significance to Islamic religious practice: see discussion of this case in section I.B. above] . . .

. . . So, the 'practice' is of little significance from the point of view of the religion of Islam, what is more, in relation to underaged boys. Certainly, it is not a part of 'Islamic prophetic teaching' . . .

Moving to the second factor . . . ie the extent of the 'prohibition'. We are not dealing with a total prohibition of wearing of the turban. The . . . primary school students . . . are not allowed to wear the turban as part of the school uniform, ie during the school hours. They are not prevented from wearing the turban at other times. Even in school, certainly, they would not be prevented from wearing the turban when they perform, say, their 'Zohor' prayer in the school 'surau' (prayer room). But, if they join the 'Boy Scouts', it is only natural if they are required to wear the Scouts uniform during its activities. Or, when they play football, naturally they would be required to wear shorts and T-shirts. Should they be allowed to wear 'jubah' [loose fitting outfit worn by Arabs] when playing football because it was the practice of the Prophet (PBUH) to wear jubah? Following the arguments or learned counsel for the appellants, they should. Certainly, there is a place for everything.

Furthermore, there is nothing to prevent them from changing school, *eg*, to a 'pondok' school that would allow them to wear the turban.

To accept the learned counsel's argument would mean that anybody has a right to do anything, any time, anywhere which he considers to be a practice of his religion, no matter how trivial. The only limit is clause (5). To me, that cannot be the law.

Coming now to the third factor . . . ie the circumstances under which the 'prohibition' was made. Whether we like it or not, we have to accept that Malaysia is not the same as a Malay State prior to the coming of the British. She is multi-racial, multi-cultural, multi-lingual and multi-religious. It is difficult enough to keep the 14 States together. By any standard, Malaysia's success has been miraculous in terms of unity, peace and prosperity. Whatever other factors that had contributed to it, we cannot ignore the educational system that had helped to mould the minds of Malaysian boys and girls to grow up as Malaysians. Recently, we heard about 'polarization' of students at universities not only on racial and religious grounds but also among the Muslim students themselves. The polarization was considered serious and even a dangerous trend. Hence, national service was introduced. Of course, such polarization does not begin the moment the students step into the campus. The seeds were sown and grew while they were in school. Our educationists, with their experience in dealing with students on the ground, should be given some respect and credit when they formulate some regulations applicable in their schools for the general good of all the students, the society and later the nation.

Look at these three appellants . . . they were made to spend [their formative] years being different from other students, disregard the school regulations, disobey the teachers, rebel against the authorities, just because Syed Ahmad, described by the learned trial Judge as 'angkuh' [arrogant], wanted the three appellants to wear the turban to school because the turban is his family's emblem! [Considering all these factors, Article 11(1) was not breached by the prohibition on turbans.] . . .

Note and Questions

1. How would you characterise the judicial approach in *Meor Atiqulrahman*?

2. In the balancing process, what factors were relevant, and how were they weighed?

3. Was an appropriate balance struck between religious freedom and state interests?

4. See Li-ann Thio and J Ling-Chen Neo, 'Religious Dress in Schools: The Serban Controversy in Malaysia' (2006) 55 *International & Comparative Law Quarterly* 871.

B. Limits to Right to Religious Organisation – Public Order Considerations

Decision Upon the Case Where the Dissolution Order on the Grounds Provided by Article 81(1)(1) and (2) of the Law on Religious Organizations is Not Against Art 20(1) of the Constitution
1996 (ku) 8, Minshū Vol 50, No 1, at 199 (Tokyo High Court) (trans Sir Ernest Satow)

Note

A dissolution order was sought to disband the Aum Shinrikyo, a religious group that produced sarin gas with the goal of mass murder. This was challenged as infringing Article 20 of the Constitution of Japan, which reads:

> Freedom of religion is guaranteed to all. No religious organization shall receive any privileges from the State, nor exercise any political authority.

Justices Ono Motoo, Takahashi Hisako, Endo Mitsuo & Fujii Masao

The Law does not intend to interfere with the freedom of religion such as the conduct of religious rituals by the believers (Art 1(2), Law). The Dissolution Order addressed to religious organisations as provided by article 81 of the Law is designed to enable the compulsory dissolution of religious organisations by judicial procedure and the deprivation of juridical personality in cases where there was an act which is against the law and substantially harms public welfare (Art 81(1)(1), Law), an act which substantially exceeds the goal of a religious organisation (Art 81(1)(2)), or where the organisation ceased to have the substance of a religious juridical person or juridical organisation (Art 81(1)(3)–(5)), since in such cases, it is inappropriate or unnecessary to leave the religious organisation with legal capability. This is similar to the order to dissolve companies (art 58 of the Commercial Code).

Therefore, even if a religious organisation is dissolved as a result of a dissolution order, believers are not prevented from continuing a religious organisation without juridical personality or from creating such an organisation anew, nor are they prevented from conducting religious acts or from procuring new installations or equipment for the exercise of such acts. The Dissolution Order does not accompany any legal effect which prohibits or limits religious acts by the believers. Admittedly, when a dissolution order takes effect, a liquidation procedure follows (Art 49(2), Art 51, Law), and as a result, the assets of the religious organisation such as the installation for rituals and other assets used for religious acts will be disposed of (Art 50, Law), and there is a possibility of some disruption to the continuation of religious acts which the believers had been conducting by using these assets. Although legal regulations on religious organisations do not accompany the effect of legally restricting the religious acts of the believers, if there is a possibility of some disruption to them, in light of the significance of religious freedom which is one of the spiritual freedoms guaranteed by the Constitution, whether the Constitution allows such restrictions should be examined carefully . . .

. . . [T]he system of the dissolution order of religious organisations . . . is solely for an eclectic purpose, and does not intend to interfere with the spiritual and religious aspects of religious organisations or the believers, and thus, the goal of the system is reasonable . . . A, who was the representative officer of the kokoku appellant,[118] and many cadres of the organisation under the instruction of A, plotted to produce sarin, which is a poisonous gas,

---

[118] An interlocutory appeal, protest and complaint.

for the purpose of mass murder and produced it systematically in an organised manner by mobilising many believers, using the installations and financial resources of the appellant. It is evident that the kokoku appellant has acted against the law and committed an act which is substantially against public welfare and has substantially exceeded the goal of a religious organisation. In order to deal with such an act by the kokoku appellant, it is necessary and appropriate to dissolve the kokoku appellant and to deprive it of its juridical personality. On the other hand, although it is unavoidable that by the dissolution order, there is some disruption to the religious acts by Aumu Shinrikyo as a religious organisation and its believers, such a disruption remains an indirect and de facto outcome of the dissolution order. Therefore, the Dissolution Order, even when considering the effect it may have on the spiritual and religious aspects of Aumu Shinrikyo as a religious organisation and its believers, can be regarded as a necessary and unavoidable legal regulation in order to deal with the acts of the kokoku appellant.

    . . . [T]he freedom of religious acts should be respected to the maximum degree possible, but it is not absolutely limitless . . . the Order Dissolution [is not] against Article 20 of the Constitution . . .

Notes and Questions

1. What factors did the Tokyo High Court consider in deciding it was 'reasonable and necessary' to dissolve the religious group?

2. How would this compare to the decision of the Singapore Home Affairs Minister to dissolve the Jehovah's Witnesses under Order 179 of 1972 issued under the Societies Act (Cap 311), which the High Court upheld in *Chan Hiang Leng Colin v PP*.[119] The sect had been dissolved for these official reasons:

    > [The Jehovah's Witnesses'] continued existence is prejudicial to public welfare and good order in Singapore. The doctrine of the sect and nature of its propaganda are based on its claim that Satan and its dispensation are responsible for all organized Government and religion. The result of the impending 'Armageddon' will be the destruction of everyone except Jehovah's Witnesses who will inherit the earth. By virtue of this doctrine the sect claims a neutral position for its members in wartime. This has led to a number of Jehovah's Witnesses in the National Service to refuse to do any military duty. Some of them even refuse to wear uniforms.([quoted at [3]).

    Chief Justice Yong reasoned thus (at [63]–[64], [68]):

    > The appellants contended that there was no evidence produced or even alleged to show that the Jehovah's Witnesses were a threat to public order. Article 15(4) clearly envisages that the right of freedom of religion is subject to inherent limitations and is therefore not an absolute and unqualified right . . . I am of the view that religious beliefs ought to have proper protection, but actions undertaken or flowing from such beliefs must conform with the general law relating to public order and social protection. The right of freedom of religion must be reconciled with 'the right of the State to employ the sovereign power to ensure peace, security and orderly living without which constitutional guarantee of civil liberty would be a mockery' (*Commissioner, HRE v LT Swamiar* AIR 1954 SC 282). The sovereignty, integrity and unity of Singapore are undoubtedly the paramount

---

[119]   *Chan Hiang Leng Colin v PP* [1994] 3 SLR(R) 209.

mandate of the Constitution and anything, including religious beliefs and practices, which tend to run counter to these objectives must be restrained.

. . . In my view, it was not for this court to substitute its view for the Minister's as to whether the Jehovah's Witnesses constituted a threat to national security . . . the appellants had the burden of showing that the Minister had exercised his powers wrongly. This court was not here to review the merits of the decision and conclude that the Jehovah's Witnesses were or were not a threat to public order. From the evidence adduced, it appeared that the Minister was of the view that the continued existence of a group which preached as one of its principal beliefs that military service was forbidden was contrary to public peace, welfare and good order. That was, in essence, the relevant finding. I could not see how the concept of public order as envisaged under Art 15(4) is dissimilar to the notion of public peace, welfare and good order within s 24(1)(a) of the Societies Act. Therefore, Order 179 could not have contravened Art 15(1) or been ultra vires s 24(1)(a).

3. To reinforce the dissolution order, the Minister of Culture banned all Jehovah Witnesses' publications (WTBTS) under the Undesirable Publications Act. On this point, the Court determined in relation to this prohibition order (at [71]–[72], [74]):

[I]t was argued that the order was unexpected, undiscriminating, excessive and sweeping. It was contended that such power to prohibit all publications of a specified publisher should only be exercised when the publisher habitually published materials contrary to the public interest. It was argued that many of the publications could not have been regarded as contrary to the public interest. Counsel illustrated this contention by stating that the ban would extend to the King James Version of the Bible as well, as long as it was printed and published by WTBTS. It was argued that this was wholly unreasonable as the King James Version was widely circulated in Singapore. I do not see the merit of this contention. The fact that one publication is unobjectionable as to its contents, be it the King James Version or 'Alice in Wonderland', does not make the ban unreasonable per se. Instead, it was not unreasonable . . . for the Minister to prohibit all publications by WTBTS. The Minister's actions were clearly to stop the dissemination and propagation of beliefs of the Jehovah's Witnesses and this would of necessity include every publication by WTBTS. Any order other than a total blanket order would have been impossible to monitor administratively.

. . . [T]he then Minister for Culture was satisfied that the Jehovah's Witnesses' teachings and beliefs contained in publications published or printed by WTBTS would be contrary to the public interest, in that they were prejudicial to the Government's efforts in nation building, in setting up the national armed forces and in maintaining national security, unity, integrity and sovereignty . . . It was clear to me that the process of de-registration and the prohibition of the publications were a joint operation by both Ministers . . . the respective Ministers were clearly of the view that the continued existence of the Jehovah's Witnesses was prejudicial to the national interest. The basis for the de-registration clearly flowed from the danger of allowing absolute freedom of religion which might create a complete denial of a government's authority and ability to govern individuals or groups asserting a religious affiliation. The Jehovah's Witnesses were not mere conscientious objectors to national service but were engaging in conduct which was prejudicial to national security. The activities of the Jehovah's Witnesses were therefore restricted on the basis that they were against the 'public order'. Equally, the prohibition on their publications was a natural consequence and was therefore in the 'public interest'. In my view, the respective decisions were not irrational or disproportionate.

4. Evaluate the balancing approach adopted in *Chan Hiang Leng Colin v PP* and its understanding of 'public order'. What impact does this have on religious freedom? Was 'public order' (which limits religious freedom under Article 15(4)) equivalent to 'national security' concerns, which is reserved in the Singapore Constitution for emergency laws and special anti-subversion legislation, over which there is only truncated judicial review (see Article 149, Singapore Constitution).

IV. RELIGIOUS EXEMPTIONS: CONSCIENTIOUS OBJECTION

Tensions arise when an individual faces a choice between his religious and social obligations. Accommodation is necessary to find a *via media* between individual freedoms and significant civic interests, such as through exemptions from general laws. States like Singapore and Malaysia adopt statutes regulating the administration of Muslim law in relation to personal and family matters.

Religious tenets may clash with legal obligations or policies on the basis of conscientious objection, particularly where refusal to perform military service stems from pacifist religious beliefs. Article 77 of the Vietnam Constitution, for example, describes defending the homeland as 'a sacred duty', and states that 'Citizens are duty-bound to do military service and take part in building a national defence of the whole people'. Some constitutions, like section 45 of the Timor-Leste Constitution, guarantee the right to be a conscientious objector in accordance with the law.

The issue arises as to whether religious freedom includes a right to be exempted from such duties, or in the alternative to perform substitute civilian service. In Asia, as elsewhere, there have been instances where Jehovah's Witnesses have refused to participate in combative physical education programmes or military service. Courts have had to grapple with whether conscientious objection, as a facet of free conscience, is part of religious freedom guarantees, so as to supersede civil obligations, requiring exemption or accommodation.

A. Combative Sport in Schools

Matsumoto v Kobayashi
50 Minshū 469, 8 March 1996 (Supreme Court, Japan)

Facts

A Jehovah's Witness studying at Kobe Municipal Technical College refused to participate in the compulsory physical educational programme as it involved Kendo (Japanese fencing), a combative sport. The College denied his request to take alternative forms of physical education, necessary to complete an academic year, and tried to persuade him to take part in catch-up kendo practices. He was expelled under Article 31 of the School Rules ('If an individual has an inferior level of academic ability and is not expected to accomplish his/her studies . . .'). The Court did not consider the propriety of the decision itself but examined the principal's exercise of discretionary power, considering whether it had any factual foundation or was inappropriate given social views, so as to constitute abuse of discretion. It found the expulsion decision to be illegal and beyond the scope of his discretionary authority.

Article 20 of the Japan Constitution (1946) provides:

Freedom of religion is guaranteed to all . . . No person shall be compelled to take part in any religious act, celebration, rite or practice. The State and its organs shall refrain from religious education or any other religious activity.

Article 3(1) of the Basic Law on Education provides that all people should have the equal opportunity to receive an education and are not to be discriminated against, inter alia, on the basis of creed. Article 9 provides:

An attitude of tolerance towards religion and the place of religion in social life shall be respected in education. Schools established by the State and local public bodies shall refrain from religious education that is only in the interests of a particular religion or any other religious activity.

Justices Kawai Shinichi, Ohnishi Katsuya, Negishi Shigeharu & Fukuda Hiroshi (unanimously)

With a view to ensuring the national standard of education . . . it cannot be denied that in the public education curriculum, it is necessary to help students acquire a certain level of essential knowledge, ability, etc proportionate to each school year, and the completion of physical education as a subject is no exception to this need. As for technical colleges . . . it is rather hard to conclude that students should take kendo practice as a requisite, but the Court assumes that the educational purpose of physical education as a subject can . . . be accomplished in alternative ways, as its contents are concerned, and . . . neither of the said dispositions can be said to directly restrict the freedom of religion guaranteed to the Appellee; it is obvious that these two dispositions are of such a nature that the Appellee had no choice but to participate in kendo practice, which was an activity in conflict with the doctrine underlying his faith, to avoid grave disadvantages inflicted by these dispositions . . . Even if the measures taken by the Appellant did not aim at restricting his freedom of religion or religious acts specifically, or even if these measures were taken in accordance with general stipulations concerning the development of the curriculum and the way of evaluating the accomplishments thereof, so long as each of the said dispositions had said nature, the Court is of the opinion that the Appellant should have given due consideration . . . in exercising the said discretionary authority. Furthermore, it should not be automatically seen as justifiable to put the Appellee at the tremendous disadvantage [because he had chosen a school where kendo is part of PE activities] . . .

. . . [T]he Court holds that sufficient consideration should have been given to the rightness of offering any alternative activity . . . but there is no proof of any such consideration such as by participating in other PE activities . . .

[The Court rejected the argument that technical difficulties would be faced should the College have to offer alternative practices as there were other schools which offered a non-combative option without creating a sense of unfairness in other students.]

. . . [I]t can be easily clarified through investigation of external circumstances whether the refusal to participate arises for religious reasons or not, and it is not rational to assume that a large number of students refuse to attend particular classes for falsely-claimed reasons of religious faith. Moreover, the Court upholds the original determination that finds that it was unlikely that order could not be maintained in the educational setting in Kobe Technical

College or that the operation of the school as a whole might be hampered in a manner too serious to be overlooked if alternative activities were offered. Hence, it cannot be said that it was practically impossible to offer alternative activities.

[The Court rejected the argument that offering alternative measures promoted a specific religion contrary to Article 20(3).]

. . . It is not permissible for public schools to ask about or scrutinize students' religious faith, or rank religions hierarchically and treat each one differently, but when a student refuses to participate in kendo practice for reasons of religious faith, the school, in order to determine the justifiability of the reasons, makes an investigation to determine whether it is an excuse for idleness, or whether there is any rational relevance between the religious teachings explained by the student in question and the refusal to participate, which is not construed as a case that would undermine the neutrality of public education in relation to religion.

Notes and Questions

1. The Court did not decide the case on constitutional grounds but on the administrative law ground of 'abuse of discretion'. While recognising the student could either practise kendo and violate his own religious convictions or refrain and be expelled, the Court did not hold that forcing one to make such a choice was unconstitutional. In contrast, US courts have found that where religious believers had to take 'sides between God and government', the Government could release them (Souter J, *Lee v Weisman* 505 US 577, 628 (1992)). See *Sherbert v Verner* 374 US 398, 406 (1963): '[T]o condition the availability of benefits upon this appellant's willingness to violate a cardinal principle of her religious faith effectively penalizes the free exercise of her constitutional liberties.'

2. Did the Court hold that the College should impose a substitute requirement to accommodate the Jehovah's Witnesses student, so as not to benefit religion over non-religion? See Eiichiro Takahata, 'Religious Accommodation in Japan' (2007)3 *Brigham Young University Law Review* 729.

3. How did the Court reconcile granting a religious exemption with the anti-establishment clause and the need for religious neutrality in public education? Must a religious exemption be given just because a student claims one? When must accommodation be made? Japanese courts have adopted a 'purpose and effect' test to ascertain whether the anti-establishment clause has been violated by state involvement in religion, similar to the US test in *Lemon v Kurtzman* 403 US 602, 612–13 (1971), in *Kakunaga v Sekiguchi* (*Tsu City Shinto Groundbreaking Ceremony case*) 31 Minshū 533 (Sup Ct, July 13, 1977), which the Court cited in *Matsumoto*. Prohibited state involvement involves activity which promotes or suppresses religion. The three-pronged *Lemon* test stipulates that a statute must have a 'secular legislative purpose', its primary effect must not advance nor inhibit religion, and it must not foster 'an excessive government entanglement with religion'.

4. On how the European Court of Human Rights handled the refusal of a Jehovah's Witness to attend a National Parade because her pacifism required avoidance of all military events, see *Efstratious v Greece* App No 24095/94 (ECtHR, 18 December 1996).

B. Military Service

Conscientious Objection to Military Service Case
16-2(A) KCCR 141 2002Hun-Ka1, August 26, 2004 (Constitutional Court, South Korea)

Facts

Under South Korea's Military Service Act (MSA), all 19- to 35-year-old Korean men are obliged to perform military service for 21–24 months. This Act does not provide alternative service options, neither does it recognise a right to conscientious objection. Penalties include up to six months' imprisonment or a fine of two million Korean Won. A Jehovah's Witness, failing to enrol for military service after receiving notice of enlistment, challenged the Act's constitutionality. The Constitutional Court considered whether the MSA infringed the free conscience of those who objected to military service on religious grounds. Its constitutionality was upheld in a 7:2 decision.

Held

Article 19 of the Constitution provides that 'All citizens shall enjoy freedom of conscience.' . . . Collision between the legal order of the nation and the conscience of the individuals would always occur, should a minority of the citizens refuse, by asserting the freedom of conscience, to obey the legal order determined by the majority.

Conscience that is protected by the Constitution is . . . the powerful and earnest voice of one's heart, the failure to realize which in action upon judging right and wrong of a matter would destroy one's existential value as a person . . . The 'conscience' that the 'freedom of conscience' intends to protect is not synonymous to the thoughts and the values of the democratic majority; rather, it is something that is extremely subjective . . . The conscience may not be judged by its object, content or motivation . . . whether the decisions from the conscience are reasonable and rational . . . or consonant to the legal order, social norm or ethical rules may not serve as the standard that judges the existence of the conscience . . .

The freedom of conscience under Article 19 of the Constitution is largely divided into the internal realm of the formation of the conscience and the external realm of the exercise of the conscience that has been formed . . . [T]he freedom to form the conscience is an absolutely protected basic right as long as it stays within one's heart, while the freedom to exercise the conscience that is the right to externally express and realize the conscientious decisions is a relative freedom that may be restricted by the statute as it may violate the legal order or infringe upon the right of others . . .

Article 39 of the Constitution provides for the duty of national defense as the obligation of the citizens, and Article 3 of the Military Service Act . . . imposes the duty of military service upon all male citizens of the Republic of Korea [and imposes criminal punishment for non-compliance] . . .

. . . The statutory provision at issue . . . compels the conscientious objectors to act against their conscience by way of criminal punishment . . . it is a provision that restricts the 'freedom not to be forced by the state to act against one's conscience' or the 'freedom not to perform legal obligation that is against one's conscience,' that is, the right to exercise the conscience by inaction.

On the other hand, as Article 20(1) of the Constitution separately protects the freedom of religion, should the conscientious objection to military service be based upon religious doctrines or religious beliefs, the statutory provision at issue in this case restricts the freedom of religion of the conscientious objectors as well . . .

The Constitution provides in Article 5(2) that the 'guarantee of national security' and the defense of the national territory are the sacred duties of the national armed forces. The Constitution further provides in Article 39(1) for the duty of national defense as an important means to realize the guarantee of national security . . . [T]he Constitution indicates in Article 37(2) that all freedoms of the citizens may be restricted for the guarantee of national security . . . as an important constitutional legal interest . . . [which is] an indispensable prerequisite for the existence of the nation, preservation of the national territory, protection of the life and safety of the citizens, and . . . a basic prerequisite for the exercise of the freedom by all citizens . . . [noting that freedom of conscience is a constitutional right and that the existence of the nation was basic to the exercise of all freedoms such that if all individuals refused to obey the legal order on grounds of conscience regardless of whether this is] unreasonable, unethical or antisocial, the position that the 'legal order of the nation is valid only as long as it is not against the conscience of the individuals' means the disintegration of the legal order and . . . national community . . .

. . . [T]he freedom of conscience of Article 19 of the Constitution does not endow individuals with the right to refuse the performance of the duty of military service. The freedom of conscience is no more than the right to request the state to take into account and protect the individual conscience if possible, and is not the right to refuse to perform legal obligations on the ground of conscience or the right to request the provision of alternative obligations. Therefore, the right to request alternative military service may not be drawn from the freedom of conscience. Our Constitution does not have any normative expression therein that recognizes the unilateral superiority of the freedom of conscience, with respect to the duty of military service . . .

The issue of guaranteeing the freedom to exercise the conscience is the question of harmonizing the 'freedom of conscience' and the 'constitutional legal interest' or 'legal order of the state' that the restriction of the freedom of conscience intends to achieve, and the question of balancing between these two legal interests.

However, the freedom to exercise the conscience takes a special form in the balancing process between the legal interests. The general process of scrutiny of the proportionality principle that determines to which extent a fundamental right should concede on the ground of public interests, through examination of the appropriateness of the means and the least restrictive means, does not apply as unchanged to the freedom of conscience . . . [B]alancing the freedom of conscience against the public interest under the principle of proportionality and rendering the conscience relative in order for the realization of the public interest is not compatible with the essence of the freedom of conscience. Should a conscientious resolution be diminished to a state that is compatible with the public interest or be distorted and refracted in its substance in the process of balancing of the legal interests, this is not 'conscience' any more . . . Therefore, in the case of the freedom of conscience, it is not to realize both of the legal interests at the same time by reaching the state of harmony and balance through balancing between the freedom of conscience and the public interest; instead, there is only the choice between the 'freedom of conscience' and the 'public interest,' that is, the question of whether an action or inaction against conscience is 'compelled or not compelled' by the legal order.

When the individuals claim that their freedom to exercise conscience is infringed by a statute, it is the case where the statute does not give a special consideration to their unique situation of ethical conflict while imposing a legal obligation that is applicable to all citizens . . .

The question of whether the state guarantees the freedom to exercise conscience is the question of whether the legal community possesses the possibility of relieving the conscientious conflicts through a means respectful of the conscience of the individuals [and also implicates national and social tolerance towards how minorities are treated] . . .

The freedom of conscience is a basic right that imposes an obligation to establish the legal order so that the freedom of conscience may be guaranteed as much as possible, primarily upon the legislators . . . If the legislators do not present an alternative while an alternative may be presented without obstructing the public interest or the legal order, this may be unconstitutional as a unilateral compulsion of sacrifice upon the freedom of conscience. However, exempting without imposing any of the alternative obligations on those who claim the freedom of conscience from the obligation that is applicable to all citizens is equivalent to the endowment of a privilege that is not permissible under the Constitution. Therefore, if the freedom of conscience requests an exception from the obligation of the citizens, the state should offset such an unequal element through the imposition of the alternative obligations if possible, in order that the national tolerance and the permission of exceptions does not become a privilege of the few.

. . . [A]s a solution to harmonize the conflicting legal interests of the conscience and the obligation to military service, we may consider an alternative civil service system . . . under which the conscientious objectors provide service for the public interest in, for example, the state institutions, the public organizations and the social welfare facilities . . . Currently, many of the nations have actually adopted this system on the constitutional or statutory basis, thereby resolving the situation of the conflict between the conscience and the obligation to [perform] military service.

. . . [T]he constitutionality of the statutory provision at issue in this case is ultimately the question of judging 'whether the legislators may still effectively achieve the public interest of national security while permitting an exception to the duty of military service through the adoption of an alternative service system.' In judging whether or not to adopt an alternative service system, the legislators should comprehensively take into account the overall state of security of the nation, the combat capability of the nation, the demand of military resources, the quantity and the quality of the human resources subject to the conscription, the expected change in the combat capability in time of adoption of an alternative service system, the meaning and the significance of the duty of military service under the national security situation of Korea, the national and the social demand for the equal allocation of the performance of the duty of military service, the actual condition of the military service, and so forth . . .

[The Court set forth two predictions, one optimistic and one pessimistic: the optimistic one noted the relatively small number of conscientious objectors, the changing nature of warfare, the feasibility of alternative service systems adopted in other countries to resolve problems of conscience and equality.]

. . . On the other hand, however, a pessimistic prediction can be made as follows. Our nation is the only divided nation in the world that is under the state of truce, and the South and the North are still in a hostile opposition state based upon extremely strong military powers accumulated through the arms races in the past. Under this unique security situation, the duty of military service and the principle of equality in allocating the burden of military service have an important meaning that is incomparable to other nations. Although it is true that there has been a change in the concept of national defense and the aspect of the modern warfare, the proportion of the human military resources in the national defense power may still not be neglected, and the natural decrease in the military resources due to the decrease of birth-rate of these days should also be taken into consideration.

Considering the tough conditions of military service on active duty in our nation, it is not easy to secure the equivalence of the burdens through the alternative service, and there is a danger that the attempt to realize the equivalence of the burdens might render the alternative service into a measure punishing the realization of one's conscience.

In addition, although the proportion of the conscientious objectors to the overall number of individuals subject to conscription is not great at the current stage, we may not rule out the possibility that the preventive effect of deterring the evasion of military service by way of the criminal sanctions might abruptly be dissipated by the adoption of the alternative service system. In light of the past experience of our society that corruption and the trend to evade military service continued incessantly, it is too much of an optimism to expect to completely prevent solely by institutional preventive measures, the intentional evasion of military service by abusing the alternative service system. In our society where the social demand for the equality in the burden of military service is strong and absolute, should the equality in performing the obligation become a social issue due to the permission of an exception to the duty of military service, the adoption of the alternative service system might cause a serious harm to the capacity of the nation as a whole by crucially injuring the social unification and might further destabilize the backbone of the entire military service system based upon the mandatory conscription of all citizens.

Should the constitutionality of a statute restrictive of the basic right depend upon the legal effect that will be materialized in the future as in this case, the question lies in to which extent the Constitutional Court may review the predictive legislative judgment [and] to which degree the Constitutional Court may substitute its own judgment on estimation for the uncertain predictive judgment of the legislators.

The right of the legislators to make predictive judgment varies . . . The more significant the public interest intended to be achieved is, and the greater the influence on others and the national community the individuals exert through the exercise of the basic right is, that is, the greater the social relevance of the exercise of the basic right is, the broader formative power is given to the legislators. Therefore . . . the only thing . . . subject to review is whether the predictive judgment of the legislators . . . may clearly be refuted or is plainly wrong. To this extent, the judgment with respect to which means [to] employ to realize the public interest should be left to the legislators . . .

. . . [T]he public interest that the statutory provision at issue . . . intends to achieve is a very important public interest of 'national security' . . . When such an important public interest is at issue, we may not request an immoderate legislative experiment that might harm national security in order for the maximum guarantee of the liberty of the individuals. Furthermore, as the realization of one's conscience by way of refusing to perform the duty of military service is requesting an exception from the duty of military service that is applicable to all, judging from the perspective of equal allocation of the burden of the duty of military service, the pervasive effect over others and the entire social community will be great, thus a strong social relevance of the exercise of the basic right is recognized . . . [The judicial test is thus limited to] the test of 'whether the legislative judgment is conspicuously wrong.'

As a matter of principle, determining . . . important policies concerning national security is the task for the legislators [whose judgment should be respected] . . . [T]he current situation does not assure that the adoption of the alternative service system will not harm the important constitutional legal interest of national security. In order for the adoption of the alternative service system, the peaceful coexistence between South Korea and North Korea should be established, the incentives for evading military service should be eliminated through the improvement of the condition of the military service, and, further, a consensus should be formed among the members of the social community that permitting the alternative service will harm neither the realization of equality in the burden of performing the duty of military service nor the social unity, through the widespread understanding and tolerance of the conscientious objectors. At the current stage where such prerequisites are yet to be satisfied, the legislative judgment that the time is not ripe for the adoption of an alternative service system, may not be deemed to be clearly unreasonable or plainly wrong . . .

The issue of conscientious objectors has now become a major [national] issue . . . The phenomenon of rejecting military service on the ground of religious conscience has existed since a long time ago primarily among the Jehovah's Witnesses, and, recently, this phenomenon has spread among the Buddhists and the pacifists. Those who evade . . . military service are not only criminally punished . . . but also subject to significant social disadvantages such as restrictions on becoming public officials or serving as directors or officers and the prohibition on obtaining permissions, approvals and licenses for various government-licensed businesses . . . The number of conscientious objectors still remains . . . small. However, as the legislators have had so far a sufficient opportunity and time to recognize and affirm that the enforcement of the statutory provision at issue in this case collectively causes the situation of conscientious conflict, we are of the opinion that now is the time to seek a national solution of our own through a serious social discussion with respect to how to take the conscientious objectors into account, instead of neglecting [their suffering and conflict] . . .

[The Court noted that the European Union has since 1967 adopted resolutions recognising conscientious objection to military service. A 1997 UN survey found that of 93 states with mandatory conscription systems, less than half did not recognise conscientious objection.]

. . . [T]he legislators should earnestly assess whether there is a solution for eliminating the conflict relationship between the legal interests of the freedom of conscience and the national security and for enabling the coexistence of these two legal interests, whether there is an alternative to protect the conscience of the conscientious objectors while securing the realization of the public interest of national security, and whether our society is now mature enough to understand and tolerate the conscientious objectors. Even if the legislators decide not to adopt an alternative service system, the legislators should seriously consider whether to supplement the legislation in the direction that the institutions implementing the law may take measures protecting the conscience through the conscience-favoring application of the law.

. . . Therefore, it is hereby held that the statutory provision at issue in this case is not in violation of the Constitution . . .

Justices Kim Kyung-il & Jeon Hyo-sook (dissenting)

[*Note*: The dissenting opinion underscored the centrality of free conscience in realising democracy and human dignity, rejecting any relaxing of judicial scrutiny. Whether the conscience is shaped by religion (Article 19) or otherwise (Article 20), the 'extent of sincerity' must be such that to violate it 'would disintegrate the existential value of one's personality'. The dissenting judges also referred to ICCPR standards, opining that South Korea was not living up to its international obligations.]

On the Standard of Review

[W]hen there is a collision or conflict between a basic right and other constitutional values, the legislators should not seek to unilaterally realize such other constitutional values, yet, instead, should seek an alternative to avoid the collision or conflict, and, even when an alternative may not be provided and the restriction of the basic right is inevitable, such restriction should stay within the scope that is in proportion to the purpose thereof. This is the content included in the principle of the restriction of basic right under Section 2 of Article 37 of the Constitution . . .

On the Importance of Free Conscience and the Possibility of Alternative Service

[T]he ideal of peace represented in the forms of . . . non-violence, prohibition of killing, and pacifism has been sought for and respected by the human race for a long period of time . . . [T]he objection to military service by the conscientious objectors may not be deemed as an attempt to avoid the hardships of the military service or a demand for protection as free-riders while failing to perform the basic duty owed to the national community. They do not deny the sincere performance of their various other duties including that of taxation as members of the community, and sincerely petition to be provided with an alternative means of service that is no easier than the military service . . .

. . . [W]e are of the opinion that the legislators are now obligated to search for a solution to achieve harmony by settling the conflict relationship between the freedom of conscience and the equal performance of the duty of military service by way of, for example, providing an alternative solution, and, further, that it is sufficiently possible in reality to satisfy such obligation.

. . . [I]n terms of the numbers, the proportion of the conscientious objectors does not reach the extent that will cause a decrease in military power or combat capacity. In addition, the fact that they have continuously objected to enlistment or bearing arms despite criminal punishment . . . corroborates that criminal punishment may not be expected to [have a deterrent effect] . . .

. . . [T]he duty of national defense is not limited to the obligation to directly form military force by bearing arms . . . Therefore, if an obligation that is equivalent to or severer than military service on active duty in light of its duration and burden is to be imposed upon them, the equality in performing the duty of national defense may be restored and the debate over providing the conscientious objectors with an unjust privilege will also cease . . . [Other nations] such as Germany, Denmark, France, Austria, Italy, Spain, Brazil and Taiwan have resolved the issue of equality in performing the duty of military service and maintained the conscription system without any notable problems by having the conscientious objectors serve as non-combat force within the military or in the alternative civilian duties. These nations generally utilize as the alternative civilian duties tasks such as rescuing activities, patient transportation, fire-fighting, service for the disabled persons, environmental improvement, agriculture, refugee protection, service at the youth protection centers, preservation and protection of cultural heritage, service at the prisons or rehabilitation institutions . . .

It should be specifically noted that having the conscientious objectors perform support tasks necessary for the public interest of the state, public organizations or social welfare facilities, and [allowing] those with expert knowledge and abilities [to] serve the public interest by utilizing it, will [more greatly benefit] national security in the broad sense, than compelling military service on active duty by bearing arms . . .

. . . [T]his problem [of equivalence of obligations] may also be settled by obligating them to [undertake] physical training for a specific time period in lieu of military training . . . and by making the duration of service longer than that for military service on active duty reflecting the time period of military force mobilization training.

[On avoiding corruption and evasion of military service] . . . it is possible to select the true conscientious objectors from those who are not through strict preliminary review processes and post management . . . [T]he greater the burden and the hardship of the alternative service would be, the corollary would be the decrease [in the numbers] of such evaders of the military service . . .

We conclude . . . that the legislators have failed to make even the minimum effort to harmonize, by resolving a serious and long conflict, the relationship between the duty of military service and the freedom of conscience of the conscientious objectors, who are social minorities, in compelling the enforcement of the duty of military service . . . [T]he statutory provision at issue . . . is unavoidably unconstitutional to the extent that it uniformly compels enlistment and imposes criminal punishment upon the conscientious objectors.

Notes and Questions

1. The majority opinion made recommendations to legislators on conscientious objection. Could this be viewed as a dangerous judicial intrusion into legislative power? Does this reflect a dialogical rather than adversarial understanding of judicial review? See Kuk Cho, 'Conscientious Objection to Military Service in Korea: The Rocky Path from Being an Unpatriotic Crime to a Human Right' (2007) 9 *Oregon Review of International Law* 187.

2. What does the Article 19 guarantee of free conscience require of the South Korean Government? Does the substance of the belief itself matter?

3. How are constitutional rights balanced against constitutional interests in conscientious objection cases? Is there a difference between statutory and constitutional limits on rights? Why did the majority opinion reject the principle of proportionality, and what test did it propose? Were any unique factors identified?

4. Justice Lee Sang Kyung, in his separate concurring opinion, pointed out that the Constitution did not present a standard for resolving clashes of constitutional values. He considered inappropriate the passive review test espoused by the dissenting opinion, applying the standards in Article 37(2) which prioritises basic rights. He held that the Constitution's choice not to present a clear standard for settling clashes between constitutional values should be read as delegating to the National Assembly the task of making law which makes a reasonable demarcation between these conflicting values. Where the Constitution expressly authorised the restriction of a basic right to secure a particular public interest, this indicated a broader legislative discretion.

5. If a religious exemption is granted, what are the implications for equal protection under the law? How was this addressed by the South Korean Constitutional Court?

6. Two convicted Jehovah's Witnesses made complaints to the UN Human Rights Committee, which oversees the ICCPR to which South Korea is a party, in *Yeo Bum Yoon and Myung Jin Choi v Republic of Korea* Communications Nos 1321/2004 and 1322/2004. The majority Committee opinion was that the state failed to demonstrate that the restriction in question was necessary under Article 18(3) ICCPR, including not showing 'what special disadvantage would be involved' if Article 18 rights were fully respected. It noted that state respect for conscientious beliefs and manifestations were important factors 'in ensuring cohesive and stable pluralism in society' (para 8.4). Ruth Wedgewood in her dissenting opinion noted that while the provision of alternative service might be a best practice, the Covenant itself did not strictly require the right to refrain from mandatory military service.

7.   The European Court of Human Rights reversed a previous decision to hold that Article 9 ECHR ('freedom of thought, conscience and religion') protected the right to refuse to bear arms on moral or religious grounds. It considered that opposition to military service arising from deeply and genuinely held religious or other beliefs 'constitutes a conviction or belief of sufficient cogency, seriousness, cohesion and importance to attract the guarantees of Article 9'.[120] Most Council of Europe Member States have laws providing for various forms of alternative service for conscientious objectors, including Armenia under the Alternative Service Act of 17 December 2003.

8.   The inter-American human rights regime holds to the view that the American Convention protects conscientious objection only in countries where this is recognised: see *Cristián Daniel Sahli Vera v Chile*, Case 12.219, Report No 43/05, Inter-Am CHR, OEA/Ser L/V/II.124 Doc 5 (2005), Inter-American Commission on Human Rights, 10 March 2005.

Judicial Yuan Interpretation No 490
1 Oct 1999 (Constitutional Court, Taiwan) (trans Jiunn-rong Yeh)

Note

Article 13 of the Republic of China (Taiwan) Constitution guarantees that 'The people shall have freedom of religious belief', while Article 20 provides for 'the duty of performing military service in accordance with law'. The constitutionality of the Conscription Act, which requires eligible males to be drafted for military service, without exception for conscientious objection, was at issue. One refusing to perform military service is not relieved of this obligation unless he has been imprisoned for at least four years.

Reasoning

Except for the freedom of personal religious belief that shall be absolutely protected and never be infringed upon or suspended, it is permissible for relevant state laws to constrain, if necessary and to the least restrictive effect, freedoms of religious practices and association. For no one shall renounce the state and laws simply because of his/her religious belief. Thus, because believers of all religions are still people of the state, their basic responsibilities and duties to the state will not be relieved because of their respective religious beliefs.

   Protection of the people's fundamental rights such as their life and property is one of the most important functions and purposes of a state and the achievement of such function and purpose lies in the people's rendering of their basic duties to the state. In order to defend national security, it is very common for states with a conscription system to prescribe the people's duty to render military service. Article 20 of the Constitution requiring the people to perform military service pursuant to laws is precisely such type of enactment. The Constitution, however, does not specify the ways in which people should render such a duty. Important matters regarding people's military service shall be specified in laws and solely left to the Legislature's discretion with due consideration of national security and the needs of social development. Given the physical differences between males and females and the derived role differentiation in their respective social functions and lives, the Legislature enacted relevant Articles in the Conscription Act. Article 1 indicates that only male citizens

---

[120] *Bayatyan v Armenia*, App no 23459/03 (ECtHR, 7 July 2011) [110].

in accordance with laws have the duty to perform military service . . . prescribing a male citizen's duty to render military service does not violate human dignity, nor does it undermine the fundamental values in the Constitution. Most nations also prescribe such duty in their respective laws. Requiring such duty is a necessary measure to protect the people and to defend national security. As a result, it does not violate the equal protection principle of Article 7 or the protection of freedom of religious beliefs of Article 13.

Notes and Questions

1. Was this decision made through interpreting the content of religious freedom, or through balancing competing interests?

2. Of the 16 states that issued a Joint Statement on Conscientious Objection to Military Service, six were Asian states (China, Bangladesh, Myanmar, Singapore, Thailand, Vietnam). A letter dated 24 April 2002, from the Singapore Permanent Representative addressed to the Chair of the 58th Session of the Commission on Human Rights on 24 April 2002 (E/CN.4/2002/188), stated:

   2   National defence is a fundamental sovereign right under international law. Where individual beliefs or actions run counter to such a right, the right of a state to preserve national security must prevail. Article 29 of the Universal Declaration of Human Rights and Article 18 of the International Covenant on Civil and Political Rights recognise that the exercise of the rights and freedom of the individual is subject to the necessity of ensuring public order and the general welfare of the society.

   3   Where a state has established a compulsory military service system under which every citizen is legally required to serve, allowing individuals to be excused from military service would compromise the concept of collective responsibility for national defence, undermine national values and breach the principle of equal application of the law.

   4   . . . [W]e do not recognise the universal applicability of conscientious objection to military service and therefore disassociate ourselves from the resolution contained in E/CN.4/2002JL.62.

3. In Singapore's *Maintenance of Religious Harmony White Paper* (Parliament: Cmd 21 of 1989), the Government stated its policy on compulsory military service at para 26(b):

   Jehovah's Witnesses believe that their religion forbids them to do any form of National Service. Under the law this is criminal conduct, not conscientious objection. Followers of this sect who refuse to obey call-up orders are court martialled and serve jail sentences.

   In 1972, the Singapore Government de-registered the Congregation of Jehovah's Witnesses under the Societies Act because its members refused to perform compulsory military service under the Enlistment Act. As such, its 'continued existence is prejudicial to public welfare and good order in Singapore'. Jehovah's Witnesses' publications were banned under the Undesirable Publications Act. This was challenged as violating Article 15(1) of the Constitution which provides that 'Every person has the right to profess and practise his religion and to propagate it'. Clause

4 states the article 'does not authorise any act contrary to any general law relating to public order, public health or morality'. The following extract deals with this case.

Chan Hiang Leng Colin v Public Prosecutor
[1994] 3 SLR(R) 209 (Court of Appeal, Singapore)

Yong CJ

In this appeal . . . the main purpose of adducing the additional evidence was to show that the Jehovah's Witnesses were a respectable religious group whose fundamental tenets could not have been in any sense objectionable and contrary to public order and the public interest . . . [I]t must be pointed out that there had never been a suggestion that the adherents of Jehovah's Witnesses were not otherwise law-abiding citizens . . . The issue at hand was simply their belief which prohibits any form of military or national service, which is a fundamental tenet in Singapore. Anything which detracts from this should not and cannot be upheld.

. . . Mr How referred me to various judicial pronouncements in the United States on the right to freedom of religion. There is a fundamental difference between the right to freedom of religion under the First Amendment to the United States Constitution and Art 15. The American provision consists of an 'establishment clause' which proscribes any preference for a particular religion (*Congress shall make no law respecting an establishment of religion*) and a 'free exercise clause' which is based on the principle of governmental non-interference with religion (*Congress shall make no law prohibiting the free exercise thereof*). Significantly, the Singapore Constitution does not prohibit the 'establishment' of any religion. The social conditions in Singapore are, of course, markedly different from those in the United States. On this basis alone, I am not influenced by the various views as enunciated in the American cases cited to me but instead must restrict my analysis of the issues here with reference to the local context.

[The ban on the Jehovah's Witnesses] was described by the appellants as . . . a violation of the freedom of religion as enshrined in the Constitution and also a violation of international declarations of human rights. All things being said, I think that the issues here are best resolved by a consideration of the provisions of the Constitution, the Societies Act and the [Undesirable Publications Act] alone.

. . . It was then contended that there was nothing which showed that the activities of the Jehovah's Witnesses, being a small, non-violent Christian group, were in any way against public order. Mr How contended that the membership of the Jehovah's Witnesses in Singapore was small and the alleged prejudice to public welfare was therefore insignificant. Further, he submitted that there needed to be a clear and immediate danger to public order before the right of freedom of religion could be curtailed, and, in this case, the deregistration orders could not have been justified since there was no such threat at all. In my view, Mr How's submission that it must be shown that there was a clear and immediate danger was misplaced for one simple reason. It cannot be said that beliefs, especially those propagated in the name of 'religion', should not be put to a stop until such a scenario exists. If not, it would in all probability be too late as the damage sought to be prevented would have transpired. In my opinion, any administration which perceives the possibility of trouble over religious beliefs and yet prefers to wait until trouble is just about to break out before taking action must be not only pathetically naive but also grossly incompetent.

[Cites approvingly the wartime Australian case of *Adelaide Co of Jehovah's Witnesses Inc v The Commonwealth* (1943) 67 CLR 116, where the court upheld the National Security

(Subversive Associations) Regulations, which declared the Jehovah's Witnesses Adelaide Company as 'prejudicial to the defence of the Commonwealth and the efficient prosecution of war' such that the Government was empowered to take over their Adelaide premises.]

The court was of the unanimous view that Parliament was not prohibited from making laws which prohibited the advocacy of doctrines and principles which, though advocated in pursuance of religious convictions, were prejudicial to the prosecution of a war engaged by the Government.

. . . [A]dherents of the Jehovah's Witnesses clearly believed that military duty was prohibited by their religion, and, as a result, they refused to do national service. The appellants contended that there was no evidence produced or even alleged to show that the Jehovah's Witnesses were a threat to public order. Article 15(4) clearly envisages that the right of freedom of religion is subject to inherent limitations and is therefore not an absolute and unqualified right . . .

I am of the view that religious beliefs ought to have proper protection, but actions undertaken or flowing from such beliefs must conform with the general law relating to public order and social protection. The right of freedom of religion must be reconciled with 'the right of the State to employ the sovereign power to ensure peace, security and orderly living without which constitutional guarantee of civil liberty would be a mockery' (*Commissioner, HRE v LT Swamiar* AIR 1954 SC 282). The sovereignty, integrity and unity of Singapore are undoubtedly the paramount mandate of the Constitution and anything, including religious beliefs and practices, which tend to run counter to these objectives must be restrained.

I think it is useful to consider parts of the additional evidence submitted by the Prosecution. The Assistant Director of Manpower of the Ministry of Defence had stated in his affidavit that from 1972 until May 1994, 108 persons, who claimed to be Jehovah's Witnesses and who were liable to serve national service, had been disciplined under s17 of the Singapore Armed Forces Act (Cap 259) for wilfully refusing to comply with orders to put on military uniforms. Their reasons were that they were unable to render any form of military service, including obeying military orders or even saluting the flag, because their religion forbade them from doing so. The Assistant Director expressed the concern that such wilful disobedience of orders would affect the motivation of the Singapore Armed Forces and noted that 'the beliefs subscribed to by persons who profess to be Jehovah's Witnesses would, if recognised, mean that persons who enjoy the social and economic benefits of Singapore citizenship and permanent residence are excused from the responsibility of defending the very social and political institutions and structure which enable them to do so'. This concern was in fact reflected in Arts 128 and 131 of the Constitution under which a citizen may not renounce his citizenship unless he has discharged his liability for national service . . .

During the Second Reading of the Maintenance of Religious Harmony Bill (*Hansard*, 23 February 1990, p 1181), the then Minister for Trade and Industry and Second Minister for Defence (Services), BG Lee Hsien Loong noted:

National Service is clearly a secular issue in Singapore. Most religious groups recognize that. But one group maintains otherwise – the Jehovah's Witnesses. They refuse to do National Service, claiming that their religion does not allow them to do so. They do so in all sincerity, with great courage of conviction. Each year, a few dozen young men who are Jehovah's Witnesses have to be court-martialled because they refuse to do National Service, and then sentenced to detention. After two years, when they are released, the enlistment order is served upon them again. They refuse again, so we court-martial them again. They serve a second period of detention until, after two periods, we call it quits and deem it equivalent to your having served National Service. This was the first issue which I learnt about when I went into Mindef when we were dealing with these people harshly. So I asked, as a young officer, 'Why do we do that? It is a matter of conscience'.

But we have no alternative, as I learned, because they are violating the law. In many Western European countries, they would count as conscientious objectors. But the idea of conscientious objection does not apply in Singapore. There is no such tradition in Singapore. If we try to introduce the practice here, the whole system of universal National Service will come unstuck. Many other people will ask: why should I also not decide to have conscientious objections and therefore exempt myself from National Service? And of course, even in Western Europe, not all countries acknowledge conscientious objectors. In Switzerland, those who do not do National Service also go to jail. Therefore, the Enlistment Act in Singapore does not recognize conscientious objection. National Service is a secular issue, subject to government laws. Everybody accepts this, including all the other religious groups. In this case, the line between religion and politics is drawn clearly. But it is not drawn in the same place as in other countries.

. . . In my view, it was not for this court to substitute its view for the Minister's as to whether the Jehovah's Witnesses constituted a threat to national security . . . The basis for the de-registration clearly flowed from the danger of allowing absolute freedom of religion which might create a complete denial of a government's authority and ability to govern individuals or groups asserting a religious affiliation. The Jehovah's Witnesses were not mere conscientious objectors to national service but were engaging in conduct which was prejudicial to national security. The activities of the Jehovah's Witnesses were therefore restricted on the basis that they were against the 'public order'. Equally, the prohibition on their publications was a natural consequence and was therefore in the 'public interest'. In my view, the respective decisions were not irrational or disproportionate.

Notes and Questions

1. Given the Government's view that conscientious objection is not part of religious freedom, could the Court have decided otherwise? What factors were determinative in the judicial decision-making process, in relation to whether Article 15 rights were implicated?

2. What do you make of the 'balancing' process where primacy was accorded to matters of 'public order' or 'national security', which appeared to have been used interchangeably? While Article 15(4) refers to 'public order', the term 'national security' is reserved for anti-subversion or emergency legislation under Article 149, under which review is restricted to procedural grounds.

C. Refusal to Participate in Flag and Anthem Ceremonies on Grounds of Religious Objections

Nappalli Peter Williams v Institute of Technical Education
[1992] 2 SLR 569 (Court of Appeal, Singapore)

Facts

Nappalli, a Jehovah's Witnesss, was dismissed from his post at the Institute of Technical Education (ITE) for misconduct in refusing to take the National Pledge or sing the National Anthem during school assemblies, as required by ITE policy. This was unsuccessfully challenged before the High Court as violating his constitutional rights under Articles 15 and 16. He appealed.

Yong Pung How CJ (delivering the judgment of the court)

The appellant's case was as follows. He equated participation in the pledge and anthem ceremony with partaking in a religious ceremony, an act which the Jehovah's Witnesses strictly believe to be reserved for God. As such, he contended that the 1988 circular directing him to take the National Pledge and sing the National Anthem was in breach of his constitutional rights as expressed in Article 16(3). The appellant's case was that the pledge and anthem ceremony fell within the meaning of 'ceremony' used in Article 16(3)[121] . . . Article 16(3) seeks to protect persons from taking part in any ceremony or act of worship of a religion other than his own. Article 16(4)[122] leaves no doubt about this interpretation. Its purposes are to protect the position of those under 18 years of age, in respect of their choice of religion. Therefore, read together, Article 16(3) and 16(4) protect a person's right to choose his own religion. A person is entitled to refrain from participating in ceremonies of religions other than his own. For example, a Muslim cannot be 'required to take part in' a Christian ceremony such as the Holy Communion.

[The trial judge interpreted Article 16(3) to mean] that a person shall not be compelled to:

a. receive instruction in a religion other than his own;
b. take part in any ceremony in a religion other than his own; or
c. take part in any act of worship of a religion other than his own.

The trial judge then concluded that the ceremony in schools during which teachers and students take the National Pledge and sing the National Anthem was 'obviously not a religious ceremony' and rejected this submission. We agree with this ruling. In *Kruger & Ors v Commonwealth of Australia* 190 CLR 1; (1997) 146 ALR 126, the High Court of Australia had to determine whether the Aboriginals Ordinance 1918 (NT) was unconstitutional. The approach favoured by the full court of six judges, including Brennan CJ, was to ask whether the challenged provision has a purpose of achieving an object forbidden by the Constitution. Toohey J, at 190 CLR 1, 86, observed that the plaintiffs had to demonstrate that the policy complained of prohibited the free exercise of religion.

---

[121] Art 16(3): 'No person shall be required to receive instruction in or to take part in any ceremony or act of worship of a religion other than his own.'

[122] Art 16(4): 'For the purposes of clause (3), the religion of a person under the age of 18 years shall be decided by his parent or guardian.'

... [I]t has not been shown how the ITE's policy breached art 16. For example, the policy does not introduce compulsory 'Bible Knowledge' classes for all students including those under 18 years of age whose parents are not of the Christian faith. It simply enforces the pledge and anthem ceremony as part of a student's educational exposure. Clearly, the 'prescribed purpose' of the policy was to encourage and instil a student's allegiance to the nation. It did not seek to establish a religion other than the religion of one's choice.

In the same vein, the appellant relied on Article 15. He contended that the policy infringed his constitutional right to profess and practise his religion, contrary to Article 15(1). He sought to identify his conduct with that of 'conscientious objectors' in cases such as *Donald v Board of Education for the City of Hamilton* [1945] OR 518. The Canadian court in *Donald* found itself in no position to hold that their equivalent of the pledge and anthem ceremony bore no religious significance and awarded damages to the parents of children who had been expelled from school for failing to participate in the ceremony. This case does not apply to our local context. Firstly, the national anthem in *Donald* consisted of a prayer hymn. This unquestionably reflected some religious character. In contrast, the secular tenet of our Article 15 is reflected in the secular tone of the pledge and national anthem. The respect attributed to country implicit in the pledge-taking cannot be found to bear religious significance.

Secondly, the ruling in *Donald* turned on legislation which specifically provided that those who objected on religious grounds to saluting the flag or singing the national anthem were entitled to refrain from participation without forfeiting their right to attend school. This was in marked contrast to the nature of the right enshrined in Article 15 of our Constitution. The 'religion' referred to in Article 15 (and throughout the Constitution) is not about a system of belief in one's own country but about a citizen's faith in a personal God, sometimes described as a belief in a supernatural being. This can be seen in the contrast presented two clauses down in Article 15(4) – that Article 15 does not authorise any act contrary to any general law relating to public order, public health or morality. The State commands no supernatural existence in a citizen's personal belief system. Article 15 taken as a whole demonstrates that the paramount concern of the Constitution is a statement of citizen's rights framed in a wider social context of maintaining unity as one nation.

This should be distinguished from the broader definition accorded to religious belief in other jurisdictions. A belief confined to the realm of thought qualified as an absolute freedom protected by the Philippines' constitution while religious practices were held subject to regulation: *Ebralinag v Division Superintendent of Schools of Cebu* (1993) 219 SCRA 256. This acceptance that any belief or thought potentially holds religious value is, in our view, wholly misplaced. The complications of such a broad view are obvious from the comments of Justice Jackson in *West Virginia State Board of Education et al v Barnette et al* (1943) 319 US 624, at 632, that 'a person gets from a symbol the meaning he puts into it, and what is one man's comfort and inspiration is another's jest and scorn.'

In contrast, the protection of freedom of religion under our Constitution is premised on removing restrictions to one's choice of religious belief. This has been described as accommodative secularism. Obviously, not every conviction or belief, including those held with what ironically may best be described as religious fervour, qualifies as a religious belief. Indeed, we were inclined to agree with the view of the lower court in *Thomas v Review Board of the Indian Employment Security Division* (1981) 450 US 707 that such beliefs would best be philosophical choices rather than religious beliefs. In other words, although the pledge ceremony does not demand worship of the flag as a symbol, if a person held that understanding, that perception was a philosophical choice. It seemed clear to us that the appellant's interpretation of the pledge and anthem ceremony as a religious ceremony was a distortion of secular fact into religious belief. It is not accepted as a religious belief and is not entitled to protection under the Constitution of Singapore.

Indeed, to accept the appellant's interpretation would rob the Constitution of any operative effect. How can the same Constitution guarantee religious freedom if, by asking citizens to pledge their allegiance to country, it is (as the appellant suggests) coercing participation in a religious ceremony? This excruciatingly absurd interpretation cannot have been what was envisaged by the authors of the Constitution. Not only did the plaintiff fail to prove the unconstitutionality of the policy; but the irresistible conclusion for this court was that, in the present case, there was no valid religious belief protected by the Constitution.

Ebralinag v Division Superintendent of Schools of Cebu
GR No 95770, 1 March 1993, 219 SCRA 256 (1993) (Supreme Court, Philippines)

Facts

The student petitioners were Jehovah's Witnesses expelled from a Cebu public school for refusing to salute the flag, sing the national anthem and recite the patriotic pledge as required by Republic Act No 1265 of 11 July 1955, which makes the flag ceremony compulsory in all educational institutions. The Jehovah's Witnesses teach their children that such acts constitute acts of idolatry, and the petitioners claimed that to compel the flag salute and pledge transcended constitutional limitations on the state's power and invaded the sphere of the intellect and spirit which the Constitution protects against official control.

Grino Aquino J

This Court in the *Gerona vs Secretary of Education*, 106 Phil 2 (1959) case upheld the expulsion of the students, thus:

> The flag is not an image but a symbol of the Republic of the Philippines, an emblem of national sovereignty, of national unity and cohesion and of freedom and liberty which it and the Constitution guarantee and protect. Under a system of complete separation of church and state in the government, the flag is utterly devoid of any religious significance. Saluting the flag does not involve any religious ceremony. The flag salute is no more a religious ceremony than the taking of an oath of office by a public official or by a candidate for admission to the bar. In requiring school pupils to participate in the flag salute, the State through the Secretary of Education is not imposing a religion or religious belief or a religious test on said students. It is merely enforcing a non-discriminatory school regulation applicable to all alike whether Christian, Moslem, Protestant or Jehovah's Witness. The State is merely carrying out the duty imposed upon it by the Constitution which charges it with supervision over and regulation of all educational institutions, to establish and maintain a complete and adequate system of public education, and see to it that all schools aim to develop, among other things, civic conscience and teach the duties of citizenship. The children of Jehovah's Witnesses cannot be exempted from participation in the flag ceremony. They have no valid right to such exemption. Moreover, exemption to the requirement will disrupt school discipline and demoralize the rest of the school population which by far constitutes the great majority. The freedom of religious belief guaranteed by the Constitution does not and cannot mean exemption from or non-compliance with reasonable and non-discriminatory laws, rules and regulations promulgated by competent authority. (pp. 2–3)

. . . Republic Act No 1265 and the ruling in *Gerona* have been incorporated in Section 28, Title VI [which the petitioners have targetted] . . .

Our task here is extremely difficult, for the 30-year-old decision of this court in *Gerona* upholding the flag salute law and approving the expulsion of students who refuse to obey it, is not lightly to be trifled with. It is somewhat ironic however, that after the *Gerona* ruling had received legislative cachet by its in corporation in the Administrative Code of 1987, the present Court believes that the time has come to re-examine it. The idea that one may be compelled to salute the flag, sing the national anthem, and recite the patriotic pledge, during a flag ceremony on pain of being dismissed from one's job or of being expelled from school, is alien to the conscience of the present generation of Filipinos who cut their teeth on the Bill of Rights which guarantees their rights to free speech and the free exercise of religious profession and worship . . .

Religious freedom is a fundamental right which is entitled to the highest priority and the amplest protection among human rights, for it involves the relationship of man to his Creator . . . Petitioners stress, however, that while they do not take part in the compulsory flag ceremony, they do not engage in 'external acts' or behaviour that would offend their countrymen who believe in expressing their love of country through the observance of the flag ceremony. They quietly stand at attention during the flag ceremony to show their respect for the right of those who choose to participate in the solemn proceedings . . . Since they do not engage in disruptive behaviour, there is no warrant for their expulsion.

'The sole justification for a prior restraint or limitation on the exercise of religious freedom . . . is the existence of a grave and present danger of a character both grave and imminent, of a serious evil to public safety, public morals, public health or any other legitimate public interest, that the State has a right (and duty) to prevent.' Absent such a threat to public safety, the expulsion of the petitioners from the schools is not justified.

The situation that the Court directly predicted in *Gerona* that:

> The flag ceremony will become a thing of the past or perhaps conducted with very few participants, and the time will come when we would have citizens untaught and uninculcated in and not imbued with reverence for the flag and love of country, admiration for national heroes, and patriotism – a pathetic, even tragic situation, and all because a small portion of the school population imposed its will, demanded and was granted an exemption. (*Gerona*, p. 24.)

has not come to pass . . . After all, what the petitioners seek only is exemption from the flag ceremony, not exclusion from the public schools where they may study the Constitution, the democratic way of life and form of government, and learn not only the arts, sciences, Philippine history and culture but also receive training for a vocation or profession and be taught the virtues of 'patriotism, respect for human rights, appreciation for national heroes, the rights and duties of citizenship, and moral and spiritual values' (Sec 3[2], Art XIV, 1987 Constitution) as part of the curricula. Expelling or banning the petitioners from Philippine schools will bring about the very situation that this Court had feared in *Gerona*. Forcing a small religious group, through the iron hand of the law, to participate in a ceremony that violates their religious beliefs, will hardly be conducive to love of country or respect for dully constituted authorities.

As Mr Justice Jackson remarked in *West Virginia v Barnette*, 319 US 624 (1943):

> . . . To believe that patriotism will not flourish if patriotic ceremonies are voluntary and spontaneous instead of a compulsory routine is to make an unflattering estimate of the appeal of our institutions to free minds . . . Furthermore, let it be noted that coerced unity and loyalty even to the country . . . assuming that such unity and loyalty can be

attained through coercion – is not a goal that is constitutionally obtainable at the expense of religious liberty. A desirable end cannot be promoted by prohibited means. (*Meyer v Nebraska*, 262 US 390, 67 L ed 1042, 1046.)

Moreover, the expulsion of members of Jehovah's Witnesses from the schools where they are enrolled will violate their right as Philippine citizens, under the 1987 Constitution, to receive free education, for it is the duty of the State to 'protect and promote the right of all citizens to quality education . . . and to make such education accessible to all (Sec 1, Art XIV).

In *Victoriano vs Elizalde Rope Workers' Union*, 59 SCRA 54, 72–75, we upheld the exemption of members of the Iglesia ni Cristo, from the coverage of a closed shop agreement between their employer and a union because it would violate the teaching of their church not to join any labor group:

> . . . It is certain that not every conscience can be accommodated by all the laws of the land; but when general laws conflict with scruples of conscience, exemptions ought to be granted unless some 'compelling state interests' intervenes. (*Sherbert v Berner*, 374 US 398, 10 L Ed 2d 965, 970, 83 S Ct 1790.)

We hold that a similar exemption may be accorded to the Jehovah's Witnesses with regard to the observance of the flag ceremony out of respect for their religious beliefs, however 'bizarre' those beliefs may seem to others. Nevertheless, their right not to participate in the flag ceremony does not give them a right to disrupt such patriotic exercises . . . If they quietly stand at attention during the flag ceremony while their classmates and teachers salute the flag, sing the national anthem and recite the patriotic pledge, we do not see how such conduct may possibly disturb the peace, or pose 'a grave and present danger of a serious evil to public safety, public morals, public health or any other legitimate public interest that the State has a right (and duty) to prevent' (*German vs Barangan*, 135 SCRA 514, 517) . . . (expulsion orders annulled).

Cruz J (concurring)

It seems to me that every individual is entitled to choose for himself whom or what to worship or whether to worship at all. This is a personal decision . . . The individual may worship a spirit or a person or a beast or a tree (or a flag), and the State cannot prevent him from doing so. For that matter, neither can it compel him to do so. As long as his beliefs are not externalized in acts that offend the public interest, he cannot be prohibited from harbouring them or punished for doing so.

In requiring the herein petitioners to participate in the flag ceremony, the State has declared *ex cathedra* that they are not violating the Bible by saluting the flag. This is to me an unwarranted intrusion into their religious beliefs, which tell them the opposite. The State cannot interpret the Bible for them; only they can read it as they see fit. Right or wrong, the meaning they derive from it cannot be revised or reversed except perhaps by their own acknowledged superiors . . . Religion is forbidden territory that the State . . . cannot invade.

Freedom of speech includes the right to be silent . . . The salute is a symbolic manner of communication . . . As a valid form of expression, it cannot be compelled any more than it can be prohibited in the face of valid religious objections like those raised in this petition . . . This coercion of conscience has no place in the free society. The democratic system provides for the accommodation of diverse ideas, including the unconventional and even the bizarre or eccentric . . . The State cannot make the individual speak when the soul within rebels.

Resolution on Motion for Reconsideration GR No 95770 December 29, 1995
Facts: The state subsequently moved for a reconsideration of the Supreme Court's decision of 1 March 1993 above.

Kapunan J

No doubt, the State possesses what the Solicitor General describes as the responsibility 'to inculcate in the minds of the youth the values of patriotism and nationalism and to encourage their involvement in public and civic affairs.' . . . However, the government's interest in molding the young into patriotic and civic spirited citizens is 'not totally free from a balancing process' when it intrudes into other fundamental rights such as those specifically protected by the Free Exercise Clause, the constitutional right to education and the unassailable interest of parents to guide the religious upbringing of their children in accordance with the dictates of their conscience and their sincere religious beliefs . . .

The State's contentions are therefore, unacceptable, for no less fundamental than the right to take part is the right to stand apart . . . the freedom of religion enshrined in the Constitution should be seen as the rule, not the exception. To view the constitutional guarantee in the manner suggested by the petitioners would be to denigrate the status of a preferred freedom and to relegate it to the level of an abstract principle devoid of any substance and meaning in the lives of those for whom the protection is addressed. As to the contention that the exemption accorded by our decision benefits a privileged few, it is enough to re-emphasize that 'the constitutional protection of religious freedom terminated disabilities, it did not create new privileges. It gave religious equality, not civil immunity.' The essence of the free exercise clause is freedom from conformity to religious dogma, not freedom from conformity to law because of religious dogma . . .

. . . While the very concept of ordered liberty precludes this Court from allowing every individual to subjectively define his own standards on matters of conformity in which society, as a whole has important interests, the records of the case and the long history of flag salute cases abundantly supports the religious quality of the claims adduced by the members of the sect Jehovah's Witnesses . . . their refusal to participate in the flag ceremony is religious, shared by the entire community of JWs and is intimately related to their theocratic beliefs and convictions . . . It is obvious that the assailed orders and memoranda would gravely endanger the free exercise of the religious beliefs of the members of the sect and their minor children.

Furthermore, the view that the flag is not a religious but a neutral, secular symbol expresses a majoritarian view intended to stifle the expression of the belief that an act of saluting the flag might sometimes be – to some individuals – so offensive as to be worth their giving up another constitutional right – the right to education. Individuals or groups of individuals get from a symbol the meaning they put to it. Compelling members of a religious sect to believe otherwise on the pain of denying minor children the right to an education is a futile and unconscionable detour towards instilling virtues of loyalty and patriotism which are best instilled and communicated by painstaking and non-coercive methods. Coerced loyalties . . . breed resentment and dissent. Those who attempt to coerce uniformity of sentiment soon find out that the only path towards achieving unity is by way of suppressing dissent. In the end, such attempts only find the 'unanimity of the graveyard.'

. . . While conceding to the idea – adverted to by the Solicitor General – that certain methods of religious expression may be prohibited to serve legitimate societal purposes, refusal to participate in the flag ceremony hardly constitutes a form of religious expression so offensive and noxious as to prompt legitimate State intervention. It is worth repeating that the absence of a demonstrable danger of a kind which the State is empowered to protect militates against the extreme disciplinary methods undertaken by school authorities in trying to enforce regulations designed to compel attendance in flag ceremonies . . . It bears repeating that their absence from the ceremony hardly constitutes a danger so grave and imminent as to warrant the state's intervention . . . (motion denied) . . .

Bijoe Emmanuel vs State Of Kerala
[1987] AIR 748, [1986] SCR (3) 518 (Supreme Court, India)

Facts

Three Jehovah's Witnesses students in Kerala, standing in respectful silence, were expelled for refusing to sing the National Anthem during morning assembly. The High Court rejected an appeal for an order restraining the authorities from preventing the students from attending school. The case came by special leave to the Supreme Court.

Chinnappa Reddy J

It is evident that Jehovah's Witnesses, wherever they are, do hold religious beliefs which may appear strange or even bizarre to us, but the sincerity of their beliefs is beyond question . . .
. . . [W]henever the [Article 25] Fundamental Right to freedom of conscience and to profess, practise and propagate religion is invoked, the act complained of as offending the Fundamental Right must be examined to discover whether such act is to protect public order, morality and health . . . [The Court approvingly referred to Latham CJ in *Adelaide Company of Jehovah's Witnesses v The Commonwealth* (1943) 67 CLR 116]:

> The Constitution protects religion within a community organized under a Constitution, so that the continuance of such protection necessarily assumes the continuance of the community so organized. This view makes it possible to reconcile religious freedom with ordered government. It does not mean that the mere fact that the Commonwealth Parliament passes a law in the belief that it will promote the peace, order and good government of Australia precludes any consideration by a court of the question whether or not such a law infringes religious freedom. The final determination of that question by Parliament would remove all reality from the Constitutional guarantee. That guarantee is intended to limit the sphere of action of the legislature. The interpretation and application of the guarantee . . . must be left to the courts of justice to determine its meaning and to give effect to it by declaring the invalidity of laws which infringes it and by declining to enforce them . . .

. . . [T]he question is not whether a particular religious belief or practice appeals to our reason or sentiment but whether the belief is genuinely and conscientiously held [and if so], it attracts the protection of Article 25 but subject . . . to the inhibitions contained therein.
[The Court noted that Frankfurter J in *Minersville School District v Gobitis* 310 US 586 (1940) exercised judicial restraint in finding that 'the courtroom is not the arena for debating issues of educational policy' over whether a school flag ceremony best promoted patriotism. *Gobitis* was overruled in *West Virginia State Board of Education v Barnette*, [319 US 624 (1943)], where Jackson J observed:]

> . . . the compulsory flag salute and pledge requires affirmation of a belief and an attitude of mind. It is not clear whether the regulation contemplates that pupils forego any

contrary convictions of their own and become unwilling converts to the prescribed ceremony or whether it will be acceptable if they simulate assent by words without belief and by a gesture barren of meaning. It is now a commonplace that censorship or suppression of expression of opinion is tolerated by our Constitution only when the expression presents a clear and present danger of action of a kind the State is empowered to prevent and punish. It would seem that involuntary affirmation could be commanded only on even more immediate and urgent grounds than silence. But here the power of compulsion is invoked without any allegation that remaining passive during a flag salute ritual creates a clear and present danger that would justify an effort even to muffle expression . . .

. . . If there is any fixed star in our Constitutional constellation, it is that no official, high or petty, can prescribe what shall be orthodox in politics, nationalism, religion . . . or force citizens to confess by word or act their faith therein. If there are any circumstances which permit an exception, they do not now occur to us. We think the action of the local authorities in compelling the flag salute and pledge transcends constitutional limitations on their power and invades the sphere of intellect and spirit which it is the purpose of the First Amendment to our Constitution to reserve from all official control.

[After referring to Jackson, J's opinion in *West Virginia State Board of Education v Barnette* and some other cases, the Court stated] . . . For the Court to take to itself the right to say that the exercises here in question had no religious or devotional significance might well be for the Court to deny that very religious freedom which the statute is intended to provide . . .

[The Court held that the Article 25 rights of the expelled children were violated and directed the authorities to readmit the children to school, stating] . . . our tradition teaches tolerance; our philosophy preaches tolerance; our constitution practices tolerance; let us not dilute it.

Notes and Questions

1. The Philippines Supreme Court in *People v Lagman*[123] rejected an attempt to avoid military duties on non-conscientious objector grounds, such as not wanting to be killed. The National Defense Law was held constitutional by dint of Article II Section 2 of the Constitution requiring citizens to render personal military or civil service to enable the Government to defend the state.

2. Are courts engaging in theological questions in determining whether flag salute requirements constitute coercion in a religious activity? How do the Singapore, Indian and Philippines courts differ in defining religion/religious obligation, or in determining whether an activity is 'sacred' or 'secular'? Compare their 'balancing' and interest prioritisation approaches. Do the courts apply abstract rules or adopt a contextualised enquiry? Which judicial approach best serves religious liberty? See Thio Li-ann, 'Courting Religion: The Judge between Caesar and God in Asian Courts' (2009) *Singapore Journal of Legal Studies* 52.

---

[123] *People v Lagman* 66 Phil 13 (1938).

V. THE DIVERSITY OF RELIGION–STATE CONSTITUTIONAL ARRANGEMENTS

A. Introduction

There is a wide diversity of state–religion constitutional arrangements[124] in Asia, influenced by factors such as history, colonial experience, political systems, the dominant religion's tenets, the informal power it may wield,[125] the intensity of commitment to 'strong religion' and its social role in shaping public life, conceptions of secularity and receptivity to religious human rights based on free conscience.

Asia is a region fraught with religious persecution,[126] where religion is taken seriously, debunking the 'secularisation' thesis[127] that modernity inaugurated Religion's demise. Religion may be accommodated through schemes of legal pluralism[128] or form part of public law. Where integral to national or group identity, conversions may be viewed as a threat. The oppressive treatment of religious minorities is exacerbated where ethnicity and religion are conflated. The maintenance of religious harmony[129] and social stability is a dominant motif in Asian religion and state discourse.

State–religion relationships, whether antagonistic, benevolent, agnostic or protectionist, shape the scope of religious liberty and how religious minorities are treated. States may establish or endorse a religion, accommodate[130] or co-operate[131] with religion in selected areas, or maintain a strict separation of religion and state. The attitude in secular democracies towards religion may vary depending on the activity: govern-

---

[124] See Ran Hirschl's nine archetypical models: R Hirschl, 'Comparative Constitutional Law and Religion' in T Ginsburg and R Dixon (eds), *Comparative Constitutional Law* (Edward Elgar, 2012) 422; WC Durham, 'Perspectives on Religious Liberty: A Comparative Framework' in JD Vyver and J Witte (eds), *Religious Human Rights in Global Perspective* (Boston, Mass: Martinus Nijhoff, 1996) 1.

[125] A *fatwa* (opinion on religious law) may not be legally binding but exerts influence as a form of non-state law. Eg, the Indonesian Ulema Council declared the presence of sperm banks *haram* (prohibited): 'Sperm bank prohibited: Indonesian Ulema Council', *Jakarta Post*, 28 July 2010. Enacted legislation may give a *fatwa* legal effect: the Syariah Criminal Offences (Terengganu) Enactment 2001 makes it an offence to propagate opinions contrary to an existing fatwa: *Sulaiman bin Takrib v Kerajaan Negeri Terengganu* [2009] 6 MLJ 354 (Federal Court, Malaysia).

[126] Eg attacks against Muslim and Christian minorities in Gujurat (2002) and Orissa (2008), India; the violent killing of Ahmadis and Christians in Muslim-majority Indonesia, or militant Buddhists in Sri Lanka demolishing Muslim and Christian places of worship: 'India hit over religious violence', *BBC News*, 13 August 2009; 'No model for Muslim democracy', *New York Times*, 21 May 2012; '"Buddhists behaving badly": What zealotry is doing to Sri Lanka', *Foreign Affairs*, 2 August 2012.

[127] 'The world today, with some exceptions . . . is as furiously religious as it ever was, and in some place more so than ever.' P Berger, 'Secularism in Retreat' (1996/7) 46 *National Interest* 3, 3.

[128] Muslim communities may be exempt from general laws through statutes permitting the limited operation of religious personal and customary laws. Thus, Singapore and Indonesian Muslim men may exceptionally practise polygamy, over the objections of women activists: 'Indonesian Constitutional Court upholds polygamy restrictions', *Digital Journal*, 3 October 2007, at <http://www.digitaljournal.com/article/236255>.

[129] Art 51A of the Indian Constitution obliges citizens to 'promote harmony and the spirit of common brotherhood amongst all the people of India transcending religious, linguistic and regional or sectional diversities'.

[130] Accommodationist regimes may allow religious symbols in public and recognise religious holidays, while not providing financial subsidies.

[131] Eg providing financial support for religious funds. In Bangladesh, where Islam is the state religion, the Religious Affairs Ministry provides funding for religious and cultural activities. In June 2011, the Hindu Welfare Trust received 180 million taka while the Buddhist Welfare Trust received 50 million taka: Executive Summary, US State Department Report 2011 at <http://www.state.gov/documents/organization/193131.pdf>.

ments may subsidise hospitals or schools run by religious groups, while remaining wary of religiously-based political parties or the 'abuse of religion for political purposes'.[132] Constitutional orders may treat religion in various ways. They may:

(a) identify a national or official religion: Islam in Brunei (Article 3), Malaysia (Article 3), Bangladesh (Part I Article 2A) and Pakistan (Article 2); Buddhism in Cambodia (Article 43);

(b) give special status to a preferred religion: special recognition is accorded to Buddhism in Sri Lanka (Article 9), Myanmar (Article 361) and Thailand (Section 79);

(c) contain general theistic references: eg the Philippines Constitutional preamble invokes 'Almighty God'; Article 29 of the Indonesian Constitution provides that 'The state shall be based upon the belief in the One and Only God';[133]

(d) stipulate the dominant religious sect, eg Shafeite sect, Islam: Brunei (Part II Section 3);

(e) define what falls outside an official religion: eg the Pakistan Constitution states that Ahmadis are not Muslims (Article 260(3));

(f) define what falls within a religion: eg Sikhs, Jains and Buddhists are considered to be 'Hindu' in India (Article 25(2));

(g) acknowledge the special role of a religion/religious group without according it official status: eg Catholicism in Timor-Leste (Section 11); Buddhism in Laos (Article 9);

(h) accord de facto recognition to a religion through a formal institutional role: eg the Pakistan President and Prime Minister must be Muslim (Articles 41(2), 91(3)); the Thai and Bhutan Kings are Buddhist (Chapter II, Section 9 and Article 9 respectively).

Constitutions like those of Nepal (Article 4, 2007 Interim) and India (preamble) expressly declare a principle of secularity; such principles are implicit elsewhere, as in Singapore, which adopted a modified version of the Malaysian Constitution, deleting the 'Islam' clause, upon secession. Constitutional clauses stipulating religion's autonomy from the state and disqualifying religious organisations from wielding political authority (Article 20, Japan; Article 9, Mongolia) reflect secular values. Clauses may expressly reject an official religion (eg Article 20(2) of the South Korean Constitution).

State involvement or detachment from religion must be examined contextually, not *in abstracto*; binary 'separation/entanglement' models are un-illuminating. Freedom of religion is distinct from values like secularism and pluralism; the European Court of Human Rights considers it must enforce religious freedom and conscience, but must not 'bully States into secularism or . . . coerce countries into schemes of religious neutrality', leaving individual states to decide 'whether, and to what extent, to separate Church and governance'.[134]

---

[132] Art 364 of the Myanmar Constitution forbids this.

[133] The Indonesian state ideology of Pancasila, which advocates monotheism, is a 'compromise between secularism, where no single religion predominates in the state, and religiosity, where religion (especially Islam) becomes one of the important pillars of the state'. N Hosen, 'Religion and the Indonesian Constitution: A Recent Debate' (2005) 36(3) *Journal of Southeast Asian Studies* 419, 424.

[134] Judge Bonello (Concurring), *Lautsi v Italy* App no 30814/06 (ECtHR, 18 March 2011) [2.5]: 'Freedom of religion is *not* secularism. Freedom of religion is *not* the separation of Church and State. Freedom of religion is *not* religious equidistance . . . In Europe, secularism is optional, freedom of religion is not.'

B. Secular Constitutional Models and Constitutional Theocracies

i. Secular Liberal Constitutional Models

In general, a secular liberal constitutional order[135] assumes that the ultimate good is to maximise individual choice through individual rights. Four pillars of liberal constitutionalism in relation to religion may be identified. First, a non-religious state espousing a rationalist worldview, that strives to be 'neutral' (or hostile) towards religion. There must be 'a minimal threshold' of institutional, organisational and role differentiation between state and (organised) religion, most aggressively expressed in Turkish or French *laïcité*. The state role in guaranteeing democratic rights is respected and ultimate authority is located in supreme constitutions or popular sovereignty, curbing religion's influence on state power.[136] Its commitment to secularity would oppose a constitutional order based on religious tenets, for fear of chauvinism undermining a 'reason' based society.[137] Religion, recognised for historical reasons, is confined to a form of ceremonial deism. A liberal state claiming genuine religious neutrality must minimise the extent to which it encourages or discourages belief or disbelief.[138] Secondly, the constitution guarantees freedom of conscience and the right to have or to reject religious belief (freedom from religion). Thirdly, it protects religious minorities from majorities[139] and, lastly, it guarantees to treat religions equally, ensure mutual tolerance and secures for religious groups freedom from state regulation. In *Metropolitan Church of Bessarabia v Moldova*,[140] the European Court of Human Rights observed that religious freedom under Article 9 ECHR excludes state assessment of the legitimacy of religious beliefs or their manner of expression. In addition, state measures 'favouring a particular leader or specific organs of a divided religious community or seeking to compel the community or part of it to place itself, against its will, under a single leadership' infringe the principle of religious neutrality.

Courts in secular liberal orders like the Philippines hold that the state will not intervene in 'ecclesiastical affairs', which

> involves the relationship between the church and its members and relate to matters of faith, religious doctrines, worship and governance of the congregation. Concrete examples of so-called ecclesiastical affairs which the State cannot meddle in include proceedings for excommunication, ordinations of religious ministers, administration of sacraments and other activities with attached religious significance.[141]

---

[135] A Sajó, 'Preliminaries to a Concept of Constitutional Secularism' (2008) 6 *I•CON* 617; L Zucca, 'The Crisis of the Secular State – A Reply to Professor Sajó' (2009) 7(3) *I•CON* 499.

[136] B Berger, 'The Limits of Belief: Freedom of Religion, Secularism, and the Liberal State' (2002) 17 *Canadian Journal of Law and Society* 39, 49.

[137] A liberal state's assumption of neutrality between competing goods itself 'rests on untestable faith'. S Idleman, 'The Role of Religious Values in Decision Making' (1993) 68 *Indiana Law Journal* 433, 446.

[138] D Laycock, 'Formal, Substantive, and Disaggregated Neutrality Toward Religion' (1990) 39 *DePaul Law Review* 993, 1001.

[139] V Bader, 'Constitutionalizing secularism, alternative secularisms or liberal-democratic constitutionalism? A critical reading of some Turkish, ECtHR and Indian Supreme Court cases on "secularism"' (2010) 6(3) *Utrecht Law Review* 1, 22.

[140] *Metropolitan Church of Bessarabia v Moldova* App no 45701/99 (ECtHR, 13 December 2001) at [117].

[141] *Pastor Dionisio Austria v National Labor Relations Commission* GR No 124382 (16 August 1999), at < http://sc.judiciary.gov.ph/jurisprudence/1999/aug99/124382.htm>.

Where a church terminates the employment of a minister rather than excommunicating him, this has been deemed to be a 'purely secular' issue without religious significance. Further, the court in *G Long and Almeria v Basa*[142] held that a state should not interfere where members of a religious corporation are expelled for holding contrarian doctrines, even if church by-laws lacked prior notice requirements. Sandoval-Gutierrez J stated that membership in a religious corporation was based on the 'absolute adherence to a common religious or spiritual belief'; if this ceased, membership ceased, and civil courts treat the expulsion decisions of church authorities as conclusive.

The Western secular principle of church–state separation[143] is not universally accepted; for example, some Islamists view this principle as the root cause of the moral and spiritual decline in many Western/Western-orientated governments and societies.[144] In contrast, a non-liberal constitutional order prioritises community interests and identifies freedoms, duties and responsibilities as the social matrix for the outworking of liberties; states may actively promote or celebrate a favoured vision of communal life or identity, which may draw from a religion(s) or an anti-theistic ideology like communism or socialism.

ii. Secular Socialist Constitutions and Religion

Communism and socialism are anti-theistic ideologies. Socialist states like China, Vietnam and Laos – where the Community Party is supreme – are suspicious of religion as an ideological competitor or Trojan horse for foreign interference. This results in intrusive regulatory regimes to consolidate political control, secure good order and promote a humanist mindset.

In Document 19 of 1982,[145] the Chinese Communist Party (CCP) set out its religious policy. This pragmatic document showed a shift away from the oppressive Cultural Revolution era (1966–76) measures banning religion, towards a more tolerant regime that anticipates the demise of religion with the advent of the modern, mature socialist system. This seems increasingly unlikely in modern China, given the trends towards growing religiosity.[146] In an era of economic growth, the CCP greatly values social harmony and courts the support of religious followers to this end.[147] However, the document proclaims: 'We communists are atheists and must unremittingly propagate atheism.'[148] Party members must be atheists.

---

[142]   *G Long and Almeria v Basa* GR Nos 134963-64 (27 Sep 2001).

[143]   The rationale for non-establishment in the US context is captured by Black J in *Engel v Vitale* 370 US 421, 432 (1962). The unity of government and religion 'tends to destroy government and to degrade religion'; English and US history showed that government alliance with a religion inevitably incurred 'the hatred, disrespect and even contempt' of those holding contrary beliefs, and tended towards religious persecution. The US model reflected the belief 'that religion is too personal, too sacred, too holy, to permit its "unhallowed perversion" by a civil magistrate'.

[144]   S Santos, Jr, *The Moro Islamic Challenge: Constitutional Rethinking for the Mindanao Peace Process* (Quezon City: University of the Philippines Press, 2001) at 18.

[145]   'The Basic Viewpoint and Policy on the Religious Question during Our Country's Socialist Period', Central Committee, CCP, 31 March 1982, in D MacInnis, *Religion in China Today: Policy and Practice* (NY: Orbis Books, 1989) 8–26, at <http://www.purdue.edu/crcs/itemResources/PRCDoc/pdf/Document_no._19_1982.pdf>.

[146]   Chen Huanzhong, 'A Brief Overview of Law and Religion in the People's Republic of China' (2003) 2 *Brigham Young University Law Review* 465.

[147]   'Chinese official confident atheist Communist Party can "unite God's followers"', *Xinhua*, 22 September 2011, at <http://english.peopledaily.com.cn/90785/7602370.html>.

[148]   Document 19, Part IV, 'The Party's Present Policy toward Religion' in MacInnis, above n 145 available: http://www.religlaw.org/content/religlaw/documents/doc19relig1982.htm.

a. Patriotic Religion and Socialist Ideology

Despite the formal recognition of religious freedom in China, extensive limitations apply to ensure that religion is 'patriotic', does not 'oppose the party's leadership or the socialist system' or threaten to 'destroy national or ethnic unity'.[149]

The Vietnam Constitution entrenches the primacy of the Vietnam Communist Party (CPV). According to founding father Ho Chi Minh, serving God is closely associated with service to country.[150] The Vietnam Fatherland Front,[151] as part of the CPV-led political system, composes social organisations which represent all ethnic groups, classes and religions. It is the vehicle by which the state tries to control the political orientation of religious groups and ensure 'political and moral cohesion' among the people.[152] Examples of patriotic religious charters include: 'Dharma-Nation-Socialism' (Vietnam Buddhism Church);[153] 'Living the Gospel within the nation for the happiness of fellow Vietnamese' (Catholic); 'The Nation is glorious, the Way enlightens' (Caodaism). In the *doi moi* (renovation) era, the Government has sought to co-opt religion to promote ethnic unity and to enlist religious believers 'in the cause of renovation, building and defense of the Homeland'.[154]

b. Recognition of Officially-sanctioned Religious Groups

Various agencies under China's Religious Affairs Bureau (RAB) regulate officially recognised religious groups, including the Catholics, Buddhists, Taoists and the Protestant Three-Self Patriotic Movement (TSPM).[155] Document 19 of 31 March 1982 states that these Patriotic Religious Organisations are

> to assist the Party and the government to implement the policy of freedom of religious belief, to help the broad mass of religious believers and persons in religious circles to continually raise their patriotic and socialist consciousness, to represent the lawful rights and interest of religious circles, to organize normal religious activities, and to manage religious affairs well.

All patriotic religious organisations should follow the Party's and Government's leadership so that they can have 'a positive influence', acting as bridges between the Party and religious citizens.[156] The CCP also sought to educate a new generation of patriotic

---

[149] Ibid.

[150] Socialist Republic of Vietnam Government Committee for Religious Affairs, 'Religion and Policies Regarding Religion in Vietnam' (2006) at < http://vietnamembassy-usa.org/docs/Vietnam%20White%20 Paper%20on%20Religion.pdf> and < http://www.docstoc.com/docs/76533863/Vietnam-White-Paper-on-Religion>.

[151] Law on Vietnam Fatherland Front (No 14/1999/QH10, 12 June 1999); and M Bouquet, 'Vietnamese Party-State and Religious Pluralism since 1986: Building the Fatherland?' (2010) 25(1) *Sojourn: Journal of Social Issues in Southeast Asia* 90.

[152] Art 9, 1999 Decree No 26 ND-CP on Religious Activities.

[153] Hoàng Thị Thơ, 'Buddhism Tolerance for the common good of the nation: From Aspect of Buddhist Philosophy' (2008) 2(4) *Religious Studies Review* 35, 53.

[154] *The Report on the Religious Affairs in the New Situation* (the Report of the Politburo in the 7th Congress of the Central Executive Committee) quoted in Nguyen Hong Duong, 'Some Religious Problems in Vietnam' (2010) 4(3) *Religious Studies Review* 3, 5.

[155] The three principles of self-governance, self-support (financial independence from foreigners) and self-propagation (indigenous missionary work).

[156] Document No 19, Part VI, 'Restoration and Administration of Churches, Temples and Other Religious Buildings' in MacInnis, above n 145 available: < http://www.purdue.edu/crcs/itemResources/PRCDoc/pdf/Document_no._19_1982.pdf>.

religious personnel who will 'loyally implement the Party's religious policy' as part of the plan to 'win over' the religious.[157] While the RAB administratively controls all places of worship, the religious organisations are responsible for their management.

However, not all religious groups are willing to join a patriotic association, such as the unregistered Chinese house churches (*jiating jiahui*),[158] numbering up to 100 million members, who view the officially sanctioned groups as CCP tools. These groups challenge the state-run religious system, where the CPP decides the content of religious truths. The Government tolerates their existence[159] while exerting pressure that hinders religious freedom, such as causing landlords to terminate leases over halls rented by churches. This happened to the 1,000-member Shouwang Church in Beijing, which had worshipped openly since April 2011, after eviction from its hall. When it tried to register, it was told to join the TSPM.[160] After their eviction, 17 underground churches from across China jointly issued their first government petition seeking legal reform of the laws regulating religion.[161]

Vietnam Resolution 24-NQ/TW ('Strengthening Religious Affairs in the New Situation') of 16 October 1990 was adopted just before *doi moi* recognised that religion is an objective spiritual need of the Vietnamese and would co-exist with socialism. This was affirmed in 2006 ('Compatriots of *different religions* constitute an all-important component of the country's larger national unity').[162] The Resolution provides that religious groups whose religious practices had 'deep attachment' to the nation, espoused purposes 'compatible with state laws' and had 'appropriate organizational apparatus' over religious and non-religious activities, 'shall be allowed by the states'.[163] A 2004 Ordinance exhorts religious groups to conduct activities which are 'safe, thrifty, compatible with the national traditions and cultural identity, and preserve and protect the environment'.[164]

[157] Document No 19, Part VIII, 'Educating a New Generation of Clergy', ibid.

[158] Document 19, Part VI, above n 145: 'As for Protestants gathering in homes for worship services, in principle this should not be allowed, yet this prohibition should not be too rigidly enforced. Rather, persons in the patriotic religious organizations should make special efforts to persuade the mass of religious believers to make more appropriate arrangements.' See further M Cheng, 'House Church Movements and Religious Freedom in China' (2003) 1(1) *China: An International Journal* 16.

[159] 'Church in China experiencing "tremendous" growth,' *Christian Today*, 3 August 2010, at <http://www.christiantoday.com/article/church.in.china.experiencing.tremendous.growth/26420.htm.>;   Hongyi Harry Lai, 'The Religious Revival in China' (2003) 18 *Copenhagen Journal of Asian Studies* 40; R Madsen, *The Upsurge of Religion in China* (2010) 21(4) *Journal of Democracy* 58.

[160] B Spegele, 'China's Banned Churches Defy Regime', 2 July 2011, *Asian Wall Street Journal*, at <http://online.wsj.com/article/SB10001424052702304567604576451913744126214.html>.

[161] 'Why Beijing's Largest House Church Refuses to Stop Meeting Outdoors', *Christianity Today*, 26 April 2011, at <http://www.christianitytoday.com/ct/2011/aprilwebonly/beijinghousechurch.html?start=2>.

[162] 'Religion and Policies Regarding Religion in Vietnam', Socialist Republic of Vietnam Government Committee for Religious Affairs, Hanoi 2006, at <http://www.presscenter.org.vn/en//images/Relegion_and_Policies_regarding_Religion_in_Vietnam.doc>.

[163] See Đỗ Quang Hưng, 'The Solution to Religious Issue: From the Democratic Republic of Vietnam to the Socialist Republic of Vietnam' (2010) 4 *Religious Studies Review* 3.

[164] Art 14, Ordinance on Beliefs and Religions (No 21/2004/PL-UBTVQH11), Standing Committee of National Assembly, at <http://moj.gov.vn/vbpq/en/Lists/Vn%20bn%20php%20lut/View_Detail.aspx?ItemID=7818>.

However, unregistered groups in Vietnam, such as the Montagnards,[165] suffer religious persecution, where police disperse religious gatherings, destroy churches, detain members on charges of violating national security or confiscate their literature. Reportedly, despite Decree 22, which 'strictly forbids coercion of citizens to convert or renounce one's religion' and states that 'all acts of violation shall be dealt with by the law' (Article 2), there have been government campaigns to force Dega Protestants and other Montagnard Christians to recant their religion as threats to national security or solidarity;[166] public denunciation ceremonies were required as a condition for returning to their community.[167] Such groups are associated with separatist movements whom the Government accuses of abusing 'Protestantism to incite people to act subversively', warranting a ban.[168]

c. Broad Regulatory Discretion Over 'Normal Religious Activities'[169] and 'Abuse of Religion'

Article 36 of the Constitution of China provides that citizens 'enjoy freedom of religious belief' and that the state protects 'normal religious activities' which must not 'disrupt public order, impair the health of citizens or interfere with the educational system of the state'. Normal religious activities do not extend to 'criminal and anti-revolutionary activities',[170] and superstitious activities such as witchcraft, fortune-telling and geomancy are discouraged, consonant with Marxist scientific materialism.

Article 70 of the Vietnam Constitution (1992) prohibits anyone from misusing beliefs and religion to contravene the law and state policies. This vague clause leaves it to state authorities to determine what 'misuse' constitutes. Article 30, which protects national culture, bans 'reactionary and depraved ideologies and culture' and provides that 'superstition is to be driven out'. It is unclear how 'superstition' is to be distinguished from 'religion', but some guidance may be obtained from Article 247 of the Penal Code (1999): 'Exercise of superstitious practices: any person who practices divination, acts as a medium, or pursues other superstitious practices . . .'. This represents an attempt to rationalise religion.

---

[165] 'Vietnam persecutes Christian minority, Report says', *New York Times*, 31 March 2011; see Human Rights Watch, *Montagnard Christians in Vietnam: A Case Study in Religious Repression* (USA: Human Rights Watch, March 2011), available: < http://www.hrw.org/sites/default/files/reports/vietnam0311Web. pdf>.

[166] Decree 22/2005/ND-CP, 'Instructions for Implementing the New Ordinance on Beliefs and Religions', March 2005.

[167] Xuan Hoang and Van Tu, 'Abandon "Dega Protestantism" to return to the community' (*Bo 'Tin Lanh De Ga', ve voi cong dong*), Quan Doi Nhan Dan (People's Army), 25 September 2010, at <http://www.qdnd. vn/qdndsite/vi-VN/61/43/7/24/24/124799/Default.aspx>

[168] Instruction of the Prime Minister No 01/2005/CT-TTG (4 Feb 2005) on Some Tasks Regarding to Protestantism; see 'PM's instruction on Protestant affairs strengthens consistency in religious policy' at <http://www.vietnamembassy-algerie.org/vnemb.vn/tinkhac/ns050218145623?b_start:int=45>.

[169] 'The Party will consistently implement its policy of respecting the right to enjoy freedom of belief, to follow or not to follow a religion and the right to take part in normal religious activities according to the law.' Vietnamese Communist Party, *The Document of the 7th Congress of the Central Committee* (Hanoi: National Politics Publishing House, 2003) 84.

[170] Document 19, Part X, 'Criminal and Counter-Revolutionary Activities under the Cover of Religion' in MacInnis, above n 145.

d. Intervention in Affairs of Religious Body

Religious groups need to be registered, operate under approved guidelines and are subject to state supervision. This may include having objectives not harmful to the state, an adequate organisational structure, conducting activities at approved venues, compliance with general regulations on religious publications and charitable activities, and obtaining permission to open religious schools and to invite foreign individuals or religious groups.[171] For example, the Vietnam Government Religious Committee established a Religious Publishing House in 2001 to publish the literature of religious organisations the state permits to operate, and other books 'serving the propagation and education of religious legislation, guidelines and policies of the Party and the State'.[172] In Laos, the Ministry of Propaganda and Culture's authorisation and the approval of the Central Committee of the Lao Front for National Construction (LFNC) is needed to print and distribute religious literature.[173] The Government wields extensive powers and has powers of approval over the building of new churches or pagodas, printing books and disseminating teachings to believers; it also regulates foreign assistance, as provided in the 2002 Decree Regarding Governance and Protection of Religious Activity in the Lao PDR.[174] The LFNC Central Committee, a constitutional body, is empowered to promote theology and issue instructions regarding the activities of religious communities, interfering with religious group autonomy.

e. Regulating Religious Leadership

The Chinese state's approval is needed in declaring the living Buddha's successor, this being a high religious office in Tibetan Buddhism. China presents itself as respecting this unique form of succession, with the state involved in identifying the reincarnation of religious leaders such as the Tenth Panchen Lama, enthroning the Eleventh Panchen Lama 'after lot-drawing from a golden urn according to the established religious rituals and historical conventions of Tibetan Buddhism, with the approval of the State Council'.[175] The exiled Fourteenth Dalai Lama disputed this.[176]

iii. Constitutional Theocracies

A non-liberal or illiberal model may accord constitutional status to religious bodies;[177] it may confer preferential treatment to one religion, including assimilationist schemes

---

[171]   Eg Decree No 26/1999/ND-CP (19 April 1999) on Religious Activities, at <http://moj.gov.vn/vbpq/en/Lists/Vn%20bn%20php%20lut/View_Detail.aspx?ItemID=1058>; Decree N0 22/2005/ND-CP (Decree Implementing Beliefs and Religious Ordinance, 1 March 2005), Implementing Decree 22 (2005); An Dang, 'Vietnam: government proposes further legal restrictions on religion', *Independent Catholic News*, 22 May 2011.

[172]   Decision 83/2001/QD-TTg (30 May 2001): establishment of the Religious Publishing House.

[173]   Art 14, Prime Minister's Decree No 92/PM on Management and Protection of Religious Activities, *Report*, Special Rapporteur on freedom of religion or belief – Mission: Lao People's Democratic Republic (A/HRC/13/40/Add.4).

[174]   Prime Minister's Decree No 92/PM.

[175]   'Protection of the Right to Freedom of Religious Belief for Ethnic Minorities' in *Freedom of Religious Belief in China* (Beijing: Information Office of the PRC State Council, 1997) available at <http://english.peopledaily.com.cn/features/religion/religion5.html>.

[176]   M Goldstein, *The Snow Lion and the Dragon: China, Tibet, and the Dalai Lama* (Berkeley, Cal: University of California Press, 1997) 100–01.

[177]   Art 203C of the Pakistan Constitution establishes the Federal Shariat Court.

to propagate its tenets or safeguard religious orthodoxy. Religious conversion may be perceived as a public order threat rather than individual choice. Religious minorities may be treated in a disadvantageous fashion, especially where religious uniformity rather than protecting religious diversity is deemed the basis for social stability. This reflects the close interaction rather than strict separation of religion and state. Most constitutions are 'mixed', having both liberal and illiberal elements.[178]

An idealised constitutional theocracy, which challenges 'the great universalist constitutional projects of Anglo-European society'[179] predicated on structural and substantive separation of state and religion, may contain these features:[180]

(a) First, it must be distinguished from an absolute theocracy, as there is some separation, not conflation, of political and religious authority, as mandated by contemporary constitutionalism. Nonetheless, religion is linked to the authority of governing bodies through constitutional directive, incorporating religious references in public office oaths or giving religious leaders constitutional governance roles.[181]

(b) Secondly, constitutional theocracies support and accord constitutional status to an official religion/denomination which may constitute national identity, as where the Bhutan constitutional preamble refers to the 'Triple Gem' of Buddhism (Buddha, Dharma, Sangha); they may provide for some religious tolerance in allowing other religions to be practised in peace and harmony (Article 2A, Bangladesh Constitution; Article 3, Malaysian Constitution); the degree of state identification with a religion affects the scope of religious liberty by favouring the majority through financial and non-pecuniary support, as Bhutan does for the monastic bodies (Article 3(7)), which disfavours minorities. In safeguarding religious orthodoxy, a constitutional theocracy may enter theological disputes by banning deviant sects or implementing blasphemy and apostasy laws, to the detriment of individual freedoms.

(c) Thirdly, a religion may be a source of public law, affecting legislative content and adjudication.[182] For example, a resolution passed by the 57th Bhutan National Assembly banning animal sacrifice during religious ceremonies is consonant with Buddhist tenets (the Central Monastic Body representative likened this to 'killing a son and offering him to the mother') but may prejudice, say, Muslim ceremonies.[183] It informs the collective identity or metanarrative of the polity and may shape the scope of rights. For example, Article 8(1A) of the Bangladesh

---

[178] J Patrick, 'Religion and New Constitutions: Recent Trends of Harmony and Divergence' (5 June 2012), available at SSRN <http://ssrn.com/abstract=2077274> or <http://dx.doi.org/10.2139/ssrn.2077274>.

[179] L Catá Backer, 'God(s) Over Constitutions: International and Religious Transnational Constitutionalism in the 21st Century' (2007) 27 *Mississippi College Law Review* 11, 19.

[180] R Hirschl, *Constitutional Theocracy* (Cambridge, Mass: Harvard University Press, 2010) at 2–3.

[181] Eg, in Iran, religious jurists who interpret Islamic law continue their historic guardianship role as a 'type of Fourth Branch to an Islamic constitutional government'. I Rabb, ' "We the Jurists": Islamic Constitutionalism in Iraq' (2007–2008) 10 *University of Pennsylvania Journal of Constitutional Law* 527, 577.

[182] Arguably, state enforcement of *shariah* (religious law) would 'necessarily be the political will of the state and not the religious law of Islam', such that voluntary Muslim compliance is preferable: A An-Naim, *Islam and the Secular State: Negotiating the Future of Sharia* (Cambridge, Mass: Harvard University Press, 2008) 1.

[183] 'Matter regarding sacrifice of animals during religious ceremonies', National Assembly 57th Session, 1982, available at <http://www.nab.gov.bt/downloads/3557th%20Session.pdf> at 17.

Constitution provides that 'absolute trust and faith in the Almighty Allah shall be the basis of all actions', as part of the Fundamental Principles of State Policy. Article 227 of the Pakistan Constitution provides for existing laws to be brought into conformity with 'the injunctions of Islam as laid down in the Holy Quran and Sunnah', but exempts the personal laws of non-Muslim citizens.

(d) Fourthly, an idealised constitutional theocracy accommodates the co-existence of religious and civil courts, vested with regional or subject matter-based jurisdiction. For example, in their constitutions, criminal and personal laws, Pakistan, Bangladesh, Malaysia and Indonesia's Aceh province have incorporated Islamic precepts.[184]

The following reading presents 10 principles identified as integral to Islamic constitutionalism, deducing these from the relevant Quranic verses and Traditions of the Prophet, which are referenced but not reproduced. This may be contrasted with models based on constitutional secularism.

Sayyid Abul Ala Maududi, 'Fundamentals of Islamic Constitution' in *The Islamic Law and Constitution,* **Khurshid Ahmad (ed & trans) (Lahore: Islamic Publications Ltd, 1955) ch 7, 271–91 (summary)**

Source of Sovereignty: . . . [T]he authority of giving commands and the title to sovereignty is the sole prerogative of Allah [whose Sovereignty] is directly addressed to mankind and is obviously all inclusive. It comprehends all spheres of human life: the doctrinal, moral, legal as well as political. The Qur'an itself specifically states that all these spheres of sovereignty belong to Allah alone, and that Allah is not only the Sustainer and the Lord of mankind but also its Sovereign and Ruler . . . a state becomes Islamic only when it recognises in clear terms the political and legal sovereignty of Allah and binds itself to His obedience and acknowledges Him as the Paramount Power whose commands must be upheld . . . (Al Quran, XII: 40 CXIV: 1–3; III:26; XVIII: 111; VII: 54; VII: 3; V: 44)

Prophets as representatives of sovereignty of God: the Prophets of God are entitled to the obedience of those who accept God as their Sovereign . . . the second fundamental principle of the Islamic Constitution [is that] it must also recognize the *Sunnah* of the Prophet as the source of law and must incorporate a specific article to the effect that no government branch may issue orders or enact laws or pronounce verdicts contrary to the *Sunnah.* (Al Quran, IV: 80, LIX: 7, IV: 65; IV: 64; IV: 105)

Qualified Sovereignty and Popular Viceregency: (Al Quran: XXIV): This verse enunciates two important constitutional principles: (1) The real status of an Islamic State is not that of a Sovereign but that of a viceregent. (2) In an Islamic State, the powers of 'vicegerency' are vested not in any one individual or family or group but in the whole Muslim community where such possesses an independent state. . . . Thus the 'vicegerency' in an Islamic State is popular . . . and it is the 'popular vicegerency' that forms the basis of democracy in an Islamic State while 'popular sovereignty' is its basis in a secular state. . . . In the Islamic polity . . . the government can be formed only with the consent of all the Muslims or

---

[184] Art 15 delineates the Aceh government's mandate over matters like organising educational content after Islamic syar'at, the role of *ulama* in determining regional policy and co-ordinating religious life by implementing Islamic syariat: Law of the Republic of Indonesia (No 11 of 2006), at <http://www.ifrc.org/docs/idrl/968EN.pdf>. See 'Shariah law: Aceh's morality police seek greater power', *Global Post*, 7 February 2012.

their majority and can function and remain in power only as long as it enjoys their confidence.

Popular Viceregency in action: collective affairs are performed by mutual consultation (Al Quran: XLII: 38) . . . whose modality is left to the discretion, of' Muslims . . . guided by three essential principles: (1) the rule of mutual consultation applies at first instance to the appointment of the Head of State . . . ruling out monarchy, despotism and dictatorship. The Head of State may not suspend the constitution at will . . . (2) all concerned people should be consulted directly or through their trusted representatives; (3) The consultation should be free, impartial and genuine. . . . There should be mechanisms to select leaders who are trustworthy and pious, well-loved by the people (Al Quran IV; 58 XLIX: 13)

Woman cannot be entrusted with positions of responsibility in an Islamic state (Al Quran IV:34 'Men are in charge of women:') In Islam there is a functional distribution between men and women . . . the fields of politics and administration belong to the men's sphere of responsibilities . . . it will not be in keeping with the teachings of Islam to drag women into these affairs.

Objectives of an Islamic State: Unlike a Secular State, its duty is not merely to maintain internal order, to defend the frontiers and to work for the material prosperity of the country. Rather, its first and foremost obligation is to establish the systems of *salat (worship)* and *zakat (tithes for the poor)*, to propagate and establish those things which are considered to be 'virtues' by God and His Messenger, and to eradicate those things which have been declared to be 'vice' by them. . . . Thus a state which does not take interest in establishing virtue and eradicating vice and in which adultery, drinking, gambling, obscene literature, indecent films, vulgar songs, immoral display of beauty, promiscuous mingling of men and women, co-education etc flourish without let or hindrance, cannot be called an Islamic state. (Al Quran XXII: 41)

Constitutional Principles from Al Quran IV:59: 'O you who believe, obey Allah and obey His Messenger and those from among yourselves who hold authority, and if there is any dispute between you concerning any matter, refer it to Allah and His Messenger, if you (really) believe in Allah and the Last Day. This is the best course (in itself) and better as regards the result.' (1) Muslims are bound to obey Allah and His Messenger individually and as a community, and this obedience must be given priority to every other obedience . . . Muslims have no obligation to obey laws, orders and cases contrary to the Quran and Sunnah . . . (2) Muslims alone can be the rulers in an Islamic State; (3) The verse gives the people the right to differ with their rulers. In that case, the verdict of Allah and His Messenger is to be taken as final both by the rulers and the ruled. This implies that there must be some institution for deciding such disputes in the light of the Qur'an and the Sunnah. But the Shari'ah does not prescribe any definite form for this purpose. It may be a body of Ulama or it may be in the form of a Supreme Court.

An Islamic state must do justice: (Al Quran: IV: 58. V: 8) Cites various traditions relating to guarantees of the sanctity of life, property and honour within the limits of Islamic law . . . it is agreed principle of Islamic Shari'ah that all non-Muslims who live under the protection of an Islamic states are entitled to the same civic rights that Muslims enjoy . . . the Islamic conception of justice does not allow that the executive be given the powers to arrest or imprison or exile or suppress the rights of belief, opinion, expression of anybody without the due process of law that meets the ends of justice . . . we learn from authentic traditions that Islam does not allow any differentiation or discrimination between the rulers and the ruled or the high and the low in matters of law and justice . . .

Duty of the Islamic state to establish the system of zakat and to shoulder the responsibility of providing for all those who are destitute and helpless.(Al Quran LI:19; IX:103)

VI. MODELS OF SECULARISM IN ASIA:
WHAT SEPARATION OF RELIGION AND STATE ENTAILS

'Secularism' is a protean term. It may be anti-theistic or anti-theocratic in nature, a 'saviour' as a framework for the pacific co-existence of many religious groups, or a substantive humanist ideology (secular fundamentalism), a 'subverter' displacing competing views. Baxi identified two types of approaches towards secularism: first, a rights-orientated secularism, the core value of which is individual agency expressed through free conscience, the exercise of which may be regulated by various public goods; secondly, a governance-orientated approach which codifies the limits to which politics may appeal to religion to acquire political power, to preserve the integrity of secular governance structures and processes.[185]

Secularism entails maintaining a principled distance or separation between religion and state, but this is more a question of degree than a binary dichotomy, given the 'mission impossible'[186] of distinguishing 'religion' and 'politics' in the absence of objective criteria and an impartial arbiter. The nature of this separation varies between secular polities and has yielded a diversity of models in Asia.

A. India and Ameliorative Secularism

i. History of the Constitutional Principle of Secularity in India

The principle of secularity, now recognised as a basic feature,[187] was not in the original constitutional preamble, having been introduced during emergency rule by the 42nd Amendment (1976). The founders deliberately omitted the word, fearing its use would imply the anti-religious tone associated with Western secularism.[188]

'Secularism' in India connotes not irreligion but respect for all religions; its state-religion model is not one of strict separation but accommodation, not requiring the removal of religion from the public sphere. There were divergent internal views towards secularism, broadly divided between Nehru's view that religion was backward super-

---

[185] U Baxi, 'Commentary' in R Sen (ed) *Legalizing Religion: The Indian Supreme* (East-West Center Washington, Policy Studies 30, 2007), 48. Available: < http://scholarspace.manoa.hawaii.edu/bitstream/handle/10125/3499/PS030.pdf?sequence=1>.

[186] S Fish, 'Mission Impossible: Settling the Just Bounds between Church and State' in S Feldman (ed), *Law and Religion: A Critical Anthology* (New York: New York University Press, 2000).

[187] *Kesavananda Bharati v The State of Kerala* [1973] AIR SC 1461; *SR Bommai v Union of India* [1994] AIR SC 1918.

[188] PN Bhagwati, 'Religion and Secularism Under the Indian Constitution' in RD Baird (ed), *Religion and Law in Independent India*, 2nd edn (New Delhi: Manohar, 2005) at 37; S Reddy, 'What Would Your Founding Fathers Think? What India's Constitution Says – And What Its Framers Would Say – About the Current Debate Over the Uniform Civil Code' (2009) 41 *George Washington International Law Review* 405.

stition and secularism was rational and modern, and Gandhi's view that in religion was found moral grounding and truths. Under this pluralistic conception of secularism, the state should protect all religions (*sarva dharma rakshata*). Ramashwami J in *Bommai* argued that secularism 'represents faiths born out of the exercise of rational faculties', 'the imperative requirements for human progress'; it 'improves the material conditions of human life, but also liberates the human spirit from bondage of ignorance, superstition, irrationality, injustice, fraud, hypocrisy and oppressive exploitations'.[189]

a. Characteristics of Indian Secularism

The courts have identified various traits of Indian secularism.[190] First, the fear of ethno-religious chauvinism is real, and to prevent abuses of religion for political gain, some degree of separation of religion and politics is required. In *Bommai*,[191] the Court held that the constitutional requirement that the state be secular in thought and action also applied to political parties. Reddy J stated that 'no party or Organisation can simultaneously be a political and a religious party. It has to be either.'[192] Thus, a party's manifesto had to abide by constitutional injunctions, including secularism. This requirement not to mix religion with secular activity reflects the principle that the state should not patronise any religion as the state religion overtly or covertly, but should demonstrate religious neutrality or impartiality. It is linked to the workings of democracy, as secularism is considered 'essential for successful working of the democratic form of government' which would be thwarted if 'anti-secular forces' were able to divide followers of different religions for political gain. Secularism was characterised as the 'saviour of the people from the dangers of supposed fusion of religion with political and economic activities'[193] as the rise 'of fundamentalism and communalisation of politics are anti-secularism'.[194] Secularism is viewed as a bulwark against disintegrative chauvinism and religious fundamentalism.

Secondly, religious impartiality means the state is to consider an individual's faith irrelevant, to ensure equal treatment to all groups and promote religious tolerance.[195] Further, secularism was a constitutionally chosen 'vehicle to establish an egalitarian social order'.[196]

Thirdly, the courts are quick to clarify that secularism 'does not mean that the State has no say whatsoever in matters of religion'.[197] Secularism was not 'anti-God' nor the 'antithesis of religious devoutness',[198] and the state was not 'irreligious or antireligion'.[199]

---

[189] *SR Bommai v Union of India* [1994] AIR SC 1918 [179].
[190] G Jacobsohn, *The Wheel of Law: India's Secularism in Comparative Constitutional Context* (Princeton, NJ: Princeton University Press, 2003).
[191] *SR Bommai v Union of India* [1994] AIR SC 1918.
[192] Ibid at [310].
[193] Per Ramaswamy J, ibid at [177].
[194] Ibid at [197].
[195] Per Sawant J, ibid at [151].
[196] Per Ramaswamy J, ibid at [186].
[197] Per Reddy J, ibid at [350].
[198] Per Ramaswamy J, ibid at [177], [182].
[199] Per Reddy J, ibid at [350].

India does not have a wall of separation between religion and state;[200] Article 25 empowers the state to intervene in Hindu religious institutions pursuant to social reform. This form of 'ameliorative secularism' is not religiously neutral but attempts to modernise and reform faith,[201] as reflected in the abolition of 'untouchability', an abhorrent tenet of the Hindu caste system, under Article 17. The state 'has a missionary role to reform the Hindu society, Hindu social order and dilute the beliefs of caste hierarchy'.[202]

Article 25(b) constitutionally mandates this reformist agenda, which is at odds with the idea of religious neutrality. While Article 25 guarantees a person's rights to profess, practise and propagate religion, clause (b) provides for the 'throwing open of Hindu religious institutions of a public character to all classes and sections of Hindus (including persons professing the Sikh, Jaina or Buddhist religion) ' . Thus the Supreme Court upheld an Act which removed the disability of Harijans from entering public Hindu temples, authorising all Hindus to enter a temple.[203] So too, the inclusion of religious topics (Sanskrit, Vedic Maths and Astrology) within a school curriculum was not considered contrary to secularism, as secularism (*sarva dharma samabhav*) meant not apathy towards religion or its negation but equal treatment and respect for all religions.[204] This overlooked the fact that only one kind of religious teaching was involved, attracting criticism that this case promoted Hindu nationalism (*hindutva*). The courts have rejected equating *hindutva* with 'narrow fundamentalist Hindu religious bigotry', preferring to view it as 'the way of life of the people in the sub-continent', thus espousing a mono rather than pluralist view of secularism.

Fourthly, treating all citizens equally through securing a uniform civil code under Article 44 was viewed as an expression of 'secularism' as the Court considered 'there is no necessary connection between religion and personal law in a civilised society'.[205] This remains unrealised and controversial, particularly given Muslim resistance to changes in their religiously-based personal laws.[206]

---

[200] *Narayanan Nambudripad v Madras* [1954] AIR Madras 385, noting that the Indian Constitution substantially departed from the American model in not enacting a general legislative prohibition against the 'establishment of religion' and through provisions inconsistent with the theory of 'a wall of separation between Church and State'. Eg, Arts 16(5) and 28(2) relate to state management of religious/educational institutions. The Court rejected the American view 'that the State should have nothing to do with religious institutions and endowments'.

[201] M Galanter, 'Secularism: East and West' in R Bhargava (ed), *Secularism and its Critics* (New Delhi: Oxford University Press, 1999) at 4; R Dhavan, 'The Road to Xanadu: India's Quest for Secularism' in G Larson (ed), *Religion and Personal Law in Secular India* (Bloomington, Ind: Indiana University Press 2001).

[202] Per Ramaswamy J, *SR Bommai v Union of India* [1994] AIR SC 1918 [185].

[203] *Sri Venkataramana Devaru v State of Mysore* [1958] AIR SC 255. It referred in para [23] to the goal of Hindu social reformers to address untouchability: 'A custom which denied to large sections of Hindus the right to use public roads and institutions to which all the other Hindus had a right of access, purely on grounds of birth could not be considered reasonable and defended on any sound democratic principle, and efforts were being made to secure its abolition by legislation. This culminated in the enactment of Article 17 ...'

[204] *Aruna Roy v Union of India* (2002) 7 SCC 368. The Court held that the teaching of Vedic astrology at graduate level did not 'saffronise' education or otherwise violate secularism: *PM Bhargava v University* [2004] AIR SC 3478.

[205] Per RM Sahai J in *Smt Sarla Mugdal, President v Union of India* [1995] AIR 1531.

[206] *Mohd Ahmed Khan v Shah Bano Begum* [1985] AIR 945: The Supreme Court cited a questionable *Hadith* (Islamic teaching) in concluding that nothing in Muslim personal law conflicted with the statutory provisions for maintaining divorced wives, in deciding whether a practice was essential to Islam. This resort to scriptural interpretation was criticised as unduly interventionist.

The following case speaks to how 'tolerance' is understood within the Indian secular order.

Hinsa Virodhak Sangh vs Mirzapur Moti Kuresh Jamat & Ors
AIR 2008 SC 1892 Appeal (Civil) 5469 of 2005 (Supreme Court, India)

Facts

The State government ordered the temporary closure of municipal slaughter houses during the Paryushan festival in Ahmedabad, to serve the public interest of promoting mutual respect for each group's religious beliefs. Here, it was in deference to the religious sentiments of Jainists and their pacific Ahinsa ideology advocating kindness to all living creatures. The court found this restriction reasonable under Article 19, referring to the importance of secularism as a method of promoting tolerance and religious diversity

Markandey Katju J

[T]he closure of the slaughter house is only for 9 days . . . [which] is a very short time and surely the non-vegetarians can become vegetarians during those 9 days out of respect for the feeling of the Jain community. Also, the dealers in meat can do their business for 356 days in a year . . . Surely this is not an excessive restriction, particularly since such closure has been observed for many years . . . Courts must act with a sense of responsibility and self-restraint with the sobering reflection that the Constitution is meant not only for people of their way of thinking but for all, and the majority of the elected representatives of the people have in authorizing the imposition of the restrictions considered them to be reasonable.

. . . India is a multi-cultural pluralistic society with tremendous diversity. There are a large number of religions, castes, languages, ethnic groups, cultures, etc in our country [comparing India to China, which had twice the land area, there being 'broad homogeneity in China'] . . . it is absolutely essential if we wish to keep our country united to have tolerance and respect for all communities and sects. It was due to the wisdom of our founding fathers that we have a Constitution which is secular in character, and which caters to the tremendous diversity in our country [by giving] equal respect to all communities, sects, lingual and ethnic groups, etc in the country.

The architect of modern India was the great Mughal Emperor Akbar who gave equal respect to people of all communities and appointed them to the highest offices on their merits irrespective of their religion, caste, etc . . . The Emperor Akbar held discussions with scholars of all religions and gave respect not only to Muslim scholars, but also to Hindus, Christians, Parsis, Sikhs, etc . . . The Emperor declared his policy of *Suleh-e-Kul*, which means universal tolerance of all religions and communities . . . Thus, as stated in the *Cambridge History of India* (Vol IV: The Mughal Period) Emperor Akbar conceived the idea of becoming the father of all his subjects, rather than the leader of only the Muslims, and he was far ahead of his times [in creating] a sense of oneness among the diverse elements of India . . .

In 1582, the Emperor invited and received a Jain delegation . . . its doctrine of non-violence, made a profound impression on him and influenced his personal life. He curtailed his food and drink and ultimately abstained from flesh diet altogether for several months in the year. He renounced hunting which was his favorite pastime, restricted the practice of fishing and released prisoners and caged birds. Slaughter of animals was prohibited on certain days and ultimately in 1587 for about half the days in the year.

If the Emperor Akbar could forbid meat eating for six months in a year in Gujarat, is it unreasonable to abstain from meat for nine days in a year in Ahmedabad today? Emperor Akbar was a propagator of *Suleh-i-Kul* (universal toleration) at a time when Europeans were indulging in religious massacres eg the St Bartholomew Day massacre in 1572 of Protestants (called Huguenots) in France by the Catholics, the burning at the stake of Protestants by Queen Mary of England, the massacre by the Duke of Alva of millions of people for their resistance to Rome and the burning at the stake of Jews during the Spanish Inquisition. We may also mention the subsequent massacre of the Catholics in Ireland by Cromwell, and the mutual massacre of Catholics and Protestants in Germany during the thirty year war from 1618 to 1648 in which the population of Germany was reduced from 18 million to 12 million. Thus, Emperor Akbar was far ahead of even the Europeans of his times.

It was because of the wise policy of toleration of the Great Emperor Akbar that the Mughal empire lasted for so long, and hence the same wise policy of toleration alone can keep our country together despite so much diversity . . . the great Emperor Akbar himself used to remain a vegetarian for a few days every week out of respect for the vegetarian section of the Indian society and out of respect for his Hindu wife. We too should have similar respect for the sentiments for others, even if they are a minority sect.

Note and Questions

1. In 2012, the Gujurat High Court ruled that chicken and fish were meat, and that their sale during Paryushon would frustrate the decision of the Supreme Court decision and hurt the religious sentiments of Jains: 'No sale of chicken, fish, during Jain festival, rules HC', *Express India News Service*, 20 September 2012.

2. Does this understanding of secular tolerance promote multi-culturalism? Is secularism understood as the binary opposite of communalism, implying a tolerance of other religious communities, the equality of religions and state religious neutrality?[207] For a comment on the case, see M Tundawala and A Sarkar, 'Hinsa Virodhak Sang v Mirzapur Modi Kuresh Jamat: A Critique of the State Enforcement of Toleration' [2009] 1 *Journal of Indian Law and Society* 105–28.

ii. Hindu Bias in the Indian Constitution and Threat of Hindutva

The Indian Constitution has been criticised for containing Hindu elements, institutionalising communalism and diluting a commitment to secularism. The Article 1 reference to 'Bharat' hails back to a glorious, pre British/Muslim Hindu past; recognising Hindi as official language (Article 343) may alienate non-Hindus.[208] Article 25(2)(b), in empowering the state to undertake social welfare to reform Hinduism, presumably to prevent the exodus of Dalits from the Hindu fold, accords Hinduism preferential treatment. The Article 48 directive that the state take steps to prohibit the slaughter of cows favours upper-caste Hindus, as cows are not sacred to Dalits.

Hindu nationalism and the promotion of Hindutva threatens Indian secularism, fuelling communal riots, as where a Hindu mob demolished a mosque built over a

---

[207] T Murshid, *The Sacred and the Secular* (Calcutta: Oxford University Press, 1995) 5.
[208] P Singh, 'Hindu Bias in India's "Secular" Constitution: probing flaws in the instruments of governance' (2005) 26(6) *Third World Quarterly* 909, 911.

Hindu Temple at Ayodhya. The courts have judicially determined the meaning of 'Hindutva' in cases involving section 123(3A) of the Representation of the People Act (1951), which makes it a corrupt practice to appeal for votes on the basis of the candidate's religion, race, caste or community, or to use religious symbols, causing feelings of enmity or hatred between different classes of Indian citizens.

Dr Ramesh Yeshwant Prabhoo v Shri Prabhakar Kashinath Kunte (1996) SCC (1) 130 (Supreme Court, India)

Facts

Prabhoo, who was Mayor of Bombay, and his election agent, Bal Thackaray, were found guilty of corruption under section 123 of the Representation of the People Act (RPA) 1951. Prabhoo was charged with making derogatory speeches about Muslims, calling them 'snakes', and stating they only wanted the Hindu votes since 'this country belongs to Hindus'. He also declared, 'You will find Hindu temples underneath if all the mosques are dug out.' One question which arose was whether the appeal to 'Hindutva' was effectively an appeal to Hinduism, which was contrary to section 123(3A) of the RPA.

Verma J

It cannot be doubted that a speech with a secular stance alleging discrimination against any particular religion and promising removal of the imbalance cannot be treated as an appeal on the ground of religion as its thrust is for promoting secularism . . . [M]ention of religion as such in an election speech is not forbidden by sub-section (3) so long as it does not amount to an appeal to vote for a candidate on the ground of his religion or to refrain from voting for any other candidate on the ground of his religion. When it is said that politics and religion do not mix, it merely means that the religion of a candidate cannot be used for gaining political mileage by seeking votes on the ground of the candidate's religion or alienating the electorate against another candidate on the ground of the other candidate's religion. It also means that the state has no religion and the State practises the policy of neutrality in the matter of religion . . .

   [Of section 123] . . . [t]he provision is made with the object of curbing the tendency to promote or attempt to promote communal, linguistic or any other factional enmity or hatred to prevent the divisive tendencies . . . Our Constitution-makers certainly intended to set up a secular democratic Republic . . . Our political history made it particularly necessary that these differences [religion, race, caste, language etc] which can generate powerful emotions depriving people of their powers of rational thought and action, should not be permitted to be exploited lest the imperative conditions for the preservation of democratic freedoms are disturbed. It seems to us that Section 123 RPA . . . was enacted to eliminate, from the electoral process, appeals to those divisive factors which arouse irrational passions that run counter to the basic tenets of our Constitution . . . The line has to be drawn by the Courts, between what is permissible and what is prohibited . . .

   . . . [O]ur democracy can only survive if those who aspire to become people's representatives and leaders understand the spirit of secular democracy . . . For such a spirit to prevail, candidates at elections have to try to persuade electors by showing them the light of reason and not by inflaming their blind and disruptive passions. Heresy-hunting propaganda or professedly religious grounds directed against a candidate at an election may be permitted in a theocratic state but not in a secular republic like ours . . . if such propaganda was permitted here, it would injure the interests of members of religious minority groups more than those of others.

[On the use of 'Hindutva' the Court noted that its mere use did not bring into within the scope of section 123, as this was a question of fact.] Both sides referred copiously to the meaning of the word 'Hindutva' and 'Hinduism' with reference to several writings. Shri Jethmalani referred to them for the purpose of indicating the several meanings of these words and to emphasise that the word 'Hindutva' relates to Indian culture based on the geographical division known as Hindustan, ie, India. On the other hand, Shri Ashok Desai emphasised that the term 'Hindutva' used in election speeches is an emphasis on Hindu religion . . . and the term can relate to Indian culture.

[Discussing various precedents and scholarly opinions] . . . We find it difficult, if not impossible, to define Hindu religion or even adequately describe it. Unlike other religions in the world, the Hindu religion does not claim any one prophet; it does not worship any one God; it does not subscribe to any one dogma; it does not believe in any one philosophic concept; it does not follow any one set of religious rites or performances; in fact, it does not appear to satisfy the narrow traditional features of any religion or creed. It may broadly be described as a way of life and nothing more . . . The term 'Hindu', according to Dr Radhakrishnan (*The Hindu View of Life*), had originally a territorial and not a credal significance. It implied residence in a well-defined geographical area . . . The history of Indian thought emphatically brings out the fact that the development of Hindu religion has always been inspired by an endless quest of the mind for truth based on the consciousness that truth has many facets . . . This knowledge inevitably bred a spirit of tolerance and willingness to understand and appreciate the opponent's point of view . . . The Constitution-makers were fully conscious of this broad and comprehensive character of Hindu religion [noting that the Article 25 reference 'Hindu' encompassed persons of the Sikh, Jain and Buddhist religion] . . .

. . . In *Encyclopaedia Britannica* (15th Edition), the term 'Hinduism' has been defined as meaning 'the civilization of Hindus (originally, the inhabitants of the land of the Indus River). It properly denotes the Indian civilization of approximately the last 2,000 years, which gradually evolved from Vedism, the religion of the ancient Indo-European who settled in India in the last centuries of the 2nd millennium BC. Because it integrates a large variety of heterogeneous elements, Hinduism constitutes a very complex but largely continuous whole, and since it covers the whole of life, it has religious, social, economic, literary, and artistic aspects. As a religion, Hinduism is an utterly diverse conglomerate of doctrines, cults, and way of life . . . The Hindu is inclined to revere the divine in every manifestation . . . and is doctrinally tolerant . . . A Hindu may embrace a non-Hindu religion without ceasing to be a Hindu, and since the Hindu is disposed to think synthetically and to regard other forms of worship, strange gods, and divergent doctrines as inadequate rather than wrong or objectionable, he tends to believe that the highest divine powers complement each other for the well-being of the world and mankind . . . Hinduism is then both a civilization and a conglomerate of religions, with neither a beginning, a founder, nor a central authority, hierarchy, or organization.

. . . In *Bhagwan Koer v JC Bose*, (1904 ILR 31 Cal 11), it was held that Hindu religion is marvelously catholic and elastic. Its theology is marked by eclecticism and tolerance and almost unlimited freedom of private worship . . . These Constitution Bench decisions . . . indicate that no precise meaning can be ascribed to the terms 'Hindu', 'Hindutva' and 'Hinduism'; and no meaning in the abstract can confine it to the narrow limits of religion alone, excluding the content of Indian culture and heritage . . . It is difficult to appreciate how in the face of these decisions the term 'Hindutva' or 'Hinduism' per se, in the abstract, can be assumed to mean and be equated with narrow fundamentalist Hindu religious bigotry, or be construed to fall within the prohibition in sub-sections (3) and/or (3A) of Section 123, RPA . . . Ordinarily, Hindutva is understood as a way of life or a state of mind and it is not to be equated with, or understood as religious Hindu fundamentalism . . . the word 'Hindutva' is used and understood as a synonym of 'Indianisation', ie, development of uniform culture by obliterating the differences between all the cultures co-existing in the country . . .

. . . Unless the context of a speech indicates a contrary meaning or use, in the abstract these terms ['Hinduism' and 'Hindutva'] are indicative more of a way of life of the Indian people and are not confined merely to describe persons practising the Hindu religion as a faith. Considering the terms 'Hinduism' or 'Hindutva' per se as depicting hostility, enmity or intolerance towards other religious faiths or professing communalism, proceeds from an improper appreciation and perception of the true meaning of these expressions emerging from the detailed discussion in earlier authorities of this Court . . . The mischief resulting from the misuse of the terms by anyone in his speech has to be checked and not its permissible use. It is indeed very unfortunate, if in spite of the liberal and tolerant features of 'Hinduism' recognised in judicial decisions, these terms are misused by anyone during the elections to gain any unfair political advantage. Fundamentalism of any colour or kind must be curbed with a heavy hand to preserve and promote the secular creed of the nation. Any misuse of these terms must, therefore, be dealt with strictly. It is, therefore, a fallacy and an error of law to proceed on the assumption that any reference to Hindutva or Hinduism in a speech makes it automatically a speech based on the Hindu religion as opposed to the other religions or that the use of words 'Hindutva' or 'Hinduism' per se depict an attitude hostile to all persons practising any religion other than the Hindu religion . . . It may well be, that these words are used in a speech to promote secularism or to emphasise the way of life of the Indian people and the Indian culture or ethos, or to criticise the policy of any political party as discriminatory or intolerant . . . [concluding that the speeches were corrupt practices under section 123 RPA].

Notes and Questions

1. 'Inclusivist' and 'exclusivist' Hinduism may be distinguished: the former views Hinduism as a universal and tolerant Vedas-based religion, a way of life instead of a form of thought, broad enough to encompass the theist, atheist and agnostic who accept the Hindu system of culture and life. This is consonant with founding Prime Minister Jawaharlal Nehru's conception of Hinduism as a vague, amorphous faith, and is reflected in the Supreme Court's judgment in *Yagnapurushdasji*.[209] This view has propelled judicial decisions, rejecting the view put forth by various Hindu sects that they are a separate religion (eg the *Arya Samaj* and *Ramakrishna Mission*[210]). An 'exclusivist' view is associated with Hindu nationalism, where the concept of Hindu is territorially bound with a 'holy land' concept. The founder of contemporary Hindu nationalism, VD Savarkar, described the term he coined as referring to 'a theory or code more or less based on spiritual or religious dogma or system'. See VD Savarkar, *Hindutva: Who is a Hindu?* (Bombay: Veer Savarkar Prakashan, 1969) at 4. Hinduism was a subset of Hindutva which 'embraces all the departments of thought and activity of the whole Being of our Hindu race'.

[209] *Yagnapurushdasji v. Muldas* AIR 1966 SC 1119 at 1227.
[210] *Arya Samaj* [1971] AIR SC 1731; *Ramakrishna Mission* [1995] AIR SC 2089.

Three core elements of Hindutva were *rashtra* (common nation), *jati* (common race) and *sanskriti* (common civilisation). Saravak's conception of Hinduism was both racial and territorial, his concern being the political goal of creating a Hindu nation, as opposed to the reform of Hinduism, a spiritual project. See R Sen, *Legalizing Religion: The Indian Supreme Court* (Washington DC: East-West Center Washington, 2007, Policy Studies 30) at 30–32.

2. Did the Court conflate Hinduism and Hindutva? Hindu nationalist groups like the BJP considered the Supreme Court's refusal to equate Hindutva with exclusive sectarianism as vindicating their ideology in equating it with 'Indianisation' and apparently approving a Hindu Nationalist conception of the nation. The case was criticised for ignoring the association of Hindutva with Savarkar's philosophy, the political context, and for assuming that 'Hinduism, the religion of the majority of Indians, had come to reflect the way of life of all Indians': B Cossman and R Kapur, *Secularism's Last Sigh: The Hindu Right and the (Mis)rule of Law* (New Delhi, Oxford University Press, 1999) at 33.

3. The Supreme Court used 'Hinduism' and 'Hindutva' interchangeably in *Manohar Joshi v Nitin Bhaurao Patil*,[211] restoring Joshi's election, despite his statement that 'the first Hindu state will be established in Maharashtra', as this was considered an expression of hope rather than an appeal for votes on grounds of religion contrary to section 123 of the RPA.

B. Philippines Secularism: Accommodation through Exemptions and Exceptions

i. Church and State in the Philippines

Catholicism was the state religion of the Philippines under Spanish rule and the 1876 Constitution. This was removed with the introduction of the American constitutional model of religion and church.[212] Section 5 of the 1902 Philippines Bill 'caused the complete separation of church and state, and the abolition of all special privileges'.[213] The Catholic Church continues to be informally influential in a country where 81 per cent of the people are Catholics.[214] Section 5 of the 1987 Constitution reads:

> No law shall be made respecting an establishment of religion, or prohibiting the free exercise thereof. The free exercise and enjoyment of religious profession and worship, without discrimination or preference, shall forever be allowed. No religious test shall be required for the exercise of civil or political rights.

Religious freedom in the Philippines as constitutionally mandated 'is not inhibition of profound reverence for religion and is not denial of its influence in human affairs'. As the Supreme Court noted in *Aglipay v Ruiz*,[215] the inclusion in the preamble of the line

---

[211] *Manohar Joshi v Nitin Bhaurao Patil* (1996) SCC (1) 169.

[212] R Pangalangan, 'Transplanted Constitutionalism: The Philippine Debate on the Secular State and the Rule of Law' (2008) 82 *Philippines Law Journal* 1.

[213] Per Justice Trent in *US v Balcorta*, GR No 8722, 10 Sep 1913.

[214] J Bautista, 'Church and State in the Philippines: Tackling Life Issues in a "Culture of Death"' (2010) 25(1) *Sojourn: Journal of Social Issues in Southeast Asia* 29.

[215] *Aglipay v Ruiz* 64 Phil 201 (1937).

imploring 'the aid of Divine Providence' to establish an ideal government, was a manifestation of the Filipino People's 'reliance upon Him who guides the destinies of men and nations'.[216]

Alejandro Estrada v Soledad Escritor
AM No P-02-1651 22 June 2006 (En Banc) (Supreme Court, Philippines)

Facts

The Supreme Court held that a court interpreter could not be dismissed for 'disgraceful and immoral conduct' under the 1987 Administrative Code. Her conjugal arrangements were consonant with her religious beliefs as a Jehovah's Witness; Escritor was not married to but cohabited with one Luciano Quilapio Jr; her Church had formally recognised their relationship as both had entered into a Declaration of Pledging Faithfulness, under which they were to have their union legally recognised, if the opportunity arose. Escritor's husband had abandoned her and Quilapio was still married to another woman. The Court had to determine the scope of religious freedom under Article III, Section 5, measured against the state interest in protecting marriage, the family and the integrity of the court in relation to its employees. In so doing, it considered the relevance of US jurisprudence.

Puno J

In our decision dated August 4, 2003, after a long and arduous scrutiny into the origins and development of the religion clauses in the United States (US) and the Philippines, we held that in resolving claims involving religious freedom (1) benevolent neutrality or accommodation, whether mandatory or permissive, is the spirit, intent and framework underlying the religion clauses in our Constitution; and (2) in deciding respondent's plea of exemption based on the Free Exercise Clause (from the law with which she is administratively charged), it is the compelling state interest test, the strictest test, which must be applied . . . [The complaint was remanded so the Government could demonstrate compelling interest on the facts.] We review the highlights of our decision . . .

1. Old World Antecedents . . .

We delved into the conception of religion from primitive times . . . when the authority and power of the state were ascribed to God. Then, religion developed on its own and became superior to the state, its subordinate, and even becoming an engine of state policy . . . We ascertained two salient features in the review of religious history: First, with minor exceptions, the history of church–state relationships was characterized by persecution, oppression, hatred, bloodshed, and war, all in the name of the God of Love and of the Prince of Peace. Second . . . this history witnessed the unscrupulous use of religion by secular powers to promote secular purposes and policies, and the willing acceptance of that role by the vanguards of religion in exchange for the favors and mundane benefits conferred by ambitious princes . . . This was the context in which the unique experiment of the principle of religious freedom and separation of church and state saw its birth in American constitutional democracy and in human history. [Discusses the US First Amendment clause which reads: 'Congress shall make no law respecting an establishment of religion or prohibiting the free exercise thereof.'] . . .

---

[216] F Hilbay, 'The Establishment Clause: An Anti-Establishment View' (2008) 82 *Philippines Law Journal* 24.

The Establishment and Free Exercise Clauses . . . were not designed to serve contradictory purposes. They have a single goal – to promote freedom of individual religious beliefs and practices. In simplest terms, the Free Exercise Clause prohibits government from inhibiting religious beliefs with penalties for religious beliefs and practice, while the Establishment Clause prohibits government from inhibiting religious belief with rewards for religious beliefs and practices . . . the two religion clauses were intended to deny government the power to use either the carrot or the stick to influence individual religious beliefs and practices . . .

2. Religion Clauses in the US Context

The Court then turned to the religion clauses' interpretation and construction in the United States, not because we are bound by their interpretation, but because the US religion clauses are the precursors to the Philippine religion clauses, although we have significantly departed from the US interpretation [noting the volatility and inconsistency within American jurisprudence] . . .

US history has produced two identifiably different, even opposing, strains of jurisprudence on the religion clauses. . . . A brief review of each theory is in order.

a. Strict Separation and Strict Neutrality/Separation

The *Strict Separationist* believes that the Establishment Clause was meant to protect the state from the church, and the state's hostility towards religion allows no interaction between the two. According to this Jeffersonian view, an absolute barrier to formal interdependence of religion and state needs to be erected. Religious institutions could not receive aid, whether direct or indirect, from the state. Nor could the state adjust its secular programs to alleviate burdens the programs placed on believers. Only the complete separation of religion from politics would eliminate the formal influence of religious institutions and provide for a free choice among political views, thus a strict 'wall of separation' is necessary [noting that such rigidly never existed in practice, as direct or indirect aid flows between government and religion, and that Congress after adopting the First Amendment endorsed a resolution supporting a presidential proclamation for a national day of Thanksgiving and Prayer to God Almighty] . . .

The tamer version of the strict separationist view, the *strict neutrality* or *separationist* view (or, the *governmental neutrality* theory) finds basis in *Everson v Board of Education* 330 US 1 (1946) . . . [This view] believes that the 'wall of separation' does not require the state to be their adversary . . . The *strict neutrality* approach is not hostile to religion, but it is strict in holding that religion may not be used as a basis for classification for purposes of governmental action, whether the action confers rights or privileges or imposes duties or obligations. Only secular criteria may be the basis of government action. It does not permit, much less require, accommodation of secular programs to religious belief . . . The problem with the strict neutrality approach . . . [as] pointed out by Justice Goldberg in his concurring opinion in *Abington School District v Schempp* 374 US 203 (1963) [is that it] could lead to 'a brooding and pervasive devotion to the secular and a passive, or even active, hostility to the religious' . . .

Thus, the dilemma of the separationist approach . . . is that while the Jeffersonian wall of separation 'captures the spirit of the American ideal of church-state separation,' in real life, church and state are not and cannot be totally separate . . .

b. Benevolent Neutrality/Accommodation

The theory of *benevolent neutrality* or *accommodation* is premised on a different view of the 'wall of separation,' associated with Williams, founder of the Rhode Island colony . . . [where] the wall is meant to protect the church from the state. This doctrine was expressed in *Zorach v Clauson* 343 US 306, 312–314 (1951):

> The First Amendment . . . does not say that in every and all respects there shall be a separation of Church and State. Rather, it studiously defines the manner, the specific ways, in which there shall be no concert or union or dependency one or the other . . . Otherwise, the state and religion would be aliens to each other – hostile, suspicious, and even unfriendly. Churches could not be required to pay even property taxes . . . Policemen who helped parishioners into their places of worship would violate the Constitution . . . 'so help me God' in our courtroom oaths – these and all other references to the Almighty that run through our laws, our public rituals, our ceremonies would be flouting the First Amendment. A fastidious atheist or agnostic could even object to the supplication with which the Court opens each session: 'God save the United States and this Honorable Court . . .'

We are a religious people whose institutions presuppose a Supreme Being. We guarantee the freedom to worship as one chooses . . . When the state encourages religious instruction or cooperates with religious authorities by adjusting the schedule of public eveFnts, it follows the best of our traditions. For it then respects the religious nature of our people and accommodates the public service to their spiritual needs. To hold that it may not would be to find in the Constitution a requirement that the government show a callous indifference to religious groups . . . But we find no constitutional requirement which makes it necessary for government to be hostile to religion and to throw its weight against efforts to widen their effective scope of religious influence.

Benevolent neutrality recognizes that religion plays an important role in the public life of the US as shown by many traditional government practices which, to *strict neutrality*, pose Establishment Clause questions. Among these are the inscription of 'In God We Trust' on American currency; the recognition of America as 'one nation under God' in the official pledge of allegiance to the flag . . .; and the practice of Congress and every state legislature of paying a chaplain, usually of a particular Protestant denomination, to lead representatives in prayer. These practices clearly show the preference for one theological viewpoint – the existence of and potential for intervention by a god – over the contrary theological viewpoint of atheism. Church and government agencies also cooperate in the building of low-cost housing and in other forms of poor relief, in the treatment of alcoholism and drug addiction, in foreign aid and other government activities with strong moral dimensions . . .

(1) Legislative Acts and the Free Exercise Clause

. . . [T]he more difficult religion cases involve legislative acts which have a secular purpose and general applicability, but may incidentally or inadvertently aid or burden religious exercise. Though the government action is not religiously motivated, these laws have a 'burdensome effect' on religious exercise.

The benevolent neutrality theory believes that with respect to these governmental actions, accommodation of religion may be allowed, not to promote the government's favored form of religion, but to allow individuals and groups to exercise their religion without hindrance. The purpose of accommodations is to remove a burden on, or facilitate the exercise of, a person's or institution's religion . . . what is sought . . . is not a declaration of unconstitutionality of a facially neutral law, but an exemption from its application or its 'burdensome effect' . . .

(2) Free Exercise Jurisprudence: Sherbert, Yoder and Smith

The pinnacle of free exercise protection and the theory of accommodation in the US blossomed in the case of *Sherbert v Verner* 374 US 398, 403 (1963) . . . Sherbert, a Seventh Day Adventist, claimed unemployment compensation under the law as her employment was terminated for refusal to work on Saturdays on religious grounds . . . This germinal case of *Sherbert* firmly established the exemption doctrine, *viz*:

> It is certain that not every conscience can be accommodated by all the laws of the land; but when general laws conflict with scruples of conscience, exemptions ought to be granted unless some 'compelling state interest' intervenes.

. . . After *Sherbert*, this strict scrutiny balancing test resulted in court-mandated religious exemptions from facially-neutral laws of general application whenever unjustified burdens were found [discusses *Wisconsin v Yoder* 406 US 205 (1972) where the Court carved out an exemption for Amish parents for violating a facially neutral general law carrying a criminal penalty relating to compulsory school attendance].

. . . The *Sherbert-Yoder* doctrine had five main components. First, action was protected – conduct beyond speech, press, or worship was included in the shelter of freedom of religion . . . Second, indirect impositions on religious conduct such as the denial of twenty-six weeks of unemployment insurance benefits to Adel Sherbert . . . were prohibited. Third . . . the protection granted was extensive. Only extremely strong governmental interests justified impingement on religious conduct, as the absolute language of the test of the Free Exercise Clause suggests. Fourth, the strong language was backed by a requirement that the government provide proof of the important interest at stake and of the dangers to that interest presented by the religious conduct at issue. Fifth, in determining the injury to the government's interest, a court was required to focus on the effect that exempting religious claimants from the regulation would have, rather than on the value of the regulation in general . . . Together, the fourth and fifth elements required that facts, rather than speculation, had to be presented concerning how the government's interest would be harmed by excepting religious conduct from the law being challenged.

Thus, the strict scrutiny and compelling state interest test significantly increased the degree of protection afforded to religiously motivated conduct . . . [T]his general test (compelling secular justification) established a strong presumption in favor of the free exercise of religion . . . The 1990 case of *Employment Division, Oregon Department of Human Resources v Smith* 494 US 872 (1990) drastically changed all that. [Native Americans challenged an Oregon law prohibiting the use of peyote, a hallucinogenic drug, in religious rituals, resulting in their dismissal from employment and disqualification from unemployment benefits. The Court noted noted that Justice Scalia declared 'that the right of free exercise does not relieve an individual of the obligation to comply with a 'valid and neutral law of general applicability of the ground that the law proscribes (or prescribes) conduct that his religion prescribes (or proscribes)'.] The Court expressly rejected the use of strict scrutiny for challenges to neutral laws of general applicability that burden religion [and said] those seeking religious exemptions from laws should look to the democratic process for protection, not the courts [such laws were subject only to the rational basis test] . . .

Criticism of *Smith* was intense and widespread . . . The *Smith* doctrine is highly unsatisfactory in several respects . . . First, the First Amendment was intended to protect minority religions from the tyranny of the religious and political majority. Critics of *Smith* have worried about religious minorities, who can suffer disproportionately from laws that enact majoritarian mores . . . and *Smith* virtually wiped out their judicial recourse for exemption. Second, *Smith* leaves too much leeway for pervasive welfare-state regulation to burden religion while satisfying neutrality. After all, laws not aimed at religion can hinder observance just as effectively as those that target religion . . . If the Free Exercise Clause could not afford protection to inadvertent interference, it would be left almost meaningless. Third, the *Reynolds-Gobitis-Smith* doctrine simply defies common sense. The state should not be allowed to interfere with the most deeply held fundamental religious convictions of an individual in order to pursue some trivial state economic or bureaucratic objective. This is especially true when there are alternative approaches for the state to effectively pursue its objective without serious inadvertent impact on religion.

At bottom, the Court's ultimate concern in *Smith* appeared to be two-fold: (1) the difficulty in defining and limiting the term 'religion' in today's pluralistic society, and (2) the belief that courts have no business determining the significance of an individual's religious beliefs. For the *Smith* Court, these two concerns appear to lead to the conclusion that the Free Exercise Clause must protect everything or it must protect virtually nothing. As a result, the Court perceives its only viable options are to leave free exercise protection to the political process or to allow a 'system in which each conscience is a law unto itself.' [The Court noted the criticism that between these two options lay a 'middle ground'.[217]]

. . . *Smith*, while expressly recognizing the power of legislature to give accommodations, is in effect contrary to the benevolent neutrality or accommodation approach . . . *Smith* is dangerous precedent because it subordinates fundamental rights of religious belief and practice to all neutral, general legislation . . .

c. *Accommodation under the Religion Clauses*

A free exercise claim could result in three kinds of accommodation . . .

Mandatory accommodation results when the Court finds that accommodation is required by the Free Exercise Clause, ie, when the Court itself carves out an exemption. This accommodation occurs when all three conditions of the compelling interest test are met . . . the Court finds that the injury to religious conscience is so great and the advancement of public purposes is incomparable that only indifference or hostility could explain a refusal to make exemptions. Thus, if the state's objective could be served as well or almost as well by granting an exemption to those whose religious beliefs are burdened by the regulation, the Court must grant the exemption . . . In permissive accommodation, the Court finds that the State may, but is not required to, accommodate religious interests . . . Finally, when the Court finds no basis for a mandatory accommodation, or it determines that the legislative accommodation runs afoul of the establishment or the free exercise clause, it results to a prohibited accommodation. In this case, the Court finds that establishment concerns prevail over potential accommodation interests. To say that there are valid exemptions buttressed by the Free Exercise Clause does not mean that all claims for free exercise exemptions are valid. An example where accommodation was prohibited is *McCollum v Board of Education* 333 US 203 (1948) where the Court ruled against optional religious instruction in the public school premises.

Given that a free exercise claim could lead to three different results, the question now remains as to how the Court should determine which action to take. In this regard, it is the strict scrutiny-compelling state interest test which is most in line with the benevolent neutrality-accommodation approach.

---

[217] I Bodensteiner, 'The Demise of the First Amendment As a Guarantor of Religious Freedom' (2005) 27 *Whittier Law Review* 415, 419.

Under the benevolent-neutrality theory, the principle underlying the First Amendment is that freedom to carry out one's duties to a Supreme Being is an inalienable right, not one dependent on the grace of legislature. Religious freedom is seen as a substantive right and not merely a privilege against discriminatory legislation. With religion looked upon with benevolence and not hostility, benevolent neutrality allows accommodation of religion under certain circumstances.

Considering that laws nowadays are rarely enacted specifically to disable religious belief or practice, free exercise disputes arise commonly when a law that is religiously neutral and generally applicable on its face is argued to prevent or burden what someone's religious faith requires, or alternatively, requires someone to undertake an act that faith would preclude . . . [F]ree exercise arguments contemplate religious exemptions from otherwise general laws. [Notes the compelling state interest test has three steps, discussed below.]

3. Religion Clauses in the Philippine Context: Constitution, Jurisprudence and Practice

a. US Constitution and jurisprudence vis-à-vis Philippine Constitution

By juxtaposing the American Constitution and jurisprudence against that of the Philippines, it is immediately clear that one cannot simply conclude that we have adopted – lock, stock and barrel – the religion clauses as embodied in the First Amendment, and therefore, the US Court's interpretation of the same. Unlike in the US where legislative exemptions of religion had to be upheld by the US Supreme Court as constituting *permissive accommodations*, similar exemptions for religion are mandatory accommodations under our own Exhibit AExhibitPageconstitutions. Thus, our 1935, 1973 and 1987 Constitutions contain provisions on tax exemption of church property, salary of religious officers in government institutions, and optional religious instruction. Our own preamble also invokes the aid of a divine being. These constitutional provisions are wholly ours and have no counterpart in the US Constitution or its *amendments*. They all reveal without doubt that the Filipino people, in adopting these constitutions, manifested their adherence to the benevolent neutrality approach that requires accommodations in interpreting the religion clauses . . .

We therefore reject Mr Justice Carpio's total adherence to the US Court's interpretation of the religion clauses to effectively deny accommodations on the sole basis that the law in question is neutral and of general application . . . our own Constitutions have made significant changes to accommodate and exempt religion. Philippine jurisprudence shows that the Court has allowed exemptions from a law of general application, in effect, interpreting our religion clauses to cover both mandatory and permissive accommodations.

Having established that benevolent neutrality-accommodation is the framework by which free exercise cases must be decided, the next question then turned to the test that should be used in ascertaining the limits of the exercise of religious freedom. In our Decision dated August 4, 2003, we reviewed our jurisprudence, and ruled that in cases involving purely conduct based on religious belief, as in the case at bar, the compelling state interest test, is proper, *viz:*

> Philippine jurisprudence articulates several tests to determine these limits . . . [where speech is implicated, a clear and present test is appropriate as speech has immediate effects] . . . The 'compelling state interest' test is proper where conduct is involved, for the whole gamut of human conduct has different effects on the state's interests: some effects may be immediate and short-term while others delayed and far-reaching. A test that would protect the interests of the state in preventing a substantive evil, whether immediate or delayed, is therefore necessary. However, not any interest of the state would suffice to prevail over the right to religious freedom as this is a fundamental right

[which is] sacred, for an invocation of the Free Exercise Clause is an appeal to a higher sovereignty. The entire constitutional order of limited government is premised upon an acknowledgment of such higher sovereignty, thus the Filipinos implore the 'aid of Almighty God in order to build a just and humane society and establish a government.' As held in *Sherbert*, only the gravest abuses, endangering paramount interests can limit this fundamental right . . . In determining which shall prevail between the state's interest and religious liberty, reasonableness shall be the guide. The 'compelling state interest' serves the purpose of revering religious liberty while at the same time affording protection to the paramount interests of the state.

[Rejecting Justice Carpio's support for the *Smith* test and pointing out that it cannot be used as a test to determine the claims of religious exemptions directly under the Free Exercise Clause because *Smith* does not recognise such exemptions, only legislative accommodations . . .]

. . . Mr Justice Carpio's advocacy of the *Smith* doctrine would effectively render the Free Exercise protection – a fundamental right under our Constitution – nugatory because he would deny its status as an independent source of right.

b. The Compelling State Interest Test

As previously stated, the compelling state interest test involves a three-step process . . .

. . . First, '[H]as the statute or government action created a burden on the free exercise of religion?' The courts often look into the sincerity of the religious belief, but without inquiring into the truth of the belief because the Free Exercise Clause prohibits inquiring about its truth as held in *Ballard* and *Cantwell*. The sincerity of the claimant's belief is ascertained to avoid the mere claim of religious beliefs to escape a mandatory regulation . . .

Second, the court asks: '[I]s there a sufficiently compelling state interest to justify this infringement of religious liberty?' In this step, the government has to establish that its purposes are legitimate for the state and that they are compelling. Government must do more than assert the objectives at risk if exemption is given; it must precisely show how and to what extent those objectives will be undermined if exemptions are granted.

Third, the court asks: '[H]as the state in achieving its legitimate purposes used the least intrusive means possible so that the free exercise is not infringed any more than necessary to achieve the legitimate goal of the state?' [ie one that 'imposes as little as possible on religious liberties . . .']

Again, the application of the compelling state interest test could result to three situations of accommodation (mandatory, permissive, prohibited) . . . One of the central arguments in Mr Justice Carpio's dissent is that only permissive accommodation can carve out an exemption from a law of general application. He posits the view that the law should prevail in the absence of a legislative exemption, and the Court cannot make the accommodation or exemption. Mr Justice Carpio's position is clearly not supported by Philippine jurisprudence. The cases of *American Bible Society*, *Ebralinag*, and *Victoriano* demonstrate that our application of the doctrine of benevolent neutrality-accommodation covers not only the grant of permissive, or legislative accommodations, but also mandatory accommodations. Thus, an exemption from a law of general application is possible, even if anchored directly on an invocation of the Free Exercise Clause alone, rather than a legislative exemption.

Moreover, it should be noted that while there is no Philippine case as yet wherein the Court granted an accommodation/exemption to a religious act from the application of general *penal* laws, permissive accommodation based on religious freedom has been granted with respect to one of the crimes penalized under the Revised Penal Code, that of bigamy. [Unlike US law which did not grant Mormons an exemption from a general law criminalising polygamy: *Reynolds v United States*, 98 US 145 (1878)] . . . Philippine law accommodates the same practice among Moslems, through a legislative act (Art 180, Code of Muslim Personal Laws) . . . Mr Justice Carpio recognized this accommodation when, in his dissent in our Decision dated August 4, 2003 and citing *Sulu Islamic Association of Masjid Lambayong v Malik* AM No MTJ-92-691, September 10, 1993, 226 SCRA 193 he stated that a Muslim Judge 'is not criminally liable for bigamy because Shari'a law allows a Muslim to have more than one wife.' [Concludes that Mr Justice Carpio's reliance on the *Smith* doctrine (permissive accommodation only) is infirmed as the benevolent neutrality approach allowing both mandatory and permissive accommodations was unequivocally adopted by Philippines jurisprudence.] . . . Parenthetically, it should be pointed out that a 'permissive accommodation-only' stance is the antithesis to the notion that religion clauses, like the other fundamental liberties found in the Bill of Rights, is a preferred right and an independent source of right . . .

. . . We hold that the Constitution itself mandates the Court [to make exemptions in cases involving general criminal law] for the following reasons. First, . . . while the US religion clauses are the precursors to the Philippine religion clauses, the benevolent neutrality-accommodation approach in Philippine jurisdiction is more pronounced and given leeway than in the US. Second, the whole purpose of the accommodation theory . . . was to address the 'inadvertent burdensome effect' that an otherwise facially neutral law would have on religious exercise. Just because the law is criminal in nature . . . should not bring it out of the ambit of the Free Exercise Clause . . . Third, there is wisdom in accommodation made by the Court as this is the recourse of minority religions who are likewise protected by the Free Exercise Clause. Mandatory accommodations are particularly necessary to protect adherents of minority religions from the inevitable effects of majoritarianism, which include ignorance and indifference and overt hostility to the minority . . . Fourth, exemption from penal laws on account of religion is not entirely an alien concept [noting Moslem polygamy exempted from the crime of bigamy] . . . Finally, we must consider the language of the Religion Clauses *vis-à-vis* the other fundamental rights in the Bill of Rights. It has been noted that unlike other fundamental rights like the right to life, liberty or property, the Religion Clauses are stated in absolute terms, unqualified by the requirement of 'due process,' 'unreasonableness,' or 'lawful order.' Only the right to free speech is comparable in its absolute grant. Given the unequivocal and unqualified grant couched in the language, the Court cannot simply dismiss a claim of exemption based on the Free Exercise Clause, solely on the premise that the law in question is a general criminal law. If the burden is great and the sincerity of the religious belief is not in question, adherence to the benevolent neutrality-accommodation approach requires that the Court make an individual determination and not dismiss the claim outright.

At this point, we must emphasize that the adoption of the benevolent neutrality-accommodation approach does not mean that the Court ought to grant exemptions every time a free exercise claim comes before it. This is an erroneous reading of the framework which the dissent of Mr Justice Carpio seems to entertain. Although benevolent neutrality is the lens with which the Court ought to view religion clause cases, the interest of the state should also be afforded utmost protection. This is precisely the purpose of the test – to draw the line between mandatory, permissible and forbidden religious exercise . . .

Current Proceedings

[The respondent's sincerity of religious belief was accepted, shifting the burden to the Government to demonstrate that the law or practice justified a compelling secular objective and that it was the least restrictive means of achieving that objective.]

A look at the evidence that the OSG (Office of the Solicitor General) has presented fails to demonstrate 'the gravest abuses, endangering paramount interests' which could limit or override respondent's fundamental right to religious freedom. Neither did the government exert any effort to show that the means it seeks to achieve its legitimate state objective is the least intrusive means . . . [T]he OSG contends that the State has a compelling interest to override respondent's claimed religious belief and practice, in order to protect marriage and the family as basic social institutions. The Solicitor General, quoting the Constitution (Art II Sec 12)[218] and the Family Code,[219] argues that marriage and the family are so crucial to the stability and peace of the nation that the conjugal arrangement embraced in the Declaration of Pledging Faithfulness should not be recognized or given effect, as 'it is utterly destructive of the avowed institutions of marriage and the family for it reduces to a mockery these legally exalted and socially significant institutions which in their purity demand respect and dignity.' . . .

[In applying the compelling state interest test] . . . it is not the State's broad interest in 'protecting the institutions of marriage and the family,' or even 'in the sound administration of justice' that must be weighed against respondent's claim, but the State's narrow interest in refusing to make an exception for the cohabitation which respondent's faith finds moral . . . This, the Solicitor General failed to do.

To paraphrase Justice Blackmun's application of the compelling interest test, the State's interest in enforcing its prohibition, in order to be sufficiently compelling to outweigh a free exercise claim, cannot be merely abstract or symbolic. The State cannot plausibly assert that unbending application of a criminal prohibition is essential to fulfill any compelling interest, if it does not, in fact, attempt to enforce that prohibition. In the case at bar, the State has not evinced any concrete interest in enforcing the concubinage or bigamy charges against respondent or her partner. The State has never sought to prosecute respondent nor her partner. The State's asserted interest thus amounts only to the symbolic preservation of an unenforced prohibition [noting the view that to deny the exemption would break up a 25-year union and defeat 'the very substance of marriage and the family'] . . .

The Solicitor General also argued against respondent's religious freedom on the basis of morality, ie, that 'the conjugal arrangement of respondent and her live-in partner should not be condoned because adulterous relationships are constantly frowned upon by society'; and 'that State laws on marriage, which are moral in nature, take clear precedence over the religious beliefs and practices of any church, religious sect or denomination on marriage . . .'

The above arguments are mere reiterations of the arguments raised by Mme Justice Ynares-Santiago in her dissenting opinion to our Decision dated August 4, 2003, which she offers again *in toto*. These arguments have already been addressed in our decision dated August 4, 2003. In said Decision, we noted that Mme Justice Ynares-Santiago's dissenting opinion dwelt more on the standards of morality, without categorically holding that religious freedom is not in issue. We, therefore, went into a discussion on morality, in order to show that:

---

[218] 'The State recognizes the sanctity of family life and shall protect and strengthen the family as a basic autonomous social institution.'

[219] Family Code, Art 149, which provides: 'The family, being the foundation of the nation, is a basic social institution which public policy cherishes and protects. Consequently, family relations are governed by law and no custom, practice or agreement destructive of the family shall be recognized or given effect.'

(a) The public morality expressed in the law is necessarily secular for in our constitutional order, the religion clauses prohibit the state from establishing a religion, including the morality it sanctions. Thus, when the law speaks of 'immorality' in the Civil Service Law or 'immoral' in the Code of Professional Responsibility for lawyers, or 'public morals' in the Revised Penal Code, or 'morals' in the New Civil Code, or 'moral character' in the Constitution, the distinction between public and secular morality on the one hand, and religious morality, on the other, should be kept in mind;

(b) Although the morality contemplated by laws is secular, benevolent neutrality could allow for accommodation of morality based on religion, provided it does not offend compelling state interests;

(c) The jurisdiction of the Court extends only to public and secular morality. Whatever pronouncement the Court makes in the case at bar should be understood only in this realm where it has authority.

(d) Having distinguished between public and secular morality and religious morality, the more difficult task is determining which immoral acts under this public and secular morality fall under the phrase 'disgraceful and immoral conduct' for which a government employee may be held administratively liable. Only one conduct is in question before this Court, ie, the conjugal arrangement of a government employee whose partner is legally married to another which Philippine law and jurisprudence consider both immoral and illegal.

(e) While there is no dispute that under settled jurisprudence, respondent's conduct constitutes 'disgraceful and immoral conduct,' the case at bar involves the defense of religious freedom, therefore none of the cases cited by Mme Justice Ynares-Santiago apply. There is no jurisprudence in Philippine jurisdiction holding that the defense of religious freedom of a member of the Jehovah's Witnesses under the same circumstances as respondent will not prevail over the laws on adultery, concubinage or some other law. We cannot summarily conclude therefore that her conduct is likewise so 'odious' and 'barbaric' as to be immoral and punishable by law.

. . . Mr Justice Carpio's slippery slope argument, on the other hand, is non-*sequitur*. If the Court grants respondent exemption from the laws which respondent Escritor has been charged to have violated, the exemption would not apply to Catholics who have secured church annulment of their marriage even without a final annulment from a civil court. First, unlike Jehovah's Witnesses, the Catholic faith considers cohabitation without marriage as immoral. Second, but more important, the Jehovah's Witnesses have standards and procedures which must be followed before cohabitation without marriage is given the blessing of the congregation. This includes an investigative process whereby the elders of the congregation verify the circumstances of the declarants. Also, the Declaration is not a blanket authority to cohabit without marriage because once all legal impediments for the couple are lifted, the validity of the Declaration ceases, and the congregation requires that the couple legalize their union.

At bottom, the slippery slope argument of Mr Justice Carpio is speculative. Nevertheless, insofar as he raises the issue of equality among religions, we look to the words of the Religion Clauses, which clearly single out religion for both a benefit and a burden: 'No law shall be made respecting an establishment of religion, or prohibiting the free exercise thereof . . .' On its face, the language grants a unique advantage to religious conduct, protecting it from governmental imposition; and imposes a unique disadvantage, preventing the government from supporting it. To understand this as a provision which puts religion on an equal footing with other bases for action seems to be a curious reading. There are no 'free exercise' of 'establishment' provisions for science, sports, philosophy, or family relations. The language itself thus seems to answer whether we have a paradigm of equality or liberty; the language of the Clause is clearly in the form of a grant of liberty.

In this case, the government's conduct may appear innocent and nondiscriminatory but in effect, it is oppressive to the minority. In the interpretation of a document, such as the Bill of Rights, designed to protect the minority from the majority, the question of which perspective is appropriate would seem easy to answer. Moreover, the text, history, structure and values implicated in the interpretation of the clauses, all point toward this perspective. Thus, substantive equality – a reading of the religion clauses which leaves both politically dominant and the politically weak religious groups equal in their inability to use the government (law) to assist their own religion or burden others – makes the most sense in the interpretation of the Bill of Rights, a document designed to protect minorities and individuals from mobocracy in a democracy . . .

. . . [I]n arguing that respondent should be held administratively liable as the arrangement she had was 'illegal *per se* because, by universally recognized standards . . . it is inherently . . . immoral . . .,' the Solicitor General failed to appreciate that benevolent neutrality could allow for accommodation of morality based on religion, provided it does not offend compelling state interests . . .

Thus . . . respondent Escritor's conjugal arrangement cannot be penalized as she has made out a case for exemption from the law based on her fundamental right to freedom of religion . . . In the area of religious exercise as a preferred freedom, however, man stands accountable to an authority higher than the state, and so the state interest sought to be upheld must be so compelling that its violation will erode the very fabric of the state that will also protect the freedom. In the absence of a showing that such state interest exists, man must be allowed to subscribe to the Infinite.

[Complaint dismissed.]

Questions

1. In his dissenting opinion, Justice Carpio pointed out that the majority failed to distinguish between mandatory and permissive accommodation in US jurisprudence. The former entails the idea that the free exercise clause requires exemptions from generally applicable laws, while the latter refers to exercises of political discretion that benefit religion, which the Constitution neither requires nor forbids. In other words, legislative accommodation could protect religious exercise. See MW McConnell, 'Accommodation of Religion: An Update and a Response to the Critics' (1992) 60(3) *George Washington Law Review* 685.

2. What are the differing conceptions of 'rights' held by the 'permissive accommodation only' as opposed to the 'mandatory/permissive accommodation approach' warranted by benevolent neutrality?

3. Justice Carpio stated in his dissenting opinion in *Estrada v Escritor*, available at <http://www.lawphil.net/judjuris/juri2006/jun2006/am_p-02-1651_2006.html>:

   The majority opinion will make every religion a separate republic, making religion a haven for criminal conduct that otherwise would be punishable under the law of the land. Today concubinage, tomorrow bigamy, will enjoy protection from criminal sanction under the new doctrine foisted by the majority opinion.

To what extent did the majority decision hold that religious beliefs excused a person from liability when he violated a general criminal law? Did it push the limits of religious liberty too far?

4.   How does one distinguish between 'public' morality and 'religious' morality? Is the Supreme Court's approach somewhat artificial, based on a separationist view that religiously based convictions have no effect in shaping public morality? Contrast this with the view expressed by Ian Chin J in *The Ritz Hotel Casino v Datuk Seri Osu Haji Sukam* [2005] 6 MLJ 760 (High Court, Kota Kinabalu, Malaysia) that religious tenets shaped public policy, noting that 'Belief in God' is 'one of the principles of our national philosophy [*Rukun Negara*].' or In concluding that gambling was injurious to public welfare, he stated that enforcing judgment for a gambling debt was 'against the Rukun Negara,' as gambling was forbidden to Muslims (citing Quran 2:219), prohibited by the Bible (citing Proverbs 28:22) and frowned upon by Hindus (citing the Tikukural 931–40) and Buddhists (citing *Buddhism in Practice*, Peter Della Santina), and pointing out that Chinese dynasties have struggled with banning gambling. He stated 'Malaysians are a God-fearing people', that gambling was a vice leading one away 'from the path God has shown us' and would be against the principle of 'Belief in God', which means 'eschewing gambling since it is a form of covetousness'. Which approach is preferable, and why?

C. Secular Government and *Halal* Certification

Singapore and the Philippines are secular states without an official religion, with multi-religious societies. Their legal systems provide for some degree of legal pluralism, eg in the form of religious or *syariah* courts which administer Muslim personal laws. Muslims comprise about 9 per cent and 15 per cent of the Philippines and Singapore population respectively.

Article 153 of the Singapore Constitution obliges the Legislature to adopt legislation to regulate Muslim religious affairs and to constitute a Council to advise the President on matters relating to Islam. This was the basis of the Administration of Muslim Law Act ('AMLA') which deals with personal Muslim laws. This establishes the Majlis Ugama Islam or MUIS (Islamic Religious Council), a statutory body charged with various matters such as collecting *zakat* (tithes) and *halal* certification. The Government has a role in appointing up to seven MUIS members. The Constitution has no anti-establishment clause; the Government is neither obliged to nor proscribed from lending financial or other support to a constitutionally identified religious group. The MUIS's role in *halal* certification has not been challenged as breaching secularity; civil courts have a role in enforcing laws that make it a strict liability offence to sell uncertified *halal* food, which centralises the administration of Muslim dietary rules (*Angliss Singapore Pte Ltd v PP*[220]).

In contrast to the pragmatic Singapore policy which does not bar a statutory body from performing a function with religious implications, a stricter conception of sepa-

---

[220] *Angliss Singapore Pte Ltd v PP* [2006] 4 SLR 653.

ration applies in the Philippines. The issue as to whether Executive Order 46, which conferred 'exclusive power to classify food products as *halal* to the Office of Muslim Affairs (OMA), contravened Article II Section 6',[221] came before the Court in *Islamic Da'Wah Council of the Philippines Inc v Office of the Executive Secretary*.

Islamic Da'Wah Council of the Philippines Inc v Office of the Executive Secretary
GR No 153888, 9 July 2003 (Supreme Court, Philippines)

Facts

Food manufacturers received letters from the OMA directing them to secure OMA *halal* certification; consequently, the petitioner, a non-government organisation claiming to be a federation of national Islamic organisations, accredited by international bodies such as the Regional Islamic Da' Wah Council of Southeast Asia and the Pacific (RISEAP) to issue *halal* certification in the Philippines, lost revenue.

Corona J

Petitioner contends . . . it is unconstitutional for the government to formulate policies and guidelines on the halal certification scheme because said scheme is a function only religious organizations, entity or scholars can lawfully and validly perform for the Muslims . . . a food product becomes halal only after the performance of Islamic religious ritual and prayer. Thus, only practicing Muslims are qualified to slaughter animals for food . . .

. . . OMA was created in 1981 through Executive Order No 697 (EO 697) 'to ensure the integration of Muslim Filipinos into the mainstream of Filipino society *with due regard to their beliefs*, customs, traditions, and institutions.' OMA deals with the societal, legal, political and economic concerns of the Muslim community *as a 'national cultural community' and not as a religious group* . . . the State must make sure that OMA does not intrude into purely religious matters lest it violate the non-establishment clause and the 'free exercise of religion' provision found in Article III, Section 5 of the 1987 Constitution.

Freedom of religion was accorded preferred status by the framers of our fundamental law . . . classifying a food product as *halal* is a religious function because the standards used are drawn from the Qur'an and Islamic beliefs. By giving OMA the exclusive power to classify food products as *halal*, EO 46 encroached on the religious freedom of Muslim organizations . . . to interpret for Filipino Muslims what food products are fit for Muslim consumption [effectively forcing] Muslims to accept [the state's] own interpretation of the Qur'an and Sunnah on *halal* food.

[The Court disagreed with the Government's justification that delegating authority to the OMA to issue *halal* certification was to secure Muslim Filipinos' health and that religious freedom was subservient to the state's police powers.] . . . Only the prevention of an immediate and grave danger to the security and welfare of the community can justify the infringement of religious freedom. If the government fails to show the seriousness and immediacy of the threat, State intrusion is constitutionally unacceptable. In a society with a democratic framework like ours, the State must minimize its interference with the affairs of its citizens and instead allow them to exercise reasonable freedom of personal and religious activity.

. . . [W]e find no compelling justification for the government to deprive Muslim organizations . . . of their religious right to classify a product as *halal* . . . The protection

---

[221] Art II, Sec 6, Philippines Constitution: 'The separation of Church and State shall be inviolable.'

and promotion of the Muslim Filipinos' right to health are already provided for in existing laws and ministered to by government agencies charged with ensuring that food products released in the market are fit for human consumption, properly labeled and safe. *Unlike EO 46, these laws do not encroach on the religious freedom of Muslims* . . . With these regulatory bodies given detailed functions on how to screen and check the quality and safety of food products, the perceived danger against the health of Muslim and non-Muslim Filipinos alike is totally avoided. Of great help are the provisions on labeling of food products (Articles 74 to 85) of RA 7394 [which] . . . informs the consuming public of the contents of food products released in the market. Stiff sanctions are imposed on violators of said labeling requirements . . .

Through the laws on food safety and quality, therefore, the State *indirectly* aids Muslim consumers in differentiating food from non-food products . . . through the labeling provisions enforced by the DTI (Department of Trade and Industry), Muslim consumers are adequately apprised of the products that contain substances or ingredients that, according to their Islamic beliefs, are not fit for human intake. These are the non-secular steps put in place by the State to ensure that the Muslim consumers' right to health is protected. The *halal* certifications issued by petitioner and similar organizations come forward as the *official religious approval* of a food product fit for Muslim consumption.

We do not share respondents' apprehension that the absence of a central administrative body to regulate *halal* certifications might give rise to schemers who, for profit, will issue certifications for products that are not actually *halal*. Aside from the fact that Muslim consumers can actually verify through the labels whether a product contains non-food substances, we believe that they are discerning enough to know who the reliable and competent certifying organizations in their community are . . . (EO 46 declared null and void)

D. Japan: From State Shinto to a Secular State and Ceremonial Shinto[222]

Shinto was inextricably entangled with government in ancient Japan, which Emperors invoked to justify their political authority. The 1889 'Meiji' Constitution[223] provided that the Empire 'shall be reigned over and governed by a line of Emperors unbroken for ages eternal' (Article 1) and that the Emperor was 'sacred and inviolable' (Article 3). The Emperor was both the highest Shinto priest and governor, and was considered a living god. After World War II, the Japanese Government received from the Headquarters of the Supreme Commander for the Allied Powers the 'Directive on the Abolition of Governmental Sponsorship, Support, Perpetuation, Control, and Dissemination of State Shinto and Shrine Shinto'. The Constitution of Japan (3 November 1946) provides:

> Art 1: The Emperor shall be the symbol of the State and of the unity of the People, deriving his position from the will of the people with whom resides sovereign power.

---

[222] See Shigenori Matsui, 'Japan: The Supreme Court and the separation of church and state' (2004) 2(3) *I•CON* 534; B White, 'Reexamining Separation: The Construction of Separation of Religion and State in Post-war Japan' (2004) 22 *UCLA Pacific Basin Law Journal* 29.

[223] Hirobumi Ito, *Commentaries on the Constitution of the Empire of Japan* (trans Miyoji Ito) (Tokyo: Igirisu-horitsu gakko, 22nd year of Meiji, 1889), available at <http://history.hanover.edu/texts/1889con.html>.

Art 20:

(1) Freedom of religion is guaranteed to all. No religious organization shall receive any privileges from the State, nor exercise any political authority.
(2) No person shall be compelled to take part in any religious act, celebration, rite or practice.
(3) The State and its organs shall refrain from religious education or any other religious activity.

Art 89: No public money or other property shall be expended or appropriated for the use, benefit or maintenance of any religious institution or association, or for any charitable, educational or benevolent enterprises not under the control of public authority.

The following case relates to the distance the state must maintain from religion (Shinto), and the Japanese conception of separation of religion and state.

*Kakunaga v Sekiguchil (The Tsu City Shinto Ground-breaking Ceremony Case)*224
31 Minshū 533 13 July 1977 (Supreme Court, Japan)

Facts

The Tsu City Mayor expended public funds for Shinto priests to hold a ground-breaking ceremony at the Tsu City Gymnasium site. The question was whether this was a 'religious activity' contravening Articles 20(3) and 89 of the Constitution. The Court of Appeals espoused a strict separation of religion and state, finding this ceremony to be religious, and not merely folk, in nature, thus violating Article 20(3).

Majority Opinion

i. The Constitutional Principle of Separation of Religion and State

In general, the principle of religion–State separation has been understood to mean the secularity or religious neutrality of the State; . . . because questions of religion and faith are matters of individual conscience that transcend the dimension of politics, the State (including local public entities . . .), as the holder of secular authority, should place such questions beyond the realm of public power and refrain from interfering in matters of religion.

The relationship of religion and State differs between countries and is a product of their historical and social conditions. The Constitution of the Empire of Japan [1889] (hereinafter 'Meiji Constitution') contained a provision that guaranteed freedom of religion (Article 28), but the same Article restricted that guarantee 'within limits not prejudicial to peace and order, and not antagonistic to [the peoples'] duties as subjects.' Moreover, State Shinto was virtually established as the national religion; belief therein was sometimes demanded, and certain other religious groups were severely persecuted. Thus, the Meiji Constitution's guarantee of religious freedom was incomplete [noting post-World War II developments where Shrine Shinto bore the same legal status as other religions and how the 1946 Constitution guaranteed unconditional freedom of belief and established the Provisions on Religion–State Separation 'to secure State secularity and religious neutrality by adopting the ideal of complete separation of religion and State.']

The Provisions on Religion–State Separation are essentially an institutional guarantee [attempting] to guarantee it indirectly by securing a system in which religion and the State

---

224 Source: LW Beer and H Itoh (eds), *The Constitutional Law of Japan 1970–1990* (Seattle, Wash: University of Washington Press, 1996) at 478–91.

are separate. However, religion involves more than private, personal belief; it is accompanied by a broad array of external social aspects and thus comes into contact with many sectors of social life, including education, social welfare, culture, and folk customs. As a natural result of this contact, the State cannot avoid association with religion as it regulates social life or implements policies to subsidize and support education, social welfare, or culture. Thus, complete separation between religion and State is virtually impossible . . .

Furthermore, to attempt complete separation would inevitably lead to anomalies in every area of social life. For example, it would cast doubt on the propriety of extending to religiously affiliated private schools the same subsidies that are given to nonreligious private schools, and it would call into question the propriety of State assistance to religious groups for the maintenance and preservation of cultural assets such as shrine and temple buildings, Buddhist statues . . . To deny such support would amount to imposing a disadvantage on these entities because of their religious affiliation; in other words, it would amount to discrimination on religious grounds. Similarly, to prohibit all prison chaplaincy activities of a religious nature would severely restrict inmates' freedom of worship . . . [T]here are [thus] certain inherent and inevitable limits to the religion–State separation guaranteed by the Provisions. When the principle of religion–State separation is embodied in an actual system of government, given that the State must accept some degree of involvement with religion according to the particular societal and cultural characteristics of the nation, the question then becomes [a balancing of interests]: under what circumstances and to what degree can such a relationship be accepted while remaining consistent with the guarantee of religious freedom which is the fundamental objective of the system . . . [T]he principle of religion–State separation . . . demands that the State be religiously neutral but does not prohibit all connection of the State with religion. Rather, it should be interpreted as prohibiting conduct that brings about State connection with religion only if that connection exceeds a reasonable standard determined by consideration of the conduct's purpose and effects in the totality of the circumstances.

ii. Religious Activity Prohibited by Article 20, Paragraph 3

. . . 'religious activity' [in Article 20(3)] should not be taken to mean all activities of the State and its organs which bring them into contact with religion, but only those which bring about contact exceeding the aforesaid reasonable limits and which have a religiously significant purpose, or the effect of which is to promote, subsidize, or, conversely, interfere with or oppose religion. The prime example of such activities is the propagation or dissemination of religion, such as religious education, which is explicitly prohibited in Article 20(3); but other religious activities like celebrations, rites, and ceremonies are not automatically excluded if their purpose and effects are as stated above. Thus, in determining whether a particular act constitutes proscribed religious activity, external aspects such as whether a religious figure officiates or whether the proceedings follow a religiously prescribed form should not be the only factors considered. The totality of the circumstances, including the place of the activity, whether the average person views it as a religious act, the actor's intent, purpose, and degree (if any) of religious consciousness, and the effects on the average person, should be taken into consideration to reach an objective judgment based on socially accepted ideas.

[Noting that the meaning of 'religious act' and 'religious activity' in clause 2 and clause 3 respectively differs, as the former is a direct guarantee of religious freedom against majoritarianism while the latter is an indirect guarantee which prohibits a range of state activities . . .]

. . . Even if a particular religious celebration, rite, or ceremony is deemed not to be included in 'religious activity' under Paragraph 3, if the State coerced a person to participate who would otherwise choose not to take part on grounds of religious belief, this would . . . infringe that person's religious freedom and would violate Paragraph 2. For that reason, the above interpretation of 'religious activity' prohibited under Article 20(3) does not in itself endanger the freedom of belief of religious minorities.

iii. The Ground-breaking Ceremony

. . . [A]lthough the ground-breaking ceremonies (known as *jichinsai*, among other names) that are traditionally performed at the start of construction work to pray for a stable foundation and workers' safety had religious origins in their intent to pacify the gods of the land, there can be no doubt that this religious significance has gradually waned over time [with the proceedings becoming a] formality perceived as almost completely devoid of religious meaning. Even if the ceremony is performed in the style of an existing religion, as long as it remains within the bounds of well-established and widely practiced usage, most people would perceive it as a secularized ritual without religious meaning . . . Although the Ground-breaking Ceremony was conducted as a Shrine Shinto rite, for most citizens, and for the Mayor of Tsu City and others involved in sponsoring the event, it was a secular occasion with no particular religious meaning . . . it is clear that the building owner had a very secular motive for holding the customary ground-breaking ceremony: meeting the demand of construction workers to observe a social formality that has become customary at the start of work, thereby ensuring its smooth progress . . .

The Japanese public in general does not display a great interest in religion. They reveal, instead, a mixed religious consciousness: as members of the community, many people are believers in Shinto, and as individuals, believers in Buddhism . . . Shrine Shinto is characterized by its close attention to ceremonial form and the virtual absence of outreach activities such as the active proselytizing seen in other religions. These circumstances taken together with the public attitude to ground-breaking ceremonies discussed above render it unlikely that a ground-breaking ceremony at a construction site, even when performed by Shinto priests according to the rituals of Shrine Shinto, would raise the religious consciousness of those attending or of people in general, or that it would have the effect of assisting, fostering, or promoting Shinto. This is equally true even when the sponsor of such a ceremony is the State, acting in the same capacity as a private citizen. It is inconceivable that such sponsorship would result in the development of a special relationship between the State and Shrine Shinto . . .

Considering the totality of the circumstances, although the Ground-breaking Ceremony is undeniably connected with religion, we deem it to be a secular ceremony conducted in accordance with general social custom . . . Its effects do not subsidize or promote Shinto, or, conversely, suppress or interfere with any other religion. Therefore, it does not constitute prohibited religious activity under Article 20(3) . . .

Justices Fujibayashi Ekizo, Yoshida Yutaka, Dando Shigemitsu, Hattori Takaaki & Tamakai Shoichi (dissenting)

1. The Constitutional Principle of Separation of Religion and State

A declaration of unconditional religious freedom is insufficient by itself to guarantee that freedom. To accomplish that guarantee it is essential . . . to sever all ties between religion and State. As long as such ties exist, there is a great risk that they will lead either to religious influence over the State or, conversely, to State interference in religious matters and, ultimately, suppression of religious dissent and violation of the freedom of belief. This risk is clearly illustrated by the history of Japan since the Meiji Restoration.

In the first year of the Meiji Period (1868), the new government proclaimed the unity of religious ritual and government administration. It reinstated the classical Office of Shinto Worship and announced a plan to establish Shinto as the State religion, whereby all the shrines and Shinto priests in Japan were placed under direct government control. It then issued a series of orders for the separation of Shinto and Buddhism, which were designed to purify Shinto and make it independent while attacking Buddhism. Meanwhile, the government maintained virtually unchanged the Tokugawa shogunate's policy of suppression of Christianity.

In 1870, the government issued the Proclamation of the Great Doctrine, which declared the 'way of the gods' [as the guiding state principle]. In 1872, the Ministry of Religion appointed Shinto priests to the Agency for Spiritual Guidance and issued 'three rules for teaching': (1) Observe a spirit of reverence for the gods and love of country; (2) Reveal the laws of nature and the way of humanity; (3) Revere the Emperor and obey the Imperial court. The government thus promulgated a political ideology imbued with religious character, centered on Emperor worship and belief in Shrine Shinto, and took steps to have the people instructed therein.

In 1871, the government declared that shrines were sites for the observance of 'national rites' and were not the private property of individuals or families (Grand Council of State Decree No 234). In the same year, it issued the Grand Council of State Decree No 235, 'Allocations for Government Shrines and Other Shrines and Employment Regulations, Etc, for Shinto Priests,' which established a ranking system for all the shrines in Japan . . . The decree also gave Shinto priests the status of public officials, a privilege not accorded to other religions. In 1875, the government prohibited joint Shinto–Buddhist proselytizing and ordered each religious sect to proselytize independently. While giving verbal assurances to Shinto and Buddhist sects that it would allow freedom of belief, in 1882 the government abolished the status of Shinto priests as officials of the Agency for Spiritual Guidance and ordered them to cease officiating at funerals (Ministry of Home Affairs Notices [Otsu] No 7 and [Tei] No 1). By requiring Shrine Shinto to engage solely in ritual observances, the government was able to adopt the official position that it was not a religion, and on that basis it consolidated a system which, in effect, established it as the national religion or State Shinto.

[Notes that under the Meiji Constitution, Shrine Shintoism continued to be effectively established even if there was no official state religion, shrine worship was considered a civic duty and under various laws, shrines were financially dependent on state or local public entities.] . . .

The de facto status of Shrine Shinto as a State religion, therefore, was maintained until Japan's defeat in 1945. During that period, other religious groups such as Omoto, Hitonomichi, Soka Kyoiku Gakkai [the pre-war name of Soka Gakkai], and the United Church of Christ in Japan were subjected to strict governmental control and repression. Religions were officially sanctioned only insofar as they did not conflict with the concept of a State Shinto-centered 'national polity.' Worship at shrines was, in effect, compulsory [noting this violated religious freedom and that 'State Shinto also formed the spiritual basis of militarism'] . . .

The Majority Opinion holds that complete separation of religion and State is merely an unrealizable ideal . . . The problem . . . is that the meaning of State connection with religion in the Majority Opinion is not entirely clear, and it is also unclear when such contact would exceed reasonable limits. In our opinion, the majority's interpretation of the separation principle poses the danger that State–religion ties will be readily tolerated and the guarantee of religious freedom itself will be weakened.

Notes and Questions

1. Stating that 'religious activity' under Article 20(3) should not be limited to evangelism but include holding religious ceremonies, including customs that retain their religious character, the Minority Opinion considered the ground-breaking ceremony, involving priests and ritual offerings to the gods at an altar, a distinct Shinto religious ceremony and not a 'secular convention', such that the sponsorship by the Mayor constituted preferential treatment and subsidisation of Shrine Shinto; it disagreed with how the Majority 'treated its religious significance lightly and underestimated its effects.

2. Have the courts adopted a dogmatic or a pragmatic approach towards interpreting the constitutional separation of religion and state in the post-war Constitution of Japan?

3. Does the Majority's 'purpose and effect' test or the Minority's 'nature' test more strictly uphold separation of state and religion? Does the Majority's 'reasonableness' test sufficiently protect religious freedom by ensuring no subjection to an official religion?

4. Dissenting Judge Fujibayashi Elizo acknowledged that the American First Amendment was 'probably the greatest influence' in enacting Article 20(1) and (3) of the Japan Constitution, which provisions 'go even further in their proclamation of the principles of religious freedom and separation of religion and State and indeed are so exhaustive that there is nothing comparable among the constitutions of the world'. How does the Japanese model compare with the *Zorach v Clauson* 'laissez–faire' model of state–religion relations?[225] This case involved a New York law permitting public schools to release students during school hours to receive religious instruction at religious centres, on written parental request. The US Supreme Court held:

    > [S]o far as interference with the 'free exercise' of religion and an 'establishment' of religion are concerned, the separation must be complete and unequivocal . . . The First Amendment . . . does not say that, in every and all respects there shall be a separation of Church and State. Rather, it studiously defines the manner, the specific ways, in which there shall be no concert or union or dependency one on the other . . . Otherwise the state and religion would be aliens to each other – hostile, suspicious, and even unfriendly. Churches could not be required to pay even property taxes . . . the proclamations making Thanksgiving Day a holiday; 'so help me God' in our courtroom oaths – these and all other references to the Almighty that run through our laws, our public rituals, our ceremonies would be flouting the First Amendment . . . We would have to press the concept of separation of Church and State to these extremes to condemn the present law on constitutional grounds.
    >
    > We are a religious people whose institutions presuppose a Supreme Being. We guarantee the freedom to worship as one chooses. We make room for as wide a variety of beliefs and creeds as the spiritual needs of man deem necessary. We sponsor an attitude on the part of government that shows no partiality to any one group and that lets each flourish according to the zeal of its adherents and the appeal of its dogma. When the state encourages religious instruction or cooperates with religious authorities by

---

[225] *Zorach v Clauson* 343 US 306 (1952).

adjusting the schedule of public events to sectarian needs, it follows the best of our traditions. For it then respects the religious nature of our people and accommodates the public service to their spiritual needs. To hold that it may not would be to find in the Constitution a requirement that the government show a callous indifference to religious groups. That would be preferring those who believe in no religion over those who do believe. Government may not finance religious groups nor undertake religious instruction nor blend secular and sectarian education nor use secular institutions to force one or some religion on any person. But we find no constitutional requirement which makes it necessary for government to be hostile to religion and to throw its weight against efforts to widen the effective scope of religious influence. The government must be neutral when it comes to competition between sects. It may not thrust any sect on any person. It may not make a religious observance compulsory. It may not coerce anyone to attend church, to observe a religious holiday, or to take religious instruction. But it can close its doors or suspend its operations as to those who want to repair to their religious sanctuary for worship or instruction. No more than that is undertaken here.[226]

5. The Japanese Supreme Court in a 13:2 majority applied the 'purpose and effect' test adopted in the *Tsu City* case to Article 89 in *Anzai v Shiraishi* or the *Ehime Tamagushi-ryo case*.[227] The Court found Article 89 was violated where the government of Ehime prefecture provided a small amount from public funds to the Yasakuni and Gokuku shrines to honour deceased Japanese soldiers, as this was state support for a particular religion. It was a prohibited religious activity under Article 20(3) as the offerings had 'religious significance', effectively promoting a specific religion such that the local government–Yasakuni shrine relationship caused by such offerings 'exceeded the reasonable limit under the social and cultural conditions of Japan', the disbursements being illegal. Is this case consistent with *Tsu City*? Subsequently in 2002, there were two cases involving state officials attending a rice crop offering to the Emperor (*Daijosai*). The *Tsu City* precedent was applied in finding attendance a matter of social courtesy and a traditional ceremony of the Imperial House, albeit having religious implications, without the purpose and effect of supporting Shinto.[228]

Judgment Upon Constitutionality of the Prefecture's Expenditure from Public Funds to Religious Corporations Which Held Ritual Ceremonies (Yasakuni Shrine Case)
1992 (Gyo-Tsu) No 156, 2 April 1997 (Supreme Court, Japan, Grand Bench)

Facts

The question at issue here was whether public fund contributions by the Ehime prefectural to the national Yasakuni shrine, a religious corporation, for its Spring and Autumn ceremony, and the affiliated prefectural gokoku shrine, violated Article 20(3) or Article 89 of the Constitution. The army managed this shrine before 1946, which is associated with a militaristic national ethos. The High Court held that the offerings were a social custom, a small sum made to support the bereaved war families without religious intent. The

---

[226] Ibid at 312–14.

[227] *Anzai v Shiraishi* or the *Ehime Tamagushi-ryo case* 51 Minshüo 1673 (Sup Ct Apr 2, 1997).

[228] *Kohno v Hiramatsu* 56 Minshül 204 (Sup Ct July 9, 2002); *Higo v Tsuchiya*, 56 Minshül 204 (Sup Ct July 11, 2002).

Supreme Court applied the 'purpose and effects' test in holding that only activities exceeding 'reasonable limits' and which supported or interfered with a religion would be prohibited.

Judgment

[I]t is clear that the prefecture was involved in important religious ceremonies held by specific religious groups. And generally, making such offerings as *tamagushiryo* at a time when important traditional ceremonies are held by the shrines within their precincts is much different from holding a ground-breaking ceremony . . . within a construction site . . . [which is] only a secular social event whose religious significance has gradually weakened over time. The offerings in this case can hardly be thought of as just a secular social courtesy by an average person . . . the contributors of such offerings as *tamagushiryo* usually think that they have some religious meanings, and so do the appellees in this case . . . the fact that the prefecture was intentionally involved in the specific religious groups cannot be denied, since the prefecture had never made offerings to the same kind of religious rites held by other religious groups. According to these analyses, if a local government has a special involvement with a specific religious group . . . the average person is impressed that the prefecture especially supports this specific religious group [with the effect that] interest in the specific religion will be stimulated.

The appellees contended that this expenditure did not violate the Constitution, because it was just a social custom with a secular purpose to mourn for the war dead and to console the bereaved families and an administrative act intended to support the bereaved families. We find that a great number of persons who are enshrined in Yasukuni Shrine and Gokoku Shrine are the war dead of World War II. We also find that not a few of the local residents of Ehime Prefecture, including the bereaved families, wish the local government to mourn for the war dead enshrined in Yasukuni Shrine or other shrines officially. Some of them wish so because of their desire to mourn for the war dead, not because of their religious beliefs. In response to such wishes, this offering of *tamagushiryo* could be assumed to be conventional . . . We consider that it is possible to mourn for the war dead and to console the bereaved families without such a special relationship with a specific religion . . . [W]e do not consider that the offering of *tamagushiryo* to a shrine's ceremonies has become a social courtesy.

. . . [I]t is reasonable to assume that these offerings by a local government to Yasukuni Shrine or Gokoku Shrine [which are religious organisations as stipulated under Article 89] . . . constitute prohibited religious activities under Article 20(3) of the Constitution, because the purpose of the offerings had religious significance and the effect of the offerings led to support or promotion of a specific religion, and the relationship between the local government and Yasukuni Shrine or other shrines caused by these offerings exceeded the reasonable limit under the social and cultural conditions of Japan. Thus, these disbursements were illegal . . .

Justice Masao Ono (Supplementary Opinion)

It may be possible to argue that the offering in this case did not necessarily support or promote the religion from an economic point of view, as its amount was between 5,000 yen and 10,000 yen a time . . . However, in considering application of the principle of separation of state and religion, one should not be bound only by the outward and economic aspects of the conduct in question but should see its substance in the light of social and historical conditions, and one should also consider its immaterial or spiritual effect and influence on society. From this point of view, it is incontrovertible that the influence or effect of the conduct in this case is important . . .

. . . Various religions have developed and are existing pluralistically in this country, and each religious group holds memorial services for the war dead following its own doctrines and ceremonial forms. If a local government supports only memorial services held by Yasukuni Shrine, it is difficult to deny that such a conduct gives an impression to the general public that the local government has selected these rituals, giving them priority over others, and takes their religious value as most important. Thus, it is incontrovertible to say that the local government gives important symbolic advantage to a specific religious group . . .

[While ceremonies may have lost their religious significance such that no one takes them as support for a specific religion, these may maintain good social relations. While noting some might hold the Yasakuni Shrine in awe as the central institution for consolation of the war dead, others belonging to different religious groups and those who were previously forced to worship at the Shrine as part of the national religion or who are disquieted that it contains few ordinary citizens may feel antipathy to it.] If a public institution conducts religious activities and widely exerts such an effect on society, the public institution will be involved in religious conflict, and, at the same time, religion will be involved in secular conflicts. It is obvious that this will transcend the permissible limits as social courtesies and customs and that this is likely to do harm to both the public institution and the religious group. Avoiding such a situation will conform to the purpose of the Constitution, which adopts the strict principle of separation of state and religion . . .

Justice Toru Miyoshi (dissenting)

Yasukuni Shrine and other Gokoku Shrines are nothing but Shinto institutions, and it is needless to say that they treat visitors as those who act based on religious belief. However, in light of the national sentiment mentioned above, they are principally special institutions to remember and honor the war dead, and the majority of people consider these shrines as rather symbolic institutions for the nation's war deads' souls than those of a specific religion.

. . . Additionally, from the practical point of view, it is possible to say that, if we went to honor the war dead, we cannot find any other institutions that symbolize all of the souls of them than Yasukuni Shrine or any other institutions that symbolize all of the souls of the war dead who have some relationship with specific prefectures than the Gokoku Shrine in that prefecture . . . Some people propose that a new public nonreligious institution for the war dead should be built. This might be a point worth considering . . .

Many people demand that representatives of the national or municipal governments honor the war dead at Yasukuni Shrine and Gokoku Shrines . . . [M]any cabinet members have visited Yasukuni Shrine on spring and autumn Reitaisai or on the memorial day of the end of World War II since October 18, 1951, the day of the first autumn Reitaisai after World War II, when Japan was still under occupation, and it was exceptional that the prime minister did not visit Yasukuni Shrine till a certain time. Most of them professed that their visit to Yasukuni Shrine was what is called an official visit; it is said that some of the ministers who visited Yasukuni Shrine were Christians . . .

. . . [I]t is quite natural for people to mourn the war dead; it is quite polite, even obligatory in terms of morality, for the state, the local government, or a representative to do so. Yasukuni Shrine and Gokoku Shrine have been considered as the main facilities for the mourning of the war dead, as well as the symbol of their holy spirits. As a matter of fact, there does not exist any other facility like these two shrines . . . the expenses for Yasukuni Shrine and Ehime Gokoku [underwrote the conduct of a periodic ritual that both the Shrines as well as most people considered essential in religious terms to remember and mourn the war dead]. The expense for Yasukuni Shrine was done in a very businesslike manner: that for Ehime Gokoku Shrine can be considered as a donation to the Ehime Prefecture Association for Bereaved Families of the War Dead, forming a part of the aid for the war bereaved. So it is very questionable to conclude that the expenses were for Ehime Gokoku Shrine. Even if we can conclude so, the expenses are indirect. We cannot necessarily see any religious intent or purpose even though the offerings were called *tama-gushiryo* or *kentoryo* and the title on the envelope was *kumotsuryo*. We cannot necessarily say ordinary people are conscious of this expense as religious. The amount of the expenses, which are offered in the name of the local government or its governor, are the minimum as a courtesy for these kind of ceremonies, so it has little to do with religion . . .

Additionally, in Japan not a few families have both a household Shinto altar and a Buddhist altar in their homes, and there are many houses displaying seals of other gods. In some cases their boys and girls go to mission schools. Moreover, we can see that the same memorial ceremony is held in [the] Shinto or Buddhist manner alternately every other year by the same war bereaved association . . . These factors mean that in Japan several different religions coexist in harmony in the daily lives of most people, as well as in their senses. This coexistence is affirmative and comfortable. Generally speaking, in our society we are magnanimous toward religious differences, because we do not have special feelings toward any specific religion. This situation should not be criticized but rather valued . . . Taking these circumstances into consideration, I think that those who deeply believe in a specific religion are also required to be magnanimous to some extent on this kind of matter.

When we take all of these circumstances into consideration, I believe that the expenses were made as a part of the war bereaved aid activity [and the relationship between the Ehime Prefecture and shrines brought about by the expenses is not beyond the admissible extent under Japan's socio-cultural circumstances] . . .

. . . Concerning the relationship between Yasukuni Shrine or Gokoku Shrine and the national or local governments, some people are worried about a revival of State Shinto or militarism . . . Under the new Constitution . . . it cannot happen that we see State Shinto revive. Our Constitution, which has pacifism as a main principle, can fully prevent militarism from reviving. Article 2 of the private rules of Yasukuni Shrine declares that its main purpose is to establish everlasting peace and contribute to realize a peaceful nation. I cannot help feeling that [in fearing] . . . the revival of State Shinto or militarism in terms of the connection between Yasukuni Shrine or Gokoku Shrine . . . the government is too hasty and suspicious about the common sense of the Japanese people . . .

. . . [T]he fact that A-class war criminals are enshrined [in Yasukuni Shrine] does not have anything to do with the mourning [of] and consoling for almost two and a half million war dead, nor does it have anything to do with the question of whether expenses are beyond an admissible extent or not . . .

Notes and Questions

1. In his dissenting opinion, Justice Tsuneo Kabe criticised the application of the *Tsu City* four points 'purpose and effect' test to the *Yasakuni Shrine* decision. He found the first factor (place where the *jichinsai* (Shinto ceremony) was held) inapplicable, as religious rites are bound to be held within the grounds of a religious corporation. Secondly (the religious evaluation of the activity by the ordinary person), he considered it impossible for anyone to deny that the offering of *tama-gushiryo* had the character of social protocol which diminished the religious significance of the act. Thirdly (intention and purpose of the city that held *jichinsai*),

he found no substance to the argument the state was promoting Shintoism and considered the majority opinion 'excessively fears the shadow of a national religion'. Lastly, in terms of affecting ordinary people, the majority opinion stated that the average person 'is impressed that the prefecture especially supports this specific religious group . . . such that interest in the specific religion will be stimulated'; he found this to be 'too abstract', a 'groping for an ideal reference to support, promote and encourage' based on the conclusion 'that the shrine should be criticized and considered not good, based on the history of having forced people to worship shrines before and during World War II'.

2.   Does Article 20(3) hold out total separation as an ideal? How strict is the separation of church and state envisaged in the *Yasakuni Shrine* case? How are 'reasonable limits' ascertained in terms of state–religion interaction? Is a categorical or a balancing approach adopted? Do Japanese courts advocate a cautious approach towards state involvement with religion and, if so, why?

3.   Is there any significance in the majority judgment's emphasis on what connection between state and religion is 'tolerated' as opposed to 'prohibited', given the ideal of the total separation of religion and state? Justice Yukinobu Ozaki criticised the majority's interpretive approach towards Article 20(3) as being unfaithful to the history of the establishment clause and the rule's meaning: 'Its test to judge constitutionality is to consider various factors collectively, so that the test is vague and lacks objectivity and clarity. Consequently, it is not proper.' He observed:

> To read the text to prohibit 'any religious activity' honestly, it is very clear . . . that all activities that connect with religion are prohibited, and it is a matter of course to take up the position that a religious activity is 'prohibited in principle but tolerated exceptionally.' . . . The idea that 'religious activity' bears a similar restriction seems to have been born in our country as well, [as] a case that adopted the purpose-and-effect test for a clause similar to the US First Amendment which influenced Article 20(3) of the Constitution, ruled that this clause prohibits activities that have a certain purpose and effect. However, this idea neglects the difference between the clause of the US Constitution and that of our country. The US Constitution provides that 'Congress shall make no law respecting an establishment of religion, or prohibiting the free exercise thereof . . .,' and prohibits only activities establishing national religion or prohibiting the free exercise of religion. So it is necessary to define the extent of prohibited activities. The case therefore set a test to determine prohibited activities . . . our Constitution directly prohibits all religious activities, so it is natural to set a test to prohibit every religious activity univocally and to tolerate special cases. According to the difference between the clauses of both constitutions, the different approach to set a test fits each constitutional text.

Judgment on the Enshrinement of a Dead SDF Officer to Gokoku Shrine (Self Defence Force Officer Enshrinement Case)
1 June 1988, 1982(O) No 902 (Supreme Court, Japan)

Facts

Takafumi, an agnostic Self Defence Force (SDF) officer, was buried with Buddhist rites. His Christian widow brought an Article 20 challenge against the local SDF Veteran

Association's application, facilitated by the Regional Office, to have the deceased jointly enshrined as a deity with 27 other SDF members who died in the course of duty, at the Gokoku Shrine of Yamaguchi Prefecture. The enshrinement took place against her will. The SDF Association and Yamaguchi Gokoku Shrine were both private organisations.

Judgment (Majority Opinion)

[T]he joint enshrinement of the twenty-seven dead SDF members including Takafumi in Gokoku Shrine was basically realized through the efforts of the Veterans Association, who had acted upon requests of the families of the dead SDF members and had negotiated with the shrine, and also through the decision of the shrine for the joint enshrinement. Therefore, although it is true that the Regional Office cooperated with the Veterans Association by performing clerical work, the application which was made under the name of the Veterans Association was filed independently in its substance and could not be regarded as a joint action of the Regional Office staff and the Veterans Association nor be considered that the office staff themselves applied for it . . .

To be examined next is the issue of whether the cooperation of the Regional Office staff with the Veterans Association for the application was a religious activity under Article 20(3) of the Constitution . . . [J]oint enshrinement is to be conducted by independent decisions of the shrines and therefore an application by someone for it does not constitute a prerequisite for it . . . The actual actions of the Regional Office staff cooperating with the Veterans Association up until the application . . . had indirect relation with the religion and their purpose and intention was assumed to be to raise the social status and morale of SDF members . . . hence it should be said that they had little religious feelings and that it was not the activity which would be considered by the general public as having effect of drawing attention to a specific religion or of sponsoring, promoting, encouraging a specific religion or suppressing or interfering with other religions. Therefore the actions of the Regional Office staff cannot be regarded as constituting religious activities though they did relate to religion . . .

Next, we examine whether the legal interest of the Appellee was infringed. [S]ince the enshrinement itself was conducted by Gokoku Shrine, we should examine the issue of infringement from the viewpoint of the relationship between the shrine and the Appellee in private law. When the freedom of religion (under Article 20(1)(3)) is infringed upon among individuals to the extent that exceeds a socially acceptable degree, depending on its situation, legal remedies should be provided by appropriate application of Article 1 or Article 90 of the Civil Code, general provisions of controlling private autonomy, or by that of provisions of torts . . . However, when one's religious peacefulness is disturbed by religious activity of others, though it is natural for him to feel uncomfortable for that and to wish not to be disturbed any more, if we admit such a person to seek legal relief such as compensation or injunction on the ground of infringement of religious feelings, then, instead, it will obviously come to harm the religious freedom of others. The guarantee of freedom of religion requires tolerance for religious activities of others that are inconsistent with the religion that one believes in as long as such activity does not disturb his or her freedom of religion through compulsion or by giving rise to disadvantages . . .

. . . Takafumi's enshrinement by Gokoku Shrine was left free for the shrine under the freedom of religion and, in itself, it did not infringe legal interests of anyone. And, the Appellee had never been compelled to attend the shrine's religious ceremonies . . . and the Appellee does not assert any facts that any disadvantage was suffered because she did not attend the ceremonies nor any facts that she was prohibited, restricted, suppressed or intervened in any way to believe in Christianity or to mourn her late husband based on her religious faith. The letter of Gokoku Shrine's chief priest concerning Eitai-Meinichi-Sai (relating to annual Shinto prayers to be held in memory of Takafumi) . . . did not interfere with the Appellee's religious belief in any way. Therefore it should be concluded that the legal interest of the Appellee was not infringed at all.

Notes and Questions

1. Justice Masam Ito (dissenting) held that the Regional Office's conduct did consti-
    tute 'religious activity' under Article 20(3). Its role in negotiating for the enshrine-
    ment made the application for enshrinement and the act itself inseparable. While
    the purpose was to promote the social status of SDF members, the enshrining of
    dead SDF members as Shinto deities was completely different from ceremonies
    which are customary for society and was clearly religious. While the application
    did not apparently suppress Christianity, the issue was whether it promoted
    Shintoism, especially for Gokoku shrine. While Justice Ito found that the appellee
    might have a tortious claim for mental distress (religious peace of mind), her dam-
    aged interests had not sufficiently 'matured' such that the conduct of the Regional
    Office towards her was lawful.

2. Who was responsible for the enshrinement application: the Veterans Association,
    the Regional Office or both? Why was state action found to be absent? Was the
    Regional Office's role in enshrinement direct or indirect? What was the 'secular'
    objective of the Regional Office such that its role fell outside Article 20(3)?

3. Does the case, by widening the range of reasonable state–religion relations, endan-
    ger religious freedom? Can the anti-establishment clause give rise to a constitu-
    tional claim or infringe the legal interest of an individual person? When does state
    involvement with religion not constitute an unlawful action in relation to indi-
    vidual persons? Does the constitution affect private law actions, like tort?

4. What duties are constitutionally required of members of one religious group
    towards another? Does the Japanese Constitution adequately protect religious
    minorities?

VII. STATE AND RELIGION – THE PROTECTIONIST STATE

A. The Protection of Religious Orthodoxy and State Regulation of Religious 'Words'

'Protectionist' states may be vested with safeguarding and promoting religious orthodoxy and the dominance of a religious majority, manifested in the application of laws
regulating blasphemy, apostasy and evangelism.

i. Use of Religious Words

Titular Roman Catholic Archbishop of Kuala Lumpur v Menteri Dalam Negeri
[2010] 2 MLJ 78 (High Court, Malaysia)

Facts

Islam is the religion of the Malaysian Federation. The question arose as to whether Government-issued conditional publications permits prohibiting the *Catholic Herald* magazine from using the word 'Allah' (name of the Muslim deity) in its Malay language section, were constitutional. The *Herald* contended that 'Allah' is the Arabic word for 'the God'. Previously, the Home Ministry had allowed the conditional use of 'Allah' and other religious terms in Christian publications, provided the front of a document contained the bold words 'For Christianity'. The applicant challenged this condition as erroneous at administrative law and inconsistent with various constitutional articles relating to religion, speech and religious education. The respondent argued that the applicant's use of 'Allah' in its publication endangered public order and national security, as it was exclusive to Islam.

Article 11(1) of the Malaysian Constitution provides:

> Every person has the right to profess and practice his religion and, subject to Clause (4), to propagate it. Clause 4 authorises the states to enact legislation to 'control or restrict the propagation of any religious doctrine or belief among persons professing the religion of Islam.

Ten states have enacted such laws, and section 9 of the various state Enactments makes the use of certain words, including 'Allah', an offence. The Court found that the respondent, in exercising its discretion, failed to consider various relevant considerations, such that the decision should be quashed. This includes the fact that the word 'Allah' is the correct Bahasa Malaysia word for 'God' and in the Bahasa Malaysian Bible translation, 'God' is translated as 'Allah' and 'Lord' is translated as 'Tuhan'; that Christians and Muslims in Arabic-speaking countries have for 15 centuries used 'Allah' to refer to the One God; that the Malay language has been the *lingua franca* for many Catholic believers for several centuries living within Malaysia, who have a culture of speaking and praying in Malay; that the word 'Allah' has been used continuously since the 1629 edition of Matthew's Gospel and the first complete Malay Bible in 1833; that the publication was for the Catholic Church in Malaysia and elsewhere, and was not made available or sold outside the Church, especially with respect to persons professing Islam, etc. It also found the permit condition to be an unreasonable restriction on free expression under Article 10.

Lau Bee Lan J

The applicant's grounds for the reliefs of certiorari and declaration is premised on the unconstitutional acts and conduct being inconsistent with arts 3(1), 10, 11 and 12 of the Federal Constitution namely:

(i)   The Applicant's legal right to use the word 'Allah' in the said publication stems from the Applicant's constitutional rights to freedom of speech and expression and religion, to practise its religion in peace and harmony in any part of the Federation and to manage its own religious affairs and to instruct and educate the Catholic congregation in the Christian religion as enshrined in Articles 3, 10, 11 and 12 of the Federal Constitution. The exercise of these rights extends to propagating the faith amongst the non-English speaking faithful in Malaysia especially the Indonesians and the Arabic-speaking of the Christian faith . . .;

(ii) The Applicant has a very important role in instructing and educating the Catholic congregation in the Christian religion in various languages and the said publication serves as a very effective avenue and medium by which the teachings of the Catholic Church are imparted to the Catholic faithful throughout Malaysia and elsewhere [thus the publication condition in question would deprive the applicant of a 'very important teaching tool, violating the Applicant's constitutional right under Article 12] . . .

. . . I cannot accept the respondents' contention [that the applicants failed to demonstrate that the condition left them unable to profess and practise their faith as it only made things more difficult to instruct their Malay-speaking congregants, and that the prohibition had obstructed the integral practice of the religion, following *Meor Atiqulrahman bin Ishak v Fatimah bte Sihi* [2006] 4 CLJ 1]. Firstly, it is to be noted art 3(1) reads 'Islam is the official religion of the Federation; but other religions may be practised in peace and harmony in any part of the Federation' . . . Applying the principles enunciated in *Meor Atiqulrahman bin Ishak*, there is no doubt that Christianity is a religion. The next question is whether the use of the word 'Allah' is a practice of the religion of Christianity. In my view there is uncontroverted historical evidence . . . which is indicative that use of the word 'Allah' is a practice of the religion of Christianity. From the evidence it is apparent the use of the word 'Allah' is an essential part of the worship and instruction in the faith of the Malay (*Bahasa Malaysia*) speaking community of the Catholic church in Malaysia and is integral to the practice and propagation of their faith. The next consideration is the circumstances under which the 'prohibition' was made. The circumstances to my mind would be the factors which the respondents rely on to justify the impugned decision . . . I have shown unchallenged evidence that there is a well established practice for the use of the 'Allah' amongst the Malay speaking community of the Catholic faith in Peninsular Malaysia, Sabah and Sarawak . . .

Considering all the factors . . . the imposition of the condition in the publication permit prohibiting the use of the word 'Allah' in the said publication, 'Herald – the Catholic Weekly' pursuant to the first respondent's exercise of powers under the Act contravenes the provision of arts 3(1), 11(1) and 11(3) of the Federal Constitution . . .

. . . [A] common thread runs through like a tapestry in the respondents' treatment of restricting the use of the word 'Allah' which appears in the Al Kitab[229] are (i) that it is not meant for Muslims; (ii) to be in the possession or use of Christians and in churches only . . . there is a . . . maxim '*Omne majus continet in se minus*' which means 'The greater contains the less'. One would have thought having permitted, albeit with the usual restrictions, the Catholic Church to use the word 'Allah' for worship and in the Al-Kitab, it would only be logical and reasonable for the respondents to allow the use of the word 'Allah' in the said publication . . .

The respondents submitted [that states had under Article 11(4) enacted laws controlling and restricting the propagation of religious doctrine among Muslims such that if the respondent allowed the use of the word 'Allah', this would be illegal in contravening these laws.] . . . [O]ne of the reasons for the decision is to avoid confusion and misunderstanding among Muslims; there is no guarantee that the said publication will be circulated only among Christians and will not fall into the hands of Muslims and it has gone online and is accessible to all . . . [The judge noted the offences enacted by the legislation of 10 states on the use of the word 'Allah', as well as the need to interpret fundamental liberties generously to ensure that their exercise is not rendered ineffective or illusory.]

---

[229] 'Book of John the Baptist'.

Mr Royan (for the applicant) [drawing attention to Article 11(4), pointed out that] s 9 of the state Enactments make it an offence for a person who is not a Muslim to use the word 'Allah' except by way of quotation or reference; so it appears that a Christian would be committing an offence if he uses the word 'Allah' to a group of non-Muslims or to a non-Muslim individual. Mr Royan then argues that that cannot be the case [because Article 11(4) restricts propagation of another faith only to Muslims] . . . I am persuaded such an interpretation would be ludicrous as the interpretation does not accord with the object and ambit of art 11(4) of the Federal Constitution.

I find there is merit in Mr Royan's submission that unless we want to say that s 9 is invalid or unconstitutional to that extent . . ., the correct way of approaching s 9 is it ought to be read with Article 11(4) [such that] . . . a non-Muslim could be committing an offence if he uses the word 'Allah' to a Muslim *but* there would be no offence if it was used to a non-Muslim. Indeed Article 11(1) reinforces this position . . . So long as he does not propagate his religion to persons not professing the religion of Islam, he commits no offence . . . [The judge found this construction permissible and persuasive as the state Enactment sought to address only the mischief set out in Article 11(4) ie restriction and propagation among persons professing the religion of Islam. Otherwise, the applicant's fundamental rights would be illusory.]

. . . The other approach of interpretation which I would adopt is the doctrine of proportionality which is housed in the equal protection limb, the second limb of Article 8(1) advocated in *Sivarasa Rasiah*[230] . . . His Lordship Gopal Sri Ram FCJ (speaking on behalf of the Federal Court) stated the test is whether the legislative state action which includes executive and administrative acts of the state is disproportionate to the object it seeks to achieve and in determining whether the limitation is arbitrary or excessive the threefold test is applicable – 'whether legislative or executive acts that infringe a fundamental right must (i) have an objective that is sufficiently important to justify limiting the right in question; (ii) the measures designed by the relevant state action to meet its objective must have a rational nexus with that objective; and (iii) the means used by the relevant state action to infringe the right asserted must be proportionate to the object it seeks to achieve'.

Applying the said test to the factual matrix of the present case the court has to bear in mind the constitutional and fundamental rights of persons professing the Christian faith to practise their religion and to impart their faith/religion to persons within their religious group and in this case, the Catholic Church comprises a large section of people from Sabah and Sarawak whose medium of instruction is *Bahasa Malaysia* and they have for years used religious material in which their god is called 'Allah'; for that matter there is a large community who are *Bahasa Malaysia* speaking from Penang and Malacca. On the other hand the object of Article 11(4) and the state Enactments is to protect or restrict propagation to persons of the Islamic faith. Seen in this context by no stretch of imagination can one say that s 9 of the state Enactments may well be proportionate to the object it seeks to achieve and the measure is therefore arbitrary and unconstitutional . . .

As to the concern of the respondents there is no guarantee that the magazine would be circulated only among Christians and it will not fall into the hand of Muslims, I agree with Mr Royan there is no requirement any guarantee be given by anyone in order to profess and practise and even to propagate it. In my view if there are breaches of any law the relevant authorities may take the relevant enforcement measures. We are living in a world of information technology; information can be readily accessible. Are guaranteed rights to be sacrificed at the altar just because the Herald has gone online and is accessible to all? One must not forget there is the restriction in the publication permit which serves as an additional

[230] *Sivarasa Rasiah v Badan Peguam Malaysia* [2010] 2 MLJ 333.

safeguard which is, the word 'TERHAD'[231] is to be endorsed on the front page and the said publication is restricted to churches and to followers of Christianity only . . .

. . . [L]earned SFC (Senior Federal Counsel) further submits the grounds of public security, public order and religious sensitivity are legal, rational and reasonable . . . and the court is not in a position to question the issue and must accept these reasons . . . The respondents also allege the applicant did not file any affidavit to dispute the facts, hence security reasons are deemed admitted by the applicant citing *Ng Hee Thoong & Anor v Public Bank Bhd* [1995] 1 MLJ 281. I find this submission is inaccurate as the applicant has at para 60 of the applicant's affidavit averred:

> 60. I wish to state that the First Respondent's reported statement that the continued use of the word 'Allah' in the said publication will bring about confusion or unease to other faith communities is clearly unfounded as the Applicant has no intentions or has never done anything to bring about any such conflict, discord or misunderstanding. Further, I reiterate that the reality of the matter is that in the last 14 years of the said publication there has never been any untoward incident arising out of the use of the word 'Allah' in the said publication . . .

There is merit in the applicant's argument that the respondents . . . sought to justify imposing the condition in purported exercise of his powers . . . on a mere statement that the use of the word 'Allah' is a security issue which is causing much confusion and which threatens and endangers public order, without any supporting evidence . . . [which is] not sufficient in law . . . [The cases] do not spell out there ought to be total prohibition of interference from the court, rather it ought to be slow to intervene . . .

I agree with the applicant there is no material to support the respondents' argument that the use of the word 'Allah' is a threat to national security or from which an inference of prejudice to national security may be inferred; all there is before the court is a mere *ipse dixit* of the first respondent . . . Therefore I am of the view that this ground ought to be rejected.

I find there is merit in Mr Dawson's argument that the court ought to take judicial notice that in other Muslim countries even in the Middle East where the Muslim and the Christian communities together use the word 'Allah', yet one hardly hear of any confusion arising . . . Further, I am incline to agree that the court has to consider the question of 'avoidance of confusion' as a ground very cautiously so as to obviate a situation where a mere confusion of certain persons within a religious group can strip the constitutional right of another religious group to practise and propagate their religion under Article 11(1) and to render such guaranteed right as illusory.

[The Court granted an order of certiorari to quash the respondents' decision on the publication permit, and declarations that this decision was void and that Article 3(1) did not authorise the respondent to prohibit the use of 'Allah' by the *Catholic Herald*, and that the right to use the word 'Allah' was one pursuant to Article 10 (free expression) and Article 11 (religious freedom, including the right to manage one's own religious affairs). Further, pursuant to Articles 11 and 12, the use of the word 'Allah' in the *Herald* was part of the right of instructing and educating the Catholic congregation in the Christian religion.]

Notes and Questions

1. Did the application of a proportionality review test sufficiently reconcile the competing interests?

---

[231] 'Limited'.

2. Churches were bombed in 2010 after this decision, with the Government and Opposition uniting to condemn such attacks as contrary to Islamic teachings: 'Church attacked in Malaysian "Allah" dispute', *New York Times*, 8 January 2010. The case is currently on appeal. Reportedly, the Malaysian Government blocked imports of Malay language bibles: 'Christians protest: government blocks 30 thousand Bibles in Malay', 2 December 2011, *AsiaNews.it,* available at <http://www.asianews.it/news-en/Christians-protest:-government-blocks-30-thousand-Bibles-in-Malay-21010.html>. The Selangor Sultan issued a 'fatwa', banning followers of faiths other than Islam from using 'Allah' to describe their gods, raising questions on whether fatwas apply to non-Muslims: 'Questions over "fatwa" effect on non-Muslims after Selangor Sultan's "Allah" decree', *Malaysian Insider*, 9 January 2013.

B. Blasphemy Laws and Protectionist Regimes

Junaid K Doja, International Book Agency Limited, Dhaka v The State (2001) 21 BLD 573 (Supreme Court, Bangladesh)

Facts

The Government issued an order under section 99A of the Bangladesh Penal Code to forfeit copies of *Newsweek* containing an article entitled 'Mysterious Women, Threatening Men, Bolstering stock images of the Muslim world', which featured Persian calligraphy on the soles of someone's feet. It was alleged that this illustration deliberately and maliciously outraged the religious feelings of the Muslims, as the Persian script resembled Arabic script which Muslims considered sacred. Section 295A of Bangladesh's Penal Code (1860) reads:

> Whoever, with deliberate and malicious intention of outraging the religious feelings of any class of the citizens of Bangladesh, by words, either spoken or written, or by visible representations insults or attempts to insult the religion or the religious feelings of that class, shall be punished with imprisonment of either description for a term which may extend to two years, or with fine, or with both.

The High Court upheld the order, rejecting the argument that the publication was meant only for *Newsweek* readers, not the common man.

Amirual Kabir Chowdhury J

The citizens of this country are generally not so literate to be able to differentiate the Persian from the Arabic. They are ignorant and unwary. On seeing the picture/calligraphy, the Muslim citizens of this country would . . . take the same to be Arabic because they (Muslim citizens) are not conversant with Persian language; but the Muslims, irrespective of being educated or not, normally love Arabic and . . . the writings at first sight greatly resemble the Arabic language . . . Arabic being the language of the Holy Quran is considered sacred language to the Muslims. Any attempt as a result of which the language is put to ridicule . . . outrages the feelings of the Muslims.

We have considered the other writings in the article . . . [involving] issues surrounding Islam and its spirituality [which] are very complicated [and] give rise to an adverse reaction [among Muslims and will] likely wound the feelings of the Muslims who would take it as insult to their religious beliefs. Who told him to quote Neshat saying: 'It is impossible to separate the ideas of spirituality, politics and violence in Islam?' Should spirituality in Islam be identified with violence?

. . . We have given our anxious consideration to the article and the picture/calligraphy and are of the view that the same is bound to be regarded by any reasonable man as grossly offensive and provocative and are maliciously intended to be regarded as such, as a result of which an offence punishable under section 295A of the Penal Code appears to have been committed.

Notes and Questions

1. In legally protecting wounded feelings and religious sensitivities, does the law assume it is dealing with the 'Reasonable Man' (a product of the European enlightenment) or the 'Emotional Man'? What are the implications with respect to free speech? Would this include a right to offend?

2. Do blasphemy laws serve to protect religious feelings or marginalise dissenting voices through state-sanctioned religious orthodoxy? Do they reinforce an intolerant version of a majoritarian religious view, rather than promote communal harmony and religious tolerance?

3. Blasphemy laws have been used to persecute not only non-believers in a majority faith, but also members of that faith: see S Hossain, ' "Apostates" ', Ahmadis and Advocates: Use and Abuse of Offences against Religion in Bangladesh' (December 2004) WLUML Publications 83, available at <http://www.wluml.org/sites/wluml.org/files/import/english/pubs/pdf/wsf/10.pdf>.

4. The Bangladesh High Court has held that books based on Sufi Mysticism insulted the Muslim religion, causing their authors to breach section 295A of the Penal Code; the Government seized their books lawfully under section 99A of the Code of Criminal Procedure: *Dr (Homeo) Baba Jahangir Beiman al-Shuresari v The State* (1996) 16 BLD 140. The Government has also banned books by the Ahmadis as objectionable materials which would hurt the sentiments of the Muslim majority.[232]

i. Cults and Deviant Sects

Non-liberal states may undertake measures to deal with 'cults' or deviant sects for varied motives. For secular constitutional orders, this may be to preserve national security; in constitutional orders with theocratic elements, efforts may be directed to preserving religious orthodoxy to avoid confusing members of a privileged faith community, or to stymie competitor ideologies.

Arguably, if states cannot define religion, there would be no need for the category, 'cult'. If a state proscribes a religion and invalidates the integrity of its belief, it necessarily discriminates against a belief system and contravenes the religious neutrality principle. Official state bodies or religious authorities operating with state sanction

---

[232] 'Bangladesh bans Islam sect books', *BBC News*, 9 January 2004, at <http://news.bbc.co.uk/2/hi/south_asia/3382931.stm>.

engaged in identifying cults or deviant sects apply theological criteria in their work, which renders religious minorities, which may be 'new religious movements', vulnerable; alternatively, states may adopt an approach transcending the binary dichotomy of 'religion' and 'cult', where the focus is on identifying the presence of 'instrumental' factors like the 'potential of danger'. This may include groups which cause mental destabilisation, exert exorbitant financial demands, propagate anti-social ideas, cause public order disturbances, or which engage in crimes or human rights violations such as sexual abuse, slavery etc.[233]

ii. Instrumentalism: Keeping Law and Order

In China, Article 36(1) of the Constitution protects 'freedom of religious belief', with the Chinese Communist Party (CCP) officially recognising Buddhism, Taoism, Islam, Catholicism and Protestantism.[234] Clause (3) provides that the State protects 'normal religious activities', and that religion may not be used 'to engage in activities that disrupt public order, impair the health of citizens or interfere with the educational system of the state'. Religious doctrine is irrelevant in labelling certain groups 'evil cults' (*xiejiao*) operating beyond the pale of 'normal religious activities'. Notably, Falun Gong, a Chinese spiritual movement founded by Li Hongzhi in 1992, which claimed 100 million followers in 1999, denies being a religious group,[235] despite espousing quasi-religious doctrines pertaining to salvation and mystical powers.[236] It was seen as a political threat, rising to international prominence when 10,000 of its followers on 25 April 1999 converged upon the CCP Beijing headquarters to protest against an article painting the group in a negative light. By July 1999, the Ministry of Civil Administration had denounced the group and declared it an 'illegal organisation' and threat to public order. The official position is encapsulated thus:

> Falun Gong is nothing but an evil cult that has all the inherent characteristics of a cult: worship of its leader, systematic mind control, spreading heretic ideas, amassing wealth, secret organization and endangering the society. For example, its ringleader Li Hongzhi fabricated and spread such fallacies as 'doomsday' and 'earth explosion'. Many Falun Gong practitioners were driven into such intense fear by these heresies that they became insane and even committed suicide or killed their loved ones. Li amassed $5.4 million through illegal publication of Falun Gong materials and tax evasion. 1400 followers died as a result of practising Falun Gong and refusing medical attention when falling ill. Falun Gong disrupted public order and stability by staging illegal demonstrations around media agencies and government organs.[237]

---

[233] See, eg, *Summary of the Report of the French National Assembly Committee of Inquiry on Cults* (December 1995), referenced by the Joint Meeting on Cults, European Parliament Committee on Civil Liberties and Internal Affairs, and representatives of the relevant national parliamentary committees, Brussels, 21 November 1996. Research and Documentation Papers, People's Europe Series W-10, 3–97, available at <http://aei.pitt.edu/4915/1/4915.pdf>, 'Annex 1: Resolution on cults in Europe'.

[234] *Freedom of Religious Belief in China* (October 1997), Information Office of the State Council of the PRC, June 1996, Beijing, at <http://www.china.org.cn/e-white/Freedom/f-1.htm>.

[235] See <http://www.facts.org.cn/krs/sofg/200810/t84638.htm>.

[236] 'Former Falun Gong Activist Denounces "Mystical Powers" of Cult Leader', *People's Daily Online*, 16 November 1999, at <http://english.peopledaily.com.cn/special/fagong/1999111600F113.html>.

[237] 'Falun Gong: An Evil Cult', Unpublished Letter sent to the Editor of the *Washington Post*, 10 January 2000, archived at PRC Embassy in the United States, available at <http://www.china-embassy.org/eng/zt/ppflg/t36582.htm>.

On 30 October 1999, the National People's Congress Standing Committee (NPCSC) adopted the Resolution on Banning Heretic Cult Organizations, Preventing and Punishing Evil Cult Activities, in order to outlaw and punish Falun Gong and other cult organizations:[238]

To maintain social stability, protect the interests of the people, safeguard reform and opening up and the construction of a modern socialist country, it is necessary to ban heretic cult organizations and prevent and punish cult activities.

Based on the constitution and other related laws, the following decision is hereby made:

1. Heretic cult organizations shall be resolutely banned according to law and all of their criminal activities shall be dealt with severely.

    Heretic cults, operating under the guise of religion, Qigong or other illicit forms, which disturb social order and jeopardize people's life and property, must be banned according to law and punished resolutely.

    People's courts, people's procuratorates, public security, national security and judicial administrative agencies shall fulfil their duties in carrying out these tasks.

    To be severely dealt with according to law are those who manipulate members of cult organizations to violate national laws and administrative regulations, organize mass gatherings to disrupt social order and fool others, cause deaths, rape women, swindle people out their money and property or commit other crimes with superstition and heresy.

2. The principle of combining education with punishment should be followed in order to unify and instruct the majority of the deceived public and to mete out severe punishment to the handful of criminals.

    During the course of handling cult groups according to law, people who joined cult organizations but were unaware of the lies being spread by the group shall be differentiated from criminal elements who organize and take advantage of cult groups for illegal activities and/or to intentionally destroy social stability.

    The majority of the deceived members shall not be prosecuted, while those organizers, leaders and core members who committed crimes shall be investigated for criminal conduct; those who surrender to the authorities or contribute to the investigations shall be given lesser punishments in accordance with the law or be exempt from punishment.

3. Long-term, comprehensive instruction on the constitution and the law should be carried out among all citizens, knowledge of science and technology should be popularized and the national literacy level raised.

    Banning cult organizations and punishing cult activities according to law goes hand in hand with protecting normal religious activities and people's freedom of religious belief.

    The public should be exposed to the inhumane and anti-social nature of heretic cults, so they can knowingly resist influences of cult organizations, enhance their awareness of the law and abide by it.

4. All corners of society shall be mobilized in preventing and fighting against cult activities, and a comprehensive management system should be put in place.

    People's governments and judicial bodies at all levels should be held responsible for guarding against the creation and spread of cult organizations and combating cult activities.

This is an important, long-term task that will ensure social stability.

---

[238] Available at <http://www.cesnur.org/testi/falun_005.htm>.

Notes and Questions

1. What methods are advocated by the 1999 NPCSC Resolution? Who decides consistency with Article 36 of the Chinese Constitution? Article 300 of the Chinese Criminal Law[239] provides that anyone organising or utilising 'superstitious sects, secret societies and evil religious organizations' to sabotage the implementation of state laws and executive regulations, to cheat others and cause the deaths of people, to have illicit sexual relations with women and to defraud others of money and property may be punished with imprisonment. When 'circumstances are particularly serious', a minimum seven-year term of imprisonment applies.

2. *A Judicial Explanation on Crimes by Cult*, by the Supreme People's Court and Supreme People's Procuratorate,[240] provided:

    > Under the explanations, those who organize and use sects and commit one of the following activities should be penalized according to Section 1, Article 300 in the criminal law:
    >
    > I.   gathering people together to besiege and charge government organs, enterprises or institutions, and disrupt their work, production and teaching and research activities;
    > II. holding illegal assembly, demonstrations to incite or deceive, or organize their members or others to besiege, charge, seize, disrupt public places or places for religious activities, or disrupt social order;
    > III. resisting departments concerned to ban their groups, or resuming the banned groups, or establishing other sects, or continuing their activities;
    > IV. instigating, deceiving or organizing their members or others to refuse fulfilling their legal obligations, and the case is serious;
    > V.   publishing, printing, duplicating or distributing publications spreading malicious fallacies, and printing symbols of their sects; and
    > VI. other activities that violate the state law or administrative regulations.
    >
    > According to the explanations, a case is regarded as 'serious' if it involves any of the following while conducting the activities in the previous article:
    >
    > I.   setting up organizations or recruiting members across provinces, autonomous regions and municipalities that are under direct administration of the central government;
    > II. collaborating with overseas groups, organizations and individuals for sect-related activities;
    > III. publishing, printing, duplicating and distributing, either in terms of volumes or sales values, a large amount of publications spreading fallacious ideas and printing symbols of sects; and
    > IV. instigating, deceiving or organizing their members or others to violate state laws, administrative regulations, and resulting in serious consequences.

    The explanation goes on to provide that offences under Article 300(2) and (3), which include the use of sects to spread superstition, deceive members to fast, cause self-inflicted wounds, commit suicide or prevent patients from taking normal

---

[239] Available at <http://www.fmprc.gov.cn/ce/cgvienna/eng/dbtyw/jdwt/crimelaw/t209043.htm>.
[240] Embassy of the PRC in the USA, 30 October 1999, at <http://www.china-embassy.org/eng/zt/ppflg/t36568.htm>.

medical treatments, resulting in deaths, would be punished under the criminal law. Further, those who use sects to carry out schemes to split China, to endanger the reunification of China or subvert the socialist system would be dealt with under state safety offences. It also provides that those who surrendered themselves to law enforcement departments or performed meritorious services would be given lenient penalties or even exempted. In addition, those deceived or coerced into sects but who had withdrawn would not be considered offenders.

What is the impact of such regulations on religious freedom and other civil liberties, and what is the basis of their curtailment?

3.   On Falun Gong in China, see Guobin Zhu, 'Persecuting "Evil Cults": A Critical Examination of Law Regarding Freedom of Religious Belief in Mainland China' (2010) 32(3) *Human Rights Quarterly* 471; R Keith and Zhiqiu Lin, 'The *"Falun Gong* Problem": Politics and the Struggle for the Rule of Law in China' (2003) 175 *The China Quarterly* 623.

iii. Intrinsic Reasons for Preserving Orthodoxy

Constitutional orders with theocratic elements may expressly identify certain groups as deviant sects. The Malaysian Government defends the dominant Sunni school of Islam and seeks to regulate religious orthodoxy in declaring various Islamic sects 'heretical'. For example, state government departments have raided Shi'ite Muslims prayer meetings whose members fear being charged in syariah courts with adhering to deviationist teachings.[241] Some Shi'ite Muslims have been preventively detained under the Internal Security Act, and the Islamic Affairs Departments of certain states have reportedly issued anti-Shi'ite sermons to be read in all mosques.[242] Members of the Sky Kingdom ('teapot cult') in Terengganu endured a police raid in July 2005, and many were arrested and charged under the Criminal Offences Enactment (2001) even though they claim not to be Muslims. The commune was later demolished. The Malaysian Government worked closely with the National Fatwa Council to disband the Al-Arqam group and ban its publications on the basis that it promulgated false teachings and a mystical brand of Islam, having some 100,000 followers at its height in 1994.[243] When the Islamic Religious Council of Singapore, a statutory body, asked the Government to ban Al-Arqam literature as it would threaten familial and societal unity, the ministerial response was that 'as a matter of principle, my ministry has no theological views on who is heretical and who is not',[244] reflecting its brand of secular democracy. The banning of publications could not be on grounds of content, 'as there is religious freedom', but only on instrumental concerns like internal security. Secular states like Singapore, in dealing with religious 'cults' like Falun Gong, do so on the

---

[241] 'Malaysia's Shiite Muslims demanded apology from authorities', *AhlulBayt News Agency* 30 Dec 2010, http://abna.ir/data.asp?lang=3&Id=219052; 'Malaysia breaks up Shia celebrations', *PressTV* 24 May 2011at http://www.presstv.ir/detail/181481.html

[242] 'Malaysian Shiites faces growing persecution', *Freemalaysiatoday.com*, 14 January 2012, at <http://www.freemalaysiatoday.com/category/nation/2012/01/14/malaysian-shiites-face-growing-persecution/>.

[243] A An-Naim, 'The Cultural Mediation of Human Rights: The Al Arqam Case in Malaysia' in J Bauer and D Bell (eds), *The East Asian Challenge for Human Rights* (Cambridge: Cambridge University Press, 1999).

[244] 'Certain controls necessary to keep peace', *Straits Times*, 10 December 1995, at 4.

basis of general laws, such as public assembly laws, remaining above issues of religious doctrinal purity or deviance.[245]

iv. On Blasphemy in General

Blasphemy involves words or actions that insult or treat with contempt God or sacred things. The rationale for laws punishing blasphemy may include punishing the causing of offence to God, preventing social disorder by the provocation of religious sensitivities, preserving religious orthodoxy, or recognising a religion as part of the general law and thus equating the reproach of a religion with a subversion of the law.[246] This has often entailed an alliance between church/mosque and state.

Western commentators have considered blasphemy a 'fascinating anachronism'.[247] Blasphemy laws applicable only to the Anglican Church are thought to be a dead letter[248] or obsolete in multicultural England,[249] and were considered unconstitutional under the American First Amendment in *Joseph Burstyn Inc v Wilson*.[250] In Australia, the continued existence of blasphemy laws was questioned as being incompatible with the section 116 constitutional anti-establishment clause and a pluralist, multi-religious society, where 'respect across religions and cultures is such that, coupled with an appropriate capacity to absorb the criticism or even the jibes of others, deep offence is neither intended nor taken'.[251]

Nonetheless, in jurisdictions where religion is taken seriously and the European Enlightenment not taken as a universal truth, blasphemy laws remain resilient, even expanded upon, as in Pakistan, where the British colonial authorities first introduced them to protect religious feelings. Even in Europe, the issue of blasphemy, which threatens the liberal canon of equal treatment of religions and concern against overburdening free speech, has gained contemporary resonance through incidents such as the *Jyllands-Posten* Mohammad Cartoons controversy of September 2005 originating in Denmark, and attempts to internationalise such laws through advocacy by Islamic states for the recognition of 'defamation of religions' (an ideology, not a person). The competing view is that the liberal response of expecting religionists to show restraint, demonstrate mutual respect and not to take offence from degrading depictions of their sacred symbols, is unrealistic in the face of continuing acts of violence arising from offended religious feelings, as it envisions a 'rational, passionless Utopia that has no parallel in any human society'.[252] Another facet of the debate is whether it would be desirable to abolish blasphemy laws which protect one or some religions, in favour of general religious vilification laws. This would remove questions of religious orthodoxy

---

[245] Ho Peng Kee, 71 *Singapore Parliamentary Debates*, 6 March 2000 (Oral Questions on Cults) col 1141.

[246] *Taylor's Case* (1676) 1 Vent 293.

[247] D Nash, *Blasphemy in Modern Britain: 1789 to the Present* (London: Ashgate, 1999) 1.

[248] Lord Denning, quoted by the General Assembly of Unitarian and Free Christian Churches, *House of Lords – Religious Offences in England and Wales – Written Submissions* (2002), at <http://www.parliament. the-stationery-office.co.uk/pa/ld200203/ldselect/ldrelof/95/95w35.htm>, 5 April 2006.

[249] The last prosecution was *Whitehouse v Lemon* [1979] 2 WLR 281. See *R v Chief Metropolitan Stipendiary Magistrate, ex p Choudhury* [1991] 1 QB 429.

[250] *Joseph Burstyn Inc v Wilson* 343 US 495 (1952).

[251] Per Harper J, *Pell v The Council of Trustees of the National Gallery of Victoria* [1998] 2 VR 391, 393.

[252] Reid Mortensen, 'Art, Expression and the Offended Believer' in *Law and Religion*, Rex Adhar (ed), (Ashgate, 2000) 181 at 190

from the hands of state authorities and focus on causes of violence against a group of persons, rather than protecting an ideology.

Notes and Questions

1. On the common law offence of blasphemy, see the discussion in the House of Lords First Report, *Religious Offences in England and Wales*, Committee Publications (Session 2002–2003). An excellent report on operational blasphemy laws is Human Rights First, *Blasphemy Laws Exposed: The Consequences of Criminalizing 'Defamation of Religions*, March 2012, available at <http://www.humanrightsfirst. org/wp-content/uploads/Blasphemy_Cases.pdf>; see also *Policing Belief: The Impact of Blasphemy Laws on Human Rights*, Freedom House Special Report (October 2010), available at <http://expression.freedomhouse.org/sites/default/files/ policing_belief_full.pdf>.

2. Do blasphemy laws increase religious respect and tolerance? Can they be used to harass and suppress religious minority rights and democratic debate, quelling both religious and political diversity? Can they breed religious extremism and violence, including mortal intimidation? What do you think of the argument that religious differences should incite argument, not violence? Consider these questions in light of the following passage:

    > Just as the ancient Roman eventually learned that executing Christians did not suppress Christianity, modern governments should realize that forbidding people to talk about certain topics does not encourage public stability. It only creates martyrs. Punishing people for speech does not discourage speech; it only drives it underground and encourages conspiracy. In the battle for public order, free speech is the ally, not the enemy.[253]

v. Pakistan, Blasphemy and the Ahmadis

The Ahmadiyya Muslim Community (Qadianism) (or Ahmadis), which considers itself a Muslim group, is a contemporary messianic movement founded by Punjab-born Mirza Ghulam Ahmad (1835–1908) in 1889. Mainstream Muslims consider Qadianism a cult, and Ghulam's claim to be the *Mujaddid* (Divine Reformer), 'Promised Messiah' and a post-Muhammad prophet blasphemous. Ahmadis have been labelled by constitutional, statutory or policy mandate as a deviant group in countries like Indonesia and Pakistan.

Article 2 of the Pakistan Constitution provides: 'Islam shall be the State religion of Pakistan.' The Muslim concept of the finality of the prophethood of Muhammad, a theological doctrine which chiefly differentiates Muslims and Ahmadis, was the basis of the 1974 constitutional amendment which declared Ahmadis to be non-Muslim under Article 260(3). A non-Muslim was one who did not believe in the 'absolute and unqualified finality of the Prophet or claims to be a Prophet in any sense of the word or of any description whatsoever, after Muhammad (pbh) or recognises such a claimant as a Prophet or a Religious Reformer'. This was buttressed by Article 160, which added 'persons of the Qadiani Group or the Lahori Group (who call themselves

---

[253] *Whitney v California*, 274 US 357, 47 S Ct 641, 71 L Ed 1095.

Ahmadis') to the list of reserved seats in the Provincial Assemblies for non-Muslims, ie Christians, Hindu, Sikh, Buddhist and Parsi Communities. Despite these constitutional amendments, the Ahmadis persist in calling themselves Muslims and affirming their faith in Islam.

In the following case, the Federal Shariat Court considered whether Ahmadis were Muslim in light of the Quran and Sunnah, and concluded that all claims of Prophethood after Muhammad would be false, noting that Jesus had been commissioned as a Prophet long before Muhammad. This judgment also elaborates upon the Muslim conception of religious liberty, including the right to religious propagation, and tolerance.

Majibur Rehman v Federal Government of Pakistan
**PLD 1985 Federal Shariat Court 8 Vol XXXVII,
at 71–72, 76–82, 87, 99–101, 114–15, 118–19**

Facts and Issues

The Court considered whether the anti-Ahmadi legislation (Ordinance No XX of 1984; Anti-Islamic Activities of Qadiani Group; Lahori Group and Ahmadis (Prohibition and Punishment) Ordinance 1984) was contrary to the Quran. In its judgment, the Court addressed the question about the status of persons who did not believe Muhammad to have been the final prophet.

Fakhre Alam CJ

The Qadianis who are followers of Mirza Ghulam Ahmad of Qadian (hereinafter to be called Mirza Sahib) are divided into two groups both of whom are however called by the name of Ahmadis. One group which is generally known as Qadiani group believes that Mirza Sahib was the promised Mehdi, the promised Messiah and a Prophet. The Lahori group says that he was a Mujaddid (revivalist) the Mehdi and the promised Messiah.

 . . . It is established from the citations from the writings of Mirza Sahib and his successors that Mirza Sahib had made an unequivocal claim of being a Prophet and had condemned all those who did not accept his claims as Kafirs (heretics). Now what is the view in Islam regarding those people who ignore or close their eyes to the patent heresies of a heretic and believe in him as Mamoorun-Minallah (appointed by Allah), Mujaddid (revivalist of the true Islam), the Promised Messiah or Mehdi which he cannot be on account of his being beyond the pale of Islam? Is not the support of heresy an act of heresy?

 . . . The quality of a Momin or Muslim is that he should believe in Allah and disbelieve in or deny Taghut (the devil, one who leads astray) which would include a false Prophet. It would follow that a person who does not deny a false Prophet, . . . a person who founds a religion which is a deviation from Islam, cannot be a Muslim despite his belief in Allah . . . To save the Ummah from disintegration . . . such misguided person should be held to be beyond the pale of Islam since it is to keep the mischief of belief in Taghut away from the Muslim Umman (community).

 . . . One of the meanings of Islam is submission and obedience; Muslim means one who is submissive. The verse points out that those who submit would form one Ummah or that the Muslims, by virtue of their Islam (submission) shall integrate into one nation. Thus the common bond of Islam will constitute them an Ummah because the principle is that persons with common aspirations and ideologies form the nation. This is clear from Q3: 104;

Q7: 181 . . . It is not difficult to conclude from these injunctions that it is the duty of the Muslim ummah to keep the banner of Islam flying and for this purpose it must be well knit . . . The Muslims are brothers among themselves without distinction of race, colour or country . . . The murder of one is the murder of all and saving one from death is the saving of all . . .

It cannot be denied that faith is a stronger stimulant towards the achievement of co-operation, fellow-feeling, comradeship and ideological cohesion irrespective of colour, ethereal, racial, linguistic and cultural barriers. The emotional fervour and the instinct of attachment to and affinity with the ideological base generates fraternal feeling which it is not difficult to demonstrate from Islamic History . . . There is however a big difference between a nation of the modern era and a religious Ummah. A nation is combination of a group of·persons but in that combination the main motive and the driving force is self-interest . . . The factors which helped the formation and cohesion of the Muslim ummah are the humanitarian character of Islam, its emphasis on equality of all rich and poor, master and slave, men and women irrespective of distinction of country, colour, race or culture, its stress on fraternity and the individual freedoms guaranteed by it. The armies of Islam were the torch-bearers of these qualities and spread the spirit of tolerance and for-bearance, love for education and research, though unfortunately in the eras of their politi-cal weakness they were the victims of savagery and religious intolerance. The love of their heritage and the pride of their history are some other factors for their fusion in an Ummah.

All these factors related to the teachings of religion and the excellence of Islam as a vital force. But the most important factor is the love and respect of the Muslims for the Holy Prophet (pbh) through whom all these blessings were conferred upon the Ummah . . . To obey him is to love him but the love which transcends obedience to him is the emotional and sentimental attachment to the Holy Prophet (pbh). The finality of Prophethood is an article of faith with each Muslim on account of the intense love for the Holy Prophet (pbh) and the belief in the finality of Prophethood is the most important element in the integra-tion of the Ummah . . . As such, they have resented all encroachments on the nexus between Islam and the finality of the Prophethood

. . . The Qadianis are not a part of the Muslim Ummah. This is already proved by their own conduct. In their opinion all the Muslims are unbelievers. They constitute a separate Ummah . . . The question who are members of the Muslim Ummah could be left unre-solved because of the absence of forum in British India but in an Islamic state in which there are institutions to determine the issue, this matter does not present any difficulty. The Legislature as well as the Federal Shariat Court are competent to resolve it.

[On the Qadianis considering non-Ahmadis non-Muslims] . . . There is nothing strange in this approach of Qadianis since it has been a world-wide phenomenon that members of each religion consider the members of any other religion to be infidels, heretics or beyond the pale of their religion. It is the same way with Jews, Christians, Magians, Hindus and others. This is not only true about the religious communities but also the secular ideological groups like Communists and Socialists . . . [A]s Sir Zafarullah Khan (ex Foreign Minister as Ahmadi) put it, either the majority of people living in Pakistan are unbelievers (Kafir) or the Qadianis are unbelievers . . . The Qadianis have been held to be a threat to the inte-gration of the Muslim Ummah . . .

. . . It is laid down in Article 203-D of the Constitution that the function of this Court is to eliminate the discrepancy and repugnance with the Quran and the Sunnah of the Holy Prophet from any law over which the Court's jurisdiction extends. . . . It appears to be cor-rect that to the extent of its constitutional jurisdiction, the Court is an Institution as con-templated in Tarjamanul Quran Vol 1, page 98 which can decide a dispute in respect of vires of a law vis-à-vis the Injunction in the Qur'an and the Sunnah of the Holy Prophet.

[After reviewing various Qurannic verses] . . . The sum and substance of all the arguments based on these verses is that there is no compulsion in matters of religion and this is not the scheme of Allah that all persons should believe. The Holy Prophet was sent only for the purpose of making His message known; it was never intended that he should compel people to accept Islam. There is nothing in the Quran and the Sunnah which may permit placing of restrictions upon non-believers against believing in the unity of God, the truthfulness of the message and reason of the Holy Prophet, the message of the Quran or making the Quran their grundnorm. Similarly it is not lawful to turn a person by force out of the religion he wishes to stick to.

. . . It was argued that to restrain the Ahmadis from calling themselves Muslims or posing as such amounts to turning them out of their religion, which according to them is Islam. We have . . . reached the conclusion that the Quadianis of either persuasion are not Muslims but are non-Muslims. The Ordinance therefore restrains them from calling themselves what they are not, since they cannot be allowed to deceive anybody especially the Muslim Ummah by passing off as Muslims . . .

[Noting that the Quadianis had called Muslims 'non-Muslims'] . . . This cannot be tolerated and non-Muslims cannot be allowed to encroach upon the rights and privileges of the Muslim community to the utter disintegration of the Ummah. Moreover, this does not affect the rights of the Quadianis to profess their faith in Mirza Sahib whether as a Prophet or as a Muhaddid, Promised Mehdi or Promised Messiah nor does it interfere with their right to practise their religion . . .

. . . Article 260(3) declares the Quadianis as non-Muslims for the purpose of the Constitution and the law. Article 20 guarantees to the citizens of Pakistan the right, inter alia, to profess their religion . . . Read with Article 260(3) . . . Article 20 will mean that the Quadianis can profess that they believe in the unity of Allah and/or the prophethood of Mirza Sahib, but they cannot profess themselves to be Muslims or their faith to be Islam . . .

[Noting that the Ordinance bans Quadianis from using epithets which are exclusive for the companions of the Prophet, his wives and the members of his family, as this would enable them to pose as Muslims directly or indirectly] . . . The Quadianis achieved some little success among members of the Muslim Ummah mainly in the Punjab because of their strategy in calling themselves Muslims and assuring them that acceptance of Ahmadis did not mean relinquishment of Islam or conversion from belief to unbelief, but gave them an option to become better Muslims. For this purpose, they touch the usual chord of the educated Muslims' distaste for the intense sectarianism and persistent rigidity of the Ulema and tend to draw them towards what they preach to be liberalism in Islam. This strategy which paid some little bonus bears strong resemblance to the passing off by a trader of his inferior goods as the superior well known goods of a reputed firm. Let the Quadianis accept that their preaching is for conversion to a religion other than Islam; even the unwary among the Muslims may be loathe to change his belief for unbelief.

We are in agreement with Professor Tahir-ul-Qadri that if the Quadianis had taken steps to implement the Constitutional provisions the promulgation of this Ordinance might not have been required. This is one reason why the propagation of the religion had to be banned. Another important reason was that the Quadianis by posing themselves as Muslims try to propagate their religion to every Muslim they come across. They outrage his feelings by calling Mirza Sahib a Prophet because every Muslim believes in the finality of prophethood of Muhammad. This creates a feeling of resentment and hostility among the Muslims which gives rise to law and order problems.

Section 298-C of the Pakistan Penal Code prohibits the outraging of the feelings of the Muslims which furnishes proof of the restlessness and anger of the Muslims on matters ultimately prohibited by the Ordinance . . .

... The right to propagate other religions in an Islamic state cannot be unlimited on account of the principle of Irtidad (conversion of a Muslim into another religion. Quotes Q5: 54, 2: 217) ... [It has] been the established practice of all religions that the conversion of a person from one religion to another was never looked with less than hostility by his co-religionists. An example in point is the antagonism shown by the Hindus – including those in power in the so-called secular State – on group conversion of the Scheduled Castes to Islam. It is possible that the reason may be that such secession from one religion to another is likely to be a disintegrating force for that religious community. In the Quadianis' Literature also, any person converted from Islam to Quadianism and then re-converted to Islam is known as Murtad and is believed to be liable to torture in hell like a non-Muslim. In this situation it is difficult to lay down that Islam confers a fundamental right upon non-Muslims to propagate their religion among Muslims unconditionally. [The court cites Qurannic verses asserting the Muslim's duty to preach to non-Muslims but to allow the non-Muslim through free discourse to raise good points about his religion so that the Muslim can refute these points and so 'demonstrate the superiority of Islam over the conceptual philosophy of the other religion'.]

... There is a conclusive presumption that the arguments of the Quran cannot be refuted. No argument favourable to unbelief is possible. This negates the possibility of the conversion of the Muslim by being influenced by the discourse of the non-Muslim in favour of his religion. The verses only apply to the form of persuasion which is required for propagation of Islam before the non-Muslim. These verses cannot be turned for the benefit of the non-Muslims in support of their claim to propagate their religion. As such, there is nothing in the Holy Quran, the Sunnah of the Holy Prophet or the commentaries on them recognising the right of a non-Muslim to propagate or preach his religion among Muslims ... Despite this, it is for the Islamic State to allow the non-Muslims to preach their religion as has been done in Article 20 of the Constitution but this can be allowed if the non-Muslims preach as non-Muslims and not by passing off as Muslims. It is for the Legislature to lay down other conditions also. [Noting that the 'Declaration of Human Rights' issued by the Islamic Council does not include the right to propagate one's religion.]

[Noting that Muslims in India and Pakistan were agitated by Mirza Sahib's claim to Prophethood in 1901, leading to Martial Law (1953) in the latter state] ... This however did not succeed in quietening the Muslim's demand as voiced by the Ulema in their 22 point programme for incorporating in the Constitution the non-Muslim and minority status of the Quadianis [which led to the 1974 constitutional amendment declaring the Quadianis non-Muslims under Article 260(3) and the associated Article 106, after a full hearing by Muslim representatives of the public in Parliament which heard the Chief of the Quadiani Sect, Mirza Basir Ahmad].

[Concluding that the Article 20 right to profess, practise and propagate religion is subject to public order and that the Ordinance] appears to be covered by the exception in Article 20 ...

Notes and Questions

1. What do you make of the understanding in *Majibur Rehman* that Islam allows Muslims to preach to non-Muslims but not vice versa?

2. Does this Muslim conception of religious freedom protect freedom of conscience and evangelism? What role is envisaged for the state in relation to sustaining religious freedom?

Blasphemy is an extremely sensitive subject in Pakistan, where 97 per cent of the 180 million population are Muslims, and allegations of insulting Islam or the Prophet provoke furious public reactions, including killings. Pakistan's blasphemy laws are part of its Penal Code, introduced in 1860 by the British into an undivided but religiously heterogeneous India. They were designed to prevent the various religious sects in India from engaging in speech and action disruptive to the social order, by establishing a stringent rule of law. The section 295 offence required intent to insult a religion.

In the 1980s, in order to legitimise his military rule, President Zia-ul-Haq introduced Presidential Ordinance 1 of 1982, a series of Islam-specific amendments to the Pakistan Penal Code ('PPC') (Act XLV of 1860), such as section 295-B, which provides life imprisonment for wilfully defiling the Quran. Section 298A provides for imprisonment and fines for derogatory written or spoken words which 'defile a sacred name of any wife (Ummul Mumineen), or members of the family (Ahle-bait), of the Holy Prophet (PBUH), or any of the righteous caliphs (FKhulafa-e-Rashideen) or companions (Sahaaba) of the Holy Prophet'. Ordinance No XX of 1984 targeted Ahmadis and was designed 'to amend the law to prohibit the Quadiani group, Lahori group and Ahmadis from indulging in anti-Islamic activities', introducing new provisions in sections 298-B and 298-C (restrictions on Qadianis calling themselves Muslims or propagating their faith by passing themselves off as Muslim).

President Zia also initiated the creation of the Federal Shariat Court in 1980 with jurisdiction to ensure that existing laws were not repugnant to Islam. In 1986 a further amendment introduced section 295-C [254] which provides that the use of written or spoken words, including innuendo, defiling the sacred name of the Prophet Muhammad is punishable by death or with life imprisonment[255] and a fine.[256] This has no *mens rea* requirement and is broad enough to encompass accidental speech without deliberate intent or malice. In 1991, the Federal Sharia Court in *Muhammad Ismail Qureshi v Pakistan*[257] held that life imprisonment was repugnant to Islamic injunctions, effectively making the death penalty mandatory for those convicted under these laws, under which both Muslims and non-Muslims have been charged, accompanied by violent vigilantism, exacerbating the insecure environment in which judges operate.

Political opposition to blasphemy laws has elicited assassination, including that of Pakistan's Minister for Religious Minorities Shahbaz Bhatti, the Cabinet's sole Federal Minister in March 2011, and the murder of Punjab Governor Salman Taseer.[258] In June 2011, the Jamiat Ulema-e-Islami (JUI) Party petitioned to have The Bible banned from Pakistan as it violated national blasphemy laws by showing figures like Abraham

---

[254] In 1994, the Lahore High Court declared that if section 295-C of the PPC were struck down, the old system of killing a culprit on the spot could be revived. Can the claim that section 295-C prevents non-state violence against blasphemers and suspects survive an empirical study?

[255] While the text of the law provides for the punishment of death or imprisonment for life, a Federal Shariat Court Judgment, reported in 1991, declared the latter possibility void, thus making the death penalty mandatory for those convicted under this law. See further at <http://harvardhrj.com/2011/11/osama-siddique-interview-part-i/>.

[256] In a Preface to *Namoos-i-Risalat*, an account of the making of s 95-C by Advocate Ismail Qureshi, (Lahore: Al Faisal Publishers, 1994), former Supreme Court judge and former President Rafiq Tarar declared: 'If this law is not there the doors to courts will be closed on the culprits and the petitioners provoked by them, and then everyone will take the law in his own hands and exact revenge from the criminals. As a result anarchy will prevail in the country.' See at <http://archives.dawn.com/archives/19261>.

[257] *Muhammad Ismail Qureshi v Pakistan* (1991) 43 PLD 10.

[258] 'Q&A: Pakistan's controversial blasphemy laws', *BBC News*, 2 September 2012.

and Solomon, whom Muslims regard as prophets, to be engaging in 'a variety of moral crimes',[259] unless the offending passages were removed. This worsened existing pressures on the oppressed Christian minority. Most recently, there were calls for the Government to consider having a separate province for Pakistan's two million Christians so that they could enjoy equal rights, after seven Christians were reportedly burnt to death in Punjab for allegedly desecrating the Koran.[260] Notably, the blasphemy laws do not contain provisions to punish a false accuser or witness. These laws raise the issue of the limits of religious freedom (and whether the state may determine how a religious minority should express this) in the face of public order considerations, as discussed below.

Zaheeruddin v The State
(1993) 26 SCMR 1718 (Supreme Court, Pakistan)

Facts

Ahmadi community members issued eight appeals challenging the constitutionality of Ordinance XX and sections 295-B and 298-C, PPC.

A plan of the Ahmadis Community (Quadianis) to celebrate their religion's centenary was thwarted when the Home Secretary (Punjab) issued an order banning these celebrations. The Jhang District Manager passed another order under the Criminal Procedure Code prohibiting Quadianis from undertaking celebratory activities, such as raising slogans, using loudspeakers, holding processions and distributing sweets, which were in the public eye, to maintain law and order. The complaint was that this law violated the constitutional rights of religious minorities under Article 20 which reads:

Subject to law, public order and morality:–

(a) every citizen shall have the right to profess, practise and propagate his religion; and
(b) every religious denomination and every sect thereof shall have the right to establish, maintain and manage its religious institutions.

Abdul Qadeer Chaudhry, Muhammad Afzal Lone, Wali Muhammad Khan JJ (Majority Opinion)

The case came up before a learned Judge of the Lahore High Court who . . . has rendered a very balanced judgment [relying] on precedents from jurisdiction[s], which are either secular or claim to be the champions of human rights. The controversy raised before the Court is, undoubtedly, of very sensitive nature, concerning one's faith and belief and need[s] a very dispassionate and careful approach, in order to inspire confidence and lend its judgment the necessary independence.

The main question involved is whether the impugned orders passed under Section 144 Cr PC (Criminal Procedure Code) and the Ordinance XX of 1984 are violative of the Fundamental Right (Art 20) as given in the Constitution of Pakistan, 1973 . . .

[Noting that some of the words, names and epithets listed in Section 298B had been used in the Quran for specific persons while others had been used exclusively by Muslims for

---

[259] 'Pakistan's Bible Ban', 14 June 2011, *Frontpage Magazine*, at <http://frontpagemag.com/2011/frank-crimi/banning-bibles/>.

[260] R Crilly, ' Christians demand separate province in Pakistan to protect them from persecution', *Telegraph* (UK), 30 August 2012.

1,400 years] . . . These epithets carry special meaning, are part of the Muslim belief and used for reverence. Any person using them for others, in the same manner, may be conveying the impression to others that they are concerned with Islam when the fact may be otherwise. [The judge noted there were laws beyond Pakistan protecting the use of words and phrases with special meanings, whose misuse would mislead people, such as the term 'Crown', 'Imperial', 'Commonwealth' in English company law; the law of trade marks, which prevents the registration of names too similar to that of an existing company, the basic principle being 'do not deceive and do not violate the property rights of others'.]

In our case, a law has been made to protect even the title of Quaid-e-Azam, without any challenge from any quarter. However, in this Ideological State, the appellants, who are non-Muslims, want to pass off their faith as Islam? It must be appreciated that in this part of the world, faith is still the most precious thing to a Muslim believer, and he will not tolerate a government which is not prepared to save him from such deceptions or forgeries.

The appellants . . . insist not only on a license to pass off their faith as Islam but they also want to attach the exclusive epithets and descriptions etc, of the very revered Muslim personages to heretic non-Muslims who are considered not even a patch on them[, which Muslims consider] as defiling and desecration of those personages [and may even deceive others]. If a religious community insists on deception as its fundamental right and wants assistance of the courts in doing the same, then God help it. The US Supreme Court in *Cantwell vs Connecticut* (310 US 296 at 306) held that 'the cloak of religion or religious belief does not protect anybody in committing fraud upon the public'.

If the appellants or their community have no designs to deceive, why do not they coin their own epithets etc? Do they not realize that relying on the 'Shaairs' and other exclusive signs, marks and practices of other religions will betray the hollowness of their own religion? It may even mean that their new religion cannot progress or expand on its own strength, worth and merit but has to rely on deception? After all there are many other religions in the world and none of them ever usurped the epithets etc, of Muslims or others. Rather, they profess and present their own beliefs proudly and eulogize their heroes their own way . . . there is no law in Pakistan which forbids Ahmadis to coin their own epithets . . .

It was argued that the finding of the Federal Shariat Court that the Ordinance is not contrary to Quran and Sunnah is of no consequence, so far as this Court is concerned. The contention, however, has no merit. The Ahmadis have been declared non-Muslims by Article 260(3)(b) of the Constitution. This fact has further been affirmed by the Federal Shariat Court of Pakistan in *Mujibur Rehman v Federal Government of Pakistan* (PLD 1985 FSC 8), for the reason that the Ahmadia do not believe in the finality of prophethood of Muhammad (Peace be upon him); they falsify a clear and general verse of Holy Quran by resort to its 'Taweel'; and import into Islam, heretic concepts like shadowism, incarnation and transmigration. They were . . . asked to restrain themselves from directly or indirectly posing as Muslims or claiming legal rights of Muslims. [The Court noted that the Federal Shariat Court held that the Ordinance provisions banning Quadianis from using Islamic epithets implemented constitutional objectives.] . . .

As regards 'Shaa'ir of Islam' (distinctive characteristics), the Court held that Islamic Sharia does not allow a non-Muslim to adopt them; an Islamic State that allows a non-Muslim to adopt them (without embracing Islam) . . . fails to discharge its duties. An Islamic state, like a secular state, has the power to legislate, to prevent non-Muslims from adopting Shaa'ire' Islam, to propagate their own beliefs . . . [S]uch restriction is meant to prevent unscrupulous and fraudulent non-Muslims from using the effective and attractive features of Islam to attract other non-Muslims not to Islam but to their own heretic fold [finding that Federal Shariat Court decisions bind even the Supreme Court if not challenged in the Shariat appellate bench of the Supreme Court]. . . .

The next point needing consideration is whether Ordinance XX of 1984 . . . is total denial of religious freedom guaranteed under Article 20 of the Constitution to the Ahmadi citizens of Pakistan? . . . [The Court noted that religious freedom was not absolute but the phrase 'subject to law' did not confer unlimited power to legislate away fundamental rights.] . . . A balance has to be struck between the two, by resorting to a reasonable interpretation, keeping in view the peculiar circumstances of each case (See *Cantwell v Connecticut*, 310 US 296 and *Tikamdas v Divisional Evacuee Trust Committee, Karachi*, PLD 1968 Kar 703 (FB).

The US Supreme Court in *Reynolds v US* 98 US 145 held that 'Congress was deprived of all legislative power over mere opinion, but was left free to reach actions which were in violation of social duties or subversive of good order . . . Laws are made for the government of actions, and while they cannot interfere with mere religious beliefs and opinions, they may with practices.' . . . [T]he Supreme Court felt justified to ban polygamy, as it was being practiced by the Mormons sect on the ground that it was a duty imposed on them by their religion and was not a religious belief or opinion. It must be noted here that the observations [above] are peculiar to America where the people and not Allah are the sovereign. [Discusses cases from India, Australia and the US supporting the view that constitutional guarantees of free speech and religion are not absolutes and may reasonably be restricted to protect the community and social order.]

[Noting that the Pakistan Constitution does not define 'religion',] but its meaning may be gathered from the definitions of 'Muslim' and 'non-Muslim', in its Article 260(3)(a) and (b):

260(3) In the Constitution and all enactments and other legal instruments, unless there is anything repugnant in the subject or context:

(a) 'Muslim' means a person who believes in the unity and oneness of Almighty Allah, in the absolute and unqualified Prophethood of Muhammed, the last of prophets and does not believe in, or recognize as a prophet or religious reformer, any person who claimed or claims to be a prophet, in the sense of the word or any description whatsoever, after Muhammad; and

(b) 'non-Muslim' means a person who is not a Muslim and includes a person belonging to the Christian, Hindu, Sikh, Buddhist or Parsi community, a person of the Quadiani Group or Lahori Group (who call themselves 'Ahmadis' or by any other name) or a Bahai, and a person belonging to any of the Scheduled Castes.

There is no definition of the term 'religion', in the Constitutions of India or America or Australia either. [Having approvingly considered and adopted various Indian Supreme Court decisions noting that 'religion' has been interpreted to include both belief and rituals, observances and ceremonies 'regarded as integral parts of the religion'] . . . what was an 'essential' part of a religion was primarily to be ascertained by reference to religious doctrine such that prescription of food offerings which involved monetary expenditure if essential would not make such acts secular: religious practices were still subject to constitutional restrictions and Indian courts did not need to refer to foreign authorities to decide what fell within the purview of religion: *Commissioner HRE v Lakshmindra Swamiar* (AIR 1954 SC 282); further a 'superstition' would not be protected as religious practice if not essential to it: Gajendragadkar J, *Durghah Committee v Hussain Ali* (AIR 1961 SC 1402); the Court affirmed its power to determine the essentiality of a religious rite or observance: *Jagdishwaranand v Police Commissioner, Calcutta* (AIR 1984 SC1) . . . these practices have to be stated and proved . . . from the authentic sources of the religion to the satisfaction of the court.

. . . The appellants, however, have not explained how the epithets etc, and the various planned ceremonies are an essential part of their religion and that they have to be performed only in public or in the public view, on the roads and streets or at the public places.

. . . [I]f the impugned law is a valid piece of legislation, and the respondents had taken the impugned actions, in the interest of law and order, unless it can be shown that the same were taken mala fide or without factual justification, the question of denial of fundamental rights may not arise. The law on the point has been well settled in various jurisdictions and it may be useful to cite them. [Cites Latham CJ in *Jehovah's Witnesses case, Adelaide vs Commonwealth* (1943) 67 CLR 116, dealing with the 'free exercise of any religion' clause embodied in section 116 of the Australian Constitution, for the proposition that a law imposing civic duties could not be characterised as infringing religious freedom, and that the refusal of religious minorities to perform military obligations prejudiced the defence of the community and was not immunised by section 116; so too the High Court was arbiter of when legislation unduly infringed religious freedom. It referred to the US decision of *Willis Cox v New Hampshire* 312 US 569 (1941) for the proposition that statutes requiring special licenes for conducting parades were not an unconstitutional interference with religious practice.]

We have referred to the above view from such countries, which claim to be the secular and liberal, and not religious or fundamentalists. The same principles were applied by the Indian Supreme Court in *Muhammad Hanif Qureshi v State of Bihar*, AIR 1958 SC 731 to hold that certain laws banning slaughter of certain animals, did not violate the fundamental rights of Muslims under Article 25(l), as there was no material to substantiate the claim that the sacrifice of a cow on Bakr-ld-Day, was enjoined or sanctioned by Islam, to exhibit a Mussalman's belief and idea. The same Court in *Acharya Jagdishwaranand Avadhutta v Commissioner of Police, Calcutta,* (AIR 1984 SC 51) held [that the desire to perform tandava dance in public was not a religious rite of Anada Marg].

The American Court held in the following cases that there was no violation of the constitutional guarantee of freedom of exercise of religion. Mr S Sharifuddin Pirzada in his book *Fundamental Rights and Constitutional Remedies in Pakistan* (1966 Edition) at pp 313–314 and 317 has observed as follows:

(i) In *Hamilton v Board of Regents of University of California,* (1934) 293 US 245, where students appealed to the Supreme Court that the act of the university to make a regulation for compulsory military training was contrary to their religious belief, the court rejected the contention, holding that the 'Government owes a duty to the people within its jurisdiction to preserve itself in adequate strength to maintain peace and order and assure the enforcement of law. And every citizen owes the reciprocal duty, according to his capacity, to support and defend the Government against all enemies.'

(ii) The plea of fundamental right was rejected in *Commonwealth vs Plaisted* (1889) 148 Mass 375 by the Massachusetts Supreme Court in a case where law prohibits the use of streets for religious meetings, or the beating of drums though it is a part of religious ceremony of such organization as the Salvation Army.

(iii) Where the statute requires a parent to provide medical treatment for a child suffering from disease even if not in accordance with religious belief of the parents.

(iv) Freedom of religion does not necessarily imply absolute equality of treatment, and in fact regard must be had to the special position of the Church of England. (*The United Kingdom* by GW Keeton and D Lloyd, pp 67–68.)

The above views . . . do go to show that freedom of religion would not be allowed to interfere with the law and order or public peace and tranquility. It is based on the principle that the state will not permit anyone to violate or take away the fundamental rights of others, in the enjoyment of his own rights and that no one can be allowed to insult, damage or defile the religion of any other class or outrage their religious feelings, so as to give rise to law and order situation [which the state may take minimum preventive measures to ensure] . . .

The Muslims think that the birth of this Ahmadia community during the English rule in the sub-continent among the Muslim society was a serious and organized attack on its ideological frontiers. They consider it a permanent threat to their integrity and solidarity, because the socio-political organization of the Muslim society is based on its religion. In that situation their using the above given epithets etc, in a manner which to the Muslim mind looks like a deliberate and calculated act of defiling and desecration of their holy personages, is a threat to the integrity of 'Ummah' and tranquility of the nation, and it is also bound to give rise to a serious law and order situation, like it happened many a time in the past . . . As a matter of fact, the Ahmadis, internally had declared themselves the real Muslim community, by alienating and excommunicating the main body of Muslims [as infidels for rejecting] Mirza Ghulam Ahmad as the prophet and the promised Messiah . . . [according to his teachings] . . . There are scores of other similar writings, not only by Mirza Sahib himself but his so called 'calipha' and followers proving, without any shadow of doubt, that they are religiously and socially, a community separate and different from the Muslims . . . Mirza Ghulam Ahmad had forbidden his followers from marrying their daughters with non-Ahmadis and from praying along with them. According to him the main body of the Muslims could, at the most, be treated like Christians. In fact Mirza Bashiruudin Ahmad, the second caliph and son of Mirza Sahib, is reported to have said:

> that through an emissary, I requested an English Officer that our separate rights be determined like those of the Parsees and Christians. The officer replied that they are minorities while you are an religious sect. On that I said that even Parsees and Christians are religious communities and if they can be given separate rights why not we.' (*Alfazal* Nov 13, 1946).

. . . The main body of Muslims never wanted to stand with Ahmadis on the same pedestal. Way back, as reported above, the Ahmadis were prepared even to be treated as a minority with separate and distinct rights. They, as a religious community [have] declared the whole Muslim 'Ummah' as infidels . . . However, they being an insignificant minority could not impose their will. On the other hand, the main body of Muslims, who had been waging a campaign against their (Ahmadis') religion since its inception made a decision in 1974, and declared them instead, a non-Muslim minority under the Constitution itself . . . The Ahmadis are, therefore, non-Muslims; legally and constitutionally, and are of their own choice a minority opposed to Muslims . . . [T]he right to oust dissidents has been recognized, in favor of the main body of a religion or a denomination by the courts, and a law prohibiting such an action was declared *ultra vires* the fundamental rights, by the Indian Supreme Court. Reference may be made to the case of *Sardar Syena Taher Saifudin Sahib v State of Bombay* (AIR 1962 SC 853) [which held that an Act removing the power of a religious community's head to excommunicate on the basis of creed violated Article 26(b) of the Indian Constitution which protects the management of a community by its religious head. Although excommunication might entail the loss of civil rights (enjoyment of properties owned by a religious group), Article 26(b) was not 'made subject to preservation of civil rights', only 'subject to public order, morality and health] . . .

. . . [The Ahmadis always wanted to be a separate entity, of their own choice, religiously and socially. Normally, they should have been pleased on achieving their objective, particularly when it was secured for them by the Constitution itself. Their disappointment is that they wanted to oust the rest of the Muslims as infidels and retain the tag of Muslims. Their grievance is that they have been excommunicated and branded as non-Muslims, unjustly. The reason of their frustration and dismay may be that now . . . they cannot operate successfully their scheme of conversion of the unwary and non-Muslims to their faith. Maybe, it is for this reason that they want to usurp the Muslim epithets, descriptions etc and display 'Kalima' and say 'Azan' so as to pose as Muslims and preach and propagate in the garb of Muslims with attractive tenets of Islam. The label of non-Muslim seems to have become counter productive [for a Quadiani to hold out that he is Muslim, without first denouncing his faith, is not only a clear violation of the Ordinance but also the Constitution] . . .

[Rejects the contention that the impugned Ordinance is vague and oppressive in relation to the section 298C phrase 'who, directly or indirectly, poses himself as a Muslim or calls, or refers to, his faith as Islam'] . . . the law addresses the members of Quadiani or Lahori group. They have a historical background of serious conflict with the main body of Muslims . . . The Ahmadis claim Mirza Sahib is himself a prophet and those who do not believe in and follow him are infidels. The right to the use of the above mentioned epithets etc, by the Ahmadis, for those connected with Mirza Sahib is on account of that connection alone . . . The appellants are, undoubtedly Ahmadis, and are non-Muslims according to the Constitution. Their use of the 'Shaa'ire Islam' etc, thus amounts to either posing as Muslims or to deceive others or to ridicule. In any case, the fact whether they were posing as such can be clearly proved . . . Undoubtedly, there is no vagueness in the law at all . . .

. . . [L]egislation just to preserve law and order has never been considered oppressive in any country of the world. Again, no legal system in the world will allow a community, howsoever vocal, organized, affluent or influential it may be, to cheat others of their faith or rights, usurp their heritage and to deliberately and knowingly do such acts or take such measures as may create law and order situation.

[The Court was not impressed by the appellant's submission that the word 'law' in Article 20 meant 'positive law' and not Islamic law.] . . . The term 'positive law', according to Black's Law Dictionary, is the law actually enacted or adopted by proper authority for the government of an organized jural society . . . all the above noted cases were decided prior to the induction of Article 2A in the Constitution:

> 2A. Objectives Resolution to form part of substantive provisions. The principles and provisions set out in the Objective Resolution reproduced in the Annex are hereby made substantive part of the Constitution and shall have effect accordingly.

It was for the first time in the constitutional history of Pakistan, that the Objective Resolution, which henceforth formed part of every constitution as a preamble, was adopted and incorporated in the Constitution, in 1985, and made its effective part. This was an act of the adoption of a body of law by reference . . . It is generally done whenever a new legal order is enforced. Here in this country, it had been done after every martial law was imposed or the constitutional order restored after the lifting of martial law. The legislature in the British days had also adopted the Muslim and other religious and customary laws in the same manner and they were considered as the positive laws. This was the stage, when the chosen representatives of people, for the first time accepted the sovereignty of Allah, as the operative part of the Constitution, to be binding on them and vowed that they will exercise only the delegated powers, within the limits fixed by Allah . . .

The above mentioned constitutional change has been acknowledged and accepted as effective by the Supreme Court. Mr Justice Nasim Hasan Shah, considering the changed authority of the representatives of the people, in *Pakistan v Public at Large*, (PLD 1987 SC 304 at p 356), stated as follows:

Accordingly, unless it can be shown definitely that the body of Muslims sitting in the legislature have enacted something which is forbidden by Almighty Allah in the Holy Quran or by the Sunnah of the Holy Prophet or of some principle emanating by necessary intendment therefrom no Court can declare such an enactment to be un-Islamic.

. . . It is thus clear that the Constitution has adopted the injunctions of Islam as contained in Quran and Sunnah of the Holy Prophet as the real and the effective law (ie, positive law) . . . Article 2A, made effective and operative the sovereignty of Almighty Allah and it is because of that Article that the legal provisions and principles of law, as embodied in the Objectives Resolution, have become effective and operative. Therefore, every man-made law must now conform to the injunctions of Islam as contained in Quran and Sunnah of the Holy Prophet (pbuh). Therefore, even the Fundamental Rights as given in the Constitution must not violate the norms of Islam.

. . . It is not correct to say that 'Azan' (Islamic call to prayer) is not mentioned in the Ordinance. In fact sub-section (2) of Section 298B is exclusively devoted to it. As for the use of 'Kalima' by the Ahmadis, in the light of the Ordinance, reference be made to Section 298C. The 'Kalima' is a covenant, on reciting which a non-believer enters the fold of Islam. It is in Arabic form, is exclusive to Muslims who recite it, not only as proof of their faith but very often, for spiritual well being. The 'Kalima' means there is no God but Allah and Muhammad is His Prophet. The belief of Quadianis is that Mirza Ghulam Ahmad is (God forbid) Muhammad incarnate . . . there is general consensus among Muslims that whenever an Ahmadi recites or displays 'Kalima', he proclaims that Mirza Ghulam Ahmad is the Prophet who should be obeyed and the one who does not do that is an infidel. In the alternative, they pose as Muslims and deceive others. Lastly, they either ridicule Muslims or deny that the teachings of the Holy Prophet (pbuh) do not govern the situation [proving the commission of the offence] . . .

Not only did Mirza Sahib in his writings belittle the glory and grace of the Holy Prophet (pbuh), he even ridiculed him occasionally [cites illustrative writings] . . . It is the cardinal faith of every Muslim to believe in the Prophet and praise him. Therefore, if anything is said against the Prophet, it will injure the feelings of a Muslim and may even incite him to the breach of peace, depending on the intensity of the attack. The learned Judge in the High Court has quoted extensively from the Ahmadi literature to show how Mirza Ghulam Ahmad belittled the other Prophets, particularly, Jesus Christ, whose place he wanted to occupy . . . Mirza Ghulam Ahmad wrote:

The miracles that the other Prophets possessed individually were all granted to Muhammad (pbuh). They all were then given to me as I am his shadow. It is for this reason that my names are Adam, Abraham, Moses, Noha, David, Joseph, Soloman, John, and Jesus Christ . . . (Matfoozaat Vol 3, page 270, Printed Rabwah).

About Jesus Christ he stated:

The ancestors of Jesus Christ were pious and innocent? His three paternal grandmothers and maternal grandmothers were prostitutes and whores and that is the blood he represents. (Appendix Anjaame Atham, note 7).

Quran, on the other hand, praises Jesus Christ, his mother and his family. (See 3: 33–37, 3:45–47, 19:16–32). Can any Muslim utter anything against Quran and can anyone who does so claim to be a Muslim? How then can Mirza Ghulam Ahmed or his followers claim to be Muslims? . . . Mirza Sahib could have been convicted and punished by an English Court, for the offense of blasphemy, under the Blasphemy Act, 1679, with a term of imprisonment.

Again, as for the Holy Prophet Muhammad (pbuh) is concerned:

> . . . every Muslim who is firm in his faith, must love him more than his children, family, parents and much more than any one else in the world. (See Al-Bukhari, Kitabul Eeman, Bab Hubbul Rasool Min-al Eeman).

Can than anyone blame a Muslim if he loses control of himself on hearing, reading or seeing such blasphemous material as produced by Mirza Sahib?

It is in this background that one should visualize the public conduct of Ahmadis, at the centenary celebrations and imagine the reaction that it might have attracted from the Muslims. So, if an Ahmadi is allowed by the administration or the law to display or chant in public, the Shaa're Islam, it is like 'creating a Rushdi' out of him. Can the administration in that case guarantee his life, liberty and property and if so at what cost? Again, if this permission is given to a procession or assembly, on the streets or a public place, it is like permitting civil war. It is not a mere guesswork. It has happened, in fact many a time, in the past, and had been checked at cost of colossal loss of life and property (For details, Munir's report may be seen.) The reason is that when an Ahmadi or Ahmadis display in public, on a placard, a badge or a poster or write on walls or ceremonial gates or huntings, the 'Kalima', or chant other 'Shaa'ire Islam' it would amount to publicly defiling the name of Holy Prophet (pbuh) and also other Prophets, and exalting the name of Mirza Sahib, thus infuriating and instigating the Muslims so that there may be a serious cause for disturbance of the public peace, order and tranquillity and it may result in loss of life and property. The preventive actions in such situations are imperative in order to maintain law and order and save loss or damage to life and property particularly of Ahmadis. In that situation, the decisions of the concerned local authorities cannot be overruled by this Court; in this jurisdiction, they are the best Judges unless contrary is proved in law or fact.

. . . [T]he holding of centenary celebrations on the roads and streets was not shown to be the essential and integral part of their religion . . . [and even essential practices] . . . have been sacrificed at the altar of public safety and tranquility. It is stated by the appellants that they wanted to celebrate the 100 years Ahmadia movement in a harmless and innocent manner, inter alia, by offering special thanksgiving prayers, distribution of sweets amongst children, and serving food to the poor. We do not find any order stopping these activities, in private. The Ahmadis like other minorities are free to profess their religion in this country and no one can take away that right of theirs, either by legislation or executive orders. They must, however, honor the Constitution and the law and should neither desecrate or defile the pious personage of any other religious including Islam . . .

We also do not think that the Ahmadis will face any difficulty in coining new names, epithets, titles and descriptions for their personages, places and practices. After all, Hindus, Christians, Sikhs and other communities have their own epithets etc, and are celebrating their festivals peacefully and without any law and order problem and trouble . . .

. . . [T]he learned single Judge has passed a detailed and well-reasoned order and has sagaciously and candidly taken into consideration judgments from such foreign jurisdictions which would infuse confidence in this hypersensitive, non-Muslim minority, ie Ahmadis . . . [W]e adopt his reasoning also. The Ordinance is thus held to be not *ultra vires* of the Constitution [dismisses appeal].

Notes and Questions

1. In his Presidential address to the Pakistan Constituent Assembly on 11 August 1947, Muhammad Ali Jinnah expressed this aspiration:

> You are free; you are free to go to your temples, you are free to go to your mosques or to any other place or worship in this State of Pakistan. You may belong to any religion or caste or creed that has nothing to do with the business of the State . . . We are starting in the days where there is no discrimination, no distinction between one community and another, no discrimination between one caste or creed and another. We are starting with this fundamental principle that we are all citizens and equal citizens of one State . . . Now I think we should keep that in front of us as our ideal and you will find that in course of time Hindus would cease to be Hindus and Muslims would cease to be Muslims, not in the religious sense, because that is the personal faith of each individual, but in the political sense as citizens of the State.

See G Allana, *Pakistan Movement Historical Documents* (Karachi: University of Karachi, c 1969) at 408.

2. What is the Pakistan Government's role in relation to Islam within an Islamic state? Who is sovereign within the Islamic state, given that the preambular reference to the sovereignty of Allah became positive law under Article 2A? Is the locus of sovereignty in Pakistan and, say, the USA significant?

3. Is the Pakistan Constitution involved in theology, ie an act of excommunication? Is the Court so involved, in its application of the imported Indian test of essentiality? What was the attitude of the Court towards propositions in cases from 'secular' jurisdictions like India, USA and Australia? Why the resort to foreign cases?

4. Section 295C PPC has been criticised for its great coercive and exploitative potential. Does a liberal paradigm have anything to offer to the question of religious sensitivities, or is it too parochial to manage the view that blasphemy against sacred personalities should be criminalised?

5. Was the case simply a conventional one of balancing religious rights against public order considerations ('creating a Rushdi out of him', 'permitting civil war') or was there more involved, in terms of deciding whether religious freedom was implicated? On what basis was it said that the religious freedom of Ahmadis was not curtailed? Were the rights of Ahmadis limited to protecting their other rights (eg life, property)?

6. A common rationale for blasphemy laws is to prevent division within a heterogeneous society. What is the impact of blasphemy law on understandings of religious tolerance? What impact does it have on other rights, such as free speech? Can it be used by extremists to legitimate violence, stifle dissenting views and to harass rivals to settle private disputes and vendettas?

7. Was it appropriate for Judge Chaudhry to draw an analogy between *Cantwell v Connecticut*, which involved restricting religious practice through a neutral licensing statute (soliciting funds for religious purposes) relating to time, place and manner, in the name of public order, and the Pakistani non-neutral anti-blasphemy law, which is designed to protect society? See AM Khan, 'Misuse and Abuse of Legal Argument by Analogy in Transjudicial Communication: The Case of Zaheeruddin v State' (2011) 10(4) *Richmond Journal of Global Law and Business* 497; and AM Khan, 'Persecution of the Ahmadiyya Community in Pakistan: An Analysis under International Law and International Relations (2003) 16 *Harvard Human Rights Journal* 17.

8. The *Zaheeruddin* decision has been criticised as indirectly inciting violence against Ahmadis, particularly by misquoting and presenting false statements allegedly made by Mirza Ghulam Ahmad. How does this square with the Court's perception that the rights of religious minorities were adequately safeguarded? See M Nadeem Siddiq, 'Enforced Apostasy: Zaheeruddin v State and the Official Persecution of the Ahmadiyya Community in Pakistan' (1995) 14 *Law & Inequality* 275, 279; T Mahmud, 'Freedom of Religion and Religious Minorities in Pakistan: a Study of Judicial Practice' (1995) 19 *Fordham International Law Journal* 40 (noting the evolving approach of the courts from protecting Ahmadis to abdicating this role). For a review of all Pakistani reported cases on blasphemy from 1960–2007, see O Siddique and Z Hayat, 'Unholy Laws & Holy Speech: Blasphemy Laws in Pakistan – Controversial Origins, Design Defects and Free Speech Implications' (2008) 17 *Minnesota Journal of International Law* 303 (noting that mala fide motivations underlying allegations of blasphemy included, as the courts uncovered, personal vendettas, property disputes, professional or personal rivalries, or marital disagreements).

9. Blasphemy laws remain a controversial issue in Pakistan. In 2012, a case (DIR no 134/12) for arresting Facebook CEO Mark Zuckerberg was registered with a Jhang police station, when an advocate filed a petition before the District Session Judge seeking a ban on websites like Facebook, Youtube and Google allegedly demeaning Prophet Muhammad under section 295-A of the Pakistan Penal Code: 'Blasphemy: Arrest Mark Zuckerberg, Fleming Rose, says petitioner', *The Express Tribune*, 26 February 2012. Facebook had drawn the ire of Muslims, who alleged that Islamic values were violated and religious hatred promoted through such initiatives as Facebook's 'Draw Muhammad Day'. See 'LHC seeks reply from govt, IT Ministry over imposing ban on Facebook', *Daily Times*, 26 May 2011, at <http://www.dailytimes.com.pk/default.asp?page=2011\05\26\story_26-5-2011_pg13_8>. See also 'Pakistan minister murdered for criticism of Islam blasphemy law', *Washington Times*, 2 March 2011.

10. Unlike Bangladeshi and Pakistan courts which operate within Islamic constitutional orders, Indian courts functioning within a secular state have regarded Ahmadis as Muslims. In *Narantakath Avullah v Parakkal Mammu*,[261] Krisnan J was of the opinion that Ahmadis were merely a 'reformed sect' of Muslims; Oldfield J noted that the Ahmadi belief involved 'a plenary acceptance of Muhammedanism' (at [6]–[7]). In *Shihabuddin Imbichi Koya Thangal v KP Ahammed Koya*,[262] the issue was whether a Muslim by birth, on accepting the Ahmadiyya persuasion, had ceased being a Muslim. The Court held (at [1]): 'Religion is not amenable to reason and theological disputes cannot be decided by secular Courts. So my duty is as embarrassing as my jurisdiction is limited.' Thus, the Court refused to evaluate whether a religious claim is false or true, instead proceeding to test its reality by its universal acceptance by the community and its affirmation in the past in courts of law (at [3]). The Court examined the doctrinal beliefs of the Ahmadis and various legal precedents. It was held that the Ahmadiyya sect was 'of Islam and not alien' (at [13]). Which approach is

---

[261] *Narantakath Avullah v Parakkal Mammu* [1923] AIR Mad 171 [14].
[262] *Shihabuddin Imbichi Koya Thangal v KP Ahammed Koya* [1971] AIR Ker 206.

preferable, from the point of view of religious freedom, considering the different conceptions of this liberty?

vi. Indonesia, Blasphemy and the Ahmadis

Indonesia has no official religion but formally recognises six (Islam, Roman Catholicism, Hinduism, Buddhism, Protestantism and Confucianism). In 2009, the population of Indonesia was 88.7 per cent Muslim, 5.7 per cent Protestant, 3.02 per cent Catholic, 1.7 per cent Hindu, 0.6 per cent Buddhist, 0.09 per cent Confucian and 0.11 per cent 'other'.[263] The national ideology of 'Pancasila' includes the precept, 'Belief in the one and only God' (*Ketuhanan Yang Maha Esa*).[264]

Presidential Decree No 1/PNPS/1965 on the Prevention of the Misuse/Insulting of a Religion Made into a Law by Law 5/1969

Note

The 'Blasphemy Law' was enacted during the autocratic 'Guided Democracy' era, before various constitutional amendments strengthened human rights protection by incorporating into Chapter XA (Human Rights) various international norms.

> **Section 1**: 'Every person is prohibited from deliberately speaking in public, recommending in public, or garnering public support, for the purposes of interpreting any religion that is adhered to in Indonesia or conducting religious activities that are similar to the activities of the religions adhered to in Indonesia, if the interpretation and activity deviate from the central teachings of that religion.'

Official Explanation:

'*a religion that is adhered to in Indonesia*' means Islam, Christianity, Catholicism, Hinduism, Buddhism, or Confucianism. This can be proven by the historical development of the religions in Indonesia. These six religions are the religions that are adhered to by almost all of the residents of Indonesia. On top of the protection guaranteed by Article 29(2) of the 1945 Constitution, these six religions are also further protected by Section 1 of the Blasphemy Law.

'*central teachings of a religion*' means religious teachings that could be known by the Ministry of Religious Affairs, which has the tools or means to investigate such teachings. Paragraph 4 of the general explanation of the Blasphemy Law provides that the main objective of the Blasphemy Law is to prevent deviations from religious teachings that are considered as central teachings by the leaders of the respective religions.

> **Section 2(1)** 'Whosoever violates Section 1 shall be given an order and a stern warning to stop his action in a joint decision of the Minister of Religious Affairs, the Minister/ Attorney-General, and the Minister of Home Affairs.'

---

[263] 'Table 1: Population by Religion 2009', Ministry of Religion, at <kemenag.go.id>.

[264] The term for 'God' used here is '*Tuhan*', the Indonesian word for God used by all religions. For a discussion of the choice of this term over '*Allah*', the Arabic term for God commonly used by Muslims, in the Pancasila, see E Darmaputera, *Pancasila and the Search for Identity and Modernity in Indonesian Society: A Cultural and Ethical Analysis* (Brill: Leiden & New York, 1988) 153.

2(2) 'If any Organization or belief group violates subsection (1), then the President of the Republic of Indonesia may dissolve such Organization and declare that the Organization or belief group is a forbidden Organization or belief group after receiving the input of the Minister of Religious Affairs, the Attorney-General, and the Minister of Home Affairs.'

Section 3 'If, after the Minister of Religious Affairs, the Attorney-General, and the Minister of Home Affairs have jointly, or the President of Republic of Indonesia has, taken action in accordance with Section 2 against a person, organization or belief group, but the person, Organization, or belief group continues to violate Section 1, then such person, follower, member and/or committee member of the Organization/belief group, may be sentenced to a maximum imprisonment term of five years.'

Section 4: 'The following provision shall be inserted into the Criminal Code:

Article 156a Any person who deliberately and publicly expresses any feeling or behaves in a manner that:

(a) which in essence is hostile towards, or is a misuse or desecration of, any of the adhered religions in Indonesia
(b) has the intention that a person should not practise any religion at all that is based on Belief in Almighty God,

shall be sentenced to a maximum of five years jail.'

Decision of the Constitutional Court on the Blasphemy Law
No 140/PUU-VII/2009, 19 April 2010 (Constitutional Court, Indonesia) [unofficial trans M Virgiany]

Facts

The constitutionality of the Blasphemy Law was challenged before the Indonesian Constitutional Court which delivered its seminal decision in 2010. It was argued that the Law violated various Articles, including Articles 28E and 29 of the Constitution:

28E (1) Every person shall be free to choose and to practice the religion of his/her choice
. . .
    (2) Every person shall have the right to the freedom to believe his/her faith (kepercayaan), and to express his/her views and thoughts, in accordance with his/her conscience.
29 (1) The State shall be based upon the belief in the One and Only God.
    (2) The State guarantees all persons the freedom of worship, each according to his/her own religion or belief.

The Applicants also relied on Article 28I(1), which includes freedom of thought and conscience and freedom of religion as 'human rights that cannot be limited under any circumstances', which is reiterated in Law No 39 of 1999 on Human Rights (Articles 4 and 22(2)).

References to international provisions were made during the course of the proceedings, including Article 18 UDHR, Article 18 ICCPR (ratified by Law No 12 of 2005) and the 1981 UN Declaration on the Elimination of All Forms of Intolerance and Discrimination Based on Religion or Belief.

One of the arguments raised supporting the application was that in the history of religions, differences in interpretation of religious texts was

a logical consequence of the development of a religion [as] . . . each religion is a deviation from another religion. Christianity deviates from Jewish teachings in many cases
for sure, such as the fact that eating pork or not being circumcised is allowed in
Christianity . . . Islam is a real deviation from Christianity that believes that Jesus is
God, whereas Islam only considers Jesus as a prophet. If we refer back to history, then
all religions came about as a form of deviation from the previous traditional religious
doctrines [1j].

It was argued that

precisely because there is a claim of truth from each religious interpretation that each
interpretation deserves to exist. Indeed, all interpretations are linked to the instinct of
men, who are endowed with reason, to always seek the truth. Due to that, each interpretation has the potential to be true, but also the potential to be false. Limiting a group of
people's chance to interpret means closing the possibility for the emergence of a possibly better interpretation. This is not only a form of tyranny because it hinders the truth
to come to light, but it also betrays human nature. [1j].

Further,

if it is legal to interpret, then it is also legal to publicize the results of religious interpretation. This is to give the opportunity for the public to accept the truest truth. Limiting
the publication of interpretation is the akin to closing the possibility of the right interpretation to be publicized, or closing the possibility of truth. Because of that the State
cannot limit it. [1j]

Opinion of the Court

The Court would like to first note the following:

That Pancasila has been the foundation of the State which has to be accepted by all citizens. Pancasila contains five principles which are interrelated to each other as a whole.
Therefore, every citizen, whether as an individual or as a nation collectively, should be able
to accept the Belief in God Almighty which animates the other principles of just and civilized humanity, unity of Indonesia, democracy guided by the wisdom in deliberation/
representation, and social justice for all Indonesian people;

That the drafters of the 1945 Constitution have included the following provisions on the
religious values in the 1945 Constitution: (references provisions relating to religion: third
and fourth preambular paragraphs, Articles 9(1), 28E(1)(2), 28I(1), 28J(2), 29(1), 31(3) . . .);

That since independence, the Laws on the Powers of the Indonesian Judiciary, such as
Law No 19 of 1964, Law No 14 of 1970, Law No 4 of 2003, Law No 48 of 2009 on Judicial
Powers, as well as Law No 24 of 2003 on the Constitutional Court, have always emphasized
that 'Adjudication is done for justice based on One God Almighty.' The constitutional and
normative provisions above clearly show that Indonesia is a nation that believes in God,
not an atheist nation;

The principle of Belief in One God Almighty is the basis of the law that requires each
educational institution to teach religious education as a subject, in accordance with their
respective religions. Teaching religious education means teaching the truth of religious
belief to those being educated, namely the students. In reality, such practice has existed for
a long time and its legality is not questioned. Therefore, the domain of belief in One God
Almighty is the *forum internum* domain, which is a consequence of the acceptance of
Pancasila as the foundation of the State. Every propaganda that distances the citizens from
Pancasila cannot be accepted by good citizens . . . [Notes that Indonesia's religious educa-

tion policy since the 1960s is to require public schools to provide religious studies for their students, in contrast with the United States where 'teaching religion in public schools is unconstitutional because there is freedom to hold a religion and freedom to not hold a religion. Belief in a religion or no religion is *forum internum* for each citizen which the State cannot interfere with'];

On the basis of the above philosophical perspective on freedom of religion, in Indonesia, which is a Pancasila state, there cannot be any activity or practice that distances citizens from Pancasila. In the name of freedom, a person or a group cannot erode the society's religiosity that has been inherited as values that animate various legal provisions in Indonesia;

. . . The provisions on blasphemy are not only seen from the juridical aspect, but also the philosophical aspect that places freedom of religion in an Indonesian perspective, so the religious practices that take place in Indonesia are different from the religious practices in other countries which cannot be equated with Indonesia . . .

Considering that Indonesia is a state based on Belief in One God Almighty (paragraph IV of the Preamble and Article 29(1) of the 1945 Constitution). Indonesia also acknowledges that its independence was achieved not only through the long struggle of the whole of the nation, but also through the grace of God Almighty (preambular paragraph III, 1945 Constitution). This formulation of Indonesia's basic philosophy, which is contained in the Preamble of the 1945 Constitution, was the result of a compromise between two schools of thought that had developed during the formulation of the state foundation in BPUPK.[265] One school of thought wanted a secular state whereas the other wanted an Islamic state.[266] Both were rejected, but the Plenary Meeting of BPUPK unanimously agreed that Indonesia was a state based on the belief in God, with obligations to carry out Islamic law principles for all Muslims, which was then passed during the PPKI[267] Plenary Meeting on 18 August 1945 by changing the phrase 'Belief in God with the obligation to carry out Islamic law principles for the adherents' to 'state based on the Belief in One God Almighty' [now embodied in Article 29(1), 1945 Constitution] . . .

. . . On the level of state practice, the State formed a special ministry in charge of religious affairs, namely the Ministry of Religious Affairs. It is state practice to respect religious holidays. Religious laws are also respected; in this case Islamic laws regarding marriage, divorce, reconciliation, inheritance, grants, wills, endowments, economic syari'ah, etc have become the laws of the state applicable to adherents of Islam; . . . Indonesia's respect for various conventions and international legal rules, including on human rights, must still be based on the philosophy and constitution of the Republic of Indonesia;

. . . The principles of the legal state of Indonesia should be seen with the perspective of the 1945 Constitution, which is a legal state that places the principle of Belief in One God Almighty as the main principle, and religious values that underlie the life motion of the nation and state, not a state that separates state from religion, and does not merely adhere to the principle of individualism or principle of communalism. The Constitution of the Republic of Indonesia does not provide for the possibility of a campaign for the freedom of not having a religion, freedom to promote anti-religion, and does not allow any insult or defilement of any religious teachings or books that are the source of religious beliefs or

---

[265] Committee for Preparatory Work for Independence (*Badan Penyelidik Usaha Persiapan Kemerdekaan*).

[266] Certain Muslims feared that not including 'Islam' as the official religion would damage it: 'If Pancasila has to be regarded, not merely as the foundation of the state but as the basis of human life, then the religion revealed by Almighty God (or so perceived) will have to be exchanged for an ideology, an ideology that claims not to be a religion but which acts as though it wants to replace existing religions.' 'Sjafruddin Prawiranegara: don't let Pancasila kill Islam', in D Bourchier and VR Hadiz (eds), *Indonesian Politics and Society: A Reader* (London: Routledge-Curzon, 2003) at 144–45.

[267] Preparatory Committee for Indonesian Independence (*Panitia Persiapan Kemerdekaan Indonesia*).

defile the name of God. This is one of the elements that mark the main difference between the legal state of Indonesia and the legal state in the West, such that in the running of the state government, the formulation of laws, and the administration of justice, the basis of belief in God and religious teachings and values become a measuring device to determine which laws are good and which are bad, and also to determine which laws are constitutional and which are not. According to the thought framework described above, limiting human rights on the basis of 'religious values', as stated in Article 28J(2) of the 1945 Constitution, is one of the considerations to limit the implementation of human rights. This is different from Article 18 ICCPR which does not provide for religious values as a restriction of individual freedoms [discusses recognition of human right of religious freedom and permissible limits, noting Article 19(3) ICCPR];

From the perspective of human rights, freedom of religion that is granted to every human being is not a freedom that is free from values . . . as such, but a freedom that is accompanied by social responsibility to realize every person's human rights. In this case, the State has a role to balance human rights and the fundamental obligation to realize human rights that are just. The State has a role to ensure that in the exercise of freedom of religion, no one hurts or violates the freedom of religion of others . . . When looking at religion, often times interpretation is based on the concept of religion as an individual and personal experience of the presence of God, which is merely a private aspect. Yet religion also has sociological, cultural, and historical aspects, a unique identity as the belief of a particular community or society. Therefore, in addition to having individual and personal values, religion also has social and communal values.

Indonesia's philosophy, as embodied in the Preamble of the 1945 Constitution . . . is to 'protect the whole of Indonesia'. This protection can be interpreted as the protection of cultural identity, ethnicity, religion, and uniqueness of Indonesia whether individually or communally. Restrictions do not always have to be interpreted as discrimination. As long as the restrictions provided for are in the form of protection of the rights of others and the orderliness of the life in society, nation, and state (see Article 28J(1) of the 1945 Constitution), then they are a form of protection of the human rights of others as well as a form of or fundamental obligation for others;

. . .

. . . [A]lthough at the concrete level the Applicants are testing the constitutionality of the provisions of the Blasphemy Law, in essence the Court is of the view that the Applicants' objective is to find the form and interpretation of freedom of religion in Indonesia . . . [I]n assessing the substance of this case, the Court deals with aspects that are very sensitive and considered as sacred by the Indonesian society, namely religion, and the Court is of the view that it is necessary to consider the development of the strength of human rights protection in Indonesia after amendments to the 1945 Constitution were made and gave rise to new discourses regarding the relationship between State and religion.

In giving its opinion based on law and justice, which the Court will uphold when deciding on the Applicants' application, the Court's opinion is not going to be based on only freedom of religion, but also other perspectives, namely the perspective of a legal state, democracy, human rights, public order, and religious values that are adhered to in Indonesia . . .

Before giving an opinion related to the Applicants' arguments, the Court has to first lay out the main issues as follows:

First, is the listing down of the six religions in Indonesia in the explanation to Section 1 of the Blasphemy Law a form of discrimination against religions and beliefs other than those six religions? . . .

Second, does the State have the right to intervene in the interpretation of the faith or belief of an individual or group by preventing that individual or group from spreading the religious teaching that has been followed and giving a label to that organization or sect as forbidden in the name of public order?

Third, is the Blasphemy Law as a Presidential Decree, which was historically enacted during a state of emergency, still relevant in light of the different conditions today . . .? Is the substance of the Blasphemy Law no longer relevant to Indonesia's more mature and diverse current religious scene?

Fourth, are the restrictions to religious interpretation and prohibitions against an individual or group's belief a form of human rights violation? Do the 1945 Constitution and other international legal instruments, such as the UDHR and ICCPR, view the restrictions as unjustified restrictions?

Fifth, is the threat of criminal prosecution provided for in Section 1 *juncto* Section 3 of the Blasphemy Law and Article 156a paragraphs (a) and (b), which were added by Section 4 of the Blasphemy Law and provides for five-year imprisonment, a form of criminalization of freedom of thought, opinion, and expression on the topic of religion and belief? This question arises because criminalization on the basis of misuse or desecration of religion is difficult to prove, such that it can be used by the ruling regime to criminalize minority religious groups, and therefore is against the principle of a legal state?

Six, does the legal instrument of Joint Decree/Joint Decision (*Surat Keputusan Bersama* or *SKB*) issued by the Minister of Religious Affairs, Minister/A-G, and Minister of Home Affairs, as mentioned in Section 2 subsections (1) and (2) of the Blasphemy Law, not ensure legal certainty in Indonesia?

. . . [T]he Applicants' claim that the provisions of the Blasphemy Law are unconstitutional is based on the following reasons:

The Blasphemy Law is a disharmonious and unconstitutional law because it is filled with violations of constitutional guarantees for all citizens, or in substance contrary to the 1945 Constitution, in particular Chapter XA on human rights and Chapter XI on religion;

The Blasphemy Law does not safeguard the existence of followers of beliefs who have lived in Indonesia for a long time, as they are often discriminated against and victimized;

The Blasphemy Law has given rise to legal uncertainty because it can be a tool for the majority to force what they think is true on the minority;

The Blasphemy Law is no longer relevant to the present condition because it is better for the State to only regulate the citizen's behaviour and not determine which religious interpretation is right and which is wrong;

The Blasphemy Law is drafted in such a way that allows for multiple interpretations such that it is feared that the state may intervene in the matter of religion. There does not have to be state intervention when a religion is desecrated, as internal guidance is sufficient;

. . . [T]he Applicants' arguments have been rejected by both the Parliament and the Government, both of which are supported by eighteen related parties . . . These parties argue that the Blasphemy Law is constitutional and should be retained essentially for the following reasons:

. . . [T]he Blasphemy Law provides protection and legal certainty to every individual and religious adherent in exercising his constitutional rights in accordance with Pancasila and the 1945 Constitution;

That freedom of thought, interpreted in carrying out out a religion, is not an absolute freedom without any limit, but can be restricted in accordance with law or legislation as provided for in Article 28J(2),1945 Constitution and Article 18(3), ICCPR;

That the repeal of the Blasphemy Law would lead to the loss of guarantee of public protection such that it is feared that the society would turn into a vigilante society when the law enforcers lose their legal basis in preventing the misuse and/or desecration of religion;

That no religion is prohibited by the Blasphemy Law, what is prohibited is desecration of religion;

Considering that out of 24 related parties, there are two related parties, namely Komnas HAM and Matakin [submitting the view that while the Blasphemy Law did not adequately guarantee religious freedom, it was still needed and should not be repealed in the absence of more comprehensive new legislation as this would give way to 'horizontal conflicts, anarchism, and misuse of religion in society'];

. . . [T]he Applicants also question the formality of the Blasphemy Law which was historically formed during an emergency revolution period . . . the Court is of the opinion that the substance of the Blasphemy Law is still needed to control public order to maintain religious harmony;

. . . According to the Applicants, the formulation of [section 1 of the Blasphemy Law] has given rise to legal uncertainty due to phrases such as 'interpretation that deviates' and 'central teachings of that religion'. These are phrases that can have multiple interpretations, which can be used to limit the freedom of religion of others. In this regard, the Applicants submitted that religious interpretation and religious belief are things that are very private and individual, such that the State is not entitled to judge one's belief or religion. If the State takes the interpretation of a majority group in a religion, then the State has sidelined the fundamental rights to religious interpretation of the minority and given rise to discrimination;

. . .

The Blasphemy Law does not prohibit anyone from interpreting a religious teaching or performing a religious activity that resembles a religion that is adhered to in Indonesia individually (in private). What is prohibited is to deliberately speak in public, recommend in public, or garner public support, to interpret a religion that is adhered to in Indonesia or conduct a religious activity that resembles a religious activity of that religion adhered to in Indonesia, which interpretation and activity deviate from the central teachings of the religion adhered to in Indonesia (Section 1 of the Blasphemy Law). If such matter is not governed, it is feared that clashes and horizontal conflicts may arise, unrest may be caused, as well as disunity and hostility in society;

. . .

In the Court's opinion, the Blasphemy law does not restrict one's belief (forum *internum*) but only restricts the expression of his thoughts and attitudes according to his conscience in public (forum *externum*) which deviates from the central teachings of the religions adhered to in Indonesia, expression of feelings or performance of actions that are essentially hostile in nature, or amount to a misuse or desecration of a religion adhered to in Indonesia;

In the Court's opinion, interpreting a teaching or rule is part of everyone's freedom of thought. By interpreting, one can gain a belief in something, so interpretation can lead to the truth although there is a potential for errors. Although the interpretation of a religious teaching is part of a forum *internum* freedom, such interpretation must be in line with central religious teachings, arrived at through the right methodology based on the source of religious teachings, namely the religion's respective holy book, such that the freedom to interpret a religion is not absolute. An interpretation that is not based on a methodology that is publicly acknowledged by the adherents of the religion and is not based on the respective holy book will give rise to reactions that threaten public security and order if expressed or performed in public. Therefore the Court is of the opinion that restrictions can be imposed. This is also in accordance with Article 18 of the ICCPR . . . Therefore, in the Court's opinion, restrictions on the religious expression (forum *externum*) that is provided for by Sections 1 and 4 of the Blasphemy Law are valid according to the 1945 Constitution and international standards;

That with regard to the Applicants' argument that the State cannot determine the right interpretation of a religious teaching, the Court is of the opinion that each religion has central teachings that are generally accepted within that religion internally, hence the religious group is the one deciding on its own central teachings. Indonesia as a state that adopts the view that religion is inseparable from the state, has a Ministry of Religious Affairs that serves and protects the healthy growth and development of religions; the Ministry of Religious Affairs has organizations and devices to gather various opinions from each of the religious groups. So in this regard the State does not autonomously determine the central teachings of a religion, but only based on the internal agreement of the respective religious groups. Hence the Court is of the opinion that there is no *étatisme (state involvement)* in the determination of central religious teachings in the Blasphemy Law.

Considering that with regard to the Applicants' argument that the Blasphemy Law is discriminatory because it only acknowledges six religions, namely Islam, Christianity, Catholicism, Hinduism, Buddhism, and Confucianism, the Court is of the opinion that it is not correct, because the Blasphemy Law does not limit the acknowledgement or protection to those six religions but acknowledges all religions adhered to by the people of Indonesia, as explained clearly in the general explanation to the Blasphemy Law, which states, 'This does not mean that other religions, such as Judaism, Zoroastrianism, Shinto, Taoism, are prohibited in Indonesia. These religions are given full protection by Article 29(2) of the 1945 Constitution and will be left the way they are as long as they do not violate the provisions of the Blasphemy Law or other laws.'

In the Court's view, the word '*dibiarkan*' (left the way they are) in the explanation to Section 1 paragraph 3 of the Blasphemy Law should be interpreted as not hindered and even given the right to grow and develop, and not left the way they are in the sense of being abandoned. Therefore, all religions, whether they are provided for in the explanation to Section 1(1) or (3) of the Blasphemy Law, are left the way they are to grow, develop, treated equally, and not hindered. With regard to the content of the explanation to Section 1(3) of the Blasphemy Law that the government should direct spiritual bodies and groups/sects towards a healthy view and in the direction of Belief in One God Almighty, the Court thinks it is right. The reason is, the rule is not intended to prohibit spiritual groups/sects but to direct them so that they progress according to the Belief in One God Almighty. This can be understood in the context that in the past (around 1960s), there were savage groups/sects, such as groups/sects that required human sacrifices at certain times or certain ceremonies. Therefore, there is no discrimination in the listing down of religions in the Blasphemy Law.

Furthermore, the Court is of the opinion that the Blasphemy Law does not put an end to the religious plurality that exists and grows in Indonesia, because all religious adherents receive the same acknowledgement and guarantee of protection. The listing down of the religions in the explanation is just a factual and sociological acknowledgement that such religions existed in Indonesia at the time the Blasphemy Law was drafted . . .

. . . [I]t is not true that the State discriminates against certain groups because the Blasphemy Law . . . provides that the determination of whether an interpretation or activity deviates from the central teachings of a religion is not based on the State's interpretation, but the interpretation of the leaders of the respective religions and the process of interpretation involves those who are experts in the particular issue at hand;

That believing and practicing a religion, such as Islam, will form a community (*umat*) that is based on such belief and practice. Sociologically, the religious leaders or theologians (*ulama*) are the leaders and representatives of the respective religious followers; the religious leaders have the knowledge and authority in interpreting their religious teachings.

When a person performs an interpretation or activity that is considered to be deviant by the religious leader who has the authority, and that person deliberately speaks in public, recommends in public, or garners public support to perform the deviant interpretation and activity, then that will clearly disturb the religious peace of those religious adherents, such that it may give rise to reactions from the adherents, which in the end will lead to social unrest, because the adherents feel their religion is being desecrated and insulted by the deviant interpretation.

If the State lets the above happen, then the State does not satisfy its obligation to realize the security and order in society. Therefore, the State rightly enacted the Blasphemy Law, whose objectives are to foster religious peace, prevent deviations from central teachings, and protect religious peace from desecration or insult;

. . . [T]he activity of interpreting a holy book of a religion in order to gain an understanding is a part of forum *internum*, but deliberately 'speaking, recommending, or garnering public support' is in the realm of forum *externum* because it involves the human rights of others, societal life, public interests, and the interests of the State. . . .

That in light of such consideration the Court is of the view that the State has an interest in legislating, here through the Blasphemy Law, as a form of carrying out its responsibility to uphold and protect human rights in accordance with the principle of a legal state. The Blasphemy Law is an implementation of the restrictions provided for by Article 28J(2) of the 1945 Constitution . . .

The Court is of the view that the Blasphemy Law is still needed and not against the protection of human rights under the 1945 Constitution . . . [T]he Court agrees with the expert of Nahdlatul Ulama General Management (PBNU), KH Hasyim Muzadi, who submitted; firstly, the Blasphemy Law is not a law on freedom of religion as a human right but a law on the prohibition against desecration of religion. Secondly, the Blasphemy Law anticipates the possibility of anarchy when the adherents of a religion feel their religion has been desecrated. With the Blasphemy Law, if such a problem arises, then it can be resolved through an existing legal avenue. Additionally, section 1 of the Blasphemy Law is not meant to restrain freedom of religion, but to provide guidelines to prevent its misuse and/or desecration of religion. Blasphemy or desecration of religion is also a form of crime that is prohibited by many countries in the world. Substantively, Section 1 of the Blasphemy Law cannot be interpreted as a form of forum *externum* restraint against one's forum *internum* freedom of religion.

The Court is of the view that the formulation of Section 1 of the Blasphemy Law which prohibits everyone from publishing a different interpretation of a religion that is adhered to in Indonesia is a form of preventive action against the possibility of horizontal conflicts among the people of Indonesia. The Court understands that religion is a sacred and sensitive subject for most people. The existence of a religion is not just an absolute transcendental personal relationship but has a social role. History has proven that religion is capable of building its own civilization in Indonesia and cannot be separated from the life of Indonesian society.

That religious freedom of an individual is a human right that is inherent in every human since he is born. However, in the context of a nation or state, freedom of religion has also become the society's collective right to carry out their religious teachings peacefully without any disturbance from other parties. Therefore, the Court is of the view that religion in the context of individual human rights cannot be separated from religious freedom in the communal context (see the Constitutional Court's Decision No 012-016-019/PUU-IV/2006 dated 19 December 2006).

Restrictions on rights from religious values as the society's communal values are constitutionally valid restrictions. The religious tradition in Indonesia is unique which the state cannot intervene with. However, the Court does not deny that there are religious organizations which have taken root and have a historical foundation as the parent organizations of the religions that are recognized in Indonesia. These parent organizations are the ones which may partner with the State to create religious public order and respect and tolerance for one another.

. . . The Court is of the opinion that Section 1 of the Blasphemy Law is an inseparable part of the purpose of protecting the people of Indonesia's religious right as provided in the Blasphemy Law, which is to prevent the misuse and desecration of religion, to ensure the harmonious living of state and nation [finds section 1 constitutional]; . . .

[The Court rejected the argument that Section 2(1) of the Blasphemy Law gives rise to coercion against religious freedom and results in discrimination.] . . . This is because the State has a function as a social controller and is given the authority based on the mandate of the people and the Constitution to organise societal life . . .

If Section 2(1) of the Blasphemy Law is repealed, then the State no longer has a role as a law enforcer with regard to deviant activities that misuse and/or desecrate religion, which violates the law and disturbs public order . . . repealing Section 2(1) of the Blasphemy Law will in fact give rise to anarchy that is more dangerous to the community.

. . . In the Court's view, the State does not have a right to not recognize the existence of a religion, because the State has to guarantee and protect religions that are adhered to by the people of Indonesia. The Court agrees with expert Yusril Ihaza Mahendra who submitted that materially, the substance of the Blasphemy Law is in line with and does not violate the Constitution, but from the perspective of organization and formulation, its legal rules need to be refined . . .

Recent conditions in Indonesia shows that there is a group of people in society who commit acts of vigilantism because they feel their religion has been desecrated. However, in reality the law enforcers who offer legal resolution through the Blasphemy Law are deemed by some people to have performed a repressive act. Therefore, in the interest of public protection (general protection) and anticipation against [horizontal or vertical social] conflicts, the existence of the Blasphemy Law becomes very important;

. . . [T]he Court does not have the power to make editorial or substantive amendments, but can only declare whether it is constitutional or unconstitutional; recalling that the substance of the Blasphemy Law as a whole is constitutional, the Court cannot repeal or amend it . . . it is within the power of the drafters of the laws [to improve the Blasphemy Law] through the normal legislative process; . . . the Court adopts the 'middle way' by giving an official interpretation of the Blasphemy Law without repealing it . . .

[Application rejected]

Notes and Questions

1. The Blasphemy Law was adopted at the height of the Communist threat and the emergence of mystical belief organisations which threatened existing religions. In 1954, the Government established an Inter-Departmental Committee to monitor 'mystical beliefs' (*kepercayaan*) as distinct from 'religion' (*agama*), a distinction maintained by the Ministry of Religion, created in 1946. This was replaced by a Co-ordinating Board for Monitoring Mystical Beliefs in Society, established by law in 1984. See M Crouch, 'Law and Religion in Indonesia: The Constitutional Court and the Blasphemy Law' (2012) 7(1) *Asian Journal of Comparative Law* 1, noting there were up to 120 cases (allegations proceeding to court) between 1998 and 2011.

2. What is the utility and danger of the Blasphemy Law? Would a mere difference in belief constitute blasphemy? Does the Law protect or restrict religious freedom? Is it necessary to maintain interreligious harmony? What insight does this decision cast on the nature of Indonesian secularism, where Indonesia is said to be neither a secular nor a religious state (*negara agama*) but a religious country where the Government has a protective duty towards (recognised) religion?

3. What is the nature of the Pancasila state's involvement in religion, particularly through the Ministry of Religious Affairs? Does the state decide whether a belief is 'deviant', or is this theological question delegated to official or dominant religious authorities? What is the effect of the Blasphemy Law on religious or ideological minorities? Note that in 2008, a Joint Ministerial Decision – Joint Decree of the Minister of Religion, the Attorney-General and the Minister of Home Affairs No 3/2008; No KEP033/A/JA/6/2008; No 199/2008 was issued. This warned the followers, members, and/or leaders of the Jemaat Ahmadiyah Indonesian (JAI) and the general public not to promote 'deviant teachings,' subject to penalties under existing laws; it also warned the public that vigilante action against Ahmadiyya would not be tolerated.

4. Justice Maria Farida in her dissenting opinion ([308]–[320]) found that the Blasphemy Law violated religious freedom and that the mention of only six recognised religions in the Elucidation, by excluding *aliran* (mystical beliefs), was discriminatory. How did the majority deal with this point and conclude that no discrimination was involved? Does the state privilege monotheistic faiths?

5. What unique features of the Indonesian polity did the Constitutional Court emphasise? Did it consider the Blasphemy Law a curtailment of religious freedom, or did it conceptualise it as something else? Are deviant beliefs a threat to religious freedom or a necessary aspect of it? Does the state have a legitimate interest in addressing religious heresy or deviancy?

6. Indonesian secularism apparently does not protect the right to propagate atheism (freedom not to have a religion), in contrast with other secular states like Singapore which has had an anti-theistic humanist society since 2010. An atheist in West Sumatra, Alexander Aan, was jailed for using the Quran to denounce the existence of God on his Facebook page ('God does not exist'). He was reported to the police by the Indonesia Council of Ulema and was found to have tainted religion (Islam), sentenced to a jail term of two-and-a-half years, and fined for professing atheism on the Internet.[268] Notably, the Indonesian Ulama Council, a religious body, has issued a form of non-state law through promulgating *fatwas* (religious rulings), including a 2005 *fatwa* stating that it was forbidden (*haram*) for Muslims to follow the ideology of pluralism, liberalism or secularism. Do you agree with the views of former Indonesian President Wahid on how to respond to religious slights?

---

[268] 'Indonesia "internet atheist" given jail term', *Al Jazeera*, 15 June 2012.

10

Socio-Economic Rights

I. INTRODUCTION

The long-standing debate over whether socio-economic rights (SERs)[1] should be embedded constitutionally is replicated in Asia. The chief reservations towards the judicial enforcement of SERs relate to institutional competence and propriety. First, courts lack both the technical expertise and the ability to monitor continuing situations and systemic inadequacies in reviewing rights implicating educational, housing or healthcare policy. Secondly, democratically-elected governments bear final responsibility in deciding how to allocate scarce resources to service socio-welfare programmes, which engage a polycentric range of issues.

Civil and political rights (CPRs) impose negative obligations on states,[2] and their violations typically engage judicial remedies (eg writ of habeas corpus for unlawful detentions). However, SERs often require positive state duties to realise human welfare objectives progressively. As such, the content and level of enjoyment of, say, the right to housing, will differ between wealthy and developing states. The realisation of SERs depends on available resources and is implemented through non-judicial and judicial measures. Generally speaking, SERs impose a higher financial cost on the state than CPRs.[3]

The juridical status of SERs is settled if they are given explicit constitutional expression. Human rights law espouses the indivisibility and mutually reinforcing nature of CPRs and SERs, and constitutional courts have developed a rich jurisprudence in South Africa, Canada, and various European and Latin American countries.[4] Certain Asian constitutional courts have also been known to intervene and interfere with government policy, as when an Indonesian electricity privatisation scheme was held unconstitutional on grounds that the poor would be detrimentally affected if electricity was not priced as a social good. Courts have become a forum for promoting rights

---

[1] See DM Davis, 'Socio-Economic Rights' in M Rosenfeld and A Sajó (eds) *The Oxford Handbook of Comparative Constitutional Law* (Oxford: Oxford University Press 2012) 1020.

[2] Like other associational rights, the freedom to join a trade union is an immediate obligation requiring non-interference by the state. Ensuring non-discrimination in disbursing welfare benefits is clearly immediate and judicially reviewable.

[3] Van Hoof argues that for poorer countries, the costs of setting up a functioning judicial and legal system may be considerable: F Van Hoof, 'The Legal Nature of Economic, Social and Cultural Rights: A Rebuttal of some Traditional Views' in P Alston and K Tomasewski (eds), *The Right to Food* (Leiden: Martinus Nijhoff, 1984).

[4] See eg F Coomans (ed), *Justiciability of Economic and Social Rights: Experiences from Domestic Systems* (Cambridge: Intersentia, 2006); V Gauri and D Brinks, *Courting Social Justice: Judicial Enforcement of Social and Economic Rights in the Developing World* (Cambridge: Cambridge University Press, 2008); M Langford (ed), *Social Rights Jurisprudence: Emerging Trends in International and Comparative Law* (Cambridge: Cambridge University Press, 2008).

consciousness and social reform for systemic problems, such as the right to food in India. Asian courts have creatively reviewed rights found in non-justiciable sections of the constitution, addressed questions of expertise and developed follow-up schemes to oversee implementation, altering the very nature of the judicial function.

Given crushing problems of poverty and socio-economic privation in many Asian states, their courts have to reconcile the need to secure minimum living standards out of finite resources with the imperative of economic growth which makes possible the enjoyment of social welfare rights and programmes. Many Asian states are party to various human rights treaties containing SERs, especially the International Covenant on Economic, Social and Cultural Rights (ICESCR).[5] The ICESCR Committee[6] considers the Covenant 'neutral' towards socialist and capitalist systems, provided the government is democratic and the indivisibility of human rights is respected.

Few Asian constitutions contain a comprehensive list of justiciable socio-economic rights such as that found in Part II of the Timor-Leste Constitution (2008). However, many do provide guarantees in the form of Directive Principles of State Policy (DPSP), which are theoretically non-justiciable, aspirational guidelines directed to the political branches. Economic rights recognised include the right to form a trade union, the right to strike, equal remuneration for equal work, and rights to employment-related social security and a minimum standard of living. Social rights include non employ-ment-related social security rights like old age pensions or disability benefits, rights to health care, housing, a healthy environment, and access to food and water.

Courts derive implied justiciable socio-economic rights in three main ways:

(a) Adopting a liberal reading of DPSP in conjunction with existing fundamental rights like the 'right to life' in jurisdictions like India, Pakistan and Bangladesh.
(b) Relying on certain DPSP guarantees *simpliciter*, based on their fundamental qual-ity and rights-language formulation.
(c) Drawing inspiration from Indian cases, as was done by the Malaysian courts which found within Article 5 ('right to life') a right to livelihood.

Other constitutions, like those of China and Vietnam, contain a list of SERs that are non-justiciable and thus operate more like directive principles. Certain constitu-tions, like those of Hong Kong,[7] Macau[8] and Timor,[9] explicitly refer to international treaties or instruments such as the ICESCR, to which courts may give effect in domes-tic adjudications. States with developmentalist priorities like Singapore purposely exclude SERs from their constitutions despite proposals for their inclusion,[10] as these

---

[5] ICESCR states parties include: Bangladesh, Cambodia, China, Democratic Republic of Korea, India, Indonesia, Japan, Lao, Nepal, Pakistan, the Philippines, Republic of Korea, Thailand, Timor-Leste and Vietnam.

[6] Committee on Economic, Social & Cultural Rights, *General Comment 3: The Nature of State Parties' Obligations* (Art 2, para 1), Fifth Session, 1990.

[7] Art 39 of the Hong Kong Basic Law incorporates the ICESCR and ICCPR.

[8] Art 40, Macau Basic Law.

[9] Sec 18(2) Timor-Leste Constitution: 'Children shall enjoy all rights that are universally recognised, as well as all those that are enshrined in international conventions commonly ratified or approved by the State.'

[10] An Indian group making representations before the 1966 Constitutional Commission had called for the inclusion of a list of constitutional SERs akin to the European Social Charter. These included the right to work, to organise, collective bargaining, social security, social and medical assistance, family rights to special protection and the rights of migrant workers. See 'Indians ask for seven basic rights in S'pore Charter', *Straits Times*, 3 March 1966, at 5.

are considered non-justiciable. This evinces a human welfare maximisation approach[11] – that allows trade off of different values and centralises responsibility and power in the hands of the legislative and executive branches – rather than a rights-orientated approach.

This chapter focuses on the contributions of Asian courts to the realisation of SERs, whether through strong or weaker forms of judicial review, and the judicial self-perception of its role in this field. Strong review would involve striking down legislation or holding government policy illegal in cases where the court's decision is final. In some cases, decisions may substantially restructure an entire health services system.[12] Weak review entails applying the administrative law test of 'reasonableness', or ensuring that the decision-maker has taken into account all relevant considerations.

This role of courts as secondary enforcer, to ensure fair procedure and require reasonable justifications for policy choices and administrative acts, is exemplified by the South African case of *Republic of South Africa v Grootboom*.[13] In considering housing policy, the South African Constitutional Court underscored the need always to have an emergency contingency plan for the poorest, most vulnerable sectors of society, resources notwithstanding. Courts may, among other things, identify a a 'minimum core' of SERs; identify criteria for compliance and violation; stipulate benchmarks to be met; elaborate on SER obligations; and apply proportionality review to balance interests. Thus, courts may not only hold government to account, but also serve as a venue for a co-operative dialogue about public values. Comparatively, the practice of Asian states helps shed light on how SERs are measured and monitored.

II. EXPRESS SOCIO-ECONOMIC RIGHTS: JUDICIAL REVIEW

Where socio-economic policies are involved, courts have adopted a more restrained version of review, as striking balances between competing interests 'is by nature a political job for the government and the legislature with the involvement of public opinion'.[14]

---

[11] See E Posner, 'Human welfare, not Human Rights' (2008) 108 *Columbia Law Review* 1857. See Thio Li-ann, 'More Matter with Less Art: Human Rights and Human Development within Singapore' in T Chong (ed), *Management of Success: Singapore Reassessed*, 2nd edn (Singapore: ISEAS, 2009) 355; see also Thio Li-ann, '"Pragmatism and Realism do not mean abdication": A Critical Inquiry into Singapore's Engagement with International Human Rights Law' (2004) 8 *Singapore Yearbook of International Law* 41.

[12] See the landmark decision of the Columbian Constitutional Court in T760/08 (Judgment of 31 July 2008); A Ely Yamin, 'The role of courts in defining health policy: The case of the Columbian Constitutional Court', available at <http://www.law.harvard.edu/programs/hrp/documents/Yamin_Parra_working_paper.pdf>.

[13] *Republic of South Africa v Grootboom* (2000) (11) BCLR 1169 (CC).

[14] Per A Cheung J, *Kong Yunming v Director of Social Welfare* [2009] HKLRD 382 [118].

A. Non-Discrimination Involving Fundamental Rights and Socio-Economic Considerations

Fok Chun Wa v The Hospital Authority
[2012] HKCFA 34, [2012] 2 HKC 413 (Court of Final Appeal, HKSAR)

Facts

The Hospital Authority's policy of charging pregnant women who are not Hong Kong residents higher rates for obstetric services was challenged in a series of cases for unlawful discrimination. It was argued that this policy violated the equal treatment guarantee under Article 25 of the Basic Law and Article 22 of the Hong Kong Bill of Rights. At first instance, one ground of challenge was that the policy violated the right to social welfare under Article 36 of the Basic Law (1997), Chapter III of which contains both CPRs and SERs.

Chief Justice Ma

[F]inancial resources are limited and decisions have to be made by the Government as to how Hong Kong's finite resources are to be utilized. Thus, socio-economic policies have to be devised and periodically revised in order to allocate public funds to the various sectors of society requiring them: . . . education, housing, welfare, infrastructure and the area which provides the background to the present case, public health. Such policies have to take into account manifold considerations and the allocation of public funds to various sectors are inter-related. At times, a fine balancing exercise may have to be struck, always against the background of limited financial resources and long-term considerations. If increased funds are given to one sector over others, this may have the consequence of reducing the funds available to those other sectors. Limited resources are not confined to the question of financial resources either. Manpower resources are also finite: there is no limitless supply of professional or skilled people. In the area of health, for example, there is a limited supply of doctors, nurses, midwives and other medical helpers. All these factors are legitimate factors to be taken into account in devising socio-economic policies.

[The Court set forth the test for justified differential treatment: that this must pursue a legitimate aim based on a genuine need to establish a difference, the difference had to be rationally connected to that aim and the difference in treatment had to be no more than is necessary to accomplish the legitimate aim. It fell to the Chief Executive under Article 48(4), Basic Law, to decide on government policies, including determining budgets under Article 62, which would involve the Executive considering many different factors and the legislature making 'a difficult collective judgment taking into account the rights of individuals as well as the interests of the society' (Chief Justice Li, *Lau Cheong v HKSAR* (2002) HKCFAR 415 at, 449C [105]).]

. . . [I]t would not usually be within the province of the courts to adjudicate on the merits or demerits of government socio-economic policies [but] where appropriate . . . the court will intervene, this being a part of its responsibility to ensure that any measure or policy is lawful and constitutional. . . .

In *International Transport Roth GmbH v Secretary of State for the Home Department* [2003] QB 728, at 767B–E, Laws LJ referred to decisions in the area of macro-economic policy as being relatively remote from judicial control [noting this fell within the legislative province, and citing various other English decisions] . . . In *Carson* (in the Court of Appeal [2003] 3 All ER 577) at 608c–d (para [73]), Laws LJ said:

In the field of what may be called macro-economic policy, certainly including the distribution of public funds upon retirement pensions, the decision-making power of the
elected arms of government is all but at its greatest, and the constraining role of the
courts, absent a florid violation by government of established legal principles, is correspondingly modest. I conceive this approach to be wholly in line with our responsibilities under the Human Rights Act 1998. In general terms I think it reflects a recurrent
theme of the Strasbourg jurisprudence, the search for a fair balance between the
demands of the general interest of the community and the protection of individual
rights: see *Sporrong v Sweden* (1982) 5 EHRR 35

. . . In the area of healthcare, where resources are also limited and the demands from many
different interests heavy, the courts are not equipped (nor is it their role) to make the 'difficult and agonizing judgments' (Sir Thomas Bingham MR in *R v Cambridge Health
Authority ex parte B* [1995] 1 WLR 898, at 906E–F) that have to be made allocating funds
to one sector or another [noting that in the European Court of Human Rights context, the
margin of discretion is wider when assessing priorities in allocating finite funds, eg a health
insurance fund's refusal to provide a robotic limb, despite claims this violated the Article 8
right to respect for private and family life: *Sentges v The Netherlands*, App no 27677/ 8 July
2003] . . .

In this area where limited public funds are involved, the courts have recognized that lines
have had to be drawn by the executive or the legislature. On the whole, save where the line
has been drawn in contravention of core values . . . or where it is shown to be manifestly
without reasonable foundation, the courts have left it to the authorities to identify the relevant line to be drawn . . . In the area of qualification for social benefits or social welfare, the
courts have consistently upheld legislation or acts which have drawn the line at residence
status: see for example *Mathews v Diaz* at 78–80, 83, 85; *R (Westminster City Council) v
National Asylum Support Service* [2002] 1 WLR 2956, at 2962D–F (paras 19–20); *Carson* at
183C–E (para 18) . . . [W]here governments have at their disposal only finite resources with
which to devise an economic or social strategy, they should be left to decide (1) whether
to have any social or welfare scheme in the first place, (2) the extent of such a scheme and
(3) where such a scheme is devised, to choose who is to benefit under it.

. . . [W]hen a line is drawn between those who are entitled to a benefit and those who are
not, the court can legitimately take into account the clarity of the line and the administrative convenience of implementing the policy . . . Naturally, this factor must be weighed
against other factors, but where, for instance, the line is drawn so vaguely or ambiguously
that the underlying policy or scheme may effectively be undermined, if not frustrated, this
is a factor that can be considered by the courts . . . Drawing the line at resident status is a
clear line and also convenient to administer.

In this context of socio-economic policies, there may be open to the authorities a number
of solutions to any perceived problem. In the present case, for example, as we have seen, the
Government considered a number of options to deal with the problems of Mainland
women giving birth in Hong Kong public hospitals . . . In such situations, the approach of
the court will not be to try to find a better solution or alternative itself . . .

Where a number of alternative solutions are open to the executive, legislature or other
authority in dealing with any particular problem, how far must the court go in inquiring as
to the alternative that is least intrusive into the constitutional protected right in question?
This is a question that particularly arises when one is dealing with the third limb of the
justification test, [requiring] any difference in treatment be 'no more than necessary'
to accomplish the legitimate aim. This question at one stage caused me some concern, for
this third limb seemed at first blush to require the court, even in a socio-economic policy

context, to embark on an exercise of searching for the best alternative among different alternative solutions. On reflection, this concern is unfounded. In the socio-economic context, where policy considerations are best left to the executive, legislative and other authority, the position is as follows:–

(1) While the third limb of the justification test does on occasion call for a comparison between the different options that may be available, the purpose of the exercise must be borne in mind: it is to see whether the relevant act or decision satisfies the justification test. The justification test is similar in nature to the test for proportionality: see *Yau Yuk Lung* (2007) 10 HKCFAR 335 at 349D–E (para 20). To ask whether a difference in treatment is justified is the same as asking whether [the act or decision is] a proportionate response to the legitimate aim.

(2) The recognition of the respective roles of the judiciary, the executive and the legislature (. . . the margin of appreciation) is relevant at all three stages of the justification test.

(3) Where a number of alternative, but reasonable, solutions to a problem exist, the court will not put itself in the place of the executive or legislature or other authority to decide which is the best option . . . The court will only interfere where the option chosen is clearly beyond the spectrum of reasonable options . . .

(4) This view is supported by authority (cites two Canadian decisions *Robert Libman Equality Party v AG of Quebec* 1997 3 RCS 569; *RJR – McDonald Inc v Attorney General of Canada* [1995] 3 SCR 199).

. . .

(6) . . . [O]utside the area of socio-economic or other general policy matters, where fundamental concepts or core-values are involved, the court will be particularly stringent or intense in the application of the justification test [noting that attempts to search for alternative solutions in general policy matters should be discouraged] . . .

   . . . It is, however, important to put what has just been discussed into proper perspective. The proposition that the courts will allow more leeway when socio-economic policies are involved, does not lead to the consequence that they will not be vigilant when it is appropriate to do so or that the authorities have some sort of carte blanche. After all, the courts have the ultimate responsibility of determining whether acts are constitutional or lawful. It would be appropriate for the courts to intervene (indeed they would be duty bound to do so) where, even in the area of socio-economic or other government policies, there has been any disregard for core-values. This requires a little elaboration. Where, for example, the reason for unequal treatment strikes at the heart of core-values relating to personal or human characteristics (such as race, colour, gender, sexual orientation, religion, politics, or social origin), the courts would extremely rarely (if at all) find this acceptable. These characteristics involve the respect and dignity that society accords to a human being. They are fundamental societal values . . . where other characteristics or status which do not relate to such notions or values are involved, and here I would include residence status, the courts will hesitate much more before interfering; . . . residence status . . . has less to do with personal characteristics . . . than with social and economic considerations. . . .

   . . . [W]here the subject matter of the challenge has to do with fundamental concepts, in contradistinction to rights associated with purely social and economic policies, the courts will be particularly vigilant to protect the rights associated with such concepts, and consequently much less leeway or margin of appreciation will be accorded to the authority concerned. These fundamental concepts are those which go to the heart of any society. They include, for example, the right to life, the right not to be tortured, the right not to be held in slavery, the freedom of expression and opinion, freedom of religion . . . Fundamental concepts also include the right to a fair trial and the presumption of innocence. Here, the courts have been vigilant to ensure that the proportionality or justification test is satisfied . . . The entitlement to social welfare or to subsidized health services is not a fundamental concept . . . It is a right that is inextricably bound with socio-economic considerations and therefore to be considered in such light. The subject matter of the present case involves entitlement to subsidized obstetric services in public hospitals in Hong Kong. While the applicants have made reference to the right to family life and family unity, this argument has obvious limits. The three Decisions in the present case do not prevent women [in the relevant group from having children] . . .

Notes and Questions

1. What factors determine the variable intensities of review? Is there an implicit value judgement that CPRs are of more weight than SERs? Is this justified?

2. See further K Kong, 'Adjudicating Social Welfare Rights in Hong Kong' (2012) 10(2) *I•CON* 588. Kong made the point that the court defers to the political branches not merely because socio-economic policies are involved, but also because of their financial implications. The more significant these are, the weaker the form of review: see M Tushnet, *Weak Court, Strong Rights: Judicial Review and Social Welfare Rights in Comparative Constitutional Law* (Princeton, NJ: Princeton University Press, 2008) at 247. Thus where the financial implications are relatively small, the Canadian courts have given a low degree of deference to the Government (*Eldridge v British Columbia (Attorney-General)*,[15] failure to provide interpreters for deaf hospital patients which would cost $150,000 or 0.0025 per cent of the health budget). Where the financial implications are larger, courts have been more deferential (*Newfoundland (Treasury Board) v NAPE*,[16] involving $24 million or a 10 per cent budget deficit through deferring wage adjustment payments designed to achieve wage equity between male and female employees).

B. Judicial Review of the Quantum of Social Benefits

Shigeru Asahi v Minister of Health and Welfare
Case Number Gyo Tsu No 14 of 1964 (Judgment of May 24, 1967)

Facts

The Director of Welfare's Office ordered the reduction of the medical benefits and commodity allowances for a tuberculosis patient, Asahi, who was hospitalised at the National Okayama Sanatorium, after discovering that he was receiving 1,500 yen/month from a living elder brother and was not without relatives or income as previously thought. The patient commenced an administrative action against the Minister of Heath and Welfare (MHW), arguing that the 600 yen/month reduction for commodity expenses was too low

---

[15] *Eldridge v British Columbia (Attorney-General)* [1997] 3 SCR 624.
[16] *Newfoundland (Treasury Board) v NAPE* [2004] 3 SCR 381.

for him to maintain a healthy and cultural standard of living as prescribed by Article 25 of the Japan Constitution (1946). The suit was terminated on 14 February 1964 when the appellant died. The Court held that the right to receive livelihood protection, not being 'a benefit given merely as a grace of the State or a reflection of a social policy', was personal in nature and extinguished by Asahi's death even if the Government was in arrears. This was because the benefits were only to satisfy 'the needs for minimum standard of living of the protected' and could not become 'an object of inheritance'. The Court gave a supplementary opinion on the constitutional issues engaged with respect to the propriety of ministerial determination of the livelihood protection schedule.

Judgment

Article 25 (a) of the Constitution provides that 'All the people shall enjoy the right to maintain healthy, cultural and minimum standard of living.' This provision merely proclaims that it is a duty of the State to administer the national policy to enable all the people to enjoy at least the healthy, cultural and minimum standard of living, and it does not grant the individual people any concrete rights . . . It may be said that the concrete right materializes only through the provisions of the Livelihood Protection Law enacted to realize the objectives prescribed in the provisions of the Constitution. The Livelihood Protection Law provides that any person who satisfies 'the requirements prescribed for by this Law' is entitled to 'the protection prescribed for by this Law' (*cf* Article 2), and such protection is to be given according to the schedule set by the MHW . . . therefore . . . the concrete right consists of a right to receive such protection as is stipulated in the schedule which the MHW establishes on the belief that the schedule is sufficient to maintain the minimum standard of living . . . [S]uch a standard should be set in accordance with the requirements enumerated in Article 8 (b) of the Law and therefore be appropriate to maintain the healthy, cultural and minimum standard of living guaranteed by the Constitution. The concept of healthy, cultural and minimum standard of living is a rather abstract and relative one. Its substance must be improved in proportion to the development of culture and national economy. It can be determined only after taking into synthetic consideration all these and other uncertain elements. [Thus] . . . the authority to determine what constitutes the healthy, cultural and minimum standard of living is first vested in the discretionary power of the MHW; his decision does not directly produce an issue of illegality, although it might produce an issue of propriety leading to a political debate about governmental responsibility. Only in cases where such decision is made as an abuse of the power bestowed by the law, against the objects of the Constitution and the Livelihood Protection Law, by ignoring the real condition of life and establishing extremely low standard [for the] schedule, would such decision be subject to judicial review as an illegal action.

The judgment below interpreted the law of establishing the standard of protection as a restricted [exercise of administrative discretion]. It pointed out that it is left to the expert discretion of the MHW to determine what the healthy, cultural and minimum standard of living is; . . . further . . . a mistake made in such judgment is merely a question of propriety as long as it does not deviate from the aims and purposes of the law. Even . . . restricted discretionary action allows some room for the administrative office to exercise its discretionary power. The judgment below did not entail any illegal contradictory reasoning when regarding the law which establish[ed] standards of aid as an exercise of limited discretion, while admitting some room for expert discretion of the MHW . . . Moreover the judgment below allegedly took into consideration matters indirectly related to maintaining life in judging the propriety of the aid schedule in this case; these included such factors as the existing national income or the national financial condition as reflected by such income, general standard of living, difference in standard of urban and rural livings, living standard of low income class and the percentage of people belonging to this class among the whole population, the sentiment of some people that it is unjust to allow better living condition to those who receive livelihood protection than the mass of people who do not receive protection, and the priorities of the national budget. It is within the discretion of the Minister to consider these factors. . . .

[Noting that the livelihood protected scheme was established in July 1953] . . . The minimum standard of living guaranteed by the Livelihood Protection Law should be of such a level which would make it possible to maintain healthy, cultural standard of living (*cf* Article 3), and the substance of the protection offered should be determined efficiently and properly with due consideration given to the actual needs of the beneficiary himself and of his family (*cf* Article 9); but at the same time, it should not be more than what is required to satisfy the minimum requirements of living (*cf* Article 8(b)). Concerning the beneficiary who was an in-patient like the appellant in this case, there are certain restrictions arising from his special situation, such as long term hospitalization and from medical reasons. In this instance, it cannot be denied that there is certain relationship between the amount of commodity expense and the effective cure of the disease; and the shortage of the amount has a grave bearing upon the patient which cannot be overlooked. The law prescribes the types of aid to satisfy the minimum need of patients and also provides appropriate aid; the law divides the protective scheme into single and double benefits, and enables in-patients to receive medical aid including meals and livelihood aid. There is a difference between the medical and livelihood benefits, both in nature and in operation; and in addition there is a system for rehabilitation aid. Therefore, attacks against the livelihood aid schedule as being illegal must not be allowed on the ground that no expenditure is [made for] daily expenses to . . . effect cures, or to fill the gap in the present medical and nursing systems, or that it is necessary to maintain one's livelihood after leaving the hospital.

The quantity of articles of daily necessities consumed by the patients . . . depends on the degree of individual frugality and the quality of articles concerned. The type of articles needed also differs from patient to patient depending upon the seriousness of the illness; and among certain categories of patients, they may be used interchangeably. Consequently, in examining the appropriateness of the livelihood aid schedule which contains the general and abstract yardstick by which to measure the daily needs of patients . . . one cannot do so by analyzing the quantity or unit cost of each individual item but must determine this against the overall picture . . . Furthermore, the daily articles for in-patients can be classified into those of ordinary need and those of extraordinary need; it is left to the MHW's discretion to determine whether to put extraordinary expenditure under the ordinary schedule, special schedule, contingency benefits or a loan system.

[Thus], the livelihood aid schedule determined by the MHW to be sufficient to meet the minimum daily needs of the in-patient under the set of facts as found by the court of original jurisdiction, cannot be said to have gone beyond the discretionary power granted under the law or [to be] an abuse of such power and therefore illegal. . . .

Notes and Questions

1. In his Supplementary Opinion, Justice Kenichi Okuno held that Article 25 was based on 'an objective minimum standard of living' not susceptible to policy change with the change of governments. As the amount of aid varied with the development of the national economy, requiring schedule adjustments, the disparity between the

schedule and 'reality of life' at the time of review would not constitute an illegality 'if it happens within the period necessary to revise the schedule', provided it did not overly deviate from constitutional purposes. Judge Jiro Tanaka, who dissented on another point, described the gap between the aid schedule and realities as 'an unavoidable evil . . . as long as the adoption of a schedule system is admitted as a reasonable means of administration'. Article 25 obliged the Government to 'conduct constant investigation' to ensure the aid schedule kept pace with changing realities, and to implement it with some 'practical discretion' to mitigate any disparities.

2.   The court essentially required the Government to review its policy regularly to ensure the needs of aid recipients were met; it did not pronounce on the scope and content on the SER in question. This form of weak review was also evident in *Mazibuko v City of Johannesburg*,[17] where the Constitutional Court declined to specify a minimum core of the right to water enshrined in Section 27 of the South African Constitution. In contrast, the German Federal Constitutional Court, in the *Hartz IV* case, which derived an implied right (sufficiency of unemployment benefits) from the principle of human dignity (Article 1, Basic Law read in conjunction with Article 20 (*sozialstaat*)), refused to specify a quantum of social assistance. It did examine a statistical model from the legislature and found it contrary to Article 1. It ordered a fresh procedure to re-compute the quantum needed to satisfy the material conditions indispensable to the physical existence of a needy person and his ability to participate in public life.[18] See C Bittner, 'Human Dignity as a Matter of Legislative Consistency in an Ideal World' (2011) 12(11) *German Law Journal* 1941.

C. Prioritising Competing Rights: Right to Smoke versus the Right to Avoid Smoke as a Facet of the Right to Life and Health

No-smoking Zone and Right to Smoke Cigarette
16-2(A) KCCR 355, 2003Hun-Ma457, 26 Aug 2004
(Constitutional Court, Korea)

Facts

A constitutional complaint challenged the National Health Promotion Act Enforcement Rule requiring owners of facilities used by the public either to make them smoke-free, or to designate a no-smoking zone. This geographical restriction on cigarette smoking allegedly violated constitutional Articles 10 (human dignity and right to pursue happiness) and 17 (right to privacy). The Constitutional Court unanimously dismissed the complaint.

Held (from the Summary of the Decision)

The Court recognised that both the smoker's right to freely smoke cigarettes and the non-smoker's right to avert or avoid cigarette smoking were protected under Articles 10 and 17

---

[17]   *Mazibuko v City of Johannesburg* [2009] ZACC 28.
[18]   Judgment of 9 February 2010, Bundesverfassungsgericht [BVerfG] [Federal Constitutional Court] 1 BVL 1/09, 1 BVL 3/09, 1 BVL 4/09 of 9 Feb 2010 (*Hartz IV*).

of the Constitution. Further, the right to avoid cigar smoking was also recognised, based on the constitutionally guaranteed right to health and the right to life,[19] as the health and life of non-smokers exposed to indirect cigarette smoking was endangered. It considered there was no clash in basic rights where a smoker smokes cigarettes in a way which did not affect the non-smoker, although clashes were inevitable where cigarettes were smoked in a space inhabited by both the smoker and non-smoker.

In such a case, as the right to avert cigarette smoking is based not only upon the right to privacy but also upon the right to life which is the premise of all basic rights and lies at the highest position, the right to avert cigarette smoking is the basic right of the higher position compared with the right to smoke cigarettes. Where there is a collision between the basic rights one of which is superior to the other in hierarchy, the basic right in inferior position may be restricted pursuant to the principle of priority of the basic right in superior position. Therefore . . . the right to smoke cigarettes may be recognized to the extent that it does not violate the right to avert cigarette smoking.

Furthermore, cigarette smoking concerns the public welfare common to the entire citizenry beyond the private interest of the individuals, in that cigarette smoking harms the health of the public including the smokers themselves and harms the environment by polluting the air. Therefore, pursuant to Article 37(2) of the Constitution that permits the restriction of the freedom and the right of the individuals for the sake of public welfare, cigarette smoking may be restricted by statute.

The relevant provision had a legitimate purpose, to protect the health of the citizenry, and it was an appropriate and effective method to designate no-smoking zones in places where the smokers and the non-smokers share their lives. The public interest in the health of the citizenry is greater than the private interest of the right to smoke cigarettes restricted thereby, and the provision at issue in this case specifically requires that facilities used by the public have designated no-smoking zones. Therefore, this provision does not violate the principle of prohibition against excessive restriction.

Note and Questions

1. How did the Court decide which right was superior? Did this turn on how many rights could be invoked by one side and/or a principle of proportionality?

2. The Indian Supreme Court banned smoking in public places to prevent air pollution and avoid inconvenience to non-smokers: *Murli S Deora v Union of India* [2002] AIR SC 40. A petitioner before the Lahore High Court in *Pakistan Chest Foundation v Government of Pakistan* (1997) CLC 1379, sought and obtained a ban on cigarette commercials on TV, since the younger generation was entitled to protection under the law from the hazards of exposure to smoking, by dint of Article 4(2)(a) (no action detrimental to the life, liberty, body, reputation or property of any person shall be taken except in accordance with law). Citizens could obtain protection under Article 9, which encompasses quality of life.

---

[19] Art 34(1): 'All citizens shall be entitled to a life worthy of human beings.'; Art 35(1): 'All citizens shall have the right to a healthy and pleasant environment.'; Art 36(1) 'The health of all citizens shall be protected by the State.'

D. Social Insurance Schemes: Competing Rights

A social insurance scheme needs to be funded. Where this is mandatory, this will restrict freedom, and in the South Korean context, contractual freedom is a facet of the constitutional 'right to pursue happiness'. Courts have sought to reconcile these interests, while appropriately deferring to the political branches.

Compulsory Subscription to the National Pension Plan
13-1 KCCR 301, 99Hun-Ma365, 22 Feb 2001

Facts

Under Article 34(2), the Korean state is obliged to 'promote social security and welfare'. This required the creation of a social insurance scheme. Articles 75 and 79 of the National Pension Act (NPA) mandate the coercive collection of a pension premium from insured persons and employers, based on compulsory subscription to the pension programme. With approval from the Minister of Health and Welfare, the National Pension Corporation (NPC) – which collected monthly premiums – was to collect premium arrears in the prescribed manner. The public pension program was based on a guaranteed minimum standard of living, which combined considerations of individual equality and social adequacy.

The Act was challenged on various grounds, including whether it violated the constitutional right to pursue happiness (Article 10),[20] the right to property (Article 23)[21] and the constitutional market economy principle (Article 119), which stipulates respect for the freedom and creative initiative of individuals in economic affairs. The complainants argued that 'All citizens are free to make their own plans for their lives without any restriction, and the state only needs to guarantee such individual freedom, including the freedom of choice in preparing for the future.' Beyond a minimal system of making provision for those who could not self-support because of old age and illness, any further income redistribution scheme would be 'excessive' and 'a socialist policy' contrary to Article 119(1). The MHW and NPC Chair argued that the Program was 'in accordance with Article 34(1) of the Constitution which provides the basis for the right to a humane livelihood [and] Article 34(2) of the Constitution which stipulates the State's responsibility to promote social security and welfare of its citizens'. Further, the state was empowered by Article 119(2) to regulate and co-ordinate economic affairs.

Review (Justices Yun Young-chul (presiding), Lee Young-mo, Ha Kyung-chull, Kim Young-il, Kwon Seong, Kim Hyo-jong, Kim Kyoung-il (assigned) and Song In-jun

History, Nature, and Current Status of the National Pension Program

. . . The objective of the National Pension Program (NPP) is to contribute to the stabilization of livelihood and promotion of welfare of citizens by paying pensions for old age, invalidity or death of citizens (Art 1, NPC). It is a social insurance program which devises relief through the national insurance system by dissipating a financial burden put on

---

[20] Art 10: 'All citizens shall be assured of human dignity and worth and have the right to pursue happiness. It shall be the duty of the State to confirm and guarantee the fundamental and inviolable human rights of individuals.'

[21] Art 23 provides that the 'right to property of all citizens' shall be guaranteed, its contents and limits determined by legislation, and the exercise of these rights must conform to public welfare.

an individual when the aforementioned events occur. Article 34(1) of the Constitution stipulates that 'all citizens shall be entitled to a life worthy of human beings,' thereby guaranteeing the right to livelihood, and Article 34(2) provides the ground for the State's responsibility to promote social security and welfare. Article 34(5) declares the State's duty to protect citizens incapable of earning a livelihood. In order to clearly define the constitutional stipulations on social security, the National Assembly enacted the Framework Act on Social Security, articulating basic elements of a social security program. Article 3[1] of the Act defines 'social security' as 'social insurance, public aid, social welfare service, and other related welfare systems, which are provided to protect citizens from social danger, such as illness, disability, ageing, unemployment and death, to overcome poverty, and to improve every citizen's quality of life,' thereby classifying social insurance as an element of social security. Article 3[2] of the Act defines 'social insurance' as 'a system of insurance, which guarantees citizens' health and income from social dangers that can harm the citizens by means of an insurance system.'

Social security programs began with social insurance, and social insurance is still the most widely used social security program. Social insurance began with worker's compensation insurance. In the beginning, worker's insurance only protected workers who had permanently lost their labor abilities, but over the years, worker's insurance extended its coverage to workers who had temporarily lost labor opportunities. Social insurance shares the principles and objectives of worker's insurance but is not limited to workers. Considering the objectives of social insurance, it can be said that the following principles are generally adopted in any social insurance program:

(i)   The minimum income guaranteed by social insurance shall be above the minimum cost of living;

(ii) The instituted program will redistribute income by requiring individuals in high-income brackets to contribute more and receive less than individuals in low-income brackets. The extent of the redistribution of income will be decided by the State with due consideration to social efficiency and individual equality;

(iii) In order to achieve unity among its members and bring about national solidarity, all citizens shall be made subject to the program . . . Funds necessary for the social insurance program will be allocated and raised by employers, workers, and the State.

(iv) The UK, Germany, France, the USA, Japan, and other developed nations around the world have adopted social insurance programs incorporating the above principles.

Currently, all citizens residing in the Republic of Korea whose age is not less than eighteen and is less than sixty are to become insured under the NPP, and the insured are classified into workplace insured persons, locally insured persons, voluntarily insured persons, and voluntarily and continuously insured persons. . . . The pension premium collected from insured persons and employers make up the principal source of funding for the national pension service. . . .

Violation of the Principle of Statutory Taxation and the Right to Property

(1) The NPP is designed to give monetary benefits to its members based on the payment made by insured persons during their subscription period. . . . [I]t is not a form of taxation which can be defined as a coercive collection of money by the government without entailing performance of a specific deed in return. Although Article 79 NPA stipulates coercive collection of pension premiums, through disposition of arrears, it is because of the strong social or public nature of the NPP, not because the pension premium is classified as taxation. . . . [The Court found the right to property under Article 23(3) was not violated as

there was no usurpation and transfer of purchasing power from high- to low-income groups under the NPP, which brought about some redistribution of income.]

Violation of the Right to Pursue Happiness

[While noting that the Article 10 right to pursue happiness included the freedom of contract, both to enter and not to form a contract, and that while the Act limited personal choice] . . . all liberties and rights of people may be restricted by a statute when such restriction is necessary for national security, maintenance of order, or for public welfare, as long as the statute is not in violation of the rule against excessive restriction. The NPP purports to contribute to the stabilization of livelihood and promotion of welfare of citizens by paying pension for the old age, invalidity or death of citizens (Art 1, NPA). Such purpose of the NPP is in accordance with Article 34(1) of the Constitution providing for the general right to life and Article 34(2) stipulating the State's duty to promote social security and welfare. Therefore, the NPP has a legitimate purpose. The NPP is a social insurance program which aims to diversify risks utilizing national insurance system when citizens come across obstacles such as old age, disability, and death of family members, and it is appropriate as the means. [The Court noted that in calculating pension premiums, it was assumed that insured persons earned a maximum of 3.6 million won, such that they] are free to use excess income any way they want. Therefore, the present NPP restricts the freedom of choice using the least restrictive means. The public interest sought by the NPP, which upholds the principle of social insurance to make all citizens subject to the program and dissipates social dangers of individual citizens among all members of the society, thereby playing the role of a social safety net for retirees and their families, is a far greater interest than the private interest that the complainants assert, namely, respect for individual's personal choice to use personal savings in order to prepare for the future [holding Article 10 was not violated].

Violation of the Market Economy

Article 119(1) of the Constitution states that 'the economic order of the Republic of Korea shall be based on a respect for the freedom and creative initiative of enterprises and individuals in economic affairs,' thereby declaring the adoption of a free-market economy based on the right to private property, the principle of private autonomy, and the principle that the liabilities for general torts are allocated according to fault. Article 119(2) provides that 'the State may regulate and coordinate economic affairs in order to maintain balanced growth and stability of the national economy, to ensure proper distribution of income, to prevent the domination of the market and the abuse of economic power, and to democratize the economy through harmony among the economic agents.' Furthermore, Article 34(1) stipulates that 'all citizens shall be entitled to a life worthy of human beings,' and Article 34(5) pronounces that 'citizens who are incapable of earning a livelihood due to a physical disability, disease, old age or other reasons shall be protected by the State under the conditions as prescribed by Act.' Such provisions reflect the fact that the Constitution has adopted the principles of a social state. In sum, the Constitution declares the free-market economy as a foundation, but has also adopted the principles of a social state to allow governmental interference to achieve substantial freedom and equality of all citizens (10-1 KCCR 522, 533–534, 96Hun-Ka4 and etc, May 28, 1998). . . . [W]hile the economic order adopted by the Constitution can be classified as a free-market economy based on the protection of the right to private property and respect for free competition, it also has characteristics of a social market economy in that the Constitution allows regulation and coordination of the State to rid the adverse effects of the free-market economy, to promote social welfare, and to achieve social justice (8-1 KCCR 370, 380, 92Hun-Ba47, April 25, 1996) . . . The NPP, which brings about the redistribution of income between high-income groups and low-income groups, working people and retirees, and current generations and future generations, is in accordance with the social market economy, and the complainants' argument that the NPP is in violation of the economic order adopted by the Constitution is without basis. *Request for adjudication denied.*

Notes and Questions

1. How did the court balance the competing individual rights and state duties? Was a test of proportionality adopted? Does the constitutional vision of the economy affect how this is applied?

2. The courts have been criticised for allowing the Government an over-broad discretion in determining livelihood standards for the poor to ensure minimum standards of living, being conscious of the impact of public benefits policy on the state's economic and fiscal policies: see *Livelihood Protection Standard Case* 9-1 KCCR 543, 94Hun-Ma33, 29 May 1997, in *Twenty Years of The Constitutional Court of Korea* (Constitutional Court of Korea, 2008) 418, available at <http://www.ccourt. go.kr/home/att_file/library/20year.pdf>.

3. On whether the pursuit of happiness clause is an appropriate basis for challenging the constitutionality of legislation, see Lim, J 'Pursuit of Happiness Clause in the Korean Constitution' (2001) 1 *Journal of Korean Law* 71.

E. Regulation of Worker's Economic Rights and Collective Bargaining

Constitutional Complaint against the Proviso of Trade Union and Labor Relations Adjustment Act Article 81 Item 2
17-2 KCCR 392, 2002Hun-Ba95·96, 2003Hun-Ba9 (consolidated)
24 Nov 2005

Facts

Article 81 of the Trade Union and Labour Relations Adjustment Act (TULAA) required unions that represented at least two-thirds of workers at a relevant workplace to organise through a Union Shop or collective bargaining agreement. Under this agreement, the relevant company was to dismiss workers who refused to join or withdraw from the labour union. Two taxi-drivers from Taxi Companies A and B left such a union (Union C) to join Union D. Upon Union C's request, A and B dismissed the petitioners, who argued that TULAA violated Article 33(1) of the Constitution. Article 33(1) reads: 'To enhance working conditions, workers shall have the right to independent association, collective bargaining and collective action.' The Constitutional Court held (7:2) that the Act was constitutional.

Justices Yun Young-chul (presiding), Kim Hyo-jong, Kim Kyung-il, Song In-jun (assigned), Choo Sun-hoe, Jeon Hyo-sook & Lee Kong-hyun

[Noting that Article 81 TULAA is an exception to the prohibition of unfair labour practices, as it allows collective bargaining agreements to be concluded with the dominant labour union commanding at least two-thirds of the workers in the concerned workplace to strengthen its power of organisation.]

Whether the Worker's Right to Organize and Other Rights are Infringed

Generally, compulsory organization of a labor union has an aspect of maintaining and strengthening the organization of a labour union by forcing the worker to join any labor union or a particular one. On the other hand, it restricts the individual worker's freedom not to organize or the freedom to choose whether to join a labor union. This problem of restricting the individual worker's right to organize appears to conflict with the collective right to organize of the Instant Provision, which regulates the compulsory organization of a labor union. . . . Therefore, it is important to resolve the conflict between the two basic rights.

Solution to conflict among basic rights . . . To resolve the conflict between two basic rights, we have discussed a hierarchy theory of basic rights, the principle of balancing competing interests, the principle of substantive harmonization (ie an interpretation favoring harmonization of norms), etc. The Constitutional Court has resolved the problem of conflicts among basic rights by choosing an appropriate solution for each case according to the characteristics and mode of the conflicting basic rights (discusses the *No-smoking Zone and Right to Smoke Cigarette* case, 2003Hun-Ma457). . . .

The conflict between workers' freedom not to organize and the labor union's positive right to organize . . . [T]here is a conflict between the workers' right not to organize and the labor union's right to positive organization (right to compulsory organization). [In relation to Article 33(1)], our Court's precedents rule that the workers' right to organize guaranteed by the Constitution only indicates the freedom to organize and not the freedom not to organize, the so-called negative right to organize (see 11-2 KCCR 614, 623-624, 98Hun-Ma141, November 25, 1999).

Therefore, the freedom of workers not to form, forcibly join or to withdraw from a labor union . . . cannot find its basis . . . within the right to organize guaranteed to workers. Rather, they find their basis from the general freedom of action derived from the right to pursue happiness under Article 10 or the freedom of association under Article 21(1) of the Constitution. Therefore, even though the conflict between workers' right not to organize and the labor union's positive right to organize is not a conflict between rights to organization, the matter of conflict can be posed between basic rights – general freedom of action or freedom of association and the positive right to organize. . . .

From the fact that workers can affect the formation of working conditions through forming an equal power with the employer by opposing the employer as a group through formation of a workers' organization such as a labor union, the right to organize has a characteristic of a 'liberty right performing the function of social protection' or a 'liberty right with the characteristic of a social right' (see 10-1 KCCR 32, 44, 94Hun-Ba13 et al, 27 Feb 1998). It is set up as a right different in quality from general civic liberty rights and is constitutionally acknowledged as a right of special status, on its own, separate from the freedom of association.

Compared to such rights, the general freedom of action, being a concrete expression implied in the right to pursue happiness under Article 10 of the Constitution, is a so-called supplementary liberty right (see 10-2 KCCR 621, 633, 97Hun-Ma345, 29 Oct 1998; 14-2 KCCR 410, 428, 99Hun-Ba76, 31 Oct 2002). Therefore, even when the freedom not to organize and the positive right to organize conflict, it can be seen that the positive right to organize has a more special meaning than the freedom not to organize. Also, the labor union's right to compulsory organization is also a right to livelihood . . . and is given more importance than the individual worker's freedom not to organize. Therefore, it cannot be concluded that granting a labor union the positive right to organize violates the essential aspect of the workers' right not to organize.

Conflict Between Workers' Right to Choose Organization and Labour Union's Collective Right to Organize

. . . [W]here the individual and the collective right to organize conflict, it cannot be concluded from the ranking of basic rights theory or the principle of balancing competing interests which basic right is superior. This is because, while the individual right to organize is the foundation of the constitutional right to organize and the prerequisite of the collective right to organize, the collective right to organize is a *sine qua non* for workers to actually maintain an equal relationship with the employer through an organization organized and strengthened through the individual right to organize. . . .

. . . [I]n order to maintain the uniformity of the Constitution, we must seek a harmonious method that allows all conflicting basic rights to exhibit their function and effect. . . .

The purpose of the principle of compulsory organization contemplated by the Instant Provision is to . . . maintain and strengthen the structure of a labour union . . . to contribute to elevating the standing of the whole body of workers. The principle coincides with the constitutional ideal of guaranteeing the right to organize. Therefore, the legitimacy of its purpose is secured. Workers' substantive freedom and rights can only be effectively secured by organization through a labor union. The Instant Provision exists to effectively guarantee such labor union's right to compulsory organization. Also, such system cannot be said to directly violate the essential aspect of the workers' right to choose an organization. Our Court already made clear that a certain degree of compulsory organization or compulsory association must accompany a labor union in order to secure its bargaining power (11-2 KCCR 614, 624, 98Hun-Ma141, 25 Nov 1999).

A labor union enters into a collective bargaining agreement, which requires workers to join a particular labor union as a pre-condition of employment, to maintain organizational strength . . . Compulsory organization through a collective bargaining agreement is a common and universal phenomenon that appeared in the development process of labor movements in various countries such as the US and Germany despite differences in form and degree. Also, it is not easy to contrive an effective alternative means besides using an organizing provision, such as a union shop agreement, in the collective bargaining agreement. Nonetheless, as the labor union's compulsory organization is inherently accompanied by restriction on the workers' right to choose an organization, there is a need to seek a balance between competing interests . . . a certain limit must be established so as not to excessively violate an individual worker's right to choose an organization and maintain the same in harmony.

. . . [T]he Instant Provision limits the scope of a labor union that can legally and validly enforce compulsory organization through collective bargaining agreement to a certain extent. It requires the labor union to be a sufficiently dominant organization [representing two-thirds of the workers minimally] to justify the principle of compulsory organization or there would be its negative consequences . . . such as withdrawing from the labour union. . . .

Also, to protect individual workers from abuse of authority by the labor union in a dominant position, TULAA limits the workers' right to choose an organization to the necessary minimum by prohibiting the employer from imposing disadvantages in worker's status for the reason that he or she has been expelled by the dominant labor union. In other words, the Instant Provision allows the restriction of the workers' right to choose an organization, by compulsory organization, to only when the worker voluntarily withdraws from or does not join a labor union.

Moreover, ultimately, workers can form and strengthen a labor union and can be guaranteed the substantive right to organize through that labor union's activities. Also, individual workers who do not want entry into the dominant labor union, receive the fruits of such activities of the labor union – the working conditions acquired by the labor union.

Therefore, although the labor union's compulsory organization, contemplated by the Instant Provision, partly has an aspect of restricting individual workers' right to choose an organization, the Instant Provision seeks balance between the workers' right to choose organization and the labor union's collective right to organize (right to compulsory organization) through means such as granting the power of compulsory organization only to dominant labor unions. Thereby, it maintains appropriate proportionality between two mutually conflicting and restricting basic rights.

Selective Discretion Through Legislation

. . . [T]he Instant Provision constitutes a statutory means of giving effect to the principle of compulsory organization through a collective bargaining agreement such as a union shop agreement to guarantee labor union's collective right to organize. Although it has an aspect of conflicting with the workers' right to choose an organization, generally it achieves rational harmony between two conflicting basic rights. Also, the restriction maintains appropriate proportionality and the essential aspect of the workers' right to choose an organization cannot be said to be violated. [Article 33(1) not violated; also found that the equality guarantee in Article 11(1) was not violated by the different treatment of dominant and minority worker unions, given the reasonable basis of classification.]

Justices Kwon Seong & Cho Dae-hyen (dissenting)

[As Article 81(2) TULAA] allows the discharge of a worker who does not join a particular labor union by requiring the entry into a particular labor union as a precondition of employment, it essentially violates the worker's freedom not to organize and right to livelihood.

Free democracy, one of the basic principles of our Constitution, aims to respect all people and to achieve coexistence and prosperity of all people. The purpose of Article 33(1) is to secure a worker's right to livelihood and improve working conditions. Therefore, a worker's right to organize and the labor union's right to strengthen organization and right to collective bargaining should be exercised in ways that seek every worker's coexistence and prosperity. They are constitutionally protected only when exercised for such purpose. As the labor union's right to strengthen organization and right to collective bargaining are acknowledged for the improvement of all workers' status, it cannot adopt discharge, which fundamentally threatens the worker's right to livelihood, as a means even for the improvement of working conditions. Even if a labor union is a dominant one with more than two-thirds of the workers, that labor union cannot have the authority to request the discharge of a worker for not joining or withdrawing from it. Firing a worker, thus, fundamentally denying his or her status as a worker, for the reason of not joining or withdrawing from a particular labor union runs directly counter to the purpose of Article 33(1) which seeks to guarantee a worker's right to livelihood and enhancement in status. It is also against the principle of coexistence and prosperity and the principle of protection of minorities – principles that free democracy strives for.

Note and Questions

1. How would you characterise the method of review used by the Court? Is this a form of strong or weak review? A 'minimum restriction' rule approach as a facet of pro-portionality balancing was applied in *Refusal of Collective Bargaining Case* (14-2 KCCR 824, 2002Hun-Ba12, 18 Dec 2002) where a provision in the TULAA was upheld which prohibited employers from refusing to engage in collective bargaining without a justifiable reason. As such, their freedom of contract and of entrepre-neurial activities was not violated, neither was the principle of proportionality.

2. The Constitutional Court upheld an Act which restricted the labour rights of public servants by prohibiting or limiting their joining of labour organisations or other forms of collective action. This was on the basis of the public nature of their job and their special status as public servants. Engagement in industrial action like strikes would undermine the normal business operation of the public service and impede the interests of the people who would suffer loss and inconvenience; as such, Article 33(2) was not violated: *The Establishment of Public Employees' Union Case* 20-2(B) KCCR 666, 2005Hun-Ma971·1193, 2006Hun-Ma198 (con-solidated), 26 Dec 2008.

3. The Supreme Court of India has not recognised a fundamental right to strike in relation to government employees who owe a duty to society, as strikes create 'chaos and total maladministration' thereby causing the public at large to suffer as a result: *TK Rangarajan v Government of Tamil Nadu* [2003] AIR SC 3032. In Japan, despite the Article 28 constitutional guarantee of the right to strike, all public workers are prohibited from striking, regardless of the nature of their jobs or their rank, under the National Public Workers Act, Law No 120 of 1947. The Supreme Court, in *All Agricultural and Forest Workers, Police Office Act Amendment Opposition Case* Saikō Saibansho [Sup Ct] 25 Apr 1973; Sho 43 (A) no 2780, 27 Saikō Saibansho Keiji Hanreishu [Keishu] 547 (Grand Bench), held that a strike by public workers suspending public services would seriously impact the public and contravene representative democracy by pressurising the legislature to reconsider the employment situation. Shifting from its more generous approach towards the rights of public workers in the earlier *All Postal Workers, Tokyo Central Post Office Case* Saikō Saibansho [Sup Ct] 26 Oct 1966, Sho 39 (A) no 296, 20 Saikō Saibansho Keiji Hanreishu [Keishu] 901 (Grand Bench), the Supreme Court concluded that union leaders could be prosecuted for soliciting an illegal strike.

III. JUDICIAL REVIEW AND THE ENFORCEMENT OF DIRECTIVE PRINCIPLES: IMPLIED RIGHTS AND LEGISLATIVE–EXECUTIVE ACCOUNTABILITY

Constitutional norms articulating directive principles of state policy are generally addressed to the legislative and executive branch, but certain courts have enforced them where the rights of the people are implicated.

JY Interpretation No 578
21 May 2004 (Constitutional Court, Taiwan)

Facts

The Labor Standards Act (LSA) was enacted to realise the fundamental national policy in Article 153(1) of the Constitution, which requires the state to enact laws and implement policies to improve the livelihood of labourers and to upgrade their productivity. A question arose as to the constitutionality of Articles 55 and 56 of the LSA, which required employers to pay for their workers' retirement pensions.

Held

Legislators possess a certain amount of discretion in determining the substance and methods of working conditions for workers' protection. But when a law has the effect of restricting the fundamental rights of the people as a result, the constitutional principle of proportionality should still be followed.

Articles 55 and 56 of the LSA required employers to make money deductions to feed a special account which was the reserve fund of workers' retirement pensions (separating the pension funds from the corporate accounts to prevent misappropriation). These provisions, as one of the means to ensure workers' livelihood, help protect workers' rights and interests, strengthen employment relationships, promote overall social stability and economic development, and thereby do not exceed the scope of legislative discretion. The resulting restriction on employers' rights to freely determine the contents of employment contracts and to use and dispose of assets at their own discretion shall be deemed proper under the Constitution, since such restriction helps to accomplish the state's goal of caring for workers and takes into account the fiscal capabilities of the government, as well as confirming the obligation of the employers – as the recipients of workers' labor – to take care of their employees. The Act imposes fines on employers who violate the aforesaid compulsory provisions in order to compel employers to fulfill their retirement payment obligations, so as to ensure the livelihood and sustenance of workers after their retirement. In consideration of factors such as the context of the legislation, labor relations, the nature and impact of the interference with legitimate interests, and so forth, it is therefore necessary for the state to prescribe criminal fines. Such a compulsory provision, conforming to the principle of proportionality under Article 23[22] of the Constitution, does not contradict the constitutional purpose of protecting people's freedom to enter into contracts or violate people's property rights protected by Article 15 of the Constitution.[23]

. . . The pension system for workers put in place by legislators entails prioritized choices and designs, reflecting legislators' evaluation of the objective socio-economic situations as well as the effective distribution of state resources . . . the Constitution does not prohibit the state from adopting means other than the provision of social insurance to accomplish the goal of protecting workers. Legislators, therefore, enjoy a certain degree of discretion in designing the overall system for workers' protection. Both the old-age benefits prescribed under the Labor Insurance Act and the retirement pension prescribed under the Labor

[22] Art 23, Constitution of the Republic of China (Taiwan): 'All the freedoms and rights enumerated in the preceding Articles shall not be restricted by law except by such as may be necessary to prevent infringement upon the freedoms of other persons, to avert an imminent crisis, to maintain social order or to advance public welfare.'

[23] Art 15, Constitution of the Republic of China (Taiwan): 'The right of existence, the right of work, and the right of property shall be guaranteed to the people.'

Standards Act help to achieve the constitutional purpose of protecting the livelihood of workers. Since the two systems are different in nature, adoption of both systems can hardly be regarded as a violation of the Constitution. Nonetheless, legislators should consider the overall social changes and accordingly from time to time review the options regarding protecting the livelihood of workers. The Act was enacted and implemented in 1984, and issues such as whether the current workers' pension system has been effectively implemented, whether this approach needs to be examined, and how it can be improved to correspond to the overall social changes in order to keep up with the pace of changes and to be consistent with the constitutional goal of labor protection, should be reviewed at appropriate times. The decision of whether to integrate the existing workers retirement system and social insurance system in response to the emerging graying trend should also be considered, as such trends result from the changing demographic composition and are likely to impact the socio-economic structure and the welfare system in the future, and such decisions will include everyone's interests and involve the issue of the distribution of social resources and the financial capabilities of the state to shoulder such burdens. The relevant authorities should, in addition to striking a balance between retaining the existing protection enjoyed by workers and noting the ability of employers to pay for workers' retirement pensions and the operational costs of enterprises, conduct a comprehensive examination of the current scheme in accordance with the fundamental principle of the Constitution to protect workers and the purpose of supporting and preserving the survival and development of small and medium-sized businesses. The provisions of international labor conventions and the overall development of the nation shall also be taken into account.

Notes and Questions

1. How does the Court envisage its role in relation to supervising the implementation of fundamental national policy pertaining to social security under Chapter XIII (Fundamental National Policies) of the Constitution?

2. Art II (Declaration of Principles and State Policies Principles) Sections 8–24 and, Articles XIII–XV (Social Justice and Human Rights) of the 1987 'People's Power' Constitution have been described as the 'heart of the new Charter',[24] and have been much influenced by the ICESCR.[25] These provisions have generally functioned as aspirational guidelines since directive principles are not 'self-executing principles ready for enforcement through the courts'.[26] They also serve as judicial aids to interpretation and in the enactment of legislative policy; they 'do not embody judicially enforceable constitutional rights'[27] as constitutional principles need legislative enactments to implement them.[28] The remedy for failure to implement these principles is to be political, not legal. Under Article VIII Section 1, the judicial duty is 'to settle actual controversies which are legally demandable and

[24] *ARIS Inc v National Labor Relations Commission* GR No 90501 (SC 5 Aug 1991).
[25] *Simon v Commission on Human Rights* GR No 100150 (SC 5 Jan 1994) (the framers were aware of the ICESCR when drafting the Social Justice provisions).
[26] *Tanada v Angara* GR No 118295, 2 Ma 1997 (challenging accession to the WTO as violating the constitutional mandate under Art II, Sec 19 'to develop a self-reliant and independent national economy effectively controlled by Filipinos' as the WTO requires products of Member States to be placed on equal footing as local products.
[27] *Kilosbayan, Incorporated v Morato* 246 SCRA 540, 564, July 17, 1995.
[28] *Basco v Pagcor* 197 SCRA 52, 68, May 14, 1991.

enforceable' and to determine grave abuses of discretion. The Court may promulgate rules concerning the enforcement of constitutional rights under Article VIII, Section 5(5).

The following decision is a seminal case, not only for its broad reading of standing to include inter-generational claimants, but also for the method through which it found a constitutional right to health under Article II Section 16 of the Philippines Constitution, rather than through Article III (Bill of Rights) which contains justiciable CPRs.

Oposa et al v Fulgencio S Factoran Jr et al
GR No 101083 (Supreme Court, Philippines)

Facts

The petitioners were Filipino children, who represented themselves and unborn generations, seeking the cancellation of all timber licence agreements (TLAs) issued by the Secretary for the Department of Environment and Natural Resources. Their claim focused on the right to a balanced and healthful ecology in Section 16, Article II, which contains non-traditional welfare rights, motivated by the harmful effects of accelerated deforestation.

Davide Jr J

In a broader sense, this petition bears upon the right of Filipinos to a balanced and healthful ecology which the petitioners dramatically associate with the twin concepts of 'inter-generational responsibility' and 'inter-generational justice.' Specifically, it touches on the issue of whether the said petitioners have a cause of action to 'prevent the misappropriation or impairment' of Philippine rainforests and 'arrest the unabated haemorrhage of the country's vital life-support systems and continued rape of Mother Earth.' . . .

. . . The complaint was instituted as a taxpayers' class suit and alleges that the plaintiffs 'are all citizens of the Republic of the Philippines, taxpayers, and entitled to the full benefit, use and enjoyment of the natural resource treasure that is the country's virgin tropical rainforests.' The same was filed for themselves and others who are equally concerned about the preservation of said resource but are 'so numerous that it is impracticable to bring them all before the Court.' The minors . . . asseverate that they 'represent their generation as well as generations yet unborn.' . . .

. . . [T]he distortion and disturbance of this balance as a consequence of deforestation have resulted in a host of environmental tragedies [including water shortages, salinization of the water table, soil erosion, endangerment of rare flora and fauna, river siltation, drought, increased typhoon speeds in the absence of windbreaks, flooding of lowlands etc] . . .

[The plaintiffs pleaded that] . . . at the present rate of deforestation, ie about 200,000 hectares per annum or 25 hectares per hour/night-time, Saturdays, Sundays and holidays included, the Philippines will be bereft of forest resources after the end of this ensuing decade, if not earlier. [If the defendant continued to allow TLA holders to cut down trees, this would be] a misappropriation and/or impairment of the natural resource property he holds in trust for the benefit of plaintiff minors and succeeding generations.

Plaintiffs have a clear and constitutional right to a balanced and healthful ecology and are entitled to protection by the State in its capacity as the *parens patriae* . . . Defendant's refusal to cancel the aforementioned TLAs is manifestly contrary to the public policy enunciated in the Philippine Environmental Policy which, in pertinent part, states that it is the policy of the State:

(a) to create, develop, maintain and improve conditions under which man and nature can thrive in productive and enjoyable harmony with each other;
(b) to fulfill the social, economic and other requirements of present and future generations of Filipinos and;
(c) to ensure 'the attainment of an environmental quality that is conducive to a life of dignity and well-being' (PD 1151, 6 June 1977).

Furthermore, defendant's continued refusal to cancel the aforementioned TLAs is contradictory to the Constitutional policy of the State to

(a) effect 'a more equitable distribution of opportunities, income and wealth' and 'make full and efficient use of natural resource . . .' (Section 1, Article XII of the Constitution);
(b) 'protect the nation's marine wealth.' (Section 2, ibid);
(c) 'conserve and promote the nation's cultural heritage and resources . . .' (Section 14, Article XIV, id.);
(d) 'protect and advance the right of the people to a balanced and healthful ecology in accord with the rhythm and harmony of nature.' (Section 16, Article II, id.)

Finally, defendant's act is contrary to the highest law of humankind: the natural law and violative of plaintiffs' right to self-preservation and perpetuation.

Petitioners contend that the complaint clearly and unmistakably states a cause of action as it contains sufficient allegations concerning their right to a sound environment based on Articles 19, 20 and 21 of the Civil Code (Human Relations), Section 4 of Executive Order (EO) No 192 creating the DENR, Section 3 of Presidential Decree (PD) No 1151 (Philippine Environmental Policy), Section 16, Article II of the 1987 Constitution recognizing the right of the people to a balanced and healthful ecology, the concept of generational genocide in Criminal Law and the concept of man's inalienable right to self-preservation and self-perpetuation embodied in natural law. Petitioners likewise rely on the respondent's correlative obligation, per Section 4 of EO No 192, the safeguard the people's right to a healthful environment.

[On the point of standing, the Court accepted that this was a class suit and that the personality of the petitioners to sue on behalf of future generations need 'only be based on the concept of intergenerational responsibility insofar as the right to a balanced and healthful ecology is concerned'. This related to the judicious disposition, use and conservation of natural resources to ensure equitable access for present and future generations. Further, 'the minors' assertion of their right to a sound environment constitutes, at the same time, the performance of their obligation to ensure the protection of that right for the generations to come'.]

[Finding for the petitioners] . . . We do not agree with the trial court's conclusion that the plaintiffs failed to allege with sufficient definiteness a specific legal right involved or a specific legal wrong committed . . . The complaint focuses on one specific fundamental legal right – the right to a balanced and healthful ecology which, for the first time in our nation's constitutional history, is solemnly incorporated in the fundamental law. Section 16, Article II of the 1987 Constitution explicitly provides:

Sec 16. The State shall protect and advance the right of the people to a balanced and healthful ecology in accord with the rhythm and harmony of nature.

This right unites with the right to health which is provided for in the preceding section of the same Article:

Sec 15. The State shall protect and promote the right to health of the people and instill health consciousness among them.

While the right to a balanced and healthful ecology is to be found under the Declaration of Principles and State Policies and not under the Bill of Rights, it does not follow that it is less important than any of the civil and political rights enumerated in the latter. Such a right belongs to a different category of rights altogether for it concerns nothing less than self-preservation and self-perpetuation, aptly and fittingly stressed by the petitioners, the advancement of which may even be said to predate all governments and constitutions. As a matter of fact, these basic rights need not even be written in the Constitution for they are assumed to exist from the inception of humankind. If they are now explicitly mentioned in the fundamental charter, it is because of the well-founded fear of its framers that unless the rights to a balanced and healthful ecology and to health are mandated as state policies by the Constitution itself, thereby highlighting their continuing importance and imposing upon the state a solemn obligation to preserve the first and protect and advance the second, the day would not be too far when all else would be lost not only for the present generation, but also for those to come; generations which stand to inherit nothing but parched earth incapable of sustaining life. The right to a balanced and healthful ecology carries with it the correlative duty to refrain from impairing the environment. [Discusses debates before 1986 Constitutional Commission] . . .

. . . Conformably with the enunciated right to a balanced and healthful ecology and the right to health, as well as the other related provisions of the Constitution concerning the conservation, development and utilization of the country's natural resources, then President Corazon C Aquino promulgated on 10 June 1987 EO No 192, 14 Section 4 of which expressly mandates that the Department of Environment and Natural Resources (DENR) 'shall be the primary government agency responsible for the conservation, management, development and proper use of the country's environment and natural resources . . . in order to ensure equitable sharing of the benefits derived therefrom for the welfare of the present and future generations of Filipinos.' Section 3 thereof makes the following statement of policy:

SEC. 3. Declaration of Policy. – It is hereby declared the policy of the State to ensure the sustainable use, development, management, renewal, and conservation of the country's forest, mineral, land, off-shore areas and other natural resources, including the protection and enhancement of the quality of the environment, and equitable access of the different segments of the population to the development and use of the country's natural resources, not only for the present generation but for future generations as well. It is also the policy of the state to recognize and apply a true value system including social and environmental cost implications relative to their utilization; development and conservation of our natural resources.

This policy declaration is substantially re-stated in Title XIV, Book IV of the Administrative Code of 1987 . . . Thus, the right of the petitioners (and all those they represent) to a balanced and healthful ecology is as clear as the DENR's duty – under its mandate and by virtue of its powers and functions under EO No 192 and the Administrative Code of 1987 – to protect and advance the said right. A denial or violation of that right by the other who has the correlative duty or obligation to respect or protect the same gives rise to a cause of action. Petitioners maintain that the granting of the TLAs, which they claim was done with grave abuse of discretion, violated their right to a balanced and healthful ecology; hence, the full protection thereof requires that no further TLAs should be renewed or granted. [Court found a prima facie violation of petitioners' rights] . . .

The foregoing considered, Civil Case No 90-777 cannot be said to raise a political question. Policy formulation or determination by the executive or legislative branches of Government is not squarely put in issue. What is principally involved is the enforcement of a right vis-à-vis policies already formulated and expressed in legislation. It must, nonetheless, be emphasized that the political question doctrine is no longer the insurmountable obstacle to the exercise of judicial power or the impenetrable shield that protects executive and legislative actions from judicial inquiry or review. [Noting the broader power of the court under Article VIII Section 1(2) to determine whether there had been 'a grave abuse of discretion amounting to lack or excess of jurisdiction on the part of any branch or instrumentality of the Government'. The petition was granted, the order of the respondent Judge dismissing the earlier case was set aside and complaints could be amended to include TLA holders.]

Separate Concurring Opinion of Justice Feliciano

. . . The Court has also declared that the complaint has alleged and focused upon 'one specific fundamental legal right – the right to a balanced and healthful ecology' . . . There is no question that 'the right to a balanced and healthful ecology' is 'fundamental' and that, accordingly, it has been 'constitutionalized.' But although it is fundamental in character, I suggest, with very great respect, that it cannot be characterized as 'specific,' without doing excessive violence to language. It is in fact very difficult to fashion language more comprehensive in scope and generalized in character than a right to 'a balanced and healthful ecology.' The list of particular claims which can be subsumed under this rubric appears to be entirely open-ended: prevention and control of emission of toxic fumes and smoke from factories and motor vehicles; of discharge of oil, chemical effluents, garbage and raw sewage into rivers, inland and coastal waters by vessels, oil rigs, factories, mines and whole communities; of dumping of organic and inorganic wastes on open land, streets and thoroughfares; failure to rehabilitate land after strip-mining or open-pit mining; kaingin or slash-and-burn farming; destruction of fisheries, coral reefs and other living sea resources through the use of dynamite or cyanide and other chemicals; contamination of ground water resources; loss of certain species of fauna and flora . . .

. . . When substantive standards as general as 'the right to a balanced and healthy ecology' and 'the right to health' are combined with remedial standards as broad ranging as 'a grave abuse of discretion amounting to lack or excess of jurisdiction,' the result will be, it is respectfully submitted, to propel courts into the uncharted ocean of social and economic policy making. At least in respect of the vast area of environmental protection and management, our courts have no claim to special technical competence and experience and professional qualification. Where no specific, operable norms and standards are shown to exist, then the policy making departments – the legislative and executive departments – must be given a real and effective opportunity to fashion and promulgate those norms and standards, and to implement them before the courts should intervene.

Notes and Questions

1. In practice, the Supreme Court has applied the directive clauses no differently from the Bill of Rights, so long as a directive clause uses the word 'right' such as in Article II Section 15 (right to health of the people). Other potentially justiciable Article II rights may include the right of workers, and the rights of indigenous cultural communities within the framework of national unity and development. See D Desierto,

'Justiciability of Socio-Economic Rights: Comparative Powers, Roles and Practices in the Philippines and South Africa' (2009) 11(1) *Asia-Pacific Law & Policy Journal* 114. On Filipino judicial activism, see R Pangalangan, 'Government by Judiciary in the Philippines: Ideological and Doctrinal Framework' in T Ginsburg and AHY Chen (eds), *Administrative Law and Governance in Asia: Comparative Perspectives* (London: Routledge, 2009) and R Pangalangan, 'The Philippines: The Persistence of Rights Discourse vis-à-vis Substantive Social Claims' in R Pereenboom, CJ Peterson and ACY Chen (eds), *Human Rights in Asia: A Comparative Legal Study of Twelve Asian Jurisdictions, France and the USA* (London: Routledge, 2006); and G Sembrano, 'Mechanisms and Avenues for Judicial and Quasi-Judicial Implementation of ESC Rights: The Philippines Experience' in F Coomans (ed), *Justiciability of Economic and Social Rights: Experiences from Domestic Systems* (Cambridge: Intersentia, 2006) 269.

2.   Did Judge Feliciano correctly identify the problem of expanded judicial power with respect to the enforceability of constitutional norms? Is this form of judicialised governance a useful corrective measure for the failings of democratic government? Or does this hold dangers of its own?

3.   In general, there appears to be a presumption that a constitutional provision may be self-executing if the text is framed in such a way that the provision is complete in itself, sufficiently clear and can become operative without enabling legislation.[29] In the *Manila Prince Hotel* case, the court allowed a losing Filipino bidder to match the winning bid of a Malaysian, in relation to the sale of an historic hotel, as an aspect of the nationalistic 'Filipino First' policy under Section 10(2) of Article XII of the Constitution.

4.   In the Bangladesh case of *M Farooque v Bangladesh*,[30] the petitioner cited the *Oposa* case to advance the idea of intergenerational responsibility and 'intergenerational justice', ie that they represented themselves and unborn generations. The court disagreed on the basis that in *Oposa*, the minors' standing was allowed since 'the right to a balanced and healthful ecology' was considered a fundamental right in the Philippines Constitution while the Bangladesh Constitution did not expressly provide such right.

IV. ECONOMIC POLICY, PRIVATISATION AND JUDICIAL REVIEW IN INDONESIA

The Indonesian Constitutional Court, established in 2003, has jurisdiction to determine a range of SERs, some of which are expressly justiciable and others of which are directive principles, and to ensure the constitutionality of legislation. The Second Amendment (2000) to the 1945 Constitution introduced Chapter XA (Human Rights), which includes the right of a person to 'to develop him/herself through the fulfillment of his/her basic needs' (Article 28C), 'the right to live in physical and spiritual prosperity, to have a home and to enjoy a good and healthy environment, and

---

[29] *Manila Prince Hotel v Government Service Insurance System* GR No 122156 (SC 3 Feb 1997) (*en banc*).
[30] *M Farooque v Bangladesh* (1997) 49 DLR (AD) 1.

[to] have the right to obtain medical care' and 'the right to social security in order to develop oneself fully as a dignified human being'.[31] A Fourth Amendment (2004) requires the state to spend a minimum of 20 per cent of the State Budget to implement national education (Article 31(4)). Under Article 34, the State is obliged to take care of impoverished persons and abandoned children, to 'develop a system of social security for all of the people' and to 'provide sufficient medical and public service facilities'. Under Article 24C, the Constitutional Court has the 'final power of decision in reviewing laws against the Constitution', and any decision of the Court 'shall take full legal force and effect upon its pronouncement in a plenary hearing open to the public'.[32] Article 56 of Law No 24 provides that judicial review extends to ascertaining whether a relevant law contravenes the Constitution; it does not include instructing the Government on how to implement laws. Article 60 provides that no review may be conducted on the material substance of a law or any legal norm which has already been subject to review.

The following cases deal with attempts to privatise the electricity industry and water resources, with implications for the impact on the poor, and the state's duties under the directive principles to ensure minimal standards of living and basic necessities.

Judicial Review of the Electricity Law (No 20/2002)
Case No 001-021-022/PUU-I/2003 (Constitutional Court, Indonesia)

Facts

In 2002, the Indonesian legislature adopted the Electricity Law which sought to deregulate, restructure and liberalise the electricity sector. Under the Law, PLN, the state-owned electricity company, would be just another actor in the market, and certain areas designated as competition areas would be free of monopolistic practices. The Government would remain involved in policy-making and in budgeting subsidies to those unable to afford electricity, and provision was made for a multi-buyer/seller system. It also stipulated environmental responsibilities for producers. A group of NGOs, including PLN's trade union, sought judicial review to challenge the constitutionality of the Electricity Law for breaching various constitutional provisions, including Article 33(2), which reads:

> Sectors of production which are important for the country and affect the life of the people shall be under the powers of the State. [Chapter XIV: The National Economy and Social Welfare]

The Court adopted a liberal approach towards standing, noting that 'the impairment of the constitutional rights does not always have to be actual, but can also be potential in nature. In fact, every tax-paying citizen has the constitutional right to question every law that relates to the economic field that affects his or her welfare.' The extract from the judgment, delivered by nine constitutional court justices, deals with substantive issues.

Held

Considering whereas to conduct a judicial review against Article 33(2) of the 1945 Constitution, the Court considers it necessary to first provide a definition or meaning of

---

[31] Art 28H(1)(3), Constitution of the Republic of Indonesia.
[32] Art 47, Law No 24 of 2003, Constitutional Court.

'controlled by the state'. . . Article 33(2) of the 1945 Constitution has a normative effective force as follows:

1. The Constitution gives authority to the state to control production branches vital to the state and which control the livelihood of the public; ('vital production branches')
2. The aforementioned authority is directed to both those who will manage and those who have managed the 'vital production branches' [which the state shall manage and control, with individuals or private entities prohibited from working in such branches] . . .;
3. With respect to the production branches that have been managed by individuals or private entities [which are 'vital production branches'], the state under Article 33(2) of the Constitution can take these over through appropriate means in accordance with just rules of law;

   . . . [T]he provision of the 1945 Constitution that gives authority to the state to control 'vital production branches' is not intended merely for the sake of the state's authority alone, but is intended for the state to be able to fulfill its obligations as mentioned in the Preamble to the 1945 Constitution, '. . . *to protect the entire Indonesian nation and the entire Indonesian motherland, and in order to promote general welfare . . .*' and also '. . . *creating social justice for all the people of Indonesia*'. The mission set forth . . . is that the state shall exercise control over the production branches to fulfill three aspects of the public interest, namely: (1) adequate availability, (2) even distribution, and (3) affordable prices for the public. The relationship between the state's control over 'vital production branches' and the purpose for state control constitutes an integral paradigm established in the 1945 Constitution . . . The question as to whether these three aspects can be fulfilled by the market economy system, and whether such aspects should therefore just be surrendered to market mechanism must surely be answered in a normative manner, namely that the 1945 Constitution does not choose such a system as reflected in Article 33(4). [This] choice is not without reason at all. The assumption that the market mechanism can automatically fulfill these three aspects is a logical simplification which is far from reality . . . [as] a perfect market mechanism does not exist, as observed by Joseph E Stiglitz:

   . . . presumption that markets, by themselves, lead to efficient outcomes, failed to allow for desirable government interventions in the market and make everyone better off'. (*Globalization and Its Discontents*, page xii);

Considering whereas based on historical interpretation, as included in the Elucidation of the 1945 Constitution before the amendment, the meaning of the provision concerned is

   The economy is based on a economic democracy, prosperity for all the people. Therefore production branches which are important to the state and which affect the livelihood public must be controlled by the state. Otherwise, the control over production falls in the hands of a few powerful people and many people will be oppressed by them. Only companies that do not affect the livelihood of the public may be left in the hands of individuals.

This explanation still leaves questions, as to what 'vital production branches' are, and what 'managed by the state' means;
   . . . Mohammad Hatta as one of the founding fathers describes the definition of control by the state as follows:

   The aspiration embedded in Article 33 of the 1945 Constitution is that massive productions whenever possible are conducted by the Government with the assistance of foreign capital loan. If this scheme does not succeed, it is also necessary to give opportunities to foreign businesses to invest in Indonesia with the requirements determined by the Government . . . Such is the way that we thought of how to carry out economic development on the basis of Article 33 . . . If national manpower and national capital are insufficient, then borrow foreign manpower and foreign capital to make production go smoothly. If other nations are unwilling to lend their capital then opportunities are given to them to invest in our motherland according to requirements determined by the Government of Indonesia itself . . .

. . . [T]he Minister of State Owned Enterprises (BUMN) in his written statement . . . interpreted 'controlled by the state' as meaning that the state shall be the regulator, facilitator, and operator . . . whereas Prof Dr Harun Alrasid, SH interpreted 'controlled by the state' as being 'owned by the state'.

. . . [T]he Court considered expert opinions that in reality, there is no economic system [which is fully liberal or fully in the nature of a command or planned economy]. Therefore, Article 33 of the 1945 Constitution must still serve as a reference, and is not in any way interpreted as anti market economy; the market economy does not preclude state intervention when there is a distortion and injustice, because the dynamic judicial interpretation of Article 33 is carried out with the optimum observance of the strategic changes in national and global environment;

. . . [T]hus the interpretation of 'controlled by the state' in Article 33 contains a higher or broader interpretation than ownership in the civil law conception. The conception of control by the state is a public legal conception which is related to the principle of the sovereignty of the people in the 1945 Constitution, in the field of politics (political democracy) and economy (economic democracy). The principle of popular sovereignty recognises the people as the source, owner and holder of the highest power in a state, in accordance with the doctrine of 'from the people, by the people and for the people'. In the interpretation of the highest power, the interpretation of public ownership by the people collectively is also included.

. . . [I]f the phrase 'controlled by the state' is just interpreted as ownership in the civil (private) sense, it will not suffice to meet the goal of using 'control' to achieve the 'greatest prosperity of the people'. Therefore the constitutional preambular mandate to 'promote public welfare' and to 'implement social justice for all the people' . . . will be impossible to realize.

However, the civil ownership conception itself must be recognised as one of the logical consequences of control by the state, which also includes the interpretation of the collective public ownership by the people of the resources concerned. The expression 'controlled by the state' cannot be interpreted simply as the right to regulate, because it is automatically inherent in the functions of the state without needing specific constitutional mention . . . therefore the phrase 'controlled by the state' must be interpreted to include the interpretation of control by the state in the broad sense based on the conception of the sovereignty of the Indonesian people over all of the resources consisting of the 'land and water and natural resources contained therein'.

Included in it is the interpretation of the collective public ownership by the people of the resources concerned. The people collectively through the 1945 Constitution give the mandate to the state to make policy (*beleid*) and perform administration (*bestuursdad*), regulation (*regelendaad*), management (*beheersdaad*) and oversight (*toezichthoudensdaad*) with the purpose of the greatest prosperity of the people. The function of administration (*bestuursdaad*) by the state is carried out by the government in issuing and revoking permit facilities (*vergunning*), licensing (*licentie*), and concession (*concessie*). The state's regulatory function (*regelendaad*) is performed through the legislative authority of the People's Legislative

Assembly together with the government, and regulation by the government (*eksekutif*). The management function (*beheersdaad*) is performed through share holding mechanism and/or through direct involvement in the management of the State Enterprises as instruments through which the state will exercise its control over the natural resources for the greatest prosperity of the people. The function of oversight by the state (*toezichthoudensdaad*) is performed by supervising and controlling the vital branches of production . . .;

. . . [T]hrough this framework of interpretation, control in the sense of civil ownership (private), which originates from the conception of public ownership, in relation to 'vital production branches' which according to Article 33(2) shall be controlled by the state, depends upon the dynamics of the condition of development of each branch of production. Those subject to state control are (i) a branch of production which is important for the state and affects the livelihood of many people, (ii) important to the state but does not control the livelihood of many people, or (iii) not important for the state but affects the livelihood of many people . . . it is up to the government with the people's representative institution to assess whether and when a branch of production is important to the state and/or affects the livelihood of many people. A branch of production which at a certain time is important for the state and controls the livelihood of many people, may at other point in time become no longer important for the state and does not affect the livelihood of many people. However, the Court has the authority to assess by reviewing it against the 1945 Constitution if in fact there are parties who claim to have been impaired constitutionally by such assessment of the legislators; [if the Government and People's Legislative Assembly consider the production of electricity unimportant, they may transfer its regulation and oversight to the market; but if it is still important and/or involves the livelihood of many] the state is still required to take control of the concerned production branch by regulating, administering, managing and supervising to ensure that it is being used truly for the greatest prosperity of the people. 'Taking control' would include maintaining civil ownership . . . Therefore, the conception of the state's private shareholding in enterprises which concern 'vital production branches' must not be dichotomised or substituted with the conception of state regulation. Both are included in the interpretation of control by the state. Therefore, the state does not have the authority to regulate or determine rules which prohibit itself from owning shares in an enterprise which is important for the government and which affects the livelihood of many people as instruments or means for the state to maintain its control over resources . . .

Considering in addition, to guarantee the efficiency with justice principle as referred to in Article 33(4) which states, 'the national economy shall be organized based on economic democracy with the principles of togetherness, efficiency with justice, sustainability, environmental insight, independence, and by keeping the balance between the progress and the unity of the national economy', control in terms of private ownership must also be understood as being relative in nature in the sense that it does not have to be absolutely 100% at all times, provided that the state properly maintains control over the management of the resources . . .

Even though the government only owns relative majority shares, divestment or privatization of the Government's ownership of shares in the related state-owned enterprises is not contrary to Article 33 provided it still determines the policy making process in the enterprise concerned. Therefore, the Court is of the opinion that Article 33 does not preclude privatisation [or the idea of competition between business actors], as long as the state determines the main policy of the enterprise in the production branches which are important to the state and/or which affect the livelihood of many people.

Considering whereas in reviewing the *a quo* law, the court also considers the government statement which contains the driving factor, scope, philosophy and the conception of Law Number 20 of 2002, briefly as follows:

1. Limited government funding in developing the electrical power sector;
2. The supply of electricity in a more transparent, efficient, and fair manner with private participation to be carried out through competition mechanism to ensure equal treatment for all business actors;
3. The need to anticipate change at the national, regional and global level and observing legal reform or development in the related sectors;
4. The state's control in electrical power sector is implemented with the authority of the state in setting policies, regulation and supervision of business implementation;
5. The effort to provide electrical power is intended to ensure the availability of electrical power in sufficient quantity, with good quality and reasonable price to justly and evenly improve the welfare and prosperity of the people and to drive the continuous improvement of the economy, with the efficient supply of the electrical power through strong regulation, business competition and transparency in a healthy business climate, for the creation of efficiency;
6. The electrical power industry structure can be formed in a vertically integrated manner or separated based on the functions. In areas which technically and economically allow competition, the functions of generation, transmission, distribution and retail are separate businesses, with the exception of any business area which naturally has to be performed by monopoly, namely transmission and distribution. For areas in which competition cannot/cannot yet be applied, the supply of electrical power is carried out through monopoly;
7. The establishment of the electric rate is directed at cost based/cost recovery approach and the monitoring of the implementation of the tariff establishment by the market. The retail price of electrical power for competitive areas is established through market mechanism. The rental price for transmission and distribution is established by the Electrical Power Market Supervisory Board;
8. The state administration system as regulated in Article 33 of the 1945 Constitution [provides] that the government has the function of a regulator, which is performed by technical ministers, and the function as an operator, which is carried out by the office of the state minister who supervises and guides the running of businesses such as State Owned Enterprises (BUMN). In time, the government must focus more as the regulator and gradually releases its function as an operator, in accordance with the principle: 'Government function is to Govern';
9. Controlled by the state has the interpretation that the (1) Ownership (2) Regulation, development, and supervision and (3) the administration of the business activities are performed by the Government itself;
10. The philosophy of 'state control' is the creation of national resilience in the field of energy (oil and gas, electricity etc) in the Unitary State of the Republic of Indonesia with the main aim of supplying and distributing energy domestically;
11. Deregulation is efficiency through competition . . . Competition does not guarantee the lowest price at a certain time, competition [tends towards the recovery of] . . . production costs in the long run including reasonable capital return. Competition will also minimize the average cost for production and the average cost for the users;

[The statements of government expert witnesses are as follows]:

1. The electricity market will stand under one authority, which is called the Bapetal, based on certain rules which are called the market rules. There are successful and unsuccessful markets, the problem is the market rules, namely how the rules of the game must be performed. By studying the market rules we can suit the rules to our interests, as mandated by the constitution that the national economy is to be conducted based on the

principle of efficiency with justice. The interpretation of efficiency with justice in the electrical power world has a special meaning. Efficiency is the achievement of economic equilibrium that is a competition balance where the price is determined on the basis of supply and demand. The efficiency with justice is achieved in one competition system if the average price used by the supplier is the best which is eventually affordable in terms of the users, and the supplier and consumer surplus meet;

2. The parameters which are used to assess whether the law being reviewed is favorable or unfavorable are as follows:

   a. **The first parameter, efficiency;** The economic theory efficiency shows that only competitions will enable the achievement of efficiency. However, electricity has a unique characteristic, a natural monopoly so that it can not be fully released into the market. Unbundling is a means of efficiency . . .

   b. **The second parameter, tax contribution;** The tax contribution from the State Owned Electricity Company (PLN), has suffered losses for three consecutive years, only this year it acquired a profit which is relatively small compared to its large assets;

   c. **The third parameter, unfavorable to the public or not;** There are two indicators namely public accessibility and price. It is very difficult to achieve 100% electrification ratio by simply relying on the State Owned Electricity Company (PLN), thus opportunities have to be provided to anyone to increase the accessibility, as low access does not benefit the public. Those who do not have access to electricity have to pay costs 4 or 5 times more expensive than those with access. Those who do not have access are people who are poor;

3. The role of Electricity as a commodity can be viewed in three large groups, namely electricity as public service, as infrastructure, and as part of the state revenue. In the public service context, electricity is only second in importance to the need for food, which means that citizens' rights will be violated without electricity. Therefore, easily accessible electricity with reasonable price has become the need of a state. It is not adequate to simply rely on the State Owned Electricity Company (PLN) to fulfill the rights for electricity. Therefore the supply of electricity has become a priority. The new Law on Electrical Power has encouraged the effort, without having to solely rely on the State Owned Electricity Company (PLN) but also relying on private investors, cooperatives or Region Owned Enterprise (BUMD) with due observance of the regulations issued by the supervisory board . . .;

[Petitioners' expert witnesses]:

1. Electricity as public utility cannot be surrendered to the free market mechanism [where] . . . the parties make decisions based on supply and demand, whereas the market in essence is based on the purchasing power and supplying power. If that happens, the real measurement of each transaction that takes place is the profit [made by] certain parties based on supply and demand, the process of which is based more on less supply and more demand which eventually yields profit to the electrical power producers or generators;

2. In the free market mechanism, those who benefit are the capital owners; in economic terms, [this entails] individual welfare gains and not social welfare gains, [giving rise to] social welfare losses . . . Efficiency and competition are not characteristics of the free market, because a free market is a free fight . . . whereby the strong wins. Efficiency with justice at the micro and macro level is based on the [effectiveness] of government administration for the sake of social welfare and not for the efficiency of investors';

3.   If the electricity system is put into competition, the capital will go into the Jamali system (Java, Madura and Bali) whose market has been formed for 90 years, and not to outside of Java, while we have to give gross subsidy for regions outside Jamali, which can only be done if it is performed by a State Owned Enterprise /BUMN (the State Owned Electricity Company/PLN). The electrical power business is capital and technology intensive. If it is given to the private sector, the mindset will be to maximize profit and then to return the capital quickly, which is different from a State Owned Enterprise/BUMN (the State Electricity Company/BUMN);

4.   [An expert gave evidence of the effects of restructuring in England] . . . The restructuring in England, in terms of electricity price compared to other countries in fact did not bring down the electricity price. It is true that in the short term, efficiency and productivity improved, but it was mainly caused by the reduction in manpower. The laborers as the stakeholders suffered the greatest loss as a consequence of termination of employment, whereas the capital owners with a bigger capital received higher profit. The current fact in England is that private companies tend to reintegrate those which were previously unbundled by the English government through restructuring program. This resulted in only five electricity companies which are vertically integrated and those previously unbundled were then reintegrated. Study indicates that electricity contracts with the private electricity companies were based on long term contracts and were very expensive. They were guaranteed by the government and often as a consequence, the government and the state enterprise had to shoulder very expensive cost and this created heavy financial burden. The study concluded that it is not wise to restructure the electricity sector, as it will create many problems and obviate other more flexible policies in terms of long term development of the electric sector. Recently, there were four countries which postponed or cancelled to restructure its electrical power sector ie Thailand, South Korea, Brazil and Mexico;

[Recalling the issues raised by the various petitioners, including the argument that privatisation of electricity, an important production branch affecting the livelihood of many, should be state-controlled, otherwise constitutional rights would be impaired. Further, the 'unbundling' policy of separating aspects of the electricity supply business (transmission, distribution, sales, etc) into the hands of separate business entities would encourage privatisation and treatment of electricity as a market commodity, such that the majority of people unable to afford it would lack protection. Further, leaving selling prices to be established by competition was out of line with Article 33 which is orientated to the people's welfare. The principal issue was whether the conduct of the electricity power business separately by different business entities under Law No 20 was constitutional.]

Considering whereas with respect to the first problem whether the electrical power is an important branch for the state and affects the livelihood of many people, it is evident from the following:

1.   During the hearings, in their written and oral statements, the government and the People's Legislative Assembly did not deny the argument of the Petitioners that electricity is a production branch which is important for the state and which affects the livelihood of many people;

2.   Whereas electricity's being an important production branch is also admitted by the legislators. This can be concluded from the 'Considering' section Sub-Article a of Law Number 20 Year 2002 on Electrical Power which states, 'whereas the electrical power is very useful in promoting public welfare, improving the intellectual life of the nation, and improving the economy in the context of realizing a just and prosperous society in both material and spiritual terms evenly based on Pancasila and the 1945 Constitution';

3.   Whereas the Experts presented by the government also admitted that electricity is very
     important for the state, whether as a commodity which is a source of revenue or as
     infrastructure which is necessary in implementing the tasks of development as needed
     by the people and which affects the livelihood of many people. As public service, the
     electricity is only second in importance to the need for food;

Considering whereas with the above facts, it has been proven that electricity is a 'vital
production branch' . . . which in accordance with Article 33(2) must be controlled by the
state; . . .

. . . [T]he interpretation of the Court on control by the government must be assessed based
on Article 33, including the administration of national economy based on economic democracy, the principle of togetherness, efficiency with justice, and environmental insight which is
interpreted to mean that control by the state also includes private ownership, which does not
always have to be 100%. This means the government in its ownership of shares in a business
related to a 'vital production branch' can be in the nature of an absolute majority (above
50%) or relative majority (under 50%), insofar as the government as the relative majority
shareholder, still legally holds a key position in the decision making of the enterprise;

It must be understood that even though the government only owns relative majority
shares in the State Owned Enterprise (BUMN), the state's key position must be maintained
in the decision-making for setting policy in the enterprise concerned. This illustrates the
control of the state which includes regulation, administration, management and supervision; [the meaning of 'control by the state' would be reduced if it is treated equally with
private and foreign enterprises in the competition system];

Considering whereas the experts are of the opinion that competition and unbundling
will only take place at JAMALI area (Java, Madura and Bali) as a market which has already
been formed. Competition will be won by businesses which are financially and technologi-
cally solid. Whereas areas outside Java, Madura and Bali whose market has not been
formed will become the responsibility of the government to supply electricity in an integrated manner. This cannot be accomplished without cross subsidy from the profitable
market at JAMALI. Therefore, the obligation to implement the greatest prosperity and
welfare for all of the Indonesian people will not be achieved because private business players will be oriented towards profit-making . . .;

. . . [T]he Court is of the opinion that to save, protect and further develop a more sound
State-Owned Enterprise (BUMN) as an asset of the state and nation which has been providing commercial and non-commercial electricity services to the Indonesian public, nation
and state as a form of control by the state, the provision of Article 16 of Law Number 20
of 2002 which orders the separation/split of the electric power business system (unbundling
system) with different business actors will aggravate the State Owned Enterprise (BUMN)
leading to the absence of guaranteed commercial and non commercial electricity supply for
all elements of the public. Therefore, it will be unfavorable for the public, nation, and state.
The statements of experts presented by the Petitioner have explained empirical experience
in Europe, Latin America, Korea and Mexico where electricity sector restructuring in fact
was not beneficial and became a heavy state burden. Therefore, the Court is of the opinion
that it is contradictory to Article 33 . . .;

. . . [T]he Court is of the opinion that the legislators also assess that the electricity sector
is currently a 'vital production branch' which according to Article 33(2) must remain within
state control through a state enterprise financed by the government or in partnership with
foreign or national private companies with foreign and domestic loan. Another alternative
is by involving national/foreign private capital in a good and mutual partnership system.
This means that only a State Owned Enterprise (BUMN) can manage the electricity sector,

whereas national or foreign private companies may only participate upon invitation from the State Enterprise (BUMN), through partnership, shareholding, capital loan etc. The problem is whether the task to manage the electricity sector solely belongs to the State Owned Enterprise (BUMN), in this case the State Owned Electricity Company (PLN), or whether it can be shared with other state enterprise, or even with Region Owned Enterprise (BUMD), in line with the regional autonomy spirit. The Court is of the opinion that, if the State Owned Electricity Company (PLN) is still capable and can be more efficient, the task should still be assigned to the it; otherwise, the tasks should be shared with other State Owned Enterprise (BUMN) or Region Owned Enterprise (BUMD) with State Owned Electricity Company (PLN) as the holding company;

. . . [F]urthermore by referring to the views of Hatta and the experts in relation to the meaning of Article 33, it can be briefly concluded that the interpretation of control by the state is that the state has to strengthen the production branch that it owns, so that gradually it will be able to independently provide for the needs which concern the livelihood of many people and replace the positions of the national and foreign private companies;

. . . [T]he inefficiency of the State Owned Enterprise (BUMN) which arises due to mis-management factors and corruption, collusion and nepotism (KKN) must not be made as an excuse to ignore Article 33, as the Indonesian idiom says 'buruk muka cermin dibelah' (equivalent to the English idiom 'an ill bird fouls its own nest'). Improvements made must reinforce the state control to be able to perform its constitutional obligations . . .

. . . [T]he provisions viewed as being contradictory to the constitution basically are Articles 16, 17 Paragraphs 3 and Article 68, which concern unbundling and competition, and are in fact the *heart* of Law Number 20 Year 2002 . . . That matter is not in accordance with the soul and spirit of Article 33(2), which is the basic norm of the Indonesian national economy; *Law No 20 of 2002 declared contradictory to 1945 Indonesian Constitution.*

Notes and Questions

1. The Constitutional Court held that all contracts and permits issued under Law No 20 of 2002 remained valid until they expired. It also reinstated the old Law No 15 of 1985 regarding Electrical Power to avoid a legal vacuum. Law No 20 of 2002 was held unconstitutional in its entirety to avoid legal uncertainty, and it was recommended that the legislators prepare a new draft law on electrical power that was in accordance with Article 33. Notably, electricity production is not treated as an individual right but as a concern for the people's welfare, and as a matter of natural resource management in accordance with socialist or familial constitutional norms set out in Chapter XIV (The National Economy and Social Welfare) of the Constitution.

2. What is the nature of the state's duties in relation to electricity production? Does it go beyond regulation? What is its relation to the idea of popular sovereignty over natural resources? Did the Court's decision contribute to the realisation of a right to an adequate standard of living?

3. Did the Constitutional Court sufficiently demonstrate that it lacked the competence to deal with complex economic issues? For example, did it adequately consider the admission by PLN that it could not meet the government target for electricity production? To what extent does the Indonesian Constitution permit the privatisation of this sector?

Judicial Review of the Law of the Republic of Indonesia Number 7 Year 2004
regarding Water Resources (Law Number 7 Year 2004)
Case Number 058-059-060-063/PUU-II/2004; Case Number 008/PUU-III/2005
(Constitutional Court, Indonesia)

Facts

The 2004 Water Resources Law[33] sought to decentralise water management and allow for
private sector management of water resources. This was controversial in so far as it was
seen as advancing a World Bank agenda of privatisation. Under the new legislation, the
Government was empowered not only to make policy but to determine and manage the
water resource management scheme and grant permits for exploiting water at various government levels. Between 2004 and 2005, a number of NGOs and individuals sought judicial
review, challenging the constitutionality of the law for threatening the people's right to
water by making it a profit-orientated business. The relevant constitutional provision was
Article 33(3), which requires that the economy be organised 'as a common endeavour based
upon the principles of the family system'. The right to water was treated as a human rights
issue, though there is no such express constitutional right.

Held (majority view)

Water is absolutely vital for human life, to such an extent that the United Nation refers to
the right to water as a Human Rights (HAM); every person has an interest in the existence
of legal provisions able to guarantee and protect the human right to water. Thus, every
Indonesian citizen, as a human being also has . . . the legal standing to question the constitutionality of the Water Resources Law deemed to have harmed him/her; . . . water [is] . . .
as important as the need of living beings for oxygen (air). The access to clean water supply
has been recognized as a human right [refers to the WHO Formation Charter (1946),
Article 25 UDHR ('Right to standard of living adequate for the health and well-being of
himself and of his family'), Article 12 ICESCR, Article 24(1) CRC (right of child to enjoyment of highest attainable standard of health)] . . .
   In 2000, the United Nation Committee for Economic, Social, and Cultural Rights
accepted the General Comment regarding the right for health which formulated the normative interpretation as indicated in Article 12(1) ICESCR which reads as follows:

> The States Parties to the present Covenant recognize the right of everyone to the enjoy-
> ment of the highest attainable standard of physical and mental health.

[This] interprets the right for health as [an] inclusive right which consists of not only continuous and appropriate medical services but also the determining factors for good health,
including . . . access to safe drinking water. Furthermore, in 2002, the Committee recognized the access to water as a separate human right.
   . . . [T]he recognition of the access to water as a human right [has] two aspects; on the one
hand, it is a recognition of the fact that water is such an important need for human life, on
the other hand, every person's access to water needs to be protected [and as such] the right
to water shall be affirmed as the highest right in law, namely, human rights. The further
issues that arise concern the position of the state in relation to water as public goods or
social goods which has been recognized as part of human rights . . . [which the state is
obliged] to respect, protect, and fulfil . . .

---

[33] The text of the 'Law on Water Resources – Indonesia' can found in (2006) 2(1) *Law, Environment and
Development Journal* 118.

... [W]ater resources exist in nature like other natural resources; [their] availability is very much influenced by the condition of the natural surroundings where people live. . . . The nature of water is different from the nature of air resource, which relatively can be obtained freely everywhere . . . the presence or absence of water supply in one location does not reduce the human need for water. Men have been working for a long time to intervene in the hydrological cycle for the purpose of making water available for their needs by utilizing the simplest to the very advanced technology. For example, water reservoir and water flow management have been utilized to fulfill a variety of needs, for drinking water, fish farm, or agriculture, and also for the power plant.

... [T]he founding fathers have appropriately laid a visionary foundation for water management in [Articles 33(3)[34] and 28H[35] of the 1945 Constitution] which lays the foundation for the recognition of the right to water as part of the right to live a physically and mentally prosperous life, which is the substance of the human rights; . . . if the respect for the human right to water is interpreted as the strict prohibition of state's involvement in water affairs, many conflicts will surely occur due to the competition to obtain water . . . [Thus], the protection of the right to water is concerned not only with the protection of rights enjoyed by a person against any violation by another person, but also with the guarantee that as a human right, it can truly be enjoyed . . . the protection of right in this aspect is inseparable from the fulfillment of the right; [thus], the fulfillment of the right to water [entails a state obligation] to guarantee that every individual's need of water can be fulfilled. [States in meeting the three aspects of human rights obligations, to respect, protect and fulfil a right] . . . are concerned not only with the present need but also the guarantee of continuation in the future, as it is directly related to the human existence. The state needs to be actively involved in the planning of water resources management, for the purpose of guaranteeing the availability of water for the community . . . [which involves many matters such as] water resources conservation. . . .

... [W]ater is needed not only to fulfill the immediate necessities of life [but also] other necessities, such as irrigation for agriculture, power plant, and for industrial needs. The utilization of . . . water resources also plays an important part in the development of human beings, and is a significant factor for human beings to live a decent life. One of the means to fulfill the availability of food, the necessities of energy/electricity is through the utilization of water resources . . . [which must be managed to meet] these secondary needs. . . .

... The Court is of the opinion that Article 5 of the Water Resources Law (WRL) which reads as follows: 'The State shall guarantee the right of every person to obtain water for minimum daily basic needs to have a healthy, hygienic, and productive life,' is [an adequate] legal formulation to describe the right to water as the right guaranteed by the Constitution. Although [this] guarantee . . . has not been reformulated in the form of responsibilities of the Government and the Provincial Government as referred to in Articles 14 and 15 of the WRL, [the Government, Provincial Government and Second Level Regional/City Government are all responsible for fulfilling] the minimal daily basic needs for water for the community of their regions [through their programmes, which] has to be reflected in the implementing regulations of the WRL.

... [It is no longer sufficient for] water supply to fulfill daily basic needs . . . to be directly obtained from the water sources managed by the community, [as this now] depends on the distribution channels . . . [T]he state is obligated [under Article 5 of the WRL] to guarantee the right of every individual to obtain water for the purpose of fulfilling the minimal daily

---

[34] Art 33(3): 'The land, the waters and the natural resources within shall be under the powers of the State and shall be used to the greatest benefit of the people.'

[35] Art 28H(1): 'Every person shall have the right to live in physical and spiritual prosperity, to have a home and to enjoy a good and healthy environment, and shall have the right to obtain medical care.'

basic needs, including the needs of community depending on distribution channels. The Court is of the opinion that the Government is obligated to fulfill the right to water other than the user rights as reflected in:

(1) The responsibilities of the Government, Provincial Governments, and Second Level Regional/City Governments described in Articles 14, 15, and 16 of the WRL, namely the responsibilities to regulate, stipulate, and to grant permits for the supply, allocation, utilization, and exploitation of the water resources in the river areas. The Government is obligated to prioritize untreated water to fulfill the daily needs for every individual through water resources utilization management.

(2) The provision of Article 29(3) of the WRL which states as follows, 'Water provision to fulfill daily basic needs and for the irrigation of people's smallholdings in the existing irrigation system shall be the main priority of water resources provision above all needs'.

(3) The provision of Article 26 (7) which reads as follows, 'The utilization of water resources shall be conducted by giving priority to social function to realize justice by taking into account the principle of payment by water users for water resources management service charges and by involving communities.' . . . The participation of community which constitutes the implementation of the principle of democracy in water management shall be prioritized in the management of PDAM (Drinking Water Regional Company), because the good or poor performance of the PDAM in water supply service for the community directly reflect the good or poor performance of the state in carrying out its obligation to fulfill the right to water.

The principle of 'water users shall pay the service charges for water resources management' treats water not [as an economic commodity but as] '*res commune*' . . . [such that] water consumers should pay [a lower] price than . . . if the water is valued in price in the economic respect, because if the latter occurs, the users have to pay not only the price of water but also the production cost along with the profit of the water management. PDAM has to position itself as the state's operational unit to realize the state's obligation as stipulated in Article 5 of the Water Resources Law, and not as the company which is economically profit-oriented. Although . . . Article 80(1) of the WRL states that in order to meet their daily basic needs and for people's smallholdings, water resource users shall be exempted from the service charge for water resources management, this provision is applicable [where] the daily basic needs and the people's smallholdings are obtained directly from water resources. It means that if the water for daily basic needs and the people's smallholdings is obtained from distribution channels, the principle of 'water users shall pay the service charges for water resources management' applies. However, this matter cannot be used as the basis to apply expensive costs for citizens whose fulfillment of their daily basic needs depends on PDAM through the distribution channel.

The amount of water resources management service charges has to be transparent and must involve the element of community in its calculation. Due to the fact that water is very vital and directly related to human rights, the implementing regulations of the WRL must contain the obligation of the Regional Government to allocate the budget for financing the water resources management in its Regional Revenues and Expenditures Budget (APBD);

[Under Article 40, the Government and Regional Governments are responsible for developing a drinking water provision system which shall be administered in an integrated fashion with the development of infrastructure and sanitation facilities; private legal entities and the community may participate only in matters the Government cannot perform by itself and the Government must remain capable of exercising its authority in the management, implementation and supervision of the overall management of water resources; it is also in charge of water conservation, in which task the fulfilment of the right to water is to be prioritised as the main right; considering these provisions] . . . the Court is of opinion that the WRL has sufficiently obligated the Government to respect, protect, and fulfill the right to water; in [implementing these regulations], the Government must take into account the opinion of the Court [such that] if [the Law is implemented in a manner] different from that which is intended in the above considerations of the Court then another petition for review of the Law is not impossible (*conditionally constitutional*);

Control of Water by the State

Considering whereas water is *res commune*, and therefore that has to be subject to the provision of Article 33(3), so that the management of water has to be included in the public legal system which cannot be made the object of ownership in the concept of civil law. [This concept accords with the fact that the management of water is an aspect of the right to water as a constitutionally stipulated human right.] The Court is of opinion that the concept of water use rights as formulated in the WRL has to be interpreted as being derived from the right to life[36] guaranteed by the 1945 Constitution;

Considering whereas therefore, except for water use rights, every exploitation of water must be subject to the state's right to control. [For water to be utilized beyond a water user's rights, a permit has to be obtained from the Government who may issue a] permit for water utilization either as untreated water or as the utilization of water resources;

Considering whereas due to the particular nature or characteristic of water compared to the other resources such as oil or other mined goods, and due to the implementation of two legal provisions on water, namely Article 28H and Article 33(3) the 1945 Constitution, the management of water has a special feature; . . .

Considering whereas although the state has the right to control water, due to the existence of human rights aspect with respect to water, the management of water shall be conducted in a transparent manner, namely by including the participation of community, and still respecting the right to water of customary law community, so as to develop democratization in the water resources system management. [under Article 11(3), both the community and business community are to be involved through inputs on planning of water resources management implementation but the role of the state controlling water implemented by the Government or Regional Government under Article 33(3) of the Constitution 'shall not be transferred to business community or private sector'].

. . . [T]he Petitioners argue the WRL contains articles encouraging privatization namely, Articles 9, 10, 26, 45. 46 and 80, which are therefore contradictory to Article 33(3) of the 1945 Constitution. The Court is of the opinion that the WRL regulates the principal matters in the water resources management, and although the WRL opens the opportunities for private participation to obtain the Right on Commercial Use of Water and the permit of exploitation of water resources, the aforementioned matters will not cause the control of water exploitation to fall into the hands of private parties. The state, in the exercising the right of water exploitation, conducts the following activities: (1) to formulate policies (*beleid*), (2) to conduct acts of administration (*bestuursdaad*), (3) to regulate (*regelendaad*), (4) to manage (*beheersdaad*), (5) to supervise (*toezichthoudendaad*);

. . . The existence of this permit system [for exploitation in relation to the right of commercial use of water] will allow the Government to control the exploitation of water

---

[36] Art 28A: 'Every person shall have the right to live and to defend his/her life and existence.' Art 28I provides that 'rights to life, freedom from torture' are 'all human rights that cannot be limited under any circumstances'.

resources. . . . The principle 'users shall pay the service charges for water resources manage-ment' is performed in a flexible manner by not applying similar calculation without consid-ering the type of water resources utilization. The implementation of this principle is not applied to water users for daily basic needs fulfillment, or to social interest and public safety. Water-users [who are farmers or people with smallholdings] are exempt from the obligation to finance the water resources management service charge. The utilization of water resources to support the small-scale economy of the community shall have different regulation from the regulation for water resources utilization for large-scale industries. Therefore, the implementation of this principle has considered the value of justice. If this principle is not implemented, meaning that there is no obligation to support the water resources management service charge at all by water users, it will clearly benefit those who utilize considerable quantities of water, namely large-scale private industries, which will definitely lead to injustice. Such regulation shall be included in the implementing regula-tions of the WRL. The purpose of this principle is the continuous implementation of water resources management, and not to generate profits. [Finding the principle not contradic-tory to Article 33(3).]

. . . The Court is of the opinion that the WRL has stipulated sufficient requirements for water exploitation for other countries provided by the central Government based on the recommendation of the Regional Government. The Government can only provide water exploitation permit for other countries if the provision of water for various necessities has been fulfilled. The needs are, among other things, basic needs, needs for environmental sanitation, needs in the field of agriculture, employment, industry, mining, transportation, forestry and biological diversity, sports, recreation and tourism, ecosystem, aesthetics, and other purposes. It means that there is real water excess in a river area, and if such excess is not utilized it will be a waste of resources. The Court is of the opinion that water exploita-tion for other countries is only possible if there is real water excess in a river area, and the principle of 'benefit receivers shall pay the management fee' must also be applied, and the benefit receivers shall be obligated to pay the charge for the aforementioned water. State revenues originating from water exploitation for other countries must be allocated for the greatest prosperity of the people; Therefore the Court is of the opinion that Article 49(4) WRL is not contradictory to the 1945 Constitution.

Notes and Questions

1. Indonesia ratified the ICCPR and ICESCR on 30 September 2005. How influen-tial was international human rights on the Court's finding a human right to water in the Indonesian Constitution, and in which article(s) was this grounded? How did the Court use constitutional prescriptions in relation to economic policy in interpreting the content of rights?

2. In his dissenting opinion, Justice A Mukthie Fadjar noted that since the Water Resources Law had received 'great resistance from the people', it should be 'revised first in order to meet the accurate paradigm . . . [of] giving more focus [to the] social and environmental dimension instead of economic dimension', to avoid being contrary to Article 33(3) of the 1945 Constitution.

3. Did the Court treat water, a recognised human right, in a way that required a more stringent implementation regime than other natural resources? How did it conclude that the right to water was a human right? Did it draw on the text, international

standards or both? What were the state's duties in relation to the realisation of this right and the public good?

4.   Given that the holding was 'conditionally constitutional', does the Court have the capacity to monitor the situation? What might be the role of NGOs in this respect? See generally P Venning, 'Determination of Economic, Social and Cultural Rights by the Indonesian Constitutional Court' [2008] *Australian Journal of Asian Law* 100.

5.   Is this form of what Tushnet described as 'strong form' judicial review, where the court intervenes in socio-economic policy and its reasonable interpretation prevails over the legislature's reasonable interpretation, desirable or an instance of institutional incapacity and over-extension? See M Tushnet, *Weak Courts, Strong Rights: Judicial Review and Social Welfare Rights in Comparative Constitutional Law* (Princeton, NJ: Princeton University Press, 2009) at 21. Would this depend on context, such as whether the situation is one of a mature democracy with a robust welfare system, or a transitional democracy facing corruption problems and ineffective government?

V.   JUDICIAL CONSTRUCTION: READING DIRECTIVE PRINCIPLES TO EXPAND THE 'RIGHT TO LIFE' TO INCLUDE SOCIO-ECONOMIC RIGHTS

The Constitutions of Bangladesh,[37] Pakistan,[38] and India[39] have separate chapters for fundamental rights, which are mostly civil-political in nature and do not contain an extended list of SERs, though state policy deals with socio-welfare concerns. Exceptionally, Article 25A of the Pakistan Constitution, introduced by the Eighteenth Amendment, provides for 'free and compulsory education' to children between the ages of five and 16. The chapters on directive principles of state policy (DPSP) are not meant to be justiciable. Part III of the Indian Constitution contains justiciable basic rights facilitated by Articles 32 and 226. While Part IV is considered fundamental to the governance of the country, Article 37 provides that Part IV provisions 'shall not be enforceable by any court', though the state is duty-bound 'to apply these principles in making laws'. They must, as such, be realised progressively.

The 'right to life' conventionally implicates issues like abortion, euthanasia and the death penalty,[40] and is classified as a fundamental CPR. This is the position of Article 9[41] jurisprudence in Singapore.[42] Courts in certain South Asian jurisdictions in hearing cases brought by public interest litigation[43] have expansively construed the right to life

---

[37]   Pt II 'Fundamental Principles of State Policy'; Pt III 'Fundamental Rights'.

[38]   Pt II ch 1 'Fundamental Rights' and ch 2 'Principles of Policy'.

[39]   Pt III 'Fundamental Rights'; Pt IV 'Directive Principles of State Policy'.

[40]   See, eg, D Korff, 'The Right to Life: A Guide to the Implementation of Article 2 of the European Convention on Human Rights', *Council of Europe: Human Rights Handbook No 8*. (Counciln of Europe, 2006) available: < http://book.coe.int/sysmodules/RBS_fichier/admin/download.php?fileid=3015>.

[41]   Art 9 reads: 'No person shall be deprived of life or personal liberty save in accordance with law'.

[42]   'Personal liberty' has been narrowly construed to mean absence of physical restraint: *Lo Pui Sang v Mamata Kapildev* [2008] 4 SLR(R) 754.

[43]   Eg, Martin Lau, 'The Islamization of Laws in Pakistan - Impact on the Independence of Judiciary', published in Eugene Cotran & Mai Yamani (eds), *The Rule of Law in the Middle East and the Islamic World (Human Rights and the Judicial Process)* (London: IB Tauris Publishers, 2000).

in a manner which transcends personal security to encompass matters pertaining to the quality of life. Read in conjunction with DPSP which speak to socio-welfare concerns, this has been a fruitful source for effectively developing a slew of SERs. Article 21 of the Indian Constitution reads: 'No person shall be deprived of his life or personal liberty except according to procedure established by law.' Article 9 and Article 32 of the Pakistan and Bangladesh Constitutions respectively differ in providing: 'No person shall be deprived of life or liberty save in accordance with law.'

The activism of the Indian Supreme Court in reading Article 21 to find SERs led the way. This path was first laid out in *Maneka Gandhi v Union of India*,[44] where personal liberty was found to cover not merely physical restraint but also a right to travel. Krishna Iyer J noted:

> It is a mark of interpretative respect for the higher norms our founding fathers held dear in affecting the dearest rights of life and liberty so to read Art 21 as to result in a human order lined with human justice.[45]

The Supreme Court held that the DPSP should be used as a code of interpretation, to help the courts determine the substance of fundamental rights.[46] A flood of Article 21-related litigation ensued.[47] In *Francis Mullin v Administrator, Union Territory of Delhi*,[48] the Court found that the right to life included 'the bare necessities of life such as adequate nutrition, clothing and shelter and facilities for reading, writing and expressing oneself in diverse forms'. In *Bandhua Mukti Morcha v Union of India*,[49] the Supreme Court stated that the 'right to live with human dignity enshrined in Article 21 derives its life breath from the Directive Principles of State Policy' and included

> protection of the health and strength of workers, men and women, and of the tender age of children against abuse, opportunities and facilities for children to develop in a healthy manner and in conditions of freedom and dignity, educational facilities, just and humane conditions of work and maternity relief.

While the Supreme Court stated that the DPSP were not judicially enforceable and that it could not compel the Government to enact laws or policies, it would give 'concrete reality and content' to *existing* legislation to meet these basic requirements. As such, state non-compliance could violate the Article 21 right to live with human dignity.

Courts have found that the right to life includes the right to livelihood, right to work,[50] the right to basic necessities, including the right to food, clothing, a decent environment, a right to shelter,[51] and reasonable accommodation,[52] a right to road

---

[44] *Maneka Gandhi v Union of India* [1978] AIR 597, [1978] SCR (2) 621.

[45] [1978] AIR 597, 726.

[46] *Akhil Bhartiya Soshit Karmachari Sangh v Union of India* [1981] AIR SC 298.

[47] See, eg, J Cassels, 'Judicial Activism and Public Interest Litigation in India: Attempting the Impossible? (1989) 37 *American Journal of Comparative Law* 495.

[48] *Francis Mullin v Administrator, Union Territory of Delhi* [1981] AIR 746.

[49] *Bandhua Mukti Morcha v Union of India* [1984] AIR 802, [1984] SCR (2) 67.

[50] *Delhi Development Horticulture Employee's Union v Delhi Administration* [1992] AIR SC 789.

[51] *Chameli Singh v. State of Uttar* [1996] AIR SC 1051, where the Supreme Court referred to UN General Resolution No 35/76 for its treatment of the problem of homeless people in developing countries. 'Shelter' went beyond protection of life and limb to encompass a place where a person had opportunities to grow physically, mentally, intellectually and spiritually. It therefore includes adequate living space, a safe and decent structure, clean and decent surroundings, sufficient light, pure air and water, electricity, sanitation and other civic amenities like roads, etc.

[52] *Shantisar Builder v Narayanan Khumlal Totame* [1990] AIR SC 630.

access in a hilly region,[53] the right of enjoyment of pollution-free water and air,[54] and a right to a safe working environment free from sexual harassment.[55] This transcends mere physical existence to engage the qualitative dimension of living.

Effectively, SERs were smuggled in the back door through expansive readings of 'right to life' clauses, drawing from DPSP. Some major cases (excerpted below), throw into sharp relief the role of courts in social policy and reform, the difficulties involved in judicial monitoring of programmes and how unelected judges address technical issues or matters of financial constraint.

A. Right to Life and Livelihood: Housing and Unlawful Eviction

Olga Tellis & Ors v Bombay Municipal Council
[1985] 2 Supp SCR 51, [1986] AIR SC 180 (Supreme Court, India)

Facts

In 1981, the Bombay Municipal Council decided to evict all pavement and slum dwellers from the city of Bombay. The residents claimed such action would violate their right to life, since a home in the city allowed them to attain a livelihood, and demanded that adequate resettlement be provided if the evictions proceeded.

Chandhandrachud CJ

These Writ Petitions portray the plight of lakhs[56] of persons who live on pavements and in slums in the city of Bombay. They constitute nearly half the population of the city. The first group of petitions relates to pavement dwellers while the second group relates to both pavement and Basti or Slum dwellers. Those who have made pavements their homes exist in the midst of filth and squalor . . . Rabid dogs in search of stinking meat and cats in search of hungry rats keep them company. They cook and sleep where they ease, for no conveniences are available to them. Their daughters, come of age, bathe under the nosy gaze of passers by, unmindful of the feminine sense of bashfulness. The cooking and washing over, women pick lice from each others' hair. The boys beg. Menfolk, without occupation [commit crimes] . . .

It is these men and women who have come to this Court to ask for a judgment that they cannot be evicted from their squalid shelters without being offered alternative accommodation. They rely for their rights on Article 21 of the Constitution which guarantees that no person shall be deprived of his life except according to procedure established by law. They do not contend that they have a right to live on the pavements. Their contention is that they have a right to live, a right which cannot be exercised without the means of livelihood. They have no option but to flock to big cities like Bombay, which provide the means of bare

---

[53] *State of HP v Umed Ram Sharma* (1986) 2 SCC 68 ('Access to road was held to be an access to life itself in that state').

[54] *Subhash Kumar v State of Bihar* [1991] AIR SC 420.

[55] *Vishaka v State of Rajasthan* (1997) 6 SCC 241, [1997] AIR SC 3011. The Supreme Court of Nepal adopted a similar tack in promulgating guidelines against sexual harassment where Parliament failed to act: *Prakash Mani Sharma v Ministry of Women, Children and Social Welfare*, SCN, Writ No 2822 of 2062 (28 Nov 2008).

[56] A unit equal to 100,000.

subsistence. They only choose a pavement or a slum which is nearest to their place of work. In a word, their plea is that the right to life is illusory without a right to the protection of the means by which alone life can be lived. And, the right to life can only be taken away or abridged by a procedure established by law, which has to be fair and reasonable, not fanciful or arbitrary such as is prescribed by the Bombay Municipal Corporation Act or the Bombay Police Act. They also rely upon their right to reside and settle in any part of the country which is guaranteed by Article 19(1)(e) . . .

. . . [T]he question which we have to consider [assuming eviction entails deprivation of livelihood] . . . is whether the right to life includes the right to livelihood. We see only one answer to that question, namely, that it does. The sweep of the right to life conferred by Article 21 is wide and far reaching. It does not mean merely that life cannot be extinguished or taken away as, for example, by the imposition and execution of the death sentence, except according to procedure established by law. That is but one aspect of the right to life. An equally important facet of that right is the right to livelihood because, no person can live without the means of living, that is, the means of livelihood. If the right to livelihood is not treated as a part of the constitutional right to life, the easiest way of depriving a person of his right to life would be to deprive him of his means of livelihood to the point of abrogation. Such deprivation would not only denude the life of its effective content and meaningfulness but it would make life impossible to live. And yet, such deprivation would not have to be in accordance with the procedure established by law, if the right to livelihood is not regarded as a part of the right to life. That, which alone makes it possible to live, leave aside what makes life livable, must be deemed to be an integral component of the right to life. Deprive a person of his right to livelihood and you shall have deprived him of his life. Indeed, that explains the massive migration of the rural population to big cities. They migrate because they have no means of livelihood in the villages . . . [in a] struggle for life. So unimpeachable is the evidence of the nexus between life and the means of livelihood. They have to eat to live: Only a handful can afford the luxury of living to eat. That they can do, namely, eat, only if they have the means of livelihood. That is the context in which it was said by Douglas J in *Baksey* that the right to work is the most precious liberty because, it sustains and enables a man to live and the right to life is a precious freedom. 'Life', as observed by Field J in *Munn v Illinois* (1877) 94 US 113, means something more than mere animal existence and the inhibition against the deprivation of life extends to all those limits and faculties by which life is enjoyed. This observation was quoted with approval by this Court in *Kharak Singh v The State of UP* [1964] 1 SCR 332.

Article 39(a) of the Constitution, which is a Directive Principle of State Policy, provides that the State shall, in particular, direct its policy towards securing that the citizens, men and women equally, have the right to an adequate means of livelihood. Article 41, which is another Directive Principle, provides, inter alia, that the State shall, within the limits of its economic capacity and development, make effective provision for securing the right to work in cases of unemployment and of undeserved want. Article 37 provides that the Directive Principles, though not enforceable by any court, are nevertheless fundamental in the governance of the country. The Principles contained in Articles 39 (a) and 41 must be regarded as equally fundamental in the understanding and interpretation of the meaning and content of fundamental rights. If there is an obligation upon the State to secure to the citizens an adequate means of livelihood and the right to work, it would be sheer pedantry to exclude the right to livelihood from the content of the right to life. The State may not, by affirmative action, be compellable to provide adequate means of livelihood or work to the citizens. But, any person, who is deprived of his right to livelihood except according to just and fair procedure established by law, can challenge the deprivation as offending the right to life conferred by Article 21.

. . . [Expert studies indicate that a main reason for] the emergence and growth of squat-ter-settlements in big Metropolitan cities like Bombay, is the availability of job opportuni-ties which are lacking in the rural sector. The undisputed fact that even after eviction, the squatters return to the cities affords proof of that position . . . It is estimated that about 200 to 300 people enter Bombay every day in search of employment. These facts constitute empirical evidence to justify the conclusion that persons in the position of petitioners live in slums and on pavements because they have small jobs to nurse in the city and there is nowhere else to live. Evidently, they choose a pavement or a slum in the vicinity of their place of work, the time otherwise taken in commuting and its cost being forbidding for their slender means. To lose the pavement or the slum is to lose the job. The conclusion, therefore, in terms of the constitutional phraseology is that the eviction of the petitioners will lead to deprivation of their livelihood and [life].

. . . Two conclusions emerge from this discussion: one, that the right to life which is con-ferred by Article 21 includes the right to livelihood and two, that it is established that if the petitioners are evicted from their dwellings, they will be deprived of their livelihood. But the Constitution does not put an absolute embargo on the deprivation of life or personal liberty, by Article 21, such deprivation has to be according to procedure established by law . . .

. . . To summarise, we hold that no person has the right to encroach, by erecting a struc-ture or otherwise, on footpaths, pavements or any other place reserved or ear-marked for a public purpose like, for example, a garden or a playground; that the provision contained in section 314 of the Bombay Municipal Corporation Act is not unreasonable in the circum-stances of the case; . . . We have referred to the assurances given by the State Government in its pleadings here which, we repeat, must be made good. Stated briefly, pavement dwell-ers who were censused or who happened to be censused in 1976 should be given, though not as a condition precedent to their removal, alternative pitches at Malavani or at such other convenient place as the Government considers reasonable but not farther away in terms of distance; slum dwellers who were given identity cards and whose dwellings were numbered in the 1976 census must be given alternate sites for their re-settlement; slums which have been in existence for a long time, say for twenty years or more, and which have been improved and developed will not be removed unless the land on which they stand or the appurtenant land, is required for a public purposes, in which case, alternate sites or accommodation will be provided to them, the 'Low Income Scheme Shelter Programme' which is proposed to be undertaken with the aid of the World Bank will be pursued ear-nestly; and, the Slum Upgradation Programme (SUP) under which basic amenities are to be given to slum dwellers will be implemented without delay. In order to minimise the hard-ship involved in any eviction, we direct that the slums, wherever situated, will not be removed until one month after the end of the current monsoon season, that is, until October 31, 1985 and, thereafter, only in accordance with this judgment. If any slum is required to be removed before that date, parties may apply to this Court. Pavement dwellers, whether censused or uncensused, will not be removed until the same date viz October 31, 1985.

Notes and Questions

1. Is the 'right' established in *Olga Tellis* truncated by the holding that evictions would be reasonable if a hearing was held beforehand? In *Occupiers of St Olivia Road v City of Johannesburg*,[57] the South African Constitutional Court, working

---

[57] *Occupiers of St Olivia Road v City of Johannesburg* (2008) 5 BCLR 475 (CC).

on the express constitutional right to housing (Section 26), required a two-way engagement process with affected persons before the City undertook evictions, which it had sought without making re-housing arrangements. The Court provided a useful remedy in requiring both parties to report on their engagement by filing further affidavits.

2.   Did the right to life include a right to housing, or a right to be provided with a job? Does the case illustrate the institutional limits of courts in addressing far-reaching social problems stemming from structural deficiencies? In *Ahmedabad Municipal Corporation v Nawab Khan Gulah Khan*,[58] the Court held that the state 'has the constitutional duty to provide adequate facilities and opportunities by distributing its wealth and resources for settlement of life and erection of shelter over their heads to make the right to life meaningful'. What is the use of declaratory judgments, urging housing authorities to developing housing schemes for the poor in a planned manner, as required by directive principles such as Articles 38, 39 and 46?

Bangladesh Legal Aid and Services Trust and others v Government of Bangladesh
Writ Petition No 5915 of 2005 (Supreme Court, Bangladesh)

Facts

A human rights NGO filed a writ petition in the public interest on behalf of the petitioners, some 127 families, (shopkeepers, small traders, maidservants, labourers, rickshaw drivers) living in Basti for some 20 years, developing the lowlands by making tiny slums over bamboo platforms. Various government ministries and NGOs operated programmes to alleviate their distressed conditions, providing primary health care and micro credit programmes. The Government had acquired the land for some housing projects. Sara Hossain, advocate for the petitioners, argued they had acquired a vested and legal right to be treated in accordance with the law by paying rent and bills, and through peaceful possession of the land. A *rule nisi* required the respondents to show cause why their threatened eviction of the slum dwellers, whom they argued were illegal occupants, from their peaceful possession of their homestead without due process of law should not be declared invalid, being contrary to their right to life after Article 32 of the Constitution.

Syed Md Ziaul Karim J

There is a clear and positive duty cast upon the Government under the Constitution to provide for the people inter alia, the basic necessities of life (including food, clothing, shelter, education and medical care), the right to work and the rights of social security, which read together, with the fundamental rights guaranteed by the Constitution, assured to the petitioner[s] . . . and the other dwellers of the Basti, the protection of their right to life. In spite of such part taken by the Government, some of the interested persons are trying to evict the inhabitants of the Basti immediately . . .

[Referring to Indian cases cited by petitioners including *Olga Tellis v Bombay Municipal Corporation* [1986] AIR SC 180 for the principle that the right to life includes the right to livelihood] . . . the inhabitants of any slum are the [unfortunates of society], homeless and provisionless; maybe due to river erosion, flood, drought, natural calamity, etc [they] became a floating rural population, having no profession, no provision for food, shelter and

---

[58] *Ahmedabad Municipal Corporation v Nawab Khan Gulah Khan* [1997] AIR SC 123, 133.

being poverty-stricken migrate to the urban area in quest of those necessities for their living on the earth . . . Their impoverishment leads them to float and flock together in certain areas where vacant space is available, to construct huts in slums, engaging themselves in the jobs of rickshaw-pulling, day labourers and garments workers, maids etc. The Government and the non-Government organizations sometimes come to their succour in a very unplanned manner for their rehabilitation, making some poor [people] turn into misguided terrorist/mastaans/drug traders/traffickers and violent arms cadre. So, the misfortune remains with them until their death.

Our Constitution, both in the Directive State Policy and in the preservation of the fundamental rights, provided that the State shall direct its policy towards securing that the citizens have the right to life, living and livelihood. Thus our country is pledge bound within its economic capacity and in an attempt for development to make effective provision for securing the right to life, livelihood, etc. As to the fundamental State Policy which is not enforceable and regarding fundamental rights, the Indian Supreme Court held in the case of *Olga Tellis vs Bombay Municipal Corporation* AIR 1986 SC 180; (1985) 3 SCC 454 that Article 37 provides that the directive principles, though not enforceable by any Court, are nevertheless fundamental in the governance of the Country. The principles contained in Articles 39(a) and 41 must be regarded as equally fundamental in the understanding and interpretation of the meaning and content of fundamental rights. If there is an obligation upon the State to secure to the citizen an adequate means of livelihood and the right to work, it would be sheer pedantry to exclude the right to livelihood from the content of the right to life. The State may not, by affirmative actions, be compellable to provide adequate means of livelihood or work to the citizens. But any person, who is deprived of his right to livelihood, except according to just and fair procedure established by law, can challenge the deprivation as offending the right to live conferred by Article 21.

The merits and demerits of the existence of slums in the Metropolitan City of Dhaka have not been disputed but the slum dwellers of necessity . . . have flocked together forming slums on the land of the Government and some other semi-Government or autonomous body, mostly on the road side, way side, wall side and near the railway lines. Their type of living not only endangers themselves but also renders the life of the City dwellers hazardous. They no doubt are contributing to the national economy by engaging as day labourers, rickshaw pullers, garment workers, handicrafts workers and as housemaids etc. But for a peaceful growth of City life for a country like ours, they have to be taken away from their slums and should be rehabilitated as far as possible in the spirit of our constitutional commitments attaining democracy, socialism, realising through democratic process a socialistic society free from exploitation, honouring the rule of law, fundamental human rights and freedom securing equality and justice.

. . . [T]he petitioners have alleged that the only provision for eviction of the slum dwellers is section 5 of the East Pakistan Government Land and Building (Recovery of Possession) Ordinance, 1970 by serving notice asking them to vacate the premises in occupation within the period of thirty days from the date of service thereof; but under the prevailing circumstances of the slum dwellers, [it is not possible to serve the notice] . . . due to their floating nature . . . as they live mostly in basti and have no fixed number and address. The Government has asserted that they have notified them of eviction. It is true that in the facts and circumstances of the present case, it was not possible to issue notice to all slum dwellers under the provision of section 5 of the Ordinance; but it may be that these slum dwellers are [the sector of society] which a poor country like ours is most concerned with, such that they need to be evicted under certain specific rehabilitation programmes, which should work as a guideline in the matter. There should be a survey of all the families residing in any particular slum. There should be a master plan or rehabilitation scheme or pilot projects to rehabilitate the slum dwellers. The slum dwellers should be given the option either to go and live at their respective rural villages or to stay in urban area. If they opt to go to the urban areas, they must be provided with funds/loan for construction of houses and small scale income generating projects for sustainance [*sic*], with proper and regular monitoring by the State; until they are fully rehabilitated in any profession, they should if possible be provided with food under the VGF project of the government. Similarly in the case of slum dwellers who do not opt to go to the rural home because of their dislocation by flood and river erosion, natural calamity, etc they should be given the choice either to live in the slum or to go elsewhere . . . [If they choose] to stay in slums, they should be rehabilitated bearing in mind the vicinity of their working place and communication facilities; if they are not employed, [they should be provided for] by erecting huts in any localised area earmarked for rehabilitation to start with; subsequently they should be rehabilitated [by providing them with] any low cost flats/ houses at nominal price, with arrangements made for vocational training or any work or employment on the basis of the principle: from each according to his ability to each according to his work, by the authority concerned.

There may be a good number of old, inferior crippled and retarded people living in the slums. They being incapable of moving/carrying on their livelihood are dependent on others. The government should arrange for their rehabilitation by constructing huts/infirm homes/retarded homes providing food, shelter, medical facilities and clothing; they should be given vocational training so that they could earn their own livelihood in due course.

In an identical matter, this Court, in the case of *Ain O Salish Kendro (ASK) v Government of Bangladesh* reported in 19 BLD 488 at paragraph 17 laid down some guidelines [which they] referred . . . to [guide] the Government [in rehabilitating] the slum dwellers, which reads:

> The Government should undertake a master plan for rehabilitation schemes or pilot projects for rehabilitation of the slum dwellers and undertake eviction of the slum dwellers according to the capacity of their available abode and with option to the dwellers either to go to their village home or to stay back leading an urban life, otherwise the wholesale demolition of slums may not solve the problem because the evicted persons from one slum may flock together to another place forming a slum or slums and thereby mounting problems for the government and the country. We have been told that ECNEC has also approved construction of residential apartments for the slum dwellers and lower income people. We appreciate the Government anxiety but considering the human aspects that is attached to the slum dwellers, we provided the guidelines to the Government to undertake a master plan rehabilitation scheme/pilot programme for rehabilitation by evicting the slums phase by phase, otherwise the wholesale removal will give rise to multiple problems for the society and the State.

We are in respectful agreement . . . Moreover, in *Kalam v Bangladesh* reported in 21 BLD-446, at paragraph no 6, his Lordship Mr Justice A.B.M. Khairul Haque observed that:

> Bangladesh came into being as a fulfillment of the dreams of the millions of Bangalis so that they can breathe in an independent country of their own. They knew that their country is not rich but expected that social justice shall be established and the people shall be provided with the bare minimum necessities of life. Admittedly, the petitioner nos 1–5 and other slum dwellers do not claim any property right on any land. They are only begging for a place to hide their heads so that they can themselves earn their own livelihood just to survive in this world, created by God. It should not be forgotten that God in His unbounded mercy provides sunshine, air, water, food and all other amenities of life for all, high or low, rich or poor, for every living being, without any discrimination. The Constitution of the People's Republic of Bangladesh envisages a welfare state and

makes all citizens equal in the eye of law. As such, all citizens have got equal rights in every sphere of life including food, shelter, health-care, education and so forth which is fundamental in nature. It is not the fault of the petitioners and slum dwellers that their Government fails to provide them with such bare necessities of life. They are only struggling [in] a losing battle to earn for themselves and to care and provide the bare minimum necessities of life to their children which are the primary objectives of any democratic Government. After all the slum dwellers, poorest of the poor they may be, without any future or dreams for tomorrow, whose every day ends with a saga of struggle with a bleak hope for survival tomorrow . . . are also citizens of this Country, theoretically at least, with equal rights. Their fundamental rights may not be fully honoured because of the limitations on the part of the State but they should not be treated, for any reason, as slaves or chattels, rather as equal human beings, and they have got a right to be treated fairly and with dignity, otherwise all commitments made in the sacred Constitution of the People's Republic, shall prove to be a mere mockery.

[Concluding that the slum-dwellers] shall not be evicted without their rehabilitation under government programmes, to be given effect to within two years from the date of eviction; no order for costs] . . .

Notes and Questions

1. The Court recommended resettlement but did not find this to be a right. In *Ain o Salish Kendra (ASK) v Government of Bangladesh*,[59] the Court laid down some guidelines for rehabilitation of slum-dwellers in demolition cases, such as giving reasonable notice before eviction, allowing eviction to proceed in phases and developing resettlement projects. However, the Government has continued to effect forcible eviction without providing alternative accommodation: see 'Forced Evictions in Bangladesh: We didn't stand a chance' (Centre on Housing Rights and Evictions and Asian Coalition of Housing Rights Mission Report, 2000).

2. In *Society for the Enforcement of Human Rights (BSEHR) v Government of Bangladesh*,[60] sex workers who were residents of Nimtali and Tanbazar brothels in Narayangaj were forcibly evicted from their rented dwelling with their children during a police raid conducted around 3–4 am while they were asleep. They were bussed with their children and detained against their will at various vagrant homes. This wholesale eviction was done to 'rehabilitate the sex workers'. Several human rights NGOs commenced public interest litigation through a writ petition, challenging this action and their detention without lawful authority. Under Article 18(2), the state is to 'adopt effective measures' to prevent prostitution, which is not criminalised. The Court referred to the Indian decision of *Olga Tellis v Bombay Municipal Corporation* AIR 1986 (SC) 180 and held:

    The evicted prostitutes of Nimtali and Tanbazar are citizens of Bangladesh, are enrolled as voters and do exercise the right of franchise. Though prostitution is not a socially recognized profession in Bangladesh . . . the prostitutes initially get themselves enrolled with the local administration, sometimes swearing an affidavit expressing the desire to be

[59] *Ain o Salish Kendra (ASK) v Government of Bangladesh* 19 BLD (1999) 488.
[60] *Society for the Enforcement of Human Rights (BSEHR) v Government of Bangladesh* 53 DLR (2001) 1.

a prostitute and get themselves confined to the place called brothel and get the required protection to continue in their profession from the local and police administration, in spite of the provisions of the Suppression of Immoral Traffic Act, 1933. [As the sex workers] are maintaining their earnings/livelihood, the State in the absence of any prohibitory legislation, has a duty to protect this and a citizen has the right to enforce that right enshrined in Articles 31 and 32 of the Constitution. Article 11 provides for the dignity of human person [but is] not enforceable, but the sex workers as citizens have enforceable rights under Articles 31 and 32.[61]

The Court observed that the sex workers through the wholesale eviction were deprived of their livelihood, which was tantamount to an unconstitutional deprivation of their right to life, censuring as shameful the police's failure to fulfil their obligations to protect the rights of the sex workers. In addition, the Court reaffirmed that 'nobody could violate the privacy of the inmates of any house or trespass into it except in accordance with law'. In this instance, 'the fundamental right of the citizen to be secured in his home against entry has definitely been breached/violated' by interested parties or the police themselves. In addition, any rehabilitation scheme

> must not be incompatible with their dignity and worth as human persons but be designed to uplift personal morals and family life and provision for jobs, giving them option to be rehabilitated or to be with their relations and providing facilities for better education, family connection and economic opportunities in order to do much to minimize the conditions that gave rise to prostitution.[62]

The authorities were directed to release the prostitutes.

3. In Pakistan, in *Chakar Ali Khan Rind v Government of Balochistan*,[63] the government authorities were obliged to build a wall to protect residents of an area susceptible to floods caused by dam construction, under the Article 9 guarantee of life and liberty.

4. In Malaysia, the Court of Appeal, in *Tan Tek Seng v Suruhanjaya Perkhidmatan Pendidikan*,[64] concerning the dismissal of a public servant which affected his livelihood, construed Article 5 ('No person shall be deprived of life . . . save in accordance with the law') liberally, drawing from Indian precedents which affirmed that 'life' entailed something more than mere animal existence, citing cases like *Bandhua Mukti Morcha v Union of India*,[65] *Olga Tellis v Bombay Municipal Corp*[66] and *Frances Mullin's case*,[67] which drew a distinct link between the Indian right to life clause (Article 21) and its DPSP, and the power of the court to review existing legislation designed to protect workers' rights for non-compliance. However, the Malaysian Constitution itself does not have a preamble, neither is Indian case law binding as precedent, merely persuasive. In reading the Court's attempt to justify

---

[61] Ibid, [11].
[62] Ibid, [36].
[63] *Chakar Ali Khan Rind v Government of Balochistan*, Constitutional Petition No 635 of 2009, 2011 CLC 601.
[64] *Tan Tek Seng v Suruhanjaya Perkhidmatan Pendidikan* [1996] 1 MLJ 261.
[65] *Bandhua Mukti Morcha v Union of India* [1984] AIR SC 802, 811–12.
[66] *Olga Tellis v Bombay Municipal Corp* [1986] AIR SC 180.
[67] *Frances Coralie Mullin v WC Khambra* [1980] AIR SC 849.

its application of Indian precedent, can you make sense of why reference was made to both the 'true intention' of the constitutional framers and the constitution as a 'living document?' Gopal Sri Ram SCJ held:

[T]he Federal Constitution, unlike the Indian Constitution, does not contain any Directive Principles of State Policy. Nevertheless, it is plain from the copious and continuous stream of beneficial legislation that is presented at almost every sitting of Parliament and from the voluminous subsidiary legislation that is promulgated periodically, that the elected government is set on improving the lot of the common man. Almost on a daily basis we see regulations being made to better the living and working conditions of our labour force. There are ceaseless and untiring efforts by the elected government, through its several agencies, to provide basic amenities and to improve the quality of life of the masses. Steps are being constantly taken to guard against any deterioration in the quality of the environment in which the populace live and work. Indeed, it is the declared policy of the government to provide housing, water, electricity and communication systems to the far flung areas of our country. And one can plainly see the ceaseless exertions on the part of the elected government to achieve the targeted policy.

In my judgment, the courts should keep in tandem with the national ethos when interpreting provisions of a living document like the Federal Constitution, lest they be left behind while the winds of modern and progressive change pass them by. Judges must not be blind to the realities of life. Neither should they wear blinkers when approaching a question of constitutional interpretation. They should, when discharging their duties as interpreters of the supreme law, adopt a liberal approach in order to implement the true intention of the framers of the Federal Constitution. Such an objective may only be achieved if the expression 'life' in art 5(1) is given a broad and liberal meaning.

. . . [T]he expression 'life' appearing in art 5(1) does not refer to mere existence. It incorporates all those facets that are an integral part of life itself and those matters which go to form the quality of life [including] the right to seek and be engaged in lawful and gainful employment and to receive those benefits that our society has to offer to its members. It includes the right to live in a reasonably healthy and pollution free environment. For the purposes of this case, it encompasses the right to continue in public service subject to removal for good cause by resort to a fair procedure.[68]

In *Bato Bagi v Kerajaan Negeri Sarawak*,[69] the Malaysian Federal Court held that the Sarawak Land Code, which extinguished Native Customary Rights (NCR) over land needed to build the Bakun Dam and pulpwood mill, did not violate Articles 5 or 13 of the Constitution. Article 13 protects the right to property, which cannot be compulsorily acquired for a public purpose without 'adequate compensation' or without public purpose. Although not fully argued, it was put forward that by extinguishing NCR, given the natives' relationship with the land and their total dependency on it for their livelihood, this destroyed their livelihood contrary to Article 5, following *Tan Tek Seng*. The Constitution mandated compensation for deprivation of property, which the Court accepted could include livelihood as well. In calculating the amount of compensation, not for the land but what was above the land,[70] the Court could consider how the right to life/livelihood of the natives was affected.

---

[68] *Tan Tek Seng v Suruhanjaya Perkhidmatan Pendidikan* [1996] 1 MLJ 261, 287 [66].
[69] *Bato Bagi v Kerajaan Negeri Sarawak* [2011] 6 MLJ 297.
[70] Following *Adong bin Kuwau v Kerajaan Negeri Johor* [1997] 1 MLJ 418.

B. Right to Life and the Right to Food

People's Union for Civil Liberties v Union of India & Ors
Writ Petition (Civil) No 196 of 2001 (Supreme Court, India)

Facts

The People's Union for Civil Liberties (PUCL) in April 2001 filed a petition before the Supreme Court to enforce the food distribution schemes and the Famine Code (permitting release of grain during famines), following death by starvation in Rajasthan state, even though the country's food stocks were at a high. This petition was based on the right to food, derived from the Article 21 right to life and the failure of the relevant Central and State governments to deal with the drought situation. The Court has since issued various Interim Orders.

Interim Order of 28th November 2001

After hearing learned counsel for the parties, we issue, as an interim measure, the following directions:

1 Targeted Public Distribution Scheme (TPDS)

i.   It is the case of the Union of India (UOI) that there has been full compliance with regard to the allotment of food grain in relation to the TPDS. However, if any of the States gives a specific instance of non-compliance, the UOI will do the needful within the framework of the Scheme.
ii.   The States are directed to complete the identification of BPL (Below Poverty Line) families, issuing of cards and commencement of distribution of 25 kgs grain per family per month latest by 1st January, 2002.
iii. The Delhi Government will ensure that the TPDS application forms are freely available and are given and received free of charge and there is an effective mechanism in place to ensure speedy and effective redressal of grievances.

2 Antyodaya Anna Yojana (ration card)

i.   It is the case of the UOI that there has been full compliance with regard to the allotment of foodgrain in relation to Antyodaya Anna Yojana. However, if any of the States gives a specific instance of non-compliance, the Union of India will do the needful within the framework of the scheme.
ii.   We direct the States and the Union Territories to complete identification of beneficiaries, issuing of cards and distribution of grain under this scheme latest by 1st January, 2002.
iii. It appears that some Antyodaya beneficiaries may be unable to lift grain because of penury. In such cases, the Centre, the States and the Union Territories are requested to consider lifting the quota fee after satisfying itself in this behalf.

3 Mid Day Meal Scheme (MDMS)

i.   It is the case of the UOI that there has been full compliance with regard to the Mid Day Meal scheme (MDMS), However, if any of the States gives a specific instance of non-compliance, the Union of India will do the needful within the framework of the Scheme.

ii. We direct the state Governments/ Union Territories to implement the Mid Day Meal Scheme by providing every child in every Government and Government assisted Primary Schools with a prepared mid day meal with a minimum content of 300 calories and 8–12 grams of protein each day of school for a minimum of 200 days. Those Governments providing dry rations instead of cooked meals must within three months start providing cooked meals in all Government and Government-aided primary schools in all half Districts of the state (in order of poverty) and must within a further period of three months extend the provision of cooked meals to the remaining parts of the state.

iii. We direct the UOI and the FCI to ensure provision of fair average quality grain for the Scheme on time. The states/Union Territories and the FCI are directed to do joint inspection of food grains. If the food grain is found, on joint inspection, not to be of fair average quality, it will be replaced by the FCI prior to lifting.

4 National Old Age Pension Scheme (NOAPS)

[Direction to identify the beneficiaries and to make payments by 1st January 2002 latest.]

5 Annapurna Scheme

The States/Union Territories are directed to identify the beneficiaries and distribute the grain latest by 1st January, 2002.

6 Integrated Child Development Scheme (ICDS)

We direct the state Governments/Union Territories to implement the Integrated Child Development Scheme (ICDS) in full and to ensure that every ICDS disbursing centre in the country shall provide as under:

i. Each child up to 6 years of age to get 300 calories and 8–10 grams of protein;
ii. Each adolescent girl to get 500 calories and 20–25 grams of protein;
iii. Each pregnant woman and each nursing mother to get 500 calories and 20–25 grams of protein;
iv. Each malnourished child to get 600 calories and 16–20 grams of protein;
v. Have a disbursement centre in every settlement.

7 National Maternity Benefit Scheme (NMBS)

We direct the state Governments/Union Territories to implement the National Maternity Benefit scheme (NMBS) by paying all BPL pregnant women Rs. 500/- through the Sarpanch, 8–12 weeks prior to delivery for each of the first two births . . .

8 National Family Benefit Scheme (NFBS)

We direct the State Governments/Union Territories to implement the National Family Benefit Scheme and pay a BPL family Rs. 10,000/- within four weeks through a local Sarpanch, whenever the primary bread winner of the family dies.

I. We direct that a copy of this order be translated in regional languages and in English by the respective States/Union Territories and prominently displayed in all Gram Panchayats, Government School Buildings and Fair Price Shops.

II. In order to ensure transparency in selection of beneficiaries and their access to these Schemes, the Gram Panchayats will also display a list of all beneficiaries under the various schemes. Copies of the schemes and the list of beneficiaries shall be made available by the Gram Panchayats to members of public for inspection.

III. We direct Doordarshan and AIR to adequately publicise various Schemes and this order.

IV. We direct the Chief Secretaries of each of the States and Union Territories to ensure compliance of this order. They will report compliance by filing affidavits in this court within 8 weeks from today with copies to the AG and counsel for the petitioner.

V. We grant liberty to the Union of India to file affidavit pursuant to the order of this Court dated 21st November, 2001. List the matter for further orders on 11th February, 2002. In the meanwhile, liberty is granted to the parties to apply for further directions, if any.

Text of the Order, 8th May 2002

... (2) On a complaint being made to the Chief Executive Officer of the Zila Panchayat (CEO)/Collector regarding noncompliance of the orders of this Court the concerned CEO/Collector shall record the salient features of the complaint in a register maintained for this purpose, acknowledge receipt of the complaint and forthwith secure compliance with this Court's order.

(3) The CEO/Collector of all the Districts in the States and territories shall scrutinize the action taken by all the implementing agencies within their jurisdiction to ensure compliance with this court's orders and report to the Chief Secretary.

(4) The responsibility for implementation of the order of this Court shall be that of the CEO/Collector. The Chief Secretary will ensure compliance with the order of this Court.

(5) Dr NC Saxena, former planning secretary, government of India, and Mr SR Shankaran, former secretary, rural development, Government of India, shall function as Commissioners of this Court for the purpose of looking into any grievance that may persist after the above-mentioned grievance resolution procedure has been exhausted.

(6) On the Commissioner's recommending a course of action to ensure compliance with this Court's order, the State Government/UT administrations, shall forthwith act upon such recommendation and report compliance.

Interim Order of May 2, 2003

In this petition that was filed little more than two years back various issues have been framed many of which may have a direct and important relevance to the very existence of poor people; their right to life and the right of food of those who can ill-afford to provide to their families two meals day. Their misfortune becomes further grave during the times of famines and drought. The petitioner has sought directions for enforcement of Famine Code. The petitioner seeks immediate release of surplus food-grains lying in the stocks of Union of India for drought affected areas. Directions are also sought requiring the Government to frame fresh schemes of Public Distribution for Scientific and Reasonable Distribution of food-grains. In order that any meaningful and immediate relief is given by the Central Government and the State Government without any delay various applications have been filed by the petitioner. Considering the importance of the matter particularly in relation to those who are Below Poverty Line (BPL) an order was made by this Hon'ble Court on 3rd March, 2003 requiring the respondents to file replies to the applications and place on record the requisite materials, while adjourning the case to the 8th April, 2003. In respect of the directions that the Central Government shall formulate the scheme to extend the benefits of the Antyodaya Anna Yojana (AAY) to destitute sections of the population, learned Attorney General stated on the last date of hearing which was on 3rd March, 2003 that for the budget for the year 2003–2004 a provision has been made for it. Despite the order of this Court the document has not been placed on record. The approach of Government is more distressing since this matter which was to come up on 8th April, 2002, has come up today after nearly four weeks of the scheduled date but neither the documents have been filed . . .

This Court in various orders passed in the last two years has expressed its deep concern and it has been observed, in one of the orders, that what is of utmost importance is to see that food is provided to the aged, infirm, disabled, destitute women, destitute men who are in danger of starvation, pregnant and lactating women and destitute children, especially in cases where they or members of their family do not have sufficient funds to provide food for them. In case of famine, there may be shortage of food, but here the situation is that amongst plenty there is scarcity. Plenty of food is available, but distribution of the same amongst the very poor and the destitute is scarce and non-existent leading to malnutrition, starvation and other related problems. The anxiety of the Court is to see that poor and the destitute and the weaker sections of the society do not suffer from hunger and starvation. The prevention of the same is one of the prime responsibilities of the Government – whether Central or the State. Mere schemes without any implementation are of no use. What is important is that the food must reach the hungry.

Article 21 of the Constitution of India protects for *every* citizen a right to live with human dignity. Would the very existence of life of those families which are below poverty line not come under danger for want of appropriate schemes and implementation thereof, to provide requisite aid to such families? Reference can also be made to Article 47 which inter alia provides that the State shall regard the raising of the level of nutrition and the standard of living of its people and the improvement of public health as among its primary duties.

[The Court issued directions for temporary relief for May–July 2003 including the enforcement of the Famine Code.]

. . . [I]t is necessary to issue immediate directions to evolve a system whereby eligible BPL families, which may not be on BPL list, are so included as also regarding the ration shops and other outlets remaining open and giving deliveries of food-grains to those who are on the list and hold the requisite cards. To facilitate the supply of the grain, we issue the following directions:

(1) Licensees, who

   (a) do not keep their shops open throughout the month during the stipulated period;
   (b) fail to provide grain to BPL families strictly at BPL rates and no higher;
   (c) keep the cards of BPL households with them;
   (d) make false entries in the BPL cards;
   (e) engage in black-marketing or siphoning away of grains to the open market and hand over such ration shops to such other person/organizations

   shall make themselves liable for cancellation of their licences. The concerned authorities/functionaries would not show any laxity on the subject.
(2) Permit the BPL household to buy the ration in instalments.
(3) Wide publicity shall be given so as to make BPL families aware of their entitlement of food-grains.

. . . We direct the Government of India to place on AAY (Antyodaya Anna Yozana) category the following groups of persons:–

(1) aged, infirm, disabled, destitute men and women, pregnant and lactating women;
(2) widows and other single women with no regular support;
(3) old persons (aged 60 or above) with no regular support and no assured means of subsistence;
(4) households with a disabled adult and assured means of subsistence;
(5) households where due to old age, lack of physical or mental fitness, social customs, need to care for a disabled, or other reasons, no adult member is available to engage in gainful employment outside the house;
(6) primitive tribes.

Regarding the 28 November 2001 directions on Mid Day Meal

. . . Some States in implementation of the said direction are supplying a cooked mid day meal to the students. We are, however, told that despite the fact that 1½ years has passed, some of the States have not even made a beginning. Particular reference has been made to States of Bihar, Jharkhand and Uttar Pradesh. It is not in dispute that in these three States even beginning has not been made whereas some of the other States are fully implementing directions for supply of cooked Mid Day Meal. Counsel for Uttar Pradesh and Jharkhand could not give any satisfactory reason for non-implementation. No reply or affidavit was filed by the said State. In so far as the State of Bihar is concerned, Mr BB Singh has drawn our attention to the affidavit filed by Secretary and Relief Commissioner, Relief and Rehabilitation Department, Government of Bihar, inter alia stating that the State Government proposes to implement this scheme in few blocks on a pilot basis through panchayat, pending settlement of the issue regarding funding of conversion cost and to establish the capacity of the panchayat raj institution to supply hygienic cooked meals to all eligible students on a regular basis, without compromising teaching activities. The affidavit could not be more vague than what it is. When they propose to start, in how many districts they propose to start, what scheme has been formulated and every other conceivable detail is missing from the affidavit. We are told that there are 38 districts in the State of Bihar. For the present, we direct the said State to implement the cooked Mid Day Meal Scheme in terms of the directions of this Court in at least 10 Districts, which may be most poor according to the State's perception.

We also direct the State of Uttar Pradesh, Jharkhand and other States to make a meaningful beginning of the cooked Mid Day Meal Scheme in at least 25% of the District, which may be most poor.

Text of the Order of 20th April, 2004

[Concerning the affidavits filed by States as to the implementation of the Mid-Day Meals Scheme.]

Mid Day Meals Scheme

Some of the States which claim that they have made a beginning and are partially implementing the scheme have also not given the full and complete details so that this Court could know the extent of the implementation. Most of the affidavits only set out the number of schools and the students where the scheme was being implemented. What was required to be done was to simply state as to how many schools in a particular State/Union Territory would be covered under the directions for supply of cooked Mid Day Meals, how many students in the said school would be eligible for the benefit and then give the number of the schools and the students who are being supplied cooked meals. The affidavits provide only a part of information without specifying the number of eligible schools and students.

[With respect to the Commissioners' report] . . . after the said Report, there has been some improvement by a token beginning having been made by some of the States. The report of the Commissioners, on the basis of their earlier experience, states that nutritious Mid Day Meals at schools can be a highly effective way of protecting children from hunger and can also boost school attendance among girls. It also notices some of the areas where such meals are supplied even during the school vacations, especially in drought affected areas. None can question the desirability of extension of this facility even during vacations in drought affected areas where children are deprived of even one daytime meal.

It is a matter of anguish that despite a lapse of nearly three and half years, the order dated 28th November, 2001 has not been fully implemented by all the States and Union Territories . . . It is a constitutional duty of every State and Union Territory to implement in letter and spirit the directions contained in the order dated 28th November, 2001 . . .

1. All such States and Union Territories who have not fully complied with the order dated 28th November, 2001 shall comply with the said directions fully in respect of the entire State/Union Territory, preferably, on the re-opening of the primary schools after a long vacation of 2004 and, in any case, not later than 1st September, 2004.

2. All Chief Secretaries/Administrators are directed to file compliance reports in regard to direction No 1 on or before 15th September, 2004.

3. The conversion costs for a cooked meals, under no circumstances, shall be recovered from the children or their parents.

4. In appointment of cooks and helpers, preference shall be given to Dalits, Scheduled Castes and Scheduled Tribes.

5. The Central Government shall make provisions for construction of kitchen sheds and shall also allocate funds to meet with the conversion costs of food-grains into cooked Mid Day Meals. It shall also periodically monitor the low take up of the food-grains.

6. In respect of the State of Uttarakhand, it has been represented that the scheme is being implemented in all the schools. It would be open to the Commissioners to inspect and bring it to the notice of the Court, if it is otherwise.

7. In drought affected areas, Mid Day Meals shall be supplied even during summer vacations.

8. An affidavit shall be filed by the Government of India, within three months, stating as to when it is possible to extend the scheme up to 10th standard in compliance with the announcement made by the Prime Minister. The affidavit shall also state the time frame within which the Government proposes to implement the recommendations of Abhijit Sen committee in respect whereof the modalities have been discussed with the concerned Ministries and Planning Commission.

9. Attempts shall be made for better infrastructure, improved facilities (safe drinking water etc), closer monitoring (regular inspection etc) and other quality safeguards as also the improvement of the contents of the meal so as to provide a nutritious meal to the children of the primary schools.

Notes and Questions

1. The Court considered that the Central Government was responsible for monitoring the implementation of the Mid Day Meal Scheme and directed it to file an affidavit concerning how it meant to manage, monitor and evaluate the programme; State governments were to claim cooking costs from the Central Government. The Court's Commissioners continued to make their reports, and the Court demanded compliance reports with its directions from States and Union Territories.[71] See generally *Supreme Court Orders on the Right to Food: A Tool for Action* (New Delhi: Right to Food Campaign, 2008), available at <http://www.righttofoodindia.org/data/scordersprimeratoolforaction.pdf>.

2. What role does the Court play in the realisation of the right to food? How effective is its follow-up mechanism?

3. The decision catalysed an India-wide movement for the implementation of food programmes, and was in no small measure aided by civil society movements seeking to transform government policy into justiciable rights of the people. See *Report of the Special Rapporteur on the Right to Food: Mission to India*, UN Doc E/CN.4/2006/44/Add.2 (2006).

4. Socio-economic rights impose three different levels of state obligations: the obligation to respect requires states not to interfere with the enjoyment of rights; the obligation to protect requires states to prevent third party rights violations; the obligation to fulfil requires States to take appropriate legislative, administrative, budgetary, judicial and other measures towards the full realisation of such rights. One might add to this the obligation to promote a right, to undertake measures to serve long-term objectives, such as training programmes to, say, help raise agricultural productivity in service of the right to food. See *Maastricht Guidelines on Violations of Economic, Social and Cultural Rights* UN Doc E/C.12/2000/13 (Maastricht, January 22–26, 1997). Which obligation did the Supreme Court deal with in the *PUCL* case? Did it specify a 'minimum core' of the right to food, and spell out both obligations of conduct and result?

5   The Indian Supreme Court has protected the right to livelihood of traditional fisherfolk and farmers against the shrimping industry, as shrimp farms had brought about severe environmental and socio-economic consequences. It held that the conversion of agricultural land into coastal aquaculture units infringed the fundamental right to life and livelihood. The Court banned high-tech shrimp farms within 500 metres of the high-tide line or within 1,000 metres of public lands. That is, all industrial shrimp aquaculture farms operating within the Coastal Regulation Zone had to cease operations. The Court affirmed the acceptance as part of the law of the land of the precautionary and 'polluter pays' principles.[72] A similar case was heard in Bangladesh.[73]

---

[71] Eg *People's Union for Civil Liberties v Union of India & Ors* [2009] INSC 811 (22 April 2009).
[72] *Jagannath v Union of India* (1997) 2 SCC 87.
[73] *Khushi Kabir v Government of Bangladesh* (WP No 3091 of 2000).

C. Right to Life and Right to Health

The right to health is enshrined as a right in various constitutions: Indonesia,[74] Nepal,[75] Thailand,[76] Timor-Leste.[77] In some other constitutions, states are compelled to provide health services or improve public health through legislation and administrative pro-grammes, treating health as a socio-economic objective rather than a justiciable right: Myanmar,[78] Sri Lanka,[79] India,[80] Bhutan[81] and Bangladesh.[82] Socialist constitutions like that of Vietnam may provide that 'Citizens are entitled to health care',[83] but these are non-justiciable. In countries like Malaysia, where the right to health is neither an express right nor a judicially recognised implicit one, SERs such as the right to health have been promoted in non-judicial settings like SUHAKAM, the National Human Rights Commission.[84]

South Asian courts like India have read DPSP into Article 21 to declare a right to health. In *Consumer Education & Research v Union of India*,[85] Article 21 of the Indian Constitution was found to contain a right to health and to medical aid to protect a worker's health and vigour during and after employment, read with Articles 39(3), 41, 43, 48A (directive principles) as well as human rights, to make the life of the workman meaningful and purposeful with the dignity of a person. Lack of health 'denudes his livelihood'. This case concerned the exposure of workers to asbestos. The Court directed industries to maintain health records for a minimum 40-year period, private factories were directed compulsorily to insure worker health coverage and the relevant governments were to review standards of permissible exposure every 10 years. Another facet of human health and public sanitation was evident in *Dr KC Malhotra v State of Madhya Pradesh*,[86] where the Madhya Pradesh High Court, in reading Article 21 with Article 47 (improving public health), ordered the relevant municipal corporation to deal with the open sewers problem by covering open drains, constructing extra public latrines, taking steps to educate backward classes like the *dalits* about measures to prevent water pollution and providing a sewage line separate from the drinking water pipeline. Such measures 'improve the life conditions of the weaker sections of society', ensuring them social justice in having fresh and non-contaminated water.

---

[74] Art 28H, Constitution of the Republic of Indonesia. See generally B Susanti, 'The Implementation of the Rights to Health Care and Education in Indonesia' in V Gauri and DM Brins (ed), *Courting Social Justice: Judicial Enforcement of Social and Economic Rights in the Developing World* (Cambridge: Cambridge University Press, 2008) 224.

[75] Art 16, Interim Constitution of Nepal.

[76] Pt 9, Sec 51, Constitution of the Kingdom of Thailand.

[77] Sec 57, Constitution of Timor Leste.

[78] Art 28, Constitution of Myanmar.

[79] Art 27, Constitution of Sri Lanka.

[80] Arts 39 and 47, Constitution of the Union of India.

[81] Art 9, Constitution of Bhutan.

[82] Art 18, Constitution of Bangladesh.

[83] Art 61, Constitution of Vietnam.

[84] 'New program supports action on ESCR rights', *Asia Pacific Forum*, 20 November 2012, available at <http://www.asiapacificforum.net/carousel/news/new-program-supports-action-on-esc-rights>.

[85] *Consumer Education & Research v Union of India* [1995] AIR 922, [1995] SCC (3) 42.

[86] *Dr KC Malhotra v State of Madhya Pradesh* [1994] AIR MP 43.

Laxmi Mandal v Deen Dayal Harinagar Hospital
WP(C) 8853/2008 (Supreme Court, India)

Note and Issue

A petition was bought on behalf of Shanti Devi, a poor Dalit woman living below the poverty line, who died after she was repeatedly denied adequate maternal healthcare. This was despite the fact that she qualified for existing state-sponsored schemes to reduce infant and maternal mortality, because her husband was unable to provide the relevant ration card. Devi was forced to carry a dead foetus in her womb for five days and died after giving birth at home, without medical attention. The Supreme Court in *PUCL v Union of India* Writ Petition No 196 of 2001 (excerpted above) recognised the interrelatedness of schemes relating to maternity benefit, family benefit and food. The schemes were designed to promote institutional delivery among poor pregnant women, and to promote safe motherhood and post-natal care. Other schemes provided for cash assistance, child nutrition, health education and services. The Antyodaya Anna Yojana scheme provided food rations to identified beneficiaries who were given cards to receive distributed grain.

Justice Muralidhar

Although the chief protagonists in the two petitions are the two mothers and their babies, the petitions highlight the gaps in implementation that affect a large number of similarly placed women and children elsewhere in the country. The petitions reveal the unsatisfactory state of implementation of the schemes in the two 'high performing states' of Haryana and the National Capital Territory of Delhi (NCT of Delhi). These petitions . . . focus on two inalienable survival rights that form part of the right to life. One is the right to health, which would include the right to access government (public) health facilities and receive a minimum standard of treatment and care. In particular this would include the enforcement of the reproductive rights of the mother and the right to nutrition and medical care of the newly born child and continuously thereafter till the age of about six years. The other facet is the right to food which is seen as integral to the right to life and right to health.

The right to health forming an inalienable component of the right to life under Article 21 of the Constitution has been settled in two important decisions of the Supreme Court: *Pt Parmanand Katara v UOI* (1989) 4 SCC 286 and *Paschim Banga Khet Majoor Samiti v State of West Bengal* (1996) 4 SCC 37. The orders in the *PUCL Case* are a continuation of the efforts of the Supreme Court at protecting and enforcing the right to health of the mother and the child and underscoring the interrelatedness of those rights with the right to food. This is consistent with the international human rights law which is briefly discussed hereafter. [Discusses Article 25 UDHR and Articles 10 (special protection for mothers before and after childbirth) and 12 ICESCR ('right to everyone to the enjoyment of the highest attainable standard of physical and mental health', including taking steps to reduce the stillbirth rate and infant mortality)] . . .

The Committee on Economic Social and Cultural Rights has in its General Comment No 14 of 2000 on the right to health under the ICESCR explained the scope of the rights as under:

8. The right to health is not to be understood as a right to be healthy. The right to health contains both freedoms and entitlements. The freedoms include the right to control one's health and body, including sexual and reproductive freedom, and the right to be free from interference, such as the right to be free from torture, non-consensual medical treatment and experimentation. By contrast, the entitlements include the right

to a system of health protection which provides equality of opportunity for people to enjoy the highest attainable level of health . . .

. . .

11. The Committee interprets the right to health, as defined in Article 12.1, as an inclusive right extending not only to timely and appropriate health care but also to the underlying determinants of health, such as access to safe and potable water and adequate sanitation, an adequate supply of safe food, nutrition and housing, healthy occupational and environmental conditions, and access to health-related education and information, including on sexual and reproductive health. A further important aspect is the participation of the population in all health-related decision-making at the community, national and international levels . . .

. . . 14. 'The provision for the reduction of the stillbirth rate and of infant mortality and for the healthy development of the child' (art 12.2 (a)) may be understood as requiring measures to improve child and maternal health, sexual and reproductive health services, including access to family planning, pre- and post-natal care, emergency obstetric services and access to information, as well as to resources necessary to act on that information.

[Discusses reproductive rights (Article 12) and the rights of rural women (Article 14) in CEDAW, and the rights of the newly born and young child in Articles 24, 27 CRC] . . . International human rights norms as contained in the Conventions which have been ratified by India are binding on India to the extent they are not inconsistent with the domestic law norms. The Protection of Human Rights WP(C) Nos 8853 of 2008 & 10700 of 2009 page 18 of 51 Act, 1993 (PHRA) recognises that the above Conventions are now part of the Indian human rights law. Section 2(d) PHRA defines 'human rights' to mean 'the rights relating to life, liberty, equality and dignity of the individual guaranteed by the Constitution or embodied in the International Covenants and enforceable by courts in India' and under Section 2(f) PHRA 'International Covenants' means 'the International Covenant on Civil and Political Rights and the International Covenant on Economic, Social and Cultural Rights adopted by the General Assembly of the United Nations on the 16th December, 1966.'

The orders in the *PUCL Case* implicitly recognize and enforce the fundamental right to life under Article 21 of the Constitution of the child and the mother. This includes the right to health, reproductive health and the right to food. In effect, the Supreme Court has spelt out what the 'minimum core' of the right to health and food is, and also spelt out, consistent with international human rights law, the 'obligations of conduct' and the 'obligations of result' of the Union of India, the States and the Union Territories. While recognizing the indivisibility of civil rights and social and economic rights, the Supreme Court has made them enforceable in courts of law by using the device of a 'continuing mandamus.' On their part, the High Courts in this country would be obligated to carry forth the mandate of the orders of the Supreme Court to ensure the implementation of those orders within the States and Union Territories.

[Aside from monetary relief and making available the benefits of the schemes to the relevant parties, the Court noticed certain shortcomings in the working of the schemes and called for various improvements in relation to ensuring those with a BPL card would have access to public healthcare services wherever such person moves, the need for the Central Government to issue clarifications to all State governments to ensure pregnant women country-wide were not denied cash assistance, a consolidated place where a pregnant women could go to obtain the benefits of various schemes, setting up monthly camps in identified places in rural areas for health check-ups, and improvement of ambulance services; it also called for instructions to be given to recognise, under a scheme which disbursed payment of Rs 10,000 in the event of the death of the 'primary breadwinner', that a woman in the family who is a homemaker was also a breadwinner for this purpose. The Central Government and various State governments were generally to put corrective measures in place. Other general directions required the State health departments to devise formats of registers by which a proper log of a pregnant woman's visits would be maintained, to provide a checklist of available benefits during ante- and post-natal care, and to assign officers to visit and persuade reluctant women to go in for institutional delivery. The Court said that it would be ideal if special cells were set up within health departments of the Central and State governments regularly to monitor the implementation of these schemes. The relevant government bodies were to file affidavits by way of compliance to the Court within eight weeks.]

Notes and Questions

1. This case demonstrates the gap between rights on paper and their actual enjoyment. To what extent can domestic courts give effect to international human rights obligations? Can a judicial decision meaningfully kick-start the reformation of health services and the improvement of health policy?

2. Did this decision give effect to the principle of the indivisibility of human rights, by using a social-economic principle and international law to inform the content of a civil-political right to life?

Paschim Banga Khet Mazdoor Samity & Ors v State of West Bengal & Anor [1996] AIR SC 2426, [1996] 4 SCC 37 (Supreme Court, India)

Notes and Issue

A man, Hakim Seikh, sustained serious head injuries falling off a train. He was refused medical treatment at six successive state hospitals, owing to a lack of vacant beds or inadequate facilities. He was finally admitted to a private hospital, incurring Rs 17,000 in medical costs. The issue was whether the non-availability of facilities for treatment of the serious injuries sustained constituted a denial of Seikh's Article 21 rights. The State Committee appointed a committee of enquiry which suggested various remedial measures.

SC Agrawal J

The Constitution envisages the establishment of a welfare state at the federal level as well as at the state level. In a welfare state the primary duty of the Government is to secure the welfare of the people. Providing adequate medical facilities for the people is an essential part of the obligations undertaken by the Government in a welfare state. The Government discharges this obligation by running hospitals and health centres which provide medical care to the person seeking to avail those facilities. Article 21 imposes an obligation on the State to safeguard the right to life of every person. Preservation of human life is thus of paramount importance. The Government hospitals run by the State and the medical officers employed therein are duty bound to extend medical assistance for preserving human life. Failure on the part of a Government hospital to provide timely medical treatment to a person in need of such treatment results in violation of his right to life guaranteed under Article 21. In the present case there was breach of the said right of Hakim Seikh guaranteed under Article 21 when he was denied treatment at the various Government hospitals which were approached even though his condition was very serious at that time and he was in need of immediate medical attention. Since the said denial of the right of Hakim Seikh guaranteed under Article 21 was by officers of the State in hospitals run by the State the State cannot avoid its responsibility for such denial of the constitutional right of Hakim Seikh. In respect of deprivation of the constitutional rights guaranteed under Part III of the Constitution the position is well settled that adequate compensation can be awarded by the court for such violation by way of redress in proceedings under Articles 32 and 226 of the Constitution. Hakim Seikh should, therefore, be suitably compensated for the breach of his right guaranteed under Article 21 of the Constitution [fixing a sum of Rs 15,000].

. . . [Considering the Committee's report and the submissions of counsel] in order that proper medical facilities are available for dealing with emergency cases it must be that:

1. Adequate facilities are available at the Primary Health Centres where the patient can be given immediate primary treatment so as to stabilize his condition;
2. Hospitals at the District level and Sub-Division level are upgraded so that serious cases can be treated there;
3. Facilities for giving specialist treatment are increased and are available at the hospitals at District level and Sub-Division level having regard to the growing needs.
4. In order to ensure availability of beds in an emergency at State level hospitals there is a centralized communication system so that the patient can be sent immediately to the hospital where a bed is available in respect of the treatment which is required.
5. Proper arrangement of ambulance is made for transport of a patient from the Primary Health Centre to the District hospital or Sub-Division hospital and from the District hospital or Sub Division hospital to the State hospital.
6. The ambulance is adequately provided with necessary equipment and medical personnel.
7. The Health Centres and the hospitals and the medical personnel attached to these Centres and hospitals are geared to deal with larger number of patients needing emergency treatment on account of higher risk of accidents on certain occasions and in certain seasons.

It is no doubt true that financial resources are needed for providing these facilities. But at the same time it cannot be ignored that it is the constitutional obligation of the State to provide adequate medical services to the people. Whatever is necessary for this purpose has to be done. In the context of the constitutional obligation to provide free legal aid to a poor accused this Court has held that the State cannot avoid its constitutional obligation in that regard on account of financial constraints. [See *Khatri (II) v State of Bihar* [1981] (1) SCC 627 at 631.] The said observations would apply with equal, if not greater, force in the matter of discharge of constitutional obligation of the State to provide medical aid to preserve human life. In the matter of allocation of funds for medical services the said constitutional obligation of the State has to be kept in view. It is necessary that a time-bound plan for providing these services should be chalked out keeping in view the recommendations of the Committee as well as the requirements for ensuring availability of proper medical services in this regard as indicated by us and steps should be taken to implement the same. The State of West Bengal alone is a party to these proceedings. Other States, though not parties, should also take necessary steps in the light of the recommendations made by the Committee, the directions contained in the Memorandum of the Government of West Bengal dated August 22, 1995 and the further directions given herein . . .

Notes and Questions

1. How should a court deal with the issue of SERs and financial constraints? Are inadequate resources a justifiable excuse for not fulfilling a right?

2. Did the Court identify part of the 'minimum core' of the right to life by finding an obligation to provide timely emergency medical treatment in cases of serious injury?

3. The South African Constitutional Court distinguished this case in *Soobramoney v Minister of Health Kwazulu-Natal*[87] on the facts. The South African Constitution contains an explicit right not to be refused emergency treatment (Article 27(3)). While *Paschim* dealt with a person suffering a sudden catastrophe, *Soobramoney* was concerned not with immediate remedial treatment but with a patient suffering chronic renal failure, an on-going state of affairs, and an inadequate number of dialysis machines. As such, a demand to receive dialysis treatment at a state hospital had to be determined under Article 27(1) and (2), which entitle every one to have access to healthcare services within the available resources of the state.

D. Right to Education

Unni Krishnan, JP v State of Andhra Pradesh
[1993] AIR 217, [1993] SCR (1) 594 (Supreme Court, India)

Facts

The issue was whether private educational institutions running professional courses like engineering and medicine could charge higher fees than government institutions. This challenged state laws regulating capitation fees. The question arose as to whether the Article 21 right to life included a fundamental right to education, drawing from Articles 41, 45 and 46 (directive principles).

Sharma CJ

[W]e hold, agreeing with the statement in *Bandhua Mukti Morcha* [1984] 2 SCR 67, that right to education is implicit in and flows from the right to life guaranteed by Article 21. That the right to education has been treated as one of transcendental importance in the life of an individual has been recognised not only in this country since thousands of years, but all over the world. In *Mohini Jain* the importance of education has been duly and rightly stressed . . . we agree with the observation that without education being provided to the citizens of this country, the objectives set forth in the Preamble to the Constitution cannot be achieved. The Constitution would fail . . . The importance of education was emphasised in the 'Neethishatakam' by Bhartruhari (First Century BC) in the following words:

> Translation: Education is the special manifestation of man; Education is the treasure which can be preserved without the fear of loss; Education secures material pleasure, happiness and fame; Education is the teacher of the teacher; Education is God incarnate; Education secures honour at the hands of the State, not money – A man without education is equal to an animal.

---

[87] *Soobramoney v Minister of Health Kwazulu-Natal* (CCT32/97) [1997] ZACC 17, 1998 (1) SA 765 (CC).

The fact that right to education occurs in as many as three Articles in Part IV viz, Articles 41, 45 and 46, shows the importance attached to it by the founding fathers. Even some of the Articles in Part III viz, Articles 29 and 30 speak of education . . .

The right to education further means that a citizen has a right to call upon the State to provide educational facilities to him within the limits of its economic capacity and development. By saying so, we are not transferring Article 41 from Part IV to Part III, we are merely relying upon Article 41 to illustrate the content of the right to education flowing from Article 21. We cannot believe that any State would say that it need not provide education to its people even within the limits of its economic capacity and development [which is a matter] . . . within the subjective satisfaction of the State.

. . . The right to free education is available only to children until they complete the age of 14 years. Thereafter, the obligation of the State to provide education is subject to the limits of its economic capacity and development. Indeed, we are not stating anything new. This aspect has already been emphasised in *Francis Coralie Mullin v Administrator, Union Territory of Delhi* [1981] 2 SCR 516; 1981 AIR 746. While elaborating the scope of the right guaranteed under Article 21, this court stated:

> . . . We think that the right to life includes right to live with human dignity and all that goes along with it viz, the bare necessities of life such as adequate nutrition, clothing and shelter and facilities for reading, writing and expressing oneself in diverse forms, freely moving about the mixing and commingling with fellow human beings. Of course, the magnitude and content of the components of this right would depend upon the extent of the economic development of the country, but it must in any view of the matter, include a right to the basic necessities of life and also the right to carry on such functions and activities as constitute the bare minimum expression of the human self.

We must hasten to add that just because we have relied upon some of the directive principles to locate the parameters of the right to education implicit in Article 21, it does not follow automatically that each and every obligation referred to in Part IV gets automatically included within the purview of Article 21. We have held the right to education to be implicit in the right to life because of its inherent fundamental importance. As a matter of fact, we have referred to Articles 41, 45 and 46 merely to determine the parameters of the said right.

. . . Now coming to life: this Court interpreted in *Bandhua Mukti Morcha v Union of India* (1984) 3 SCC 161, at 183–184:

> It is the fundamental right of everyone in this country, assured under the interpretation given to Article 21 by this Court in *Francis Mullin's* case, to live with human dignity, free from exploitation [which right] derives its life breath from the Directive Principles of State Policy and particularly clauses (e) and (f) of Article 39 and Article 41 and 42 and at the least, therefore, it must include protection of the health and strength of workers, men and women, and of the tender age of children against abuse, opportunities and facilities for children to develop in a healthy manner and in conditions of freedom and dignity, educational facilities, just and humane conditions of work and maternity relief. These are the minimum requirements which must exist in order to enable a person to live with human dignity and neither the Central Government nor any State Government has the right to take any action which will deprive a person of the enjoyment of these basic essentials. Since the Directive Principles of State Policy contained in clauses (e) and (f) of Article 39, Articles 41 and 42 are not enforceable in a court of law, it may not be possible to compel the State through the judicial process to make provision by statutory enactment or executive fiat for ensuring these basic

essentials which go to make up a life of human dignity but where legislation is already enacted by the State providing these basic requirements to the workmen and thus investing their right to live with basic human dignity, with concrete reality and content, the State can certainly be obligated to ensure observance of such legislation for inaction on the part of the State in securing implementation of such legislation would amount to denial of the right to live with human dignity enshrined in Article 21, more so in the context of Article 256 which provides that the executive power of every State shall be so exercised as to ensure compliance with the laws made by Parliament and any existing laws which apply in that State.

[Discussing *Olga Tellis*] . . . If thus, personal liberty and life have come to be given expanded meaning, the question to be addressed is whether life, which means to live with dignity, will take within it education as well? . . . Now, coming to *Mohini Jain's* case [(1992) SCR (3) 658] it was observed at pages 679–80:

> 'Right to life' is the compendious expression for all those rights which the courts must enforce because they are basic to the dignified enjoyment of life. It extends to the full range of conduct which the individual is free to pursue. The right to education flows directly from right to life. The right to life under Article 21 and the dignity of an individual cannot be assured unless it is accompanied by the right to education. The State Government is under an obligation to make endeavour to provide educational facilities at all levels to its citizens.

Education is enlightenment. It is the one that lends dignity to a man . . . If 'life' is so interpreted as to bring within it right to education, it has to be interpreted in the light of directive principles. This Court has uniformly taken the view that harmonious interpretation of the fundamental rights vis-à-vis the directive principles must be adopted . . .

[Discussing Article 45 of the Constitution which states:] 'Provision for free and compulsory education for children. The State shall endeavour to provide, within a period of ten years from the commencement of this Constitution, for free and compulsory education for all children until they complete the age of fourteen years.'

Fourteen years, spoken to under the Article, had long ago come to an end. We are in the 43rd year of Independence. Yet, if Article 45 were to be a pious wish and a fond hope, what good of it having regard to the importance of primary education? A time limit was prescribed under this Article . . . If, therefore, endeavour has not been made till now to make this Article reverberate with life and articulate with meaning, we should think the Court should step in . . .

[Referencing Article 13 ICESCR] . . . Higher education calls heavily on national economic resources. The right to it must necessarily be limited in any given country by its economic and social circumstances. The State's obligation to provide it is, therefore, not absolute and immediate . . . It has to take steps to the maximum of its available resources with a view to achieving progressively the full realization of the right of education by all appropriate means. But, with regard to the general obligation to provide education, the State is bound to provide the same, if it deliberately starved its educational system by resources that it manifestly had available unless it could show that it was allocating them to some even more pressing programme. For, by holding education as a fundamental right up to the age of 14 years, this Court is not determining the priorities. On the contrary, [it is reminding the state] of the solemn endeavour it has to take under Article 45 within a prescribed time, which time limit was expired long ago.

. . . Thus, it has to be concluded that the right to free education up to the age of 14 years is a fundamental right.

Notes and Questions

1. This decision modified *Mohini Jain v State of Karnataka*[88] in so far as it held that the right to education was a fundamental right which the state was obliged to provide at all levels. What does the decision in *Unni Krishnan* demonstrate about the character of SERs?

2. The Eighty-Sixth Amendment to the Constitution (2002) introduced Article 21A, which provides for the fundamental right of education for children between the ages of six and 14. Various states have enacted laws making education compulsory, but some have remained unenforced owing to financial and administrative constraints. See V Sripathi and AK Thiruvengadam, 'India: Constitutional Amendment Making the Right to Education a Fundamental Right' (2004) 2 *I·CON* 148. In *Ashok Kumar Thakur v Union of India*,[89] the Court stated that Article 21A might be the most important fundamental right, 'as one's ability to enforce one's fundamental rights flows from one's education'. In 2009, Parliament enacted The Right of Children to Free and Compulsory Education Act.

3. Pakistani cases have drawn from Indian cases in affirming the link between the right of life and education, the former composing 'a sum total of rights which an individual in a State may require to enjoy a dignified existence. In this modern age, dignified existence may not be possible without a certain level of education and the State has to play a role in ensuring by positive action that the citizens enjoy this right'.[90]

E. Right to Life and Right to a Healthy Environment

The Pakistani Supreme Court has stated that Article 9[91] is not to be restrictively construed but extends to 'right of enjoyment of life, maintaining an adequate level of living for full enjoyment of freedom and rights'.[92] The Pakistan Constitution does not contain a right to environment, but in the seminal decision of *Shehla Zia*, the Supreme Court found that the right to live in an unpolluted environment was contained within the right to life and the dignity of man.[93]

Shehla Zia v WAPDA (Water and Power Development Authority)
PLD 1994 SC 693, 712 (Supreme Court, Pakistan)

Facts

The issue raised through public interest litigation was that the construction of an electricity grid station in Islamabad posed a health hazard by: (a) exposing people in the vicinity to

---

[88] *Mohini Jain v State of Karnataka* (1992) 3 SCC 666.
[89] *Ashok Kumar Thakur v Union of India* (2008) 6 SCC 1.
[90] *Ahmed Abdullah v Government of Punjab* PLD 2003 Lahore 752, citing *St Xaviers College v State of Gujarat* [1974] AIR SC 1389.
[91] Art 9 reads: 'No person shall be deprived of life or liberty save in accordance with law.'
[92] *Employees of the Pakistan Law Commission v Ministry of Works* (1994) SCMR 1548.
[93] Art 14, Constitution of Pakistan.

electromagnetic fields; (b) damaging the greenbelt; and (c) negatively affecting the environment, thus violating constitutional rights, including Article 9. The Government cited expert opinions that there was no conclusive finding that electric lines or wiring would seriously affect the health of human beings. The petitioners filed evidence in the form of articles from research journals, magazines and scientific opinion to show how electromagnetic radiation and fields could affect human beings, including concerns of a rise in diseases like leukaemia, brain tumours, depression and suicide.

The Court noted that from the material presented, scientists and scholars had not reached a definite conclusion but 'the trend is in support of the fact that there may be likelihood of adverse effects of electromagnetic fields on human health. It is for this reason that in all the developed countries special care is being taken to establish organizations for carrying on further research on the subject'. Further, the material presented by WAPDA was old and 'based on studies carried out two decades back', while the petitioners presented 'the latest researches'. WAPDA was advised 'to employ better resources and personnel engaged in research and study to keep themselves up to date in scientific and technical knowledge and adopt all such measures which are necessary for safety from adverse effect of magnetic and electric fields'.

Saleem Ahktar J

At this stage it is not possible to give a definite finding on the claims of either side. There is a state of uncertainty and in such a situation the authorities should observe the rules of prudence and precaution. The rule of prudence is to adopt such measures which may avert the so-called danger, if it occurs. The rule of precautionary policy is to first consider the welfare and safety of the human beings and the environment and then to pick up a policy and execute the plan which is more suited to obviate the possible dangers of make such alternate precautionary measures which may ensure safety. To stick to a particular plan on the basis of old studies or inconclusive research cannot be said to be a policy of prudence and precaution. There are instances in American Studies that the power authorities have been asked to alter and mould their programme and planning in such a way that the intensity and the velocity is kept at the lowest level. It is highly technical subject upon which the Court would not like to give a definite finding particularly when the experts and technical evidence produced is inconclusive. In these circumstances the balance should be struck between the rights of the citizens and also the plans which are executed by the power authorities for welfare, economic progress and prosperity of the country.

Dr Parvez Hasan, learned counsel for the petitioners contended that the Rio Declaration on Environment and Development has recommended the precautionary approach contained in principle No 15, which reads as follows:

> Principle 15.–In order to protect the environment, the precautionary approach shall be widely applied by States according to their capabilities. Where there are threats of serious or irreversible damage lack of full scientific certainty shall not be used as a reason for postponing cost-effective measures to prevent environmental degradation.

The concern for protecting environment was first internationally recognised when the declaration of United Nations Conference on the Human Environment was adopted at Stockholm on 16-6-1972. Thereafter it had taken two decades to create awareness and consensus among the countries when in 1992 Rio Declaration was adopted. Pakistan is a signatory to this declaration and according to Dr Pervez Hasan although it has not been ratified or enacted, the principle so adopted has its own sanctity and it should be implemented, if not in letter, at least in spirit [the Court noted that this document had 'a persuasive value and command respect' being an 'almost consensus declaration' dealing with transboundary problems] . . .

Coming back to the present subject, it would not be out of place to mention that Principle No 15 envisages rules of precaution and prudence. According to it, if there are threats of serious damage, effective measures should be taken to control it and it should not be postponed merely on the ground that scientific research and studies are uncertain and not conclusive. It enshrines the principle that prevention is better than cure. It is a cautious approach to avert a catastrophe at the earliest stage. Pakistan is a developing country. It cannot afford the researches and studies made in developed countries on scientific problems particularly the subject at hand. However, the researches and their conclusions with reference to specific cases are available, the information and knowledge is at hand and we should take benefit out of it. In this background if we consider the problem faced by us in this case, it seems reasonable to take preventive and precautionary measures straightaway instead of maintaining status quo because there is no conclusive finding on the effect of electromagnetic fields on human life. One should not wait for conclusive finding as it may take ages to find it out and, therefore, measures should be taken to avert any possible danger and for that reason one should not go to scrap the entire scheme but could make such adjustments, alterations or additions which may ensure safety and security or at least minimise the possible hazards.

The issue raised in this petition involves the welfare and safety of the citizens at large because the network of high tension wires is spread throughout the country. One cannot ignore that energy is essential for present-day life, industry, commerce, and day-to-day affairs. The more energy is produced and distributed, the more progress and economic development become possible. Therefore, a method should be devised to strike balance between economic progress and prosperity and to minimise possible hazards. In fact a policy of sustainable development should be adopted. It will thus require a deep study into the planning and the methods adopted by WAPDA for construction of the grid station. The studies in the USA referred to above have suggested that certain modes can be adopted by which high tension frequency can be decreased. This is purely scientific approach which has to be dealt with and decided by the technical and scientific persons involved in it. It is for this reason that both the parties have agreed that NESPAK should be appointed as a Commissioner to examine the plan made by the petitioners and submit its report and if necessary to suggest any alteration or addition which may be economically possible for constructing a grid station. The location should also be examined and report submitted at the earliest possible time.

At this stage it may be pointed out that in all the developed countries great importance has been given to energy production. Our need is greater as it is bound to affect our economic development, but in the quest of economic development one has to adopt such measures which may not create hazards to life, destroy the environment and pollute the atmosphere. From the comments filed by WAPDA it seems that they in consultation with the Ministry of Water and Power have prepared a plan for constructing a grid station for distribution of power. While making such a plan, no public hearing is given to the citizens nor any opportunity is afforded to the residents who are likely to be affected by the high tension wires running near their locality. It is only a one-sided affair with the Authority which prepares and executes its plan. Although WAPDA and the Government may have been keeping in mind the likely dangers to the citizens health and property, no due importance is given to seek opinion or objections from the residents of the locality where the grid station is constructed or from where the high tension wires run. In the USA a Public Service Commission has been appointed for the purposes of regulating and formulating the plans and permission for establishing a grid station. It hears objections and decides them before giving permission to construct such a power station. No such procedure has been adopted in our country. Being a developing country we will need many such grid stations and lines for transmission of power. It would, therefore, be proper for the Government to establish an Authority or Commission manned by internationally known and recognised scientists having no bias and prejudice to be members of such Commission whose opinion or permission should be obtained before any new grid station is allowed to be constructed. Such Commission should also examine the existing grid stations and the distribution lines from the point of view of health hazards and environmental pollution. If such a step is taken by the Government in time much of the problem in future can be avoided.

The learned counsel for the respondent has raised the objection that the facts of the case do not justify intervention under Article 184 of the Constitution. The main thrust was that the grid station and the transmission line are being constructed after a proper study of the problem taking into consideration the risk factors, the economic factors and also necessity and requirement in a particular area. It is after due consideration that planning is made and is being executed according to rules. After taking such steps, the possibility of health hazard is ruled out and there is no question of affecting property and health of a number of citizens nor is any fundamental right violated which may warrant interference under Article 184. So far as the first part of the contention regarding health hazards is concerned, sufficient discussion has been made in the earlier part of the judgment and need not be repeated. So far as the fundamental rights are concerned, one has not to go too far to find the reply.

Article 9 of the Constitution provides that no person shall be deprived of life or liberty save in accordance with the law. The word 'life' is very significant as it covers all facts of human existence. The word 'life' has not been defined in the Constitution but it does not mean nor can it be restricted only to the vegetative or animal life or mere existence from conception to death. Life includes all such amenities and facilities which a person born in a free country is entitled to enjoy with dignity, legally and constitutionally. For the purposes of present controversy suffice it to say that a person is entitled to protection of law from being exposed to hazards of electromagnetic fields or any other such hazards which may be due to installation and construction of any grid station, any factory, power station or such like installations. Under the common law a person whose right of easement, property or health is adversely affected by any act of omission or commission of a third person in the neighbourhood or at a far off place, is entitled to seek an injunction and also claim damages, but the Constitutional rights are higher than the legal rights conferred by law be it municipal law or the common law. Such a danger as depicted, the possibility of which cannot be excluded, is bound to affect a large number of people who may suffer from it unknowingly because of lack of awareness, information and education and also because such sufferance is silent and fatal and most of the people who would be residing near, under or at a dangerous distance of the grid station or such installation do not know that they are facing any risk or are likely to suffer by such risk. Therefore, Article 184 can be invoked because a large number of citizens throughout the country cannot make such representation and may not like to make it due to ignorance, poverty and disability. Only some conscientious citizens aware of their rights and the possibility of danger come forward and this has happened so in the present case.

According to *Oxford Dictionary*, 'life' means state of all functional activity and continual 'change peculiar to organised matter and specially to the portion of it constituting an animal or plant before death and animate existence'. In Black's Law Dictionary, 'life' means 'that state of animals, humans, and plants or of an organised being, in which its natural functions and motions are performed, or in which its organs are capable of performing their functions. The interval between birth and death. The sum of the forces by which death is resisted.' 'Life' protected by the Federal Constitution includes all personal rights and their enjoyment of the faculties, acquiring useful knowledge, the right to marry, establish a home and bring up children, freedom of worship, conscience, contract, occupation, speech, assembly and press.

The Constitutional Law in America provides an extensive and wide meaning to the word 'life' which includes all such rights which are necessary and essential for leading a free, proper, comfortable and clean life. The requirement of acquiring knowledge, to establish home, the freedoms as contemplated by the Constitution, the personal rights and their enjoyment are nothing but part of life. A person is entitled to enjoy his personal rights and to be protected from encroachments on such personal rights, freedom and liberties. Any action taken which may create hazards of life will be encroaching upon the personal rights of a citizen to enjoy the life according to law. In the present case this is the complaint the petitioners have made. In our view the word 'life' constitutionally is so wide that the danger and encroachment complained of would impinge fundamental right of a citizen. In this view of the matter the petition is maintainable.

Dr Pervez Hasan, learned counsel has referred to various judgments of the Indian Supreme Court in which the term 'life' has been explained with reference to public interest litigation. In *Kharak Singh v State of UP* (AIR 1963 SC 1295) for interpreting the word 'life' used in Article 21 of the Indian Constitution reliance was placed on the judgment of Field J in *Munn v Ilinois* (1876) 94 US 113 at page 142 where it was observed that '"life" means not merely the right to the continuance of a person's animal existence but a right to the possession of each of his organs – his arms and legs etc.' In *Francis Corali v Union Territory or Delhi* (AIR 1981 SC 746) Bhagvati J observed that right to life includes right to live with human dignity and all that goes along with it, namely, the bare necessities of life such as adequate nutrition, clothing and shelter and facilities for reading and writing in diverse form. The same view has been expressed in *Olga Tellis v Bombay Municipal Corporation* (AIR 1986 SC 180) and *State of Himachal Pradesh v Umed Ram Sharma* (AIR 1986 SC 847). In the first case right to life under the Constitution was held to mean right to livelihood. In the latter case the definition has been extended to include the 'quality of life' and not mere physical existence. It was observed that 'for residents of hilly areas, access to road is access to life itself.' Thus, apart from the wide meaning given by US Courts, the Indian Supreme Court seems to give a wider meaning which includes the quality of life, adequate nutrition, clothing and shelter and cannot be restricted merely to physical exist- ence. The word 'life' in the Constitution has not been used in a limited manner. A wide meaning should be given to enable a man not only to sustain life but to enjoy it. Under our Constitution, Article 14 provides that the dignity of man and subject to law the privacy of home shall be inviolable. The fundamental right to preserve and protect the dignity of man under Article 14 is unparalleled and could be found only in few Constitutions of the world. The Constitution guarantees dignity of man and also right to 'life' under Article 9 and if both are read together, question will arise whether a person can be said to have dignity of man if his right to life is below bare necessity like without proper food, clothing, shelter, education, health care, clean atmosphere and unpolluted environment. Such questions will arise for consideration which can be dilated upon in more detail in a proper proceeding involving such specific questions.

Dr Pervaz Hasan has also referred to several judgments of the Indian Supreme Court in which issues relating to environment and ecological balance were raised and relief was granted as the industrial activity causing pollution had degraded the quality of life. In *Rural Litigation & Entitlement Kendra v State of UP* (AIR 1985 SC 652) mining operations carried out through blasting was stopped and directions were issued to regulate it. The same case came up for further consideration and concern was shown for the preservation and protection of environment and ecology. However, considering the defence needs and for earning foreign exchange, some quarries were allowed to be operated in a limited manner subject to strict control and regulations. These judgments are reported in AIR 1987 SC 359 and 2426 and AIR 1988 SC 2187 and AIR 1989 SC 594. In *Shri Sachidanand Pandy v State of West Bengal* (AIR 1987 SC 1109) part of land of zoological garden was given to Taj Group of Hotels to build a five-star hotel. This transaction was challenged in the High Court without success. The appeal was dismissed. Taking note of the fact that society's interaction with nature is so extensive that the 'environmental question has assumed proportion affecting all humanity', it was observed that:

> Obviously, if the Government is alive to the various considerations requiring thought and deliberation and has arrived at a conscious decision after taking them into account, it may not be for this Court to interfere in the absence of mala fides. On the other hand, if relevant considerations are not borne in mind and irrelevant considerations influence the decision, the Court may interfere in order to prevent a likelihood of prejudice to the public.

In *MC Mehta v Union of India* (AIR 1988 SC 1115) and *MC Mehta v Union of India* (AIR 1988 SC 1037) the Court on petition filed by a citizen taking note of the fact that the municipal sewage and industrial effluents from tanneries were being thrown in River Ganges whereby it was completely polluted, the tanneries were closed down. These judgments go a long way to show that in cases where life of citizens is degraded, the quality of life is adversely affected and health hazards are created affecting a large number of people, the Court in exercise of its jurisdiction under Article 184(3) of the Constitution may grant relief to the extent of stopping the functioning of factories which create pollution and environmental degradation.

In the problem at hand the likelihood of any hazard to life by magnetic field effect cannot be ignored. At the same time the need for constructing grid stations which are necessary for industrial and economic development cannot be lost sight of. From the material produced by the parties it seems that while planning and deciding to construct the gird station WAPDA and the Government Department acted in a routine manner without taking into consideration the latest research and planning in the field nor any thought seems to have been given to the hazards it may cause to human health. In these circumstances, before passing any final order, with the consent of both the parties we appoint NESPAK as Commissioner to examine and study the scheme, planning, device and technique employed by WAPDA and report whether there is any likelihood of any hazard or adverse effect on health of the residents of the locality. NESPAK may also suggest variations in the plan for minimizing the alleged danger. WAPDA shall submit all the plans, scheme and relevant information to NESPAK. The petitioners will be at liberty to send NESPAK necessary documents and material, as they desire these documents should reach NESPAK within two weeks. NESPAK is authorised to call for such documents or information from WAPDA and the petitioners which in their opinion is necessary to complete their report. The report should be submitted within four weeks from the receipt of the order after which further proceeding shall be taken. WAPDA is further directed that in future prior to installing or constructing any grid station and/or transmission line, they should issue public notice in newspapers, radio and television inviting objections and to finalise the plan after considering the objections, if any, by affording public hearing to the persons filing objections. This procedure shall be adopted and continued by WAPDA till such time the Government constitutes any commission or authority as suggested above.

Notes and Questions

1. This was the first Pakistani case to discuss environmental issues at length, which sought expert opinion and consulted relevant Indian case law: W Menski et al, *Public Interest Litigation in Pakistan* (Karachi: Pakistan Law House, 2000) at 93. What guidelines were laid down for future similar cases? Did these go to the substance of the right to life/health, or were these procedure-orientated? See P Hassan, 'Shehla Zia vs WAPDA: Ten Years Later' (2005) 48 *Pakistan Law Journal* 48,; P Hassan and A Azfar, 'Securing Environmental Rights through Public Interest Litigation in South Asia' (2004) 22 *Virginia Environmental Law Journal* 215.

2. How did the Court deal with technical and scientific issues beyond its competence? In *Suo Moto Case No 25 of 2009 (Lahore Canal Bank Case)*,[94] the Supreme Court considered a challenge to a canal widening project in Lahore which the petitioner said threatened to cause environmental degradation to a green belt and which would not solve traffic congestion. The Court appointed a mediator who formed a committee of experts, which produced a report with the consensus view that the residents of Lahore had been excluded from the project, which had serious flaws, and made various recommendations, including declaring the Canal Road area a heritage urban park and measures to improve public transport and traffic management, to preserve the ecosystem and restore communal life on Canal Road. The Court held thus:

    > The Canal Road Project is neither a plant omitting hazardous gases nor releasing pollutants in the canal water. It aims at widening the road on both sides of the Canal Bank which of necessity would cause some damage to the green belt and thereby affect environment. The apprehended change or damage which has neither been quantified nor ascertained per se may not be violative of Fundamental Right of Right to Life (Article 9 of the Constitution) unless it is shown by placing incontrovertible material before this Court that it would lead to hazardous effects on environment and ecology to an extent that it would seriously affect human living.[95]

    The Court concluded that the relevant authorities had carried out environment viability studies, assessed the feasibility of other solutions and suggested mitigating measures. As such, the project did not violate Article 9 (fundamental right to life) or Article 14 (human dignity). It noted:

    > Every project of this kind would have some adverse impact on environment but that would be negligible as compared to the ameliorative effects it is expected to have on traffic congestion and convenience of commuters and on improvement in traffic safety levels. When challenge is thrown to such projects, the Courts have to take into consideration the issues and problems that would remain unresolved and the resultant hardship of the people if the road is not widened and project is stayed. The ecological and environmental concerns, on the one hand, and hardship of the city commuters, on the other, faced with traffic congestions pose a dilemma. A balance needs to be struck between these two competing issues. The Courts may not be ideally suited for striking such a balance because such an exercise would entail factual enquiry, research work and

---

[94] *Suo Moto Case No 25 of 2009 (Lahore Canal Bank Case)*, available at < http://www.supremecourt.gov. pk/web/user_files/File/SMCNo25of2009.pdf>.
[95] Ibid.

expert knowledge of specialists in the relevant field. The Court noted that when NESPAK carried out the requisite EIA, it held a public hearing, considered the objections of the petitioners, examined the alternative solutions suggested and found that the project in hand was preferable to all other solutions suggested. The report submitted by NESPAK (National Engineering Services of Pakistan) in turn was placed before the EPA-Punjab (Environmental Protection Agency), which granted approval and environmental clearance to the Canal Road Project. This approval was neither mechanical nor without conscious application of mind, rather the precautionary principles of environmental regulations reiterated by this Court in *Shehla Zia* were fully kept in view.[96]

3.   '[T]he use of judicial commissions is by no means a panacea as the technique can only work effectively where expert opinion is not divided and there is a fair chance that a consensus can emerge amongst the diverse group of stakeholders. Even though the advent of public interest litigation and innovative procedural pathways such as judicial commissions threaten to obliterate the law/policy divide, the successes of the new approach in India and Pakistan have been welcomed by a public that has long been used to an apathetic legislature and a weak executive. As long as environmental protection remains a low priority item for the political establishment and the state machinery, courts in Pakistan will increasingly be called upon to give practical significance to the fundamental rights guaranteed under the Constitution. However, it should be borne in mind that the activism of the courts is not a substitute for proper policy making and implementation as judicial intervention is by its very nature reactive and hemmed in by the procedural pathways that are peculiar to the legal process. The countries of South Asia are still in the early stages of environmental consciousness and although public awareness of environmental issues is improving with each passing year, prioritizing environmental concerns in national planning and steady implementation of laws and policies is of paramount importance.'[97] Can expert committees help reduce judicial arbitrariness and promote institutional legitimacy?

4.   Deprivation of 'life' in the Pakistani context has been interpreted to include access to public parks, which the construction of a commercial complex threatened to block,[98] and the non-payment of living wages to low-paid employees.[99] It has extended to public health issues, such as unserviceable sewerage systems, where highway construction caused dirty water to enter dwelling houses, endangering human life through disease.[100] It includes 'the right to have unpolluted water' wherever a person lives.[101] The qualitative dimension of the Article 9 'right to life' was affirmed in *Mst Sajida Bibi v Incharge Chouki No 2 Police Station Saddar, Saihwal*,[102] which cited *Shehla Zia* approvingly. The Court held that 'life' 'also means a happy life which a married couple is entitled to lead and enjoy'; Article 9

---

[96]   Ibid, [17].
[97]   See P Hassan, 'The Role of the Judiciary and Judicial Commissions on Sustainable Development Issues in Pakistan' 2006 *All Pakistan Legal Decisions Journal* 45, 56–57: See also Hassan, at <http://www.supremecourt.gov.pk/ijc/Articles/9/7.pdf>.
[98]   *Muhammad Tariq Abbassi v Defence Housing Authority* (2007) CLC 1358 [Karachi].
[99]   *Ghulam Umar Qazi v General Manager & others*, 2006 PLC (CS) 1143.
[100]   *Ameer Bano v SE Highways*, PLD 1996 Lahore 592.
[101]   *General Secretary, West Pakistan Salt Miners Labour Union (CBA) Khewara, Jhelum v The Director, Industries and Mineral Development* (1994) SCMR 2061 (Pak).
[102]   *Mst Sajida Bibi v Incharge Chouki No 2 Police Station Saddar, Saihwal*, PLD 1997 Lahore 666 at 670E.

would be violated if a duly married couple were compelled to live separately against their wishes. The police were obliged to protect and not hinder marital life by facilitating the couple's involuntary separation at the wishes of unhappy parents who disapproved of the match between two Muslims and sought to recover their daughter forcibly. Indeed, the application of the *Shehla Zia* precedent has extended beyond environmental concerns to political abuses, such as telephone-tapping and eaves-dropping,[103] as well as the right to have non-corrupt authorities.[104] Has the category become a catch-all for social injustices, and is this a good thing?

F. Right to Life Defined by Reference to ICESCR

Clean Air Foundation Ltd v The Government of the HKSAR
[2007] HKCFI 757 (Court of First Instance, HKSAR, No 35 of 2007)

Facts

The Government's failure to improve Hong Kong's air quality was challenged by judicial review. It was asserted that the polluted air poisoned residents and shortened their lives, and harmed Hong Kong as a business centre. The argument was that the right to life of all citizens, which included the best possible health care, as guaranteed under the Basic Law, Bill of Rights and applicable International Covenant, was violated. The alleged failings lay in not adopting more stringent steps through legislative or policy measures to combat air pollution. These were in nature immediate (not rationalising bus routes and services to facilitate higher transport occupancy, not providing better ventilation in constructing underground bus terminals), medium-term (not requiring all diesel vehicles to move to Euro IV and Euro V standards) and long-term (policy failures in not providing a specific fraction of the construction cost of new rail lines as a direct grant to rail companies to allow them to alleviate congestion through more services).

Hartmann J

I was concerned that, despite the importance of the subject matter, it did not engage the supervisory jurisdiction of this court [as] . . . the application . . . was in reality an attack on Government policy. But matters of policy, of course, provided they are lawfully determined and executed, are not matters for this court. In a recent judgment, Reyes J, in dismissing an application for leave to apply for judicial review, said the following; in my view, a succinct and entirely correct statement of principle –

> I fully sympathise with Mr Ng's concerns about the deteriorating quality of the environment around Tai Kok Tsui, where he lives. But the Court can only apply law. The Judiciary cannot manage the environment. That is the role of the Executive. [*Ng Ngau Chai v The Town Planning Board* (unreported) HCAL 64/2007 dated 4 July 2007]

---

[103] *Benazir Bhutto v President of Pakistan* PLD 1988 Supreme Court 377 at 619.
   PLD 2000 Supreme Court 77 Review Petition No 6 of 1998 in Constitutional Petition No 59 of 1996, decided on 11th October, 1999.
[104] *Benazir Bhutto v President of Pakistan* PLD 1998 SC 607.

. . . The applicants have sought two declarations. The first declaration is intended to be a 'foundation' declaration, setting out the exact nature of the Government's obligations under the Basic Law, the Bill of Rights and the international conventions. It is to the following effect:

'Article 28 of the Basic Law[105] and/or Article 2 of the Hong Kong Bill of Rights Ordinance,[106] in providing for protection of a 'right to life' and the 'right to health', as provided by Article 12 of the International Covenant on Economic, Social and Cultural Rights, imposes upon the Government an affirmative duty to protect the residents and the economy of Hong Kong from the known harmful effects of air pollution . . .'

Art 28 of the Basic Law and art 2 of the Bill of Rights provide for the right to life in the context of detention, trial and punishment. The question arises, therefore, of whether, on a purposive interpretation, the constitutional protection can be extended to matters of air pollution control . . . [L]eading counsel for the applicants has referred to an emerging international jurisprudence to the effect that the right to life may, depending on the circumstances, impose on public authorities an obligation outside of the context of crime and punishment; for example, to provide vaccines in the case of epidemics or to protect against identified environmental hazards such as nuclear waste. I accept therefore that it is at least *prima facie* arguable that the constitutional right to life may apply in the circumstances advocated by the applicants; that is, by imposing some sort of duty on the Government to combat air pollution.

As for art 12 of the ICESCR, it is more directly in point. It reads:

1. The States Parties to the present Covenant recognize the right of everyone to the enjoyment of the highest attainable standard of physical and mental health.
2. The steps to be taken by the States Parties to the present Covenant to achieve the full realization of this right shall include those necessary for:
   (b) The improvement of all aspects of environmental and industrial hygiene;

Art 12, of course, looks to the progressive achievement of the highest attainable standard of health . . . it recognises that Rome wasn't built in a day . . . I accept that it must be *prima facie* arguable that it imposes some sort of duty on state authorities to combat air pollution even if it cannot be an absolute duty to ensure with immediate effect the end of all pollution . . .

. . . Art 62 of the Basic Law provides that it is for the Government to formulate and implement policies. Art 48 provides that it is for the Chief Executive, once a policy has been formulated, to decide whether, and to what degree, it should be executed. A policy may, of course, be unlawful. But because a policy is considered to be unwise, short-sighted or retrogressive does not make it unlawful. It has long been accepted that policy is a matter for policy-makers and that to interfere with the lawful discretion given to policy-makers would amount to an abuse of the supervisory jurisdiction vested in the courts.

[The Assistant Director of the Environment Department made an affirmation averring to the complexity of air pollution control in the HKSAR, pointing out that emissions from power plants, vehicles etc in the Pearl River Delta (PRD) affected the HKSAR air quality such that the HKSAR had to work within the Guangdong Provincial Government to

---

[105] Art 28 of the Basic Law: 'The freedom of the person of Hong Kong residents shall be inviolable. No Hong Kong resident shall be subjected to arbitrary or unlawful arrest, detention or imprisonment. Arbitrary or unlawful search of the body of any resident or deprivation or restriction of the freedom of the person shall be prohibited. Torture of any resident or arbitrary or unlawful deprivation of the life of any resident shall be prohibited.'

[106] Art 2(1), Hong Kong Bill of Rights Ordinance reads: ' Every human being has the inherent right to life. This right shall be protected by law. No one shall be arbitrarily deprived of this life.'

reduce emissions in the entire PRD region. He noted the costliness of certain air pollution control measures which would impact a wide range of issues and policy areas including energy, transportation, industrial production and the livelihood of citizens in general.]

. . . Deciding on the relevant emphasis in respect of this complex, interlocking mix of legislation, administrative schemes and political initiatives is a matter of policy. And policy, as I have said, is for Government . . . While issues of importance to the community may have been raised, it is not for this court to determine those issues. They are issues for the political process.

Notes and Questions

1. How influential were international human rights in the determination of this case?

2. Do courts have a role in ensuring that government policies do not unjustifiably restrict constitutional freedoms, or should they adhere to the separation of powers to preserve the distinction between law and policy? Would this require a shift from an adversarial proceeding to a more inquisitorial role? Would judicial review, applying administrative law principles such as relevancy, avoid concerns regarding institutional propriety? Contrast the view of the Indian Supreme Court, that environmental concerns were equal in importance to human rights, and both were rooted in Article 21, with the environmental aspects concerning 'life' and the human rights aspect concerning 'liberty': *AP State Pollution Control Board v MV Nayudu & Ors* (affirming that the right to access to drinking water is fundamental to life and the state was duty-bound under Article 21 to provide clean drinking water to its citizens).[107] The Inter-American Commission on Human Rights has found that the right to life is impaired by not taking measures to prevent environmental damage: see *Yanomani Indians v Brazil*.[108]

3. The European Court of Human Rights has held that Article 8 ECHR might be violated by environmental degradation which would affect an individual's well-being and deprive him of his enjoyment of private and family life.[109]

G. Right to a Healthy Environment and Sustainable Development

The Nepal Interim Constitution (2007) provides that 'every person has the right to live in a clean environment'.[110] In the Sri Lanka Constitution (1978), this is couched as a state duty to 'protect, preserve and improve the environment for the benefit of the community'.[111] Article 5 of the Bhutan Constitution (2008) states that it is a fundamental duty of every citizen to protect the natural environment and natural resources for present and future generations. The Government is obliged to prevent pollution,

---

[107] *AP State Pollution Control Board v MV Nayudu & Ors* 2000(3) SCALE 354, 2000 Supp 5 SCR 249.
[108] *Yanomani Indians v Brazil* Inter-American Commission on Human Rights 7615 OEA/SerLV/II/66 Doc 10 rev 1 (1985).
[109] *Lopez Ostra v Spain* (1994) Series A no 303-C at [51].
[110] Art 16, Nepal Interim Constitution.
[111] Art 27(14), Sri Lanka Constitution.

ensure a safe and healthy environment and develop ecologically sustainable development, and is required to ensure that at least 60 per cent of the total land shall be under
forest cover for all time.[112] Bangladeshi courts have liberally construed the fundamental right to life in Articles 31 and 32[113] to include the right to a healthy environment
which can sustain a meaningful 'existence of life'. In *Farooque v Bangladesh*,[114] a Flood
Action Plan was challenged as harming the environment and people by displacement,
damage of natural habitant and soil damage. Chowdhury J stated:

> Although we do not have any provision like Article 48A of the Indian Constitution for
> protection of environment, Articles 31 and 32 of our Constitution protect right to life as a
> fundamental right. It encompasses within its ambit, the protection and preservation of
> environment, ecological balance free from pollution of air and water, sanitation without
> which, life can hardly be enjoyed. Any act or omission contrary thereto will violate the said
> right to life.[115]

A 2011 constitutional amendment obliges the Bangladesh Government under Article
18A to protect and improve the environment.

The right to a healthy environment conflicts with other competing interests in developing land resources, and the courts have been conscious of the need to reconcile these
competing interests. The Indian courts touted the concept of 'sustainable development' as 'a viable concept to eradicate poverty and improve the quality of human life
while living within the carrying capacity of the supporting ecosystem', in *Vellore
Citizen's Welfare Forum v Union of India*.[116] This concerned a petition against the discharge of untreated effluent from Tamil Nadu tanneries into waterways and agricultural fields, causing environmental degradation and polluting drinking-water wells.
The tanneries, despite notices, had failed to control the pollution they generated.
Kuldip Singh J for the Supreme Court noted that the leather industry was important
to India as a foreign exchange earner, and that Tamil Nadu accounted for 80 per cent
of India's production. However, the industry

> has no right to destroy the ecology, degrade the environment and pose as a health hazard. It
> cannot be permitted to expand or even to continue with the present production unless it
> tackles by itself the problem of pollution . . . The traditional concept that development and
> ecology are opposed to each other, is no longer acceptable. 'Sustainable Development' is the
> answer. [117]

> The Court traced the development of the concept in the international sphere from the 1972
> Stockholm Declaration, the 1992 Rio Declaration and Agenda 21 programme, holding that
> 'sustainable development', 'as a balancing concept between ecology and development', was a
> customary international law norm. In particular, two key principles were the precautionary
> principle (lack of scientific certainty is no reason to postpone adopting measures to prevent
> environment degradation) and the polluter pays principle (bearing absolutely liability for

---

[112] On commitments safeguarding against deforestation, see also Art 22, Constitution of the Maldives
(2008); Art 15, Constitution of Afghanistan (2004); Art 48A, Constitution of India (1950, through a 1976
amendment).

[113] Art 31 protects every citizen from 'action detrimental to the life, liberty, body, reputation, or property',
unless taken in accordance with law, violation of which must be compensated. Art 32 states that 'No person
shall be deprived of life or personal liberty save in accordance with law'.

[114] *Farooque v Bangladesh* (1997) 49 *Dhaka Law Reports* (AD) 1.

[115] Ibid at [101].

[116] *Vellore Citizen's Welfare Forum v Union of India* AIR 1996 SC 2715.

[117] Ibid, 2720.

environmental harm which includes compensating the victims and the costs of restoration), The Court found that these two principles were 'accepted as part of the law of the land'. It noted as part of the constitutional mandate to protect and improve the environment, Article 21 of the Constitution guaranteed life and personal liberty; Article 47 involved the state duty to raise standard of living and improve public health; Article 48A(g) the duty to protect the environment, safeguard forests and wild life; and Article 51A(g) the duty to protect and improve the natural environment and have compassion for living creatures. There were also many relevant legislative acts to prevent water and environmental pollution. Aside from these constitutional and statutory sources to fresh air, clean water and a pollution-free environment, India had adopted the British legal system and, with it, the inalienable common law right of clean environment. The Court ordered the Central Government to constitute an authority to deal with tanneries in Tamil Nadu headed by a retired High Court judge; with expert advice, it would implement the 'polluter pays' and precautionary principles, identify the victims of pollution and assess their losses. These would be recovered by the Collector/District Magistrate as land revenue arrears and forwarded to the affected persons. Refusal to pay compensation could bring about the closure of the polluter's industry. The authority would frame schemes to reverse ecological damage, to be executed by the State government under supervision of the Central Government. Subsequently, the Court noted the tension between inter-generational interests in ecological impact and the need for development, given 'the dire need which the society urgently requires'.[118] Article 21 guaranteed a right to a decent environment, and the parameters of this 'would essentially be a legislative policy'.[119]

However, Rajagopal Balakrishnan[120] has criticised the Indian courts for being pro-development rather than pro-poor, for being concerned about environmental issues of concern to urban-dwellers, like water pollution, but showing less attention to rural livelihoods, land and forest issues. This is exemplified in *Narmada Bachao Andolan v Union of India*.[121] At issue was the plan to build the Sardar Sarovar dam which would irrigate 1.8 million hectares and provide water to drought-prone areas in Gujarat. This would displace some 320,000 people living in the river basin, submerge forests, destroy the local environment and affect the livelihood of thousands. The Supreme Court held that the displacement of tribal peoples did not 'per se result in the violation of their fundamental or other rights' including Article 21, and ordered that the planned 136.5 metre dam should be constructed up to 90 metres, in tandem with dealing with the relief and rehabilitation of the landless community living in the vicinity. This decision was criticised for a variety of reasons, including the fact that it discounted environmental concerns and sanctioned the forced eviction of tribal peoples. The majority had lauded the effect the dam would have on the national economy, water supply and food security. It stated that it was for elected governments to decide what projects to

---

[118] *Bombay Dyeing & Mfg Co Ltd v Bombay Environmental Action Group* (2006) 3 SCC 434, [2006] AIR SC 1489 ('Consideration of ecological aspects from the court's point of view cannot be one sided. It depends on the fact situation in each case. Whereas the court would take a very strict view as regards setting up of an industry which is of a hazardous nature but such a strict construction may not be resorted to in the case of town planning.')

[119] Ibid.

[120] B Rajagopal, 'Judicial Governance and the Ideology of Human Rights from a Social Movement Perspective' in CR Kumar and K Chockalingam (eds), *Human Rights, Justice and Constitutional Empowerment* (New Delhi: Oxford University Press, 2006) 204.

[121] *Narmada Bachao Andolan v Union of India* [1999] AIR SC 3345. See P Culletf, 'Human Rights and Displace: The Indian Supreme Court Decision on Sardar Sarovar in International Perspective' (2001) 50(4) *ICLQ* 973; J Razzaque, 'Linking Human Rights, Development and Environment: Experiences from Litigation in South Asia' (2007) 16 *Fordham Environmental Law Review* 587.

undertake for the benefit of the people, and in the absence of a blatant illegality, the Court should not interfere with their execution. In 2006, the Supreme Court upheld the continuing construction of the dam despite the inadequacy of relief and rehabilitation measures.[122] Rajagopal argues that the courts, by assuming governance functions such as monitoring the implementation of programmes, had imbibed the ideology of statism and developmentalism, and had effectively become an 'executive judiciary'[123] in favouring the larger good of development over issues of human rights and the environment.

Note and Questions

1. Are there any objections to courts making value judgements on what is best for the community? Or is the fact that judges are unelected and able to consider long-run implications, being above short-term electoral politicking, a virtue?

2. Socio-economic rights, the historical origins of which date back to the eighteenth century in Prussia and Bavaria, were included in the French Constitution of 1793, the 1917 Mexican Constitution and the 1919 Weimar Constitution. These were more broadly inserted into constitutions after World War II, and have been included in late twentieth-century and twenty-first-century Asian constitutions (eg Cambodia, 1993; Thailand, 2007; Nepal (Interim), 2008; Timor-Leste, 2008). The inclusion of such 'second-generation' rights, which require active state intervention as the agent of the people's welfare and happiness, focuses on marginalised sectors of society, the nature of the broader community and social solidarity, as opposed to the fixation of CPRs on the individual rights-holder. While seeking judicial enforcement of SERs may not provide a strong remedy, owing to competing interests and limited resources, it provides a forum for the poor and marginalised to articulate their concerns. This compels the political branches to enter into a dialogue with the courts, in working out the truism that 'Necessitous men are not freemen'[124] and encouraging the adoption of ameliorative measures.

---

[122] K Ramachandra, 'Sardar Sarovar: An Experience Retained?' (2006) 19 *Harvard Human Rights Journal* 275.

[123] Rajagopal, above n 120, at 204.

[124] US President Franklin D Roosevelt, State of the Union Address calling for an Economic Bill of Rights, 90 *Congressional Record* 55, 57 (1944).

Index

References such as '178–9' indicate (not necessarily continuous) discussion of a topic across a range of pages. Wherever possible in the case of topics with many references, these have either been divided into sub-topics or only the most significant discussions of the topic are listed. Because the entire work is about the 'constitutional law' and 'Asia', the use of these terms (and certain others which occur constantly throughout the book) as entry points has been minimised. Information will be found under the corresponding detailed topics.

AAY, *see* Antyodaya Anna Yojana
abode, right of 227, 229–30, 314, 317, 320–2, 421–3, 428–9, 640
aboriginal peoples 560–4, 572
abortion 106–7, 626–9, 983
absentee voting 453, 528
absolute equality 548–9, 604, 608, 613, 925
absolute freedoms 835, 850
  of religion 835, 850
absolute monarchy 37, 260
absolute power 37, 40, 58, 70, 211, 244, 266, 289
absolute theocracies 867
absolute trust 105, 110–11, 868
absolute truth 804, 816
abstract review 329–31, 334, 343, 399
abstract symmetry 596, 598–9
abuse 152, 154, 211, 214, 436, 538, 695, 950–1
  of discretion 273, 837–8
    grave 376, 402–3, 520, 964, 966–7
  grave 376, 402, 520, 964, 966–7
  gravest 885, 887
  political 538, 1017
  of power 154, 166, 268, 285, 294, 669
  of religion 111, 860, 865
  sexual 439, 723, 728, 911
accommodation 215, 475, 477, 738, 836, 838, 870, 878–86
  benevolent neutrality-accommodation 883–6
  judicial 251
  legislative 883, 885, 889
  mandatory 883–6
  models of 215
  of morality 888–9
  permissive 883–6, 889
accommodative secularism 798, 852
accountability 74, 120–1, 141–2, 181, 187–9, 195, 203, 369
  democratic 463
  judicial 373–4
  political 369, 705
  politics of 141–2, 187–9
accused persons 305, 407, 451, 602, 676–7
Ackerman, Bruce 155, 181, 215, 255, 270, 658
Acting Presidents 54, 185, 247, 376–8
activism, judicial 282, 291, 968

additional judges 376, 379–80, 382, 412
  appointment 376, 382
  non-appointment 379, 412
administration 152, 177–9, 199–200, 692, 760, 770, 971, 976
  general interest of 598–9
  judicial 358, 369, 389, 391–2, 396, 457
  national 483, 522–3
  public 2, 31, 93–4, 96, 178, 376, 522, 525
administration of justice 382–3, 437–8, 674, 676, 688–9, 691–6, 698–9, 736
administrative agencies 71, 178, 191, 513, 596, 648, 765, 912
administrative authorities 458, 620, 646–7, 754, 786
administrative courts 365–6, 392, 458, 581, 648, 727, 763–4
administrative discretion 74, 577, 950
administrative districts 469, 472–3, 477, 764
administrative orders 166, 206, 363
administrative power 93–4, 96, 201, 208, 291
administrative punishment 458
administrative reforms 16, 178, 193
administrative regulations 177, 319, 347–8, 357, 361, 912–13
  constitutionality 310, 348
administrative rules 349, 356–8, 360, 364, 765
  constitutionality 356–7, 444
  judicial review 356–61
administrative supervision 388–9, 512
administrative unity 140–4, 186, 190, 468, 477
adolescents 85, 650–1
advertisements 628, 649–50, 656, 663–4, 666, 669, 734
advocacy of communism 749–50, 753
affidavits 693, 695, 697, 783–5, 988, 991, 996, 998–1000
agencies 141–2, 186–8, 190–2, 454–5, 657, 727, 764–5, 812–13
  government 90, 175, 329–30, 334, 358, 366, 414, 443
  independent 141–3, 186–9, 455
  state 330–1, 353, 425, 583, 619
agnosticism 782, 812, 859, 877, 881
Agong, *see* Yang di-Pertuan Agong

agriculture 572, 779, 781, 844, 979, 982
Ahmadis 859–60, 910
  Indonesia 932–42
  Pakistan 916–32
Ainu 566–75, 577
  culture 569, 571, 573–6
  language 571, 574
air pollution 1017–19
alienation 124, 162, 294–5, 560, 563, 565, 584
Allah 115, 790, 868–9, 905–9, 917, 919, 924, 927–8
  Almighty 105, 110–11, 868, 924, 928
allegiance 530, 853, 881
  dual 529–30
allurement 154, 156, 808, 810–11, 821–2
Almighty Allah 105, 110–11, 868, 924, 928
ambiguity 264, 322, 420, 423, 428, 745
ameliorative secularism 870–8
amending power 283, 285–7, 289, 351
amendment, power of 257, 285–6, 292
amendment procedures 219–20, 257–61, 280, 351
American test of equality 607, 610–19
amparo, write of 348, 443
anarchy 64, 266, 921, 940–1
ancestral lands 561–2
ancillary jurisdictions 337–42
ancillary powers 329, 337–9, 341–2, 344, 404
anthem ceremonies 771, 851–8
anti-constitutionalism 5, 68, 278
anti-establishment clauses 838, 890, 904
anti-hopping laws 481, 490–3
anti-propagation legislation 782, 805–8, 810, 816
Antyodaya Anna Yojana (AAY) 994, 997–8, 1002
apologies 734–9, 829
  forced 733, 737–8
apostasy 780, 782–6, 788–9, 792–5, 797, 904
  certificate of 796–7
apostates 784, 790, 910
appointed officials 608–10, 612
appointing power, *see* powers, appointment
appointment 94–5, 136–7, 181–6, 188–9, 369–71,
    375–81, 478–9, 658–9
  executive 93, 374
  judicial 166, 189, 369, 371, 373, 375–6, 379,
    381–2
  power 17, 159, 186, 189, 371, 378, 658
  processes 182, 189–90, 512
  supreme court justices 185, 378, 394
  temporary 185, 376–7
apportionment 468–70, 474–5, 477
appropriateness 132, 207, 363, 439–40, 526, 622,
    840, 951
Aquino
  Benigno 55, 248, 252
  Corazon 'Cory' 55–6, 158–9, 251, 401–2, 632,
    966
arbitrary discrimination 552, 596
armed attack 198, 237–8
armed forces 157–8, 162, 165–6, 176, 197–202,
    208, 236–8, 252
  foreign 198, 237
  national 165, 177, 835, 840
arrest 28, 44, 90, 267–8, 408, 418, 555, 673

artistic quality 724, 729
assembly
  freedom of 641–2, 740, 749, 753–4
    peaceful 743, 747
  outdoor assemblies 740–1, 749–51, 753–4
  peaceful, *see* peaceful assembly
  public 739, 752–4
  right to 739–55
assent 131, 148, 250, 257, 266, 346–7, 698
assets 414, 833, 962, 976
assimilationist policies 571–2, 574
association, right of 756–7, 761, 763, 769
associations, rights and freedoms of 763–70
attorneys 375, 389, 420, 688, 690, 708, 724
Aung San 29–30
Aurobindo, Sri 774
Australia 2, 34, 253, 547, 562, 915, 924, 930
authoritarian governments 23, 54, 74–5
authorities
  administrative 458, 620, 646–7, 754, 786
  competent 212, 314, 386, 439, 458, 740, 749–51,
    753
  constitutional 326, 354, 384–5, 389, 538
  governing 581, 763–4, 770
  immigration 314, 320–1
  judicial 353, 372, 394–6, 403
  legislative 207–8, 364, 971
  local 334, 761, 858, 929
  political 97, 118, 546, 776, 833, 860, 892–3
  religious 777–8, 786, 798, 867, 881, 897, 910
  secular 774, 893
autonomous regions 176, 319, 913
autonomy 24, 29–30, 36, 59, 156, 227, 231, 255
  fiscal 386–8
  high degree of 228, 230, 315–16, 325, 428–9
  individual 79, 101, 118, 121, 465, 642, 782, 828
  judicial 369, 391–2
  private 638, 903, 956

bad faith 361, 691–3
Baer, Susanne 2, 4
balance of power 161–2, 187, 255, 294–5
balancing approach 836, 902
balancing process 832, 840, 850, 856
balancing test 741, 882
Bali 52, 54, 300, 975–6
  bombers 299–300
ballots 250, 485, 507, 515–17, 519
Balochistan 253, 992
Bangladesh 3, 5
  caretaker government 180
  constitution making 18
  constitutional change 243–7, 251, 257, 260, 290
  constitutional culture 70, 79, 86, 105, 110, 113,
    115–16
  democracy and right to political
    participation 493–4, 496, 518, 537
  free speech 642, 652, 687, 704, 711, 768, 770
  government system 128, 144–5, 174, 180–1
  judicial review 309, 313, 328, 350–1, 389–90,
    393–4, 433–4, 440–1
  religion 828–30, 847, 859–60, 867–8, 909–10

right to equality and equal protection 550, 554, 556–7, 605, 625, 635
from secular to Islamic Republic and back 110–16
socio-economic rights 944, 968, 983, 988, 990–1, 1000–1, 1020
banks 193, 445–6, 618, 757
Bao Dai 46–7
bare necessities of life 984, 990–1, 1007, 1013
Barisan Nasional (BN) 492–3
basic features 113–15, 209, 245, 280, 288–90, 292–3, 298–9, 351
doctrine 282, 299
basic humanity 434–5
basic order of free democracy 172, 242, 360, 621, 672
basic rights 84–5, 368, 526–7, 613–14, 620, 638, 953, 958–60
basic structure 113–14, 279–80, 282–3, 288–92, 295, 298, 351, 389–90
doctrine 283, 290–1, 295, 298–9, 351
Beer, Lawrence Ward 3, 14, 18–19, 37, 46, 53, 70, 554
belief
freedom of 853, 863, 865, 895–6, 911
in god 890, 935
groups 933
inner 622, 737
mistaken but justified 710
mystical 774, 941–2
personal 773, 775, 814, 894
systems 771–4, 852, 910
believers 777, 779, 782, 833–4, 838, 863–4, 866, 895
benevolent neutrality 879, 881, 883–4, 886, 888–9
benevolent neutrality-accommodation 883–6
Bengal Famine 289–90
best interests 361, 617, 665
bestiality 723, 728
Bharatiya Janata Party (BJP) 807, 878
Bhumibol, King 135
Bhutan 5
constitution making 58
constitutional culture 70, 77–8, 80, 82, 103–4, 106–7
equality 550, 556–7, 635
free speech 683
government system 128–9
judicial review 309
religion 802–5, 867
socio-economic rights 1001
Bhutto, Benazir 252–3, 1017
bias 94, 117, 691, 699, 795, 1012
Bible 799, 835, 855, 890, 909, 921
bigamy 886, 889
Bihar 152–3, 754, 772, 781, 925, 985, 998, 1005
Biman 768–9
bisexuals 482, 487–8, 629–30, 633
BJP (Bharatiya Janata Party) 807, 878
blasphemy 110, 915–16, 921, 928, 930–2, 935, 940, 942
in general 915–16

Indonesia 932–42
laws 643, 909–42
Pakistan 916–32
blind persons 581, 588
blogs 651, 677
BN (Barisan Nasional) 492–3
bona fides 253, 414, 416, 597, 691, 698, 781
Borneo 18, 34, 36
North 34–6
broadcasting 654–6, 667, 730
Brunei 3, 5, 7
constitution making 26, 34–7, 58
constitutional change 221, 257, 260
equality 550
free speech 683
government system 128, 144, 205
judicial review 309, 312, 440
religion 860
Sultan 37, 135, 172, 205, 440
Buddha Sasana, *see* Buddhism
Buddhism 104–9, 772, 774–5, 805, 807–8, 816–17, 819–20, 822–3
Tibetan 97, 802, 866
Buddhist monks 107–8, 799
Buddhist theocracy 106, 802
Buddhists 107–9, 115–16, 799–800, 802, 804–5, 816, 819, 859–60
budgetary powers 178, 196
budgets 145, 148, 159, 161, 177, 369, 371, 386–7
national 190, 193, 196, 951
and policy 190–6
bumiputeras 577–8
bureaucracy 127–8, 147, 155, 175, 177–8, 534
buried assets protection 576
Burma 2, 99, 552, 711; *see also* Myanmar
constitution making 18, 20, 26, 29–30, 34, 58, 60, 64
business 204, 209–10, 378–80, 478–9, 580–1, 593, 679, 976
activities 583, 648, 973
entities 588, 649, 975
private 209, 588

cabinet ministers 48, 147, 172
cabinet system 13–14, 134, 257, 354
cabinets 131, 133, 135–7, 146–52, 205–6, 237–8, 374, 402
calamities 80, 195, 203–4, 215, 225, 579, 988, 990
Cambodia 5, 18, 38
constitution making 50–1, 56, 58, 60
constitutional change 221–2, 257, 260, 280
constitutional culture 79–81, 83, 86, 120
democracy 466
equality 557, 625
free speech 683
government system 127–8, 144–5, 189, 205
judicial review 309–10, 328–30, 334–5, 338, 350, 370–1, 432
religion 860
Sihanouk, King 50–1, 56
socio-economic rights 944, 1022
Cambodian People's Party (CPP) 56, 864

Canada 2, 72, 324, 327, 426, 546, 561–2, 681
candidacy 534, 607, 611
    certificates of 530, 607–9, 611
candidates 141–2, 186–8, 482–5, 501–3, 507–11,
    529–30, 533–6, 875
    independent 137, 296, 484–5, 533–4
    presidential 23, 532
capital punishment 132–3, 526, 555
capitalist economy 25, 480
Cappelletti, Mauro 3–4, 307–8
caretaker governments 174, 180–1, 247
    non-party 180, 247
Carlyle, Thomas 652
caste 112, 114, 557–8, 808, 829, 872–3, 875, 930
    scheduled castes 113, 467, 493–7, 559–60, 577,
    920, 924, 999
Catholic Church 86, 107, 776, 878, 906–7
Catholics 863, 874, 876, 878, 888, 906
CCP (Chinese Communist Party) 37, 40–5, 101,
    121, 173–8, 862–3, 911
censorship 643–5, 647, 649–51, 653, 657, 678, 686,
    724
Central Authorities 178, 229, 314, 316–19, 322,
    326
central government 288, 319, 380–1, 384–5, 627–8,
    996–7, 999–1000, 1003–4
centralised systems 327–8, 342, 347–9, 352, 356,
    405, 443, 447
    judicial review 308–11, 348, 365
ceremonial functions 128–9, 139
ceremonial powers 135, 140
ceremonial presidency 144, 195
ceremonial Shinto 892
ceremonies 772, 813, 815, 851–2, 854, 893–5,
    900–1, 903–4
    anthem 771, 851–2
    religious 807, 851–3, 867, 897, 903, 925
    traditional 569, 574, 898–9
certificate of apostasy 796–7
certificates of candidacy 530, 607–9, 611
certification 358, 524–5, 591, 892
certiorari 286, 443, 509, 514, 516, 519–20, 905,
    908
Ceylon 2, 222, 298; *see also* Sri Lanka
    constitution making 18, 26, 29–31, 60
chaos 216, 256, 284–5, 450, 453, 517, 776, 786
Chat Kasertrakorn Thai Party 506
Chat Prachachon Party 506
Chat Samakkee Party 506
Chatniyom Party 506
checks and balances 142–3, 181, 184, 187–8, 190,
    196, 278, 395
Chiang Kai-shek 21, 39–40, 349
Chief Election Commissioner 154, 511, 515, 518
children 79–80, 84–5, 439–40, 730–1, 852–3, 999,
    1002–3, 1007–9
chilling effect 267, 651, 671, 711
China 3, 5–6
    CCP (Chinese Communist Party) 37, 40–5, 101,
    121, 173–8, 862–3, 911
    constitution making 10, 12–14, 17, 20–2, 25,
    38–46, 51, 53

constitutional change 221–2, 224, 226–9, 260,
    277, 281
constitutional culture 75, 78–80, 86–7, 92, 95–7,
    99–101, 104, 121–4
democracy 482, 497, 543
equality 547, 550–1, 578, 592, 613–16, 625–6,
    629, 637
free speech 701–3, 711, 764
government system 128–9, 139–40, 144, 173–8,
    204–5
Hong Kong SAR, *see* Hong Kong
judicial review 312–15, 318–20, 322–4, 328, 425,
    428, 431, 441
religion 847, 862–4, 866, 873, 911, 913–14
socio-economic rights 944, 962
Taiwan, *see* Taiwan
Chinese Communist Party, *see* CCP
Chinese nationality 314, 319–20, 612
Chinese People's Political Consultative Conference,
    see CPPCC
choice 267–9, 484–5, 513–15, 611–12, 783–6,
    790–1, 810, 836–8
    freedom of 267–8, 786, 809–10, 880, 954, 956
    individual 59, 782, 861, 867
    occupational 581, 585
    personal 782, 785, 828, 956
Christian institutions 800, 817
Christianity 800, 802–3, 807–8, 811, 819–21, 906,
    908, 934
    growth of 803–4
Chulalongkorn, King 16
circular letters 376, 379–81, 411–12
citizen petitions 464, 543–4
citizenry 101, 165, 202, 272, 641, 709, 760–1, 953
citizens 76–84, 122–3, 405–7, 529–32, 550–3,
    839–42, 953–6, 1006–14
    dual 530
    good 79–80, 101, 934
    individual 331, 333–4, 591, 956
    natural-born 375, 377, 381
    naturalized 381, 530, 638
citizenship 69, 76, 79, 377, 528–30, 606, 849, 853–4
    dual 529–30, 615
    equal 76, 426
    foreign 530, 616
civic associations 641, 763–4, 770
civic duties 78, 896, 925
civic responsibility 101, 683
civil administrative executive services 393–4
civil and political rights (CPRs) 303, 429, 433, 638,
    641, 943, 946, 949
civil associations 187, 189, 765
civil contempt 396, 687
civil courts 734, 784, 788–92, 797, 862, 868, 888,
    890
civil liberties 37, 55, 295, 299, 703, 834, 911, 914
civil ownership 971–2
civil penalties 508, 659
civil rights 19, 94, 590–1, 926, 1003
civil service 11, 27, 147, 179, 389, 606, 609, 858
civil society 282, 373, 497, 700
    and freedom of association 755–70

civil wars 21, 40, 42, 46, 61, 223–4, 227, 929–30
classes 413, 428–9, 551–3, 589–601, 608–12, 630–1,
    676, 755–6
  working 41, 48, 100–1, 173–4
classification 317, 553–4, 557, 589–92, 595–602,
    605–7, 609–11, 618–19
  condition 229, 317, 322, 429
  doctrine of 589
  legislative 606, 611, 619
  rational 589–622
  reasonable 553, 591, 594, 598–600, 605, 607–8
clean environment 1019, 1021
clean water 978, 1019, 1021
clear and present danger 79, 440, 670, 688–9, 750,
    858
clemency 119, 131–3, 397
  power 131–3
co-regulation 118, 825
coalition government 49, 147, 149
coercion 28, 741, 802, 804, 810–11, 855, 858, 865
coercive powers 275–6
coexistence 76, 104, 775, 843, 868, 901, 960
  peaceful 80, 105, 826
cohabitation 887–8
Cold War 23, 57, 74, 238, 328
collective bargaining 758, 761, 944, 957, 960–1
  agents 768–9
  agreements 957–60
collective leadership 121, 176
collective leadership system 174, 176
collective responsibility 157, 847
collective security arrangements 198, 237
colonial powers 14–15, 45, 53, 59
colonial rule 58, 195, 222, 230, 328, 478
colonialism 17, 86–8, 117, 120, 196, 230, 793
combative sport in schools 836–8
COMELEC (Commission on Elections) 468, 474,
    486–90, 507, 512–20, 541, 607, 668
Commission on Elections, *see* COMELEC
committal 693–4
  orders of 437, 690
commodity expenses 949, 951
common good, visions of 69, 77–82
common law 228–9, 311, 422–3, 437, 560–2,
    564–5, 694–5, 712
  contempt of court 695–6
  countries/jurisdictions 133, 433, 436, 438, 687–8,
    694, 705, 712
common values 727–8
Commonwealth 27, 35, 145, 780, 848–9, 857, 923,
    925
  jurisdictions 79, 120, 440
communal harmony 678, 910
communism 17, 25, 37–8, 101, 196, 238, 763–4,
    862
  advocacy of 749–50, 753
Communist Party of Malaya (CPM) 207
Communist Party of Vietnam 100, 173, 863
Communist revolutions 37–51, 621
communist states 38, 75, 178, 309, 313
communitarian democracies 70, 463, 465–6, 494,
    642–3

communities 303, 665, 731, 800–2, 873, 923–7,
    929–31, 979–82
  cultural 105, 486, 559, 967
  Muslim 89, 786, 790–1, 794, 859, 868, 891, 919
  religious 792, 801, 866, 874, 918, 920, 923, 926
community expectations 825–6
community interests 465, 642, 701–2, 862
community values 303, 465, 467, 642
compelling state interests 557, 855, 882, 885, 888–9
  test 814, 879, 882, 884–5, 887
compensation 560–1, 563, 565–6, 706, 728, 734–5,
    739, 903
  monetary 439, 709, 737
competence 164, 244, 291, 329–30, 334, 977, 1015
  disputes 182–3, 328–30, 334
competent authorities 212, 314, 386, 439, 458, 740,
    749–51, 753
competing interests 64, 576, 612, 710, 908, 945,
    1020, 1022
  principle of balancing 958–9
competing rights 6, 91, 438, 783, 801, 952–3
  social insurance schemes 954–7
competition 99, 155, 485, 586–7, 652, 656, 972–7,
    979
  free 359, 956
  political 121, 262
compromise 44, 59, 241, 256, 414, 444, 663, 738
  political 217, 262, 304
compulsion 790, 818, 858, 903, 919
compulsory education 531, 983, 1008
compulsory military service 91, 847
compulsory organization 958–60
concrete review 329, 331–5, 337
concubinage 887–9
conduct 394–6, 440, 630–1, 694–6, 698, 703,
    747–9, 899–900
  criminal 439, 847, 889, 912
  disgraceful and immoral 879, 888
  expressive 683, 700
  homosexual 488
  of public affairs 521, 525, 531, 536
  religious 882, 888
confidence 63, 65, 148–9, 151, 172–3, 538, 540,
    604–5
  public, *see* public confidence
  referenda 160, 171–2, 537–8
  votes 151, 354, 537–9
confirmation 22, 142, 182, 184, 188, 281, 354, 532
  power 354
Confucian constitutionalism 96–8, 120, 123, 328
Confucianism 67, 95–6, 100–1, 118, 120, 122, 550,
    932
confusion 114, 308, 454, 517–18, 786, 789, 906,
    908
conscience 620–2, 733–5, 737–8, 788, 808–10, 812,
    839–44, 854–7
  free 782–3, 799, 801, 808–9, 816, 818, 836, 843–5
  freedom of 620–2, 734, 738, 788, 808–9, 812,
    839–41, 843–4
  religious 843, 883
  right of 738, 814
  scruples of 855, 882

conscientious objection 91, 835–58
conscription 616, 841–4, 846
consensus 60, 89–90, 103, 139, 780, 787, 1010,
    1015–16
  national 65, 217, 226, 272, 274
  political 217–18, 226, 260, 282
consent 163–5, 182–4, 284, 370–1, 379–83, 405,
    420, 596
  parliamentary 370, 374
consistency 228, 315, 324–5, 348, 452, 457, 760,
    865
constituencies 469–71, 475–6, 480, 482, 494, 509,
    515–16
  delimitation 469, 475–6, 509
  functional 97, 467, 478–80, 525
constituent assemblies 30–3, 41, 56, 58, 60–1, 254,
    552, 556
constituent power 59, 235, 282, 289
constituents 165, 202, 480, 612, 709
constitution making 9–64, 74, 100, 127, 222,
    230–1, 235, 239–40
  Bangladesh 18
  Bhutan 58
  Brunei 34–7, 58
  Burma 18, 20, 26, 29–30, 34, 58, 60, 64
  Cambodia 50–1, 56, 58, 60
  Ceylon 18, 26, 29–31, 60
  China 10, 12–14, 17, 20–2, 25, 38–46, 51, 53
  colonisation and decolonisation 17–37
  epochs of 57–8
  incremental 239–40
  India 17, 20, 26, 31–3
  Indonesia 20, 36, 52–4, 58, 60–1
  Japan 9–14, 16–20, 23, 57–8, 61
  Laos 18, 38, 48–50
  Malaysia 26, 34–7, 58
  Mongolia 14, 37, 52, 57–8
  Myanmar 58
  Nepal 58, 61
  North Korea 24–5
  Pakistan 26, 31–4, 58, 60, 64
  Philippines 14–15, 18, 22, 36, 51, 54–6
  Singapore 18, 20, 26–8, 34–7, 58, 63
  South Korea 18, 20, 22–4, 51, 58, 61
  Sri Lanka 29–30, 58
  Taiwan 12, 18, 20, 20–31, 40, 58
  Thailand 14, 16–17, 49–50, 58, 64
  Vietnam 18, 38, 45–8, 50, 63
constitutional adjudication 4, 342, 352, 355, 359,
    424, 426, 431
constitutional amendments 135, 219–20, 255–8,
    260–4, 279–83, 290–1, 295–7, 349–52
  impugned 351–2, 477
  judicial review 349–52
  and procedure 256–65
  unconstitutional 220, 282, 291
constitutional authorisation, express 342, 344, 350,
    357, 361, 364
constitutional authorities 326, 354, 384–5, 389,
    538
constitutional change 7, 17, 107, 219–305, 927
  Bangladesh 243–7, 251, 257, 260, 290

Brunei 221, 257, 260
Cambodia 221–2, 257, 260, 280
China 221–2, 224, 226–9, 260, 277, 281
  during revolutions and emergencies 247–55
  Hong Kong 227, 229–30, 257, 274, 276–7, 280–1
  imposed and autonomous 230–9
  India 221–2, 246, 253, 257, 260, 283, 286,
    288–90
  Indonesia 221, 240, 258, 260, 280–1, 299–300,
    302–4
  Japan 221–2, 231–2, 234–9, 243, 247, 260
  and judicial decisions 270–8
  Laos 221–2, 258, 260
  limits to 278–305
    implied 280–99
    international law and transnational
      constitutionalism 299–305
  Malaysia 221, 235, 258, 260, 271, 280–1, 298–9,
    309
  methods 255–78
  Mongolia 221–2, 239–40, 260
  Myanmar 221–2
  Nepal 258, 260
  Pakistan 221–2, 245–6, 248, 251–2, 254–5
  Philippines 221–2, 231, 239–40, 248, 251,
    258–61, 266–9
  Singapore 221–2, 235, 259–60, 298–9
  South Korea 221–2, 235, 239–41, 243, 258, 260,
    271–3
  Sri Lanka 259–60, 262–5, 291, 293, 295
  Taiwan 221–6, 240, 260, 262
  Thailand 221–2, 240, 251, 259–60, 280–1
  Vietnam 221–2, 259–60
constitutional conventions 15, 258, 260, 266, 268,
    274, 400–1, 424
constitutional courts 328–30, 334–5, 337–41,
    349–50, 369–70, 399, 404, 447–8
constitutional crises 181–2, 216, 262, 271, 362, 492
constitutional cultism 102–3
constitutional cultures 7, 65–125
  Bangladesh 70, 79, 86, 105, 110, 113, 115–16
  Bhutan 70, 77–8, 80, 82, 103–4, 106–7
  Cambodia 79–81, 83, 86, 120
  China 75, 78–80, 86–7, 92, 95–7, 99–101, 104,
    121–4
  and courts 65, 68, 71, 90–1, 112, 115, 117–21,
    123
  functional approach 76–94
  India 70, 79, 112
  Indonesia 75, 78, 88–9, 91–2, 106
  influence on style of constitutionalism 118–25
  and instrumentalism 85–103
  Japan 67, 72, 74–5, 81, 83, 106
  Laos 86, 104, 106
  Malaysia 70, 74, 76, 79, 89, 92, 105–6,
    116–17
  Mongolia 78, 80
  Myanmar 106
  Nepal 109–10
  North Korea 102–3
  Pakistan 70, 108, 110–12, 117
  Philippines 70, 75, 81–2, 107

Singapore 74, 82, 90–2, 103–4, 116, 118–19, 124–5
South Korea 67, 73, 75, 84, 86, 120
Sri Lanka 80, 106–8
Taiwan 75, 87, 92, 120, 123
Thailand 75, 78, 80–1, 86, 99–100, 106, 108–9
Vietnam 75, 78, 80, 100–1, 104, 106, 120, 122–3
constitutional democracy 92, 95, 139, 192, 225, 497, 661
constitutional development 7, 11–12, 18, 21, 30, 35, 38, 74–5
constitutional durability and adaptability 220–55
constitutional government 2, 11–13, 39, 55, 59, 62, 88, 209
constitutional guarantees 109, 422, 428–9, 435, 712, 715, 856–7, 924–5
constitutional identity 105, 121, 239–40
constitutional immunity 167, 169
constitutional intent 142, 188, 387, 455, 491, 750–1
constitutional interpretation 335, 337, 342–3, 355, 388–9, 417–43, 460, 786–7
   historically-based approach 424–6
   purposive approach 426–31
   text-based approach 417–23
   use of foreign and international law 431–43
constitutional legitimacy 59, 62, 64, 68
constitutional monarchy 12–13, 16–17, 49, 56, 58, 92, 95, 134–5
constitutional patriotism 85–7
constitutional petitions 252, 333–4, 537, 992, 1017
constitutional politics 62, 235, 255
constitutional principles 68, 70, 74–5, 239–40, 299, 340, 472, 962–3
   fundamental 187, 279, 460
   general 538, 672
constitutional protection 491, 520, 558, 670, 700, 709, 764, 856
constitutional reform 16, 23, 35, 75, 100, 157, 166, 328
constitutional review 120, 277–8, 309–12, 325, 329–32, 334, 365, 620
   centralised system 416
constitutional revision 19, 254–5, 260–1, 264, 272–3, 296–7, 338–9, 349–51
   frequent 246–7, 264
constitutional rights 122–3, 333–4, 348, 407–8, 410–11, 442–3, 746–7, 851
constitutional supremacy 117, 326, 798
   clauses 308, 793
constitutional theocracies 866–9
constitutional traditions 67, 240, 274, 417, 630
constitutional transformation 219, 739
constitutional validity 212, 288, 304, 379, 381–5, 412, 630
constitutional values 76, 86, 120, 211, 270, 282, 843, 845
constitutionalism 1–6, 12–14, 65–6, 68–70, 74–5, 118–25, 219–21, 282–3
   Confucian 96–8, 120, 123, 328
   development 70, 231
   Islamic 867–8
   and legitimacy 58–63

liberal 5, 82, 120, 643, 861
   modern 270, 313, 349, 369
   political 118, 120
   rights-based 79, 120
   transnational 279, 299, 417
constitutionality 197–9, 237–8, 243–4, 328–36, 341–5, 366–8, 387–90, 442–4
   administrative regulations 310, 348
   administrative rules 356–7, 444
   limited 366, 443–4, 447
   partial 366, 445
construction 191–2, 509, 511, 574–7, 647, 649, 708, 1011–12
   judicial 983, 985, 987, 989, 991, 993, 995, 997
consultation 119, 127, 267, 374, 378–80, 382–5, 390–1, 412
   effective 381–5
consumers 81, 83, 581, 649
contempt 437–8, 440, 642–3, 670, 674–6, 683, 687–8, 690–9
   civil 396, 687
   common law 695–6
   criminal 396, 687–8, 695
   law of 438, 696, 700
contempt of court 396, 437–8, 642–3, 670, 682–3, 687–8, 690, 692–9
contemptuous speech 688, 699
continuity 37, 59, 98, 104, 171, 178–9, 265, 470
   institutional 76, 221
   legal 24, 63, 234–5
contraception 107
contract 159, 163, 365, 405, 588–9, 657, 956, 961–2
   freedom of 588–9, 956, 961
control 39–40, 45, 152–3, 635–6, 656–8, 970–2, 976–7, 981
   social 284–5
   state 101, 970, 972–3, 976–7
Control Yuan 22, 39, 184, 225, 310, 391, 396, 424–5
convenience 508, 748, 752, 947, 985, 1015
conversion 785, 789–91, 793, 796, 798, 859, 919–20, 927
   forced 808, 810, 813, 816, 821
   mass 800
   and propagation 798–826
   as public order issue 785–98
   unethical 808, 817
convertees 804, 811, 813–15
cooperation 68, 96, 103, 251, 741, 903, 918
cooperatives 88, 974
corporate governance 445
corporate voting 479–80
corruption 54, 93, 154, 156–7, 172, 178, 251, 606
   acts of 251, 606
cosmopolitanism 85–6
costs 327, 508, 573–4, 646, 656, 929, 943, 949
coup leaders 16–17
coups 16–17, 47, 53–4, 241, 243, 245, 248, 466
   successful 56, 241–2, 360
courtesy 225, 901
   social 898–900

courts 241–55, 307–18, 396–407, 410–24, 434–57, 687–700, 943–57, 979–94
  constitutional 328–30, 334–5, 337–41, 349–50, 369–70, 399, 404, 447–8
  and constitutional cultures 65, 68, 71, 90–1, 112, 115, 117–21, 123
  highest 207, 286, 288, 343, 349, 369, 401, 449–50
  lower 316, 331–2, 344–5, 389, 391–2, 396, 706–7, 738
  ordinary 168, 309, 325, 332–5, 348–9, 356–9, 365–6, 372–3
  role in mediating political conflicts 216–18
  structure 389–96
  syariah 784–6, 788–92, 794–8, 890, 914
cow slaughter 781–2, 874
CPM (Communist Party of Malaya) 207
CPP (Cambodian People's Party) 56, 864
CPPCC (Chinese People's Political Consultative Conference) 40–2
CPRs, *see* civil and political rights
credible elections 180, 517–18
crimes 170, 232–3, 243, 300–3, 440, 526–7, 554–5, 683–4
crimes against humanity 301–2
criminal conduct 439, 847, 889, 912
criminal contempt 396, 687–8, 695
criminal defamation 684, 705, 708–9, 711
criminal punishment 439, 572, 728, 730–1, 734, 742, 839, 844–5
criminalization 301, 937
criminals 299, 303, 392, 526–7, 865, 868, 912, 921
  convicted 439–40
  habitual 434, 597
  war 246, 301, 901
criticism, fair 690–1
cultism 102–3
cults 24, 773, 876, 910–16
cultural communities 105, 486, 559, 967
cultural diversity 82, 804, 828
cultural heritage 69, 76–7, 104, 543, 635–6, 844, 965
cultural identities 62, 235, 731–2, 799, 864, 936
cultural interests 559, 578
cultural legitimacy 97
cultural life 77, 613, 625
cultural norms 70, 76, 122, 130, 806
cultural traditions 90, 105, 635, 803, 806
cultural values 76, 713
culture 66–73, 75–7, 79–80, 103–5, 121–2, 566–7, 569, 573–5
  constitutional, *see* constitutional cultures
  ethnic 568–9, 571, 574–5
  governing institutional interactions through 103–9
  legal 9, 59, 68–73, 75, 374, 403
  national 76–7, 104–5, 865
  as normative matrix 77–85
  and paths of institutional interaction 103–24
  as platform for political ideology 100–2
  political 253, 720–1
  unique 79, 440, 568–9, 571

customs 104–5, 458, 562, 572, 635–6, 774–5, 777, 779
  lifestyle 574–5
cybercrime 711–12

damages 322–3, 591, 639, 690–1, 704, 707, 721, 735–7
  quantum of 119, 721
daughters 628, 638, 926, 985, 1017
de-registration 835, 848, 850
death sentence, *see* capital punishment
debts 134, 445–6
decentralised systems 356, 369
  judicial review 308–9, 327–8, 342–9, 443
deception 112, 507, 923
decision-making powers 136, 178, 327, 947
declarations of emergency 22, 214
declarations of unconstitutionality 330, 443, 447, 450, 454
decolonisation 17, 19, 21, 23, 25–7, 29, 31, 33
decrees 54–5, 206–7, 250, 330, 332, 363–4, 400, 865–6
  emergency 23, 47, 157–8, 193–4, 204–7, 349, 356, 361–4
  presidential 266, 300, 349, 387, 400, 932, 937, 965
deed poll 790, 792
deemed-resigned provisions 608, 610–12
defamation 642–3, 664–5, 670, 684–6, 704–5, 707–12, 714, 716–17
  criminal 684, 705, 708–9, 711
  intentional 683–4
  political 90, 704–21
deference 165, 202, 477, 519–20, 873, 949
  judicial 330, 364, 459, 477, 519
deforestation 964, 1020
degradation, environmental 99, 416, 1010, 1014–15, 1019–20
delegated powers 325, 927
delegation 209, 257, 327, 392, 519, 596
deliberate intention 671, 688, 698
deliberative democracy 463, 651
democracy 52–3, 74–5, 91–2, 96, 107–11, 280, 289, 463–544
  Bangladesh 493–4, 496, 518, 537
  Cambodia 466
  China 482, 497, 543
  concepts and types 464–5
  constitutional 92, 95, 139, 192, 225, 497, 661
  deliberative 463, 651
  direct 172, 464, 535, 538, 540
  economic 970–2, 976
  electoral 463, 465
  free 387, 617, 960
  guided 53, 61, 932
  Hong Kong 467, 478–80, 521, 524, 531
  India 465, 475, 477, 493–7, 504–5, 509, 515
  Indonesia 464, 466, 498, 501, 532
  Japan 465, 468, 470, 481–3, 521–3, 535, 537, 540
  liberal 9, 56, 120, 280, 463–7, 476–7, 642–3, 653
  Malaysia 465, 492–3, 499
  militant 350, 497–8, 505

Mongolia 464, 537
Pakistan 465, 493, 533, 536–7
parliamentary 17, 52, 58, 89–90, 130, 145, 148, 253
Philippines 464–8, 473–4, 481–2, 486–9, 512–16, 519–20, 536–7, 540–1
pluralistic 56, 281
principle of 172, 296, 484, 980
representative 165, 202, 273, 464, 467, 498, 508, 527
secular 798, 859, 875, 914
Singapore 465, 478–9, 481, 490, 492, 537
socialist 463–4
South Korea 464–7, 472–3, 476–7, 481–2, 484, 498, 501, 540–1
Sri Lanka 465, 537, 539
Taiwan 464, 466–7, 481–2, 489–90, 493, 498, 501, 534
Thailand 464–7, 482, 498, 500–2, 511, 514, 537
transitional 239, 983
Vietnam 537
democratic accountability 463
democratic elections 54, 181
democratic governance 466, 511, 520, 641, 721, 739, 742
democratic government 16, 38, 40, 251, 345, 968, 991
democratic institutions 4, 6, 510
democratic legitimacy 62, 141, 171, 432, 436, 461, 464, 527
democratic polity 464, 534, 656, 705
democratic processes 295, 507, 652, 683, 882, 989
Democratic Progressive Party, *see* DPP
democratic republic 297, 352, 464, 467, 590
Democratic Republic of Vietnam, *see* DRV
democratic revolutions 51–8, 64
democratic society 303, 686–8, 698, 700, 702, 742–3, 748, 750
democratic transitions 143, 155, 166, 222, 224, 227, 239–40, 295
Taiwan 226, 261
democratisation 134, 217, 224, 226, 239, 241, 459, 463–97
waves of 465–7
demonstrations 359, 686, 693, 700, 703, 744, 749, 753–5
student 217, 226
Deng Xiaoping 43–4, 139, 175
deposits 457–8, 533–4, 593, 618
deprivation of life 526, 986–7
descent 533, 557, 607, 622, 625, 638
desecration 441, 700–2, 923, 926, 933, 938, 940
flag 701–3
of religion 937–8, 940–1
desecration of religion 937–8, 940–1
detention 134, 148, 204, 408, 418, 654, 849, 1018
development
economic 6, 62–3, 70, 74–5, 82, 1007, 1011, 1014
socio-economic 560, 804
developmentalism 57, 1022
deviant sects 867, 910–11, 914
dialogue 120, 124, 166, 273, 442, 713, 826, 1022

judicial 442, 711
dictatorship 25, 41, 103, 215, 243, 251, 463, 869
people's 42, 173
differential treatment 589, 610, 613, 617, 620–1
differentiation 592, 601–2, 604, 613, 869
dignity 287–90, 394–5, 683–4, 697, 699, 991–2, 1007–9, 1012–13
human 83, 85, 279–80, 737–8, 952, 954, 984, 1007–8
diplomacy 203, 355, 537
diplomatic immunities 555
diplomats 97, 555
direct democracy 172, 464, 535, 538, 540
direct election 54, 61, 128, 247, 478, 481, 484–5, 494–5
directive principles 285, 287, 961, 963, 967–9, 986, 988–9, 1006–8
Directive Principles of State Policy, *see* DPSP
disability 116, 411–12, 531, 582–3, 588, 624, 736, 955–6
physical 581–2, 956
visual 586
disabled persons 582–3, 587–9, 844
disadvantaged people 414, 456, 559
discretion 273–4, 435, 469, 514, 645–6, 742–4, 962, 966–7
administrative 74, 577, 950
exercise of 267, 724
lawful 200, 1018
legislative 142, 188, 366, 472–3, 508, 528, 583, 750
limited 744, 752, 950
personal 131, 148
statutory 500, 743–4
unprincipled 499, 767
discretionary authority 538, 566, 837
discretionary powers 130, 134–6, 148, 154, 198, 237, 346–7, 950–1
discrimination 582–4, 597–8, 600–2, 613–16, 619–20, 623–7, 631–2, 634–5
against aliens or foreigners 637–40
against indigenous peoples 634–7
against women 624–6
arbitrary 552, 596
gender 557, 624–34, 828–9
hostile 591–2, 594, 608
positive 558–78
prohibited categories 557
and protection of minorities 622–40
racial 638, 681
religious 109, 112
discriminatory legislation 557, 606–7, 615, 884
discriminatory treatment 579, 582, 589, 617, 624
disease 581–2, 925, 951, 956, 1010, 1016
disgraceful and immoral conduct 879, 888
dismissals 79, 95, 154, 170, 178, 250, 252, 882
disorder 124, 517, 650, 670, 825
public 743, 776, 814
social 676, 915
disqualification 492, 529–30, 532, 761, 882
dissent 116, 250, 612, 641, 856, 886

dissenting opinions/judgments 269, 272, 447, 590–1, 843, 845, 887, 889
dissolution 136–7, 148–54, 156, 161–2, 339–40, 402–3, 501–2, 504–6
  orders 501, 833–5
  of parliament 133, 161–2, 180, 294
  of political parties 329, 337, 339–40, 392, 497, 501–2, 505
  power of 152, 156, 161–2, 294
disturbances 198, 238, 251, 303, 563, 741, 745, 810
diversity 60, 66, 125, 189, 568, 798–9, 870, 873–4
  cultural 82, 804, 828
  religious 867, 873
divorce 600–1, 689, 793, 796, 935
dominant religion 787–9, 824, 859
domination 17, 20, 33, 49, 104, 546, 956
donations 172, 514, 776, 901
Dorsen, Norman 2, 4, 463, 670, 700, 740
DPP (Democratic Progressive Party) 22, 141, 172, 297, 466
DPSP (Directive Principles of State Policy) 413, 944, 983–5, 992–3, 1001, 1007
dress codes 827–9
drinking water 978–9, 999, 1019
drought 964, 988, 994, 996, 999, 1021
drug trafficking 397, 713
DRV (Democratic Republic of Vietnam) 46, 48, 864
dual allegiance 529–30
dual citizens 530
dual citizenship 529–30, 615
Dutch East Indies 18, 20, 52–3, 58
duties 80, 83–4, 284–6, 315–17, 567, 744–5, 846–7, 853–5
  civic 78, 896, 925
  constitutional 133, 182–4, 356, 988, 999
  judicial 688, 695, 963
  military 834, 849, 858
  of military service 839–42, 844–5
  of national defense 839–40, 844
  official 164, 171, 537, 617
  positive 667, 744
  religious 801, 808

East Pakistan 112, 605, 637
East Timor 128, 205, 260, 280, 304, 431–2
  President 129, 205
ecological balance 1013, 1020
ecology 772, 1013, 1015, 1020
  healthful 415, 964–8
economic and legal legitimacy 62–3
economic crises 47, 58, 75, 158, 194, 203–4, 206, 291
economic democracy 970–2, 976
economic development 6, 62–3, 70, 74–5, 82, 1007, 1011, 1014
economic policy 78, 967–9, 971, 973, 975, 977, 979, 981–2
economic rights 45, 55–6, 413, 552, 943–4, 1001, 1003
economy 45, 81, 88, 158, 193–4, 401–2, 673–4, 970–1

national 82, 194, 950–1, 956, 972–3, 976–7, 989, 1021
Edo Shogunate 570–1
education 84–5, 322–3, 530 1, 578–9, 760–2, 837, 852–3, 855–8
  compulsory 531, 983, 1008
  free 855, 1007–8
  health 1002–3
  physical 836–7
  religious 837, 893–4, 905, 934
  right to 1006–9
educational agencies 760–1
educational facilities 984, 1007–8
educational institutions 559, 578, 830, 853, 934
  private 829, 1006
educational value 723, 728, 733
effective consultation 381–5
effective enforcement 436, 460
effectiveness 13, 62, 206, 363, 460, 541, 709, 974
efficiency 94, 209, 445, 452, 542, 972–6
elected officials 607–12
elected Presidents 98, 103, 133–4, 138, 144, 172–3, 195, 342–3
elected representatives 30, 41, 58, 96, 119, 523, 531, 533
election campaigns 28, 484, 507, 514, 661, 759–60
election candidates, *see* candidates
election commissions 497, 505, 511–20
  functions 514–20
  independence 511–14
election disputes 367, 404, 519–20
election-fixing 517–18
election(s) 340–1, 470–2, 476–87, 489–91, 507–17, 519–23, 526–7, 529–33
  credible 180, 517–18
  democratic 54, 181
  direct 54, 61, 128, 247, 478, 481, 484–5, 494–5
  fair 56, 74, 290, 454, 489, 503, 523
  free 497, 508, 516, 529
  general 52–4, 151–2, 180, 252–4, 470–1, 481, 504–5, 508
  local 454, 527–8, 533
  national 122, 171, 224, 297, 534, 607
  presidential 156, 166, 172–3, 184–5, 376–8, 525–6, 532, 534
  vacancy 507–8
electoral disputes 329, 340–2
electoral districts 468, 472–3, 477, 484–5, 489
electoral politics 467, 493, 497
electorates 155, 252, 480, 503, 507, 517–18, 609, 612
electors 259, 472, 476, 485, 518, 521, 523, 533–4
electricity 573, 943, 969, 972–7, 984, 993
electronic media 656–7, 668–9
embezzlement 89, 169, 342, 423, 597
emergencies, constitutional change during 247–55
emergency 134, 203–10, 212, 214–15, 247–8, 251–2, 361–4, 650
  declarations of 22, 214
  decrees 23, 47, 157–8, 193–4, 204–7, 349, 356, 361–4
  judicial review 361–5

legislation 203, 850
measures 207, 363
powers 2, 22, 47, 148, 180–1, 203–16, 295, 364–5
proclamations of 134, 204–5, 210, 212, 214, 252, 361–2, 364
states of 204–5, 207–10, 212, 214, 216, 246–8, 280–1, 364
emperor worship 106, 896
employees 216, 535, 588, 607, 609, 693, 757–8, 879
government 142, 535, 776, 888, 961
employers 460, 589, 592, 756–9, 768–9, 954–5, 958–9, 962–3
employment 580, 582–5, 588–9, 625, 757–8, 822, 829, 882
right of 581
enforcement 232–4, 285–6, 412–15, 435–6, 459–60, 627–8, 963–4, 996–7
effective 436, 460
fair 142, 187–8, 659
of fundamental rights 204, 253, 444
entitlements 72–3, 314, 562, 949, 997, 1002
environment 80, 416, 584, 966, 1009–11, 1015, 1017, 1019–22
clean 1019, 1021
healthy 404, 944, 968, 979, 1009, 1020
natural 80, 1019, 1021
environmental degradation 99, 416, 1010, 1014–15, 1019–20
environmental protection 967, 1013, 1016, 1020
equal citizenship 76, 426
equal protection 2, 7, 15, 283, 357, 545–640, 796, 798
clauses 407, 553, 556, 590, 595–7, 607–10, 618, 624
equal rights 112, 479, 548–9, 559, 624, 659, 812, 991
equal treatment 112, 114, 204, 604, 613–14, 624, 871–2, 915
equal work 623, 944
equality 280, 467–9, 471–3, 545–56, 588–91, 601, 623–6, 841–2
absolute 548–9, 604, 608, 613, 925
American test 607, 610–19
Bangladesh 550, 554, 556–7, 605, 625, 635
before the law 550–5, 595, 598, 601, 618
Bhutan 550, 556–7, 635
Cambodia 557, 625
China 547, 550–1, 578, 592, 613–16, 625–6, 629, 637
clauses 545–7, 550–1, 597, 607, 619
racial 547, 623
constitutional principle 359, 470–1, 613, 621
gender 273, 415, 435–6, 460, 827
Hong Kong 557, 640
India 552, 554, 556–8, 590, 625–9, 637, 642, 644
Indonesia 550, 556, 625
Japan 547, 550, 554, 557, 567–8, 573–5, 577, 637–8
Laos 550, 625
and the law 545–50

Malaysia 550–1, 554, 556–64, 577–8, 606, 625–6, 629
Mongolia 550, 557, 625
moral 546, 804
Myanmar 550, 556–7, 625
Nepal 550, 557–8, 625, 629, 632, 634
North Korea 550, 557, 621, 625
Pakistan 550, 554, 556, 605, 625–6, 629
Philippines 550, 556–8, 607, 640
political 340, 477, 481, 546
principle 455, 457–8, 484–5, 589, 591, 613–14, 616–17, 619
and privilege 579–89
right to 288, 358–9, 445, 472–3, 484, 509, 531, 545–640
Singapore 550, 552, 554, 556–60, 565, 578, 625, 629
South Korea 555, 557, 581, 584, 588, 612–16, 619–22, 625
Sri Lanka 550, 556–7, 605–6, 625
Taiwan 550, 579, 584, 588, 617, 619, 625, 636
Thailand 550, 556–7, 618, 625
Vietnam 550, 625
equitable access to resources 965–6
establishment clauses 824, 848, 879–80, 902
establishment of religion 848, 872, 878–9, 888, 902
eternity clauses 220, 279–80
ethics 77–8, 88, 101, 395, 727, 732, 737
professional 395, 652
societal cultural 723, 727
ethnic culture 568–9, 571, 574–5
ethnic groups 100–1, 104, 568, 571, 574, 675, 863, 873
ethnic origin 551, 557, 638, 681
ethnic unity 863
ethnicity 106, 108, 465, 568, 575, 623, 637, 680
evangelism 782, 798, 801–2, 897, 904, 920
evictions 864, 985–92
evidence 137, 274, 276, 361, 479–80, 569–71, 690–1, 706–7
examination power 95
exceptional circumstances 210, 242, 360, 453, 459, 736, 757
excess of jurisdiction 402, 520, 967
excessive restriction 439, 582, 586, 588, 730, 734, 953, 956
excluded provisions 229, 316–17, 321–2, 429
exclusive jurisdiction 135, 344–5, 520, 785, 789, 792, 795
exclusive powers 145, 230, 264, 324, 891
excommunication 861, 926, 930
executive acts 164, 228, 313, 315, 325, 594, 907
executive branch of government 48, 190, 196
executive orders 164, 166, 178–80, 452, 591, 609, 891, 929
executive power 142–4, 155, 157–9, 161–2, 166, 186–8, 191, 293–4
in parliamentary systems 146–8
executive presidency 160, 263
Executive Yuan 141–3, 186–9, 191–2, 206, 354–5, 362–4, 403, 425

exemptions 76, 105, 551, 827, 836, 853–6, 878–9, 882–9
  legislative 884–5
  religious 836–9, 841, 843, 845, 847, 849, 851, 884–5
exile 12, 46, 49–51, 158, 251, 401, 869
exit polls 517–18
expectations
  community 825–6
  legitimate 436, 451–2
expenses 143, 246, 442, 585, 705, 711, 737, 900–1
  commodity 949, 951
expert knowledge 844, 1016
experts 141–2, 187–8, 686–7, 939–40, 975–7, 987, 1010, 1015
express constitutional authorisation 342, 344, 350, 357, 361, 364
express socio-economic rights, judicial review 945–61
expression, freedom of 437, 641–3, 650–1, 660–1, 681, 700–4, 715, 828–9
expressive conduct 683, 700
expropriation 197, 199, 201, 560, 566, 577
expulsions 265, 806, 837, 853–5, 862
extrinsic materials 422–3, 428
Ezochi, *see* Hokkaido

Facebook 931
facilitation functions 524–5
factories 93, 757–8, 967, 1012, 1014
fair comment
  defence of 705, 712–18
  right of 712, 720
fair criticism 690–1
fair elections 56, 74, 290, 454, 489, 503, 523
fair enforcement 142, 187–8, 659
fair trial 301, 433, 594, 949
fairness 188, 190, 451–2, 523, 528, 661, 754, 767
faith 799–802, 804, 821–4, 837–8, 904–7, 917–19, 921–3, 927–9
Falun Gong 773, 911, 914
families 72, 560–1, 565, 804–5, 887, 928–9, 988–9, 994–7
family life 84, 887, 947, 949, 992, 1019
famines 994, 996–7
fathers 21, 25, 46, 51, 80, 245, 377, 554; *see also* parents
fatwas 772, 776, 778, 790, 859, 909, 942
favouritism 590, 602
Federation of Malaysia, *see* Malaysia
female infanticide 626–8
females, *see* women
feudal monarchy 242, 360
Filipino citizens 82, 377, 414, 487, 530
  natural-born 376–7, 381
  naturalized 377
final decisions 160, 241–2, 325, 330, 339, 377, 379, 384–5
final power of decision 311, 331, 969
finality 211, 268, 365, 435, 788, 916, 918
  of prophethood 918–19, 923
finance 19, 36, 147, 149, 177, 193–4, 389, 393

financial crises 192–3, 446
financial institutions 194
financial reforms 192–3
financial resources 192, 834, 946, 1005
financial support/assistance 194, 501, 583–4, 587, 652, 859
fiscal autonomy 386–8
fishing 572–3, 575, 873
fitnah 776–7
flag ceremonies 851–8
flags 26, 91, 246, 683–4, 701, 771, 849, 852–6
  desecration 701–3
  national 87, 280–1, 683, 700–2
  regional 441, 700–2
floods 590, 984, 988, 990, 992
followers 106, 781, 809, 812, 815, 818, 823–4, 911
food 649–50, 891–2, 943–4, 990, 994, 996–7, 1000, 1002–3
  grains 994–7, 999
  halal 890–1
  right to 943–4, 984, 994–1000, 1002–3
  security 290, 1021
force of law 193, 207–8, 829
forced apologies 733, 737–8
forced conversion 808, 810, 813, 816, 821
foreign armed forces 198, 237
foreign citizenship 530, 616
foreign domestic workers 639–40
foreign law, use in constitutional interpretation 431–43
foreign nationalities 613–16
foreign policy 29, 80, 163, 196–203
foreign relations 38, 159, 163, 196, 238, 268, 433
foreigners 96, 521–2, 527–8, 533, 535, 614–16, 669, 686
  discrimination against 637–40
former presidents 217, 242–3, 360
forum externum 782, 798, 826, 938, 940
France 13, 15, 45–6, 50, 82, 101, 120, 127
franchise 15, 293, 494, 528, 991
fraternity 93, 112–13, 289, 545, 918
fraud 153, 503, 517–18, 808, 811–12, 814–15, 821, 871
free choice 809, 880
free competition 359, 956
free conscience 782–3, 799, 801, 808–9, 816, 818, 836, 843–5
free democracy 387, 617, 960
  basic order of 172, 242, 360, 621, 672
free education 855, 1007–8
free elections 497, 508, 516, 529
free exercise clause 782, 848, 856, 879–83, 885–6, 889
free expressions 242, 360, 521, 529, 820, 829, 905, 908
free press 16, 118, 652, 667–8
free speech 7, 79, 437, 641–770, 910, 915–16, 924, 930
  Bangladesh 642, 652, 687, 704, 711, 768, 770
  Cambodia 683
  China 701–3, 711, 764
  guarantees 641–2, 660, 670, 693, 800–1

Hong Kong 688, 692–3, 700–3, 713, 733, 735, 738, 741–3
India 651, 653, 655, 723, 725–6, 732, 751, 753
Indonesia 653, 683–5, 711, 770
Japan 683, 686, 705–8, 721, 723, 728–9, 742, 744
judicially enforced apologies 643, 733–9
Laos 652
lèse majesté, contempt of court and symbolic speech 682–703
Malaysia 642–3, 645, 671–4, 687–8, 693–7, 704, 761–2, 766–7
Nepal 642, 670, 687, 704
obscenity and pornography 722–33
Pakistan 642, 687, 696, 704, 711
Philippines 642, 652, 668–9, 687, 711, 713
political defamation 90, 704–21
press, media and right to reply 652–69
prior restraints on 643–51
protection 438, 641–2, 654, 699, 711, 721
religious 798, 824
sedition and hate speech 669–82
Singapore 642–3, 668–9, 671–2, 687–90, 711–12, 716–17, 719–21, 746–8
South Korea 648, 650–2, 710–11, 730, 733–4, 738, 740, 753
Sri Lanka 643, 687, 697, 704, 756
Taiwan 642, 644, 648, 653–4, 658, 733, 740–1, 762–4
Thailand 643, 652–3, 683, 686–7, 711
freedom 642–5, 659–63, 733–9, 749–51, 787–91, 839–41, 846–9, 935–8
    absolute 782, 852, 937
    of assembly 641–2, 740, 749, 753–4
    of association 204, 446, 641, 693, 767–8, 770, 958
        and civil society 755–70
        rights of individuals to associate/disassociate 756–62
    of belief 853, 863, 865, 895–6, 911
    of choice 267–8, 786, 809–10, 880, 954, 956
    of conscience 620–2, 734, 738, 788, 808–9, 812, 839–41, 843–4
    of contract 588–9, 956, 961
    of expression 437, 641–3, 650–1, 660–1, 681, 686, 700–4, 828–9
    fundamental freedoms 433, 437, 619, 700, 797
    individual 836, 867, 918, 936, 954
    inner 621–2, 788
    of movement 44, 204, 565
    of occupation 359, 582, 584–8, 614
    of peaceful assembly 743, 747
    of political party membership 759–60
    press 652–3, 662, 672
    of religion 785–7, 789–93, 799–803, 807–11, 823–5, 891–7, 935–6, 940–2
        absolute 835, 850
        content 782–805
        propagation, *see* propagation
        right to practice 826–36
        right to profess 783–5
    religious, *see* freedom, of religion
    of silence 733–4

of speech 438, 644–6, 649–50, 653–8, 663–6, 678–9, 708–9, 747–8
of worship 894, 933, 1013
freedoms of other persons 618–19, 648, 962
full and identical facts 379, 384–5
full independence 14, 27, 29–30, 35, 50
functional constituencies 97, 467, 478–80, 525
functional representation 478–81
functions 166–9, 187–8, 274–6, 390–1, 418–20, 512–14, 518–20, 971–3
    core 352, 460
    election commissions 514–20
    facilitation 524–5
    judicial 198, 238, 350, 393, 396, 698–9, 754, 944
    social 469, 846, 980
fundamental freedoms 433, 437, 619, 700, 797
fundamental laws 45, 114, 176, 220, 254, 268, 349, 541
fundamental liberties 44, 91, 797, 829, 886, 906
fundamental principles 39, 110, 112, 115, 172–3, 293, 339–40, 345
fundamental rights 283–7, 290–1, 351–2, 435–6, 581–5, 924–6, 983–4, 988–9
    enforcement 204, 253, 444
    protection 350, 584, 743
fundamental values 69, 220, 278–9, 825, 847, 948

gender 557–8, 613, 618, 622, 625–6, 629, 633, 732–3
    discrimination 557, 624–34, 828–9
    equality 273, 415, 435–6, 460, 827
    identity 487, 546, 632–3
    quotas 496
gender selection 626–9
general elections 52–4, 151–2, 180, 252–4, 470–1, 481, 504–5, 508
general interest of administration 598–9
general law 105, 782, 786, 834, 836, 848–9, 852, 915
general rules of interpretation 366, 445
general welfare 159, 303, 701–2, 748, 847, 970
generous interpretation 91, 422, 429, 668, 700, 743
genocide 300–2, 665
Germany 4, 335, 339, 682, 730, 874, 955, 959
gerrymandering 472, 474
girls 627–8, 827, 829, 832, 901, 999
Gneist, Rudolph 11
GNH (Gross National Happiness) 82, 105
GNP (Gross National Product) 82, 182
God 89–90, 106–7, 772–3, 780–1, 867–9, 879, 905, 932–6
    existence of 772, 942
    personal 771, 775, 852
    sovereignty of 96, 868
    word of 811–12
Gokoku Shrines 899–901, 903–4
good citizens 79–80, 101, 934
good faith 133, 164, 503, 598–9, 602, 690, 696, 698
good governance 74–5, 78, 82, 103, 157, 248, 251
good government 62, 91, 411, 857
good morals 78, 501, 728

governance 128, 130, 568, 571, 719–20, 860–1, 983, 986
 corporate 445
 democratic 466, 511, 520, 641, 721, 739, 742
 good 74–5, 78, 82, 103, 157, 248, 251
governing authorities 581, 763–4, 770
government action 308, 880–1, 885
government agencies 90, 175, 329–30, 334, 358, 366, 414, 443
government branches 48, 127–8, 173, 175, 186, 189, 298, 371
 executive 48, 190, 196
 legislative 145, 155, 163, 181, 309, 313, 315, 454
government employees 142, 535, 776, 888, 961
government institutions 69, 224, 683, 753, 884, 1006
government officials 39, 78, 93–4, 337–8, 799, 826
government organs 41, 98, 161, 293–5, 332, 334–5, 418, 911
government policies 178, 652, 675, 943, 946, 948, 1017, 1019
government system, Taiwan 127–8, 140–1, 143–4, 157–8, 169–71, 182–3, 190–1, 203–6
government systems 39, 44, 127–218, 309, 423, 563, 701, 894
 Bangladesh 128, 144–5, 174, 180–1
 Bhutan 128–9
 Brunei 128, 144, 205
 Cambodia 127–8, 144–5, 189, 205
 China 128–9, 139–40, 144, 173–8, 204–5
 Hong Kong 144, 174, 178–80, 205
 India 127–8, 140, 144, 146, 152–3, 156–7, 204, 210
 Indonesia 127–8, 144, 157–8, 170–2, 189, 205
 Japan 127–8, 135–6, 139, 144–51, 156, 196–201, 205, 217
 Laos 128, 134, 173–4, 205
 Malaysia 127–9, 131, 134–7, 144–5, 156, 204–5, 207
 Mongolia 128–9, 144–5, 189, 205, 216–17
 Myanmar 134, 144, 203
 Nepal 127–8, 134, 140, 149, 205
 Pakistan 144, 180, 204, 212
 Philippines 127–8, 157–9, 163–4, 166–7, 171, 185, 204–5, 208
 Singapore 127–8, 130–1, 133, 138, 144–8, 156, 195–6, 203
 South Korea 127–8, 156–8, 160, 165–6, 189–90, 192, 201–2, 204–5
 Sri Lanka 127–8, 144, 157–8, 160–1, 167–8, 205
 Thailand 127–8, 135, 139, 144–5, 193–4, 203, 205, 216–17
 Vietnam 128–9, 144, 173, 205
government(s) 87–98, 143–8, 293–5, 673–6, 896–8, 966–73, 978–82, 987–91
 authoritarian 23, 54, 74–5
 caretaker, *see* caretaker governments
 central 288, 319, 380–1, 384–5, 627–8, 996–7, 999–1000, 1003–4
 coalition 49, 147, 149
 constitutional 2, 11–13, 39, 55, 59, 62, 88, 209
 democratic 16, 38, 40, 251, 345, 968, 991

 elected 62, 96, 993, 1021
 heads of 128–9, 140, 143, 155, 157, 159
 limited 6, 9, 59, 62, 885
 local 19, 290, 329, 334, 589, 611, 758, 899–901
 organs of 161, 293–5
 parliamentary 11, 16, 32, 127, 145, 151–2, 209, 211
 republican 13, 30, 95, 280–1, 641
 stable 14–15, 74, 362
grand constitution revision 239–40
grave abuse of discretion 376, 402–3, 520, 964, 966–7
grave danger 459, 600–1, 891
gravity 171, 529, 532, 693, 735
 degree of 733, 736
Greece 615, 805, 818–19, 838
grievances 117, 515, 543–4, 739, 927, 994, 996
Gross National Happiness, *see* GNH
Gross National Product, *see* GNP
gross partiality 674–5
ground-breaking ceremonies 774–5, 893, 895, 897, 899
group identities 138, 643, 799, 859
guarantees
 constitutional 109, 422, 428–9, 435, 712, 715, 856–7, 924–5
 free speech 641–2, 660, 670, 693, 800–1
guided democracy 53, 61, 932
Gujarat 382, 626–7, 874, 1009, 1021

habeas corpus 248–50, 252, 267, 270, 286, 348, 443, 943
habeas data 348, 443
habitual criminals 434, 597
Hahm, Chaihark 61, 122, 235, 341–2
halal food 890–2
happiness 83–5, 160, 548–9, 568, 952, 954, 956, 958
 Gross National 82, 105
 right to pursue 83–5, 160, 472, 549, 952, 954, 956, 958
harassment 168, 625, 692–3, 735–6, 829–30, 916
 sexual 415, 435–6, 459–60, 625, 828–9, 985
hardship 844, 987, 1015
harm 438, 461, 651, 669–70, 711, 722, 822, 842
 moral 722
 political 670
harmony 105–6, 124–5, 773, 775, 786–90, 867, 905–6, 965
 communal 678, 910
 religious 90, 124–5, 134, 670–1, 817, 824–6, 859, 938
 social 118, 120, 124, 738, 799, 808, 862
hate speech 642–3, 669, 671, 681
heads of government 128–9, 140–4, 155, 157, 159
heads of state 44, 46–7, 128–40, 157, 159, 163, 166, 175–6
health 82–3, 649–50, 891–2, 952–5, 964–7, 978, 1001–3, 1010–12
 care 944, 1001, 1013
 centres 1004–5
 education 1002–3

hazards 1009, 1012, 1014, 1020
  mental 978, 1002, 1018
  public, *see* public health
  right to, *see* rights, to life (and health)
healthful ecology 415, 964–8
healthy environment 404, 944, 968, 979
  right to a 404, 1009–17, 1019–20
hegemonic self-preservation 327
heirs 281, 414, 566, 683
helplessness 411–12
heresy 783, 911–12, 917–18, 942
heritage
  cultural 69, 76–7, 104, 543, 635–6, 844, 965
  spiritual 106, 802, 804
high schools 84, 803
highest courts 207, 286, 288, 343, 349, 369, 401,
  449–50
Himachal Pradesh 810, 815, 1013
Hindu culture 765, 800, 877
Hindu nationalism 807, 872, 874, 877
Hinduism 772, 774, 780–1, 800, 807–8, 816, 875–8,
  932
Hindus 677, 780, 800, 804–5, 807, 816, 872–4,
  876–7
Hindutva 872, 874–8
Hirschl, Ran 307, 327, 859, 867
historical legitimacy 98–9
Ho Chi Minh 45–6, 63, 77, 86, 100–1, 863
Hokkaido 570–3, 577, 639
holidays 897, 964
  religious 859, 898, 935
Holy Prophet 918–21, 928–9
Holy Quran, *see* Quran
homeland 86–7, 497, 836, 863
homosexual conduct 488
homosexuals 488, 629–34
honesty 503, 514, 719–20
Hong Kong 3, 18, 45
  constitutional change 227, 229–30, 257, 274,
    276–7, 280–1
  Court of Final Appeal 324–5, 418, 479–80, 712,
    720, 740, 742, 752–3
  democracy 467, 478–80, 521, 524, 531
  equality 557, 640
  free speech 688, 692–3, 700–3, 713, 733, 735,
    738, 741–3
  government system 144, 174, 178–80, 205
  handover 314, 703
  judicial review 313–14, 316, 318, 320–2, 325–6,
    328, 421–2, 428–31
  one country two systems 178–9
  permanent residents 320, 421, 479
  socio-economic rights 944, 946–7, 949,
    1017–18
honor 394–5, 549, 900, 929
hostile discrimination 591–2, 594, 608
hostility 671, 674–6, 680, 682, 823, 825, 883–4,
  919–20
house arrest 12, 54
housing 55–6, 63, 943–4, 946, 988, 993, 1003
human dignity 83, 85, 279–80, 737–8, 952, 954,
  984, 1007–8

human life 106, 868, 871, 978, 1004–5, 1011, 1016,
  1020
human resources 548, 841
human rights 78–9, 301–4, 634–5, 667, 845–8,
  935–7, 978–81, 1019
  fundamental 233, 276, 387, 989
  inalienable 279
  indivisibility of 944, 1004
  obligations 979, 1004
  protection of 278, 280, 304, 433, 936, 940
humane livelihood 582–5, 954
hybrid models 344, 347–8, 368

identity 61–2, 69–70, 292, 548–9, 569, 571, 599,
  799
  constitutional 105, 121, 239–40
  cultural 62, 235, 731–2, 799, 864, 936
  disclosure system 439–40
  gender 487, 546, 632–3
  group 138, 643, 799, 859
  national 6, 77, 85–100, 105, 109, 231, 235, 732
  political 77, 86
  religious 782–3, 785, 807
ideology 53, 87–90, 92, 109–10, 782, 807, 915–16,
  935
  national 87, 90, 104, 118, 465, 932
  political 6, 70, 89, 100, 379, 417, 465, 896
  socialist 100, 102, 104, 863
  state 24, 643, 731–2
illegality 115, 522, 527–8, 575, 577, 664, 950,
  952
imbalances 142, 188, 475, 477, 585, 875
immigration authority 314, 320–1
immorality 482, 487, 555, 628, 661, 698, 888–9
immunity 161, 168–9, 242, 263–5, 360, 420, 555–6,
  712
  constitutional 167, 169
  diplomatic 555
impartiality 142, 188–9, 262, 270, 369, 437–8, 691,
  694
  political 511, 658, 760, 762
impeachment 170–1, 173, 329–30, 337–9, 341–2,
  384, 388, 537
  adjudication 171, 329, 338–9, 537
  motions 170, 172, 339
  Presidents 157, 169, 170–3, 338, 341
imperialism 41, 86–7, 96, 196, 546
important public interests 456, 579–81, 654, 740,
  842
imports 420, 542, 602, 671–2, 923
imposed and autonomous constitutional
  change 230
imprisonment 451–2, 525–6, 531–2, 671–2, 680–1,
  685–6, 688, 741
  life 243, 451–2, 554, 713, 921
improper motives 691, 694–6
improper proselytism 805, 818
impropriety 566, 576, 691
impugned laws 331–5, 366, 404, 443–4, 447–8, 450,
  455–6, 604
incitement 623, 642, 665, 670–1, 681, 747
income 523, 563, 949–50, 955–6, 965

inconsistency 162, 228, 309, 315, 324–5, 436, 460, 790–1
inconvenience 450, 452, 664, 741, 953, 961
incremental constitution-making 239–40
incremental constitutional revisions 239–40
incumbent Presidents 166, 186, 250, 378
independence 14–15, 31, 49–50, 58–9, 187, 369, 387–8, 934–5
  election commissions 511–14
  institutional 369, 393
  judicial 189–90, 213, 369, 373–5, 382, 386, 388–93, 396
independent agencies 141–3, 186–9, 455
independent candidates 137, 296, 484–5, 533–4
independent judiciary 33, 47, 121, 387, 463
independent regulatory commissions 140, 143, 186, 455, 658
India 2–3, 5
  ameliorative secularism 870–8
  British 32–3, 918
  Chief Justice of India 378–81, 383–5, 412, 420
  constitution making 17, 20, 26, 31–3, 58
  constitutional change 221–2, 246, 253, 257, 260, 283, 286, 288–90
  constitutional culture 70, 79, 112
  democracy 465, 475, 477, 493–7, 504–5, 509, 515
  equality 552, 554, 556–8, 590, 625–9, 637, 642, 644
  free speech 651, 653, 655, 723, 725–6, 732, 751, 753
  government system 127–8, 140, 144, 146, 152–3, 156–7, 204, 210
  judicial review 350–1, 374, 376, 378, 382–3, 412, 429–30, 448–9
  religion 787–8, 800–1, 806–8, 810–12, 830–1, 859–60, 872–6, 920–1
  socio-economic rights 944, 983–5, 994, 996, 998–1004, 1006, 1009, 1020–1
  Supreme Court 414–15, 459–60, 553–4, 589, 653–4, 753–4, 770–1, 1013
Indian test 589–607, 777, 930
indigenous peoples 104, 558–78, 634–7
indigenous rights 105, 559–60, 569, 577, 967
indigenous villagers 521, 524–5
individual autonomy 79, 101, 118, 121, 465, 642, 782, 828
individual citizens 331, 333–4, 591, 956
individual freedoms 836, 867, 918, 936, 954
individual personality 586–7, 641
individualism 72–3, 87–8, 90, 568, 935
Indonesia 2–3, 5–6
  and Ahmadis 932–42
  Bali, *see* Bali
  blasphemy 932–42
  constitution making 20, 36, 52–4, 58, 60–1
  constitutional change 221, 240, 258, 260, 280–1, 299–300, 302–4
  Constitutional Court 299, 305, 331, 365, 368, 373, 683, 685
  constitutional culture 75, 78, 88–9, 91–2, 106
  democracy 464, 466, 498, 501, 532

economic policy, privatisation and judicial review 968–83
equality 550, 556, 625
free speech 653, 683–5, 711, 770
government system 127–8, 144, 157–8, 170–2, 189, 205
judicial review 310–12, 328–9, 332–3, 338–9, 365, 367, 370–2, 968–83
Pancasila 88–9, 91–2, 860, 932, 934–5, 937, 975
religion 774, 823, 868, 916, 932–42, 944
search for stability 87
socio-economic rights 968–83, 1001
Suharto 54, 92, 172, 466
Sukarno 53–4, 61, 88
Supomo 87–8
inducement 731, 802, 804, 808, 810–15
inequality 480, 485, 545, 548, 550, 590, 598, 600–1; *see also* equality
infant mortality 1002–3
infanticide, female 626–8
infidels 918, 926–8
influence, political 99, 142, 186–8, 762
information 414, 516–17, 655–6, 659, 684–5, 730–1, 1003, 1011–12
inherent tendency test 438, 440, 688–9, 698–9
initiative 19, 39, 257–8, 261, 460, 464, 535–6, 540–3
  creative 954, 956
  legislative 258, 352
  local 541–2
injunctions 9, 137, 377, 539, 644, 646–7, 649, 918
  of Islam 868, 921, 928
  preliminary 460–1
injury 404, 614, 616, 622, 715–16, 735, 737–9, 882–3
  public 413
  serious 1004, 1006
injustice 73, 240, 302, 435, 449, 452, 545, 558
inner belief 622, 737
inner freedom 621–2, 788
institutional continuity 76, 221
institutional design 307, 325, 333, 337, 365, 368, 373, 540
institutional independence 369, 393
institutional structures 69, 124, 636
institutions 76–7, 97–9, 213–14, 307–8, 327–9, 722, 900, 918
  democratic 4, 6, 510
  financial 194
  Islamic 117, 787, 789
  majoritarian 327
  political 39, 122, 324, 331, 342, 356, 459, 465
  for political representation 497–520
  religious 109, 872, 880, 893, 922
  representative 165, 202, 972
  state 53, 98, 311, 332, 334, 356, 410, 682–3
instructions 131, 176, 250, 695, 851, 865–6, 898, 906–7
instrumentalism
  and constitutional cultures 85–103
  and religion 911–14
insult 683, 686–7, 909–10, 915, 921, 926, 935, 940

integralists 87–9
integrity, moral 90, 119, 737
intelligentsia 104, 173–4
intent 169–70, 193, 421–4, 427–8, 706–7, 715–16,
     728, 741–2
   constitutional 142, 188, 387, 455, 491, 750–1
   legislative 319–22, 418, 422, 426–7, 445, 447,
        490, 496
   original 276, 373, 419, 765
   religious 898, 901
intention 219–20, 347, 483–4, 691, 696, 698,
     715–16, 786
   deliberate 671, 688, 698
intentional defamation 683–4
inter-religious harmony, *see* religious harmony
interests 404, 413–15, 564–6, 581–3, 656–8, 701–4,
     747–8, 884–7
   best 361, 617, 665
   common 96, 410–11, 479
   commonality of 475, 477
   community 465, 642, 701–2, 862
   competing, *see* competing interests
   cultural 559, 578
   legal 526–7, 564, 840–3, 903–4
   legally protected 411–12, 749–51, 753
   legitimate 201, 558, 669, 682–3, 942, 962
   national 103, 135, 140, 159, 202, 267, 414, 490–1
   of national security 204, 361, 739, 743, 757
   political 94, 327, 808
   private 497, 527, 566, 585, 587, 741, 953, 956
   prurient 723, 727–8, 731, 733
   public, *see* public interest
   social 479, 526, 679, 681, 982
   sufficient 405–7, 411, 413–14, 416
interference 187, 335, 345, 383, 388–9, 405, 891,
     897
   political 141, 230, 375
intergenerational justice 964, 968
intergenerational responsibility 415, 965, 968
intermediate scrutiny 557, 618
internal security 35, 914
international community 192, 202, 224, 251, 280,
     299, 301, 303–4
international law
   as limit to constitutional change 299–305
   use in constitutional interpretation 431–43
international obligations 433, 638, 843
international peace 38, 81, 115, 196, 198, 200–1,
     238
international terrorism 304
interpretation 228–30, 275–7, 316–26, 421–2,
     426–30, 932–4, 938–40, 971–4
   constitutional, *see* constitutional interpretation
   generous 91, 422, 429, 668, 700, 743
   judicial 186, 220, 255–6, 277, 279, 324, 617, 619
   literal 417, 419
   power of 277, 313, 315–16, 318, 325
   proper 227, 230, 274, 276, 314, 789
   purposive 275–6, 347, 417, 426–31, 787, 1018
   religious 934, 937–8
interpretive methods 337, 417–18
intersexuals 633

intolerance 236, 549, 801, 804–5, 824, 877,
     918
intra-party democracy in socialist states 121–2
invalidation 232, 234, 325, 443, 447–8, 456, 459,
     483
invalidity 201, 228, 315, 325, 450, 489, 954, 956
Ip, Eric 92
Iraq 163, 165, 201–2, 231, 867
Ireland 2, 28, 874
irrigation 979–80
Islam 115–17, 246–7, 777–9, 785–96, 798, 905–7,
     916–21, 923
   Allah. *see* Allah
   renunciation of 792–3, 795–6
   Sunnah 779, 868–9, 891, 917–20, 923, 928
   Surah 777, 790
   syariah, *see* syariah
   ulama/ulema 779, 868–9, 919–20, 939, 942
   zakat 795, 869–70, 890
Islamd, Ahmadis, *see* Ahmadis
Islamic Constitutionalism 867–8
Islamic institutions 117, 787, 789
Islamic law 117, 784–6, 788, 791, 793, 795–7, 867,
     869
Islamic solidarity 86, 115
Islamic state 88–9, 117, 795, 868–70, 918, 920,
     923, 930
Islamic teachings 776–7, 872, 909
Italy 4, 13, 253, 308, 335, 528–9, 844

Japan 3–5
   constitution making 9–14, 16–20, 23, 57–8,
        61
   constitutional change 221–2, 231–2, 234–9,
        243, 247, 260
   constitutional culture 67, 72, 74–5, 81, 83,
        106
   democracy 465, 468, 470, 481–3, 521–3, 535,
        537, 540
   equality 547, 550, 554, 557, 567–8, 573–5, 577,
        637–8
   free speech 683, 686, 705–8, 721, 723, 728–9,
        742, 744
   government system 127–8, 135–6, 139, 144–51,
        156, 196–201, 205, 217
   judicial review 328, 335, 344, 374–5, 400, 402,
        405, 409
   religion 774–5, 836, 838, 860, 892–904
   security 198–200, 238
   socio-economic rights 944, 955, 961
   from State Shinto to secular state and
        ceremonial Shinto 892–904
   Supreme Court 136, 236, 238, 344, 476–7,
        527–8, 535, 666–7
Japanese citizens 409, 522–3, 527–8
Japanese language 571–2
Jefferson, Thomas 83, 219, 545
Jehovah's Witnesses 91, 834–6, 838–9, 847–51,
     853, 855, 857, 888
Jews 680, 682, 779, 811, 874, 918
Jiang 96–9
journalists 28, 652, 709, 716

judges 212–14, 335–6, 371–5, 378–88, 390–6,
    417–21, 602–4, 688–96
  appointment, *see* judicial appointment
  ordinary court 358, 371–3, 376
  permanent 379–81, 412, 459
judicial accountability 373–4
judicial activism 282, 291, 968
judicial administration 358, 369, 389, 391–2, 396,
    457
judicial appointment 166, 189, 307, 325, 369–82,
    519
judicial authorities 353, 372, 394–6, 403
judicial branch 143, 201, 270, 298, 308
judicial construction 983, 985, 987, 989, 991, 993,
    995, 997
judicial decisions 270–1, 367–8, 443–5, 447, 449,
    451, 453, 455
  and constitutional change 270–8
  forms 443–61
  judicial review 365–8
judicial deference 330, 364, 459, 477, 519
judicial duty 688, 695, 963
judicial functions 198, 238, 350, 393, 396, 698–9,
    754, 944
judicial independence 189–90, 213, 369, 373–5,
    382, 386, 388–93, 396
judicial interpretation 186, 220, 255–6, 277, 279,
    324, 617, 619
judicial law-making 461
judicial legislation 299, 426
judicial power 228, 293–4, 298, 307–9, 315, 327,
    344–5, 372–3
judicial process 404, 415, 609, 983, 1007
judicial redress 412–13, 415
judicial review 118–20, 131–3, 210–11, 270–1,
    307–461, 945, 949–51, 969
  administrative rules 356–61
  Bangladesh 309, 313, 328, 350–1, 389–90,
    393–4, 433–4, 440–1
  Bhutan 309
  Brunei 309, 312, 440
  Cambodia 309–10, 328–30, 334–5, 338, 350,
    370–1, 432
  centralised systems 308–11, 328–42, 348, 365
  China 312–15, 318–20, 322–4, 328, 425, 428,
    431, 441
  constitutional amendments 349–52
  decentralised systems 308–9, 327–8, 342–9,
    443
  emergency decrees 361–5
  and enforcement of directive principles 961–8
  express socio-economic rights 945–61
  Hong Kong 313–14, 316, 318, 320–2, 325–6,
    328, 421–2, 428–31
  India 350–1, 374, 376, 378, 382–3, 412, 429–30,
    448–9
  individual complaints 333–4
  Indonesia 310–12, 328–9, 332–3, 338–9, 365,
    367, 370–2, 968–83
  institutional design 327–49
  Japan 328, 335, 344, 374–5, 400, 402, 405, 409
  judicial decisions 365–8

judicial power and assertion of judicial review
    powers 311–27
Laos 309, 313
laws or parliamentary resolutions 352–6
Malaysia 309, 312, 361–2, 364, 397, 405, 448,
    450
Mongolia 328–30, 332, 334, 338, 350, 353–4,
    365, 370–1
Myanmar 328–9, 331, 334–5, 338, 370–1, 374
nature 307–27
Nepal 309, 466
North Korea 313
Pakistan 309, 313, 328, 374, 391, 440, 444
Philippines 348, 350, 374–7, 385–9, 397–8,
    400–4, 413, 415
power 198, 200, 210, 270–1, 307, 311, 313, 325
quantum of social benefits 949–52
scope 151, 356, 507
Singapore 398–9, 405–7, 427, 432, 436–8, 440,
    448, 451
South Korea 328–30, 332–4, 338–9, 341–2,
    357–9, 365–6, 370–1, 444–5
Sri Lanka 328, 331, 343, 350, 440
subject of 307, 349–68
Taiwan 328–35, 337–9, 350–3, 355–6, 361–2,
    385–6, 423–4, 459–60
Thailand 310–11, 328–9, 331–3, 336–40, 354,
    357, 370–1
Vietnam 309, 312–13
judicial scrutiny 208, 784, 612, 843
judicial supervision 350, 356, 364
judicial transfer 382–5
judicial warnings 443, 456, 459
Judicial Yuan 22, 310, 335–6, 366, 381, 391–2,
    396, 457
judicialisation of politics 256, 341
judicialization 341–2
judicially enforced apologies 643, 733–9
judiciary 189, 213–14, 276–7, 382–3, 386–9,
    459–60, 692, 698–9
  independent 33, 47, 121, 387, 463
juridical personality 833–4
jurisdiction(s) 228–9, 315–16, 328–35, 343–5,
    388–92, 783–6, 789–92, 796–7
  ancillary 337–8
  appellate 291, 515, 519
  excess of 402, 520, 967
  exclusive 135, 344–5, 520, 785, 789, 792, 795
  primary 328–9, 337
juristic persons 503, 750
juristocracy 217, 256, 307, 327
jus sanguinis 529–30, 615
jus soli 529–30
justice
  administration of 382–3, 437–8, 674, 676, 688–9,
    691–6, 698–9, 736
  intergenerational 964, 968
  political 114, 289, 291
  social 88–9, 105, 110–11, 113, 413–14, 957,
    970–1, 1001
  transitional 217, 240–1, 243
justiciability 249, 264, 307, 362, 396–417

justification 89–90, 475, 477, 513–14, 580, 582,
 642–3, 722
 reasonable 614, 945
 test 947–9

kangaroo courts 690–2
kendo practice 837–8
Kerala 283, 286, 292, 313, 351, 504, 811, 857
Khmer Rouge 51, 56
Kingdom of Thailand, *see* Thailand
KMT (Kuomintang) 21–2, 38, 40, 140–1, 172–3,
 184, 186, 466
knowledge 101, 104, 580, 632–3, 817–18, 820,
 1011, 1013
 expert 844, 1016
 public 68, 237, 301
Korea, *see* North Korea; South Korea
Korean War 1, 23, 196, 344
Kuomintang, *see* KMT

labour 36, 55, 101–2, 193, 360, 478, 747, 756–7
labour movement 146, 478–9
labour unions, *see* trade unions
land 196–7, 199–201, 560–3, 565–6, 571–3, 601–4,
 987–90, 993
 ownership 88, 283
 reform 40, 56, 283, 289–91
landowners 197, 200, 283, 290
language 66, 322, 418–23, 428–9, 552–3, 557–8,
 567, 635
 Japanese 571–2
Lao People's Revolutionary Party (LPRP) 50, 100,
 104, 174
Laos 5
 constitution making 18, 38, 48–50
 constitutional change 221–2, 258, 260
 constitutional culture 86, 104, 106
 equality 550, 625
 free speech 652
 government system 128, 134, 173–4, 205
 judicial review 309, 313
 religion 799, 860, 862, 866
 socio-economic rights 944
law enforcement agencies 672, 710
lawful discretion 200, 1018
lawfulness 199–200
lawmakers 94, 142, 188, 422, 485, 542, 615
lawyers 7, 26–8, 68, 177, 326, 451, 717, 726
LDP (Liberal Democratic Party) 147, 149, 156,
 234, 507, 663–4
leadership 32, 41, 46, 50–1, 92, 100, 102, 119
 collective 121, 176
 political 25, 251
Lee Kuan Yew (LKY) 28, 705, 716, 719, 721
legal continuity 24, 63, 234–5
legal culture 9, 59, 68–73, 75, 374, 403
legal effect 138, 232–3, 242, 248, 355, 360, 833,
 842
legal history 30, 72, 703, 794
legal interests 526–7, 564, 840–3, 903–4
legal legitimacy 44, 59, 62–3, 72
legal obligations 576, 635, 638, 836, 839–40, 913

legal order 72, 219, 230–1, 234, 432–3, 452, 622,
 839–41
legal status 160, 177, 179, 431, 535, 607, 612–13,
 615
legal validity 117, 151, 402, 793
legality 57, 59, 149–50, 248, 261–2, 303, 305,
 356–8
legally protected interests 411–12, 749–51, 753
legislation
 discriminatory 557, 606–7, 615, 884
 judicial 299, 426
legislative authority 207–8, 364, 971
legislative branch of government 145, 155, 163,
 181, 309, 313, 315, 454
legislative classification 606, 611, 619
legislative discretion 142, 188, 366, 472–3, 508,
 528, 583, 750
legislative districts 258, 468, 474, 490, 536, 540
legislative-formative power 619–20
legislative intent 319–22, 418, 422, 426–7, 445, 447,
 490, 496
legislative policy 209, 403, 522, 719, 963, 1021
legislative powers 47, 178–80, 187–8, 208–9, 277–8,
 280, 293, 388–9
 in parliamentary systems 145–6
legislative purpose 439, 484, 526, 582–4, 587,
 615–16, 622, 754
 legitimate 498, 526, 613, 741
legislators 489, 508–9, 579–80, 582–3, 585, 841–5,
 962–3, 975–7
legitimacy 37–8, 42, 72, 96–7, 99, 220, 223–7,
 369
 constitutional 59, 62, 64, 68
 and constitutionalism 58–63
 crises of 223–4
 cultural 97
 democratic 62, 141, 171, 432, 436, 461, 464,
 527
 economic and legal 62–3
 historical 98–9
 legal 44, 59, 62–3, 72
 political 64, 96, 99
 sacred 97
legitimate expectations 436, 451–2
legitimate interests 201, 558, 669, 682–3, 942,
 962
legitimate legislative purpose 498, 526, 613, 741
legitimate public interest 854–5
legitimate purpose 498, 600, 743–4, 752, 885, 953,
 956
legitimate state interest 488, 557, 589
lesbians 482, 487–8, 629–31, 633
lèse majesté 643, 682–3, 685–6
liability 438, 446, 553, 561, 595, 598–9, 605, 609
libel 694–5, 704, 706, 711, 718, 721, 738
 political 119, 704
liberal constitutionalism 5, 82, 120, 643, 861
liberal democracy 9, 56, 120, 280, 463–7, 476–7,
 642–3, 653
Liberal Democratic Party, *see* LDP
liberalisation 239, 310, 670, 711
liberalism 73, 919, 942

liberty 78, 83–4, 93, 603–4, 644–5, 889, 958,
       1012–14
   constitutional 204, 825, 838
   fundamental 44, 91, 797, 829, 886, 906
   personal 408, 828, 983–4, 987, 1008, 1020–1
licences 359, 558, 580–1, 592–3, 596, 653, 655–6,
       658
licenses, massager 583–4, 587
life, right to, *see* rights, to life (and health)
life imprisonment 243, 451–2, 554, 713, 921
lifestyle 569, 571
   customs 574–5
lifting of martial law 21–2, 927
limited constitutionality 366, 443–4, 447
limited discretion 744, 752, 950
limited government 6, 9, 59, 62, 885
limited unconstitutionality 366–7, 444–5, 447
lineal ascendants 554–5
litigation 125, 330, 332, 334, 403, 405, 458, 577
   public interest 414–17, 630, 983, 991, 1009,
       1013, 1016
livelihood 582–8, 959–60, 962, 970, 972, 975–7,
       984–90, 992–3
   humane 582–5, 954
   stabilization of 954, 956
living conditions 561, 570, 588, 951
LKY, *see* Lee Kuan Yew
local authorities 334, 761, 858, 929
local government 19, 290, 329, 334, 589, 611, 758,
       899–901
   units 474–5, 542
local initiative 541–2
local ordinances 540–1
Locke, John 73, 144–5, 546, 549
locus standi 253–4, 307, 396–7, 399, 404–17
   individuals 404–10
   public interest litigation and taxpayer suits
       411–17
loyalty 80, 86, 90, 99, 116, 128, 854, 856
LPRP (Lao People's Revolutionary Party) 50, 100,
       104, 174
Lutz, Donald S 70, 104, 256

MacArthur, Douglas 19–20, 686
Macau 18, 79, 105, 550, 557, 625, 944
Madhya Pradesh 210, 212, 808, 814, 818, 1001
Madison, James 63, 118, 122, 181, 219–20, 307,
       311, 313
Madras 27, 379, 771, 779, 800–1, 810, 872
Maharashtra 627–8, 725, 878
Majelis Permusyawaratan Rakyat, *see* MPR
majoritarian institutions 327
majoritarian legitimacy 59–62
majority judgments/opinions 272, 288, 343, 795–7,
       889, 893, 896, 902–3
majority vote 15, 173, 257–9, 264, 364, 526
Malacca 34, 787, 907
Malay language 559, 578, 792, 905, 909
Malays 117, 558–60, 562, 577–8, 673–7, 789,
       792–3, 905–6
Malaysia 3, 5–6
   constitution making 26, 34–7, 58

constitutional change 221, 235, 258, 260, 271,
       280–1, 298–9, 309
constitutional culture 70, 74, 76, 79, 89, 92,
       105–6, 116–17
   democracy 465, 492–3, 499
   equality 550–1, 554, 556–64, 577–8, 606, 625–6,
       629
   free speech 642–3, 645, 671–4, 687–8, 693–7,
       704, 761–2, 766–7
   government system 127–9, 131, 134–7, 144–5,
       156, 204–5, 207
   judicial review 309, 312, 361–2, 364, 397, 405,
       448, 450
   religion 776–8, 785–7, 789–90, 792–3, 795,
       797–9, 905–7, 914
   socio-economic rights 944, 968, 992–3, 1001
   Islam 116–17
   Rukunegara declaration 89–92, 890
   Supreme Court 405, 492, 688, 699, 741, 762
Malaysians 76, 271, 550, 772, 777, 783, 795, 832
malice 704–5, 711–12, 714–15, 921
management 175, 177, 445–6, 580, 756, 966–7,
       971–2, 980
   water resources 978–82
mandamus 164, 286, 435, 443, 509, 541, 628, 632
manipulation, political 141, 149, 173, 183, 376
Mao Tse Tung 42–5, 123, 139, 173
Marcos regime 55, 158–9, 251, 266, 269, 400–2,
       413–14
market economy 25, 81, 86, 101, 956, 970–1
   social 956–7
market mechanisms 581, 970, 973–4
markets 10, 580, 587, 641, 669, 892, 969–70, 972–6
marriage 40, 73, 722, 732, 790, 793, 796, 887–8
martial law 21, 23, 55, 224–5, 244–6, 248–51,
       253–4, 266–7
   instruments 244–5
   lifting of 21–2, 927
   proclamations/declarations of 115, 244, 247–8,
       250
Marxism-Leninism 25, 100–1, 173
mass media 121, 123, 517–18, 651–3, 655 7,
       659–61, 665–9, 717–21
mass murder 833–4
massage business 579–81, 583–7
media, *see* mass media
meetings, public 748, 751–2
mental health 978, 1002, 1018
Mid Day Meal Scheme (MDMS) 994–5, 998–1000
midnight appointments 184, 190, 376
militant democracy 350, 497–8, 505
military 47, 80–1, 99, 251, 304, 309, 844, 848
military duties 834, 849, 858
military rule 243, 245, 247, 921
military service 91, 101
   compulsory 91, 847
   conscientious objection 91, 835–58
   duty of 839–42, 844–5
ministers 95, 128–9, 180, 182, 329–30, 652, 716,
       900
minorities 566–9, 622–5, 633–5, 637, 839–40, 889,
       926, 937–8

protection 622–40, 682, 960
  religious 578, 782, 816, 859, 861, 922, 925, 931
minority groups 493–4, 526, 546, 569, 575, 675
minority rights 623, 636–7
Mirza Sahib 917, 919, 926–9
mischief 427, 605–7, 790, 809, 877, 917
misconduct 93–4, 271, 363, 851
missionaries 800, 810–11, 816
mistaken but justified belief 710
misuse 268, 627–8, 877, 923, 930, 933, 937–8,
  940–1
mitigating factors 688, 697–8
modern constitutionalism 270, 313, 349, 369
monarchs 50, 64, 98–9, 128–31, 134–6, 138–9, 144,
  280
monarchy 37–8, 58, 61, 99–100, 127–8, 134–5,
  139–40, 686–7
  absolute 37, 260
  constitutional 12–13, 16–17, 49, 56, 58, 92, 95,
    106
  feudal 242, 360
  theocratic 109
monetary compensation 439, 709, 737
Mongolia 5
  constitution making 14, 37, 52, 57–8
  constitutional change 221–2, 239–40, 260
  Constitutional Court 216, 352
  constitutional culture 78, 80
  democracy 464, 537
  equality 550, 557, 625
  government system 128–9, 144–5, 189, 205,
    216–17
  judicial review 328–30, 332, 334, 338, 350,
    353–4, 365, 370–1
  religion 860
monks 106, 108–9
monopolies 81, 359, 580, 583–4, 587, 656, 661,
  973
moral equality 546, 804
moral harm 722
moral integrity 90, 119, 737
moral or virtuous constitution 77–9
moral rights 284, 737
morality 78, 83, 97–8, 724, 733, 737–8, 762, 887–9
  public 722, 729, 762, 830, 888, 890
  religious 888–90
  sexual 16, 723, 727–8
morals 66, 78, 701, 714, 739, 743, 888
  good 78, 501, 728
  public 488, 642, 722, 854–5, 888
mosques 112, 778–9, 874–5, 914, 930
Mosse, Alfred 11
motherland 87, 101, 616, 971
mothers 83, 377, 626, 867, 928, 1002–3; *see also*
  parents
motives 143, 248, 421, 514, 602, 692, 712, 714–15
  improper 691, 694–6
MPR (Majelis Permusyawaratan Rakyat) 54, 172,
  258, 304, 339
multi-religious society 125, 130, 794, 805, 824,
  890, 915
multiculturalism 578, 637, 827

municipalities 176, 319, 469, 473–4, 528, 542, 611,
  913
murder 336, 434, 554–5, 627, 918, 921
  dowry 629
  mass 833–4
murtad 788, 790, 795, 920
Muslim community 89, 786, 790–1, 794, 859, 868,
  891, 919
Myanmar 5
  constitution making 58
  constitutional change 221–2
  constitutional culture 106
  equality 550, 556–7, 625
  government system 134, 144, 203
  judicial review 328–9, 331, 334–5, 338, 370–1,
    374
  religion 847, 860
  socio-economic rights 1001
mystical beliefs 774, 941–2

national anthem 851–5, 857
national budgets 190, 193, 196, 951
National Communications Commission, *see* NCC
national consensus 65, 217, 226, 272, 274
national culture 76–7, 104–5, 865
national defence 41, 197, 203, 236, 537, 836, 841,
  847
  duty of 839–40, 844
National Economic Policy (NEP) 90
national economy 82, 194, 950–1, 956, 972–3,
  976–7, 989, 1021
national elections 122, 171, 224, 297, 534, 607
national emergency, *see* emergency
national flag 87, 280–1, 683, 700–2
national identity 6, 77, 85–100, 105, 109, 231, 235,
  732
national ideology 87, 90, 104, 118, 465, 932
national interests 103, 135, 140, 159, 202, 267, 414,
  490–1
National People's Congress, *see* NPC
national referenda 160, 258, 272, 281, 341, 346,
  453–4, 537–9
national religion 105, 108, 775, 893, 896, 900, 902
national representatives 224–6, 455
national security 687, 750, 835–6, 840–4, 846–8,
  850, 865, 908
  interests of 204, 361, 739, 743, 757
national service 832, 834–5, 847–50
national territory 403, 763–4, 770, 840
national unity 89, 105, 123, 467, 497, 702, 827, 853
nationalisation 288, 291
nationalism 16, 102, 105, 110–11, 134, 295, 856,
  858
  Hindu 807, 872, 874, 877
nationality 103–4, 375, 377, 613, 615–16, 623, 635,
  638–9
  Chinese 314, 319–20, 612
  foreign 613–16
natural-born citizens 375, 377, 381
natural calamities, *see* calamities
natural environment 80, 1019, 1021
natural law 72, 278, 965

natural resources 35, 81, 88, 965–6, 971–2, 977, 979, 982
natural rights 284, 549
naturalized citizens 381, 530, 638
NCC (National Communications Commission) 140–3, 186–9, 455, 658–9
necessary or expedient 642, 747–8
necessities of life, bare 984, 990–1, 1007, 1013
necessity 154, 200–1, 232, 237, 248–9, 603–4, 650–1, 979
 condition 229, 317, 322, 743
 doctrine 452–3, 742, 749
 scope of 737, 764
negotiations 29–30, 62, 163–4, 223, 247, 414, 663, 787
 political 241, 282, 478
NEP (National Economic Policy) 90
Nepal 5
 constitution making 58, 61
 constitutional change 258, 260
 constitutional culture 109–10
 equality 550, 557–8, 625, 629, 632, 634
 free speech 642, 670, 687, 704
 government system 127–8, 134, 140, 149, 205
 from Hindu kingdom to secular state 109–10
 judicial review 309, 466
 religion 806, 860
 socio-economic rights 944, 1001, 1022
Netherlands 20, 51–3, 528, 947
neutrality 79–80, 116, 642, 824, 838, 861, 883
 benevolent, *see* benevolent neutrality
 political 760, 762
 religious 838, 860–1, 871–2, 874, 893, 910
 strict 114, 880–1
newspapers 659–60, 663, 666, 668–9, 677–9, 707–8, 710, 720–1
Ngo Dinh Diem 46–7
NGOs (non-governmental organisations) 415, 417, 627, 630, 806, 969, 978, 983
no-confidence
 motion 148 9
 vote of 148–9, 151–2
nominal authority 142, 188
nominations 142, 184, 188–9, 342, 371, 375, 381, 390
nominees 184–5, 374, 378, 381, 484–5
 party 484–5, 532–4
non-believers 910, 919, 928
non-citizens 533, 553, 606, 640
non-discrimination 109, 590, 829, 943
non-governmental organisations, *see* NGOs
non-Malays 116, 792, 798
non-Muslims 792, 794–5, 907, 909, 916–17, 919–21, 923–4, 926–7
non-party caretaker governments 180, 247
non-smokers 952–3
non-violence 106, 844, 873
nonretroactive principle 300–1
normal politics 255, 265, 270
normal religious activities 863, 865, 911
normative values 70, 465, 762
North Borneo 34–6

North Korea
 constitution making 24–5
 constitutional change 202
 constitutional cultism 102–3
 equality 550, 557, 621, 625
 judicial review 313
North Vietnam 47–8
NPC (National People's Congress) 41–5, 121, 175–7, 228–9, 257, 309, 312–21, 324–5
Nullum Delictum 303
nutrition 984, 997, 1002–3, 1007, 1013

oaths 212–13, 397, 401, 520, 530
 of office 180, 213–14, 520, 788, 853
obiter 449, 610, 653
objective standards 723, 727–8
obligations 79–80, 199–200, 841–2, 844, 980, 1000, 1004, 1006–8
 human rights 979, 1004
 international 433, 638, 843
 legal 576, 635, 638, 836, 839–40, 913
 positive 667, 787
 social 661, 836
obscene speech 643, 722, 729
obscenity 83, 704, 722–33, 869
 test of 726
occupation 231–4, 359, 557, 562–3, 580–1, 583–7, 985, 989
 freedom of 359, 582, 584–8, 614
occupational associations 763, 770
occupational choice 581, 585
occupational freedom, *see* freedom, of occupation
offerings 779, 897–9, 901, 924
official duties 164, 171, 537, 617
official religion 105–6, 108, 787, 794–5, 798–9, 860, 932, 935
officials 27, 94–5, 500–1, 522, 602, 608–9, 612, 705
 appointed 608–10, 612
 government 39, 78, 93–4, 337–8, 799, 826
 public 171, 178, 507–9, 521–3, 614, 700, 704–5, 759–60
 state 78, 123, 799, 822, 898
Okinawa 196–7, 199, 201
old age 581–2, 954, 956, 998
oligarchies 463–4
ombudsmen 329, 331, 333, 387, 391, 457, 490, 511
omissions 89, 168–9, 268, 413, 421, 424, 1012, 1020
one person one vote 468, 475, 477, 484, 494
operation of art 346–7
operation of law 491, 769
opposition 16, 36, 53, 103, 148–9, 167, 405–6, 716
 parties 22, 56, 141, 148–9, 218, 234, 267, 481
 political 74, 466, 921
 politicians 22, 90, 397
oppression 41, 104, 112–13, 236, 303, 608, 879
ordinary courts 168, 309, 325, 332–5, 348–9, 356–9, 365–6, 372–3
ordinary majority vote 324
ordinary meaning 427, 525, 601, 720
ordinary reasonable person 717–18, 721
organisations of state 128–43

Oriental constitutionalism 94
original intent 276, 373, 419, 765
Orissa 696, 800, 808–11, 813–14, 816, 859
orthodoxy, religious 682, 867, 904, 910, 914–15
outdoor assemblies 740–1, 749–51, 753–4
overruling
  prospective 285, 290, 448–50, 452
  retrospective 448
overseas voting 409, 523–4
ownership 445–6, 649, 654, 659, 971, 973, 976, 981
  civil 971–2
  of land 88, 283
  private 81, 972, 976
  proof of 648–9
  public 101, 971–2

Paen Din Thai Party 501–2
Pakistan 2, 5, 7, 251
  and Ahmadis 916–32
  blasphemy 916–32
  constitution making 26, 31–4, 58, 60, 64
  constitutional change 221–2, 245–6, 248, 251–2,
    254–5
  constitutional culture 70, 108, 110–12, 117
  democracy 465, 493, 533, 536–7
  equality 550, 554, 556, 605, 625–6, 629
  free speech 642, 687, 696, 704, 711
  government system 144, 180, 204, 212
  judicial review 309, 313, 328, 374, 391, 440, 444
  religion 826, 860, 868, 916–32
  socio-economic rights 944, 953, 983, 992,
    1009–11, 1015–16
  Supreme Court 108, 212, 248, 252, 254, 348, 533
Pancasila 88–9, 91–2, 860, 932, 934–5, 937, 975
parades 739–42, 745–6, 749–51, 753–4, 925
parents 80, 84–5, 227, 320–1, 627–9, 791–2, 798,
  851–2; *see also* fathers; mothers
parliamentary and executive enactment 328, 342,
  349, 399, 443
parliamentary consent 370, 374
parliamentary democracy 17, 52, 58, 89–90, 130,
  145, 148, 253
parliamentary government 11, 16, 32, 127, 145,
  151–2, 209, 211
parliamentary privileges 344, 642, 670, 747
parliamentary sovereignty 120, 147
parliamentary supremacy 120, 324–6
parliamentary systems 127, 129–30, 134, 138,
  144–57, 160, 172, 195
  executive power in 146–8
  legislative power in 145–6
parole 620–2
parole review 620–2
Parti Sosialis Malaysia, *see* PSM
partial constitutionality 366, 445
partial ratification 207, 363
partiality, gross 674–5
parties 146–9, 337–41, 481–92, 497–507, 534,
  663–4, 758–64, 862–6
  dissolution 329, 337, 339, 392, 497, 501–2, 505
  major 103, 143, 254, 297
  opposition 22, 56, 141, 148–9, 218, 234, 267, 481

religion-based 108, 110, 115–16
  unconstitutional 328, 339–40, 404
partisan politics 181, 295, 658
partition 31, 46, 109, 112, 679, 763, 770
party-list system 486–8, 490, 520
party nominees 484–5, 532–4
party politics 93, 162, 181, 485, 498–9, 534, 540
passive review test 845
patriotism 55, 80, 101, 128, 854, 856
  constitutional 85–7
Pattana Chart Thai Party 502
peace 105–6, 116–17, 125, 197–200, 236–8, 786–8,
  802–4, 824–5
  international 38, 81, 115, 196, 198, 200–1, 238
  public 204, 651, 661, 746–7, 749, 835, 925, 929
  religious 904, 940
peace loving people 197, 236, 238
peaceful assembly, right of 739, 743–4
peaceful coexistence 80, 105, 826
penalties 233–4, 302, 668, 672, 709, 711, 742, 745
  administrative 648, 654
pensions 387–8, 944, 947, 954, 956, 962–3
people power 6, 55, 74, 94, 158, 251, 266, 541
people's dictatorship 42, 173
People's Republic of China (PRC), *see* China
people's sovereignty 60, 242, 360, 491, 508–9,
  521–2, 538
perceptions 327, 666, 773, 806, 852, 877
  social 633, 775–6
permanent residence 314, 616, 640, 849
permanent residents 227, 314, 317, 319–22, 421–2,
  428–9, 521–2, 640
permission 123, 487, 572, 586, 745, 748–51, 841–2,
  1011–12
permissive accommodations 883–6, 889
persecution 111, 113, 879, 922, 930
  religious 859, 862, 865
personal belief 773, 775, 814, 894
  systems 771, 852
personal choice 782, 785, 828, 956
personal data 83, 348, 443
personal discretion 131, 148
personal God 771, 775, 852
personal interest 404, 414, 526
personal law(s) 449, 601, 796, 868, 872, 890
personal liberty 408, 828, 983–4, 987, 1008, 1020–1
personal security 708, 984
personality 24–5, 62, 84–5, 584, 586, 589, 662, 734
  individual 586–7, 641
  juridical 833–4
personnel 142, 187–8, 389, 455, 1010
  affairs 141–2, 186–9
persuasion 122, 138, 798, 801–2, 809–10, 825, 919–20
petitioners 163–4, 367–8, 410–14, 677–8, 684–5,
  853–6, 964–6, 987–91
petitions 253–4, 332–6, 343–5, 367–8, 399, 410–11,
  540–1, 543–4, 684–5
  citizen 464, 543–4
  constitutional 252, 333–4, 537, 992, 1017
  popular 123–4
  writ 380–2, 384–5, 413, 415–16, 985, 988, 991,
    994

Philippines 3, 5–6
    constitution making 14–15, 18, 22, 36, 51, 54–6
    constitutional change 221–2, 231, 239–40, 248,
        251, 258–61, 266–9
    constitutional culture 70, 75, 81–2, 107
    democracy 464–8, 473–4, 481–2, 486–9, 512–16,
        519–20, 536–7, 540–1
    equality 550, 556–8, 607, 640
    free speech 642, 652, 668–9, 687, 711, 713
    government system 127–8, 157–9, 163–4, 166–7,
        171, 185, 204–5, 208
    judicial review 348, 350, 374–7, 385–9, 397–8,
        400–4, 413, 415
    religion 824, 852–3, 861, 878–9, 884, 890–1
    secularism 878–90
    socio-economic rights 944, 964, 968
    Supreme Court 157, 185, 248, 351, 377, 400,
        403, 711–12
philosophy 109, 301, 304, 548, 774, 800, 807,
        972–3
    political 87, 100, 102, 121, 722
photographs 690–2, 726, 728–9, 732
physical disability 581–2, 956
physical education 836–7
physical restraint 983–4
piety 83, 778, 823
plebiscites 15, 55, 59, 259, 267, 474–5, 536, 540
pluralistic democracy 56, 281
pluralistic society 89, 821, 873, 883
police 706, 740, 742, 746–7, 749, 751–3, 756, 781
policy and budgets 190–6
political accountability 369, 705
political actions 220, 256, 265–70, 461
political activities 108, 470, 504, 663–4, 760
political authorities 97, 118, 546, 776, 833, 860,
        892–3
political branches 120, 144, 146, 181, 203, 215–17,
        369, 506
    conflict and conciliation 181–90
political change 157, 248, 739
political clout 142, 188, 251, 612, 659
political competition 121, 262
political compromise 217, 262, 304
political conflicts 181, 216, 223, 240, 262, 291,
        341–2, 697
political consensus 217–18, 226, 260, 282
political control 186, 189, 569, 862
political culture 253, 720–1
political defamation 90, 704–21
political equality 340, 477, 481, 546
political harms 670
political identity 77, 86
political ideologies 6, 70, 89, 100, 379, 417, 465,
        896
political impartiality 511, 658, 760, 762
political influence 99, 142, 186–8, 762
political institutions 39, 122, 324, 331, 342, 356,
        459, 465
political interests 94, 327, 808
political interference 141, 230, 375
political justice 114, 289, 291
political leadership 25, 251

political legitimacy 64, 96, 99
political libel 119, 704
political manipulation 141, 149, 173, 183, 376
political negotiations 241, 282, 478
political neutrality 760, 762
political opposition 74, 466, 921
political participation, right to 7, 520–35, 756, 762
political parties, *see* parties
political philosophy 87, 100, 102, 121, 722
political power 93–4, 97, 99, 122, 129, 664, 673–4,
        760
political process 652, 739, 741, 743, 745, 747, 749,
        751
political protests 21, 216, 700
political question doctrine 196, 251, 268–9, 340,
        351, 396, 400–4, 967
political reform 54, 175–6, 310–11, 466
political representation 463, 467, 479, 493
    forms 467–77
    institutions for 497–520
political systems 62, 93, 96, 100, 154, 157, 174–5,
        178
political theories 93, 95, 294, 424, 426, 479, 550
political trust 663–4
politicians 26–7, 102, 108, 150, 406, 705, 715–16,
        721
politics 25–6, 91–2, 106–8, 175, 341–2, 545, 760,
        869–71
    of accountability 141–2, 187–9
    electoral 467, 493, 497
    judicialisation of 256, 341
    normal 255, 265, 270
    partisan 181, 295, 658
    party 93, 162, 181, 485, 498–9, 534, 540
    regional 239, 271, 299
    transitional 241, 282, 505
polling 509–10, 515, 517
pollution 993, 1012–14, 1018–21
    air 1017–19
    water 1001, 1021
popular petitions 123–4
popular sovereignty 139, 145, 278–9, 523, 527,
        861, 971, 977
populist constitutionalism 123–4
pornography 722, 724, 726, 731–3; *see also*
        obscenity
Portugal 17–18, 58, 253, 787
positive discrimination 558–78
positive duties 667, 744
positive law 70, 300, 724, 927–8, 930
poverty 56, 210, 402, 411–12, 415, 601, 1012, 1020
power-sharing mechanisms 189, 205, 369, 371, 373
power(s) 92–100, 130–8, 140–7, 149–59, 181–91,
        273–91, 293–8, 338–51
    absolute 37, 40, 58, 70, 211, 244, 266, 289
    abstract review 331, 399, 443
    abuse of 154, 166, 268, 285, 294, 669
    administrative 93–4, 96, 201, 208, 291
    amending 283, 285–7, 289, 351
    of amendment 257, 285–6, 292
    ancillary 329, 337–9, 341–2, 344, 404
    appointment 17, 159, 186, 189, 371, 378, 658

balance of 161–2, 187, 255, 294–5
budgetary 178, 196
ceremonial 135, 140
constituent 59, 235, 282, 289
decision-making 136, 178, 327, 947
delegated 325, 927
discretionary 130, 134–6, 148, 154, 198, 237,
  346–7, 950–1
of dissolution 152, 156, 161–2, 294
examination 95
exclusive 145, 230, 264, 324, 891
executive 142–4, 146–8, 155, 157–9, 161–2,
  186–8, 191, 293–4
government 88, 118, 127–8, 293, 295, 393, 466,
  544
of interpretation 277, 313, 315–16, 318, 325
investigative 353, 447
judicial 228, 293–4, 298, 307–9, 315, 327, 344–5,
  372–3
of judicial review 198, 200, 210, 270–1, 307, 311,
  313, 325
legislative 145–6, 178–80, 187–8, 208–9, 277–8,
  280, 293, 388–9
legislative-formative 619–20
political 93–4, 97, 99, 122, 129, 664, 673–4, 760
prerogative 133, 179
presidential 53, 130–1, 157–9, 175, 185, 190,
  214, 346
primary 205, 341
public 118–20, 160, 893
of ratification 207, 363
relinquishment of 161–2, 294–5, 919
separation of 142, 144, 187–8, 290, 294, 298,
  401, 403
sovereign 39, 198, 237–8, 277, 298, 523, 612, 834
state, *see* state power
statutory 166, 362, 499, 562, 767, 797
supervisory 95, 389, 391–2, 512
symbolic 98, 128–9
PR, *see* proportional representation
Prajadhipok, King 16
prayers 775, 778–80, 808, 831, 880–1, 891, 928
PRC, *see* China
precautionary principle 1016, 1020–1
precedence 84, 135, 154, 183, 250, 577, 787, 793
precedents 32, 284, 335, 417, 504, 609–10, 725,
  795
preferential treatment 81, 388, 555, 582, 584–5,
  866, 874, 897
pregnant women 995, 1002–3
preliminary injunctions 460–1
preliminary review 330, 844
prerogative powers 133, 179
presidential decrees 266, 300, 349, 387, 400, 932,
  937, 965
presidential elections 156, 166, 172–3, 184–5,
  376–8, 525–6, 532, 534
presidential immunity 157, 167–70, 342, 423
presidential impeachment 157, 169, 170–3, 338,
  341
presidential powers 53, 130–1, 157–9, 175, 185,
  190, 214, 346

presidential systems 14, 75, 127, 144, 155–73, 178,
  190, 195
  domestic affairs 157–62
  foreign affairs 163–6
presidentialism 127, 155, 165–6
Presidents 129–34, 157–72, 182–6, 202–6, 209–12,
  338–44, 376–85, 536–40
  Acting 54, 185, 247, 376–8
  elected 98, 103, 133–4, 138, 144, 172–3, 195,
    342–3
  former 217, 242–3, 360
  impeachment 157, 169, 170–3, 338, 341
  incumbent 166, 186, 250, 378
press freedoms 652–3, 662, 672
prestige 17, 21, 128, 168, 507
presumptions 119, 444, 593, 596, 600, 602, 968,
  970
primary jurisdiction 328–9, 337
primary powers 205, 341
Prime Ministers 130, 133–5, 147, 149, 182–3,
  204–5, 216, 252–4
printers 646, 677–8, 697
printing 643, 645–6, 649, 677–8, 707, 720, 913
prior approval 498, 513, 644, 648, 654, 658, 763–4,
  770
prior restraints 643–4, 646–7, 649, 740, 854
prison 525, 648, 693–4, 844
prisoners 451, 521, 525–8
privacy 44, 662, 669, 777–8, 813–14, 816, 829,
  952–3
private autonomy 638, 903, 956
private educational institutions 829, 1006
private individuals 268, 588, 686, 704–5, 721
private interests 497, 527, 566, 585, 587, 741, 953,
  956
private ownership 81, 972, 976
private property 46, 55, 200, 290, 752, 896, 956
privatisation 943, 968, 972, 975, 977–8
privilege(s) 249–50, 267, 553, 556, 598–9, 613–16,
  713–14, 841
  and equality 579–89
  parliamentary 344, 642, 670, 747
  special 90, 388, 553, 675, 713, 724, 878
privileged treatment 107, 550, 558
procedural safeguards 131, 133, 364
processions 693, 701, 743–4, 752, 929
proclamations
  of emergency 134, 204–5, 210, 212, 214, 252,
    361–2, 364
  of martial law 115, 244, 247–8, 250
professional ethics 395, 652
profit 55, 652, 726, 892, 974–5, 980, 982
prohibited religious activities 895, 898–9
proof of ownership 648–9
propaganda 24, 26, 681, 801, 834, 866, 875, 934
  hate 681
propagation 116, 124, 726, 786–9, 835, 905–7, 917,
  919–20
  anti-propagation legislation 782, 805–8, 810, 816
  constitutionalisation of right to propagate
    799–802
  and conversion 798–826

proper interpretation 227, 230, 274, 276, 314, 789
property 556–7, 564–5, 567, 780, 912–13, 929–30,
     953–5, 1011–12
  private 46, 55, 200, 290, 752, 896, 956
  public 123, 656–7
prophethood 916–20
  finality of 918–19, 923
prophets 868, 876, 922, 924, 926–9, 934
proportional representation 281, 467, 481–90, 493,
     496, 520
  systems 281, 409, 481–5, 489, 522–4
proportionality 469, 528, 619–22, 702, 907, 948–9,
     957, 961–2
  principle 527, 580–1, 618–19, 621–2, 654–5, 740,
     840, 961–2
  reviews 827, 945
  test 743–4, 957
propriety 122, 601, 691, 814, 836, 894, 943, 950
prosecution 169–70, 241, 407–8, 673, 675, 686,
     710–11, 849
  threat of 710, 721, 937
prosecutors 169–70, 217, 242–3, 330, 336, 360,
     418–19, 710
proselytism 801, 804–5, 818
  improper 805, 818
proselytization 805, 811
prospective effect 447–8, 450–2
prospective overruling 285, 290, 443, 447–50, 452
prosperity 53, 62, 123, 125, 960, 970, 973, 1010–11
prostitution 78, 83, 455, 625, 704, 828, 928, 991–2
protection
  constitutional 491, 520, 558, 670, 700, 709, 764,
     856
  environmental 967, 1016
  equal, *see* equal protection
  of free speech 438, 641–2, 654, 699, 711, 721
  of fundamental rights 350, 584, 743
  of human rights 278, 280, 304, 433, 936, 940
  of minorities 622–40, 682, 960
  of personal data 348, 443
  of public order 700–2
  of religious orthodoxy 904–9
  special 56, 105, 236, 262, 388, 534, 584, 686
protectionist state 904–5, 907, 909, 911, 913, 915,
     917, 919
protests 23, 39, 135, 169, 458, 701, 749, 755
  peaceful 746–7
  political 21, 216, 700
  street 217, 226, 626, 739
prudence 165, 202, 717, 826, 1010–11
prurient interest 723, 727–8, 731, 733
PSM (Parti Sosialis Malaysia) 499–500, 766, 768
public administration 2, 31, 93–4, 96, 178, 376,
     522, 525
public affairs 463, 521, 525, 528, 532–3, 536, 641,
     667
  conduct of 521, 525, 531, 536
public apologies 734, 737, 739
public benefits 566, 573, 577, 780
public confidence 142, 187–8, 190, 438, 659, 687–9,
     691–2, 699
  impairment of 438, 699

public discourse 124, 710, 719–20
public disorder 743, 776, 814
public figures 704, 711, 721
public functionaries 386, 392, 617, 741–2
public funds 167, 414, 666, 709, 893, 898, 946–7
public health 701, 739, 743, 848, 852, 854–5, 997,
     1001
public hearings 259, 1011, 1014, 1016
public injury 413
public interest 209–10, 383–4, 585–7, 705–7,
     711–13, 715–17, 719–20, 840–2
  critical 580
  important 456, 579–81, 654, 740, 842
  legitimate 854–5
  litigation 414–17, 630, 983, 991, 1009, 1013,
     1016
public knowledge 68, 237, 301
public law 74–5, 337, 341, 409, 412, 637, 644, 859
  arguments 432–3
public life 69, 465, 524, 527, 533, 642, 825, 829
public meetings 748, 751–2
public morality 722, 729, 762, 830, 888, 890
public morals 488, 642, 722, 854–5, 888
public office 107, 521, 529, 531, 533–5, 612, 614,
     617
public officials 171, 178, 507–9, 521–3, 614, 700,
     704–5, 759–60
public opinion 39, 50, 123, 192, 217–18, 652–3,
     656, 661–2
public order 302–3, 678–9, 743–4, 747–8, 810,
     814–15, 834–6, 847–50
  maintenance of 286, 644, 743, 748, 810
public ownership 101, 971–2
public parks 740, 744, 1016
public peace 204, 651, 661, 746–7, 749, 835, 925,
     929
public policy 63, 72, 75, 260, 414, 553, 641, 758–9
public powers 118–20, 160, 893
public property 123, 656–7
public prosecutors 91, 207–8, 298, 313, 450–1, 606,
     673, 676
public referenda 343, 349–50, 400
public safety 185, 376–7, 656, 739, 741, 743, 750,
     854–5
public schools 756, 762, 771, 827, 830, 838, 853–4,
     935
public security 215, 728, 908, 912, 938
public service 130, 133–4, 178–80, 185, 376–7, 558,
     560, 961
public trust 90, 119, 172, 186, 538
public utilities 209–10, 974
  privately-owned 204, 210
public values 527, 945
public welfare 132, 568, 618–19, 698, 750, 833–4,
     847–8, 953–4
publishers 644–6, 648–9, 677–8, 708, 716–18, 723,
     730, 835
punishment 132, 232–4, 300–3, 384, 434–5, 525–6,
     554–5, 912
  administrative 458
  criminal 439, 572, 728, 730–1, 734, 742, 839,
     844–5

Punjab 283, 286–7, 290–1, 350, 677–8, 680, 780, 922
purpose and effect test 838, 897–8, 901
purposive interpretation 275–6, 347, 417, 426–31, 787, 1018

Quadianis 916–22, 924, 927–8
qualifications 355, 376, 410–11, 487, 519–21, 533, 580, 586
qualified persons 376, 378–9, 412
qualified privilege 705, 712–14, 718, 720
quantum of damages 119, 721
quo warranto 286, 443, 628
quotas 15, 227, 314, 467, 493–7
    gender 496
Quran 776–8, 782, 784, 790, 868–9, 890–1, 917–23, 928

race 551–3, 557–8, 567, 671, 673–7, 680–1, 823–4, 828–9
racial discrimination 638, 681
racial groups 465, 671, 677, 682, 825, 827
racial harmony 124, 467, 680, 825
radio 653, 657, 661, 665, 669, 713, 1014
Rajasthan 79, 210, 290, 415, 435, 459, 985
ratification 163–4, 183, 203, 205–7, 250, 266–7, 363, 400
    partial 207, 363
    power of 207, 363
rational classification 589–622
re-election 166, 225–6, 455, 507–8
real risk test 437–8, 440, 688–90, 698
reasonable classification 553, 591, 594, 598–600, 605, 607–8
reasonable courtesy 696, 699
reasonable nexus test 589–622
reasonable person, ordinary 717–18, 721
reasonable restrictions 499, 656–7, 665, 670, 678–9, 751–2, 761–2, 770
reasonableness 442, 498, 591, 593, 602, 610–11, 620, 642
    test 489, 897
rebellion 63, 167, 169–70, 249–50, 360
    state of 249–50
recall 39, 93–4, 98, 169–70, 173, 176, 339, 342
recidivism 622, 654
reconciliation 124, 159, 708, 825, 935
recruitment 179–80, 249, 394, 765
redress, judicial 412–13, 415
referenda 39, 162, 256–7, 259–68, 271–3, 293, 329–30, 535–43
    confidence 160, 171–2, 537–8
    disputes 264, 340–2, 344
    national 160, 258, 272, 281, 341, 346, 453–4, 537–9
    public 343, 349–50, 400
reform 12, 14–15, 17, 19, 21, 100–1, 193–4, 304
    administrative 16, 178, 193
    constitutional 16, 23, 35, 75, 100, 157, 166, 328
    financial 192–3
    land 40, 56, 283, 289–91
    political 54, 175–6, 310–11, 466
regional politics 239, 271, 299

regionalism 106, 138
registered voters 258, 536, 540–2
regulations 178–80, 348–9, 356–9, 398–9, 512–13, 762–6, 830–2, 971–4
    administrative, *see* administrative regulations
regulatory commissions, independent 140, 143, 186, 455, 658
rehabilitation 194, 989–91, 1021
    schemes 989–90, 992
    vocational 583–4
relational constitutionalism 124–5, 824–5
religion 104–17, 124–5, 551–3, 557–8, 567, 622–3, 676–7, 771–942
    abuse of 111, 860, 865
    apostasy, *see* apostasy
    Bangladesh 828–30, 847, 859–60, 867–8, 909–10
    blasphemy laws 643, 909–42
    Buddhism, *see* Buddhism
    Cambodia 860
    China 847, 862–4, 866, 873, 911, 913–14
    clauses 879–80, 883–4, 886, 888–9
    definition 771–82
    desecration of 937–8, 940–1
    establishment of 848, 872, 878–9, 888, 902
    freedom of, *see* freedom, of religion
    Hinduism, *see* Hinduism
    India 787–8, 800–1, 806–8, 810–12, 830–1, 859–60, 872–6, 920–1
    Indonesia 774, 823, 868, 916, 932–42, 944
    and instrumentalism 911–14
    intrinsic reasons for preserving orthodoxy 914–15
    Japan 774–5, 836, 838, 860, 892–904
    Laos 799, 860, 862, 866
    Malaysia 776–8, 785–7, 789–90, 792–3, 795, 797–9, 905–7, 914
    Mongolia 860
    Myanmar 847, 860
    national 105, 108, 775, 893, 896, 900, 902
    Nepal 806, 860
    official 105–6, 108, 787, 794–5, 798–9, 860, 932, 935
    Pakistan 826, 860, 868, 916–32
    Philippines 824, 852–3, 861, 878–9, 884, 890–1
    propagation, *see* propagation
    protection of religious orthodoxy 904–9
    protectionist State 904–42
    religion–state constitutional arrangements 859–69
    secular liberal constitutional models 861–2
    and secular socialisat constitutions 862–6
    secularism, *see* secularism
    separation of religion and state 109, 859, 867, 871, 892–3
    Singapore 798, 823–5, 827, 830, 834–6, 847–51, 858, 860
    South Korea 839, 841, 843, 845
    Sri Lanka 816–17, 819–22, 859
    and state 771–942
    state 70, 110, 115, 247, 822, 828, 871, 896
    Taiwan 844, 846
    Thailand 847, 860
    Vietnam 847, 862–6

religion-based political parties 108, 110, 115–16
religious activities 772, 774, 837, 866, 891, 893–5,
    902–4, 938
  normal 863, 865, 911
  prohibited 895, 898–9
religious affairs 786, 789, 791, 863–4, 932–3, 935,
    937, 939
religious authorities 777–8, 786, 798, 867, 881,
    897, 910
religious beliefs 846–9, 852–7, 861, 865–6, 879–80,
    883–7, 910–12, 923–5
  choice of 798, 852
  freedom of 853, 863, 911
religious bodies 772, 785, 820, 866, 942
religious ceremonies 807, 851–3, 867, 897, 903,
    925
religious communities 792, 801, 866, 874, 918, 920,
    923, 926
religious conduct 882, 888
religious conversions, *see* conversion
religious discrimination 109, 112
religious diversity 867, 873
religious doctrine 116, 786, 789, 839, 861, 905–6,
    911, 924
religious dress 827–8
serban 777–8, 830
religious duty 801, 808
religious education 837, 893–4, 905, 934
religious exemptions 836–58, 882, 884–5
religious faith, *see* faith
religious feelings 903, 909–10, 915, 926
religious free speech 798, 824
religious freedom, *see* freedom, of religion
religious groups 124–5, 771–2, 821–2, 824–6,
    863–4, 866, 898–900, 907–8
religious harmony 90, 124–5, 134, 670–1, 817,
    824–6, 859, 938
religious holidays 859, 898, 935
religious identity 782–3, 785, 807
religious institutions 109, 872, 880, 893, 922
religious instruction 796, 881, 897–8
  optional 883–4
religious intent 898, 901
religious interpretation 934, 937–8
religious law 76, 105–6, 777, 859, 867, 935
religious liberty 125, 794, 802, 805, 855, 858–9,
    885, 890; *see also* freedom, of religion
  scope of 859, 867
religious minorities 578, 782, 816, 859, 861, 922,
    925, 931
religious morality 888–90
religious neutrality 838, 860–1, 871–2, 874, 893,
    910
religious organisations 803–4, 833–4, 860, 863–4,
    866, 891, 893, 899
religious orthodoxy 682, 867, 904, 910, 914–15
  protection of 904–9
religious peace 904, 940
religious persecution 859, 862, 865
religious practices 777–8, 780–1, 799, 811–12, 826,
    830–1, 924–5, 935
religious propagation, *see* propagation

religious rites/rituals 776, 781, 876, 882, 896, 899,
    901, 924–5
religious sects, *see* sects
religious sensitivities 908, 910, 915, 930
religious sentiments 804, 873–4
religious speech 643, 801
religious teachings 776, 838, 872, 932, 935–40
  central 938–9
religious tenets 780, 836, 861, 890
religious tolerance 89, 114, 806, 825, 867, 871,
    910, 930
religious traditions 635, 827, 940
religious values 302, 574, 733, 852, 861, 900,
    934–6, 940
religious violence 802, 859
relinquishment of powers 161–2, 294–5, 919
remedies 443–61
remuneration 136, 150, 371, 382, 385–7, 394, 402
  security of 386, 396
renunciation of Islam 792–3, 795–6
reply, right of 660, 666–7
representation 253–4, 467, 475, 481, 486–7, 489,
    510–11, 875
  political, *see* political representation
  proportional, *see* proportional representation
  sectoral 55, 478–81
representations 500, 671, 682, 697, 736, 768, 909,
    944
representative democracy 165, 202, 273, 464, 467,
    498, 508, 527
representative institutions 165, 202, 972
representative review 207, 363
representativeness 508–9
representatives 34, 136, 150–2, 182–3, 224–6,
    469–71, 489–90, 520–2
  elected 30, 41, 58, 96, 119, 523, 531, 533
  national 224–6, 455
  proportional 484–6
repression 88–9, 301, 896
Republic of Indonesia, *see* Indonesia
Republic of Korea, *see* South Korea
Republic of Singapore, *see* Singapore
republican form of government 13, 30, 280–1
republicanism 38, 92, 251, 590
reputation 304–5, 646–7, 701, 704–5, 710, 718–21,
    733–4, 736–7
  good 90–1
  personal/individual 687, 704, 709
  right of 642, 647
  women 83, 704
res commune 980–1
res publica 7, 641–770
research 77, 104, 221, 416, 435, 615, 1010–11, 1014
reservations 207, 247, 494–5, 558–60, 564, 578,
    626, 645
residence 522, 533, 613–14, 616, 749
  permanent 314, 616, 640, 849
  status 616, 640, 947–8
resignation 148–9, 151–2, 265, 342, 381, 466, 483
resources 546, 548–9, 635–6, 945, 947, 964–5,
    971–2, 981–2
  financial 192, 834, 946, 1005

finite 944, 946–7
natural 35, 81, 88, 965–6, 971–2, 977, 979, 982
water 969, 978–82
responsibilities 316–17, 319, 321–2, 558–9, 578,
    664, 869–70, 979–80
civic 101, 683
collective 157, 847
intergenerational 415, 965, 968
restraints 73, 97, 122–3, 125, 132, 214–15, 267, 651
physical 983–4
restrictions 525–9, 580–2, 679, 700–2, 741–3,
    747–50, 752–7, 936–8
excessive 439, 582, 586, 588, 730, 734, 953, 956
reasonable 499, 656–7, 665, 670, 678–9, 751–2,
    761–2, 770
substantive 279, 671, 823
unreasonable 525, 752, 767, 905
retroactivity 243, 301–2, 449–50
review
abstract, *see* abstract review
concrete 329, 331–5, 337
constitutional, *see* constitutional review
judicial, *see* judicial review
parole 620–2
power of 150, 519
preliminary 330, 844
representative 207, 363
substantive 749–50, 764
weak 945, 952, 961
revision 13, 20, 23, 239–40, 247, 256–9, 280–1,
    456–7
comprehensive 239–40
constitutional, *see* constitutional revision
revolutions 13, 16, 37, 58–9, 63–4, 247–8, 285,
    287
Communist 37–51, 621
constitutional change during 247–55
democratic 51, 54, 57–8, 64
Green 290
Reynolds-Gobitis-Smith doctrine 883
Reynolds privilege 712, 718–20
rights
to assembly 739–55
    prior notification or approval 740–2
    restrictions on 742–55
of associations 763–70
civil 19, 94, 590–1, 926, 1003
consciousness 68, 73
economic 45, 55–6, 413, 552, 943–4, 1001, 1003
to education 1006–9
of employment 581
equal 112, 479, 548–9, 559, 624, 659, 812, 991
of equal protection 579–80
to equality 288, 358–9, 445, 472–3, 484, 509,
    531, 545–640
fundamental, *see* fundamental rights
guaranteed 58, 518, 735–6, 907
to health, *see* rights, to life (and health)
to a healthy environment 404, 1009–17, 1019–22
human, *see* human rights
indigenous 105, 559–60, 569, 577, 967
of individuals to associate/disassociate 756–62

to life (and health) 944, 952–3, 981, 983–9,
    992–4, 1000–9, 1013, 1015–20
    defined by reference to ICESCR 1017–19
    expansion to include socio-economic
        rights 983–1022
minority 623, 636–7
moral 284, 737
natural 284, 549
to organize 958–60
to political participation 7, 520–35, 756, 762
to profess 783–5
to pursue happiness 83–5, 160, 472, 549, 952,
    954, 956, 958
to reply 652–3, 659–60, 662, 666–7
of reputation 642, 647
of self-defense 198, 237
social welfare 944, 949, 983
socio-economic, *see* socio-economic rights
traditional 524–5, 560
rights-based constitutionalism 79, 120
roads 406, 740, 745–6, 925, 929, 984–5, 1013, 1015
Roesler, Hermann 11
Rose-Ackerman, Susan 140, 143, 196
Rosenfeld, Michel 2, 4
Ru 97
Rukunegara declaration 89–92, 890
rule of law 6, 64–5, 74–5, 101–2, 230–1, 280,
    452–4, 459

Sabah 34, 36, 137, 558, 560, 577–8, 906–7
sacred legitimacy 97
safeguards 108, 495, 497, 558–9, 680, 687, 712, 715
objective 715
procedural 131, 133, 364
Sajó, András 2, 4, 143, 149, 463, 467, 658, 861
salaries 371, 383, 385–6, 388, 394, 884
saluting 91, 852–6
Samak Sundaravej 156, 216
sanctions 124, 527, 530, 593, 647, 709, 741, 813
sange daibiao 101, 121
Sapporo 566, 572, 637, 646–7
Sarawak 34–6, 362, 558, 560, 577–8, 906–7
scheduled castes and tribes 113, 467, 493–7,
    559–60, 577, 920, 924, 999
schools 84–5, 322–3, 760, 827–9, 831–2, 836–8,
    851–5, 998–9
high 84, 803
primary 760, 827, 995, 999
public 756, 762, 771, 827, 830, 838, 853–4,
    935
scrutiny
intermediate 557, 618
judicial 208, 284, 612, 843
strict 495, 557, 620, 882
secession 59, 235, 637, 749–50, 753, 860, 920
second-class citizens 109, 112
sectoral representation 55, 478–81
sects 114, 834, 856, 873, 896, 898, 913–14, 937
deviant 867, 910–11, 914
secular authorities 774, 893
secular democracies 798, 859, 875, 914
secular liberal constitutional models 861–2

secular state 109, 116–17, 787–8, 795, 801, 867–9, 920, 923
secularism 109–17, 860–1, 868, 870–5, 877–9, 881, 883, 885
  accommodative 798, 852
  ameliorative 870–8
  India 870–8
  models of 870–904
  Philippines 878–90
  principle of 111, 114–15
secularity 859–61, 870, 893
security 81, 194, 196–201, 204–5, 236–8, 302, 458, 617
  collective 198, 237
  forces 198, 238, 300
  internal 35, 914
  national, *see* national security
  personal 708, 984
  public 215, 728, 908, 912, 938
  of tenure 371, 382, 393, 609
security of remuneration and judicial budget 385–9
sedition 21, 643, 646, 669–71, 673–4, 676–7, 682, 823
seditious tendency 671, 673–6, 680, 823
seditious words 670–1, 673, 682
Selangor 397, 499, 563, 766, 909
self-defense 81, 236, 238
  right of 198, 237
self-determination 84, 231, 569, 634 7
self-government 27, 29, 34–6, 220, 641
  local 153, 495, 522
self-interest 327, 918
self-preservation 965–6
separation
  of powers 128, 144, 181, 187–90, 280–1, 294–5, 298, 403–4
    and government systems 143–81
  of religion and state 109, 774, 859, 867, 870–904
SERs, *see* socio-economic rights
sexual abuse 439, 723, 728, 911
sexual exploitation 439, 730
sexual harassment 415, 435–6, 459–60, 625, 828–9, 985
sexual morality 16, 723, 727–8
sexual orientation 487, 546, 622, 631–4, 763, 948
sexual transactions 455–6, 730–1
Shaa'ire Islam 927, 929
shame 701, 723–5, 727–9
Sharif, Mian Nawaz 252
Shinawatra, Thaksin 135 139, 222
Shinto 67, 774, 892–904, 939
  ceremonial 892
  priests 774–5, 893, 895–6
  Shrine 775, 892–3, 895–7
  State 892–3, 896, 901
shrines 139, 775, 892–903; *see also* temples
Siam 14, 16–17; *see also* Thailand
Sihanouk, King 50–1, 56
Sikhs 780, 805, 827–8, 872–3, 876, 917, 924, 929
silence 313, 601, 722, 733–4, 738, 857–8
  freedom of 733–4

sincerity 102, 724, 739, 757, 843, 849, 857, 885–7
Singapore 436–8, 556–60, 578, 668–9, 676, 687–90, 719–21, 847–51
  citizens 36, 606, 669, 676, 747, 755, 763, 824
  constitution making 18, 20, 26–8, 34–7, 58, 63
  constitutional change 221–2, 235, 259–60, 298–9
  constitutional culture 74, 82, 90–2, 103–4, 116, 118–19, 124–5
  Court of Appeal 79, 405, 440, 653, 712, 721, 771
  democracy 465, 478–9, 481, 490, 492, 537
  equality 550, 552, 554, 556–60, 565, 578, 625, 629
  free speech 642–3, 668–9, 671–2, 687–90, 711–12, 716–17, 719–21, 746–8
  government system 127–8, 130–1, 133, 138, 144–8, 156, 195–6, 203
  judicial review 398–9, 405–7, 427, 432, 436–8, 440, 448, 451
  religion 798, 823–5, 827, 830, 834–6, 847–51, 858, 860
  secular government and Halal certification 890–2
  shared values 90–1
  socio-economic rights 944–5, 983
slum dwellers 985, 987–91
Smith doctrine 882, 885–6
social control 284–5
social courtesy 898–900
social disorder 676, 915
social functions 469, 846, 980
social harmony 118, 120, 124, 738, 799, 808, 862
social insurance 962; *see also* social security
  competing rights 954–7
social interest 479, 526, 679, 681, 982
social justice 88–9, 105, 110–11, 113, 413–14, 957, 970–1, 1001
social life 95, 469, 800, 837, 894
social obligations 661, 836
social order 64, 95, 618–19, 749–50, 871–2, 912–13, 921, 924
social perceptions 633, 775–6
social protection 834, 849, 958
social security 55, 354, 581–2, 587–8, 944, 954–6, 963, 969
social solidarity 120, 124, 1022
social stability 803, 805, 859, 867, 912, 962
social status 79, 523, 551, 579, 613, 622, 704, 903–4
social trust 186, 825–6
social values 70, 647, 681, 710
social welfare 290, 584, 588, 894, 945–7, 949, 974, 977
  rights 944, 949, 983
socialism 42–5, 50, 52, 70, 101–2, 110–11, 862, 864
socialist constitutions 46, 50, 52, 57, 80, 100, 104, 123
socialist democracy 463–4
socialist ideology 100, 102, 104, 863
Socialist Republic of Vietnam, *see* Vietnam
socialist road 101, 173
socialist states 6, 38, 101, 121, 173, 222, 260, 464
  intra-party democracy 121–2
socialist systems 25, 86, 173–4, 863, 914

societal cultural ethics 723, 727
socio-economic development 560, 804
socio-economic policies 945–9, 983
socio-economic rights (SERs) 6–7, 251, 943–1022;
    see also *individual rights*
  Bangladesh 944, 968, 983, 988, 990–1, 1000–1,
    1020
  Bhutan 1001
  Cambodia 944, 1022
  China 944, 962
  express, judicial review 945–61
  Hong Kong 944, 946–7, 949, 1017–18
  India 944, 983–5, 994, 996, 998–1004, 1006,
    1009, 1020–1
  Indonesia 968–83, 1001
    economic policy, privatisation and judicial
      review 968–83
  Japan 944, 955, 961
  judicial construction 983–1022
  judicial review and enforcement of directive
    principles 961–8
  Laos 944
  Malaysia 944, 968, 992–3, 1001
  Myanmar 1001
  Nepal 944, 1001, 1022
  Pakistan 944, 953, 983, 992, 1009–11, 1015–16
  Philippines 944, 964, 968
  Singapore 944–5, 983
  South Korea 944, 952, 955–6, 975–6
  Sri Lanka 1001
  Taiwan 962
  Thailand 944, 975, 1001, 1022
  Vietnam 944, 1001
soft constitutional law 65, 89, 91, 103, 220, 270–1
soft constitutional law/norms 65, 89, 91, 124, 220,
    271, 825
solidarity 86–7, 103, 115, 124–5, 472, 623, 825, 865
  Islamic 86, 115
  social 120, 124, 1022
Souphanouvong, Prince 49
South Korea 5–6
  constitution making 18, 20, 22–4, 51, 58, 61
  constitutional change 221–2, 235, 239–41, 243,
    258, 260, 271–3
  Constitutional Court 241, 243, 274, 331, 528,
    733, 753–4, 957
  constitutional culture 67, 73, 75, 84, 86, 120
  democracy 464–7, 472–3, 476–7, 481–2, 484,
    498, 501, 540–1
  equality 555, 557, 581, 584, 588, 612–16,
    619–22, 625
  free speech 648, 650–2, 710–11, 730, 733–4, 738,
    740, 753
  government system 127–8, 156–8, 160, 165–6,
    189–90, 192, 201–2, 204–5
  judicial review 328–30, 332–4, 338–9, 341–2,
    357–9, 365–6, 370–1, 444–5
  religion 839, 841, 843, 845
  socio-economic rights 944, 952, 955–6, 975–6
South Vietnam 46–7
sovereign powers 39, 198, 237–8, 277, 298, 523,
    612, 834

sovereignty 91, 95–6, 223–4, 293–7, 670, 684–5,
    793, 868
  of Allah 927, 930
  of God 96, 868
  parliamentary 120, 147
  people's 60, 242, 360, 491, 508–9, 521–2, 538
  popular 139, 145, 278–9, 523, 527, 861, 971, 977
Soviet Union 4, 14, 23–4, 37, 42–3, 52, 57–8, 368
SPA (Supreme People's Assembly) 24–5, 50
special protection 56, 105, 236, 262, 388, 534, 584,
    686
specialty premiums 386–7
speech
  freedom of 438, 644–6, 649–50, 653–8, 663–6,
    678–9, 708–9, 747–8
  hate 642–3, 669, 671, 681
  obscene 643, 722, 729
  religious 643, 801
  symbolic 643, 682–3, 700, 703
Spencer, Herbert 11
spiritual heritage 106, 802, 804
spirituality 82, 636, 773, 909–10
spite 119, 200, 664, 714–16, 726, 877, 988, 992
Sri Lanka 5
  constitution making 29–30, 58
  constitutional change 259–60, 262–5, 291, 293,
    295
  constitutional culture 80, 106–8
  democracy 465, 537, 539
  equality 550, 556–7, 605–6, 625
  free speech 643, 687, 697, 704, 756
  government system 127–8, 144, 157–8, 160–1,
    167–8, 205
  judicial review 328, 331, 343, 350, 440
  religion 816–17, 819–22, 859
  socio-economic rights 1001
  Supreme Court 161, 265, 291, 343–4, 399, 650,
    688
stability 62, 71, 134–5, 139, 247, 256, 447, 449
  social 803, 805, 859, 867, 912, 962
stable government 14–15, 74, 362
stakeholders 479–80, 975, 1016
state agencies 330–1, 353, 425, 583, 619
state control 101, 970, 972–3, 976–7
State Council 38, 44, 48, 104, 175–7, 202, 205, 319
state ideology 24, 643, 731–2
state institutions 53, 98, 311, 332, 334, 356, 410,
    682–3
state interests
  compelling, *see* compelling state interests
  legitimate 488, 557, 589
state officials 78, 123, 799, 822, 898
state organs 87, 176, 187, 213, 298, 311, 386, 394
state policy 81–2, 486–7, 865, 868, 961, 966, 983–4,
    986
  fundamental principles 105, 111, 114
state power 41, 45, 88, 99, 102, 121, 123, 538
  highest organ of 176, 228, 315
state regulation 779, 798, 826, 861, 904, 972
state religion 70, 110, 115, 247, 822, 828, 871, 896;
    see also official religion
State Shinto 892–3, 896, 901

states of emergency 204–5, 207–10, 212, 214, 216,
    246–8, 280–1, 364
status, social 79, 523, 551, 579, 613, 622, 704,
    903–4
statutory discretion 500, 743–4
statutory powers 166, 362, 499, 562, 767, 797
street protests 217, 226, 626, 739
strict neutrality 114, 880–1
strict scrutiny 495, 557, 620, 882
student demonstrations 217, 226
subordination 75, 496, 546, 722, 732
substantial equality 458, 584–5
successful treason 242, 248, 360
sufficient interests 405–7, 411, 413–14, 416
Suharto 54, 92, 172, 466
Sukarno 53–4, 61, 88
Sultan of Brunei 37, 135, 172, 205, 440
Sun Yat-sen 13, 38–40, 92–6, 100, 424–6
Sunnah 779, 868–9, 891, 917–20, 923, 928
supermajorities 189, 215, 260–1, 343, 349, 444
superstition 549, 774, 780, 865, 871, 912–13, 924
supervision 372–3, 390, 392, 394–6, 457–8, 973,
    976, 980
    administrative 388–9, 512
    judicial 350, 356, 364
supervisory jurisdiction 1017–18
supervisory powers 95, 389, 391–2, 512
Supomo 87–8
supremacy 18, 47, 152, 288, 290, 324–5
    constitutional 117, 326, 798
    judicial 197, 324
    parliamentary 120, 324–6
supreme authority 25, 45, 229
supreme law 77, 252, 262, 296, 299, 308–9, 342,
    349
Supreme People's Assembly, *see* SPA
Surah 777, 790
suspension 178, 194, 204, 212, 249–50, 267, 324,
    452–3
sustainable development 1011, 1019–22
syariah
    courts 784–6, 788–92, 794–8, 890, 914
    law 108, 786, 788–9, 791
symbolic powers 98, 128–40
symbolic speech 643, 682–3, 700, 703
symbols 128, 134, 164, 166, 852–3, 856, 892,
    900
    religious 827, 859, 875
    of state 40, 280, 702

Taiwan 3, 5
    Chiang Kai-shek 21, 39–40, 349
    constitution making 12, 18, 20, 20–31, 40, 58
    constitutional change 221–6, 240, 260, 262
    constitutional culture 75, 87, 92, 120, 123
    Control Yuan 22, 39, 184, 225, 310, 391, 396,
        424–5
    democracy 464, 466–7, 481–2, 489–90, 493, 498,
        501, 534
    equality 550, 579, 584, 588, 617, 619, 625, 636
    Executive Yuan 141–3, 186–9, 191–2, 206,
        354–5, 362–4, 403, 425

free speech 642, 644, 648, 653–4, 658, 733,
    740–1, 762–4
government system 127–8, 140–1, 143–4, 157–8,
    169–71, 182–3, 190–1, 203–6
judicial review 328–35, 337–9, 350–3, 355–6,
    361–2, 385–6, 423–4, 459–60
Judicial Yuan 22, 310, 335–6, 366, 381, 391–2,
    396, 457
religion 844, 846
socio-economic rights 962
Taiwanp 264, 296–7
Tamil Nadu 504, 767, 800, 961, 1020–1
Taoism 90, 772, 911, 939
taxation 192, 275, 366, 593, 844, 955
taxpayers 272, 411, 413–14, 473, 512, 964
teachers 85, 91, 756, 760, 762, 827–9, 832, 1006
telecasting 655–8, 665
television 73, 653, 656, 661, 665, 1014
temples 112, 775, 811, 863, 872, 875, 930; *see also*
    shrines
temporal validity 447–8
temporary validity 452–6
tenure 23, 128–9, 168, 369, 371, 393, 396, 609
    security of 371, 382, 393, 609
terrorism 208, 299, 301, 303–4
    international 304
terrorist attacks 203, 214, 299–300, 364
Thai Rak Thai Party 501–2
Thailand 3, 5–6, 374, 376, 382, 389
    1932 Revolution 16–17
    constitution making 14, 16–17, 49–50, 58, 64
    constitutional change 221–2, 240, 251, 259–60,
        280–1
    Constitutional Court 216, 311, 333, 340, 399
    constitutional culture 75, 78, 80–1, 86, 99–100,
        106, 108–9
    democracy 464–7, 482, 498, 500–2, 511, 514,
        537
    equality 550, 556–7, 618, 625
    free speech 643, 652–3, 683, 686–7, 711
    government system 127–8, 135, 139, 144–5,
        193–4, 203, 205, 216–17
    judicial review 310–11, 328–9, 331–3, 336–40,
        354, 357, 370–1
    religion 847, 860
    socio-economic rights 944, 975, 1001, 1022
    Shinawatra, Thaksin 135, 139, 222
Thaksin Shinawatra (see Shinawatra, Thaksin)
theocracies
    absolute 867
    constitutional 866–9
theocratic monarchy 109
theocratic State 113–14, 787, 875
Tibetan Buddhism 97, 802, 866
timber licence agreements, *see* TLAs
Timor-Leste 5, 58, 60, 76–7, 80–1, 86, 550, 557
TLAs (timber licence agreements) 404, 964, 966
tolerance 125, 803–5, 824, 827, 837, 873–4, 876–7,
    916–18
    religious 89, 114, 806, 825, 867, 871, 910, 930
totalitarian rule 284–5
trade 17–18, 27, 101, 204, 273, 430, 570–1, 679

trade unions 23, 693, 744, 755–62, 768–9, 943–4, 957–9
  registered 756, 768–9
traditional ceremonies 569, 574, 898–9
traditional rights 524–5, 560
traditional values 77, 92
traditions 57, 60, 69–71, 120, 122, 603–4, 633, 635–6
  constitutional 67, 240, 274, 417, 630
  cultural 90, 105, 635, 803, 806
  religious 635, 827, 940
traffic order 745–6, 749, 752
tranquility 650, 679, 810, 925–6, 929
transformation, constitutional 219, 739
transgendered individuals 482, 487
transition 28, 68–9, 74, 184, 193, 222, 225, 239–41
  political 143, 222
transitional democracies 239, 983
transitional justice 217, 240–1, 243
transitional politics 241, 282, 505
transnational constitutionalism 279, 417
  as limit to constitutional change 299–305
transnational lawyering 417
transparency 74, 103, 196, 255, 296, 973, 996
treason 167, 169–70, 242, 360
  successful 242, 248, 360
trust 90–1, 115, 118–20, 124, 143, 151–2, 162, 294–6
  absolute 105, 110–11, 868
  political 663–4
  social 186, 825–6
truth 549, 662–3, 667–8, 681–2, 709–10, 714–16, 801–2, 934
  religious 798, 807, 864
truthfulness 661, 709, 919
tudung 827–8
turban 777–9, 827–8, 830–2

ulama/ulema 779, 868–9, 919–20, 939, 942
ultimate authority 132, 428, 541, 861
unconstitutional constitutional amendment 220, 282, 291
unconstitutional declaration without invalidation 456, 459
unconstitutional law 305, 348–9, 407–8, 937
unconstitutional political parties 328, 339–40, 404
unconstitutionality 200–1, 329, 332, 336, 443, 446–7, 450, 454–5
  declarations of 330, 443, 447, 450, 454
  limited 366–7, 444–5, 447
  unqualified 366, 444
unique culture 79, 440, 568–9, 571
unique rights 83–5
unitary State 53, 281, 291–2, 351, 973
United Kingdom 2, 4, 33, 35, 65, 324, 437, 441
United Nations (UN) 115–16, 236–7, 303–4, 431, 433, 561, 624, 636
United States 196–201, 236–8, 556, 590–3, 595–7, 703–4, 878–84, 923–5
  Supreme Court 143, 311, 556, 562, 660, 670, 723, 731
unity 88, 90–1, 288–90, 814, 832, 854, 856, 919

administrative 140–1, 143, 186, 190, 468, 477
  ethnic 863
  national 89, 105, 123, 467, 497, 702, 827, 853
universal application 598, 600, 605, 610
unprincipled discretion 499, 767
unqualified unconstitutionality 366, 444
unreasonableness 284, 471, 797, 886
US, *see* United States
Uttar Pradesh 426, 429, 504, 553, 998

vacancies 185–6, 265, 374, 376–8, 381, 507
vacancy election 507–8
valid votes 259, 486, 504, 508–9
validity 228, 230, 233–4, 244–5, 252–4, 324, 598–9, 768–9
  constitutional 212, 288, 304, 379, 381–5, 412, 630
  temporary 452–6
values 68–9, 76–7, 467–8, 471–3, 476, 484–5, 574, 935–6
  common 727–8
  community 303, 465, 467, 642
  constitutional 76, 86, 120, 211, 270, 282, 843, 845
  cultural 76, 713
  educational 723, 728, 733
  fundamental 69, 220, 278–9, 825, 847, 948
  normative 70, 465, 762
  public 527, 945
  religious 302, 574, 733, 852, 861, 900, 934–6, 940
  social 70, 647, 681, 710
  traditional 77, 92
Vatikiotis, Michael RJ 92
Vice-Presidents 19, 48, 56, 247, 338–9, 353, 611, 684–5
Vietminh 45–6, 49
Vietnam 3, 5–6
  constitution making 18, 38, 45–8, 50, 63
  constitutional change 221–2, 259–60
  constitutional culture 75, 78, 80, 100–1, 104, 106, 120, 122–3
  democracy 537
  DRV (Democratic Republic of Vietnam) 46, 48, 864
  equality 550, 625
  government system 128–9, 144, 173, 205
  judicial review 309, 312–13
  North 47–8
  religion 847, 862–6
  socio-economic rights 944, 1001
  South 46–7
violence 402, 670–1, 728, 732, 816, 818–19, 910, 916
  religious 802, 859
visions of the common good 69, 77–82
visual impairment 582, 584–7
vocational rehabilitation 583–4
von Stein, Lorenz 11
voters 173, 258, 260, 267, 468–70, 481–6, 507–9, 517–18
  registered 258, 536, 540–2
  registration of 514, 521

votes 182–3, 257–60, 409, 453–4, 472–3, 479–86,
    521–3, 525–8
  value of 468–72, 476–7
votes of no-confidence 148–52
voting 257, 259, 467–8, 480–1, 492–3, 508, 523,
    525–8
  corporate 479–80
  overseas 409, 523–4
vulnerable groups/people 442, 819–21

war 45–7, 49–50, 157–8, 165, 196–203, 209–10,
    236–8, 899–901
war criminals 246, 301, 901
war potential 81, 197–8, 236–8
warnings, judicial 443, 456, 459
Watch Tower Bible and Tract Society, *see* WTBTS
water 944, 952, 971, 978–82, 984, 990, 993, 1020–1
  drinking 978–9, 999, 1019
  pollution 1001, 1021
  resources 969, 978–82
wealth 79, 90, 402, 414, 549, 557, 568, 625
welfare 55–6, 560, 583, 586–7, 617, 835, 954–6,
    1010–11
  general 159, 303, 701–2, 748, 847, 970
  policies 582–5
  public 132, 568, 618–19, 698, 750, 833–4, 847–8,
    953–4
  social 290, 584, 588, 894, 945–7, 949, 974, 977
  state 72, 279, 287–8, 588, 990, 1004
West Bengal 414, 589, 597, 605, 810, 1002, 1004–5,
    1014
witnesses 274–6, 433, 821, 922
women 493–4, 496, 633, 722, 732–4, 776–7,
    828–30, 984–6
  discrimination against 624–6
  lactating 997–8
  pregnant 995, 1002–3
  reputation 83, 704
  working 56, 415, 435–6, 459–60
word of God 811–12
work 2–3, 29–34, 43, 59, 111, 586–8, 723–5,
    986–90
  equal 623, 944
  humane conditions of 984, 1007
workers 686, 757–8, 761, 768, 955, 957–60, 962–3,
    967
working class 41, 48, 100–1, 173–4
working conditions 56, 957–8, 960, 962, 993
working women 56, 415, 435–6, 459–60
workplaces 625, 829, 955, 958
worship 112–13, 775, 851–2, 854–5, 876, 881–2,
    896–8, 906
  freedom of 894, 933, 1013
  shrine 775, 896
writ petitions 380–2, 384–5, 413, 415–16, 985, 988,
    991, 994
written constitutions 11, 16, 65, 72, 133, 256,
    270–4, 311–12
WTBTS (Watch Tower Bible and Tract
    Society) 406, 835

Yang di-Pertuan Agong 134–5, 138, 207–8, 361,
    558, 674, 694, 788
Yasukuni Shrine 139, 899–901

zakat 795, 869–70, 890